In 1996 the United Nations celebrated its fiftieth birthday. During the last half century it has played a pivotal role in the establishment of friendly relations between States, dispute resolution, disarmament and peacekeeping, development, self-determination and the development of humanitarian law. It has also played a central role in international co-operation to prevent crimes such as terrorism and drug smuggling. This gigantic task has involved the passing of nearly 8000 resolutions and the creation of a mountain of documentation. This book is the only collection to offer an authoritative selection of the most important resolutions from these first fifty years. It will be invaluable for those studying, teaching or practising in international law or international relations and also for politicians, diplomats and staff members of international organizations.

Key Resolutions of the United Nations General Assembly 1946–1996

Key Resolutions of the United Nations General Assembly 1946–1996

edited by

Dietrich Rauschning
Professor of Law

Katja Wiesbrock
Research Associate

Martin Lailach
Research Associate

Institut für Völkerrecht der Universität Göttingen

CAMBRIDGE
UNIVERSITY PRESS

PUBLISHED BY THE PRESS SYNDICATE OF THE UNIVERSITY OF CAMBRIDGE
The Pitt Building, Trumpington Street, Cambridge CB2 1RP, United Kingdom

CAMBRIDGE UNIVERSITY PRESS
The Edinburgh Building, Cambridge, CB2 2RU, United Kingdom
40 West 20th Street, New York, NY 10011–4211, USA
10 Stamford Road, Oakleigh, Melbourne 3166, Australia

First published 1997

Printed in the United Kingdom at the University Press, Cambridge

A catalogue record for this book is available from the British Library

ISBN 0 521 59287 9 hardback
ISBN 0 521 59704 8 paperback

CONTENTS

02.12 NUCLEAR WEAPONS

02.13 OTHER WEAPONS

02.20 PEACE-KEEPING AND OTHER OPERATIONS

02.30 COOPERATION OF THE UNITED NATIONS WITH REGIONAL ARRANGEMENTS

02.40 OBSERVATION OF ELECTIONS

03.00 DEVELOPMENT AND STRENGTHENING OF INTERNATIONAL LAW

06.00 HUMAN RIGHTS

06.10 GENERAL MATTERS

06.20 RACIAL DISCRIMINATION AND APARTHEID

06.30 RELIGIOUS DISCRIMINATION

06.40 GROUPS REQUIRING SPECIAL PROTECTION

06.41 WOMEN

06.42 CHILDREN AND YOUTH

PREFACE

The United Nations has now been functioning as the global political organization for half a century, and the General Assembly has become a forum for practically all States. During its 50 sessions, 9 emergency sessions and 18 special sessions, the General Assembly has adopted 7981 resolutions. The collection of the printed text fills a bookshelf, although more recent resolutions are available on CD-ROM or the internet. This multitude of resolutions tends to obscure the legal content of a number of important resolutions of the General Assembly. The significant influence of those resolutions on many international issues cannot be denied: on friendly relations between States and peaceful settlement of their disputes, on disarmament and peace-keeping, on self-determination and decolonization, on development and economic cooperation, on the protection of human rights and the development of humanitarian law, on international social problems such as the protection of health and the international cooperation in the prevention of crimes - especially terrorism and drug trafficking - and finally on the global protection of the environment. Consequently, the main topics of political, social and legal development cannot be seriously discussed without referring to the resolutions of the United Nations General Assembly.

For any research into or discussion of these areas, it is essential to have access to the relevant discussions. The task of the selection presented here is to provide easy access to these documents. The volume is intended on the one hand to support politicians and diplomats and even staff members of international organizations, and on the other hand to help scholars and lecturers in the fields of international law, of political science specializing in international relations, and of contemporary history in their research and lecturing. It should also be useful and interesting to students, to journalists and to all those interested in international relations.

The collection is limited to one volume so that it can be used at home or a desk, or even during a lecture; more detailed information may be obtained by using a library or a data-bank. In the selection of material, general declarations used by the General Assembly with the intention of restating and developing rules of international law were given priority; political declarations and plans of action are also necessarily included. As the view of the member states on the content of international law emerges on the basis of particular cases, some resolutions concerning these are included. Where the General Assembly has passed several resolutions on the same subject in various sessions, the most recent resolution, or the one containing the most information or including an annex, has been reproduced.

These principles of selection have resulted in a collection of 419 resolutions. They are arranged in chronological order under a series of systematic headings. As many resolutions concern different topics and every resolution is printed only once, the reader might question the classification under one or the other heading. Using the index should resolve this difficulty. The table of contents, arranged according to the numbers of the resolutions, enables the reader to check easily whether a resolution is included in the collection.

The Institute of Public International Law in Göttingen has been planning this volume for some years. In the early stages of the project former members of the Institute, Brigitte Daum, Sonja Köhler, née Maas, and Dr Margit Sigmund worked on the concept and selection of resolutions. The current version has initially been drawn up by Martin Lailach. The work has been intensively discussed with CUP; in particular its referee, Professor James Crawford, has helped with appropriate classification, and has given some advice on the choice of resolutions to be adopted in the volume.

When Martin Lailach left the Institute in Summer 1996 Katja Wiesbrock took over the editorial work on the volume, with the support of Katrin Weschke and Thomas Jelitte. The difficult task of the EDV word processing has been handled by Silvia Geßner and especially Christiane Becker, who has also done the complete layout. In their struggle against the persistent printing errors the editors have been supported by Wiebke Dörre, Melanie Gatzsch, Louise Müller, Claas de Boer and Albrecht Prestel. Without all this help and commitment the publication of the volume would not have been possible. Thanks to all who have helped complete the task! The responsibility, however, remains with the editors.

Dietrich Rauschning　　Katja Wiesbrock　　Martin Lailach

01.00 PRINCIPLES GOVERNING INTERNATIONAL RELATIONS

01.10 GENERAL PRINCIPLES

375 (IV). Draft Declaration on Rights and Duties of States

Committee: 6
Vote: 39 - 0 - 12
Ref.: 596(VI), 378(V), 178(II), 38(I)

The General Assembly,

Having received the draft Declaration on Rights and Duties of States[1] prepared by the International Law Commission in pursuance of the instruction given to it by the General Assembly in resolution 178 (II) of 21 November 1947,

Considering that it is a responsibility of the United Nations, and more especially of the General Assembly, under Article 13 of the Charter, to encourage the progressive development of international law and its codification,

Considering that at the present time it has encountered some difficulties in formulating basic rights and duties of States in the light of new developments of international law and in harmony with the Charter of the United Nations, and recognizing the need of continuing study with regard to this subject,

1. *Notes* the draft Declaration on Rights and Duties of States prepared by the International Law Commission and expresses to the Commission its appreciation for its work on the draft Declaration;

2. *Deems* the draft Declaration a notable and substantial contribution towards the progressive development of international law and its codification and as such commends it to the continuing attention of Member States and of jurists of all nations;

3. *Resolves* to transmit to Member States, for consideration, the draft Declaration together with all the documentation relating thereto produced during the present session of the General Assembly, and to request them to furnish their comments and suggestions at the latest by 1 July 1950;

4. *Requests* Member States to furnish at the same time comments on the following questions:

(*a*) Whether any further action should be taken by the General Assembly on the draft Declaration;

(*b*) If so, the exact nature of the document to be aimed at and the future procedure to be adopted in relation to it;

5. *Requests* the Secretary-General to prepare and publish the suggestions and comments furnished by Member States, for such use as the General Assembly may find desirable;

6. *Directs* that the text of the draft Declaration be annexed to the present resolution.

270th plenary meeting
6 December 1949

Annex

Draft Declaration on Rights and Duties of States

Whereas the States of the world form a community governed by international law,

Whereas the progressive development of international law requires effective organization of the community of States,

Whereas a great majority of the States of the world have accordingly established a new international order under the Charter of the United Nations, and most of the other States of the world have declared their desire to live within this order,

Whereas a primary purpose of the United Nations is to maintain international peace and security, and the reign of law and justice is essential to the realization of this purpose, and

Whereas it is therefore desirable to formulate certain basic rights and duties of States in the light of new developments of international law and in harmony with the Charter of the United Nations,

The General Assembly of the United Nations adopts and proclaims this Declaration on Rights and Duties of States:

Article 1

Every State has the right to independence and hence to exercise freely, without dictation by any other State, all its legal powers, including the choice of its own form of government.

Article 2

Every State has the right to exercise jurisdiction over its territory and over all persons and things therein, subject to the immunities recognized by international law.

Article 3

Every State has the duty to refrain from intervention in the internal or external affairs of any other State.

Article 4

Every State has the duty to refrain from fomenting civil strife in the territory of another State, and to prevent the organization within its territory of activities calculated to foment such civil strife.

Article 5

Every State has the right to equality in law with every other State.

Article 6

Every State has the duty to treat all persons under its jurisdiction with respect for human rights and fundamental freedoms, without distinction as to race, sex, language, or religion.

Article 7

Every State has the duty to ensure that condition prevailing in its territory do not menace international peace and order.

Article 8

Every State has the duty to settle its disputes with other States by peaceful means in such a manner that international peace and security, and justice, are not endangered.

Article 9

Every State has the duty to refrain from resorting to war as an instrument of national policy, and to refrain from the threat or use of force against the territorial integrity or political independence of another State, or in any other manner inconsistent with international law and order.

Article 10

Every State has the duty to refrain from giving assistance to any State which is acting in violation of article 9, or against which the United Nations is taking preventive or enforcement action.

Article 11

Every State has the duty to refrain from recognizing any territorial acquisition by another State acting in violation of article 9.

Article 12

Every State has the right of individual or collective self-defence against armed attack.

---

1 See *Official Records of the General Assembly, Fourth Session, Supplement No. 10*, p. 8.

Article 13

Every State has the duty to carry out in good faith its obligations arising from treaties and other sources of international law, and it may not invoke provisions in its constitution or its laws as an excuse for failure to perform this duty.

Article 14

Every State has the duty to conduct its relations with other States in accordance with international law and with the principle that the sovereignty of each State is subject to the supremacy of international law.

378 (V). Duties of States in the Event of the Outbreak of Hostilities

Committee: 1
Vote: A: 45 - 5 - 1; B: 59 - 5 - 1

A

The General Assembly,

Reaffirming the Principles embodied in the Charter, which require that the force of arms shall not be resorted to except in the common interest, and shall be not used against the territorial integrity or political independence of any State,

Desiring to create a further obstacle to the outbreak of war, even after hostilities have started, and to facilitate the cessation of the hostilities by the action of the parties themselves, thus contributing to the peaceful settlement of disputes,

1. *Recommends*:

(*a*) That if a State becomes engaged in armed conflict with another State or States, it take all steps practicable in the circumstances and compatible with the right of self-defence to bring the armed conflict to an end at the earliest possible moment;

(*b*) In particular, that such State shall immediately, and in any case not later than twenty-four hours after the outbreak of the hostilities, make a public statement wherein it will proclaim its readiness, provided that the States with which it is in conflict will do the same, to discontinue all military operations and withdraw all its military forces which have invaded the territory or territorial water of another State or crossed a demarcation line, either on terms agreed by the parties to the conflict or under conditions to be indicated to the parties by the appropriate organs of the United Nations;

(*c*) That such State immediately notify the Secretary-General, for communication to the Security Council and to the Members of the United Nations, of the statement made in accordance with the preceding subparagraph and of the circumstances in which the conflict has arisen;

(*d*) That such State, in its notification to the Secretary-General, invite the appropriate organs of the United Nations to dispatch the Peace Observation Commission[1] to the area in which the conflict has arisen, if the Commission is not already functioning there;

(*e*) That the conduct of the States concerned in relation to the matters covered by the foregoing recommendations be taken into account in any determination of responsibility for the breach of the peace or act of aggression in the case under consideration and in all other relevant proceedings before the appropriate organs of the United Nations;

2. *Determines* that the provisions of the present resolution in no way impair the rights and obligations of States under the Charter of the United Nations nor the decisions or recommendations of the Security Council, the General Assembly or any other competent organ of the United Nations.

308th plenary meeting
17 November 1950

[1] See resolution 377 A (V), section B.

B

The General Assembly,

Considering that the question raised by the proposal[2] of the Union of Soviet Socialist Republics can better be examined in conjunction with matters under consideration by the International Law Commission, a subsidiary organ of the United Nations,

Decides to refer the proposal of the Union of Soviet Socialist Republics and all the records[3] of the First Committee dealing with this question to the International Law Commission, so that the latter may take them into consideration and formulate its conclusions as soon as possible.

308th plenary meeting
17 November 1950

1236 (XII). Peaceful and Neighbourly Relations among States

Committee: 1
Vote: 77 - 0 - 1
Ref.: 1301(XIII), 504(VI)

The General Assembly,

Considering the urgency and the importance of strengthening international peace and of developing peaceful and neighbourly relations among States irrespective of their divergences or the relative stages and nature of their political, economic and social development,

Recalling that among the fundamental objectives of the Charter of the United Nations are the maintenance of international peace and security and friendly cooperation among States,

Realizing the need to promote these objectives and to develop peaceful and tolerant relations among States in conformity with the Charter, based on mutual respect and benefit, non-aggression, respect for each other's sovereignty, equality and territorial integrity and non-intervention in one another's internal affairs, and to fulfil the purposes and principles of the Charter,

Recognizing the need to broaden international cooperation, to reduce tensions and to settle differences and disputes among States by peaceful means,

Calls upon all States to make every effort to strengthen international peace, and to develop friendly and cooperative relations and settle disputes by peaceful means as enjoined in the Charter of the United Nations and as set forth in the present resolution.

731st plenary meeting
14 December 1957

2160 (XXI). Strict Observance of the Prohibition of the Threat or Use of Force in International Relations, and of the Right of Peoples to Self-Determination

Committee: -
Vote: 98 - 2 - 8

The General Assembly,

I

Drawing the attention of States to the fundamental obligations incumbent upon them in accordance with the Charter of the United Nations to refrain in their international relations from the threat or use of force against the territorial integrity or political independence of any State, or in any other manner inconsistent with the purposes of the United Nations and to develop friendly relations among nations based on respect for the principle of equal rights and self-determination of peoples,

Deeply concerned at the existence of dangerous situations in the world constituting a direct threat to universal peace and security, due to the arbitrary use of force in international relations,

Reaffirming the right of peoples under colonial rule to exercise their

[2] See document A/C.1/608 Appendix 1, p. 257.

[3] See *Official Records of the General Assembly, Fifth Session, First Committee*, 384th to 390th meetings inclusive.

right to self-determination and independence and the right of every nation, large or small, to choose freely and without any external interference its political, social and economic system,

Recognizing that peoples subjected to colonial oppression are entitled to seek and receive all support in their struggle which is in accordance with the purposes and principles of the Charter,

Firmly convinced that it is within the power and in the vital interest of the nations of the world to establish genuinely sound relations between States, based on justice, equality, mutual understanding and cooperation,

Recalling the declarations contained in its resolutions 1514 (XV) of 14 December 1960 and 2131 (XX) of 21 December 1965,

1. *Reaffirms* that:

(*a*) States shall strictly observe, in their international relations, the prohibition of the threat or use of force against the territorial integrity or political independence of any State, or in any other manner inconsistent with the purposes of the United Nations. Accordingly, armed attack by one State against another or the use of force in any other form contrary to the Charter of the United Nations constitutes a violation of international law giving rise to international responsibility;

(*b*) Any forcible action, direct or indirect, which deprives peoples under foreign domination of their right to self-determination and freedom and independence and of their right to determine freely their political status and pursue their economic, social and cultural development constitutes a violation of the Charter of the United Nations. Accordingly, the use of force to deprive peoples of their national identity, as prohibited by the Declaration on the Inadmissibility of Intervention in the Domestic Affairs of States and the Protection of Their Independence and Sovereignty contained in General Assembly resolution 2131 (XX), constitutes a violation of their inalienable rights and of the principle of non-intervention;

2. *Urgently appeals* to States:

(*a*) To renounce and to refrain from any action contrary to the above-stated fundamental principles and to assure that their activities in international relations are in full harmony with the interests of international peace and security;

(*b*) To exert every effort and to undertake all necessary measures with a view to facilitating the exercise of the right of self-determination of peoples under colonial rule, lessening international tension, strengthening peace and promoting friendly relations and cooperation among States;

3. *Reminds* all Members of their duty to give their fullest support to the endeavours of the United Nations to ensure respect for and the observance of the principles enshrined in the Charter and to assist the Organization in discharging its responsibilities as assigned to it by the Charter for the maintenance of international peace and security;

II

Considering that the above principles, together with the other five principles of friendly relations and cooperation among States, have been the object of a study with a view to their progressive development and codification[1] on the basis of General Assembly resolutions 1815 (XVII) of 18 December 1962, 1966 (XVIII) of 16 December 1963 and 2103 (XX) of 20 December 1965,

Requests the Secretary-General to include the present resolution and the records of the debate on the item entitled "Strict observance of the prohibition of the threat or use of force in international relations, and of the right of peoples to self-determination" in the documentation to be considered in the further study of the principles of international law concerning friendly relations and cooperation among States in accordance with the Charter of the United Nations, with a view to the early adoption of a declaration containing an enunciation of these principles.

1482nd plenary meeting
30 November 1966

1 *Official Records of the General Assembly, Twenty-first Session, Annexes,* agenda item 87, document A/6230.

2625 (XXV). Declaration on Principles of International Law Concerning Friendly Relations and Cooperation among States in Accordance with the Charter of the United Nations

Committee: 6
Vote: Adopted without a vote

The General Assembly,

Recalling its resolutions 1815 (XVII) of 18 December 1962, 1966 (XVIII) of 16 December 1963, 2103 (XX) of 20 December 1965, 2181 (XXI) of 12 December 1966, 2327 (XXII) of 18 December 1967, 2463 (XXIII) of 20 December 1968 and 2533 (XXIV) of 8 December 1969, in which it affirmed the importance of the progressive development and codification of the principles of international law concerning friendly relations and cooperation among States,

Having considered the report of the Special Committee on Principles of International Law concerning Friendly Relations and Cooperation among States,[2] which met in Geneva from 31 March to 1 May 1970,

Emphasizing the paramount importance of the Charter of the United Nations for the maintenance of international peace and security and for the development of friendly relations and cooperation among States,

Deeply convinced that the adoption of the Declaration on Principles of International Law concerning Friendly Relations and Cooperation among States in accordance with the Charter of the United Nations or the occasion of the twenty-fifth anniversary of the United Nations would contribute to the strengthening of world peace and constitute a landmark in the development of international law and of relations among States, in promoting the rule of law among nations and particularly the universal application of the Principle embodied in the Charter,

Considering the desirability of the wide dissemination of the text of the Declaration,

1. *Approves* the Declaration on Principles of International Law concerning Friendly Relations and Cooperation among States in accordance with the Charter of the United Nations, the text of which is annexed to the present resolution;

2. *Expresses its appreciation* to the Special Committee on Principles of International Law concerning Friendly Relations and Cooperation among States for its work resulting in the elaboration of the Declaration;

3. *Recommends* that all efforts be made so that the Declaration becomes generally known.

1883rd plenary meeting
24 October 1970

Annex

Declaration on Principles of International Law Concerning Friendly Relations and Cooperation among States in Accordance with the Charter of the United Nations

Preamble

The General Assembly,

Reaffirming in the arms of the Charter of the United Nations that the maintenance of international peace and security and the development of friendly relations and cooperation between nations are among the fundamental purposes of the United Nations,

Recalling that the peoples of the United Nations are determined to practise tolerance and live together in peace with one another as good neighbours,

Bearing in mind the importance of maintaining and strengthening international peace founded upon freedom, equality, justice and respect for fundamental human right and of developing friendly

2 *Official Records of the General Assembly, Twenty-fifth Session, Supplement No. 18* (A/8018).

relations among nations irrespective of their political economic and social systems or the levels of their development,

Bearing in mind also the paramount importance of the Charter of the United Nations in the promotion of the rule of law among nations,

Considering that the faithful observance of the principles of international law concerning friendly relations and cooperation among States and the fulfilment in good faith of the obligation assumed by States, in accordance with the Charter, is of the greatest importance for the maintenance of international peace and security and for the implementation of the other purposes of the United Nations,

Noting that the great political, economic and social changes and scientific progress which have taken place in the world since the adoption of the Charter give increased importance to these principles and to the need for their more effective application in the conduct of States wherever carried on,

Recalling the established principle that outer space, including the Moon and other celestial bodies, is not subject to national appropriation by claim of sovereignty, by means of use or occupation, or by any other means, and mindful of the fact that consideration is being given in the United Nations to the question of establishing other appropriate provisions similarly inspired,

Convinced that the strict observance by States of the obligation not to intervene in the affairs of any other State is an essential condition to ensure that nations live together in peace with one another, since the practice of any form of intervention not only violates the spirit and letter of the Charter, but also leads to the creation of situations which threaten international peace and security,

Recalling the duty of States to refrain in their international relations from military, political, economic or any other form of coercion aimed against the political independence or territorial integrity of any State,

Considering it essential that all States shall refrain in their international relations from the threat or use of force against the territorial integrity or political Independence of any State, or in any other manner inconsistent with the purposes of the United Nations,

Considering it equally essential that all States shall settle their international disputes by peaceful means in accordance with the Charter,

Reaffirming, in accordance with the Charter, the basic importance of sovereign equality and stressing that the purposes of the United Nations can be implemented only if States enjoy sovereign equality and comply fully with the requirements of this principle in their international relations,

Convinced that the subjection of peoples to alien subjugation, domination and exploitation constitutes a major obstacle to the promotion of international peace and security,

Convinced that the principle of equal rights and self-determination of peoples constitutes a significant contribution to contemporary international law, and that its effective application is of paramount importance for the promotion of friendly relations among States, based on respect for the principle of sovereign equality,

Convinced in consequence that any attempt aimed at the partial or total disruption of the national unity and territorial integrity of a State or country or at its political independence is incompatible with the purposes and principles of the Charter,

Considering the provisions of the Charter as a whole and taking into account the role of relevant resolutions adopted by the competent organs of the United Nations relating to the content of the principles,

Considering that the progressive development and codification of the following principles:

(*a*) The principle that States shall refrain in their international relations from the threat or use of force against the territorial integrity or political independence of any State, or in any other manner inconsistent with the purposes of the United Nations,

(*b*) The principle that States shall settle their international disputes by peaceful means in such a manner that international peace and security and justice are not endangered,

(*c*) The duty not to intervene in matters within the domestic jurisdiction of any State in accordance with the Charter,

(*d*) The duty of States to cooperate with one another in accordance with the Charter,

(*e*) The principle of equal rights and self-determination of peoples,

(*f*) The principle of sovereign equality of States

(*g*) The principle that States shall fulfil in good faith the obligations assumed by them in accordance with the Charter,

so as to secure their more effective application within the international community, would promote the realization of the purposes of the United Nations,

Having considered the principles of international law relating to friendly relations and cooperation among States,

1. *Solemnly proclaims* the following principles:

The Principle that States shall refrain in their international relations from the threat or use of force against the territorial integrity or political independence of any State, or in any other manner inconsistent with the purposes of the United Nations

Every State has the duty to refrain in its international relations from the threat or use of force against the territorial integrity or political independence of any State, or in any other manner inconsistent with the purposes of the United Nations. Such a threat or use of force constitutes a violation of international law and the Charter of the United Nations and shall never be employed as a means of settling international issues.

A war of aggression constitutes a crime against the peace, for which there is responsibility under international law.

In accordance with the purposes and principles of the United Nations, States have the duty to refrain from propaganda for wars of aggression.

Every State has the duty to refrain from the threat or use of force to violate the existing international boundaries of another State or as a means of solving international disputes, including territorial disputes and problems concerning frontiers of States.

Every State likewise has the duty to refrain from the threat or use of force to violate international lines of demarcation, such as armistice lines, established by or pursuant to an international agreement to which it is a party or which it is otherwise bound to respect. Nothing in the foregoing shall be construed as prejudicing the positions of the parties concerned with regard to the status and effects of such lines under their special régimes or as affecting their temporary character.

States have a duty to refrain from acts of reprisal involving the use of force. Every State has the duty to refrain from any forcible action which deprives peoples referred to in the elaboration of the principle of equal rights and self-determination of their right to self-determination and freedom and independence.

Every State has the duty to refrain from organizing or encouraging the organization of irregular forces or armed bands, including mercenaries, for incursion into the territory of another State.

Every State has the duty to refrain from organizing, instigating, assisting or participating in acts of civil strife or terrorist acts in another State or acquiescing in organized activities within its territory directed towards the commission of such acts when the acts referred to in the present paragraph involve a threat or use of force.

The territory of a State shall not be the object of military occupation resulting from the use of force in contravention of the provisions of the Charter. The territory of a State shall not be the object of acquisition by another State resulting from the threat or use of force. No territorial acquisition resulting from the threat or use of force shall be recognized as legal. Nothing in the foregoing shall be construed as affecting:

(*a*) Provisions of the Charter or any international agreement prior to the Charter régime and valid under international law; or

(*b*) The powers of the Security Council under the Charter.

All States shall pursue in good faith negotiations for the early conclusion of a universal treaty on general and complete disarmament under effective international control and strive to adopt appropriate measures to reduce international tensions and strengthen confidence among States.

All States shall comply in good faith with their obligations under the generally recognized principles and rules of international law with respect to the maintenance of international peace and security, and shall endeavour to make the United Nations security system based on the Charter more effective.

Nothing in the foregoing paragraphs shall be construed as enlarging or diminishing in any way the scope of the provisions of the Charter concerning crises in which the use of force is lawful.

The principle that States shall settle their international disputes by peaceful means in such a manner that international peace and security and justice are not endangered

Every State shall settle its international disputes with other States by peaceful means in such a manner that international peace and security and justice are not endangered.

States shall accordingly seek early and just settlement of their international disputes by negotiation, inquiry, mediation, conciliation, arbitration, judicial settlement, resort to regional agencies or arrangements or other peaceful means of their choice. In seeking such a settlement the parties shall agree upon such peaceful means as may be appropriate to the circumstances and nature of the dispute.

The parties to a dispute have the duty, in the event of failure to reach a solution by any one of the above peaceful means, to continue to seek a settlement of the dispute by other peaceful means agreed upon by them.

States parties to an international dispute, as well as other States, shall refrain from any action which may aggravate the situation so as to endanger the maintenance of international peace and security and shall act in accordance with the purposes and principles of the United Nations.

International disputes shall be settled on the basis of the sovereign equality of States and in accordance with the principle of free choice of means. Recourse to, or acceptance of, a settlement procedure freely agreed to by States with regard to existing or future dispute to which they are parties shall not be regarded as incompatible with sovereign equality.

Nothing in the foregoing paragraphs prejudices or derogates from the applicable provision of the Charter, in particular those relating to the pacific settlement of international disputes.

The principle concerning the duty not to intervene in matters within the domestic jurisdiction of any State, in accordance with the Charter

No State or group of States has the right to intervene directly or indirectly, for any reason whatever, in the internal or external affairs of any other State. Consequently, armed intervention and all other forms of interference or attempted threats against the personality of the State or against its political, economic and cultural elements, are in violation of international law.

No State may use or encourage the use of economic, political or any other type of measures to coerce another State in order to obtain from it the subordination of the exercise of its sovereign rights and to secure from it advantages of any kind. Also, no State shall organize, assist, foment, finance, incite or tolerate subversive, terrorist or armed activities directed towards the violent overthrow of the régime of another State, or interfere in civil strife in another State.

The use of force to deprive peoples of their national identity constitutes a violation of their inalienable rights and of the principle of non-intervention.

Every State has an inalienable right to choose its political, economic, social and cultural systems, without interference in any form by another State.

Nothing in the foregoing paragraphs shall be construed as affecting the relevant provisions of the Charter relating to the maintenance of international peace and security.

The duty of States to cooperate with one another in accordance with the Charter

State have the duty to cooperate with one another, irrespective of the differences in their political, economic and social systems, in the various spheres of international relations, in order to maintain international peace and security and to promote international economic stability and progress, the general welfare of nations and international cooperation free from discrimination based on such differences.

To this end

(*a*) States shall cooperate with other States in the maintenance of international peace and security;

(*b*) States shall cooperate in the promotion of universal respect for, and observance of, human rights and fundamental freedoms for all, and in the elimination of all forms of racial discrimination and all forms of religious intolerance;

(*c*) States shall conduct their international relations in the economic, social, cultural, technical and trade fields in accordance with the principles of sovereign equality ad non-intervention;

(*d*) States Members of the United Nations have the duty to take joint and separate action in cooperation with the United Nations in accordance with the relevant provisions of the Charter.

States should cooperate in the economic, social and cultural fields as well as in the field of science and technology and for the promotion of international cultural and educational progress. States should cooperate in the promotion of economic growth throughout the world, especially that of the developing countries.

The principle of equal rights and self-determination of peoples

By virtue of the principle of equal rights and self-determination of peoples enshrined in the Charter of the United Nations, all peoples have the right freely to determine, without external interference, their political status and to pursue their economic, social and cultural development, and every State has the duty to respect this right in accordance with the provisions of the Charter.

Every Sate has the duty to promote, through joint and separate action, realization of the principle of equal rights and self-determination of peoples, in accordance with the provisions of the Charter, and to render assistance to the United Nations in carrying out the responsibilities entrusted to it by the Charter regarding the implementation of the principle, in order:

(*a*) To promote friendly relations and cooperation among States; and

(*b*) To bring a speedy end to colonialism, having due regard to the freely expressed will of the peoples concerned;

and bearing in mind that subjection of peoples to alien subjugation, domination and exploitation constitutes a violation of the principle, as well as a denial of fundamental human rights, and is contrary to the Charter.

Every State has the duty to promote through joint and separate action universal respect for and observance of human rights and fundamental freedoms in accordance with the Charter.

The establishment of a sovereign and independent State, the free association or integration with an independent State or the emergence into any other political status freely determined by a people constitute modes of implementing the right of self-determination by that people.

Every State has the duty to refrain from any forcible action which deprives peoples referred to above in the elaboration of the present principle of their right to self-determination and freedom and independence. In their actions against, and resistance to, such forcible action in pursuit of the exercise of their right to self-determination, such peoples are entitled to seek and to receive support in accordance with the purposes and principles of the Charter.

The territory of a colony or other Non-Self-Governing Territory has, under the Charter, a status separate and distinct from the territory of the State administering it; and such separate and distinct status under the Charter shall exist until the people of the colony or Non-Self-Governing Territory have exercised their right of self-determination in accordance with the Charter, and particularly its purposes and principles.

Nothing in the foregoing paragraphs shall be construed as authorizing or encouraging any action which would dismember or impair, totally or in part, the territorial integrity or political unity of sovereign and independent State conducting themselves in compliance with the principle of equal rights and self-determination of peoples as described above and thus possessed of a government representing the whole people belonging to the territory without distinction as to race, creed or colour.

Every State shall refrain from any action aimed at the partial or total disruption of the national unity and territorial integrity of any other State or country.

The principle of sovereign equality of States

All States enjoy sovereign equality. They have equal rights and duties and are equal members of the international community, notwithstanding differences of an economic, social, political or other nature.

In particular, sovereign equality includes the following elements:

(*a*) States are juridically equal;

(*b*) Each State enjoys the rights inherent in full sovereignty;

(*c*) Each State has the duty to respect the personality of other States;

(*d*) The territorial integrity and political independence of the State are inviolable;

(*e*) Each State has the right freely to choose and develop its political, social, economic and cultural systems;

(*f*) Each State has the duty to comply fully and in good faith with its international obligations and to live in peace with other States.

The principle that States shall fulfil in good faith the obligations assumed by them in accordance with the Charter

Every State has the duty to fulfil in good faith the obligations assumed by it in accordance with the Charter of the United Nations.

Every State has the duty to fulfil in good faith its obligations under the generally recognized principles and rules of international law.

Every State has the duty to fulfil in good faith its obligations under international agreements valid under the generally recognized principles and rules of international law.

Where obligations arising under international agreements are in conflict with the obligations of Members of the United Nations under the Charter of the United Nations, the obligations under the Charter shall prevail.

General Part

2. *Declares* that:

In their interpretation and application the above principles are interrelated and each principle should be construed in the context of the other principles.

Nothing in this Declaration shall be construed as prejudicing in any manner the provisions of the Charter or the rights and duties of Member States under the Charter or the rights of peoples under the Charter, taking into account the elaboration of these rights in this Declaration.

3. *Declares* further that:

The principles of the Charter which are embodied in this Declaration constitute basic principles of international law, and consequently appeals to all States to be guided by these principles in their international conduct and to develop their mutual relations on the basis of the strict observance of these principles.

34/103. Inadmissibility of the Policy of Hegemonism in International Relations

Committee: 1
Vote: 111 - 4 - 26

The General Assembly,

Recognizing the primary responsibility of the United Nations to promote and strengthen international peace and security on the basis of strict respect for the principles of the Charter of the United Nations, especially the principle of sovereignty, sovereign equality and national independence of States,

Recalling the duty of States to refrain in their international relations from military, political, economic or any other form of coercion aimed against the sovereignty, political independence or territorial integrity of any State,

Noting that hegemonism is a manifestation of the policy of a State, or a group of States, to control, dominate and subjugate, politically, economically, ideologically or militarily, other States, peoples or regions of the world,

Considering that imperialism, colonialism, neo-colonialism, racism including zionism and apartheid are all forces which seek to perpetuate unequal relations and privileges acquired by force and are, therefore, different manifestations of the policy and practice of hegemonism,

Concerned that hegemonism, global as well as regional, pursued in the context of the policy of division of the world into blocs or by individual States, manifests itself in the use or threat of use of force, foreign domination and intervention,

Concerned also that hegemonism seeks to limit the freedom of States to determine their political systems and pursue economic, social and cultural development without intimidation, hindrance or pressure,

Convinced that hegemonism, global and regional, in all its different forms, leads to a serious threat to international peace and security,

Considering that it is the common desire of all peoples to oppose hegemonism and to preserve the sovereignty and national independence of all States,

Bearing in mind the importance and urgency of creating a new and equitable system of international relations based on the equal participation of all States in the solution of international problems and the maintenance of international peace and security, one which ensures equal security for all States, and progress and prosperity for all peoples, through the establishment of the new international economic order,

1. *Condemns* hegemonism in all its manifestations, including that conducted at the global, regional or subregional level, pursued in the context of the policy of division of the world into blocs or by individual States;

2. *Declares* that no State or group of States shall, under any circumstance or for any reason whatsoever, pursue hegemony in international relations or seek a position of dominance, either globally or in any region of the world;

3. *Rejects* all forms of domination, subjugation, interference or intervention and all forms of pressure, whether political, ideological, economic, military or cultural, in international relations;

4. *Resolutely condemns* policies of pressure and use or threat of use of force, direct or indirect aggression, occupation and the growing practice of interference and intervention, overt or covert, in the internal affairs of States;

5. *Resolutely condemns* imperialism, colonialism, neocolonialism, apartheid, racism including zionism and all other forms of foreign aggression, occupation, domination and interference, as well as the creation of spheres of influence and the division of the world into antagonistic political and military blocs;

6. *Calls upon* all States, in the conduct of international relations, to observe strictly the principles of the Charter of the United Nations and those regarding respect for the sovereignty, sovereign equality, national independence, unity and territorial integrity of States, non-interference in their internal affairs, non-aggression, peaceful settlement of disputes and cooperation, as well as the right of peoples under colonial and alien domination to self-determination;

7. *Calls* for the withdrawal of all occupation forces back to their own territories, so as to enable the peoples of all States to determine and administer their own affairs;

8. *Further calls* for strict respect for the right of all States to determine their political and socio-economic systems and pursue their national economic, social and other policies without intimidation, hindrance or interference from outside;

9. *Resolves* to continue the endeavour to establish a new and equitable system of international relations based on the equal participation of all States in the solution of international problems and the maintenance of international peace and security;

10. *Further resolves* to continue the endeavour for the establishment of the new international economic order, so as to ensure the economic emancipation and freedom of all nations, in particular the developing countries.

103rd plenary meeting
14 December 1979

42/22. Declaration on the Enhancement of the Effectiveness of the Principle of Refraining from the Threat or Use of Force in International Relations

Committee: 6
Vote: Adopted without a vote
Ref.: 40/70, 39/81, 38/133, 37/105, 36/31, 35/50, 34/13, 33/96, 32/150, 31/9

The General Assembly,

Recalling its resolution 41/76 of 3 December 1986, in which it decided that the Special Committee on Enhancing the Effectiveness of the Principle of Non-Use of Force in International Relations should complete a draft declaration on the enhancement of the effectiveness of the principle, including, as appropriate, recommendations on the peaceful settlement of disputes, and submit its final report containing a draft declaration to the General Assembly at its forty-second session,

Taking note of the report of the Special Committee, which met in New York from 9 to 27 March 1987,[1]

Considering that the Special Committee has completed a draft Declaration on the Enhancement of the Effectiveness of the Principle of Refraining from the Threat or Use of Force in International Relations and has decided to submit it to the General Assembly for consideration and adoption,

Convinced of the need for the effective universal application of the principle of refraining from the threat or use of force in international relations and of the importance of the role of the United Nations in this regard,

Convinced also that the adoption of the Declaration on the Enhancement of the Effectiveness of the Principle of Refraining from the Threat or Use of Force in International Relations should contribute to the improvement of international relations,

1. *Approves* the Declaration on the Enhancement of the Effectiveness of the Principle of Refraining from the Threat or Use of Force in International Relations, the text of which is annexed to the present resolution;

2. *Expresses its appreciation* to the Special Committee on Enhancing the Effectiveness of the Principle of Non-Use of Force in International Relations for completing its work by elaborating the Declaration;

3. *Recommends* that every effort should he made so that the Declaration becomes generally known.

73rd plenary meeting
18 November 1987

Annex

Declaration on the Enhancement of the Effectiveness of the Principle of Refraining from the Threat or Use of Force in International Relations

The General Assembly,

Recalling the principle that States shall refrain in their international relations from the threat or use of force against the territorial integrity or political independence of any State, or in any other manner inconsistent with the purposes of the United Nations,

Recalling that this principle is enshrined in Article 2, paragraph 4, of the Charter of the United Nations and has been reaffirmed in a number of international instruments,

Reaffirming the Declaration on Principles of International Law Concerning Friendly Relations and Cooperation among States in accordance with the Charter of the United Nations,[2] the Definition of Aggression[3] and the Manila Declaration on the Peaceful Settlement of International Disputes,[4]

Reaffirming the obligation to maintain international peace and security in conformity with the purposes of the United Nations,

Expressing deep concern at the continued existence of situations of conflict and tension and the impact of the persistence of violations of the principle of refraining from the threat or use of force on the maintenance of international peace and security, as well as at the loss of human life and material damage in the countries affected, the development of which may thereby be set back,

Desiring to remove the risk of new armed conflicts between States by promoting a change in the international climate from confrontation to peaceful relations and cooperation and by taking other appropriate measures to strengthen international peace and security,

Convinced that, in the present world situation, in which nuclear weapons exist, there is no reasonable alternative to peaceful relations among States,

Fully aware that the question of general and complete disarmament is of the utmost importance and that peace, security, fundamental freedoms and economic and social development are indivisible,

Noting with concern the pernicious impact of terrorism on international relations,

Stressing the need for all States to desist from any forcible action aimed at depriving peoples of their right to self-determination, freedom and independence,

Reaffirming the obligation of States to settle their international disputes by peaceful means,

Conscious of the importance of strengthening the United Nations system of collective security,

Bearing in mind the universal significance of human rights and fundamental freedoms as essential factors for international peace and security,

Convinced that States have a common interest in promoting a stable and equitable world economic environment as an essential basis for world peace and that, to that end, they should strengthen international cooperation for development and work towards a new international economic order,

Reaffirming the commitment of States to the basic principle of the sovereign equality of States,

Reaffirming the inalienable right of every State to choose its political, economic, and social and cultural systems without interference in any form by another State,

Recalling that States are under an obligation not to intervene directly or indirectly, for any reason whatever, in the internal or external affairs of any other State,

Reaffirming the duty of States to refrain in their international relations from military, political, economic or any other form of coercion aimed against the political independence or territorial integrity of any State,

Reaffirming the principle of equal rights and self-determination of peoples enshrined in the Charter,

Reaffirming that States shall fulfil in good faith all their obligations under international law,

Aware of the urgent need to enhance the effectiveness of the principle that States shall refrain from the threat or use of force in order to contribute to the establishment of lasting peace and security for all States,

---

1 *Official Records of the General Assembly, Forty-second Session, Supplement No. 41* (A/42/41).

2 Resolution 2625 (XXV), annex.

3 Resolution 3314 (XXIX), annex.

4 Resolution 37/10, annex.

1. *Solemnly declares* that:

I

1. Every State has the duty to refrain in its international relations from the threat or use of force against the territorial integrity or political independence of any State, or in any other manner inconsistent with the purposes of the United Nations. Such a threat or use of force constitutes a violation of international law and of the Charter of the United Nations and entails international responsibility.

2. The principle of refraining from the threat or use of force in international relations is universal in character and is binding, regardless of each State's political, economic, social or cultural system or relations of alliance.

3. No consideration of whatever nature may be invoked to warrant resorting to the threat or use of force in violation of the Charter.

4. States have the duty not to urge, encourage or assist other States to resort to the threat or use of force in violation of the Charter.

5. By virtue of the principle of equal rights and self-determination enshrined in the Charter, all peoples have the right freely to determine, without external interference, their political status and to pursue their economic, social and cultural development, and every State has the duty to respect this right in accordance with the provisions of the Charter.

6. States shall fulfil their obligations under international law to refrain from organinzing, instigating, or assisting or participating in paramilitary, terrorist or subversive acts, including acts of mercenaries, in other States, or acquiescing in organized activities within their territory directed towards the commission of such acts.

7. States have the duty to abstain from armed intervention and all other forms of interference or attempted threats against the personality of the State or against its political, economic and cultural elements.

8. No State may use or encourage the use of economic, political or any other type of measures to coerce another State in order to obtain from it the subordination of the exercise of its sovereign rights and to secure from it advantages of any kind.

9. In accordance with the purposes and principles of the United Nations, States have the duty to refrain from propaganda for wars of aggression.

10. Neither acquisition of territory resulting from the threat or use of force nor any occupation of territory resulting from the threat or use of force in contravention of international law will be recognized as legal acquisition or occupation.

11. A treaty is void if its conclusion has been procured by the threat or use of force in violation of the principles of international law embodied in the Charter.

12. In conformity with the Charter and in accordance with the relevant paragraphs of the Declaration on Principles of International Law concerning Friendly Relations and Cooperation among States in accordance with the Charter of the United Nations, States shall fulfil in good faith all their international obligations.

13. States have the inherent right of individual or collective self-defence if an armed attack occurs, as set forth in the Charter.

II

14. States shall make every effort to build their international relations on the basis of mutual understanding, trust, respect and cooperation in all areas.

15. States should also promote bilateral and regional cooperation as one of the important means to enhance the effectiveness of the principle of refraining from the threat or use of force in international relations.

16. States shall abide by their commitment to the principle of peaceful settlement of disputes, which is inseparable from the principle of refraining from the threat or use of force in their international relations.

17. States parties to international disputes shall settle their disputes exclusively by peaceful means in such a manner that international peace and security, and justice, are not endangered. For this purpose they shall utilize such means as negotiation, inquiry, mediation, conciliation, arbitration, judicial settlement, resort to regional agencies or arrangements, or other peaceful means of their own choice, including good offices.

18. States shall take effective measures which, by their scope and by their nature, constitute steps towards the ultimate achievement of general and complete disarmament under strict and effective international control.

19. States should take effective measures in order to prevent the danger of any armed conflicts, including those in which nuclear weapons could be used, to prevent an arms race in outer space and to halt and reverse it on Earth, to lower the level of military confrontation and to enhance global stability.

20. States should cooperate in order to undertake active efforts aimed at ensuring the relaxation of international tensions, the consolidation of the international legal order and the respect of the system of international security established by the Charter of the United Nations.

21. States should establish appropriate confidence-building measures aimed at preventing and reducing tensions and at creating a better climate among them.

22. States reaffirm that the respect for effective exercise of all human rights and fundamental freedoms and protection thereof are essential factors for international peace and security, as well as for justice and the development of friendly relations and cooperation among all States. Consequently, they should promote and encourage respect for human rights and fundamental freedoms for all, without distinction as to race, sex, language or religion, *inter alia*, by strictly complying with their international obligations and considering, as appropriate, becoming parties to the principal international instruments in this field.

23. States shall cooperate at the bilateral, regional and international levels in order to:

(*a*) Prevent and combat international terrorism;

(*b*) Contribute actively to the elimination of the causes underlying international terrorism.

24. States shall endeavour to take concrete measures and promote favourable conditions in the international economic environment in order to achieve international peace, security and justice; they will take into account the interest of all in the narrowing of the differences in the levels of economic development, and in particular the interest of developing countries throughout the world.

III

25. The competent United Nations organs should make full use of the provisions of the Charter of the United Nations in the field of the maintenance of international peace and security with a view to enhancing the effectiveness of the principle of refraining from the threat or use of force in international relations.

26. States should cooperate fully with the organs of the United Nations in supporting their action relating to the maintenance of international peace and security and to the peaceful settlement of international disputes in accordance with the Charter. In particular, they should enhance the role of the Security Council so that it can fully and effectively discharge its duties. In this regard, the permanent members of the Council have a special responsibility under the Charter.

27. States should strive to enhance the effectiveness of the collective security system through the effective implementation of the provisions of the Charter, particularly those relating to the special responsibilities of the Security Council in this regard. They should also fully discharge their obligations to support United Nations peacekeeping operations decided upon in accordance with the Charter. States shall accept and carry out the decisions of the Council in accordance with the Charter.

28. States should give the Security Council every possible type of assistance in all actions taken by it for the just settlement of crisis situations and regional conflicts. They should strengthen the part the Council can play in preventing disputes and situations the continuation of which is likely to endanger the maintenance of international

peace and security. They should facilitate the task of the Council in reviewing situations of potential danger for international peace and security at as early a stage as possible.

29. The fact-finding capacity of the Security Council should be enhanced on an *ad hoc* basis in accordance with the Charter.

30. States should give full effect to the important role conferred by the Charter on the General Assembly in the area of peaceful settlement of disputes and the maintenance of international peace and security.

31. States should encourage the Secretary-General to exercise fully his functions with regard to the maintenance of international peace and security and the peaceful settlement of disputes, in accordance with the Charter, including those under Articles 98 and 99, and fully cooperate with him in this respect.

32. States should take into consideration that legal disputes should, as a general rule, be referred by the parties to the International Court of Justice in accordance with the provisions of the Statute of the Court as an important factor for strengthening the maintenance of international peace and security. The General Assembly and the Security Council should consider making use of the provisions of the Charter concerning the possibility of requesting the Court to give an advisory opinion on any legal question.

33. States parties to regional arrangements or agencies should consider making greater use of such arrangements and agencies for dealing with such matters relating to the maintenance of international peace and security as are appropriate, pursuant to Article 52 of the Charter;

2. *Declares* that nothing in the present Declaration shall be construed as:

(*a*) Enlarging or diminishing in any way the scope of the provisions of the Charter concerning cases in which the use of force is lawful;

(*b*) Prejudicing in any manner the relevant provisions of the Charter or the rights and duties of Member States or the scope of the functions and powers of the United Nations organs under the Charter, in particular those relating to the threat or use of force;

3. *Declares* that nothing in the present Declaration could in any way prejudice the right to self-determination, freedom and independence, as derived from the Charter, of peoples forcibly deprived of that right and referred to in the Declaration on Principles of International Law concerning Friendly Relations and Cooperation among States in accordance with the Charter of the United Nations, particularly peoples under colonial and racist régimes or other forms of alien domination; nor the right of these peoples to struggle to that end and to seek and receive support, in accordance with the principles of the Charter and in conformity with the above-mentioned Declaration;

4. *Confirms* that, in the event of a conflict between the obligations of Members of the United Nations under the Charter and their obligations under any other international agreement, their obligations under the Charter will prevail in accordance with Article 103 of the Charter.

46/62. Development and Strengthening of Good-Neighbourliness Between States

Committee: 6
Vote: Adopted without a vote
Ref.: 43/171, 42/158, 41/84, 39/78, 38/126, 37/117, 36/101, 34/99

The General Assembly,

Recalling that, in the Preamble to the Charter of the United Nations, living together in peace with one another as good neighbours is one of the means by which the ends of the United Nations are to be achieved,

Recalling the Declaration on Principles of International Law concerning Friendly Relations and Cooperation among States in accordance with the Charter of the United Nations, approved by its resolution 2625 (XXV) of 24 October 1970,

Considering that the great changes of a political, economic and social nature, as well as the scientific and technological advances that have taken place in the world and led to unprecedented interdependence of nations, have given new dimensions to good-neighbourliness in the conduct of States and increased the need to develop and strengthen it,

Bearing in mind that good-neighbourliness should continue to be taken into account by United Nations bodies in their efforts to promote and strengthen the rule of law,

1. *Reaffirms* that, by acting as good neighbours, States can help to ensure that the ends for which the United Nations was established are achieved;

2. *Emphasizes* that States should act as good neighbours whether or not they are contiguous;

3. *Calls upon* all States to keep in mind the need to act as good neighbors both in their dealings with other States and when taking decisions that could affect them;

4. *Expresses the conviction* that good-neighbourliness is best fostered by each State respecting the rule of law in its international relations, and by practical measures designated to promote good relations with other States;

5. *Decides* that the question of development and strengthening of good-neighbourliness between States should continue to guide States as a goal to be pursued in their consideration of the issues before the United Nations, and notes that it could be considered in the future.

67th plenary meeting
9 December 1991

01.20 PEACE AND SECURITY

290 (IV). Essentials of Peace

Committee: 1
Vote: 53 - 5 - 1

The General Assembly

1. *Declares* that the Charter of the United Nations, the most solemn pact of peace in history, lays down basic principles necessary for an enduring peace; that disregard of these principles is primarily responsible for the continuance of international tension; and that it is urgently necessary for all Members to act in accordance with these principles in the spirit of cooperation on which the United Nations was founded;

Calls upon every nation

2. *To refrain* from threatening or using force contrary to the Charter;

3. *To refrain* from any threats or acts, direct or indirect, aimed at impairing the freedom, independence or integrity of any State, or at fomenting civil strife and subverting the will of the people in any State;

4. *To carry out* in good faith its international agreements;

5. *To afford* all United Nations bodies full cooperation and free access in the performance of the tasks assigned to them under the Charter;

6. *To promote*, in recognition of the paramount importance of preserving the dignity and worth of the human person, full freedom for the peaceful expression of political opposition, full opportunity for the exercise of religious freedom and full respect for all the other fundamental rights expressed in the Universal Declaration of Human Rights;

7. *To promote* nationally and through international cooperation, efforts to achieve and sustain higher standards of living for all peoples;

8. *To remove* the barriers which deny to peoples the free exchange of information and ideas essential to international understanding and peace;

Calls upon every Member

9. *To participate* fully in all the work of the United Nations;

Calls upon the five permanent members of the Security Council

10. *To broaden* progressively their cooperation and to exercise restraint in the use of the veto in order to make the Security Council a more effective instrument for maintaining peace;

Calls upon every nation

11. *To settle* international disputes by peaceful means and to cooperate in supporting United Nations efforts to resolve outstanding problems;

12. *To cooperate* to attain the effective international regulation of conventional armaments; and

13. *To agree* to the exercise of national sovereignty jointly with other nations to the extent necessary to attain international control of atomic energy which would make effective the prohibition of atomic weapons and assure the use of atomic energy for peaceful purposes only.

261st plenary meeting
1 December 1949

380 (V). Peace Through Deeds

Committee: 1
Vote: 50 - 5 - 1

The General Assembly,

Recognizing the profound desire of all mankind to live in enduring peace and security, and in freedom from fear and want,

Confident that, if all governments faithfully reflect this desire and observe their obligations under the Charter, lasting peace and security can be established,

Condemning the intervention of a State in the internal affairs of another State for the purpose of changing its legally established government by the threat or use of force,

1. *Solemnly* reaffirms that, whatever the weapons used, any aggression, whether committed openly, or by fomenting civil strife in the interest of a foreign Power, or otherwise, is the gravest of all crimes against peace and security throughout the world;

2. *Determines* that for the realization of lasting peace and security it is indispensable:

(*1*) That prompt united action be taken to meet aggression wherever it arises;

(*2*) That every nation agree:

(*a*) To accept effective international control of atomic energy, under the United Nations, on the basis already approved[1] by the General Assembly in order to make effective the prohibition of atomic weapons;

(*b*) To strive for the control and elimination, under the United Nations, of all other weapons of mass destruction;

(*c*) To regulate all armaments and armed forces under a United Nations system of control and inspection, with a view to their gradual reduction;

(*d*) To reduce to a minimum the diversion for armaments of its human and economic resources and to strive towards the development of such resources for the general welfare, with due regard to the needs of the under-developed areas of the world;

1 See resolution 1 (I), 41 (I), 191 (III), 192 (III), 290 (IV) and 299 (IV).

3. *Declares* that these goals can be attained if all the Members of the United Nations demonstrate by their deeds their will to achieve peace.

308th plenary meeting
17 November 1950

381 (V). Condemnation of Propaganda Against Peace

Committee: 1
Vote: 49 - 0 - 7

The General Assembly,

1. *Reaffirms* its resolutions 110 (II) and 290 (IV), paragraph 8, which condemn all propaganda against peace and recommend the free exchange of information and ideas as one of the foundations of good-neighbourly relations between the peoples;

2. *Declares* that such propaganda includes:

(*1*) Incitement to conflicts or acts of aggression;

(*2*) Measures tending to isolate the peoples from any contact with the outside world, by preventing the Press, radio and other media of communication from reporting international events, and thus hindering mutual comprehension and understanding between peoples;

(*3*) Measures tending to silence or distort the activities of the United Nations in favour of peace or to prevent their peoples from knowing the views of other States Members.

308th plenary meeting
17 November 1950

2037 (XX). Declaration on the Promotion among Youth of the Ideals of Peace, Mutual Respect and Understanding Between Peoples

Committee: 3
Vote: Adopted without a vote
Ref.: 3023(XXVIII), 1965(XVIII), 1842(XVII), 1838(XVII), 1572(XV)

The General Assembly,

Recalling that under the terms of the Charter of the United Nations the peoples have declared themselves determined to save succeeding generations from the scourge of war,

Recalling further that in the Charter the United Nations has affirmed its faith in fundamental human rights, in the dignity of the human person and in the equal rights of men and nations,

Reaffirming the principles embodied in the Universal Declaration of Human Rights,[2] the Declaration on the Granting of Independence to Colonial Countries and Peoples,[3] the United Nations Declaration on the Elimination of All Forms of Racial Discrimination,[4] General Assembly resolution 110 (II) of 3 November 1947 condemning all forms of propaganda designed or likely to provoke or encourage any threat to the peace, the Declaration of the Rights of the Child,[5] and General Assembly resolution 1572 (XV) of 18 December 1960, which have a particular bearing upon the upbringing of young people in a spirit of peace, mutual respect and understanding among peoples,

Recalling that the purpose of the United Nations Educational, Scientific and Cultural Organization is to contribute to peace and security by promoting collaboration among nations through education, science and culture, and recognizing the role and contributions of that organization towards the education of young people in the spirit of international understanding, cooperation and peace,

Taking into consideration the fact that in the conflagrations which have afflicted mankind it is the young people who have had to suffer most and who have had the greatest number of victims,

2 Resolution 217 A (III) of 10 December 1948.

3 Resolution 1514 (XV) of 14 December 1960.

4 Resolution 1904 (XVIII) of 20 November 1963.

5 Resolution 1386 (XIV) of 20 November 1959.

Convinced that young people wish to have an assured future and that peace, freedom and justice are among the chief guarantees that their desire for happiness will be fulfilled,

Bearing in mind the important part being played by young people in every field of human endeavour and the fact that they are destined to guide the fortunes of mankind,

Bearing in mind furthermore that, in this age of great scientific, technological and cultural achievements, the energies, enthusiasm and creative abilities of the young should be devoted to the material and spiritual advancement of all peoples,

Convinced that the young should know, respect and develop the cultural heritage of their own country and that of all mankind,

Convinced furthermore that the education of the young and exchanges of young people and of ideas in a spirit of peace, mutual respect and understanding between peoples can help to improve international relations and to strengthen peace and security,

Proclaims this Declaration on the Promotion among Youth of the Ideals of Peace, Mutual Respect and Understanding between Peoples and calls upon Governments, non-governmental organizations and youth movements to recognize the principles set forth therein and to ensure their observance by means of appropriate measures:

Principle I

Young people shall be brought up in the spirit of peace, justice, freedom, mutual respect and understanding in order to promote equal rights for all human beings and all nations, economic and social progress, disarmament and the maintenance of international peace and security.

Principle II

All means of education, including as of major importance the guidance given by parents or family, instruction and information intended for the young should foster among them the ideals of peace, humanity, liberty and international solidarity and all other ideals which help to bring peoples closer together, and acquaint them with the role entrusted to the United Nations as a means of preserving and maintaining peace and promoting international understanding and cooperation.

Principle III

Young people shall be brought up in the knowledge of the dignity and equality of all men, without distinction as to race, colour, ethnic origins or beliefs, and in respect for fundamental human rights and for the right of peoples to self-determination.

Principle IV

Exchanges, travel, tourism, meetings, the study of foreign languages, the twinning of towns and universities without discrimination and similar activities should be encouraged and facilitated among young people of all countries in order to bring them together in educational, cultural and sporting activities in the spirit of this Declaration.

Principle V

National and international associations of young people should be encouraged to promote the purposes of the United Nations, particularly international peace and security, friendly relations among nations based on respect for the equal sovereignty of States, the final abolition of colonialism and of racial discrimination and other violations of human rights.

Youth organizations in accordance with this Declaration should take all appropriate measures within their respective fields of activity in order to make their contribution without any discrimination to the work of educating the young generation in accordance with these ideals.

Such organizations, in conformity with the principle of freedom of association, should promote the free exchange of ideas in the spirit of the principles of this Declaration and of the purposes of the United Nations set forth in the Charter.

All youth organizations should conform to the principles set forth in this Declaration.

Principle VI

A major aim in educating the young shall be to develop all their faculties and to train them to acquire higher moral qualities, to be deeply attached to the noble ideals of peace, liberty, the dignity and equality of all men, and imbued with respect and love for humanity and its creative achievements. To this end the family has an important role to play.

Young people must become conscious of their responsibilities in the world they will be called upon to manage and should be inspired with confidence in a future of happiness for mankind.

1390th plenary meeting
7 December 1965

2734 (XXV). Declaration on the Strengthening of International Security

Committee: 1
Vote: 120 - 1 - 1
Ref.: 48/83, 45/80, 44/216, 43/88, 42/92, 41/90, 40/158, 39/156, 39/155, 39/154, 38/190, 37/118, 36/103, 35/158, 34/100, 33/75, 3389(XXX), 3185(XXVIII), 2993(XXVII), 809(IX), 703(VII), 503(VI)

The General Assembly,

Recalling the determination of the peoples of the United Nations, as proclaimed by the Charter, to save succeeding generations from the scourge of war, and to this end to live together in peace with one another as good neighbours and to unite their strength to maintain international peace and security,

Considering that in order to fulfil the purposes and principles of the United Nations Member States must strictly abide by all provisions of the Charter,

Recalling its resolution 2606 (XXIV) of 16 December 1969 in which the General Assembly, *inter alia*, expressed the desire that the twenty-fifth year of the Organization's existence should be marked by new initiatives to promote peace, security, disarmament and economic and social progress for all mankind and the conviction of the urgent need to make the United Nations more effective as an instrument for maintaining international peace and security,

Mindful of the observations, proposals and suggestions advanced during the debate at the twenty-fourth session of the General Assembly or presented subsequently by Governments of Member States concerning the attainment of this objective, and of the report submitted by the Secretary-General in conformity with paragraph 5 of resolution 2606 (XXIV),[1]

Having in mind the Declaration on Principles of International Law concerning Friendly Relations and Cooperation among States in accordance with the Charter of the United Nations, adopted unanimously at the current session,[2]

Conscious of its duty to examine in depth the present international situation and to study the means and recourses provided by the relevant provisions of the Charter in order to build peace, security and cooperation in the world,

1. *Solemnly reaffirms* the universal and unconditional validity of the purposes and principles of the Charter of the United Nations as the basis of relations among States irrespective of their size, geographical location, level of development or political, economic and social systems and declares that the breach of these principles cannot be justified in any circumstances whatsoever;

2. *Calls upon* all States to adhere strictly in their international relations to the purposes and principles of the Charter, including the principle that States shall refrain in their international relations from the threat or use of force against the territorial integrity or political independence of any State or in any other manner inconsistent with

---

1 A/7922 and Add.1-6.

2 Resolution 2625 (XXV).

the purposes of the United Nations; the principle that States shall settle their international disputes by peaceful means in such a manner that international peace and security and justice are not endangered; the duty not to intervene in matters within the domestic jurisdiction of any State, in accordance with the Charter; the duty of States to cooperate with one another in accordance with the Charter; the principle of equal rights and self-determination of peoples; the principle of sovereign equality of States; and the principle that States shall fulfil in good faith the obligations assumed by them in accordance with the Charter;

3. *Solemnly reaffirms* that, in the event of a conflict between the obligations of the Members of the United Nations under the Charter and their obligations under any other international agreement, their obligations under the Charter shall prevail;

4. *Solemnly reaffirms* that States must fully respect the sovereignty of other States and the right of peoples to determine their own destinies, free of external intervention, coercion or constraint, especially involving the threat or use of force, overt or covert, and refrain from any attempt aimed at the partial or total disruption of the national unity and territorial integrity of any other State or country;

5. *Solemnly reaffirms* that every State has the duty to refrain from the threat or use of force against the territorial integrity and political independence of any other State, and that the territory of a State shall not be the object of military occupation resulting from the use of force in contravention of the provisions of the Charter, that the territory of a State shall not be the object of acquisition by another State resulting from the threat or use of force, that no territorial acquisition resulting from the threat or use of force shall be recognized as legal and that every State has the duty to refrain from organizing, instigating, assisting or participating in acts of civil strife or terrorist acts in another State;

6. *Urges* Member States to make full use and seek improved implementation of the means and methods provided for in the Charter for the exclusively peaceful settlement of any dispute or any situation, the continuance of which is likely to endanger the maintenance of international peace and security, including negotiation, inquiry, mediation, conciliation, arbitration, judicial settlement, resort to regional agencies or arrangements, good offices including those of the Secretary-General, or other peaceful means of their own choice, it being understood that the Security Council in dealing with such disputes or situations should also take into consideration that legal disputes should as a general rule be referred by the parties to the International Court of Justice in accordance with the provisions of the Statute of the Court;

7. *Urges* all Member States to respond to the immediate need to agree on guidelines for more effective peace-keeping operations in accordance with the Charter, which could increase the effectiveness of the United Nations in dealing with situations endangering international peace and security, and consequently to support the efforts of the Special Committee on Peace-keeping Operations to reach agreement on all questions relating to such operations, as well as on provisions for their appropriate and equitable financing;

8. *Recognizes* the need for effective, dynamic and flexible measures, in accordance with the Charter, to prevent and remove threats to the peace, suppress acts of aggression or other breaches of the peace, and in particular for measures to build, maintain and restore international peace and security;

9. *Recommends* that the Security Council take steps to facilitate the conclusion of the agreements envisaged in Article 43 of the Charter in order fully to develop its capacity for enforcement action as provided for under Chapter VII of the Charter;

10. *Recommends* that the Security Council consider, in conformity with Article 29 of the Charter, whenever appropriate and necessary, the desirability of establishing subsidiary organs, on an *ad hoc* basis, and with the participation of the parties concerned, when conditions so warrant, to assist the Council in the performance of its functions as defined in the Charter;

11. *Recommends* that all States contribute to the efforts to ensure peace and security for all nations and to establish, in accordance with the Charter, an effective system of universal collective security without military alliances;

12. *Invites* Member States to do their utmost to enhance by all possible means the authority and effectiveness of the Security Council and of its decisions;

13. *Calls upon* the Security Council, including the permanent members, to intensify efforts to discharge, in conformity with the Charter, its primary responsibility for the maintenance of international peace and security;

14. *Recommends* that Member States support the efforts of the Special Committee on the Question of Defining Aggression to bring its work to a successful conclusion, thus achieving the definition of aggression as soon as possible;

15. *Reaffirms* its competence under the Charter to discuss and recommend measures for the peaceful adjustment of any situation which it deems likely to impair the general welfare or friendly relations among States, including situations resulting from a violation of the provisions of the Charter setting forth the purposes and principles of the United Nations;

16. *Urges* all Member States to implement the decisions of the Security Council in accordance with their obligations under Article 25 of the Charter and to respect, as provided for in the Charter, the resolutions of United Nations organs responsible for the maintenance of international peace and security and the peaceful settlement of disputes;

17. *Urges* Member States to reaffirm their will to respect fully their obligations under international law in accordance with the relevant provisions of the Charter and to continue and intensify the efforts towards the progressive development and codification of international law;

18. *Calls upon* all States to desist from any forcible or other action which deprives peoples, in particular those still under colonial or any other form of external domination, of their inalienable right to self-determination, freedom and independence and to refrain from military and repressive measures aimed at preventing the attainment of independence by all dependent peoples in accordance with the Charter and in furtherance of the objectives of General Assembly resolution 1514 (XV) of 14 December 1960, and render assistance to the United Nations and, in accordance with the Charter, to the oppressed peoples in their legitimate struggle in order to bring about the speedy elimination of colonialism or any other form of external domination;

19. *Affirms* its belief that there is a close connexion between the strengthening of international security, disarmament and the economic development of countries, so that any progress made towards any of these objectives will constitute progress towards all of them;

20. *Urges* all States, particularly the nuclear-weapon States, to make urgent and concerted efforts within the framework of the Disarmament Decade and through other means for the cessation and reversal of the nuclear and conventional arms race at an early date, the elimination of nuclear weapons and other weapons of mass destruction and the conclusion of a treaty on general and complete disarmament under effective international control, as well as to ensure that the benefits of the technology of the peaceful use of nuclear energy shall be available to all States, to the maximum extent possible, without discrimination;

21. *Emphatically reiterates* the need to undertake, within the framework of the Second United Nations Development Decade, urgent and concerted international action based on a global strategy aimed at reducing and eliminating as soon as possible the economic gap between developed and developing countries, which is closely and essentially correlated to the strengthening of the security of all nations and the establishment of lasting international peace;

22. *Solemnly reaffirms* that universal respect for and full exercise of human rights and fundamental freedoms and the elimination of the violation of those rights are urgent and essential to the strengthening of international security, and hence resolutely condemns all forms of oppression, tyranny and discrimination, particularly racism and racial discrimination, wherever they occur;

23. *Resolutely condemns* the criminal policy of apartheid of the Government of South Africa and reaffirms the legitimacy of the struggle of the oppressed peoples to attain their human rights and fundamental freedoms and self-determination;

24. *Expresses its conviction* that the achievement of universality of the United Nations, in accordance with the Charter, would increase its effectiveness in strengthening international peace and security;

25. *Considers* that the promotion of international cooperation, including regional, subregional and bilateral cooperation among States, in keeping with the provisions of the Charter and based on the principle of equal rights and on strict respect for the sovereignty and independence of States, can contribute to the strengthening of international security;

26. *Welcomes* the decision of the Security Council[1] to hold periodic meetings in accordance with Article 28, paragraph 2, of the Charter and expresses the hope that these meetings will make an important contribution to the strengthening of international security;

27. *Emphasizes* the need for the United Nations to exert continuous efforts for the strengthening of international peace and security and requests the Secretary-General to submit a report to the General Assembly at its twenty-sixth session on steps taken in pursuance of the present Declaration.

1932nd plenary meeting
16 December 1970

3314 (XXIX). Definition of Aggression

Committee: 6
Vote: Adopted without a vote
Ref.: 3105(XXVIII), 2967(XXVII), 2781(XXVI), 2644(XXV), 2549(XXIV), 2420(XXIII), 2330(XXII), 1181(XII), 895(IX), 688(VII), 599(VI)

The General Assembly,

Having considered the report of the Special Committee on the Question of Defining Aggression, established pursuant to its resolution 2330 (XXII) of 18 December 1967, covering the work of its seventh session held from 11 March to 12 April 1974, including the draft Definition of Aggression adopted by the Special Committee by consensus and recommended for adoption by the General Assembly,[2]

Deeply convinced that the adoption of the Definition of Aggression would contribute to the strengthening of international peace and security,

1. *Approves* the Definition of Aggression, the text of which is annexed to the present resolution;

2. *Expresses its appreciation* to the Special Committee on the Question of Defining Aggression for its work which resulted in the elaboration of the Definition of Aggression;

3. *Calls upon* all States to refrain from all acts of aggression and other uses of force contrary to the Charter of the United Nations and the Declaration on Principles of International Law concerning Friendly Relations and Cooperation among States in accordance with the Charter of the United Nations;[3]

4. *Calls the attention* of the Security Council to the Definition of Aggression, as set out below, and recommends that it should, as appropriate, take account of that Definition as guidance in determining, in accordance with the Charter, the existence of an act of aggression.

2319th plenary meeting
14 December 1974

1 See *Official Records of the Security Council, Twenty-fifth Year,* 1544th meeting.

2 *Official Records of the General Assembly, Twenty-ninth Session, Supplement No. 19* (A/9619 and Corr.1).

3 Resolution 2625 (XXV), annex.

Annex

Definition of Aggression

The General Assembly,

Basing itself on the fact that one of the fundamental purposes of the United Nations is to maintain international peace and security and to take effective collective measures for the prevention and removal of threats to the peace, and for the suppression of acts of aggression or other breaches of the peace,

Recalling that the Security Council, in accordance with Article 39 of the Charter of the United Nations, shall determine the existence of any threat to the peace, breach of the peace or act of aggression and shall make recommendations, or decide what measures shall be taken in accordance with Articles 41 and 42, to maintain or restore international peace and security,

Recalling also the duty of States under the Charter to settle their international disputes by peaceful means in order not to endanger international peace, security and justice,

Bearing in mind that nothing in this Definition shall be interpreted as in any way affecting the scope of the provisions of the Charter with respect to the functions and powers of the organs of the United Nations,

Considering also that, since aggression is the most serious and dangerous form of the illegal use of force, being fraught, in the conditions created by the existence of all types of weapons of mass destruction, with the possible threat of a world conflict and all its catastrophic consequences, aggression should be defined at the present stage,

Reaffirming the duty of States not to use armed force to deprive peoples of their right to self-determination, freedom and independence, or to disrupt territorial integrity,

Reaffirming also that the territory of a State shall not be violated by being the object, even temporarily, of military occupation or of other measures of force taken by another State in contravention of the Charter, and that it shall not be the object of acquisition by another State resulting from such measures or the threat thereof,

Reaffirming also the provisions of the Declaration on Principles of International Law concerning Friendly Relations and Cooperation among States in accordance with the Charter of the United Nations,

Convinced that the adoption of a definition of aggression ought to have the effect of deterring a potential aggressor, would simplify the determination of acts of aggression and the implementation of measures to suppress them and would also facilitate the protection of the rights and lawful interests of, and the rendering of assistance to, the victim,

Believing that, although the question whether an act of aggression has been committed must be considered in the light of all the circumstances of each particular case, it is nevertheless desirable to formulate basic principles as guidance for such determination,

Adopts the following Definition of Agression:[4]

Article 1

Aggression is the use of armed force by a State against the sovereignty, territorial integrity or political independence of another State, or in any other manner inconsistent with the Charter of the United Nations, as set out in this Definition.

Explanatory note: In this Definition the term "State":

(*a*) Is used without prejudice to questions of recognition or to whether a State is a member of the United Nations;

(*b*) Includes the concept of a "group of States" where appropriate.

4 Explanatory notes on articles 3 and 5 are to be found in paragraph 20 of the Report of the Special Committee on the Question of Defining Aggression *(Official Records of the General Assembly, Twenty-ninth Session, Supplement No. 19* (A/9619 and Corr.1). Statements on the Definition are contained in paragraphs 9 and 10 of the report of the Sixth Committee (A/9890).

Article 2

The first use of armed force by a State in contravention of the Charter shall constitute *prima facie* evidence of an act of aggression although the Security Council may, in conformity with the Charter, conclude that a determination that an act of aggression has been committed would not be justified in the light of other relevant circumstances, including the fact that the acts concerned or their consequences are not of sufficient gravity.

Article 3

Any of the following acts, regardless of a declaration of war, shall, subject to and in accordance with the provisions of article 2, qualify as an act of aggression:

(*a*) The invasion or attack by the armed forces of a State of the territory of another State, or any military occupation, however temporary, resulting from such invasion or attack, or any annexation by the use of force of the territory of another State or part thereof;

(*b*) Bombardment by the armed forces of a State against the territory of another State or the use of any weapons by a State against the territory of another State;

(*c*) The blockade of the ports or coasts of a State by the armed forces of another State;

(*d*) An attack by the armed forces of a State on the land, sea or air forces, or marine and air fleets of another State;

(*e*) The use of armed forces of one State which are within the territory of another State with the agreement of the receiving State, in contravention of the conditions provided for in the agreement or any extension of their presence in such territory beyond the termination of the agreement;

(*f*) The action of a State in allowing its territory, which it has placed at the disposal of another State, to be used by that other State for perpetrating an act of aggression against a third State;

(*g*) The sending by or on behalf of a State of armed bands, groups, irregulars or mercenaries, which carry out acts of armed force against another State of such gravity as to amount to the acts listed above, or its substantial involvement therein.

Article 4

The acts enumerated above are not exhaustive and the Security Council may determine that other acts constitute aggression under the provisions of the Charter.

Article 5

1. No consideration of whatever nature, whether political, economic, military or otherwise, may serve as a justification for aggression.

2. A war of aggression is a crime against international peace. Aggression gives rise to international responsibility.

3. No territorial acquisition or special advantage resulting from aggression is or shall be recognized as lawful.

Article 6

Nothing in this Definition shall be construed as in any way enlarging or diminishing the scope of the Charter, including its provisions concerning cases in which the use of force is lawful.

Article 7

Nothing in this Definition, and in particular article 3, could in any way prejudice the right to self-determination, freedom and independence, as derived from the Charter, of peoples forcibly deprived of that right and referred to in the Declaration on Principles of International Law concerning Friendly Relations and Cooperation among States in accordance with the Charter of the United Nations, particularly peoples under colonial and racist régimes or other forms of alien domination: nor the right of these peoples to struggle to that end and to seek and receive support, in accordance with the principles of the Charter and in conformity with the above-mentioned Declaration.

Article 8

In their interpretation and application the above provisions are interrelated and each provision should be construed in the context of the other provisions.

3384 (XXX). Declaration on the Use of Scientific and Technological Progress in the Interests of Peace and for the Benefit of Mankind

Committee: 3
Vote: 97 - 0 - 20
Ref.: 3269(XXIX), 3150(XXVIII)

The General Assembly,

Noting that scientific and technological progress has become one of the most important factors in the development of human society,

Taking into consideration that, while scientific and technological developments provide ever increasing opportunities to better the conditions of life of peoples and nations, in a number of instances they can give rise to social problems, as well as threaten the human rights and fundamental freedoms of the individual,

Noting with concern that scientific and technological achievements can be used to intensify the arms race, suppress national liberation movements and deprive individuals and peoples of their human rights and fundamental freedoms,

Also noting with concern that scientific and technological achievements can entail dangers for the civil and political rights of the individual or of the group and for human dignity,

Noting the urgent need to make full use of scientific and technological developments for the welfare of man and to neutralize the present and possible future harmful consequences of certain scientific and technological achievements,

Recognizing that scientific and technological progress is of great importance in accelerating the social and economic development of developing countries,

Aware that the transfer of science and technology is one of the principal ways of accelerating the economic development of developing countries,

Reaffirming the right of peoples to self-determination and the need to respect human rights and freedoms and the dignity of the human person in the conditions of scientific and technological progress,

Desiring to promote the realization of the principles which form the basis of the Charter of the United Nations, the Universal Declaration of Human Rights, the International Covenants on Human Rights, the Declaration on the Granting of Independence to Colonial Countries and Peoples, the Declaration on Principles of International Law concerning Friendly Relations and Cooperation among States in accordance with the Charter of the United Nations, the Declaration on Social Progress and Development, and the Charter of Economic Rights and Duties of States,

Solemnly proclaims that:

1. All States shall promote international cooperation to ensure that the results of scientific and technological developments are used in the interests of strengthening international peace and security, freedom and independence, and also for the purpose of the economic and social development of peoples and the realization of human rights and freedoms in accordance with the Charter of the United Nations.

2. All States shall take appropriate measures to prevent the use of scientific and technological developments, particularly by the State organs, to limit or interfere with the enjoyment of the human rights and fundamental freedoms of the individual as enshrined in the Universal Declaration of Human Rights, the International Covenants on Human Rights and other relevant international instruments.

3. All States shall take measures to ensure that scientific and technological achievements satisfy the material and spiritual needs of all sectors of the population.

4. All States shall refrain from any acts involving the use of scientific and technological achievements for the purposes of violating the

sovereignty and territorial integrity of other States, interfering in their internal affairs, waging aggressive wars, suppressing national liberation movements or pursuing a policy of racial discrimination. Such acts are not only a flagrant violation of the Charter of the United Nations and principles of international law, but constitute an inadmissible distortion of the purposes that should guide scientific and technological developments for the benefit of mankind.

5. All States shall cooperate in the establishment, strengthening and development of the scientific and technological capacity of developing countries with a view to accelerating the realization of the social and economic rights of the peoples of those countries.

6. All States shall take measures to extend the benefits of science and technology to all strata of the population and to protect them, both socially and materially, from possible harmful effects of the misuse of scientific and technological developments, including their misuse to infringe upon the rights of the individual or of the group, particularly with regard to respect for privacy and the protection of the human personality and its physical and intellectual integrity.

7. All States shall take the necessary measures, including legislative measures, to ensure that the utilization of scientific and technological achievements promotes the fullest realization of human rights and fundamental freedoms without any discrimination whatsoever on grounds of race, sex, language or religious beliefs.

8. All States shall take effective measures, including legislative measures, to prevent and preclude the utilization of scientific and technological achievements to the detriment of human rights and fundamental freedoms and the dignity of the human person.

9. All States shall, whenever necessary, take action to ensure compliance with legislation guaranteeing human rights and freedoms in the conditions of scientific and technological developments.

2400th plenary meeting
10 November 1975

32/155. Declaration on the Deepening and Consolidation of International Détente

Committee: 1
Vote: Adopted without a vote

The General Assembly,

Adopts the following Declaration:

Declaration on the deepening and consolidation of international détente

The States Members of the United Nations,

Reaffirming their full commitment to the purposes and principles of the Charter of the United Nations and their resolve to ensure conditions in which all peoples can live and prosper in peace with justice,

Recalling the Declaration on Principles of International Law concerning Friendly Relations and Cooperation among States in accordance with the Charter of the United Nations of 24 October 1970,[1] the Declaration on the Strengthening of International Security of 16 December 1970,[2] as well as the Declaration on the Granting of Independence to Colonial Countries and Peoples of 14 December 1960[3] and the Definition of Aggression of 14 December 1974,[4]

Recognizing that, in order to resolve effectively international problems, an ever increasing degree of harmony and cooperation among nations is called for,

Anxious to create conditions whereby all States can put all their resources to the task of improving the living conditions of their peoples without fear of coercion, threat or use of force,

Noting with satisfaction a growing interest in and increased desire for relaxation of tension in recent years,

Convinced of the urgent need to exert additional efforts to extend this trend to encompass all regions of the world and facilitate the settlement of outstanding international problems by peaceful means through participation of and cooperation among States,

Recognizing that the continuation of the policies of confrontation and rivalry among States or groups of States is incompatible with the relaxation of international tension,

Reaffirming the indivisibility of peace and security in all parts of the world and the increasing interdependence among nations, and anxious therefore to work towards the removal of all sources of tension and friction,

Convinced that confidence-building measures could contribute to the relaxation of international tension,

Convinced also that progress in arms control and disarmament negotiations, particularly in the nuclear field, and the elimination of the threat of war are of great importance for the continued relaxation of tension and for further development of friendly relations among States,

Convinced that the establishment of just and equitable economic relations among States is an important condition for genuine and lasting peace and for harmony among nations,

Convinced also of the need to eliminate all forms of aggression, foreign occupation and interference in the internal affairs of other States, to ensure respect for human rights, to eliminate colonialism through the free exercise of the right of self-determination and to eradicate racism and apartheid and other forms of injustice,

Guided, therefore, by the need for all States, in the supreme interest of peace and the future of mankind, to continue their efforts towards further reduction of tension, the promotion of better relations among themselves and the strengthening and widening of détente, and, to that end,

Declare their determination:

1. To adhere firmly to and promote the implementation of the provisions of the Charter of the United Nations, as well as the universally accepted principles and declarations aimed at enhancing world peace and security and the development of friendly and cooperative relations among States, and to fulfil their obligations arising from multilateral treaties and agreements serving the achievement of these objectives;

2. To consider taking new and meaningful steps, both in bilateral and multilateral arms control negotiation forums, aimed at achieving the objective of a cessation of the arms race, in particular the nuclear arms race, at an early stage and realization of disarmament measures, especially nuclear disarmament, with the ultimate objective of general and complete disarmament under strict and effective international control;

3. To facilitate the peaceful and speedy settlement of outstanding international problems and to strive to remove both causes and effects of international tension so that relations among all States may evolve in the direction of cooperation and friendship in order to prevent the recurrence of situations which might endanger international peace and security;

4. To strengthen the role of the United Nations as a primary instrument in the maintenance of international peace and security by reinforcing both the peace-making and peace-keeping capabilities of the Organization;

5. To refrain from the threat or use of force and to abide in their relations with other States by the principles of sovereign equality, territorial integrity, inviolability of international frontiers, inadmissibility of the acquisition and occupation of the territories of other States by force, settlement of disputes - including frontier disputes - strictly by peaceful means, non-intervention and non-interference in the internal affairs of other States, respect for human rights, respect for the right of all nations to choose freely their social, political and economic systems and to develop their external relations in the way they deem best for the interest of their respective peoples in conformity with the Charter of the United Nations;

---

1 Resolution 2625 (XXV), annex.

2 Resolution 2734 (XXV).

3 Resolution 1514 (XV).

4 Resolution 3314 (XXIX), annex.

6. To ensure the free exercise of the right of the peoples under colonial and alien domination to self-determination and to promote majority rule, especially where racial oppression, in particular apartheid, has deprived peoples from exercising their inalienable rights;

7. To work towards the establishment and development of just and balanced economic relations among States and to strive to narrow the gap between the developed and developing countries, in accordance with the resolutions of the General Assembly adopted by consensus at its sixth and seventh special sessions on the establishment of the new international economic order;[1]

8. To encourage and promote respect for human rights and fundamental freedoms for all in conformity with the Universal Declaration of Human Rights and other relevant international treaties and instruments, including the International Covenants on Human Rights;[2]

9. To foster mutual understanding and trust among peoples by promoting and facilitating cultural exchanges, freer movement and contacts among them both on an individual and a collective basis;

10. To develop further their relations and cooperation in conformity with the purposes and principles of the Charter of the United Nations and to observe the principles set forth above which derive from the Charter, recognizing that nothing in the present Declaration could either alter or detract from obligations they might have undertaken in relation to other States in accordance with the principles of international law and the Charter.

106th plenary meeting
19 December 1977

33/73. Declaration on the Preparation of Societies for Life in Peace

Committee: 1
Vote: 138 - 0 - 2
Ref.: 42/91, 39/157, 36/104

The General Assembly,

Recalling that in the Charter the peoples of the United Nations proclaimed their determination to save succeeding generations from the scourge of war and that one of the fundamental purposes of the United Nations is to maintain international peace and security,

Reaffirming that, in accordance with General Assembly resolution 95 (I) of 11 December 1946, planning, preparation, initiation or waging of a war of aggression are crimes against peace and that, pursuant to the Declaration on Principles of International Law concerning Friendly Relations and Cooperation among States in accordance with the Charter of the United Nations, of 24 October 1970,[3] and the Definition of Aggression of 14 December 1974,[4] a war of aggression constitutes a crime against the peace,

Reaffirming the right of individuals, States and all mankind to life in peace,

Aware that, since wars begin in the minds of men, it is in the minds of men that the defences of peace must be constructed,

Recognizing that peace among nations is mankind's paramount value, held in the highest esteem by all principal political, social and religious movements,

Guided by the lofty goal of preparing societies for and creating conditions of their common existence and cooperation in peace, equality, mutual confidence and understanding,

Recognizing the essential role of Governments, as well as governmental and non-governmental organizations, both national and international, the mass media, educational processes and teaching methods, in promoting the ideals of peace and understanding among nations,

Convinced that, in the era of modern scientific and technological progress, mankind's resources, energy and creative talents should be directed to the peaceful economic, social and cultural development of all countries, should promote the implementation of the new international economic order and should serve the raising of the living standards of all nations,

Stressing with utmost concern that the arms race, in particular in the nuclear field, and the development of new types and systems of weapons, based on modern scientific principles and achievements, threaten world peace,

Recalling that, in the Final Document of the Tenth Special Session of the General Assembly,[5] the States Members of the United Nations solemnly reaffirmed their determination to make further collective efforts aimed at strengthening peace and international security and eliminating the threat of war, and agreed that, in order to facilitate the process of disarmament, it was necessary to take measures and pursue policies to strengthen international peace and security and to build confidence among States,

Reaffirming the principles contained in the Declaration on the Granting of Independence to Colonial Countries and Peoples, of 14 December 1960,[6] the Declaration on the Strengthening of International Security, of 16 December 1970[7] and the Declaration on the Deepening and Consolidation of International Détente, of 19 December 1977,[8]

Recalling the Declaration on the Promotion among Youth of the Ideals of Peace, Mutual Respect and Understanding between Peoples, of 7 December 1965,[9]

Further recalling the Universal Declaration of Human Rights, of 10 December 1948,[10] as well as the International Covenant on Civil and Political Rights, of 16 December 1966,[11] and bearing in mind that the latter states, *inter alia*, that any propaganda for war shall be prohibited by law,

I

Solemnly invites all States to guide themselves in their activities by the recognition of the supreme importance and necessity of establishing, maintaining and strengthening a just and durable peace for present and future generations and, in particular, to observe the following principles:

1. Every nation and every human being, regardless of race, conscience, language or sex, has the inherent right to life in peace. Respect for that right, as well as for the other human rights, is in the common interest of all mankind and an indispensable condition of advancement of all nations, large and small, in all fields.

2. A war of aggression, its planning, preparation or initiation are crimes against peace and are prohibited by international law.

3. In accordance with the purposes and principles of the United Nations, States have the duty to refrain from propaganda for wars of aggression.

4. Every State, acting in the spirit of friendship and good-neighbourly relations, has the duty to promote all-round, mutually advantageous and equitable political, economic, social and cultural cooperation with other States, notwithstanding their socio-economic systems, with a view to securing their common existence and cooperation in peace, in conditions of mutual understanding of and respect for the identity and diversity of all peoples, and the duty to take up actions conducive to the furtherance of the ideals of peace, humanism and freedom.

5. Every State has the duty to respect the right of all peoples to self-determination, independence, equality, sovereignty, the territorial integrity of States and the inviolability of their frontiers, including

1 Resolutions 3201 (S-VI), 3202 (S-VI) and 3362 (S-VII).

2 Resolution 2200 A (XXI), annex.

3 Resolution 2625 (XXV), annex.

4 Resolution 3314 (XXIX), annex.

5 Resolution S-10/2.

6 Resolution 1514 (XV).

7 Resolution 2734 (XXV).

8 Resolution 32/155.

9 Resolution 2037 (XX).

10 Resolution 217 A (III).

11 Resolution 2200 A (XXI), annex.

the right to determine the road of their development, without interference or intervention in their internal affairs.

6. A basic instrument of the maintenance of peace is the elimination of the threat inherent in the arms race, as well as efforts towards general and complete disarmament, under effective international control, including partial measures with that end in view, in accordance with the principles agreed upon within the United Nations and relevant international agreements.

7. Every State has the duty to discourage all manifestations and practices of colonialism, as well as racism, racial discrimination and apartheid, as contrary to the right of peoples to self-determination and to other human rights and fundamental freedoms.

8. Every State has the duty to discourage advocacy of hatred and prejudice against other peoples as contrary to the principles of peaceful co-existence and friendly cooperation.

II

Calls upon all States, in order to implement the above principles:

(*a*) To act perseveringly and consistently, with due regard for the constitutional rights and the role of the family, the institutions and the organizations concerned:

(i) To ensure that their policies relevant to the implementation of the present Declaration, including educational processes and teaching methods as well as media information activities, incorporate contents compatible with the task of the preparation for life in peace of entire societies and, in particular, the young generations;

(ii) Therefore, to discourage and eliminate incitement to racial hatred, national or other discrimination, injustice or advocacy of violence and war;

(*b*) To develop various forms of bilateral and multilateral cooperation, also in international, governmental and non-governmental organizations, with a view to enhancing preparation of societies to live in peace and, in particular, exchanging experiences on projects pursued with that end in view;

III

1. *Recommends* that the governmental and non-governmental organizations concerned should initiate appropriate action towards the implementation of the present Declaration;

2. *States* that a full implementation of the principles enshrined in the present Declaration calls for concerted action on the part of Governments, the United Nations and the specialized agencies, in particular the United Nations Educational, Scientific and Cultural Organization, as well as other interested international and national organizations, both governmental and non-governmental;

3. *Requests* the Secretary-General to follow the progress made in the implementation of the present Declaration and to submit periodic reports thereon to the General Assembly, the first such report to be submitted not later than at its thirty-sixth session.

85th plenary meeting
15 December 1978

37/63. Declaration on the Participation of Women in Promoting International Peace and Cooperation

Committee: 3
Vote: Adopted

The General Assembly,

Considering that the Charter of the United Nations expresses the determination of the peoples of the United Nations to reaffirm faith in the equal rights of men and women and to practise tolerance and live together in peace with one another as good neighbours,

Considering also that the Universal Declaration of Human Rights[1] proclaims that the inherent dignity and of the equal and inalienable rights of all members of the human family is the foundation of freedom, justice and peace in the world,

Considering further that the International Covenants on Human Rights[2] provide for the equal right of men and women to the enjoyment of all economic, social, cultural, civil and political rights,

Reaffirming the objectives of the United Nations Decade for Women: Equality, Development and Peace,

Taking into account the resolutions, declarations, conventions, programmes and recommendations of the United Nations and the specialized agencies and international conferences designed to eliminate all forms of discrimination and to promote equal rights for men and women,

Recalling that the Declaration of Mexico on the Equality of Women and Their Contribution to Development and Peace, 1975,[3] states that women have a vital role to play in the promotion of peace in all spheres of life: in the family, the community, the nation and the world,

Recalling that the Convention on the Elimination of All Forms of Discrimination against Women declares that discrimination against women violates the principles of equality of rights and respect for human dignity, is an obstacle to the participation of women, on equal terms with men, in the political, social, economic and cultural, civil and political life of their countries and makes more difficult the full development of the potentialities of women in the service of their countries and of humanity,

Recalling also that the Convention on the Elimination of All Forms of Discrimination against Women affirms that the strengthening of international peace and security, the relaxation of international tension, mutual cooperation among all States irrespective of their social and economic systems, general and complete disarmament and in particular nuclear disarmament under strict and effective international control, the affirmation of the principles of justice, equality and mutual benefit in relations among countries and the realization of the right of peoples under alien and colonial domination and foreign occupation to self-determination and independence, as well as respect for national sovereignty and territorial integrity, will promote social progress and development and as a consequence will contribute to the attainment of full equality between men and women,

Recognizing that the Convention on the Elimination of All Forms of Discrimination against Women obligates States Parties to take all appropriate measures to eliminate discrimination against women in all its forms and in every field of human endeavour, including politics, economic activities, law, employment, education, health care and domestic relations,

Noting that, despite progress towards the achievement of equality between men and women, considerable discrimination against women continues to exist, thereby impeding the active participation of women in promoting international peace and cooperation,

Welcoming the contribution which women have nevertheless made towards promoting international peace and cooperation, the struggle against colonialism, apartheid, all forms of racism and racial discrimination, foreign aggression and occupation and all forms of alien domination, and towards the unrestricted and effective enjoyment of human rights and fundamental freedoms,

Welcoming also the contribution of women towards a just restructuring of international economic relations and the achievement of a new international economic order,

Convinced that women can play an important and increasing role in thcsc areas,

Solemnly proclaims the Declaration on the Participation of Women in Promoting International Peace and Cooperation set forth in the annex to the present resolution.

90th plenary meeting
3 December 1982

1 Resolution 217 A. (III).

2 Resolution 2200 A (XXI), annex.

3 *Report of the World Conference of the International Women's Year, Mexico City, 19 June-2 July 1975* (United Nations publication, Sales No. E.76.IV.1), chap. I.

Annex

Declaration on the Participation of Women in Promoting International Peace and Cooperation

Part I

Article 1

Women and men have an equal and vital interest in contributing to international peace and cooperation. To this end, women must be enabled to exercise their right to participate in the economic, social, cultural, civil and political affairs of society on an equal footing with men.

Article 2

The full participation of women in the economic, social, cultural, civil and political affairs of society and in the endeavour to promote international peace and cooperation is dependent on a balanced and equitable distribution of roles between men and women in the family and in society as a whole.

Article 3

The increasing participation of women in the economic, social, cultural, civil and political affairs of society will contribute to international peace and cooperation.

Article 4

The full enjoyment of the rights of women and men and the full participation of women in promoting international peace and cooperation will contribute to the eradication of apartheid, of all forms of racism, racial discrimination, colonialism, neo-colonialism, aggression, foreign occupation and domination and interference in the internal affairs of States.

Article 5

Special national and international measures are necessary to increase the level of women's participation in the sphere of international relations so that women can contribute, on an equal basis with men, to national and international efforts to secure world peace and economic and social progress and to promote international cooperation.

Part II

Article 6

All appropriate measures shall be taken to intensify national and international efforts in respect of the participation of women in promoting international peace and cooperation by ensuring the equal participation of women in the economic, social, cultural, civil and political affairs of society through a balanced and equitable distribution of roles between men and women in the domestic sphere and in society as a whole, as well as by providing an equal opportunity for women to participate in the decision-making process.

Article 7

All appropriate measures shall be taken to promote the exchange of experience at the national and international levels for the purpose of furthering the involvement of women in promoting international peace and cooperation and in solving other vital national and international problems.

Article 8

All appropriate measures shall be taken at the national and international levels to give effective publicity to the responsibility and active participation of women in promoting international peace and cooperation and in solving other vital national and international problems.

Article 9

All appropriate measures shall be taken to render solidarity and support to those women who are victims of mass and flagrant violations of human rights such as apartheid, all forms of racism, racial discrimination, colonialism, neo-colonialism, aggression, foreign occupation and domination and of all other violations of human rights.

Article 10

All appropriate measures shall be taken to pay tribute to the participation of women in promoting international peace and cooperation.

Article 11

All appropriate measures shall be taken to encourage women to participate in non-governmental and intergovernmental organizations aimed at the strengthening of international peace and security, the development of friendly relations among nations and the promotion of cooperation among States and, to that end, freedom of thought, conscience, expression, assembly, association, communication and movement, without distinction as to race, political or religious belief, language or ethnic origin, shall be effectively guaranteed.

Article 12

All appropriate measures shall be taken to provide practical opportunities for the effective participation of women in promoting international peace and cooperation, economic development and social progress including, to that end:

(*a*) The promotion of an equitable representation of women in governmental and non-governmental functions,

(*b*) The promotion of an equality of opportunities for women to enter diplomatic service,

(*c*) The appointment or nomination of women, on an equal basis with men, as members of delegations to national, regional or international meetings;

(*d*) Support for increased employment of women at all levels in the secretariats of the United Nations and the specialized agencies, in conformity with Article 101 of the Charter of the United Nations.

Article 13

All appropriate measures shall be taken to establish adequate legal protection of the rights of women on an equal basis with men in order to ensure effective participation of women in the activities referred to above.

Article 14

Governments, non-governmental and international organizations, including the United Nations and the specialized agencies, as well as individuals, are urged to do all in their power to promote the implementation of the principles set forth in the present Declaration.

50/80. Maintenance of International Security

Committee: 1
Vote: Adopted without a vote

A. Permanent neutrality of Turkmenistan

The General Assembly,

Having considered the question of the permanent neutrality of Turkmenistan,

Reaffirming the sovereign right of every State to determine independently its foreign policy in accordance with the norms and principles of international law and the Charter of the United Nations,

Welcoming the legislative confirmation by Turkmenistan of its status of permanent neutrality,

Welcoming the desire of Turkmenistan to play an active and positive role in developing peaceful, friendly and mutually beneficial relations with the countries of the region and other States of the world,

Expressing the hope that the status of permanent neutrality of Turkmenistan will contribute to the strengthening of peace and security in the region,

Taking note of the support by the Movement of Non-Aligned Countries and by the Economic Cooperation Organization of the status of permanent neutrality of Turkmenistan,

Recognizing that the adoption by Turkmenistan of the status of permanent neutrality does not affect the fulfilment of its obligations under the Charter and will contribute to the achievement of the purposes of the United Nations,

1. *Recognizes and supports* the status of permanent neutrality declared by Turkmenistan;

2. *Calls upon* States Members of the United Nations to respect and support this status of Turkmenistan and also to respect its independence, sovereignty and territorial integrity.

90th plenary meeting
12 December 1995

B. Development of good-neighbourly relations among Balkan States

The General Assembly,

Recalling its resolutions 2625 (XXV) of 24 October 1970, the annex to which contains the Declaration on Principles of International Law concerning Friendly Relations and Cooperation among States in accordance with the Charter of the United Nations, 46/62 of 9 December 1991 and 48/84 B of 16 December 1993,

Affirming its determination that all nations should live together in peace with one another as good neighbours,

Emphasizing the urgency of the consolidation of the Balkans as a region of peace, security, stability and good-neighbourliness, thus contributing to the maintenance of international peace and security and so enhancing the prospects for sustained development and prosperity for all its peoples,

Noting the desire of the Balkan States to develop good-neighbourly relations among themselves and friendly relations with all nations in accordance with the Charter,

Welcoming the present international efforts aimed at achieving an overall political settlement of the conflict in the former Yugoslavia,

Having considered the report of the Secretary-General on the development of good-neighbourly relations among the Balkan States,[1]

Stressing the importance of the ongoing cooperation between the United Nations and the Organization for Security and Cooperation in Europe,

Taking note of its deliberations on the subject at its present session,

1. *Notes with interest* the views of some States on the development of good-neighbourly relations among the Balkan States contained in the report of the Secretary-General;

2. *Urges* relevant international organizations and competent bodies and organizations of the United Nations system to submit to the Secretary- General their views on the subject;

3. *Calls upon* all Balkan States to endeavour to promote good-neighbourly relations and continually to undertake unilateral and joint activities, particularly confidence-building measures as appropriate, in particular within the framework of the Organization for Security and Cooperation in Europe;

4. *Emphasizes* the importance for all Balkan States to promote mutual cooperation in all fields;

5. *Stresses* that closer engagement of Balkan States in cooperation arrangements on the European continent will favourably influence the political and economic situation in the region, as well as the good- neighbourly relations among all Balkan States;

6. *Urges* normalization of the relations among all States of the Balkan region;

7. *Requests* the Secretary-General to continue to seek the views of the Member States, particularly those from the Balkan region, and of international organizations, as well as of competent organs of the United Nations, on the development of good-neighbourly relations in the region and on measures and preventive activities aimed at the creation of a stable zone of peace and cooperation in the Balkans by the year 2000, and to submit a report to the General Assembly at the fifty-second session taking into account, *inter alia*, the views expressed by Member States;

8. *Decides* to consider the report of the Secretary-General on the subject at its fifty-second session.

90th plenary meeting
12 December 1995

01.30 PEACEFUL SETTLEMENT OF DISPUTES

37/10. Manila Declaration on the Peaceful Settlement of International Disputes

Committee: 6
Vote: Adopted without a vote
Ref.: 39/79, 36/110, 35/160, 34/102, 3283(XXIX), 603(VI), 480(V), 372(IV)

The General Assembly,

Having examined the item entitled "Peaceful settlement of disputes between States",

Recalling its resolutions 34/102 of 14 December 1979, 35/160 of 15 December 1980 and 36/110 of 10 December 1981,

Reaffirming the need to exert utmost efforts in order to settle any conflicts and disputes between States exclusively by peaceful means and to avoid any military action and hostilities, which can only make more difficult the solution of those conflicts and disputes,

Considering that the question of the peaceful settlement of disputes should represent one of the central concerns for States and for the United Nations and that the efforts to strengthen the process of the peaceful settlement of disputes should be continued,

Convinced that the adoption of the Manila Declaration on the Peaceful Settlement of International Disputes should enhance the observance of the principle of peaceful settlement of disputes in relations between States and contribute to the elimination of the danger of recourse to force or to the threat of force, to the relaxation of international tensions, to the promotion of a policy of cooperation and peace and of respect for the independence and sovereignty of all States, to the enhancing of the role of the United Nations in preventing conflicts and settling them peacefully and, consequently, to the strengthening of international peace and security,

Considering the need to ensure a wide dissemination of the text of the Declaration, [1]

1. *Approves* the Manila Declaration on the Peaceful Settlement of International Disputes, the text of which is annexed to the present resolution;

2. *Expresses its appreciation* to the Special Committee on the Charter of the United Nations and on the Strengthening of the Role of the Organization for its important contribution to the elaboration of the text of the Declarations;

3. *Requests* the Secretary-General to inform the Governments of the States Members of the United Nations or members of specialized agencies, the Security Council and the International Court of Justice of the adoption of the Declaration;

4. *Urges* that all efforts be made so that the Declaration becomes generally known and fully observed and implemented.

68th plenary meeting
15 November 1982

---

1 A/50/412 and Add.1.

Annex

Manila Declaration on the Peaceful Settlement of International Disputes

The General Assembly,

Reaffirming the principle of the Charter of the United Nations that all States shall settle their international disputes by peaceful means in such a manner that international peace and security, and justice, are not endangered,

Conscious that the Charter of the United Nations embodies the means and an essential framework for the peaceful settlement of international disputes, the continuance of which is likely to endanger the maintenance of international peace and security,

Recognizing the important role of the United Nations and the need to enhance its effectiveness in the peaceful settlement of international disputes and the maintenance of international peace and security, in accordance with the principles of justice and international law, in conformity with the Charter of the United Nations,

Reaffirming the principle of the Charter of the United Nations that all States shall refrain in their international relations from the threat or use of force against the territorial integrity or political independence of any State, or in any other manner inconsistent with the purposes of the United Nations,

Reiterating that no state or group of States has the right to intervene, directly or indirectly, for any reason whatsoever, in the internal or external affairs of any other State,

Reaffirming the Declaration on Principles of International Law concerning Friendly Relations and Cooperation among States in accordance with the Charter of the United Nations,[1]

Bearing in mind the importance of maintaining and strengthening international peace and security and the development of friendly relations among States, irrespective of their political, economic and social systems or levels of economic development,

Reaffirming the principle of equal rights and self-determination of peoples as enshrined in the Charter of the United Nations and referred to in the Declaration on Principles of International Law concerning Friendly Relations and Cooperation among States in accordance with the Charter of the United Nations and in other relevant resolutions of the General Assembly,

Stressing the need for all States to desist from any forcible action which deprives peoples, particularly peoples under colonial and racist régimes or other forms of alien domination, of their inalienable right to self-determination, freedom and independence, as referred to in the Declaration on Principles of International Law concerning Friendly Relations and Cooperation among States in accordance with the Charter of the United Nations,

Mindful of existing international instruments as well as respective principles and rules concerning the peaceful settlement of international disputes, including the exhaustion of local remedies whenever applicable,

Determined to promote international cooperation in the political field and to encourage the progressive development of international law and its codification, particularly in relation to the peaceful settlement of international disputes,

Solemnly declares that:

I

1. All States shall act in good faith and in conformity with the purposes and principles enshrined in the Charter of the United Nations with a view to avoiding disputes among themselves likely to affect friendly relations among States, thus contributing to the maintenance of international peace and security. They shall live together in peace with one another as good neighbours and strive for the adoption of meaningful measures for strengthening international peace and security.

2. Every State shall settle its international disputes exclusively by peaceful means in such a manner that international peace and security, and justice, are not endangered.

3. International disputes shall be settled on the basis of the sovereign equality of States and in accordance with the principle of free choice of means in conformity with obligations under the Charter of the United Nations and with the principles of justice and international law. Recourse to, or acceptance of, a settlement procedure freely agreed to by States with regard to existing or future disputes to which they are parties shall not be regarded as incompatible with the sovereign equality of States.

4. States parties to a dispute shall continue to observe in their mutual relations their obligations under the fundamental principles of international law concerning the sovereignty, independence and territorial integrity of States, as well as other generally recognized principles and rules of contemporary international law.

5. States shall seek in good faith and in a spirit of cooperation an early and equitable settlement of their international disputes by any of the following means: negotiation, inquiry, mediation, conciliation, arbitration, judicial settlement, resort to regional arrangements or agencies or other peaceful means of their own choice, including good offices. In seeking such a settlement, the parties shall agree on such peaceful means as may be appropriate to the circumstances and the nature of their dispute.

6. States parties to regional arrangements or agencies shall make every effort to achieve pacific settlement of their local disputes through such regional arrangements or agencies before referring them to the Security Council. This does not preclude States from bringing any dispute to the attention of the Security Council or of the General Assembly in accordance with the Charter of the United Nations.

7. In the event of failure of the parties to a dispute to reach an early solution by any of the above means of settlement, they shall continue to seek a peaceful solution and shall consult forthwith on mutually agreed means to settle the dispute peacefully. Should the parties fail to settle by any of the above means a dispute the continuance of which is likely to endanger the maintenance of international peace and security, they shall refer it to the Security Council in accordance with the Charter of the United Nations and without prejudice to the functions and powers of the Council set forth in the relevant provisions of Chapter VI of the Charter.

8. States parties to an international dispute, as well as other States, shall refrain from any action whatsoever which may aggravate the situation so as to endanger the maintenance of international peace and security and make more difficult or impede the peaceful settlement of the dispute, and shall act in this respect in accordance with the purposes and principles of the United Nations.

9. States should consider concluding agreements for the peaceful settlement of disputes among them. They should also include in bilateral agreements and multilateral conventions to be concluded, as appropriate, effective provisions for the peaceful settlement of disputes arising from the interpretation or application thereof.

10. States should, without prejudice to the right of free choice of means, bear in mind that direct negotiations are a flexible and effective means of peaceful settlement of their disputes. When they choose to resort to direct negotiations, States should negotiate meaningfully, in order to arrive at an early settlement acceptable to the parties. States should be equally prepared to seek the settlement of their disputes by the other means mentioned in the present Declaration.

11. States shall in accordance with international law implement in good faith all the provisions of agreements concluded by them for the settlement of their disputes.

12. In order to facilitate the exercise by the peoples concerned of the right to self-determination as referred to in the Declaration on Principles of International Law concerning Friendly Relations and Cooperation among States in accordance with the Charter of the United Nations, the parties to a dispute may have the possibility, if they agree to do so and as appropriate, to have recourse to the relevant

[1] Resolution 2625 (XXV), annex.

procedures mentioned in the present Declaration, for the peaceful settlement of the dispute.

13. Neither the existence of a dispute nor the failure of a procedure of peaceful settlement of disputes shall permit the use of force or threat of force by any of the States parties to the dispute.

II

1. Member States should make full use of the provisions of the Charter of the United Nations, including the procedures and means provided for therein, particularly Chapter VI, concerning the peaceful settlement of disputes.

2. Member States shall fulfil in good faith the obligations assumed by them in accordance with the Charter of the United Nations. They should, in accordance with the Charter, as appropriate, duly take into account the recommendations of the Security Council relating to the peaceful settlement of disputes. They should also, in accordance with the Charter, as appropriate, duly take into account the recommendations adopted by the General Assembly, subject to Articles 11 and 12 of the Charter, in the field of peaceful settlement of disputes.

3. Member States reaffirm the important role conferred on the General Assembly by the Charter of the United Nations in the field of peaceful settlement of disputes and stress the need for it to discharge effectively its responsibilities. Accordingly, they should:

(*a*) Bear in mind that the General Assembly may discuss any situation, regardless of origin, which it deems likely to impair the general welfare or friendly relations among nations and, subject to Article 12 of the Charter, recommend measures for its peaceful adjustment;

(*b*) Consider making use, when they deem it appropriate, of the possibility of bringing to the attention of the General Assembly any dispute or any situation which might lead to international friction or give rise to a dispute;

(*c*) Consider utilizing, for the peaceful settlement of their disputes, the subsidiary organs established by the General Assembly in the performance of its functions under the Charter;

(*d*) Consider, when they are parties to a dispute brought to the attention of the General Assembly, making use of consultations within the framework of the Assembly, with a view to facilitating an early settlement of their dispute.

4. Member States should strengthen the primary role of the Security Council so that it may fully and effectively discharge its responsibilities, in accordance with the Charter of the United Nations, in the area of the settlement of disputes or of any situation the continuance of which is likely to endanger the maintenance of international peace and security. To this end they should:

(*a*) Be fully aware of their obligation to refer to the Security Council such a dispute to which they are parties if they fail to settle it by the means indicated in Article 33 of the Charter;

(*b*) Make greater use of the possibility of bringing to the attention of the Security Council any dispute or any situation which might lead to international friction or give rise to a dispute;

(*c*) Encourage the Security Council to make wider use of the opportunities provided for by the Charter in order to review disputes or situations the continuance of which is likely to endanger the maintenance of international peace and security;

(*d*) Consider making greater use of the fact-finding capacity of the Security Council in accordance with the Charter;

(*e*) Encourage the Security Council to make wider use, as a means to promote peaceful settlement of disputes, of the subsidiary organs established by it in the performance of its functions under the Charter;

(*f*) Bear in mind that the Security Council may, at any stage of a dispute of the nature referred to in Article 33 of the Charter or of a situation of like nature, recommend appropriate procedures or methods of adjustment;

(*g*) Encourage the Security Council to act without delay, in accordance with its functions and powers, particularly in cases where international disputes develop into armed conflicts.

5. States should be fully aware of the role of the International Court of Justice, which is the principal judicial organ of the United Nations. Their attention is drawn to the facilities offered by the International Court of Justice for the settlement of legal disputes, especially since the revision of the Rules of the Court.

States may entrust the solution of their differences to other tribunals by virtue of agreements already in existence or which may be concluded in the future.

States should bear in mind:

(*a*) That legal disputes should as a general rule be referred by the parties to the International Court of Justice, in accordance with the provisions of the Statute of the Court;

(*b*) That it is desirable that they:

(i) Consider the possibility of inserting in treaties, whenever appropriate, clauses providing for the submission to the International Court of Justice of disputes which may arise from the interpretation or application of such treaties;

(ii) Study the possibility of choosing, in the free exercise of their sovereignty, to recognize as compulsory the jurisdiction of the International Court of Justice in accordance with Article 36 of its Statute;

(iii) Review the possibility of identifying cases in which use may be made of the International Court of Justice.

The organs of the United Nations and the specialized agencies should study the advisability of making use of the possibility of requesting advisory opinions of the International Court of Justice on legal questions arising within the scope of their activities, provided that they are duly authorized to do so.

Recourse to judicial settlement of legal disputes, particularly referral to the International Court of Justice, should not be considered an unfriendly act between States.

6. The Secretary-General should make full use of the provisions of the Charter of the United Nations concerning the responsibilities entrusted to him. The Secretary-General may bring to the attention of the Security Council any matter which in his opinion may threaten the maintenance of international peace and security. He shall perform such other functions as are entrusted to him by the Security Council or by the General Assembly. Reports in this connection shall be made whenever requested to the Security Council or the General Assembly.

Urges all States to observe and promote in good faith the provisions of the present Declaration in the peaceful settlement of their international disputes;

Declares that nothing in the present Declaration shall be construed as prejudicing in any manner the relevant provisions of the Charter or the rights and duties of States, or the scope of the functions and powers of the United Nations organs under the Charter, in particular those relating to the peaceful settlement of dispute;

Declares that nothing in the present Declaration could in any way prejudice the right to self-determination, freedom and independence, as derived from the Charter, of peoples forcibly deprived of that right and referred to in the Declaration on Principles of International Law concerning Friendly Relations and Cooperation among States in accordance with the Charter of the United Nations, particularly peoples under colonial and racist régimes or other forms of alien domination; nor the right of these peoples to struggle to that end and to seek and receive support, in accordance with the principles of the Charter and in conformity with the above-mentioned Declaration;

Stresses the need, in accordance with the Charter, to continue efforts to strengthen the process of the peaceful settlement of disputes through progressive development and codification of international law, as appropriate, and through enhancing the effectiveness of the United Nations in this field.

43/51. Declaration on the Prevention and Removal of Disputes and Situations which May Threaten International Peace and Security and on the Role of the United Nations in this Field

Committee: 6
Vote: Adopted without a vote

The General Assembly,

Recalling its resolutions 38/141 of 19 December 1983, 39/88 of 13 December 1984, 40/78 of 11 December 1985, 41/83 of 3 December 1986 and 42/157 of 7 December 1987,

Taking note of the report of the Special Committee on the Charter of the United Nations and on the Strengthening of the Role of the Organization,[1] which met in New York from 22 February to 11 March 1988 and completed a draft Declaration on the Prevention and Removal of Disputes and Situations Which May Threaten International Peace and Security and on the Role of the United Nations in this Field,

Convinced that the adoption of the Declaration on the Prevention and Removal of Disputes and Situations Which May Threaten International Peace and Security and on the Role of the United Nations in this Field will contribute towards strengthening the role and enhancing the effectiveness of the United Nations in maintaining international peace and security,

Considering the need to ensure a wide dissemination of the text of the Declaration,

1. *Approves* the Declaration on the Prevention and Removal of Disputes and Situations Which May Threaten International Peace and Security and on the Role of the United Nations in this Field, the text of which is annexed to the present resolution;

2. *Expresses* its appreciation to the Special Committee on the Charter of the United Nations and on the Strengthening of the Role of the Organization for its important contribution to the elaboration of the text of the Declaration;

3. *Requests* the Secretary-General to inform the Governments of the States Members of the United Nations or members of specialized agencies, and the Security Council, of the adoption of the Declaration;

4. *Urges* that every effort be made to ensure that the Declaration becomes generally known and fully implemented.

68th plenary meeting
5 December 1988

Annex

Declaration on the Prevention and Removal of Disputes and Situations which May Threaten International Peace and Security and on the Role of the United Nations in this Field

The General Assembly,

Recognizing the important role that the United Nations and its organs can play in the prevention and removal of international disputes and situations which may lead to international friction or give rise to an international dispute, the continuance of which may threaten the maintenance of international peace and security (hereafter: "disputes" or "situations"), within their respective functions and powers under the Charter of the United Nations,

Convinced that the strengthening of such a role of the United Nations will enhance its effectiveness in dealing with questions relating to the maintenance of international peace and security and in promoting the peaceful settlement of international disputes,

Recognizing the fundamental responsibility of States for the prevention and removal of disputes and situations,

Recalling that the peoples of the United Nations are determined to practise tolerance and live together in peace with one another as good neighbours,

Bearing in mind the right of all States to resort to peaceful means of their own choice for the prevention and removal of disputes or situations,

Reaffirming the Declaration on Principles of International Law concerning Friendly Relations and Cooperation among States in accordance with the Charter of the United Nations,[2] the Manila Declaration on the Peaceful Settlement of International Disputes[3] and the Declaration on the Enhancement of the Effectiveness of the Principle of Refraining from the Threat or Use of Force in International Relations,[4]

Recalling that it is the duty of States to refrain in their international relations from military, political, economic or any other form of coercion against the political independence or territorial integrity of any State,

Calling upon States to cooperate fully with the relevant organs of the United Nations and to support actions taken by them in accordance with the Charter relating to the prevention or removal of disputes and situations,

Bearing in mind the obligation of States to conduct their relations with other States in accordance with international law, including the principles of the United Nations,

Reaffirming the principle of equal rights and self-determination of peoples,

Recalling that the Charter confers on the Security Council the primary responsibility for the maintenance of international peace and security, and that the Member States have agreed to accept and carry out its decisions in accordance with the Charter,

Recalling also the important role conferred by the Charter on the General Assembly and the Secretary-General in the maintenance of international peace and security,

1. *Solemnly declares* that:

1. States should act so as to prevent in their international relations the emergence or aggravation of disputes or situations, in particular by fulfilling in good faith their obligations under international law;

2. In order to prevent disputes or situations, States should develop their relations on the basis of the sovereign equality of States and in such a manner as to enhance the effectiveness of the collective security system through the effective implementation of the provisions of the Charter of the United Nations;

3. States should consider the use of bilateral or multilateral consultations in order better to understand each others views, positions and interests;

4. States party to regional arrangements or members of agencies referred to in Article 52 of the Charter should make every effort to prevent or remove local disputes or situations through such arrangements and agencies;

5. States concerned should consider approaching the relevant organs of the United Nations in order to obtain advice or recommendations on preventive means for dealing with a dispute or situation;

6. Any State party to a dispute or directly concerned with a situation, particularly if it intends to request a meeting of the Security Council, should approach the Council, directly or indirectly, at an early stage and, if appropriate, on a confidential basis;

7. The Security Council should consider holding from time to time meetings, including at a high level with the participation, in particular, of Ministers for Foreign Affairs, or consultations to review the international situation and search for effective ways of improving it;

8. In the course of the preparation for the prevention or removal of particular disputes or situations, the Security Council should consider making use of the various means at its disposal, including the ap-

---

[1] *Official Records of the General Assembly, Forty-third Session, Supplement No. 33* (A/43/33).

[2] Resolution 2625 (XXV), annex.

[3] Resolution 37/10, annex.

[4] Resolution 42/22, annex.

pointment of the Secretary-General as rapporteur for a specified question;

9. When a particular dispute or situation is brought to the attention of the Security Council without a meeting being requested, the Council should consider holding consultations with a view to examining the facts of the dispute or situation and keeping it under review, with the assistance of the Secretary-General when needed; the States concerned should have the opportunity of making their views known;

10. In such consultations, consideration should be given to employing such informal methods as the Security Council deems appropriate, including confidential contacts by its President;

11. In such consultations, the Security Council should consider, *inter alia*:

(*a*) Reminding the States concerned to respect their obligations under the Charter;

(*b*) Making an appeal to the States concerned to refrain from any action which might give rise to a dispute or lead to the deterioration of the dispute or situation;

(*c*) Making an appeal to the States concerned to take action which might help to remove, or to prevent the continuation or deterioration of, the dispute or situation;

12. The Security Council should consider sending, at an early stage, fact-finding or good offices missions or establishing appropriate forms of United Nations presence, including observers and peace-keeping operations, as a means of preventing the further deterioration of the dispute or situation in the areas concerned;

13. The Security Council should consider encouraging and, where appropriate, endorsing efforts at the regional level by the States concerned or by regional arrangements or agencies to prevent or remove a dispute or situation in the region concerned;

14. Taking into consideration any procedures that have already been adopted by the States directly concerned, the Security Council should consider recommending to them appropriate procedures or methods of settlement of disputes or adjustment of situations, and such terms of settlement as it deems appropriate;

15. The Security Council, if it is appropriate for promoting the prevention and removal of disputes or situations, should, at an early stage, consider making use of the provisions of the Charter concerning the possibility of requesting the International Court of Justice to give an advisory opinion on any legal question;

16. The General Assembly should consider making use of the provisions of the Charter in order to discuss disputes or situations, when appropriate, and, in accordance with Article 11 and subject to Article 12 of the Charter, making recommendations;

17. The General Assembly should consider, where appropriate, supporting efforts undertaken at the regional level by the States concerned or by regional arrangements or agencies, to prevent or remove a dispute or situation in the region concerned;

18. If a dispute or situation has been brought before it, the General Assembly should consider including in its recommendations making more use of fact-finding capabilities, in accordance with Article 11 and subject to Article 12 of the Charter;

19. The General Assembly, if it is appropriate for promoting the prevention and removal of disputes or situations, should consider making use of the provisions of the Charter concerning the possibility of requesting the International Court of Justice to give an advisory opinion on any legal question;

20. The Secretary-General, if approached by a State or States directly concerned with a dispute or situation, should respond swiftly by urging the States to seek a solution or adjustment by peaceful means of their own choice under the Charter and by offering his good offices or other means at his disposal, as he deems appropriate;

21. The Secretary-General should consider approaching the States directly concerned with a dispute or situation in an effort to prevent it from becoming a threat to the maintenance of international peace and security;

22. The Secretary-General should, where appropriate, consider making full use of fact-finding capabilities, including, with the consent of the host State, sending a representative or fact-finding missions to areas where a dispute or a situation exists; where necessary, the Secretary-General should also consider making the appropriate arrangements;

23. The Secretary-General should be encouraged to consider using, at as early a stage as he deems appropriate, the right that is accorded to him under Article 99 of the Charter;

24. The Secretary-General should, where appropriate, encourage efforts undertaken at the regional level to prevent or remove a dispute or situation in the region concerned;

25. Should States fail to prevent the emergence or aggravation of a dispute or situation, they shall continue to seek a settlement by peaceful means in accordance with the Charter;

2. *Declares* that nothing in the present Declaration shall be construed as prejudicing in any manner the provisions of the Charter, including those contained in Article 2, paragraph 7, thereof, or the rights and duties of States, or the scope of the functions and the powers of United Nations organs under the Charter, in particular those relating to the maintenance of international peace and security;

3. *Also declares* that nothing in the present Declaration could in any way prejudice the right to self-determination, freedom and independence of peoples forcibly deprived of that right and referred to in the Declaration on Principles of International Law concerning Friendly Relations and Cooperation among States in accordance with the Charter of the United Nations,[1] particularly peoples under colonial or racist régimes or other forms of alien domination.

50/50. United Nations Model Rules for the Conciliation of Disputes Between States

Committee: 6
Vote: Adopted without a vote

The General Assembly,

Considering that conciliation is among the methods for the settlement of disputes between States enumerated by the Charter of the United Nations in Article 33, paragraph 1, that it has been provided for in numerous treaties, bilateral as well as multilateral, for the settlement of such disputes, and that it has proved its usefulness in practice,

Convinced that the establishment of model rules for the conciliation of disputes between States which incorporate the results of the most recent scholarly work and of experience in the field of international conciliation, as well as a number of innovations which can with advantage be made in the traditional practice in that area, can contribute to the development of harmonious relations between States,

1. *Commends* the Special Committee on the Charter of the United Nations and on the Strengthening of the Role of the Organization for having completed the final text of the United Nations Model Rules for the Conciliation of Disputes between States;[2]

2. *Draws* to the attention of States the possibility of applying the Model Rules, the text of which is annexed hereto, whenever a dispute has arisen between States which it has not been possible to solve through direct negotiations;

3. *Requests* the Secretary-General, to the extent possible and in accordance with the relevant provisions of the Model Rules, to lend his assistance to the States resorting to conciliation on the basis of those Rules;

4. *Also requests* the Secretary-General to make the necessary arrangements to distribute to Governments the text of the present resolution, including the annex.

---

1 Resolution 2625 (XXV), annex.

2 *Official Records of the General Assembly, Fiftieth Session, Supplement No. 33* (A/50/33), chap. V, sect. A.

Annex
United Nations Model Rules for the Conciliation of Disputes Between States

Chapter I
Application of the Rules

1. These rules apply to the conciliation of disputes between States where those States have expressly agreed in writing to their application.

2. The States which agree to apply these rules may at any time, through mutual agreement, exclude or amend any of their provisions.

Chapter II
Initiation of the Conciliation Proceedings

Article 2

1. The conciliation proceedings shall begin as soon as the States concerned (henceforth: the parties) have agreed in writing to the application of the present rules, with or without amendments, as well as on a definition of the subject of the dispute, the number and emoluments of members of the conciliation commission, its seat and the maximum duration of the proceedings, as provided in article 24. If necessary, the agreement shall contain provisions concerning the language or languages in which the proceedings are to be conducted and the linguistic services required.

2. If the States cannot reach agreement on the definition of the subject of the dispute, they may by mutual agreement request the assistance of the Secretary-General of the United Nations to resolve the difficulty. They may also by mutual agreement request his assistance to resolve any other difficulty that they may encounter in reaching an agreement on the modalities of the conciliation proceedings.

Chapter III
Number and Appointment of Conciliators

Article 3

There may be three conciliators or five conciliators. In either case the conciliators shall form a commission.

Article 4

If the parties have agreed that three conciliators shall be appointed, each one of them shall appoint a conciliator, who may not be of its own nationality. The parties shall appoint by mutual agreement the third conciliator, who may not be of the nationality of any of the parties or of the other conciliators. The third conciliator shall act as president of the commission. If he is not appointed within two months of the appointment of the conciliators appointed individually by the parties, the third conciliator shall be appointed by the Government of a third State chosen by agreement between the parties or, if such agreement is not obtained within two months, by the President of the International Court of Justice. If the President is a national of one of the parties, the appointment shall be made by the Vice-President or the next member of the Court in order of seniority who is not a national of the parties. The third conciliator shall not reside habitually in the territory of the parties or be or have been in their service.

Article 5

1. If the parties have agreed that five conciliators should be appointed, each one of them shall appoint a conciliator who may be of its own nationality. The other three conciliators, one of whom shall be chosen with a view to his acting as president, shall be appointed by agreement between the parties from among nationals of third States and shall be of different nationalities. None of them shall reside habitually in the territory of the parties or be or have been in their service. None of them shall have the same nationality as that of the other two conciliators.

2. If the appointment of the conciliators whom the parties are to appoint jointly has not been effected within three months, they shall be appointed by the Government of a third State chosen by agreement between the parties or, if such an agreement is not reached within three months, by the President of the International Court of Justice. If the President is a national of one of the parties, the appointment shall be made by the Vice-President or the next judge in order of seniority who is not a national of the parties. The Government or member of the International Court of Justice making the appointment shall also decide which of the three conciliators shall act as president.

3. If, at the end of the three-month period referred to in the preceding paragraph, the parties have been able to appoint only one or two conciliators, the two conciliators or the conciliator still required shall be appointed in the manner described in the preceding paragraph. If the parties have not agreed that the conciliator or one of the two conciliators whom they have appointed shall act as president, the Government or member of the International Court of Justice appointing the two conciliators or the conciliator still required shall also decide which of the three conciliators shall act as president.

4. If, at the end of the three-month period referred to in paragraph 2 of this article, the parties have appointed three conciliators but have not been able to agree which of them shall act as president, the president shall be chosen in the manner described in that paragraph.

Article 6

Vacancies which may occur in the. commission as a result of death, resignation or any other cause shall be filled as soon as possible by the method established for appointing the members to be replaced.

Chapter IV
Fundamental Principles

Article 7

The commission, acting independently and impartially, shall endeavour to assist the parties in reaching an amicable settlement of the dispute. If no settlement is reached during the consideration of the dispute, the commission may draw up and submit appropriate recommendations to the parties for consideration.

Chapter V
Procedures and Powers of the Commission

Article 8

The commission shall adopt its own procedure.

Article 9

1. Before the commission begins its work, the parties shall designate their agents and shall communicate the names of such agents to the president of the commission. The president shall determine, in agreement with the parties, the date of the commission's first meeting, to which the members of the commission and the agents shall be invited.

2. The agents of the parties may be assisted before the commission by counsel and experts appointed by the parties.

3. Before the first meeting of the commission, its members may meet informally with the agents of the parties, if necessary, accompanied by the appointed counsel and experts to deal with administrative and procedural matters.

Article 10

1. At its first meeting, the commission shall appoint a secretary.

2. The secretary of the commission shall not have the nationality of any of the parties, shall not reside habitually in their territory and shall not be or have been in the service of any of them. He may be a United Nations official if the parties agree with the Secretary-General on the conditions under which the official will exercise these functions.

Article 11

1. As soon as the information provided by the parties so permits, the commission, having regard, in particular, to the time-limit laid down in article 24, shall decide in consultation with the parties whether the parties should be invited to submit written pleadings and, if so, in what order and within what time-limits, as well as the dates when, if

necessary, the agents and counsel will be heard. The decisions taken by the commission in this regard may be amended at any later stage of the proceedings.

2. Subject to the provisions of article 20, paragraph 1, the commission shall not allow the agent or counsel of one party to attend a meeting without having also given the other party the opportunity to be represented at the same meeting.

Article 12

The parties, acting in good faith, shall facilitate the commission's work and, in particular, shall provide it to the greatest possible extent with whatever documents, information and explanations may be relevant.

Article 13

1. The commission may ask the parties for whatever relevant information or documents, as well as explanations, it deems necessary or useful. It may also make comments on the arguments advanced as well as the statements or proposals made by the parties.

2. The commission may accede to any request by a party that persons whose testimony it considers necessary or useful be heard, or that experts be consulted.

Article 14

In cases where the parties disagree on issues of fact, the commission may use all means at its disposal, such as the joint expert advisers mentioned in article 15, or consultation with experts, to ascertain the facts.

Article 15

The commission may propose to the parties that they jointly appoint expert advisers to assist it in the consideration of technical aspects of the dispute. If the proposal is accepted, its implementation shall be conditional upon the expert advisers being appointed by the parties by mutual agreement and accepted by the commission and upon the parties fixing their emoluments.

Article 16

Each party may at any time, at its own initiative or at the initiative of the commission, make proposals for the settlement of the dispute. Any proposal made in accordance with this article shall be communicated immediately to the other party by the president, who may, in so doing, transmit any comment the commission may wish to make thereon.

Article 17

At any stage of the proceedings, the commission may, at its own initiative or at the initiative of one of the parties, draw the attention of the parties to any measures which in its opinion might be advisable or facilitate a settlement.

Article 18

The commission shall endeavour to take its decisions unanimously but, if unanimity proves impossible, it may take them by a majority of votes of its members. Abstentions are not allowed. Except in matters of procedure, the presence of all members shall be required in order for a decision to be valid.

Article 19

The commission may, at any time, ask the Secretary-General of the United Nations for advice or assistance with regard to the administrative or procedural aspects of its work.

Chapter VI
Conclusion of the Conciliation Proceedings

Article 20

1. On concluding its consideration of the dispute, the commission may, if full settlement has not been reached, draw up and submit appropriate recommendations to the parties for consideration. To that end, it may hold an exchange of views with the agents of the parties, who may be heard jointly or separately.

2. The recommendations adopted by the commission shall be set forth in a report communicated by the president of the commission to the agents of the parties, with a request that the agents inform the commission, within a given period, whether the parties accept them. The president may include in the report the reasons which, in the commission's view, might prompt the parties to accept the recommendations submitted. The commission shall refrain from presenting in its report any final conclusions with regard to facts or from ruling formally on issues of law, unless the parties have jointly asked it to do so.

3. If the parties accept the recommendations submitted by the commission, a procès-verbal shall be drawn up setting forth the conditions of acceptance. The procès-verbal shall be signed by the president and the secretary. A copy thereof signed by the secretary shall be provided to each party. This shall conclude the proceedings.

4. Should the commission decide not to submit recommendations to the parties, its decision to that effect shall be recorded in a procès-verbal signed by the president and the secretary. A copy thereof signed by the secretary shall be provided to each party. This shall conclude the proceedings.

Article 21

1. The recommendations of the commission will be submitted to the parties for consideration in order to facilitate an amicable settlement of the dispute. The parties undertake to study them in good faith, carefully and objectively.

2. If one of the parties does not accept the recommendations and the other party does, it shall inform the latter, in writing, of the reasons why it could not accept them.

Article 22

1. If the recommendations are not accepted by both parties but the latter wish efforts to continue in order to reach agreement on different terms, the proceedings shall be resumed. Article 24 shall apply to the resumed proceedings, with the relevant time-limit, which the parties may, by mutual agreement, shorten or extend, running from the commission's first meeting after resumption of the proceedings.

2. If the recommendations are not accepted by both parties and the latter do not wish further efforts to be made to reach agreement on different terms, a procès-verbal signed by the president and the secretary of the commission shall be drawn up, omitting the proposed terms and indicating that the parties were unable to accept them and do not wish further efforts to be made to reach agreement on different terms. The proceedings shall be concluded when each party has received a copy of the procès-verbal signed by the secretary.

Article 23

Upon conclusion of the proceedings, the president of the commission shall, with the prior agreement of the parties, deliver the documents in the possession of the secretariat of the commission either to the Secretary-General of the United Nations or to another person or entity agreed upon by the parties. Without prejudice to the possible application of article 26, paragraph 2, the confidentiality of the documents shall be preserved.

Article 24

The commission shall conclude its work within the period agreed upon by the parties. Any extension of this period shall be agreed upon by the parties.

Chapter VII
Confidentiality of the Commission's Work and Documents

Article 25

1. The commission's meetings shall be closed. The parties and the members and expert advisers of the commission, the agents and counsel of the parties, and the secretary and the secretariat staff, shall maintain strictly the confidentiality of any documents or statements,

or any communication concerning the progress of the proceedings unless their disclosure has been approved by both parties in advance.

2. Each party shall receive, through the secretary, certified copies of any minutes of the meetings at which it was represented.

3. Each party shall receive, through the secretary, certified copies of any documentary evidence received and of experts' reports, records of investigations and statements by witnesses.

Article 26

1. Except with regard to certified copies referred to in article 25, paragraph 3, the obligation to respect the confidentiality of the proceedings and of the deliberations shall remain in effect for the parties and for members of the commission, expert advisers and secretariat staff after the proceedings are concluded and shall extend to recommendations and proposals which have not been accepted.

2. Notwithstanding the foregoing, the parties may, upon conclusion of the proceedings and by mutual agreement, make available to the public all or some of the documents that in accordance with the preceding paragraph are to remain confidential, or authorize the publication of all or some of those documents.

Chapter VIII
Obligation not to Act in a Manner which might have an Adverse Effect on the Conciliation

Article 27

The parties shall refrain during the conciliation proceedings from any measure which might aggravate or widen the dispute. They shall, in particular, refrain from any measures which might have an adverse effect on the recommendations submitted by the commission, so long as those recommendations have not been explicitly rejected by either of the parties.

Chapter IX
Preservation of the Legal Position of the Parties

Article 28

1. Except as the parties may otherwise agree, neither party shall be entitled in any other proceedings, whether in a court of law or before arbitrators or before any other body, entity or person, to invoke any views expressed or statements, admissions or proposals made by the other party in the conciliation proceedings, but not accepted, or the report of the commission, the recommendations submitted by the commission or any proposal made by the commission, unless agreed to by other parties.

2. Acceptance by a party of recommendations submitted by the commission in no way implies any admission by it of the considerations of law or of fact which may have inspired the recommendations.

Chapter X
Costs

Article 29

The costs of the conciliation proceedings and the emoluments of expert advisers appointed in accordance with article 15, shall be borne by the parties in equal shares.

87th plenary meeting
11 December 1995

01.40 NATIONAL SOVEREIGNTY AND NON-INTERVENTION

2131 (XX). Declaration on the Inadmissibility of Intervention in the Domestic Affairs of States and the Protection of Their Independence and Sovereignty

Committee: 1
Vote: 109 - 0 - 1
Ref.: 2225(XXI)

The General Assembly,

Deeply concerned at the gravity of the international situation and the increasing threat to universal peace due to armed intervention and other direct or indirect forms of interference threatening the sovereign personality and the political independence of States,

Considering that the United Nations, in accordance with their aim to eliminate war, threats to the peace and acts of aggression, created an Organization, based on the sovereign equality of States, whose friendly relations would be based on respect for the principle of equal rights and self-determination of peoples and on the obligation of its Members to refrain from the threat or use of force against the territorial integrity or political independence of any State,

Recognizing that, in fulfilment of the principle of self-determination, the General Assembly, in the Declaration on the Granting of Independence to Colonial Countries and Peoples contained in resolution 1514 (XV) of 14 December 1960, stated its conviction that all peoples have an inalienable right to complete freedom, the exercise of their sovereignty and the integrity of their national territory, and that, by virtue of that right, they freely determine their political status and freely pursue their economic, social and cultural development,

Recalling that in the Universal Declaration of Human Rights the General Assembly proclaimed that recognition of the inherent dignity and of the equal and inalienable rights of all members of the human family is the foundation of freedom, justice and peace in the world, without distinction of any kind,

Reaffirming the principle of non-intervention, proclaimed in the charters of the Organization of American States, the League of Arab States and the Organization of African Unity and affirmed at the conferences held at Montevideo, Buenos Aires, Chapultepec and Bogotá, as well as in the decisions of the Asian-African Conference at Bandung, the First Conference of Heads of State or Government of Non-Aligned Countries at Belgrade, in the Programme for Peace and International Cooperation adopted at the end of the Second Conference of Heads of State or Government of Non-Aligned Countries at Cairo, and in the declaration on subversion adopted at Accra by the Heads of State and Government of the African States,

Recognizing that full observance of the principle of the non-intervention of States in the internal and external affairs of other States is essential to the fulfilment of the purposes and principles of the United Nations,

Considering that armed intervention is synonymous with aggression and, as such, is contrary to the basic principles on which peaceful international cooperation between States should be built,

Considering further that direct intervention, subversion and all forms of indirect intervention are contrary to these principles and, consequently, constitute a violation of the Charter of the United Nations,

Mindful that violation of the principle of non-intervention poses a threat to the independence, freedom and normal political, economic, social and cultural development of countries, particularly those which have freed themselves from colonialism, and can pose a serious threat to the maintenance of peace,

Fully aware of the imperative need to create appropriate conditions which would enable all States, and in particular the developing countries, to choose without duress or coercion their own political, economic and social institutions,

In the light of the foregoing considerations, solemnly declares:

1. No State has the right to intervene, directly or indirectly, for any reason whatever, in the internal or external affairs of any other State. Consequently, armed intervention and all other forms of interference or attempted threats against the personality of the State or against its political, economic and cultural elements, are condemned.

2. No State may use or encourage the use of economic, political or any other type of measures to coerce another State in order to obtain

from it the subordination of the exercise of its sovereign rights or to secure from it advantages of any kind. Also, no State shall organize, assist, foment, finance, incite or tolerate subversive, terrorist or armed activities directed towards the violent overthrow of the régime of another State, or interfere in civil strife in another State.

3. The use of force to deprive peoples of their national identity constitutes a violation of their inalienable rights and of the principle of non-intervention.

4. The strict observance of these obligations is an essential condition to ensure that nations live together in peace with one another, since the practice of any form of intervention not only violates the spirit and letter of the Charter of the United Nations but also leads to the creation of situations which threaten international peace and security.

5. Every State has an inalienable right to choose its political, economic, social and cultural systems, without interference in any form by another State.

6. All States shall respect the right of self-determination and independence of peoples and nations, to be freely exercised without any foreign pressure, and with absolute respect for human rights and fundamental freedoms. Consequently, all States shall contribute to the complete elimination of racial discrimination and colonialism in all its forms and manifestations.

7. For the purpose of the present Declaration, the term "State" covers both individual States and groups of States.

8. Nothing in this Declaration shall be construed as affecting in any manner the relevant provisions of the Charter of the United Nations relating to the maintenance of international peace and security, in particular those contained in Chapters VI, VII and VIII.

1408th plenary meeting
21 December 1965

36/103. Declaration on the Inadmissibility of Intervention and Interference in the Internal Affairs of States

Committee: 1
Vote: 120 - 22 - 6

The General Assembly,

Recalling its resolutions 2734 (XXV) of 16 December 1970, containing the Declaration on the Strengthening of International Security and 2131 (XX) of 21 December 1965, containing the Declaration on the Inadmissibility of Intervention in the Domestic Affairs of States and the Protection of Their Independence and Sovereignty,

Recalling also its resolutions 2625 (XXV) of 24 October 1970, containing the Declaration on Principles of International Law concerning Friendly Relations and Cooperation among States in accordance with the Charter of the United Nations, and 3314 (XXIX) of 14 December 1974, containing the Definition of Aggression,

Recalling further its resolutions 31/91 of 14 December 1976, 32/153 of 19 December 1977, 33/74 of 15 December 1978, 34/101 of 14 December 1979 and 35/159 of 12 December 1980 on non-interference in the internal affairs of States,

Deeply concerned at the gravity of the international situation and the increasing threat to international peace and security owing to frequent recourse to the threat or use of force, aggression, intimidation, military intervention and occupation, escalation of military presence and all other forms of intervention or interference, direct or indirect, overt or covert, threatening the sovereignty and political independence of States, with the aim of overthrowing their Governments,

Conscious of the fact that such policies endanger the political independence of States, the freedom of peoples and their permanent sovereignty over their natural resources, adversely affecting thereby the maintenance of international peace and security,

Conscious of the imperative need for all foreign forces engaged in military occupation, intervention or interference to be completely withdrawn to their own territories, so that peoples under colonial domination, foreign occupation or racist régimes may freely and fully exercise their right to self-determination, in order to enable peoples of all States to administer their own affairs and determine their own political, economic and social systems without external interference or control,

Conscious also of the imperative need to put a complete end to any threat of aggression, any recruitment, any use of armed bands, in particular mercenaries, against sovereign States, so as to enable the peoples of all States to determine their own political, economic and social systems without external interference or control,

Recognizing that full observance of the principles of non-intervention and non-interference in the internal and external affairs of sovereign States and peoples, whether direct or indirect, overt or covert, is essential to the fulfilment of the purposes and principles of the Charter of the United Nations,

1. *Approves* the Declaration on the Inadmissibility of Intervention and Interference in the Internal Affairs of States, the text of which is annexed to the present resolution;

2. *Requests* the Secretary-General to ensure the widest dissemination of the Declaration to States, the specialized agencies and other organizations in association with the United Nations, and other appropriate bodies.

91st plenary meeting
9 December 1981

Annex

Declaration on the Inadmissibility of Intervention and Interference in the Internal Affairs of States

The General Assembly,

Reaffirming, in accordance with the Charter of the United Nations, that no State has the right to intervene directly or indirectly for any reason whatsoever in the internal and external affairs of any other State,

Reaffirming further the fundamental principle of the Charter that all States have the duty not to threaten or use force against the sovereignty, political independence or territorial integrity of other States,

Bearing in mind that the establishment, maintenance and strengthening of international peace and security are founded upon freedom, equality, self-determination and independence, respect for the sovereignty of States, as well as permanent sovereignty of States over their natural resources, irrespective of their political, economic or social systems or the levels of their development,

Considering that full observance of the principle of non-intervention and non-interference in the internal and external affairs of States is of the greatest importance for the maintenance of international peace and security and for the fulfilment of the purposes and principles of the Charter,

Reaffirming, in accordance with the Charter, the right to self-determination and independence of peoples under colonial domination, foreign occupation or racist régimes,

Stressing that the purposes of the United Nations can be achieved only under conditions where peoples enjoy freedom and States enjoy sovereign equality and comply fully with the requirements of these principles in their international relations,

Considering that any violation of the principle of non-intervention and non-interference in the internal and external affairs of States poses a threat to the freedom of peoples, the sovereignty, political independence and territorial integrity of States and to their political, economic, social and cultural development, and also endangers international peace and security,

Considering that a declaration on the inadmissibility of intervention and interference in the internal affairs of States will contribute towards the fulfilment of the purposes and principles of the Charter,

Considering the provisions of the Charter as a whole and taking into account the resolutions adopted by the United Nations relating to that principle, in particular those containing the Declaration on the Strengthening of International Security, the Declaration on the Inadmissibility of Intervention in the Domestic Affairs of States and the Protection of Their Independence and Sovereignty, the Declaration on Principles of International Law concerning Friendly Relations and

Cooperation among States in accordance with the Charter of the United Nations and the Definition of Aggression,

Solemnly declares that:

1. No State or group of States has the right to intervene or interfere in any form or for any reason whatsoever in the internal and external affairs of other States.

2. The principle of non-intervention and non-interference in the internal and external affairs of States comprehends the following rights and duties:

I

(*a*) Sovereignty, political independence, territorial integrity, national unity and security of all States, as well as national identity and cultural heritage of their peoples;

(*b*) The sovereign and inalienable right of a State freely to determine its own political, economic, cultural and social systems, to develop its international relations and to exercise permanent sovereignty over its natural resources, in accordance with the will of its people, without outside intervention, interference, subversion, coercion or threat in any form whatsoever;

(*c*) The right of States and peoples to have free access to information and to develop fully, without interference, their system of information and mass media and to use their information media in order to promote their political, social, economic and cultural interests and aspirations, based, *inter alia*, on the relevant articles of the Universal Declaration of Human Rights[1] and the principles of the new international information order;

II

(*a*) The duty of States to refrain in their international relations from the threat or use of force in any form whatsoever to violate the existing internationally recognized boundaries of another State, to disrupt the political, social or economic order of other States, to overthrow or change the political system of another State or its Government, to cause tension between or among States or to deprive peoples of their national identity and cultural heritage;

(*b*) The duty of a State to ensure that its territory is not used in any manner which would violate the sovereignty, political independence, territorial integrity and national unity or disrupt the political, economic and social stability of another State; this obligation applies also to States entrusted with responsibility for territories yet to attain self-determination and national independence;

(*c*) The duty of a State to refrain from armed intervention, subversion, military occupation or any other form of intervention and interference, overt or covert, directed at another State or group of States, or any act of military, political or economic interference in the internal affairs of another State, including acts of reprisal involving the use of force;

(*d*) The duty of a State to refrain any forcible action which deprives peoples under colonial domination or foreign occupation of their right to self-determination, freedom and independence;

(*e*) The duty of a State to refrain from any action or attempt in whatever form or under whatever pretext to destabilize or to undermine the stability of another State or of any of its institutions;

(*f*) The duty of a State to refrain from the promotion, encouragement or support, direct or indirect, of rebellious or secessionist activities within other States, under any pretext whatsoever, or any action which seeks to disrupt the unity or to undermine or subvert the political order of other States;

(*g*) The duty of a State to prevent on its territory the training, financing and recruitment of mercenaries, or the sending of such mercenaries into the territory of another State, and to deny facilities, including financing, for the equipping and transit of mercenaries;

(*h*) The duty of a State to refrain from concluding agreements with other States designed to intervene or interfere in the internal and external affairs of third States;

(*i*) The duty of States to refrain from any measure which would lead to the strengthening of existing military blocs or the creation or strengthening of new military alliances, interlocking arrangements, the deployment of interventionist forces or military bases and other related military installations conceived in the context of great-Power confrontation;

(*j*) The duty of a State to abstain from any defamatory campaign, vilification or hostile propaganda for the purpose of intervening or interfering in the internal affairs of other States;

(*k*) The duty of a State, in the conduct of its international relations in the economic, social, technical and trade fields, to refrain from measures which would constitute interference or intervention in the internal or external affairs of another State, thus preventing it from determining freely its political, economic and social development; this includes, *inter alia*, the duty of a State not to use its external economic assistance programme or adopt any multilateral or unilateral economic reprisal or blockade and to prevent the use of transnational and multinational corporations under its jurisdiction and control as instruments of political pressure or coercion against another State, in violation of the Charter of the United Nations;

(*l*) The duty of a State to refrain from the exploitation and the distortion of human rights issues as a means of interference in the internal affairs of States, of exerting pressure on other States or creating distrust and disorder within and among States or groups of States;

(*m*) The duty of a State to refrain using terrorist practices as state policy against another State or against peoples under colonial domination, foreign occupation or racist régimes and to prevent any assistance to or use of or tolerance of terrorist groups, saboteurs or subversive agents against third States;

(*n*) The duty of a State to refrain from organizing, training, financing and arming political and ethnic groups on their territories or the territories of other States for the purpose of creating subversion, disorder or unrest in other countries;

(*o*) The duty of a State to refrain from economic, political or military activity in the territory of another State without its consent;

III

(*a*) The right and duty of States to participate actively on the basis of equality in solving outstanding international issues, thus actively contributing to the removal of causes of conflict and interference;

(*b*) The right and duty of States fully to support the right to self-determination, freedom and independence of peoples under colonial domination, foreign occupation or racist régimes, as well as the right of these peoples to wage both political and armed struggle to that end, in accordance with the purposes and principles of the Charter;

(*c*) The right and duty of States to observe, promote and defend all human rights and fundamental freedoms within their own national territories and to work for the elimination of massive and flagrant violations of the rights of nations and peoples, and, in particular, for the elimination of apartheid and all forms of racism and racial discrimination;

(*d*) The right and duty of States to combat, within their constitutional prerogatives, the dissemination of false or distorted news which can be interpreted as interference in the internal affairs of other States or as being harmful to the promotion of peace, cooperation and friendly relations among States and nations;

(*e*) The right and duty of States not to recognize situations brought about by the threat or use of force or acts undertaken in contravention of the principle of non-intervention and non-interference.

3. The rights and duties set out in this Declaration are interrelated and are in accordance with the Charter.

4. Nothing in this Declaration shall prejudice in any manner the right to self-determination, freedom and independence of peoples under colonial domination, foreign occupation or racist régimes, and the right to seek and receive support in accordance with the purposes and principles of the Charter.

5. Nothing in this Declaration shall prejudice in any manner the provisions of the Charter.

6. Nothing in this Declaration shall prejudice action taken by the United Nations under Chapters VI and VII of the Charter.

---

1 Resolution 217 A (III).

01.50 DIPLOMATIC AND CONSULAR MISSIONS

2531 (XXIV). Settlement of Civil Claims in Connexion with the Convention on Special Missions

Committee: 6
Vote: 101 - 0 - 3

The General Assembly,

Noting that the Convention on Special Missions, adopted by the General Assembly on 8 December 1969,[1] provides for immunity from the jurisdiction of the receiving State of members of a special mission of the sending State,

Recalling that such immunity may be waived by the sending State,

Noting in addition that, as was recalled in the preamble to the Convention, the purpose of immunities is not to benefit individuals but to ensure the efficient performance of the functions of special missions,

Mindful of the deep concern expressed during the deliberations of the General Assembly that claims of immunity might, in certain cases, deprive persons in the receiving State of the benefit of a judicial settlement,

Recommends that the sending State should waive the immunity of members of its special mission in respect of civil claims of persons in the receiving State when it can do so without impeding the performance of the functions of the special mission, and that, when immunity is not waived, the sending State should use its best endeavours to bring about a just settlement of the claims.

1825th plenary meeting
8 December 1969

45/39. Consideration of Effective Measures to Enhance the Protection, Security and Safety of Diplomatic and Consular Missions and Representatives

Committee: 6
Vote: 148 - 1 - 0
Ref.: 49/49, 47/031, 43/167, 42/154, 41/78, 40/73, 39/83, 38/136, 37/108, 36/33, 35/168

The General Assembly,

Having considered the report of the Secretary-General,[2]

Conscious of the need to develop and strengthen friendly relations and cooperation among States,

Convinced that respect for the principles and rules of international law governing diplomatic and consular relations is a basic prerequisite for the normal conduct of relations among States and for the fulfilment of the purposes and principles of the Charter of the United Nations,

Alarmed by the repeated acts of violence against diplomatic and consular representatives, as well as against representatives to international intergovernmental organizations and officials of such organizations, which endanger or take innocent lives and seriously impede the normal work of such representatives and officials,

Recalling Security Council resolutions 664 (1990) of 18 August 1990, 667 (1990) of 16 September 1990 and 674 (1990) of 29 October 1990 regarding, *inter alia*, certain recent flagrant violations of international law concerning the protection, security and safety of diplomatic and consular missions and representatives,

Mindful of the universal condemnation of those violations during the debate on the question in the Sixth Committee at the forty-fifth session of the General Assembly,[3]

Concerned at the abuse of diplomatic or consular privileges and immunities, particularly if acts of violence are involved,

Emphasizing the duty of States to take all appropriate measures as required by international law, including measures of a preventive nature, and to bring offenders to justice,

Welcoming measures already taken by States to this end in conformity with their international obligations,

Convinced that the role of the United Nations, which includes the reporting procedures established under General Assembly resolution 35/168 of 15 December 1980 and further elaborated in later Assembly resolutions, is important in promoting efforts to enhance the protection, security and safety of diplomatic and consular missions and representatives,

Reaffirming its resolution 43/167 of 9 December 1988,

1. *Takes note* of the report of the Secretary-General;

2. *Strongly condemns* acts of violence against diplomatic and consular missions and representatives, as well as against missions and representatives to international intergovernmental organizations and officials of such organizations, and emphasizes that such acts can never be justified;

3. *Calls* for the immediate cessation of continuing violations of the protection, security and safety of diplomatic and consular missions and representatives and for respect of the right of free passage of diplomatic and consular personnel coming from or returning to the sending State;

4. *Urges* States to observe, implement and enforce the principles and rules of international law governing diplomatic and consular relations and, in particular, to ensure, in conformity with their international obligations, the protection, security and safety of the missions, representatives and officials mentioned in paragraph 2 above officially present in territories under their jurisdiction, including practical measures to prohibit in their territories illegal activities of persons, groups and organizations that encourage, instigate, organize or engage in the perpetration of acts against the security and safety of such missions, representatives and officials;

5. *Also urges* States to take all necessary measures at the national and international levels to prevent any acts of violence against the missions, representatives and officials mentioned in paragraph 2 above and to bring offenders to justice;

6. *Recommends* that States should cooperate closely through, *inter alia*, contacts between the diplomatic and consular missions and the receiving State, with regard to practical measures designed to enhance the protection, security and safety of diplomatic and consular missions and representatives and with regard to the exchange of information on the circumstances of all serious violations thereof;

7. *Calls upon* States that have not yet done so to consider becoming parties to the instruments relevant to the protection, security and safety of diplomatic and consular missions and representatives;

8. *Also calls upon* States, in cases where a dispute arises in connection with a violation of their international obligations concerning the protection of the missions or the security of the representatives and officials mentioned in paragraph 2 above, to make use of the means for peaceful settlement of disputes, including the good offices of the Secretary-General, and requests the Secretary-General, when he deems it appropriate, to offer his good offices to the States directly concerned;

9. *Requests* all States to report to the Secretary-General in accordance with paragraph 9 of resolution 42/154 of 7 December 1987;

10. *Requests* the Secretary-General to issue a report on the item, in accordance with paragraph 12 of resolution 42/154, containing also an analytical summary of the reports received under paragraph 9 above, on an annual basis, as well as to proceed with his other tasks pursuant to the same resolution;

11. *Decides* to include in the provisional agenda of its forty-seventh session the item entitled "Consideration of effective measures to enhance the protection, security and safety of diplomatic and consular missions and representatives".

48th plenary meeting
28 November 1990

---

1 Resolution 2530 (XXIV), annex, p. 305.

2 A/45/455 and Add.1-3.

3 See *Official Records of the General Assembly, Forty-fifth Session, Sixth Committee,* 5th to 7th and 45th meetings, and corrigendum.

01.60 PARTICULAR DISPUTES

01.61 SUEZ CANAL

997 (ES-I). Resolution 997 (ES-I)

Committee: -
Vote: 64 - 5 - 6
Ref.: 1003(ES-I), 1002(ES-I), 999(ES-I)

The General Assembly,

Noting the disregard on many occasions by parties to the Israel-Arab armistice agreements of 1949 of the terms of such agreements, and that the armed forces of Israel have penetrated deeply into Egyptian territory in violation of the General Armistice Agreement between Egypt and Israel of 24 February 1949,[1]

Noting that armed forces of France and the United Kingdom of Great Britain and Northern Ireland are conducting military operations against Egyptian territory,

Noting that traffic through the Suez Canal is now interrupted to the serious prejudice of many nations,

Expressing its grave concern over these developments,

1. *Urges* as a matter of priority that all parties now involved in hostilities in the area agree to an immediate cease-fire and, as part thereof, halt the movement of military forces and arms into the area;

2. *Urges* the parties to the armistice agreements promptly to withdraw all forces behind the armistice lines, to desist from raids across the armistice lines into neighbouring territory, and to observe scrupulously the provisions of the armistice agreements;

3. *Recommends* that all Member States refrain from introducing military goods in the area of hostilities and in general refrain from any acts which would delay or prevent the implementation of the present resolution;

4. *Urges* that, upon the cease-fire being effective, steps be taken to reopen the Suez Canal and restore secure freedom of navigation;

5. *Requests* the Secretary-General to observe and report promptly on the compliance with the present resolution to the Security Council and to the General Assembly, for such further action as they may deem appropriate in accordance with the Charter;

6. *Decides* to remain in emergency session pending compliance with the present resolution.

562nd plenary meeting,
2 November 1956

1000 (ES-I). Resolution 1000 (ES-I)

Committee: -
Vote: 57 - 0 - 19
Ref.: 998(ES-I)

The General Assembly,

Having requested the Secretary-General, in its resolution 998 (ES-I) of 4 November 1956, to submit to it a plan for an emergency international United Nations Force, for the purposes stated, [1]

Noting with satisfaction the first report of the Secretary-General on the plan,[2] and having in mind particularly paragraph 4 of that report,

1. *Establishes* a United Nations Command for an emergency international Force to secure and supervise the cessation of hostilities in accordance with all the terms of General Assembly resolution 997 (ES-I) of 2 November 1956;

2. *Appoints*, on an emergency basis, the Chief of Staff of the United Nations Truce Supervision Organization, Major-General E. L. M. Burns, as Chief of the Command;

3. *Authorizes* the Chief of the Command immediately to recruit, from the observer corps of the United Nations Truce Supervision Organization, a limited number of officers who shall be nationals of countries other than those having permanent membership in the Security Council, and further authorizes him, in consultation with the Secretary-General, to undertake the recruitment directly, from various Member States other than the permanent members of the Security Council, of the additional number of officers needed;

4. *Invites* the Secretary-General to take such administrative measures as may be necessary for the prompt execution of the actions envisaged in the present resolution.

565th plenary meeting
5 November 1956

1001 (ES-I). Resolution 1001 (ES-I)

Committee: -
Vote: 64 - 0 - 12

The General Assembly,

Recalling its resolution 997 (ES-I) of 2 November 1956 concerning the cease-fire, withdrawal of troops and other matters related to the military operations in Egyptian territory, as well as its resolution 998 (ES-I) of 4 November 1956 concerning the request to the Secretary-General to submit a plan for an emergency international United Nations Force,

Having established by its resolution 1000 (ES-I) of 5 November 1956 a United Nations Command for an emergency international Force, having appointed the Chief of Staff of the United Nations Truce Supervision Organization as Chief of the Command with authorization to him to begin the recruitment of officers for the Command, and having invited the Secretary-General to take the administrative measures necessary for the prompt execution of that resolution,

Noting with appreciation the second and final report of the Secretary-General[3] on the plan for an emergency international United Nations Force as requested in General Assembly resolution 998 (ES-I), and having examined that plan,

1. *Expresses its approval* of the guiding principles for the organization and functioning of the emergency international United Nations Force as expounded in paragraphs 6 to 9 of the Secretary-General's report;

2. *Concurs* in the definition of the functions of the Force as stated in paragraph 12 of the Secretary-General's report;

3. *Invites* the Secretary-General to continue discussions with Governments of Member States concerning offers of participation in the Force, toward the objective of its balanced composition;

4. *Requests* the Chief of the Command, in consultation with the Secretary-General as regards size and composition, to proceed forthwith with the full organization of the Force;

5. *Approves provisionally* the basic rule concerning the financing of the Force laid down in paragraph 15 of the Secretary-General's report;

6. *Establishes* an Advisory Committee composed of one representative from each of the following countries: Brazil, Canada, Ceylon, Colombia, India, Norway and Pakistan, and requests this Committee, whose Chairman shall be the Secretary-General, to undertake the development of those aspects of the planning for the Force and its operation not already dealt with by the General Assembly and which do not fall within the area of the direct responsibility of the Chief of the Command;

---

1 *Official Records of the Security Council, Fourth Year, Special Supplement No. 3.*

2 *Official Records of the General Assembly, First Emergency Special Session, Annexes,* agenda item 5, document A/3289.

3 *Ibid.*, document A/3302.

7. *Authorizes* the Secretary-General to issue all regulations and instructions which may be essential to the effective functioning of the Force, following consultation with the Committee aforementioned, and to take all other necessary administrative and executive action;

8. *Determines* that, following the fulfilment of the immediate responsibilities defined for it in operative paragraphs 6 and 7 above, the Advisory Committee shall continue to assist the Secretary-General in the responsibilities falling to him under the present and other relevant resolutions;

9. *Decides* that the Advisory Committee, in the performance of its duties, shall be empowered to request, through the usual procedures, the convening of the General Assembly and to report to the Assembly whenever matters arise which, in its opinion, are of such urgency and importance as to require consideration by the General Assembly itself;

10. *Requests* all Member States to afford assistance as necessary to the United Nations Command in the performance of its functions, including arrangements for passage to and from the area involved.

567th plenary meeting
7 November 1956

1120 (XI). Resolution 1120 (XI)

Committee: -
Vote: 63 - 5 - 10
Ref.: 1212(XXII), 1125(XI), 1124(XI), 1123(XI), 1121(XI)

The General Assembly,

Having received the report of the Secretary-General[1] on compliance with General Assembly resolutions 997 (ES-I) and 1002 (ES-I) of 2 and 7 November 1956,

Recalling that its resolution 1002 (ES-I) called upon Israel immediately to withdraw its forces behind the demarcation line established by the General Armistice Agreement between Egypt and Israel of 24 February 1949,[2]

Recalling further that the above-mentioned resolution also called upon France and the United Kingdom of Great Britain and Northern Ireland immediately to withdraw their forces from Egyptian territory, in conformity with previous resolutions,

1. *Notes with regret* that, according to the communications received by the Secretary-General,[3] two-thirds of the French forces remain, all the United Kingdom forces remain although it has been announced that arrangements are being made for the withdrawal of one battalion, and no Israel forces have been withdrawn behind the armistice line although a considerable time has elapsed since the adoption of the relevant General Assembly resolutions;

2. *Reiterates* its call to France, Israel and the United Kingdom of Great Britain and Northern Ireland to comply forthwith with resolutions 997 (ES-I) and 1002 (ES-I) of 2 and 7 November 1956;

3. *Requests* the Secretary-General urgently to communicate the present resolution to the parties concerned, and to report without delay to the General Assembly on the implementation thereof.

594th plenary meeting
24 November 1956

1 *Official Records of the General Assembly, Eleventh Session, Annexes,* agenda item 66, documents A/3384 and Add. 1 and 2. Appendix 27, p. 399.

2 *Official Records of the Security Council, Fourth Year, Special Supplement No. 3.*

3 *Official Records of the General Assembly, Eleventh Session, Annexes,* agenda item 66, documents A/3384 and Add. 1 and 2. Appendix 27, p. 399.

1122 (XI). Resolution 1122 (XI)

Committee: -
Vote: 52 - 9 - 13
Ref.: 1126(XI)

The General Assembly,

Having decided, in resolutions 1000 (ES-I) and 1001 (ES-I) of 5 and 7 November 1956, to establish an emergency international United Nations Force (hereafter to be known as the United Nations Emergency Force) under a Chief of Command (hereafter to be known as the Commander),

Having considered and provisionally approved the recommendations made by the Secretary-General concerning the financing of the Force in paragraph 15 of his report of 6 November 1956,[4]

1. *Authorizes* the Secretary-General to establish a United Nations Emergency Force Special Account to which funds received by the United Nations, outside the regular budget, for the purpose of meeting the expenses of the Force shall be credited, and from which payments for this purpose shall be made;

2. *Decides* that the Special Account shall be established in an initial amount of $10 million;

3. *Authorizes* the Secretary-General, pending the receipt of funds for the Special Account, to advance from the Working Capital Fund such sums as the Special Account may require to meet any expenses chargeable to it;

4. *Requests* the Secretary-General to establish such rules and procedures for the Special Account and make such administrative arrangements as he may consider necessary to ensure effective financial administration and control of that Account;

5. *Requests* the Fifth Committee and, as appropriate, the Advisory Committee on Administrative and Budgetary Questions, to consider and, as soon as possible, to report on further arrangements that need to be adopted regarding the costs of maintaining the Force.

596th plenary meeting
26 November 1956

01.62 HUNGARY

1004 (ES II). Resolution 1004 (ES II)

Committee: -
Vote: 50 - 8 - 15
Ref.: 1005(ES-II), 1006(ES-II), 1007(ES-II), 1008(ES-I)

The General Assembly,

Considering that the United Nations is based on the principle of the sovereign equality of all its Members,

Recalling that the enjoyment of human rights and of fundamental freedom in Hungary was specifically guaranteed by the Peace Treaty between Hungary and the Allied and Associated Powers signed at Paris on 10 February 1947, and that the general principle of these rights and this freedom is affirmed for all peoples in the Charter of the United Nations,

Convinced that recent events in Hungary manifest clearly the desire of the Hungarian people to exercise and to enjoy fully their fundamental rights, freedom and independence,

Condemning the use of Soviet military forces to suppress the efforts of the Hungarian people to reassert their rights,

Noting moreover the declaration of 30 October 1956 by the Government of the Union of Soviet Socialist Republics of its avowed policy of non-intervention in the internal affairs of other States,

4 *Official Records of the General Assembly, First Emergency Special Session, Annexes,* agenda-item 5, document A/3302. Appendix 29, p. 404.

Noting the communication of 1 November 1956[1] of the Government of Hungary to the Secretary-General regarding demands made by that Government to the Government of the Union of Soviet Socialist Republics for the instant and immediate withdrawal of Soviet forces,

Noting further the communication of 2 November 1956[2] from the Government of Hungary to the Secretary-General asking the Security Council to instruct the Government of the Union of Soviet Socialist Republics and the Government of Hungary to start negotiations immediately on the withdrawal of Soviet forces,

Noting that the intervention of Soviet military forces in Hungary has resulted in grave loss of life and widespread bloodshed among the Hungarian people,

Taking note of the radio appeal of Prime Minister Imre Nagy of 4 November 1956,

1. *Calls upon* the Government of the Union of Soviet Socialist Republics to desist forthwith from all armed attack on the people of Hungary and from any form of intervention, in particular armed intervention, in the internal affairs of Hungary;

2. *Calls upon* the Union of Soviet Socialist Republics to cease the introduction of additional armed forces into Hungary and to withdraw all of its forces without delay from Hungarian territory;

3. *Affirms* the right of the Hungarian people to a government responsive to its national aspirations and dedicated to its independence and well-being;

4. *Requests* the Secretary-General to investigate the situation caused by foreign intervention in Hungary, to observe the situation directly through representatives named by him, and to report thereon to the General Assembly at the earliest moment, and as soon as possible to suggest methods to bring an end to the foreign intervention in Hungary in accordance with the principles of the Charter of the United Nations;

5. *Calls upon* the Government of Hungary and the Government of the Union of Soviet Socialist Republics to permit observers designated by the Secretary-General to enter the territory of Hungary, to travel freely therein, and to report their findings to the Secretary-General;

6. *Calls upon* all Members of the United Nations to cooperate with the Secretary-General and his representatives in the execution of his functions;

7. *Requests* the Secretary-General in consultation with the heads of appropriate specialized agencies to inquire, on an urgent basis, into the needs of the Hungarian people for food, medicine and other similar supplies, and to report to the General Assembly as soon as possible;

8. *Requests* all Members of the United Nations, and invites national and international humanitarian organizations to cooperate in making available such supplies as may be required by the Hungarian people.

564th plenary meeting
4 November 1956

1131 (XI). Resolution 1131 (XI)

Committee: -
Vote: 55 - 8 - 13
Ref.: 1133(XI), 1132(XI), 1130(XI), 1129(XI), 1128(XI), 1127(XI)

The General Assembly,

Deeply concerned over the tragic events in Hungary,

Recalling those provisions of its resolutions 1004 (ES-II) of 4 November 1956, 1005 (ES-II) of 9 November 1956, 1127 (XI) of 21 November 1956 and 1130 (XI) of 4 December 1956, calling upon the Government of the Union of Soviet Socialist Republics to desist from its intervention in the internal affairs of Hungary, to withdraw its forces from Hungary and to cease its repression of the Hungarian people,

Recalling also those provisions of its resolutions 1004 (ES-II) and 1127 (XI), calling for permission for United Nations observers to enter the territory of Hungary, to travel freely therein and to report their findings to the Secretary-General,

Having received the report of the Secretary-General[3] of 30 November 1956, stating that no information is available to the Secretary-General concerning steps taken in order to establish compliance with the decisions of the General Assembly which refer to a withdrawal of troops or related political matters, and the note of the Secretary-General[4] of 7 December 1956,

Noting with grave concern that there has not been a reply to the latest appeal of the General Assembly for the admission of United Nations observers to Hungary, as contained in its resolution 1130 (XI),

Considering that recent events have clearly demonstrated the will of the Hungarian people to recover their liberty and independence,

Noting the overwhelming demand of the Hungarian people for the cessation of intervention of foreign armed forces and the withdrawal of foreign troops,

1. *Declares* that, by using its armed force against the Hungarian people, the Government of the Union of Soviet Socialist Republics is violating the political independence of Hungary;

2. *Condemns* the violation of the Charter of the United Nations by the Government of the Union Soviet Socialist Republics in depriving Hungary of its liberty and independence and the Hungarian people of the exercise of their fundamental rights;

3. *Reiterates* its call upon the Government of the Union of Soviet Socialist Republics to desist forthwith from any form of intervention in the internal affairs Hungary;

4. *Calls upon* the Government of the Union of Soviet Socialist Republics to make immediate arrangements for the withdrawal, under United Nations observation, of its armed forces from Hungary and to permit the re-establishment of the political independence of Hungary;

5. *Requests* the Secretary-General to take any initiative that he deems helpful in relation to the Hungarian problem, in conformity with the principles of the Charter and the resolutions of the General Assembly.

618th plenary meeting
12 December 1956

1312 (XIII). The Situation in Hungary

Committee: -
Vote: 54 - 10 - 15
Ref.: 1857(XVII), 1741(XVI), 1454(XIV)

The General Assembly,

Having considered the supplementary report, dated 14 July 1958, of the United Nations Special Committee[5] established by resolution 1132 (XI) of 10 January 1957 to report on the problem of Hungary,

Having considered the report, dated 9 December 1957, of the Special Representative of the General Assembly, His Royal Highness Prince Wan Waithayakon,[6] who was appointed by Assembly resolution 1133 (XI) of 14 September 1957 to take steps to achieve the objectives of Assembly resolutions 1004 (ES-II) of 4 November 1956, 1127 (XI) of 21 November 1956, 1131 (XI) of 12 December 1956 and 1132 (XI) of 10 January 1957,

1. *Expresses its appreciation* to its Special Representative, Prince Wan Waithayakon, for the efforts he has made to enter into consulta-

---

1 *Official Records of the General Assembly, Second Emergency Special Session, Annexes*, agenda item 5, document A/3251.

2 *Official Records of the Security Council, Eleventh Year, Supplement for October, November and December 1956*, document S/3726.

3 *Official Records of the General Assembly, Eleventh Session, Annexes*, agenda item 66, document A/3403. Appendix 34, p. 430.

4 *Ibid.*, document A/3435. Appendix 35, p. 432.

5 *Official Records of the General Assembly, Thirteenth Session, Annexes*, agenda item 69, document A/3849. Appendix 35, p. 410.

6 *Ibid., Twelfth Session, Annexes*, agenda item 63, document A/3774. Appendix 36, p. 421

tion with the appropriate authorities with a view to achieving the objectives of the resolutions referred to above;

2. *Endorses* the unanimous report of the Special Committee on the Problem of Hungary, dated 14 July 1958, and expresses its thanks to the Committee for its objective and efficient discharge of the tasks entrusted to it;

3. *Deplores* the continued refusal of the Government of the Union of Soviet Socialist Republics and the régime in Hungary to cooperate with the Special Representative and with the Committee in their efforts to achieve the objectives of the United Nations in accordance with the pertinent resolutions of the General Assembly;

4. *Deplores* the continuing repression in Hungary of fundamental rights of the Hungarian people and of their freedom of political expression under the shadow of the continuing presence of Soviet armed forces;

5. *Denounces* the execution of Mr. Imre Nagy, General Pál Maléter and other Hungarian patriots;

6. *Condemns* this continued defiance of the resolutions of the General Assembly;

7. *Again calls upon* the Union of Soviet Socialist Republics and the present authorities in Hungary to desist from repressive measures against the Hungarian people and to respect the liberty and political independence of Hungary and the Hungarian people's enjoyment of fundamental human rights and freedoms;

8. *Declares* that the United Nations will continue to be seized of the situation in Hungary in view of the fact that the Government of the Union of Soviet Socialist Republics and the present authorities in Hungary are disregarding the above-mentioned resolutions of the General Assembly;

9. *Decides* to appoint Sir Leslie Munro to represent the United Nations for the purpose of reporting to Member States or to the General Assembly on significant developments relating to the implementation of the Assembly resolutions on Hungary;

10. *Requests* the Secretary-General to provide the necessary facilities to assist Sir Leslie Munro in the performance of his duties.

787th plenary meeting
12 December 1958

01.63 CONGO

1474 (ES-IV). Question Considered by the Security Council at its 906th Meeting on 16 September 1960

Committee: 70 - 0 - 11
Vote:

The General Assembly,

Having considered the situation in the Republic of the Congo,

Taking note of the resolutions of 14 July,[1] 22 July[2] and 9 August 1960[3] of the Security Council,

Taking into account the unsatisfactory economic and political conditions that continue in the Republic of the Congo,

Considering that, with a view to preserving the unity, territorial integrity and political independence of the Congo, to protecting and advancing the welfare of its people, and to safeguarding international peace, it is essential for the United Nations to continue to assist the Central Government of the Congo,

1. *Fully supports* the resolutions of 14 and 22 July and 9 August 1960 of the Security Council;

2. *Requests* the Secretary-General to continue to take vigorous action in accordance with the terms of the aforesaid resolutions and to assist the Central Government of the Congo in the restoration and maintenance of law and order throughout the territory of the Republic of the Congo and to safeguard its unity, territorial integrity and political independence in the interests of international peace and security;

3. *Appeals* to all Congolese within the Republic of the Congo to seek a speedy solution by peaceful means of all their internal conflicts for the unity and integrity of the Congo, with the assistance, as appropriate, of Asian and African representatives appointed by the Advisory Committee on the Congo, in consultation with the Secretary-General, for the purpose of conciliation;

4. *Appeals* to all Member Governments for urgent voluntary contributions to a United Nations Fund for the Congo to be used under United Nations control and in consultation with the Central Government for the purpose of rendering the fullest possible assistance to achieve the objective mentioned in the preamble;

5. *Requests*:

(*a*) All States to refrain from any action which might tend to impede the restoration of law and order and the exercise by the Government of the Republic of the Congo of its authority and also to refrain from any action which might undermine the unity, territorial integrity and the political independence of the Republic of the Congo;

(*b*) All Member States, in accordance with Articles 25 and 49 of the Charter of the United Nations, to accept and carry out the decisions of the Security Council and to afford mutual assistance in carrying out measures decided upon by the Security Council;

6. Without prejudice to the sovereign rights of the Republic of the Congo, *calls upon* all States to refrain from the direct and indirect provision of arms or other materials of war and military personnel and other assistance for military purposes in the Congo during the temporary period of military assistance through the United Nations, except upon the request of the United Nations through the Secretary-General for carrying out the purposes of this resolution and of the resolutions of 14 and 22 July and 9 August 1960 of the Security Council.

863rd plenary meeting
20 September 1960

1599 (XV). The Situation in the Republic of the Congo

Committee: -
Vote: 61 - 5 - 33

The General Assembly,

Recalling its resolution 1474 (ES-IV) of 20 September 1960 and the Security Council resolutions of 14 July,[4] 22 July[5] and 9 August 1960[6] and, more particularly, that of 21 February 1961,[7] urging the immediate withdrawal and evacuation of all Belgian and other foreign military and paramilitary personnel and political advisers not under the United Nations Command, and mercenaries,

Deploring that despite all these requests the Government of Belgium has not yet complied with the resolutions and that such non-compliance has mainly contributed to the further deterioration of the situation in the Congo,

Convinced that the central factor in the present grave situation in the Congo is the continued presence of Belgian and other foreign military and paramilitary personnel and political advisers, and mercenaries, in total disregard of repeated resolutions of the United Nations,

1. *Calls upon* the Government of Belgium to accept its responsibilities as a Member of the United Nations and to comply fully and

1 *Official Records of the Security Council, Fifteenth Year, Supplement for July, August and September 1960*, document S/4387.

2 *Ibid.*, document S/4405.

3 *Ibid.*, document S/4426.

4 *Official Records of the Security Council, Fifteenth Year, Supplement for July, August and September 1960*, document S/4387.

5 *Ibid.*, document S/4405.

6 *Ibid.*, document S/4426.

7 *Ibid.*, *Sixteenth Year, Supplement for January, February and March 1961*, document S/4741.

promptly with the will of the Security Council and of the General Assembly;

2. *Decides* that all Belgian and other foreign military and paramilitary personnel and political advisers not under the United Nations Command, and mercenaries, shall be completely withdrawn and evacuated;

3. *Calls upon* all States to exert their influence and extend their cooperation to effect the implementation of the present resolution.

985th plenary meeting
15 April 1961

1600 (XV). The Situation in the Republic of the Congo

Committee: -
Vote: 60 - 16 - 23
Ref.: 1601(XV), 1599(XV), 1592(XV), 1498(XV), 1486(XV), 1480(XV)

The General Assembly,

Having considered the situation in the Republic of the Congo,

Gravely concerned at the danger of civil war and foreign intervention and at the threat to international peace and security,

Taking note of the report of the Conciliation Commission appointed in pursuance of paragraph 3 of its Resolution 1474 (ES-IV) of 20 September 1960,

Mindful of the desire of the Congolese people for a solution of the crisis in the Congo through national reconciliation and return to constitutionality without delay,

Noting with concern the many difficulties that have arisen in the way of effective functioning of the United Nations operation in the Congo,

1. *Reaffirms* its resolution 1474 (ES-IV) and the Security Council resolutions on the situation in the Congo, more particularly the Council resolution of 21 February 1961;

2. *Calls upon* the Congolese authorities concerned to desist from attempting a military solution to their problems and resolve them by peaceful means;

3. *Considers* it essential that necessary and effective measures be taken by the Secretary-General immediately to prevent the introduction of arms, military equipment and supplies into the Congo, except in conformity with the resolutions of the United Nations;

4. *Urges* the immediate release of all members of Parliament and members of provincial assemblies and all other political leaders now under detention;

5. *Urges* the convening of Parliament without delay, with safe conduct and security extended to the members of Parliament by the United Nations, so that Parliament may take the necessary decisions concerning the formation of a national government and on the future constitutional structure of the Republic of the Congo in accordance with the constitutional processes laid down in the *Loi fondamentale*;

6. *Decides* to appoint a Commission of Conciliation of seven members to be desired by the President of the General Assembly to assist the Congolese leaders to achieve reconciliation and to end the political crisis;

7. *Urges* the Congolese authorities to cooperate fully in the implementation of the resolutions of the Security Council and of the General Assembly and to accord all facilities essential to the performance by the United Nations of functions envisaged in those resolutions.

985th plenary meeting
15 April 1961

01.64 CYPRUS

2077 (XX). Question of Cyprus

Committee: 1
Vote: 47 - 5 - 54
Ref.: 1489(XV), 1287(XIII), 1013(XI), 814(IX)

The General Assembly,

Having considered the question of Cyprus,

Recalling Security Council resolutions 186 (1964) of 4 March 1964, 187 (1964) of 13 March 1964, 192 (1964) of 20 June 1964, 193 (1964) of 9 August 1964, 194 (1964) of 25 September 1964, 198 (1964) of 18 December 1964, 201 (1965) of 19 March 1965, 206 (1965) of 15 June 1965 and 207 (1965) of 10 August 1965, and the Council's consensus of 11 August 1964 with regard to Cyprus,[1]

Recalling the parts of the Declaration adopted on 10 October 1964 by the Second Conference of Heads of State or Government of Non-Aligned Countries, held at Cairo, regarding the question of Cyprus,[2]

Noting the report of the United Nations Mediator on Cyprus, submitted to the Secretary-General on 26 March 1965,[3]

Noting further that the Government of Cyprus is committed, through its Declaration of Intention and the accompanying Memorandum,[4] to:

(*a*) The full application of human rights to all citizens of Cyprus, irrespective of race or religion,

(*b*) The ensuring of minority rights,

(*c*) The safeguarding of the above rights as contained in the said Declaration and Memorandum,

1. *Takes cognizance* of the fact that the Republic of Cyprus, as an equal Member of the United Nations, is, in accordance with the Charter of the United Nations, entitled to enjoy, and should enjoy, full sovereignty and complete independence without any foreign intervention or interference;

2. *Calls upon* all States, in conformity with their obligations under the Charter, and in particular Article 2, paragraphs 1 and 4, to respect the sovereignty, unity, independence and territorial integrity of the Republic of Cyprus and to refrain from any intervention directed against it;

3. *Recommends* to the Security Council the continuation of the United Nations mediation work in conformity with Council resolution 186 (1964).

1402nd plenary meeting
18 December 1965

3212 (XXIX). Question of Cyprus

Committee: -
Vote: 117 - 0 - 0

The General Assembly,

Having considered the question of Cyprus,

Gravely concerned about the continuation of the Cyprus crisis, which constitutes a threat to international peace and security,

Mindful of the need to solve this crisis without delay by peaceful means, in accordance with the purposes and principles of the United Nations,

Having heard the statements in the debate and taking note of the report of the Special Political Committee on the question of Cyprus,[5]

---

1 *Official Records of the Security Council, Nineteenth Year,* 1143rd meeting, para. 358.

2 See A/5763.

3 *Official Records of the Security Council, Twentieth Year, Supplement for January, February and March 1965,* document S/6253.

4 *Official Records of the General Assembly, Twentieth Session, Annexes,* agenda item 93, document A/6039. Appendix 11, p. 228.

1. *Calls upon* all States to respect the sovereignty, independence, territorial integrity and non-alignment of the Republic of Cyprus and to refrain from all acts and interventions directed against it;

2. *Urges* the speedy withdrawal of all foreign armed forces and foreign military presence and personnel from the Republic of Cyprus, and the cessation of all foreign interference in its affairs;

3. *Considers* that the constitutional system of the Republic of Cyprus concerns the Greek Cypriot and Turkish Cypriot communities;

4. *Commends* the contacts and negotiations taking place on an equal footing, with the good offices of the Secretary-General, between the representatives of the two communities, and calls for their continuation with a view to reaching freely a mutually acceptable political settlement, based on their fundamental and legitimate rights;

5. *Considers* that all the refugees should return to their homes in safety and calls upon the parties concerned to undertake urgent measures to that end;

6. *Expresses the hope* that, if necessary, further efforts including negotiations can take place, within the framework of the United Nations, for the purpose of implementing the provisions of the present resolution, thus ensuring to the Republic of Cyprus its fundamental right to independence, sovereignty and territorial integrity;

7. *Requests* the Secretary-General to continue to provide United Nations humanitarian assistance to all parts of the population of Cyprus and calls upon all States to contribute to that effort;

8. *Calls upon* all parties to continue to cooperate fully with the United Nations Peace-keeping Force in Cyprus, which may be strengthened if necessary;

9. *Requests* the Secretary-General to continue to lend his good offices to the parties concerned;

10. *Further requests* the Secretary-General to bring the present resolution to the attention of the Security Council.

2275th plenary meeting
1 November 1974

37/253. Question of Cyprus

Committee: -
Vote: 103 - 5 - 20; para. 7: 89 - 5 - 27; para. 10: 86 - 8 - 25
Ref.: 34/30, 33/15, 32/15, 31/12, 3395(XXX), 3212(XXIX)

The General Assembly,

Having considered the question of Cyprus,

Recalling its resolution 3212 (XXIX) of 1 November 1974 and its subsequent resolutions on the question of Cyprus,

Recalling the high-level agreements of 12 February 1977 and 19 May 1979,

Reaffirming the principle of the inadmissibility of occupation and acquisition of territory by force,

Greatly concerned at the prolongation of the Cyprus crisis, which poses a serious threat to international peace and security,

Deeply regretting that the resolutions of the United Nations on Cyprus have not yet been implemented,

Recalling the idea of holding an international conference on Cyprus,

Deploring the fact that part of the territory of the Republic of Cyprus is still occupied by foreign forces,

Deploring the lack of progress in the intercommunal talks,

Deploring all unilateral actions that change the demographic structure of Cyprus or promote faits accomplis,

Reaffirming the need to settle the question of Cyprus without further delay by peaceful means in accordance with the provisions of the Charter of the United Nations and the relevant United Nations resolutions,

1. *Reiterates* its full support for the sovereignty, independence, territorial integrity, unity and non-alignment of the Republic of Cyprus and calls once again for the cessation of all foreign interference in its affairs;

2. *Affirms* the right of the Republic of Cyprus and its people to full and effective sovereignty and control over the entire territory of Cyprus and its natural and other resources and calls upon all States to support and help the Government of the Republic of Cyprus to exercise these rights;

3. *Condemns* any act which tends to undermine the full and effective exercise of the above-mentioned rights, including the unlawful issue of titles of ownership of property;

4. *Welcomes* the proposal for total demilitarization made by the President of the Republic of Cyprus;

5. *Expresses its support* for the high-level agreements of 12 February 1977 and 19 May 1979 and all the provisions thereof;

6. *Demands* the immediate and effective implementation of resolution 3212 (XXIX), unanimously adopted by the General Assembly and endorsed by the Security Council in its resolution 365 (1974) of 13 December 1974, and of the subsequent resolutions of the Assembly and the Council on Cyprus which provide the valid and essential basis for the solution of the problem of Cyprus;

7. *Considers* the withdrawal of all occupation forces from the Republic of Cyprus as an essential basis for a speedy and mutually acceptable solution of the problem of Cyprus;

8. *Demands* the immediate withdrawal of all occupation forces from the Republic of Cyprus;

9. *Commends* the intensification of the efforts made by the Secretary-General, while noting with concern the lack of progress in the intercommunal talks;

10. *Calls* for meaningful, result-oriented, constructive and substantive negotiations between the representatives of the two communities, under the auspices of the Secretary-General, to be conducted freely and on an equal footing, on the basis of relevant United Nations resolutions and the high-level agreements, with a view to reaching as early as possible a mutually acceptable agreement based on the fundamental and legitimate rights of the two communities;

11. *Calls* for respect of the human rights and fundamental freedoms of all Cypriots, including the freedom of movement, the freedom of settlement and the right to property, and the instituting of urgent measures for the voluntary return of the refugees to their homes in safety;

12. *Considers* that the *de facto* situation created by the force of arms should not be allowed to influence or in any way affect the solution of the problem of Cyprus;

13. *Calls upon* the parties concerned to refrain from any unilateral action which might adversely affect the prospects of a just and lasting solution of the problem of Cyprus by peaceful means and to cooperate fully with the Secretary-General in the performance of his task under the relevant resolutions of the General Assembly and the Security Council as well as with the United Nations Peace-keeping Force in Cyprus;

14. *Calls upon* the parties concerned to refrain from any action which violates or is designed to violate the independence, unity, sovereignty and territorial integrity of the Republic of Cyprus;

15. *Reiterates its recommendation* that the Security Council should examine the question of implementation, within a specified time-frame, of its relevant resolutions and consider and adopt thereafter, if necessary, all appropriate and practical measures under the Charter of the United Nations for ensuring the speedy and effective implementation of the resolutions of the United Nations on Cyprus;

16. *Welcomes* the intention of the Secretary-General, as expressed in his report,[1] to pursue a renewed personal involvement in the quest for a solution of the problem of Cyprus and, in view of this, requests the Secretary-General to undertake such actions or initiatives as he may consider appropriate within the framework of the mission of good offices entrusted to him by the Security Council for promoting

5 *Ibid., Twenty-ninth Session, Annexes,* agenda item 110, document A/9820.

1 A/37/805 and Corr.1.

a just and lasting solution of the problem and to report to the General Assembly at its thirty-eighth session on the results of his efforts;

17. *Decides* to include in the provisional agenda of its thirty-eighth session the item entitled "Question of Cyprus" and requests the Secretary-General to follow up the implementation of the present resolution and to report on all its aspects to the General Assembly at that session.

121st plenary meeting
13 May 1983

01.65 NICARAGUA

33/76. Situation in Nicaragua

Committee: 1
Vote: 85 - 2 - 45

The General Assembly,

Reaffirming its obligations with regard to the maintenance of international peace and security and the promotion of universal respect for human rights and fundamental freedoms,

Bearing in mind the statement of the President of the Republic of Costa Rica at the current session of the General Assembly on the violation of his country's sovereignty by military aircraft of Nicaragua,[1]

Noting also the message sent to the President of the General Assembly concerning this matter by the President of the Republic of Colombia and the President of the Republic of Venezuela on 27 September 1978,[2]

Considering the extreme gravity of the events that have taken place and are continuing to occur in Nicaragua, which have caused the death of thousands of people, incalculable destruction of property and repeated violations of the most basic rights and which have led some countries of the American continent to attempt to reach a peaceful solution to the internal conflict in Nicaragua by means of a friendly committee of conciliation,

1. *Censures* the repression of the civilian population of Nicaragua and the violation of the sovereignty of Costa Rica by Nicaraguan military aircraft;

2. *Expresses deep concern* over the serious turn taken by the domestic situation in Nicaragua and over its implications for peace and security in the region;

3. *Demands* that the Nicaraguan authorities stop military and other activities that endanger the security of the region, in particular those that threaten the sovereignty and territorial inviolability of neighbouring countries;

4. *Urges* the Nicaraguan authorities to ensure respect for the human rights of the citizens of Nicaragua, in accordance with their international commitments and the provisions of the Charter of the United Nations;

5. *Requests* all States to adopt the necessary measures, in accordance with their constitutional procedures, to discourage the recruitment and participation of their nationals as mercenaries in the conflict occurring in Nicaragua;

6. *Urges* the continuation of international efforts to achieve a peaceful settlement of the internal conflict in Nicaragua;

7. *Requests* the Secretary-General, through the appropriate channels, carefully to follow developments in the situation in Nicaragua and provide the assistance needed to achieve the purposes of the present resolution.

85th plenary meeting
15 December 1978

1 *Official Records of the General Assembly, Thirty-third Session, Plenary Meetings,* 11th meeting, paras. 75-126.

2 A/33/275, annex.

40/188. Trade Embargo Against Nicaragua

Committee: 2
Vote: 91 - 6 - 49

The General Assembly,

Recalling the relevant purposes and principles set forth in the Charter of the United Nations,

Reaffirming the fundamental principles that govern relations among the States of the international community,

Recalling the Universal Declaration of Human Rights,[3]

Recalling Security Council resolution 562 (1985) of 10 May 1985,

Recalling also General Assembly resolution 2625 (XXV) of 24 October 1970, in particular the principle concerning the duty not to intervene in matters within the domestic jurisdiction of any State, in accordance with the Charter of the United Nations,

Reaffirming that each country has the sovereign right to choose its own development policies and strategies,

Recalling all relevant articles of the General Agreement on Tariffs and Trade,

Recalling also General Assembly resolution 39/4 of 26 October 1984, in which the Assembly encouraged the efforts of the Contadora Group and all interested States, in particular those with ties to and interests in the region, to respect fully the purposes and principles of the Contadora Act on Peace and Cooperation in Central America of 7 September 1984,[4]

Concerned that the unilateral trade embargo and other measures imposed on Nicaragua on 1 May 1985, which have been extended and broadened as from 1 November 1985, adversely affect the economy of the country, specifically its trade, and consequently its development plans,

Deeply concerned that the said measures will not contribute to the economic and social development of Nicaragua and to the goals and objectives of the Contadora process,

Recalling the widespread concern expressed by the international community about the situation in Central America, aggravated by the trade embargo against Nicaragua,

Considering that the international community is unanimous in contributing to the economic and social progress of the countries of the area and to the reinforcing of the process of economic integration of the area, in order to contribute to the quest for a negotiated political solution to the regional crisis,

Reaffirming the sovereignty and inalienable right of Nicaragua and the rest of the States in the region to decide freely on their own political, economic and social systems to develop their international relations according to their peoples' interests, free from outside interference, subversion, direct or indirect coercion or threats of any kind,

Deeply concerned that the said trade embargo jeopardizes the principles of free trade and non-discrimination that should prevail among nations,

1. *Regrets* the recent trade embargo and other measures imposed against Nicaragua and requests that those measures be immediately revoked;

2. *Invites* all States to promote and take concrete actions of cooperation in the economic and technological spheres in Central America, in particular to help reduce the negative effects of the trade embargo and other measures imposed against Nicaragua and to contribute to economic and social development and to regional economic integration;

3 TD/RS/CONF/19, annex 11.

4 *Official Records of the Security Council, Thirty-ninth Year, Supplement for July, August and September 1984,* document S/16775, annex.

3. *Requests* the Secretary-General to report to the General Assembly at its forty-first session on the implementation of the present resolution.

119th plenary meeting
17 December 1985

44/217. Trade Embargo Against Nicaragua

Committee: 2
Vote: 82 - 2 - 47

The General Assembly,

Recalling its resolutions 40/188 of 17 December 1985, 41/164 of 5 December 1986, 42/176 of 11 December 1987 and 43/185 of 20 December 1988, as well as its resolutions 42/204 of 11 December 1987, 42/231 of 12 May 1988 and 43/210 of 20 December 1988,

Taking note of the report of the Secretary-General on the trade embargo against Nicaragua,[1]

1. *Deplores* the continuation of the trade embargo contrary to its resolutions 40/188, 41/164, 42/176 and 43/185 and to the Judgment of the International Court of Justice of 27 June 1986,[2] and once again requests that those measures be immediately revoked,

2. *Requests* the Secretary-General to report to the General Assembly at its forty-fifth session on the implementation of the present resolution.

85th plenary meeting
22 December 1989

01.66 OTHER CASES

508 (VI). Threats to the Political Independence and Territorial Integrity of Greece

Committee: P
Vote: A: 48 - 5 - 1; B: 48 - 5 - 1
Ref.: 382(V), 288(IV), 193(III), 109(II)

A

The General Assembly,

Having considered the report[3] of the United Nations Special Committee on the Balkans,

1. *Approves* the said report;

2. *Expresses* its deep appreciation of the invaluable services rendered for the preservation of peace and security in the Balkans by the members of the Special Committee;

3. *Expresses* its warm gratitude for the gallantry with which the observers of the Special Committee have carried out their difficult and dangerous task;

4. *Decides* to discontinue the Special Committee within sixty days after the adoption of the present resolution.

351st plenary meeting
7 December 1951

B

The General Assembly,

Recalling its resolution 377A(V) ("Uniting for peace"), section B, establishing a Peace Observation Commission which could observe and report on the situation in any area where there exists international tension, the continuance of which is likely to endanger the maintenance of international peace and security,

Considering that the situation in the Balkans may require prompt establishment of observations as contemplated in resolution 377A(V), section B,

Resolves to request the Peace Observation Commission to establish a Balkan sub-commission composed of not less than three nor more than five members, with its seat at the United Nations Headquarters, with authority:

(*a*) To dispatch such observers as it may deem necessary to any area of international tension in the Balkans on the request of any State or States concerned, but only to the territory of States consenting thereto;

(*b*) To visit, if it deems necessary, any area in which observation requested under sub-paragraph (a) is being conducted;

(*c*) To consider such data as may be submitted to it by its members or observers and to make such reports as it deems necessary to the Peace Observation Commission and to the Secretary General for the information of Member States.

351st plenary meeting
7 December 1951

815 (IX). Complaint by the Union of Burma Regarding Aggression Against it by the Government of the Republic of China

Committee: P
Vote: 56 - 0
Ref.: 717(VIII), 707(VII)

The General Assembly,

Having considered the report[4] dated 27 September 1954 of the Government of the Union of Burma on the situation relating to the presence of foreign forces in its territory,

Having taken note of the report[5] of the Joint Military Committee for the Evacuation of Foreign Forces from Burma the efforts of which were directed to securing the removal of these foreign forces,

1. *Notes with satisfaction* that nearly 7,000 persons, both foreign forces and their dependants, have been evacuated from Burma and that this constitutes a substantial contribution to the solution of the problem pursuant to the recommendations of the General Assembly;

2. *Expresses its appreciation* of the efforts of the Governments of the United States of America and of Thailand in helping to bring about this evacuation;

3. *Deplores* the fact that considerable foreign forces with a significant quantity of arms still remain in the territory of the Union of Burma and have failed to respond to the declarations of the General Assembly that they should either leave the territory of the Union of Burma or submit to internment;

4. *Declares* once more that these forces should submit to disarmament and internment;

5. *Assures* the Government of the Union of Burma of its continuing sympathy with and support of the efforts of that Government to bring about a complete solution of this serious problem;

6. *Urges* all States to take all necessary steps to prevent the furnishing of any assistance which may enable foreign forces to remain in the territory of the Union of Burma or to continue their hostile acts against that country;

7. *Invites* the Government of the Union of Burma to report on the situation to the General Assembly as appropriate.

496th plenary meeting
29 October 1954

---

1 A/44/581.

2 See *Military and Paramilitary Activities in and against Nicaragua* (Nicaragua v. United States of America), Merits, Judgment, *I.C.J. Reports 1986*, p. 14.

3 See *Official Records of The General Assembly, Sixth Session, Supplement No. 11.*

4 See *Official Records of the General Assembly, Ninth Session, Annexes*, agenda item 63, document A/ 2739. Appendix 6, p. 269.

5 *Ibid.*, document A/2740. Appendix 7, p. 270.

1622 (S-III). Consideration of the Grave Situation in Tunisia Obtaining since 19 July 1961

Committee: -
Vote: 66 - 0 - 30
Ref.: 1112(XI), 813(IX), 611(VII)

The General Assembly,

Having examined the grave situation prevailing in Tunisia since 19 July 1961 which was the subject matter of Security Council consideration in its meetings of 21, 22, 28 and 29 July 1961,[1]

Noting with concern and regret that France has not fully complied with the provisions of the interim resolution adopted by the Security Council on 22 July 1961,[2]

Noting that the Security Council has failed to take further appropriate action,

Convinced that the presence of French armed forces in Tunisian territory against the express will of the Tunisian Government and people constitutes a violation of Tunisia's sovereignty, is a permanent source of international friction and endangers international peace and security,

1. *Reaffirms* the Security Council's interim resolution and urges the Government of France to implement fully the provisions of operative paragraph 1 thereof;

2. *Recognizes* the sovereign right of Tunisia to call for the withdrawal of all French armed forces present on its territory without its consent;

3. *Calls upon* the Governments of France and Tunisia to enter into immediate negotiations to devise peaceful and agreed measures in accordance with the principles of the Charter of the United Nations for the withdrawal of all French armed forces from Tunisian territory.

1006th plenary meeting
25 August 1961

2793 (XXVI). Question Considered by the Security Council at its 1606th, 1607th and 1608th Meetings on 4, 5 and 6 December 1971

Committee: -
Vote: 104 - 11 - 10

The General Assembly,

Noting the reports of the Secretary-General of 3 and 4 December 1971[3] and the letter from the President of the Security Council[4] transmitting the text of Council resolution 303 (1971) of 6 December 1971,

Gravely concerned that hostilities have broken out between India and Pakistan which constitute an immediate threat to international peace and security,

Recognizing the need to deal appropriately at a subsequent stage, within the framework of the Charter of the United Nations, with the issues which have given rise to the hostilities,

Convinced that an early political solution would be necessary for the restoration of conditions of normalcy in the area of conflict and for the return of the refugees to their homes,

Mindful of the provisions of the Charter, in particular of Article 2, paragraph 4,

Recalling the Declaration on the Strengthening of International Security, particularly paragraphs 4, 5 and 6,

Recognizing further the need to take immediate measures to bring about an immediate cessation of hostilities between India and Pakistan and effect a withdrawal of their armed forces to their own side of the India-Pakistan borders,

Mindful of the purposes and principles of the Charter and of the General Assembly's responsibilities under the relevant provisions of the Charter and of Assembly resolution 377 A (V) of 3 November 1950,

1. *Calls upon* the Governments of India and Pakistan to take forthwith all measures for an immediate cease-fire and withdrawal of their armed forces on the territory of the other to their own side of the India-Pakistan borders;

2. *Urges* that efforts be intensified in order to bring about, speedily and in accordance with the purposes and principles of the Charter of the United Nations, conditions necessary for the voluntary return of the East Pakistan refugees to their homes;

3. *Calls* for the full cooperation of all States with the Secretary-General for rendering assistance to and relieving the distress of those refugees;

4. *Urges* that every effort be made to safeguard the lives and well-being of the civilian population in the area of conflict;

5. *Requests* the Secretary-General to keep the General Assembly and the Security Council promptly and currently informed on the implementation of the present resolution;

6. *Decides* to follow the question closely and to meet again should the situation so demand;

7. *Calls upon* the Security Council to take appropriate action in the light of the present resolution.

2003rd plenary meeting
7 December 1971

ES-6/2. The Situation in Afghanistan and its Implications for International Peace and Security

Committee: -
Vote: 104 - 18 - 18

The General Assembly,

Taking note of Security Council resolution 462 (1980) of 9 January 1980, calling for an emergency special session of the General Assembly to examine the question contained in document S/Agenda/2185,

Gravely concerned at the recent developments in Afghanistan and their implications for international peace and security,

Reaffirming the inalienable right of all peoples to determine their own future and to choose their own form of government free from outside interference,

Mindful of the obligation of all States to refrain in their international relations from the threat or use of force against the sovereignty, territorial integrity and political independence of any State or in any other manner inconsistent with the purposes and principles of the Charter of the United Nations,

Recognizing the urgent need for immediate termination of foreign armed intervention in Afghanistan so as to enable its people to determine their own destiny without outside interference or coercion,

Noting with profound concern the large outflow of refugees from Afghanistan,

Recalling its resolutions on the strengthening of international security, on the inadmissibility of intervention in the domestic affairs of States and the protection of their independence and sovereignty and on the principles of international law concerning friendly relations and cooperation among States in accordance with the Charter of the United Nations,

Expressing its deep concern at the dangerous escalation of tension, intensification of rivalry and increased recourse to military intervention and interference in the internal affairs of States, which are detrimental to the interests of all nations, particularly the non-aligned countries,

---

1. *Official Records of the Security Council, Sixteenth Year,* 961st to 966th meetings.
2. *Ibid., Supplement for July, August and September 1961,* document S/4882.
3. *Official Record of the Security Council, Twenty-sixth Year, Supplement for October, November and December 1971,* documents S/10410 and Add.1 and S/10412.
4. *Official Records of the General Assembly, Twenty-sixth Session, Annexes,* agenda item 102, document A/8555.

Mindful of the purposes and principles of the Charter and of the responsibility of the General Assembly under the relevant provisions of the Charter and of Assembly resolution 377 A (V) of 3 November 1950,

1. *Reaffirms* that respect for the sovereignty, territorial integrity and political independence of every State is a fundamental principle of the Charter of the United Nations, any violation of which on any pretext whatsoever is contrary to its aims and purposes;

2. *Strongly deplores* the recent armed intervention in Afghanistan, which is inconsistent with that principle;

3. *Appeals* to all States to respect the sovereignty, territorial integrity, political independence and non-aligned character of Afghanistan and to refrain from any interference in the internal affairs of that country;

4. *Calls* for the immediate, unconditional and total withdrawal of the foreign troops from Afghanistan in order to enable its people to determine their own form of government and choose their economic, political and social systems free from outside intervention, subversion, coercion or constraint of any kind whatsoever;

5. *Urges* all parties concerned to assist in bringing about, speedily and in accordance with the purposes and principles of the Charter, conditions necessary for the voluntary return of the Afghan refugees to their homes;

6. *Appeals* to all States and national and international organizations to extend humanitarian relief assistance with a view to alleviating the hardship of the Afghan refugees in coordination with the United Nations High Commissioner for Refugees;

7. *Requests* the Secretary-General to keep Member States and the Security Council promptly and concurrently informed on the progress towards the implementation of the present resolution;

8. *Calls upon* the Security Council to consider ways and means which could assist in the implementation of the present resolution.

7th plenary meeting
14 January 1980

46/23. The Situation in Afghanistan and its Implications for International Peace and Security

Committee: -
Vote: Adopted without a vote
Ref.: 50/88, 49/140, 48/208, 47/119, 45/12, 44/15, 43/20, 42/15, 41/33, 40/12, 39/13, 38/29, 37/37, 36/34, 35/37

The General Assembly,

Having considered the item entitled "The situation in Afghanistan and its implications for international peace and security",

Recalling its resolutions 43/20 of 3 November 1988, 44/15 of 1 November 1989 and 45/12 of 7 November 1990,

Reaffirming the purposes and principles of the Charter of the United Nations and the obligation of all States to refrain in their international relations from the threat or use of force against the sovereignty, territorial integrity and political independence of any State,

Reaffirming also the inalienable right of all peoples to determine their own form of government and to choose their own economic, political and social system free from outside intervention, subversion, coercion or constraint of any kind whatsoever,

Gravely concerned about the situation in Afghanistan, which resulted from the violation of principles of the Charter and of the recognized norms of inter-State conduct,

Recalling the conclusion at Geneva, on 14 April 1988, of the Agreements on the Settlement of the Situation Relating to Afghanistan, and the completion of the withdrawal of foreign troops in accordance with those Agreements,

Aware of the continuing concern of the international community about the sufferings of the Afghan people and the magnitude of the social and economic problems posed to Pakistan and Iran by the presence on their soil of millions of Afghan refugees,

Deeply conscious of the urgent need for a comprehensive political solution of the situation in respect of Afghanistan,

Conscious that a successful final political settlement of the Afghanistan problem would have a favourable impact on the international situation and provide an impetus for the resolution of other acute regional conflicts,

Expressing its appreciation to the Secretary-General and his Personal Representative for their efforts to bring about peace and security,

Supporting the statement of the Secretary-General on Afghanistan of 21 May 1991,

Taking note of the report of the Secretary-General and the status of the process of political settlement,

1. *Emphasizes* the importance of the Agreements on the Settlement of the Situation Relating to Afghanistan, hereinafter referred to as the "Geneva Agreements", concluded at Geneva on 14 April 1988 under United Nations auspices, which constitute an important step towards a comprehensive political solution of the Afghanistan problem;

2. *Expresses its deep appreciation* to the Secretary-General and his Personal Representative for their constant efforts to achieve a political solution of the Afghanistan problem;

3. *Calls* for scrupulous respect for and faithful implementation of the Geneva Agreements by all parties concerned who should fully abide by their letter and spirit;

4. *Calls upon* all parties concerned to promote actively the search for ways towards a political solution, acceptable to the Afghan people, on the basis of principles contained in the statement of the Secretary-General on Afghanistan;

5. *Reiterates* that the preservation of the sovereignty, territorial integrity, political independence and non-aligned and Islamic character of Afghanistan is essential for a peaceful solution of the Afghanistan problem;

6. *Reaffirms* the right of the Afghan people to determine their own form of government and to choose their economic, political and social system free from outside intervention, subversion, coercion or constraint of any kind whatsoever;

7. *Calls upon* all parties concerned to work urgently for the achievement of a comprehensive political solution, the cessation of hostilities and the creation of the necessary conditions of peace and normalcy that would enable the Afghan refugees to return voluntarily to their homeland in safety and honour;

8. *Emphasizes* the need for an early start of the intra-Afghan dialogue for the establishment, through democratic procedures acceptable to the Afghan people, including free and fair elections, of a broad-based government to ensure the broadest support and immediate participation of all segments of the Afghan people;

9. *Also calls upon* all parties concerned to exert every effort to promote a political settlement acceptable to the Afghan people in order to bring to an end the protracted conflict that has prevailed in Afghanistan for the past several years;

10. *Requests* the Secretary-General and his Personal Representative to continue to encourage and facilitate the early realization of a comprehensive political settlement in Afghanistan in accordance with the provisions of the Geneva Agreements and of the present resolution;

11. *Expresses its appreciation* for the efforts of the United Nations High Commissioner for Refugees aimed at providing humanitarian assistance to the Afghan refugees and facilitating their voluntary return, and appeals to the parties concerned to take all necessary measures to ease their lot;

12. *Renews its appeal* to all States and national and international organizations to continue to extend humanitarian relief assistance with a view to alleviating the hardship of the Afghan refugees, in coordination with the High Commissioner;

13. *Expresses its appreciation* for the efforts of the Coordinator for Humanitarian and Economic Assistance Programmes Relating to Afghanistan and calls upon all States to provide to the Coordinator adequate financial and material resources for the purposes of achieving the speedy repatriation and rehabilitation of the Afghan refugees, as well as for the economic and social reconstruction of the country;

14. *Requests* the Secretary-General to keep Member States and the Security Council informed of progress towards the implementation of the present resolution and to submit to the General Assembly at its forty-seventh session a report on the situation in Afghanistan and on progress achieved in the implementation of the Geneva Agreements and the political settlement relating to Afghanistan;

15. *Decides* to include in the provisional agenda of its forty-seventh session the item entitled "The situation in Afghanistan and its implications for international peace and security".

64th plenary meeting
5 December 1991

37/3. Consequences of the Prolongation of the Armed Conflict between Iran and Iraq

Committee: -
Vote: 119 - 1 - 15

The General Assembly,

Having considered the item entitled "Consequences of the prolongation of the armed conflict between Iran and Iraq",

Noting the Preamble of the Charter of the United Nations, in which all States expressed their determination to live together in peace with one another as good neighbours,

Reaffirming the principles that no State should acquire or occupy territories by the use of force, that whatever territories had been acquired in this way should be returned, that no act of aggression should be committed against any State, that the territorial integrity and the sovereignty of all States should be respected, that no State should try to interfere or intervene in the internal affairs of other States and that all differences or claims which may exist between States should be settled by peaceful means in order that peaceful relations should prevail among Member States,

Recalling resolutions 479 (1980) of 28 September 1980, 514 (1982) of 12 July 1982 and 522 (1982) of 4 October 1982 on the question entitled "The situation between Iran and Iraq", unanimously adopted by the Security Council,

Further recalling the statements made by the President of the Security Council on 5 November 1980[1] and 15 July 1982,[2]

Taking note of the report of the Secretary-General of 7 October 1982,[3]

Considering that the Security Council has already called for an immediate cease-fire and an end to all military operations,

Considering further that the prolongation of the conflict constitutes a violation of the obligations of Member States under the Charter,

1. *Considers* that the conflict between Iran and Iraq and its prolongation and recent escalation, resulting in heavy losses in human lives and considerable material damage in a politically and economically strategic region, endanger international peace and security;

2. *Affirms* the necessity of achieving an immediate cease-fire and withdrawal of forces to internationally recognized boundaries as a preliminary step towards the settlement of the dispute by peaceful means in conformity with the principles of justice and international law;

3. *Calls upon* all other States to abstain from all actions which could contribute to the continuation of the conflict and to facilitate the implementation of the present resolution;

4. *Requests* the Secretary-General to continue his efforts, in consultation with the parties concerned, with a view to achieving a peaceful settlement;

5. *Further requests* the Secretary-General to keep Member States informed on the implementation of the present resolution.

41st plenary meeting
22 October 1982

41/12. Armed Israeli Aggression Against the Iraqi Nuclear Installations and its Grave Consequences for the Established International System Concerning the Peaceful Uses of Nuclear Energy, the Non-Proliferation of Nuclear Weapons and International Peace and Security

Committee: -
Vote: 86 - 5 - 55
Ref.: 40/6, 39/14, 38/9, 37/18, 36/27

The General Assembly,

Having considered the item entitled "Armed Israeli aggression against the Iraqi nuclear installations and its grave consequences for the established international system concerning the peaceful uses of nuclear energy, the non-proliferation of nuclear weapons and international peace and security",

Recalling the relevant resolutions of the Security Council and the General Assembly,

Taking note of the relevant resolutions of the International Atomic Energy Agency,

Viewing with deep concern Israel's refusal to comply with Security Council resolution 487 (1981) of 19 June 1981,

Concerned that armed attacks on nuclear facilities raise fears about the safety of present and future nuclear installations,

Aware that all States developing nuclear energy for peaceful purposes need assurances against armed attacks on nuclear facilities,

1. *Calls upon* Israel urgently to place all its nuclear facilities under International Atomic Energy Agency safeguards in accordance with resolution 487 (1981) adopted unanimously by the Security Council;

2. *Considers* that Israel has not yet committed itself not to attack or threaten to attack nuclear facilities in Iraq or elsewhere, including facilities under International Atomic Energy Agency safeguards;

3. *Reaffirms* that Iraq is entitled to compensation for the damage it has suffered as a result of the Israeli armed attack on 7 June 1981;

4. *Requests* the Conference on Disarmament to continue negotiations with a view to reaching an immediate conclusion of the agreement on the prohibition of military attacks on nuclear facilities as a contribution to promoting and ensuring the safe development of nuclear energy for peaceful purposes;

5. *Decides* to include in the provisional agenda of its forty-second session the item entitled "Armed Israeli aggression against the Iraqi nuclear installations and its grave consequences for the established international system concerning the peaceful uses of nuclear energy, the non-proliferation of nuclear weapons and international peace and security".

51st plenary meeting
29 October 1986

41/38. Declaration of the Assembly of Heads of State and Government of the Organization of African Unity on the Aerial and Naval Military Attack Against the Socialist People's Libyan Arab Jamahiriya by the Present United States Administration in April 1986

Committee: -
Vote: 79 - 28 - 33

The General Assembly,

Having heard the statement of the representative of the Socialist People's Libyan Arab Jamahiriya,

Reaffirming the purposes and principles of the Charter of the United Nations and the obligation of all States to refrain from the threat or use of force in their international relations and to settle their disputes by peaceful means,

---

1 S/14244. For the printed text, see *Official Records of the Security Council, Thirty-fifth Year, Resolutions and Decisions.*

2 S/15296. For the printed text, see *Official Records of the Security Council, Thirty-seventh Year, Resolutions and Decisions.*

3 *Official Records of the Security Council, Thirty-seventh Year, Supplement for October, November and December 1982,* document S/15449.

Reaffirming also the inalienable right of all peoples to determine their own form of government and to choose their political, social and economic system without any interference, subversion, coercion or constraint of any kind whatsoever,

Recalling its resolution 40/157 of 16 December 1985 on the strengthening of security and cooperation the Mediterranean region,

Deeply concerned at the threats and aggressive provocations, and the imposition of comprehensive cultural and economic sanctions, including the freezing of assets and properties, carried out against the Libyan Arab Jamahiriya,

Deeply concerned also at the series of disinformation campaigns carried out against the Libyan Arab Jamahiriya,

Gravely concerned at the aerial and naval military attack perpetrated against the cities of Tripoli and Benghazi on 15 April 1986, which constitutes a serious threat to peace and security in the Mediterranean region,

Noting with concern that the Security Council has been prevented from discharging its responsibilities owing to the negative vote of certain permanent members,

Taking into consideration the Declaration adopted by the Assembly of Heads of State and Government of the Organization of African Unity at its twenty-second ordinary session, held at Addis Ababa from 28 to 30 July 1986,[1]

Taking note of the Political Declaration adopted by the Eighth Conference of Heads of State or Government of Non-Aligned Countries, held at Harare from 1 to 6 September 1986,[2] and other relevant declarations of the Movement of Non-Aligned Countries in this context,

Taking note also of the final communiqué adopted at the Coordination Meeting of the Ministers for Foreign Affairs of the Organization of the Islamic Conference, held in New York on 2 October 1986,[3]

1. *Condemns* the military attack perpetrated against the Socialist People's Libyan Arab Jamahiriya on 15 April 1986, which constitutes a violation of the Charter of the United Nations and of international law;

2. *Calls upon* the Government of the United States in this regard to refrain from the threat or use of force in the settlement of disputes and differences with the Libyan Arab Jamahiriya and to resort to peaceful means in accordance with the Charter of the United Nations;

3. *Calls upon* all States to refrain from extending any assistance or facilities for perpetrating acts of aggression against the Libyan Arab Jamahiriya;

4. *Affirms* the right of the Libyan Arab Jamahiriya to receive appropriate compensation for the material and human losses inflicted upon it;

5. *Requests* the Security Council to remain seized of the matter and requests the Secretary-General to report thereon to the General Assembly at its forty-second session.

78th plenary meeting
20 November 1986

44/22. The Situation in Kampuchea

Committee: -
Vote: 124 - 17 - 12

The General Assembly,

Recalling its resolutions 34/22 of 14 November 1979, 35/6 of 22 October 1980, 36/5 of 21 October 1981, 37/6 of 28 October 1982, 38/3 of 27 October 1983, 39/5 of 30 October 1984, 40/7 of 5 November 1985, 41/6 of 21 October 1986, 42/3 of 14 October 1987 and 43/19 of 3 November 1988,

Recalling also the Declaration on Kampuchea[4] and resolution 1 (I)[5] adopted by the International Conference on Kampuchea,

Taking note of the report of the Secretary-General on the implementation of General Assembly resolution 43/19,[6]

Deploring foreign armed intervention and occupation in Kampuchea, the cause of continuing hostilities in that country, seriously threatening international peace and security,

Noting the continued and effective struggle of the Kampuchean people under the leadership of Samdech Norodom Sihanouk to achieve the independence, sovereignty, territorial integrity and neutral and non-aligned status of Kampuchea,

Taking note of Economic and Social Council decision 1989/156 of 24 May 1989 on the right of peoples to self-determination and its application to peoples under colonial or alien domination or foreign occupation,

Greatly disturbed that the continued fighting and instability in Kampuchea have forced an additional large number of Kampucheans to flee to the Thai-Kampuchean border in search of food and safety,

Recognizing that the assistance extended by the international community has continued to reduce the food shortages and health problems of the Kampuchean people,

Emphasizing that it is the inalienable right of the Kampuchean people who have sought refuge in neighbouring countries to return safely to their homeland,

Emphasizing also that no effective solution to the humanitarian problems can be achieved without a comprehensive political settlement of the Kampuchean conflict,

Seriously concerned about reported demographic changes imposed in Kampuchea as a result of foreign occupation,

Convinced that, to bring about lasting peace in South-East Asia and reduce the threat to international peace and security, there is an urgent need for the international community to find a comprehensive political settlement of the Kampuchean problem, with effective guarantees, that must include the total withdrawal of all foreign forces from Kampuchea under supervision and control of the United Nations and will provide for the creation of an interim administering authority, the promotion of national reconciliation among all Kampucheans under the leadership of Samdech Norodom Sihanouk and the non-return to the universally condemned policies and practices of a recent past and ensure respect for the sovereignty, independence, territorial integrity and neutral and non-aligned status of Kampuchea, as well as the right of the Kampuchean people to self-determination free from outside interference,

Recognizing that the informal meetings held at Jakarta from 25 to 28 July 1988[7] and from 19 to 21 February 1989[8] have made a significant contribution towards achieving a comprehensive political settlement of the Kampuchean problem,

Recognizing also that the Paris Conference on Cambodia, which met from 30 July to 30 August 1989, made progress in elaborating a wide variety of elements necessary for reaching a comprehensive settlement, although it was not yet possible to achieve a comprehensive political settlement, and that the Conference should be reconvened in due time after consultations by the Co-Presidents with the participants,

Noting the announced withdrawal of foreign forces from Kampuchea, but emphasizing that it has not been verified under supervision and control of the United Nations and is not within the framework of a comprehensive political settlement,

---

1 See A/41/654, annex II, declaration AHG/Decl. 2 (XXII).

2 A/41/697-S/18392, annex, sect. I, paras. 215-217.

3 A/41/740-S/18418, annex, para. 23.

4 *Report of the International Conference on Kampuchea, New York, 13-17 July 1981* (United Nations publication, Sales No. E.81.I.20), annex I.

5 *Ibid.*, annex II.

6 A/44/670.

7 See A/43/493-S/20071; see *Official Records of the Security Council, Forty-third Year, Supplement for July, August and September 1988*, document S/20071.

8 See A/44/138-S/20477 and Corr. 1; see *Official Records of the Security Council, Forty-fourth Year, Supplement for January, February and March 1989*, document S/20477.

Reiterating its conviction that, after the comprehensive political settlement of the Kampuchean question through peaceful means, the countries of the South-East Asian region can pursue efforts to establish a zone of peace, freedom and neutrality in South-East Asia so as to lessen international tensions and to achieve lasting peace in the region,

Reaffirming the need for all States to adhere strictly to the principles of the Charter of the United Nations, which call for respect for the national independence, sovereignty and territorial integrity of all States, non-intervention and non-interference in the internal affairs of States, non-recourse to the threat or use of force and peaceful settlement of disputes,

1. *Reaffirms* its resolutions 34/22, 35/6, 36/5, 37/6, 38/3, 39/5, 40/7, 41/6, 42/3 and 43/19 and calls for their full implementation;

2. *Reiterates its conviction* that the withdrawal of all foreign forces from Kampuchea under supervision and control of the United Nations, the creation of an interim administering authority, the promotion of national reconciliation among all Kampucheans under the leadership of Samdech Norodom Sihanouk, the non-return to the universally condemned policies and practices of a recent past, the restoration and preservation of the independence, sovereignty, territorial integrity and neutral and non-aligned status of Kampuchea, the reaffirmation of the right of the Kampuchean people to determine their own destiny and the commitment by all States to non-interference and non-intervention in the internal affairs of Kampuchea, with effective guarantees, are the principal components of any just, lasting and comprehensive political settlement of the Kampuchean problem;

3. *Emphasizes* that the Kampuchean people should be allowed to exercise their inalienable right to self-determination through internationally supervised free, fair and democratic elections;

4. *Affirms* that any withdrawal of foreign forces from Kampuchea without United Nations supervision, control and verification is not within the framework of a comprehensive political settlement;

5. *Calls upon* all parties concerned to intensify urgently all efforts towards ensuring that the Kampuchean problem be resolved through a comprehensive political settlement in order to prevent further hostilities and subsequent loss of life and the continued suffering of the Kampuchean people, and to ensure the independence, sovereignty, territorial integrity, neutral and non-aligned status of Kampuchea and the non-return to the universally condemned policies and practices of a recent past;

6. *Takes note with appreciation* of the report of the *Ad Hoc Committee* of the International Conference on Kampuchea on its activities during 1988-1989[1] and requests that the Committee continue its work;

7. *Authorizes* the *Ad Hoc Committee* to convene when necessary and to carry out the tasks entrusted to it in its mandate;

8. *Reaffirms* its commitment to reconvene the Conference at an appropriate time, in accordance with Conference resolution 1 (I), and its readiness to support any other conference of an international nature under the auspices of the Secretary-General;

9. *Requests* the Secretary-General to continue to consult with and assist the Conference and the *Ad Hoc Committee* and to provide them on a regular basis with the necessary facilities to carry out their functions;

10. *Expresses its appreciation* once again to the Secretary-General for taking appropriate steps in following the situation closely and requests him to continue to do so and to exercise his good offices in order to contribute to a comprehensive political settlement;

11. *Invites* the Co-Presidents of the Paris Conference on Cambodia to intensify their consultations with a view to reconvening the Conference and its committees at an appropriate time;

12. *Expresses its deep appreciation once again* to donor countries, the United Nations and its agencies and other humanitarian organizations, national and international, that have rendered relief assistance to the Kampuchean people, and appeals to them to continue to provide emergency assistance to those Kampucheans who are still in need, especially along the Thai-Kampuchean border and in the various encampments in Thailand;

13. *Reiterates its deep appreciation* to the Secretary-General for his efforts in coordinating humanitarian relief assistance and in monitoring its distribution, and requests him to intensify such efforts as necessary;

14. *Urges* the States of South-East Asia, once a comprehensive political settlement to the Kampuchean conflict is achieved, to exert renewed efforts to establish a zone of peace, freedom and neutrality in South-East Asia;

15. *Reiterates* the hope that, following a comprehensive political settlement, an intergovernmental committee will be established to consider a programme of assistance to Kampuchea for the reconstruction of its economy and for the economic and social development of all States in the region;

16. *Requests* the Secretary-General to report to the General Assembly at its forty-fifth session on the implementation of the present resolution;

17. *Decides* to include in the provisional agenda of its forty-fifth session the item entitled "The situation in Kampuchea".

58th plenary meeting
16 November 1989

46/18. The Situation in Cambodia

Committee: -
Vote: Adopted without a vote

The General Assembly,

Having considered the item entitled "The situation in Cambodia",

Recalling its resolution 45/3 of 15 October 1990 and Security Council resolutions 668 (1990) of 20 September 1990, 717 (1991) of 16 October 1991 and 718 (1991) of 31 October 1991,

Recalling also the support and assistance of the international community, the participants in the Paris Conference on Cambodia and all interested States and parties, especially the humanitarian aid rendered to the Cambodian people since 1978,

Welcoming the agreements on a comprehensive political settlement of the Cambodia conflict, signed at the Paris Conference on Cambodia on 23 October 1991,

Taking note of the report of the Secretary-General,

Noting with appreciation the continuing efforts of the Secretary-General and his staff towards the implementation of the agreements on a comprehensive political settlement of the Cambodia conflict,

1. *Expresses its full support* for the agreements on a comprehensive political settlement of the Cambodia conflict, hereinafter referred to as the "Paris Agreements", which, *inter alia*, would maintain, preserve and guarantee the sovereignty, independence, territorial integrity and inviolability, neutrality and national unity of Cambodia;

2. *Supports* the efforts of the Secretary-General to set up an effective United Nations Transitional Authority in Cambodia as soon as possible, with the aim of restoring peace and stability in Cambodia and to implement the Paris Agreements;

3. *Welcomes* the fact that commitment to self-determination for the Cambodian people through free and fair elections organized and conducted by the United Nations and full respect for human rights have been incorporated in the provisions of the settlement;

4. *Calls upon* all parties concerned to ensure respect for and full observance of the human rights and fundamental freedoms of the Cambodian people and to assist them to exercise their right to self-determination through free and fair elections, as provided for in the Paris Agreements;

5. *Also calls upon* all parties concerned to comply fully with the cease-fire that entered into force at the time of the signature of the Paris Agreements;

[1] A/CONF.109/15.

6. *Urges* all parties concerned to implement fully the terms of the Paris Agreements, in close cooperation with the United Nations Transitional Authority in Cambodia;

7. *Expresses its deep appreciation* to the international community, the Co-Presidents of the Paris Conference on Cambodia, the permanent members of the Security Council, States in the region, other States and the Cambodian parties themselves, in particular His Royal Highness Samdech Norodom Sihanouk, for their invaluable contributions over the past decade to restore and maintain peace and unity in Cambodia and to promote national reconciliation;

8. *Expresses its deep appreciation also* to donor countries, the United Nations agencies and other national and international humanitarian organizations that have rendered assistance to the Cambodian people and urges them to continue their support for the process of repatriation of the Cambodian refugees and displaced persons under the leadership and coordination of the United Nations High Commissioner for Refugees, and for the rehabilitation and reconstruction of Cambodia;

9. *Reiterates its deep appreciation* to the Secretary-General and his staff for their continuing efforts in helping to implement the Paris Agreements;

10. *Reiterates also its deep appreciation* to the Secretary-General for his efforts in coordinating humanitarian relief assistance and in monitoring its distribution, and requests him to continue such efforts as necessary.

50th plenary meeting
20 November 1991

44/240. Effects of the Military Intervention by the United States of America in Panama on the Situation in Central America

Committee: -
Vote: 75 - 20 - 40

The General Assembly,

Taking note of the statements made in the General Assembly and the Security Council regarding the invasion of Panama,

Reaffirming the sovereign and inalienable right of Panama to determine freely its social, economic and political system and to develop its international relations without any form of foreign intervention, interference, subversion, coercion or threat,

Recalling that, in accordance with Article 2, paragraph 4, of the Charter of the United Nations, all Member States shall refrain in their international relations from the threat or use of force against the territorial integrity or political independence of any State, or in any other manner inconsistent with the purposes of the United Nations,

Reaffirming the need to restore conditions which will guarantee the full exercise of the human rights and fundamental freedoms of the Panamanian people,

Express its profound concern at the serious consequences the armed intervention by the United States of America in Panama might have for peace and security in the Central American region,

1. *Strongly deplores* the intervention in Panama by the armed forces of the United States of America, which constitutes a flagrant violation of international law and of the independence, sovereignty and territorial integrity of States;

2. *Demands* the immediate cessation of the intervention and the withdrawal from Panama of the armed invasion forces of the United States;

3. *Demands also* full respect for and strict observance of the letter and spirit of the Torrijos-Carter Treaties;

4. *Calls upon* all States to uphold and respect the sovereignty, independence and territorial integrity of Panama;

5. *Requests* the Secretary-General to monitor the developments in Panama and to report to the General Assembly within twenty-four hours after the adoption of the present resolution.

88th plenary meeting
29 December 1989

47/19. Necessity of Ending the Economic, Commercial and Financial Embargo Imposed by the United States of America Against Cuba

Committee: -
Vote: 59 - 3 - 71
Ref.: 50/10, 49/9, 48/16

The General Assembly,

Determined to encourage strict compliance with the purposes and principles enshrined in the Charter of the United Nations,

Reaffirming, among other principles, the sovereign equality of States, non-intervention and non-interference in their internal affairs and freedom of trade and international navigation, which are also enshrined in many international legal instruments,

Concerned about the promulgation and application by Member States of laws and regulations whose extraterritorial effects affect the sovereignty of other States and the legitimate interests of entities or persons under their jurisdiction, as well as the freedom of trade and navigation,

Having learned of the recent promulgation of measures of that nature aimed at strengthening and extending the economic, commercial and financial embargo against Cuba,

1. *Calls upon* all States to refrain from promulgating and applying laws and measures of the kind referred to in the preamble to the present resolution in conformity with their obligations under the Charter of the United Nations and international law and with the commitments that they have freely entered into in acceding to international legal instruments that, *inter alia*, reaffirm the freedom of trade and navigation;

2. *Urges* States that have such laws or measures to take the necessary steps to repeal or invalidate them as soon as possible in accordance with their legal régime;

3. *Requests* the Secretary-General to submit to the General Assembly at its forty-eighth session a report on the implementation of the present resolution;

4. *Decides* to include the item in the provisional agenda of its forty-eighth session.

70th plenary meeting
24 November 1992

47/21. Complete Withdrawal of Foreign Military Forces from the Territories of the Baltic States

Committee: -
Vote: Adopted without a vote
Ref.: 48/18

The General Assembly,

Having considered the item entitled "Complete withdrawal of foreign military forces from the territories of the Baltic States",

Considering that the United Nations, pursuant to the provisions of its Charter, has a major role to play in, and responsibility for, the maintenance of international peace and security,

Recalling with particular satisfaction that independence was restored in Estonia, Latvia and Lithuania through peaceful and democratic means,

Recognizing that the stationing of foreign military forces on the territories of Estonia, Latvia and Lithuania without the required consent of those countries is a problem remaining from the past that must be resolved in a peaceful manner,

Welcoming recent agreements on the complete withdrawal of foreign military forces from the territory of Lithuania,

Welcoming also the bilateral talks on the complete withdrawal of foreign military forces from the territories of Estonia and Latvia,

Concerned about the continuing absence of any agreements for the complete withdrawal of foreign military forces from the territories of Estonia and Latvia,

Taking note of the report of the Secretary-General entitled "An Agenda for Peace",[1] pursuant to the statement of 31 January 1992 adopted at the conclusion of the meeting held by the Security Council at the level of Heads of State and Government,[2]

Mindful that the timely application of preventive diplomacy is the most desirable and efficient means to ease tensions before they result in conflict,

Welcoming the "Helsinki Document 1992 - The Challenges of Change", in particular paragraph 15, agreed upon at the Conference on Security and Cooperation in Europe, held at Helsinki on 9 and 10 July 1992,[3]

Recognizing that the Conference on Security and Cooperation in Europe is a regional arrangement in the sense of Chapter VIII of the Charter of the United Nations, and as such provides an important link between European and global security,

Recognizing also that regional organizations participating in complementary efforts with the United Nations may encourage States outside the region to act supportively,

1. *Expresses support* for the efforts made by the States participating in the Conference on Security and Cooperation in Europe to remove the foreign military forces stationed on the territories of Estonia, Latvia and Lithuania without the required consent of those countries, in a peaceful manner and through negotiations;

2. *Calls upon* the States concerned, in line with the basic principles of international law and in order to prevent any possible conflict, to conclude without delay appropriate agreements, including timetables, for the early, orderly and complete withdrawal of foreign military forces from the territories of Estonia and Latvia;

3. *Urges* the Secretary-General to use his good offices to facilitate the complete withdrawal of foreign military forces from the territories of Estonia, Latvia and Lithuania;

4. *Requests* the Secretary-General to keep Member States informed of progress towards the implementation of the present resolution and to report thereon to the General Assembly at its forty-eighth session;

5. *Decides* to include in the provisional agenda of its forty-eighth session the item entitled "Complete withdrawal of foreign military forces from the territories of the Baltic States".

72nd plenary meeting
25 November 1992

---

1 A/47/277-S/24111.

2 S/23500.

3 A/47/361-S/24370, annex.

02.00 MAINTENANCE AND RESTORATION OF PEACE AND SECURITY

02.10 DISARMAMENT

02.11 PRINCIPLES OF DISARMAMENT

41 (I). Principles Governing the General Regulation and Reduction of Armaments

Committee: 1
Vote: unanimous
Ref.: 42(I)

1. In pursuance of Article 11 of the Charter and with a view to strengthening international peace and security in conformity with the Purposes and Principles of the United Nations,

The General Assembly,
Recognizes the necessity of an early general regulation and reduction of armaments and armed forces.

2. Accordingly,

The General Assembly,
Recommends that the Security Council give prompt consideration to formulating the practical measures, according to their priority, which are essential to provide for the general regulation and reduction of armaments and armed forces and to assure that such regulation and reduction of armaments and armed forces will be generally observed by all participants and not unilaterally by only some of the participants. The plans formulated by the Security Council shall be submitted by the Secretary-General to the Members of the United Nations for consideration at a special session of the General Assembly. The treaties or conventions approved by the General Assembly shall be submitted to the signatory States for ratification in accordance with Article 26 of the Charter.

3. As an essential step towards the urgent objective of prohibiting and eliminating from national armaments atomic and all other major weapons adaptable now and in the future to mass destruction, and the early establishment of international control of atomic energy and other modern scientific discoveries and technical developments to ensure their use only for peaceful purposes,

The General Assembly,
Urges the expeditious fulfilment by the Atomic Energy Commission of its terms of reference as set forth in section 5 of the General Assembly resolution of 24 January 1946.

4. In order to ensure that the general prohibition, regulation and reduction of armaments are directed towards the major weapons of modern warfare and not merely towards the minor weapons,

The General Assembly,
Recommends that the Security Council expedite consideration of the reports which the Atomic Energy Commission will make to the security Council and that it facilitate the work of that Commission, and also that the Security Council expedite consideration of a draft convention or conventions for the creation of an international system of control and inspection, these conventions to include the prohibition of atomic and all other major weapons adaptable now and in the future to mass destruction and the control of atomic energy to the extent necessary to ensure its use only for peaceful purposes.

5. The General Assembly,
Further recognizes that essential to the general regulation and reduction of armaments and armed forces, is the provision of practical and effective safeguards by way of inspection and other means to protect complying States against the hazards of violations and evasions.

Accordingly,

The General Assembly,
Recommends to the Security Council that it give prompt consideration to the working out of proposals to provide such practical and effective safeguards in connexion with the control of atomic energy and the general regulation and reduction of armaments.

6. To ensure the adoption of measures for the early general regulation and reduction of armaments and armed forces, for the prohibition of the use of atomic energy for military purposes and the elimination from national armaments of atomic and all other major weapons adaptable now or in the future to mass destruction, and for the control of atomic energy to the extent necessary to ensure its use only for peaceful purposes,

There shall be established, within the framework of the Security Council, which bears the primary responsibility for the maintenance of international peace and security, an international system, as mentioned in paragraph 4, operating through special organs, which organs shall derive their powers and status from the convention or conventions under which they are established.

7. The General Assembly,
Regarding the problem of security as closely connected with that of disarmament,

Recommends the Security Council to accelerate as much as possible the placing at its disposal of the armed forces mentioned in Article 43 of the Charter;

Recommends the Members to undertake the progressive and balanced withdrawal, taking into account the needs of occupation, of their armed forces stationed in ex-enemy territories, and the withdrawal without delay of their armed forces stationed in the territories of Members without their consent freely and publicly expressed in treaties or agreements consistent with the Charter and not contradicting international agreements;

Further recommends a corresponding reduction of national armed forces, and a general progressive and balanced reduction of national armed forces.

8. Nothing herein contained shall alter or limit the resolution of the General Assembly passed on 24 January 1946, creating the Atomic Energy Commission.

9. The General Assembly,
Calls upon all Members of the United Nations to render every possible assistance to the Security Council and the Atomic Energy Commission in order to promote the establishment and maintenance of international peace and collective security with the least diversion for armaments of the world's human and economic resources.

Sixty-third plenary meeting
14 December 1946

502 (VI). Regulation, Limitation and Balanced Reduction of all Armed Forces and all Armaments; International Control of Atomic Energy

Committee: 1
Vote: 42 - 5 - 7
Ref.: 1148(XII), 1011(XI), 914(X), 808(IX), 715(VIII), 704(VII), 300(IV)

The General Assembly,

Moved by anxiety at the general lack of confidence plaguing the world and leading to the burden of increasing armaments and the fear of war,

Desiring to lift from the peoples of the world this burden and this fear, and thus to liberate new energies and resources for positive programmes of reconstruction and development,

Reaffirming its desire that the United Nations develop an effective collective security system to maintain the peace and that the armed forces and armaments of the world be progressively reduced in accordance with the Purposes and Principles of the Charter,

Believing that a necessary means to this end is the development by the United Nations of comprehensive and coordinated plans, under international control for the regulation, limitation and balanced reduction of all armed forces and all armaments, for the elimination of all major weapons adaptable to mass destruction, and for the effective international control of atomic energy to ensure the prohibition of atomic weapons and the use of atomic energy for peaceful purposes only,

Recognizing that a genuine system for disarmament must include all kinds of armed forces and armaments, must be accepted by all nations whose military resources are such that their failure to accept would endanger the system, and must include safeguards that will ensure the compliance of all such nations,

Noting the recommendation[1] of the Committee of Twelve established by resolution 496 (V) that the General Assembly should establish a new commission to carry forward the tasks originally assigned to the Atomic Energy Commission and the Commission for Conventional Armaments,

1. *Establishes* under the Security Council a Disarmament Commission. This Commission shall have the same membership as the Atomic Energy Commission and the Commission for Conventional Armaments, and shall function under the rules of procedure of the Atomic Energy Commission with such modifications as the Commission shall deem necessary;

2. *Dissolves* the Atomic Energy Commission and recommends to the Security Council that it dissolve the Commission for Conventional Armaments;

3. *Directs* the Disarmament Commission to prepare proposals to be embodied in a draft treaty (or treaties) for the regulation, limitation and balanced reduction of all armed forces and all armaments, for the elimination of all major weapons adaptable to mass destruction, and for effective international control of atomic energy to ensure the prohibition of atomic weapons and the use of atomic energy for peaceful purposes only. The Commission shall be guided by the following principles:

(*a*) in a system of guaranteed disarmament there must be progressive disclosure and verification on a continuing basis of all armed forces - including paramilitary, security and police forces - and all armaments including atomic;

(*b*) Such verification must be based on effective international inspection to ensure the adequacy and accuracy of the information disclosed; this inspection to be carried out in accordance with the decisions of the international control organ (or organs) to be established;

(*c*) The Commission shall be ready to consider any proposals or plans for control that may be put forward involving either conventional armaments or atomic energy. Unless a better or no less effective system is devised, the United Nations plan for the international control of atomic energy and the prohibition of atomic weapons should continue to serve as the basis for the international control of atomic energy to ensure the prohibition of atomic weapons and the use of atomic energy for peaceful purposes only;

(*d*) There must be an adequate system of safeguards to ensure observance of the disarmament programme, so as to provide for the prompt detection of violations while at the same time causing the minimum degree of interference in the internal life of each country;

(*e*) The treaty (or treaties) shall specifically be open to all States for signature and ratification or adherence. The treaty (or treaties) shall provide what States must become parties thereto before the treaty (or treaties) shall enter into force;

4. *Directs* the Commission, when preparing the proposals referred to in the preceding paragraph, to formulate plans for the establishment, within the framework of the Security Council, of an international control organ (or organs) to ensure the implementation of the treaty (or treaties). The functions and powers of the control organ (or organs) shall be defined in the treaty which establishes it;

5. *Directs* the Commission, in preparing the proposals referred to in paragraph 3 above, to consider from the outset plans for progressive and continuing disclosure and verification, the implementation of which is recognized as a first and indispensable step in carrying out the disarmament programme envisaged in the present resolution;

6. *Directs* the Commission, in working out plans for the regulation, limitation and balanced reduction of all armed forces and all armaments :

(*a*) To determine how over-all limits and restrictions on all armed forces and all armaments can be calculated and fixed;

(*b*) To consider methods according to which States can agree by negotiation among themselves, under the auspices of the Commission, concerning the determination of the over-all limits and restrictions referred to in sub-paragraph (*a*) above and the allocation within their respective national military establishments of the permitted national armed forces and armaments;

7. *Directs* the Commission to commence its work not later than thirty days from the adoption of the present resolution and to report periodically, for information, to the Security Council and to the General Assembly, or to the Members of the United Nations when the General Assembly is not in session. The Commission shall submit its first report not later than 1 June 1952;

8. *Declares* that a conference of all States should be convened to consider the proposals for a draft treaty (or treaties) prepared by the Commission as soon as the work of the Commission shall have progressed to a point where in the judgment of the Commission any part of its programme is ready for submission to governments;

9. *Requests* the Secretary-General to convene such a conference when so advised by the Commission;

10. *Requests* the Secretary-General to furnish such experts, staff and facilities as the Commission may consider necessary for the effective accomplishment of the purposes of the present resolution.

358th plenary meeting
11 January 1952

1837 (XVII). Declaration on the Conversion to Peaceful Needs of the Resources Released by Disarmament

Committee: 2
Vote: unanimous
Ref.: 2387(XXIII), 2171(XXI), 1931(XVIII)

The General Assembly,

Inspired by the ardent desire for peace and by the lofty aims of the Charter of the United Nations, and recalling its resolutions 1378 (XIV) of 20 November 1959 and 1516 (XV) of 15 December 1960,

Noting that the arms race is continuing all over the world, that military expenditures of States are enormous, that conventional, nuclear and other weapons of mass destruction are accumulating and being

[1] See *Official Records of the General Assembly, Sixth Session, Annexes,* agenda items 66 and 16, document A/ 1922. Appendix 13, p. 325.

developed, and that, as a result, an agreement on general and complete disarmament under effective international control is urgent,

Convinced that there is still time to stave off the deadly danger looming over the world and to achieve the implementation of general and complete disarmament under effective international control,

Recalling that the consultative group of experts, in its study on the economic and social consequences of disarmament,[1] estimated that the world is spending at the present time roughly $120,000 million annually on military account, a sum at least two-thirds of, and, according to some estimates, of the same order of magnitude as, the entire annual national income of all the under-developed countries,

Realizing the enormous importance which an agreement on disarmament would have for the attainment of accelerated economic and social progress for the benefit of mankind,

Recognizing that all problems of transition connected with disarmament can be met by appropriate national and international measures, that diversion to peaceful uses of the resources now in military use can be accomplished in a manner which will benefit all countries and will lead to the improvement of economic and social conditions throughout the world, and that disarmament can be accomplished in all countries not only without impairing their economies but with great advantages to the real welfare of their people,

Recalling its resolution 1710 (XVI) of 19 December 1961 on the United Nations Development Decade, which calls for proposals relating, *inter alia*, to the utilization of resources released by disarmament for the purpose of economic and social development, in particular of the under-developed countries,

Believing that the release of a portion of the savings which would follow upon an agreement on disarmament for aid to the economic growth of the less developed countries, together with their own intensified internal efforts and domestic savings, would enable countless millions of people in the less developed countries to improve substantially within a generation their present level of living standards through, *inter alia*, the development of new centres of energy and industrial activity,

Convinced that disarmament and the conversion of huge resources to peaceful uses would open up vast opportunities for the development of peaceful cooperation and trade among States on the basis of equality and mutual benefit, that the expansion of international economic exchange and mutual assistance would be beneficial to all countries, both big and small and both economically less developed and highly developed, would ensure the growth of production and provide new jobs for millions of people,

1. *Solemnly urges* the Governments of all States to multiply their efforts for a prompt achievement of general and complete disarmament under effective international control;

2. *Declares* that it firmly believes in the triumph of the principles of reason and justice, in the establishment of such conditions in the world as would forever banish wars from the life of human society, and replace the arms race, which consumes enormous resources of funds, by broad and fruitful cooperation among nations in bettering life on earth;

3. *Takes into account* the important role of the United Nations in organizing international aid to the less developed countries and in making studies of the economic and social consequences of disarmament;

4. *Expresses its appreciation* for the report of the Secretary-General transmitting the study on the economic and social consequences of disarmament presented by the consultative group of experts pursuant to resolution 1516 (XV);

5. *Endorses* the unanimous conclusion of the consultative group of experts that the implementation of general and complete disarmament will be an unqualified blessing for all mankind;

6. *Concurs* in Economic and Social Council resolution 891 (XXXIV) of 26 July 1962 and endorses the request in paragraph 6 thereof that Member States, particularly those which are significantly involved in or affected by current military programmes should devote further attention to, and conduct any necessary studies of, the detailed aspects of the economic and social consequences of disarmament, with a view to developing needed information, plans and policies for making necessary economic and social adjustments in the event of disarmament and in the successive stages towards the achievement of complete disarmament, bearing in mind the imperative needs of the developing countries;

7. *Requests* the Secretary-General to make available to the General Assembly at its eighteenth session the report prepared for the session of the Economic and Social Council pursuant to Council resolution 891 (XXXIV);

8. *Invites* the Secretary-General and the Governments of developing countries to intensify their efforts to establish and implement soundly conceived projects and well integrated development plans of a national and regional character, as indicated in General Assembly resolution 1708 (XVI) of 19 December 1961, the implementation of which may be accelerated as part of an economic programme for disarmament at such time as additional resources are released following an agreement on general and complete disarmament under effective international control, and requests the Secretary-General to present his preliminary report on this matter to the Assembly at a forthcoming session, if possible at the eighteenth session;

9. *Affirms* that, pending an agreement on general and complete disarmament under effective international control, Member States should not relax their efforts to assist the developing countries but should rather accelerate such efforts.

1197th plenary meeting
18 December 1962

[1] United Nations publication, Sales No.: 62.IX. 1.

S-10/2. Final Document of the Tenth Special Session of the General Assembly

Committee: -
Vote: Adopted without a vote
Ref.: 50/72, 49/77, 48/77, 47/54, 46/38, 45/62, 44/119, 43/78, 42/42, 41/86, 40/152, 39/148, 38/183, 37/78, 36/92, 35/152, 34/83, 33/71, 32/88

The General Assembly,

Alarmed by the threat to the very survival of mankind posed by the existence of nuclear weapons and the continuing arms race, and recalling the devastation inflicted by all wars,

Convinced that disarmament and arms limitation, particularly in the nuclear field, are essential for the prevention of the danger of nuclear war and the strengthening of international peace and security and for the economic and social advancement of all peoples, thus facilitating the achievement of the new international economic order,

Having resolved to lay the foundations of an international disarmament strategy which, through coordinated and persevering efforts in which the United Nations should play a more effective role, aims at general and complete disarmament under effective international control,

Adopts the following Final Document of this special session of the General Assembly devoted to disarmament:

Final Document of the Tenth Special Session of the General Assembly

Contents

I. Introduction

1. The attainment of the objective of security, which is an inseparable element of peace, has always been one of the most profound aspirations of humanity. States have for a long time sought to maintain their security through the possession of arms. Admittedly, their survival has, in certain cases, effectively depended on whether they could count on appropriate means of defence. Yet the accumulation of weapons, particularly nuclear weapons, today constitutes much more a threat than a protection for the future of mankind. The time

has therefore come to put an end to this situation, to abandon the use of force in international relations and to seek security in disarmament, that is to say, through a gradual but effective process beginning with a reduction in the present level of armaments. The ending of the arms race and the achievement of real disarmament are tastes of primary importance and urgency. To meet this historic challenge is in the political and economic interests of all the nations and peoples of the world as well as in the interests of ensuring their genuine security and peaceful future.

2. Unless its avenues are closed, the continued arms race means a growing threat to international peace and security and even to the very survival of mankind. The nuclear and conventional arms build-up threatens to stall the efforts aimed at reaching the goals of development, to become an obstacle on the road of achieving the new international economic order and to hinder the solution of other vital problems facing mankind.

3. The dynamic development of détente, encompassing all spheres of international relations in all regions of the world, with the participation of all countries, would create conditions conducive to the efforts of States to end the arms race, which has engulfed the world thus reducing the danger of war. Progress on détente and progress on disarmament mutually complement and strengthen each other.

4. The Disarmament Decade solemnly declared in 1969 by the United Nations is coming to an end. Unfortunately, the objectives established on that occasion by the General Assembly appear to be as far away today as they were then, or even further because the arms race is not diminishing but increasing and outstrips by far the efforts to curb it. While it is true that some limited agreements have been reached, "effective measures relating to the cessation of the nuclear arms race at an early date and to nuclear disarmament" continue to elude man's grasp. Yet the implementation of such measures is urgently required. There has not been any real progress either that might lead to the conclusion of a treaty on general and complete disarmament under effective international control. Furthermore, it has not been possible to free any amount, however modest, of the enormous resources, both material and human, which are wasted on the unproductive and spiralling arms race and which should be made available for the purpose of economic and social development, especially since such a race "places a great burden on both the developing and the developed countries".

5. The Members of the United Nations are fully aware of the conviction of their peoples that the question of general and complete disarmament is of utmost importance and that peace, security and economic and social development are indivisible, and they have therefore recognized that the corresponding obligations and responsibilities are universal.

6. Thus a powerful current of opinion has gradually formed, leading to the convening of what will go down in the annals of the United Nations as the first special session of the General Assembly devoted entirely to disarmament.

7. The outcome of this special session, whose deliberations have to a large extent been facilitated by the five sessions of the Preparatory Committee which preceded it, is the present Final Document. This introduction serves as a preface to the document which comprises also the following three sections: a Declaration, a Programme of Action and recommendations concerning the international machinery for disarmament negotiations.

8. While the final objective of the efforts of all States should continue to be general and complete disarmament under effective international control, the immediate goal is that of the elimination of the danger of a nuclear war and the implementation of measures to halt and reverse the arms race and clear the path towards lasting peace. Negotiations on the entire range of those issues should be based on the strict observance of the purposes and principles enshrined in the Charter of the United Nations, with full recognition of the role of the United Nations in the field of disarmament and reflecting the vital interest of all the peoples of the world in this sphere. The aim of the Declaration is to review and assess the existing situation, outline the objectives and the priority tasks and set forth fundamental principles for disarmament negotiations.

9. For disarmament - the aims and purposes of which the Declaration proclaims - to become a reality, it was essential to agree on a series of specific disarmament measures, selected by common accord as those on which there is a consensus to the effect that their subsequent realization in the short term appears to be feasible. There is also a need to prepare through agreed procedures a comprehensive disarmament programme. That programme, passing through all the necessary stages, should lead to general and complete disarmament under effective international control. Procedures for watching over the fulfilment of the obligations thus assumed had also to be agreed upon. That is the purpose of the Programme of Action.

10. Although the decisive factor for achieving real measures of disarmament is the "political will" of States, especially of those possessing nuclear weapons, a significant role can also be played by the effective functioning of an appropriate international machinery designed to deal with the problems of disarmament in its various aspects. Consequently, it would be necessary that the two kinds of organs required to that end, the deliberative and the negotiating organs, have the appropriate organization and procedures that would be most conducive to obtaining constructive results. The last section of the Final Document, section IV, has been prepared with that end in view.

II. Declaration

11. Mankind today is confronted with an unprecedented threat of self-extinction arising from the massive and competitive accumulation of the most destructive weapons ever produced. Existing arsenals of nuclear weapons alone are more than sufficient to destroy all life on earth. Failure of efforts to halt and reverse the arms race, in particular the nuclear arms race, increases the danger of the proliferation of nuclear weapons. Yet the arms race continues. Military budgets are constantly growing, with enormous consumption of human and material resources. The increase in weapons, especially nuclear weapons, far from helping to strengthen international security, on the contrary weakens it. The vast stockpiles and tremendous build-up of arms and armed forces and the competition for qualitative refinement of weapons of all kinds, to which scientific resources and technological advances are diverted, pose incalculable threats to peace. This situation both reflects and aggravates international tensions, sharpens conflicts in various regions of the world, hinders the process of détente, exacerbates the differences between opposing military alliances, jeopardizes the security of all States, heightens the sense of insecurity among all States, including the non-nuclear-weapon States and increases the threat of nuclear war.

12. The arms race, particularly in its nuclear aspect, runs counter to efforts to achieve further relaxation of international tension, to establish international relations based on peaceful coexistence and trust between all States, and to develop broad international cooperation and understanding. The arms race impedes the realization of the purposes, and is incompatible with the principles, of the Charter of the United Nations, especially respect for sovereignty, refraining from the threat or use of force against the territorial integrity or political independence of any State, the peaceful settlement of disputes and non-intervention and non-interference in the internal affairs of States. It also adversely affects the right of peoples freely to determine their systems of social and economic development, and hinders the struggle for self-determination and the elimination of colonial rule, racial or foreign domination or occupation. Indeed, the massive accumulation of armaments and the acquisition of armaments technology by racist régimes, as well as their possible acquisition of nuclear weapons, present a challenging and increasingly dangerous obstacle to a world community faced with the urgent need to disarm. It is, therefore, essential for purposes of disarmament to prevent any further acquisition of arms or arms technology by such régimes, especially through strict adherence by all States to relevant decisions of the Security Council.

13. Enduring international peace and security cannot be built on the accumulation of weaponry by military alliances nor be sustained by a precarious balance of deterrence or doctrines of strategic superiority. Genuine and lasting peace can only be created through the effective implementation of the security system provided for in the Charter of

the United Nations and the speedy and substantial reduction of arms and armed forces, by international agreement and mutual example, leading ultimately to general and complete disarmament under effective international control. At the same time, the causes of the arms race and threats to peace must be reduced and to this end effective action should be taken to eliminate tensions and settle disputes by peaceful means.

14. Since the process of disarmament affects the vital security interests of all States, they must all be actively concerned with and contribute to the measures of disarmament and arms limitation, which have an essential part to play in maintaining and strengthening international security. Therefore the role and responsibility of the United Nations in the sphere of disarmament, in accordance with its Charter, must be strengthened.

15. It is essential that not only Governments but also the peoples of the world recognize and understand the dangers in the present situation. In order that an international conscience may develop and that world public opinion may exercise a positive influence, the United Nations should increase the dissemination of information on the armaments race and disarmament with the full cooperation of Member States.

16. In a world of finite resources there is a close relationship between expenditure on armaments and economic and social development. Military expenditures are reaching ever higher levels, the highest percentage of which can be attributed to the nuclear-weapon States and most of their allies, with prospects of further expansion and the danger of further increases in the expenditures of other countries. The hundreds of billions of dollars spent annually on the manufacture or improvement of weapons are in sombre and dramatic contrast to the want and poverty in which two thirds of the world's population live. This colossal waste of resources is even more serious in that it diverts to military purposes not only material but also technical and, human resources which are urgently needed for development in all countries, particularly in the developing countries. Thus, the economic and social consequences of the arms race are so detrimental that its continuation is obviously incompatible with the implementation of the new international economic order based on justice, equity and cooperation. Consequently, resources released as a result of the implementation of disarmament measures should be used in a manner which will hip to promote the well-being of all peoples and to improve the economic conditions of the developing countries.

17. Disarmament has thus become an imperative and most urgent task facing the international community. No real progress has been made so far in the crucial field of reduction of armaments. However, certain positive changes in international relations in some areas of the world provide some encouragement. Agreements have been reached that have been important in limiting certain weapons or eliminating them altogether, as in the case of the Convention on the Prohibition of the Development, Production and Stockpiling of Bacteriological (Biological) and Toxin Weapons and on Their Destruction[1] and excluding particular areas from the arms race. The fact remains that these agreements relate only to measures of limited restraint while the arms race continues. These partial measures have done little to bring the world closer to the goal of general and complete disarmament. For more than a decade there have been no negotiations leading to a treaty on general and complete disarmament. The pressing need now is to translate into practical terms the provisions of this Final Document and to proceed along the road of binding and effective international agreements in the field of disarmament.

18. Removing the threat of a world war - a nuclear war - is the most acute and urgent task of the present day. Mankind is confronted with a choice: we must halt the arms race and proceed to disarmament or face annihilation.

19. The ultimate objective of the efforts of States in the disarmament process is general and complete disarmament under effective international control. The principal goals of disarmament are to ensure the survival of mankind and to eliminate the danger of war, in particular nuclear war, to ensure that war is no longer an instrument for settling international disputes and that the use and the threat of force are eliminated from international life, as provided for in the Charter of the United Nations. Progress towards this objective requires the conclusion and implementation of agreements on the cessation of the arms race and on genuine measures of disarmament, taking into account the need of States to protect their security.

20. Among such measures, effective measures of nuclear disarmament and the prevention of nuclear war have the highest priority. To this end, it is imperative to remove the threat of nuclear weapons, to halt and reverse the nuclear arms race until the total elimination of nuclear weapons and their delivery systems has been achieved, and to prevent the proliferation of nuclear weapons. At the same time, other measures designed to prevent the outbreak of nuclear war and to lessen the danger of the threat or use of nuclear weapons should be taken.

21. Along with these measures, agreements or other effective measures should be adopted to prohibit or prevent the development, production or use of other weapons of mass destruction. In this context, an agreement on elimination of all chemical weapons should be concluded as a matter of high priority.

22. Together with negotiations on nuclear disarmament measures, negotiations should be carried out on the balanced reduction of armed forces and of conventional armaments, based on the principle of undiminished security of the parties with a view to promoting or enhancing stability at a lower military level, taking into account the need of all States to protect their security. These negotiations should be conducted with particular emphasis on armed forces and conventional weapons of nuclear-weapon States and other militarily significant countries. There should also be negotiations on the limitation of international transfer of conventional weapons, based in particular on the same principle, and taking into account the inalienable right to self-determination and independence of peoples under colonial or foreign domination and the obligations of States to respect that right, in accordance with the Charter of the United Nations and the Declaration on Principles of International Law concerning Friendly Relations and Cooperation among States,[2] as well as the need of recipient States to protect their security.

23. Further international action should be taken to prohibit or restrict for humanitarian reasons the use of specific conventional weapons, including those which may be excessively injurious, cause unnecessary suffering or have indiscriminate effects.

24. Collateral measures in both the nuclear and conventional fields, together with other measures specifically designed to build confidence, should be undertaken in order to contribute to the creation of favourable conditions for the adoption of additional disarmament measures and to further the relaxation of international tension.

25. Negotiations and measures in the field of disarmament shall be guided by the fundamental principles set forth below.

26. All States Members of the United Nations reaffirm their full commitment to the purposes of the Charter of the United Nations and their obligation strictly to observe its principles as well as other relevant and generally accepted principles of international law relating to the maintenance of international peace and security. They stress the special importance of refraining from the threat or use of force against the sovereignty, territorial integrity or political independence of any State, or against peoples under colonial or foreign domination seeking to exercise their right to self-determination and to achieve independence; non-intervention and non-interference in the internal affairs of other States; the inviolability of international frontiers; and the peaceful settlement of disputes, having regard to the inherent right of States to individual and collective self-defence in accordance with the Charter.

27. In accordance with the Charter, the United Nations has a central role and primary responsibility in the sphere of disarmament. In order effectively to discharge this role and facilitate and encourage all measures in this field, the United Nations should be kept appropriately informed of all steps in this field, whether unilateral, bilateral,

---

1 Resolution 2826 (XXVI), annex.

2 Resolution 2625 (XXV), annex.

regional or multilateral, without prejudice to the progress of negotiations.

28. All the peoples of the world have a vital interest in the success of disarmament negotiations. Consequently, all States have the duty to contribute to efforts in the field of disarmament. All States have the right to participate in disarmament negotiations. They have the right to participate on an equal footing in those multilateral disarmament negotiations which have a direct bearing on their national security. While disarmament is the responsibility of all States, the nuclear-weapon States have the primary responsibility for nuclear disarmament and, together with other militarily significant States, for halting and reversing the arms race. It is therefore important to secure their active participation.

29. The adoption of disarmament measures should take place in such an equitable and balanced manner as to ensure the right of each State to security and to ensure that no individual State or group of States may obtain advantages over others at any stage. At each stage the objective should be undiminished security at the lowest possible level of armaments and military forces.

30. An acceptable balance of mutual responsibilities and obligations for nuclear and non-nuclear-weapon States should be strictly observed.

31. Disarmament and arms limitation agreements should provide for adequate measures of verification satisfactory to all parties concerned in order to create the necessary confidence and ensure that they are being observed by all parties. The form and modalities of the verification to be provided for in any specific agreement depend upon and should be determined by the purposes, scope and nature of the agreement. Agreements should provide for the participation of parties directly or through the United Nations system in the verification process. Where appropriate, a combination of several methods of verification as well as other compliance procedures should be employed.

32. All States, in particular nuclear-weapon States, should consider various proposals designed to secure the avoidance of the use of nuclear weapons, and the prevention of nuclear war. In this context, while noting the declarations made by nuclear-weapon States, effective arrangements, as appropriate, to assure no nuclear-weapon States against the use or the threat use of nuclear weapons could strengthen the security of those States and international peace and security.

33. The establishment of nuclear-weapon-free zones on the basis of agreements or arrangement freely arrived at among the States of the zone concerned and the full compliance with those agreement or arrangements, thus ensuring that the zones are genuinely free from nuclear weapons, and respect for such zones by nuclear-weapon States constitute an important disarmament measure.

34. Disarmament, relaxation of international tension, respect for the right to self-determination and national independence, the peaceful settlement of disputes in accordance with the Charter of the United Nations and the strengthening of international peace and security are directly related to each other. Progress in any of these spheres has a beneficial effect on all of them; in turn, failure in one sphere has negative effects on others.

35. There is also a close relationship between disarmament and development. Progress in the former would help greatly in the realization of the latter. Therefore resources released as a result of the implementation of disarmament measures should be devoted to the economic and social development of nations and contribute to the bridging of the economic gap between developed and developing countries.

36. Non-proliferation of nuclear weapons is a matter of universal concern. Measures of disarmament must be consistent with the inalienable right of all States, without discrimination, to develop, acquire and use nuclear technology, equipment and materials for the peaceful use of nuclear energy and to determine their peaceful nuclear programmes in accordance with their national priorities, needs and interests, bearing in mind the need to prevent the proliferation of nuclear weapons. International cooperation in the peaceful uses of nuclear energy should be conducted under agreed and appropriate international safeguards applied on a non-discriminatory basis.

37. Significant progress in disarmament, including nuclear disarmament, would be facilitated by parallel measures to strengthen the security of States and to improve the international situation in general.

38. Negotiations on partial measures of disarmament should be conducted concurrently with negotiations on more comprehensive measures and should be followed by negotiations leading to a treaty on general and complete disarmament under effective international control.

39. Qualitative and quantitative disarmament measures are both important for halting the arms race. Efforts to that end must include negotiations on the limitation and cessation of the qualitative improvement of armaments, especially weapons of mass destruction and the development of new means of warfare so that ultimately scientific and technological achievement may be used solely for peaceful purposes.

40. Universality of disarmament agreements helps create confidence among States. When multilateral agreements in the field of disarmament are negotiated every effort should be made to ensure that they are universally acceptable. The full compliance of all parties with the provisions contained in such agreements would also contribute to the attainment of that goal.

41. In order to create favourable conditions for success in the disarmament process, all States should strictly abide by the provisions of the Charter of the United Nations, refrain from actions which might adversely affect efforts in the field of disarmament, and display a constructive approach to negotiations and the political will to reach agreements. There are certain negotiations on disarmament under way at different levels, the early and successful completion of which could contribute to limiting the arms race. Unilateral measures of arms limitation or reduction could also contribute to the attainment of that goal.

42. Since prompt measures should be taken in order to halt and reverse the arms race, Member States hereby declare that they will respect the objectives and principles stated above and make every effort faithfully to carry out the Programme of Action set forth in section III below.

III. Programme of Action

43. Progress towards the goal of general and complete disarmament can be achieved through the implementation of a programme of action on disarmament, in accordance with the goals and principles established in the Declaration on disarmament. The present Programme of Action contains priorities and measures in the field of disarmament that States should undertake as a matter of urgency with a view to halting and reversing the arms race and to giving the necessary impetus to efforts designed to achieve genuine disarmament leading to general and complete disarmament under effective international control.

44. The present Programme of Action enumerates the specific measures of disarmament which should be implemented over the next few years, as well as other measures and studies to prepare the way for future negotiations and for progress towards general and complete disarmament.

45. Priorities in disarmament negotiations shall be: nuclear weapons; other weapons of mass destruction, including chemical weapons; conventional weapons, including any which may be deemed to be excessively injurious or to have indiscriminate effects; and reduction of armed forces.

46. Nothing should preclude States from conducting negotiations on all priority items concurrently.

47. Nuclear weapons pose the greatest danger to mankind and to the survival of civilization. It is essential to halt and reverse the nuclear arms race in all its aspects in order to avert the danger of war involving nuclear weapons. The ultimate goal in this context is the complete elimination of nuclear weapons.

48. In the task of achieving the goals of nuclear disarmament, all the nuclear-weapon States, in particular those among them which possess the most important nuclear arsenals, bear a special responsibility.

49. The process of nuclear disarmament should be carried out in such a way, and requires measures to ensure, that the security of all States is guaranteed at progressively lower levels of nuclear armaments, taking into account the relative qualitative and quantitative importance of the existing arsenals of the nuclear-weapon States and other States concerned.

50. The achievement of nuclear disarmament will require urgent negotiation of agreements at appropriate stages and with adequate measures of verification satisfactory to the States concerned for:

(*a*) Cessation of the qualitative improvement and development of nuclear-weapon systems;

(*b*) Cessation of the production of all types of nuclear weapons and their means of delivery, and of the production of fissionable material for weapons purposes;

(*c*) A comprehensive, phased programme with agreed time-frames, whenever feasible, for progressive and balanced reduction of stockpiles of nuclear weapons and their means of delivery, leading to their ultimate and complete elimination at the earliest possible time.

Consideration can be given in the course of the negotiations to mutual and agreed limitation or prohibition, without prejudice to the security of any State, of any types of nuclear armaments.

51. The cessation of nuclear-weapon testing by all States within the framework of an effective nuclear disarmament process would be in the interest of mankind. It would make a significant contribution to the above aim of ending the qualitative improvement of nuclear weapons and the development of new types of such weapons and of preventing the proliferation of nuclear weapons. In this context the negotiations now in progress on "a treaty prohibiting nuclear-weapon tests, and a protocol covering nuclear explosions for peaceful purposes, which would be an integral part of the treaty", should be concluded urgently and the result submitted for full consideration by the multilateral negotiating body with a view to the submission of a draft treaty to the General Assembly at the earliest possible date. All efforts should be made by the negotiating parties to achieve an agreement which, following endorsement by the General Assembly, could attract the widest possible adherence. In this context, various views were expressed by non-nuclear-weapon States that, pending the conclusion of this treaty, the world community would be encouraged if all the nuclear-weapon States refrained from testing nuclear weapons. In this connexion, some nuclear-weapon States expressed different views.

52. The Union of Soviet Socialist Republics and the United States of America should conclude at the earliest possible date the agreement they have been pursuing for several years in the second series of the strategic arms limitation talks. They are invited to transmit in good time the text of the agreement to the General Assembly. It should be followed promptly by further strategic arms limitation negotiations between the two parties, leading to agreed significant reductions of, and qualitative limitations on, strategic arms. It should constitute an important step in the direction of nuclear disarmament and, ultimately, of establishment of a world free of such weapons.

53. The process of nuclear disarmament described in the paragraph on this subject should be expedited by the urgent and vigorous pursuit to a successful conclusion of ongoing negotiations and the urgent initiation of further negotiations among the nuclear-weapon States.

54. Significant progress in nuclear disarmament would be facilitated both by parallel political or international legal measures to strengthen the security of States and by progress in the limitation and reduction of armed forces and conventional armaments of the nuclear-weapon States and other States in the regions concerned.

55. Real progress in the field of nuclear disarmament could create an atmosphere conducive to progress in conventional disarmament on a world-wide basis.

56. The most effective guarantee against the danger of nuclear war and the use of nuclear weapons is nuclear disarmament and the complete elimination of nuclear weapons.

57. Pending the achievement of this goal, for which negotiations should be vigorously pursued, and bearing in mind the devastating results which nuclear war would have on belligerents and non-belligerents alike, the nuclear-weapon States have special responsibilities to undertake measures aimed at preventing the outbreak of nuclear war, and of the use of force in international relations, subject to the provisions of the Charter of the United Nations, including the use of nuclear weapons.

58. In this context all States, in particular nuclear-weapon States, should consider as soon as possible various proposals designed to secure the avoidance of the use of nuclear weapons, the prevention of nuclear war and related objectives, where possible through international agreement, and thereby ensure that the survival of mankind is not endangered. All States should actively participate in efforts to bring about conditions in international relations among States in which a code of peaceful conduct of nations in international affairs could be agreed and which would preclude the use or threat of use of nuclear weapons.

59. In the same context, the nuclear-weapon States are called upon to take steps to assure the non-nuclear-weapon States against the use or threat of use of nuclear weapons. The General Assembly notes the declarations made by the nuclear-weapon States and urges them to pursue efforts to conclude, as appropriate, effective arrangements to assure non-nuclear-weapon States against the use or threat of use of nuclear weapons.

60. The establishment of nuclear-weapon-free zones on the basis of arrangements freely arrived at among the States of the region concerned constitutes an important disarmament measure.

61. The process of establishing such zones in different parts of the world should be encouraged with the ultimate objective of achieving a world entirely free of nuclear weapons. In the process of establishing such zones, the characteristics of each region should be taken into account. The States participating in such zones should undertake to comply fully with all the objectives, purposes and principles of the agreements or arrangements establishing the zones, thus ensuring that they are genuinely free from nuclear weapons.

62. With respect to such zones, the nuclear-weapon States in turn are called upon to give undertakings, the modalities of which are to be negotiated with the competent authority of each zone, in particular:

(*a*) To respect strictly the status of the nuclear-weapon-free zone;

(*b*) To refrain from the use or threat of use of nuclear weapons against the States of the zone.

63. In the light of existing conditions, and without prejudice to other measures which may be considered in other regions, the following measures are especially desirable:

(*a*) Adoption by the States concerned of all relevant measures to ensure the full application of the Treaty for the Prohibition of Nuclear Weapons in Latin America (Treaty of Tlatelolco),[1] taking into account the views expressed at the tenth special session on the adherence to it;

(*b*) Signature and ratification of the Additional Protocols of the Treaty for the Prohibition of Nuclear Weapons in Latin America (Treaty of Tlatelolco) by the States entitled to become parties to those instruments which have not yet done so;

(*c*) In Africa, where the Organization of African Unity has affirmed a decision for the denuclearization of the region, the Security Council of the United Nations shall take appropriate effective steps whenever necessary to prevent the frustration of this objective;

(*d*) The serious consideration of the practical and urgent steps, as described in the paragraphs above, required for the implementation of the proposal to establish a nuclear-weapon-free zone in the Middle East, in accordance with the relevant General Assembly resolutions, where all parties directly concerned have expressed their support for the concept and where the danger of nuclear-weapon proliferation exists. The establishment of a nuclear-weapon-free zone in the Middle East would greatly enhance international peace and security. Pending the establishment of such a zone in the region, States of the region should solemnly declare that they will refrain on a reciprocal basis from producing, acquiring or in any other way possessing nuclear weapons and nuclear explosive devices and from permitting

1 United Nations, *Treaty Series*, vol. 634, No. 9068.

the stationing of nuclear weapons on their territory by any third party, and agree to place all their nuclear activities under International Atomic Energy Agency safeguards. Consideration should be given to a Security Council role in advancing the establishment of a nuclear-weapon-free zone in the Middle East;

(*e*) All States in the region of South Asia have expressed their determination to keep their countries free of nuclear weapons. No action should be taken by them which might deviate from that objective. In this context, the question of establishing a nuclear-weapon-free zone in South Asia has been dealt with in several resolutions of the General Assembly, which is keeping the subject under consideration.

64. The establishment of zones of peace in various regions of the world under appropriate conditions, to be clearly defined and determined freely by the States concerned in the zone, taking into account the characteristics of the zone and the principles of the Charter of the United Nations, and in conformity with international law, can contribute to strengthening the security of States within such zones and to international peace and security as a whole. In this regard, the General Assembly notes the proposals for the establishment of zones of peace, *inter alia*, in:

(*a*) South-East Asia where States in the region have expressed interest in the establishment of such a zone, in conformity with their views;

(*b*) The Indian Ocean, taking into account the deliberations of the General Assembly and its relevant resolutions and the need to ensure the maintenance of peace and security in the region.

65. It is imperative, as an integral part of the effort to halt and reverse the arms race, to prevent the proliferation of nuclear weapons. The goal of nuclear non-proliferation is on the one hand to prevent the emergence of any additional nuclear-weapon States besides the existing five nuclear-weapon States, and on the other progressively to reduce and eventually eliminate nuclear weapons altogether. This involves obligations and responsibilities on the part of both nuclear-weapon States and non-nuclear-weapon States, the former undertaking to stop the nuclear arms race and to achieve nuclear disarmament by urgent application of the measures outlined in the relevant paragraphs of this Final Document, and all States undertaking to prevent the spread of nuclear weapons.

66. Effective measures can and should be taken at the national level and through international agreements to minimize the danger of the proliferation of nuclear weapons without jeopardizing energy supplies or the development of nuclear energy for peaceful purposes. Therefore, the nuclear-weapon States and the non-nuclear-weapon States should jointly take further steps to develop an international consensus of ways and means, on a universal and non-discriminatory basis, to prevent the proliferation of nuclear weapons.

67. Full implementation of all the provisions of existing instruments on non-proliferation, such as the Treaty on the Non-Proliferation of Nuclear Weapons[1] and/or the Treaty for the Prohibition of Nuclear Weapons in Latin America (Treaty of Tlatelolco) by States parties to those instruments will be an important contribution to this end. Adherence to such instruments has increased in recent years and the hope has been expressed by the parties that this trend might continue.

68. Non-proliferation measures should not jeopardize the full exercise of the inalienable rights of all States to apply and develop their programmes for the peaceful uses of nuclear energy for economic and social development in conformity with their priorities, interests and needs. All States should also have access to and be free to acquire technology, equipment and materials for peaceful uses of nuclear energy, taking into account the particular needs of the developing countries. International cooperation in this field should be under agreed and appropriate international safeguards applied through the International Atomic Energy Agency on a non-discriminatory basis in order to prevent effectively the proliferation of nuclear weapons.

69. Each country's choices and decisions in the field of the peaceful uses of nuclear energy should be respected without jeopardizing their respective fuel cycle policies or international cooperation, agreements and contracts for the peaceful uses of nuclear energy, provided that the agreed safeguard measures mentioned above are applied.

70. In accordance with the principles and provisions of General Assembly resolution 32/50 of 8 December 1977, international cooperation for the promotion of the transfer and utilization of nuclear technology for economic and social development, especially in the developing countries, should be strengthened.

71. Efforts should be made to conclude the world of the International Nuclear Fuel Cycle Evaluation strictly in accordance with the objectives set out in the final communiqué of its Organizing Conference.[2]

72. All States should adhere to the Protocol for the Prohibition of the Use in War of Asphyxiating, Poisonous or Other Gases, and of Bacteriological Methods of Warfare, signed at Geneva on 17 June 1925.[3]

73. All States which have not yet done so should consider adhering to the Convention on the Prohibition of the Development, Production and Stockpiling of Bacteriological (Biological) and Toxin Weapons and on Their Destruction.

74. States should also consider the possibility of adhering to multilateral agreements concluded so far in the disarmament field which are mentioned below in this section.

75. The complete and effective prohibition of the development, production and stockpiling of all chemical weapons and their destruction represent one of the most urgent measures of disarmament. Consequently, the conclusion of a convention to this end, on which negotiations have been going on for several years, is one of the most urgent tasks of multilateral negotiations. After its conclusion, all States should contribute to ensuring the broadest possible application of the convention through its early signature and ratification.

76. A convention should be concluded prohibiting the development, production, stockpiling and use of radiological weapons.

77. In order to help prevent a qualitative arms race and so that scientific and technological achievements may ultimately be used solely for peaceful purposes, effective measures should be taken to avoid the danger and prevent the emergence of new types of weapons of mass destruction based on new scientific principles and achievements. Efforts should be appropriately pursued aiming at the prohibition of such new types and new systems of weapons of mass destruction. Specific agreements could be concluded on particular types of new weapons of mass destruction which may be identified. This question should be kept under continuing review.

78. The Committee on Disarmament should keep under review the need for a further prohibition of military or any other hostile use of environmental modification techniques in order to eliminate the dangers to mankind from such use.

79. In order to promote the peaceful use of and to avoid an arms race on the sea-bed and the ocean floor and the subsoil thereof, the Committee on Disarmament is requested - in consultation with the States parties to the Treaty on the Prohibition of the Emplacement of Nuclear Weapons and Other Weapons of Mass Destruction on the Sea-Bed and the Ocean Floor and in the Subsoil Thereof,[4] and taking into account the proposals made during the 1977 Review Conference of the parties to that Treaty and any relevant technological developments - to proceed promptly with the consideration of further measures in the field of disarmament for the prevention of an arms race in that environment.

80. In order to prevent an arms race in outer space, further measures should be taken and appropriate international negotiations held in accordance with the spirit of the Treaty on Principles Governing the Activities of States in the Exploration and Use of Outer Space, including the Moon and Other Celestial Bodies.[5]

81 Together with negotiations on nuclear disarmament measures, the limitation and gradual reduction of armed forces and conventional weapons should he resolutely pursued within the framework of prog-

1 Resolution 2373 (XXII), annex.

2 See A/C.1/32/7.

3 League of Nations, *Treaty Series*, vol. XCIV (1929), No. 2138.

4 Resolution 2660 (XXV), annex.

5 Resolution 2222 (XXI), annex.

ress towards general and complete disarmament. States with the largest military arsenals have a special responsibility in pursuing the process of conventional armaments reductions.

82. In particular the achievement of a more stable situation in Europe at a lower level of military potential on the basis of approximate equality and parity, as well as on the basis of undiminished security of all States with full respect for security interests and independence of States outside military alliances, by agreement on appropriate mutual reductions and limitations would contribute to the strengthening of security in Europe and constitute a significant step towards enhancing international peace and security. Current efforts to this end should be continued most energetically

83. Agreements or other measures should be resolutely pursued on a bilateral, regional and multilateral basis with the aim of strengthening peace and security at a lover level of forces, by the limitation and reduction of armed forces and of conventional weapons, taking into account the need of States to protect their security, bearing in mind the inherent right of self-defence embodied in the Charter of the United Nations and without prejudice to the principle of equal rights and self-determination of peoples in accordance with the Charter, and the need to ensure balance at each stage and undiminished security of all States. Such measures might include those in the following two paragraphs.

84. Bilateral, regional and multilateral consultations and conferences should be held where appropriate conditions exist with the participation of all the countries concerned for the consideration of different aspects of conventional disarmament, such as the initiative envisaged in the Declaration of Ayacucho subscribed to by eight Latin American countries on 9 December 1974.[1]

85. Consultations should be carried out among major arms supplier and recipient countries on the limitation of all types of international transfer of conventional weapons, based in particular on the principle of undiminished security of the parties with a view to promoting or enhancing stability at a lower military level, taking into account the need of all States to protect their security as well as the inalienable right to self-determination and independence of peoples under colonial or foreign domination and the obligations of States to respect that right, in accordance with the Charter of the United Nations and the Declaration on Principles of International Law concerning Friendly Relations and Cooperation among States.

86. The United Nations Conference on Prohibitions or Restrictions of Use of Certain Conventional Weapons Which May Be Deemed to Be Excessively Injurious or to Have Indiscriminate Effects, to be held in 1979, should seek agreement, in the light of humanitarian and military considerations, on the prohibition or restriction of use of certain conventional weapons including those which may cause unnecessary suffering or have indiscriminate effects. The Conference should consider specific categories of such weapons, including those which were the subject-matter of previously conducted discussions.

87. All States are called upon to contribute towards carrying out this task.

88. The result of the Conference should be considered by all States, especially producer States, in regard to the question of the transfer of such weapons to other States.

89. Gradual reduction of military budgets on a mutually agreed basis, for example, in absolute figures or in terms of percentage points, particularly by nuclear-weapon States and other militarily significant States, would be a measure that would contribute to the curbing of the arms race and would increase the possibilities of reallocation of resources now being used for military purposes to economic and social development, particularly for the benefit of the developing countries. The basis for implementing this measure will have to be agreed by all participating States and will require ways and means of its implementation acceptable to all of them, taking account of the problems involved in assessing the relative significance of reductions as among different States and with due regard to the proposals of States on all the aspects of reduction of military budgets.

1 See A/10044, annex.

90. The General Assembly should continue to consider what concrete steps should be taken to facilitate the reduction of military budgets, bearing in mind the relevant proposals and documents of the United Nations on this question.

91. In order to facilitate the conclusion and effective implementation of disarmament agreements and to create confidence, States should accept appropriate provisions for verification in such agreements.

92. In the context of international disarmament negotiations, the problem of verification should be further examined and adequate methods and procedures in this field be considered. Every effort should be made to develop appropriate methods and procedures which are non-discriminatory and which do not unduly interfere with the internal affairs of other States or jeopardize their economic and social development.

93. In order to facilitate the process of disarmament, it is necessary to take measures and pursue policies to strengthen international peace and security and to build confidence among States. Commitment to confidence-building measures could significantly contribute to preparing for further progress in disarmament. For this purpose, measures such as the following and other measures yet to be agreed upon, should be undertaken:

(*a*) The prevention of attacks which take place by accident, miscalculation or communications failure by taking steps to improve communications between Governments, particularly in areas of tension, by the establishment of "hot lines" and other methods of reducing the risk of conflict;

(*b*) States should assess the possible implications of their military research and development for existing agreements as well as for further efforts in the field of disarmament;

(*c*) The Secretary-General shall periodically submit reports to the General Assembly on the economic and social consequences of the armaments race and its extremely harmful effects on world peace and security.

94. In view of the relationship between expenditure on armaments and economic and social development and the necessity to release real resources now being used for military purposes to economic and social development in the world, particularly for the benefit of the developing countries, the Secretary-General should, with the assistance of a group of qualified governmental experts appointed by him, indicate an expert study on the relationship between disarmament and development. The Secretary-General should submit an interim report on the subject to the General Assembly at its thirty-fourth session and submit the final results to the Assembly at its thirty-sixth session for subsequent action.

95. The expert study should have the terms of reference contained in the report of the *Ad Hoc* Group on the Relationship between Disarmament and Development[2] appointed by the Secretary-General in accordance with General Assembly resolution 32/88 A of 12 December 1977. It should investigate the three main areas listed in the report, bearing in mind the United Nations studies previously carried out. The study should be made in the context of how disarmament can contribute to the establishment of the new international economic order. The study should be forward-looking and policy-oriented and place special emphasis on both the desirability of a reallocation, following disarmament measures, of resources now being used for military purposes to economic and social development, particularly for the benefit of the developing countries, and the substantive feasibility of such a reallocation. A principal aim should be to produce results that could effectively guide the formulation of practical measures to reallocate those resources at the local, national, regional and international levels.

96. Taking further steps in the field of disarmament and other measures aimed at promoting international peace and security would be facilitated by carrying out studies by the Secretary-General in this field with appropriate assistance from governmental or consultant experts.

2 A/S-10/9, annex.

97. The Secretary-General shall, with the assistance of consultant experts appointed by him, continue the study of the interrelationship between disarmament and international security requested in Assembly resolution 32/87 C of 12 December 1977 and submit it to the thirty-fourth session of the General Assembly.

98. At its thirty-third and subsequent sessions the General Assembly should determine the specific guidelines for carrying out studies, taking into account the proposals already submitted including those made by individual countries at the special session, as well as other proposals which can be introduced later in this field. In doing so, the Assembly would take into consideration a report on these matters prepared by the Secretary-General.

99. In order to mobilize world public opinion on behalf of disarmament, the specific measures set forth below, designed to increase the dissemination of information about the armaments race and the efforts to halt and reverse it, should be adopted.

100. Governmental and non-governmental information organs and those of the United Nations and its specialized agencies should give priority to the preparation and distribution of printed and audio-visual material relating to the danger represented by the armaments race as well as to the disarmament efforts and negotiations on specific disarmament measures.

101. In particular, publicity should be given to the Final Document of the tenth special session.

102. The General Assembly proclaims the week starting 24 October, the day of the foundation of the United Nations, as a week devoted to fostering the objectives of disarmament.

103. To encourage study and research on disarmament, the United Nations Centre for Disarmament should intensify its activities in the presentation of information concerning the armaments race and disarmament. Also, the United Nations Educational, Scientific and Cultural Organization is urged to intensify its activities aimed at facilitating research and publications on disarmament, related to its fields of competence, especially in developing countries, and should disseminate the results of such research.

104. Throughout this process of disseminating information about developments in the disarmament field of all countries, there should be increased participation by non-governmental organizations concerned with the matter, through closer liaison between them and the United Nations.

105. Member States should be encouraged to ensure a better flow of information with regard to the various aspects of disarmament to avoid dissemination of false and tendentious information concerning armaments, and to concentrate on the danger of escalation of the armaments race and on the need for general and complete disarmament under effective international control.

106. With a view to contributing to a greater understanding and awareness of the problems created by the armaments race and of the need for disarmament, Governments and governmental and non-governmental international organizations are urged to take steps to develop programmes of education for disarmament and peace studies at all levels.

107. The General Assembly welcomes the initiative of the United Nations Educational, Scientific and Cultural Organization in planning to hold a world congress on disarmament education and, in this connexion, urges that organization to step up its programme aimed at the development of disarmament education as a distinct field of study through the preparation, *inter alia*, of teachers, guides, textbooks, readers and audio-visual materials. Member States should take all possible measures to encourage the incorporation of such materials in the curricula of their educational institutes.

108. In order to promote expertise in disarmament in more Member States, particularly in the developing countries, the General Assembly decides to establish a programme of fellowships on disarmament. The Secretary-General, taking into account the proposal submitted to the special session, should prepare guidelines for the programme. He should also submit the financial requirements of twenty fellowships to the General Assembly at its thirty-third session for inclusion in the regular budget of the United Nations, bearing in mind the savings that can be made within the existing budgetary appropriations.

109. Implementation of these priorities should lead to general and complete disarmament under effective international control, which remains the ultimate goal of all efforts exerted in the field of disarmament. Negotiations on general and complete disarmament shall be conducted concurrently with negotiations on partial measures of disarmament. With this purpose in mind, the Committee on Disarmament will undertake the elaboration of a comprehensive programme of disarmament encompassing all measures thought to be advisable in order to ensure that the goal of general and complete disarmament under effective international control becomes a reality in a world in which international peace and security prevail and in which the new international economic order is strengthened and consolidated. The comprehensive programme should contain appropriate procedures for ensuring that the General Assembly is kept fully informed of the progress of the negotiations including an appraisal of the situation when appropriate and, in particular, a continuing review of the implementation of the programme.

110. Progress in disarmament should be accompanied by measures to strengthen institutions for maintaining peace and the settlement of international disputes by peaceful means. During and after the implementation of the programme of general and complete disarmament, there should be taken, in accordance with the principles of the Charter of the United Nations, the necessary measures to maintain international peace and security, including the obligation of States to place at the disposal of the United Nations agreed manpower necessary for an international peace force to be equipped with agreed types of armaments. Arrangements for the use of this force should ensure that the United Nations can effectively deter or supress any threat or use of arms in violation of the purposes and principles of the United Nations.

111. General and complete disarmament under strict and effective international control shall permit States to have at their disposal only those non-nuclear forces, armaments, facilities and establishments as are agreed to be necessary to maintain internal order and protect the personal security of citizens and in order that States shall support and provide agreed manpower for a United Nations peace force.

112. In addition to the several questions dealt with in this Programme of Action, there are a few others of fundamental importance, on which, because of the complexity of the issues involved and the short time at the disposal of the special session, it has proved impossible to reach satisfactory agreed conclusions. For those reasons they are treated only in very general terms and, in a few instances, not even treated at all in the Programme. It should be stressed, however, that a number of concrete approaches to deal with such questions emerged from the exchange of views carried out in the General Assembly which will undoubtedly facilitate the continuation of the study and negotiation of the problems involved in the competent disarmament organs.

IV. Machinery

113. While disarmament, particularly in the nuclear field, has become a necessity for the survival of mankind and for the elimination of the danger of nuclear war, little progress has been made since the end of the Second World War. In addition to the need to exercise political will, the international machinery should be utilized more effectively and also improved to enable implementation of the Programme of Action and help the United Nations to fulfil its role in the field of disarmament. In spite of the best efforts of the international community, adequate results have not been produced with the existing machinery. There is, therefore, an urgent need that existing disarmament machinery be revitalized and forums appropriately constituted for disarmament deliberations and negotiations with a better representative character. For maximum effectiveness, two kinds of bodies are required in the field of disarmament—deliberative and negotiating. All Member States should be represented on the former, whereas the latter, for the sake of convenience, should have a relatively small membership.

114. The United Nations, in accordance with the Charter, has a central role and primary responsibility in the sphere of disarmament. Accordingly, it should play a more active role in this field and, in

order to discharge its functions effectively, the United Nations should facilitate and encourage all disarmament measures - unilateral, bilateral, regional or multilateral - and be kept duly informed through the General Assembly, or any other appropriate United Nations channel reaching all Members of the Organization, of all disarmament efforts outside its aegis without prejudice to the progress of negotiations.

115. The General Assembly has been and should remain the main deliberative organ of the United Nations in the field of disarmament and should make every effort to facilitate the implementation of disarmament measures. An item entitled "Review of the implementation of the recommendations and decisions adopted by the General Assembly at its tenth special session" shall be included in the provisional agenda of the thirty-third and subsequent sessions of the General Assembly.

116. Draft multilateral disarmament conventions should be subjected to the normal procedures applicable in the law of treaties. Those submitted to the General Assembly for its commendation should be subject to full review by the Assembly.

117. The First Committee of the General Assembly should deal in the future only with questions of disarmament and related international security questions.

118. The General Assembly establishes, as successor to the Commission originally established by resolution 502 (VI) of 11 January 1952, a Disarmament Commission, composed of all States Members of the United Nations, and decides that:

(*a*) The Disarmament Commission shall be a deliberative body, a subsidiary organ of the General Assembly, the function of which shall be to consider and make recommendations on various problems in the field of disarmament and to follow up the relevant decisions and recommendations of the special session devoted to disarmament. The Disarmament Commission should, *inter alia*, consider the elements of a comprehensive programme for disarmament to be submitted as recommendations to the General Assembly and, through it, to the negotiating body, the Committee on Disarmament;

(*b*) The Disarmament Commission shall function under the rules of procedure relating to the committees of the General Assembly with such modifications as the Commission may deem necessary and shall make every effort to ensure that, in so far as possible, decisions on substantive issues be adopted by consensus;

(*c*) The Disarmament Commission shall report annually to the General Assembly and will submit for consideration by the Assembly at its thirty-third session a report on organizational matters; in 1979, the Disarmament Commission will meet for a period not exceeding four weeks, the dates to be decided at the thirty-third session of the Assembly

(*d*) The Secretary-General shall furnish such experts, staff and services as are necessary for the effective accomplishment of the Commission's functions.

119. A second special session of the General Assembly devoted to disarmament should be held on a date to be decided by the Assembly at its thirty-third session.

120. The General Assembly is conscious of the work that has been done by the international negotiating body that has been meeting since 14 March 1962 as well as the considerable and urgent work that remains to be accomplished in the field of disarmament. The Assembly is deeply aware of the continuing requirement for a single multilateral disarmament negotiating forum of limited size taking decisions on the basis of consensus. It attaches great importance to the participation of all the nuclear-weapon States in an appropriately constituted negotiating body, the Committee on Disarmament. The Assembly welcomes the agreement reached following appropriate consultations among the Member States during the special session of the General Assembly devoted to disarmament that the Committee on Disarmament will be open to the nuclear-weapon States, and thirty-two to thirty-five other States to be chosen in consultation with the President of the thirty-second session of the Assembly; that the membership of the Committee on Disarmament will be reviewed at regular intervals; that the Committee on Disarmament will be convened in Geneva not later than January 1979 by the country whose name appears first in the alphabetical list of membership; and that the Committee on Disarmament will:

(*a*) Conduct its work by consensus;

(*b*) Adopt its own rules of procedure;

(*c*) Request the Secretary-General of the United Nations, following consultations with the Committee on Disarmament, to appoint the Secretary of the Committee, who shall also act as his personal representative, to assist the Committee and its Chairman in organizing the business and time-tables of the Committee;

(*d*) Rotate the chairmanship of the Committee among all its members on a monthly basis;

(*e*) Adopt its own agenda taking into account the recommendations made to it by the General Assembly and the proposals presented by the members of the Committee;

(*f*) Submit a report to the General Assembly annually, or more frequently as appropriate, and provide its formal and other relevant documents to the States Members of the United Nations on a regular basis;

(*g*) Make arrangements for interested States, not members of the Committee, to submit to the Committee written proposals or working documents on measures of disarmament that are the subject of negotiation in the Committee and to participate in the discussion of the subject-matter of such proposals or working documents;

(*h*) Invite States not members of the Committee, upon their request, to express views in the Committee when the particular concerns of those States are under discussion;

(*i*) Open its plenary meetings to the public unless otherwise decided.

121. Bilateral and regional disarmament negotiations may also play an important role and could facilitate negotiations of multilateral agreements in the field of disarmament.

122. At the earliest appropriate time, a world disarmament conference should be convened with universal participation and with adequate preparation.

123. In order to enable the United Nations to continue to fulfil its role in the field of disarmament and to carry out the additional tasks assigned to it by this special session, the United Nations Centre for Disarmament should be adequately strengthened and its research and information functions accordingly extended. The Centre should also take account fully of the possibilities offered by specialized agencies and other institutions and programmes within the United Nations system with regard to studies and information on disarmament. The Centre should also increase contacts with non-governmental organizations and research institutions in view of the valuable role they play in the field of disarmament. This role could be encouraged also in other ways that may be considered as appropriate.

124. The Secretary-General is requested to set up an advisory board of eminent persons, selected on the basis of their personal expertise and taking into account the principle of equitable geographical representation, to advise him on various aspects of studies to be made under the auspices of the United Nations in the field of disarmament and arms limitation, including a programme of such studies.

125. The General Assembly notes with satisfaction that the active participation of the Member States in the consideration of the agenda items of the special session and the proposals and suggestions submitted by them and reflected to a considerable extent in the Final Document have made a valuable contribution to the work of the special session and to its positive conclusion. Since a number of those proposals and suggestions,[1] which have become an integral

---

1 See *Official Records of the General Assembly, Tenth Special Session, Plenary Meetings*, 1st to 25th meetings; *ibid., Tenth Special Session, Supplement No. 1* (A/S-10/1), *Supplement No. 2* (A/S-10/2 and Corr.1), *Supplement No. 2A* (A/S-10/2/Add.1/Rev.1) and *Supplement No. 3* (A/S-10/3 and Corr.1); *ibid., Tenth Special Session, Annexes*, agenda item 7, document A/S-10/10; and *ibid., Tenth Special Session, ad hoc Committee of the Tenth Special Session*, 1st to 16th meetings, and *ibid., ad hoc Committee of the Tenth Special Session, Sessional Fascicle*, corrigendum; A/S-10/5, A/S-10/6 and Corr.1 and Add.1, A/S-10/7 and Corr.1, A/S-10/8 and Add.1 and 2,

part of the work of the special session of the General Assembly, deserve to be studied further and more thoroughly, taking into consideration the many relevant comments and observations made in both the general debate in plenary meeting and the deliberations of the *Ad Hoc Committee* of the Tenth Special Session, the Secretary-General is requested to transmit, together with this Final Document, to the appropriate deliberative and negotiating organs dealing with the questions of disarmament all the official records of the special session devoted to disarmament, in accordance with the recommendations which the Assembly may adopt at its thirty-third session. Some of the proposals put forth for the consideration of the special session are listed below:

(*a*) Text of the decision of the Central Committee of the Romanian Communist Party concerning Romania's position on disarmament and, in particular, on nuclear disarmament, adopted on 9 May 1978;[1]

(*b*) Views of the Swiss Government on problems to be discussed at the tenth special session of the General Assembly;[2]

(*c*) Proposals of the Union of Soviet Socialist Republics on practical measures for ending the arms race;[3]

(*d*) Memorandum from France concerning the establishment of an International Satellite Monitoring Agency;[4]

(*e*) Memorandum from France concerning the establishment of an International Institute for Research on Disarmament;[5]

(*f*) Proposal by Sri Lanka for the establishment of a World Disarmament Authority;[6]

(*g*) Working paper submitted by the Federal Republic of Germany entitled "Contribution to the seismological verification of a comprehensive test ban";[7]

(*h*) Working paper submitted by the Federal Republic of Germany entitled "Invitation to attend an international chemical-weapon verification workshop in the Federal Republic of Germany";[8]

(*i*) Working paper submitted by China on disarmament;[9]

(*j*) Working paper submitted by the Federal Republic of Germany concerning zones of confidence building measures as a first step towards the preparation of a world-wide convention on confidence-building measures;[10]

(*k*) Proposal by Ireland for a study of the possibility of establishing a system of incentives to promote arms control and disarmament;[11]

(*l*) Working paper submitted by Romania concerning a synthesis of the proposals in the field of disarmament;[12]

(*m*) Proposal by the United States of America on the establishment of a United Nations Peace-keeping Reserve and on confidence-building measures and stabilizing measures in various regions, including notification of manouvres, invitation of observers to manouvers, and United Nations machinery to study and promote such measures;[13]

(*n*) Proposal by Uruguay on the possibility of establishing a polemological agency;[14]

(*o*) Proposal by Belgium, Canada, Denmark, Germany, Federal Republic of, Ireland, Italy, Japan, Luxembourg, the Netherlands, New Zealand, Norway, Sweden, the United Kingdom of Great Britain and Northern Ireland and the United States of America on the strengthening of the security role of the United Nations in the peaceful settlement of disputes and peace-keeping;[15]

(*p*) Memorandum from France concerning the establishment of an International Disarmament Fund for Development;[16]

(*q*) Proposal by Norway entitled "Evaluation of the impact of new weapons on arms control and disarmament efforts";[17]

(*r*) Note verbale transmitting the text, signed in Washington on 22 June 1978 by the Ministers for Foreign Affairs of Argentina, Bolivia, Chile, Colombia, Ecuador, Panama, Peru and Venezuela, reaffirming the principles of the Declaration of Ayacucho with respect to the limitation of conventional weapons;[18]

(*s*) Memorandum from Liberia entitled "Declaration of a new philosophy on disarmament";[19]

(*t*) Statements made by the representatives of China, on 22 June 1978, on the draft Final Document of the tenth special session;[20]

(*u*) Proposal by the President of Cyprus for the total demilitarization and disarmament of the Republic of Cyprus and the implementation of the resolutions of the United Nations;[21]

(*v*) Proposal by Costa Rica on economic and social incentives to halt the arms race;[22]

(*w*) Amendments submitted by China to the draft Final Document of the tenth special session;[23]

(*x*) Proposals by Canada for the implementation of a strategy of suffocation of the nuclear arms race;[24]

(*y*) Draft resolution submitted by Cyprus, Ethiopia and India on the urgent need for cessation of further testing of nuclear weapons;[25]

(*z*) Draft resolution submitted by Ethiopia and India on the non-use of nuclear weapons and prevention of nuclear war;[26]

(*aa*) Proposal by the non-aligned countries on the establishment of a zone of peace in the Mediterranean;[27]

(*bb*) Proposal by the Government of Senegal for a tax on military budgets;[28]

(*cc*) Proposal by Austria for the transmission to Member States of working paper A/AC.187/109 and the ascertainment of their views on the subject of verification;[29]

(*dd*) Proposal by the non-aligned countries for the dismantling of foreign military bases in foreign territories and withdrawal of foreign troops from foreign territories;[30]

(*ee*) Proposal by Mexico for the opening, on a provisional basis, of an *Ad Hoc* account in the United Nations Development Programme to

---

A/S-10/9, A/S-10/11-14 and A/S-10/17; A/S-10/AC.1/1-8, A/S-10/AC.1/9 and Add.1, A/S-10/AC.1/10 and 11, A/S-10/AC.1/12 and Corr.1, A/S-10/AC.1/13-25, A/S-10/AC.1/26 and Corr.1 and 2, A/S-10/AC.1/27-36, A/S-10/AC.1/37 and Rev.1 and Corr.1 and Rev.1/Add.1, and A/S-10/AC.1/38-40; A/S-10/AC.1/L.1 and Rev.1 and A/S-10/AC.1/L.2-17.

1 A/S-10/14.

2 A/S-10/AC. 1/2.

3 A/S-10/AC.1/4.

4 A/S-10/AC.1/7

5 A/S 10/AC.1/8.

6 A/S-10/AC.1/9 and Add.1.

7 A/S-10/AC.1/12 and Corr.1.

8 A/S-10/AC.1/13.

9 A/S-10/AC.1/17.

10 A/S-10/AC.1/20.

11 A/S-10/AC.1/21.

12 A/S-10/AC.1/23.

13 A/S-10/AC.1/24.

14 A/S-10/AC.1/25.

15 A/S-10/AC.1/26 and Corr.1 and 2.

16 A/S-10/AC.1/28.

17 A/S-10/AC.1/31.

18 A/S-10/AC.1/34

19 A/S-10/AC.1/35.

20 A/S-10/AC.1/36.

21 A/S-10/AC.1/39.

22 A/S-10/AC.1/40.

23 A/S-10/AC.1/L.2-4, A/S-10/AC.1/L.7 and 8.

24 A/S-10/AC.1/L.6.

25 A/S-10/AC.1/L.10.

26 A/S-10/AC.1/L.11.

27 A/S-10/AC.1/37, para. 72.

28 *Ibid.*, para. 101.

29 *Ibid.*, para. 113.

30 *Ibid.*, para. 126.

use for development the funds which may be released as a result of disarmament measures;[1]

(*ff*) Proposal by Italy on the role of the Security Council in the field of disarmament in accordance with Article 26 of the Charter of the United Nations;[2]

(*gg*) Proposal by the Netherlands for a study on the establishment of an international disarmament organization;[3]

126. In adopting this Final Document, the States Members of the United Nations solemnly reaffirm their determination to work for general and complete disarmament and to make further collective efforts aimed at strengthening peace and international security; eliminating the threat of war, particularly nuclear war; implementing practical measures aimed at halting and reversing the arms race; strengthening the procedures for the peaceful settlement of disputes; and reducing military expenditures and utilizing the resources thus released in a manner which will help to promote the well-being of all peoples and to improve the economic conditions of the developing countries.

127. The General Assembly expresses its satisfaction that the proposals submitted to its special session devoted to disarmament and the deliberations thereon have made it possible to reaffirm and define in this Final Document fundamental principles, goals, priorities and procedures for the implementation of the above purposes, either in the Declaration or the Programme of Action or in both. The Assembly also welcomes the important decisions agreed upon regarding the deliberative and negotiating machinery and is confident that these organs will discharge their functions in an effective manner.

128. Finally, it should be borne in mind that the number of States that participated in the general debate, as well as the high level of representation and the depth and scope of that debate, are unprecedented in the history of disarmament efforts. Several Heads of State or Government addressed the General Assembly. In addition, other Heads of State or Government sent messages and expressed their good wishes for the success of the special session of the Assembly. Several high officials of specialized agencies and other institutions and programmes within the United Nations system and spokesmen of twenty-five non-governmental organizations and six research institutes also made valuable contributions to the proceedings of the session. It must be emphasized, moreover, that the special session marks not the end but rather the beginning of a new phase of the efforts of the United Nations in the field of disarmament.

129. The General Assembly is convinced that the discussions of the disarmament problems at the special session and its Final Document will attract the attention of all peoples, further mobilize world public opinion and provide a powerful impetus for the cause of disarmament.

27th plenary meeting
30 June 1978

34/88. Declaration on International Cooperation for Disarmament

Committee: 1
Vote: Adopted without a vote

The General Assembly,

Recalling once again the affirmation in the Charter of the United Nations of the determination of the peoples of the United Nations to save succeeding generations from the scourge of war and to this end to unite their strength to maintain international peace and security,

Stressing again the importance of the recommendations and decisions adopted by the General Assembly at its tenth special session, devoted to disarmament, and recalling the principles proclaimed in the Final Document of that session,[4]

Convinced that there is an urgent need for active and combined efforts further to intensify the comprehensive implementation of the recommendations and decisions unanimously adopted at the tenth special session and that, to this end, a continuing and sustained effort by all States, in a more coordinated manner and on the basis of world-wide cooperation in the interests of security and peace, is essential,

Recalling the Declaration on Principles of International Law concerning Friendly Relations and Cooperation among States in accordance with the Charter of the United Nations,[5] in which the General Assembly proclaimed the duty of all States to pursue in good faith negotiations for the early conclusion of a universal treaty on general and complete disarmament and to strive to adopt appropriate measures to reduce international tensions and strengthen confidence among States,

Stressing the inalienable right of every nation and every human being to live in peace, free from the threat of war, in freedom and independence, as was solemnly reaffirmed by the General Assembly in the Declaration on the Preparation of Societies for Life in Peace,[6] the strict observance of which is in the highest interests of mankind and is an essential prerequisite for its full development,

Conscious that a dynamic development of détente in all spheres of international relations throughout the world would contribute to the achievement of the aims of disarmament,

Deeply disturbed by the fact that international peace and security of peoples continue to be threatened by the arms race, particularly in the nuclear field, and the accumulation of stockpiles of highly destructive weapons and that, at the same time, the continuation of the arms race conflicts with the interest of the economic development and the social and spiritual progress of mankind,

Noting, in particular, that the arms race is incompatible with and contrary to the efforts directed towards the establishment of the new international economic order,

Stressing the fact that the Governments of all countries, particularly of nuclear-weapon States, bear a historic responsibility for eliminating war from human life, primarily through the adoption of effective and decisive disarmament measures aimed at the achievement of general and complete disarmament under strict and effective international control,

Noting that special responsibility for achieving general and complete disarmament, particularly nuclear disarmament, and for averting nuclear war rests with all States possessing nuclear weapons and other militarily significant States,

Proceeding from the principle that effective, constructive and continuing cooperation among all States based on mutual confidence and political will, irrespective of their social system and level of economic development, is essential for the achievement of disarmament and the attainment of its goals,

Convinced that such cooperation must be demonstrated, developed and intensified in mutual contacts and in any forum where States conduct negotiations on disarmament, particularly in the Committee on Disarmament, in order that the aims of the negotiations may be achieved as speedily as possible,

Convinced also that such cooperation must express a common determination by States to bring about a decisive shift in disarmament negotiations and, at the same time, must be sustained by the creation of a favourable atmosphere of trust in relations among States,

Bearing in mind the central role and primary responsibility of the United Nations in promoting the uniting of efforts and the establishment of cooperation among States aimed at the solution of disarmament problems,

I

Solemnly calls upon all States actively to promote the development, strengthening and intensification of international cooperation designed to achieve the goals of disarmament, as defined by the Gen-

1 *Ibid.*, para. 141.

2 *Ibid.*, para. 179.

3 *Ibid.*, para. 186.

4 Resolution S-10/2.

5 Resolution 2625 (XXV), annex.

6 Resolution 33/73.

eral Assembly at its tenth special session, and to this end, in particular:

(*a*) To take initiatives aimed at eliminating the threat of nuclear war and adopting effective new measures to halt and reverse the arms race and pave the way for the ultimate objective of the efforts in the disarmament process, namely, general and complete disarmament under effective international control;

(*b*) To exercise actively their inalienable right to take part in disarmament negotiations, as confirmed in the Final Document of the Tenth Special Session of the General Assembly;

(*c*) To participate actively, as appropriate, in measures taken in the field of disarmament, bearing in mind the interests of maintaining both international and national security in conformity with the Charter of the United Nations, and actively to promote such measures;

(*d*) To conduct disarmament negotiations in good faith on all priority items concurrently, including appropriate confidence-building measures, with a view to ensuring that such negotiations will complement one another and will be conducive to the early achievement of a decisive break-through in the sphere of disarmament;

(*e*) To make every effort to secure continuous and accelerated progress in the negotiations on halting the arms race and achieving disarmament and, to these ends, to refrain from impeding such negotiations, in particular with issues unrelated to disarmament;

(*f*) To strive in the course of disarmament negotiations to ensure that they will outstrip the qualitative development and stockpiling of weapons to which the negotiations relate and, wherever possible, to prevent the emergence of new types of weapons and weapon systems, particularly weapons of mass destruction;

(*g*) To ensure that multilateral, regional and bilateral negotiations on disarmament questions will be consistently conducted in accordance with the respective provisions of the Final Document of the Tenth Special Session, bearing in mind that the United Nations has a central role and primary responsibility in the sphere of disarmament;

(*h*) To develop joint efforts in achieving concrete disarmament measures whose implementation would progressively enable a significant portion of the resources made available through such measures to be used for social and economic needs, thus contributing to the bridging of the economic gap between developed and developing countries, taking into account the close relationship between disarmament and development;

II

Urges all States, with a view to improving further the international climate required for the full implementation of the Final Document of the Tenth Special Session of the General Assembly and accelerating the progress of the appropriate disarmament negotiations, in particular:

(*a*) To exert determined efforts to expedite measures and pursue policies to strengthen international peace and security and to build confidence among States with a view to reducing the danger of the outbreak of military conflicts and facilitating decisive advance of the process of disarmament, including the creation of a favourable international atmosphere which would be conducive to the strengthening of international peace and security;

(*b*) To take effective measures for setting in motion the security system provided for in the Charter of the United Nations and to strengthen it by eliminating tensions and settling disputes by peaceful means and to these ends, in particular, to refrain from seeking military superiority and from any other steps which might adversely affect efforts in the field of disarmament, and accordingly to refrain from using their military potential for aggressive purposes, notably the threat or use of force against the sovereignty, territorial integrity or political independence of any State or against peoples under colonial or foreign domination which are striving to exercise their right to self-determination and the achievement of independence, or for interference in the internal affairs of other States;

(*c*) To strive consistently for the repudiation of all concepts which are based on military intimidation and policies of acting from a position of strength and which lead to the intensification or perpetuation of the arms race and the further accumulation of armaments;

(*d*) To affirm, wherever possible, in their constitutional norms or by any other appropriate means, their political will and determination to promote with all their strength the cause of peace and international security and the achievement of progress in the field of disarmament;

(*e*) To intensify steps, both through the United Nations system and individually, to promote a better understanding by world opinion of the danger of the arms race and the need for disarmament, and to ensure that world opinion will exert a positive influence on the efforts of Governments to resolve disarmament issues, utilizing to this end educational systems, the mass media and all other appropriate institutions;

(*f*) On the basis of the principles of the Charter, to take all appropriate measures, including legislative ones, to prevent and prohibit propaganda for war and the arms race and the dissemination of views asserting their necessity or usefulness on political, economic or other grounds;

(*g*) To take vigorous measures, individually or collectively, to disseminate the ideals of peace, disarmament, cooperation and friendly relations between peoples;

III

Urges all States, in implementing the common political will expressed in the Final Document of the Tenth Special Session of the General Assembly, to strive to achieve concrete measures of disarmament and, in that connexion:

(*a*) To be guided, in all disarmament negotiations, by the generally recognized principles of international law, as well as by their adherence to the principles of peaceful coexistence;

(*b*) To ensure that the problems of disarmament will be solved in the spirit of the Final Document of the Tenth Special Session in such a manner that, as a result of the measures adopted, no individual State or group of States may obtain advantages over others at any stage, that both the security of the States participating in the negotiations and the security of the entire international community will be strengthened and that the principle of undiminished security of each party will not be impaired;

(*c*) To consult with one another on disarmament matters at all levels, including the highest level, in order that, in a spirit of good will and in an endeavour to harmonize their positions, they may establish the political pre-conditions for the solution of those problems, and also, in the interests of disarmament, to make maximum use of all opportunities for cooperation created by States in other fields of their relations with one another;

(*d*) To consider in a fully responsible manner and in a spirit of cooperation all proposals and initiatives aimed at promoting the achievement of mutually acceptable concrete measures of disarmament and helping to accelerate progress in disarmament negotiations;

IV

1. *Declares* that the provisions of the present Declaration are interrelated in their interpretation and implementation and that each of them is a component of a joint approach by States in their determination fully to respect and apply all the principles of the Final Document of the Tenth Special Session of the General Assembly and to develop broad international cooperation for achieving the objectives of real disarmament as defined by the Assembly at its tenth special session;

2. *Declares further* that no provision of this Declaration may be interpreted as contradicting the purposes and principles of the Charter or superseding the Final Document of the Tenth Special Session and that no provision of the Declaration may interfere with the immediate realization of the right of every State to individual or collective self-defence or its legitimate right to defend its territorial integrity, to liberate its occupied territories in accordance with the Charter, or with the right of colonial or displaced peoples to struggle by every possible means for their national freedom, independence and self-determination.

97th plenary meeting
11 December 1979

44/114. Reduction of Military Budgets

Committee: 1
Vote: A: 116 - 10 - 19; B: 127 - 0 - 15
Ref.: 49/66, 48/62, 47/54, 46/25, 43/73, 42/36, 41/57, 40/91, 39/64, 38/184, 37/95, 36/82, 35/142, 33/67, 32/85, 31/87, 3093(XXVIII)

A

Reduction of Military Budgets

The General Assembly,

Desirous of reversing the arms race and military expenditures, which constitute a heavy burden for the economies of all nations and have harmful effects on world peace and security,

Convinced that the reduction of military expenditures as a result of the progress in disarmament negotiations will have favourable consequences on the world economic and financial situation,

Reaffirming that the resources released through the reduction of military expenditures could be reallocated to the economic and social development of all States, particularly for the benefit of the developing countries,

Firmly convinced that the reduction of military expenditures will have a positive impact on the process of strengthening confidence and improving international security and cooperation among States,

Desirous of bringing its contribution to the achievement of these goals,

1. *Welcomes* the work of the Disarmament Commission on the identification and elaboration of a set of principles that should govern further action of States in the field of the freezing and reduction of military budgets;[1]

2. *Takes note* of these principles, as annexed to the present resolution, and decides to bring them to the attention of Member States and of the Conference on Disarmament as useful guidelines for further action in the field of the freezing and reduction of military budgets;

3. *Requests* the Secretary-General to submit to the General Assembly at its forty-sixth session a progress report on the implementation of the present resolution;

4. *Decides* to include in the provisional agenda of its forty-sixth session the item entitled "Reduction of military budgets".

81st plenary meeting
15 December 1989

Annex

Principles that Should Govern Further Actions of States in the Field of the Freezing and Reduction of Military Budgets

1. Concerted efforts should be made by all States, in particular by those States with the largest military arsenals and by the appropriate negotiating forums, with the objective of concluding international agreements to freeze and reduce military budgets, including adequate verification measures acceptable to all parties. Such agreements should contribute to genuine reductions of armed forces and armaments of States parties, with the aim of strengthening international peace and security at lower levels of armed forces and armaments. Definite agreements on the freezing and reduction of military expenditures are assuming special importance and should be reached within the shortest period of time in order to contribute to the curbing of the arms race, alleviate international tensions and increase the possibilities of reallocation of resources now being used for military purposes to economic and social development, particularly for the benefit of the developing countries.

2. All efforts in the field of the freezing and reduction of military expenditures should take into account the principles and purposes of the Charter of the United Nations and the relevant paragraphs of the Final Document of the Tenth Special Session of the General Assembly.

3. Pending the conclusion of agreements to freeze and reduce military expenditures, all States, in particular the most heavily armed States, should exercise self-restraint in their military expenditures.

4. The reduction of military expenditures on a mutually agreed basis should be implemented gradually and in a balanced manner, either on a percentage or on an absolute basis, so as to ensure that no individual State or group of States may obtain advantages over others at any stage, and without prejudice to the right of all States to undiminished security and sovereignty and to undertake the necessary measures of self-defence.

5. While the freezing and reduction of military budgets is the responsibility of all States, to be implemented in stages in accordance with the principle of greatest responsibility, the process should begin with those nuclear-weapon States with the largest military arsenals and the biggest military expenditures, to be followed immediately by other nuclear-weapon States and militarily significant States. This should not prevent other States from initiating negotiations and reaching agreements on the balanced reduction of their respective military budgets at any time during this process.

6. Human and material resources released through the reduction of military expenditures should be devoted to economic and social development, particularly for the benefit of the developing countries.

7. Meaningful negotiations on the freezing and reduction of military budgets would require that all parties to such negotiations have accepted and implemented transparency and comparability. The elaboration of agreed methods of measuring and comparing military expenditures between specified periods of time and between countries with different budgeting systems would be required. To this end States should utilize the reporting system adopted by the General Assembly in 1980.

8. Armaments and military activities that would be the subject of physical reductions within the limits provided for in any agreement to reduce military expenditures will be identified by every State party to such agreements.

9. The agreements to freeze and reduce military expenditures should contain adequate and efficient measures of verification, satisfactory to all parties, in order to ensure that their provisions are strictly applied and fulfilled by all States parties. The specific methods of verification or other compliance procedure should be agreed upon in the process of negotiation depending upon the purposes, scope and nature of the agreement.

10. Unilateral measures undertaken by States concerning the freezing and reduction of military expenditures, especially when they are followed by similar measures adopted by other States on the basis of mutual example, could contribute to favourable conditions for the negotiation and conclusion of international agreements to freeze and reduce military expenditures.

11. Confidence-building measures could help to create a political climate conducive to the freezing and reduction of military expenditures. Conversely, the freezing and reduction of military expenditures could contribute to the increase of confidence among States.

12. The United Nations should play a central role in orienting, stimulating and initiating negotiations on freezing and reducing military expenditures, and all Member States should cooperate with the Organization and among themselves, with a view to solving the problems implied by this process.

13. The freezing and reduction of military expenditures may be achieved, as appropriate, on a global, regional or subregional level, with the agreement of all States concerned.

14. The agreements on the freezing and reduction of military budgets should be viewed in a broader perspective, including respect for and implementation of the security system of the United Nations, and be interrelated with other measures of disarmament, within the context of progress towards general and complete disarmament under effective international control. The reduction of military budgets should therefore be complementary to agreements on the limitation of ar-

[1] See *Official Records of the General Assembly, Forty-fourth Session Supplement No. 42* (A/44/42), para. 41.

maments and disarmament and should not be considered as a substitute for such agreements.

15. The adoption of the above principles should be regarded as a means of facilitating meaningful negotiations on concrete agreements on the freezing and reduction of military budgets.

B

Military Budgets

The General Assembly,

Welcoming the encouraging progress achieved in arms limitations and disarmament,

Noting that further progress in disarmament negotiations could also lead to reductions in military expenditures,

Stressing that increased information on military matters is an important prerequisite for achieving agreements on the reduction of armed forces,

Recalling that an international system for the standardized reporting of military expenditures[1] has been introduced in pursuance of General Assembly resolution 35/142 B of 12 December 1980, and that national reports on military expenditures have been received from a number of Member States belonging to different geographic regions and having different budgeting and accounting systems,

Convinced that more transparency and comparability could be reached through broader participation in the standardized system of the United Nations for reporting military expenditures,

1. *Considers* that transparency requires also agreed methods of measuring and comparing military expenditures between specified periods of time and between countries with different budgeting systems;

2. *Accordingly calls upon* all States to make use of the reporting system adopted by the General Assembly;

3. *Decides* to include in the provisional agenda of its forty-sixth session an item entitled "Transparency and reduction of military budgets".

81st plenary meeting
15 December 1989

48/62. Reduction of Military Budgets: Transparency of Military Expenditures

Committee: 1
Vote: Adopted without a vote
Ref.: 49/66, 47/54B, 46/25

The General Assembly,

Recalling its resolutions 35/142 B of 12 December 1980, which introduced the United Nations system for the standardized reporting of military expenditures, 46/25 of 6 December 1991 and 47/54 B of 9 December 1992, dealing with the guidelines and recommendations for objective information on military matters,

Noting that since then national reports on military expenditures have voluntarily been submitted by a number of Member States belonging to different geographic regions,

Expressing its appreciation to the Secretary-General for providing Member States with the reports on military expenditures,

Welcoming the decision of the States participating in the Conference on Security and Cooperation in Europe, as contained in the Vienna Document 1990 of the negotiations on confidence- and security-building measures, to exchange information annually on their military budgets, on the basis of the categories of the United Nations standardized reporting system,

Welcoming also the recent progress achieved in arms limitations and disarmament, which, in the long term, will lead to significant reductions in military expenditures,

Convinced that the end of the East-West confrontation and the resulting improvement of international relations form a sound basis for promoting further openness and transparency on all military matters,

Emphasizing that an increased flow and exchange of information on military expenditures will contribute to the predictability of military activities, thus strengthening international peace and security on a global and regional level,

Recalling that the guidelines and recommendations for objective information on military matters stated that the United Nations system for the standardized reporting of military expenditures should continue in operation and could be further improved,

1. *Calls upon* all Member States to participate in the United Nations system for the standardized reporting of military expenditures as adopted by the General Assembly in its resolution 47/54 B;

2. *Requests* the Secretary-General to seek the views of Member States on ways and means to strengthen, and to broaden participation in, the United Nations system for the standardized reporting of military expenditures and to submit a report on the subject to the General Assembly at its forty-ninth session;

3. *Decides* to include in the provisional agenda of its forty-ninth session the item entitled "Transparency of military expenditures".

81st plenary meeting
16 December 1993

50/70. General and Complete Disarmament

Committee: 1
Vote: A: 85-18-43; B:- 140 - 0 - 19; C: 154 - 0 - 10; D: 149 - 0 - 15; E: Adopted without a vote; F: 111 - 2 - 49; G: Adopted without a vote; H: Adopted Without a vote; I: 150 - 0 - 14; J: Adopted without a vote; K: 165 - 0 - 1; L: 158 - 0 -7; M: 157 - 4 - 2; N: 105 - 37 - 20; O: Adopted without a vote; P: 106 - 39 - 17; Q: 161 - 0 - 2; R: Adopted without a vote
Ref.: 49/75, 48/75, 47/52, 46/36, 45/58, 44/116, 43/75, 42/38, 41/59, 40/94, 39/151, 38/188, 37/99, 36/97, 35/156, 34/87, 33/91, 32/87, 31/189, 3484(XXX), 3261(XXIX), 3184(XXVIII), 2932(XXVII), 2825(XXVI), 2661(XXV), 2602(XXIV), 2454(XXIII), 2342(XXII), 2162(XXI), 2031(XX), 1908(XVIII), 1884(XVIII)), 1767(XVII), 1722(XVI), 1664(XVI), 1660(XVI), 1617(XV), 1378(XIV), 1252(XIII)

A

Nuclear testing

The General Assembly,

Welcoming the easing of international tension and the strengthening of trust between States that have prevailed following the end of the cold war,

Reaffirming that the cessation of all nuclear testing will contribute to the non-proliferation of nuclear weapons in all its aspects, to the process of nuclear disarmament leading to the ultimate objective of the complete elimination of nuclear weapons and therefore to the further enhancement of international peace and security,

Convinced that the cessation of all nuclear testing will provide a favourable climate for the conclusion of negotiations on a comprehensive nuclear-test-ban treaty,

Considering that nuclear testing is not consistent with undertakings by the nuclear-weapon States at the 1995 Review and Extension Conference of the Parties to the Treaty on the Non-Proliferation of Nuclear Weapons,

Deeply concerned about the potential negative effects of underground nuclear testing on health and the environment,

Sharing alarm expressed internationally, regionally and nationally at recent nuclear tests,

---

1 See *Reduction of Military Budgets: International reporting of military expenditures* (United Nations publication, Sales No. E.81.I.9), para. 98.

1. *Commends* those nuclear-weapon States observing nuclear testing moratoria, and urges them to continue those moratoria pending the entry into force of a comprehensive nuclear-test-ban treaty;

2. *Strongly deplores* all current nuclear testing;

3. *Strongly urges* the immediate cessation of all nuclear testing.

B

Small arms

The General Assembly,

Reaffirming the role of the United Nations in the field of disarmament and the commitment of Member States to take concrete steps in order to strengthen that role,

Realizing the urgent need to resolve underlying conflicts, to diminish tensions and to accelerate efforts towards general and complete disarmament under strict and effective international control with a view to maintaining regional and international peace and security in a world free from the scourge of war and the burden of armaments,

Reaffirming the inherent right to individual or collective self-defence recognized in Article 51 of the Charter of the United Nations, which implies that States also have the right to acquire arms with which to defend themselves,

Reaffirming also the right of self-determination of all peoples, in particular peoples under colonial or other forms of alien domination or foreign occupation, and the importance of the effective realization of this right, as enunciated, *inter alia,* in the Vienna Declaration and Programme of Action, adopted by the World Conference on Human Rights on 25 June 1993,[1]

Realizing that arms obtained through the illicit arms trade are most likely to be used for violent purposes and that even small arms when so obtained, directly or indirectly, by terrorist groups, drug traffickers or underground organizations can pose a danger to regional and international security, and certainly to the security and political stability of the countries affected,

Taking note of the report of the Secretary-General to the Security Council entitled "Supplement to an Agenda for Peace",[2] which stressed the urgent need for practical disarmament in the context of the conflicts the United Nations is actually dealing with and of the weapons, most of them light weapons, that are actually killing people in the hundreds of thousands,[3] and which identified light weapons as including, *inter alia,* small arms and anti-personnel land-mines,

Recalling its resolution 49/75 G of 15 December 1994, in which it welcomed the initiative taken by Mali concerning the question of the illicit circulation of small arms and their collection in the affected States of the Saharo-Sahelian subregion, as well as the action taken by the Secretary-General in implementation of this initiative,

Noting the work of the Disarmament Commission on international arms transfers,

1. *Requests* the Secretary-General, within the existing resources, to prepare a report, with the assistance of a panel group of qualified governmental experts to be nominated by him on the basis of equitable geographical representation, on:

(*a*) The types of small arms and light weapons actually being used in conflicts being dealt with by the United Nations;

(*b*) The nature and causes of the excessive and destabilizing accumulation and transfer of small arms and light weapons, including their illicit production and trade;

(*c*) The ways and means to prevent and reduce the excessive and destabilizing accumulation and transfer of small arms and light weapons, in particular as they cause or exacerbate conflict; with particular attention to the role of the United Nations in this field and to the complementary role of regional organizations, and taking into account views and proposals of Member States and all other relevant information, for submission to the General Assembly at its fifty-second session;

2. *Also requests* the Secretary-General to seek the views and proposals of Member States on the matters mentioned in paragraph 1, to collect all other relevant information and to make them available for consideration by the panel of governmental experts referred to in paragraph 1;

3. *Decides* to include in the provisional agenda of its fifty-second session an item entitled "Small arms".

C

Nuclear disarmament with a view to the ultimate elimination of nuclear weapons

The General Assembly,

Recalling its resolution 49/75 H of 15 December 1994,

Recognizing that the end of the cold war has increased the possibility of freeing the world from the fear of nuclear war,

Appreciating the entry into force of the Treaty on the Reduction and Limitation of Strategic Offensive Arms, to which Belarus, Kazakstan, the Russian Federation, Ukraine and the United States of America are party, and looking forward to the early entry into force of the Treaty on the Further Reduction and Limitation of Strategic Offensive Arms,

Welcoming the reductions in the nuclear arsenals of other nuclear-weapon States,

Welcoming also the decision of the 1995 Review and Extension Conference of the Parties to the Treaty on the Non-Proliferation of Nuclear Weapons[4] to extend the Treaty indefinitely,[5] taken without a vote, as well as the decisions on strengthening the review process for the Treaty[6] and on the principles and objectives for nuclear non-proliferation and disarmament,[7]

Noting the reference in the decision on the principles and objectives for nuclear non-proliferation and disarmament to the importance of the following measures for the full realization and effective implementation of article VI of the Treaty on the Non-Proliferation of Nuclear Weapons, including the programme of action as reflected below:

(*a*) The completion by the Conference on Disarmament of the negotiations on a universal and internationally and effectively verifiable comprehensive nuclear-test-ban treaty no later than 1996, and utmost restraint that should be exercised by the nuclear-weapon States pending the entry into force of that treaty;

(*b*) The immediate commencement and early conclusion of negotiations on a non-discriminatory and universally applicable convention banning the production of fissile material for nuclear weapons or other nuclear explosive devices in accordance with the statement of the Special Coordinator of the Conference on Disarmament and the mandate contained therein;

(*c*) The determined pursuit by the nuclear-weapon States of systematic and progressive efforts to reduce nuclear weapons globally, with the ultimate goal of eliminating those weapons, and by all States of general and complete disarmament under strict and effective international control,

Welcoming positive developments as well as the efforts being made by the States members of the Conference on Disarmament in the negotiations on a comprehensive nuclear-test-ban treaty at the Conference on Disarmament at Geneva,

Recalling that nuclear non-proliferation and the promotion of nuclear disarmament are key elements in the maintenance of international peace and security, which is one of the most important purposes of the United Nations,

1 *Report of the World Conference on Human Rights, Vienna, 14 to 25 June 1993* (A/CONF.157/24 (Part I)), chap. III.

2 A/50/60-S/1995/1.

3 *Ibid.*, para. 60.

4 United Nations, *Treaty Series,* vol. 729, No. 10485.

5 NPT/CONF.1995/32 (Part I), annex, decision 3.

6 *Ibid.*, decision 1.

7 *Ibid.*, decision 2.

1. *Urges* States not parties to the Treaty on the Non-Proliferation of Nuclear Weapons to accede to it at the earliest possible date, recognizing the importance of universal adherence to the Treaty;

2. *Calls* for the determined pursuit by the nuclear-weapon States of systematic and progressive efforts to reduce nuclear weapons globally, with the ultimate goals of eliminating those weapons, and by all States of general and complete disarmament under strict and effective international control, and invites them to keep States Members of the United Nations duly informed of the progress and efforts made;

3. *Calls upon* all States to implement fully their commitments in the field of disarmament and non-proliferation of weapons of mass destruction.

D

Transparency in armaments

The General Assembly,

Recalling its resolutions 46/36 L of 9 December 1991, 47/52 L of 15 December 1992, 48/75 E of 16 December 1993 and 49/75 C of 15 December 1994,

Continuing to take the view that an enhanced level of transparency in armaments contributes greatly to confidence-building and security among States and that the establishment of the United Nations Register of Conventional Arms[1] constitutes an important step forward in the promotion of transparency in military matters,

Welcoming the consolidated report of the Secretary-General on the Register,[2] which includes the returns of Member States for 1994,

Welcoming also the response of Member States to the request contained in paragraphs 9 and 10 of resolution 46/36 L to provide data on their imports and exports of arms, as well as available background information regarding their military holdings, procurement through national production and relevant policies,

Stressing that the continuing operation of the Register and its further development should be reviewed in order to secure a Register that is capable of attracting the widest possible participation,

1. *Reaffirms its determination* to ensure the effective operation of the United Nations Register of Conventional Arms as provided for in paragraphs 7, 8, 9 and 10 of resolution 46/36 L;

2. *Calls upon* Member States to provide the requested data and information for the Register, on the basis of resolutions 46/36 L and 47/52 L and the annex and appendices to the report of the Secretary-General on the continuing operation of the Register and its further development[3] to the Secretary-General by 30 April annually;

3. *Reaffirms* its decision, with a view to further development of the Register, to keep the scope of and participation in the Register under review, and, to that end:

(*a*) Recalls its request to Member States to provide the Secretary-General with their views on the continuing operation of the Register and its further development and on transparency measures related to weapons of mass destruction;

(*b*) Recalls its request to the Secretary-General, with the assistance of a group of governmental experts to be convened in 1997, on the basis of equitable geographical representation, to prepare a report on the continuing operation of the Register and its further development, taking into account the work of the Conference on Disarmament, the views expressed by Member States and the report of the Secretary-General on the continuing operation of the Register and its further development,[4] with a view to a decision at its fifty-second session;

4. *Requests* the Secretary-General to ensure that sufficient resources are made available for the Secretariat to operate and maintain the Register;

5. *Invites* the Conference on Disarmament to consider continuing its work undertaken in the field of transparency in armaments;

1 See resolution 46/36 L.

2 A/50/547 and Corr.1 and Add.1.

3 A/49/316.

4 *Ibid.*

6. *Reiterates* its call upon all Member States to cooperate at the regional and subregional levels, taking fully into account the specific conditions prevailing in the region or subregion, with a view to enhancing and coordinating international efforts aimed at increased openness and transparency in armaments;

7. *Requests* the Secretary-General to report to the General Assembly at its fifty-first session on the progress made in implementing the present resolution;

8. *Decides* to include in the provisional agenda of its fifty-first session the item entitled "Transparency in armaments".

E

Prohibition of the dumping of radioactive wastes

The General Assembly,

Bearing in mind resolutions CM/Res.1153 (XLVIII) of 1988[5] and CM/Res.1225 (L) of 1989,[6] adopted by the Council of Ministers of the Organization of African Unity, concerning the dumping of nuclear and industrial wastes in Africa,

Welcoming resolution GC(XXXIV)/Res/530 establishing a Code of Practice on the International Transboundary Movement of Radioactive Waste, adopted on 21 September 1990 by the General Conference of the International Atomic Energy Agency at its thirty-fourth regular session,[7]

Welcoming also resolution GC(XXXVIII)/Res/6, adopted on 23 September 1994 by the General Conference of the International Atomic Energy Agency at its thirty-eighth regular session,[8] inviting the Board of Governors and the Director-General of the Agency to commence preparations for a convention on the safety of radioactive waste management,

Considering its resolution 2602 C (XXIV) of 16 December 1969, in which it requested the Conference of the Committee on Disarmament,[9] *inter alia,* to consider effective methods of control against the use of radiological methods of warfare,

Recalling resolution CM/Res.1356 (LIV) of 1991, adopted by the Council of Ministers of the Organization of African Unity,[10] on the Bamako Convention on the Ban on the Import of Hazardous Wastes into Africa and on the Control of Their Transboundary Movements within Africa,

Aware of the potential hazards underlying any use of radioactive wastes that would constitute radiological warfare and its implications for regional and international security, in particular for the security of developing countries,

Recalling its resolutions 43/75 Q of 7 December 1988, 44/116 R of 15 December 1989, 45/58 K of 4 December 1990, 46/36 K of 6 December 1991, 47/52 D of 9 December 1992, 48/75 D of 16 December 1993 and 49/75 A of 15 December 1994,

Desirous of promoting the implementation of paragraph 76 of the Final Document of the Tenth Special Session of the General Assembly,[11] the first special session devoted to disarmament,

1. *Takes note* of the part of the report of the Conference on Disarmament relating to a future convention on the prohibition of radiological weapons;[12]

5 A/43/398, annex I.

6 See A/44/603, annex I.

7 See International Atomic Energy Agency, *Resolutions and other Decisions of the General Conference, Thirty-fourth Regular Session,* 17-21 September 1990 (GC(XXXIV)/RESOLUTIONS(1990)).

8 *Ibid., Thirty-eighth Regular Session,* 19-23 September 1994 (GC(XXXVIII)/RES/DEC/(1994)).

9 The Conference of the Committee on Disarmament became the Committee on Disarmament as from the tenth special session of the General Assembly. The Committee on Disarmament was redesigned the Conference on Disarmament as from 7 February 1984.

10 See A/49/390, annex I.

11 Resolution S-10/2.

2. *Expresses grave concern* regarding any use of nuclear wastes that would constitute radiological warfare and have grave implications for the national security of all States;

3. *Calls upon* all States to take appropriate measures with a view to preventing any dumping of nuclear or radioactive wastes that would infringe upon the sovereignty of States;

4. *Requests* the Conference on Disarmament to take into account, in the negotiations for a convention on the prohibition of radiological weapons, radioactive wastes as part of the scope of such a convention;

5. *Also requests* the Conference on Disarmament to intensify efforts towards an early conclusion of such a convention and to include in its report to the General Assembly at its fifty-first session the progress recorded in the negotiations on this subject;

6. *Takes note* of resolution CM/Res.1356 (LIV) of 1991, adopted by the Council of Ministers of the Organization of African Unity, on the Bamako Convention on the Ban on the Import of Hazardous Wastes into Africa and on the Control of Their Transboundary Movements within Africa;

7. *Expresses the hope* that the effective implementation of the International Atomic Energy Agency Code of Practice on the International Transboundary Movement of Radioactive Waste will enhance the protection of all States from the dumping of radioactive wastes on their territories;

8. *Welcomes* current efforts of the International Atomic Energy Agency in the preparation of a draft convention on the safe arrangement of radioactive waste;

9. *Decides* to include in the provisional agenda of its fifty-first session the item entitled "Prohibition of the dumping of radioactive wastes".

F

Convening of the fourth special session of the General Assembly devoted to disarmament

The General Assembly,

Recalling its resolution 49/75 I of 15 December 1994,

Recalling also that three special sessions of the General Assembly devoted to disarmament were held in 1978, 1982 and 1988,

Bearing in mind the Final Document of the Tenth Special Session of the General Assembly,[1] the first special session devoted to disarmament, and the final objective of general and complete disarmament under effective international control,

Welcoming the recent positive changes in the international landscape, characterized by the end of the cold war, the relaxation of tensions at the global level and the emergence of a new spirit governing relations among nations,

Taking note of paragraph 108 of the Final Declaration of the Eleventh Conference of Heads of State or Government of the Non-Aligned Countries, held at Cartagena de Indias, Colombia, from 18 to 20 October 1995, which supported the convening of the fourth special session of the General Assembly devoted to disarmament in 1997, which would offer an opportunity to review, from a perspective more in tune with the current international situation, the most critical aspects of the process of disarmament and to mobilize the international community and public opinion in favour of the elimination of weapons of mass destruction and of the control and reduction of conventional weapons,

Expecting that, since negotiations and action on important disarmament issues will be completed by the end of 1996, the year 1997 would be an opportune time to review the progress in the entire field of disarmament in the post-cold-war era,

1. *Decides* to convene its fourth special session on disarmament in 1997, if possible, the exact date and agenda to be decided upon before the end of the current session of the General Assembly through consultations;

2. *Also decides* to establish a Preparatory Committee to prepare a draft agenda for the special session, to examine all relevant questions relating to that session and to submit its recommendations thereon to the General Assembly at its fifty-first session;

3. *Invites* all Member States to communicate to the Secretary-General, not later than 1 April 1996, their views on the draft agenda and other relevant questions relating to the fourth special session on disarmament;

4. *Requests* the Preparatory Committee to meet for a short organizational session before the end of the fifty-first session of the General Assembly in order, *inter alia*, to set the date for its substantive session;

5. *Also requests* the Preparatory Committee to submit its progress report to the General Assembly at its fifty-first session;

6. *Decides* to include in the provisional agenda of its fifty-first session an item entitled "Convening of the fourth special session of the General Assembly devoted to disarmament: report of the Preparatory Committee for the Fourth Special Session of the General Assembly Devoted to Disarmament".

G

Relationship between disarmament and development

The General Assembly,

Recalling the provisions of the Final Document of the Tenth Special Session of the General Assembly,[2] the first special session devoted to disarmament, concerning the relationship between disarmament and development,

Recalling also the adoption on 11 September 1987 of the Final Document of the International Conference on the Relationship between Disarmament and Development,[3]

Recalling further its resolution 49/75 J of 15 December 1994,

Bearing in mind the final documents of the Eleventh Conference of Heads of State or Government of the Non-Aligned Countries, held at Cartagena de Indias, Colombia, from 18 to 20 October 1995,

Stressing the growing importance of the symbiotic relationship between disarmament and development in current international relations,

1. *Takes note* of the note by the Secretary-General[4] and of actions taken in accordance with the Final Document of the International Conference on the Relationship between Disarmament and Development;

2. *Urges* the international community to devote part of the resources made available by the implementation of disarmament and arms limitation agreements to economic and social development, with a view to reducing the ever-widening gap between developed and developing countries;

3. *Requests* the Secretary-General to continue to take action, through appropriate organs and within available resources, for the implementation of the action programme adopted at the International Conference;[5]

4. *Also requests* the Secretary-General to submit a report to the General Assembly at its fifty-first session;

5. *Decides* to include in the provisional agenda of its fifty-first session the item entitled "Relationship between disarmament and development".

---

12 See *Official Records of the General Assembly, Fiftieth Session, Supplement No. 27* (A/50127).

1 Resolution S-10/2.

2 *Ibid.*

3 United Nations publication, Sales No. E.87.IX.8.

4 A/50/388.

5 United Nations publication, Sales No. E87.IX.8, para. 35.

H

Assistance to States for curbing the illicit traffic in small arms and collecting them

The General Assembly,

Recalling its resolutions 46/36 H of 6 December 1991, 47/52 G and 47/52 J of 9 December 1992, 48/75 H and 48/75 J of 16 December 1993 and 49/75 G of 15 December 1994,

Considering that the circulation of massive quantities of small arms throughout the world impedes development and is a source of increased insecurity,

Considering also that the illicit international transfer of small arms and their accumulation in many countries constitute a threat to the populations and to national and regional security and are a factor contributing to the destabilization of States,

Basing itself on the statement of the Secretary-General relating to the request of Mali concerning United Nations assistance for the collection of small arms,

Gravely concerned at the extent of the insecurity and banditry linked to the illicit circulation of small arms in Mali and the other affected States of the Saharo-Sahdian subregion,

Taking note of the first conclusions of the United Nations advisory missions sent to the affected countries of the subregion by the Secretary-General to study the best way of curbing the illicit circulation of small arms and ensuring their collection,

Taking note also of the interest shown by other States of the subregion in receiving the United Nations Advisory Mission,

Noting the actions taken and those recommended at the meetings of the States of the subregion held at Banjul, Algiers and Bamako to establish close regional cooperation with a view to strengthening security,

1. *Welcomes* the initiative taken by Mali concerning the question of the illicit circulation of small arms and their collection in the affected States of the Saharo-Sahelian subregion;

2. *Also welcomes* the action taken by the Secretary-General in implementation of this initiative in the context of resolution 40/151 H of 16 December 1985;

3. *Thanks* the Governments concerned in the subregion for the substantial support that they have given to the United Nations advisory missions and welcomes the declared readiness of other States to receive the Advisory Mission;

4. *Encourages* the Secretary-General to continue his efforts in the context of the implementation of resolution 49/75 G and of the recommendations of the United Nations advisory missions,[1] to curb the illicit circulation of small arms and to collect such arms in the affected States that so request, with the support of the United Nations Regional Centre for Peace and Disarmament in Africa and in close cooperation with the Organization of African Unity;

5. *Invites* Member States to implement national control measures in order to check the illicit circulation of small arms, in particular by curbing the illegal export of such arms;

6. *Invites* the international community to give appropriate support to the efforts made by the affected countries to suppress the illicit circulation of small arms, which is likely to hamper their development;

7. *Requests* the Secretary-General to continue to examine the issue and to report to the General Assembly at its fifty-first session.

I

Bilateral nuclear arms negotiations and nuclear disarmament

The General Assembly,

Recalling its previous relevant resolutions,

Recognizing the fundamental changes that have taken place with respect to international security, which have permitted agreements on deep reductions in the nuclear armaments of the States possessing the largest inventories of such weapons,

Mindful that it is the responsibility and obligation of all States to contribute to the process relaxation of international tension and to the strengthening of international peace and security,

Stressing the importance of strengthening international peace and security through general and complete disarmament, under strict and effective international control,

Stressing also that it is the responsibility of all States to adopt and implement measures towards the attainment of general and complete disarmament under strict and effective international control,

Appreciating a number of positive developments in the field of nuclear disarmament, in particular the Treaty between the United States of America and the Union of Soviet Socialist Republics on the Elimination of Their Intermediate-Range and Shorter-Range Missiles,[2] and the treaties on the reduction and limitation of strategic offensive arms,

Appreciating also the indefinite extension of the Treaty on the Non-Proliferation of Nuclear Weapons[3] and acknowledging the importance of the determined pursuit by the nuclear-weapon States of systematic and progressive efforts to reduce nuclear weapons globally, with the ultimate goal of eliminating those weapons, and by all States of general and complete disarmament under strict and effective international control,

Welcoming the steps that have already been taken by the Russian Federation and the United States of America to begin the process of reducing the number of nuclear weapons and removing such weapons from a deployed status, and bilateral agreements on the issue of detargeting strategic nuclear missiles,

Noting the new climate of relations between the United States of America and the States of the former Union of Soviet Socialist Republics, which permits them to intensify their cooperative efforts to ensure the safety, security and environmentally sound destruction of nuclear weapons,

Noting also that the Russian Federation and the United States of America concurred that, once the Treaty between them on the Further Reduction and Limitation of Strategic Offensive Arms is ratified, they would proceed to deactivate all nuclear delivery systems to be reduced under the Treaty by removing their nuclear warheads or taking other steps to remove them from alert status,

Noting further the commitment between the Russian Federation and the United States of America to intensify their dialogue to compare conceptual approaches and to develop concrete steps to adapt the nuclear forces and practices on both sides to the changed international security situation, including the possibility, after ratification of the Treaty on the Further Reduction and Limitation of Strategic Offensive Arms, of further reductions of and limitations on remaining nuclear forces,

Taking note of the joint statement of 10 May 1995 by the Russian Federation and the United States of America on the Treaty on the Limitation of Anti-Ballistic Missile Systems,

Urging the early ratification of the Treaty on the Further Reduction and Limitation of Strategic Offensive Arms and further intensification of such efforts to accelerate the implementation of agreements and unilateral decisions relating to nuclear arms reduction,

Welcoming the significant reductions made by other nuclear-weapon States, and encouraging all nuclear-weapon States to consider appropriate measures relating to nuclear disarmament,

1. *Welcomes* the entry into force of the Treaty on the Reduction and Limitation of Strategic Offensive Arms, signed in Moscow on 31 July 1991 by the former Union of Soviet Socialist Republics and the United States of America, including the Protocol to that Treaty signed at Lisbon on 23 May 1992 by the parties thereto, and the exchange of documents of ratification between the United States of

---

1 See the report of the Secretary-General (A/50/405).

2 *The United Nations Disarmament Yearbook,* vol. 12: 1987 (United Nations publication, Sales No. E.88.IX.2), appendix VII.

3 United Nations, *Treaty Series,* vol. 729, No. 10485.

America, Belarus, Kazakstan, the Russian Federation and Ukraine on 5 December 1994 at Budapest;

2. *Also welcomes* the signing of the Treaty between the Russian Federation and the United States of America on the Further Reduction and Limitation of Strategic Offensive Arms in Moscow on 3 January 1993, and urges the parties to take the steps necessary to bring that Treaty into force at the earliest possible date;

3. *Expresses its satisfaction* at the fact that the entry into force of the 1991 Treaty on the Reduction and Limitation of Strategic Offensive Arms clears the way for prompt ratification by the Russian Federation and the United States of America of the 1993 Treaty;

4. *Also expresses it satisfaction* at the continuing implementation of the Treaty on the Elimination of Intermediate-Range and Shorter-Range Missiles,[1] in particular at the completion by the parties of the destruction of all their declared missiles subject to elimination under the Treaty;

5. *Encourages* the United States of America, the Russian Federation, Belarus, Kazakstan and Ukraine to continue their cooperative efforts aimed at eliminating nuclear weapons and strategic offensive arms on the basis of existing agreements, and welcomes the contributions that other States are making to such cooperation as well;

6. *Welcomes* the accession to the Treaty on the Non-Proliferation of Nuclear Weapons[2] of Belarus, Kazakstan and Ukraine as non-nuclear-weapon States, which thereby provided a notable enhancement to the non-proliferation regime;

7. *Encourages and supports* the Russian Federation and the United States of America in their efforts to reduce their nuclear weapons and to continue to give those efforts the highest priority in order to contribute to the ultimate goal of eliminating those weapons;

8. *Invites* the Russian Federation and the United States of America to keep other States Members of the United Nations duly informed of progress in their discussions and in the implementation of their strategic offensive arms agreements and unilateral decisions.

J

Measures to curb the illicit transfer and use of conventional arms

The General Assembly,

Recalling its resolution 46/36 H of 6 December 1991 and its decision 47/419 of 9 December 1992 on international arms transfers,

Recalling also its resolutions 48/75 F and H of 16 December 1993 and 49/75 M of 15 December 1994 on measures to curb illicit transfer and use of conventional arms,

Recognizing that the availability of massive quantities of conventional weapons and especially their illicit transfer, often associated with destabilizing activities, are most disturbing and dangerous phenomena, in particular for the internal situation of affected States and the violation of human rights,

Bearing in mind that in certain situations mercenaries, terrorists and child soldiers are supplied with weapons acquired from illicit transfers of conventional arms,

Convinced that peace and security are inextricably interlinked with and in some cases imperative for economic development and reconstruction, including in war-stricken countries,

Realizing the urgent need to resolve conflicts and to diminish tension, and to accelerate efforts towards general and complete disarmament with a view to maintaining regional and international peace and security,

Recognizing the curbing of the illicit transfer of arms as an important contribution to the relaxation of tension and peaceful reconciliation processes,

Stressing the need for effective national control measures on the transfer of conventional weapons,

Convinced that effective measures to curb illicit transfer and use of conventional arms will help enhance regional and international peace, security and economic development,

1. *Invites* Member States:

(*a*) To take appropriate and effective enforcement measures to seek to ensure that illicit transfers of arms are immediately discontinued;

(*b*) To provide the Secretary-General promptly with relevant information on national control measures on arms transfers with a view to preventing illicit arms transfers;

2. *Requests* the Disarmament Commission:

(*a*) To expedite its consideration of the agenda item on international arms transfers, with special emphasis on the adverse consequences of the illicit transfer of arms and ammunition;

(*b*) To study and report on measures to curb the illicit transfer and use of conventional arms, bearing in mind concrete problems in various regions of the world;

3. *Requests* the Secretary-General:

(*a*) To seek the views of Member States on effective ways and means of collecting weapons transferred illicitly, in particular in the light of experience gained by the United Nations;

(*b*) To seek the views of Member States on concrete proposals concerning measures at the national, regional and international level to curb the illicit transfer and use of conventional arms;

(*c*) To submit to the General Assembly at its fifty-first session a report containing the views expressed by Member States;

4. *Also requests* the Secretary-General to report to the General Assembly at its fifty-first session on the effective implementation of the present resolution;

5. *Decides* to include in the provisional agenda of its fifty-first session the item entitled "Measures to curb the illicit transfer and use of conventional arms".

K

Regional disarmament

The General Assembly,

Recalling its resolutions 45/58 P of 4 December 1990, 46/36 I of 6 December 1991, 47/52 J of 9 December 1992, 48/75 I of 16 December 1993 and 49/75 N of 15 December 1994 on regional disarmament,

Believing that the efforts of the international community to move towards the ideal of general and complete disarmament are guided by the inherent human desire for genuine peace and security, the elimination of the danger of war and the release of economic, intellectual and other resources for peaceful pursuit,

Affirming the abiding commitment of all States to the purposes and principles enshrined in the Charter of the United Nations in the conduct of their international relations,

Noting that essential guidelines for progress towards general and complete disarmament were adopted at the tenth special session of the General Assembly, the first special session devoted to disarmament,[3]

Taking note of the guidelines and recommendations for regional approaches to disarmament within the context of global security adopted by the Disarmament Commission at its 1993 substantive session,[4]

Welcoming the prospects of genuine progress in the field of disarmament engendered in recent years as a result of negotiations between the two super-Powers,

Taking note of the recent proposals for disarmament and nuclear non-proliferation at the regional and subregional levels,

Recognizing the importance of confidence-building measures for regional and international peace and security,

---

1 *The United Nations Disarmament Yearbook,* vol. 12: 1987 (United Nations publication, Sales No. E.88.IX.2), appendix VII.

2 United Nations, *Treaty Series.* vol. 729, No. 10485.

3 Resolution S-10/2.

4 *Official Records of the General Assembly, Forty-eighth Session, Supplement No. 42* (A/48/42), annex II.

Convinced that endeavours by countries to promote regional disarmament, taking into account the specific characteristics of each region and in accordance with the principle of undiminished security at the lowest level of armaments, would enhance the security of smaller States and would thus contribute to international peace and security by reducing the risk of regional conflicts,

1. *Stresses* that sustained efforts are needed, within the framework of the Conference on Disarmament and under the umbrella of the United Nations, to make progress on the entire range of disarmament issues;

2. *Affirms* that global and regional approaches to disarmament complement each other and should therefore be pursued simultaneously to promote regional and international peace and security;

3. *Calls upon* States to conclude agreements, wherever possible, for nuclear non-proliferation, disarmament and confidence-building measures at the regional and subregional levels;

4. *Welcomes* the initiatives towards disarmament, nuclear non-proliferation and security undertaken by some countries at the regional and subregional levels;

5. *Supports and encourages* efforts aimed at promoting confidence-building measures at the regional and subregional levels in order to ease regional tensions and to further disarmament and nuclear non-proliferation measures at the regional and subregional levels;

6. *Decides* to include in the provisional agenda of its fifty-first session the item entitled "Regional disarmament".

L

Conventional arms control at the regional and subregional levels

The General Assembly,

Recalling its resolutions 48/75 J of 16 December 1993 and 49/75 O of 15 December 1994,

Recognizing the crucial role of conventional arms control in promoting regional and international peace and security,

Convinced that conventional arms control needs to be pursued primarily in the regional and subregional contexts since most threats to peace and security in the post-cold-war era arise mainly among States located in the same region or subregion,

Aware that the preservation of a balance in the defence capabilities of States at the lowest level of armaments would contribute to peace and stability and should be a prime objective of conventional arms control,

Desirous of promoting agreements to strengthen regional peace and security at the lowest possible level of armaments and military forces,

Believing that militarily significant States, and States with larger military capabilities, have a special responsibility in promoting such agreements for regional security,

Believing also that two of the principal objectives of conventional arms control should be to prevent the possibility of military attack launched by surprise and to avoid aggression,

1. *Decides* to give urgent consideration to the issues involved in conventional arms control at the regional and subregional levels;

2. *Requests* the Conference on Disarmament, as a first step, to consider the formulation of principles that can serve as a framework for regional agreements on conventional arms control, and looks forward to a report of the Conference on this subject;

3. *Decides* to include in the provisional agenda of its fifty-first session the item entitled "Conventional arms control at the regional and subregional levels".

M

Observance of environmental norms in the drafting and implementation of agreements on disarmament and arms control

The General Assembly,

Recognizing the importance of the observance of environmental norms in the drafting and implementation of agreements on disarmament and arms limitation,

Taking note of the relevant provisions of the Convention on the Prohibition of the Development, Production, Stockpiling and Use of Chemical Weapons and Their Destruction[1] regarding the environment,

Convinced of the importance of the environmentally sound implementation of the Convention on the Prohibition of the Development, Production and Stockpiling of Bacteriological (Biological) and Toxin Weapons and on Their Destruction,[2]

Mindful of the detrimental environmental effects of the use of nuclear weapons,

Conscious of the positive potential implications for the environment of a future comprehensive nuclear-test-ban treaty,

Desirous of banning effectively military or any other hostile use of environment modification techniques, with a view to removing the dangers for mankind that might arise from such uses,

1. *Invites* the Conference on Disarmament to take every necessary measure to include in negotiating treaties and agreements on disarmament and arms limitation the corresponding environmental norms, with a view to ensuring that the process of implementation of such treaties and agreements is environmentally sound, in particular the destruction of weapons covered by them;

2. *Emphasizes* the importance of the compliance of all States parties to the Convention on the Prohibition of the Development, Production, Stockpiling and Use of Chemical Weapons and Their Destruction, and calls upon them to cooperate and ensure that the process of implementation of the Convention in all relevant aspects is environmentally sound;

3. *Urges* all States parties to consider all relevant norms related to the protection of the environment in implementing the Convention on the Prohibition of the Development, Production and Stockpiling of Bacteriological (Biological) and Toxin Weapons and on Their Destruction;

4. *Calls upon* the Conference on Disarmament to conclude, as a task of the highest priority, a comprehensive nuclear-test-ban treaty as soon as possible in 1996;

5. *Urges* the States that are not yet party to the Convention on the Prohibition of Military or Any Other Hostile Use of Environmental Modification Techniques[3] to consider adhering to it as soon as possible, in order to assure the universality of the Convention.

N

Bilateral nuclear arms negotiations and nuclear disarmament

The General Assembly,

Recalling its previous relevant resolutions,

Recognizing the fundamental changes that have taken place with respect to international security, which have permitted agreements on deep reductions in the nuclear armaments of the States possessing the largest inventories of such weapons,

Mindful that it is the responsibility and obligation of all States to contribute to the process of the relaxation of international tension and to the strengthening of international peace and security,

Stressing the importance of strengthening international peace and security through disarmament,

---

1 *Official Records of the General Assembly, Forty-seventh Session, Supplement No. 27* (A/47/27), appendix I.

2 Resolution 2826 (XXVI), annex.

3 Resolution 31/72, annex.

Emphasizing that nuclear disarmament remains one of the principal tasks of our times,

Appreciating a number of positive developments in the field of nuclear disarmaments, in particular the treaty concluded on 8 December 1987 between the former Union of Soviet Socialist Republics and the United States of America on the elimination of their intermediate-range and shorter-range missiles,[1] and the treaties on the reduction and limitation of strategic offensive arms,

Noting that there are still significant nuclear arsenals and that the primary responsibility for nuclear disarmament, with the objective of the elimination of nuclear weapons, rests with the nuclear-weapon States, in particular those which possess the largest stockpiles,

Noting also the expressed determination by the nuclear-weapon States to pursue systematic and progressive efforts to reduce nuclear weapons globally, with the ultimate goal of eliminating those weapons within a time-bound framework,

Welcoming the steps that have already been taken by those States to begin the process of reducing the number of nuclear weapons and removing such weapons from a deployed status, and bilateral agreements on the issue of de-targeting strategic nuclear missiles,

Noting the new climate of relations between the United States of America and the States of the former Soviet Union, which permits them to intensify their cooperative efforts to ensure the safety, security and environmentally sound destruction of nuclear weapons,

Noting also that the Russian Federation and the United States of America concurred that, once the Treaty on the Further Reduction and Limitation of Strategic Offensive Arms was ratified, they would proceed to deactivate all nuclear delivery systems to be reduced under the Treaty by removing their nuclear warheads or taking other steps to remove them from alert status,

Noting further the agreement between the Russian Federation and the United States of America to intensify their dialogue to compare conceptual approaches and to develop concrete steps to adapt the nuclear forces and practices on both sides to the changed international security situation, including the possibility, after ratification of the Treaty on the Further Reduction and Limitation of Strategic Offensive Arms, of further reductions of and limitations on remaining nuclear forces,

Taking note of the joint statement of 10 May 1995 between the Russian Federation and the United States of America on the Treaty on the Limitation of Anti-Ballistic Missile Systems,

Urging the early ratification of the Treaty on the Further Reduction and Limitation of Strategic Offensive Arms and further intensification of such efforts to accelerate the implementation of agreements and unilateral decisions relating to nuclear-arms reduction,

Welcoming the reduction made by other nuclear-weapon States, in some of their nuclear-weapon programmes, and encouraging all nuclear-weapon States to consider appropriate measures relating to nuclear disarmament,

Affirming that bilateral and multilateral negotiations on nuclear disarmament should facilitate and complement each other,

1. *Welcomes* the entry into force of the Treaty on the Reduction and Limitation of Strategic Offensive Arms, signed in Moscow on 31 July 1991 by the former Union of Soviet Socialist Republics and the United States of America, including the Protocol to that Treaty signed in Lisbon on 23 May 1992 by the parties thereto, and the exchange of documents of ratification between the United States of America, Belarus, Kazakstan, the Russian Federation and Ukraine on 5 December 1994 in Budapest;

2. *Also welcomes* the signing of the Treaty between the Russian Federation and the United States of America on the Further Reduction and Limitation of Strategic Offensive Arms in Moscow on 3 January 1993, and urges the parties to take the steps necessary to bring that Treaty into force at the earliest possible date;

3. *Expresses its satisfaction* at the fact that the entry into force of the 1991 Treaty on the Reduction and Limitation of Strategic Offensive Arms clears the way to prompt ratification by the Russian Federation and the United States of America of the 1993 Treaty;

4. *Also expresses its satisfaction* at the continuing implementation of the treaty on the elimination of intermediate-range and shorter-range missiles,[2] in particular at the completion by the parties of the destruction of all their declared missiles subject to elimination under the treaty;

5. *Encourages* the United States of America, the Russian Federation, Belarus, Kazakstan and Ukraine to continue their cooperative efforts aimed at eliminating nuclear weapons and strategic offensive arms on the basis of existing agreements, and welcomes the contributions that other States are making to such cooperation as well;

6. *Encourages and supports* the Russian Federation and the United States of America in their efforts to reduce their nuclear armaments and to continue to give those efforts the highest priority in order to contribute to the objective of the elimination of nuclear weapons within a time-bound framework;

7. *Invites* the Russian Federation and the United States of America to keep other States Members of the United Nations and the Conference on Disarmament duly informed of progress in their discussions and in the implementation of their strategic offensive arms agreements and unilateral decisions;

8. *Calls* on the Conference on Disarmament to take this information into account in the negotiations to be held on nuclear disarmament and for the ultimate elimination of nuclear weapons within a time-bound framework.

O

Moratorium on the export of anti-personnel land-mines

The General Assembly,

Recalling with satisfaction its resolutions 49/75 D of 15 December 1994 and 48/75 of 16 December 1993, in which it, *inter alia,* called upon States to agree to a moratorium on the export of anti-personnel land-mines that pose grave dangers to civilian populations, and urged States to implement moratoria on the export of anti-personnel land-mines,

Also recalling with satisfaction its resolution 49/75 D of 15 December 1994, in which it, *inter alia,* established as a goal of the international community the eventual elimination of anti-personnel land-mines,

Noting that, according to the 1994 report of the Secretary-General entitled "Assistance in mine clearance",[3] it is estimated that there are more than 110 million land-mines in the ground in more than 60 countries throughout the world,

Noting also that, according to the same report, the global land-mine crisis continues to worsen as an estimated 2 to 5 million new land-mines are laid each year, while only an estimated 100,000 were cleared in 1994,

Expressing deep concern that anti-personnel land-mines kill or maim hundreds of people every week, mostly innocent and defenceless civilians, obstruct economic development and reconstruction, and have other severe consequences for years after emplacement, which include inhibiting the repatriation of refugees and the return of internally displaced persons,

Gravely concerned with the suffering and casualties caused to non-combatants as a result of the proliferation, as well as the indiscriminate and irresponsible use, of anti-personnel land-mines,

Recalling with satisfaction its resolutions 48/7 of 19 October 1993 and 49/215 A of 23 December 1994, calling for assistance in mine clearance,

Welcoming the programmes of assistance that exist for demining and humanitarian support for the victims of anti-personnel land-mines,

---

1 *The United Nations Disarmament Yearbook,* vol. 12: 1987 (United Nations publication, Sales No. E.88.IX.2), appendix VII.

2 *Ibid.,* vol. 12: 1987 (United Nations publication, Sales No. E.88.IX.2), appendix VII.

3 A/49/357 and Add. 1 and 2.

Welcoming also the International Meeting on Mine Clearance, held at Geneva from 5 to 7 July 1995, and noting the statement of the Secretary-General at the meeting that the international community must take specific and tangible steps to address the intolerable situation caused by the proliferation of anti-personnel land-mines throughout the world,

Recalling with satisfaction the report of the Secretary-General concerning progress on the initiative in resolution 49/75 D,[1]

Convinced that moratoria by States on the export of anti-personnel land-mines that pose grave dangers to civilian populations are important measures in helping to reduce substantially the human and economic costs resulting from the proliferation, as well as the indiscriminate and irresponsible use, of such devices,

Noting with satisfaction that more than twenty-five States already have declared moratoria on the export, transfer or sale of anti-personnel land-mines, with many of these moratoria being declared as a result of the aforementioned resolutions,

Believing that ongoing efforts to strengthen the Convention on Prohibitions or Restrictions on the Use of Certain Conventional Weapons Which May Be Deemed to Be Excessively Injurious or to Have Indiscriminate Effects,[2] in particular Protocol II thereto,[3] are an essential part of the overall effort to address problems caused by the proliferation, as well as the indiscriminate and irresponsible use, of antipersonnel land-mines,

Noting the efforts that were made at the Review Conference of the Convention, held at Vienna in September and October 1995, to strengthen prohibitions and restrictions in Protocol II governing land-mine use and transfer, and urging parties to build consensus towards agreement on such prohibition and restrictions when the Review Conference reconvenes in January and April 1996,

Believing that, in addition to Protocol II other measures to control the production, stockpiling and transfer of anti-personnel land-mines are also necessary to address problems caused by anti-personnel land-mines, especially the indiscriminate or illegal use of anti-personnel land-mines that continue to inflict harm on civilian populations long after emplacement,

Recognizing that States can move most effectively towards the goal of the eventual elimination of antipersonnel land-mines as viable alternatives are developed that significantly reduce the risk to the civilian population, and emphasizing the need for States to work on developing such alternatives on an urgent basis,

1. *Welcomes* the moratoria already declared by certain States on the export of anti-personnel land-mines;

2. *Urges* States that have not yet done so to declare such moratoria at the earliest possible date;

3. *Requests* the Secretary-General to prepare a report on steps taken by Member States to implement such moratoria, and to submit it to the General Assembly at its fifty-first session under the item entitled "General and complete disarmament";

4. *Emphasizes* the importance of the Convention on Prohibitions or Restrictions on the Use of Certain Conventional Weapons Which May Be Deemed to Be Excessively Injurious or to Have Indiscriminate Effects and Protocol II thereto as the authoritative international instrument governing the responsible use of anti-personnel land-mines and related devices, and urges parties to build consensus towards an agreement when the Review Conference reconvenes;

5. *Encourages* the widest possible accession to the Convention and to Protocol II thereto, and further urges all States to comply immediately and fully with the applicable rules of Protocol II;

6. *Also encourages further* immediate international efforts to seek solutions to the problems caused by anti-personnel land-mines, with a view to the eventual elimination of anti-personnel land-mines.

---

1 A/50/701.

2 See *The United Nations Disarmament Yearbook,* vol. 5: 1980 (United Nations publication, Sales No. E.81.IX.4), appendix VII.

3 *Ibid.*, Protocol on Prohibitions or Restrictions on the Use of Mines, Booby Traps and other Devices.

P

Nuclear disarmament

The General Assembly,

Reaffirming the commitment of the international community to the goal of the total elimination of nuclear weapons and the creation of a nuclear-weapon-free world,

Determined to achieve the objective of prohibiting the development, production, stockpiling and use of nuclear weapons and their destruction, and to conclude such an international treaty or treaties at an early date,

Bearing in mind paragraph 50 of the Final Document of the Tenth Special Session of the General Assembly,[4] the first special session devoted to disarmament, calling for the urgent negotiation of agreements for the cessation of the qualitative improvement and development of nuclear-weapon systems, and for a comprehensive and phased programme with agreed time-frames, wherever feasible, for progressive and balanced reduction of nuclear weapons and their means of delivery, leading to their ultimate and complete elimination at the earliest possible time,

Recognizing that a comprehensive nuclear-test-ban treaty, the proposed treaty on fissile material for nuclear weapons or other nuclear explosive devices and a convention prohibiting the use of nuclear weapons constitute important steps towards the elimination of the nuclear threat, and will contribute to the achievement of the goal of nuclear disarmament within a time-bound framework,

Recognizing also that the end of the cold war has brought about favourable conditions for creating a world free of nuclear weapons,

Welcoming the entry into force of the Treaty on the Reduction and Limitation of Strategic Offensive Arms, to which Belarus, Kazakstan, the Russian Federation, Ukraine and the United States of America are States parties, as well as the conclusion of the Treaty on the Further Reduction and Limitation of Strategic Offensive Arms by the Russian Federation and the United States of America, and looking forward to full implementation of these treaties and to further concrete steps for nuclear disarmament by all nuclear-weapon States,

Noting with appreciation the unilateral measures of nuclear-weapon States for nuclear arms limitation,

Recognizing the complementarity of bilateral and multilateral negotiations on nuclear disarmament and that bilateral negotiations can never replace multilateral negotiations in the respect,

Recognizing also that a comprehensive nuclear-test-ban treaty and the proposed treaty on fissile material for nuclear weapons or other explosive devices must both constitute disarmament measures and not only non-proliferation measures, and that they must be important steps leading to the total elimination of nuclear weapons within a time-bound framework,

Noting the support expressed in the Conference on Disarmament and in the General Assembly for the elaboration of an international convention to assure non-nuclear-weapon States against the use or threat of use of nuclear weapons, and the multilateral efforts in the Conference on Disarmament to reach agreement on such an international convention at an early date,

Recalling its resolution 49/75 E of 15 December 1994 on a step-by-step reduction of the nuclear threat,

Taking note of paragraph 84 and other relevant recommendations in the Final Document of the Eleventh Conference of Heads of State or Government of the Non-Aligned Countries, held at Cartagena de Indias, Colombia, from 18 to 20 October 1995, calling on the Conference on Disarmament to establish, on a priority basis, an *Ad Hoc* committee to commence negotiations early in 1996 on a phased programme of nuclear disarmament and for the eventual elimination of nuclear weapons within a time-bound framework,

1. *Recognizes* that, in view of the end of the cold war and recent political developments, the time is now opportune for all nuclear-weapon States to undertake effective nuclear disarmament measures

---

4 Resolution S-10/2.

with a view to the total elimination of these weapons within a time-bound framework;

2. *Also recognizes* that there is a genuine need to de-emphasize the role of nuclear weapons, and to review and revise nuclear doctrines accordingly;

3. *Urges* the nuclear-weapon States to stop immediately the qualitative improvement, development, stockpiling and production of nuclear warheads and their delivery systems;

4. *Calls upon* the nuclear-weapon States to undertake step-by-step reduction of the nuclear threat and a phased programme of progressive and balanced deep reductions of nuclear weapons, and to carry out effective nuclear disarmament measures with a view to the total elimination of these weapons within a time-bound framework;

5. *Calls upon* the Conference on Disarmament to establish, on a priority basis, an *Ad Hoc* committee on nuclear disarmament to commence negotiations early in 1996 on a phased programme of nuclear disarmament and for the eventual elimination of nuclear weapons within a time-bound framework;

6. *Expresses its support* for the efforts of the Member States of the Conference on Disarmament to this end;

7. *Requests* the Secretary-General to submit to the General Assembly at its fifty-first session a report on the implementation of the present resolution;

8. *Decides* to include in the provisional agenda of its fifty-first session the item entitled "Nuclear disarmament".

Q

1995 Review and Extension Conference of the Parties to the Treaty on the Non-Proliferation of Nuclear Weapons

The General Assembly,

Recalling its resolution 47/52 A of 9 December 1992, in which it, *inter alia,* took note of the decision of the parties to the Treaty on the Non-Proliferation of Nuclear Weapons,[1] following appropriate consultations, to form a preparatory committee for a conference to review the operation of the Treaty and to decide on its extension, as provided for in article VIII, paragraph 3, and also called for in article X, paragraph 2, of the Treaty,

Recalling also that the parties to the Treaty on the Non-Proliferation of Nuclear Weapons convened in New York from 17 April to 12 May 1995 in accordance with article VIII, paragraph 3, and article X, paragraph 2, of the Treaty,

Noting that, at the time of the Review and Extension Conference, there were one hundred and seventy-five of the one hundred and seventy-eight States parties to the Treaty present,

1. *Notes* that on 11 May 1995 the 1995 Review and Extension Conference of the Parties to the Treaty on the Non-Proliferation of Nuclear Weapons adopted three decisions on strengthening the review process for the Treaty, principles and objectives for nuclear non-proliferation and disarmament, and extension of the Treaty on the Non-Proliferation of Nuclear Weapons;[2]

2. *Takes note* of the resolution on the Middle East adopted on 11 May 1995 by the parties to the Treaty;[3]

3. *Notes* that the States party to the Treaty participating in the Review Conference:

(*a*) Agreed to strengthen the review process for the operation of the Treaty with a view to assuring that the purposes of the preamble and the provisions of the Treaty were being realized, and decided that, in accordance with article VIII, paragraph 3, the Review Conferences should continue to be held every five years, and that, accordingly, the next Review Conference should be held in the year 2000, and that the first meeting of the Preparatory Committee should be held in 1997;

(*b*) Affirmed the need to continue to move with determination towards the full realization and effective implementation of the provisions of the Treaty, and accordingly adopted a set of principles and objectives;

(*c*) Decided that, as a majority existed among States party to the Treaty for its indefinite extension, in accordance with its article X, paragraph 2, the Treaty should continue in force indefinitely;

4. *Notes* that the three decisions and the resolution were adopted without a vote.

R

Contribution to nuclear disarmament

The General Assembly,

Recalling its resolutions 49/75 H, 49/75 L and 49/75 P of 15 December 1994,

Noting with satisfaction a number of positive developments in the field of nuclear disarmament, in particular, the entry into force of the Treaty on the Reduction and Limitation of Strategic Offensive Arms,

Noting also with satisfaction the conclusion of the Treaty on the Further Reduction and Limitation of Strategic Offensive Arms,

Realizing the vital importance of further nuclear disarmament with the ultimate goals of the complete elimination of nuclear weapons and a treaty on general and complete disarmament under strict and effective international control,

Bearing in mind the results of the 1995 Review and Extension Conference of the Parties to the Treaty on the Non-Proliferation of Nuclear Weapons,[4]

Noting that the vast majority of States Members of the United Nations are now parties to the Treaty on the Non-Proliferation of Nuclear Weapons,

1. *Welcomes* the accession to the Treaty on the Non-Proliferation of Nuclear Weapons of the following States: Algeria, Argentina, Chile, Comoros, Eritrea, Marshall Islands, Micronesia (Federated States of), Monaco, Palau, Ukraine, United Arab Emirates and Vanuatu;

2. *Also welcomes* the accession on 5 December 1994 to the Treaty on the Non-Proliferation of Nuclear Weapons of Ukraine as a non-nuclear-weapon State, and in this regard acknowledges that this decision, as well as relevant decisions previously taken by Belarus and Kazakstan, contributed to the entry into force of the Treaty on the Reduction and Limitation of Strategic Offensive Arms, which is a major landmark in the process of nuclear disarmament;

3. *Acknowledges* the progress in the process of implementation of the Treaty on the Reduction and Limitation of Strategic Offensive Arms to date by the parties to the Treaty;

4. *Welcomes* the signing of the Treaty on the Further Reduction and Limitation of Strategic Offensive Arms by the Russian Federation and the United States of America, and urges the parties to take the steps necessary to bring that Treaty into force at the earliest possible date;

5. *Also welcomes* the fact that South Africa has voluntarily given up its nuclear weapon programme as well as the voluntary renunciation of nuclear weapons by Belarus, Kazakstan and Ukraine, and recognizes the significant contribution of those States to nuclear disarmament and the strengthening of regional and global security.

90th plenary meeting
12 December 1995

---

1 United Nations, *Treaty Series,* vol. 729, No. 10485.

2 See *1995 Review and Extension Conference of the Parties to the Treaty on the Non-Proliferation of Nuclear Weapons,* Final Documents, Part I (NPT/CONF.1995/32 (Part II)), para. 30.

3 *Ibid.*, para. 32.

4 See *1995 Review and Extension Conference of the Parties to the Treaty on the Non-Proliferation of Nuclear Weapons.* Part I (NPT/CONF.1995/32 (Part I)).

02.12 NUCLEAR WEAPONS

1 (I). Establishment of a Commission to Deal with the Problems Raised by the Discovery of Atomic Energy

Committee: 1
Vote: unanimous
Ref.: 191(III)

Resolved by the General Assembly of the United Nations to establish a Commission, with the composition and competence set out hereunder, to deal with the problems raised by the discovery of atomic energy and other related matters:

1. Establishment of the Commission

A Commission is hereby established by the General Assembly with the terms of reference set out under section 5 below.

2. Relations of the Commission with the Organs of the United Nations

(*a*) The Commission shall submit its reports and recommendations to the Security Council, and such reports and recommendations shall be made public unless the Security Council, in the interest of peace and security, otherwise directs. In the appropriate cases the Security Council should transmit these reports to the General Assembly and the Members of the United Nations, as well as to the Economic and Social Council and other organs within the framework of the United Nations.

(*b*) In view of the Security Council's primary responsibility under the Charter of the United Nations for the maintenance of international peace and security, the Security Council shall issue directions to the Commission in matters affecting security. On these matters the Commission shall be accountable for its work to the Security Council.

3. Composition of the Commission

The Commission shall be composed of one representative from each of those States represented on the Security Council, and Canada when that State is not a member of the Security Council. Each representative on the Commission may have such assistance as he may desire.

4. Rules of Procedure

The Commission shall have whatever staff it may deem necessary, and shall make recommendations for its rules of procedure to the Security Council, which shall approve them as a procedural matter.

5. Terms of Reference of the Commission

The Commission shall proceed with the utmost despatch and enquire into all phases of the problem, and make such recommendations from time to time with respect to them as it finds possible. In particular, the Commission shall make specific proposals:

(*a*) for extending between all nations the exchange of basic scientific information for peaceful ends;

(*b*) for control of atomic energy to the extent necessary to ensure its use only for peaceful purposes;

(*c*) for the elimination from national armaments of atomic weapons and of all other major weapons adaptable to mass destruction;

(*d*) for effective safeguards by way of inspection and other means to protect complying States against the hazards of violations and evasions.

The work of the Commission should proceed by separate stages, the successful completion of each of which will develop the necessary confidence of the world before the next stage is undertaken.

The Commission shall not infringe upon the responsibilities of any organ of the United Nations, but should present recommendations for the consideration of those organs in the performance of their tasks under the terms of the United Nations Charter.

Seventeenth plenary meeting
24 January 1946

192 (III). Prohibition of the Atomic Weapon and Reduction by One-Third of the Armaments and Armed Forces of the Permanent Members of the Security Council

Committee: 1
Vote: 43 - 6 - 1

The General Assembly,

Desiring to establish relations of confident collaboration between the States within the framework of the Charter and to make possible a general reduction of armaments in order that humanity may in future be spared the horrors of war and that the peoples may not be overwhelmed by the continually increasing burden of military expenditure,

Considering that no agreement is attainable on any proposal for the reduction of conventional armaments and armed forces so long as each State lacks exact and authenticated information concerning the conventional armaments and armed forces of other States, so long as no convention has been concluded regarding the types of military forces to which such reduction noted apply, and so long as no organ of control has been established,

Considering that the aim of the reduction of conventional armaments and armed forces can only be attained in an atmosphere of real and lasting improvement in international relations, which implies in particular the application of control of atomic energy involving the prohibition of the atomic weapon,

But noting on the other hand that this renewal of confidence would be greatly encouraged if States were placed in possession of precise and verified data as to the level of their respective conventional armaments and armed forces,

Recommends the Security Council to pursue the study of the regulation and reduction of conventional armaments and armed forces through the agency of the Commission for Conventional Armaments in order to obtain concrete results as soon as possible;

Trusts that the Commission for Conventional Armaments, in carrying out its plan of work, will devote its first attention to formulating proposals for the receipt, checking and publication, by an international organ of control within the framework of the Security Council, of full information to be supplied by Member States with regard to their electives and their conventional armaments;

Invites the Security Council to report to the Assembly no later than its next regular session on the effect given to the present recommendation, with a view to enabling it to continue its activity with regard to the regulation of armaments in accordance with the purposes and principles defined by the Charter;

Invites all nations in the Commission for Conventional Armaments to cooperate to the utmost of their power in the attainment of the abovementioned objectives.

Hundred and sixty-third plenary meeting
19 November 1948

1379 (XIV). Question of French Nuclear Tests in the Sahara

Committee: 1
Vote: 51 - 16 - 15

The General Assembly,

Conscious of the great concern throughout the world repeatedly expressed in the United Nations over the prospect of further nuclear tests and their effects upon mankind,

Noting the declared intention of the Government of France to undertake nuclear tests in the Sahara,

Considering the deep concern felt over the dangers and risks which such tests entail,

Considering that significant progress is being made in the negotiations now proceeding at Geneva concerning the discontinuance of nuclear weapons tests under an international control system,

Considering that the parties to those negotiations have facilitated their progress by voluntarily suspending such tests,

Considering that the purpose of the said negotiations is to bring about a general discontinuance of nuclear weapons tests and that it is to be hoped that, in the same spirit which inspired the present voluntary suspension of tests, no State will initiate or resume tests of this kind,

Recognizing the anxiety caused by the contemplated tests in the Sahara among all peoples, and more particularly those of Africa,

1. *Expresses* its grove concern over the intention of the Government of France to conduct nuclear tests;

2. *Requests* France to refrain from such tests.

840th plenary meeting
20 November 1959

1402 (XIV). Suspension of Nuclear and Thermo-Nuclear Tests

Committee: 1
Vote: A: 78 - 0 - 2; B: 60 - 1 - 20
Ref.: 1578(XV), 1577(XV)

A

The General Assembly,

Recalling its resolution 1252 B (XIII) of 4 November 1958,

Noting that the negotiations on the discontinuance of nuclear weapons tests and on the establishment of an appropriate international control system, which began at Geneva on 31 October 1958, are still continuing,

1. *Expresses its appreciation* to the States concerned for their efforts to reach an agreement relating to the prohibition of nuclear weapons tests and including an appropriate international control system;

2. *Expresses the hope* that these States will intensify their efforts to reach such an agreement at an early date;

3. *Urges* the States concerned in these negotiations to continue their present voluntary discontinuance of the testing of nuclear weapons;

4. *Requests* the States concerned to report to the General Assembly the results of their negotiations.

842nd plenary meeting
21 November 1959

B

The General Assembly,

Desiring to safeguard mankind from the increasing hazards resulting from tests of nuclear and thermo-nuclear weapons,

Bearing in mind the profound concern evinced by the peoples of all countries regarding the testing of nuclear and thermo-nuclear weapons,

Welcoming the endeavours at Geneva of the States concerned to reach an agreement on the discontinuance of these tests, and the progress so far achieved,

Noting with appreciation that the States concerned have voluntarily suspended such tests, enabling progress in the discussions at Geneva,

Considering that an agreement on the cessation of nuclear and thermo-nuclear tests with effective international control is urgent,

1. *Expresses its appreciation* to the States concerned for their patient and sincere efforts to reach agreement on the discontinuance of nuclear and thermo-nuclear tests with effective international control, and for the progress hitherto achieved;

2. *Expresses further* the hope that the States concerned will reach such agreement at an early date;

3. *Appeals* to the States concerned in the Geneva discussions to continue their present voluntary suspension of tests, and to other States to desist from such tests;

4. *Requests* the States concerned to report to the Disarmament Commission and to the General Assembly the results of their negotiations.

842nd plenary meeting
21 November 1959

1632 (XVI). Continuation of Suspension of Nuclear and Thermo-Nuclear Tests and Obligations of States to Refrain from their Renewal. The Urgent Need for a Treaty to Ban Nuclear Weapons Tests under Effective International Control

Committee: 1
Vote: 87 - 11 - 1
Ref.: 50/65, 49/70, 48/70, 47/47, 46/29, 45/51, 44/107, 43/64, 42, 27, 41/47, 40/81, 39/53, 38/63, 37/73, 3466(XXX), 3257(XXIX), 3078(XXVIII), 2934(XXVII), 2828(XXVI), 2663(XXV), 2604(XXIV), 2455(XXIII), 2343(XXII), 2163(XXI), 2032(XX), 1910(XVIII), 1762(XVII), 1649(XVI), 1648(XVI)

The General Assembly,

Seized of the question of halting nuclear weapons tests,

Solemnly appeals to the Government of the Union of Soviet Socialist Republics to refrain from carrying out its intention to explode in the atmosphere a 50-megaton bomb before the end of this month.

1043rd plenary meeting
27 October 1961

1653 (XVI). Declaration on the Prohibition of the Use of Nuclear and Thermo-Nuclear Weapons

Committee: 1
Vote: 55 - 20 - 26
Ref.: 2936(XXVII), 2830(XXVI), 2666(XV), 2664(XXV), 2660(XXV), 2373(XXII), 2346(XXII), 2289(XXII), 2286(XXII), 2164(XXI), 2153(XXI), 2149(XXI), 2028(XX), 1909(XVIII), 1801(XVII), 1665(XVI), 1576(XV), 1380(XIV)

The General Assembly,

Mindful of its responsibility under the Charter of the United Nations in the maintenance of international peace and security, as well as in the consideration of principles governing disarmament,

Gravely concerned that, while negotiations on disarmament have not so far achieved satisfactory results the armaments race, particularly in the nuclear and thermo-nuclear fields, has reached a dangerous stage requiring all possible precautionary measures to protect humanity and civilization from the hazard of nuclear and thermo-nuclear catastrophe,

Recalling that the use of weapons of mass destruction, causing unnecessary human suffering, was in the past prohibited, as being contrary to the laws of humanity and to the principles of international law, by international declarations and binding agreements, such as the Declaration of St. Petersburg of 1868, the Declaration of the Brussels Conference of 1874, the Conventions of The Hague Peace Conferences of 1899 and 1907, and the Geneva Protocol of 1925, to which the majority of Nations are still parties,

Considering that the use of nuclear and thermo-nuclear weapons would bring about indiscriminate suffering and destruction to mankind and civilization to an even greater extent than the use of those weapons declared by the aforementioned international declarations and agreements to be contrary to the laws of humanity and a crime under international law,

Believing that the use of weapons of mass destruction, such as nuclear and thermo-nuclear weapons, is a direct negation of the high ideals and objectives which the United Nations has been established to achieve through the protection of succeeding generations from the scourge of war and through the preservation and promotion of their cultures,

1. *Declares* that :

(*a*) The use of nuclear and thermo-nuclear weapons is contrary to the spirit, letter and aims of the United Nations and, as such, a direct violation of the Charter of the United Nations;

(*b*) The use of nuclear and thermo-nuclear weapons would exceed even the scope of war and cause indiscriminate suffering and destruction to mankind and civilization and, as such, is contrary to the rules of international law and to the laws of humanity;

(*c*) The use of nuclear and thermo-nuclear weapons is a war directed not against an enemy or enemies alone but also against mankind in general, since the peoples of the world not involved in such a war will be subjected to all the evils generated by the use of such weapons;

(*d*) Any State using nuclear and thermo-nuclear weapons is to be considered as violating the Charter of the United Nations, as acting contrary to the laws of humanity and as committing a crime against mankind and civilization;

2. *Requests* the Secretary-General to consult the Governments of Member States to ascertain their views on the possibility of convening a special conference for signing a convention on the prohibition of the use of nuclear and thermo-nuclear weapons for war purposes and to report on the results of such consultation to the General Assembly at its seventeenth session.

1063rd plenary meeting
24 November 1961

3472 (XXX). Comprehensive Study of the Question of Nuclear-Weapon-Free Zones in all its Aspects

Committee: 1
Vote: A: 126 - 0 - 2; B: 82 - 10 - 36
Ref.: 3478(XXX)

A

The General Assembly,

Recalling its resolution 3261 F (XXIX) of 9 December 1974, by which it decided to undertake a comprehensive study of the question of nuclear-weapon-free zones in all its aspects,

Having considered the special report of the Conference of the Committee on Disarmament[1] containing the comprehensive study of the question of nuclear-weapon-free zones in all its aspects,[2]

Noting the comments made by States members of the Conference of the Committee on Disarmament regarding the study,[3]

Convinced that the study will enhance further efforts concerning nuclear-weapon-free zones,

Recognizing that the establishment of nuclear-weapon-free zones can contribute to the security of members of such zones, to the prevention of the proliferation of nuclear weapons and to the goals of general and complete disarmament,

Expressing the wish that the study will be of assistance to States interested in the establishment of nuclear-weapon-free zones,

1. *Takes note* of the special report of the Conference of the Committee on Disarmament containing the comprehensive study of the question of nuclear-weapon-free zones in all its aspects;

2. *Expresses its appreciation* to the *Ad Hoc* Group of Qualified Governmental Experts for the Study of the Question of Nuclear-Weapon-Free Zones for the preparation of the study;

3. *Conveys its thanks* to the Secretary-General of the United Nations, the Director-General of the International Atomic Energy Agency and other relevant international organizations for the assistance they have given for the preparation of the study;

4. *Commends* the special report to the attention of all Governments, the International Atomic Energy Agency and other relevant international organizations;

5. *Invites* all Governments, the International Atomic Energy Agency and other international organizations concerned to transmit to the Secretary-General before 30 June 1976 such views, observations and suggestions on the special report as they may deem appropriate;

6. *Requests* the Secretary-General to prepare a report based on information received under paragraph 5 above and to submit it to the General Assembly at its thirty-first session;

7. *Requests* the Secretary-General to arrange for the reproduction of the special report as a United Nations publication and to give it the widest possible publicity in as many languages as is considered desirable and practicable;

8. *Recommends* that all Governments give a wide distribution to the special report so as to acquaint public opinion with its contents, and invites relevant international organizations to use their facilities to make the special report widely known;

9. *Decides* to include in the provisional agenda of its thirty-first session the item entitled "Comprehensive study of the question of nuclear-weapon-free zones in all its aspects".

2437th plenary meeting
11 December 1975

B

The General Assembly,

Recalling that, as set forth in the Charter of the United Nations, the Organization is based on the principle of the sovereign equality of all its Members and that, in conformity with the provisions of the Charter, international relations should be governed, among other fundamental principles, by those relating to the prohibition of the threat or use of force and to non-intervention,

Bearing in mind that nuclear-weapon-free zones constitute one of the most effective means for preventing the proliferation, both horizontal and vertical, of nuclear weapons and for contributing to the elimination of the danger of a nuclear holocaust,

Reaffirming the principle defined in its resolution 2028 (XX) of 19 November 1965, which established the necessity that there should be an acceptable balance of mutual responsibilities and obligations of the nuclear-weapon and non-nuclear-weapon States,

Reaffirming also the request made in its resolution 2153 A (XXI) of 17 November 1966 to all nuclear-weapon States to refrain from the use, or the threat of use, of nuclear weapons against States which conclude regional treaties in order to ensure the total absence of nuclear weapons in their respective territories,

Having examined the comprehensive study of the question of nuclear-weapon-free zones in all its aspects[4] carried out under the auspices of the Conference of the Committee on Disarmament by the *Ad Hoc* Group of Qualified Governmental Experts for the Study of the Question of Nuclear-Weapon-Free Zones in pursuance of General Assembly resolution 3261 F (XXIX) of 9 December 1974,

Having also examined the comments made by States members of the Conference of the Committee on Disarmament regarding that study,[5] the text of which is annexed to the special report in which the Conference transmitted the study to the General Assembly,[6]

Bearing in mind that, without prejudice to the results that may be obtained through any further examination of this matter, from the analysis of the contents of the special report it is already possible at this time to draw certain incontrovertible conclusions,

Noting that from among those conclusions it would seem advisable to stress the necessity that the General Assembly define the concept of a nuclear-weapon-free zone and the scope of the principal obligations

1 *Official Records of the General Assembly, Thirtieth Session, Supplement No. 27A* (A/10027/Add.1).

2 *Ibid.*, annex I.

3 *Ibid.*, annex II.

4 *Ibid.*, annex I.

5 *Ibid.*, annex II.

6 *Official Records of the General Assembly, Thirtieth Session, Supplement No. 27A* (A/10027/Add.1).

of the nuclear-weapon States towards such zones and towards the States included therein,

Convinced that in so doing it will strengthen the new efforts recently undertaken and the realizations already achieved for the establishment of nuclear-weapon-free zones,

Solemnly adopts the following declaration :

I. Definition of the concept of a nuclear-weapon-free zone

1. A "nuclear-weapon-free zone" shall, as a general rule, be deemed to be any zone, recognized as such by the General Assembly of the United Nations, which any group of States, in the free exercise of their sovereignty, has established by virtue of a treaty or convention whereby:

(*a*) The statute of total absence of nuclear weapons to which the zone shall be subject, including the procedure for the delimitation of the zone, is defined;

(*b*) An international system of verification and control is established to guarantee compliance with the obligations deriving from that statute.

II. Definition of the principal obligations of the nuclear-weapon States towards nuclear-weapon-free zones and towards the States included therein

2. In every case of a nuclear-weapon-free zone that has been recognized as such by the General Assembly, all nuclear-weapon States shall undertake or reaffirm, in a solemn international instrument having full legally binding force, such as a treaty, a convention or a protocol, the following obligations:

(*a*) To respect in all its parts the statute of total absence of nuclear weapons defined in the treaty or convention which serves as the constitutive instrument of the zone;

(*b*) To refrain from contributing in any way to the performance in the territories forming part of the zone of acts which involve a violation of the aforesaid treaty or convention;

(*c*) To refrain from using or threatening to use nuclear weapons against the States included in the zone.

III. Scope of the definitions

3. The above definitions in no way impair the resolutions which the General Assembly has adopted or may adopt with regard to specific cases of nuclear-weapon-free zones nor the rights emanating for the Member States from such resolutions.

2437th plenary meeting
11 December 1975

36/100. Declaration on the Prevention of Nuclear Catastrophe

Committee: 1
Vote: 81 - 19 - 41

The General Assembly,

Bearing in mind that the foremost task of the United Nations, born in the flames of the Second World War, has been, is and will be to save present and succeeding generations from the scourge of war,

Recognizing that all the horrors of past wars and all other calamities that have befallen people would pale in comparison with what is inherent in the use of nuclear weapons capable of destroying civilization on earth,

Reaffirming that the universally accepted objective is to eliminate completely the possibility of the use of nuclear weapons through the cessation of their production, followed by the destruction of their stockpiles, and that, to this end, priority in disarmament negotiations should be given to nuclear disarmament,

Convinced that, as the first step in this direction, the use of nuclear weapons and the waging of nuclear war should be outlawed,

Solemnly proclaims, on behalf of the States Members of the United Nations

1. States and statesmen that resort first to the use of nuclear weapons will be committing the gravest crime against humanity;

2. There will never be any justification or pardon for statesmen who would take the decision to be the first to use nuclear weapons;

3. Any doctrines allowing the first use of nuclear weapons and any actions pushing the world towards a catastrophe are incompatible with human moral standards and the lofty ideals of the United Nations;

4. It is the supreme duty and direct obligation of the leaders of nuclear-weapon States to act in such a way as to eliminate the risk of the outbreak of a nuclear conflict. The nuclear-arms race must be stopped and reversed by joint effort, through negotiations conducted in good faith and on the basis of equality, having as their ultimate goal the complete elimination of nuclear weapons;

5. Nuclear energy should be used exclusively for peaceful purposes and only for the benefit of mankind.

91st plenary meeting
9 December 1981

37/85. Immediate Cessation and Prohibition of Nuclear-Weapon Tests

Committee: 1
Vote: 115 - 5 - 25
Ref.: 46/29, 45/49, 44/105, 43/63, 42/26, 41/46, 40/80, 39/52, 38/72, 38/62, 37/72, 36/84

The General Assembly,

Deeply concerned over the continuing nuclear-arms race and the growing danger of nuclear war,

Convinced that an immediate cessation of nuclear-weapon tests by all States in all environments and the prohibition of such testing in the future would be a serious obstacle to the development of ever-new types and systems of nuclear weapons, as well as to the emergence of new nuclear States,

Taking note of the "Basic provisions of a treaty on the complete and general prohibition of nuclear-weapon tests", submitted by the Union of Soviet Socialist Republics at the current session,[1] the text of which is annexed to the present resolution,

1. *Urges* the Committee on Disarmament to proceed promptly to practical negotiations with a view to elaborating a draft treaty on the complete and general prohibition of nuclear-weapon tests;

2. *Refers* to the Committee on Disarmament for its consideration the basic provisions of such a treaty, submitted by the Union of Soviet Socialist Republics, the text of which is annexed to the present resolution, as well as the proposals and observations made by other States on this question in the course of the current session;

3. *Calls upon* all the nuclear-weapon States, as a gesture of goodwill and with a view to creating more favourable conditions for the formulation of a treaty on the complete and general prohibition of nuclear-weapon tests, not to conduct any nuclear explosions, starting from a date to be agreed among them and until the above-mentioned treaty is concluded, after the appropriate declarations have been made by them to that effect well in advance;

4. *Decides* to include in the provisional agenda of its thirty-eighth session the item entitled "Immediate cessation and prohibition of nuclear-weapon tests".

98th plenary meeting
9 December 1982

Annex

Basic Provisions of a Treaty on the Complete and General Prohibition of Nuclear-Weapon Tests

The objective of averting nuclear war, towards which the efforts of the Union of Soviet Socialist Republics and of other peace-loving

---

1 See A/37/243.

States are directed, makes it imperative to take such measures, *inter alia*, as would impede the development of ever-new types and systems of nuclear weapons.

One such effective measure would be the immediate cessation and prohibition of nuclear-weapon tests by all States and in all environments, which at the same time would promote the non-proliferation of nuclear weapons.

Motivated by these goals, the Soviet Union is submitting to States Members of the United Nations, for their consideration, the following basic provisions of a treaty on the complete and general prohibition of nuclear-weapon tests.

A. Scope of the prohibition

1. Each State party to this Treaty shall undertake to prohibit, to prevent, and not to carry out any nuclear-weapon test explosions at any place under its jurisdiction or control, in any environment - in the atmosphere, beyond its limits, including outer space, under water or under ground.

2. No party shall cause, encourage or in any way participate in the conduct of any nuclear-weapon test explosions anywhere.

3. A moratorium shall be declared on nuclear explosions for peaceful purposes, under which the parties to this Treaty shall refrain from causing, encouraging, or in any way participating in carrying out such explosions until the relevant procedure has been evolved.

4. Promptly after the entry into force of this Treaty, consideration shall be given to the question of procedure for carrying out nuclear explosions for peaceful purposes. Such procedure, to be agreed upon, may take the form of a special agreement or agreements constituting an integral part of this Treaty.

38/75. Condemnation of Nuclear War

Committee: 1
Vote: 95 - 19 - 30

The General Assembly,

Expressing its alarm at the growing threat of nuclear war, which can lead to the destruction of civilization on earth,

Drawing the attention of all States and peoples to the conclusions arrived at by the most eminent scientists and military and civilian experts to the effect that it is impossible to limit the deadly consequences of nuclear war if it is ever begun and that in a nuclear war there can be no victors,

Convinced that the prevention of nuclear catastrophe is the most profound aspiration of billions of people on earth,

Reaffirming its call for the conclusion of an international convention on the prohibition of the use of nuclear weapons with the participation of all the nuclear-weapon States,

1. *Resolutely unconditionally and for all time condemns* nuclear war as being contrary to human conscience and reason, as the most monstrous crime against peoples and as a violation of the foremost human right - the right to life;

2. *Condemns* the formulation, propounding, dissemination and propaganda of political and military doctrines and concepts intended to provide "legitimacy" for the first use of nuclear weapons and in general to justify the "admissibility" of unleashing nuclear war;

3. *Calls upon* all States to unite and redouble their efforts aimed at removing the threat of nuclear war, halting the nuclear-arms race and reducing nuclear weapons until they are completely eliminated.

97th plenary meeting
15 December 1983

46/28. Amendment of the Treaty Banning Nuclear Weapon Tests in the Atmosphere, in Outer Space and under Water

Committee: 1
Vote: 110 - 2 - 35

The General Assembly,

Recalling its resolutions 44/106 of 15 December 1989 and 45/50 of 4 December 1990,

Reiterating its conviction that a comprehensive nuclear-test-ban treaty is the highest-priority measure for the cessation of the nuclear arms race and for the achievement of the objective of nuclear disarmament,

Recalling also the central role of the United Nations in the field of nuclear disarmament and in particular in the cessation of all nuclear-test explosions, as well as the persistent efforts of non-governmental organizations in the achievement of a comprehensive nuclear-test-ban treaty,

Conscious of the growing environmental concerns throughout the world and of the past and potential negative effects of nuclear testing on the environment,

Recalling its resolution 1910 (XVIII) of 27 November 1963, in which it noted with approval the Treaty Banning Nuclear Weapon Tests in the Atmosphere, in Outer Space and under Water, signed on 5 August 1963, and requested the Conference of the Eighteen-Nation Committee on Disarmament to continue with a sense of urgency its negotiations to achieve the objectives set forth in the preamble to the Treaty,

Recalling also that more than one third of the parties to the Treaty requested the Depositary Governments to convene a conference to consider an amendment that would convert the Treaty into a comprehensive test-ban treaty,

Reiterating its conviction that the Amendment Conference of the States Parties to the Treaty Banning Nuclear Weapon Tests in the Atmosphere, in Outer Space and under Water will facilitate the attainment of the objectives set forth in the Treaty and thus serve to strengthen it,

Recalling further its recommendation that arrangements be made to ensure that intensive efforts continue, under the auspices of the Amendment Conference, until a comprehensive nuclear-test-ban treaty is achieved,

1. *Notes with satisfaction* that a substantive session of the Amendment Conference of the States Parties to the Treaty Banning Nuclear Weapon Tests in the Atmosphere, in Outer Space and under Water was held in New York from 7 to 18 January 1991, and takes note of its report;

2. *Takes note* of the decision adopted by the Amendment Conference to the effect that, since further work needed to be undertaken on certain aspects of a comprehensive test-ban treaty, especially those with regard to verification of compliance and possible sanctions against non-compliance, the President of the Conference should conduct consultations with a view to achieving progress on those issues and to resuming the work of the Conference at an appropriate time;

3. *Welcomes* the ongoing consultations being conducted by the President of the Amendment Conference and the holding in 1992 of more structured open-ended consultations, as well as the establishment of a group of friends of the President in order to examine various aspects of a comprehensive nuclear-test ban, with a view to resuming the work of the Conference as soon as possible thereafter;

4. *Calls upon* all parties to the Treaty Banning Nuclear Weapon Tests in the Atmosphere, in Outer Space and under Water to participate in, and to contribute to the success of, the Amendment Conference for the achievement of a comprehensive nuclear-test ban at an early date, as an indispensable measure towards implementation of their undertakings in the preamble to the Treaty;

5. *Urges* all States, especially those nuclear-weapon States which have not yet done so, to adhere to the Treaty;

6. *Recommends* that arrangements should be made to ensure the fullest possible participation of non-governmental organizations in the Amendment Conference;

7. *Reiterates its conviction* that, pending the conclusion of a comprehensive nuclear-test-ban treaty, the nuclear-weapon States should suspend all nuclear-test explosions through an agreed moratorium or unilateral moratoria;

8. *Stresses* once again the importance of ensuring adequate coordination among the various negotiating forums dealing with a comprehensive nuclear-test- ban treaty;

9. *Decides* to include in the provisional agenda of its forty-seventh session the item entitled "Amendment of the Treaty Banning Nuclear Weapon Tests in the Atmosphere, in Outer Space and under Water".

65th plenary meeting
6 December 1991

49/75 K. Request for an Advisory Opinion from the International Court of Justice on the Legality of the Threat or Use of Nuclear Weapons

Committee: 1
Vote: 78 - 43 - 38

The General Assembly,

Conscious that the continuing existence and development of nuclear weapons pose serious risks to humanity,

Mindful that States have an obligation under the Charter of the United Nations to refrain from the threat or use of force against the territorial integrity or political independence of any State,

Recalling its resolutions 1653 (XVI) of 24 November 1961, 33/71 B of 14 December 1978, 34/83 G of 11 December 1979, 35/152 D of 12 December 1980, 36/92 I of 9 December 1981, 45/59 B of 4 December 1990 and 46/37 D of 6 December 1991, in which it declared that the use of nuclear weapons would be a violation of the Charter and a crime against humanity,

Welcoming the progress made on the prohibition and elimination of weapons of mass destruction, including the Convention on the Prohibition of the Development, Production and Stockpiling of Bacteriological (Biological) and Toxin Weapons and on Their Destruction[1] and the Convention on the Prohibition of the Development, Production, Stockpiling and Use of Chemical Weapons and on Their Destruction,[2]

Convinced that the complete elimination of nuclear weapons is the only guarantee against the threat of nuclear war,

Noting the concerns expressed in the Fourth Review Conference of the Parties to the Treaty on the Non-Proliferation of Nuclear Weapons that insufficient progress had been made towards the complete elimination of nuclear weapons at the earliest possible time,

Recalling that, convinced of the need to strengthen the rule of law in international relations, it has declared the period 1990-1999 the United Nations Decade of International Law, [3]

Noting that Article 96, paragraph 1, of the Charter empowers the General Assembly to request the International Court of Justice to give an advisory opinion on any legal question,

Recalling the recommendation of the Secretary-General, made in his report entitled "An Agenda for Peace",[4] that United Nations organs that are authorized to take advantage of the advisory competence of the International Court of Justice turn to the Court more frequently for such opinions,

Welcoming resolution 46/40 of 14 May 1993 of the Assembly of the World Health Organization, in which the organization requested the International Court of Justice to give an advisory opinion on whether the use of nuclear weapons by a State in war or other armed conflict would be a breach of its obligations under international law, including the Constitution of the World Health Organization,

Decides, pursuant to Article 96, paragraph 1, of the Charter of the United Nations, to request the International Court of Justice urgently to render its advisory opinion on the following question: "Is the threat or use of nuclear weapons in any circumstance permitted under international law?".

90th plenary meeting
15 December 1994

1 Resolution 2826 (XXVI), annex.

2 See *Official Records of the General Assembly, Forty-seventh Session, Supplement No. 27* (A/47/27), appendix I.

3 Resolution 44/23.

4 A/47/277-S/24111.

50/68. Conclusion of Effective International Arrangements to Assure Non-Nuclear-Weapon States Against the Use or Threat of Use of Nuclear Weapons

Committee: 1
Vote: 122 - 0 - 44
Ref.: 49/73, 48/73, 47/50, 46/32, 45/54, 44/111, 44/110, 43/69, 43/68, 42/32, 42/31, 41/52, 41/51, 40/86, 40/85, 39/58, 39/57, 38/68, 38/67, 37/81, 37/80, 36/95, 36/94, 35/155, 35/154, 34/86, 34/85

The General Assembly,

Bearing in mind the need to allay the legitimate concern of the States of the world with regard to ensuring lasting security for their peoples,

Convinced that nuclear weapons pose the greatest threat to mankind and to the survival of civilization,

Welcoming the progress achieved in recent years in both nuclear and conventional disarmament,

Noting that, despite recent progress in the field of nuclear disarmament, further efforts are necessary towards the achievement of the goal of general and complete disarmament under effective international control,

Also convinced that nuclear disarmament and the complete elimination of nuclear weapons are essential to remove the danger of nuclear war,

Determined strictly to abide by the relevant provisions of the Charter of the United Nations on the non-use of force or threat of force,

Recognizing that the independence, territorial integrity and sovereignty of non-nuclear-weapon States need to be safeguarded against the use or threat of use of force, including the use or threat of use of nuclear weapons,

Considering that, until nuclear disarmament is achieved on a universal basis, it is imperative for the international community to develop effective measures and arrangements to ensure the security of non-nuclear-weapon States against the use or threat of use of nuclear weapons from any quarter,

Recognizing also that effective measures and arrangements to assure the non-nuclear-weapon States against the use or threat of use of nuclear weapons can contribute positively to the prevention of the spread of nuclear weapons,

Bearing in mind paragraph 59 of the Final Document of the Tenth Special Session of the General Assembly,[5] the first special session devoted to disarmament, in which it urged the nuclear-weapon States to pursue efforts to conclude, as appropriate, effective arrangements to assure non-nuclear-weapon States against the use or threat of use of nuclear weapons, and desirous of promoting the implementation of the relevant provisions of the Final Document,

Recalling the relevant parts of the special report of the Committee on Disarmament,[6] submitted to the General Assembly at its twelfth special session,[7] the second special session devoted to disarmament, and of the special report of the Conference on Disarmament submitted to the Assembly at its fifteenth special session,[8] the third special

5 Resolution S-10/2.

6 The Committee on Disarmament was redesignated the Conference on Disarmament as from 7 February 1984.

7 *Official Records of the General Assembly, Twelfth Special Session. Supplement No. 2* (A/S-12/2), sect. III.C.

8 *Ibid., Fifteenth Special Session, Supplement No. 2* (A/S-15/2), sect. III.F.

session devoted to disarmament, as well as of the report of the Conference on its 1992 session,[1]

Recalling also paragraph 12 of the Declaration of the 1980s as the Second Disarmament Decade, contained in the annex to its resolution 35/46 of 3 December 1980, which states, *inter alia,* that all efforts should be exerted by the Committee on Disarmament urgently to negotiate with a view to reaching agreement on effective international arrangements to assure non-nuclear-weapon States against the use or threat of use of nuclear weapons,

Noting the in-depth negotiations undertaken in the Conference on Disarmament and its *Ad Hoc Committee* on Effective International Arrangements to Assure Non-Nuclear-Weapon States against the Use or Threat of Use of Nuclear Weapons,[2] with a view to reaching agreement on this item,

Taking note of the proposals submitted under that item in the Conference on Disarmament, including the drafts of an international convention,

Taken note of the relevant decision of the Eleventh Conference of Heads of State or Government of Non-Aligned Countries, held at Cartagena de Indias, Colombia, from 18 to 20 October 1995, and also of the decision adopted by the Tenth Conference of Heads of State or Government of Non-Aligned Countries, held at Jakarta from 1 to 6 September 1992,[3] as well as the relevant recommendations of the Organization of the Islamic Conference reiterated in the Final Communiqué of the Twentieth Islamic Conference of Foreign Ministers, held at Istanbul in August 1991,[4] calling upon the Conference on Disarmament to reach an urgent agreement on an international convention to assure non-nuclear-weapon States against the use or threat of use of nuclear weapons,

Taking note further of the unilateral declarations made by all nuclear-weapon States on their policies of non-use or non-threat of use of nuclear weapons against non-nuclear-weapon States,

Noting the support expressed in the Conference on Disarmament and in the General Assembly for the elaboration of an international convention to assure non-nuclear-weapon States against the use or threat of use of nuclear weapons, as well as the difficulties pointed out in evolving a common approach acceptable to all,

Noting also the greater willingness to overcome the difficulties encountered in previous years,

Noting further Security Council resolution 984 (1995) of 11 April 1995 and the views expressed on it,

Recalling its relevant resolutions adopted in previous years, in particular resolutions 45/54 of 4 December 1990, 46/32 of 6 December 1991, 47/50 of 9 December 1992, 48/73 of 16 December 1993 and 49/73 of 15 December 1994,

1. *Reaffirms* the urgent need to reach an early agreement on effective international arrangements to assure non-nuclear-weapon States against the use or threat of use of nuclear weapons;

2. *Notes with satisfaction* that in the Conference on Disarmament there is no objection, in principle, to the idea of an international convention to assure non-nuclear-weapon States against the use or threat of use of nuclear weapons, although the difficulties as regards evolving a common approach acceptable to all have also been pointed out;

3. *Appeals* to all States, especially the nuclear-weapon States, to work actively towards an early agreement on a common approach and, in particular, on a common formula that could be included in an international instrument of a legally binding character;

4. *Recommends* that further intensive efforts should be devoted to the search for such a common approach or common formula and that the various alternative approaches, including, in particular, those considered in the Conference on Disarmament, should be further explored in order to overcome the difficulties;

5. *Also recommends* that the Conference on Disarmament should actively continue intensive negotiations with a view to reaching early agreement and concluding effective international arrangements to assure non-nuclear-weapon States against the use or threat of use of nuclear weapons, taking into account the widespread support for the conclusion of an international convention and giving consideration to any other proposals designed to secure the same objective;

6. *Decides* to include in the provisional agenda of its fifty-first session the item entitled "Conclusion of effective international arrangements to assure non-nuclear-weapon States against the use or threat of use of nuclear weapons".

90th plenary meeting
12 December 1995

50/245. Comprehensive Nuclear-Test-Ban Treaty

Committee: -
Vote: 158 - 3 - 5
Ref.: 50/65, 49/70, 48/70, 47/47, 46/29, 45/51, 44/107, 43/64, 42, 27, 41/47, 40/81, 39/53, 38/63, 37/73, 3466(XXX), 3257(XXIX), 3078(XXVIII), 2934(XXVII), 2828(XXVI), 2663(XXV), 2604(XXIV), 2455(XXIII), 2343(XXII), 2163(XXI), 2032(XX), 1910(XVIII), 1762(XVII), 1649(XVI), 1648(XVI)

The General Assembly,

Recalling its resolution 50/65 of 12 December 1995, in which the Assembly declared its readiness to resume consideration of the item "Comprehensive test-ban treaty", as necessary, before its fifty-first session in order to endorse the text of a comprehensive nuclear-test-ban treaty,

1. *Adopts* the Comprehensive Nuclear-Test-Ban Treaty, as contained in document A/50/1027;

2. *Requests* the Secretary-General, as depositary of the Treaty, to open it for signature, at United Nations Headquarters, at the earliest possible date;

3. *Calls upon* all States to sign and, thereafter, according to their respective constitutional processes, to become parties to the Treaty at the earliest possible date;

4. *Also requests* the Secretary-General, as depositary of the Treaty, to report to the General Assembly at its fifty-second session on the status of signature and ratifications of the Treaty.

125th plenary meeting
10 September 1996

02.13 OTHER WEAPONS

3464 (XXX). Napalm and other Incendiary Weapons and all Aspects of their Possible Use

Committee: 1
Vote: Adopted without a vote
Ref.: 32/152, 31/64, 3255(XXIX), 3076(XVIII)

The General Assembly,

Convinced that the suffering of civilian populations and combatants could be significantly reduced if general agreement can be attained on the prohibition or restriction for humanitarian reasons of the use of specific conventional weapons, including any which may be deemed to be excessively injurious or to have indiscriminate effects,

Mindful that positive results in this regard are likely to facilitate subsequent substantive disarmament negotiations with a view to the

---

1 *Ibid., Forty-seventh Session, Supplement No. 27* (A/47/27), sect. III.F.

2 *Ibid., Forty-eighth Session, Supplement No. 27* (A/48/27), para. 39.

3 See A/47/675-S/24816, annex, chap. II, para. 47; see *Official Records of the Security Council, Forty-seventh Year, Supplement for October. November and December 1992.* document S/24816.

4 See A/46/486-S/23055, annex I; see *Official Records of the Security Council, Forty-sixth Year, Supplement for July, August and September 1991,* document S/23055.

elimination of production, stockpiling and proliferation of the weapons in question, which should be an ultimate objective,

Recalling that the issue of prohibitions or restrictions for humanitarian reasons of the use of specific conventional weapons has been the subject of serious and substantive discussion at the level of government experts at the Conference of Government Experts, held at Lucerne, from 24 September to 18 October 1974, under the auspices of the International Committee of the Red Cross and of government representatives at the Diplomatic Conference on the Reaffirmation and Development of International Humanitarian Law Applicable in Armed Conflicts and in the General Assembly,

Aware that the discussions, as well as the proposals and suggestions which have been advanced, have regard not only to napalm and other incendiary weapons but to a number of other specific kinds of conventional weapons, such as various small-calibre projectiles, certain blast and fragmentation weapons, as well as some delayed-action weapons and perfidious weapons,

Conscious of the need to continue discussion and for supplementary data to enable Governments to reach further conclusions and to seek broad agreement,

Noting with satisfaction that the issue will be before a second Conference of Government Experts, to be held under the auspices of the International Committee of the Red Cross at Lugano from 28 January to 26 February 1976, with a view to focusing on such weapons as have been or might become the subject of proposed bans or restrictions and to studying the possibility, contents and form of such proposed bans or restrictions and that, thereafter, the issue will come before the third session of the Diplomatic Conference on the Reaffirmation and Development of International Humanitarian Law Applicable in Armed Conflicts, to be held at Geneva from 21 April to 11 June 1976,

Trusting that this further work will be inspired by a sense of urgency and a wish to attain concrete results,

1. *Takes note* of the reports of the Secretary-General on the work of the Diplomatic Conference on the Reaffirmation and Development of International Humanitarian Law Applicable in Armed Conflicts as regards the work of the Conference relevant to the present resolution;[1]

2. *Invites* the Diplomatic Conference to continue its consideration of the use of specific conventional weapons, including any which may be deemed to be excessively injurious or to have indiscriminate effects, and its search for agreement for humanitarian reasons on possible rules prohibiting or restricting the use of such weapons;

3. *Requests* the Secretary-General, who has been invited to attend the Diplomatic Conference as an observer, to report to the General Assembly at its thirty-first session on aspects of the work of the Diplomatic Conference and of the Conference of Government Experts, to be held at Lugano, relevant to the present resolution;

4. *Decides* to include in the provisional agenda of its thirty-first session an item entitled "Incendiary and other specific conventional weapons which may be the subject of prohibitions or restrictions of use for humanitarian reasons".

2437th plenary meeting
11 December 1975

3475 (XXX). Prohibition of Action to Influence the Environment and Climate for Military and other Hostile Purposes, which are Incompatible with the Maintenance of International Security, Human Well-Being and Health

Committee: I
Vote: Adopted without a vote

The General Assembly,

Recalling that in its resolution 3264 (XXIX) of 9 December 1974 it requested the Conference of the Committee on Disarmament to proceed as soon as possible to achieving agreement on the text of a convention on the prohibition of action to influence the environment for military and other hostile purposes,

Convinced that the conclusion of such a convention would serve to spare mankind from the potential dangers of the use of environmental modification techniques for military and other hostile purposes, and thereby contribute to strengthening peace and averting the threat of war,

Convinced also that such a convention should not affect the use of environmental modification techniques for peaceful purposes, which should contribute to the preservation and improvement of the environment for the benefit of present and future generations,

Taking into account the report of the Conference of the Committee on Disarmament[2] as it relates to this question,

Noting with satisfaction that the delegations of the Union of Soviet Socialist Republics and the United States of America submitted at the Conference of the Committee on Disarmament identical drafts of a convention on the prohibition of military or any other hostile use of environmental modification techniques[3] and that other delegations offered suggestions and preliminary observations regarding those drafts,

1. *Requests* the Conference of the Committee on Disarmament to continue negotiations, bearing in mind existing proposals and suggestions as well as relevant discussion by the General Assembly, with a view to reaching early agreement, if possible during the 1976 session of the Conference, on the text of a convention on the prohibition of military or other hostile use of environmental modification techniques, and to submit a special report on the results achieved for consideration by the Assembly at its thirty-first session;

2. *Requests* the Secretary-General to transmit to the Conference of the Committee on Disarmament all documents relating to the discussion by the General Assembly at its thirtieth session of the item entitled "Prohibition of action to influence the environment and climate for military and other hostile purposes, which are incompatible with the maintenance of international security, human well-being and health";

3. *Decides* to include in the provisional agenda of its thirty-first session an item entitled "Convention on the prohibition of military or any other hostile use of environmental modification techniques: report of the Conference of the Committee on Disarmament".

2437th plenary meeting
11 December 1975

3479 (XXX). Prohibition of the Development and Manufacture of New Types of Weapons of Mass Destruction and New Systems of Such Weapons

Committee: I
Vote: 112 - 1 - 15
Ref.: 48/61, 45/66, 43/72, 40/90, 39/96, 38/182, 37/77, 36/89, 35/149, 34/75, 33/66, 32/84, 31/74

The General Assembly,

Striving to strengthen international peace and security,

Conscious of the interest of nations in continuing efforts to save mankind from the danger of the use of new means of mass destruction, to limit the arms race and to bring about disarmament,

Bearing in mind that modern science and technology have reached a level where a serious danger arises of the development of new, still more destructive types of weapons of mass destruction and of new systems of such weapons,

Convinced that the prohibition of the development and manufacture of new, still more destructive types of weapons of mass destruction would serve the goal of strengthening peace and preventing the threat of war,

---

1 A/10195 and Corr.1, A/10222.

2 *Official Records of the General Assembly, Thirtieth Session, Supplement No. 27* (A/10027).

3 *Ibid.*, annex II, documents CCD/471 and CCD/472.

1. *Considers it necessary* to take effective steps, by concluding an appropriate international treaty or agreement, for the prohibition of the development and manufacture of new types of weapons of mass destruction and new systems of such weapons;

2. *Takes note* of the draft agreement on the prohibition of the development and manufacture of new types of weapons of mass destruction and new systems of such weapons, submitted to the General Assembly by the Union of Soviet Socialist Republics, the text of which is annexed to the present resolution, as well as points of view and suggestions put forward during the discussion of this question;

3. *Requests* the Conference of the Committee on Disarmament to proceed as soon as possible, with the assistance of qualified governmental experts, to work out the text of such an agreement and to submit a report on the results achieved for consideration by the General Assembly at its thirty-first session;

4. *Requests* the Secretary-General to transmit to the Conference of the Committee on Disarmament all documents relating to the discussion by the General Assembly at its thirtieth session of the item entitled "Prohibition of the development and manufacture of new types of weapons of mass destruction and new systems of such weapons";

5. *Decides* to include in the provisional agenda of its thirty-first session the item entitled "Prohibition of the development and manufacture of new types of weapons of mass destruction and new systems of such weapons".

2437th plenary meeting
11 December 1975

Annex

Union of Soviet Socialist Republics Draft Agreement on the Prohibition of the Development and Manufacture of new Types of Weapons of Mass Destruction and new Systems of such Weapons

The States Parties to this agreement,

Guided by the interests of strengthening international peace and security,

Desiring to contribute to saving mankind from the danger of the use of new means of warfare, to limiting the arms race and to bringing about disarmament,

Recognizing that modern science and technology have reached a level where a serious danger arises of the development of new, still more destructive types of weapons of mass destruction and of new systems of such weapons,

Conscious that the development and manufacture of such weapons are fraught with the most serious consequences for the peace and security of nations,

Bearing in mind that recent years have seen the conclusion of a number of important agreements concerning limitation of the arms race and disarmament, including those related to the prohibition of weapons of mass destruction,

Expressing the profound interest of States and peoples in the adoption of measures to prevent the use of the achievements of modern science and technology for the development and manufacture of the above-mentioned weapons of mass destruction,

Desiring to promote the strengthening of confidence among nations and the further improvement of the international situation,

Seeking to contribute to the realization of the lofty purposes and principles of the Charter of the United Nations,

Having agreed on the following:

Article I

1. Each State Party to this Agreement undertakes not to develop or manufacture new types of weapons of mass destruction or new systems of such weapons, including those utilizing the latest achievements of modern science and technology. New types of weapons of mass destruction and new systems of such weapons shall include (to be specified through negotiations on the subject).

2. In the event that new areas of development and manufacture of weapons of mass destruction and systems of such weapons not covered by this Agreement emerge after the entry into force of the Agreement, the Parties shall conduct negotiations with a view to extending the prohibition provided for in this Agreement to cover such potential new types and systems of weapons.

3. Each State Party to this Agreement undertakes not to assist, encourage or induce any other State, group of States or international organizations to engage in activities contrary to the provisions of paragraph 1 of this article.

Article II

Each State Party to this Agreement undertakes, in accordance with its constitutional procedures, to take the necessary measures to prohibit and prevent any activities contrary to the provisions of this Agreement within the territory of such State or in any territory under its jurisdiction or under its control, wherever it may be.

Article III

1. In the event that any State Party to this Agreement has any suspicions that another State Party has violated the provisions of this Agreement, the Parties concerned undertake to consult one another and cooperate in solving the problems which arise.

2. If the consultations referred to in paragraph 1 of this article fail to produce results mutually acceptable to the Parties concerned, the State which has such suspicions may lodge a complaint with the Security Council of the United Nations.

Such complaint must include evidence confirming its validity, as well as a request for its consideration by the Security Council.

3. Each State Party to this Agreement undertakes to cooperate in carrying out any investigation which the Security Council may initiate, in accordance with the provisions of the Charter of the United Nations, on the basis of the complaint received by the Council. The Security Council shall inform the States Parties to the Agreement of the results of the investigation.

4. Each State Party to this Agreement undertakes to provide or support assistance, in accordance with the Charter of the United Nations, to any State Party to the Agreement which so requests, if the Security Council decides that such State Party has been exposed to danger as a result of violation of the Agreement.

Article IV

1. Nothing in this Agreement shall be interpreted as affecting the inalienable right of all the States Parties to the Agreement to develop and use scientific research and discoveries exclusively for peaceful purposes without any discrimination.

2. The States Parties to this Agreement undertake to facilitate scientific and technological cooperation in the use of the latest achievements and discoveries of science and technology for peaceful purposes.

Article V

Each State Party to this Agreement undertakes to pursue in good faith negotiations on effective measures to limit the arms race in all its forms and put an end to it, as well as on a treaty on general and complete disarmament under strict and effective international control.

Article VI

1. Any State Party may propose amendments to this Agreement. Each proposed amendment shall be submitted to the depositary Governments and circulated by them to all Parties to the Agreement, which shall inform the depositary Governments of acceptance or rejection as soon as possible after its receipt.

2. The amendment shall enter into force for each State Party accepting the amendment upon its acceptance by a majority of the States Parties to the Agreement, including the depositary Governments, and thereafter for each remaining State Party on the date of its acceptance of the amendment.

Article VII

1. This Agreement shall be of unlimited duration.

2. Each State Party to this Agreement shall, in the exercise of its national sovereignty, have the right to withdraw from the Agreement if it decides that extraordinary circumstances, connected with the subject-matter of this Agreement, have jeopardized its supreme interests. It shall give notice of such withdrawal to all other States Parties to the Agreement and to the Security Council of the United Nations three months in advance. Such notice shall include a statement of the extraordinary circumstances which it regards as having jeopardized its supreme interests.

Article VIII

1. This Agreement shall be open to all States for signature. Any State which does not sign the Agreement before its entry into force in accordance with paragraph 3 of this article may accede to it at any time.

2. This Agreement shall be subject to ratification by signatory States. Instruments of ratification and accession shall be deposited with the Governments of ......, which are hereby designated the depositary Governments.

3. This Agreement shall enter into force upon the deposit of the instruments of ratification by .... Governments including the Governments designated the depositary Governments of the Agreement.

4. For States whose instruments of ratification or accession are deposited subsequent to the entry into force of this Agreement, it shall enter into force on the date of the deposit of their instruments of ratification or accession.

5. The depositary Governments shall promptly inform all signatory and acceding States of the date of each signature, the date of deposit of each instrument of ratification or accession and the date of the entry into force of this Agreement and of the receipt of other notices.

6. This Agreement shall be registered by the depositary Governments pursuant to Article 102 of the Charter of the United Nations.

Article IX

This Agreement, the Chinese, English, French, Russian and Spanish texts of which are equally authentic, shall be deposited in the archives of the depositary Governments. Duly certified copies of the Agreement shall be transmitted by the depository Governments to the Governments of the signatory and acceding States.

IN WITNESS WHEREOF the undersigned, duly authorized for the purpose, have signed this Agreement.

DONE in .... copies, at ..... on the .... day of ...., ...

02.20 PEACE-KEEPING AND OTHER OPERATIONS

377 (V). Uniting for Peace

Committee: 1
Vote: 52 - 5 - 2

A

The General Assembly,

Recognizing that the first two stated Purposes of the United Nations are:

> "To maintain international peace and security, and to that end: to take effective collective measures for the prevention and removal of threats to the peace, and for the suppression of acts of aggression or other breaches of the peace, and to bring about by peaceful means, and in conformity with the principles of justice and international law, adjustment or settlement of international disputes or situations which might lead to a breach of the peace", and
>
> "To develop friendly relations among nations based on respect for the principle of equal rights and self-determination of peoples, and to take other appropriate measures to strengthen universal peace",

Reaffirming that it remains the primary duty of all Members of the United Nations, when involved in an international dispute, to seek settlement of such a dispute by peaceful means through the procedures laid down in Chapter VI of the Charter, and recalling the successful achievements of the United Nations in this regard on a number of previous occasions,

Finding that international tension exists on a dangerous scale,

Recalling its resolution 290 (IV) entitled "Essentials of peace", which states that disregard of the Principles of the Charter of the United Nations is primarily responsible for the continuance of international tension, and desiring to contribute further to the objectives of that resolution,

Reaffirming the importance of the exercise by the Security Council of its primary responsibility for the maintenance of international peace and security, and the duty of the permanent members to seek unanimity and to exercise restraint in the use of the veto,

Reaffirming that the initiative in negotiating the agreements for armed forces provided for in Article 43 of the Charter belongs to the Security Council, and desiring to ensure that, pending the conclusion of such agreements, the United Nations has at its disposal means for maintaining international peace and security,

Conscious that failure of the Security Council to discharge its responsibilities on behalf of all the Member States, particularly those responsibilities referred to in the two preceding paragraphs, does not relieve Member States of their obligations or the United Nations of its responsibility under the Charter to maintain international peace and security,

Recognizing in particular that such failure does not deprive the General Assembly of its rights or relieve it of its responsibilities under the Charter in regard to the maintenance of international peace and security,

Recognizing that discharge by the General Assembly of its responsibilities in these respects calls for possibilities of observation which would ascertain the fact and expose aggressors; for the existence of armed forces which could be used collectively; and for the possibility of timely recommendation by the General Assembly to Members of the United Nations for collective action which, to be effective, should be prompt,

A

1. *Resolves* that if the Security Council, because of lack of unanimity of the permanent members, fails to exercise its primary responsibility for the maintenance of international peace and security in any case when there appears to be a threat to the peace, breach of the peace, or act of aggression, the General Assembly shall consider the matter immediately with a view to making appropriate recommendations to Members for collective measures, including in the case of a breach of the peace or act of aggression the use of armed force where necessary, to maintain or restore international peace and security. If not in session at the time, the General Assembly may meet in emergency special session within twenty-four hours of the request therefor. Such emergency special session shall be called if requested by the Security Council on the vote of any seven members, or by a majority of the Members of the United Nations;

2. *Adopts* for this purpose the amendments to its rules of procedure set forth in the annex to the present resolution;

B

3. *Establishes* a Peace Observation Commission which, for the calendar years 1951 and 1952, shall be composed of fourteen Members, namely: China, Colombia, Czechoslovakia, France, India, Iraq, Israel, New Zealand, Pakistan, Sweden, the Union of Soviet Socialist Republics, the United Kingdom of Great Britain and Northern Ire-

land, the United States of America and Uruguay, and which could observe and report on the situation in any area where there exists international tension the continuance of which is likely to endanger the maintenance of international peace and security. Upon the invitation or with the consent of the State into whose territory the Commission would go, the General Assembly, or the Interim Committee when the Assembly is not in session, may utilize the Commission if the Security Council is not exercising the functions assigned to it by the Charter with respect to the matter in question. Decisions to utilize the Commission shall be made on the affirmative vote of two-thirds of the members present and voting. The Security Council may also utilize the Commission in accordance with its authority under the Charter;

4. *Decides* that the Commission shall have authority in its discretion to appoint sub-commissions and to utilize the services of observers to assist it in the performance of its functions;

5. *Recommends* to all governments and authorities that they cooperate with the Commission and assist it in the performance of its functions;

6. *Requests* the Secretary-General to provide the necessary staff and facilities, utilizing, where directed by the Commission, the United Nations Panel of Field Observers envisaged in General Assembly resolution 297 B (IV);

C

7. *Invites* each Member of the United Nations to survey its resources in order to determine the nature and scope of the assistance it may be in a position to render in support of any recommendations of the Security Council or of the General Assembly for the restoration of international peace and security;

8. *Recommends* to the States Members of the United Nations that each Member maintain within its national armed forces elements so trained, organized and equipped that they could promptly be made available, in accordance with its constitutional processes, for service as a United Nations unit or units, upon recommendation by the Security Council or the General Assembly, without prejudice to the use of such elements in exercise of the right of individual or collective self-defence recognized in Article 51 of the Charter;

9. *Invites* the Members of the United Nations to inform the Collective Measures Committee provided for in paragraph 11 as soon as possible of the measures taken in implementation of the preceding paragraph;

10. *Requests* the Secretary-General to appoint, with the approval of the Committee provided for in paragraph 11, a panel of military experts who could be made available, on request, to Member States wishing to obtain technical advice regarding the organization, training, and equipment for prompt service as United Nations units of the elements referred to in paragraph 8;

D

11. *Establishes* a Collective Measures Committee consisting of fourteen Members, namely: Australia, Belgium, Brazil, Burma, Canada, Egypt, France, Mexico, Philippines, Turkey, the United Kingdom of Great Britain and Northern Ireland, the United States of America, Venezuela and Yugoslavia, and directs the Committee, in consultation with the Secretary-General and with such Member States as the Committee finds appropriate, to study and make a report to the Security Council and the General Assembly, not later than 1 September 1951, on methods, including those in section C of the present resolution, which might be used to maintain and strengthen international peace and security in accordance with the Purposes and Principles of the Charter, taking account of collective self-defence and regional arrangements (Articles 51 and 52 of the Charter);

12. *Recommends* to all Member States that they cooperate with the Committee and assist it in the performance of its functions;

13. *Requests* the Secretary-General to furnish the staff and facilities necessary for the effective accomplishment of the purposes set forth in sections C and D of the present resolution;

14. *Is fully conscious* that, in adopting the proposals set forth above, enduring peace will not be secured solely by collective security arrangements against breaches of international peace and acts of aggression, but that a genuine and lasting peace depends also upon the observance of all the Principles and Purposes established in the Charter of the United Nations, upon the implementation of the resolutions of the Security Council, the General Assembly and other principal organs of the United Nations intended to achieve the maintenance of international peace and security, and especially upon respect for and observance of human rights and fundamental freedoms for all and on the establishment and maintenance of conditions of economic and social well-being in all countries; and accordingly

15. *Urges* Member States to respect fully, and to intensify, joint action, in cooperation with the United Nations, to develop and stimulate universal respect for and observance of human rights and fundamental freedoms, and to intensify individual and collective efforts to achieve conditions of economic stability and social progress, particularly through the development of under-developed countries and areas.

Annex

The rules of procedure of the General Assembly are amended in the following respects:

1. The present text of rule 8 shall become paragraph (*a*) of that rule, and a new paragraph (*b*) shall be added to read as follows:

"Emergency special sessions pursuant to resolution 377 A (V) shall be convened within twenty-four hours of the receipt by the Secretary-General of a request for such a session from the Security Council, on the vote of any seven members thereof, or of a request from a majority of the Members of the United Nations expressed by vote in the Interim Committee or otherwise, or of the concurrence of a majority of Member as provided in rule 9."

2. The present text of rule 9 shall become paragraph (a) of that rule and a new paragraph (b) shall be added to read as follows:

"This rule shall apply also to a request by any Member for an emergency special session pursuant to resolution 377 A (V). In such a case the Secretary-General shall communicate with other Members by the most expeditious means of communication available."

3. Rule 10 is amended by adding at the end thereof the following:

"... In the case of an emergency special session convened pursuant to rule 8 (*b*), the Secretary-General shall notify the Members of the United Nations at least twelve hours in advance of the opening of the session."

4. Rule 16 is amended by adding at the end thereof the following:

"... The provisional agenda of an emergency special session shall be communicated to the Members of the United Nations simultaneously with the communication summoning the session."

5. Rule 19 is amended by adding at the end thereof the following:

"... During an emergency special session additional items concerning the matters dealt with in resolution 377 A (V) may be added to the agenda by a two-thirds majority of the Members present and voting."

6. There is added a new rule to precede rule 65 to read as follows:

"Notwithstanding the provisions of any other rule and unless the General Assembly decides otherwise, the Assembly, in case of an emergency special session, shall convene in plenary session only and proceed directly to consider the item proposed for consideration in the request for the holding of the session, without previous reference to the General Committee or to any other Committee, the President and Vice-Presidents for such emergency special sessions shall be, respectively, the Chairman of those delegations from which were elected the President and Vice-Presidents of the previous session."

302nd plenary meeting
3 November 1950

B

For the purpose of maintaining international peace and security, in accordance with the Charter of the United Nations, and, in particular, with Chapters V, VI and VII of the Charter,

The General Assembly,

Recommends to the Security Council:

That it should take the necessary steps to ensure that the action provided for under the Charter is taken with respect to threats to the peace, breaches of the peace or acts of aggression and with respect to the peaceful settlement of disputes or situations likely to endanger the maintenance of international peace and security;

That it should devise measures for the earliest application of Articles 43, 45, 46 and 47 of the Charter of the United Nations regarding the placing of armed forces at the disposal of the Security Council by the States Members of the United Nations and the effective functioning of the Military Staff Committee;

The above dispositions should in no manner prevent the General Assembly from fulfilling its functions under resolution 377 A (V).

302nd plenary meeting
3 November 1950

C

The General Assembly,

Recognizing that the primary function of the United Nations Organization is to maintain and promote peace, security and justice among all nations,

Recognizing the responsibility of all Member States to promote the cause of international peace in accordance with their obligations as provided in the Charter,

Recognizing that the Charter charges the Security Council with the primary responsibility for maintaining international peace and security,

Reaffirming the importance of unanimity among the permanent members of the Security Council on all problems which are likely to threaten world peace,

Recalling General Assembly resolution 190 (III) entitled "Appeal to the Great Powers to renew their efforts to compose their differences and establish a lasting peace",

Recommends to the permanent members of the Security Council that:

(*a*) They meet and discuss, collectively or otherwise, and, if necessary, with other States concerned, all problems which are likely to threaten international peace and hamper the activities of the United Nations, with a view to their resolving fundamental differences and reaching agreement in accordance with the spirit and letter of the Charter;

(*b*) They advise the General Assembly and, when it is not in session, the Members of the United Nations, as soon as appropriate, of the results of their consultations.

302nd plenary meeting
3 November 1950

503 (VI). Methods which Might be Used to Maintain and Strengthen International Peace and Security in Accordance with the Purposes and Principles of the Charter

Committee: 1
Vote: A: 51 - 5 - 3; B: 57 - 0 - 2
Ref.: 809(IX), 703(VII)

A

The General Assembly,

Reaffirming that it is one of the foremost Purposes of the United Nations to "take effective collective measures for the prevention and removal of threats to the peace and for the suppression of acts of aggression or other breaches of the peace",

Recognizing that the establishment of an effective collective security system is in harmony with other United Nations Purposes and Principles as embodied in the Charter, in particular those relating to the pacific settlement of disputes, which must be fulfilled if an enduring peace is to be secured,

Reaffirming its desire, as expressed in its resolution 377 A (V) entitled "Uniting for peace", to ensure that the United Nations has at its disposal means for maintaining international peace and security pending the conclusion of agreements provided for in Article 43 of the Charter,

Recognizing that the ability and readiness of States to contribute armed forces and other assistance and facilities in support of United Nations collective action are essential to an effective security system,

Having received the report[1] of the Collective Measures Committee rendered in accordance with paragraph 11 of resolution 377 A (V),

Noting the responses[2] from Member States to its recommendation contained in that resolution that they maintain elements within their national armed forces which could be made available for United Nations service,

Convinced, moreover, that additional action should be taken by States and further study undertaken by the United Nations for the establishment of an effective system of collective security under the authority of the United Nations,

Recognizing that regional and collective self-defence arrangements concluded in accordance with the terms of the Charter can and should constitute an important contribution to the universal collective security system of the United Nations,

Recognizing that United Nations collective action, to be most effective, should be as nearly universal as possible and that in the event of need States not Members of the United Nations should unite their strength with that of the United Nations to maintain international peace and security in accordance with the Purposes and Principles of the Charter,

1. *Takes note* of the report of the Collective Measures Committee and of its conclusions and expresses its appreciation of the Committee's constructive work in the study of collective security;

2. *Recommends* to Member States that, in accordance with paragraph 8 of resolution 377 A (V), each take such further action as is necessary to maintain within its national armed forces elements so trained, organized and equipped that they could promptly be made available, in accordance with its constitutional processes and to the extent to which in its judgment its capacity permits it to do so, for service as a United Nations unit or units without prejudice to the use of such elements in exercise of the right of individual or collective self-defence recognized in Article 51 of the Charter and without prejudice likewise to internal security;

3. *Recommends* to Member States that they take such steps as are necessary to enable them, in accordance with their constitutional processes and to the extent to which in their judgment their capacity permits them to do so, to provide assistance and facilities to United Nations armed forces engaged in collective military measures undertaken by the Security Council or by the General Assembly;

4. *Recommends* to Member States that they determine, in the light of their existing legislation, the appropriate steps for carrying out promptly and effectively United Nations collective measures in accordance with their constitutional processes;

5. *Recommends* to Member States that they continue the survey of their resources provided for in paragraph 7 of resolution 377 A (V);

6. *Recommends* to Members of the United Nations which belong to other international bodies, or which are parties to international arrangements concluded in accordance with the Charter, that, in addition to their individual participation in the collective security system of the United Nations, they seek to obtain, when appropriate, in and through such bodies and arrangements within the constitutional limitations and the other provisions of those bodies and arrangements, all possible support for collective measures undertaken by the United Nations;

---

1 See *Official Records of the General Assembly, Sixth Session, Supplement No. 13.*

2 *Ibid.*

7. *Invites* States not Members of the United Nations to take note of the report of the Collective Measures Committee and consider ways and means, in the economic as well as in other fields, whereby they could contribute most effectively to collective measures undertaken by the United Nations in accordance with the Purposes and Principles of the Charter;

8. *Requests* the Secretary-General to appoint as soon as possible the members of the panel of military experts provided for in paragraph 10 of resolution 377 A (V), to the end that they can be made available on request to States wishing to obtain technical advice regarding the training, organization and equipment of the United Nations units referred to in paragraph 2 above;

9. *Directs* the Collective Measures Committee, in consultation with the Secretary-General and with such States as the Committee finds appropriate, to continue for another year its studies on methods which might be used to maintain and strengthen international peace and security in accordance with the Purposes and Principles of the Charter, taking account of both regional and collective self-defence arrangements, and to report thereon to the Security Council and to the General Assembly before the seventh session of the General Assembly;

10. *Recognizes* that nothing in the present resolution shall be construed to permit any measures to be taken in any State without the free and express consent of that State.

359th plenary meeting
12 January 1952

B

The General Assembly,

Considering that a basic task of the United Nations is to secure and strengthen international peace and security, and bearing in mind that under the Charter the main responsibility for the maintenance of international peace and security has been conferred on the Security Council,

Recommends that the Security Council, in accordance with Article 28 of the Charter, should convene a periodic meeting to consider what measures might ensure the removal of the tension at present existing in international relations and the establishment of friendly relations between countries whenever such a meeting would usefully serve to remove such tension and establish such friendly relations in furtherance of the Purposes and Principles of the Charter.

359th plenary meeting
12 January 1952

1874 (S-IV). General Principles to Serve as Guide Lines for the Sharing of the Costs of Future Peace-Keeping Operations Involving Heavy Expenditures

Committee: 5
Vote: 92 - 11 - 3
Ref.: 382(V), 288(IV), 193(III), 109(II)

The General Assembly,

Noting with appreciation the report of the Working Group on the Examination of the Administrative and Budgetary Procedures of the United Nations,[1] submitted pursuant to General Assembly resolution 1854 B (XVII) of 19 December 1962,

Recognizing the necessity of sharing equitably the financial burden of peace-keeping operations to the extent not otherwise covered by agreed arrangements,

1. *Affirms* that the following principles, *inter alia*, shall serve as guidelines for the equitable sharing, by assessed or voluntary contributions or a combination thereof, of the costs of peace-keeping operations involving heavy expenditures that may be initiated in the future:

(*a*) The financing of such operations is the collective responsibility of all States Members of the United Nations;

(*b*) Whereas the economically more developed countries are in a position to make relatively larger contributions, the economically less developed countries have a relatively limited capacity to contribute towards peace-keeping operations involving heavy expenditures;

(*c*) Without prejudice to the principle of collective responsibility, every effort should be made to encourage voluntary contributions from Member States;

(*d*) The special responsibilities of the permanent members of the Security Council for the maintenance of peace and security should be borne in mind in connexion with their contributions to the financing of peace and security operations;

(*e*) Where circumstances warrant, the General Assembly should give special consideration to the situation of any Member States which are victims of, and those which are otherwise involved in, the events or actions leading to a peace-keeping operation;

2. *Considers* that suitable administrative procedures should be established to ensure that provision for the financing of a peace-keeping operation is made by the General Assembly at the time the operation is authorized;

3. *Requests* the Secretary-General to review in consultation with the Advisory Committee on Administrative and Budgetary Questions, as appropriate, suitable administrative procedures designed to improve the financial procedures to be followed by the General Assembly at the time peace-keeping operations are authorized, and to report to the Assembly at its eighteenth session on the results of this review and any recommendations he may wish to make regarding procedures to be followed in the future.

1205th plenary meeting
27 June 1963

46/59. Declaration on Fact-Finding by the United Nations in the Field of the Maintenance of International Peace and Security

Committee: 6
Vote: Adopted without a vote
Ref.: 2329(XXII), 2128(XXI), 2104(XX), 1967(XVIII)

The General Assembly,

Recalling its resolutions 43/170 of 9 December 1988, 44/37 of 4 December and 45/44 of 28 November 1990,

Taking note of the report of the Special Committee on the Charter of the United Nations and on the Strengthening of the Role of the Organization,[2] which met in New York from 4 to 22 February 1991 and completed a draft Declaration on Fact-finding by the United Nations in the Field of the Maintenance of International Peace and Security,

Convinced that the adoption of the draft Declaration will contribute to strengthening the role of the United Nations and enhancing its effectiveness in maintaining international peace and security,

Considering the need to ensure a wide dissemination of the text of the Declaration,

Considering the Declaration to be an important and concrete contribution of the Special Committee to the United Nations Decade of International Law,

1. *Approves* the Declaration on Fact-finding by the United Nations in the Field of the Maintenance of International Peace and Security, the text of which is annexed to the present resolution;

2. *Expresses* its appreciation to the Special Committee on the Charter of the United Nations and on the Strengthening of the Role of the organization for its important contribution to the elaboration of the text of the Declaration;

3 *Requests* the Secretary-General to inform the Governments of the States Members of the United Nations or members of specialized

---

1 *Official Records of the General Assembly, Forty-sixth Session*, agenda item 7, document A/5407.

2 *Official Records of the General Assembly, Fourth Special Session, Supplement No. 33* and corrigendum (A/46/33 and Corr. 1).

agencies, and the Security Council, of the adoption of the Declaration;

4. *Urges* that all efforts be made so that the Declaration becomes generally known and fully implemented.

67th plenary meeting
9 December 1991

Annex

Declaration on Fact-Finding by the United Nations in the Field of the Maintenance of International Peace and Security

The General Assembly,

Recalling the Declaration on Principles of International Law concerning Friendly Relations and Cooperation among States in accordance with the Charter of the United Nations,[1] the Manila Declaration on the Peaceful Settlement of International Disputes,[2] the Declaration on the Enhancement of the Effectiveness of the Principle of Refraining from the Threat or Use of Force in International Relations,[3] the Declaration on the Prevention and Removal of Disputes and Situations Which May Threaten International Peace and Security and on the Role of the United Nations in this Field,[4] and their provisions regarding fact-finding,

Emphasizing that the ability of the United Nations to maintain international peace and security depends to a large extent on its acquiring detailed knowledge about the factual circumstances of any dispute or situation, the continuance of which might threaten the maintenance of international peace and security (hereinafter, "disputes or situations"),

Recognizing that the full use and further improvement of the means for fact-finding of the United Nations could contribute to the strengthening of the role of the United Nations in the maintenance of international peace and security and promote the peaceful settlement of disputes, as well as the prevention and removal of threats to peace,

Desiring to encourage States to bear in mind the role that competent organs of the United Nations can play in ascertaining the facts in relation to disputes or situations,

Recognizing the particular usefulness of fact-finding missions that the competent United Nations organs may undertake in this respect,

Bearing in mind the experience and expertise acquired by the United Nations in the field of fact-finding missions,

Recognizing the need for States, in exercising their sovereignty, to cooperate with the relevant organs of the United Nations as regards fact-finding missions undertaken by them,

Seeking to contribute to the effectiveness of the United Nations, with a view to enhancing mutual understanding, trust and stability in the world,

Solemnly declares that:

I

1. In performing their functions in relation to the maintenance of international peace and security, the competent organs of the United Nations should endeavour to have full knowledge of all relevant facts. To this end they should consider undertaking fact-finding activities.

2. For the purpose of the present Declaration fact-finding means any activity designed to obtain detailed knowledge of the relevant facts of any dispute or situation which the competent United Nations organs need in order to exercise effectively their functions in relation to the maintenance of international peace and security.

3. Fact-finding should be comprehensive, objective, impartial and timely.

4. Unless a satisfactory knowledge of all relevant facts can be obtained through the use of the information-gathering capabilities of the Secretary-General or other existing means, the competent organ of the United Nations should consider resorting to a fact-finding mission.

5. In deciding if and when to undertake such a mission, the competent United Nations organs should bear in mind that the sending of a fact-finding mission can signal the concern of the Organization and should contribute to building confidence and defusing the dispute or situation while avoiding any aggravation of it.

6. The sending of a United Nations fact-finding mission to the territory of any State requires the prior consent of that State, subject to the relevant provisions of the Charter of the United Nations.

II

7. Fact-finding missions may be undertaken by the Security Council, the General Assembly and the Secretary-General, in the context of their respective responsibilities for the maintenance of international peace and security in accordance with the Charter.

8. The Security Council should consider the possibility of undertaking fact-finding to discharge effectively its primary responsibility for the maintenance of international peace and security in accordance with the Charter.

9. The Security Council should, wherever appropriate, consider the possibility of providing in its resolutions for recourse to fact-finding.

10. The General Assembly should consider the possibility of undertaking fact-finding for exercising effectively its responsibilities under the Charter for the maintenance of international peace and security.

11. The General Assembly should, wherever appropriate, consider the possibility of providing for recourse to fact-finding in its resolutions relevant to the maintenance of international peace and security.

12. The Secretary-General should pay special attention to using the United Nations fact-finding capabilities at an early stage in order to contribute to the prevention of disputes and situations.

13. The Secretary-General, on his own initiative or at the request of the States concerned, should consider undertaking a fact-finding mission when a dispute or a situation exists.

14. The Secretary-General should prepare and update lists of experts in various fields who would be available for fact-finding missions. He should also maintain and develop, within existing resources, capabilities for mounting emergency fact-finding missions.

15. The Security Council and the General Assembly should, in deciding to whom to entrust the conduct of a fact-finding mission, give preference to the Secretary-General, who may, *inter alia*, designate a special representative or a group of experts reporting to him. Resort to an *Ad Hoc* subsidiary body of the Security Council or the General Assembly may also be considered.

16. In considering the possibility of undertaking a fact-finding mission, the competent United Nations organ should bear in mind other relevant fact-finding efforts, including those undertaken by the States concerned and in the framework of regional arrangements or agencies.

17. The decision by the competent United Nations organ to undertake fact-finding should always contain a clear mandate for the fact-finding mission and precise requirements to be met by its report. The report should be limited to a presentation of findings of a factual nature.

18. Any request by a State to a competent organ of the United Nations for the sending of a United Nations fact-finding mission to its territory should be considered without undue delay.

III

19. Any request by a competent organ of the United Nations for the consent of a State to receive a fact-finding mission within its territory should be given timely consideration by that State. That State should inform the organ of its decision without delay.

20. In the event a State decides not to admit a United Nations fact-finding mission to its territory, it should, if it deems it appropriate,

1 Resolution 2625 (XXV), annex.
2 Resolution 37/10, annex.
3 Resolution 42/22, annex.
4 Resolution 43/51, annex.

indicate the reasons for its decision. It should also keep the possibility of admitting the fact-finding mission under review.

21. States should endeavour to follow a policy of admitting United Nations fact-finding missions to their territory.

22. States should cooperate with United Nations fact-finding missions and give them, within the limits of their capabilities, the full and prompt assistance necessary for the exercise of their functions and the fulfilment of their mandate.

23. Fact-finding missions should be accorded all immunities and facilities needed for discharging their mandate, in particular full confidentiality in their work and access to all relevant places and persons, it being understood that no harmful consequences will result to these persons. Fact-finding missions have an obligation to respect the laws and regulations of the State in which they exercise their functions; such laws and regulations should not however be applied in such a way as to hinder missions in the proper discharge of their functions.

24. The members of fact-finding missions, as a minimum, enjoy the privileges and immunities accorded to experts on missions by the Convention on the Privileges and Immunities of the United Nations. Without prejudice to their privileges and immunities, members of fact-finding missions have an obligation to respect the laws and regulations of the State in the territory in which they exercise their functions.

25. Fact-finding missions have an obligation to act in strict conformity with their mandate and perform their task in an impartial way. Their members have an obligation not to seek or receive instructions from any Government or from any authority other than the competent United Nations organ. They should keep the information acquired in discharging their mandate confidential even after the mission has fulfilled its task.

26. The States directly concerned should be given an opportunity, at all stages of the fact-finding process, to express their views in respect of the facts the fact-finding mission has been entrusted to obtain. When the results of fact-finding are to be made public, the views expressed by the States directly concerned should, if they so wish, also be made public.

27. Whenever fact-finding includes hearings, appropriate rules of procedure should ensure their fairness.

IV

28. The Secretary-General should monitor the state of international peace and security regularly and systematically in order to provide early warning of disputes or situations which might threaten international peace and security. The Secretary-General may bring relevant information to the attention of the Security Council and, where appropriate, of the General Assembly.

29. To this end, the Secretary-General should make full use of the information-gathering capabilities of the Secretariat and keep under review the improvement of these capabilities.

V

30. The sending of a United Nations fact-finding mission is without prejudice to the use by the States concerned of inquiry or any similar procedure or of any means of peaceful settlement of disputes agreed by them.

31. Nothing in the present Declaration is to be construed as prejudicing in any manner the provisions of the Charter.

47/120. An Agenda for Peace: Preventive Diplomacy and Related Matters

Committee: -
Vote: Adopted without a vote

The General Assembly,

Recalling the statement of 31 January 1992, adopted at the conclusion of the first meeting held by the Security Council at the level of Heads of State and Government,[1] in which the Secretary-General was invited to prepare, for circulation to the States Members of the United Nations by 1 July 1992, an "analysis and recommendations on ways of strengthening and making more efficient within the framework and provisions of the Charter the capacity of the United Nations for preventive diplomacy, for peacemaking and for peace-keeping",

Welcoming the timely presentation of the forward-looking report of the Secretary-General entitled "An Agenda for Peace",[2] in response to the summit meeting of the Security Council, as a set of recommendations that deserve close examination by the international community,

Recognizing the need to maintain the increased interest in and momentum for revitalization of the Organization to meet the challenges of the new phase of international relations in order to fulfil the purposes and principles of the Charter of the United Nations,

Stressing that the implementation of the concepts and proposals contained in "An Agenda for Peace" should be in strict conformity with the provisions of the Charter, in particular its purposes and principles,

Recalling also its resolution 2625 (XXV) of 24 October 1970, the annex to which contains the Declaration on Principles of International Law concerning Friendly Relations and Cooperation among States in accordance with the Charter of the United Nations, and its resolution 43/51 of 5 December 1988, the annex to which contains the Declaration on the Prevention and Removal of Disputes and Situations Which May Threaten International Peace and Security and on the Role of the United Nations in this Field,

Emphasizing that international peace and security must be seen in an integrated manner and that the efforts of the Organization to build peace, justice, stability and security must encompass not only military matters, but also, through its various organs within their respective areas of competence, relevant political, economic, social, humanitarian, environmental and developmental aspects,

Stressing the need for international action to strengthen the socio-economic development of Member States as one of the means of enhancing international peace and security and, in this regard, recognizing the need to complement "An Agenda for Peace" with "An Agenda for Development",

Acknowledging that timely application of preventive diplomacy is the most desirable and efficient means of easing tensions before they result in conflict,

Recognizing that preventive diplomacy may require such measures as confidence-building, early-warning, fact-finding and other measures in which consultations with Member States, discretion, confidentiality, objectivity and transparency should be combined as appropriate,

Emphasizing the need to strengthen the capacity of the United Nations in the field of preventive diplomacy, through, *inter alia*, allocating appropriate staff resources and financial resources for preventive diplomacy, in order to assist Member States to resolve their differences in a peaceful manner,

Reaffirming the fundamental importance of a sound and secure financial basis for the United Nations in order, *inter alia*, to enable the Organization to play an effective role in preventive diplomacy,

Emphasizing the importance of cooperation between the United Nations and regional arrangements and organizations for preventive diplomacy within their respective areas of competence,

Emphasizing also that respect for the principles of sovereignty, territorial integrity and political independence of States is crucial to any common endeavour to promote international peace and security,

Recalling further other resolutions adopted by the Assembly during its forty-seventh session concerning various aspects of "An Agenda for Peace",

Emphasizing the need for all organs and bodies of the United Nations, as appropriate, to intensify their efforts to strengthen the role of the Organization in preventive diplomacy, peacemaking, peace-

---

1 S/23500.

2 A/47/277-S/24111.

keeping and peace-building and to continue the discussion of the report of the Secretary-General with a view to adequate action being taken,

Stressing the need for adequate protection of personnel involved in preventive diplomacy, peacemaking, peace-keeping and humanitarian operations, in accordance with relevant norms and principles of international law,

Noting the definition of preventive diplomacy provided by the Secretary-General in his report entitled "An Agenda for Peace",[1]

I. Peaceful Settlement of Disputes

Emphasizing the need to promote the peaceful settlement of disputes,

1. *Invites* Member States to seek solutions to their disputes at an early stage through such peaceful means as provided for in the Charter of the United Nations;

2. *Decides* to explore ways and means for a full utilization of the provisions of the Charter whereby the General Assembly may recommend measures for the peaceful adjustment of any situation, regardless of origin, which is deemed likely to impair the general welfare or friendly relations among nations;

3. *Encourages* the Security Council to utilize fully the provisions of Chapter VI of the Charter on procedures and methods for peaceful settlement of disputes and to call upon the parties concerned to settle their disputes peacefully;

4. *Encourages* the Secretary-General and the Security Council to engage at an early stage in close and continuous consultation in order to develop, on a case-by-case basis, an appropriate strategy for the peaceful settlement of specific disputes, including the participation of other organs, organizations and agencies of the United Nations system, as well as regional arrangements and organizations as appropriate, and invites the Secretary-General to report to the General Assembly on such consultations;

II. Early Warning, Collection of Information and Analysis

Recognizing the need to strengthen the capacity of the United Nations for early-warning, collection of information and analysis,

1. *Encourages* the Secretary-General to set up an adequate early-warning mechanism for situations which are likely to endanger the maintenance of international peace and security, in close cooperation with Member States and United Nations agencies, as well as regional arrangements and organizations, as appropriate, making use of the information available to these organizations and/or received from Member States, and to keep Member States informed of the mechanism established;

2. *Invites* the Secretary-General to strengthen the capacity of the Secretariat for the collection of information and analysis to serve better the early-warning needs of the Organization and, to that end, encourages the Secretary-General to ensure that staff members receive proper training in all aspects of preventive diplomacy, including the collection and analysis of information;

3. *Invites* Member States and regional arrangements and organizations to provide timely early-warning information, on a confidential basis when appropriate, to the Secretary-General;

4. *Encourages* the Secretary-General to continue, in accordance with Article 99 of the Charter of the United Nations, to bring to the attention of the Security Council, at his discretion, any matter which in his opinion may threaten the maintenance of international peace and security, together with his recommendations thereon;

5. *Invites* Member States to support the efforts of the Secretary-General in preventive diplomacy, including by providing assistance he may require;

6. *Encourages* the Secretary-General, in accordance with the relevant provisions of the Charter, to notify the General Assembly, as appropriate, of any situation which is potentially dangerous or might lead to international friction or dispute;

7. *Invites* the Secretary-General to bring to the attention of Member States concerned, at an early stage, any matter which in his opinion may adversely affect relations between States;

III. Fact-Finding

Recalling the statements made by the President of the Security Council, on behalf of the Council, on 29 October[2] and 30 November 1992,[3] and its own resolutions 1967 (XVIII) of 16 December 1963, 2104 (XX) of 20 December 1965, 2182 (XXI) of 12 December 1966 and 2329 (XXII) of 18 December 1967 on the question of methods of fact-finding,

1. *Reaffirms* its resolution 46/59 of 9 December 1991, the annex to which contains the Declaration on Fact-Finding by the United Nations in the Field of the Maintenance of International Peace and Security, particularly its guidelines;

2. *Recommends* to the Secretary-General that he should continue to utilize the services of eminent and qualified experts in fact-finding and other missions, selected on as wide a geographical basis as possible, taking into account candidates with the highest standards of efficiency, competence and integrity;

3. *Invites* Member States to submit names of suitable individuals whom the Secretary-General might wish to use at his discretion in fact-finding and other missions;

4. *Recommends* that a request by a Member State for the dispatch of a fact-finding mission to its territory should be considered expeditiously;

5. *Invites* the Secretary-General to continue to dispatch fact-finding and other missions in a timely manner in order to assist him in the proper discharge of his functions under the Charter of the United Nations;

IV. Confidence-Building Measures

Recognizing that the application of appropriate confidence-building measures, consistent with national security needs, would promote mutual confidence and good faith, which are essential to reducing the likelihood of conflicts between States and enhancing prospects for the peaceful settlement of disputes,

Recalling its resolutions 43/78 H of 7 December 1988 and 45/62 F of 4 December 1990, as well as its resolution 47/54 D of 9 December 1992 on the implementation of the guidelines for appropriate types of confidence-building measures,

Recognizing that confidence-building measures may encompass both military and non-military matters, including political, economic and social matters,

Stressing the need to encourage Member States, and regional arrangements and organizations where relevant and in a manner consistent with their mandates, to play a leading role in developing confidence-building measures appropriate to the region concerned and to coordinate their efforts in this regard with the United Nations in accordance with Chapter VIII of the Charter of the United Nations,

1. *Invites* Member States and regional arrangements and organizations to inform the Secretary-General through appropriate channels about their experiences in confidence-building measures in their respective regions;

2. *Supports* the intention of the Secretary-General to consult on a regular basis with Member States and regional arrangements and organizations on further confidence-building measures;

3. *Encourages* the Secretary-General to consult with parties to existing or potential disputes, the continuance of which is likely to endanger the maintenance of international peace and security, and with other interested Member States and regional arrangements and organizations, as appropriate, on the possibility of initiating confidence-building measures in their respective regions and to keep Member States informed thereon in consultation with the parties concerned;

1 A/47/277-S/24111.

2 S/24728.

3 S/24872.

4. *Commends* such confidence-building measures as the promotion of openness and restraint in the production, procurement and deployment of armaments, the systematic exchange of military missions, the possible formation of regional risk reduction centres, arrangements for the free flow of information and the monitoring of regional arms control and disarmament agreements;

V. Humanitarian Assistance

Recalling its resolution 45/100 of 14 December 1990 on humanitarian assistance to victims of natural disasters and similar emergency situations and its resolution 46/182 of 19 December 1991 on the strengthening of the coordination of emergency humanitarian assistance of the United Nations,

Welcoming the increasing role of the United Nations system in providing humanitarian assistance,

Noting that, in certain circumstances, programmes of impartially-provided humanitarian assistance and peace-keeping operations can be mutually supportive,

1. *Encourages* the Secretary-General to continue to strengthen the capacity of the Organization in order to ensure coordinated planning and execution of humanitarian assistance programmes, drawing upon the specialized skills and resources of all parts of the United Nations system, as well as those of non-governmental organizations, as appropriate;

2. *Also encourages* the Secretary-General to continue to address the question of coordination, when necessary, between humanitarian assistance programmes and peace-keeping or related operations, preserving the non-political, neutral and impartial character of humanitarian action;

3. *Invites* the Secretary-General to bring to the attention of appropriate organs of the United Nations any situation requiring urgent humanitarian assistance in order to prevent its deterioration, which might lead to international friction or dispute;

VI. Resources and Logistical Aspects of Preventive Diplomacy

Recognizing the need for adequate resources in support of the United Nations efforts in preventive diplomacy,

1. *Invites* Member States to provide political and practical support to the Secretary-General in his efforts for the peaceful settlement of disputes, including early-warning, fact-finding, good offices and mediation;

2. *Also invites* Member States, on a voluntary basis, to provide the Secretary-General with any necessary additional expertise and logistical resources that he might require for the successful execution of these functions of increasing importance;

VII. Role of the General Assembly in Preventive Diplomacy

Emphasizing that, together with the Security Council and the Secretary-General, it has an important role in preventive diplomacy,

Recognizing that, having an important role in preventive diplomacy, it has to work in close cooperation and coordination with the Security Council and the Secretary-General in accordance with the Charter of the United Nations and consistent with their respective mandates and responsibilities,

Decides to explore ways and means to support the recommendations of the Secretary-General in his report entitled "An Agenda for Peace"[1] to promote the utilization of the General Assembly, in accordance with the relevant provisions of the Charter of the United Nations, by Member States so as to bring greater influence to bear in pre-empting or containing any situation which is potentially dangerous or might lead to international friction or dispute;

VIII. Future Work

Bearing in mind that owing to time constraints it could not examine all the proposals contained in the report of the Secretary-General entitled "An Agenda for Peace",

1. *Decides* to continue early in 1993 its examination of other recommendations on preventive diplomacy and related matters contained in the report of the Secretary-General entitled "An Agenda for Peace", including preventive deployment, demilitarized zones and the International Court of Justice, as well as implementation of the provisions of Article 50 of the Charter of the United Nations, in conformity with the Charter and taking into account the relevant developments and practices in the competent organs of the United Nations;

2. *Also decides* to discuss and consider other proposals contained in "An Agenda for Peace".

91st plenary meeting
18 December 1992

47/217. Establishment of a Peace-keeping Reserve Fund

Committee: 5
Vote: Adopted without a vote

The General Assembly,

Having considered with appreciation the report of the Secretary-General entitled "An agenda for peace",

Having considered with appreciation also the reports of the Secretary-General and the Advisory Committee on Administrative and Budgetary Questions,

Noting that the Organization is confronted with increasing demands and challenges in the area of peace-keeping operations,

Recognizing the unpredictable nature of peace-keeping operations and the consequent necessity of giving the Secretary-General adequate resources to respond in a timely manner to a crisis,

Recognizing also that it is essential to provide peace-keeping operations, especially in their start-up phases, with the necessary financial resources to enable the timely, full and effective implementation of their mandates,

Decides:

(*a*) To establish under the authority of the Secretary-General effective 1 January 1993 a Peace-keeping Reserve Fund as a cash flow mechanism to ensure the rapid response of the Organization to the needs of peace-keeping operations;

(*b*) To authorize the Secretary-General to advance from the Fund such sums as may be necessary to finance:

(i) Unforeseen and extraordinary expenses relating to peace-keeping operations within the commitment authority established by the General Assembly;

(ii) Budgetary appropriations, including start-up costs, approved by the General Assembly for new, expanded or renewed peace-keeping operations pending the collection of assessed contributions;

(*c*) That the advances authorized in accordance with subparagraph (b) above shall be reimbursed as soon as receipts from contributions are available for these purposes;

(*d*) That the level of the Fund shall be 150 million United States dollars;

(*e*) That Member States' shares of the Fund shall remain fixed and shall be calculated on the basis of the *Ad Hoc* apportionment as set out in General Assembly resolution 45/247 of 21 December 1990;

(*f*) That the Fund shall be financed as follows:

(i) By the transfer of the balance of the excess of income over expenditures in the special accounts for the United Nations Transition Assistance Group and the United Nations Iran-Iraq Military Observer Group after the credits to Member States have been applied in accordance with General Assembly resolutions 45/265 of 17 May 1991 and 47/206 and 47/207 of 22 December 1992, based on the latest rates of apportionment applied for the Transition Assistance Group and the Military Observer Group;

(ii) By the transfer of whatever portion of the amount of 154,881,112 dollars retained in the General Fund pursuant to

[1] A/47/277-S/24111.

General Assembly resolution 42/216 A of 21 December 1987 is needed for each Member State to reach its fixed share of the Peace-keeping Reserve Fund based on the *Ad Hoc* apportionment set out in Assembly resolution 45/247;

(*g*) That States which become Members of the United Nations following the date of the adoption of the present resolution and which do not have a claim to a share in the Fund shall contribute to the Fund in accordance with the scale of apportionment for peace-keeping operations in effect on the date of their first assessment for United Nations peace-keeping operations;

(*h*) That all outstanding contributions to the United Nations Transition Assistance Group and/or the United Nations Iran-Iraq Military Observer Group at the date of the final liquidation of these accounts shall be transferred as receivable assets to the Fund;

(i) (i) That the sum referred to in subparagraph (f) (i) above shall become credits available to Member States that have paid their assessed contributions in full to the United Nations Transition Assistance Group and/or the United Nations Iran-Iraq Military Observer Group upon the liquidation of the Fund;

(ii) That the sum referred to in subparagraph (f) (ii) above shall reduce the credits available to Member States in the General Fund by the amounts transferred to the Peace-keeping Reserve Fund and shall become credits to Member States which have no unpaid assessed contributions to the regular budget for the biennium 1986-1987, upon the liquidation of the Peace-keeping Reserve Fund;

(*j*) To address the issue of the imputation of interest income earned in the Fund at the earliest opportunity during its forty-seventh session;

(*k*) That the Fund shall be administered in accordance with the Financial Regulations and Rules of the United Nations, without prejudice to the funding of the activities of the regular budget;

(*l*) To request the Secretary-General to report on actions taken to implement the present resolution at the earliest opportunity during its forty-seventh session.

94th plenary meeting
23 December 1992

48/7. Assistance in Mine Clearance

Committee: -
Vote: Adopted without a vote
Ref.: 50/82, 49/215

The General Assembly,

Gravely alarmed by the increasing presence of mines and other unexploded devices resulting from armed conflicts,

Dismayed by the high number of victims of mines, especially among civilian populations, and taking note in this context of resolution 1993/83 of the Commission on Human Rights of 10 March 1993, on the effects of armed conflicts on children's lives,

Gravely concerned by the serious humanitarian, social, economic and ecological disruption which can be caused by the failure to remove mines and other unexploded devices,

Bearing in mind the serious threat which mines and other unexploded devices pose to the safety, the health and the lives of personnel participating in humanitarian, peace-keeping and rehabilitation operations,

Aware that mines constitute an obstacle to reconstruction and economic development as well as to the restoration of normal social conditions,

Considering that, in addition to the responsibilities incumbent upon States, there is scope for the United Nations to strengthen its contribution to the solution of problems relating to mine clearance,

Taking note with interest, in this regard, of the recommendations made by the Secretary-General in paragraph 58 of his report of 17 June 1992 entitled "An Agenda for Peace", as well as in his report of 15 June 1993,

Recalling its resolution 47/120 B of 20 September 1993 on the "Agenda for Peace",

Taking note of the statement made by the President of the Security Council on 26 February 1993,

Recalling also its resolution 47/56 of 9 December 1992 on the Convention on Prohibitions or Restrictions on the Use of Certain Conventional Weapons Which May Be Deemed to Be Excessively Injurious or to Have Indiscriminate Effects, and in particular on the Protocol on Prohibitions or Restrictions on the Use of Mines, Booby Traps and Other Devices (Protocol II),

Noting with interest, in this regard, the convening by the Secretary-General of a review conference to amend the above-mentioned Convention and in particular its Protocol II,

Noting with satisfaction the inclusion in the mandate of several peace-keeping operations of provisions relating to mine clearance,

Commending the activities already undertaken by the United Nations system, the International Committee of the Red Cross and non-governmental organizations to address the solution of problems relating to the presence of mines,

Welcoming the establishment, within the Secretariat, of a coordinated mine-clearance programme,

1. *Deplores* the adverse consequences which can be caused by the failure to remove mines and other unexploded devices remaining in place after armed conflicts, and considers it a matter of urgency to correct the situation;

2. *Stresses the importance* of coordination by the United Nations of activities, including those by regional organizations, related to mine clearance, in particular those activities relating to information and training with a view to improving the effectiveness of operations in the field;

3. *Invites* all relevant programmes and bodies, multilateral or national, to include, in a coordinated manner, activities related to mine clearance in their humanitarian, social and economic assistance activities;

4. *Requests* the Secretary-General to submit to the General Assembly, before its forty-ninth session, a comprehensive report on the problems caused by the increasing presence of mines and other unexploded devices resulting from armed conflicts and on the manner in which the United Nations contribution to the solution of problems relating to mine clearance could be strengthened;

5. *Also requests* the Secretary-General to include in his report consideration of the financial aspects of activities related to mine clearance and, in this context, of the advisability of establishing a voluntary trust fund to finance, in particular, information and training programmes relating to mine clearance and to facilitate the launching of mine-clearance operations;

6. *Urges* all Member States to extend full assistance and cooperation to the Secretary-General in this respect and to provide him with any information and data which could be useful in drawing up the above-mentioned report;

7. *Decides* to include in the provisional agenda of its forty-ninth session the item entitled "Assistance in mine clearance".

32nd plenary meeting
19 October 1993

48/210. Economic Assistance to States Affected by the Implementation of the Security Council Resolutions Imposing Sanctions Against the Federal Republic of Yugoslavia (Serbia and Montenegro)

Committee: 2
Vote: Adopted without a vote

The General Assembly,

Recalling the provisions of Articles 25, 48, 49 and 50 of the Charter of the United Nations,

Recalling also its resolution 47/120 B of 20 September 1993 entitled "An Agenda for Peace", and in particular section IV thereof,

Recalling further Security Council resolutions 713 (1991) of 25 September 1991, 724 (1991) of 15 December 1991, 757 (1992) of 30

May 1992, 787 (1992) of 16 November 1992, and 820 (1993) of 17 April 1993, in which the Council decided to impose an arms embargo against the territory of the former Socialist Federal Republic of Yugoslavia and a comprehensive set of trade and economic sanctions against the Federal Republic of Yugoslavia (Serbia and Montenegro),

Taking note of Security Council resolution 843 (1993) of 18 June 1993, in which the Council entrusted the Committee established pursuant to its resolution 724 (1991) concerning Yugoslavia with the task of examining requests for assistance under the provisions of Article 50 of the Charter, as well as other relevant resolutions,

Commending the efforts of the Security Council Committee established pursuant to resolution 724 (1991) aimed at improving the efficiency of its work,

Expressing concern at the special economic problems confronting States and in particular the States that border the Federal Republic of Yugoslavia (Serbia and Montenegro), the other Danube riparian States and other States in the region adversely affected by the severance of their economic relations with the Federal Republic of Yugoslavia (Serbia and Montenegro) and the disruption of traditional transport and communications links in that part of Europe,

Noting the information provided by States regarding the measures taken to give full effect to the sanctions as laid down in the relevant Security Council resolutions, as well as the information concerning the special economic problems they have been confronted with as a result of the implementation of those measures,

Recalling the recommendations adopted by the Security Council Committee established pursuant to resolution 724 (1991) with regard to the States confronted with special economic problems arising from the application of sanctions against the Federal Republic of Yugoslavia (Serbia and Montenegro) pursuant to Security Council resolutions 757 (1992), 787 (1992) and 820 (1993),

Recognizing that the continued full implementation of Security Council resolutions 713 (1991), 724 (1991), 757 (1992), 760 (1992) of 18 June 1992, 787 (1992) and 820 (1993) by all States will support measures to ensure compliance with these and other relevant resolutions,

Taking note of the report of the Secretary-General prepared pursuant to the note by the President of the Security Council regarding the question of special economic problems of States as a result of sanctions imposed under Chapter VII of the Charter,

1. *Commends* the States bordering on the Federal Republic of Yugoslavia (Serbia and Montenegro), the other Danube riparian States and all other States for the measures they have taken to comply with Security Council resolutions 713 (1991), 724 (1991), 757 (1992), 760 (1992), 787 (1992) and 820 (1993), and urges all States to continue to observe those resolutions strictly;

2. *Recognizes* the urgent need to assist States in coping with their special economic problems arising from the implementation of sanctions against the Federal Republic of Yugoslavia (Serbia and Montenegro), *inter alia*, through consideration of assistance for the promotion of the exports of the affected countries and for the promotion of investments in those countries;

3. *Supports* the recommendations of the Security Council Committee established pursuant to resolution 724 (1991) concerning Yugoslavia, in response to requests for assistance received by the Security Council from certain States confronting special economic problems under the provisions of Article 50 of the Charter of the United Nations, in which the Committee, *inter alia*:

(*a*) Appealed to all States on an urgent basis to provide immediate technical, financial and material assistance to the affected States to mitigate the adverse impact on their economies of the application by those States of sanctions against the Federal Republic of Yugoslavia (Serbia and Montenegro) pursuant to Security Council resolutions 757 (1992), 787 (1992) and 820 (1993);

(*b*) Invited the competent organs and specialized agencies of the United Nations system, including the international financial institutions and the regional development banks, to consider how their assistance programmes and facilities might be helpful to the affected States, with a view to alleviating their special economic problems arising from the application of sanctions against the Federal Republic of Yugoslavia (Serbia and Montenegro) pursuant to Security Council resolutions 757 (1992), 787 (1992) and 820 (1993);

4. *Appeals* to all States and invites the competent organs and specialized agencies of the United Nations system to fulfil these recommendations of the Security Council Committee established pursuant to resolution 724 (1991);

5. *Requests* the Secretary-General to seek on a regular basis information from States and the concerned organs and agencies of the United Nations system on action taken to alleviate the special economic problems of the affected States and to report thereon to the Security Council, as well as to submit a report on the implementation of the present resolution to the General Assembly at its forty-ninth session.

86th plenary meeting
21 December 1993

49/37. Comprehensive Review of the Whole Question of Peace-keeping Operations in all their Aspects

Committee: 4
Vote: Adopted without a vote
Ref.: 50/30, 48/42, 47/72, 46/48, 45/75, 44/49, 43/59, 42/161, 41/67, 40/163, 39/97, 38/81, 37/93, 36/37, 35/121, 34/53, 33/114, 32/106, 31/105, 3457(XXX), 3239(XXIX), 3091(XXVIII), 2965(XXVII), 2835(XXVI), 2670(XXV), 2576(XXIV), 2451(XXIII), 2308(XXII), 2249(S-V), 2220(XXI), 2053

The General Assembly,

Recalling its resolution 2006 (XIX) of 18 February 1965 and all other relevant resolutions,

Recalling in particular its resolutions 48/42 and 48/43 of 10 December 1993,

Welcoming the progress made by the Special Committee on Peace-keeping Operations during its recent sessions,

Convinced that peace-keeping operations constitute a considerable part of the efforts by the United Nations to maintain international peace and security and to enhance the effectiveness of the United Nations in this regard,

Recognizing that the peacemaking activities of the Secretary-General and of organs of the United Nations, which are actions to bring hostile parties to agreement essentially through peaceful means such as those foreseen in Chapter VI of the Charter of the United Nations, constitute an essential function of the United Nations and are among the important means for the prevention, containment and resolution of disputes, the continuance of which is likely to endanger the maintenance of international peace and security,

Taking note of the statements of the President of the Security Council of 3 May[1] and 4 November 1994,[2] and, in particular, welcoming the improvements in respect of consultations with troop-contributing countries reported therein.

Bearing in mind that the increase in activities in the field of United Nations peace-keeping requires both increasing and better managed human, financial and material resources for the Organization,

Taking note also of the report of the Secretary-General on the work of the Organization,[3] having examined the report of the Special Committee on Peace-keeping Operations,[4] and taking note further of the report of the Secretary-General[5] and the statement of the Presi-

---

1 S/PRST/1994/22; see *Official Records of the Security Council, Forty-ninth Year,* Resolutions and Decisions of the Security Council 1994.

2 S/PRST/1994/62; see *Official Records of the Security Council, Forty-ninth Year,* Resolutions and Decisions of the Security Council 1994.

3 *Official Records of the General Assembly, Forty-ninth Session, Supplement No. 1* (A/49/1).

4 A/149/136.

5 S/1994/777; see *Official Records of the Security Council, Forty-ninth Year, Supplement for April, May and June 1994.*

dent of the Security Council of 27 July 1994[1] concerning stand-by peace-keeping arrangements,

Noting the various proposals and ideas regarding United Nations peace-keeping put forward during the general debate at its forty-ninth session,

Noting also the existence of humanitarian activities in support of certain United Nations peace-keeping operations and the usefulness of bilateral arrangements between concerned Member States for consultations on providing legal protection to the personnel participating in such activities,

1. *Welcomes* the report of the Special Committee on Peace-keeping Operations;

Definition and implementation of mandates

2. *Emphasizes* that respect for the principles of sovereignty, territorial integrity and political independence of States and non-intervention in matters that are essentially within the domestic jurisdiction of any State is crucial to common efforts, including peace-keeping operations, to promote international peace and security;

3. *Stresses* the need to address effectively the underlying causes of conflict;

4. *Also stresses* that peace-keeping operations contribute to, but are not a substitute for, political settlement of disputes and should be preceded and accompanied, as appropriate, by the use of all possible means for the peaceful settlement of disputes in accordance with the provisions of the Charter of the United Nations, and urges parties involved in long-standing operations to find political solutions to outstanding disputes;

5. *Expresses its belief* that it is of paramount importance that there be a clear and precise formulation of the mandate of peace-keeping operations, based on a comprehensive analysis and assessment of the situation on the ground by the Secretary-General and the Security Council and incorporating objectives achievable within a clear time-frame, which objectives should contribute to a political solution and be clearly related to the availability of the resources essential for their implementation;

6. *Underlines* the importance of considering, on a case-by-case basis, the establishment of demilitarized zones and the use of preventive deployment of troops, as indicated its resolution 47/120 B of 20 September 1993;

7. *Stresses* the importance, taking into account the principles that have guided peace-keeping operations and the increasingly complex nature of those operations. of the elaboration of a set of principles and guidelines and the need to consider on a case-by-case basis the coordination between political, military, civilian and humanitarian aspects, as well as the need for United Nations peace-keeping operations to continue to fulfil their mandates impartially and requests the Secretary-General, in consultation with Member States, to develop further common definitions of terms used in peace-keeping and related activities;

Consultation and coordination mechanisms

8. *Stresses* that, while the Security Council bears primary responsibility for the maintenance of international peace and security, the Charter also provides for General Assembly functions and powers in this regard and that, in addition to its responsibility for financing peace-keeping operations, the Assembly could, *inter alia*, recommend, in accordance with relevant articles of Chapter IV of the Charter, principles and guidelines for the conduct of peace-keeping operations, for their effective management and, consistent with the Charter, for encouraging support of their mandates;

9. *Notes* that the views of troop-contributing countries[2] are of critical importance, and calls for enhanced arrangements for consultations and exchange of information with troop-contributing countries regarding peace-keeping operations, including their planning, management and coordination, throughout the duration of those operations;

10. *Welcomes* the recent practice of members of the Security Council, including its President, of attending meetings between the Secretariat and troop-contributing countries, agrees with the Secretary-General that this constitutes a step towards the development of improved mechanisms for effective consultation, and considers that such consultations are particularly important when the Council is considering changes to or significant extensions of the mandates of existing missions;

11. *Also welcomes* the statement of the President of the Security Council of 4 November 1994 on consultations between members of the Council, troop-contributing countries and the Secretariat;[3]

12. *Notes* the important role played by countries of the region concerned in supporting peace-keeping operations, welcomes the recognition, in the statement of the President of the Security Council of 4 November 1994, of the practice of informal communication between the President of the Council or Council members and non-members, and encourages the inclusion of countries of the region concerned, on a case-by-case basis, in those communications when they relate to decisions regarding a peace-keeping operation that may affect them directly;

13. *Recommends* the regular transmission of situation reports to troop-contributing countries, members of the Security Council and, where possible, other Member States on all peace-keeping operations;

Evaluation of operations

14. *Requests* the Secretary-General, once again, to provide periodically to Member States analytic reports on the performance of all peace-keeping operations;

15. *Takes note* of the progress report of the Secretary-General on the start-up phase of the in-depth evaluation of peace-keeping,[4] and expresses its belief that a continuing process of in-depth evaluation of various phases and aspects of peace-keeping operations is important to the deliberations on improving the capacity of the United Nations for peace-keeping;

Command and control

16. *Stresses* the need for a unified and well-defined United Nations command and control structure, incorporating a clear delineation of functions between United Nations Headquarters and the field, and notes that while operational matters should essentially be the responsibility of the force commander, Headquarters is responsible for overall control and political direction;

17. *Confirms*, as a leading principle, that a peace-keeping operation should be under the operational control of the United Nations in accordance with its mandate, taking into account the intended tasks of the unit provided and according to the agreement between the Secretary-General and the troop-contributing countries and that the appropriate channel for raising specific national concerns regarding the course of actions pursued in an operation is through Headquarters;

18. *Also stresses* the need for effective coordination between the field headquarters and contingent commanders on issues affecting the planning and management of a peace-keeping operation;

19. *Urges* that immediate steps be taken to strengthen current arrangements in the United Nations for political direction, military command and control and consultations, as well as to improve coordination, when required, with the humanitarian and other civilian aspects of peace-keeping operations, both at Headquarters and in the field;

---

1 S/PRST/1994/36; see *Official Records of the Security Council, Forty-ninth Year,* Resolutions and Decisions of the Security Council 1994.

2 It was understood that the Secretariat interpreted the term "troopcontributing" in a broad sense, including contributions of various sorts, not only troops.

3 S/PRST/1994/62; see *Official Records of the Security Council, Forty-ninth Year,* Resolutions and Decisions of the Security Council 1994.

4 E/AC.51/199413 and Corr.l.

Enhancing the capacity of the United Nations for peace-keeping

Finances

20. *Reaffirms* that the financing of peace-keeping operations is the collective responsibility of all Member States in accordance with Article 17, paragraph 2, of the Charter and reiterates its call upon all Member States to pay their assessed contributions in full and on time, commends those Members States which have offered voluntary contributions in addition to their assessed ones, and encourages other Member States, including those directly concerned in a dispute that has resulted in deployment of a peace-keeping operation, to do the same, including contributions in kind in accordance with their financial capacity and the Financial Regulations and Rules of the United Nations;

21. *Expresses deep concern* about the adverse effect that the deteriorating financial situation has on the reimbursement of troop contributors, many of which are developing countries, placing an additional burden on all troop-contributing countries and putting at risk the continuing supply of troops to United Nations peace-keeping operations and, consequently, the effective implementation of the mandates;

22. *Takes note* of the important proposals on rationalization of the budgetary process contained in section V of the report of the Secretary-General on improving the capacity of the United Nations for peace-keeping[1] and the proposals in the report of the Secretary-General on the effective planning, budgeting and administration of peace-keeping operations;[2]

23. *Recommends* that decisions on the allocation of additional resources for peace-keeping operations should be taken without prejudice to decisions on the allocation of future resources intended for international cooperation for development;

24. *Calls for* a better mechanism of financial control, including reinforcement of audit and inspection mechanisms, and recalls its establishment of the Office of Internal Oversight Services by resolution 48/218 B of 29 July 1994;

25. *Stresses* the need to delegate the appropriate degree of financial and administrative authority to force commanders or special representatives, while ensuring that measures relating to responsibility and accountability are strengthened in order to increase the capacity of missions to adjust to new situations and specific requirements;

26. *Requests* the Secretary-General to continue his consultations with Member States with a view to concluding, as soon as possible, his current review of the rates of reimbursement for depreciation of contingent-owned equipment deployed at the request of the United Nations and to report thereon to the General Assembly;

27. *Stresses* the importance attached to the ongoing review of current arrangements for compensation for death, injury or illness attributable to peace-keeping service, intended to develop equitable arrangements, takes note of the report of the Secretary-General in this regard,[3] and encourages appropriate forums to consider this matter on an urgent basis;

Resources

28. *Welcomes* the work of the Stand-by Forces Unit of the Planning Division of the Department of Peace-keeping Operations of the Secretariat and notes that some Member States have made commitments to the Secretary-General in this regard, looks forward to the completion of the compilation of lists of units, forces, capabilities or resources that Member States would in principle be prepared to put at the disposal of the United Nations on a case-by-case basis, subject to the agreement of the Government concerned and recommends that the list be periodically updated and brought to the attention of Member States;

29. *Recognizes* the need to enhance the United Nations logistics capability, considers that a first step is the operational support manual for all areas of logistics support, and in this connection looks forward to the completion of all chapters of that manual and their issue to troop contributors;

30. *Considers* that all the implications of creating limited stockpiles of equipment should be examined in the appropriate bodies of the United Nations;

31. *Notes* the growing weight of the civilian component in peace-keeping operations, requests, in this respect, the Secretary-General to develop a proposal for regularly updated data banks recording the type and availability of resources that Member States could provide, at the request of the United Nations, for civilian duties, and encourages the Secretary-General to continue his efforts to include civilian personnel, such as police, in the current stand-by arrangements and planning;

32. *Urges* the Secretary-General to consider the endowment of a memorial medal honouring civilian participants in order to encourage their activities;

Planning, organization and effectiveness

33. *Encourages* the Secretary-General to continue with his plans to strengthen the Department of Peace-keeping Operations in order to ensure the best structure and capacity for successfully managing such operations, bearing in mind the need to give due regard to the principle of equitable geographical representation, and notes the organizational approach of the Secretary-General as set out in his report on improving the capacity of the United Nations for peace-keeping;

34. *Welcomes* the creation of a Policy and Analysis Unit and a Planning Division within the Department of Peace-keeping Operations, and considers that those units should be further developed to improve the capacity of the United Nations to manage peace-keeping;

35. *Considers* it important that force commanders and other key personnel be associated with the planning of peace-keeping operations from the outset and that they should, where feasible, participate in preparatory technical missions to the field, which should be designed with clear terms of reference, and also considers that deployment of some of the members of technical missions to the field at an early stage of an operation is useful;

36. *Requests* the Secretary-General to strengthen further the civilian police function within the Department of Peace-keeping Operations, with particular attention to planning, training, logistical support and standardized doctrine and procedures, noting, in this connection, the views expressed in his progress report on the startup phase of the in-depth evaluation of peace-keeping;[4]

37. *Requests* the Secretariat immediately to make all necessary arrangements for the updating and reissue of The Blue Helmets[5] in 1995;

Safety and security of United Nations personnel

38. *Stresses* the need for security of personnel to be an integral part of the planning of any peace-keeping operation, and stresses also that appropriate measures should be taken to ensure their safety and security;

39. *Welcomes* the adoption by its Sixth Committee of the Convention on the Safety of United Nations and Associated Personnel;[6]

40. *Recognizes* that overall responsibility for the safety and security of the members of a peace-keeping operation lies with the Secretary-General, who also has to follow the development of the situation, make timely adjustments in the safety and security arrangements when the situation so requires and cooperate closely with troop-contributing countries and the Security Council in this regard, and urges the Secretary-General to initiate a dialogue with Member States on possible additional safety measures that can be taken in situations where current measures are deemed inadequate;

---

1 A/48/403-S/26450; see *Official Records of the Security Council, Forty-ninth Year, Supplement for January, February and March 1994*, document S/26450.

2 A/48/945 and Corr. 1.

3 A/48/945 and Corr. 1.

4 E/AC. 51/1994/3 and Corr. 1.

5 United Nations publication, Sales No. E.90.1.18.

6 The text is contained in the annex to resolution 49/59, adopted by the General Assembly on 9 December 1994.

41. *Requests* the Secretary-General to keep troop-contributing countries and the members of the Security Council informed as appropriate on evacuation plans and arrangements;

42. *Urges* the Secretary-General to strengthen the Office of the United Nations Security Coordinator, within existing resources, in order to facilitate better coordination to ensure the security of the personnel participating in peace-keeping operations;

Model agreement

43. *Notes* the importance of concluding arrangements between the United Nations and troop contributing countries before deployment occurs, and stresses that, as far as possible, those arrangements should be along the lines of the model agreement outlined in the report of the Secretary-General of 23 May 1991;[1]

Public information

44. *Stresses* the need for the United Nations to adopt a more proactive approach to public information policy for peace-keeping operations, to keep local populations informed of the nature of United Nations operations, with a view, *inter alia*, to facilitating constructive communication between the parties to provide, where possible, troop-contributing countries with materials on peace-keeping operations that may assist them in their domestic public information efforts and to provide the international media with objective information so as to promote a more accurate understanding of United Nations actions; and encourages the Committee on Information to review ways to strengthen public information activities in support of peace-keeping;

45. *Requests* the Secretary-General to improve support for the planning and implementation of public affairs programmes in peace-keeping missions, including their print and broadcast needs, and, drawing upon the experience of the United Nations and national expertise to develop programmes and materials to train public affairs officers;

46. *Also requests* the Secretary-General to train Headquarters and mission staff in dealing with the media, in presenting the case for a peace-keeping operation and commenting on it as it progresses;

Training

47. *Recognizes* that, while the training of personnel for peace-keeping operations is essentially the responsibility of Member States, the United Nations should establish basic guidelines and performance standards and provide descriptive materials;

48. *Welcomes* the efforts of the Secretary-General to develop manuals, including a curriculum module, and a programme of correspondence instruction which will enable Member States to train personnel provided for United Nations peace-keeping operations in a standardized and cost-effective manner in accordance with agreed common standards, skills, practices and procedures, and looks forward to those manuals and other materials being made available to Member States;

49. *Requests* the Secretary-General to investigate the means to strengthen the leadership cadre available for peace-keeping, *inter alia*, by coordinating relevant training for potential force commanders and other senior military and civilian personnel for peace-keeping leadership and management duties;

50. *Also requests* the Secretary-General to establish, on a trial basis, a peace-keeping training coordination programme; such a programme, administered by the United Nations, could include training-the-trainer workshops, specialized training in community relations and conflict resolution, arrangements to organize and rapidly dispatch training teams, at the request of Member States to assist in national training efforts seminars in mission management and short orientation courses at Headquarters or in the field for staff officers before deployment to a new mission;

51. *Encourages* Member States that have peace-keeping training programmes to share information and experience and, if requested, to enable personnel from other Member States to participate in the work of national staff colleges to help in the development of training programmes and to receive personnel from other Member States interested in such programmes;

52. *Encourages* the establishment of peace-keeping training centres, on a national or regional basis as deemed appropriate, for military and civilian personnel;

53. *Recommends* that the Training Unit, as the focal point for peace-keeping training in the Department of Peace-keeping Operations, act as a coordinating centre on peace-keeping training matters between the United Nations and national and international peace-keeping training centres to develop links with counterpart bodies and to encourage the exchange of training materials with and between Member States;

54. *Encourages* Member States to examine the feasibility of developing, in their regions, small short-term training teams from Member States experienced in peace-keeping to assist other Member States;

55. *Encourages* the Secretary-General to examine the feasibility of establishing a training advisory group providing a link to national and regional peace-keeping training institutions to assist the Department of Peace-keeping Operations in the periodic review of training requirements;

Cooperation with regional organizations

56. *Stresses* the need, bearing in mind the provisions of Chapter VIII of the Charter, to enhance the cooperation and coordination between the United Nations and those regional arrangements and organizations able to assist it in its peace-keeping activities in accordance with their respective mandates, scope and composition, and encourages the Secretary-General and Member States to consider ways and means to assist those regional arrangements and organizations in the activities described above;

57. *Notes* the recent initiative of the Secretary-General to convene an informal meeting at Headquarters with representatives of regional arrangements and organizations and with other inter-governmental organizations;

58. *Also notes* the recent work of the Special Committee on the Charter of the United Nations and on the Strengthening of the Role of the Organization in elaborating the text of the Declaration on the Enhancement of Cooperation between the United Nations and Regional Arrangements or Agencies in the Maintenance of International Peace and Security;[2]

59. *Recommends* that, should any of the proposals contained in the present resolution result in budgetary implications for the biennium 1994-1995, such additional costs should be accommodated within the appropriation level approved by the General Assembly for that biennium;

60. *Decides* that the Special Committee on Peace-keeping Operations, in accordance with its mandate, should continue its efforts for a comprehensive review of the whole question of peace-keeping operations in all their aspects;

61. *Requests* the Special Committee on Peace-keeping Operations to submit a report on its work to the General Assembly at its fiftieth session;

62. *Invites* Member States to submit further observations and suggestions on peace-keeping operations to the Secretary-General by 1 March 1995, outlining practical proposals on specific items in order to allow for more detailed consideration by the Special Committee;

63. *Requests* the Secretary-General to prepare, within existing resources, a compilation of the above-mentioned observations and suggestions and to submit it to the Special Committee by 30 March 1995;

64. *Decides* to include in the provisional agenda of its fiftieth session the item entitled "Comprehensive review of the whole question of peace-keeping operations in all their aspects".

83rd plenary meeting
9 December 1994

1 A/46/185 and Corr. 1, annex.

2 The text is contained in the annex to resolution 49/57, adopted by the General Assembly on 9 December 1994.

50/51. Implementation of Charter Provisions Related to Assistance to Third States Affected by the Application of Sanctions

Committee: 6
Vote: Adopted without a vote

The General Assembly,

Concerned with the special economic problems confronting certain States arising from the carrying out of preventive or enforcement measures taken by the Security Council against other States, and taking into account the obligation of Members of the United Nations under Article 49 of the Charter of the United Nations to join in affording mutual assistance in carrying out the measures decided upon by the Security Council,

Recalling the right of third States confronted with special economic problems of that nature to consult the Security Council with regard to a solution to those problems, in accordance with Article 50 of the Charter,

Recalling also the 1994[1] and 1995[2] reports of the Special Committee on the Charter of the United Nations and on the Strengthening of the Role of the Organization containing sections on the consideration by the Committee of the proposals presented on the question of the implementation of the provisions of the Charter of the United Nations related to assistance to third States affected by the application of sanctions under Chapter VII of the Charter,

Recalling further:

(*a*) The report of the Secretary-General, entitled "An Agenda for Peace",[3] in particular paragraph 41 thereof;

(*b*) Its resolutions 47/120 A of 18 December 1992, entitled "An Agenda for Peace: preventive diplomacy and related matters", and 47/120 B of 20 September 1993, entitled "An Agenda for Peace", in particular section IV thereof, entitled "Special economic problems arising from the implementation of preventive or enforcement measures";

(*c*) The position paper of the Secretary-General, entitled "Supplement to An Agenda for Peace";[4]

(*d*) The statement of the President of the Security Council of 22 February 1995;[5]

(*e*) The report of the Secretary-General prepared pursuant to the note by the President of the Security Council[6] regarding the question of special economic problems of States as a result of sanctions imposed under Chapter VII of the Charter of the United Nations;[7]

(*f*) The reports of the Secretary-General on "Economic assistance to States affected by the implementation of the Security Council resolutions imposing sanctions against the Federal Republic of Yugoslavia (Serbia and Montenegro)",[8]

Taking note of the report of the Secretary-General on the implementation of the provisions of the Charter related to assistance to third States affected by the application of sanctions under Chapter VII of the Charter,[9]

Recalling that the question of assistance to third States affected by the application of sanctions has been addressed recently in several forums, including the General Assembly and its subsidiary organs and the Security Council,

Recalling also the Security Council's intention expressed in the statement of the President of the Security Council of 16 December 1994[10] as part of the Council's effort to improve the flow of information and the exchange of ideas between members of the Council and other States Members of the United Nations that there should be increased recourse to open meetings, in particular at an early stage in its consideration of a subject,

Stressing that in the formulation of sanctions regimes, due account should be taken of the potential effects of sanctions on third States,

Stressing also in this context the powers of the Security Council under Chapter VII of the Charter and the Council's principal responsibility under Article 24 of the Charter for the maintenance of international peace and security in order to ensure prompt and effective action by the United Nations,

Recalling that, under Article 31 of the Charter, any Member of the United Nations which is not a member of the Security Council may participate, without vote, in the discussion of any question brought before the Security Council whenever the latter considers that the interests of that Member are specially affected,

Recognizing that assistance to third States affected by the application of sanctions would further contribute to an effective and comprehensive approach by the international community to mandatory sanctions imposed by the Security Council,

Recognizing also the importance of taking into account in international mechanisms of cooperation and of economic and financial assistance special economic problems of States arising from the implementation of sanctions imposed under Chapter VII of the Charter,

1. *Underlines* the importance of consultations under Article 50 of the Charter of the United Nations, as early as possible, with third States which may be confronted with special economic problems arising from the carrying out of preventive or enforcement measures imposed by the Security Council under Chapter VII of the Charter and of early and regular assessments, as appropriate, of their impact on such States, and, for this purpose, invites the Security Council to consider appropriate ways and means for increasing the effectiveness of its working methods and procedures applied in the consideration of the requests by the affected countries for assistance, in the context of Article 50;

2. *Welcomes* the measures taken by the Security Council aimed at increasing the effectiveness and transparency of the sanctions committees, and strongly recommends that the Council continue its efforts further to enhance the functioning of those committees, to streamline their working procedures and to facilitate access to them by representatives of States which find themselves confronted with special economic problems arising from the carrying out of sanctions;

3. *Requests* the Secretary-General, within existing resources, to ensure that the Security Council and its sanctions committees are able to carry out their work expeditiously, and to make appropriate arrangements in the relevant parts of the Secretariat, in order to carry out, in a coordinated way, the following functions:

(*a*) To collate, assess and analyse information, at the request of the Security Council and its organs, on the effects of sanctions regimes in third States which are or may be specially affected by the implementations of sanctions and the resulting needs of such States, and keep the Security Council and its organs informed;

(*b*) To provide advice to the Security Council and its organs at their request on specific needs or problems of those third States and present possible options so that, while maintaining the effectiveness of the sanctions regimes, appropriate adjustments may be made to the administration of the regime or the regime itself with a view to mitigating the adverse effects on such States;

(*c*) To collate and coordinate information about international assistance available to third States affected by the implementations of sanctions and to make it officially available to the interested member States;

1 *Official Records of the General Assembly, Forty-ninth Session, Supplement No. 33* (A/49/33).

2 *Ibid., Fiftieth Session, Supplement No. 33* (A/50/33).

3 A/47/277-S/24111.

4 A/50/60-S/1995/1.

5 S/PRST/1995/9.

6 S/25036.

7 A/48/573 -S/26705.

8 A/49/356 and A/50/423.

9 A/50/361.

10 S/PRST/1994/81.

(*d*) To explore innovative and practical measures of assistance to the affected third States through cooperation with relevant institutions and organizations inside and outside the United Nations system;

4. *Requests* the Secretary-General to report to the General Assembly, at its fifty-first session, on the implementation of paragraph 3 and on possible guidelines which might be adopted on technical procedures to be used by the appropriate parts of the Secretariat:

(*a*) For providing better information and early assessments for the Security Council and its organs about the actual or potential effects of sanctions on third States which invoke Article 50 of the Charter;

(*b*) For developing a possible methodology for assessing the consequences actually incurred by third States as a result of the implementation of preventive or enforcement measures;

(*c*) For coordination of information about international economic or other assistance potentially available to those third States;

5. *Stresses* the important role of the General Assembly, the Economic and Social Council and the Committee for Programme and Coordination in mobilizing and monitoring, as appropriate, the economic assistance efforts by the international community and the United Nations system to States confronted with special economic problems arising from the carrying out of preventive or enforcement measures imposed by the Security Council;

6. *Invites* the organizations of the United Nations system, international financial institutions, other international organizations, regional organizations and States Members to continue to take into account and to address more specifically and directly, where appropriate, special economic problems of third States affected by sanctions imposed under Chapter VII of the Charter and, for this purpose, to consider ways and means for improving procedures for consultations in order to maintain a constructive dialogue with such States, including through regular and frequent meetings as well as, where appropriate, special meetings between the affected third States and the donor community, with the participation of United Nations agencies and other international organizations;

7. *Requests* the Special Committee on the Charter of the United Nations and on the Strengthening of the Role of the Organization, at its session in 1996, to continue to consider on a priority basis the question of the implementation of the provisions of the Charter related to assistance to third States affected by the application of sanctions under Chapter VII of the Charter taking into consideration the report of the Secretary-General,[1] the proposals presented on this subject, the debate on this question which took place in the Sixth Committee at the fiftieth session of the General Assembly and, in particular, the implementation of the provisions of the present resolution.

87th plenary meeting
11 December 1995

02.30 COOPERATION OF THE UNITED NATIONS WITH REGIONAL ARRANGEMENTS

46/109. The Situation in Central America: Threats to International Peace and Security and Peace Initiatives

Committee: -
Vote: A + B adopted without a vote
Ref.: 50/132, 49/137, 48/161, 47/118

A

Procedures for the establishment of a firm and lasting peace in Central America

The General Assembly, [1]

Recalling Security Council resolutions 530 (1983) of 19 May 1983, 562 (1985) of 10 May 1985, 637 (1989) of 27 July 1989, 644 (1989) of 7 November 1989, 650 (1990) of 27 March 1990, 653 (1990) of 20 April 1990, 654 (1990) of 4 May 1990, 656 (1990) of 8 June 1990 and 719 (1991) of 6 November 1991, and its resolutions 38/10 of 11 November 1983, 39/4 of 26 October 1984, 41/37 of 18 November 1986, 42/1 of 7 October 1987, 43/24 of 15 November 1988, 44/10 of 23 October 1989, 44/44 of 7 December 1989 and 45/15 of 20 November 1990,

Aware that the agreement on "Procedures for the establishment of a firm and lasting peace in Central America" signed at Guatemala City on 7 August 1987 by the Presidents of the Republics of Costa Rica, El Salvador, Guatemala, Honduras and Nicaragua, at the Esquipulas II summit meeting, is the outcome of the decision by Central Americans to take up fully the historical challenge of forging a peaceful destiny for Central America,

Convinced that the peoples of Central America wish to achieve peace, reconciliation, development and justice, without outside interference, in accordance with their own decision and their own historical experience, and without sacrificing the principles of self-determination and non-intervention,

Aware also of the political will which inspires them to settle their differences by means of dialogue, negotiation and respect for the legitimate interests of all States, establishing commitments to be fulfilled in good faith, through the verifiable performance of actions aimed at achieving peace, democracy, security, cooperation and respect for human rights,

Taking note of the second report of the United Nations Observer Mission in El Salvador of 15 November 1991 and of the report of the Secretary-General of 28 October 1991 concerning the United Nations Observer Group in Central America,

Taking note with satisfaction of the work carried out in the region by the Group in verifying the security commitments entered into by the Central American Governments under the agreement signed at the Esquipulas II summit meeting, and of the work of the International Support and Verification Commission in the repatriation and relocation of displaced persons and refugees, which it has undertaken with the cooperation of the Office of the United Nations High Commissioner for Refugees and the United Nations Development Programme, and of the United Nations Observer Mission in El Salvador, which is monitoring compliance with human rights commitments,

Convinced that the National Conciliation Agreement on Economic and Social Matters reached in Nicaragua on 26 October 1990 and phase II thereof, signed on 15 August 1991, constitute positive and promising contributions to strengthening the process of democratization, development and peace in Nicaragua and in the region,

Observing with satisfaction that the Government of El Salvador and the Frente Farabundo Martí para la Liberación Nacional are continuing the negotiating process, begun on 4 April 1990 under the auspices of the Secretary-General, with a view to putting an end, once and for all, to the armed conflict by political means in the shortest possible time, as well as promoting the democratization of the country, guaranteeing unrestricted respect for human rights and reunifying Salvadorian society,

Observing also with satisfaction the progress of the talks between the Government of Guatemala and the Unidad Revolucionaria Nacional Guatemalteca aimed at ending the internal armed confrontation and bringing about reconciliation and full respect for the human rights of all Guatemalans, which have taken place under the auspices of the National Reconciliation Commission of Guatemala, in the presence of the Representative of the Secretary-General,

Recognizing the unfailing determination of the Rio Group to achieve peace in Central America and the valuable contribution made by its member States throughout the regional peace effort,

1 S/25036.

1. *Commends* the effort made by the Central American countries to achieve peace through the implementation of the agreement on "Procedures for the establishment of a firm and lasting peace in Central America" signed at Guatemala City on 7 August 1987, as well as of the agreements adopted at subsequent summit meetings;

2. *Expresses its strongest support* for these agreements and urges the Governments to continue their efforts to consolidate firm and lasting peace in Central America;

3. *Requests* the Secretary-General to continue to afford the fullest possible support to the Central American Governments in their efforts to consolidate peace, especially by taking the measures necessary for the maintenance, establishment and effective functioning of the appropriate verification machinery;

4. *Welcomes* the implementation of phases I and II of the National Conciliation Agreement on Economic and Social Matters concluded in Nicaragua on 26 October 1990 and 15 August 1991 and endorses, in particular, the provision concerning exceptional circumstances and the invitation made in phase I to the international community and the international funding agencies to provide effective and efficient support for the implementation of the Agreement, and also supports the agreements reached in phase II regarding property rights and privatization;

5. *Fully endorses* the efforts of the Secretary-General to bring about peace in Central America and in particular his active role as an intermediary in Guatemala and El Salvador;

6. *Urges* the Government of El Salvador and the Frente Farabundo Martí para la Liberación Nacional to step up the confidence-building and security measures unilaterally adopted by them in order to maintain the suspension of the armed confrontation pending the conclusion in the shortest possible time of political agreements which will put an end to the armed conflict once and for all and will achieve the other goals laid down in the Geneva Agreement of 4 April 1990;

7. *Expresses its support* for the process of negotiation between the Government of Guatemala and the Unidad Revolucionaria Nacional Guatemalteca, which has given rise to the agreements signed at Mexico City on 26 April 1991 and the Querétaro Agreement signed at Querétaro, Mexico, on 25 July 1991, and encourages both parties to continue their efforts to reach a political solution to the long process of confrontation experienced by Guatemala;

8. *Requests* the Secretary-General to submit a report to the General Assembly at its forty-seventh session on progress made in implementing the present resolution.

75th plenary meeting
17 December 1991

B

Central America: Region of peace, freedom, democracy and development

The General Assembly,

Bearing in mind the importance of the commitments assumed by the Central American Presidents under the agreement signed at Guatemala City on 7 August 1987 at the Esquipulas II summit meeting; the declarations adopted at Alajuela, Costa Rica, on 16 January 1988 and at Costa del Sol, El Salvador, on 14 February 1989; the agreements concluded at Tela, Honduras, on 7 August 1989, at Montelimar, Nicaragua, on 3 April 1990, at Antigua, Guatemala, on 17 June 1990 and at Puntarenas, Costa Rica, on 17 December 1990; and the Declaration of San Salvador of 17 July 1991,

Recognizing the importance of all aspects of the peace-keeping operations which have been carried out in Central America, pursuant to the decisions of the Security Council and with the support of the Secretary-General, and the need to preserve and enhance the results obtained,

Considering that at their meetings at Montelimar, Nicaragua, and Antigua, Guatemala, the Central American Presidents reaffirmed their determination to set Central America on the road to a stable peace through the establishment of democratic regimes throughout the region, the individual and collective forging of a better economic and social future for the area, and the design of specific mechanisms and courses of action for the peaceful settlement of disputes or possible conflicts between the States of the region,

Considering also that, at the Puntarenas summit meeting, the Presidents declared Central America to be a region of peace, freedom, democracy and development, and that in the Declaration of San Salvador they agreed to update the legal framework of the Organization of Central American States and to work for the inclusion of Central America in a world order marked by interdependence, the emergence of new forms of integration and cooperation and the effective implementation of international law,

Considering the commitments which have been entered into during the negotiations on security, verification, and control and limitation of arms and military personnel, within the Security Commission established under the agreement signed at the Esquipulas II summit meeting, for the purpose of achieving a stable and lasting peace in Central America,

Taking into consideration that the force of the new democratic spirit prevailing in Central America has created a sphere of political action which makes it feasible to resume with greater momentum the process of regional integration, as the basis for a firm and lasting peace in the region, taking into account the specific circumstances of each country,

Bearing in mind the political determination in Central America to strengthen the process of cooperation in the political, economic and social fields, which complements the progressive steps towards pacification, reconciliation and democratization,

Reaffirming the belief that peace is one, undivided and indivisible, and thus inseparable from freedom, democracy and development, and that these goals are essential for consolidating the transformations which will guarantee sustained, participatory and equitable development in Central America and redefining the manner in which the Central American economies are linked to the rest of the world,

Recognizing the valuable and effective contribution of the United Nations and of various governmental and non-governmental mechanisms to the process of democratization, pacification and development in Central America,

Recognizing also the importance for the progressive transformation of Central America into a region of peace, freedom, democracy and development of both the political dialogue and the economic cooperation set in motion by the Ministerial Conference on Political Dialogue and Economic Cooperation between the European Community and the Central American countries and the joint initiative of the industrialized countries (Group of Twenty-four) and the group of cooperating countries (Group of Three), in Latin America, through a Partnership for Democracy and Development in Central America,

Bearing in mind that there remain in Central America major obstacles to the full exercise of peace, freedom, democracy and development, the final overcoming of which requires a global frame of reference which would enable the international community to focus its support on efforts towards collective affirmation and democratic progress being made by the Central American countries,

1. *Reaffirms* the decision of the Presidents of the Central American countries to declare Central America a region of peace, freedom, democracy and development;

2. *Encourages* the initiatives of the Central American countries to consolidate Governments which genuinely represent the will of their people and which base their development on democracy, peace, cooperation and strict respect for human rights and on security, verification, and control and limitation of arms and military personnel;

3. *Welcomes with satisfaction* the agreements reached and progress made by the Security Commission in the creation of a new security model based on coordination, communication and prevention, confidence-building between the States of the region, and the presentation of an inventory of weapons present in Central America;

4. *Stresses* the importance that the outcome of the political dialogue and economic cooperation between the European Community and its member States, the States of Central America and Panama and the

group of cooperating countries (Group of Three) as well as the initiative of the industrialized countries (Group of Twenty-four) and the group of cooperating countries (Group of Three), through the Partnership for Democracy and Development in Central America, have for the efforts of the Central American countries to achieve peace and to consolidate democracy and economic development;

5. *Requests* the Secretary-General and the organizations of the United Nations system to provide, as appropriate and within the available resources, the necessary technical and financial support to the Central American Governments for the purpose of consolidating the processes of peace, freedom, democratization and development in the region;

6. *Reiterates* the importance that the Special Plan of Economic Cooperation for Central America, which the General Assembly welcomed in its resolution 42/231, has for the implementation of this resolution, in particular because it provides the underpinning for the execution of the Central American Economic Plan of Action, which the Central American Presidents approved at their meeting held at Antigua, Guatemala, in June 1990;

7. *Decides* to include in the provisional agenda of its forty-seventh session an item entitled "The situation in Central America: procedures for the establishment of a firm and lasting peace and progress in fashioning a region of peace, freedom, democracy and development";

8. *Requests* the Secretary-General to submit a report to the General Assembly at its forty-seventh session on progress made in implementing the present resolution.

75th plenary meeting
17 December 1991

49/57. Declaration on the Enhancement of Cooperation Between the United Nations and Regional Arrangements or Agencies in the Maintenance of International Peace and Security

Committee: 6
Vote: Adopted without a vote

The General Assembly,

Recalling its resolutions 46/58 of 9 December 1991, 47/38 of 25 November 1992 and 48/36 of 9 December 1993,

Taking note of the report of the Special Committee on the Charter of the United Nations and on the Strengthening of the Role of the Organization,[1] which met in New York from 7 to 25 March 1994 and completed a draft declaration on the enhancement of cooperation between the United Nations and regional arrangements or agencies in the maintenance of international peace and security,

Convinced that the adoption of the declaration will contribute towards strengthening the role and enhancing the effectiveness of the United Nations and of the regional arrangements or agencies in the maintenance of international peace and security,

Considering the need to ensure a wide dissemination of the text of the declaration,

Convinced also that the declaration will be a major and specific contribution of the Special Committee to the activities within the United Nations Decade of International Law,

1. *Approves* the Declaration on the Enhancement of Cooperation between the United Nations and Regional Arrangements or Agencies in the Maintenance of International Peace and Security, the text of which is annexed to the present resolution;

2. *Expresses its appreciation* to the Special Committee on the Charter of the United Nations and on the Strengthening of the Role of the Organization for its important contribution to the elaboration of the text of the Declaration;

3. *Requests* the Secretary-General to inform the Governments of the States Members of the United Nations or members of specialized agencies, the Security Council and regional arrangements or agencies which have observer status in the General Assembly of the adoption of the Declaration;

4. *Urges* that every effort be made to ensure that the Declaration becomes generally known and fully implemented.

84th plenary meeting
9 December 1994

Annex

Declaration on the Enhancement of Cooperation Between the United Nations and Regional Arrangements or Agencies in the Maintenance of International Peace and Security

The General Assembly,

Recalling the provisions of the Charter of the United Nations concerning the role of regional arrangements or agencies in the maintenance of international peace and security, in particular the provisions of Chapter VIII of the Charter,

Recalling also that resort to regional arrangements or agencies is among the means referred to in Chapter VI of the Charter for the peaceful settlement of disputes,

Recognizing that regional arrangements or agencies can play an important role in preventive diplomacy and in enhancing regional and international cooperation,

Recognizing also the importance of the role of regional arrangements or agencies in dealing with such matters relating to the maintenance of international peace and security as are appropriate for regional action, provided that such arrangements or agencies and their activities are consistent with the purposes and principles of the United Nations,

Taking into account the experience gained and the favourable results achieved by regional arrangements or agencies in the peaceful settlement of disputes in different parts of the world,

Bearing in mind the variety of mandates, scope and composition of regional arrangements or agencies,

Considering that action at the regional level can contribute to the maintenance of international peace and security,

Emphasizing that respect for the principles of sovereignty, territorial integrity and political independence of States and non-intervention in matters which are essentially within the domestic jurisdiction of any State is crucial to any common endeavour to promote international peace and security,

Emphasizing also that peace-keeping activities undertaken by regional arrangements or agencies should be conducted with the consent of the State in whose territory such activities are carried out,

Stressing the primary responsibility of the Security Council, under Article 24 of the Charter, for the maintenance of international peace and security,

Emphasizing further that the efforts made by regional arrangements or agencies, in their respective fields of competence, in cooperation with the United Nations can usefully complement the work of the Organization in the maintenance of international peace and security,

Stressing the need to enhance cooperation between the United Nations and regional arrangements or agencies in the maintenance of international peace and security,

Considering that such enhanced cooperation between the United Nations and regional arrangements or agencies would promote collective security in accordance with the Charter,

Solemnly declares that:

1. In accordance with the provisions of the Charter of the United Nations concerning the role of regional arrangements or agencies in the maintenance of international peace and security, in particular Chapter VIII of the Charter:

(*a*) The Members of the United Nations entering into such arrangements or constituting such agencies shall make every effort to achieve pacific settlement of local disputes through such regional

1 *Official Records of the General Assembly, Forty-fifth Session, Supplement No. 33* (A/49/33).

arrangements or by such regional agencies before referring them to the Security Council;

(*b*) The Security Council shall encourage the development of pacific settlement of local disputes through such regional arrangements or by such regional agencies either on the initiative of the States concerned or by reference from the Council;

(*c*) The above provisions in no way impair the application of Articles 34 and 35 of the Charter;

(*d*) The Security Council shall, where appropriate, utilize such regional arrangements or agencies for enforcement action under its authority, but no enforcement action shall be taken under regional arrangements or by regional agencies without the authorization of the Council;

(*e*) The Security Council shall at all times be kept fully informed of activities undertaken or in contemplation under regional arrangements or by regional agencies for the maintenance of international peace and security;

2. Regional arrangements or agencies can, in their fields of competence and in accordance with the Charter, make important contributions to the maintenance of international peace and security, including, where appropriate, through the peaceful settlement of disputes, preventive diplomacy, peacemaking, peace-keeping and post-conflict peace-building;

3. Cooperation between regional arrangements or agencies and the United Nations in the maintenance of international peace and security may take various forms, including, *inter alia*:

(*a*) Exchange of information and the holding of consultations at all levels;

(*b*) Participation as appropriate in the work of the United Nations organs, in accordance with the applicable rules of procedure and practices;

(*c*) Making available personnel, material and other assistance, where appropriate;

4. Cooperation between regional arrangements or agencies and the United Nations should be in accordance with their respective mandates, scope and composition and should take place in forms that are suited to each specific situation, in accordance with the Charter;

5. Regional efforts undertaken by regional arrangements or agencies in the area of the maintenance of international peace and security, within their respective fields of competence and in accordance with the purposes and principles of the Charter, should be encouraged and, where appropriate, supported by the Security Council;

6. States participating in regional arrangements or agencies are encouraged to consider the possibility of increasing efforts at the regional level for the maintenance of international peace and security in accordance with the Charter;

7. States participating in regional arrangements or agencies are encouraged to promote confidence-building at the regional level for the maintenance of international peace and security;

8. States participating in regional arrangements or agencies are encouraged to consider the possibility of using or, where appropriate, establishing or improving at the regional level procedures and mechanisms for the early detection, the prevention and the peaceful settlement of disputes, in close coordination with the preventive efforts of the United Nations;

9. Regional arrangements or agencies are encouraged to consider, as appropriate, in their fields of competence, ways and means for promoting closer cooperation and coordination with the United Nations with the aim of contributing to the fulfilment of the purposes and principles of the Charter, including in the fields of preventive diplomacy, peacemaking and post-conflict peace-building, and where appropriate, peace-keeping;

10. Regional arrangements or agencies are encouraged to consider, in their fields of competence, the possibility of establishing and training groups of military and civilian observers, fact-finding missions and contingents of peace-keeping forces, for use as appropriate, in coordination with the United Nations and, when necessary, under the authority or with the authorization of the Security Council, in accordance with the Charter;

11. The Declaration on Principles of International Law concerning Friendly Relations and Cooperation among States in accordance with the Charter of the United Nations,[3] the Manila Declaration on the Peaceful Settlement of International Disputes,[4] the Declaration on the Enhancement of the Effectiveness of the Principle of Refraining from the Threat or Use of Force in International Relations,[5] the Declaration on the Prevention and Removal of Disputes and Situations Which May Threaten International Peace and Security and on the Role of the United Nations in this Field[6] and the Declaration on Fact-finding by the United Nations in the Field of the Maintenance of International Peace and Security[7] are hereby reaffirmed together with their provisions concerning the activities of regional arrangements or agencies in the maintenance of international peace and security;

12. Nothing in the present Declaration is to be construed as prejudicing in any manner the provisions of the Charter.

84th plenary meeting
9 December 1994

02.40 OBSERVATION OF ELECTIONS

47/114. Report of the Secretary-General Concerning a Request to the United Nations to Observe the Referendum Process in Eritrea

Committee: 3
Vote: Adopted without a vote
Ref.: 617(VII), 530(VI), 390(V)

The General Assembly,

Having considered the report of the Secretary-General concerning a request to the United Nations to observe the referendum process in Eritrea,[1]

Recalling that the authorities directly concerned have registered their commitment to respect the results of the referendum in Eritrea,[2]

Taking into account that the authorities directly concerned have requested the involvement of the United Nations to verify the referendum in Eritrea,

1. *Takes note* of the report of the Secretary-General[8] and of the recommendations contained therein for the establishment of a United Nations observer mission to verify the referendum scheduled to take place in Eritrea in April 1993;

2. *Decides* to authorize the Secretary-General to establish the United Nations Observer Mission to Verify the Referendum in Eritrea, which will have terms of reference as provided for in paragraph 7 of the report of the Secretary-General, and to appoint, as a matter of ur-

1 A/47/544.
2 See A/C.3/47/5.

3 Resolution 2625 (XXV), annex.
4 Resolution 37/10, annex.
5 Resolution 42/22, annex.
6 Resolution 43/51, annex.
7 Resolution 46/59, annex.
8 A/47/544.

gency, a Special Representative for the referendum, who will head the Observer Mission;

3. *Requests* the Secretary-General to arrange, as soon as possible, for the deployment of the Observer Mission so that it may commence its verification functions;

4. *Calls upon* the authorities directly concerned to extend their fullest cooperation to the Observer Mission in order to facilitate the accomplishment of its task, as requested by the United Nations;

5. *Requests* the Secretary-General to report to the General Assembly at its forty-eighth session on the implementation of the present resolution.

89th plenary meeting
16 December 1992

50/172. Respect for the Principles of National Sovereignty and Non-Interference in the Internal Affairs of States in their Electoral Processes

Committee: 3
Vote: 91 - 57 - 21
Ref.: 49/180, 48/124, 47/130, 46/130, 45/151, 44/147

The General Assembly,

Reaffirming the purpose of the United Nations to develop friendly relations among nations based on respect for the principle of equal rights and self-determination of peoples and to take other appropriate measures to strengthen universal peace,

Recalling its resolution 1514 (XV) of 14 December 1960, containing the Declaration on the Granting of Independence to Colonial Countries and Peoples,

Recalling also its resolution 2625 (XXV) of 24 October 1970, by which it approved the Declaration on Principles of International Law concerning Friendly Relations and Cooperation among States in accordance with the Charter of the United Nations,

Recalling further the principle enshrined in Article 2, paragraph 7, of the Charter of the United Nations, which establishes that nothing contained in the Charter shall authorize the United Nations to intervene in matters which are essentially within the domestic jurisdiction of any State or shall require the Members to submit such matters to settlement under the Charter,

Reaffirming the obligation of Member States to comply with the principles of the Charter of the United Nations and the resolutions of the United Nations regarding the right to self-determination, by virtue of which all peoples can freely determine, without external interference, their political status and freely pursue their economic, social and cultural development,

Reaffirming also in this context, the right of the Palestinian people to self-determination,

Recognizing that the principles of national sovereignty and non-interference in the internal affairs of any State should be respected in the holding of elections,

Recognizing also that there is no single political system or single universal model for electoral processes equally suited to all nations and their peoples, and that political systems and electoral processes are subject to historical, political, cultural and religious factors,

Convinced that the establishment of the necessary mechanisms and means to guarantee full and effective popular participation in electoral processes corresponds to States,

Recalling all its resolutions in this regard,

Welcoming the Vienna Declaration and Programme of Action,[1] adopted by the World Conference on Human Rights, held at Vienna from 14 to 25 June 1993, in which the Conference reaffirmed that the processes of promoting and protecting human rights should be conducted in conformity with the purposes and principles of the Charter,

1 *Report of the World Conference on Human Rights, Vienna, 14-25 June 1993* (A/CONF.157/24 (Part I)), chap. III.

1. *Reiterates* that, by virtue of the principle of equal rights and self-determination of peoples enshrined in the Charter of the United Nations, all peoples have the right, freely and without external interference, to determine their political status and to pursue their economic, social and cultural development, and that every State has the duty to respect that right in accordance with the provisions of the Charter;

2. *Reaffirms* that it is the concern solely of peoples to determine methods and to establish institutions regarding the electoral process, as well as to determine the ways for its implementation according to their constitution and national legislation, and that, consequently, States should establish the necessary mechanisms and means to guarantee full and effective popular participation in those processes;

3. *Reaffirms also* that any activities that attempt, directly or indirectly, to interfere in the free development of national electoral processes, in particular in the developing countries, or that are intended to sway the results of such processes, violate the spirit and letter of the principles established in the Charter and in the Declaration on Principles of International Law concerning Friendly Relations and Cooperation among States in accordance with the Charter of the United Nations;

4. *Reaffirms further* that electoral assistance to Member States should be provided by the United Nations only at the request and with the consent of specific sovereign States, by virtue of resolutions adopted by the Security Council or the General Assembly in each case, in strict conformity with the principles of sovereignty and non-interference in the internal affairs of States, or in special circumstances such as cases of decolonization, or in the context of regional or international peace processes;

5. *Strongly appeals* to all States to refrain from financing or providing, directly or indirectly, any other form of overt or covert support for political parties or groups and from taking actions to undermine the electoral processes in any country;

6. *Condemns* any act of armed aggression or threat or use of force against peoples, their elected Governments or their legitimate leaders;

7. *Reaffirms* that all countries have the obligation under the Charter of the United Nations to respect the right of others to self-determination and to determine freely their political status and pursue their economic, social and cultural development;

8. *Decides* to consider this question at its fifty-second session under the item entitled "Human rights questions".

99th plenary meeting
22 December 1995

50/185. Strengthening the Role of the United Nations in Enhancing the Effectiveness of the Principle of Periodic and Genuine Elections and the Promotion of Democratization

Committee: 3
Vote: 156 - 0 - 15
Ref.: 49/190, 48/131, 47/138, 46/137, 45/150, 44/146

The General Assembly,

Recalling its previous resolutions on the subject, especially resolutions 48/131 of 20 December 1993 and 49/190 of 23 December 1994,

Recalling also the Vienna Declaration and Programme of Action, adopted by the World Conference on Human Rights, held at Vienna from 14 to 25 June 1993,[2] especially the recognition therein that assistance provided upon the request of Governments for the conduct of free and fair elections, including assistance in the human rights aspects of elections and public information about elections, is of particular importance in the strengthening and building of institutions relating to human rights and the strengthening of a pluralistic civil society, and that special emphasis should be given to measures that assist in achieving those goals,[3]

2 *Report of the World Conference on Human Rights, Vienna, 14-25 June 1993* (A/CONF.157/24 (Part I)), chap. III.

3 *Ibid.*, sect. II, para. 67.

Reaffirming that electoral assistance and support for the promotion of democratization are provided only at the specific request of the Member State concerned,

Recognizing the usefulness of a comprehensive and balanced approach in the activities carried out by the United Nations in this field in order to contribute to the strengthening of both democracy and human rights within the country concerned,

Welcoming the support provided by States to the electoral assistance activities of the United Nations, *inter alia*, through the provision of experts and electoral observers, as well as through contributions to the United Nations Trust Fund for Electoral Observation,

Having considered the report of the Secretary-General,[1]

Noting the continuing high level and evolving nature of requests for electoral assistance by Member States,

1. *Takes note* of the report of the Secretary-General on United Nations activities aimed at enhancing the effectiveness of the principle of periodic and genuine elections;[2]

2. *Commends* the electoral assistance provided to Member States at their request by the United Nations, requests that such assistance continue on a case-by-case basis in accordance with the guidelines on electoral assistance, recognizing that the fundamental responsibility of organizing free and fair elections lies with Governments, and also requests the Electoral Assistance Division of the Department of Political Affairs of the Secretariat to continue to inform Member States on a regular basis about the requests received, responses given to those requests and the nature of the assistance provided;

3. *Requests* that the United Nations continue its efforts to ensure, before undertaking to provide electoral assistance to a requesting State, that there is adequate time to organize and carry out an effective mission for providing such assistance, that conditions exist to allow a free and fair election and that provisions can be made for adequate and comprehensive reporting of the results of the mission;

4. *Commends* the steps taken by the United Nations to ensure the continuation and consolidation of the democratization process in certain Member States requesting assistance, including the provision of assistance before and after elections have taken place and needs-assessment missions aimed at recommending programmes which might contribute to the consolidating of the democratization process, and requests that such efforts be strengthened;

5. *Recommends* that the Electoral Assistance Division provide post-election assistance, as appropriate, to requesting States and electoral institutions, in order to contribute to the stability and continuity of their dectoral processes, as provided for in the report of the Secretary-General, and that it study, in cooperation with relevant United Nations offices, ways of defining more clearly the activities related to democratic consolidation which the United Nations might usefully undertake in assisting the efforts of interested States in this regard;

6. *Requests* the Secretary-General to take further steps to support States which request assistance by, *inter alia,* enabling the United Nations High Commissioner for Human Rights, in accordance with his mandate and through the Centre for Human Rights of the Secretariat, to support democratization activities related to human rights concerns, including, *inter alia,* human rights training and education, assistance for human rights related legislative reform, strengthening and reform of the judiciary, assistance to national human rights institutions and advisory services on treaty accession, reporting and international obligations as related to human rights;

7. *Commends* the programmes of assistance carried out by the United Nations Development Programme for civil service reform, and for governance, especially those for strengthening participation and linkages between concerned sectors of society and Governments;

8. *Recalls* the establishment by the Secretary-General of the United Nations Trust Fund for Electoral Observation, and calls upon Member States to consider contributing to the Fund;

9. *Stresses* the importance of coordination within the United Nations system, including cooperation with the Centre for Human Rights, the Department for Development Support and Management Services of the Secretariat and the United Nations Development Programme, which provide advisory services and technical assistance to requesting Member States, and encourages the Electoral Assistance Division to strengthen its collaboration with the Centre, including through an exchange of personnel when appropriate, and with the Department and the Programme and to continue to inform them of requests submitted in the area of electoral assistance;

10. *Notes with appreciation* additional efforts being made to enhance cooperation with other international, governmental and non-governmental organizations in order to facilitate more comprehensive and need-specific responses to requests for electoral assistance;

11. *Requests* the Secretary-General to provide the Electoral Assistance Division with adequate human and financial resources, under the regular budget of the Organization and within existing resources, to allow it to carry out its mandate, and to continue to ensure that the Centre for Human Rights is able to respond, within its mandate and in close coordination with the Electoral Assistance Division, to the increasing number of requests from Member States for advisory services;

12. *Takes note* of the evolution in the nature of requests for assistance and the growing need for specific types of expert assistance aimed at supporting and strengthening the existing capability of the requesting Government, in particular, through enhancing the capacity of electoral institutions;

13. *Recommends* that the Secretary-General consider ways to continue to improve coordination and to strengthen further the efforts of the Electoral Assistance Division, the Centre for Human Rights and the United Nations system in general to respond to its increased and evolving responsibilities and enlarged mandate in the field of electoral assistance and democratization as reflected in the present resolution, and to include his recommendations in this regard in his report to the General Assembly at its fifty-second session;

14. *Requests* the Secretary-General to report to the General Assembly at its fifty-second session on the implementation of resolution 49/190 and the present resolution, in particular on the status of requests from Member States for electoral assistance and verification, and on his efforts to enhance the Organization's support of the democratization process in Member States.

99th plenary meeting
22 December 1995

---

1 A/50/736.

2 *Ibid.*

03.00 DEVELOPMENT AND STRENGTHENING OF INTERNATIONAL LAW

23 (I). Registration of Treaties and International Agreements

Committee: 6
Vote: Adopted without a vote
Ref.: 34/149, 33/141, 1092(XI), 966(X), 482(V), 364(IV), 254(III), 172(II), 97(I)

The Executive Secretary sent a circular letter to the Members of the United Nations on 8 November 1945 informing them that from the date of the entry into force of the Charter treaties and international agreements would be received and filed on a provisional basis until the adoption of detailed regulations prescribing the procedure to be followed in the registration and publication of treaties and international agreements under the provisions of Article 102 of the Charter. The Executive Secretary also invited the Governments of Members to transmit to the Secretariat for filing and publication treaties and international agreements not included in the treaty series of the League of Nations and entered into in recent years before the date of the entry into force of the Charter.

It is desirable, as a matter of practical convenience, that arrangements should be made for the publication of any treaties or international agreements which non-member States may voluntarily transmit and which have not been included in the treaty series of the League of Nations. These arrangements should not, however, extend to treaties or international agreements transmitted by any non-member State such as Spain, the Government of which has been founded with the support of the Axis powers and does not, in view of its origin, its nature, its record and its close association with the aggressor States, possess qualifications necessary to justify membership in the United Nations under the provisions of the Charter.

Therefore, the General Assembly instructs the Secretary General:

1. To submit to the General Assembly proposals for detailed regulations and other measures designed to give effect to the provisions of Article 102 of the Charter;

2. To invite the governments of Members of the United Nations to transmit to the Secretary-General for filing and publication, treaties and international agreements entered into in recent years, but before the date of entry into force of the Charter, which had not been included in the League of Nations treaty series, and to transmit for registration and publication treaties and international agreements entered into after the date of entry into force of the Charter;

3. To receive, from the governments of non-member States, treaties and international agreements entered into both before and after the date of entry into force of the Charter, which have not been included in the League of Nations treaty series and which they may voluntarily transmit for filing and publication; and to dispose of them in accordance with the foregoing provisions, and subject to such detailed regulations and other measures as may hereafter be adopted.

Twenty-eighth plenary meeting
10 February 1946

94 (I). Progressive Development of International Law and its Codification

Committee: 6
Vote: unanimous
Ref.: 2669(XXV), 1686(XVI), 1505(XV)

The General Assembly,

Recognizes the obligation laid upon it by Article 13, paragraph 1, sub-paragraph a, of the Charter to initiate studies and make recommendations for the purpose of encouraging the progressive development of international law and its codification;

Realizes the need for a careful and thorough study of what has already been accomplished in this field as well as of the projects and activities of official and unofficial bodies engaged in efforts to promote the progressive development and formulation of public and private international law, and the need for a report on the methods whereby the General Assembly may most effectively discharge its obligations under the above-mentioned provision:

Therefore,

Resolves to establish a Committee of seventeen Members of the United Nations to be appointed by the General Assembly on the recommendation of the President, each of these Members to have one representative on the Committee;

Directs the Committee to study:

(*a*) The methods by which the General Assembly should encourage the progressive development of international law and its eventual codification;

(*b*) Methods of securing the cooperation of the several organs of the United Nations to this end;

(*c*) Methods of enlisting the assistance of such national or international bodies as might aid in the attainment of this objective;

and to report to the General Assembly at its next regular session.

Requests the Secretary-General to provide such assistance as the Committee may require for its work.

Fifty-fifth plenary meeting
11 December 1946

487 (V). Ways and Means for Making the Evidence of Customary International Law More Readily Available

Committee: 6
Vote: 50 - 0
Ref.: 686(VII), 602(VI)

The General Assembly,

Noting part II (Ways and means for making the evidence of customary international law more readily available) of the report[1] of the International Law Commission on the work of its second session,

Appreciating the work of the International Law Commission on this subject,

Invites the Secretary-General, in preparing his future programme of work in this field, to consider and report to the General Assembly upon the recommendations contained in paragraphs 90, 91 and 93 of part II of the report of the International Law Commission, in the light of the discussion[2] held and the suggestions made thereon in the Sixth Committee.

320th plenary meeting
12 December 1950

1903 (XVIII). Participation in General Multilateral Treaties Concluded under the Auspices of the League of Nations

Committee: 6
Vote: 79 - 0 - 22
Ref.: 2021(XX), 1766(XVII)

The General Assembly,

Having considered the question of extended participation in general multilateral treaties concluded under the auspices of the League of Nations, and the report of the International Law Commission thereon,[3]

Noting that there are twenty-one such treaties of a technical and non-political character which by their terms authorized the Council of the

---

1 See *Official Records of the General Assembly, Fifth Session, Supplement No. 12.*

2 *Ibid., Sixth Committee*, 230th and 231st meetings.

3 *Official Records of the General Assembly, Eighteenth Session, Supplement No. 9*, Chapter III.

League of Nations to invite additional States to become parties, and thus were not intended to be closed to new States,

Further noting that since the Council of the League ceased to exist a large number of new States have come into being and that many of them have been unable to become parties to the treaties in question for lack of an invitation to accede,

Recalling the recommendation made by the Assembly of the League of Nations at its final session that its Members should facilitate in every way the assumption by the United Nations of functions and powers entrusted to the League of Nations under international agreements of a technical and non-political character,[1]

Further recalling that the General Assembly, in resolution 24 (I) of 12 February 1946, declared that the United Nations was willing in principle to assume the exercise of certain functions and powers previously entrusted to the League of Nations under international agreements,

1. *Decides* that the General Assembly is the appropriate organ of the United Nations to exercise the power conferred by multilateral treaties of a technical and nonpolitical character on the Council of the League of Nations to invite States to accede to those treaties;

2. *Records* that those Members of the United Nations which are parties to the treaties referred to above assent by the present resolution to the decision set forth in paragraph 1 above and express their resolve to use their good offices to secure the cooperation of the other parties to the treaties so far as this may be necessary;

3. *Requests* the Secretary-General:

(*a*) As depositary of the treaties referred to above, to bring to the notice of any party which is not a Member of the United Nations the terms of the present resolution;

(*b*) To transmit copies of the present resolution to States Members of the United Nations which are parties to those treaties;

(*c*) To consult, where necessary, with the States referred to in subparagraphs (a) and (b) above and with the United Nations organs and the specialized agencies concerned as to whether any of the treaties in question have ceased to be in force, have been superseded by later treaties, have otherwise ceased to be of interest for accession by additional States, or require action to adapt them to contemporary conditions;

(*d*) To report on these matters to the General Assembly at its nineteenth session;

4. *Further requests* the Secretary-General to invite each State which is a Member of the United Nations or member of a specialized agency or a party to the Statute of the International Court of Justice, or has been designated for this purpose by the General Assembly, and which otherwise is not eligible to become a party to the treaties in question, to accede thereto by depositing an instrument of accession with the Secretary-General of the United Nations;

5. *Decides* to place on the provisional agenda of its nineteenth session an item entitled "General multilateral treaties concluded under the auspices of the League of Nations".

1259th plenary meeting
18 November 1963

[1] League of Nations, *Official Journal, Special Supplement No. 194*, p. 57 (resolution of 18 April 1946).

50/43. United Nations Programme of Assistance in the Teaching, Study, Dissemination and Wider Appreciation of International Law

Committee: 6
Vote: Adopted without a vote
Ref.: 48/29, 46/50, 44/28, 42/148, 40/66, 38/129, 36/108, 34/144, 32/146, 3502(XXX), 3106(XXVIII), 2838(XXVI), 2698(XXV), 2550(XXIV), 2464(XXIII), 2313(XXII), 2204(XXI), 2099(XX), 1968(XVIII), 1816(XVII)

The General Assembly,

Recalling paragraph 17 of its resolution 48/29 of 9 December 1993, paragraph 1 of section IV of the annex to its resolution 47/32 of 25 November 1992 and paragraph 1 of section IV of the annex to its resolution 49/50 of 9 December 1994,

Taking note with appreciation of the report of the Secretary-General on the implementation of the United Nations Programme of Assistance in the Teaching, Study, Dissemination and Wider Appreciation of International Law[2] and the guidelines and recommendations on future implementation of the Programme within the framework of the United Nations Decade of International Law, which were adopted by the Advisory Committee on the Programme and are contained in section III of that report,

Bearing in mind that the encouragement of the teaching, study, dissemination and wider appreciation of international law is one of the main objectives of the United Nations Decade of International Law, as declared in its resolution 44/23 of 17 November 1989 and further reaffirmed and expanded in section IV of the programme for the activities for the first term (1990-1992), the second term (1993-1994) and the third term (1995-1996) annexed to resolutions 45/40 of 28 November 1990, 47/32, and 49/50,

Considering that international law should occupy an appropriate place in the teaching of legal disciplines at all universities,

Noting with appreciation the efforts made by States at the bilateral level to provide assistance in the teaching and study of international law,

Convinced, nevertheless, that States and international organizations and institutions should be encouraged to give further support to the Programme and increase their activities to promote the teaching, study, dissemination and wider appreciation of international law, in particular those activities which are of special benefit to persons from developing countries,

Reaffirming its resolutions 2464 (XXIII) of 20 December 1968, 2550 (XXIV) of 12 December 1969, 2838 (XXVI) of 18 December 1971, 3106(XXVIII) of 12 December 1973, 3502 (XXX) of 15 December 1975, 32/146 of 16 December 1977, 36/108 of 10 December 1981 and 38/129 of 19 December 1983, in which it stated or recalled that in the conduct of the Programme it was desirable to use as far as possible the resources and facilities made available by Member States, international organizations and others, as well as its resolutions 34/144 of 17 December 1979, 40/66 of 11 December 1985, 42/148 of 7 December 1987, 44/28 of 4 December 1989, 46/50 of 9 December 1991 and 48/29, in which, in addition, it expressed or reaffirmed the hope that, in appointing lecturers for the seminars to be held within the framework of the fellowship programme in international law, account would be taken of the need to secure representation of major legal systems and balance among various geographical regions,

1. *Approves* the guidelines and recommendations contained in section III of the report of the Secretary-General and adopted by the Advisory Committee on the United Nations Programme of Assistance in the Teaching, Study, Dissemination and Wider Appreciation of International Law, in particular those designed to achieve the best possible results in the administration of the Programme within a policy of maximum financial restraint;

2. *Authorizes* the Secretary-General to carry out in 1996 and 1997 the activities specified in his report, including the provision of:

[2] A/50/726.

(*a*) A number of international law fellowships in both 1996 and 1997, to be determined in the light of the overall resources for the Programme and to be awarded at the request of Governments of developing countries;

(*b*) A minimum of one scholarship in both 1996 and 1997 under the Hamilton Shirley Amerasinghe Memorial Fellowship on the Law of the Sea, subject to the availability of new voluntary contributions made specifically to the fellowship fund;

(*c*) Subject to the overall resources for the Programme, assistance in the form of a travel grant for one participant from each developing country, who would be invited to possible regional courses to be organized in 1996 and 1997; and to finance the above activities from provisions in the regular budget, when appropriate, as well as from voluntary financial contributions earmarked for each of the activities concerned, which would be received as a result of the requests set out in paragraphs 13, 14 and 15 below;

3. *Expresses its appreciation* to the Secretary-General for his constructive efforts to promote training and assistance in international law within the framework of the Programme in 1994 and 1995, in particular for the organization of the thirtieth[1] and thirty-first[2] sessions of the International Law Seminar, held at Geneva from 20 May to 10 June 1994 and from 22 May to 9 June 1995, respectively, and for the activities of the Office of Legal Affairs of the Secretariat related to the fellowship programme in international law and to the Hamilton Shirley Amerasinghe Memorial Fellowship on the Law of the Sea, carried out, respectively, through its Codification Division and its Division for Ocean Affairs and the Law of the Sea;

4. *Requests* the Secretary-General to consider the possibility of admitting, for participation in the various components of the Programme of Assistance, candidates from countries willing to bear the entire cost of such participation;

5. *Also requests* the Secretary-General to consider the relative advantages of using available resources and voluntary contributions for regional, subregional or national courses, as against courses organized within the United Nations system;

6. *Invites* interested States to consider the option of financing the translation and publication of the Judgments of the International Court of Justice;

7. *Welcomes* the efforts undertaken by the Office of Legal Affairs to bring up to date the *United Nations Treaty Series* and the *United Nations Juridical Yearbook*;

8. *Expresses its appreciation* to the United Nations Institute for Training and Research for its participation in the Programme through the activities described in the report of the Secretary-General;

9. *Also expresses its appreciation* to the United Nations Educational, Scientific and Cultural Organization its participation in the Programme through the activities described in the report of the Secretary-General;

10. *Further expresses its appreciation* of the Hague Academy of International Law for the valuable contribution it continues to make to the Programme which has enabled candidates under the international law fellowship programme to attend and participate in the Programme in conjunction with the Academy courses;

11. *Notes with appreciation* the contributions of the Hague Academy of International Law to the teaching, study, dissemination and wider appreciation of international law, and calls on Member States and interested organizations to give favourable consideration to the appeal of the Academy for a continuation of support and a possible increase in their financial contributions, to enable the Academy to carry out its activities, particularly those relating to the summer courses, regional courses and programmes of the Centre for Studies and Research in International Law and International Relations;

12. *Urges* all States and relevant international organizations, whether regional or universal, to make all possible efforts to implement the goals and carry out the activities contemplated in section IV of the programme of activities for the third term (1995-1996) of the United Nations Decade of International Law, dealing with the encouragement of the teaching, study, dissemination and wider appreciation of international law and contained in the annex to its resolution 49/50;

13. *Requests* the Secretary-General to continue to publicize the Programme and periodically to invite Member States, universities, philanthropic foundations and other interested national and international institutions and organizations, as well as individuals, to make voluntary contributions towards the financing of the Programme or otherwise to assist in its implementation and possible expansion;

14. *Reiterates its request* to Member States and to interested organizations and individuals to make voluntary contributions, *inter alia*, for the International Law Seminar, for the fellowship programme in international law and for the Hamilton Shirley Amerasinghe Memorial Fellowship on the Law of the Sea, and expresses its appreciation to those Member States, institutions and individuals which have made voluntary contributions for this purpose;

15. *Urges* in particular all Governments to make voluntary contributions for the organization of regional refresher courses in international law by the United Nations Institute for Training and Research, especially with a view to covering the amount needed for the financing of the daily subsistence allowance for up to twenty-five participants in each regional course, thus alleviating the burden on prospective host countries and making it possible for the Institute to continue to organize the regional courses;

16. *Requests* the Secretary-General to report to the General Assembly at its fifty-second session on the implementation of the Programme during 1996 and 1997 and, following consultations with the Advisory Committee on the United Nations Programme of Assistance in the Teaching, Study, Dissemination and Wider Appreciation of International Law, to submit recommendations regarding the execution of the Programme in subsequent years;

17. *Decides* to appoint twenty-five Member States, six from Africa, five from Asia, three from Eastern Europe, five from Latin America and the Caribbean and six from Western Europe and other States, as members of the Advisory Committee on the United Nations Programme of Assistance in the Teaching, Study, Dissemination and Wider Appreciation of International Law, for a period of four years beginning on 1 January 1996;[3]

18. *Decides* to include in the provisional agenda of its fifty-second session the item entitled "United Nations Programme of Assistance in the Teaching, Study, Dissemination and Wider Appreciation of International Law".

87th plenary meeting
11 December 1995

50/44. United Nations Decade of International Law

Committee: 6
Vote: Adopted without a vote
Ref.: 49/50, 48/30, 46/53, 45/40, 44/23

The General Assembly,

Recalling its resolution 44/23 of 17 November 1989, by which it declared the period 1990-1999 the United Nations Decade of International Law,

Recalling also that the main purposes of the Decade, according to resolution 44/23, should be, *inter alia*:

(*a*) To promote acceptance of and respect for the principles of international law;

1 See *Official Records of the General Assembly, Forty-ninth Session, Supplement No. 10* (A/49/10), chap. VI, sect. G.

2 *Ibid., Fiftieth Session, Supplement No. 10* (A/50/10), chap. VII, sect. E.

3 States appointed members of the Advisory Committee on the United Nations Programme of Assistance in the Teaching, Study, Dissemination and Wider Appreciation of International Law are the following: Canada, Colombia, Cyprus, Czech Republic, Ethiopia, France, Germany, Ghana, Iran, Italy, Jamaica, Kenya, Lebanon, Malaysia, Mexico, Nigeria, Pakistan, Portugal, Russian Federation, Sudan, Trinidad and Tobago, Ukraine, United Republic of Tanzania, United States and Uruguay.

(*b*) To promote means and methods for the peaceful settlement of disputes between States, including resort to and full respect for the International Court of Justice;

(*c*) To encourage the progressive development of international law and its codification;

(*d*) To encourage the teaching, study, dissemination and wider appreciation of international law,

Recalling further its resolution 49/50 of 9 December 1994, to which was annexed the programme for the activities for the third term (1995-1996) of the Decade,

Expressing its appreciation to the Secretary-General for his report[1] submitted pursuant to resolution 49/50,

Having considered the above-mentioned report,

Recalling that at its forty-fifth session the Sixth Committee established the Working Group on the United Nations Decade of International Law with a view to preparing generally acceptable recommendations on the programme of activities for the Decade,

Noting that at its forty-sixth, forty-seventh, forty-eighth, forty-ninth and fiftieth sessions the Sixth Committee reconvened the Working Group to continue its work in accordance with resolutions 45/40 of 28 November 1990, 46/53 of 9 December 1991, 47/32 of 25 November 1992, 48/30 of 9 December 1993 and 49/50,

Having considered the oral report of the Chairman of the Working Group submitted to the Sixth Committee,[2]

1. *Expresses its appreciation* for the work done on the United Nations Decade of International Law at the current session, and requests the Working Group of the Sixth Committee to continue its work at the fifty-first session in accordance with its mandate and methods of work;

2. *Also expresses its appreciation* to States and international organizations and institutions that have undertaken activities in implementation of the programme for the third term (1995-1996) of the Decade, including sponsoring conferences on various subjects of international law;

3. *Further expresses its appreciation* to the Secretary-General for the successful organization of the United Nations Congress on Public International Law, held from 13 to 17 March 1995, noting with satisfaction that the Congress emphasized the importance of all aspects of international law and focused on the four main purposes of the Decade, as well as on new challenges and expectations for the twenty-first century, and requests the Secretary-General, within existing resources, to make the proceedings widely available;

4. *Strongly welcomes* the recent advances made by the Treaty Section of the Office of Legal Affairs in its programme of computerization of the Multilateral Treaties Deposited with the Secretary-General and the United Nations Treaty Series and looks forward to the early effective availability of the former on the Internet and the latter online to Member States and other users;

5. *Invites* all States and international organizations and institutions referred to in the programme to provide, update or supplement information on activities they have undertaken in implementation of it, as appropriate, to the Secretary-General, as well as to submit their views on possible activities for the next term of the Decade;

6. *Requests* the Secretary-General to submit, on the basis of such information as well as of new information on the activities of the United Nations relevant to the progressive development of international law and its codification, a report to the General Assembly at its fifty-first session on the implementation of the programme;

7. *Encourages* States to disseminate at the national level, as appropriate, information contained in the report of the Secretary-General;

8. *Appeals* to States, international organizations and non-governmental organizations working in the field of international law and to the private sector to make financial contributions or contributions in kind for the purpose of facilitating the implementation of the programme;

9. *Encourages* the Office of Legal Affairs to continue in its efforts to bring up to date the publication of the United Nations Treaty Series and the United Nations Juridical Yearbook:

10. *Once again requests* the Secretary-General to bring to the attention of States and international organizations and institutions working in the field of international law the programme annexed to resolution 49/50;

11. *Invites* the International Committee of the Red Cross to continue to report on activities undertaken by the Committee and other relevant bodies with regard to the protection of the environment in times of armed conflict, so that the information received may be included in the report to be prepared pursuant to paragraph 6 of the present resolution;

12. *Decides* to include in the provisional agenda of its fifty-first session the item entitled "United Nations Decade of International Law".

87th plenary meeting
11 December 1995

---

[1] A/50/368 and Add.1 and 2.

[2] See A/C.6/50/SR.45.

04.00 PROBLEMS OF STATEHOOD

04.10 NON-SELF-GOVERNING TERRITORIES AND TRUST TERRITORIES

9 (I). Non-Self-Governing Peoples

Committee: 4
Vote: unanimous

The United Nations, meeting in its first General Assembly, is keenly aware of the problems and political aspirations of the peoples who have not yet attained a full measure of self-government and who are not directly represented here.

Chapters XI, XII and XIII of the Charter recognize the problems of the non-self-governing peoples as of vital concern to the peace and general welfare of the world community.

By Chapter XI, all the Members of the United Nations which have or assume responsibilities for the administration of territories whose peoples have not yet attained a full measure of self-government recognize the principle that the interests of the inhabitants of these territories are paramount. They accept, as a sacred trust, the obligation to promote to the utmost the well-being of the inhabitants of these territories. To that end they accept certain specific obligations, including the obligation to develop self-government and to assist the inhabitants in the progressive development of their free political institutions.

By Chapters XII and XIII, the Charter provides for the establishment of an international trusteeship system, the basic objectives of which are, among others, to promote the political, economic, social and educational advancement of the inhabitants of trust territories, and to promote their progressive development towards self-government or independence.

The General Assembly regrets that the Trusteeship Council cannot be brought into being at this first part of the first session, not because of any lack of desire to do so but because, before the Trusteeship Council can be established, trusteeship agreements must be concluded.

The General Assembly holds the view that any delay in putting into effect the system of international trusteeship prevents the implementation of the principles of the trusteeship system, as declared in the Charter, and deprives the populations of such territories as may be brought under the trusteeship system of the opportunity of enjoying the advantages arising from the implementation of these principles.

With a view to expediting the conclusion of these agreements and the establishment of the Trusteeship Council, the Preparatory Commission recommended that the General Assembly should call on those Members of the United Nations which are now administering territories held under mandate to undertake practical steps, in concert with the other States directly concerned, for the implementation of Article 79 of the Charter.

Without waiting for the recommendation of the Preparatory Commission to be considered by the General Assembly, the Members of the United Nations administering territories held under mandate took the initiative in making declarations in regard to these territories.

Therefore
with respect to Chapter XI of the Charter, the General Assembly:

1. *Draws* attention to the fact that the obligations accepted under Chapter XI of the Charter by all Members of the United Nations are in no way contingent upon the conclusion of trusteeship agreements or upon the bringing into being of the Trusteeship Council and are, therefore, already in full force.

2. *Requests* the Secretary-General to include in his annual report on the work of the Organization, as provided for in Article 98 of the Charter, a statement summarizing such information as may have been transmitted to him by Members of the United Nations under Article 73(e) of the Charter relating to economic, social and educational conditions in the territories for which they are responsible other than those to which Chapters XII and XIII apply.

with respect to Chapters XII and XIII of the Charter, the General Assembly:

3. *Welcomes* the declarations, made by certain States administering territories now held under mandate, of an intention to negotiate trusteeship agreements in respect of some of those territories and, in respect of Transjordan, to establish its independence.

4. *Invites* the States administering territories now held under mandate to undertake practical steps, in concert with the other States directly concerned, for the implementation of Article 79 of the Charter (which provides for the conclusion of agreements on the terms of trusteeship for each territory to be placed under the trusteeship system), in order to submit these agreements for approval, preferably not later than during the second part of the first session of the General Assembly.

In conclusion, the General Assembly:

5. *Expects* that the realization of the objectives of Chapters XI, XII and XIII will make possible the attainment of the political, economic, social and educational aspirations of non-self-governing peoples.

Twenty-seventh plenary meeting
9 February 1946

742 (VIII). Factors which Should be Taken into Account in Deciding whether a Territory is or is not a Territory whose People have Nnt yet Attained a Full Measure of Self-Government

Committee: 4
Vote: 32 - 19 - 6
Ref.: 648(VII), 567(VI), 334(IV)

The General Assembly,

Bearing in mind the principles embodied in the Declaration regarding Non-Self-Governing Territories and the objectives set forth in Chapter XI of the Charter,

Recalling the provisions of resolutions 567 (VI) and 648 (VII), adopted by the General Assembly on 18 January and 10 December 1952 respectively, indicating the value of establishing a list of factors which should be taken into account in deciding whether a Territory has or has not attained a full measure self-government,

Having regard to the competence of the General Assembly to consider the principles that should guide the United Nations and the Member States in the implementation of obligations arising from Chapter XI of the Charter and to make recommendations in connexion with them,

Having examined the report[1] of the *Ad Hoc Committee* on Factors (Non-Self-Governing Territories) set up by resolution 648 (VII),

1. *Takes note* of the conclusions of the report of the *Ad Hoc Committee* on Factors (Non-Self-Governing Territories);

2. *Approves* the list of factors as adopted by the Fourth Committee;

3. *Recommends* that the annexed list of factors should be used by the General Assembly and the Administering Members as a guide in determining whether any Territory, due to changes in its constitutional status, is or is no longer within the scope of Chapter XI of the Charter, in order that, in view of the documentation provided under resolution 222 (III) of 3 November 1948, a decision may be taken by

1 See document A/2428. Appendix 33, p. 491.

the General Assembly on the continuation or cessation of the transmission of information required by Chapter XI of the Charter;

4. *Reasserts* that each concrete case should be considered and decided upon in the light of the particular circumstances of that case and taking into account the right of self-determination of peoples;

5. *Considers* that the validity of any form of association between a Non-Self-Governing Territory and a metropolitan or any other country essentially depends on the freely expressed will of the people at the time of the taking of the decision;

6. *Considers* that the manner in which Territories referred to in Chapter XI of the Charter can become fully self-governing is primarily through the attainment of independence, although it is recognized that self-government can also be achieved by association with another State or group of States if this is done freely and on the basis of absolute equality;

7. *Reaffirms* that the factors, while serving as a guide in determining whether the obligations as set forth in Chapter XI of the Charter shall exist, should in no way be interpreted as a hindrance to the attainment of a full measure of self-government by a Non-Self-Governing Territory;

8. *Further reaffirms* that, for a Territory to be deemed self-governing in economic, social or educational affairs, it is essential that its people shall have attained a full measure of self-government;

9. *Instructs* the Committee on Information from Non-Self-Governing Territories to study any documentation transmitted hereafter under resolution 222 (III) in the light of the list of factors approved by the present resolution, and other relevant considerations which may arise from each concrete case of cessation of information;

10. *Recommends* that the Committee on Information from Non-Self-Governing Territories take the initiative of proposing modifications at any time to improve the list of factors, as may seem necessary in the light of circumstances.

459th plenary meeting
27 November 1953

Annex

List of Factors

Factors Indicative of the Attainment of Independence or of Other Separate Systems of Self-Government

First part

Factors Indicative of the Attainment of Independence

A. International status

1. *International responsibility.* Full international responsibility of the Territory for the acts inherent in the exercise of its external sovereignty and for the corresponding acts in the administration of its internal affairs.

2. *Eligibility for membership in the United Nations.*

3. *General international relations.* Power to enter into direct relations of every kind with other governments and with international institutions and to negotiate, sign and ratify international instruments.

4. *National defence.* Sovereign right to provide for its national defence.

B. Internal self-government

1. *Form of government.* Complete freedom of the people of the Territory to choose the form of government which they desire.

2. *Territorial government.* Freedom from control or interference by the government of another State in respect of the internal government (legislature, executive, judiciary, and administration of the Territory).

3. *Economic, social and cultural jurisdiction.* Complete autonomy in respect of economic, social and cultural affairs.

Second part

Factors Indicative of the Attainment of Other Separate Systems of Self-Government

A. General

1. *Opinion of the population.* The opinion of the population of the Territory, freely expressed by informed and democratic processes, as to the status or change in status which they desire.

2. *Freedom of choice.* Freedom of choosing on the basis of the right of self-determination of peoples between several possibilities, including independence.

3. *Voluntary limitation of sovereignty.* Degree of evidence that the attribute or attributes of sovereignty which are not individually exercised will be collectively exercised by the larger entity thus associated and the freedom of the population of a Territory which has associated itself with the metropolitan country to modify at any time this status through the expression of their will by democratic means.

4. *Geographical considerations.* Extent to which the relations of the Non-Self-Governing Territory with the capital of the metropolitan government may be affected by circumstances arising out of their respective geographical positions, such as separation by land, sea or other natural obstacles; and extent to which the interests of boundary States may be affected bearing in mind the general principle of good-neighbourliness referred to in Article 74 of the Charter.

5. *Ethnic and cultural considerations.* Extent to which the populations are of different race, language or religion or have a distinct cultural heritage, interests or aspirations, distinguishing them from the peoples of the country with which they freely associate themselves.

6. *Political advancement.* Political advancement of the population sufficient to enable them to decide upon the future destiny of the Territory with due knowledge.

B. International status

1. *General international relations.* Degree or extent to which the Territory exercises the power to enter freely into direct relations of every kind with other governments and with international institutions and to negotiate, sign and ratify international instruments freely. Degree or extent to which the metropolitan country is bound, through constitutional provisions or legislative means, by the freely expressed wishes of the Territory in negotiating, signing and ratifying international conventions which may influence conditions in the Territory.

2. *Change of political status.* The right of the metropolitan country or the Territory to change the political status of that Territory in the light of the consideration whether that Territory is or is not subject to any claim or litigation on the part of another State.

3. *Eligibility for membership in the United Nations.*

C. Internal self-government

1. *Territorial government.* Nature and measure of control or interference, if any, by the government of another State in respect of the internal government, for example, in respect of the following:

Legislature: The enactment of laws for the Territory by an indigenous body whether fully elected by free and democratic processes or lawfully constituted in a manner receiving the free consent of the population;

Executive: The selection of members of the executive branch of the government by the competent authority in the Territory receiving consent of the indigenous population, whether that authority is hereditary or elected, having regard also to the nature and measure of control, if any, by an outside agency on that authority, whether directly or indirectly exercised in the constitution and conduct of the executive branch of the government;

Judiciary: The establishment of courts of law and the selection of judges.

2. *Participation of the population.* Effective participation of the population in the government of the Territory: (a) Is there an adequate and appropriate electoral and representative system? (b) Is this

electoral system conducted without direct or indirect interference from a foreign government?

3. *Economic, social and cultural jurisdiction.* Degree of autonomy in respect of economic, social and cultural affairs, as illustrated by the degree of freedom from economic pressure as exercised, for example, by a foreign minority group which, by virtue of the help of a foreign Power, has acquired a privileged economic status prejudicial to the general economic interest of the people of the Territory; and by the degree of freedom and lack of discrimination against the indigenous population of the Territory in social legislation and social developments.

Third part

Factors Indicative of the Free Association of a Territory on Equal Basis with the Metropolitan or other Country as an Integral Part of that Country or in any Other Form

A. General

1. *Opinion of the population.* The opinion of the population of the Territory, freely expressed by informed and democratic processes, as to the status or change in status which they desire.

2. *Freedom of choice.* The freedom of the population of a Non-Self-Governing Territory which has associated itself with the metropolitan country as an integral part of that country or in any other form to modify this status through the expression of their will by democratic means.

3. *Geographical considerations.* Extent to which the relations of the Territory with the capital of the central government may be affected by circumstances arising out of their respective geographical positions, such as separation by land, sea or other natural obstacles. The right of the metropolitan country or the Territory to change the political status of that Territory in the light of the consideration whether that Territory is or is not subject to any claim or litigation on the part of another State.

4. *Ethnic and cultural considerations.* Extent to which the population are of different race, language or religion or have a distinct cultural heritage, interests or aspirations, distinguishing them from the peoples of the country with which they freely associate themselves.

5. *Political advancement.* Political advancement of the population sufficient to enable them to decide upon the future destiny of the Territory with due knowledge.

6. *Constitutional considerations.* Association by virtue of a treaty or bilateral agreement affecting the status of the Territory, taking into account (i) whether the constitutional guarantees extend equally to the associated Territory, (ii) whether there are powers in certain matters constitutionally reserved to the Territory or to the central authority, and (iii) whether there is provision for the participation of the Territory on a basis of equality in any changes in the constitutional system of the State.

B. Status

1. *Legislative representation.* Representation without discrimination in the central legislative organs on the same basis as other inhabitants and regions.

2. *Participation of the population.* Effective participation of the population in the government of the Territory (a) Is there an adequate and appropriate electoral and representative system? (b) Is this electoral system conducted without direct or indirect interference from a foreign government?[1]

3. *Citizenship.* Citizenship without discrimination on the same basis as other inhabitants.

4. *Government officials.* Eligibility of officials from the Territory to all public offices of the central authority, by appointment or election, on the same basis as those from other parts of the country.

C. Internal constitutional conditions

1. *Suffrage.* Universal and equal suffrage, and free periodic elections, characterized by an absence of undue influence over and coercion of the voter or of the imposition of disabilities on particular political parties.[2]

2. *Local rights and status.* In a unitary system equal rights and status for the inhabitants and local bodies of the Territory as enjoyed by inhabitants and local bodies of other parts of the country; in a federal system an identical degree of self-government for the inhabitants and local bodies of all parts of the federation.

3. *Local officials.* Appointment or election of officials in the Territory on the same basis as those in other parts of the country.

4. *Internal legislation.* Local self-government of the same scope and under the same conditions as enjoyed by other parts of the country.

5. *Economic, social and cultural jurisdiction.* Degree of autonomy in respect of economic, social and cultural affairs, as illustrated by the degree of freedom from economic pressure as exercised, for example, by a foreign minority group which, by virtue of the help of a foreign Power, has acquired a privileged economic status prejudicial to the general economic interest of the people of the Territory; and by the degree of freedom and lack of discrimination against the indigenous population of the Territory in social legislation and social developments.

1541 (XV). Principles which Should Guide Members in Determining whether or not an Obligation Exists to Transmit the Information Called for under Article 73 e of the Charter

Committee: 4
Vote: 69 - 2 - 21
Ref.: 50/32, 40/51, 39/41, 38/49, 37/29, 36/49, 35/26, 34/33, 32/33, 31/29, 3420(XXX), 3293(XXIX), 3110(XXVIII), 2978(XXVII), 2870(XXVI), 2701(XXV), 2558(XXIV), 2422(XXIII), 2351(XXII), 2233(XXI), 2109(XX), 1745(XVI), 1645(XVI), 1644(XVI), 1542(XV), 1468(XIV), 1467(XIV), 1052(XI), 930(X)848(IX), 751(VIII), 551(VI), 447(V), 446(V), 335(IV), 327(IV), 218(III), 144(II), 143(II), 142(II)

The General Assembly,

Considering the objectives set forth in Chapter XI of the Charter of the United Nations,

---

1 For example, the following questions would be relevant

(i) Has each adult inhabitant equal power (subject to special safeguards for minorities) to determine the character of the government of the Territory?

(ii) Is this power exercised freely, i.e., is there an absence of undue influence over and coercion of the voter and of the imposition of disabilities on particular political parties?

Some tests which can be used in the application of this factor are as follows

(a) The existence of effective measures to ensure the democratic expression of the will of the people.

(b) The existence of more than one political party in the Territory.

(c) The existence of a secret ballot.

(d) The existence of legal prohibitions on the exercise of undemocratic practices in the course of elections.

(e) The existence for the individual elector of a choice between candidates of differing political parties.

(f) The absence of "martial law" \band similar measures at election times;

(iii) Is each individual free to express his political opinions to support or oppose any political party or cause, and to criticize the government of the day?

2 For example, the following tests would be relevant

(a) The existence of effective measures to ensure the democratic expression of the will of the people.

(b) The existence of more than one political party in the Territory.

(c) The existence of a secret ballot;

(d) The existence of legal prohibitions on the exercise of undemocratic practices in the course of elections;

(e) The existence for the individual elector of a choice between candidates of differing political parties.

(f) The absence of "martial law" \band similar measures at election times.

(g) Freedom of each individual to express his political opinions, to support or oppose any political party or cause, and to criticize the government of the day.

Bearing in mind the list of factors annexed to General Assembly resolution 742 (VIII) of 27 November 1953,

Having examined the report of the Special Committee of Six on the Transmission of Information under Article 73 e of the Charter,[1] appointed under General Assembly resolution 1467 (XIV) of 12 December 1959 to study the principles which should guide Members in determining whether or not an obligation exists to transmit the information called for in Article 73 e of the Charter and to report on the results of its study to the Assembly at its fifteenth session,

1. *Expresses its appreciation* of the work of the Special Committee of Six on the Transmission of Information under Article 73 e of the Charter;

2. *Approves* the principles set out in section V, part B, of the report of the Committee, as amended and as they appear in the annex to the present resolution;

3. *Decides* that these principles should be applied in the light of the facts and the circumstances of each case to determine whether or not an obligation exists to transmit information under Article 73 e of the Charter.

948th plenary meeting
15 December 1960

Annex

Principles which Should Guide Members in Determining whether or not an Obligation Exists to Transmit the Information Called for in Article 73 e of the Charter of the United Nations

Principle I

The authors of the Charter of the United Nations had in mind that Chapter XI should be applicable to territories which were then known to be of the colonial type. An obligation exists to transmit information under Article 73 e of the Charter in respect of such territories whose peoples have not yet attained a full measure of self-government.

Principle II

Chapter XI of the Charter embodies the concept of Non-Self-Governing Territories in a dynamic state of evolution and progress towards a "full measure of self-government". As soon as a territory and its peoples attain a full measure of self-government, the obligation ceases. Until this comes about, the obligation to transmit information under Article 73 e continues.

Principle III

The obligation to transmit information under Article 73 e of the Charter constitutes an international obligation and should be carried out with due regard to the fulfillment of international law.

Principle IV

Prima facie there is an obligation to transmit information in respect of a territory which is geographically separate and is distinct ethnically and/or culturally from the country administering it.

Principle V

Once it has been established that such a *prima facie* case of geographical and ethnical or cultural distinctness of a territory exists, other elements may then be brought into consideration. These additional elements may be, *inter alia* of an administrative, political, juridical, economic or historic nature. If they affect the relationship between the metropolitan State and the territory concerned in a manner which arbitrarily places the latter in a position or status of subordination, they support the presumption that there is an obligation to transmit information under Article 73 e of the Charter.

Principle VI

A Non-Self-Governing Territory can be said to have reached a full measure of self-government by:

(*a*) Emergence as a sovereign independent State;
(*b*) Free association with an independent State; or
(*c*) Integration with an independent State.

Principle VII

(*a*) Free association should be the result of a free and voluntary choice by the peoples of the territory concerned expressed through informed and democratic processes. It should be one which respects the individuality and the cultural characteristics of the territory and its peoples, and retains for the peoples of the territory which is associated with an independent State the freedom to modify the status of that territory through the expression of their will by democratic means and through constitutional processes.

(*b*) The associated territory should have the right to determine its internal constitution without outside interference, in accordance with due constitutional processes and the freely expressed wishes of the people. This does not preclude consultations as appropriate or necessary under the terms of the free association agreed upon.

Principle VIII

Integration with an independent State should be on the basis of complete equality between the peoples of the erstwhile Non-Self-Governing Territory and those of the independent country with which it is integrated. The peoples of both territories should have equal status and rights of citizenship and equal guarantees of fundamental rights and freedoms without any distinction or discrimination; both should have equal rights and opportunities for representation and effective participation at all levels in the executive, legislative and judicial organs of government.

Principle IX

Integration should have come about in the following circumstances:

(*a*) The integrating territory should have attained an advanced stage of self-government with free political institutions, so that its peoples would have the capacity to make a responsible choice through informed and democratic processes;

(*b*) The integration should be the result of the freely expressed wishes of the territory's peoples acting with full knowledge of the change in their status, their wishes having been expressed through informed and democratic processes, impartial conducted and based on universal adult suffrage. The United Nations could, when it deems it necessary, supervise these processes.

Principle X

The transmission of information in respect of Non-Self-Governing Territories under Article 73e of the Charter is subject to such limitation as security and constitutional considerations may require. This means that the extent of the information may be limited in certain circumstances, but the limitation in Article 73 e cannot relieve a Member State of the obligations of Chapter XI. The "limitation" can relate only to the quantum of information of economic, social and educational nature to be transmitted.

Principle XI

The only constitutional considerations to which Article 73 e of the Charter refers are those arising from constitutional relations of the territory with the Administering Member. They refer to a situation in which the constitution of the territory gives it self-government in economic, social and educational matters through freely elected institutions. Nevertheless, the responsibility for transmitting information under Article 73 e continues, unless these constitutional relations preclude the Government or parliament of the Administering Member from receiving statistical and other information of a technical nature relating to economic, social and educational conditions in the territory.

1 *Official Records of the General Assembly, Fifteenth Session*, agenda item 38, document A/4526, Appendix 8, p. 367.

Principle XII

Security considerations have not been invoked in the past. Only in very exceptional circumstances can information on economic, social and educational conditions have any security aspect. In other circumstances, therefore, there should be no necessity to limit the transmission of information on security grounds.

46/70. Cooperation and Coordination of Specialized Agencies and the International Institutions Associated with the United Nations in their Assistance to Non-Self-Governing Territories

Committee: 4
Vote: Adopted without a vote
Ref.: 145(II)

The General Assembly,

Aware that in addition to general problems facing developing countries, the remaining Non-Self-Governing Territories, many of which are small island Territories, also suffer handicaps arising from the interplay of such factors as their size, remoteness, geographical dispersion, vulnerability to natural disasters, the fragility of their ecosystems, constraints in transport and communications, great distances from market centres, a highly limited internal market, lack of natural resources, weak indigenous technological capacity, the acute problem of obtaining freshwater supplies, heavy dependence on imports and a small number of commodities, depletion of non-renewable resources, migration, particularly of personnel with high-level skills, shortage of administrative personnel and heavy financial burdens,

Recalling resolution 24 (XI), on the Programme of Assistance to Small Island Developing Countries, adopted by the eleventh session of the Caribbean Development and Cooperation Committee on 22 November 1988, in which the Committee directed its secretariat to continue to examine the access of the non-independent Caribbean countries to programmes and activities of the United Nations system with the aim of identifying areas within that system which could provide technical and other assistance to those countries in the furtherance of their development process, and other resolutions of the Caribbean Development and Cooperation Committee,

Taking note of the report of the Meeting of Governmental Experts of Island Developing Countries and Donor Countries and Organizations which was held in New York from 25 to 29 June 1990,

Mindful of the growing importance that the General Assembly attaches to the contributions of specialized agencies and the international institutions to the economic and social development of Non-Self-Governing Territories,

Welcoming the role being played by the United Nations Development Programme and the specialized agencies in that regard,

Recalling its resolution 44/211 of 22 December 1989, entitled "Comprehensive triennial policy review of operational activities for development of the United Nations system",

Taking into account the suggestions made by Member States during the general debate on the relevant item,

1. *Invites* the specialized agencies and the international institutions associated with the United Nations to increase their participation in the debates of the General Assembly on the remaining Non-Self-Governing Territories, with a view to apprising the Assembly of their development programmes in those Territories and thereby facilitating more informed comments on their work;

2. *Requests* the Secretary-General to take the necessary measures for promoting and expanding cooperation and coordination among the specialized agencies and the international institutions associated with the United Nations in their assistance to Non-Self-Governing Territories and to report to the General Assembly at its forty-seventh session on the implementation of the present resolution;

3. *Decides* to keep this question under review.

68th plenary meeting
11 December 1991

04.20 PRINCIPLE OF DECOLONIZATION

1514 (XV). Declaration on the Granting of Independence to Colonial Countries and Peoples

Committee: -
Vote: 89 - 0 - 9

The General Assembly,

Mindful of the determination proclaimed by the peoples of the world in the Charter of the United Nations to reaffirm faith in fundamental human rights, in the dignity and worth of the human person, in the equal rights of men and women and of nations large and small and to promote social progress and better standards of life in larger freedom,

Conscious of the need for the creation of conditions of stability and well-being and peaceful and friendly relations based on respect for the principles of equal rights and self-determination of all peoples, and of universal respect for, and observance of, human rights and fundamental freedoms for all without distinction as to race, sex, language or religion,

Recognizing the passionate yearning for freedom; all dependent peoples and the decisive role of such peoples in the attainment of their independence,

Aware of the increasing conflicts resulting from this denial of or impediments in the way of the freedom such peoples, which constitute a serious threat to world peace,

Considering the important role of the United Nations in assisting the movement for independence in Trust and Non-Self-Governing Territories,

Recognizing that the peoples of the world ardently desire the end of colonialism in all its manifestations,

Convinced that the continued existence of colonialism prevents the development of international economic cooperation, impedes the social, cultural and economic development of dependent peoples and militates against the United Nations ideal of universal peace,

Affirming that peoples may, for their own ends, free dispose of their natural wealth and resources without prejudice to any obligations arising out of international economic cooperation, based upon the principle mutual benefit, and international law,

Believing that the process of liberation is irresistible and irreversible and that, in order to avoid serious crises an end must be put to colonialism and all practices a segregation and discrimination associated therewith,

Welcoming the emergence in recent years of a large number of dependent territories into freedom and independence, and recognizing the increasingly powerful trends towards freedom in such territories which have not yet attained independence,

Convinced that all peoples have an inalienable right to complete freedom, the exercise of their sovereignty and the integrity of their national territory,

Solemnly proclaims the necessity of bringing to a speedy and unconditional end colonialism in all its forms and manifestations;

And to this end

Declares that:

1. The subjection of peoples to alien subjugation, domination and exploitation constitutes a denial of fundamental human rights, is contrary to the Charter of the United Nations and is an impediment to the promotion of world peace and cooperation.

2. All peoples have the right to self-determination; by virtue of that right they freely determine their political status and freely pursue their economic, social and cultural development.

3. Inadequacy of political, economic, social or educational preparedness should never serve as a pretext for delaying independence.

4. All armed action or repressive measures of all kinds directed against dependent peoples shall cease in order to enable them to exercise peacefully and freely their right to complete independence, and the integrity of their national territory shall be respected.

5. Immediate steps shall be taken, in Trust and Non-Self-Governing Territories or all other territories which have not yet attained independence, to transfer all powers to the peoples of those territories, without any conditions or reservations, in accordance with their freely expressed will and desire, without any distinction as to race, creed or colour, in order to enable them to enjoy complete independence and freedom.

6. Any attempt aimed at the partial or total disruption of the national unity and the territorial integrity of a country is incompatible with the purposes and principles of the Charter of the United Nations.

7. All States shall observe faithfully and strictly the provisions of the Charter of the United Nations, the Universal Declaration of Human Rights and the present Declaration on the basis of equality, non-interference in the internal affairs of all States, and respect for the sovereign rights of all peoples and their territorial integrity.

947th plenary meeting
14 December 1960

2621 (XXV). Programme of Action for the Full Implementation of the Declaration on the Granting of Independence to Colonial Countries and Peoples

Committee: -
Vote: 86 - 5 - 15

The General Assembly,

Having decided to hold a special commemorative session on the occasion of the tenth anniversary of the Declaration on the Granting of Independence to Colonial Countries and Peoples,

Considering that, by arousing world public opinion and promoting practical action for the speedy liquidation of colonialism in all its forms and manifestations, the Declaration has played and will continue to play an important role in assisting the peoples under colonial domination in their struggle for freedom and independence,

Conscious of the fact that, although many colonial countries and peoples have achieved freedom and independence in the last ten years, the system of colonialism continues to exist in many areas of the world,

Reaffirming that all peoples have the right to self-determination and independence and that the subjection of the peoples to alien domination constitutes a serious impediment to the maintenance of international peace and security and the development of peaceful relations among nations,

1. *Declares* the further continuation of colonialism in all its forms and manifestations a crime which constitutes a violation of the Charter of the United Nations, the Declaration on the Granting of Independence to Colonial Countries and Peoples and the principles of international law;

2. *Reaffirms* the inherent right of colonial peoples to struggle by all necessary means at their disposal against colonial Powers which suppress their aspiration for freedom and independence;

3. *Adopts* the following programme of action to assist in the full implementation of the Declaration on the Granting of Independence to Colonial Countries and Peoples:

(1) Member States shall do their utmost to promote, in the United Nations and the international institutions and organizations within the United Nations system, effective measures for the full implementation of the Declaration on the Granting of Independence to Colonial Countries and Peoples in all Trust Territories, Non-Self-Governing Territories and other colonial Territories, large and small, including the adoption by the Security Council of effective measures against Governments and regimes which engage in any form of repression of colonial peoples, which would seriously impede the maintenance of international peace and security.

(2) Member States shall render all necessary moral and material assistance to the peoples of colonial Territories in their struggle to attain freedom and independence.

(3) (*a*) Member States shall intensify their efforts to promote the implementation of the resolutions of the General Assembly and the Security Council relating to Territories under colonial domination.

(*b*) In this connexion, the General Assembly draws the attention of the Security Council to the need to continue to give special attention to the problems of southern Africa by adopting measures to ensure the full implementation of General Assembly resolution 1514 (XV) of 14 December 1960 and its own resolutions, and in particular:

(i) To widen the scope of the sanctions against the illegal regime of Southern Rhodesia by declaring mandatory all the measures laid down in Article 41 of the Charter of the United Nations;

(ii) To give careful consideration to the question of imposing sanctions upon South Africa and Portugal, in view of their refusal to carry out the relevant decisions of the Security Council;

(iii) To give urgent consideration, with a view to promoting the speedy elimination of colonialism, to the question of imposing fully and unconditionally, under international supervision, an embargo on arms of all kinds to the Government of South Africa and the illegal regime of Southern Rhodesia;

(iv) To consider urgently the adoption of measures to prevent the supply of arms of all kinds to Portugal, as such arms enable that country to deny the right of self-determination and independence to the peoples of the Territories under its domination.

(*c*) Member States shall also intensify their efforts to oppose collaboration between the regimes of South Africa and Portugal and the illegal racist regime of Southern Rhodesia for the preservation of colonialism in southern Africa and to end the political, military, economic and other forms of aid received by the above-mentioned regimes, which enables them to persist in their policy of colonial domination.

(4) Member States shall wage a vigorous and sustained campaign against activities and practices of foreign economic, financial and other interests operating in colonial Territories for the benefit and on behalf of colonial Powers and their allies, as these constitute a major obstacle to the achievement of the goals embodied in resolution 1514 (XV). Member States shall consider the adoption of necessary steps to have their nationals and companies under their jurisdiction discontinue such activities and practices; these steps should also aim at preventing the systematic influx of foreign immigrants into colonial Territories, which disrupts the integrity and social, political and cultural unity of the peoples under colonial domination.

(5) Member States shall carry out a sustained and vigorous campaign against all military activities and arrangements by colonial Powers in Territories under their administration, as such activities and arrangements constitute an obstacle to the full implementation of resolution 1514 (XV).

(6) (*a*) All freedom fighters under detention shall be treated in accordance with the relevant provisions of the Geneva Convention relative to the Treatment of Prisoners of War, of 12 August 1949.[1]

(*b*) The specialized agencies and international institutions associated with the United Nations shall intensify their activities related to the implementation of resolution 1514 (XV).

(*c*) Representatives of liberation movements shall be invited, whenever necessary, by the United Nations and other international organizations within the United Nations system to participate in an appropriate capacity in the proceedings of those organs relating to their countries.

(*d*) Efforts shall be intensified to provide increased educational opportunities for the inhabitants of Non-Self-Governing Territories.

---

1 United Nations, *Treaty Series*, vol. 75 (1950), No. 972.

All States shall render greater assistance in this field, both individually through programmes in the countries concerned and collectively by contributions through the United Nations.

(7) All States shall undertake measures aimed at enhancing public awareness of the need for active assistance in the achievement of complete decolonization and, in particular, creating satisfactory conditions for activities by national and international non-governmental organizations in support of the peoples under colonial domination.

(8) The United Nations as well as all States shall intensify their efforts in the field of public information in the area of decolonization through all media, including publications, radio and television. Of special importance will be programmes relating to United Nations activities on decolonization, the situation in colonial Territories and the struggle being waged by colonial peoples and the national liberation movements.

(9) The Special Committee on the Situation with regard to the Implementation of the Declaration on the Granting of Independence to Colonial Countries and Peoples shall continue to examine the full compliance of all States with the Declaration and with other relevant resolutions on the question of decolonization. The question of territorial size, geographical isolation and limited resources should in no way delay the implementation of the Declaration. Where resolution 1514 (XV) has not been fully implemented with regard to a given Territory, the General Assembly shall continue to bear responsibility for that Territory until such time as the people concerned has had an opportunity to exercise freely its right to self-determination and independence in accordance with the Declaration. The Special Committee is hereby directed:

(*a*) To continue to assist the General Assembly in finding the best ways and means for the final liquidation of colonialism;

(*b*) To continue to give special consideration to the views expressed orally or in written communications by representatives of the peoples in the colonial Territories;

(*c*) To continue to send visiting missions to the colonial Territories and to hold meetings at places where it can best obtain first-hand information on the situation in colonial Territories, as well as to continue to hold meetings away from Headquarters as appropriate;

(*d*) To assist the General Assembly in making arrangements, in cooperation with the administering Powers, for securing a United Nations presence in the colonial Territories to participate in the elaboration of the procedural measures for the implementation of the Declaration and to observe the final stages of the process of decolonization in the Territories;

(*e*) To prepare draft rules and regulations for visiting missions for approval by the General Assembly.

1862nd plenary meeting
12 October 1970

46/64. Activities of Foreign Economic and other Interests which Are Impeding the Implementation of the Declaration on the Granting of Independence to Colonial Countries and Peoples in Territories under Colonial Domination and Efforts to Eliminate Colonialism, Apartheid and Racial Discrimination in Southern Africa

Committee: 4
Vote: 109 - 34 - 16
Ref.: 49/40, 48/46, 45/17, 44/84, 43/29, 42/74, 41/14, 40/52, 39/42, 38/50, 37/31, 36/51, 35/28, 34/41, 33/40, 32/35, 31/7, 3398(XXX), 3299(XXIX), 3117(XXVIII), 2979(XXVII), 2873(XXVI), 2703(XXV), 2554(XXIV), 2425(XXIII), 2288(XXII)

The General Assembly,

Having considered the item entitled "Activities of foreign economic and other interests which are impeding the implementation of the Declaration on the Granting of Independence to Colonial Countries and Peoples in Territories under colonial domination and efforts to eliminate colonialism, apartheid and racial discrimination in southern Africa",

Having examined the chapter of the report of the Special Committee on the Situation with regard to the Implementation of the Declaration on the Granting of Independence to Colonial Countries and Peoples relating to the item,

Recalling its resolution 1514 (XV) of 14 December 1960, containing the Declaration on the Granting of Independence to Colonial Countries and Peoples, as well as all its other resolutions on this subject, including, in particular, resolution 43/47 of 22 November 1988, declaring the period 1990-2000 as the International Decade for the Eradication of Colonialism,

Reaffirming the solemn obligation of the administering Powers under the Charter of the United Nations to promote the political, economic, social and educational advancement of the inhabitants of the Territories under their administration and to protect the human and natural resources of those Territories against abuses,

Reaffirming also that those economic and other activities which impede the implementation of the Declaration on the Granting of Independence to Colonial Countries and Peoples and obstruct efforts aimed at the elimination of colonialism, apartheid and racial discrimination in South Africa and in colonial Territories are in direct violation of the rights of the inhabitants and of the principles of the Charter and all relevant resolutions of the United Nations,

Seriously concerned about the activities of those foreign economic, financial and other interests which continue to exploit the natural resources that are the heritage of the indigenous populations of the colonial and Non-Self-Governing Territories in the Caribbean, the Pacific and other regions, as well as their human resources, to the detriment of their interests, thus depriving them of their right to control the resources of their Territories and impeding the realization by those peoples of their legitimate aspirations for self-determination and independence,

Bearing in mind the relevant provisions of the final documents of the successive Conferences of Heads of State or Government of Non-Aligned Countries and of the resolutions adopted by the Assembly of Heads of State and Government of the Organization of African Unity,

Gravely concerned that certain countries, transnational corporations and international financial institutions have continued their economic relations with South Africa,

Recognizing the crucial and decisive role that the imposition of international sanctions has played in applying the necessary pressure on the South African régime to undertake significant measures towards the eradication of apartheid,

1. *Approves* the chapter of the report of the Special Committee on the Situation with regard to the Implementation of the Declaration on the Granting of Independence to Colonial Countries and Peoples relating to the item;[1]

2. *Reaffirms* the inalienable right of the peoples of colonial and Non-Self-Governing Territories to self-determination and independence and to the enjoyment of the natural resources of their Territories, as well as their right to dispose of those resources in their best interests;

3. *Reiterates* that any administering or occupying Power that deprives the colonial peoples of the exercise of their legitimate rights over their natural resources or subordinates the rights and interests of those peoples to foreign economic and financial interests violates the solemn obligations it has assumed under the Charter of the United Nations;

4. *Reaffirms* its concern over the activities of those foreign economic, financial and other interests which continue to exploit the natural resources that are the heritage of the indigenous populations of the colonial and Non-Self-Governing Territories in the Caribbean, the Pacific and other regions, as well as their human resources, to the detriment of their interests, thus depriving them of their right to control the resources of their Territories and impeding the realization by those peoples of their legitimate aspirations for self-determination and independence;

---

1 *Official Records of the General Assembly, Forty-sixth Session, Supplement No. 23* (A/46/23), chap. VI.

5. *Condemns* those activities of foreign economic and other interests in the colonial Territories which are impeding the implementation of the Declaration on the Granting of Independence to Colonial Countries and Peoples, contained in General Assembly resolution 1514 (XV), and the efforts to eliminate colonialism, apartheid and racial discrimination;

6. *Strongly condemns* the collaboration with the South African régime by certain countries as well as transnational corporations that continue to make new investments in South Africa and supply the racist régime with armaments, nuclear technology and all other materials that are likely to buttress it and thus aggravate the threat to world peace;

7. *Calls upon* all States to maintain the existing measures against the apartheid régime as specified in the Declaration on Apartheid and its Destructive Consequences in Southern Africa, annexed to General Assembly resolution S-16/1 of 14 December 1989;

8. *Calls once again* upon all Governments that have not yet done so to take, in accordance with the relevant provisions of General Assembly resolution 2621 (XXV) of 12 October 1970, legislative, administrative or other measures in respect of their nationals and the bodies corporate under their jurisdiction that own and operate enterprises in colonial Territories that are detrimental to the interests of the inhabitants of those Territories, in order to put an end to such enterprises and to prevent new investments that run counter to the interests of the inhabitants of those Territories;

9. *Calls upon* those oil-producing and oil-exporting countries that have not yet done so to take effective measures against the oil companies concerned so as to terminate the supply of crude oil and petroleum products to the racist régime of South Africa;

10. *Reiterates* that the exploitation and plundering of the marine and other natural resources of colonial and Non-Self-Governing Territories by foreign economic interests, in violation of the relevant resolutions of the United Nations, is a grave threat to the integrity and prosperity of those Territories;

11. *Invites* all Governments and organizations of the United Nations system to take all possible measures to ensure that the permanent sovereignty of the peoples of colonial and Non-Self-Governing Territories over their natural resources is fully respected and safeguarded;

12. *Urges* the administering Powers concerned to take effective measures to safeguard and guarantee the inalienable right of the peoples of the colonial and Non-Self-Governing Territories to their natural resources and to establish and maintain control over the future development of those resources, and requests the administering Powers to take all necessary steps to protect the property rights of the peoples of those Territories;

13. *Calls upon* the administering Powers concerned to ensure that no discriminatory and unjust wage systems or working conditions prevail in the Territories under their administration and to apply in each Territory a uniform system of wages to all the inhabitants without any discrimination;

14. *Requests* the Secretary-General to continue, through the Department of Public Information of the Secretariat, to inform world public opinion of those activities of foreign economic and other interests which are impeding the implementation of the Declaration on the Granting of Independence to Colonial Countries and Peoples;

15. *Appeals* to mass media, trade unions and non-governmental organizations, as well as individuals, to continue their efforts in the struggle against apartheid and the mobilization of international public opinion against the policy pursued by the South African apartheid régime and to oppose the relaxation of existing measures against the régime, in order to accelerate the process of constitutional change;

16. *Decides* to continue to monitor closely the situation in the colonial and Non-Self-Governing Territories so as to ensure that all economic activities in those Territories are aimed at strengthening and diversifying their economies in the interest of the indigenous peoples and at promoting the economic and financial viability of those Territories, in order to facilitate and accelerate the exercise by the peoples of those Territories of their right to self-determination and independence;

17. *Requests* the Special Committee on the Situation with regard to the Implementation of the Declaration on the Granting of Independence to Colonial Countries and Peoples to continue to examine this question and to report thereon to the General Assembly at its forty-seventh session.

68th plenary meeting
11 December 1991

50/34. Implementation of the Declaration on the Granting of Independence to Colonial Countries and Peoples by the Specialized Agencies and the International Institutions Associated with the United Nations

Committee: 4
Vote: 107 - 0 - 50
Ref.: 49/41, 48/47, 47/16, 46/65, 45/18, 44/85, 43/30, 42/75, 41/15, 40/53, 39/43, 38/51, 37/32, 36/52, 35/29, 34/42, 33/41, 32/36, 31/30, 3421(XXX), 3300(XXIX), 3118(XXVIII), 2980XXVII), 2874(XXVI), 2704(XXV), 2555(XXIV), 2426(XXIII), 2311(XXII)

The General Assembly,

Having considered the item entitled "Implementation of the Declaration on the Granting of Independence to Colonial Countries and Peoples by the specialized agencies and the international institutions associated with the United Nations",

Having also considered the reports submitted on the item by the Secretary-General[1] and the Chairman of the Special Committee on the Situation with regard to the Implementation of the Declaration on the Granting of Independence to Colonial Countries and Peoples,[2]

Having examined the chapter of the report of the Special Committee on the Situation with regard to the Implementation of the Declaration on the Granting of Independence to Colonial Countries and Peoples relating to the item,[3]

Recalling its resolutions 1514 (XV) of 14 December 1960 and 1541 (XV) of 15 December 1960, and resolutions of the Special Committee on the Situation with regard to the Implementation of the Declaration on the Granting of Independence to Colonial Countries and Peoples, as well as other relevant resolutions and decisions of the United Nations,

Bearing in mind the relevant provisions of the final documents of the successive Conferences of Heads of State or Government of Non-Aligned Countries and of the resolutions adopted by the Assembly of Heads of State and Government of the Organization of African Unity, the South Pacific Forum and the Caribbean Community,

Conscious of the need to facilitate the implementation of the Declaration on the Granting of Independence to Colonial Countries and Peoples, contained in its resolution 1514 (XV),

Noting that the large majority of the remaining Non-Self-Governing Territories are small island Territories,

Welcoming the assistance extended to Non-Self-Governing Territories by certain specialized agencies and other organizations of the United Nations system, in particular the United Nations Development Programme,

Stressing that, because the development options of small island Non-Self-Governing Territories are limited, there are special challenges to planning for and implementing sustainable development and that those Territories will be constrained in meeting the challenges without the continuing cooperation and assistance of the specialized agencies and other organizations of the United Nations system,

Stressing also the importance of securing necessary resources for funding expanded assistance programmes for the peoples concerned and the need to enlist the support of all major funding institutions within the United Nations system in that regard,

Reaffirming the mandates of the specialized agencies and other organizations of the United Nations system to take all the appropriate

---

1 A/50/212 and Add.1.

2 A/AC.109/L.1838.

3 A/50/23 (Part IV), chap. VII.

measures, within their respective spheres of competence, to ensure the full implementation of resolution 1514 (XV) and other relevant resolutions,

Expressing its appreciation to the Organization of African Unity, the South Pacific Forum and the Caribbean Community, as well as other regional organizations, for the continuing cooperation and assistance they have extended to the specialized agencies and other organizations of the United Nations system in this regard,

Expressing its conviction that closer contacts and consultations between and among the specialized agencies and other organizations of the United Nations system and regional organizations help to facilitate the effective formulation of assistance programmes for the peoples concerned,

Mindful of the imperative need to keep under continuous review the activities of the specialized agencies and other organizations of the United Nations system in the implementation of the various United Nations decisions relating to decolonization,

Bearing in mind the extremely fragile economies of the Non-Self-Governing small island Territories and their vulnerability to natural disasters, such as hurricanes, cyclones and sea-level rise, and recalling its relevant resolutions,

Recalling its resolution 49/41 of 9 December 1994 on the implementation of the Declaration on the Granting of Independence to Colonial Countries and Peoples by the specialized agencies and the international institutions associated with the United Nations,

1. *Takes note* of the report of the Chairman of the Special Committee on the Situation with regard to the Implementation of the Declaration on the Granting of Independence to Colonial Countries and Peoples on his consultations with the President of the Economic and Social Council[1] and endorses the observations and suggestions arising therefrom;[2]

2. *Recommends* that all States intensify their efforts in the specialized agencies and other organizations of the United Nations system to ensure implementation of the Declaration on the Granting of Independence to Colonial Countries and Peoples and other relevant resolutions of the United Nations;

3. *Reaffirms* that the specialized agencies and other organizations and institutions of the United Nations system should continue to be guided by the relevant resolutions of the United Nations in their efforts to contribute to the implementation of the Declaration and other relevant General Assembly resolutions;

4. *Reaffirms also* that the recognition by the General Assembly and other United Nations organs of the legitimacy of the aspiration of the peoples of Non-Self-Governing Territories to exercise their right to self-determination entails, as a corollary, the extension of all appropriate assistance to those peoples;

5. *Expresses its appreciation* to those specialized agencies and other organizations of the United Nations system that have continued to cooperate with the United Nations and the regional and subregional organizations in the implementation of General Assembly resolution 1514 (XV) and other relevant resolutions of the United Nations;

6. *Requests* the specialized agencies and the international institutions associated with the United Nations, as well as regional organizations, to examine and review conditions in each Territory so as to take appropriate measures to accelerate progress in the economic and social sectors of the Territories and strengthen existing measures of support, and, in that regard, to formulate appropriate programmes of assistance to the remaining Non-Self-Governing Territories, within the framework of their respective mandates;

7. *Recommends* that the executive heads of the specialized agencies and other organizations of the United Nations system formulate, with the active cooperation of the regional organizations concerned, concrete proposals for the full implementation of the relevant resolutions of the United Nations and submit the proposals to their governing and legislative organs;

8. *Also recommends* that the specialized agencies and other organizations of the United Nations system continue to review at the regular meetings of their governing bodies the implementation of resolution 1514 (XV) and other relevant resolutions of the United Nations;

9. *Welcomes* the continuing initiative exercised by the United Nations Development Programme in maintaining close liaison among the specialized agencies and other organizations of the United Nations system and in providing assistance to the peoples of Non-Self-Governing Territories;

10. *Encourages* Non-Self-Governing Territories to take steps to establish and/or strengthen disaster preparedness and management institutions and policies;

11. *Requests* the administering Powers concerned to facilitate the participation of appointed and elected representatives of Non-Self-Governing Territories in the relevant meetings and conferences of specialized agencies and other organizations so that the Territories may benefit from the related activities of those agencies and other organizations of the United Nations system;

12. *Recommends* that all Governments intensify their efforts in the specialized agencies and other organizations of the United Nations system of which they are members to ensure the full and effective implementation of resolution 1514 (XV) and other relevant resolutions of the United Nations and, in that connection, accord priority to the question of providing assistance to the peoples of the Non-Self-Governing Territories;

13. *Requests* the Secretary-General to continue to assist the specialized agencies and other organizations of the United Nations system in working out appropriate measures for implementing the relevant resolutions of the United Nations and to prepare for submission to the relevant bodies, with the assistance of those agencies and organizations, a report on the action taken in implementation of the relevant resolutions, including the present resolution, since the circulation of his previous report;

14. *Commends* the Economic and Social Council for its debate[3] and its resolution 1995/58 of 28 July 1995 on this issue, and requests it to continue to consider, in consultation with the Special Committee, appropriate measures for coordination of the policies and activities of the specialized agencies and other organizations of the United Nations system in implementing the relevant resolutions of the General Assembly;

15. *Requests* the specialized agencies to report periodically to the Secretary-General on the implementation of the present resolution;

16. *Requests* the Secretary-General to transmit the present resolution to the governing bodies of the appropriate specialized agencies and international institutions associated with the United Nations so that those bodies may take the necessary measures to implement the resolution, and also requests the Secretary-General to report to the General Assembly at its fifty-first session on the implementation of the present resolution;

17. *Requests* the Special Committee to continue to examine the question and to report thereon to the General Assembly at its fifty-first session.

82nd plenary meeting
6 December 1995

1 A/AC. 109/L. 1838.

2 E/1995/85.

3 See *Official Records of the Economic and Social Council, 1995, Plenary Meetings,* 57th meeting (E/1995/SR.57).

50/39. Implementation of the Declaration on the Granting of Independence to Colonial Countries and Peoples

Committee: -
Vote: 130 - 4 - 26
Ref.: 49/89, 48/52, 47/23, 46/71, 45/34, 44/101, 43/45, 42/71, 41/41, 40/57, 39/91, 38/54, 37/35, 36/68, 35/119, 34/94, 33/44, 32/42, 31/143, 3481(XXX), 3328(XXIX), 3163(XXVIII), 2908(XXVII), 2878(XXVI), 2708(XXV), 2548(XXIV), 2465(XXIII), 2326(XXII), 2189(XXI), 2105(XX), 1956(XVIII), 1810(XVII), 1654(XVI)

The General Assembly,

Having examined the report of the Special Committee on the Situation with regard to the Implementation of the Declaration on the Granting of Independence to Colonial Countries and Peoples,[1]

Recalling its resolution 1514 (XV) of 14 December 1960, containing the Declaration on the Granting of Independence to Colonial Countries and Peoples, and all its subsequent resolutions concerning the implementation of the Declaration, most recently resolution 49/89 of 16 December 1994, as well as the relevant resolutions of the Security Council,

Recognizing that the eradication of colonialism is one of the priorities of the Organization for the decade that began in 1990,

Deeply conscious of the need to take, speedily, measures to eliminate the last vestiges of colonialism by the year 2000, as called for in its resolution 43/47 of 22 November 1988,

Reiterating its conviction of the need for the elimination of colonialism, as well as of the need for the total eradication of racial discrimination and violations of basic human rights,

Noting with satisfaction the achievements of the Special Committee in contributing to the effective and complete implementation of the Declaration and other relevant resolutions of the United Nations on decolonization,

Stressing the importance of the participation of the administering Powers in the work of the Special Committee,

Also noting with satisfaction the cooperation and active participation of some administering Powers in the work of the Special Committee, as well as their continued readiness to receive United Nations visiting missions in the Territories under their administration,

Noting with concern the negative impact which the non-participation of certain administering Powers has had on the work of the Special Committee, depriving it of an important source of information on the Territories under their administration,

Aware of the pressing need of newly independent and emerging States for assistance from the United Nations and its system of organizations in the economic, social and other fields,

Aware also of the pressing need of the remaining Non-Self-Governing Territories, including particularly the small island Territories, for economic, social and other assistance from the United Nations and the organizations within its system,

Taking special note of the fact that, during its 1995 session, the Special Committee carried out a midterm review of the Plan of Action for the International Decade for the Eradication of Colonialism in the context of the commemoration of the fiftieth anniversary of the United Nations in which further options for self-determination were explored,

1. *Reaffirms* its resolution 1514(XV) and all other resolutions on decolonization, including its resolution 43/47, in which it declared the decade that began in 1990 as the International Decade for the Eradication of Colonialism, and calls upon the administering Powers, in accordance with those resolutions, to take all necessary steps to enable the peoples of the Territories concerned to exercise fully as soon as possible their right to self-determination, including independence;

2. *Affirms once again* that the continuation of colonialism in any form or manifestation - including economic exploitation - is incompatible with the Charter of the United Nations, the Universal Declaration of Human Rights[2] and the Declaration on the Granting of Independence to Colonial Countries and Peoples;

3. *Reaffirms* its determination to continue to take all steps necessary to bring about the complete and speedy eradication of colonialism and the faithful observance by all States of the relevant provisions of the Charter, the Declaration on the Granting of Independence to Colonial Countries and Peoples and the Universal Declaration of Human Rights;

4. *Affirms once again* its support for the aspirations of the peoples under colonial rule to exercise their right to self-determination including independence;

5. *Approves* the report of the Special Committee on the Situation with regard to the Implementation of the Declaration on the Granting of Independence to Colonial Countries and Peoples covering its work during 1995, including the programme of work envisaged for 1996;[3]

6. *Calls upon* all States, in particular the administering Powers, as well as the specialized agencies and other organizations of the United Nations system, to give effect within their respective spheres of competence to the recommendations of the Special Committee for the implementation of the Declaration and other relevant resolutions of the United Nations;

7. *Calls upon* the administering Powers to ensure that no activity of foreign economic and other interests in the Non-Self-Governing Territories under their administration hinders the peoples of those Territories from exercising their right to self-determination, including independence;

8. *Takes note* of the decision of some of the administering Powers to close or downsize some of the military bases in the Non-Self-Governing Territories;

9. *Calls upon* the administering Powers to eliminate the remaining military bases in the Non-Self-Governing Territories in compliance with the relevant resolutions of the General Assembly, and urges them not to involve those Territories in any offensive acts or interference against other States;

10. *Urges* all States, directly and through their action in the specialized agencies and other organizations of the United Nations system, to provide moral and material assistance to the peoples of colonial Territories, and requests that the administering Powers, in consultation with the Governments of the Territories under their administration, take steps to enlist and make effective use of all possible assistance, on both a bilateral and a multilateral basis, in the strengthening of the economies of those Territories;

11. *Requests* the Special Committee to continue to seek suitable means for the immediate and full implementation of the Declaration and to carry out those actions approved by the General Assembly regarding the International Decade for the Eradication of Colonialism in all Territories that have not yet exercised their right to self-determination, including independence, and in particular:

(*a*) To formulate specific proposals for the elimination of the remaining manifestations of colonialism and to report thereon to the General Assembly at its fifty-first session;

(*b*) To continue to examine the implementation by Member States of resolution 1514 (XV) and other relevant resolutions on decolonization;

(*c*) To continue to pay special attention to the small Territories, in particular through the dispatch of regular visiting missions, and to recommend to the General Assembly the most suitable steps to be taken to enable the populations of those Territories to exercise their right to self-determination and independence;

(*d*) To take all necessary steps to enlist world-wide support among Governments, as well as national and international organizations, for the achievement of the objectives of the Declaration and the implementation of the relevant resolutions of the United Nations;

---

1 *Official Records of the General Assembly, Fiftieth Session, Supplement No. 23* (A/50/23).

2 Resolution 217 A (III).

3 *Official Records of the General Assembly, Fiftieth Session, Supplement No. 23* (A/50/23), chap. I, sect. J.

12. *Calls upon* the administering Powers to continue to cooperate with the Special Committee in the discharge of its mandate and to receive visiting missions to the Territories to secure first-hand information and ascertain the wishes and aspirations of their inhabitants;

13. *Also calls upon* the administering Powers that have not participated in the work of the Special Committee to do so at its 1996 session;

14. *Requests* the Secretary-General, the specialized agencies and other organizations of the United Nations system to provide economic, social and other assistance to the Non-Self-Governing Territories and to continue to do so, as appropriate, after they exercise their right to self-determination, including independence;

15. *Requests* the Secretary-General to provide the Special Committee with the facilities and services required for the implementation of the present resolution, as well as of the other resolutions and decisions on decolonization adopted by the General Assembly and the Special Committee.

82nd plenary meeting
6 December 1995

04.30 RIGHT OF SELF-DETERMINATION

637 (VII). The Right of Peoples and Nations to Self-Determination

Committee: 3
Vote: A: 40 - 14 - 6; B: 39 - 12 - 5; C: 42 - 7 - 8
Ref.: 33/24, 32/14, 31/34, 3382(XXIX), 3246(XXIX), 3070(XXVIII), 2955(XXII), 2787(XXVI), 2649(XXV), 1314(XIII), 1188(XII), 837(IX), 738(VIII), 545(VI)

A

Whereas the right of peoples and nations to self-determination is a prerequisite to the full enjoyment of all fundamental human rights,

Whereas the Charter of the United Nations, under Articles 1 and 55, aims to develop friendly relations among nations based on respect for the equal rights and self-determination of peoples in order to strengthen universal peace,

Whereas the Charter of the United Nations recognizes that certain Members of the United Nations are responsible for the administration of Territories whose peoples have not yet attained a full measure of self-government, and affirms the principles which should guide them,

Whereas every Member of the United Nations, in conformity with the Charter should respect the maintenance of the right of self-determination in other States,

The General Assembly recommends that:

1. The States Members of the United Nations shall uphold the principle of self-determination of all peoples and nations;

2. The States Members of the United Nations shall recognize and promote the realization of the right of self-determination of the peoples of Non-Self-Governing and Trust Territories who are under their administration and shall facilitate the exercise of this right by the peoples of such Territories according to the principles and spirit of the Charter of the United Nations in regard to each Territory and to the freely expressed wishes of the peoples concerned the wishes of the people being ascertained through plebiscites or other recognized democratic means, preferably under the auspices of the United Nations;

3. The States Members of the United Nations responsible for the administration of Non-Self-Governing and Trust Territories shall take practical steps, pending the realization of the right of self-determination and in preparation thereof, to ensure the direct participation of the indigenous populations in the legislative and executive organs of government of those Territories, and to prepare them for complete self-government or independence.

403rd plenary meeting
16 December 1952

B

The General Assembly,

Considering that one of the conditions necessary to facilitate United Nations action to promote respect for the right of self-determination of peoples and nations, in particular with regard to the peoples of Non-Self-Governing Territories, is that the competent organs of the United Nations should be in possession of official information on the government of these Territories,

Recalling its resolution 144 (II) of 3 November 1947 in which it declared that the voluntary transmission of such information was entirely in conformity with the spirit of Article 73 of the Charter, and should therefore be encouraged,

Recalling its resolution 327 (IV) of 2 December 1949 in which it expressed the hope that such of the Members of the United Nations as had not done so might voluntarily include details on the government of Non-Self-Governing Territories in the information transmitted by them under Article 73 e of the Charter,

Considering that at the present time such information has not yet been furnished in respect of a large number of Non-Self-Governing Territories,

1. *Recommends* States Members of the United Nations responsible for the administration of Non-Self-Governing Territories voluntarily to include in the information transmitted by them under Article 73 e of the Charter details regarding the extent to which the right of peoples and nations to self-determination is exercised by the peoples of those Territories, and in particular regarding their political progress and the measures taken to develop their capacity for self-administration, to satisfy their political aspirations and to promote the progressive development of their free political institutions;

2. *Decides* to place the present resolution on the agenda of the Committee on Information from Non-Self-Governing Territories for its next session in 1953.

403rd plenary meeting
16 December 1952

C

The General Assembly,

Considering that it is necessary to continue the study of ways and means of ensuring international respect for the right of peoples to self-determination,

Considering that the recommendations it has adopted at its seventh session do not represent the only steps that can be taken to promote respect for such right,

1. *Requests* the Economic and Social Council to ask the Commission on Human Rights to continue preparing recommendations concerning international respect for the right of peoples to self-determination, and particularly recommendations relating to the steps which might be taken, within the limits of their resources and competence, by the various organs of the United Nations and the specialized agencies to develop international respect for the right of peoples to self-determination;

2. *Requests* the Commission on Human Rights to submit through the Economic and Social Council its recommendations to the General Assembly.

403rd plenary meeting
16 December 1952

47/82. Importance of the Universal Realization of the Right of Peoples to Self-Determination and of the Speedy Granting of Independence to Colonial Countries and Peoples for the Effective Guarantee and Observance of Human Rights

Committee: 3
Vote: 107 - 22 - 33
Ref.: 50/139, 49/148, 48/93, 46/87, 45/130, 44/79, 43/106, 42/95, 41/101, 40/25, 40/24, 39/18, 39/17, 38/17, 38/16, 37/43, 37/42, 36/10, 36/9, 35/36, 35/35, 34/44, 33/24, 32/14, 31/34, 3382(XXX), 3246(XXIX), 3070(XXVIII), 2955(XXVII), 2787(XXVI), 2649(XXV)

The General Assembly,

Reaffirming its faith in the importance of the implementation of the Declaration on the Granting of Independence to Colonial Countries and Peoples contained in its resolution 1514 (XV) of 14 December 1960,

Reaffirming also the importance of the universal realization of the right of peoples to self-determination, national sovereignty and territorial integrity and of the speedy granting of independence to colonial countries and peoples as imperatives for the full enjoyment of all human rights,

Reaffirming further the obligation of all Member States to comply with the principles of the Charter of the United Nations and the resolutions of the United Nations regarding the exercise of the right to self-determination by peoples under colonial and foreign domination,

Recalling its resolution 1514 (XV) and all relevant resolutions concerning the implementation of the Declaration on the Granting of Independence to Colonial Countries and Peoples,

Considering the urgent need of Namibia for assistance in its efforts to reconstruct and strengthen its fledgling economic and social structures,

Recalling with satisfaction the adoption at Harare on 21 August 1989 of the Declaration of the *Ad Hoc Committee* of the Organization of African Unity on Southern Africa on the question of South Africa[1] and its subsequent endorsement by the Ninth Conference of Heads of State or Government of Non-Aligned Countries, held at Belgrade from 4 to 7 September 1989,[2] as well as the report of the Monitoring Group of the *Ad Hoc Committee* of the Organization of African Unity on Southern Africa,[3] and the Declaration on Apartheid and its Destructive Consequences in Southern Africa,[4] adopted by the General Assembly on 14 December 1989,

Welcoming Security Council resolution 765 (1992) of 16 July 1992, and Council resolution 772 (1992) of 17 August 1992 which, *inter alia*, provides the basis for action by the Secretary-General in South Africa in order to assist the people of South Africa in ending the violence in that country,

Recalling the Abuja Declaration on South Africa, adopted by the Assembly of Heads of State and Government of the Organization of African Unity at its twenty-seventh ordinary session, held at Abuja from 3 to 5 June 1991,[5]

Reaffirming that the system of apartheid imposed on the South African people constitutes a violation of the fundamental rights of that people, a crime against humanity and a threat to regional peace and security,

Deeply concerned that, in spite of the National Peace Accord signed on 14 September 1991,[6] acts of assassination of members and leaders of national liberation movements in South Africa are still continuing,

Recalling its resolution 46/79 A, adopted by consensus on 13 December 1991, in which, *inter alia*, it reaffirmed the need for the full implementation of the provisions of the Declaration on Apartheid and its Destructive Consequences in Southern Africa that were not yet fulfilled,

Noting with concern that, while significant legal and political measures in the right direction have been undertaken by the Government of South Africa, there remain various pieces of security legislation that restrict the possibilities for free and peaceful political activity, and that apartheid remains in place,

Noting also with concern that political trials and the detention of opponents of apartheid continue in South Africa in total disregard of the provisions of the Declaration on Apartheid and its Destructive Consequences in Southern Africa,

Deeply concerned about the current wave of violence in South Africa resulting from the continued existence of apartheid policies, practices and structures as well as from actions of those forces opposed to the democratic transformation of the country,

Gravely concerned that a number of South African patriots remain on death row,

Welcoming the signing of the General Peace Agreement for Mozambique,[7] at Rome on 4 October 1992, which provides for the termination of the armed conflict in that country,

Reaffirming the national unity and territorial integrity of the Comoros,

Recalling the Geneva Declaration on Palestine and the Programme of Action for the Achievement of Palestinian Rights, adopted by the International Conference on the Question of Palestine,[8]

Considering that the continuation of the Israeli oppressive measures and the denial of the inalienable rights of the Palestinian people to self-determination, sovereignty, independence and return to Palestine constitute a serious threat to international peace and security,

Bearing in mind United Nations resolutions related to the question of Palestine and the rights of the Palestinian people,

Deeply concerned and alarmed at the deplorable consequences of Israel's acts of aggression against Lebanon and its practices in and its continuing occupation of parts of southern Lebanon, as well as its refusal to implement the relevant resolutions of the Security Council, in particular resolution 425 (1978) of 19 March 1978,

1. *Calls upon* all States to implement fully and faithfully all the relevant resolutions of the United Nations regarding the exercise of the right to self-determination and independence by peoples under colonial and foreign domination;

2. *Reaffirms* the legitimacy of the struggle of peoples for independence, territorial integrity, national unity and liberation from colonial domination, apartheid and foreign occupation, in all its forms and by all available means;

3. *Reaffirms also* the inalienable right of the Palestinian people and all peoples under foreign occupation and colonial domination to self-determination, national independence, territorial integrity, national unity and sovereignty without foreign interference;

4. *Calls upon* those Governments which do not recognize the right to self-determination and independence of all peoples still under colonial domination, alien subjugation and foreign occupation to do so;

5. *Calls upon* Israel to refrain from the constant, deliberate violations of the fundamental rights of the Palestinian people, which constitute an obstacle to the achievement of self-determination and independence by the Palestinian people and the ongoing efforts towards comprehensive peace in the region;

6. *Urges* all States, the specialized agencies and organizations of the United Nations system, as well as other international organizations, to extend their support to the Palestinian people through its sole and legitimate representative, the Palestine Liberation Organization, in its struggle to regain its right to self-determination and independence in accordance with the Charter of the United Nations;

---

1 See A/44/697, annex.

2 See A/44/551-S/20870, annex.

3 A/44/963, annex.

4 Resolution S-16/1, annex.

5 A/46/390, annex II.

6 See Centre Against Apartheid, *Notes and Documents*, No. 23/91.

7 S/24635, annex.

8 *Report of the International Conference on the Question of Palestine, Geneva, 29 August - 7 September 1983* (United nations publication, Sales No. E.83.I.21), chap. I.

7. *Urgently appeals* to all States, the organizations of the United Nations system and other international organizations to render assistance to Namibia in order to enhance its efforts to promote democracy and economic development;

8. *Reaffirms* its rejection of the so-called "tri-cameral constitution" of 1983 as null and void, and reiterates that peace in South Africa can be guaranteed only by the establishment of majority rule through the full and free exercise of adult suffrage by all the people in a united and undivided South Africa;

9. *Strongly urges* the Government of South Africa to take additional steps to implement fully the provisions of the Declaration of the *Ad Hoc Committee* of the Organization of African Unity on Southern Africa on the question of South Africa,[1] and the Declaration on Apartheid and its Destructive Consequences in Southern Africa;[2]

10. *Calls* for an immediate end to violence and calls upon the Government of South Africa to exercise its responsibility to end it through, *inter alia*, strict adherence to the National Peace Accord;

11. *Calls upon* all signatories to the National Peace Accord to manifest their commitment to peace by fully implementing its provisions and calls upon all other parties to contribute to the attainment of its objectives;

12. *Strongly condemns* the establishment and use of armed groups with a view to pitting them against the national liberation movements;

13. *Demands* that the Government of South Africa repeal the security legislation that remains in force, which inhibits free and peaceful political activity;

14. *Requests* the Secretary-General to act speedily to implement Security Council resolution 772 (1992) in its entirety, including those parts pertaining to the investigation of criminal conduct and the monitoring of all armed formations in the country;

15. *Demands* the full application of the mandatory arms embargo against South Africa, imposed under Security Council resolution 418 (1977) of 4 November 1977, by all countries and more particularly by those countries which maintain military and nuclear cooperation with the Government of South Africa and continue to supply it with related materiel;

16. *Expresses its deep concern* about the actions by certain countries whose premature relaxation of existing measures against the South African regime, in flagrant violation of the United Nations consensus declaration, encourages the regime to persist in its oppression of the Black majority with regard to their right to self-determination;

17. *Strongly urges* the international community, pursuant to General Assembly resolution 46/87 of 16 December 1991, to continue to extend maximum assistance to Lesotho to enable it to fulfil its international humanitarian obligations towards refugees;

18. *Pays tribute* to the Government and people of Angola for their noble contribution to the evolving climate of peace in southern Angola;

19. *Demands* that the Government of South Africa pay compensation to Angola for damages caused, in accordance with the relevant decisions and resolutions of the Security Council;

20. *Demands also* that the Government of South Africa pay full and adequate compensation to Botswana for the loss of life and damage to property resulting from the unprovoked and unwarranted military attacks of 14 June 1985, 19 May 1986 and 20 June 1988 on the capital of Botswana;

21. *Calls upon* the international community to extend its generous support to the ongoing efforts aimed at ensuring respect for and the successful implementation of the General Peace Agreement for Mozambique and at assisting the Government of Mozambique[3] in the establishment of lasting peace and democracy and in the promotion of an effective programme of national reconstruction in that country;

22. *Fully supports* the Secretary-General in his efforts to implement the plan for the settlement of the question of Western Sahara by organizing, in cooperation with the Organization of African Unity, a referendum for the self-determination of the people of Western Sahara;

23. *Notes* the contacts between the Government of the Comoros and the Government of France in the search for a just solution to the problem of the integration of the Comorian island of Mayotte into the Comoros, in accordance with the resolutions of the Organization of African Unity and the United Nations on the question;

24. *Strongly condemns* the continued violation of the human rights of the peoples still under colonial domination and alien subjugation;

25. *Calls* for a substantial increase in all forms of assistance given by all States, United Nations organs, the specialized agencies and non-governmental organizations to the victims of racism, racial discrimination and apartheid through anti-apartheid organizations and national liberation movements recognized by the Organization of African Unity;

26. *Reaffirms* that the practice of using mercenaries against sovereign States and national liberation movements constitutes a criminal act, and calls upon the Governments of all countries to enact legislation declaring the recruitment, financing and training of mercenaries in their territories and the transit of mercenaries through their territories to be punishable offences and prohibiting their nationals from serving as mercenaries, and to report on such legislation to the Secretary-General;

27. *Demands* the immediate and unconditional release of all persons detained or imprisoned as a result of their struggle for self-determination and independence, full respect for their fundamental individual rights and compliance with article 5 of the Universal Declaration of Human Rights,[1] under which no one shall be subjected to torture or to cruel, inhuman or degrading treatment;

28. *Expresses its appreciation* for the material and other forms of assistance that peoples under colonial rule continue to receive from Governments, organizations of the United Nations system and other intergovernmental organizations, and calls for a substantial increase in that assistance;

29. *Urges* all States, the specialized agencies and other competent organizations of the United Nations system to do their utmost to ensure the full implementation of the Declaration on the Granting of Independence to Colonial Countries and Peoples and to intensify their efforts to support peoples under colonial, foreign and racist domination in their just struggle for self-determination and independence;

30. *Decides* to consider this question at its forty-eighth session under the item entitled "Right of peoples to self-determination".

89th plenary meeting
16 December 1992

---

[1] See A/44/697, annex.

[2] Resolution S-16/1, annex.

[3] S/24635, annex.

04.40 PARTICULAR CASES OF DECOLONIZATION AND SELF-DETERMINATION

04.41 TERRITORIES UNDER PORTUGUESE ADMINISTRATION

1699 (XVI). Non-Compliance of the Government of Portugal with Chapter XI of the Charter of the United Nations and with General Assembly Resolution 1542 (XV)

Committee: 4
Vote: 90 - 3 - 2

The General Assembly, [1]

Recalling that by resolution 1542 (XV) of 15 December 1960 it declared that an obligation exists on the part of the Government of Portugal to transmit information under Chapter XI of the Charter of the United Nations concerning Non-Self-Governing Territories under its administration, and that this obligation should be discharged without further delay,

Noting with deep regret that the Government of Portugal has refused and still continues to refuse to submit information on its Non-Self-Governing Territories or to participate in the work of the Committee on Information from Non-Self-Governing Territories, as called for by General Assembly resolution 1542 (XV) and Chapter XI of the Charter,

Recalling further the principles set forth in its resolution 1514 (XV) of 14 December 1960 entitled "Declaration on the granting of independence to colonial countries and peoples",

Considering that the provisions of the said Declaration and any decision of the General Assembly concerning its implementation are fully applicable to the Territories under Portuguese administration equally with other Non-Self-Governing Territories,

Noting the continuing deterioration of the situation in the Territories under Portuguese administration,

1. *Condemns* the continuing non-compliance of the Government of Portugal with its obligations under Chapter XI of the Charter of the United Nations and with the terms o f General Assembly resolution 1542 (XV) and its refusal to cooperate in the work of the Committee on Information from Non-Self-Governing Territories;

2. *Considers* it necessary that, pending the fulfilment of these obligations by the Government of Portugal, the General Assembly must, for its part, continue to discharge its own obligations and responsibilities towards the inhabitants of the Non-Self-Governing Territories under Portuguese administration;

3. *Decides* to establish a Special Committee of seven members to be elected by the General Assembly to examine as a matter of urgency, within the context of Chapter XI of the Charter and relevant resolutions of the Assembly, such information as is available concerning Territories under Portuguese administration, and to formulate its observations, conclusions and recommendations for the consideration of the Assembly and any other body which the Assembly may appoint to assist it in the implementation of its resolution 1514 (XV);

4. *Requests* the Secretary-General, pending the compliance by Portugal with its obligations under Chapter XI of the Charter to transmit information on conditions in the Territories under its administration, to prepare for the use of the Special Committee, on the basis of available information, background papers containing information on conditions prevailing in the Territories under the administration of Portugal;

5. *Authorizes* the Special Committee, in order that information available to it may be as up to date and authentic as possible, to receive petitions and hear petitioners concerning conditions prevailing in Portuguese Non-Self-Governing Territories;

6. *Requests* the Secretary-General to furnish the Special Committee with such necessary secretarial and other assistance as it may require in the performance of its tasks;

7. *Requests* Member States to use their influence to secure the compliance of Portugal with its obligations under the Charter and the relevant resolutions of the General Assembly;

8. *Further requests* Member States to deny Portugal any support and assistance which it may use for the suppression of the peoples of its Non-Self-Governing Territories.

1083rd plenary meeting
19 December 1961

3113 (XXVIII). Question of Territories under Portuguese Administration

Committee: 4
Vote: 105 - 8 - 16
Ref.: 2918(XXVII), 2795(XXVI), 2707(XXV), 2507(XXIV), 2395(XXIII), 2270(XXII), 2184(XXI), 2107(XX), 1913(XVIII), 1807(XVII)

The General Assembly,

Having considered the question of Territories under Portuguese domination,

Having examined the relevant chapters of the report of the Special Committee on the Situation with regard to the Implementation of the Declaration on the Granting of Independence to Colonial Countries and Peoples,[2] including in particular the views expressed by the representatives of the national liberation movements of the Territories concerned who participated as observers in the relevant proceedings of the Special Committee,[3]

Having examined the report of the Secretary-General concerning the present item,[4]

Having heard the statements of the representatives of the Frente Nacional para a Libertaço de Angola and the Frente de Libertaço de Moçambique, who participated in an observer capacity in the Fourth Committee's consideration of the item[5] in accordance with the decision taken by the General Assembly at its 2139th plenary meeting, on 3 October 1973,

Recalling its resolution 1514 (XV) of 14 December 1960, containing the Declaration on the Granting of Independence to Colonial Countries and Peoples, and its resolution 2621 (XXV) of 12 October 1970, containing the programme of action for the full implementation of the Declaration, as well as all other resolutions relating to the question of Territories under Portuguese domination adopted by the General Assembly, the Security Council and the Special Committee,

Recalling, in particular, the provisions of its resolution 2918 (XXVII) of 14 November 1972, and of Security Council resolution 322 (1972) of 22 November 1972 in which the Government of Portugal was called upon, *inter alia*, to enter into negotiations with the parties concerned, with a view to achieving a solution to the armed confrontation that exists in the African Territories under its domination and permitting the peoples of those Territories to exercise freely their right to self-determination and independence, and deeply deploring the refusal of that Government to comply with those provisions,

Taking into consideration the programme of action adopted by the International Conference of Experts for the Support of Victims of

1 Resolution 217 A(III).

2 See *Official Records of the General Assembly, Twenty-eighth Session, Supplement No. 23* (A/9023/Rev.1), chaps. I, IV-VI and IX.

3 A/AC.109/PV.915 and Corr.1, 917, 920, 921 and 929.

4 A/9132 and Add.1 and 2.

5 *Official Records of the General Assembly, Twenty-eighth Session, Fourth Committee,* 2028th and 2055th meetings.

Colonialism and Apartheid in Southern Africa held at Oslo from 9 to 14 April 1973,[1]

Bearing in mind the Declaration on Territories under Portuguese Domination, adopted by the Assembly of Heads of State and Government of the Organization of African Unity at its tenth ordinary session, held at Addis Ababa from 27 to 29 May 1973,

Condemning the continued collaboration of Portugal, South Africa and the illegal racist minority regime in Southern Rhodesia, designed to perpetuate colonialist and racialist domination in the region, and the persistent intervention against the peoples of the Territories concerned by police and armed forces, as well as by mercenaries from South Africa and Southern Rhodesia,

Condemning the repeated acts of aggression committed by the armed forces of Portugal against independent African States, which constitute a violation of the sovereignty and territorial integrity of those States and seriously disturb international peace and security in the African continent, as reaffirmed in Security Council resolution 312 (1972) of 4 February 1972,

Condemning any attempt by Portugal to place any of the facilities in the Territories under its domination at the disposal of the North Atlantic Treaty Organization or any of its members on a bilateral basis for military purposes,

Strongly deploring the policies of those States, particularly some of the military allies of Portugal, which, in defiance of repeated requests addressed to them by the United Nations, continue to provide Portugal with military and other assistance both within the context of the North Atlantic Treaty Organization and bilaterally, without which Portugal could not pursue its policies of colonial domination and oppression of the peoples of Angola and Mozambique,

Deeply disturbed by the intensified activities of those foreign economic, financial and other interests which, contrary to the relevant resolutions of the General Assembly, are assisting Portugal in its colonial wars and obstructing the realization by the peoples of the Territories under Portuguese domination of their legitimate aspirations for freedom and independence,

Noting with appreciation the concrete programmes of assistance being extended to the national liberation movements of those Territories by a number of Governments, as well as those initiated by organizations within the United Nations system and several non-governmental organizations,

Noting with satisfaction the progress towards national independence and freedom being made by the national liberation movements in those Territories, both through their struggle and through reconstruction programmes, particularly in the liberated areas of Angola and Moçambique,

Noting also with satisfaction the intention of the Special Committee to send a visiting mission to the liberated areas of Angola and Moçambique,

1. *Reaffirms* the inalienable right of the peoples of Angola and Mozambique and other Territories under Portuguese domination to self-determination and independence, as recognized by the General Assembly in its resolution 1514 (XV), and the legitimacy of their struggle by all ways and means at their disposal to achieve that right;

2. *Reaffirms* that the national liberation movements of Angola and Mozambique are the authentic representatives of the true aspirations of the peoples of those Territories and recommends that, pending the accession of those Territories to independence, all Governments, the specialized agencies and other organizations within the United Nations system and the United Nations bodies concerned should, when dealing with matters pertaining to the Territories, ensure the representation of those Territories by the liberation movements concerned in an appropriate capacity and in consultation with the Organization of African Unity;

3. *Condemns* in the strongest possible terms the persistent refusal of the Government of Portugal to comply with the provisions of the relevant resolutions of the United Nations and, in particular, the intensified armed repression by Portugal of the peoples of the Territories under its domination, including the brutal massacre of villagers, the mass destruction of villages and property and the ruthless use of napalm and chemical substances, in order to stifle the legitimate aspirations of those peoples for freedom and independence;

4. *Demands* that the Government of Portugal should cease forthwith its colonial wars and all acts of repression against the peoples of Angola and Moçambique, withdraw its military and other forces and discontinue all practices which violate the inalienable rights of those populations, including the eviction from their homes and the regrouping of the African populations in aldeamentos and the settlement of foreign immigrants in the Territories;

5. *Demands* that the Government of Portugal treat the freedom fighters of Angola and Mozambique captured during the struggle for freedom as prisoners of war in accordance with the principles of the Geneva Convention relative to the Treatment of Prisoners of War, of 12 August 1949,[2] and in that connexion invites the International Committee of the Red Cross to continue to maintain close contact with the liberation movements as parties to the conflict, to provide reports on conditions in prisoner-of-war camps and on the treatment of prisoners of war detained by Portugal and to make the necessary arrangements to secure the exchange of prisoners of war;

6. *Appeals* to all Governments, the specialized agencies and other organizations within the United Nations system and non-governmental organizations to render to the peoples of Angola, Mozambique and other Territories under Portuguese domination, in particular the populations in the liberated areas of those Territories, all the moral, material and economic assistance necessary to continue their struggle for the achievement of their inalienable right to freedom and independence;

7. *Urges* all Governments, particularly those members of the North Atlantic Treaty Organization which continue to render assistance to Portugal, to withdraw any assistance that enables Portugal to prosecute the colonial war in Angola and Mozambique, and to prevent the sale or supply of all arms and military materiel to Portugal, including civil aircraft, ships and other means of transport capable of being used for transporting military material and personnel, as well as supplies, equipment and material for the manufacture or maintenance of weapons and ammunition that it uses to perpetuate its colonial domination in Africa;

8. *Appeals* to all States to refrain from any collaboration with Portugal involving the use of any of the Territories under its domination for military purposes;

9. *Calls upon* all States to take forthwith all possible measures:

(*a*) To put an end to any activities that help to exploit the Territories under Portuguese domination and the peoples therein;

(*b*) To discourage their nationals and the bodies corporate under their jurisdiction from entering into any transactions or arrangements that contribute to Portugal's domination over those Territories;

(*c*) To exclude Portugal from taking part on behalf of Angola and Mozambique in any bilateral or multilateral treaties or agreements relating particularly to external trade in the products of those Territories;

10. *Draws the attention* of the Security Council, having regard to the explosive situation resulting from the policies of Portugal in the colonial Territories under its domination and from its constant provocations against the independent African States bordering those Territories, and in the light of the outright disregard by Portugal of the relevant resolutions of the United Nations, particularly Council resolutions 312 (1972) and 322 (1972), to the urgent need for taking, as a matter of priority, all effective steps with a view to securing the full and speedy implementation of General Assembly resolution 1514 (XV) and of the related decisions of the United Nations;

11. *Requests* the Secretary-General to follow the implementation of the present resolution and to report thereon to the General Assembly at its twenty-ninth session;

12. *Invites* the Secretary-General, bearing in mind the urgent need for mobilizing world public opinion against the criminal war of repres-

[1] A/9061, annex, sect. IV.

[2] United Nations, *Treaty Series*, vol. 75, No. 972, p. 135.

sion being waged by the Government of Portugal against the peoples of the Territories under its domination, to continue to take effective and concrete measures through all the media at his disposal to give widespread and continuous publicity to the critical situation obtaining in those Territories and the heroic struggle of their peoples towards freedom and independence;

13. *Decides* to keep the situation in these Territories under continuous review and to include in the agenda of its twenty-ninth session an item entitled "Question of Territories under Portuguese domination".

2198th plenary meeting
12 December 1973

3294 (XXIX). Question of Territories under Portuguese Domination

Committee: 4
Vote: Adopted without a vote

The General Assembly,

Having considered the question of Territories under Portuguese domination,

Having examined the relevant chapters of the report of the Special Committee on the Situation with regard to the Implementation of the Declaration on the Granting of Independence to Colonial Countries and Peoples,[1]

Having heard the statements made by the administering Power,[2] in particular the important statement made by the Head of State of Portugal on 17 October 1 974,[3]

Having heard the statements of the representatives of the Movimento de Libertaçao de Sao Tomé e Príncipe, the Frente Nacional para a Libertaçao de Angola, the Frente de Libertaçao de Moçambique, the Movimento Popular de Libertaçao de Angola and the Partido Africano da Indepêndencia de Guiné e Cabo Verde,[4] who participated in an observer capacity in the Fourth Committee's consideration of the item,

Taking into account the important statement made by the current Chairman of the Assembly of Heads of State and Government of the Organization of African Unity before the General Assembly on 9 October 1974 in which he referred to the present item,[5]

Recalling its resolution 1514 (XV) of 14 December 1960, containing the Declaration on the Granting of Independence to Colonial Countries and Peoples and its resolution 2621 (XXV) of 12 October 1970 containing the programme of action for the full implementation of the Declaration, as well as all other resolutions relating to the item adopted by the General Assembly, the Security Council and the Special Committee,

Welcoming the declaration of the Government of Portugal accepting to fulfil its obligations under the relevant provisions of the Charter of the United Nations and recognizing the right of the peoples to self-determination and independence, as well as Portugal's express readiness to cooperate in the work of the competent United Nations bodies, as stated by the Government of Portugal in its declarations before the General Assembly on 23 September and 17 October 1974,[6]

Cognizant that the changes in the policy of Portugal towards its colonial Territories were brought about mainly as a consequence of the heroic struggle and persistent resistance of the peoples of the Territories concerned, led by their national liberation movements, for the achievement of their independence and the restoration of their human rights,

Cognizant also that the action carried out in Portugal by the movement of 25 April 1974 represents a fundamental step in the process of decolonization occurring in the Territories

Reiterating that only total decolonization will restore peace in the Territories,

Deeply concerned at the activities of the fascist and reactionary groups still in existence in Angola, Cape Verde and Mozambique, which are trying to obstruct the realization by the peoples of these Territories of their aspirations for freedom and independence and which are provoking racial confrontations that have resulted on several occasions in deplorable incidents causing death and injuries among the inhabitants,

Mindful of the responsibility of the United Nations to continue to render all moral and material aid to the peoples of the Territories under Portuguese domination and their national liberation movements recognized by the Organization of African Unity in their efforts to consolidate national unity and to reconstruct their countries,

1. *Reaffirms* the inalienable right of the peoples of the Territories under Portuguese domination to self-determination and independence in accordance with the Declaration on the Granting of Independence to Colonial Countries and Peoples, contained in its resolution 1514 (XV);

2. *Welcomes* with satisfaction the acceptance by the new Government of Portugal of the sacred principle of self-determination and independence and its unqualified applicability to all the peoples under Portuguese colonial domination;

3. *Notes with particular satisfaction* that, as a result of the consultations held between the Government of Portugal and the national liberation movements of the Territories concerned:

(*a*) Mozambique will accede to independence on 25 June 1975;[7]

(*b*) Sao Tome and Principe will accede to independence on 12 July 1975;[8]

(*c*) Provisional governments will be established in Angola and Cape Verde with a view to the attainment by these Territories during 1975 of the goals set forth in the Charter of the United Nations and in the Declaration;[9]

4. *Strongly deplores* the subversive and criminal activities of the fascist and reactionary groups in Angola, Cape Verde, Mozambique and Sao Tomé and Príncipe, which are attempting to obstruct the realization by the peoples of the Territories of their aspirations for freedom and independence, and requests the Government of Portugal to continue and strengthen its efforts to put an end to all such activities;

5. *Reiterates* its affirmation that the national unity and territorial integrity of these Territories must be preserved, taking note in this connexion of the statement delivered by the administering Power;[10]

6. *Reaffirms* its total support of, and constant solidarity with, the peoples of the Territories under Portuguese domination in their legitimate struggle to achieve without further delay freedom and independence under the leadership of their national liberation movements - the Frente Nacional para a Libertaçao de Angola, the Movimento Popular de Libertaçao de Angola, the Partido Africano da Independência da Guiné e Cabo Verde, the Frente de Libertaçao de Moçambique and the Movimento de Libertaçao de Sao Tomé e Príncipe - which are authentic representatives of the peoples concerned;

7. *Calls upon* the Government of Portugal to pursue the necessary steps to ensure the full implementation of the Declaration contained in resolution 1514 (XV) and all other resolutions of the United Nations relating to the Territories concerned, as well as other recent measures geared towards total decolonization, namely, the agree-

1 *Official Records of the General Assembly, Twenty-ninth Session, Supplement No. 23* (A/9623/Rev.1), chaps. IV-VII.

2 *Ibid., Twenty-ninth Session, Plenary Meetings,* 2233rd, 2239th, 2269th and 2309th meetings and *Ibid.*, Fourth Committee, 2080th and 2092th meetings.

3 *Ibid., Plenary Meetings,* 2269th meeting.

4 *Ibid., Fourth Committee,* 2080th, 2081st, 2084th and 2088th meetings.

5 *Ibid.*, Plenary Meetings, 2262nd meeting.

6 *Ibid.*, 2239th and 2269th meetings.

7 A/9769, annex I.

8 A/9885.

9 A/9885.

10 See *Official Records of the General Assembly, Twenty-ninth Session, Fourth Committee,* 2080th meeting.

ments concluded in Algiers and in Lusaka and the continuation of the negotiations with the above-mentioned national liberation movements, in their capacity of qualified counterparts, for the total transfer of powers to representatives of the peoples concerned, by adopting forthwith all necessary measures to remove any obstacle to the full and free exercise of their inalienable right to self-determination and independence;

8. *Requests* the Government of Portugal to keep the United Nations informed of the action taken or envisaged in the implementation of paragraphs 4 and 7 above and of the related developments in these Territories;

9. *Invites* all Governments to increase their efforts with a view to contributing to the acceleration of the process of decolonization in the Territories concerned;

10. *Appeals* to all Governments and the specialized agencies and other institutions associated with the United Nations to render to the peoples of the Territories concerned all moral and material assistance towards the achievement of their national independence and the reconstruction of their countries;

11. *Requests* the Special Committee on the Situation with regard to the Implementation of the Declaration on the Granting of Independence to Colonial Countries and Peoples to keep the situation in these Territories under continuous review, in particular through the dispatch of visiting missions as appropriate, and to report thereon to the General Assembly at its thirtieth session.

2318th plenary meeting
13 December 1974

1819 (XVII). The Situation in Angola

Committee: -
Vote: 57 - 14 - 18
Ref.: 31/44, 1819(XVII), 1742(XVI), 1603(XV)

The General Assembly,

Having considered the critical situation in Angola,

Having considered the report of the Special Committee on Territories under Portuguese Administration,[1] established under General Assembly resolution 1699 (XVI) of 19 December 1961,

Having considered the report of the Sub-Committee on the Situation in Angola,[2] established under General Assembly resolution 1603 (XV) of 20 April 1961,

Resolutely condemning the mass extermination of the indigenous population of Angola and other severe repressive measures being used by the Portuguese colonial authorities against the people of Angola,

Deploring the armed action being taken by Portugal for the suppression of the people of Angola and the use in this process of arms supplied to Portugal by certain Member States,

Noting that in the Territory of Angola, as in other Portuguese colonies, the indigenous population is denied all fundamental rights and freedoms, that racial discrimination is in fact widely practised and that the economic life of Angola is to a large extent based on forced labour,

Convinced that the colonial war being carried on by the Government of Portugal in Angola, the violation by that Government of the Security Council resolution of 9 June 1961,[3] its refusal to implement the provisions of the Declaration on the granting of independence to colonial countries and peoples contained in General Assembly resolution 1514 (XV) of 14 December 1960, and its refusal to implement resolutions 1542 (XV) of 15 December 1960, 1603 (XV) of 20 April 1961, 1654 (XVI) of 27 November 1961 and 1742 (XVI) of 30 January 1962, constitute a source of international conflict and tension as well as a serious threat to world peace and security,

Bearing in mind the principles embodied in resolution 1514 (XV),

1. *Expresses its satisfaction* to the Sub-Committee on the Situation in Angola for the work it has accomplished;

2. *Solemnly reaffirms* the inalienable right of the people of Angola to self-determination and independence, and supports their demand for immediate independence;

3. *Condemns* the colonial war being carried on by Portugal against the people of Angola and demands that the Government of Portugal put an end to it immediately;

4. *Again calls upon* the Portuguese authorities to desist forthwith from armed action and repressive measures against the people of Angola;

5. *Urges* the Government of Portugal, without any further delay:

(*a*) To release all political prisoners;

(*b*) To lift the ban on political parties;

(*c*) To undertake extensive political, economic and social measures that would ensure the creation of freely elected and representative political institutions and transfer of power to the people of Angola in accordance with the Declaration on the granting of independence to colonial countries and peoples;

6. *Requests* Member States to use their influence to secure the compliance of Portugal with the present resolution;

7. *Requests* all Member States to deny Portugal any support or assistance which may be used by it for the suppression of the people of Angola, and in particular to terminate the supply of arms to Portugal;

8. *Reminds* the Government of Portugal that its continued non-implementation of the resolutions of the General Assembly and of the Security Council is inconsistent with its membership in the United Nations;

9. *Requests* the Security Council to take appropriate measures, including sanctions, to secure Portugal's compliance with the present resolution and with the previous resolutions of the General Assembly and of the Security Council.

1196th plenary meeting
18 December 1962

3061 (XXVIII). Illegal Occupation by Portuguese Military Forces of Certain Sectors of the Republic of Guinea-Bissau and Acts of Aggression Committed by Them Against the People of the Republic

Committee: -
Vote: 93 - 7 - 30
Ref.: 3205(XXIX)

The General Assembly,

Recognizing the inalienable right of all peoples to self-determination and independence in accordance with the principles of the Charter of the United Nations and the Declaration on the Granting of Independence to Colonial Countries and Peoples,

Deeply concerned at the explosive situation resulting from the continued illegal occupation by the armed forces of Portugal of certain sectors of the Republic of Guinea-Bissau and the intensified acts of aggression committed by them against the people of Guinea-Bissau,

Mindful that all States should, in conformity with Article 2, paragraph 4, of the Charter, refrain in their international relations from the threat or use of force against the territorial integrity or national independence of any State or from taking any action inconsistent with the purposes and principles of the Charter,

Noting with satisfaction that the State of Guinea-Bissau assumes the sacred duty to expel the forces of aggression of Portuguese colonialism from that part of the territory of Guinea-Bissau which they still occupy and to intensify the struggle in the Cape Verde Islands, which form an integral and inalienable part of the national territory of the people of Guinea-Bissau and Cape Verde,

---

1 *Official Records of the General Assembly, Seventeenth Session, Annexes,* agenda item 54, documents A/5160 and Add.1 and 2.

2 *Ibid.*, agenda item 29, document A/5286.

3 *Official Records of the Security Council, Sixteenth Year, Supplement for April, May and June 1961,* document S/4835.

Aware of the urgent need of the people of the newly established State of Guinea-Bissau for all possible international assistance in its national reconstruction programmes,

1. *Welcomes* the recent accession to independence of the people of Guinea-Bissau, thereby creating the sovereign State of the Republic of Guinea-Bissau;

2. *Strongly condemns* the policies of the Government of Portugal in perpetuating its illegal occupation of certain sectors of the Republic of Guinea-Bissau and the repeated acts of aggression committed by its armed forces against the people of Guinea-Bissau and Cape Verde;

3. *Demands* that the Government of Portugal desist forthwith from further violation of the sovereignty and territorial integrity of the Republic of Guinea-Bissau and from all acts of aggression against the people of Guinea-Bissau and Cape Verde by immediately withdrawing its armed forces from those territories;

4. *Draws the attention* of the Security Council, in conformity with Article 11, paragraph 3, of the Charter of the United Nations, to the critical situation resulting from the illegal presence of Portugal in Guinea-Bissau and to the urgent need for taking, as a matter of priority, all effective steps to restore the territorial integrity of the Republic;

5. *Invites* all Member States, the specialized agencies and other organizations within the United Nations system to render all necessary assistance to the Government of Guinea-Bissau in its national reconstruction and development programmes;

6. *Decides* to keep the situation under continuous review.

2163rd plenary meeting
2 November 1973

3485 (XXX). Question of Timor

Committee: 1
Vote: 120 - 0 - 22
Ref.: 31/53

The General Assembly,

Recognizing the inalienable right of all peoples to self-determination and independence in accordance with the principles of the Charter of the United Nations and of the Declaration on the Granting of Independence to Colonial Countries and Peoples, contained in its resolution 1514 (XV) of 14 December 1960,

Having examined the chapter of the report of the Special Committee on the Situation with regard to the Implementation of the Declaration on the Granting of Independence to Colonial Countries and Peoples relating to the question of Timor,[1]

Having heard the statements of the representatives of Portugal, as the administering Power,[2] concerning developments in Portuguese Timor and the implementation with regard to that Territory of the relevant provisions of the Charter and the Declaration, as well as those of General Assembly resolution 1541 (XV) of 15 December 1960,

Bearing in mind the responsibility of the administering Power to undertake all efforts to create conditions enabling the people of Portuguese Timor to exercise freely their right to self-determination, freedom and independence and to determine their future political status in accordance with the principles of the Charter and the Declaration, in an atmosphere of peace and order,

Mindful that all States should, in conformity with Article 2, paragraph 4, of the Charter, refrain in their international relations from the threat or use of force against the territorial integrity or national independence of any State, or from taking any action inconsistent with the purposes and principles of the Charter,

Deeply concerned at the critical situation resulting from the military intervention of the armed forces of Indonesia in Portuguese Timor,

1. *Calls upon* all States to respect the inalienable right of the people of Portuguese Timor to self-determination, freedom and independence and to determine their future political status in accordance with the principles of the Charter of the United Nations and the Declaration on the Granting of Independence to Colonial Countries and Peoples;

2. *Calls upon* the administering Power to continue to make every effort to find a solution by peaceful means through talks between the Government of Portugal and the political parties representing the people of Portuguese Timor;

3. *Appeals* to all the parties in Portuguese Timor to respond positively to efforts to find a peaceful solution through talks between them and the Government of Portugal in the hope that such talks will bring an end to the strife in that Territory and lead towards the orderly exercise of the right of self-determination by the people of Portuguese Timor;

4. *Strongly deplores* the military intervention of the armed forces of Indonesia in Portuguese Timor;

5. *Calls upon* the Government of Indonesia to desist from further violation of the territorial integrity of Portuguese Timor and to withdraw without delay its armed forces from the Territory in order to enable the people of the Territory freely to exercise their right to self-determination and independence;

6. *Draws the attention* of the Security Council, in conformity with Article 11, paragraph 3, of the Charter, to the critical situation in the Territory of Portuguese Timor and recommends that it take urgent action to protect the territorial integrity of Portuguese Timor and the inalienable right of its people to self-determination;

7. *Calls upon* all States to respect the unity and territorial integrity of Portuguese Timor;

8. *Requests* the Government of Portugal to continue its cooperation with the Special Committee on the Situation with regard to the Implementation of the Declaration on the Granting of Independence to Colonial Countries and Peoples and requests the Committee to send a fact-finding mission to the Territory as soon as possible, in consultation with the political parties in Portuguese Timor and the Government of Portugal.

2439th plenary meeting
12 December 1975

32/34. Question of East Timor

Committee: 4
Vote: 67 - 26 - 47

The General Assembly,

Recognizing the inalienable right of all peoples to self-determination and independence in accordance with the principles of the Charter of the United Nations and of the Declaration on the Granting of Independence to Colonial Countries and Peoples, contained in its resolution 1514 (XV) of 14 December 1960,

Having examined the chapter of the report of the Special Committee on the Situation with regard to the Implementation of the Declaration on the Granting of Independence to Colonial Countries and Peoples relating to the Territory,[3]

Having heard the statements of the representatives of Portugal[4] and Indonesia,[5]

Having also heard the statements of the representatives of the Frente Revolucionaria de Timor Leste Independente,[6]

---

1 *Official Records of the General Assembly, Thirtieth Session, Fourth Committee, Supplement No. 23* (A/10023/ Rev.l), chap. VIII.

2 *Ibid., Thirtieth Session, Fourth Committee,* 2178th, 2184th and 2185th meetings.

3 *Official Records of the General Assembly, Thirty-second Session, Supplement No. 23* (A/32/23/Rev.l), vol. II, chap. X.

4 *Ibid., Thirty-second Session, Fourth Committee,* 12th meeting, paras. 22-26.

5 *Ibid.,* 19th meeting, paras. 4-58.

Mindful that all States should, in conformity with Article 2, paragraph 4, of the Charter, refrain in their international relations from the threat or use of force against the territorial integrity or national independence of any State, or in any other manner inconsistent with the purposes of the United Nations,

Deeply concerned at the continuing critical situation in the Territory, resulting from the persistent refusal on the part of the Government of Indonesia to comply with the provisions of the resolutions of the General Assembly and the Security Council,

Recalling its resolutions 3485 (XXX) of 12 December 1975 and 31/53 of 1 December 1976 and Security Council resolutions 384 (1975) of 22 December 1975 and 389 (1976) of 22 April 1976,

1. *Reaffirms* the inalienable right of the people of East Timor to self-determination and independence. and the legitimacy of their struggle to achieve that right;

2. *Reaffirms* its resolutions 3485 (XXX) and 31/ 53 and Security Council resolutions 384 (1975) and 389 (1976);

3. *Rejects* the claim that East Timor has been integrated into Indonesia, inasmuch as the people of the Territory have not been able to exercise freely their right to self-determination and independence;

4. *Requests* the Special Committee on , the Situation with regard to the Implementation of the Declaration on the Granting of Independence to Colonial Countries and Peoples to keep the situation in the Territory under active consideration, to follow the implementation of the present resolution, to dispatch to the Territory as soon as possible a visiting mission with a view to the full and speedy implementation of the Declaration and to report thereon to the General Assembly at its thirty-third session;

5. *Requests* the Secretary-General in consultation with the Chairman of the Special Committee, in the meantime to send urgently a special representative to East Timor for the purpose of making a thorough, on-the-spot assessment of the existing situation in the Territory and of establishing contact with the representatives of the Frente Revolucionaria de Timor Leste Independente and the Government of Indonesia, as well as the Governments of other States concerned, in order to prepare the ground for a visiting mission of the Special Committee, and to report thereon to the Special Committee;

6. *Draws the attention* of the Security Council, in conformity with Article 11, paragraph 3, of the Charter of the United Nations, to the critical situation in the Territory of East Timor and recommends that it should take all effective steps for the implementation of its resolutions 384 (1975) and 389 (1976) with a view, to securing the full exercise by the people of East Timor of their right to self-determination and independence;

7. *Calls upon* the Government of Indonesia and the leadership of the Frente Revolucionaria de Timor Leste Independente to facilitate the entry into East Timor of the International Committee of the Red Cross and other relief organizations in order to assist the people of the Territory;

8. *Decides* to include in the provisional agenda of its thirty-third session the item entitled "Question of East Timor".

83rd plenary meeting
28 November 1977

37/30. Question of East Timor

Committee: 4
Vote: 50 - 46 - 50
Ref.: 36/50, 35/27, 34/40, 33/39

The General Assembly,

Recognizing thc inalicnable right of all peoples to self-determination and independence in accordance with the principles of the Charter of the United Nations, the Declaration on the Granting of Independence to Colonial Countries and Peoples, contained in its resolution 1514 (XV) of 14 December 1960, and other relevant United Nations resolutions,

Having examined the chapter of the report of the Special Committee on the Situation with regard to the Implementation of the Declaration on the Granting of Independence to Colonial Countries and Peoples relating to East Timor[1] and other relevant documents,

Taking note of the report of the Secretary-General on the question of East Timor,[2]

Taking note of resolution 1982/20[3] adopted by the Sub-Commission on Prevention of Discrimination and Protection of Minorities on 8 September 1982,

Having heard the statement of the representative of Portugal,[4] as the administering Power,

Having heard the statement of the representative of Indonesia,[5]

Having heard the statements of the representative of the Frente Revolucionaria de Timor Leste Independente and of various petitioners, as well as of the representatives of non-governmental organizations,[6]

Bearing in mind that Portugal, the administering Power, has stated its full and solemn commitment to uphold the right of the people of East Timor to self-determination and independence,

Bearing in mind also its resolutions 3485 (XXX) of 12 December 1975, 31/53 of 1 December 1976, 32/34 of 28 November 1977, 33/39 of 13 December 1978, 34/40 of 21 November 1979, 35/27 of 11 November 1980 and 36/50 of 24 November 1981,

Concerned at the humanitarian situation prevailing in the Territory and believing that all efforts should be made by the international community to improve the living conditions of the people of East Timor and to guarantee to those people the effective enjoyment of their fundamental human rights,

1. *Requests* the Secretary-General to initiate consultations with all parties directly concerned, with a view to exploring avenues for achieving a comprehensive settlement of the problem and to report thereon to the General Assembly at its thirty-eighth session;

2. *Requests* the Special Committee on the Situation with regard to the Implementation of the Declaration on the Granting of Independence to Colonial Countries and Peoples to keep the situation in the Territory under active consideration and to render all assistance to the Secretary-General with a view to facilitating the implementation of the present resolution;

3. *Calls upon* all specialized agencies and other organizations of the United Nations system, in particular the World Food Programme, the United Nations Children's Fund and the Office of the United Nations High Commissioner for Refugees, immediately to assist, within their respective fields of competence, the people of East Timor, in close consultation with Portugal, as the administering Power;

4. *Decides* to include in the provisional agenda of its thirty-eighth session the item entitled "Question of East Timor".

77th plenary meeting
23 November 1982

---

6 *Ibid.*, 11th meeting, paras. 135-155, and 20th meeting, paras. 101-130.

---

1 *Official Records of the General Assembly, Thirty-Seventh Session, Supplement No. 23* (A/37/23/Rev.1), chap. X.

2 A/37/538.

3 See E/CN.4/1983/4-E/CN.4/Sub.2/1982/43 and Corr.1, chap. XXI.

4 *Official Records of the General Assembly, Thirty-seventh Session, Fourth Committee*, 14th meeting, paras. 17-19.

5 *Ibid.*, 23rd meeting, paras. 22-37.

6 *Ibid.*, 15th-18th meetings.

04.42 NAMIBIA

65 (I). Future Status of South West Africa

Committee: 4
Vote: 37 - 0 - 9

The General Assembly,

Having considered the statements of the delegation of the Union of South Africa regarding the question of incorporating the mandated territory of South West Africa in the Union;

Noting with satisfaction that the Union of South Africa, by presenting this matter to the United Nations, recognizes the interest and concern of the United Nations in the matter of the future status of territories now held under mandate;

Recalling that the Charter of the United Nations provides in Articles 77 and 79 that the trusteeship system shall apply to territories now under mandate as may be subsequently agreed;

Referring to the resolution of the General Assembly of 9 February 1946, inviting the placing of mandated territories under trusteeship;

Desiring that agreement between the United Nations and the Union of South Africa may hereafter be reached regarding the future status of the mandated territory of South West Africa;

Assured by the delegation of the Union of South Africa that, pending such agreement, the Union Government will continue to administer the territory as heretofore in the spirit of the principles laid down in the mandate;

Considering that the African inhabitants of South West Africa have not yet secured political autonomy or reached a stage of political development enabling them to express a considered opinion which the Assembly could recognize on such an important question as incorporation of their territory:

The General Assembly, therefore,

Is unable to accede to the incorporation of the territory of South West Africa in the Union of South Africa; and

Recommends that the mandated territory of South West Africa be placed under the international trusteeship system and invites the Government of the Union of South Africa to propose for the consideration of the General Assembly a trusteeship agreement for the aforesaid territory.

Sixty-fourth plenary meeting
14 December 1946

338 (IV). Question of South West Africa: Request for an Advisory Opinion of the International Court of Justice

Committee: 4
Vote: 40 - 7 - 4
Ref.: 934(X), 337(IV), 227(III), 141(II)

The General Assembly,

Recalling its previous resolutions 65 (I) of 14 December 1946, 141 (II) of 1 November 1947 and 227 (III) of 26 November 1948 concerning the Territory of South West Africa,

Considering that it is desirable that the General Assembly, for its further consideration of the question, should obtain an advisory opinion on its legal aspects,

1. *Decides* to submit the following questions to the International Court of Justice with a request for an advisory opinion which shall be transmitted to the General Assembly before its fifth regular session, if possible:

"What is the international status of the Territory of South West Africa and what are the international obligations of the Union of South Africa arising therefrom, in particular:

"(*a*) Does the Union of South Africa continue to have international obligations under the Mandate for South West Africa and, if so, what are those obligations?

"(*b*) Are the provisions of Chapter XII of the Charter applicable and, if so, in what manner, to the Territory of South West Africa?

"(*c*) Has the Union of South Africa the competence to modify the international status of the Territory of South West Africa, or, in the event of a negative reply, where does competence rest to determine and modify the international status of the Territory?"

2. *Requests* the Secretary-General to transmit the present resolution to the International Court of Justice, in accordance with Article 65 of the Statute of the Court, accompanied by all documents likely to throw light upon the question.

The Secretary-General shall include among these documents, the text of article 22 of the Covenant of the League of Nations; the text of the Mandate[1] for German South West Africa, confirmed by the Council of the League on 17 December 1920; relevant documentation concerning the objectives and the functions of the Mandates System; the text of the resolution[2] adopted by the League of Nations on the question of Mandates on 18. April 1946; the text of Articles 77 and 80 of the Charter and data on the discussion of these Articles in the San Francisco Conference and the General Assembly; the report of the Fourth Committee and the official records, including the annexes, of the consideration of the question of South West Africa at the fourth session of the General Assembly.

269th plenary meeting
6 December 1949

749 (VIII). Question of South West Africa

Committee: 4
Vote: A: 46 - 1 - 12; B: 47 - 1 - 11
Ref.: 1246(XIII), 1141(XII), 1061(XI), 1055(XI), 940(X), 852(IX), 651(VII), 570(VI), 449(V)

A

The General Assembly,

Having accepted, by resolution 449 A (V) of 13 December 1950 and by resolution 570 (VI) of 19 January 1952, the advisory opinion of the International Court of Justice with respect to South West Africa,

Recalling that the advisory opinion[3] of the International Court of Justice with respect to the Territory of South West Africa sets forth, *inter alia*, that:

(*a*) The Territory of South West Africa is a Territory under the international Mandate assumed by the Union of South Africa on 17 December 1920,

(*b*) The Union of South Africa acting alone has not the competence to modify the international status of the Territory of South West Africa, and that the competence to determine and modify the international status of the Territory rests with the Union of South Africa acting with the consent of the United Nations,

(*c*) The Union of South Africa continues to have the international obligations stated in Article 22 of the Covenant of the League of Nations and in the Mandate for South West Africa as well as the obligation to transmit petitions from the inhabitants of that Territory, the supervisory functions to be exercised by the United Nations to which the annual reports and the petitions are to be submitted,

Considering that, in accordance with the opinion of the International Court of Justice, the Union of South Africa is under an obligation to accept the compulsory jurisdiction of the Court as provided by Article 37 of the Statute of the International Court of Justice, by Article 80, paragraph 1, of the Charter of the United Nations and by article 7 of the Mandate for South West Africa,

---

1 See *Terms of League of Nations Mandates* (document A/70).

2 See League of Nations *Official Journal, Special Supplement No. 194*, Records of the twentieth (conclusion) and twenty-first ordinary sessions of the Assembly, p. 58.

3 See *International Status of South West Africa, Advisory Opinion*: I.C.J. Reports 1950, p. 128.

Having reconstituted the *Ad Hoc Committee* on South West Africa, consisting of the representatives of Norway, Syria, Thailand, the United States of America and Uruguay, by General Assembly resolution 570 A (VI) of 19 January 1952 and, by General Assembly resolution 651 (VII) of 20 December 1952, having continued it on the same basis as before,

Having considered the reports of the aforesaid *Ad Hoc Committee*, i.e., document A/2261 submitted on 21 November 1952 and documents A/2475 and Adds.l and 2 submitted on 16 September, 8 October and 9 November 1953,

1. *Commends* the *Ad Hoc Committee* on South West Africa for its earnest and constructive efforts to find a mutually satisfactory basis of agreement;

2. *Records* with deep regret that the Government of the Union of South Africa continues in its refusal to assist in the implementation of the advisory opinion of the International Court of Justice concerning South West Africa, and continues to maintain that the Union of South Africa has no international commitments as the result of the demise of the League of Nations, and that the Government of the Union of South Africa is prepared only to enter into new arrangements for the Territory of South West Africa with the Principal Allied and Associated Powers of the First World War (France, the United Kingdom and the United States of America), and not with the United Nations;

3. *Notes with concern* that, as required by paragraph 6 of General Assembly resolution 570 A (VI), the *Ad Hoc Committee* was unable to examine reports on the administration of the Territory of South West Africa because again no such reports were submitted by the Government of the Union of South Africa;

4. *Notes with further regret* that the Union of South Africa has refused to cooperate with the United Nations concerning the submission of petitions in accordance with the procedures of the Mandates System;

5. *Notes* the contents of the communications relating to South West Africa received by the *Ad Hoc Committee* in 1951, 1952 and 1953 from sources within and outside the Territory of South West Africa and contained in the aforesaid reports of the *Ad Hoc Committee*;

6. *Affirms* that, in order to implement the advisory opinion of the International Court of Justice with regard to South West Africa,

(*a*) The supervision of the administration of South West Africa, though it should not exceed that which applied under the Mandates System, should be exercised by the United Nations; judicial supervision by the International Court of Justice, which the Union Government is prepared to accept, is not in accordance with the advisory opinion expressed by that Court and accepted by the General Assembly;

(*b*) The Union Government should assume its obligations to the United Nations and not, as proposed by the Union Government, to the three Powers (France, the United Kingdom and the United States of America) as principals;

7. *Appeals solemnly* to the Government of the Union of South Africa to reconsider its position, and urges it to continue negotiations with the Committee on South West Africa, established under paragraph 12 below, in accordance with the aforesaid principles for the purpose of concluding an agreement providing for the full implementation of the advisory opinion of the International Court of Justice; and urges it further to resume submission of reports on the administration of the Territory of South West Africa and to transmit to the United Nations petitions from individuals or groups of the population of the Territory;

8. *Recalls and reaffirms* that the Territory of South West Africa is a Territory under the international Mandate assumed by the Union of South Africa on 17 December 1920;

9. *Reaffirms further* that the Union of South Africa continues to have the international obligations stated in Article 22 of the Covenant of the League of Nations and in the Mandate for South West Africa as well as the obligation to transmit petitions from the inhabitants of that Territory, the supervisory functions to be exercised by the United Nations to which the annual reports and the petitions are to be submitted;

10. *Considers* that without United Nations supervision the inhabitants of the Territory are deprived of the international supervision envisaged by the Covenant of the League of Nations;

11. *Believes* that it would not fulfil its obligation towards the inhabitants of South West Africa if it were not to assume the supervisory responsibilities with regard to the Territory of South West Africa which were formerly exercised by the League of Nations;

12. *Establishes*, until such time as an agreement is reached between the United Nations and the Union of South Africa, a Committee on South West Africa, consisting of seven Members, and requests this Committee to:

(*a*) Examine, within the scope of the Questionnaire adopted by the Permanent Mandates Commission of the League of Nations in 1926, such information and documentation as may be available in respect of the Territory of South West Africa;

(*b*) Examine, as far as possible in accordance with the procedure of the former Mandates System, reports and petitions which may be submitted to the Committee or to the Secretary-General;

(*c*) Transmit to the General Assembly a report concerning conditions in the Territory taking into account, as far as possible, the scope of the reports of the Permanent Mandates Commission of the League of Nations;

(*d*) Prepare, for the consideration of the General Assembly, a procedure for the examination of reports and petitions which should conform as far as possible to the procedure followed in this respect by the Assembly, the Council and the Permanent Mandates Commission of the League of Nations;

13. *Authorizes* the Committee to continue negotiations with the Union of South Africa in order to implement fully the advisory opinion of the International Court of Justice regarding the question of South West Africa;

14. *Requests* the Committee to submit reports on its activities to the General Assembly at its regular sessions.

460th plenary meeting
28 November 1953

* * *

At its 467th plenary meeting on 3 December 1953, the General Assembly, on the recommendation of the Fourth Committee to the President, approved the nomination of the following Members to serve on the Committee on South West Africa: Brazil, Mexico, Norway, Pakistan, Syria, Thailand and Uruguay.

B

The General Assembly,

Having recommended, by its resolutions 65 (I) of 14 December 1946, 141 (II) of 1 November 1C947, 227 (III) of 26 November 1948, 337 (IV) of 6 December 1949, 449 B (V) of 13 December 1950 and 570 B (VI) of 19 January 1952, that the Mandated Territory of South West Africa be placed under the International Trusteeship System, and having repeatedly invited the Government of the Union of South Africa to propose, for the consideration of the General Assembly, a Trusteeship Agreement for South West Africa,

Having accepted, by resolution 449 A (V) of 13 December 1950, the advisory opinion of 11 July 1950 of the International Court of Justice concerning South West Africa, *inter alia*, to the effect that:

(*a*) While "the provisions of Chapter XII of the Charter do not impose on the Union of South Africa a legal obligation to place the Territory under the Trusteeship System", they "are applicable to the Territory of South West Africa in the sense that they provide a means by which the Territory may be brought under the Trusteeship System",

(*b*) " ... the Union of South Africa acting alone has not the competence to modify the international status of the Territory of South West Africa", and "... the competence to determine and modify the international status of the Territory rests with the Union of South Africa acting with the consent of the United Nations",

Considering that, in accordance with Chapter XII of the Charter, all Mandated Territories which have not achieved independence have been brought under the Trusteeship System with the sole exception of the Territory of South West Africa,

1. *Reiterates* its resolutions 65 (I) of 14 December 1946, 141 (II) of 1 November 1947, 227 (III) of 26 November 1948, 337 (IV) of 6 December 1949, 449 B (V) of 13 December 1950 and 570 B (VI) of 19 January 1952, to the effect that the Territory of South West Africa be placed under the International Trusteeship System;

2. *Reasserts* that the normal way of modifying the international status of the Territory would be to place it under the Trusteeship System by means of a Trusteeship Agreement in accordance with the provisions of Chapter XII of the Charter.

460th plenary meeting
28 November 1953

844 (IX). Procedure for the Examination of Reports and Petitions Relating to the Territory of South West Africa

Committee: 4
Vote: 33 - 3 - 15

The General Assembly,

Having received a report[1] of the Committee on South West Africa concerning the procedure for the examination by the Assembly of reports and petitions relating to the Territory of South West Africa,

Having in mind the advisory opinion[2] of the International Court of Justice on South West Africa,

Desiring to apply, as far as possible, and pending the conclusion of an agreement between the United Nations and the Union of South Africa, the procedure followed in that respect by the Council of the League of Nations,

Adopts the following special rules:

Procedure with Regard to Reports

Special rule A: The General Assembly shall receive annually from the Committee on South West Africa the report on South West Africa submitted to the Committee by the Union of South Africa (or a report on conditions in the Territory of South West Africa prepared by the Committee in accordance with paragraph 12 (c) of General Assembly resolution 749 A (VIII)) together with the observations of the Committee on the report as well as the comments of the duly authorized representative of the Union of South Africa, should that Government decide to follow the General Assembly's recommendation and appoint such a representative.

Special rule B: The General Assembly shall, as a rule, be guided by the observations of the Committee on South West Africa and shall base its conclusions as far as possible, on the Committee's observations.

Procedure with Regard to Petitions

Special rule C: The General Assembly shall receive annually from the Committee on South West Africa a report with regard to petitions submitted to it. The summary records of the meetings at which the petitions were discussed shall be attached.

Special rule D: The General Assembly shall, as a rule, be guided by the conclusions of the Committee on South West Africa and shall base its own conclusions, as far as possible, on the conclusions of the Committee.

Private Meetings

Special rule E: Having regard to rule 62 of the rules of procedure of the General Assembly, meetings at which decisions concerning persons are considered shall be held in private.

Voting Procedure

Special rule F: Decisions of the General Assembly on questions relating to reports and petitions concerning the Territory of South West Africa shall be regarded as important questions within the meaning of Article 18, paragraph 2, of the Charter of the United Nations.

494th plenary meeting
11 October 1954

904 (IX). Voting Procedure on Questions Relating to Reports and Petitions Concerning the Territory of South West Africa: Request for an Advisory Opinion from the International Court of Justice

Committee: -
Vote: 25 - 11 - 21
Ref.: 934(X)

The General Assembly,

Having accepted, by resolution 449 A (V) of 13 December 1950, the advisory opinion[3] of the International Court of Justice of 11 July 1950 with respect to South West Africa,

Having regard, in particular, to the Court's opinion on the general question, namely, "that South-West Africa is a territory under the international Mandate assumed by the Union of South Africa on December 17th, 1920", and to the Court's opinion on question (a), namely, "that the Union of South Africa continues to have the international obligations stated in Article 22 of the Covenant of the League of Nations and in the Mandate for South-West Africa as well as the obligation to transmit petitions from the inhabitants of that Territory, the supervisory functions to be exercised by the United Nations, to which the annual reports and the petitions are to be submitted, and the reference to the Permanent Court of International Justice to be replaced by a reference to the International Court of Justice, in accordance with Article 7 of the Mandate and Article 37 of the Statute of the Court;",

Having expressed, in resolution 749 A (VIII) of 28 November 1953, its opinion "that without United Nations supervision the inhabitants of the Territory are deprived of the international supervision envisaged by the Covenant of the League of Nations" and its belief "that it would not fulfil its obligation towards the inhabitants of South West Africa if it were not to assume the supervisory responsibilities with regard to the Territory of South West Africa which were formerly exercised by the League of Nations",

Having regard to the opinion of the International Court of Justice that "The degree of supervision to be exercised by the General Assembly should not ... exceed that which applied under the Mandates System, and should conform as far as possible to the procedure followed in this respect by the Council of the League of Nations" and that "These observations are particularly applicable to annual reports and petitions",

Having adopted, by resolution 844 (IX) of 11 October 1954, a special rule F on the voting procedure to be followed by the General Assembly in taking decisions on questions relating to reports and petitions concerning the Territory of South West Africa,

Having adopted this rule in a desire "to apply, as far as possible, and pending the conclusion of an agreement between the United Nations and the Union of South Africa, the procedure followed in that respect by the Council of the League of Nations",

Considering that some elucidation of the advisory opinion is desirable,

---

[1] See *Official Records of the General Assembly, Ninth Session, Supplement No. 14* and documents A/2666/Corr.l and A/2666/Add.l Appendix 16, p. 321.

[2] See *International Status of South West Africa, Advisory Opinion*: I.C.J Reports 1950.

[3] See *International Status of South West Africa, Advisory Opinion*: I.C.J. Reports 1950, p. 128.

Requests the International Court of Justice to give an advisory opinion on the following questions:

"(*a*) Is the following rule on the voting procedure to be followed by the General Assembly a correct interpretation of the advisory opinion of the International Court of Justice of 11 July 1950:

"'Decisions of the General Assembly on questions relating to reports and petitions concerning the Territory of South West Africa shall be regarded as important questions within the meaning of Article 18, paragraph 2, of the Charter of the United Nations.'"

"(*b*) If this interpretation of the advisory opinion of the Court is not correct, what voting procedure should be followed by the General Assembly in taking decisions on questions relating to reports and petitions concerning the Territory of South West Africa?"

501st plenary meeting
23 November 1954

942 (X). Question of the Admissibility of Oral Hearings by the Committee on South West Africa: Request for an Advisory Opinion from the International Court of Justice

Committee: 4
Vote: 32 . 5 . 19
Ref.: 1047(XI)

The General Assembly,

Having been requested by the Committee on South West Africa to decide whether or not the oral hearing of petitioners on matters relating to the Territory of South West Africa is admissible before that Committee,[1]

Having instructed the Committee, in General Assembly resolution 749 A (VIII) of 28 November 1953, to examine petitions as far as possible in accordance with the procedure of the former Mandates System,

Requests the International Court of Justice to give an advisory opinion on the following question:

"Is it consistent with the advisory opinion[2] of the International Court of Justice of 11 July 1950 for the Committee on South West Africa, established by General Assembly resolution 749 A (VIII) of 28 November 1953, to grant oral hearings to petitioners on matters relating to the Territory of South West Africa?"

550th plenary meeting
3 December 1955

2145 (XXI). Question of South West Africa

Committee: -
Vote: 114 - 2 - 3
Ref.: 2074(XX), 1979(XVIII), 1899(XXVIII), 1805(XVII), 1702(XVI), 1596(XV), 1568(XV), 1360(XIV), 1359(XIV), 1356(XIV), 1059(XI)

The General Assembly,

Reaffirming the inalienable right of the people of South West Africa to freedom and independence in accordance with the Charter of the United Nations, General Assembly resolution 1514 (XV) of 14 December 1960 and earlier Assembly resolutions concerning the Mandated Territory of South West Africa,

Recalling the advisory opinion of the International Court of Justice of 11 July 1950,[3] accepted by the General Assembly in its resolution 449 A (V) of 13 December 1950, and the advisory opinions of 7 June 1955[4] and 1 June 1956[5] as well as the judgement of 21 December 1962,[6] which have established the fact that South Africa continues to have obligations under the Mandate which was entrusted to it on 17 December 1920 and that the United Nations as the successor to the League of Nations has supervisory powers in respect of South West Africa,

Gravely concerned at the situation in the Mandated Territory, which has seriously deteriorated following the judgment of the International Court of Justice of 18 July 1966,[7]

Having studied the reports of the various committees which had been established to exercise the supervisory functions of the United Nations over the administration of the Mandated Territory of South West Africa,

Convinced that the administration of the Mandated Territory by South Africa has been conducted in a manner contrary to the Mandate, the Charter of the United Nations and the Universal Declaration of Human Rights,

Reaffirming its resolution 2074 (XX) of 17 December 1965, in particular paragraph 4 thereof which condemned the policies of apartheid and racial discrimination practised by the Government of South Africa in South West Africa as constituting a crime against humanity,

Emphasizing that the problem of South West Africa is an issue falling within the terms of General Assembly resolution 1514 (XV),

Considering that all the efforts of the United Nations to induce the Government of South Africa to fulfil its obligations in respect of the administration of the Mandated Territory and to ensure the well-being and security of the indigenous inhabitants have been of no avail,

Mindful of the obligations of the United Nations towards the people of South West Africa,

Noting with deep concern the explosive situation which exists in the southern region of Africa,

Affirming its right to take appropriate action in the matter, including the right to revert to itself the administration of the Mandated Territory,

1. *Reaffirms* that the provisions of General Assembly resolution 1514 (XV) are fully applicable to the people of the Mandated Territory of South West Africa and that, therefore, the people of South West Africa have the inalienable right to self-determination, freedom and independence in accordance with the Charter of the United Nations;

2. *Reaffirms further* that South West Africa is a territory having international status and that it shall maintain this status until it achieves independence;

3. *Declares* that South Africa has failed to fulfil its obligations in respect of the administration of the Mandated Territory and to ensure the moral and material well-being and security of the indigenous inhabitants of South West Africa and has, in fact, disavowed the Mandate;

4. *Decides* that the Mandate conferred upon His Britannic Majesty to be exercised on his behalf by the Government of the Union of South Africa is therefore terminated, that South Africa has no other right to administer the Territory and that henceforth South West Africa comes under the direct responsibility of the United Nations;

5. *Resolves* that in these circumstances the United Nations must discharge those responsibilities with respect to South West Africa;

6. *Establishes* an *Ad Hoc Committee* for South West Africa - composed of fourteen Member States to be designated by the President of the General Assembly - to recommend practical means by which South West Africa should be administered, so as to enable the people of the Territory to exercise the right of self-determination and to

---

1 *Official Records of the General Assembly, Tenth Session, Annexes*, agenda item 30, document A/2913/Add.2. Appendix 50, p. 469.

2 *International Status of South-West Africa, Advisory Opinion*: I.C.J. Reports 1950, p. 128.

3 *Ibid.*

4 *South West Africa-Voting procedure, Advisory Opinion of June 7th, 1955*: I.C.J. Reports 1955, p. 67.

5 *Admissibility of hearings of petitioners by the Committee on South West Africa, Advisory Opinion of June 1st, 1956*: I.C.J. Reports 1956, p. 23.

6 *South West Africa Cases (Ethiopia v. South Africa; Liberia v. South Africa), Preliminary Objections, Judgment of 21 December 1962*: I.C.J. Reports 1962, p. 319.

7 *South West Africa, Second Phase, Judgment*: I.C.J. Reports 1966, p. 6.

achieve independence, and to report to the General Assembly at a special session as soon as possible and in any event not later than April 1967;

7. *Calls upon* the Government of South Africa forthwith to refrain and desist from any action, constitutional, administrative, political or otherwise, which will in any manner whatsoever alter or tend to alter the present international status of South West Africa;

8. *Calls the attention* of the Security Council to the present resolution;

9. *Requests* all States to extend their whole-hearted cooperation and to render assistance in the implementation of the present resolution;

10. *Requests* the Secretary-General to provide all the assistance necessary to implement the present resolution and to enable the *Ad Hoc Committee* for South West Africa to perform its duties.

1454th plenary meeting
27 October 1966

2248 (S-V). Question of South West Africa

Committee: -
Vote: 85 - 2 - 30

The General Assembly,

Having considered the report of the *Ad Hoc Committee* for South West Africa,[1]

Reaffirming its resolution 1514 (XV) of 14 December 1960 containing the Declaration on the Granting of Independence to Colonial Countries and Peoples,

Reaffirming its resolution 2145 (XXI) of 27 October 1966, by which it terminated the Mandate conferred upon His Britannic Majesty to be exercised on his behalf by the Government of the Union of South Africa and decided that South Africa had no other right to administer the Territory of South West Africa,

Having assumed direct responsibility for the Territory of South West Africa in accordance with resolution 2145 (XXI),

Recognizing that it has thereupon become incumbent upon the United Nations to give effect to its obligations by taking practical steps to transfer power to the people of South West Africa,

I

Reaffirms the territorial integrity of South West Africa and the inalienable right of its people to freedom and independence, in accordance with the Charter of the United Nations, General Assembly resolution 1514 (XV) and all other resolutions concerning South West Africa;

II

1. *Decides* to establish a United Nations Council for South West Africa (hereinafter referred to as the Council) comprising eleven Member States to be elected during the present session and to entrust to it the following powers and functions, to be discharged in the Territory:

(*a*) To administer South West Africa until independence, with the maximum possible participation of the people of the Territory;

(*b*) To promulgate such laws, decrees and administrative regulations as are necessary for the administration of the Territory until a legislative assembly is established following elections conducted on the basis of universal adult suffrage;

(*c*) To take as an immediate task all the necessary measures, in consultation with the people of the Territory, for the establishment of a constituent assembly to draw up a constitution on the basis of which elections will be held for the establishment of a legislative assembly and a responsible government;

(*d*) To take all the necessary measures for the maintenance of law and order in the Territory;

(*e*) To transfer all powers to the people of the Territory upon the declaration of independence;

2. *Decides* that in the exercise of its powers and in the discharge of its functions the Council shall be responsible to the General Assembly;

3. *Decides* that the Council shall entrust such executive and administrative tasks as it deems necessary to a United Nations Commissioner for South West Africa (hereinafter referred to as the Commissioner), who shall be appointed during the present session by the General Assembly on the nomination of the Secretary-General;

4. *Decides* that in the performance of his tasks the Commissioner shall be responsible to the Council;

III

1. *Decides* that:

(*a*) The administration of South West Africa under the United Nations shall he financed from the revenues collected in the Territory;

(*b*) Expenses directly related to the operation of the Council and the Office of the Commissioner - the travel and subsistence expenses of members of the Council, the remuneration of the Commissioner and his staff and the cost of ancillary facilities - shall be met from the regular budget of the United Nations;

2. *Requests* the specialized agencies and the appropriate organs of the United Nations to render to South West Africa technical and financial assistance through a coordinated emergency programme to meet the exigencies of the situation;

IV

1. *Decides* that the Council shall be based in South West Africa;

2. *Requests* the Council to enter immediately into contact with the authorities of South Africa in order to lay down procedures, in accordance with General Assembly resolution 2145 (XXI) and the present resolution, for the transfer of the administration of the Territory with the least possible upheaval;

3. *Further requests* the Council to proceed to South West Africa with a view to:

(*a*) Taking over the administration of the Territory;

(*b*) Ensuring the withdrawal of South African police and military forces;

(*c*) Ensuring the withdrawal of South African personnel and their replacement by personnel operating under the authority of the Council;

(*d*) Ensuring that in the utilization and recruitment of personnel preference be given to the indigenous people;

4. *Calls upon* the Government of South Africa to comply without delay with the terms of resolution 2145 (XXI) and the present resolution and to facilitate the transfer of the administration of the Territory of South West Africa to the Council;

5. *Requests* the Security Council to take all appropriate measures to enable the United Nations Council for South West Africa to discharge the functions and responsibilities entrusted to it by the General Assembly;

6. *Requests* all States to extend their whole-hearted cooperation and to render assistance to the Council in the implementation of its task;

V

Requests the Council to report to the General Assembly at intervals not exceeding three months on its administration of the Territory, and to submit a special report to the Assembly at its twenty-second session concerning the implementation of the present resolution;

VI

Decides that South West Africa shall become independent on a date to be fixed in accordance with the wishes of the people and that the Council shall do all in its power to enable independence to be attained by June 1968.

1518th plenary meeting,
19 May 1967

1 *Official Records of the General Assembly, Fifth Special Session, Annexes*, agenda item 7, document A/6640.

2372 (XXII). Question of South West Africa

Committee: -
Vote: 96 - 2 - 18

The General Assembly,

Having considered the report of the United Nations Council for South West Africa,[1]

Recalling its resolutions 1514 (XV) of 14 December 1960, 2145 (XXI) of 27 October 1966, 22448 (S-V) of 19 May 1967 and 2324 (XXII) and 2325 (XXII) of 16 December 1967,

Noting with grave concern that the refusal of the Government of South Africa to withdraw its administration from the Territory of South West Africa has obstructed the attainment of independence by the Territory in accordance with the relevant United Nations resolutions,

Mindful of the serious consequences of the continued foreign occupation by South Africa of the Territory of South West Africa, which constitutes a grave threat to international peace and security,

Concerned that the continued refusal of the Government of South Africa to comply with its obligations to the United Nations and to the international community as a whole, making it impossible for the United Nations Council for South West Africa to perform effectively the functions that were entrusted to it by the General Assembly, constitutes a flagrant defiance of the authority of the United Nations,

Deploring the defiance by the Government of South Africa of General Assembly resolution 2324 (XXII) and Security Council resolutions 245 (1968) of 25 January 1968 and 246 (1968) of 14 March 1968 concerning the illegal arrest, deportation, trial and conviction of South West African patriots engaged in the struggle for independence,

Conscious of the special and direct responsibility of the United Nations towards the people and the Territory of South West Africa, in accordance with the provisions of General Assembly resolutions 2145 (XXI) and 2248 (S-V),

Recalling Security Council resolution 246 (1968), in particular its last preambular paragraph, in which the Security Council took cognizance of its special responsibility towards the people and the Territory of South West Africa,

Taking into account the views expressed by representatives of the people of South West Africa in their consultations with the United Nations Council for South West Africa,

1. *Proclaims* that, in accordance with the desires of its people, South West Africa shall henceforth be known as "Namibia";

2. *Takes note* of the report of the United Nations Council for South West Africa and expresses its appreciation for the Council's efforts to discharge the responsibilities and functions entrusted to it;

3. *Decides* that the United Nations Council for South West Africa shall be called "United Nations Council for Namibia" and that the United Nations Commissioner for South West Africa shall be called "United Nations Commissioner for Namibia";

4. *Decides* that, taking into account the provisions of General Assembly resolution 2248 (S-V), the United Nations Council for Namibia shall perform, as a matter of priority, the following functions:

(*a*) In consultation and cooperation with the specialized agencies and other appropriate organs of the United Nations, which under section III, paragraph 2, of resolution 2248 (S-V) were requested to render technical and financial assistance to Namibia, the Council shall assume responsibility for establishing a coordinated emergency programme for rendering such assistance, in order to meet the exigencies of the present situation;

(*b*) The Council shall organize a training programme for Namibians, in consultation with those Governments which indicate their interest and concern, so that a cadre of civil servants and of technical and professional personnel may be developed who would be in a position to undertake the public administration and the social, political and economic development of the State;

(*c*) The Council shall continue with a sense of urgency its consultations on the question of issuing to Namibians travel documents enabling them to travel abroad;

5. *Reaffirms* the inalienable right of the Namibian people to freedom and independence and the legitimacy of their struggle against foreign occupation;

6. *Condemns* the Government of South Africa for its persistent refusal to comply with the resolutions of the General Assembly and the Security Council, its refusal to withdraw from Namibia and its obstruction of the efforts of the United Nations Council for Namibia to proceed to Namibia;

7. *Condemns* the action of the Government of South Africa designed to consolidate its illegal control over Namibia and to destroy the unity of the people and the territorial integrity of Namibia;

8. *Condemns* the actions of those States which by their continued political, military and economic collaboration with the Government of South Africa have encouraged that Government to defy the authority of the United Nations and to obstruct the attainment of independence by Namibia;

9. *Calls upon* all States to desist from those dealings with the Government of South Africa which would have the effect of perpetuating South Africa's illegal occupation of Namibia and to take effective economic and other measures with a view to securing the immediate withdrawal of the South African administration from Namibia;

10. *Further calls upon* all States to provide the necessary moral and material assistance to the Namibian people in their legitimate struggle for independence and to assist the United Nations Council for Namibia in the discharge of its mandate;

11. *Considers* that the continued foreign occupation of Namibia by South Africa in defiance of the relevant United Nations resolutions and of the Territory's established international status constitutes a grave threat to international peace and security;

12. *Reiterates* its demand that the Government of South Africa withdraw from Namibia, immediately and unconditionally, all its military and police forces and its administration;

13. *Recommends* the Security Council urgently to take all appropriate steps to secure the implementation of the present resolution and to take effective measures in accordance with the provisions of the Charter of the United Nations to ensure the immediate removal of the South African presence from Namibia and to secure for Namibia its independence in accordance with General Assembly resolution 2145 (XXI);

14. *Requests* the Secretary-General to continue to provide all possible assistance to enable the United Nations Council for Namibia to perform its duties;

15. *Requests* the Secretary-General to report to the General Assembly and to the Security Council on the implementation of the present resolution.

1671st plenary meeting,
12 June 1968

S-9/2. Declaration on Namibia and Programme of Action in Support of Self-Determination and National Independence for Namibia

Committee: -
Vote: 119 - 0 - 2

The General Assembly,

Gravely concerned at the threat to international peace and security posed by the continued illegal occupation of Namibia by South Africa,

Conscious of its responsibilities under its resolutions 2145 (XXI) of 27 October 1966 and 2248 (S-V) of 19 May 1967 and its subsequent resolutions relating to the question of Namibia,

---

1 *Official Records of the General Assembly, Twenty-second Session, Annexes*, agenda item 64, document A/7088.

Recalling the Declaration of Dakar on Namibia and Human Rights,[1] adopted by the International Conference on Namibia and Human Rights, held at Dakar from 5 to 8 January 1976,

Recalling further the Maputo Declaration in Support of the Peoples of Zimbabwe and Namibia and the Programme of Action for the Liberation of Zimbabwe and Namibia,[2] adopted by the International Conference in Support of the Peoples of Zimbabwe and Namibia, held at Maputo from 16 to 21 May 1977,

Bearing in mind the 1978 Lusaka Declaration of the United Nations Council for Namibia,[3] adopted on 23 March 1978,

Reaffirming that the Territory and people of Namibia are the direct responsibility of the United Nations and that the Namibian people under the leadership of the South West Africa People's Organization, their sole and authentic representative, must be enabled to attain self-determination, freedom and genuine independence within a united Namibia, including Walvis Bay,

Cognizant that the deteriorating situation in Namibia, resulting from the attempts of South Africa to perpetuate its illegal occupation of the Territory and its increased acts of aggression and repression against the people of Namibia, necessitated the convening of the current special session of the General Assembly in order urgently to initiate action which would speedily bring about the genuine independence of the Territory of Namibia,

Adopts the following Declaration on Namibia and Programme of Action in Support of Self-Determination and National Independence for Namibia:

I. Declaration on Namibia

1. The General Assembly reiterates that Namibia is the direct responsibility of the United Nations until genuine self-determination and national independence are achieved in the Territory and, for this purpose, reaffirms the mandate given to the United Nations Council for Namibia as the legal Administering Authority for Namibia until independence.

2. The General Assembly reaffirms the inalienable rights of the Namibian people to self-determination, freedom and national independence in a united Namibia, in accordance with the Charter of the United Nations and as declared in Assembly resolutions 1514 (XV) of 14 December 1960 and 2145 (XXI) of 27 October 1966, as well as in its subsequent resolutions and those of the Security Council relating to Namibia, and the legitimacy of their struggle by all means at their disposal against the illegal occupation of Namibia by South Africa.

3. The General Assembly stresses its commitment to end South Africa's illegal occupation of Namibia by ensuring its complete and unconditional withdrawal to enable the Namibian people, under the leadership of the South West Africa People's Organization, to exercise freely their right to self-determination and independence.

4. The General Assembly strongly condemns the colonialist and racist régime of South Africa for its continued illegal occupation of Namibia in defiance of repeated demands by the Assembly and the Security Council for its withdrawal from the Territory, and further condemns South Africa for its attempts to perpetuate its illegal occupation of Namibia and for its escalated brutal repression of the Namibian people.

5. The General Assembly expresses its grave concern that, in complete defiance of continued demands by the international community, members of the South West Africa People's Organization and its supporters continue to be constantly harassed, intimidated and humiliated. There has been an escalation of the arbitrary mass arrest, torture, detention and imprisonment of members of the South West Africa People's Organization. Prolonged illegal and fraudulent trials of its members are being conducted to undermine it and drain its financial resources.

6. The General Assembly condemns the creation of tribal armies in Namibia by South Africa as a measure of ensuring its control of the Territory after independence. It is imperative that all tribal armies be dissolved in order to prevent additional sources of conflict within the Territory.

7. The General Assembly condemns the military build-up of South Africa in Namibia in preparation for a major confrontation with the liberation forces led by the South West Africa People's Organization. In order to increase its military activities in Namibia, South Africa is intensifying the recruitment of mercenaries and organizing tribal armies in the Territory. South Africa has increased the shipment into Namibia of large numbers of tanks and large quantities of ammunition and is constructing additional army barracks.

8. The General Assembly strongly condemns South Africa for exploiting the uranium resources of Namibia and for pursuing policies of nuclear adventurism with incalculable consequences for the people of Namibia and Africa as a whole.

9. The General Assembly strongly deprecates any collaboration with South Africa in the development of nuclear weapons that could enable it to intimidate neighbouring African States and thus perpetuate its colonialist and racist régime in Namibia.

10. The aggressive policies of the South African occupation régime in Namibia are further reflected in its repeated acts of aggression against, military incursions into, and violations of the territorial integrity of, the neighbouring States, in particular Angola and Zambia, causing considerable loss of human life and damage to property. These activities have the immediate objective of consolidating the position of the occupation régime and of carrying out its hegemonistic ambitions in the region.

11. The General Assembly reiterates that Walvis Bay is an integral part of Namibia and condemns South Africa in the strongest possible terms for its decision to annex Walvis Bay, thus violating the principle of the territorial integrity of Namibia, which is embodied in relevant resolutions of the Assembly and the Security Council, including Council resolution 385 (1976) of 30 January 1976. It further reiterates that this decision is illegal, null and void and that it is an act of aggression against the Namibian people. The existence of South African military bases in Walvis Bay is a threat to the national security of Namibia. The illegal annexation of Walvis Bay, the main port and vital economic avenue of Namibia, is a deliberate attempt to undermine the territorial integrity, economic independence and national security of Namibia.

12. The General Assembly reiterates that South Africa's illegal occupation of Namibia constitutes a continued act of aggression against the Namibian people and against the United Nations. The militarization of Namibia by South Africa, its development of nuclear weapons, its brutal use of force against the Namibian people, its attempts to undermine the South West Africa People's Organization, the vanguard of the Namibian liberation struggle, its attempts to destroy the national unity and territorial integrity of Namibia and its acts of aggression against neighbouring independent African States clearly constitute a serious threat to peace and security in the region and to international peace and security.

13. The General Assembly strongly condemns South Africa for its continued exploitation and plundering of the natural resources of Namibia in complete disregard of the legitimate interests of the Namibian people. The exploitation and plundering of those resources by South African and other foreign economic interests, in violation of the relevant resolutions of the Assembly and the Security Council and of Decree No. 1 for the Protection of the Natural Resources of Namibia enacted by the United Nations Council for Namibia on 27

---

1 *Official Records of the General Assembly, Thirty-first Session, Supplement No. 24* (A/31/24) vol. II, annex II, para. 51.

2 A/32/109/Rev.l-S/12344/Rev.l, annex V. For the printed text, see *Official Records of the Security Council, Thirty-second Year, Supplement for July, August and September 1977.*

3 A/S-9/2-S/12631, annex. For the printed text of the Declaration, see *Official Records of the General Assembly, Ninth Special Session, Supplement No. 1* (A/S-9/4), chap. VI.

September 1974,[1] is illegal and contributes to the maintenance of the illegal occupation régime.

14. The General Assembly expresses its full support for the armed liberation struggle of the Namibian people under the leadership of the South West Africa People's Organization, its sole and authentic representative. It expresses its conviction that the intensified armed liberation struggle by the Namibian people continues to be a decisive factor in the efforts to achieve self-determination, freedom and national independence in a united Namibia.

15. The General Assembly commends the valiant people of Namibia, under the leadership of the South West Africa People's Organization, for having intensified the armed struggle for the liberation of their country from the illegal occupation of South Africa.

16. The General Assembly supports the political and diplomatic efforts of the South West Africa People's Organization to secure genuine independence for Namibia, in accordance with all relevant resolutions of the Assembly and the Security Council, and commends that organization for its willingness to enter into negotiations for the achievement of genuine independence for Namibia, in conformity with Council resolution 385 (1976) in its entirety.

17. The General Assembly notes that the South West Africa People's Organization has made farreaching and substantive concessions to facilitate a negotiated settlement. On the other hand, South Africa, by its continued intransigence and inflexibility, has refused to demonstrate any good faith or willingness to enter seriously into meaningful negotiations for its withdrawal from Namibia.

18. The General Assembly rejects the idea that South Africa, as the illegal occupier of Namibia, has any legitimate interest in Namibia about which the South West Africa People's Organization should be pressed to make concessions in any negotiated and internationally acceptable settlement. South Africa has no right whatsoever to remain in Namibia or to procrastinate and prevaricate in any negotiating process on the question of genuine independence for Namibia.

19. The General Assembly declares that, unless effective political, economic and diplomatic pressures are demonstrably brought to bear on South Africa, no negotiation will succeed. Moreover, any genuine attempt to resolve the problem of Namibia by negotiation must not undermine the position of the South West Africa People's Organization or diminish the role of the United Nations or the United Nations Council for Namibia as the legal Administering Authority for the Territory until its independence. It is imperative that any negotiated settlement be arrived at with the agreement of the South West Africa People's Organization and within the framework of the resolutions of the United Nations.

20. The General Assembly strongly condemns the intensified preparation by South Africa to impose in Namibia a so-called "internal settlement", designed to give a semblance of power to a puppet régime and a cover of legality to the racist occupation, to foster civil war and to propagate the fiction that the struggle of the Namibian people for the liberation of the Territory would be aggression perpetrated from the outside.

21. The General Assembly, in this regard, expresses grave concern that South Africa is continuing to promote its puppets and quislings of the Turnhalle tribal gathering as an alternative to the South West Africa People's Organization, which is fighting for the genuine national and social liberation of Namibia as a united political entity.

22. The General Assembly approves the activities of the United Nations Council for Namibia and the policies and programmes defined by the Council in cooperation with the South West Africa People's Organization for the implementation of the mandate which has been entrusted to the Council to promote the cause of self-determination and independence of the Namibian people.

23. The General Assembly declares that it will continue to carry out its responsibilities in regard to the Territory until genuine independence has been attained. These responsibilities will be discharged through the United Nations Council for Namibia, in its capacity as the legal Administering Authority for Namibia, until the Council informs the Assembly that genuine independence has been attained. In this regard, the Council must be associated with any solution in which the United Nations is involved.

24. The General Assembly declares that membership of the United Nations Council for Namibia in the specialized agencies and other organizations and bodies within the United Nations system, in conformity with the recommendations of the Assembly, is an indispensable element in the fulfilment of the responsibilities of the international community towards the people of Namibia, represented by the South West Africa People's Organization, their sole and authentic liberation movement. The Council's membership in the Food and Agriculture Organization of the United Nations is a significant step in achieving this objective. Further and more vigorous initiatives must be taken, however, in order to meet fully the responsibility of the United Nations towards Namibia.

25. The General Assembly reaffirms its determination to continue its efforts towards increased assistance to Namibians in the context of the Nationhood Programme for Namibia, the Institute for Namibia at Lusaka, the United Nations Fund for Namibia and all other projects and programmes designed to prepare the Namibian people in the skills needed to build a prosperous and independent Namibia.

26. The General Assembly expresses its satisfaction with the effective work being accomplished by the Institute for Namibia in training Namibian cadres to administer an independent Namibia and in conducting research into basic problems relating to the human and natural resources of Namibia. These activities should be further intensified and widened.

27. The General Assembly endorses the initiatives of the United Nations Council for Namibia, in accordance with its 1978 Lusaka Declaration,[2] to implement the Nationhood Programme for Namibia, and notes with appreciation the cooperation of the specialized agencies and other organizations and bodies within the United Nations system in the planning and implementation of the Programme.

28. The General Assembly decides that, in the event of the Security Council's inability to adopt concrete measures to compel South Africa to end its illegal occupation by withdrawing from Namibia, it will urgently consider necessary action in accordance with the Charter of the United Nations, cognizant of the fact that this is a unique instance in which the United Nations has assumed direct responsibility for promoting self-determination, freedom and national independence for Namibia.

II. Programme of Action in Support of Self-Determination and National Independence for Namibia

29. The General Assembly reiterates its commitment to discharge the solemn obligation it has assumed to assist the Namibian people to achieve self-determination and independence.

30. The General Assembly, recognizing the role and scope of the activities of the United Nations Council for Namibia in furtherance of the attainment of self-determination by the people of Namibia, appeals to Member States to extend full support to those activities.

31. The General Assembly calls upon those countries which have not yet done so to recognize the South West Africa People's Organization as the sole and authentic representative of the Namibian people.

32. The General Assembly appeals to all Member States to render increased and sustained support and assistance to the South West Africa People's Organization to enable it to intensify its struggle for the liberation of Namibia.

33. The General Assembly calls upon Member States and the international community as a whole to reject unequivocally all maneuvers engineered to deprive the Namibian people of their legitimate right to achieve genuine national independence in a united Namibia and to undermine and destroy the achievements of the liberation struggle of the South West Africa People's Organization.

1 *Official Records of the General Assembly, Twenty-ninth Session, Supplement No. 24A* (A/9624/Add.1), para. 84. The Decree has been issued in final form in Namibia Gazette No. 1.

2 A/S-9/2-S/12631, annex. For the printed text of the Declaration, see *Official Records of the General Assembly, Ninth Special Session, Supplement No.* 1 (A/S-9/4), chap. VI.

34. The General Assembly calls upon the Governments of Member States and governmental and non-governmental organizations to give all possible assistance to the Nationhood Programme for Namibia and the Institute for Namibia and to increase contributions to the United Nations Fund for Namibia.

35. The General Assembly is fully convinced that, at this decisive stage in the struggle of the Namibian people, the international community must take definitive action to ensure the complete and unconditional withdrawal of South Africa from Namibia and thus eliminate the dangerous threat to international peace and security created by South Africa. To this end, it strongly urges the Security Council to take the most vigorous measures, including sanctions provided for under Chapter VII of the Charter of the United Nations, particularly comprehensive economic sanctions, an oil embargo and an arms embargo.

36. The General Assembly calls upon the international community, especially all Member States, to refrain from extending any recognition to, or cooperation with, any régime which the illegal South African administration may impose upon the Namibian people in disregard of the provisions of Security Council resolution 385 (1976).

37. The General Assembly urges all States to do their utmost to compel South Africa to renounce its spurious claims to Walvis Bay, to respect the territorial integrity of Namibia and to withdraw immediately from the entire Namibian Territory.

38. The General Assembly urges all States to cease and desist from any form of direct or indirect military consultation, cooperation or collaboration with South Africa.

39. The General Assembly urges all States to refrain from any collaboration with South Africa in the nuclear field, including the production and development of nuclear weapons.

40. The General Assembly requests the Security Council to take appropriate, effective and urgent steps to prevent South Africa from acquiring or developing nuclear weapons and from exploding nuclear devices, and to ensure the dismantling of the nuclear-test installations in the Kalahari Desert, all of which endanger international peace and security.

41. The General Assembly calls upon all States to take effective measures to prevent the recruitment of mercenaries for service in Namibia or South Africa.

42. The General Assembly urges once again all States to take steps to ensure the termination of all arms-licensing agreements with South Africa and to prohibit the transfer to it of all information relating to arms and armaments.

43. The General Assembly urges once again all Member States to take all appropriate measures to ensure the full application of, and compliance with, the provisions of Decree No. 1 for the Protection of the Natural Resources of Namibia.

44. The General Assembly calls upon States to compel transnational corporations under their jurisdiction to comply with all pertinent resolutions of the United Nations by immediately abstaining from making any investment in Namibia, by withdrawing current investments from the Territory and by terminating their cooperation with the illegal South African administration in Namibia.

45. The General Assembly calls upon the International Atomic Energy Agency and appeals to the members of the General Agreement on Tariffs and Trade to apply, within their respective spheres of competence, the resolutions of the Assembly and the Security Council on Namibia and to ensure that South Africa does not represent Namibia in those organizations and thereby benefit from its participation in them.

15th plenary meeting
3 May 1978

ES-8/2. Question of Namibia

Committee: -
Vote: 117 - 0 - 25

The General Assembly,

Having considered the question of Namibia at an emergency special session,

Declaring that the illegal occupation of Namibia by South Africa together with the repeated acts of aggression committed by South Africa against neighboring States constitute a breach of international peace and security,

Noting with regret and concern that the Security Council failed to exercise its primary responsibility for the maintenance of international peace and security when draft resolutions proposing comprehensive mandatory sanctions against South Africa under Chapter VII of the Charter of the United Nations were vetoed by the three Western permanent members of the Council on 30 April 1981,[1]

Noting further with grave concern that the Security Council failed on 31 August 1981,[2] on account of the veto of the United States of America, to exercise its responsibilities in the face of unprovoked massive armed aggression against Angola,

Taking note of the memorandum of the United Nations Council for Namibia dated 2 September 1981,[3]

Having heard the statement by the President of the United Nations Council for Namibia,[4] the legal Administering Authority of the Territory until genuine independence is achieved,

Having heard the statement by the Secretary for Foreign Relations of the South West Africa People's Organization,[5] the sole and authentic representative of the Namibian people,

Having heard the statements by African Ministers and by Ministers of the Movement of Non-Aligned Countries,

1. *Reaffirms* the inalienable right of the people of Namibia to self-determination, freedom and national independence in a united Namibia, in accordance with the Charter of the United Nations and General Assembly resolution 1514 (XV) of 14 December 1960, as well as the subsequent relevant resolutions and decisions of the Assembly and the Security Council;

2. *Reaffirms* that Namibia is the legal responsibility of the United Nations until genuine self-determination and national independence are achieved in terms of the relevant resolutions of the General Assembly, in particular resolutions 2145 (XXI) of 27 October 1966 and 2248 (S-V) of 19 May 1967;

3. *Reaffirms* its support for the South West Africa People's Organization, the sole and authentic representative of the Namibian people, and for its armed struggle to achieve self-determination, freedom and national independence;

4. *Strongly condemns* South Africa for its continued illegal occupation of Namibia and its persistent refusal to comply with the resolutions and decisions of the General Assembly and the Security Council, thus violating the principles of the Charter and defying the authority of the United Nations;

5. *Condemns* South Africa for its increased oppression of the Namibian people, for the massive militarization of Namibia and for its armed attacks against neighbouring States, particularly Angola;

6. *Calls upon* Member States, specialized agencies and other international organizations to render increased and sustained support and material, financial, military and other assistance to the South West Africa People's Organization to enable it to intensify its struggle for the liberation of Namibia;

---

1 See *Official Records of the Security Council, Thirty-sixth Year,* 2277th meeting.

2 *Ibid.*, 2300th meeting.

3 A/ES-8/3, annex.

4 *Official Records of the General Assembly, Eighth Emergency Special Session, Plenary Meetings,* 3rd meeting, paras. 33-48.

5 *Ibid.*, paras. 68-117.

7. *Calls upon* the international community to extend, as a matter of urgency, all support and assistance, including military assistance, to the front-line States in order to enable them to defend their sovereignty and territorial integrity against the renewed acts of aggression by South Africa;

8. *Strongly condemns* the exploitation and plunder of the natural resources of Namibia by South Africa and Western transnational corporations, in violation of Decree No. 1 for the Protection of the Natural Resources of Namibia, enacted by the United Nations Council for Namibia on 27 September 1974;[1]

9. *Reaffirms* that Security Council resolution 435 (1978) of 29 September 1978, in which the Council endorsed the United Nations plan for the independence of Namibia, is the only basis for a peaceful settlement;

10. *Firmly rejects* the latest maneuvers by certain members of the Western contact group aimed at undermining the international consensus embodied in Security Council resolution 435 (1978) and depriving the oppressed Namibian people of their hard-won victories in the struggle for national liberation;

11. *Demands* the immediate commencement of the unconditional implementation of Security Council resolution 435 (1978) without any prevarication qualification or modification and not later than December 1981;

12. *Strongly urges* the Security Council, in the light of the serious threat to international peace and security posed be South Africa, to respond positively to the overwhelming demand of the international community by immediately imposing against that country comprehensive mandatory sanctions as provided for in Chapter VII of the Charter;

13. *Calls upon* all States, in view of the threat to international peace and security posed by South Africa, to impose against that country comprehensive mandatory sanctions in accordance with the provisions of the Charter;

14. *Also strongly* urges States to cease forthwith, individually and collectively, all dealings with South Africa in order totally to isolate it politically economically, militarily and culturally;

15. *Requests* the United Nations Council for Namibia to monitor the boycott of South Africa and to bring instances Of contacts between Member States and South Africa to the attention of the General Assembly as necessary;

16. *Requests* the United Nations Council for Namibia to study the modalities for monitoring this boycott of South Africa and to report to the General Assembly at its thirty-sixth session on the arrangements which may be required;

17. *Requests* all States to report to the Secretary-General on measures taken by them to implement the relevant provisions of the present resolution;

18. *Requests* the Secretary-General to report to the General Assembly as appropriate, but not later than 31 December 1981, on the implementation of the present resolution

12th plenary meeting
14 September 1981

1 *Ibid.*, *Thirty-fifth Session, Supplement No. 24* (A/35/24), vol. I, annex II.

43/26. Question of Namibia

Committee: -
Vote: A: 130 - 0 - 23; B: 140 - 0 - 13; C: 147 - 0 - 6; D: 129 - 0 - 23; E: 148 - 0 - 5
Ref.: 42/14, 41/39, S-14/1, 40/97, 39/50, 38/36, 37/233, 36/121, 35/227, 34/92, 33/182, 32/9, 31/146, 31/148, 31/149, 31/150, 31/151, 3399(XXX), 3295(XXIX), 3111(XXVIII), 3031(XXVII), 2871(XXVI), 2678(XXV), 2498(XXIV), 2517(XXIV), 2403(XXIII)

A

Situation in Namibia resulting from the illegal occupation of the Territory by South Africa

The General Assembly,

Recalling its resolution 1514 (XV) of 14 December 1960, containing the Declaration on the Granting of Independence to Colonial Countries and Peoples,

Recalling also its resolution 2145 (XXI) of 27 October 1966, by which it terminated the Mandate of South Africa over Namibia and placed the Territory under the direct responsibility of the United Nations,

Recalling further its resolution 2248 (S-V) of 19 May 1967, by which it established the United Nations Council for Namibia as the legal Administering Authority for Namibia until independence,

Having examined the report of the United Nations Council for Namibia,[2]

Having examined also the relevant chapter of the report of the Special Committee on the Situation with regard to the Implementation of the Declaration on the Granting of Independence to Colonial Countries and Peoples,[3]

Recalling other resolutions and decisions declaring the illegality of the continued occupation of Namibia by South Africa, in particular Security Council resolutions 284 (1970) of 29 July 1970 and 301 (1971) of 20 October 1971, and the advisory opinion of the International Court of Justice of 21 June 1971,[4]

Recalling its resolutions 3111 (XXVIII) of 12 December 1973 and 31/146 and 31/152 of 20 December 1976, by which, *inter alia*, it recognized the South West Africa People's Organization as the sole and authentic representative of the Namibian people and granted observer status to it,

Recalling also its resolutions ES-8/2 of 14 September 1981 and 36/121 B of 10 December 1981, by which it called upon States to cease forthwith, individually and collectively, all dealings with South Africa in order totally to isolate it politically, economically, militarily and culturally,

Recalling further the debates held at its special session on the question of Namibia and its resolution S-14/1 of 20 September 1986, adopted at that session,

Taking note of debates held by the Security Council from 28 to 30 October 1987 on the question of Namibia,[5] and of its resolution 601 (1987) of 30 October 1987,

Welcoming the final documents and communiqués of the Assembly of Heads of State and Government of the Organization of African Unity at its twenty-fourth ordinary session, held at Addis Ababa from 25 to 28 May 1988, the Fifth Islamic Summit Conference, held at Kuwait from 26 to 29 January 1987,[6] the Conference of Foreign Ministers of Non-Aligned Countries, held at Nicosia from 7 to 10

2 *Official Records of the General Assembly, Forty-third Session, Supplement No. 24* (A/43/24).

3 *Ibid., Supplement No. 23* (A/43/23), chap. VIII.

4 *Legal Consequences for States of the Continued Presence of South Africa in Namibia (South West Africa) notwithstanding Security Council Resolution 276 (1970), Advisory Opinion*, I.C.J. Reports 1971, p. 16.

5 See *Official Records of the Security Council, Forty-second Year*, 2755th to 2759th meetings.

6 A/42/178-S/18753, annexes I and II.

September 1988,[1] the Council of Ministers of the Organization of African Unity at its forty-seventh and forty-eighth ordinary sessions, held at Addis Ababa from 22 to 27 February 1988[2] and from 19 to 23 May 1988, respectively, the Seminar on the International Responsibility for Namibia's Independence, held at Istanbul, Turkey, from 21 to 25 March 1988,[3] and the Seminar on Efforts to Implement the United Nations Plan for the Independence of Namibia, held at Toronto, Canada, from 7 to 11 September 1988,[4]

1. *Approves* the report of the United Nations Council for Namibia;

2. *Reaffirms* the inalienable right of the people of Namibia to self-determination, freedom and national independence in a united Namibia, in accordance with the Charter of the United Nations and as recognized by the General Assembly in its resolutions 1514 (XV) and 2145 (XXI) and in subsequent resolutions of the Assembly relating to Namibia;

3. *Strongly condemns* the South African régime for its continued illegal occupation of Namibia in defiance of the resolutions of the United Nations relating to Namibia;

4. *Declares* that South Africa's illegal occupation of Namibia constitutes an act of aggression against the Namibian people in terms of the Definition of Aggression contained in General Assembly resolution 3314 (XXIX) of 14 December 1974, and supports the legitimate struggle of the Namibian people by all means at their disposal, under the leadership of the South West Africa People's Organization, to repel South Africa's aggression and to achieve self-determination, freedom and national independence in a united Namibia;

5. *Declares also* that the liberation struggle in Namibia is a conflict of an international character in terms of article 1, paragraph 4, of Additional Protocol I to the Geneva Conventions of 12 August 1949,[5] and demands that South Africa accord prisoner-of-war status to all captured freedom fighters as called for by the Geneva Convention relative to the Treatment of Prisoners of War[6] and the Additional Protocol thereto;

6. *Reiterates* that, in accordance with its resolution 2145 (XXI), Namibia is the direct responsibility of the United Nations until genuine self-determination and national independence are achieved in the Territory and reaffirms the mandate of the United Nations Council for Namibia as the legal Administering Authority for Namibia until independence under its resolution 2248 (S-V) and subsequent resolutions of the General Assembly;

7. *Reaffirms* its decision that the United Nations Council for Namibia, in pursuance of its mandate, should proceed to establish its administration in Namibia with a view to terminating racist South Africa's illegal occupation of the Territory;

8. *Also reaffirms* that the South West Africa People's Organization, the national liberation movement of Namibia, is the sole and authentic representative of the Namibian people and only with its direct and full participation can the genuine independence of Namibia be achieved;

9. *Solemnly reaffirms* that Namibia's independence must be with its territorial integrity intact, including Walvis Bay, the Penguin Islands and other offshore islands, and reiterates that, in accordance with the resolutions of the United Nations, any attempt by South Africa to annex them is, therefore, illegal, null and void;

10. *Calls upon* the Security Council to declare categorically that Walvis Bay is an integral part of Namibia and that the question should not be left as a matter for negotiation between an independent Namibia and South Africa;

11. *Reaffirms* its solidarity with, and support for, the South West Africa People's Organization, the sole and authentic representative of the Namibian people, and pays tribute to that organization for the sacrifices that it has made in the field of battle and also for the spirit of statesmanship, cooperation and far-sightedness that it has displayed in the political and diplomatic arena despite the most extreme provocations on the part of the racist Pretoria régime;

12. *Commends* the South West Africa People's Organization for its continued intensification of the struggle on all fronts, including the armed struggle, and for its commitment to embrace all Namibian patriots in an effort further to strengthen national unity so as to ensure the territorial integrity and sovereignty of a united Namibia, and welcomes the consolidation of unity in action by the patriotic forces in Namibia, as clearly demonstrated by the combined actions of workers, youth, students, parents, churches and various professional organizations during this critical phase of their struggle for national and social liberation;

13. *Reaffirms* that the United Nations plan for the independence of Namibia, embodied in Security Council resolutions 385 (1976) of 30 January 1976 and 435 (1978) of 29 September 1978, is the only internationally accepted basis for a peaceful settlement of the Namibian question and demands its immediate implementation without precondition or modification;

14. *Strongly condemns* South Africa for obstructing the implementation of the resolutions of the United Nations, in particular Security Council resolutions 385 (1976), 435 (1978), 439 (1978) of 13 November 1978, 532 (1983) of 31 May 1983, 539 (1983) of 28 October 1983, 566 (1985) of 19 June 1985 and 601 (1987), and for its maneuvers, in contravention of these resolutions, designed to consolidate its colonial and neo-colonial interests at the expense of the legitimate aspirations of the Namibian people for genuine self-determination, freedom and national independence in a united Namibia;

15. *Expresses its dismay* at the failure to date of the Security Council to discharge effectively its responsibilities for the maintenance of peace and security in southern Africa, owing to the vetoes of two of its Western permanent members;

16. *Urges* the Security Council to act decisively in fulfilment of the direct responsibility of the United Nations over Namibia and to take, without further delay, appropriate action to ensure that the United Nations plan, as embodied in Council resolution 435 (1978), is not undermined or modified in any way and that it is fully respected and implemented;

17. *Reiterates* its conviction that racist South Africa's continued illegal occupation of Namibia, its defiance of the resolutions of the United Nations, its brutal repression of the Namibian people, its acts of destabilization and aggression against independent African States and its policies of apartheid constitute a threat to international peace and security;

18. *Denounces* all fraudulent constitutional and political schemes by which the illegal racist régime of South Africa attempts to perpetuate its colonial domination of Namibia, and, in particular, calls upon the international community to refrain from according any recognition or extending any cooperation to any régime imposed by the illegal South African administration upon the Namibian people in violation of Security Council resolutions 385 (1976), 435 (1978), 439 (1978), 532 (1983), 539 (1983), 566 (1985) and 601 (1987) and of other relevant resolutions of the General Assembly and of the Council;

19. *Strongly condemns* the Pretoria régime for the imposition of the so-called interim government in Namibia on 17 June 1985, declares this measure null and void and affirms that it constitutes a direct affront and a clear defiance of the resolutions of the Security Council, particularly resolutions 435 (1978) and 439 (1978), and further affirms that this manoeuvre by South Africa of creating puppet institutions subservient to the interests of the racist régime is intended to consolidate Pretoria's colonial stranglehold over Namibia and to prolong the oppression of the Namibian people;

20. *Reiterates* that there are only two parties to the conflict in Namibia, namely, the Namibian people represented by the South West Africa People's Organization, their sole and authentic representative, and the racist régime of South Africa, which illegally occupies Namibia;

---

1 See A/43/667-S/20212, annex.

2 See A/AC.131/292.

3 See A/AC.131/279.

4 A/AC.131/294.

5 United Nations, *Treaty Series*, vol. 75, Nos. 970-973.

6 *Ibid.*, vol. 75, No. 972.

21. *Strongly rejects and condemns* the persistent attempts made by the Pretoria régime and its ally to establish a "linkage" between the implementation of Security Council resolution 435 (1978) and extraneous and irrelevant issues, particularly the presence of Cuban forces in Angola, which is a ploy intended to delay the independence of Namibia and to jeopardize the responsibility of the United Nations for this Territory and constitutes interference in the internal affairs of that independent and sovereign State;

22. *Expresses its appreciation* to the front-line States and the South West Africa People's Organization for their statesmanlike and constructive attitude in the efforts aimed at implementing Security Council resolution 435 (1978);

23. *Rejects* all attempts to distort the question of Namibia by portraying it as part of a global East-West confrontation rather than one of decolonization that must be resolved in accordance with the provisions of the Charter and the Declaration on the Granting of Independence to Colonial Countries and Peoples;

24. *Firmly condemns and rejects* the policy of "constructive engagement", which encourages the racist régime of South Africa to continue its defiance of the decisions of the international community on Namibia, and its policy of apartheid, which is a crime against humanity;

25. *Strongly condemns* the continuing collaboration between South Africa and certain Western and other States in the political, economic, diplomatic, military, cultural and financial fields, and expresses its conviction that such collaboration helps to prolong South Africa's domination and control over the people and Territory of Namibia;

26. *Deplores*, in this context, the establishment and operation by racist South Africa of the so-called Namibia information offices in France, the Federal Republic of Germany, the United Kingdom of Great Britain and Northern Ireland and the United States of America, aimed at legitimizing its puppet institutions in Namibia, in particular the so-called interim government for which the racist régime has been condemned by the Security Council and the international community, and demands their immediate closure;

27. *Strongly condemns also* the sinister and slanderous campaign of disinformation by the racist régime of South Africa and its agents, including the so-called International Society for Human Rights, against the just struggle of the Namibian people for self-determination and national independence;

28. *Notes with appreciation* the measures taken by some States, international organizations, parliamentarians, institutions and non-governmental organizations to exert pressure on the racist régime of South Africa and calls upon them to redouble and intensify their efforts to force the racist régime to comply with the resolutions and decisions of the United Nations relating to Namibia and South Africa;

29. *Calls once again upon* all Governments, especially those that have close links with South Africa, to support, in cooperation with the United Nations Council for Namibia, the actions of the United Nations to defend the national rights of the Namibian people until independence and to isolate the racist régime of South Africa;

30. *Urges* Governments that have in the past used their veto or cast negative votes in the Security Council in regard to the question of the imposition of comprehensive and mandatory sanctions against South Africa to support and respond positively to the international call to isolate racist South Africa;

31. *Calls upon* the members of the European Economic Community to strengthen and extend, as a matter of urgency, the economic sanctions that they have imposed on the Pretoria régime, so as to include their application to illegally occupied Namibia;

32. *Calls upon* the Government of the Federal Republic of Germany, as a measure of its recognition of the direct responsibility of the United Nations over Namibia and the United Nations Council for Namibia as the sole legal Administering Authority for the Territory until independence, to discontinue all programmes of development aid and assistance to illegally occupied Namibia, and urges all States to consult the United Nations Council for Namibia regarding any such assistance, in order to ensure that it will not prolong the illegal occupation of Namibia by the Pretoria régime and the colonial institutions in the Territory;

33. *Strongly condemns* South Africa for its use of mercenaries to suppress the Namibian people and to carry out its military attacks against independent African States, and reiterates its call upon all States to take legislative and other appropriate measures to prohibit the recruitment, training, financing and transit of mercenaries for service in Namibia;

34. *Strongly condemns* South Africa for its military buildup in Namibia, its imposition of military conscription of all Namibian males between seventeen and fifty-five years of age into the occupying colonial army, its forcible displacement of Namibians from their homes and its proclamation of a so-called security zone in Namibia, and declares that all such measures taken by racist South Africa are illegal, null and void;

35. *Demands once again* that South Africa immediately release all Namibian political prisoners, including all those imprisoned or detained under the so-called internal security laws, martial law or any other arbitrary measures, whether such Namibians have been charged or tried or are being held without charge in Namibia or South Africa;

36. *Demands* that South Africa account for all "disappeared" Namibians and declares that South Africa shall be liable to compensate the victims, their families and the future lawful Government of an independent Namibia for the losses sustained;

37. *Calls upon* Member States to render sustained and increased support, as well as material, financial, military and other assistance, to the South West Africa People's Organization so as to enable it to intensify its struggle for the liberation of Namibia;

38. *Calls upon* the specialized agencies and other organizations of the United Nations system to render sustained and increased material, financial and other assistance to the South West Africa People's Organization so as to enable it to intensify its struggle for the liberation of Namibia;

39. *Urges* all Governments and the specialized agencies and other intergovernmental organizations to provide increased material assistance to the thousands of Namibian refugees who have been forced by the oppressive policies of the apartheid régime to flee Namibia, especially into the neighbouring front-line States;

40. *Reaffirms* its conviction that the solidarity and support of the front-line States for the Namibian cause continue to be factors of paramount importance in the efforts to bring genuine independence to the Territory;

41. *Strongly condemns* the racist régime of South Africa for its utilization of the illegally occupied international Territory of Namibia as a springboard for perpetrating armed invasions, subversion, destabilization and aggression against neighbouring African States, in particular Angola;

42. *Denounces* the acts of aggression by the racist régime against Angola, Botswana, Mozambique, Zambia and Zimbabwe, declares that the Pretoria régime's policy of aggression and destabilization not only undermines the peace and stability of the southern African region but also constitutes a threat to international peace and security, and calls upon South Africa to cease all acts of aggression against the neighbouring African States;

43. *Strongly urges* the international community to increase, as a matter of urgency, humanitarian assistance and financial, material, military and political support to the front-line States so as to enable them to resolve their own economic difficulties, which are largely a consequence of the Pretoria régime's policies of aggression and subversion, and to defend themselves better against South Africa's persistent attempts to destabilize them;

44. *Requests* Member States urgently to extend all necessary assistance to Angola and other front-line States in order to enable them to strengthen their defence capacities against acts of aggression by South Africa;

45. *Expresses its grave concern* at the acquisition of nuclear-weapon capability by the racist régime of South Africa and declares that such acquisition constitutes a threat to peace and security in Africa while posing a danger to all mankind;

46. *Condemns*, and calls for an immediate end to, the continuing military collaboration on the part of certain Western countries with the racist régime of South Africa, and expresses its conviction that such collaboration, in addition to strengthening the aggressive military machinery of the Pretoria régime, thereby constituting a hostile action against the people of Namibia and the front-line States, is also in violation of the arms embargo imposed against South Africa under Security Council resolution 418 (1977) of 4 November 1977;

47. *Declares* that such collaboration encourages the Pretoria régime in its defiance of the international community and obstructs efforts to eliminate apartheid and bring South Africa's illegal occupation of Namibia to an end, and calls for the immediate cessation of such collaboration;

48. *Calls upon* the Security Council to adopt the necessary measures to tighten the arms embargo imposed against South Africa under Council resolution 418 (1977), to ensure its application to illegally occupied Namibia and to ensure strict compliance with the embargo by all States;

49. *Further calls upon* the Security Council to implement, as a matter of urgency, the recommendations contained in the report of the Security Council Committee established in pursuance of Council resolution 421 (1977) of 9 December 1977;[1]

50. *Condemns* all collaboration with the Pretoria régime in the nuclear field, and calls upon all States that do so to terminate such collaboration, including refraining from supplying the racist minority régime of South Africa, directly or indirectly, with installations, equipment or material that might enable it to produce uranium, plutonium or other nuclear materials or reactors;

51. *Endorses* the decision taken by the United Nations Council for Namibia[2] that it will, in the exercise of its rights under the United Nations Convention on the Law of the Sea, proclaim an exclusive economic zone for Namibia, the outer limit of which shall be 200 miles, and states that any action for the implementation of that decision should be taken in consultation with the South West Africa People's Organization, the representative of the Namibian people;

52. *Reaffirms* that the natural resources of Namibia, including its marine resources, are the inviolable heritage of the Namibian people, and expresses its deep concern at the depletion of these resources, particularly its uranium deposits, as a result of their plunder by South Africa and certain Western and other foreign economic interests, in violation of the pertinent resolutions of the General Assembly and of the Security Council, of Decree No. 1 for the Protection of the Natural Resources of Namibia,[3] enacted by the United Nations Council for Namibia on 27 September 1974, and in disregard of the advisory opinion of the International Court of Justice of 21 June 1971; 53. Declares that all activities of foreign economic interests in Namibia are illegal under international law and that all the foreign economic interests operating in Namibia are liable to pay damages to the future legitimate Government of an independent Namibia;

53. *Declares* that all activities of foreign economic interests in Namibia are illegal under international law and that all the foreign economic interests operating in Namibia are liable to pay damages to the future legitimate Government of an independent Namibia;

54. *Calls upon* the United Nations Council for Namibia, in pursuance of the relevant provisions of Decree No. 1 for the Protection of the Natural Resources of Namibia, to continue to take the necessary steps to compile statistical information on the wealth illegally extracted from Namibia with a view to assessing the extent of compensation eventually due to an independent Namibia;

55. *Strongly condemns* the activities of all foreign economic interests operating in Namibia which are illegally exploiting the resources of the Territory, and demands that these interests comply with all the relevant resolutions and decisions of the United Nations by immediately withdrawing from the Territory and by putting an end to their cooperation with the illegal South African administration;

56. *Declares* that, by their incessant exploitation of the human and natural resources of the Territory and their continued accumulation and repatriation of huge profits, the foreign economic, financial and other interests operating in Namibia constitute a major obstacle to its independence;

57. *Once again requests* all Member States, particularly those States whose corporations are engaged in the exploitation of Namibian resources, to take all appropriate measures, including legislative and enforcement action, to ensure the full application of, and compliance by all corporations and individuals within their jurisdiction with, the provisions of Decree No. 1 for the Protection of the Natural Resources of Namibia;

58. *Calls upon* the Governments of all States, particularly those whose corporations are involved in the mining and processing of Namibian uranium, to take all appropriate measures in compliance with resolutions and decisions of the United Nations and Decree No. 1 for the Protection of the Natural Resources of Namibia, including the practice of requiring negative certificates of origin, to prohibit State-owned and other corporations, together with their subsidiaries, from dealing in Namibian uranium and from engaging in any uranium-prospecting activities in Namibia;

59. *Reiterates* its approval of the initiation by the United Nations Council for Namibia of legal proceedings in the domestic courts of States against corporations or individuals involved in the exploitation, transport, processing or purchase of Namibia's natural resources, as part of its efforts to give effect to Decree No. 1 for the Protection of the Natural Resources of Namibia;

60. *Requests* the Governments of the Federal Republic of Germany, the Netherlands and the United Kingdom of Great Britain and Northern Ireland, which operate the Urenco uranium-enrichment plant, to have Namibian uranium specifically excluded from the Treaty of Almelo,[4] which regulates the activities of Urenco;

61. *Urges* the United Nations Council for Namibia, in its capacity as the legal Administering Authority for Namibia until independence, to consider the promulgation of additional legislation in order to protect and promote the interests of the people of Namibia and to implement effectively all its legislation;

62. *Calls upon* all specialized agencies, in particular the International Monetary Fund, to ensure the termination of all collaboration with, and assistance to, the racist régime of South Africa, since such assistance serves to augment the military capability of the Pretoria régime, thus enabling it not only to continue the brutal repression in Namibia and South Africa itself, but also to commit acts of aggression against independent neighbouring States;

63. *Requests* all States that have not already done so, pending the imposition of comprehensive and mandatory sanctions against South Africa, to take legislative, administrative and other measures individually and collectively, as appropriate, in order effectively to isolate South Africa politically, economically, militarily and culturally, in accordance with General Assembly resolutions ES-8/2 and 36/121 B, and its resolution 37/233 A of 20 December 1982;

64. *Requests* the United Nations Council for Namibia, in its implementation of paragraph 15 of General Assembly resolution ES-8/2 and of the relevant provisions of Assembly resolutions 36/121 B and 37/233 A, to continue to monitor the boycott of South Africa and to submit to the Assembly at its forty-fourth session a comprehensive report on all contacts between Member States and South Africa containing an analysis of the information received from Member States and other sources on the continuing political, economic, financial and other relations of States and their economic and other interest groups with South Africa and of measures taken by States to terminate all dealings with the racist régime of South Africa;

65. *Requests* all States to cooperate fully with the United Nations Council for Namibia in the fulfilment of its task concerning the implementation of General Assembly resolutions ES-8/2, 36/121 B

1 *Official Records of the Security Council, Thirty-fifth Year, Supplement for July, August and September 1980*, document S/14179.

2 See *Official Records of the General Assembly, Fortieth Session, Supplement No. 24* (A/40/24), para.513.

3 *Ibid., Thirty-fifth Session, Supplement No. 24* (A/35/24), vol. I, annex II.

4 United Nations, *Treaty Series*, vol. 795, No. 11326.

and 37/233 A and to report to the Secretary-General by the forty-fourth session of the Assembly on the measures taken by them in the implementation of those resolutions;

66. *Strongly urges* the Security Council, in view of the persistent refusal by the racist régime of South Africa to comply with the resolutions and decisions of the United Nations on the question of Namibia, particularly Council resolutions 385 (1976), 435 (1978), 539 (1983) and 566 (1985), and, in the light of the serious threat to international peace and security posed by South Africa, to impose comprehensive and mandatory sanctions against that régime as provided for in Chapter VII of the Charter;

67. *Expresses* its appreciation to the Secretary-General for his personal commitment to Namibia's independence and for his efforts aimed at the implementation of resolutions and decisions of the United Nations on the question of Namibia, particularly Security Council resolution 435 (1978), and urges him to continue those efforts;

68. *Requests* the Secretary-General to report to the General Assembly at its forty-fourth session on the implementation of the present resolution.

54th plenary meeting
17 November 1988

B

Implementation of Security Council resolution 435 (1978)

The General Assembly,

Noting that the Secretary-General has reported that all the necessary conditions for the implementation of Security Council resolution 435 (1978) of 29 September 1978 have already been fulfilled,

Indignant that ten years after the adoption of Security Council resolution 435 (1978) the Namibian people have not yet exercised their right to self-determination and attained independence;

Expressing grave concern at the lack of progress in implementing Security Council resolution 435 (1978), as indicated in the further reports of the Secretary-General dated 29 December 1983,[1] 6 June 1985,[2] 6 September 1985,[3] 26 November 1985,[4] 31 March 1987[5] and 27 October 1987[6] concerning the implementation of Council resolution 435 (1978) and resolution 439 (1978) of 13 November 1978,

Recalling Security Council resolution 601 (1987) of 30 October 1987 by which the Council, *inter alia*, decided to authorize the Secretary-General to proceed to arrange a cease-fire between South Africa and the South West Africa People's Organization in order to undertake the administrative and other practical steps necessary for the emplacement of the United Nations Transition Assistance Group,

1. *Reiterates* that Security Council resolutions 385 (1976) of 30 January 1976 and 435 (1978), embodying the United Nations plan for the independence of Namibia, constitute the only internationally accepted basis for a peaceful settlement of the question of Namibia and demands their immediate and unconditional implementation;

2. *Strongly condemns* racist South Africa for obstructing the implementation of Security Council resolutions 385 (1976), 435 (1978), 439 (1978), 532 (1983) of 31 May 1983, 539 (1983) of 28 October 1983, 566 (1985) of 19 June 1985 and 601 (1987);

3. *Demands* that South Africa urgently comply fully and unconditionally with the resolutions of the Security Council, in particular resolutions 385 (1976) and 435 (1978) and subsequent resolutions of the Council relating to Namibia;

4. *Emphasizes once again* that the only parties to the conflict in Namibia are, on the one hand, the Namibian people represented by the South West Africa People's Organization, their sole and authentic representative, and, on the other, the racist régime of South Africa which illegally occupies the Territory;

5. *Strongly condemns* the racist régime of South Africa for the installation of a so-called interim government in Namibia on 17 June 1985, in defiance of resolutions and decisions of the United Nations, and declares this measure null and void, and reiterates its call upon the international community to continue to refrain from according any recognition or extending any cooperation to any régime imposed by the illegal South African administration upon the Namibian people;

6. *Firmly rejects and condemns* the president attempts to establish a "linkage" or "parallelism" between the independence of Namibia and any extraneous and irrelevant issues, in particular the presence of Cuban forces in Angola, and emphasizes unequivocally that all such attempts are designed to delay further the independence of Namibia in accordance with Security Council resolution 435 (1978), and that they constitute a gross and unwarranted interference in the internal affairs of Angola;

7. *Urgently calls upon* the international community to act resolutely against the intransigent stance of the Pretoria régime, and stresses the responsibility of the Security Council concerning the implementation of its resolutions on Namibia in view of the threat to regional and international peace and security created by the racist régime of South Africa;

8. *Notes with satisfaction* the statement by the Security Council on the occasion of the tenth anniversary of the adoption of resolution 435 (1978) in which the members of the Council, *inter alia*, strongly urged South Africa to comply forthwith with the resolutions and decisions of the Security Council, particularly resolution 435 (1978), and to cooperate with the Secretary-General in its immediate, full and definitive implementation;[7]

9. *Expresses its appreciation* to the Secretary-General for his personal commitment to the independence of Namibia and for his efforts aimed at the implementation of Resolutions and decisions of the United Nations on the question of Namibia, particularly Security Council resolution 435 (1978), and urges him to continue those efforts;

10. *Requests* the Secretary-General to report to the General Assembly at its forty-fourth session on the implementation of the present resolution.

54th plenary meeting
17 November 1988

C

Programme of work of the United Nations Council for Namibia

The General Assembly,

Having examined the report of the United Nations Council of Namibia,

Convinced of the need for continued consultations with the South West Africa People' s Organization in the formulation and implementation of the programme of work of the United Nations Council of Namibia, as well as in any matter of interest to the Namibian people,

1. *Approves* the report of the United Nations Council for Namibia, including the recommendations contained therein, and decides to make adequate financial provision for their implementation;

2. *Decides* that the United Nations Council for Namibia, in the discharge of its responsibilities as the legal Administering Authority for Namibia until independence, shall:

---

1 *Official Records of the Security Council, Thirty-eighth Year, Supplement for October, November and December 1983,* document S/16237.

2 *Ibid., Fortieth Year, Supplement for April, May and June 1985,* document S/17242.

3 *Ibid., Supplement for July, August and September 1985,* document S/17442.

4 *Ibid., Supplement for October, November and December 1985,* document S/17658.

5 *Ibid., Forty-second Year, Supplement for January, February and March 1987,* document S/18767.

6 *Ibid., Supplement for October, November and December 1987,* document S/19234.

7 See S/20208. For the printed text; see *Resolutions and Decisions of the Security Council, 1988.*

(*a*) Continue to mobilize international support in order to press for the speedy withdrawal of the illegal South African administration from Namibia in accordance with the resolutions of the United Nations relating to Namibia;

(*b*) Counter the policies of South Africa against the Namibian people and the United Nations, as well as against the United Nations Council for Namibia as the legal Administering Authority for Namibia;

(*c*) Denounce and seek the rejection by all States of all kinds of schemes through which South Africa attempts to perpetuate its illegal presence in Namibia;

(*d*) Ensure non-recognition of any administration or entity installed in Namibia not ensuring from free elections conducted under the supervision and control of the United Nations, in accordance with the relevant resolutions of the Security Council, in particular resolutions 385 (1976) of 30 January 1976, 435 (1978) of 29 September 1978, 439 (1978) of 13 November 1978, 532 (1983) of 31 May 1983, 539 (1983) of 28 October 1983, 566 (1985) of 19 June 1985, and 601 (1987) of 30 October 1987;

(*e*) Make a concerted effort to counter the attempts to establish a "linkage" or "parallelism" between the independence of Namibia and extraneous issues, such as the withdrawal of Cuban forces from Angola;

3. *Decides* that the United Nations Council for Namibia shall hold extraordinary plenary meetings in Latin America or Southern Africa and that such meetings provided with verbatim records;

4. *Decides also* that the United Nations Council for Namibia shall send missions of consultation to Governments in order to coordinate efforts for the implementation of resolutions of the United Nations on the question of Namibia and to mobilize support for the Namibian cause;

5. *Decides further* that the United Nations Council for Namibia shall represent Namibia at United Nations conferences and meetings of intergovernmental and non-governmental organizations, bodies and conferences to ensure that the rights and interests of Namibia shall be adequately protected;

6. *Decides* that Namibia, represented by the United Nations Council for Namibia, shall participate as a full member in all conferences and meetings organized by the United Nations to which all States or, in the case of regional conferences and meetings, all African States are invited;

7. *Requests* all committees and other subsidiary bodies of the General Assembly and of the Economic and Social Council to continue to invite the United Nations Council for Namibia to participate whenever the rights and interests of Namibians are discussed, and to consult closely with the United Nations Council for Namibia before submitting any draft resolution that may involve such rights and interests;

8. *Reiterates* its request to all specialized agencies and other organizations of the United Nations system to grant full membership to Namibia, represented by the United Nations Council for Namibia, so that the Council may participate as the legal Administering Authority for Namibia in the work of those agencies and organizations;

9. *Reiterates* its request to all specialized agencies and other organizations of the United Nations system that have not yet done so to grant a waiver of the assessment of Namibia during the period in which it is represented by the United Nations Council for Namibia;

10. *Again requests* all intergovernmental organizations, bodies and conferences to ensure that the rights and interests of Namibia are protected and to invite Namibia, to participate as a full member, whenever such rights and interests are involved;

11. *Requests* the United Nations Council for Namibia, in its capacity as the legal Administering Authority for Namibia, to accede to any international conventions as it may deem appropriate in close consultation with the South West Africa People's Organization;

12. *Decides* that the United Nations Council for Namibia shall:

(*a*) Consult regularly with the leaders of the South West Africa People's Organization by inviting them to New York and by sending high-level missions to the provisional headquarters of that organization, which will visit Namibian refugee centres whenever necessary;

(*b*) Prepare and publish reports on the political, economic, military and social situation in and relating to Namibia;

(*c*) Review the progress of the liberation struggle in Namibia in its political, military and social aspects and prepare comprehensive and analytical periodic reports related thereto;

(*d*) Review the compliance of Member States with the relevant resolutions and decisions of the United Nations relating to Namibia and, taking into account the advisory opinion of the International Court of Justice of 21 June 1971, prepare annual reports on the subject with a view to recommending appropriate policies to the General Assembly, in order to counter the support that some States give to the illegal South African administration in Namibia;

(*e*) Continue taking measures to ensure the full implementation of Decree No. 1 for the Protection of the Natural Resources of Namibia, including legal proceedings in the domestic courts of States, in accordance with paragraph 59 of resolution 43/26 A;

(*f*) Consider the illegal activities of foreign economic interests, particularly the transnational corporations operating in Namibia, including the exploitation of and trade in Namibian uranium, with a view to recommending appropriate policies to the General Assembly, in order to put an end to such activities;

(*g*) Take measures to ensure the closure of the so-called information offices created by the illegal South African occupation régime in certain Western countries for promoting its puppet institutions in Namibia, in violation of resolutions and decisions of the United Nations on the question of Namibia;

(*h*) Notify the Governments of States whose corporations, whether public or private, operate in Namibia of the illegality of such operations and urge them to take measures to end such operations;

(*i*) Consider sending missions of consultations to Governments of States whose corporations have investments in Namibia in order to persuade them to take all possible measures to terminate such investments;

(*j*) Contact institutions and municipalities to encourage them to divest themselves of their investments in Namibia and South Africa;

(*k*) Contact specialized agencies and other international institutions associated with the United Nations, in particular the International Monetary Fund, with the view to protecting Namibia's interests;

(*l*) Draw the attention of States, the specialized agencies and private corporations to Decree No. 1 for the Protection of the Natural Resources of Namibia, with a view to ensuring their compliance with the Decree;

(*m*) Organize international and regional activities, as required, in order to obtain relevant information on all aspects of the situation in and relating to Namibia, in particular the exploitation of the people and resources of Namibia by South African and other foreign economic interests, and to expose such activities, with a view to intensifying active supports for the Namibian cause;

(n) Secure the territorial integrity of Namibia as a unitary State, including Walvis Bay, the Penguin Islands and other offshore islands of Namibia;

13. *Decides* to make adequate financial provision in the section of the programme budget of the United Nations relating to the United Nations Council for Namibia for the financing of the office of the South West Africa People's Organization in New York, in order to ensure appropriate representation of the people of Namibia at the United Nations through the South West Africa People's Organization;

14. *Decides also* to continue to defray the expenses of representatives of the South West Africa People's Organization, whenever the United Nations Council for Namibia so decides;

15. *Requests* the United Nations Council for Namibia to continue to consult with the South West Africa People's Organizations in the formulation and implementation of its programme of work, as well as on all matters of interest to the Namibian people;

16. *Also requests* the United Nations Council for Namibia to facilitate the participation of the liberation movements recognized by the Organization of African Unity in meetings of the Council away from

United Nations Headquarters, whenever such participation is deemed necessary;

17. *Decides* that, in order to expedite the training of the personnel required for an independent Namibia, qualified Namibians should be given opportunities to develop further their skills in the work of the United Nations Secretariat and the specialized agencies and other organizations of the United Nations Council for Namibia, in consultation with the South West Africa People's Organization, to take, on an urgent basis, necessary action towards that end;

18. *Takes note* of the consolidation of the Office of the United Nations Commissioner for Namibia and the secretariat of the United Nations Council for Namibia and in this regard requests the Secretary-General, in consultation with the President of the United Nations Council for Namibia, to ensure that the Council is provided with adequate secretariat assistance to help it to continue to discharge fully and effectively all tasks and functions arising out of its mandate.

54th plenary meeting
17 November 1988

D

Dissemination of information and mobilization of international public opinion in support of the immediate independence of Namibia

The General Assembly,

Gravely concerned at the total black-out of news on Namibia imposed by the illegal régime of South Africa, in particular regarding the increased repression of the Namibian people by that régime,

Gravely concerned at the campaign of slander and disinformation against the United Nations and the liberation struggle of the Namibian people for self-determination and national independence led by the South West Africa People's Organization, their sole and authentic representative,

Stressing the urgent need to mobilize international public opinion on a continuous basis with a view to assisting effectively the people of Namibia in the achievement of self-determination, freedom and independence in a united Namibia and, in particular, to intensify the world-wide and continuous dissemination of information on the struggle for liberation being waged by the people of Namibia under the leadership of the South West Africa People's Organization,

Reiterating the importance of intensifying publicity on all aspects of the question of Namibia as an instrument for furthering the mandate given by the General Assembly to the United Nations Council for Namibia,

Recognizing the important role that non-governmental organizations are playing in the dissemination of information on Namibia and in the mobilization of international public opinion in support of the immediate independence of Namibia,

1. *Requests* the United Nations Council for Namibia, in cooperation with the Department of Public Information of the Secretariat and in consultation with the South West Africa People's Organization, the sole and authentic representative of the Namibian people, in pursuance of its international campaign in support of the struggle of the Namibian people for national independence:

(*a*) To continue to consider effective ways and means of increasing the dissemination of information relating to Namibia in order to intensifying the international campaign in favour of the cause of Namibia;

(*b*) To focus its activities towards greater mobilization of public opinion in Western countries, particularly the United States of America, the United Kingdom of Great Britain and Northern Ireland and the Federal Republic of Germany, as well as in Japan;

(*c*) To counteract the total news black-out on Namibia imposed by the illegal South African régime, which forbids foreign journalists from entering and reporting from the Territory;

(*d*) To intensify the international campaign for the imposition of comprehensive and mandatory sanctions against South Africa under Chapter VII of the Charter of the United Nations;

(*e*) To organize an international campaign to boycott products from Namibia and South Africa, in cooperation with non-governmental organizations;

(*f*) To expose and denounce collaboration with the racist régime of South Africa in all fields;

(*g*) To organize exhibitions on Namibia and the struggle of the Namibian people for independence;

(*h*) To prepare and disseminate publications on the political, economic, military and social consequences of the illegal occupation of Namibia by South Africa, on legal matters, on the question of the territorial integrity of Namibia and on contacts between Member States and South Africa;

(*i*) To prepare periodic reports on the brutalities committed by the racist régime of South Africa against the Namibian people and ensure their widest possible distribution;

(*j*) To produce and disseminate radio and television programmes designed to draw the attention of world public opinion to the current situation in and around Namibia;

(*k*) To produce and disseminate, in both the English language and the local languages of Namibia, radio programmes designed to counter the hostile propaganda and disinformation campaign of the racist régime of South Africa;

(*l*) To produce and disseminate posters;

(*m*) To ensure full coverage through advertisements in newspapers and magazines, press releases, press conferences and press briefings of all activities of the United Nations regarding Namibia in order to maintain a constant flow of information to the public on all aspects of the question of Namibia;

(*n*) To prepare and disseminate a thematic atlas on Namibia;

(*o*) To reproduce and disseminate the comprehensive economic map of Namibia;

(*p*) To produce and disseminate booklets on the activities of the Council;

(*q*) To update and disseminate widely a compendium of resolutions of the General Assembly and of the Security Council relating to Namibia and of relevant documents of the Movement of Non-Aligned Countries and the Organization of African Unity, as well as decisions, declarations and communiqués of the front-line States on the question of Namibia;

(*r*) To update, publize and distribute the indexed reference book on transnational corporations that plunder the human and natural resources of Namibia, and on the profits they extract from the Territory;

(*s*) To produce and disseminate widely, on a monthly basis, a bulletin containing analytical and updated information intended to mobilize maximum support for the Namibian cause;

(*t*) To produce and disseminate, on a weekly basis, an information newsletter containing updated information on developments in and relating to Namibia, in support of the Namibian cause;

(*u*) To acquire books, pamphlets and other materials relating to Namibia for dissemination;

(*v*) To prepare, in consultation with the South West Africa People's Organization, a list of Namibian political prisoners;

(*w*) To assist the South Africa People's Organization in the production and distribution of material on Namibia;

2. *Also requests* the United Nations Council for Namibia to continue to organize, in cooperation with the Department of Public Information, media encounters on developments relating to Namibia, particularly prior to activities of the Council during 1989;

3. *Further requests* the United Nations Council for Namibia to exert all efforts to counteract the campaign of slander and disinformation against the United Nations and the liberation struggle in Namibia carried out by South African agents from the so-called information offices established in several Western countries;

4. *Requests* the United Nations Council for Namibia to cooperate closely with relevant intergovernmental organizations, in order to increase the awareness of the international community of the direct

responsibility of the United Nations over Namibia and the continued illegal occupation of that Territory by the racist régime of South Africa;

5. *Calls upon* the United Nations Council for Namibia to continue to cooperate with non-governmental organizations in its efforts to mobilize international public opinion in support of the liberation struggle of the Namibian people, under the leadership of the South West Africa People's Organization;

6. *Also requests* the United Nations Council for Namibia to prepare, update and disseminate lists of non-governmental organizations, in particular those in the major Western countries, in order to ensure better cooperation and coordination among non-governmental organizations working in support of the Namibian cause and against apartheid;

7. *Further requests* the United Nations Council for Namibia to organize workshops for non-governmental organizations, parliamentarians, trade unionists, academics and media representatives at which the participants will consider how they can contribute to the implementation of the decisions of the United Nations relating to the dissemination of information on Namibia;

8. *Decides* to allocate the sum f $ 500,000 to be used by the United Nations Council for Namibia for its programme of cooperation with non-governmental organizations, including support to conferences and workshops in solidarity with Namibia arranged by those organizations, dissemination of conclusions of such conferences and workshops and support to such other activities as will promote the cause of the liberation struggle of the Namibian people, subject to decisions to be taken by the Council in each individual case in consultation with the South West Africa People's Organization;

9. *Requests* the United Nations Council for Namibia to continue to contact and inform leading opinion makers, media leaders, academic institutions, trade unions, legislators and parliamentarians, cultural organizations, support groups and other concerned persons and non-governmental organizations about the objectives and functions of the United Nations Council for Namibia and the struggle of the Namibian people under the leadership of the South West Africa People's Organization;

10. *Also requests* the United Nations Council for Namibia to cooperate with the spezialized agencies and other organizations of the United Nations system in the promotion of a campaign of information on the question of Namibia, in their respective fields;

11. *Appeals* to non-governmental organizations and associations, institutions, support groups and individuals sympathetic to the Namibian cause:

(*a*) To increase the awareness of their national communities and legislative bodies concerning South Africa's illegal occupation of Namibia, the liberation struggle being waged by the Namibian people under the leadership of the South West Africa People's Organization, the gross violation of basic human rights by the South West African régime in Namibia and the plunder of the Territory's resources by foreign economic interests;

(*b*) To mobilize in their countries broad public support for the national liberation of Namibia by holding hearings, seminars and public presentations on various aspects of the Namibian question, as well as by producing and distributing pamphlets, films and other information material;

(*c*) To expose and campaign against the political, economic, financial, military and cultural collaboration of certain Western Governments with the South African régime, as well as official visits to and from South Africa;

(*d*) To intensify public pressure for the immediate withdrawal from Namibia of foreign economic interests that are exploiting the human and natural resources of the Territory;

(*e*) To continue and develop campaign and research work, in order to expose the involvement and operations of certain Western-based oil companies in the supply of petroleum products to Namibia and South Africa;

(*f*) To step up their efforts to persuade universities, local governments, trade unions and churches and other institutions to divest themselves of all investments in firms doing business in Namibia and South Africa;

(*g*) To intensify the campaign for the immediate and unconditional release of all Namibian political prisoners and detainees and the granting of prisoner-of-war status to all Namibian freedoms fighters, in accordance with the Geneva Convention relative to the Treatment of Prisoners of War and the Additional Protocol thereto;

12. *Requests* Member States to broadcast programmes on their national radio and television networks and to publish material in their official news media about the situation in and around Namibia and the obligation of Governments and peoples to assist in every possible way in the struggle of the Namibian people for independence;

13. *Requests* the Secretary-General to direct the Department of Public Information to assist the United Nations Council for Namibia in the implementation of its programme of dissemination of information and to ensure that all activities of the United Nations on dissemination of information on the question of Namibia follow the policy guidelines laid down by the United Nations Council for Namibia as the legal Administering Authority for the Territory;

15. *Requests* the Secretary-General to continue to assist, as a matter of priority, the United Nations Council for Namibia in the implementation of its programme of dissemination of information;

16. *Also requests* the Secretary-General to provide the United Nations Council for Namibia with the work programme of the Department of Public Information for 1989 covering the activities of dissemination of information on the question of Namibia, followed by periodic reports on the programme undertaken, including details of expenses incurred;

17. *Further requests* the Secretary-General to direct the Department of Public Information to disseminate, in 1989, the list of Namibian political prisoners prepared by the United Nations Council for Namibia in consultation with the South West Africa People's Organization, in order to intensify international pressure for their immediate and unconditional release.

54th plenary meeting
17 November 1988

E

United Nations Fund for Namibia

The General Assembly,

Having examined the parts of the report of the United Nations Council for Namibia relating to the United Nations Fund for Namibia,[1]

Recalling its resolution 2679 (XXV) of 9 December 1970, by which it established the United Nations Fund for Namibia,

Recalling its resolution 3112 (XXVIII) of 12 December 1973, by which it appointed the United Nations Council for Namibia trustee of the United Nations Fund for Namibia,

Recalling also its resolution 31/153 of 20 December 1976, by which it decided to launch the Nationhood Programme for Namibia,

Recalling further its resolution 34/92 A of 12 December 1979, by which it approved the charter of the United Nations Institute for Namibia, and its resolution 37/233 E of 20 December 1982, by which it approved amendments to the charter,[2]

1. *Takes note* of the relevant parts of the report of the United Nations Council for Namibia;

2. *Decides* that the United Nations Council for Namibia shall:

(*a*) Continue to formulate policies of assistance to Namibians and coordinate assistance for Namibia provided by the specialized agen-

---

1 *Official Records of the General Assembly, Forty-third Session, Supplement No. 24* (A/43/24), part four, chap. III and chap. IV, sect. B.

2 For the text of the charter of the United Nations Institute for Namibia, as amended, see *Official Records of the General Assembly, Thirty-seventh Session, Supplement No. 24* (A/37/24), annex IV.

cies and other organizations and institutions of the United Nations system;

(*b*) Continue to act as trustee of the United Nations Fund for Namibia and, in this capacity, administer and manage the Fund;

(*c*) Continue to provide broad guidelines and formulate principles and policies for the United Nations Institute for Namibia;

(*d*) Continue to coordinate, plan and direct the Nationhood Programme for Namibia, in consultation with the South Africa People's Organization, with the aim of consolidating all measures of assistance by the specialized agencies and other organizations and institutions of the United Nations system into a comprehensive assistance programme;

(*e*) Continue to consult with the South West Africa People's Organization in the formulation and implementation of assistance programmes for Namibians;

(*f*) Reports to the General Assembly at its forty-fourth session on the programmes and activities undertaken through the United Nations Fund for Namibia;

3. *Decides* that the United Nations Fund for Namibia, which comprises the General Account, the United Nations Institute for Namibia Account and the Nationhood Programme Account, shall be the primary source of development assistance to Namibians;

4. *Expresses its appreciation* to all States, specialized agencies and other organizations of the United Nations system, governmental and non-governmental organizations and individuals that have made contributions to the United Nations Fund for Namibia to support the activities under the General Account, the activities of the United Nations Institute for Namibia and the Nationhood Programme for Namibia, and calls upon them to increase their assistance to Namibians through those channels;

5. *Requests* the Secretary-General and the President of the United Nations Council for Namibia to intensify appeals to Governments, intergovernmental and non-governmental organizations and individuals for more generous voluntary contributions to the General Account, the Nationhood Programme Account and the United Nations Institute for Namibia Account of the United Nations Fund for Namibia in view of the increased activities undertaken through the Fund for Namibia, and, in this connection, emphasizes the need for contributions in order to increase the number of scholarships awarded to Namibians under the United Nations Fund for Namibia;

6. *Invites* Governments to appeal once more to their national organizations and institutions for voluntary contributions to the United Nations Fund for Namibia;

7. *Decides* to allocate as a temporary measure to the United Nations Fund for Namibia the sum of 1.5 million dollars from the regular budget of the United Nations for 1989;

8. *Requests* the United Nations Commissioner for Namibia, in order to mobilize additional resources, to continue to formulate, in consultation with the South West Africa People's Organization, projects of assistance to the Namibian people to be co-financed by Governments and non-governmental organizations;

9. *Requests* the specialized agencies and other organizations and institutions of the United Nations system, in the light of the urgent need to strengthen the programmes of assistance to the Namibian people, to make every effort to expedite the execution of projects under the Nationhood Programme for Namibia and other projects in favour of Namibians on the basis of procedures which will reflect the role of the United Nations Council for Namibia as the legal Administering Authority for Namibia;

10. *Expresses its appreciation* to those specialized agencies and other organizations and institutions of the United Nations system that have contributed to the Nationhood Programme for Namibia, and calls upon them to continue their participation in the Programme by:

(*a*) Implementing projects approved by the United Nations Council for Namibia;

(*b*) Planning and initiating new project proposals in cooperation with, and at the request of, the Council;

(*c*) Allocating fund from their own financial resources for the implementation of the projects approved by the Council;

11. *Commends* the progress made in the implementation of the pre-independence components of the Nationhood Programme for Namibia, and requests the United Nations Council for Namibia to continue to elaborate and consider policies and contingency plans regarding the transitional and post-independence phases of the Programme;

12. *Requests* the United Nations Council for Namibia to continue and to intensify its field attachment programme, enabling Namibians trained under various programmes to gain practical on-the-job experience in Governments, and institutions in diverse countries, particularly in Africa;

13. *Appeals* to all Governments, specialized agencies and other organizations and institutions of the United Nations system, non-governmental organizations and individuals to make generous contributions to the United Nations Fund for Namibia in order to support the field attachment programme and to meet its financial requirements;

14. *Expresses its appreciation* to the United Nations Development Programme for its increased contribution to the financing and administrations of the Nationhood Programme for Namibia and the financing of the United Nations Institute for Namibia, and calls upon it to continue to allocate, at the request of the United Nations Council for Namibia, funds from the indicative planning figure for Namibia for the projects under the Nationhood Programme and for the Institute, taking into consideration that Namibia remains a unique responsibility of the United Nations, and to exercise maximum flexibility and understanding in approving projects funded from the indicative planning figure;

15. *Expresses its appreciation* for the assistance provided by the United Nations Children's Fund, the Office of the United Nations High Commissioner for Refugees and the World Food Programme to Namibian refugees, and requests them to expand their assistance in order to provide for the basic needs of the refugees;

16. *Expresses its appreciation* to those specialized agencies and other organizations of the United Nations system which have waived agency support costs in respect of projects in favour of Namibians, financed from the United Nations Fund for Namibia and other sources, and urges those that have not yet done so to take appropriate steps in this regard;

17. *Decides* that Namibians shall continue to be eligible for assistance through the United Nations Educational and Training Programme for Southern Africa and the United Nations Trust Fund for South Africa;

18. *Commends* the United Nations Institute for Namibia for the effectiveness of its training programmes for Namibians and its research activities on Namibia, which contribute substantially to the struggle for freedom of the Namibian people and to the establishment of an independent State of Namibia;

19. *Urges* the specialized agencies and other organizations and institutions of the United Nations system to cooperate closely with the United Nations Institute for Namibia in strengthening its programme of activities;

20. *Requests* the United Nations Council for Namibia, in consultation with the South West Africa People's Organization, to finalize and publish, at an early date, a demographic study of the Namibian population;

21. *Requests* the Secretary-General to continue to provide the Office of the United Nations Commissioner for Namibia with the necessary resources for the performance of the responsibilities entrusted to it by the United Nations Council for Namibia as the coordinating authority for the implementation of the Nationhood Programme for Namibia, as well as other assistance programmes.

54th plenary meeting
17 November 1988

44/243. Question of Namibia

Committee: -
Vote: Adopted without a vote
Ref.: 43/26

A

Dissolution of the United Nations Council for Namibia

The General Assembly,

Recalling its resolution 2248 (S-V) of 19 May 1967, by which it decided to establish a United Nations Council for South West Africa[1] as the legal Administering Authority for the Territory until independence,

Recalling also its resolution S-18/1 of 23 April 1990, by which it admitted the Republic of Namibia to membership in the United Nations,

Taking note of the declaration of the United Nations Council for Namibia adopted at its special plenary meetings, held at Windhoek from 9 to 11 April 1990,[2] by which the Council decided to recommend to the General Assembly its own dissolution as a result of Namibia's attainment of freedom and independence,

Taking note also of the decision taken by the United Nations Council for Namibia at its special plenary meetings immediately to arrange, with the agreement of the Government of the Republic of Namibia, to coordinate the smooth transfer of the relevant programmes and activities of the Council to the Government of Namibia,

Taking note further of the decision of the United Nations Council for Namibia requesting the Office of the United Nations Commissioner for Namibia and the United Nations Institute for Namibia to organize in Namibia a seminar on programme planning for the national reconstruction and development of Namibia,

1. *Commends* the United Nations Council for Namibia, as the legal Administering Authority for the Territory until independence, for the fulfilment of the important responsibilities entrusted to it by the General Assembly in its resolution 2248 (S-V) and for its unrelenting efforts to ensure the attainment by the Namibian people of self-determination and national independence;

2. *Decides* that the United Nations Council for Namibia, having fulfilled the important mandate entrusted to it by General Assembly resolution 2248 (S-V) relating to the Territory, is hereby dissolved;

3. *Requests* the Secretary-General to continue to provide the necessary resources in order to complete the implementation of the programme activities approved by the United Nations Council for Namibia for 1990, as set forth in annex I to the present resolutions;

4. *Requests* the Secretary-General immediately to arrange, in consultation with the Government of Namibia, to coordinate the transfer to the Government of Namibia of the programmes, activities and assets of the United Nations Council for Namibia, including archival collections consisting of, *inter alia*, major resolutions and decisions of the United Nations on the question of Namibia and other relevant documents and official correspondence, as well as, in particular, those relating to the implementation of Decree No. 1 for the Protection of the Natural Resources of Namibia[3] and to the accession to international conventions and representation of Namibia in specialized agencies of the United Nations and intergovernmental organizations;

5. *Requests* the Secretary-General, in recognition of the unique and direct responsibility that the United Nations had assumed over Namibia prior to independence, to ensure the continued role of the United Nations in the reconstruction and development of the newly independent State of Namibia by providing the necessary resources and staff within the Secretariat for the delivery of such programmes of assistance;

6. *Also requests* the Secretary-General to provide assistance as may be requested by the Government of Namibia in the preparation of a comprehensive national census in order to determine accurate demographic and other relevant socio-economic statistics on Namibia;

7. *Further requests* the Secretary-General to consider as a matter of priority the redeployment within the United Nations Secretariat and other organizations of the United Nations system of the staff of the Office of the United Nations Commissioner for Namibia.

96th plenary meeting
11 September 1990

B

United Nations Fund for Namibia

The General Assembly,

Having examined the parts of the report of the United Nations Council for Namibia relating to the United Nations Fund for Namibia,[4]

Recalling its resolution 2679 (XXV) of 9 December 1970, by which it established the United Nations Fund for Namibia,

Recalling also its resolution 3112 (XXVIII) of 12 December 1973, by which it appointed the United Nations Council for Namibia trustee of the United Nations Fund for Namibia,

Recalling further its resolution 31/153 of 20 December 1976, by which it decided to launch the Nationhood Programme for Namibia, a comprehensive assistance programme within the United Nations system, covering both the period of the struggle for independence and the initial years of independence of Namibia,

Noting that the current programmes under the General Account, the United Nations Institute for Namibia Account and the Nationhood Programme Account of the United Nations Fund for Namibia should be completed,

1. *Takes note* of the relevant parts of the report of the United Nations Council for Namibia;

2. *Takes note also* of the declaration of the United Nations Council for Namibia adopted at its special plenary meetings held at Windhoek from 9 to 11 April 1990, by which the Council recognized that some of its current programmes and activities remain incomplete;

3. *Decides* that the United Nations Fund for Namibia shall continue to operate in order to ensure the orderly completion of all programmes and activities currently financed from it and as set forth in annex II to the present resolutions and that a report in this respect shall be made to the General Assembly at an appropriate time;

4. *Decides also* that the United Nations Fund for Namibia shall operate under the custody of the Secretary-General;

5. *Decides further* to establish the United Nations Trust Committee for the United Nations Fund for Namibia, the composition and guidelines of which shall follow the pattern of the Committee on the United Nations Fund for Namibia, to serve as the trustee of the Fund until its dissolution;

6. *Requests* the Committee, with the agreement of the Government of Namibia, to take the necessary measures to ensure the completion of ongoing programmes and activities currently financed from the United Nations Fund for Namibia;

7. *Decides* that the United Nations Institute for Namibia, having fulfilled its mandate to provide substantive support in its areas of competence in the struggle for freedom of the Namibians and the establishment of an independent Namibia and in view of the critical financial difficulties which it is experiencing, shall cease its operations on 30 September 1990;

---

1 By its resolution 2372 (XXII) of 12 June 1968, the General Assembly proclaimed that South West Africa should thenceforth be known as "Namibia". By the same resolution, the Assembly decided that the United Nations Council for South Africa should be called "United Nations Council for Namibia".

2 A/44/940-S/21270, annex.

3 *Official Records of the General Assembly, Thirty-fifth Session, Supplement No. 24* (A/35/24), vol. I, annex II.

4 *Ibid., Forty-fourth Session, Supplement No. 24* (A/44/24), part four, chaps. III and IV, sect. B.

8. *Requests* the Secretary-General, in consultation with the United Nations Trust Committee for the United Nations Fund for Namibia, and in cooperation with the Governments of Namibia and Zambia, to implement the closure of the United Nations Institute for Namibia as provided for in paragraph 7 above, and to liquidate its assets and discharge its liabilities and, having regard to the needs of Namibia and the successor institution to the Institute, to make available any residual net assets for utilization by such successor institution;

9. *Expresses its deep appreciation* to the Government of Zambia for accommodating the United Nations Institute for Namibia prior to Namibia's independence and extending services, courtesies and privileges to facilitate the Institute's operations in Zambia;

10. *Requests* the Secretary-General, in cooperation with the Governments concerned, to coordinate the transfer to Namibia of the United Nations Vocational Training Centre for Namibia at Cuacra, Angola, and to determine the future status of the Namibia Secondary Technical School at Loudima, the Congo, and expresses its deep appreciation to the Governments of Angola and the Congo for the courtesies and hospitality that they have extended to these institutions;

11. *Expresses its appreciation* to all States, specialized agencies and other organizations and institutions of the United Nations system, and to governmental and non-governmental organizations that have made contributions to the United Nations Fund for Namibia, as well as to all individuals who have done so;

12. *Requests* the Secretary-General to appeal to Governments, intergovernmental and non-governmental organizations and individuals for voluntary contributions to the United Nations Fund for Namibia;

13. *Invites* Governments to appeal once more to their national organizations and institutions for voluntary contributions to the United Nations Fund for Namibia;

14. *Expresses its appreciation* to the United Nations Development Programme for its contribution to the financing and administration of the Nationhood Programme for Namibia and the financing of the United Nations Institute for Namibia, and calls upon it to continue its contribution to the United Nations Fund for Namibia;

15. *Decides* that Namibians currently benefiting from assistance through the United Nations Educational and Training Programme for Southern Africa and through the United Nations Trust Fund for South Africa shall continue to be eligible for such assistance until they complete their programmes;

16. *Requests* the Secretary-General to credit as soon as possible to the United Nations Fund for Namibia the sum of 1.5 million United States dollars already appropriated for 1990 under the regular budget;

17. *Requests* the Secretary-General to continue to provide the necessary resources for the performance of the activities financed from the United Nations Fund for Namibia.

96th plenary meeting
11 September 1990

Annex I

Programme Activities Approved by the United Nations Council for Namibia for 1990 to be Carried out Following the Dissolution of the Council

The United Nations Council for Namibia approved the programme activities enumerated below for 1990:

1. Preparation of reports on the political, military and social situation in Namibia, and on the activities of foreign economic interests in the Territory, for the period from 1 April 1989 until independence;

2. Preparation of a report on contacts between Member States and South Africa to cover the period from 1 April 1989 until independence;

3. Preparation of a report on the activities of the Council for the period from 1 September 1989 until independence;

4. Organization of a seminar on programme planning for the national reconstruction and development of Namibia and preparation of its final report;

5. Preparation of draft chapters on Namibia for inclusion in the Yearbook of the United Nations for the years 1986 to 1990;

6. Preparation of a draft study of Article 81 of the Charter of the United Nations for inclusion in Supplement No. 7 of the Repertory of Practice of United Nations Organs;

7. Compilation of archival materials relating to United Nations action on Namibia and deemed to be of use or interest to Namibia, including major resolutions and decisions of the United Nations on the question of Namibia and other relevant documents and official correspondence;

8. Drafting of a historical account of the responsibilities and programmes undertaken by the Council since its inception.

Annex II

Programmes and Activities Financed from the United Nations Fund For Namibia

A. Nationhood Programme Account

1. The Nationhood Programme Account of the Fund finances sixteen training and education projects for Namibians in various fields of study. Two of these projects provide funding for the United Nations Vocational Training Centre for Namibia at Cuacra, Angola, which is to be relocated to Namibia in late 1990 or early 1991.

B. General Account

2. The individual scholarship programme of the General Account provides sponsorship for one hundred eighty-five Namibian students, the majority of whom are studying at university level in the United States of America.

3. The General Account also supports six training projects similar to those of the Nationhood Programme and one project that makes a major contribution to the operating expenses of the Namibia Secondary Technical School at Loudima, the Congo.

4. The General Account provides social and medical assistance for expatriate Namibians in need, generally students, and covers the return travel expenses of scholarship holders who have completed their degrees.

C. Institute for Namibia Account

5. The Institute for Namibia Account of the Fund provided most of the funding for the budget of the United Nations Institute for Namibia at Lusaka. The Institute shall cease its operations on 30 September 1990.

04.43 PALESTINE

181 (II). Future Government of Palestine[1]

Committee: Ad Hoc Committee on Palestine
Vote: 33 - 13 - 10
Ref.: 107(S-1), 106(S-1), 105(S-1), 104(S-1)

A

The General Assembly,

Having met in special session at the request of the mandatory Power to constitute and instruct a special committee to prepare for the consideration of the question of the future government of Palestine at the second regular session;

Having constituted a Special Committee and instructed it to investigate all questions and issues relevant to the problem of Palestine, and to prepare proposals for the solution of the problem, and

1 A map of the Plan of Partition and a map of the proposed Boundaries of the City of Jerusalem as annexed to this resolution are not printed in this volume.

Having received and examined the report of the Special Committee (document A/364)[1] including a number of unanimous recommendations and a plan of partition with economic union approved by the majority of the Special Committee,

Considers that the present situation in Palestine is one which is likely to impair the general welfare and friendly relations among nations;

Takes note of the declaration by the mandatory Power that it plans to complete its evacuation of Palestine by 1 August 1948;

Recommends to the United Kingdom, as the mandatory Power for Palestine, and to all other Members of the United Nations the adoption and implementation, with regard to the future government of Palestine, of the Plan of Partition with Economic Union set out below;

Requests that

(*a*) The Security Council take the necessary measures as provided for in the plan for its implementation;

(*b*) The Security Council consider, if circumstances during the transitional period require such consideration, whether the situation in Palestine constitutes a threat to the peace. If it decides that such a threat exists, and in order to maintain international peace and security, the Security Council should supplement the authorization of the General Assembly by taking measures, under Articles 39 and 41 of the Charter, to empower the United Nations Commission, as provided in this resolution, to exercise in Palestine the functions which are assigned to it by this resolution;

(*c*) The Security Council determine as a threat to the peace, breach of the peace or act of aggression, in accordance with Article 39 of the Charter, any attempt to alter by force the settlement envisaged by this resolution;

(*d*) The Trusteeship Council be informed of the responsibilities envisaged for it in this plan;

Calls upon the inhabitants of Palestine to take such steps as may be necessary on their part to put this plan into effect;

Appeals to all Governments and all peoples to refrain from taking any action which might hamper or delay the carrying out of these recommendations, and

Authorizes the Secretary-General to reimburse travel and subsistence expenses of the members of the Commission referred to in Part I, Section B, paragraph 1 below, on such basis and in such form as he may determine most appropriate in the circumstances, and to provide the Commission with the necessary staff to assist in carrying out the functions assigned to the Commission by the General Assembly.

B

The General Assembly

Authorizes the Secretary-General to draw from the Working Capital Fund a sum not to exceed $2,000,000 for the purposes set forth in the last paragraph of the resolution on the future government of Palestine.

Hundred and twenty-eighth plenary meeting
29 November 1947

At its hundred and twenty-eighth plenary meeting on 29 November 1947 the General Assembly, in accordance with the terms of the above resolution, elected the following members of the United Nations Commission on Palestine:

Bolivia, Czechoslovakia, Denmark, Panama and Philippines.

[1] See *Official Records of the second session of the General Assembly, Supplement No. 11*, Volumes I-IV.

Plan of Partition with Economic Union

Part I

Future constitution and government of Palestine

A. Termination of Mandate, Partition and Independence

1. The Mandate for Palestine shall terminate as soon as possible but in any case not later than 1 August 1948.

2. The armed forces of the mandatory Power shall be progressively withdrawn from Palestine, the withdrawal to be completed as soon as possible but in any case not later than 1 August 1948.

The mandatory Power shall advise the Commission, as far in advance as possible, of its intention to terminate the Mandate and to evacuate each area.

The mandatory Power shall use its best endeavours to ensure that an area situated in the territory of the Jewish State, including a seaport and hinterland adequate to provide facilities for a substantial immigration, shall be evacuated at the earliest possible date and in any event not later than 1 February 1948.

3. Independent Arab and Jewish States and the Special International Régime for the City of Jerusalem, set forth in part III of this plan, shall come into existence in Palestine two months after the evacuation of the armed forces of the mandatory Power has been completed but in any case not later than 1 October 1948. The boundaries of the Arab State, the Jewish State, and the City of Jerusalem shall be as described in parts II and III below.

4. The period between the adoption by the General Assembly of its recommendation on the question of Palestine and the establishment of the independence of the Arab and Jewish States shall be a transitional period.

B. Steps Preparatory to Independence

1. A Commission shall be set up consisting of one representative of each of five Member States. The Members represented on the Commission shall be elected by the General Assembly on as broad a basis, geographically and otherwise, as possible.

2. The administration of Palestine shall, as the mandatory Power withdraws its armed forces, be progressively turned over to the Commission, which shall act in conformity with the recommendations of the General Assembly, under the guidance of the Security Council. The mandatory Power shall to the fullest possible extent coordinate its plans for withdrawal with the plans of the Commission to take over and administer areas which have been evacuated.

In the discharge of this administrative responsibility the Commission shall have authority to issue necessary regulations and take other measures as required.

The mandatory Power shall not take any action to prevent, obstruct or delay the implementation by the Commission of the measures recommended by the General Assembly.

3. On its arrival in Palestine the Commission shall proceed to carry out measures for the establishment of the frontiers of the Arab and Jewish States and the City of Jerusalem in accordance with the general lines of the recommendations of the General Assembly on the partition of Palestine. Nevertheless, the boundaries as described in part II of this plan are to be modified in such a way that village areas as a rule will not be divided by state boundaries unless pressing reasons make that necessary.

4. The Commission, after consultation with the democratic parties and other public organizations of the Arab and Jewish States, shall select and establish in each State as rapidly as possible a Provisional Council of Government. The activities of both the Arab and Jewish Provisional Councils of Government shall be carried out under the general direction of the Commission.

If by 1 April 1948 a Provisional Council of Government cannot be selected for either of the States, or, if selected, cannot carry out its functions, the Commission shall communicate that fact to the Security Council for such action with respect to that State as the Security Council may deem proper, and to the Secretary-General for communication to the Members of the United Nations.

5. Subject to the provisions of these recommendations, during the transitional period the Provisional Councils of Government, acting under the Commission, shall have full authority in the areas under their control, including authority over matters of immigration and land regulation.

6. The Provisional Council of Government of each State, acting under the Commission, shall progressively receive from the Commission full responsibility for the administration of that State in the period between the termination of the Mandate and the establishment of the State's independence.

7. The Commission shall instruct the Provisional Councils of Government of both the Arab and Jewish States, after their formation, to proceed to the establishment of administrative organs of government, central and local.

8. The Provisional Council of Government of each State shall, within the shortest time possible, recruit an armed militia from the residents of that State, sufficient in number to maintain internal order and to prevent frontier clashes.

This armed militia in each State shall, for operational purposes, be under the command of Jewish or Arab officers resident in that State, but general political and military control, including the choice of the militia's High Command, shall be exercised by the Commission.

9. The Provisional Council of Government of each State shall, not later than two months after the withdrawal of the armed forces of the mandatory Power, hold elections to the Constituent Assembly which shall be conducted on democratic lines.

The election regulations in each State shall be drawn up by the Provisional Council of Government and approved by the Commission. Qualified voters for each State for this election shall be persons over eighteen years of age who are: (a) Palestinian citizens residing in that State and (b) Arabs and Jews residing in the State, although not Palestinian citizens, who, before voting, have signed a notice of intention to become citizens of such State.

Arabs and Jews residing in the City of Jerusalem who have signed a notice of intention to become citizens, the Arabs of the Arab State and the Jews of the Jewish State, shall be entitled to vote in the Arab and Jewish States respectively.

Women may vote and be elected to the Constituent Assemblies.

During the transitional period no Jew shall be permitted to establish residence in the area of the proposed Arab State, and no Arab shall be permitted to establish residence in the area of the proposed Jewish State, except by special leave of the Commission.

10. The Constituent Assembly of each State shall draft a democratic constitution for its State and choose a provisional government to succeed the Provisional Council of Government appointed by the Commission. The constitutions of the States shall embody chapters 1 and 2 of the Declaration provided for in section C below and include *inter alia* provisions for:

(*a*) Establishing in each State a legislative body elected by universal suffrage and by secret ballot on the basis of proportional representation, and an executive body responsible to the legislature;

(*b*) Settling all international disputes in which the State may be involved by peaceful means in such a manner that international peace and security, and justice, are not endangered;

(*c*) Accepting the obligation of the State to refrain in its international relations from the threat or use of force against the territorial integrity or political independence of any State, or in any other manner inconsistent with the purposes of the United Nations;

(*d*) Guaranteeing to all persons equal and nondiscriminatory rights in civil, political, economic and religious matters and the enjoyment of human rights and fundamental freedoms, including freedom of religion, language, speech and publication, education, assembly and association;

(*e*) Preserving freedom of transit and visit for all residents and citizens of the other State in Palestine and the City of Jerusalem, subject to considerations of national security, provided that each State shall control residence within its borders.

11. The Commission shall appoint a preparatory economic commission of three members to make whatever arrangements are possible for economic cooperation, with a view to establishing, as soon as practicable. the Economic Union and the Joint Economic Board, as provided in section D below.

12. During the period between the adoption of the recommendations on the question of Palestine by the General Assembly and the termination of the Mandate, the mandatory Power in Palestine shall maintain full responsibility for administration in areas from which it has not withdrawn its armed forces. The Commission shall assist the mandatory Power in the carrying out of these functions. Similarly the mandatory Power shall cooperate with the Commission in the execution of its functions.

13. With a view to ensuring that there shall be continuity in the functioning of administrative services and that, on the withdrawal of the armed forces of the mandatory Power, the whole administration shall be in the charge of the Provisional Councils and the Joint Economic Board, respectively, acting under the Commission, there shall be a progressive transfer, from the mandatory Power to the Commission, of responsibility for all the functions of government, including that of maintaining law and order in the areas from which the forces of the mandatory Power have been withdrawn.

14. The Commission shall be guided in its activities by the recommendations of the General Assembly and by such instructions as the Security Council may consider necessary to issue.

The measures taken by the Commission, within the recommendations of the General Assembly, shall become immediately effective unless the Commission has previously received contrary instructions from the Security Council.

The Commission shall render periodic monthly progress reports, or more frequently if desirable, to the Security Council.

15. The Commission shall make its final report to the next regular session of the General Assembly and to the Security Council simultaneously.

C. Declaration

A declaration shall be made to the United Nations by the provisional government of each proposed State before independence. It shall contain *inter alia* the following clauses:

General Provision

The stipulations contained in the declaration are recognized as fundamental laws of the State and no law, regulation or official action shall conflict or interfere with these stipulations, nor shall any law, regulation or official action prevail over them.

Chapter 1
Holy Places, religious buildings and sites

1. Existing rights in respect of Holy Places and religious buildings or sites shall not be denied or impaired.

2. In so far as Holy Places are concerned, the liberty of access, visit and transit shall be guaranteed, in conformity with existing rights, to all residents and citizens of the other State and of the City of Jerusalem, as well as to aliens, without distinction as to nationality, subject to requirements of national security, public order and decorum.

Similarly, freedom of worship shall be guaranteed in conformity with existing rights, subject to the maintenance of public order and decorum.

3. Holy Places and religious buildings or sites shall be preserved. No act shall be permitted which may in any way impair their sacred character. If at any time it appears to the Government that any particular Holy Place, religious building or site is in need of urgent repair, the Government may call upon the community or communities concerned to carry out such repair. The Government may carry it out itself at the expense of the community or communities concerned if no action is taken within a reasonable time.

4. No taxation shall be levied in respect of any Holy Place, religious building or site which was exempt from taxation on the date of the creation of the State.

No change in the incidence of such taxation shall be made which would either discriminate between the owners or occupiers of Holy Places, religious buildings or sites, or would place such owners or occupiers in a position less in relation to the general incidence of taxation than existed at the time of the adoption of the Assembly's recommendations.

5. The Governor of the City of Jerusalem shall have the right to determine whether the provisions of the Constitution of the State in relation to Holy Places, religious buildings and sites within the borders of the State and the religious rights appertaining thereto, are being properly applied and respected, and to make decisions on the basis of existing rights in cases of disputes which may arise between the different religious communities or the rites of a religious community with respect to such places, buildings and sites. He shall receive full cooperation and such privileges and immunities as are necessary for the exercise of his functions in the State.

Chapter 2
Religious and minority rights

1. Freedom of conscience and the free exercise of all forms of worship, subject only to the maintenance of public order and morals, shall be ensured to all.

2. No discrimination of any kind shall be made between the inhabitants on the ground of race, religion, language or sex.

3. All persons within the jurisdiction of the State shall be entitled to equal protection of the laws.

4. The family law and personal status of the various minorities and their religious interests, including endowments, shall be respected.

5. Except as may be required for the maintenance of public order and good government, no measure shall be taken to obstruct or interfere with the enterprise of religious or charitable bodies of all faiths or to discriminate against any representative or member of these bodies on the ground of his religion or nationality.

6. The State shall ensure adequate primary and secondary education for the Arab and Jewish minority, respectively, in its own language and its cultural traditions.

The right of each community to maintain its own schools for the education of its own members in its own language, while conforming to such educational requirements of a general nature as the State may impose, shall not be denied or impaired. Foreign educational establishments shall continue their activity on the basis of their existing rights.

7. No restriction shall be imposed on the free use by any citizen of the State of any language in private intercourse, in commerce, in religion, in the Press or in publications of any kind, or at public meetings.[1]

8. No expropriation of land owned by an Arab in the Jewish State (by a Jew in the Arab State)[2] shall be allowed except for public purposes. In all cases of expropriation full compensation as fixed by the Supreme Court shall be paid previous to dispossession.

Chapter 3
Citizenship, international conventions and financial obligations

1. *Citizenship.* Palestinian citizens residing in Palestine outside the City of Jerusalem, as well as Arabs and Jews who, not holding Palestinian citizenship, reside in Palestine outside the City of Jerusalem shall, upon the recognition of independence, become citizens of the State in which they are resident and enjoy full civil and political rights. Persons over the age of eighteen years may opt, within one year from the date of recognition of independence of the State in which they reside, for citizenship of the other State, providing that no Arab residing in the area of the proposed Arab State shall have the right to opt for citizenship in the proposed Jewish State and no Jew residing in the proposed Jewish State shall have the right to opt for citizenship in the proposed Arab State. The exercise of this right of option will be taken to include the wives and children under eighteen years of age of persons so opting.

Arabs residing in the area of the proposed Jewish State and Jews residing in the area of the proposed Arab State who have signed a notice of intention to opt for citizenship of the other State shall be eligible to vote in the elections to the Constituent Assembly of that State, but not in the elections to the Constituent Assembly of the State in which they reside.

2. *International conventions.* (*a*) The State shall be bound by all the international agreements and conventions, both general and special, to which Palestine has become a party. Subject to any right of denunciation provided for therein, such agreements and conventions shall be respected by the State throughout the period for which they were concluded.

(*b*) Any dispute about the applicability and continued validity of international conventions or treaties signed or adhered to by the mandatory Power on behalf of Palestine shall be referred to the International Court of Justice in accordance with the provisions of the Statute of the Court.

3. *Financial obligations.* (*a*) The State shall respect and fulfil all financial obligations of whatever nature assumed on behalf of Palestine by the mandatory Power during the exercise of the Mandate and recognized by the State. This provision includes the right of public servants to pensions, compensation or gratuities.

(*b*) These obligations shall be fulfilled through participation in the Joint Economic Board in respect of those obligations applicable to Palestine as a whole, and individually in respect of those applicable to, and fairly apportionable between, the States.

(*c*) A Court of Claims, affiliated with the Joint Economic Board, and composed of one member appointed by the United Nations, one representative of the United Kingdom and one representative of the State concerned, should be established. Any dispute between the United Kingdom and the State respecting claims not recognized by the latter should be referred to that Court.

(*d*) Commercial concessions granted in respect of any part of Palestine prior to the adoption of the resolution by the General Assembly shall continue to be valid according to their terms, unless modified by agreement between the concession-holder and the State.

Chapter 4
Miscellaneous provisions

1. The provisions of chapters 1 and 2 of the declaration shall be under the guarantee of the United Nations, and no modifications shall he made in them without the assent of the General Assembly of the United Nations. Any Member of the United Nations shall have the right to bring to the attention of the General Assembly any infraction or danger of infraction of any of these stipulations, and the General Assembly may thereupon make such recommendations as it may deem proper in the circumstances.

2. Any dispute relating to the application or the interpretation of this declaration shall be referred, at the request of either party, to the International Court of Justice, unless the parties agree to another mode of settlement.

D. Economic Union and Transit

1. The Provisional Council of Government of each State shall enter into an undertaking with respect to Economic Union and Transit. This undertaking shall be drafted by the Commission provided for in section B, paragraph 1, utilizing to the greatest possible extent the advice and cooperation of representative organizations and bodies from each of the proposed States. It shall contain provisions to establish the Economic Union of Palestine and provide for other matters of common interest. If by 1 April 1948 the Provisional Councils of Government have not entered into the undertaking, the undertaking shall be put into force by the Commission.

---

1 The following stipulation shall be added to the declaration concerning the Jewish state: "In the Jewish State adequate facilities shall be given to Arabic-speaking citizens for the use of their language, either orally or in writing, in the legislature, before the courts and in the administration."

2 In the declaration concerning the Arab State the words "by an Arab in the Jewish State" should be replaced by the words "by a Jew in the Arab State".

The Economic Union of Palestine

2. The objectives of the Economic Union of Palestine shall be:

(*a*) A customs union;

(*b*) A joint currency system providing for a single foreign exchange rate;

(*c*) Operation in the common interest on a nondiscriminatory basis of railways; inter-State highways; postal, telephone and telegraphic services, and ports and airports involved in international trade and commerce;

(*d*) Joint economic development, especially in respect of irrigation, land reclamation and soil conservation;

(*e*) Access for both States and for the City of Jerusalem on a non-discriminatory basis to water and power facilities.

3. There shall be established a Joint Economic Board, which shall consist of three representatives of each of the two States and three foreign members appointed by the Economic and Social Council of the United Nations. The foreign members shall be appointed in the first instance for a term of three years; they shall serve as individuals and not as representatives of States.

4. The functions of the Joint Economic Board shall be to implement either directly or by delegation the measures necessary to realize the objectives of the Economic Union. It shall have all powers of organization and administration necessary to fulfil its functions.

5. The States shall bind themselves to put into effect the decisions of the Joint Economic Board. The Board's decisions shall be taken by a majority vote.

6. In the event of failure of a State to take the necessary action the Board may, by a vote of six members, decide to withhold an appropriate portion of that part of the customs revenue to which the State, in question is entitled under the Economic Union. Should the State persist in its failure to cooperate, the Board may decide by a simple majority vote upon such further sanctions, including disposition of funds which it has withheld, as it may deem appropriate.

7. In relation to economic development, the functions of the Board shall be the planning, investigation and encouragement of joint development projects, but it shall not undertake such projects except with the assent of both States and the City of Jerusalem, in the event that Jerusalem is directly involved in the development project.

8. In regard to the joint currency system the currencies circulating in the two States and the City of Jerusalem shall he issued under the authority of the Joint Economic Board, which shall be the sole issuing authority and which shall determine the reserves to be held against such currencies.

9. So far as is consistent with paragraph 2 (*b*) above, each State may operate its own central bank, control its own fiscal and credit policy, its foreign exchange receipts and expenditures, the grant of import licenses, and may conduct international financial operations on its own faith and credit. During the first two years after the termination of the Mandate, the Joint Economic Board shall have the authority to take such measures as may be necessary to ensure that - to the extent that the total foreign exchange revenues of the two States from the export of goods and services permit, and provided that each State takes appropriate measures to conserve its own foreign exchange resources - each State shall have available, in any twelve months, period, foreign exchange sufficient to assure the supply of quantities of imported goods and services for consumption in its territory equivalent to the quantities of such goods and services consumed in that territory in the twelve months, period ending 31 December 1947.

10. All economic authority not specifically vested in the Joint Economic Board is reserved to each State.

11. There shall be a common customs tariff with complete freedom of trade between the States, and between the States and the City of Jerusalem.

12. The tariff schedules shall be drawn up by a Tariff Commission, consisting of representatives of each of the States in equal numbers, and shall be submitted to the Joint Economic Board for approval by a majority vote. In case of disagreement in the Tariff Commission, the Joint Economic Board shall arbitrate the points of difference. In the event that the Tariff Commission fails to draw up any schedule by a date to be fixed, the Joint Economic Board shall determine the tariff schedule.

13. The following items shall be a first charge on the customs and other common revenue of the Joint Economic Board:

(*a*) The expenses of the customs service and of the operation of the joint services;

(*b*) The administrative expenses of the Joint Economic Board;

(*c*) The financial obligations of the Administration of Palestine consisting of:

(i) The service of the outstanding public debt;

(ii) The cost of superannuation benefits, now being paid or falling due in the future, in accordance with the rules and to the extent established by paragraph 3 of chapter 3 above.

14. After these obligations have been met in full, the surplus revenue from the Customs and other common services shall be divided in the following manner: not less than 5 per cent and not more than 10 per cent to the City of Jerusalem; the residue shall be allocated to each State by the Joint Economic Board equitably, with the objective of maintaining a sufficient and suitable level of government and social services in each State, except that the share of either State shall not exceed the amount of that State's contribution to the revenues of the Economic Union by more than approximately four million pounds in any year. The amount granted may be adjusted by the Board according to the price level in relation to the prices prevailing at the time of the establishment of the Union. After five years, the principles of the distribution of the joint revenues may be revised by the Joint Economic Board on a basis of equity.

15. All international conventions and treaties affecting customs tariff rates, and those communications services under the jurisdiction of the Joint Economic Board, shall be entered into by both States. In these matters, the two States shall be bound to act in accordance with the majority vote of the Joint Economic Board.

16. The Joint Economic Board shall endeavour to secure for Palestine's exports fair and equal access to world markets.

17. All enterprises operated by the Joint Economic Board shall pay fair wages on a uniform basis.

Freedom of transit and visit

18. The undertaking shall contain provisions preserving freedom of transit and visit for all residents or citizens of both States and of the City of Jerusalem, subject to security considerations; provided that each State and the City shall control residence within its borders.

Termination, modification and interpretation of the undertaking

19. The undertaking and any treaty issuing therefrom shall remain in force for a period of ten years. It shall continue in force until notice of termination, to take effect two years thereafter, is given by either of the parties.

20. During the initial ten-year period, the undertaking and any treaty issuing therefrom may not be modified except by consent of both parties and with the approval of the General Assembly.

21. Any dispute relating to the application or the interpretation of the undertaking and any treaty issuing therefrom shall be referred, at the request of either party, to the International Court of Justice, unless the parties agree to another mode of settlement.

E. Assets

1. The movable assets of the Administration of Palestine shall be allocated to the Arab and Jewish States and the City of Jerusalem on an equitable basis. Allocations should be made by the United Nations Commission referred to in section B, paragraph 1, above. Immovable assets shall become the property of the government of the territory in which they are situated.

2. During the period between the appointment of the United Nations Commission and the termination of the Mandate, the mandatory Power shall, except in respect of ordinary operations, consult with the Commission on any measure which it may contemplate involving the liquidation, disposal or encumbering of the assets of the Palestine

Government, such as the accumulated treasury surplus, the proceeds of Government bond issues, State lands or any other asset.

F. Admission to Membership in the United Nations

When the independence of either the Arab or the Jewish State as envisaged in this plan has become effective and the declaration and undertaking, as envisaged in this plan, have been signed by either of them, sympathetic consideration should be given to its application for admission to membership in the United Nations in accordance with Article 4 of the Charter of the United Nations.

Part II

Boundaries

A. The Arab State

The area of the Arab State in Western Galilee is bounded on the west by the Mediterranean and on the north by the frontier of the Lebanon from Ras en Naqura to a point north of Saliha. From there the boundary proceeds southwards, leaving the built-up area of Saliha in the Arab State, to join the southernmost point of this village. Thence it follows the western boundary line of the villages of 'Alma, Rihaniya and Teitaba, thence following the northern boundary line of Meirun village to join the Acre-Safad sub-district boundary line. It follows this line to a point west of Es Sammu'i village and joins it again at the northernmost point of Farradiya. Thence it follows the sub-district boundary line to the Acre-Safad main road. From here it follows the western boundary of Kafr I'nan village until it reaches the Tiberias-Acre sub-district boundary line, passing to the west of the junction of the Acre-Safad and Lubiya-Kafr I'nan roads. From the south-west corner of Kafr I'nan village the boundary line follows the western boundary of the Tiberias sub-district to a point close to the boundary line between the villages of Maghar and Eilabun, thence bulging out to the west to include as much of the eastern part of the plain of Battuf as is necessary for the reservoir proposed by the Jewish Agency for the irrigation of lands to the south and east.

The boundary rejoins the Tiberias sub-district boundary at a point on the Nazareth-Tiberias road south-east of the built-up area of Tur'an; thence it runs southwards, at first following the sub-district boundary and then passing between the Kadoorie Agricultural School and Mount Tabor, to a point due south at the base of Mount Tabor. From here it runs due west, parallel to the horizontal grid line 230, to the north-east corner of the village lands of Tel Adashim. It then runs to the north-west corner of these lands, whence it turns south and west so as to include in the Arab State the sources of the Nazareth water supply in Yafa village. On reaching Ginneiger it follows the eastern, northern and eastern boundaries of the lands of this village to their south-west corner, whence it proceeds in a straight line to a point on the Haifa-Afula railway on the boundary between the villages of Sarid and El Mujeidil. This is the point of intersection.

The south-western boundary of the area of the Arab State in Galilee takes a line from this point, passing northwards along the eastern boundaries of Sarid and Gevat to the north-eastern corner of Nahalal, proceeding thence across the land of Kefar ha Horesh to a central point on the southern boundary of the village of 'Ilut, thence westwards along that village boundary to the eastern boundary of Beit Lahm, thence northwards and north-eastwards along its western boundary to the north-eastern corner of Waldheim and thence north-eastwards across the village lands of Shafa 'Amr to the south-eastern corner of Ramat Yohanan. From here it runs due north-north-east to a point on the Shafa 'Amr-Haifa road, west of its junction with the road to I'Billin. From there it proceeds north-east to a point on the southern boundary of I'Billin situated to the west of the I'Billin-Birwa road. Thence along that boundary to its westernmost point, whence it turns to the north, follows across the village land of Tamra to the north-westernmost corner and along the western boundary of Julis until it reaches the Acre-Safad road. It then runs westwards along the southern side of the Safad-Acre road to the Galilee-Haifa District boundary, from which point it follows that boundary to the sea.

The boundary of the hill country of Samaria and Judea starts on the Jordan River at the Wadi Malih south-east of Beisan and runs due west to meet the Beisan-Jericho road and then follows the western side of that road in a north-westerly direction to the junction of the boundaries of the sub-districts of Beisan, Nablus, and Jenin. From that point it follows the Nablus-Jenin sub-district boundary westwards for a distance of about three kilometres and then turns north-westwards, passing to the east of the built-up areas of the villages of Jalbun and Faqqu'a, to the boundary of the sub-districts of Jenin and Beisan at a point north-east of Nuris.

Thence it proceeds first north-westwards to a point due north of the built-up area of Zir'in and then westwards to the Afula-Jenin railway, thence northwestwards along the district boundary line to the point of intersection on the Hejaz railway. From here the boundary runs south-westwards, including the built-up area and some of the land of the village of Kh.Lid in the Arab State to cross the Haifa-Jenin road at a point on the district boundary between Haifa and Samaria west of El Mansi. It follows this boundary to the southernmost point of the village of El Buteimat. From here it follows the northern and eastern boundaries of the village of Ar'ara, rejoining the Haifa-Samaria district boundary at Wadi'Ara, and thence proceeding south-south-westwards in an approximately straight line joining up with the western boundary of Qaqun to a point east of the railway line on the eastern boundary of Qaqun village. From here it runs along the railway line some distance to the east of it to a point just east of the Tulkarm railway station. Thence the boundary follows a line half-way between the railway and the Tulkarm-Qalqiliya-Jaljuliya and Ras el Ein road to a point just east of Ras el Ein station, whence it proceeds along the railway some distance to the east of it to the point on the railway line south of the junction of the Haifa-Lydda and Beit Nabala lines, whence it proceeds along the southern border of Lydda airport to its south-west corner, thence in a south-westerly direction to a point just west of the built-up area of Sarafand el'Amar, whence it turns south, passing just to the west of the built-up area of Abu el Fadil to the north-east corner of the lands of Beer Ya'Aqov. (The boundary line should be so demarcated as to allow direct access from the Arab State to the airport.) Thence the boundary line follows the western and southern boundaries of Ramle village, to the north-east corner of El Na'ana village, thence in a straight line to the southernmost point of El Barriya, along the eastern boundary of that village and the southern boundary of 'Innaba village. Thence it turns north to follow the southern side of the Jaffa-Jerusalem road until El Qubab, whence it follows the road to the boundary of Abu Shusha. It runs along the eastern boundaries of Abu Shusha, Seidun, Hulda to the southernmost point of Hulda, thence westwards in a straight line to the northeastern corner of Umm Kalkha, thence following the northern boundaries of Umm Kalkha, Qazaza and the northern and western boundaries of Mukhezin to the Gaza District boundary and thence runs across the village lands of El Mismiya, El Kabira, and Yasur to the southern point of intersection, which is midway between the built-up areas of Yasur and Batani Sharqi.

From the southern point of intersection the boundary lines run north-westwards between the villages of Gan Yavne and Barqa to the sea at a point half way between Nabi Yunis and Minat el Qila, and south-eastwards to a point west of Qastina, whence it turns in a south-westerly direction, passing to the east of the built-up areas of Es Sawafir, Esh Sharqiya and Ibdis. From the south-east corner of Ibdis village it runs to a point south-west of the built-up area of Beit 'Affa, crossing the Hebron-El Majdal road just to the west of the built-up area of Iraq Suweidan. Thence it proceeds southwards along the western village boundary of El Faluja to the Beersheba sub-district boundary. It then runs across the tribal lands of 'Arab el Jubarat to a point on the boundary between the sub-districts of Beersheba and Hebron north of Kh. Khuweilifa, whence it proceeds in a south-westerly direction to a point on the Beersheba-Gaza main road two kilometres to the north-west of the town. It then turns south-eastwards to reach Wadi Sab at a point situated one kilometre to the west of it. From here it turns north-eastwards and proceeds along Wadi Sab, and along the Beersheba-Hebron road for a distance of one kilometre, whence it turns eastwards and runs in a straight line to Kh. Kuseifa to join the Beersheba-Hebron sub-district boundary. It then follows the Beersheba-Hebron boundary eastwards to a point north of Ras Ez Zuweira, only departing from it so as to cut across the base of the indentation between vertical grid lines 150 and 160.

About five kilometres north-east of Ras ez Zuweira it turns north, excluding from the Arab State a strip along the coast of the Dead Sea not more than seven kilometres in depth, as far as Ein Geddi, whence it turns due east to join the Transjordan frontier in the Dead Sea.

The northern boundary of the Arab section of the coastal plain runs from a point between Minat el Qila and Nabi Yunis, passing between the built-up areas of Gan Yavne and Barqa to the point of intersection. From here it turns south-westwards, running across the lands of Batani Sharqi, along the eastern boundary of the lands of Beit Daras and across the lands of Julis, leaving the built-up areas of Batani Sharqi and Julis to the westwards, as far as the north-west corner of the lands of Beit Tima. Thence it runs east of El Jiya across the village lands of El Barbara along the eastern boundaries of the villages of Beit Jirja, Deir Suneid and Dimra. From the south-east corner of Dimra the boundary passes across the lands of Beit Elanun, leaving the Jewish lands of Nir-Am to the eastwards. From the south-east corner of Beit Hanun the line runs south-west to a point south of the parallel grid line 100, then turns north-west for two kilometres, turning again in a south-westerly direction and continuing in an almost straight line to the north-west corner of the village lands of Kirbet Ikhza'a. From there it follows the boundary line of this village to its southernmost point. It then runs in a southerly direction along the vertical grid line 90 to its junction with the horizontal grid line 70. It then turns south-eastwards to Kh. el Ruheiba and then proceeds in a southerly direction to a point known as El Baha, beyond which it crosses the Beersheba-El 'Auja main road to the west of Kh. el Mushrifa. From there it joins Wadi El Zaiyatin just to the west of El Subeita. From there it turns to the north-east and then to the south-east following this wadi and passes to the east of 'Abda to join Wadi Nafkh. It then bulges to the south-west along Wadi Nafkh, Wadi Ajrim and Wadi Lassan to the point where Wadi Lassan crosses the Egyptian frontier.

The area of the Arab enclave of Jaffa consists of that part of the town-planning area of Jaffa which lies to the west of the Jewish quarters lying south of Tel-Aviv, to the west of the continuation of Herzl street up to its junction with the Jaffa-Jerusalem road, to the south-west of the section of the Jaffa Jerusalem road lying south-east of that junction, to the west of Mique Yisrael lands, to the north-west of Holon local council area, to the north of the line linking up the north-west corner of Holon with the north-east corner of Bat Yam local council area and to the north of Bat Yam local council area. The question of Karton quarter will be decided by the Boundary Commission, bearing in mind among other considerations the desirability of including the smallest possible number of its Arab inhabitants and the largest possible number of its Jewish inhabitants in the Jewish State.

B. The Jewish State

The north-eastern sector of the Jewish State (Eastern Galilee) is bounded on the north and west by the Lebanese frontier and on the east by the frontiers of Syria and Transjordan. It includes the whole of the Hula Basin, Lake Tiberias, the whole of the Beisan sub-district, the boundary line being extended to the crest of the Gilboa mountains and the Wadi Malih. From there the Jewish State extends north-west, following the boundary described in respect of the Arab State.

The Jewish section of the coastal plain extends from a point between Minat et Qila and Nabi Yunis in the Gaza sub-district and includes the towns of Haifa and Tel-Aviv, leaving Jaffa as an enclave of the Arab State. The eastern frontier of the Jewish State follows the boundary described in respect of the Arab State.

The Beersheba area comprises the whole of the Beersheba sub-district, including the Negeb and the eastern part of the Gaza sub-district, but excluding the town of Beersheba and those areas described in respect of the Arab State. It includes also a strip of land along the Dead Sea stretching from the Beersheba-Hebron sub-district boundary line to Ein Geddi, as described in respect of the Arab State.

C. The City of Jerusalem

The boundaries of the City of Jerusalem are as defined in the recommendations on the City of Jerusalem. (See Part III, Section B, below).

Part III

City of Jerusalem

A. Special Regime

The City of Jerusalem shall be established as a *corpus separatum* under a special international regime and shall be administered by the United Nations. The Trusteeship Council shall be designated to discharge the responsibilities of the Administering Authority on behalf of the United Nations.

B. Boundaries of the City

The City of Jerusalem shall include the present municipality of Jerusalem plus the surrounding villages and towns, the most eastern of which shall be Abu Dis; the most southern, Bethlehem; the most western, Ein Karim (including also the built-up area of Motsa); and the most northern Shu'fat, as indicated on the attached sketch-map (annex B).

C. Statute of the City

The Trusteeship Council shall, within five months of the approval of the present plan, elaborate and approve a detailed Statute of the City which shall contain *inter alia* the substance of the following provisions:

1. *Government machinery; special objectives.* The Administering Authority in discharging its administrative obligations shall pursue the following special objectives:

(*a*) To protect and to preserve the unique spiritual and religious interests located in the city of the three great monotheistic faiths throughout the world, Christian, Jewish and Moslem; to this end to ensure that order and peace, and especially religious peace, reign in Jerusalem;

(*b*) To foster cooperation among all the inhabitants of the city in their own interests as well as in order to encourage and support the peaceful development of the mutual relations between the two Palestinian peoples throughout the Holy Land; to promote the security, well-being and any constructive measures of development of the residents, having regard to the special circumstances and customs of the various peoples and communities.

2. *Governor and administrative staff.* A Governor of the City of Jerusalem shall be appointed by the Trusteeship Council and shall be responsible to it. He shall be selected on the basis of special qualifications and without regard to nationality. He shall not, however, be a citizen of either State in Palestine.

The Governor shall represent the United Nations in the City and shall exercise on their behalf all powers of administration, including the conduct of external affairs. He shall be assisted by an administrative staff classed as international officers in the meaning of Article 100 of the Charter and chosen whenever practicable from the residents of the city and of the rest of Palestine on a non-discriminatory basis. A detailed plan for the organization of the administration of the city shall be submitted by the Governor to the Trusteeship Council and duly approved by it.

3. *Local autonomy.* (*a*) The existing local autonomous units in the territory of the city (villages, townships and municipalities) shall enjoy wide powers of local government and administration.

(*b*) The Governor shall study and submit for the consideration and decision of the Trusteeship Council a plan for the establishment of special town units consisting, respectively, of the Jewish and Arab sections of new Jerusalem. The new town units shall continue to form part of the present municipality of Jerusalem.

4. *Security measures.* (*a*) The City of Jerusalem shall be demilitarized; its neutrality shall be declared and preserved, and no para-military formations, exercises or activities shall be permitted within its borders.

(*b*) Should the administration of the City of Jerusalem be seriously obstructed or prevented by the non-cooperation or interference of one or more sections of the population, the Governor shall have authority to take such measures as may be necessary to restore the effective functioning of the administration.

(*c*) To assist in the maintenance of internal law and order and especially for the protection of the Holy Places and religious buildings and sites in the city, the Governor shall organize a special police force of adequate strength, the members of which shall be recruited outside of Palestine. The Governor shall be empowered to direct such budgetary provision as may be necessary for the maintenance of this force.

5. *Legislative organization.* A Legislative Council, elected by adult residents of the city irrespective of nationality on the basis of universal and secret suffrage and proportional representation, shall have powers of legislation and taxation. No legislative measures shall, however, conflict or interfere with the provisions which will be set forth in the Statute of the City, nor shall any law, regulation, or official action prevail over them. The Statute shall grant to the Governor a right of vetoing bills inconsistent with the provisions referred to in the preceding sentence. It shall also empower him to promulgate temporary ordinances in case the Council fails to adopt in time a bill deemed essential to the normal functioning of the administration.

6. *Administration of justice.* The Statute shall provide for the establishment of an independent judiciary system, including a court of appeal. All the inhabitants of the City shall be subject to it.

7. *Economic union and economic regime.* The City of Jerusalem shall be included in the Economic Union of Palestine and be bound by all stipulations of the undertaking and of any treaties issued therefrom, as well as by the decisions of the Joint Economic Board. The headquarters of the Economic Board shall be established in the territory of the City.

The Statute shall provide for the regulation of economic matters not falling within the regime of the Economic Union, on the basis of equal treatment and non-discrimination for all Members of the United Nations and their nationals.

8. *Freedom of transit and visit; control of residents.* Subject to considerations of security, and of economic welfare as determined by the Governor under the directions of the Trusteeship Council, freedom of entry into, and residence within, the borders of the City shall be guaranteed for the residents or citizens of the Arab and Jewish States. Immigration into, and residence within, the borders of the city for nationals of other States shall be controlled by the Governor under the directions of the Trusteeship Council.

9. *Relations with the Arab and Jewish States.* Representatives of the Arab and Jewish States shall be accredited to the Governor of the City and charged with the protection of the interests of their States and nationals in connexion with the international administration of the City.

10. *Official languages.* Arabic and Hebrew shall be the official languages of the city. This will not preclude the adoption of one or more additional working languages, as may be required.

11. *Citizenship.* All the residents shall become *ipso facto* citizens of the City of Jerusalem unless they opt for citizenship of the State of which they have been citizens or, if Arabs or Jews, have filed notice of intention to become citizens of the Arab or Jewish State respectively, according to part I, section B, paragraph 9, of this plan.

The Trusteeship Council shall make arrangements for consular protection of the citizens of the City outside its territory.

12. *Freedoms of citizens.* (*a*) Subject only to the requirements of public order and morals, the inhabitants of the City shall be ensured the enjoyment of human rights and fundamental freedoms, including freedom of conscience, religion and worship, language, education, speech and Press, assembly and association, and petition.

(*b*) No discrimination of any kind shall be made between the inhabitants on the grounds of race, religion, language or sex.

(*c*) All persons within the City shall be entitled to equal protection of the laws.

(*d*) The family law and personal status of the various persons and communities and their religious interests, including endowments, shall be respected.

(*e*) Except as may be required for the maintenance of public order and good government, no measure shall be taken to obstruct or interfere with the enterprise of religious or charitable bodies of all faiths or to discriminate against any representative or member of these bodies on the ground of his religion or nationality.

(*f*) The City shall ensure adequate primary and secondary education for the Arab and Jewish communities respectively, in their own languages and in accordance with their cultural traditions.

The right of each community to maintain its own schools for the education of its own members in its own language, while conforming to such educational requirements of a general nature as the City may impose, shall not be denied or impaired. Foreign educational establishments shall continue their activity on the basis of their existing rights.

(*g*) No restriction shall be imposed on the free use by any inhabitant of the City of any language in private intercourse, in commerce, in religion, in the Press or in publications of any kind, or at public meetings.

13. *Holy Places.* (*a*) Existing rights in respect of Holy Places and religious buildings or sites shall not be denied or impaired.

(*b*) Free access to the Holy Places and religious buildings or sites and the free exercise of worship shall be secured in conformity with existing rights and subject to the requirements of public order and decorum.

(*c*) Holy Places and religious buildings or sites shall be preserved. No act shall be permitted which may in any way impair their sacred character. If at any time it appears to the Governor that any particular Holy Place, religious building or site is in need of urgent repair, the Governor may call upon the community or communities concerned to carry out such repair. The Governor may carry it out himself at the expense of the community or communities concerned if no action is taken within a reasonable time.

(*d*) No taxation shall be levied in respect of any Holy Place, religious building or site which was exempt from taxation on the date of the creation of the City. No change in the incidence of such taxation shall be made which would either discriminate between the owners or occupiers of Holy Places, religious buildings or sites, or would place such owners or occupiers in a position less favourable in relation to the general incidence of taxation than existed at the time of the adoption of the Assembly's recommendations.

14. *Special powers of the Governor in respect of the Holy Places, religious buildings and sites in the City and in any part of Palestine.* (*a*) The protection of the Holy Places, religious buildings and sites located in the City of Jerusalem shall be a special concern of the Governor.

(*b*) With relation to such places, buildings and sites in Palestine outside the city, the Governor shall determine, on the ground of powers granted to him by the Constitutions of both States, whether the provisions of the Constitutions of the Arab and Jewish States in Palestine dealing therewith and the religious rights appertaining thereto are being properly applied and respected.

(*c*) The Governor shall also be empowered to make decisions on the basis of existing rights in cases of disputes which may arise between the different religious communities or the rites of a religious community in respect of the Holy Places, religious buildings and sites in any part of Palestine.

In this task he may be assisted by a consultative council of representatives of different denominations acting in an advisory capacity.

D. Duration of the Special Regime

The Statute elaborated by the Trusteeship Council on the aforementioned principles shall come into force not later than 1 October 1948. It shall remain in force in the first instance for a period of ten years, unless the Trusteeship Council finds it necessary to undertake a re-examination of these provisions at an earlier date. After the expiration of this period the whole scheme shall be subject to re-examination by the Trusteeship Council in the light of the experience acquired with its functioning. The residents of the City shall be then free to express by means of a referendum their wishes as to possible modifications of the regime of the City.

Part IV

Capitulations

States whose nationals have in the past enjoyed in Palestine the privileges and immunities of foreigners, including the benefits of consular jurisdiction and protection, as formerly enjoyed by capitulation or usage in the Ottoman Empire, are invited to renounce any right pertaining to them to the reestablishment of such privileges and immunities in the proposed Arab and Jewish States and the City of Jerusalem.

186 (S-2). Appointment and Terms of Reference of a United Nations Mediator in Palestine

Committee: 1
Vote: 31 - 7 - 16
Ref.: 189(S-2)

The General Assembly,
Taking account of the present situation in regard to Palestine,

I

Strongly affirms its support of the efforts of the Security Council to secure a truce in Palestine and calls upon all Governments, organizations and persons to cooperate in making effective such a truce;

II

1. *Empowers* a United Nations Mediator in Palestine, to be chosen by a committee of the General Assembly composed of representatives of China, France, the Union of Soviet Socialist Republics, the United Kingdom and the United States of America, to exercise the following functions:

(*a*) To use his good offices with the local and community authorities in Palestine to:

(i) Arrange for the operation of common services necessary to the safety and well-being of the population of Palestine;

(ii) Assure the protection of the Holy Places, religious buildings and sites in Palestine;

(iii) Promote a peaceful adjustment of the future situation of Palestine;

(*b*) To cooperate with the Truce Commission for Palestine appointed by the Security Council in its resolution of 23 April 1948;[1]

(*c*) To invite, as seems to him advisable, with a view to the promotion of the welfare of the inhabitants of Palestine, the assistance and cooperation of appropriate specialized agencies of the United Nations, such as the World Health Organization, of the International Red Cross, and of other governmental or non-governmental organizations of a humanitarian and non-political character;

2. *Instructs* the United Nations Mediator to render progress reports monthly, or more frequently as he deems necessary, to the Security Council and to the Secretary-General for transmission to the Members of the United Nations;

3. *Directs* the United Nations Mediator to conform in his activities with the provisions of this resolution, and with such instructions as the General Assembly or the Security Council may issue;

4. *Authorizes* the Secretary-General to pay the United Nations Mediator an emolument equal to that paid to the President of the International Court of Justice, and to provide the Mediator with the necessary staff to assist in carrying out the functions assigned to the Mediator by the General Assembly;

III

Relieves the Palestine Commission from the further exercise of responsibilities under resolution 181 (II) of 29 November 1947.[2]

Hundred and thirty-fifth plenary meeting
14 May 1948

187 (S-2). Protection of the City of Jerusalem and its Inhabitants: Appointment of a Special Municipal Commissioner

Committee: -
Vote: 35 - 0 - 17
Ref.: 185(S-2)

The General Assembly,
Having asked the Trusteeship Council to study, with the Mandatory Power and the interested parties, suitable measures for the protection of the city of Jerusalem and its inhabitants and to submit within the shortest possible time proposals to the General Assembly to that effect,

Takes note of the conclusions and recommendations of the Trusteeship Council, as set forth in its report[3] to the General Assembly on the protection of the city of Jerusalem and its inhabitants;

Approves these conclusions and recommendations;

Recommends that the Mandatory Power appoint under Palestine legislation, before 15 May 1948, a neutral acceptable to both Arabs and Jews, as Special Municipal Commissioner, who shall, with the cooperation of the community committees already existing in Jerusalem, carry out the functions hitherto performed by the Municipal Commission;

Decides that continuing urgent attention should be given by the First Committee or its subsidiary bodies to the question of further measures for the protection of the city of Jerusalem and its inhabitants.

Hundred and thirty-fourth plenary meeting
6 May 1948

194 (III). Palestine-Progress Report of the United Nations Mediator

Committee: 1
Vote: 35 - 15 - 8
Ref.: 512(VI), 394(V)

The General Assembly,
Having considered further the situation in Palestine,

1. *Expresses* its deep appreciation of the progress achieved through the good offices of the late United Nations Mediator in promoting a peaceful adjustment of the future situation of Palestine, for which cause he sacrificed his life; and

Extends its thanks to the Acting Mediator and his stall for their continued efforts and devotion to duty in Palestine;

2. *Establishes* a conciliation Commission consisting of three State members of the United Nations which shall have the following functions;

(*a*) To assume, in so far as it considers necessary in existing; circumstances, the functions given to the United Nations Mediator on Palestine by resolution 186 (S-2) of the General Assembly of 18 May 1948;

(*b*) To carry out the specific functions and directories given to it by the present resolution and such additional functions and directives as may be given to it by the General Assembly or by the Security Council:

(*c*) To undertake, upon the request of the Security Council, any of the functions now assigned to the United Nations Mediator on Palestine

1 See document S/727.

2 See *Official Records of the second session of the General Assembly, Resolutions*, No. 181 (II), p. 322.

3 See document A/544. See apendix 14, p. 503.

or to the United Nations Truce Commission by resolutions of the Security Council; upon such request to the Conciliation Commission by the Security Council with respect to all the remaining functions of the United Nations Mediator on Palestine under Security Council resolutions, the office of the Mediator shall be terminated;

3. *Decides* that a Committee of the Assembly, consisting of China, France, the Union of Soviet Socialist Republics, the United Kingdom and the United States of America, shall present, before the end of the first part of the present session of the General Assembly, for the approval of the Assembly, a proposal concerning the names of the three States which will constitute the Conciliation Commission;

4. *Requests* the Commission to begin its functions at once, with a view to the establishment of contact between the parties themselves and the Commission at the earliest possible date;

5. *Calls upon* the Governments and authorities concerned to extend the scope of the negotiations provided for in the Security Council's resolution of 16 November 1948[1] and to seek agreement by negotiations conducted either with the Conciliation Commission or directly, with a view to the final settlement of all questions outstanding between them;

6. *Instructs* the Conciliation Commission to take steps to assist the Governments and authorities concerned to achieve a final settlement of all questions outstanding between them;

7. *Resolves* that the Holy Places - including Nazareth - religious buildings and sites in Palestine should be protected and free access to them assured, in accordance with existing rights and historical practice; that arrangements to this end should be under effective United Nations supervision; that the United Nations Conciliation Commission, in presenting to the fourth regular session of the General Assembly its detailed proposals for a permanent international regime for the territory of Jerusalem, should include recommendations concerning the Holy Places in that territory; that with regard to the Holy Places in the rest of Palestine the Commission should call upon the political authorities of the areas concerned to give appropriate formal guarantees as to the protection of the Holy Places and access to them; and that these undertakings should be presented o the General Assembly for approval;

8. *Resolves* that, in view of its association with three world religions, the Jerusalem area, including the present municipality of Jerusalem plus the surrounding villages and towns, the most eastern of which shall be Abu Dis; the most southern, Bethlehem; the most western, Ein Karim (including also the built-up area of Motsa); and the most northern, Shu'fat, should be accorded special and separate treatment from the rest of Palestine and should be placed under effective United Nations control;

Requests the Security Council to take further steps to ensure the demilitarization of Jerusalem at the earliest possible date;

Instructs the Conciliation Commission to present to the fourth regular session of the General Assembly detailed proposals for a permanent international regime for the Jerusalem area which will provide for the maximum local autonomy for distinctive groups consistent with the special international status of the Jerusalem area;

The Conciliation Commission is authorized to appoint a United Nations representative, who shall cooperate with the local authorities with respect to the interim administration of the Jerusalem area;

9. *Resolves* that, pending agreement on more detailed arrangements among the Governments and authorities concerned, the freest possible access to Jerusalem by road, rail or air should be accorded to all inhabitants of Palestine;

Instructs the Conciliation Commission to report immediately to the Security Council, for appropriate action by that organ, any attempt by any party to impede such access;

10. *Instructs* the Conciliation Commission to seek arrangements among the Governments and authorities concerned which will facilitate the economic development of the area, including arrangements for access to ports and airfields and the use of transportation and communication facilities;

11. *Resolves* that the refugees wishing to return to their homes and live at peace with their neighbours should be permitted to do so at the earliest practicable date, and that compensation should be paid for the property of those choosing not to return and for 1055 of or damage to property which, under principles of international law or in equity, should be made good by the Governments or authorities responsible;

Instructs the Conciliation Commission to facilitate the repatriation, resettlement and economic and social rehabilitation of the refugees and the payment of compensation, and to maintain close relations with the Director of the United Nations Relief for Palestine Refugees and, through him, with the appropriate organs and agencies of the United Nations;

12. *Authorizes* the Conciliation Commission to appoint such subsidiary bodies and to employ such technical experts, acting under its authority, as it mar find necessary for the effective discharge of its functions and responsibilities under the present resolution;

The Conciliation Commission will have its official headquarters at Jerusalem. The authorities responsible for maintaining order in Jerusalem will be responsible for taking all measures necessary to ensure the security of the Commission. The Secretary-General will provide a limited number of guards for the protection of the staff and premises of the Commission;

13. *Instructs* the Conciliation Commission to render progress reports periodically to the Secretary-General for transmission to the Security Council and to the Members of the United Nations;

14. *Calls upon* all Governments and authorities concerned to cooperate with the Conciliation Commission and to take all possible steps to assist in the implementation of the present resolution;

15. *Requests* the Secretary-General to provide the necessary staff and facilities and to make appropriate arrangements to provide the necessary funds required in carrying out the terms of the present resolution.

Hundred and eighty sixth plenary meeting
11 December 1948

303 (IV). Palestine: Question of an International Regime for the Jerusalem Area and the Protection of the Holy Places

Committee: P
Vote: 38 - 14 - 7

The General Assembly,

Having regard to its resolutions 181 (II) of 29 November 1947 and 194 (III) of 11 December 1948,

Having studied the reports of the United Nations Conciliation Commission for Palestine set up under the latter resolution,

I. *Decides*

In relation to Jerusalem,

Believing that the principles underlying its previous resolutions concerning this matter, and in particular its resolution of 29 November 1947, represent a just and equitable settlement of the question,

1. To restate, therefore, its intention that Jerusalem should be placed under a permanent international regime, which should envisage appropriate guarantees for the protection of the Holy Places, both within and outside Jerusalem, and to confirm specifically the following provisions of General Assembly resolution 181 (II): (1) the City of Jerusalem shall be established as a *corpus separatum* under a special international regime and shall be administered by the United Nations. (2) the Trusteeship Council shall be designated to discharge the responsibilities of the Administering Authority ...; and (3) the City of Jerusalem shall include the present municipality of Jerusalem plus the surrounding villages and towns, the most eastern of which shall be Abu Dis; the most southern, Bethlehem; the most western,

[1] See *Official Records of the Security Council,* Third Year, No. 126.

Ein Karim (including also the built-up area of Motsa); and the most northern, Shu'fat, as indicated on the attached sketch-map;[1]

2. To request for this purpose that the Trusteeship Council at its next session, whether special or regular, complete the preparation of the Statute of Jerusalem,[2] omitting the now inapplicable provisions, such as articles 32 and 39, and, without prejudice to the fundamental principles of the international regime for Jerusalem set forth in General Assembly resolution 181 (II) introducing therein amendments in the direction of its greater democratization, approve the Statute, and proceed immediately with its implementation. The Trusteeship Council shall not allow any actions taken by any interested Government or Governments to divert it from adopting and implementing the Statute of Jerusalem;

II. *Calls upon* the States concerned to make formal undertakings, at an early date and in the light of their obligations as Members of the United Nations, that they will approach these matters with good will and be guided by the terms of the present resolution.

275th plenary meeting
9 December 1949

2253 (ES-V). Measures Taken by Israel to Change the Status of the City of Jerusalem

Committee: -
Vote: 99 - 0 - 20

The General Assembly,

Deeply concerned at the situation prevailing in Jerusalem as a result of the measures taken by Israel to change the status of the City,

1. *Considers* that these measures are invalid;

2. *Calls upon* Israel to rescind all measures already taken and to desist forthwith from taking any action which would alter the status of Jerusalem;

3. *Requests* the Secretary-General to report to the General Assembly and the Security Council on the situation and on the implementation of the present resolution not later than one week from its adoption.

1548th plenary meeting
4 July 1967

2254 (ES-V). Measures Taken by Israel to Change the Status of the City of Jerusalem

Committee: -
Vote: 99 - 0 - 18

The General Assembly,

Recalling its resolution 2253 (ES-V) of 4 July 1967,

Having received the report submitted by the Secretary-General,[3]

Taking note with the deepest regret and concern of the non-compliance by Israel with resolution 2253 (ES-V),

1. *Deplores* the failure of Israel to implement General Assembly resolution 2253 (ES-V);

2. *Reiterates* its call to Israel in that resolution to rescind all measures already taken and to desist forthwith from taking any action which would alter the status of Jerusalem;

3. *Requests* the Secretary-General to report to the Security Council and the General Assembly on the situation and on the implementation of the present resolution.

1554th plenary meeting
14 July 1967

1 For the map see *Official Records of the General Assembly, Second Session*, resolution 181 (II), annex.

2 See *Official Records of the second session of the Trusteeship Council*, Third Part, Annex, p. 4.

3 A/6753. For the printed text of this document, see *Official Records of the Security Council, Twenty-second Year, Supplement for July, August and September 1967,* document S/8052.

32/5. Recent Illegal Israeli Measures in the Occupied Arab Territories Designed to Change the Legal Status, Geographical Nature and Demographic Composition of those Territories in Contravention of the Principles of the Charter of the United Nations, of Israel's International Obligations under the Fourth Geneva Convention of 1949 and of United Nations Resolutions, and Obstruction of Efforts Aimed at Achieving a Just and Lasting Peace in the Middle East

Committee: -
Vote: 131 - 1 - 7

The General Assembly,

Stressing the urgent need to achieve a just and lasting peace in the Middle East,

Expressing grave anxiety and concern over the present serious situation in the occupied Arab territories as a result of the continued Israeli occupation and the measures and actions taken by the Government of Israel, as the occupying Power, and designed to change the legal status, geographical nature and demographic composition of those territories,

Considering that the Geneva Convention relative to the Protection of Civilian Persons in Time of War, of 12 August 1949,[4] is applicable to all the Arab territories occupied since 5 June 1967,

1. *Determines* that all such measures and actions taken by Israel in the Palestinian and other Arab territories occupied since 1967 have no legal validity and constitute a serious obstruction of efforts aimed at achieving a just and lasting peace in the Middle East;

2. *Strongly deplores* the persistence of Israel in carrying out such measures, in particular the establishment of settlements in the occupied Arab territories;

3. *Calls upon* Israel to comply strictly with its international obligations in accordance with the principles of international law and the provisions of the Geneva Convention relative to the Protection of Civilian Persons in Time of War, of 12 August 1949;

4. *Calls once more upon* the Government of Israel, as the occupying Power, to desist forthwith from taking any action which would result in changing the legal status, geographical nature or demographic composition of the Arab territories occupied since 1967, including Jerusalem;

5. *Urges* all States parties to the Geneva Convention relative to the Protection of Civilian Persons in Time of War to ensure respect for and compliance with its provisions in all the Arab territories occupied by Israel since 1967, including Jerusalem;

6. *Requests* the Secretary-General:

(*a*) To undertake urgent contacts with the Government of Israel to ensure the prompt implementation of the present resolution;

(*b*) To submit a report to the General Assembly and the Security Council, not later than 31 December 1977, on the results of his contacts;

7. *Requests* the Security Council to review the situation in the light of the present resolution and of the report of the Secretary-General.

52nd plenary meeting
28 October 1977

3236 (XXIX). Question of Palestine

Committee: -
Vote: 89 - 7 - 37
Ref.: 3376(XXX)

The General Assembly,

Having considered the question of Palestine,

Having heard the statement of the Palestine Liberation Organization, the representative of the Palestinian people,[5]

4 United Nations, *Treaty Series*, vol. 75, No. 973, p. 287.

5 *Official Records of the General Assembly, Twenty-ninth Session, Plenary Meetings,* 2282nd meeting, paras. 3-83.

Having also heard other statements made during the debate,

Deeply concerned that no just solution to the problem of Palestine has yet been achieved and recognizing that the problem of Palestine continues to endanger international peace and security,

Recognizing that the Palestinian people is entitled to self-determination in accordance with the Charter of the United Nations,

Expressing its grave concern that the Palestinian people has been prevented from enjoying its inalienable rights, in particular its right to self-determination,

Guided by the purposes and principles of the Charter,

Recalling its relevant resolutions which affirm the right of the Palestinian people to self-determination,

1. *Reaffirms* the inalienable rights of the Palestinian people in Palestine, including:

(*a*) The right to self-determination without external interference;

(*b*) The right to national independence and sovereignty;

2. *Reaffirms also* the inalienable right of the Palestinians to return to their homes and property from which they have been displaced and uprooted, and calls for their return;

3. *Emphasizes* that full respect for and the realization of these inalienable rights of the Palestinian people are indispensable for the solution of the question of Palestine;

4. *Recognizes* that the Palestinian people is a principal party in the establishment of a just and lasting peace in the Middle East;

5. *Further recognizes* the right of the Palestinian people to regain its rights by all means in accordance with the purposes and principles of the Charter of the United Nations;

6. *Appeals* to all States and international organizations to extend their support to the Palestinian people in its struggle to restore its rights, in accordance with the Charter;

7. *Requests* the Secretary-General to establish contacts with the Palestine Liberation Organization on all matters concerning the question of Palestine;

8. *Requests* the Secretary-General to report to the General Assembly at its thirtieth session on the implementation of the present resolution;

9. *Decides* to include the item entitled "Question of Palestine" in the provisional agenda of its thirtieth session.

2296th plenary meeting
22 November 1974

ES-7/2. Question of Palestine

Committee: -
Vote: 112 - 7 - 24

The General Assembly,

Having considered the question of Palestine at an emergency special session,

Convinced that the failure to solve this question poses a grave threat to international peace and security,

Noting with regret and concern that the Security Council, at its 2220th meeting on 30 April 1980, failed to take a decision, as a result of the negative vote of the United States of America, on the recommendations of the Committee on the Exercise of the Inalienable Rights of the Palestinian People endorsed by the General Assembly in its resolutions 31/20 of 24 November 1976, 32/40 A of 2 December 1977, 33/28 A of 7 December 1978 and 34/65 A of 29 November 1979,

Having considered the letter dated 1 July 1980 from the Permanent Representative of Senegal to the United Nations, Chairman of the Committee on the Exercise of the Inalienable Rights of the Palestinian People,[1]

Having heard the statement by the Observer of the Palestine Liberation Organization, the representative of the Palestinian people,[2]

1. *Recalls and reaffirms* its resolutions 3236 (XXIX) and 3237 (XXIX) of 22 November 1974 and all other relevant United Nations resolutions pertinent to the question of Palestine;

2. *Reaffirms*, in particular, that a comprehensive, just and lasting peace in the Middle East cannot be established, in accordance with the Charter of the United Nations and the relevant United Nations resolutions, without the withdrawal of Israel from all the occupied Palestinian and other Arab territories, including Jerusalem, and without the achievement of a just solution of the problem of Palestine on the basis of the attainment of the inalienable rights of the Palestinian people in Palestine;

3. *Reaffirms* the inalienable right of the Palestinians to return to their homes and property in Palestine, from which they have been displaced and uprooted, and calls for their return;

4. *Reaffirms* also the inalienable rights in Palestine of the Palestinian people, including:

(*a*) The right to self-determination without external interference, and to national independence and sovereignty;

(*b*) The right to establish its own independent sovereign State;

5. *Reaffirms* the right of the Palestine Liberation Organization, the representative of the Palestinian people, to participate on an equal footing in all efforts, deliberations and conferences on the question of Palestine and the situation in the Middle East within the framework of the United Nations;

6. *Reaffirms* the fundamental principle of the inadmissibility of the acquisition of territory by force;

7. *Calls upon* Israel to withdraw completely and unconditionally from all the Palestinian and other Arab territories occupied since June 1967, including Jerusalem, with all property and services intact, and urges that such withdrawal from all the occupied territories should start before 15 November 1980;

8. *Demands* that Israel should fully comply with provisions of resolution 465 (1980) adopted unanimously by the Security Council on 1 March 1980;

9. *Further demands* that Israel should fully comply with all United Nations resolutions relevant to the historic character of the Holy City of Jerusalem, in particular Security Council resolution 476 (1980) of 30 June 1980;

10. *Expresses its opposition* to all policies and plans aimed at the resettlement of the Palestinians outside their homeland;

11. *Requests and authorizes* the Secretary-General, in consultation, as appropriate, with the Committee on the Exercise of the Inalienable Rights of the Palestinian People, to take the necessary measures towards the implementation of the recommendations contained in paragraphs 59 to 72 of the report of the Committee to the General Assembly at its thirty-first session[3] as a basis for the solution of the question of Palestine;

12. *Requests* the Secretary-General to report to the General Assembly at its thirty-fifth session on the implementation of the present resolution;

13. *Requests* the Security Council, in the event of non-compliance by Israel with the present resolution, to convene in order to consider the situation and the adoption of effective measure under Chapter VII of the Charter;

14. *Decides* to adjourn the seventh emergency special session temporarily and to authorize the President of the latest regular session of the General Assembly to resume its meetings upon request from Member States.

11th plenary meeting
29 July 1980

---

1 *Official Records of the General Assembly, Seventh Emergency Special Session*, Annexes, agenda item 5, document A/ES-7/13.

2 *Ibid., Plenary Meetings*, 1st meeting, paras. 171-217.

3 *Ibid., Thirty-first Session, Supplement No.* 35 (A/31/35).

ES-9/1. The Situation in the Occupied Arab Territories

Committee: -
Vote: 86 - 21 - 34
Ref.: 34/29

The General Assembly,

Having considered the item entitled "The situation in the occupied Arab territories" at its ninth emergency special session, in accordance with Security Council resolution 500 (1982) of 28 January 1982,

Noting with regret and concern that the Security Council, at its 2329th meeting, on 20 January 1982, failed to take appropriate measures against Israel, as requested by the Council in resolution 497 (1981) of 17 December 1981, as a result of the negative vote of a permanent member of the Council,

Recalling Security Council resolution 497 (1981);

Recalling its resolution 35/122 E of 11 December 1980,

Reaffirming its resolution 36/226 B of 17 December 1981,

Having considered the reports of the Secretary-General of 21 December 1981,[1] and 31 December 1981,[2]

Recalling its resolution 3314 (XXIX) of 14 December 1974, in which it defined an act of aggression as, *inter alia*, "the invasion or attack by the armed forces of a State of the territory of another State, or any military occupation, however temporary, resulting from such invasion or attack, or any annexation by the use of force of the territory of another State or part thereof", and provided that "no consideration of whatever nature, whether political, economic, military or otherwise, may serve as justification for aggression",

Stressing once again that the acquisition of territory by force is inadmissible under the Charter of the United Nations, the principles of international law and relevant United Nations resolutions,

Reaffirming once more the applicability of the Geneva Convention relative to the Protection of Civilian Persons in Time of War, of 12 August 1949,[3] to the occupied Syrian territory,

Noting that Israel's record and actions establish conclusively that it is not a peace-loving Member State and that it has not carried out its obligations under the Charter,

Noting further that Israel has refused, in violation of Article 25 of the Charter, to accept and carry out the numerous relevant decisions of the Security Council, the latest being resolution 497 (1981),

1. *Strongly condemns* Israel for its failure to comply with Security Council resolution 497 (1981) and General Assembly resolution 36/226 B;

2. *Declares* that Israel's decision of 14 December 1981 to impose its laws, jurisdiction and administration on the occupied Syrian Golan Heights constitutes an act of aggression under the provisions of Article 39 of the Charter of the United Nations and General Assembly resolution 3314 (XXIX);

3. *Declares* once more that Israel's decision to impose its laws, jurisdiction and administration on the occupied Syrian Golan Heights is null and void and has no legal validity and/or effect whatsoever;

4. *Determines* that all actions taken by Israel to give effect to its decision relating to the occupied Syrian Golan Heights are illegal and invalid and shall not be recognized;

5. *Reaffirms* its determination that all the provisions of the Hague Conventions of 1907[4] and the Geneva Convention relative to the Protection of Civilian Persons in Time of War, of 12 August 1949, continue to apply to the Syrian territory occupied by Israel since 1967, and calls upon all parties thereto to respect and ensure respect of their obligations under these instruments in all circumstances;

6. *Determines* that the continued occupation of the Syrian Golan Heights since 1967 and its effective annexation by Israel on 14 December 1981, following Israel's decision to impose its laws, jurisdiction and administration on that territory, constitute a continuing threat to international peace and security;

7. *Strongly deplores* the negative vote by a permanent member of the Security Council which prevented the Council from adopting against Israel, under Chapter VII of the Charter, the "appropriate measures" refereed to in resolution 497 (1981) unanimously adopted by the Council;

8. *Further deplores* any political, economic, military and technological support to Israel that encourages Israel to commit acts of aggression and to consolidate and perpetuate its occupation and annexation of occupied Arab territories;

9. *Firmly emphasizes* its demands that Israel, the occupying Power, rescind forthwith its decision of 14 December 1981 to impose its laws, jurisdiction and administration on the Syrian Golan Heights, which has resulted in the effective annexation of that territory;

10. *Reaffirms* the overriding necessity of the total and unconditional withdrawal by Israel from all the Palestinian and other Arab territories occupied since 1967, including Jerusalem, which is a primary requirement for the establishment of a comprehensive and just peace in the Middle East;

11. *Declares* that Israel's record and actions confirm that it is not a peace-loving Member State and that it has carried out neither its obligations under the Chatter nor its commitment under General Assembly resolution 273 (III) of 11 May 1949;

12. *Calls upon* all Member States to apply the following measures:

(*a*) To refrain from supplying Israel with any weapons and related equipment and to suspend any military assistance which Israel receives from them;

(*b*) To refrain from acquiring any weapons or military equipment from Israel;

(*c*) To suspend economic, financial and technological assistance to and cooperation with Israel;

(*d*) To sever diplomatic, trade and cultural relations with Israel;

13. *Also calls upon* all Member States to cease forthwith, individually and collectively, all dealings with Israel in order totally to isolate it in all fields;

14 *Urges* non-member States to act in accordance with the provisions of the present resolution;

15 *Calls upon* all specialized agencies of the United Nations system and international institutions to conform their relations with Israel to the terms of the present resolution;

16. *Requests* the Secretary-General to follow up the implementation of the present resolution and to report thereon at intervals of two months to Member States as well as to the Security Council and to submit a comprehensive report to the General Assembly at its thirty-seventh session under the item entitled "The situation in the Middle East"

12th plenary meeting
5 February 1982

38/144. Permanent Sovereignty over National Resources in the Occupied Palestinian and other Arab Territories

Committee: 2
Vote: 120 - 2 - 18
Ref.: 37/135, 36/173, 35/110, 34/136, 32/161, 31/186, 3516(XXX), 3336(XXIX)

The General Assembly,

Recalling its resolution 37/135 of 17 December 1982,

Recalling also its previous resolutions on permanent sovereignty over natural resources,

---

1 A/36/846 and Corr.1-S/14805 and Corr.1. For the printed text, see *Official Records of the Security Council, Thirty-sixth Year, Supplement for October, November and December 1981*, document S/14805.

2 *Official Records of the Security Council, Thirty-sixth Year, Supplement for October, November and December 1981*, S/14821.

3 United Nations, *Treaty Series*, vol. 75, No. 973, p. 287.

4 Carnegie Endowment for International Peace, *The Hague Conventions and Declarations of 1899 and 1907* (New York, Oxford University Press, 1915).

Bearing in mind the relevant principles of international law and the provisions of the international conventions and regulations, in particular Convention IV of The Hague of 1907,[1] and the Geneva Convention Relative to the Protection of Civilian Persons in Time of War, of 12 August 1949,[2] concerning the obligations and responsibilities of the occupying Power,

Bearing in mind also the pertinent of its resolutions 3201 (S-VI) and 3202 (S-VI) of May 1974, containing the Declaration and the Programme of Action on the Establishment of a New International Economic Order, and 3281 (XXIX) of 12 December 1974, containing the Charter of Economic Rights and Duties of States,

1. *Takes note* of the report of the Secretary-General on permanent sovereignty over national resources in the occupied Palestinian and other Arab territories;[3]

2. *Commends* the report of the Secretary-General on the implications, under international law, of the United Nations resolutions on permanent sovereignty over natural resources, on the occupied Palestinian and other Arab territories and on the obligations of Israel concerning its conduct in these territories;[4]

3. *Condemns* Israel for its exploitation of the national resources of the occupied Palestinian and other Arab territories;

4. *Reaffirms* that Convention IV of The Hague of 1907 and the Geneva Convention Relative to the Protection of Civilian Persons in Time of War, of 12 August 1949, are applicable to the occupied Palestinian and other Arab territories;

5. *Emphasizes* the right of the Palestinian and other Arab peoples whose territories are under Israeli occupation to full and effective permanent sovereignty and control over their natural and all other resources, wealth and economic activities;

6. *Also reaffirms* that all measures undertaken by Israel to exploit the human, natural and all other resources, wealth and economic activities in the occupied Palestinian and other Arab territories are illegal, and calls upon Israel to desist immediately from such measures;

7. *Further reaffirms* the right of the Palestinian and other Arab peoples subjected to Israeli aggression and occupation to the restitution of, and full compensation for the exploitation, depletion and loss of and damage to, their natural, human and all other resources, wealth and economic activities, and calls upon Israel to meet their just claims;

8. *Calls upon* all States to support the Palestinian and other Arab peoples in the exercise of their abovementioned rights;

9. *Calls upon* all States, international organizations, spezialized agencies, business corporations and all other institutions not to recognize, or cooperate with or assist in exploit the national resources of the occupied Palestinian and other Arab territories or to effect any charges in the demographic composition, the character and form of use of their natural resources or the institutional structure of those territories;

10. *Requests* the Secretary-General to elaborate on his report[5] in order to cover also, in detail, the resources exploited by the Israeli settlements and the Israeli-imposed regulations and policies hampering the economic development of the occupied Palestinian and other Arab territories, including a comparison between the practices of Israel and its obligations under international law;

11. *Also requests* the Secretary-General to submit the detailed report to the General Assembly at its thirty-ninth session, through the Economic and Social Council.

102nd plenary meeting
19 December 1983

1 Carnegie Endowment for International Peace, *The Hague Conventions and Declarations of 1899 and 1907* (New York, Oxford University Press, 1915), p. 100.

2 United Nations, *Treaty Series,* vol. 75, No. 973, p. 287.

3 A/38/282-E/1983/84.

4 A/38/265-E/1983/85.

5 A/38/265-E/1983/85.

39/101. Israel's Decision to Build a Canal Linking the Mediterranean Sea to the Dead Sea

Committee: P
Vote: 143 - 2 - 1

The General Assembly,

Recalling its resolutions 36/150 of 16 December 1981, 37/122 of 16 December 1982 and 38/85 of 15 December 1983,

Recalling the rules and principles of international law relative to the fundamental rights and duties of States,

Bearing in mind the principles of international law relative to belligerent occupation of land, including the Geneva Convention relative to the Protection of Civilian Persons in Time of War, of 12 August 1949,[6] and reaffirming their applicability to all Arab territories occupied since 1967, including Jerusalem,

Having considered the report of the Secretary-General,[7]

Recognizing that the proposed canal, to be constructed partly through the Gaza Strip, a Palestinian territory occupied in 1967, would violate the principles of international law and affect the interests of the Palestinian people,

Confident that the canal linking the Mediterranean Sea with the Dead Sea, if constructed by Israel, will cause direct, serious and irreparable damage to Jordan's rights and legitimate and vital interests in the economic, agricultural, demographic and ecological fields,

Deeply concerned at the digging activities in the Dead Sea area at the envisaged site of that end of the canal,

Noting with regret the non-compliance by Israel with General Assembly resolution 36/150,

1. *Deplores* Israel's non-compliance with General Assembly resolutions 37/122 and 38/85 and its refusal to receive the team of experts;

2. *Emphasizes* that the canal linking the Mediterranean Sea with the Dead Sea, if constructed, is a violation of the rules and principles of international law, especially those relating to the fundamental rights and duties of States and to belligerent occupation of land;

3. *Demands once again* that Israel not construct this canal and cease forthwith all actions taken and/or digging plans made towards the execution of this project;

4. *Calls upon* all States, specialized agencies and governmental and non-governmental organizations not to assist, directly or indirectly, in the preparation and execution of this project, and strongly urges national, international and multinational corporations to do likewise;

5. *Requests* the Secretary-General to monitor and assess, on a continuing basis and through a competent expert organ, all aspects - juridical, political, economic, ecological and demographic - of the adverse effects on Jordan and on the Arab territories occupied since 1967, including Jerusalem, arising from the implementation of the Israeli decision to construct this canal and to forward the findings of that organ on a regular basis to the General Assembly;

6. *Requests* the Secretary-General to report to the General Assembly at its fortieth session on the implementation of the present resolution;

7. *Decides* to include in the provisional agenda of its fortieth session the item entitled "Israel's decision to build a canal linking the Mediterranean Sea to the Dead Sea".

100th plenary meeting
14 December 1984

6 United Nations, *Treaty Series,* vol. 75, No. 973, p. 287.

7 A/39/142.

46/46. United Nations Relief and Works Agency for Palestine Refugees in the Near East

Committee: s
Vote: A: 137 - 0 - 1; B: adopted without a vote; C: adopted without a vote; D: 147 - 0 - 1; E: 143 - 2 0; F: 115 - 21 - 13; G: 115 - 2 - 32; H: 114 - 2 - 33; I: 147 - 2 - 2; J: 146 - 2 - 2; K: 151 - 2 - 0
Ref.: 50/28, 49/35, 48/40, 47/69, 45/73, 44/47, 43/57, 42/69, 41/69, 40/165, 39/99, 38/83, 37/120, 36/146, 35/13, 34/52, 33/112, 32/90, 31/15, 3419(XXX), 3331(XXIX), 3330(XXIX), 3089(XXVIII), 2969(XXVII), 2963(XXVII), 2792(XXVI), 2728(XXV), 2672(XXV), 2656(XXV), 2535(XXIV), 2452(XXIII)2341(XXII), 2145(XXI), 2052(XX), 2002(XIX), 1912(XVIII), 1856(XVII), 1789(XVII), 1725(XVI), 1604(XV), 1545(XV), 1456(XIV)

A

Assistance to Palestine refugees

The General Assembly,

Recalling its resolution 45/73 A of 11 December 1990 and all its previous resolutions on the question, including resolution 194 (III) of 11 December 1948,

Taking note of the report of the Commissioner-General of the United Nations Relief and Works Agency for Palestine Refugees in the Near East, covering the period from 1 July 1990 to 30 June 1991,[1]

1. *Notes with deep regret* that repatriation or compensation of the refugees as provided for in paragraph 11 of General Assembly resolution 194 (III) has not been effected, that no substantial progress has been made in the programme endorsed by the Assembly in paragraph 2 of its resolution 513 (VI) of 26 January 1952 for the reintegration of refugees either by repatriation or resettlement and that, therefore, the situation of the refugees continues to be a matter of serious concern;

2. *Expresses its thanks* to the Commissioner-General and to all the staff of the United Nations Relief and Works Agency for Palestine Refugees in the Near East, recognizing that the Agency is doing all it can within the limits of available resources, and also expresses its thanks to the specialized agencies and private organizations for their valuable work in assisting the refugees;

3. *Reiterates* its request that the headquarters of the Agency should be relocated to its former site within its area of operations as soon as practicable;

4. *Notes* with regret that the United Nations Conciliation Commission for Palestine has been unable to find a means of achieving progress in the implementation of paragraph 11 of General Assembly resolution 194 (III),[2] and requests the Commission to exert continued efforts towards the implementation of that paragraph and to report to the Assembly as appropriate, but no later than 1 September 1992;

5. *Directs* attention to the continuing seriousness of the financial position of the Agency, as outlined in the report of the Commissioner-General;

6. *Notes with profound concern* that, despite the commendable and successful efforts of the Commissioner-General to collect additional contributions, this increased level of income to the Agency is still insufficient to cover essential budget requirements in the present year and that, at currently foreseen levels of giving, deficits will recur each year;

7. *Calls upon* all Governments, as a matter of urgency, to make the most generous efforts possible to meet the anticipated needs of the Agency, particularly in the light of the budgetary deficit projected in the report of the Commissioner-General, and therefore urges non-contributing Governments to contribute regularly and contributing Governments to consider increasing their regular contributions.

66th plenary meeting
9 December 1991

1 *Official Records for the General Assembly, Forty-sixth Session, Supplement No. 13* and corrigendum and addendum (A/46/13 and Corr.1 and Add.1)

2 A/46/373, annex.

B

Working Group on the Financing of the United Nations Relief and Works Agency for Palestine Refugees in the Near East

The General Assembly,

Recalling its resolution 2656 (XXV) of 7 December 1970, 2728 (XXV) of 15 December 1970, 2791 (XXVI) of 6 December 1971, 45/73 B of 11 December 1990 and the previous resolutions on this question,

Recalling also its decision 36/462 of 16 March 1982, whereby it took note of the special report of the Working Group on the Financing of the United Nations Relief and Works Agency for Palestine Refugees in the Near East[3] and adopted the recommendations contained therein,

Having considered the report of the Working Group,[4]

Taking into account the report of the Commissioner-General of the United Nations Relief and Works Agency for Palestine Refugees in the Near East, covering the period from 1 July 1990 to 30 June 1991,[5]

Deeply concerned at the critical financial situation of the Agency, which has affected and affects the continuation of the provision of the necessary Agency services to the Palestine refugees, including the emergency- related programmes,

Emphasizing the continuing need for extraordinary efforts in order to maintain, at least at the present minimum level, the activities of the Agency, as well as to enable the Agency to carry out essential construction,

1. *Commends* the Working Group on the Financing of the United Nations Relief and Works Agency for Palestine Refugees in the Near East for its efforts to assist in ensuring the Agency's financial security;

2. *Takes note with approval* of the report of the Working Group;

3. *Requests* the Working Group to continue its efforts, in cooperation with the Secretary-General and the Commissioner-General, for the financing of the Agency for a further period of one year;

4. *Requests* the Secretary-General to provide the necessary services and assistance to the Working Group for the conduct of its work.

66th plenary meeting
9 December 1991

C

Assistance to persons displaced as a result of the June 1967 and subsequent hostilities

The General Assembly,

Recalling its resolution 45/73 C of 11 December 1990 and all previous resolutions on the question,

Taking note of the report of the Commissioner-General of the United Nations Relief and Works Agency for Palestine Refugees in the Near East, covering the period from 1 July 1990 to 30 June 1991,[6]

Concerned about the continued human suffering resulting from the hostilities in the Middle East,

1. *Reaffirms* its resolution 45/73 C and all its previous resolutions on the question;

2. *Endorses*, bearing in mind the objectives of those resolutions, the efforts of the Commissioner-General of the United Nations Relief and Works Agency for Palestine Refugees in the Near East to continue to provide humanitarian assistance as far as practicable, on an emergency basis and as a temporary measure, to other persons in the

3 A/36/866 and Corr.1; see also A/37/591.

4 A/46/622.

5 *Official Records for the General Assembly, Forty-sixth Session, Supplement No. 13* and corrigendum and addendum (A/46/13 and Corr.1 and Add.1).

6 *Ibid.*

area who are at present displaced and in serious need of continued assistance as a result of the June 1967 and subsequent hostilities;

3. *Strongly appeals* to all Governments and to organizations and individuals to contribute generously for the above purposes to the United Nations Relief and Works Agency for Palestine Refugees in the Near East and to the other intergovernmental and non-governmental organizations concerned.

66th plenary meeting
9 December 1991

D

Offers by Member States of grants and scholarships for higher education, including vocational training, for Palestine refugees

The General Assembly,

Recalling its resolution 212 (III) of 19 November 1948 on assistance to Palestine refugees,

Recalling also its resolutions 35/13 B of 3 November 1980, 36/146 H of 16 December 1981, 37/120 D of 16 December 1982, 38/83 D of 15 December 1983, 39/99 D of 14 December 1984, 40/165 D of 16 December 1985, 41/69 D of 3 December 1986, 42/69 D of 2 December 1987, 43/57 D of 6 December 1988, 44/47 D of 8 December 1989 and 45/73 D of 11 December 1990,

Cognizant of the fact that the Palestine refugees have, for the last four decades, lost their homes, lands and means of livelihood,

Having considered the report of the Secretary-General,[1]

Having also considered the report of the Commissioner-General of the United Nations Relief and Works Agency for Palestine Refugees in the Near East, covering the period from 1 July 1990 to 30 June 1991,[2]

1. *Urges* all States to respond to the appeal contained in its resolution 32/90 F of 13 December 1977 and reiterated in subsequent relevant resolutions in a manner commensurate with the needs of Palestine refugees for higher education, including vocational training;

2. *Strongly appeals* to all States, specialized agencies and non- governmental organizations to augment the special allocations for grants and scholarships to Palestine refugees in addition to their contributions to the regular budget of the United Nations Relief and Works Agency for Palestine Refugees in the Near East;

3. *Expresses its appreciation* to all Governments, specialized agencies and non-governmental organizations that responded favourably to its resolutions 41/69 D, 42/69 D, 43/57 D, 44/47 D and 45/73 D;

4. *Invites* the relevant specialized agencies and other organizations of the United Nations system to continue, within their respective spheres of competence, to extend assistance for higher education to Palestine refugee students;

5. *Appeals* to all States, specialized agencies and the United Nations University to contribute generously to the Palestinian universities in the Palestinian territory occupied by Israel since 1967, including, in due course, the proposed University of Jerusalem "Al-Quds" for Palestine refugees;

6. *Also appeals* to all States, specialized agencies and other international bodies to contribute towards the establishment of vocational training centres for Palestine refugees;

7. *Requests* the Agency to act as the recipient and trustee for the special allocations for grants and scholarships and to award them to qualified Palestine refugee candidates;

8. *Requests* the Secretary-General to report to the General Assembly at its forty-seventh session on the implementation of the present resolution.

66th plenary meeting
9 December 1991

1 A/46/535.

2 *Official Records for the General Assembly, Forty-sixth Session, Supplement No. 13* and corrigendum and addendum (A/46/13 and Corr.1 and Add.1).

E

Palestine refugees in the Palestinian territory occupied by Israel since 1967

The General Assembly,

Recalling Security Council resolution 237 (1967) of 14 June 1967,

Recalling also its resolutions 2792 C (XXVI) of 6 December 1971, 2963 C (XXVII) of 13 December 1972, 3089 C (XXVIII) of 7 December 1973, 3331 D (XXIX) of 17 December 1974, 3419 C (XXX) of 8 December 1975, 31/15 E of 23 November 1976, 32/90 C of 13 December 1977, 33/112 E of 18 December 1978, 34/52 F of 23 November 1979, 35/13 F of 3 November 1980, 36/146 A of 16 December 1981, 37/120 E and I of 16 December 1982, 38/83 E and J of 15 December 1983, 39/99 E and J of 14 December 1984, 40/165 E and J of 16 December 1985, 41/69 E and J of 3 December 1986, 42/69 E and J of 2 December 1987, 43/57 E of 6 December 1988, 44/47 E of 8 December 1989 and 45/73 E of 11 December 1990,

Having considered the report of the Secretary-General,[3]

Having also considered the report of the Commissioner-General of the United Nations Relief and Works Agency for Palestine Refugees in the Near East, covering the period from 1 July 1990 to 30 June 1991,[4]

Recalling the provisions of paragraph 11 of its resolution 194 (III) of 11 December 1948, and considering that measures to resettle Palestine refugees in the Palestinian territory occupied by Israel since 1967 away from their homes and property from which they were displaced constitute a violation of their inalienable right of return,

Alarmed by the reports received from the Commissioner-General that the Israeli occupying authorities, in contravention of Israel's obligation under international law, persist in their policy of demolishing shelters occupied by refugee families,

1. *Strongly reiterates* its demand that Israel desist from the removal and resettlement of Palestine refugees in the Palestinian territory occupied by Israel since 1967 and from the destruction of their shelters;

2. *Requests* the Commissioner-General of the United Nations Relief and Works Agency for Palestine Refugees in the Near East to address the acute situation of the Palestine refugees in the Palestinian territory occupied by Israel since 1967 and accordingly to extend all the services of the Agency to those refugees;

3. *Requests* the Secretary-General, in cooperation with the Commissioner-General, to resume issuing identification cards to all Palestine refugees and their descendants in the occupied Palestinian territory, irrespective of whether or not they are recipients of rations and services of the Agency;

4. *Also requests* the Secretary-General, after consulting with the Commissioner-General, to report to the General Assembly, before the opening of its forty-seventh session, on the implementation of the present resolution and in particular on Israel's compliance with paragraph 1 above.

66th plenary meeting
9 December 1991

F

Resumption of the ration distribution to Palestine refugees

The General Assembly,

Recalling its resolutions 36/146 F of 16 December 1981, 37/120 F of 16 December 1982, 38/83 F of 15 December 1983, 39/99 F of 14 December 1984, 40/165 F of 16 December 1985, 41/69 F of 3 December 1986, 42/69 F of 2 December 1987, 43/57 F of 6 December 1988, 44/47 F of 8 December 1989, 45/73 F of 11 December 1990

3 A/46/536.

4 *Official Records for the General Assembly, Forty-sixth Session, Supplement No. 13* and corrigendum and addendum (A/46/13 and Corr.1 and Add.1).

and all its previous resolutions on the question, including resolution 302 (IV) of 8 December 1949,

Having considered the report of the Secretary-General,[1]

Having also considered the report of the Commissioner-General of the United Nations Relief and Works Agency for Palestine Refugees in the Near East, covering the period from 1 July 1990 to 30 June 1991,[2]

Deeply concerned at the interruption by the Agency, owing to financial difficulties, of the general ration distribution to Palestine refugees in all fields,

1. *Regrets* that its resolutions 37/120 F, 38/83 F, 39/99 F, 40/165 F, 41/69 F, 42/69 F, 43/57 F, 44/47 F and 45/73 F have not been implemented;

2. *Calls once again upon* all Governments, as a matter of urgency, to make the most generous efforts possible and to offer the necessary resources to meet the needs of the United Nations Relief and Works Agency for Palestine Refugees in the Near East, particularly in the light of the interruption by the Agency of the general ration distribution to Palestine refugees in all fields, and therefore urges non-contributing Governments to contribute regularly and contributing Governments to consider increasing their regular contributions;

3. *Requests* the Commissioner-General of the United Nations Relief and Works Agency for Palestine Refugees in the Near East to resume on a continuing basis the interrupted general ration distribution to Palestine refugees in all fields;

4. *Requests* the Secretary-General, in consultation with the Commissioner-General, to report to the General Assembly at its forty-seventh session on the implementation of the present resolution.

66th plenary meeting
9 December 1991

G

Return of population and refugees displaced since 1967

The General Assembly,

Recalling Security Council resolution 237 (1967) of 14 June 1967,

Recalling also its resolutions 2252 (ES-V) of 4 July 1967, 2452 A (XXIII) of 19 December 1968, 2535 B (XXIV) of 10 December 1969, 2672 D (XXV) of 8 December 1970, 2792 E (XXVI) of 6 December 1971, 2963 C and D (XXVII) of 13 December 1972, 3089 C (XXVIII) of 7 December 1973, 3331 D (XXIX) of 17 December 1974, 3419 C (XXX) of 8 December 1975, 31/15 D of 23 November 1976, 32/90 E of 13 December 1977, 33/112 F of 18 December 1978, 34/52 E of 23 November 1979, ES-7/2 of 29 July 1980, 35/13 E of 3 November 1980, 36/146 B of 16 December 1981, 37/120 G of 16 December 1982, 38/83 G of 15 December 1983, 39/99 G of 14 December 1984, 40/165 G of 16 December 1985, 41/69 G of 3 December 1986, 42/69 G of 2 December 1987, 43/57 G of 6 December 1988, 44/47 G of 8 December 1989 and 45/73 G of 11 December 1990,

Having considered the report of the Secretary-General,[3]

Having also considered the report of the Commissioner-General of the United Nations Relief and Works Agency for Palestine Refugees in the Near East, covering the period from 1 July 1990 to 30 June 1991,[4]

1. *Reaffirms* the inalienable right of all displaced inhabitants to return to their homes or former places of residence in the territories occupied by Israel since 1967, and declares once more that any attempt to restrict, or to attach conditions to, the free exercise of the right to return by any displaced person is inconsistent with that inalienable right and is inadmissible;

2. *Considers* any and all agreements embodying any restriction on, or condition for, the return of the displaced inhabitants as null and void;

3. *Strongly deplores* the continued refusal of the Israeli authorities to take steps for the return of the displaced inhabitants;

4. *Calls once more upon* Israel:

(*a*) To take immediate steps for the return of all displaced inhabitants;

(*b*) To desist from all measures that obstruct the return of the displaced inhabitants, including measures affecting the physical and demographic structure of the occupied territories;

5. *Requests* the Secretary-General, after consulting with the Commissioner-General of the United Nations Relief and Works Agency for Palestine Refugees in the Near East, to report to the General Assembly, before the opening of its forty-seventh session, on the compliance of Israel with paragraph 4 above.

66th plenary meeting
9 December 1991

H

Revenues derived from Palestine refugees' properties

The General Assembly,

Recalling its resolutions 35/13 A to F of 3 November 1980, 36/146 C of 16 December 1981, 37/120 H of 16 December 1982, 38/83 H of 15 December 1983, 39/99 H of 14 December 1984, 40/165 H of 16 December 1985, 41/69 H of 3 December 1986, 42/69 H of 2 December 1987, 43/57 H of 6 December 1988, 44/47 H of 8 December 1989, 45/73 H of 11 December 1990 and all its previous resolutions on the question, including resolution 194 (III) of 11 December 1948,

Taking note of the report of the Secretary-General,[5]

Taking note also of the report of the United Nations Conciliation Commission for Palestine, covering the period from 1 September 1990 to 31 August 1991,[6]

Recalling that the Universal Declaration of Human Rights[7] and the principles of international law uphold the principle that no one shall be arbitrarily deprived of his or her private property,

Considering that the Palestine Arab refugees are entitled to their property and to the income derived therefrom, in conformity with the principles of justice and equity,

Recalling in particular its resolution 394 (V) of 14 December 1950, in which it directed the United Nations Conciliation Commission for Palestine, in consultation with the parties concerned, to prescribe measures for the protection of the rights, property and interests of the Palestine Arab refugees,

Taking note of the completion of the programme of identification and evaluation of Arab property, as announced by the United Nations Conciliation Commission for Palestine in its twenty-second progress report,[8] and of the fact that the Land Office had a schedule of Arab owners and file of documents defining the location, area and other particulars of Arab property,

1. *Requests* the Secretary-General to take all appropriate steps, in consultation with the United Nations Conciliation Commission for Palestine, for the protection and administration of Arab property, assets and property rights in Israel and to establish a fund for the receipt of income derived therefrom, on behalf of the rightful owners;

2. *Calls once more upon* Israel to render all facilities and assistance to the Secretary-General in the implementation of the present resolution;

---

1 A/46/537.

2 *Official Records for the General Assembly, Forty-sixth Session, Supplement No. 13* and corrigendum and addendum (A/46/13 and Corr.1 and Add.1)

3 A/46/538.

4 *Official Records for the General Assembly, Forty-sixth Session, Supplement No. 13* and corrigendum and addendum (A/46/13 and Corr.1 and Add.1).

5 A/46/399.

6 A/46/373, annex.

7 Resolution 217A(III).

8 *Official Records of the General Assembly, Nineteenth Session, Annex No. 11*, document A/5700.

3. *Calls upon* the Governments of all the other Member States concerned to provide the Secretary-General with any pertinent information in their possession concerning Arab property, assets and property rights in Israel, which would assist the Secretary-General in the implementation of the present resolution;

4. *Deplores* the refusal of Israel to cooperate with the Secretary-General in the implementation of the resolutions on the question;

5. *Requests* the Secretary-General to report to the General Assembly at its forty-seventh session on the implementation of the present resolution.

66th plenary meeting
9 December 1991

I

Protection of Palestine refugees

The General Assembly,

Recalling in particular recent Security Council resolutions 605 (1987) of 22 December 1987, 607 (1988) of 5 January 1988, 608 (1988) of 14 January 1988, 636 (1989) of 6 July 1989, 641 (1989) of 30 August 1989, 672 (1990) of 12 October 1990, 673 (1990) of 24 October 1990, 681 (1990) of 20 December 1990 and 694 (1991) of 24 May 1991,

Also recalling its resolutions ES-7/5 of 26 June 1982, ES-7/6 and ES-7/8 of 19 August 1982, ES-7/9 of 24 September 1982, 37/120 J of 16 December 1982, 38/83 I of 15 December 1983, 39/99 I of 14 December 1984, 40/165 I of 16 December 1985, 41/69 I of 3 December 1986, 42/69 I of 2 December 1987, 43/21 of 3 November 1988, 43/57 I of 6 December 1988, 44/47 I of 8 December 1989 and 45/73 I of 11 December 1990,

Taking note of the report of the Secretary-General dated 21 January 1988, submitted in accordance with Security Council resolution 605 (1987),[1] the report dated 31 October 1990, submitted in accordance with Council resolution 672 (1990),[2] and the report dated 9 April 1991, submitted in accordance with Council resolution 681 (1990),[3]

Having considered the report of the Secretary-General,[4]

Having also considered the report of the Commissioner-General of the United Nations Relief and Works Agency for Palestine Refugees in the Near East, covering the period from 1 July 1990 to 30 June 1991,[5]

Gravely concerned and alarmed by the deteriorating situation in the Palestinian territory occupied by Israel since 1967, including Jerusalem,

Taking into account the need to consider measures for the impartial protection of the Palestinian civilian population under Israeli occupation,

Referring to the humanitarian principles of the Geneva Convention relative to the Protection of Civilian Persons in Time of War, of 12 August 1949,[6] and to the obligations arising from the regulations annexed to the Hague Convention IV of 1907,[7]

Deeply distressed that, notwithstanding the improved security situation owing to the deployment of the Lebanese army, the Palestinian and Lebanese population are still suffering from continuing Israeli acts of aggression against Lebanon and from other hostile acts,

1. *Holds* Israel responsible for the security of the Palestine refugees in the occupied Palestinian territory, including Jerusalem, and other Arab territories occupied by Israel since 1967, and calls upon it to fulfil its obligations as the occupying Power in this regard, in accordance with the pertinent provisions of the Geneva Convention relative to the Protection of Civilian Persons in Time of War, of 12 August 1949;[8]

2. *Calls upon* all the High Contracting Parties to the Convention to take appropriate measures to ensure respect by Israel, the occupying Power, for the Convention in all circumstances, in conformity with their obligation under article 1 thereof;

3. *Strongly urges* the Security Council to consider the current situation in the occupied Palestinian territory, taking into account the recommendations contained in the reports of the Secretary-General dated 21 January 1988,[9] 31 October 1990[10] and 9 April 1991;[11]

4. *Urges* the Secretary-General and the Commissioner-General of the United Nations Relief and Works Agency for Palestine Refugees in the Near East to continue their efforts in support of the upholding of the safety and security and the legal and human rights of the Palestine refugees in all the territories under Israeli occupation since 1967;

5. *Calls once again upon* Israel to desist forthwith from acts of aggression against the Lebanese and Palestinian population in Lebanon, in violation of the Charter of the United Nations and the norms of international law;

6. *Demands* that Israel, the occupying Power, release forthwith all arbitrarily detained Palestine refugees, including the employees of the United Nations Relief and Works Agency for Palestine Refugees in the Near East;

7. *Calls once again upon* Israel to compensate the Agency for damages to its property and facilities resulting from the invasion of Lebanon by Israel in 1982, without prejudice to the responsibility of the latter for all damages resulting from that invasion, as well as for other damages resulting from the policies and practices of Israel, the occupying Power, in the occupied Palestinian territory;

8. *Requests* the Secretary-General, in consultation with the Commissioner-General, to report to the General Assembly, before the opening of its forty-seventh session, on the implementation of the present resolution.

66th plenary meeting
9 December 1991

J

University of Jerusalem "Al-Quds" for Palestine refugees

The General Assembly,

Recalling its resolutions 36/146 G of 16 December 1981, 37/120 C of 16 December 1982, 38/83 K of 15 December 1983, 39/99 K of 14 December 1984, 40/165 D and K of 16 December 1985, 41/69 K of 3 December 1986, 42/69 K of 2 December 1987, 43/57 J of 6 December 1988, 44/47 J of 8 December 1989 and 45/73 J of 11 December 1990,

Having considered the report of the Secretary-General,[12]

---

1 S/19443; see *Official Records of the Security Council, Forty-third Year, Supplement for January, February and March 1988,* document S/19443.

2 S/21919 and Corr.1; see *Official Records of the Security Council, Forty-fifth Year, Supplement for October, November and December 1990,* document S/21919.

3 S/22472; see *Official Records of the Security Council, Forty-sixth Year, Supplement for April, May and June 1991,* document S/22472.

4 A/46/539.

5 *Official Records for the General Assembly, Forty-sixth Session, Supplement No. 13* and corrigendum and addendum (A/46/13 and Corr.1 and Add.1).

6 United Nations, *Treaty Series,* vol. 75, No. 973.

7 Carnegie Endowment for International Peace, *The Hague Conventions and Declarations of 1899 and 1907* (New York, Oxford University Press, 1915), p. 100.

8 United Nations, *Treaty Series,* vol. 75, No. 973.

9 S/19443; see *Official Records of the Security Council, Forty-third Year, Supplement for January, February and March 1988,* document S/19443.

10 S/21919 and Corr.1; see *Official Records of the Security Council, Forty-fifth Year, Supplement for October, November and December 1990,* document S/21919.

11 S/22472; see *Official Records of the Security Council, Forty-sixth Year, Supplement for April, May and June 1991,* document S/22472.

12 A/46/540.

Having also considered the report of the Commissioner-General of the United Nations Relief and Works Agency for Palestine Refugees in the Near East, covering the period from 1 July 1990 to 30 June 1991,[1]

1. *Emphasizes* the need for strengthening the educational system in the Palestinian territory occupied by Israel since 5 June 1967, including Jerusalem, and specifically the need for the establishment of the proposed university;

2. *Requests* the Secretary-General to continue to take all necessary measures for establishing the University of Jerusalem "Al-Quds", in accordance with Assembly resolution 35/13 B of 3 November 1980, giving due consideration to the recommendations consistent with the provisions of that resolution;

3. *Calls once more upon* Israel, the occupying Power, to cooperate in the implementation of the present resolution and to remove the hindrances that it has put in the way of establishing the University of Jerusalem "Al-Quds";

4. *Also requests* the Secretary-General to report to the General Assembly at its forty-seventh session on the progress made in the implementation of the present resolution.

66th plenary meeting
9 December 1991

K

Protection of Palestinian students and educational institutions and safeguarding of the security of the facilities of the United Nations Relief and Works Agency for Palestine Refugees in the Near East in the occupied Palestinian territory

The General Assembly,

Recalling Security Council resolution 605 (1987) of 22 December 1987,

Recalling its resolutions 43/21 of 3 November 1988, 43/57 I of 6 December 1988, 44/2 of 6 October 1989, 44/47 K of 8 December 1989 and 45/73 K of 11 December 1990,

Taking note of the report of the Secretary-General dated 21 January 1988, submitted in accordance with Security Council resolution 605 (1987),[2] the report dated 31 October 1990, submitted in accordance with Council resolution 672 (1990),[3] and the report dated 9 April 1991, submitted in accordance with Council resolution 681 (1990),[4]

Having considered the report of the Secretary-General,[5]

Having also considered the report of the Commissioner-General of the United Nations Relief and Works Agency for Palestine Refugees in the Near East, covering the period from 1 July 1990 to 30 June 1991,[6]

Taking note, in particular, of paragraph 100 of that report, in which it is stated that during the reporting period "there were 251 incursions into Agency installations by members of the Israeli security forces in the West Bank and 367 such incursions in the Gaza Strip" and that "the Agency recorded 201 incidents in which health clinic premises were entered, including 153 in the Gaza Strip alone" and that "on 27 December 1990, members of the Israeli security forces entered the Agency's health centre in Jabalia camp, passing through the emergency section and the maternity ward where several women were about to give birth and fired shots from within the health centre compound at stone-throwers on the roof of a nearby mosque",

Gravely concerned and alarmed by the deteriorating situation in the Palestinian territory occupied by Israel since 1967, including Jerusalem,

1. *Condemns* the repeated Israeli raids on the premises and installations of the United Nations Relief and Works Agency for Palestine Refugees in the Near East and calls upon Israel, the occupying Power, to refrain from such raids;

2. *Deplores* the policy and practices of Israel, the occupying Power, which have led to the prolonged closure of educational and vocational institutions, a large number of which are operated by the Agency, and the repeated disruption of medical services;

3. *Calls upon* Israel, the occupying Power, to open immediately all closed educational and vocational institutions and to refrain from closing them thereafter;

4. *Requests* the Secretary-General to report to the General Assembly at its forty-seventh session on the implementation of the present resolution.

66th plenary meeting
9 December 1991

46/47. Report of the Special Committee to Investigate Israeli Practices Affecting the Human Rights of the Palestinian People and other Arabs of the Occupied Territories

Committee: P
Vote: A: 96 - 5 - 52; B: 153 - 1 - 3; C: 153 - 1 - 3; D: 153 - 2 - 2; E: 153 - 1 - 3; F: 152 - 1 - 4; G: 150 - 2 - 4
Ref.: 50/29, 49/36, 48/41, 47/70, 45/74, 44/48, 43/58, 42/160, 41/63, 40/161, 39/95, 38/79, 37/88, 36/147, 35/122, 34/90, 33/113, 32/91, 31/106, 3525(XXX), 3240(XXIX), 3092(XXVIII), 3005(XXVII), 2851(XXVI), 2546(XXIV)

A

The General Assembly,

Guided by the purposes and principles of the Charter of the United Nations and by the principles and provisions of the Universal Declaration of Human Rights,[7]

Aware of the uprising (*intifadah*) of the Palestinian people since 9 December 1987 against Israeli occupation, which has received significant attention and sympathy from world public opinion,

Deeply concerned about the alarming situation in the Palestinian territory occupied since 1967, including Jerusalem, as well as in the other occupied Arab territories, as a result of their continued occupation by Israel, the occupying Power, and of its persistent policies against the Palestinian people,

Bearing in mind the provisions of the Geneva Convention relative to the Protection of Civilian Persons in Time of War, of 12 August 1949,[8] as well as of other relevant conventions and regulations,

Taking into account the need to consider measures for the impartial protection of the Palestinian people under Israeli occupation,

Recalling the relevant resolutions of the Security Council, in particular resolutions 605 (1987) of 22 December 1987, 607 (1988) of 5 January 1988, 608 (1988) of 14 January 1988, 636 (1989) of 6 July 1989, 641 (1989) of 30 August 1989, 672 (1990) of 12 October 1990, 673 (1990) of 24 October 1990 and 694 (1991) of 24 May 1991,

Recalling specifically Security Council resolution 681 (1990) of 20 December 1990, in paragraph 6 of which the Council requested "the Secretary-General, in cooperation with the International Committee of the Red Cross, to develop further the idea, expressed in his report, of convening a meeting of the High Contracting Parties to the said

---

1 *Official Records for the General Assembly, Forty-sixth Session, Supplement No. 13* and corrigendum and addendum (A/46/13 and Corr.1 and Add.1).

2 S/19443; see *Official Records of the Security Council, Forty-third Year, Supplement for January, February and March 1988*, document S/19443.

3 S/21919 and Corr.1; see *Official Records of the Security Council, Forty-fifth Year, Supplement for October, November and December 1990*, document S/21919.

4 S/22472; see *Official Records of the Security Council, Forty-sixth Year, Supplement for April, May and June 1991*, document S/22472.

5 A/46/541.

6 *Official Records for the General Assembly, Forty-sixth Session, Supplement No. 13* and corrigendum and addendum (A/46/13 and Corr.1 and Add.1).

7 Resolution 217 A (III).

8 United Nations, *Treaty Series*, vol. 75, No. 973.

Convention to discuss possible measures that might be taken by them under the Convention and, for this purpose, to invite the Parties to submit their views on how the idea could contribute to the goals of the Convention, as well as on other relevant matters, and to report thereon to the Council",

Recalling also all its resolutions on the subject, in particular resolutions 32/91 B and C of 13 December 1977, 33/113 C of 18 December 1978, 34/90 A of 12 December 1979, 35/122 C of 11 December 1980, 36/147 C of 16 December 1981, ES-9/1 of 5 February 1982, 37/88 C of 10 December 1982, 38/79 D of 15 December 1983, 39/95 D of 14 December 1984, 40/161 D of 16 December 1985, 41/63 D of 3 December 1986, 42/160 D of 8 December 1987, 43/21 of 3 November 1988, 43/58 A of 6 December 1988, 44/2 of 6 October 1989, 44/48 A of 8 December 1989 and 45/74 A of 11 December 1990,

Recalling further the relevant resolutions adopted by the Commission on Human Rights, in particular its resolutions 1983/1 of 15 February 1983,[1] 1984/1 of 20 February 1984,[2] 1985/1 A and B and 1985/2 of 19 February 1985,[3] 1986/1 A and B and 1986/2 of 20 February 1986,[4] 1987/1, 1987/2 A and B and 1987/4 of 19 February 1987,[5] 1988/1 A and B and 1988/2 of 15 February 1988 and 1988/3 of 22 February 1988,[6] 1989/1 and 1989/2 of 1, February 1989 and 1989/19 of 6 March 1989,[7] 1990/1, 1990/2 and 1990/3 of 16 February 1990 and 1990/6 of 19 February 1990[8] and 1991/1 A and B, 1991/3 and 1991/6 of 15 February 1991,[9]

Having considered the reports of the Special Committee to Investigate Israeli Practices Affecting the Human Rights of the Palestinian People and Other Arabs of the Occupied Territories,[10] which contain, *inter alia*, self-incriminating public statements made by officials of Israel, the occupying Power,

Having also considered the reports of the Secretary-General of 21 January 1988,[11] 31 October 1990,[12] 9 April 1991[13] and 4 October 1991,[14]

1. *Commends* the Special Committee to Investigate Israeli Practices Affecting the Human Rights of the Palestinian People and Other Arabs of the Occupied Territories for its efforts in performing the tasks assigned to it by the General Assembly and for its impartiality;

2. *Deplores* the continued refusal by Israel to allow the Special Committee access to the occupied Palestinian territory, including Jerusalem, and other Arab territories occupied by Israel since 1967;

3. *Demands* that Israel allow the Special Committee access to the occupied territories;

4. *Reaffirms* the fact that occupation itself constitutes a grave violation of the human rights of the Palestinian people in the occupied Palestinian territory, including Jerusalem, and other Arab territories occupied by Israel since 1967;

5. *Condemns* the continued and persistent violation by Israel of the Geneva Convention relative to the Protection of Civilian Persons in Time of War, of 12 August 1949,[15] and other applicable international instruments, and condemns in particular those violations which the Convention designates as "grave breaches" thereof;

6. *Declares once more* that Israel's grave breaches of that Convention are war crimes and an affront to humanity;

7. *Reaffirms*, in accordance with the Convention, that the Israeli military occupation of the Palestinian territory including Jerusalem, and other Arab territories is of a temporary nature, thus giving no right whatsoever to the occupying Power over the territorial integrity of the occupied territories;

8. *Strongly condemns* the following Israeli policies and practices:

(*a*) Annexation of parts of the occupied Palestinian territory, including Jerusalem;

(*b*) Imposition of Israeli laws, jurisdiction and administration on the occupied Syrian Golan, which has resulted in the effective annexation of that territory;

(*c*) Illegal imposition and levy of taxes and dues;

(*d*) Establishment of new Israeli settlements and expansion of the existing ones on private and public Palestinian and other Arab lands, and transfer of an alien population thereto;

(*e*) Eviction, deportation, expulsion, displacement and transfer of Palestinians and other Arabs from the occupied territories and denial of their right to return;

(*f*) Confiscation and expropriation of private and public Palestinian and other Arab property in the occupied territories and all other transactions for the acquisition of land by Israeli authorities, institutions or nationals;

(*g*) Excavation and transformation of the landscape and the historical, cultural and religious sites, especially at Jerusalem;

(*h*) Pillaging of archaeological and cultural property;

(*i*) Destruction and demolition of Palestinian and other Arab houses;

(*j*) Collective punishment, mass arrests, administrative detention and ill-treatment of Palestinians and other Arabs;

(*k*) Torture of Palestinians and other Arabs;

(*l*) Interference with religious freedoms and practices, as well as family rights and customs;

(*m*) Interference with the system of education and with the social and economic development and health of the Palestinians and other Arabs in the occupied territories;

(*n*) Interference with the freedom of movement of individuals within the occupied Palestinian territory, including Jerusalem, and other Arab territories occupied by Israel since 1967;

(*o*) Illegal exploitation of the natural wealth, resources and labour of the occupied territories;

9. *Also strongly condemns*, in particular, the following Israeli policies and practices:

(*a*) Implementation of an "iron-fist" policy against the Palestinian people in the occupied Palestinian territory;

(*b*) Escalation of Israeli brutality since the beginning of the uprising (intifadah) on 9 December 1987;

(*c*) Ill-treatment and torture of children and minors under detention and/or imprisonment;

(*d*) Closure of headquarters and offices of trade unions and social organizations and harassment of their leaders, including through expulsion, as well as attacks on hospitals and their personnel;

(*e*) Interference with the freedom of the press, including censorship, detention or expulsion of journalists, closure and suspension of

---

1 See *Official Records of the Economic and Social Council, 1983, Supplement No. 3* and corrigendum (E/1983/13 and Corr.1), chap. XXVII, sect. A.

2 *Ibid., 1984, Supplement No. 4* and corrigendum (E/1984/14 and Corr.1), chap. II, sect. A.

3 *Ibid., 1985, Supplement No. 2* (E/1985/22), chap. II, sect. A.

4 *Ibid., 1986, Supplement No. 2* (E/1986/22), chap. II, sect. A.

5 *Ibid., 1987, Supplement No. 5* and corrigenda (E/1987/18 and Corr.1 and 2), chap. II, sect. A.

6 *Ibid., 1988, Supplement No. 2* (E/1988/12), chap. II, sect. A.

7 *Ibid., 1989, Supplement No. 2* (E/1989/20), chap. II, sect. A.

8 *Ibid., 1990, Supplement No. 2* and corrigenda (E/1990/22 and Corr.1 and 2), chap. II, sect. A.

9 *Ibid., 1991, Supplement No. 2* (E/1991/22), chap. II, sect. A.

10 A/46/65, A/46/282 and A/46/522.

11 S/19443; see *Official Records of the Security Council, Forty-third Year, Supplement for January, February and March 1988*, document S/19443.

12 S/21919 and Corr.1; see *Official Records of the Security Council, Forty-fifth Year, Supplement for October, November and December 1990,* document S/21919.

13 S/22472; see *Official Records of the Security Council, Forty-sixth Year, Supplement for April, May and June 1991,* document S/22472.

14 A/46/521.

15 United Nations, *Treaty Series*, vol. 75, No. 973.

newspapers and magazines, as well as denial of access to international media;

(*f*) Killing and wounding of defenceless demonstrators;

(*g*) Breaking of bones and limbs of thousands of civilians;

(*h*) House and/or town arrests;

(*i*) Use of toxic gas, which has resulted, *inter alia*, in the killing of many Palestinians;

10. *Condemns* the Israeli repression against and closing of the educational institutions in the occupied Syrian Golan, particularly prohibiting Syrian textbooks and the Syrian educational system, preventing Syrian students from pursuing their higher education in Syrian universities, denying the right of return to Syrian students receiving their higher education in the Syrian Arab Republic, forcing Hebrew on Syrian students, imposing courses that promote hatred, prejudice and religious intolerance and dismissing teachers, all in clear violation of the Convention;[1]

11. *Strongly condemns* the arming of Israeli settlers in the occupied territories to perpetrate and commit acts of violence against Palestinians and other Arabs, causing deaths and injuries;

12. *Requests* the Security Council to ensure Israel's respect for and compliance with all the provisions of the Convention in the occupied Palestinian territory, including Jerusalem, and other Arab territories occupied by Israel since 1967, and to initiate measures to halt Israeli policies and practices in those territories;

13. *Urges* the Security Council to consider the current situation in the Palestinian territory occupied by Israel since 1967, taking into account the recommendations contained in the reports of the Secretary-General, with a view to securing international protection for the defenceless Palestinian people until the withdrawal of Israel, the occupying Power, from the occupied Palestinian territory;

14. *Reaffirms* that all measures taken by Israel to change the physical character, demographic composition, institutional structure or legal status of the occupied territories, or any part thereof, including Jerusalem, are null and void, and that Israel's policy of settling parts of its population and new immigrants in those occupied territories constitutes a flagrant violation of the Convention and of the relevant resolutions of the United Nations;

15. *Demands* that Israel desist forthwith from the policies and practices referred to in paragraphs 8, 9, 10 and 11 above;

16. *Calls upon* Israel, the occupying Power, to allow the reopening of the Roman Catholic Medical Facility Hospice at Jerusalem in order to continue to provide needed health and medical services to the Palestinians in the city;

17. *Also calls upon* Israel, the occupying Power, to take immediate steps for the return of all displaced Arab and Palestinian inhabitants to their homes or former places of residence in the territories occupied by Israel since 1967, in implementation of Security Council resolution 237 (1967) of 14 June 1967;

18. *Urges* international organizations, including the specialized agencies, in particular the International Labour Organisation, the United Nations Educational, Scientific and Cultural Organization and the World Health Organization, to continue to examine the educational and health conditions in the occupied Palestinian territory, including Jerusalem, and other Arab territories occupied by Israel since 1967;

19. *Reiterates* its call upon all States, in particular those States parties to the Convention, in accordance with article 1 thereof, and upon international organizations, including the specialized agencies, not to recognize any changes carried out by Israel, the occupying Power, in the occupied territories and to avoid actions, including those in the field of aid, that might be used by Israel in its pursuit of the policies of annexation and colonization or any of the other policies and practices referred to in the present resolution;

20. *Urges* all the High Contracting Parties to the Convention to respond to the inquiry submitted to them by the Secretary-General in accordance with paragraph 6 of Security Council resolution 681 (1990);

21. *Requests* the Special Committee, pending early termination of the Israeli occupation, to continue to investigate Israeli policies and practices in the occupied Palestinian territory, including Jerusalem, and other Arab territories occupied by Israel since 1967, to consult, as appropriate, with the International Committee of the Red Cross according to its regulations in order to ensure that the welfare and human rights of the peoples of the occupied territories are safeguarded and to report to the Secretary-General as soon as possible and whenever the need arises thereafter;

22. *Also requests* the Special Committee to submit regularly to the Secretary General periodic reports on the present situation in the occupied Palestinian territory;

23. *Further requests* the Special Committee to continue to investigate the treatment of prisoners in the occupied Palestinian territory, including Jerusalem, and other Arab territories occupied by Israel since 1967;

24. *Condemns* Israel's refusal to permit persons from the occupied Palestinian territory to appear as witnesses before the Special Committee and to participate in conferences and meetings held outside the occupied Palestinian territory;

25. *Condemns* Israel's latest attack against the Sharia Islamic Court in occupied Jerusalem on 18 November 1991, when Israeli forces took away important documents and papers;

26. *Demands* that Israel, the occupying Power, return immediately all documents and papers that were taken away from the Sharia Islamic Court in occupied Jerusalem, to the officials of the said Court;

27. *Requests* the Secretary-General:

(*a*) To provide all necessary facilities to the Special Committee, including those required for its visits to the occupied territories, so that it may investigate the Israeli policies and practices referred to in the present resolution;

(*b*) To continue to make available such additional staff as may be necessary to assist the Special Committee in the performance of its tasks;

(*c*) To circulate regularly and periodically the reports mentioned in paragraph 21 above to Member States;

(*d*) To ensure the widest circulation of the reports of the Special Committee and of information regarding its activities and findings, by all means available, through the Department of Public Information of the Secretariat and, where necessary, to reprint those reports of the Special Committee that are no longer available;

(*e*) To report to the General Assembly at its forty-seventh session on the tasks entrusted to him in the present resolution;

28. *Decides* to include in the provisional agenda of its forty-seventh session the item entitled "Report of the Special Committee to Investigate Israeli Practices Affecting the Human Rights of the Palestinian People and Other Arabs of the Occupied Territories".

66th plenary meeting
9 December 1991

B

The General Assembly,

Recalling Security Council resolution 465 (1980) of 1 March 1980, in which, *inter alia*, the Council affirmed that the Geneva Convention relative to the Protection of Civilian Persons in Time of War, of 12 August 1949,[2] is applicable to the Arab territories occupied by Israel since 1967, including Jerusalem,

Recalling also Security Council resolutions 672 (1990) of 12 October 1990, 673 (1990) of 24 October 1990 and 681 (1990) of 20 December 1990,

Recalling further its resolutions 3092 A (XXVIII) of 7 December 1973, 3240 B (XXIX) of 29 November 1974, 3525 B (XXX) of 15 December 1975, 31/106 B of 16 December 1976, 32/91 A of 13

---

1 *Ibid.*

2 *Ibid.*

December 1977, 33/113 A of 18 December 1978, 34/90 B of 12 December 1979, 35/122 A of 11 December 1980, 36/147 A of 16 December 1981 37/88 A of 10 December 1982, 38/79 B of 15 December 1983, 39/95 B of 14 December 1984, 40/161 B of 16 December 1985, 41/63 B of 3 December 1986, 42/160 B of 8 December 1987, 43/58 B of 6 December 1988, 44/48 B of 8 December 1989 and 45/74 B of 11 December 1990,

Recalling the reports of the Secretary-General of 21 January 1988[1] and 31 October 1990,[2] and taking note of the reports of the Secretary-General of 9 April 1991[3] and 11 September 1991,[4]

Considering that the promotion of respect for the obligations arising from the Charter of the United Nations and other instruments and rules of international law is among the basic purposes and principles of the United Nations,

Bearing in mind the provisions of the Convention,[5]

Noting that Israel and the concerned Arab States whose territories have been occupied by Israel since June 1967 are parties to that Convention,

Taking into account that States parties to the Convention undertake, in accordance with article I thereof, not only to respect but also to ensure respect for the Convention in all circumstances,

1. *Reaffirms* that the Geneva Convention relative to the Protection of Civilian Persons in Time of War, of 12 August 1949, is applicable to the occupied Palestinian territory, including Jerusalem, and other Arab territories occupied by Israel since 1967;

2. *Condemns once again* the failure of Israel, the occupying Power, to acknowledge the applicability of the Convention to the territories it has occupied since 1967 including Jerusalem;

3. *Strongly demands* that Israel accept the *de jure* applicability of the Convention and comply with its provisions in the occupied Palestinian territory, including Jerusalem, and other Arab territories occupied by Israel since 1967;

4. *Urgently calls upon* all States parties to the Convention to exert all efforts in order to ensure respect for and compliance with its provisions in the occupied Palestinian territory, including Jerusalem, and other Arab territories occupied by Israel since 1967;

5. *Requests* the Secretary-General to report to the General Assembly at its forty-seventh session on the implementation of the present resolution.

66th plenary meeting
9 December 1991

C

The General Assembly,

Recalling Security Council resolutions 465 (1980) of 1 March 1980, 605 (1987) of 22 December 1987, 672 (1990) of 12 October 1990, 673 (1990) of 24 October 1990 and 681 (1990) of 20 December 1990,

Recalling also its resolutions 32/5 of 28 October 1977, 33/113 B of 18 December 1978, 34/90 C of 12 December 1979, 35/122 B of 11 December 1980, 36/147 B of 16 December 1981, 37/88 B of 10 December 1982, 38/79 C of 15 December 1983, 39/95 C of 14 December 1984, 40/161 C of 16 December 1985, 41/63 C of 3 December 1986, 42/160 C of 8 December 1987, 43/58 C of 6 December 1988, 44/48 C of 8 December 1989 and 45/74 C of 11 December 1990,

Expressing grave anxiety and concern about the serious situation prevailing in the occupied Palestinian territory, including Jerusalem, and other Arab territories occupied by Israel since 1967, as a result of the continued Israeli occupation and the measures and actions taken by Israel, the occupying Power, designed to change the legal status, geographical nature and demographic composition of those territories,

Recalling the reports of the Secretary-General of 21 January 1988[6] and 31 October 1990,[7] and taking note of the reports of the Secretary-General of 9 April 1991[8] and 11 September 1991,[9]

Confirming that the Geneva Convention relative to the Protection of Civilian Persons in Time of War, of 12 August 1949,[10] is applicable to all occupied Palestinian territory, including Jerusalem, and other Arab territories occupied by Israel since 1967,

1. *Determines* that all such measures and actions taken by Israel in the occupied Palestinian territory, including Jerusalem, and other Arab territories occupied by Israel since 1967 are in violation of the relevant provisions of the Geneva Convention relative to the Protection of Civilian Persons in Time of War, of 12 August 1949, constitute a serious obstacle to the efforts to achieve a comprehensive, just and lasting peace in the Middle East and therefore have no legal validity;

2. *Strongly deplores* the persistence of Israel in carrying out such measures, in particular the establishment of settlements in the occupied Palestinian territory, including Jerusalem, and other Arab territories occupied by Israel since 1967;

3. *Demands* that Israel comply strictly with its international obligations in accordance with the principles of international law and the provisions of the said Convention;[11]

4. *Demands once more* that Israel, the occupying Power, desist forthwith from taking any action that would result in changing the legal status, geographical nature or demographic composition of the occupied Palestinian territory, including Jerusalem, and other Arab territories occupied by Israel since 1967;

5. *Urgently calls upon* all States parties to the Convention to respect and to exert all efforts in order to ensure respect for and compliance with its provisions in all occupied Palestinian territory, including Jerusalem, and other Arab territories occupied by Israel since 1967;

6. *Requests* the Secretary-General to report to the General Assembly at its forty-seventh session on the implementation of the present resolution.

66th plenary meeting
9 December 1991

D

The General Assembly,

Recalling Security Council resolution 605 (1987) of 22 December 1987,

Recalling also its resolutions 38/79 A of 15 December 1983, 39/95 A of 14 December 1984, 40/161 A of 16 December 1985, 41/63 A of 3 December 1986, 42/160 A of 8 December 1987 43/21 of 3 November

---

1 S/19443; see *Official Records of the Security Council, Forty-third Year, Supplement for January, February and March 1988*, document S/19443.

2 S/21919 and Corr.1; see *Official Records of the Security Council, Forty-fifth Year, Supplement for October, November and December 1990,* document S/21919.

3 S/22472; see *Official Records of the Security Council, Forty-sixth Year, Supplement for April, May and June 1991,* document S/22472.

4 A/46/440.

5 United Nations, *Treaty Series,* vol. 75, No. 973.

6 S/19443; see *Official Records of the Security Council, Forty-third Year, Supplement for January, February and March 1988*, document S/19443.

7 S/21919 and Corr.1; see *Official Records of the Security Council, Forty-fifth Year, Supplement for October, November and December 1990,* document S/21919.

8 S/22472; see *Official Records of the Security Council, Forty-sixth Year, Supplement for April, May and June 1991,* document S/22472.

9 A/46/441.

10 United Nations, *Treaty Series,* vol. 75, No. 973.

11 *Ibid.*

1988, 43/58 D of 6 December 1988, 44/2 of 6 October 1989, 44/48 D of 8 December 1989 and 45174 D of 11 December 1990,

Taking note of the reports of the Special Committee to Investigate Israeli Practices Affecting the Human Rights of the Palestinian People and Other Arabs of the Occupied Territories,[1]

Recalling the reports of the Secretary-General of 21 January 1988[2] and 31 October 1990,[3] and taking note of the report of the Secretary-General of 11 September 1991,[4]

1. *Deplores* the arbitrary detention or imprisonment by Israel of thousands of Palestinians as a result of their resistance to occupation in order to attain self-determination;

2. *Calls upon* Israel, the occupying Power, to release all Palestinians and other Arabs arbitrarily detained or imprisoned;

3. *Requests* the Secretary-General to report to the General Assembly as soon as possible but not later than the beginning of its forty-seventh session on the implementation of the present resolution.

66th plenary meeting
9 December 1991

E

The General Assembly,

Recalling Security Council resolutions 605 (1987) of 22 December 1987, 607 (1988) of 5 January 1988, 608 (1988) of 14 January 1988, 636 (1989) of 6 July 1989, 641 (1989) of 30 August 1989, 672 (1990) of 12 October 1990, 673 (1990) of 24 October 1990, 681 (1990) of 20 December 1990 and 694 (1991) of 24 May 1991,

Recalling the reports of the Secretary-General of 21 January 1988[5] and 31 October 1990,[6] and taking note of the reports of the Secretary-General of 9 April 1991[7] and 11 September 1991,[8]

Alarmed by the continuing deportation of Palestinians from the occupied Palestinian territory by the Israeli authorities,

Recalling the Geneva Convention relative to the Protection of Civilian Persons in Time of War, of 12 August 1949,[9] in particular article 1 and the first paragraph of article 49, which read as follows:

Article I

"The High Contracting Parties undertake to respect and to ensure respect for the present Convention in all circumstances."

Article 49

"Individual or mass forcible transfers, as well as deportations of protected persons from occupied territory to the territory of the occupying Power or to that of any other country, occupied or not, are prohibited, regardless of their motive ...",

Reaffirming the applicability of the Convention to the occupied Palestinian territory, including Jerusalem, and other Arab territories occupied by Israel since 1967,

1. *Strongly deplores* the continuing disregard by Israel, the occupying Power, of the relevant resolutions and decisions of the Security Council and resolutions of the General Assembly;

2. *Demands* that the Government of Israel, the occupying Power, rescind the illegal measures taken by its authorities in deporting Palestinians and that it facilitate their immediate return;

3. *Calls upon* Israel, the occupying Power, to cease forthwith the deportation of Palestinians and to abide scrupulously by the provisions of the Geneva Convention relative to the Protection of Civilian Persons in Time of War, of 12 August 1949;

4. *Requests* the Secretary-General to report to the General Assembly as soon as possible but not later than the beginning of its forty-seventh session on the implementation of the present resolution.

66th plenary meeting
9 December 1991

F

The General Assembly,

Deeply concerned that the Arab territories occupied since 1967 have been under continued Israeli military occupation,

Recalling Security Council resolution 497 (1981) of 17 December 1981,

Recalling also its resolutions 36/226 B of 17 December 1981, ES-9/1 of 5 February 1982, 37/88 E of 10 December 1982, 38/79 F of 15 December 1983, 39/95 F of 14 December 1984 40/161 F of 16 December 1985, 41/63 F of 3 December 1986, 42/160 F of 8 December 1987, 43/21 of 3 November 1988, 43/58 F of 6 December 1988, 44/2 of 6 October 1989, 44/48 F of 8 December 1989 and 45/74 F of 11 December 1990,

Having considered the report of the Secretary-General of 11 September 1991,[10]

Recalling its previous resolutions, in particular resolutions 3414 (XXX) of 5 December 1975, 31/61 of 9 December 1976, 32/20 of 25 November 1977, 33/28 and 33/29 of 7 December 1978, 34/70 of 6 December 1979 and 35/122 E of 11 December 1980, in which, *inter alia*, it called upon Israel to put an end to its occupation of the Arab territories and to withdraw from all those territories,

Reaffirming once more the illegality of Israel's decision of 14 December 1981 to impose its laws, jurisdiction and administration on the occupied Syrian Golan, which has resulted in the effective annexation of that territory,

Reaffirming that the acquisition of territory by force is inadmissible under the Charter of the United Nations and that all territories thus occupied by Israel must be returned,

Recalling the Geneva Convention relative to the Protection of Civilian Persons in Time of War, of 12 August 1949,[11]

Reaffirming the applicability of that Convention to the occupied Syrian Golan,

Bearing in mind Security Council resolution 237 (1967) of 14 June 1967,

1. *Strongly condemns* Israel, the occupying Power, for its refusal to comply with the relevant resolutions of the General Assembly and the Security Council, particularly Council resolution 497 (1981), in which the Council, *inter alia*, decided that the Israeli decision to impose its laws, jurisdiction and administration on the occupied Syrian Arab Golan was null and void and without international legal effect and demanded that Israel, the occupying Power, should rescind forthwith its decision;

2. *Condemns* the persistence of Israel in changing the physical character, demographic composition, institutional structure and legal status of the occupied Syrian Golan;

3. *Determines* that all legislative and administrative measures and actions taken or to be taken by Israel, the occupying Power, that purport to alter the character and legal status of the occupied Syrian

---

1 A/46/65, A/46/282 and A/46/522.

2 S/19443; see *Official Records of the Security Council, Forty-third Year, Supplement for January, February and March 1988*, document S/19443.

3 S/21919 and Corr.1; see *Official Records of the Security Council, Forty-fifth Year, Supplement for October, November and December 1990*, document S/21919.

4 A/46/442.

5 S/19443; see *Official Records of the Security Council, Forty-third Year, Supplement for January, February and March 1988*, document S/19443.

6 S/21919 and Corr.1; see *Official Records of the Security Council, Forty-fifth Year, Supplement for October, November and December 1990*, document S/21919.

7 S/22472; see *Official Records of the Security Council, Forty-sixth Year, Supplement for April, May and June 1991*, document S/22472.

8 A//46/443.

9 United Nations, *Treaty Series*, vol. 75, No. 973.

10 A/46/444.

11 United Nations, *Treaty Series*, vol. 75, No. 973.

Golan are null and void, constitute a flagrant violation of international law and of the Geneva Convention relative to the Protection of Civilian Persons in Time of War, of 12 August 1949, and have no legal effect;

4. *Strongly condemns* Israel for its attempts forcibly to impose Israeli citizenship and Israeli identity cards on the Syrian citizens in the occupied Syrian Golan, and calls upon it to desist from its repressive measures against the population of the occupied Syrian Golan;

5. *Deplores* the violations by Israel of the Convention;

6. *Calls once again upon* Member States not to recognize any of the legislative or administrative measures and actions referred to above;

7. *Requests* the Secretary-General to report to the General Assembly at its forty-seventh session on the implementation of the present resolution.

66th plenary meeting
9 December 1991

G

The General Assembly,

Bearing in mind the Geneva Convention relative to the Protection of Civilian Persons in Time of War, of 12 August 1949,[1]

Deeply concerned about the continued and intensified harassment by Israel, the occupying Power, directed against educational institutions in the occupied Palestinian territory,

Recalling Security Council resolutions 605 (1987) of 22 December 1987, 672 (1990) of 12 October 1990, 673 (1990) of 24 October 1990 and 681 (1990) of 20 December 1990,

Recalling also its resolutions 38/79 G of 15 December 1983, 39/95 G of 14 December 1984, 40/161 G of 16 December 1985, 41/63 G of 3 December 1986, 42/160 G of 8 December 1987, 43/21 of 3 November 1988, 43/58 G of 6 December 1988, 44/2 of 6 October 1989, 44/48 G of 8 December 1989 and 45/74 G of 11 December 1990,

Recalling the reports of the Secretary-General of 21 January 1988[2] and 31 October 1990,[3] and taking note of the reports of the Secretary-General of 9 April 1991[4] and 11 September 1991,[5]

Taking note of the relevant decisions adopted by the Executive Board of the United Nations Educational, Scientific and Cultural Organization concerning the educational and cultural situation in the occupied Palestinian territory,

1. *Reaffirms* the applicability of the Geneva Convention relative to the Protection of Civilian Persons in Time of War, of 12 August 1949, to the occupied Palestinian territory, including Jerusalem, and other Arab territories occupied by Israel since 1967;

2. *Condemns* Israeli policies and practices against Palestinian students and faculty members in schools, universities and other educational institutions in the occupied Palestinian territory, especially the opening of fire on defenceless students, causing many casualties;

3. *Also condemns* the systematic Israeli campaign of repression against and closing of universities, schools and other educational and vocational institutions in the occupied Palestinian territory, in large numbers and for prolonged periods, restricting and impeding the academic activities of Palestinian universities by subjecting the selection of courses, textbooks and educational programmes, the admission of students and the appointment of faculty members to the control and supervision of the military occupation authorities, in flagrant contravention of the Convention;

4. *Demands* that Israel, the occupying Power, comply with the provisions of that Convention, rescind all actions and measures taken against all educational institutions ensure the freedom of those institutions and refrain forthwith from hindering the effective operation of the universities, schools and other educational institutions;

5. *Requests* the Secretary-General to report to the General Assembly as soon as possible but not later than the beginning of its forty-seventh session on the implementation of the present resolution.

66th plenary meeting
9 December 1991

46/76. The Uprising (*Intifadah*) of the Palestinian People

Committee: -
Vote: 142 - 2 - 5
Ref.: 45/69, 44/2, 43/21

The General Assembly,

Aware of the uprising (*intifadah*) of the Palestinian people since 9 December 1987 against Israeli occupation, which has received significant attention and sympathy from world public opinion,

Deeply concerned about the alarming situation in the Palestinian territory occupied since 1967, as a result of the continued occupation by Israel, the occupying Power, and of its persistent policies and practices against the Palestinian people,

Reaffirming that the Geneva Convention relative to the Protection of Civilian Persons in Time of War, of 12 August 1949,[6] is applicable to the Palestinian territory occupied by Israel since 1967, including Jerusalem, and to the other occupied Arab territories,

Expressing its profound shock at the continued measures by Israel, the occupying Power, including the killing and wounding of Palestinian civilians, and at the acts of violence committed by the Israeli security forces, which took place on 8 October 1990 at the Haram al-Sharif in Jerusalem, resulting in injuries and loss of human lives, and on 29 December 1990 at Rafah,

Stressing the need to promote international protection to the Palestinian civilians in the occupied Palestinian territory,

Recognizing the need for increased support to, and aid for and solidarity with, the Palestinian people under Israeli occupation,

Having considered the recommendations contained in the reports of the Secretary-General of 21 January 1988,[7] 31 October 1990[8] and 9 April 1991,[9]

Recalling its relevant resolutions as well as the relevant Security Council resolutions, in particular Council resolution 681 (1990) of 20 December 1990, in paragraph 6 of which the Council requested "the Secretary-General, in cooperation with the International Committee of the Red Cross, to develop further the idea, expressed in his report, of convening a meeting of the High Contracting Parties to the said Convention to discuss possible measures that might be taken by them under the Convention and, for this purpose, to invite the Parties to submit their views on how the idea could contribute to the goals of the Convention, as well as on other relevant matters, and to report thereon to the Council",

1. *Condemns* those policies and practices of Israel, the occupying Power, which violate the human rights of the Palestinian people in the occupied Palestinian territory, including Jerusalem, and, in par-

---

1 *Ibid.*

2 S/19443; see *Official Records of the Security Council, Forty-third Year, Supplement for January, February and March 1988*, document S/19443.

3 S/21919 and Corr.1; see *Official Records of the Security Council, Forty-fifth Year, Supplement for October, November and December 1990,* document S/21919.

4 S/22472; see *Official Records of the Security Council, Forty-sixth Year, Supplement for April, May and June 1991,* document S/22472.

5 A/46/445.

6 United Nations, *Treaty Series*, vol. 75, No. 973.

7 S/19443; see *Official Records of the Security Council, Forty-third Year, Supplement for January, February and March 1988*, document S/19443.

8 S/21919 and Corr.1; see *Official Records of the Security Council, Forty-fifth Year, Supplement for October, November and December 1990,* document S/21919.

9 S/22472; see *Official Records of the Security Council, Forty-sixth Year, Supplement for April, May and June 1991,* document S/22472.

ticular, such acts as the opening of fire by the Israeli army and settlers that result in the killing and wounding of defenceless Palestinian civilians, the beating and breaking of bones, the deportation of Palestinian civilians, the imposition of restrictive economic measures, the demolition of houses, the ransacking of real or personal property belonging individually or collectively to private persons, collective punishment and detentions, and so forth;

2. *Demands* that Israel, the occupying Power, abide scrupulously by the Geneva Convention relative to the Protection of Civilian Persons in Time of War, of 12 August 1949, and desist immediately from those policies and practices which are in violation of the provisions of the Convention;

3. *Calls upon* all the High Contracting Parties to the Convention to ensure respect by Israel, the occupying Power, for the Convention in all circumstances, in conformity with their obligation under article 1 thereof;

4. *Urges* all the High Contracting Parties to the Geneva Convention to respond to the note verbale submitted to them by the Secretary-General in accordance with paragraph 6 of Security Council resolution 681 (1990);

5. *Strongly deplores* the continuing disregard by Israel, the occupying Power, of the relevant decisions of the Security Council;

6. *Reaffirms* that the occupation by Israel of the Palestinian territory since 1967, including Jerusalem, and of the other Arab territories in no way changes the legal status of those territories;

7. *Requests* the Security Council to examine with urgency the situation in the occupied Palestinian territory with a view to considering measures needed to provide international protection to the Palestinian civilians in the Palestinian territory occupied by Israel since 1967, including Jerusalem;

8. *Invites* Member States, the organizations of the United Nations system, governmental, intergovernmental and non-governmental organizations, and the mass communications media to continue and enhance their support for the Palestinian people;

9. *Requests* the Secretary-General to examine the present situation in the Palestinian territory occupied since 1967, including Jerusalem, by all means available to him and to submit periodic reports thereon, the first such report as soon as possible.

69th plenary meeting
11 December 1991

46/82. The Situation in the Middle East

Committee: -
Vote: A: 93 - 37 - 27; B: 152 - 1 - 4
Ref.: 50/22, 50/21, 49/88, 49/87, 48/59, 48/58, 47/63, 45/083, 44/40, 43/54, 42/209, 41/162, 40/168, 39/146, 38/180, 37/123, 36/226, 35/207, 34/70, 33/29, 32/20, 31/61, 3414(XXX), 2949(XXVII), 2799(XXVI), 2628(XXV), 2257(ES-V), 2256(ES-V)

A

The General Assembly,

Having discussed the item entitled "The situation in the Middle East",

Recalling its resolutions 36/226 A and B of 17 December 1981, ES-9/1 of 5 February 1982, 37/123 F of 20 December 1982, 38/58 A to E of 13 December 1983, 38/180 A to D of 19 December 1983, 39/146 A to C of 14 December 1984, 40/168 A to C of 16 December 1985, 41/162 A to C of 4 December 1986, 42/209 A to D of 11 December 1987, 43/54 A to C of 6 December 1988, 44/40 A to C of 4 December 1989, 45/83 A to C of 13 December 1990 and 45/68 of 6 December 1990,

Recalling Security Council resolutions 425 (1978) of 19 March 1978, 497 (1981) of 17 December 1981, 508 (1982) of 5 June 1982, 509 (1982) of 6 June 1982, 701 (1991) of 31 July 1991 and other relevant resolutions,

Taking note of the reports of the Secretary-General of 22 October 1991,[1] 8 November 1991[2] and 15 November 1991,[3]

Reaffirming the need for continued collective support for the decisions adopted by the Twelfth Arab Summit Conference, held at Fez, Morocco, on 25 November 1981 and from 6 to 9 September 1982,[4] which were confirmed by subsequent Arab summit conferences, including the Extraordinary Arab Summit Conference held at Casablanca, Morocco, from 23 to 26 May 1989,

Reiterating its previous resolutions on the question of Palestine and its support for the Palestine Liberation Organization as the sole legitimate representative of the Palestinian people,

Welcoming all efforts contributing towards the realization of the inalienable rights of the Palestinian people through the achievement of a comprehensive, just and lasting peace in the Middle East, in accordance with the United Nations resolutions relating to the question of Palestine and to the situation in the Middle East, including Security Council resolutions 242 (1967) of 22 November 1967 and 338 (1973) of 22 October 1973,

Welcoming also the world-wide support extended to the just cause of the Palestinian people and the other Arab countries in their struggle against Israeli aggression and occupation in order to achieve a comprehensive, just and lasting peace in the Middle East and the full exercise by the Palestinian people of its inalienable national rights, as affirmed by previous resolutions of the General Assembly on the question of Palestine and on the situation in the Middle East,

Gravely concerned that the Palestinian territory occupied since 1967, including Jerusalem, and the other occupied Arab territories still remain under Israeli occupation, that the relevant resolutions of the United Nations have not been implemented and that the Palestinian people is still denied the restoration of its land and the exercise of its inalienable national rights in conformity with international law, as reaffirmed by resolutions of the United Nations,

Reaffirming the applicability of the Geneva Convention relative to the Protection of Civilian Persons in Time of War, of 12 August 1949,[5] to the Palestinian territory occupied since 1967, including Jerusalem, and the other occupied Arab territories,

Reaffirming also all relevant United Nations resolutions which stipulate that the acquisition of territory by force is inadmissible under the Charter of the United Nations and the principles of international law and that Israel must withdraw unconditionally from the Palestinian territory occupied since 1967, including Jerusalem, and the other occupied Arab territories,

Gravely concerned also at Israeli policies involving the escalation and expansion of the conflict in the region, which further violate the principles of international law and endanger international peace and security,

Reaffirming further the imperative necessity and urgency of establishing a comprehensive, just and lasting peace in the region, based on full respect for the Charter and the principles of international law,

1. *Reaffirms its conviction* that the question of Palestine is the core of the conflict in the Middle East and that no comprehensive, just and lasting peace in the region will be achieved without the full exercise by the Palestinian people of its inalienable national rights and the immediate, unconditional and total withdrawal of Israel from the Palestinian territory occupied since 1967, including Jerusalem, and the other occupied Arab territories;

---

1 A/46/586.

2 A/46/623-S/23204 and Corr.1; see *Official Records of the Security Council, Forty-sixth Year, Supplement for October, November and December 1991*, document S/23204.

3 A/46/652-S/23225 and Corr.1; see *Official Records of the Security Council, Forty-sixth Year, Supplement for October, November and December 1991*, document S/23225.

4 See A/37/696-S/15510, annex. For the printed text, see *Official Records of the Security Council, Thirty-seventh Year, Supplement for October, November and December 1982*, document S/15510, annex.

5 United Nations, *Treaty Series* vol. 75, No. 973.

2. *Reaffirms* that a just and comprehensive settlement of the situation in the Middle East cannot be achieved without the participation on an equal footing of all the parties to the conflict, including the Palestine Liberation Organization, the representative of the Palestinian people;

3. *Declares once more* that peace in the Middle East is indivisible and must be based on a comprehensive, just and lasting solution of the Middle East problem under the auspices of the United Nations and on the basis of its relevant resolutions, which ensures the complete and unconditional withdrawal of Israel from the Palestinian territory occupied since 1967, including Jerusalem, and the other occupied Arab territories, and which enables the Palestinian people, under the leadership of the Palestine Liberation Organization, to exercise its inalienable rights, including the right to return and the right to self-determination, national independence and the establishment of its independent sovereign State in Palestine, in accordance with the resolutions of the United Nations relating to the question of Palestine, in particular General Assembly resolutions ES-7/2 of 29 July 1980, 36/120 A to F of 10 December 1981, 37/86 A to D of 10 December 1982, 37/86 E of 20 December 1982, 38/58 A to E of 13 December 1983, 39/49 A to D of 11 December 1984, 40/96 A to D of 12 December 1985, 41/43 A to D of 2 December 1986, 42/66 A to D of 2 December 1987, 43/54 A to C of 6 December 1988, 43/175 A to C, 43/176 and 43/177 of 15 December 1988, 44/42 of 6 December 1989 and 45/68;

4. *Considers* the Arab peace plan adopted unanimously at the Twelfth Arab Summit Conference, held at Fez, Morocco, on 25 November 1981 and from 6 to 9 September 1982,[1] which was confirmed by subsequent Arab summit conferences, including the Extraordinary Arab Summit Conference held at Casablanca, Morocco, from 23 to 26 May 1989, as an important contribution towards the realization of the inalienable rights of the Palestinian people through the achievement of a comprehensive, just and lasting peace in the Middle East;

5. *Condemns* Israel's continued occupation of the Palestinian territory occupied since 1967, including Jerusalem, and the other occupied Arab territories, in violation of the Charter of the United Nations, the principles of international law and the relevant resolutions of the United Nations, and demands the immediate, unconditional and total withdrawal of Israel from all the territories occupied since 1967;

6. *Rejects* all agreements and arrangements which violate the inalienable rights of the Palestinian people and contradict the principles of a just and comprehensive solution to the Middle East problem to ensure the establishment of a just peace in the area;

7. *Deplores* Israel's failure to comply with Security Council resolutions 476 (1980) of 30 June 1980 and 478 (1980) of 20 August 1980 and General Assembly resolutions 35/207 of 16 December 1980 and 36/226 A and B.; determines that Israel's decision to annex Jerusalem and to declare it as its "capital" as well as the measures to alter its physical character, demographic composition, institutional structure and status are null and void and demands that they be rescinded immediately; and calls upon all Member States, the specialized agencies and all other international organizations to abide by the present resolution and all other relevant resolutions and decisions;

8. *Condemns* Israel's aggression, policies and practices against the Palestinian people in the occupied Palestinian territory and outside this territory, including expropriation, establishment of settlements, annexation and other aggressive and repressive measures, which are in violation of the Charter and the principles of international law and the relevant international conventions;

9. *Strongly* condemns the imposition by Israel of its laws, jurisdiction and administration on the occupied Syrian Golan, its annexationist policies and practices, the establishment of settlements, the confiscation of lands, the diversion of water resources and the imposition of Israeli citizenship on Syrian nationals, and declares that all these measures are null and void and constitute a violation of the rules and principles of international law relative to belligerent occupation, in particular the Geneva Convention relative to the Protection of Civilian Persons in Time of War, of 12 August 1949;

10. *Calls upon* all States not to provide Israel with any assistance to be used specifically in connection with settlements in the occupied territories;

11. *Strongly deplores* the continuing and increasing collaboration between Israel and South Africa, especially in the economic, military and nuclear fields, which constitutes a hostile act against the African and Arab States and enables Israel to enhance its nuclear capabilities;

12. *Requests* the Secretary-General to report to the Security Council periodically on the development of the situation and to submit to the General Assembly at its forty-seventh session a comprehensive report covering the developments in the Middle East pertaining to the present resolution.

73rd plenary meeting
16 December 1991

B

The General Assembly,

Recalling its resolutions 36/120 E of 10 December 1981, 37/123 C of 16 December 1982, 38/180 C of 19 December 1983, 39/146 C of 14 December 1984, 40/168 C of 16 December 1985, 41/162 C of 4 December 1986, 42/209 D of 11 December 1987, 43/54 C of 6 December 1988, 44/40 C of 4 December 1989 and 45/83 C of 13 December 1990, in which it determined that all legislative and administrative measures and actions taken by Israel, the occupying Power, which had altered or purported to alter the character and status of the Holy City of Jerusalem, in particular the so-called "Basic Law" on Jerusalem and the proclamation of Jerusalem as the capital of Israel, were null and void and must be rescinded forthwith,

Recalling Security Council resolution 478 (1980) of 20 August 1980, in which the Council, *inter alia*, decided not to recognize the "Basic Law" and called upon those States that had established diplomatic missions at Jerusalem to withdraw such missions from the Holy City,

Having considered the report of the Secretary-General of 22 October 1991,[2]

1. *Determines* that Israel's decision to impose its laws, jurisdiction and administration on the Holy City of Jerusalem is illegal and therefore null and void and has no validity whatsoever;

2. *Deplores* the transfer by some States of their diplomatic missions to Jerusalem in violation of Security Council resolution 478 (1980), and their refusal to comply with the provisions of that resolution;

3. *Calls once more upon* those States to abide by the provisions of the relevant United Nations resolutions, in conformity with the Charter of the United Nations;

4. *Requests* the Secretary-General to report to the General Assembly at its forty-seventh session on the implementation of the present resolution.

73rd plenary meeting
16 December 1991

50/84. Question of Palestine

Committee: -
Vote: A: 95 - 2 - 52; B: 96 - 2 - 53; C: 142 - 2 - 7; D: 143 - 3 - 3

A

Committee on the Exercise of the Inalienable Rights of the Palestinian People

The General Assembly,

Recalling its resolutions 181 (II) of 29 November 1947, 194 (III) of 11 December 1948, 3236 (XXIX) of 22 November 1974, 3375 (XXX) and 3376 (XXX) of 10 November 1975, 31/20 of 24 Novem-

[1] See A/37/696-S/15510, annex. For the printed text, see *Official Records of the Security Council, Thirty-seventh Year, Supplement for October, November and December 1982*, document S/15510, annex.

[2] A/46/586.

ber 1976, 32/40 A of 2 December 1977, 33/28 A and B of 7 December 1978, 34/65 A of 29 November 1979 and 34/65 C of 12 December 1979, ES-7/2 of 29 July 1980, 35/169 A and C of 15 December 1980, 36/120 A and C of 10 December 1981, ES-7/4 of 28 April 1982, 37/86 A of 10 December 1982, 38/58 A of 13 December 1983, 39/49 A of 11 December 1984, 40/96 A of 12 December 1985, 41/43 A of 2 December 1986, 42/66 A of 2 December 1987, 43/175 A of 15 December 1988, 44/41 A of 6 December 1989, 45/67 A of 6 December 1990, 46/74 A of 11 December 1991, 47/64 A of 11 December 1992, 48/158 A of 20 December 1993 and 49/62 A of 14 December 1994,

Having considered the report of the Committee on the Exercise of the Inalienable Rights of the Palestinian People,[1]

Welcoming the signing of the Declaration of Principles on Interim Self-Government Arrangements, including its Annexes and Agreed Minutes, by the Government of the State of Israel and the Palestine Liberation Organization at Washington, on 13 September 1993,[2] as well as the subsequent implementation agreements, in particular the Agreement on the Gaza Strip and the Jericho Area, signed at Cairo on 4 May 1994,[3] and the Interim Agreement on the West Bank and the Gaza Strip, signed at Washington on 28 September 1995,

Reaffirming that the United Nations has a permanent responsibility with respect to the question of Palestine until the question is resolved in all its aspects in a satisfactory manner in accordance with international legitimacy,

1. *Expresses its appreciation* to the Committee on the Exercise of the Inalienable Rights of the Palestinian People for its efforts in performing the tasks assigned to it by the General Assembly;

2. *Considers* that the Committee can continue to make a valuable and positive contribution to international efforts to promote the effective implementation of the Declaration of Principles on Interim Self-Government Arrangements and to mobilize international support for and assistance to the Palestinian people during the transitional period;

3. *Endorses* the recommendations of the Committee contained in section VII of its report;

4. *Requests* the Committee to continue to keep under review the situation relating to the question of Palestine and to report and make suggestions to the General Assembly or the Security Council, as appropriate;

5. *Authorizes* the Committee to continue to exert all efforts to promote the exercise of the inalienable rights of the Palestinian people, to make such adjustments in its approved programme of work as it may consider appropriate and necessary in the light of developments, to give special emphasis to the need to mobilize support and assistance for the Palestinian people, and to report thereon to the General Assembly at its fifty-first session and thereafter;

6. *Also requests* the Committee to continue to extend its cooperation to non-governmental organizations in their contribution towards heightening international awareness of the facts relating to the question of Palestine and promoting support and assistance to meet the needs of the Palestinian people, and to take the necessary steps to involve additional non-governmental organizations in its work;

7. *Requests* the United Nations Conciliation Commission for Palestine, established under resolution 194 (III), and other United Nations bodies associated with the question of Palestine, to continue to cooperate fully with the Committee and to make available to it, at its request, the relevant information and documentation which they have at their disposal;

8. *Requests* the Secretary-General to circulate the report of the Committee to all the competent bodies of the United Nations and urges them to take the necessary action, as appropriate;

9. *Also requests* the Secretary-General to continue to provide the Committee with all the necessary facilities for the performance of its tasks.

B

Division for Palestinian Rights of the Secretariat

The General Assembly,

Having considered the report of the Committee on the Exercise of the Inalienable Rights of the Palestinian People,[4]

Taking note, in particular, of the relevant information contained in section V.B of that report,

Recalling its resolutions 32/40 B of 2 December 1977, 33/28 C of 7 December 1978, 34/65 D of 12 December 1979, 35/169 D of 15 December 1980, 36/120 B of 10 December 1981, 37/86 B of 10 December 1982, 38/58 B of 13 December 1983, 39/49 B of 11 December 1984, 40/96 B of 12 December 1985, 41/43 B of 2 December 1986, 42/66 B of 2 December 1987, 43/175 B of 15 December 1988, 44/41 B of 6 December 1989, 45/67 B of 6 December 1990, 46/74 B of 11 December 1991, 47/64 B of 11 December 1992, 48/158 B of 20 December 1993 and 49/62 B of 14 December 1994;

1. *Notes with appreciation* the action taken by the Secretary-General in compliance with its resolution 49/62 B;

2. *Considers* that the Division for Palestinian Rights of the Secretariat continues to make a useful and constructive contribution through the organization of seminars and meetings of non-governmental organizations, as well as through its research and monitoring activities, the preparation of studies and publications and the collection and dissemination of information in printed and electronic form on all issues pertaining to the question of Palestine;

3. *Requests* the Secretary-General to continue to provide the Division with the necessary resources, including for the further development of the United Nations Information System on the Question of Palestine,[5] and to ensure that it continues to discharge the tasks detailed in paragraph 1 of resolution 32/40 B, paragraph 2 (b) of resolution 34/65 D, paragraph 3 of resolution 36/120 B, paragraph 3 of resolution 38/58 B, paragraph 3 of resolution 40/96 B, paragraph 2 of resolution 42/66 B, paragraph 2 of resolution 44/41 B, paragraph 2 of resolution 46/74 B and paragraph 2 of resolution 48/158 B, in consultation with the Committee on the Exercise of the Inalienable Rights of the Palestinian People and under its guidance;

4. *Also requests* the Secretary-General to ensure the continued cooperation of the Department of Public Information and other units of the Secretariat in enabling the Division for Palestinian Rights to perform its tasks and in covering adequately the various aspects of the question of Palestine;

5. *Invites* all Governments and organizations to lend their cooperation to the Committee and the Division in the performance of their tasks;

6. *Notes with appreciation* the action taken by Member States to observe annually on 29 November the International Day of Solidarity with the Palestinian People, and requests them to continue to give the widest possible publicity to the observance, and requests the Committee to continue to organize, as part of the observance of the Day of Solidarity, an annual exhibit on Palestinian rights in cooperation with the Permanent Observer Mission of Palestine to the United Nations.

---

1 *Official Records of the General Assembly, Fiftieth Session, Supplement No. 35* (A/50/35).

2 A/48/486-S/26560, annex.

3 A/49/180-S/1994/727, annex.

4 *Official Records of the General Assembly, Fiftieth Session, Supplement No. 35* (A/50/35).

5 *Official Records of the General Assembly, Fiftieth Session, Supplement No. 35* (A/50/35), para. 99.

C

Department of Public Information of the Secretariat

The General Assembly,

Having considered the report of the Committee on the Exercise of the Inalienable Rights of the Palestinian People,[1]

Taking note, in particular, of the information contained in paragraphs 102 to 114 of that report,

Recalling its resolution 49/62 C of 14 December 1994,

Convinced that the world-wide dissemination of accurate and comprehensive information and the role of non-governmental organizations and institutions remain of vital importance in heightening awareness of and support for the inalienable rights of the Palestinian people,

Aware of the Declaration of Principles on Interim Self-Government Arrangements signed by the Government of the State of Israel and the Palestine Liberation Organization in Washington, D.C., on 13 September 1993,[2] and of the subsequent implementation agreements, in particular the Interim Agreement on the West Bank and Gaza Strip on 28 September 1995, and their positive implications,

1. *Takes note with appreciation* of the action taken by the Department of Public Information of the Secretariat in compliance with General Assembly resolution 49/62 C;

2. *Considers* that the special information programme on the question of Palestine of the Department of Public Information is very useful in raising the awareness of the international community concerning the complexities of the question and the situation in the Middle East in general, including the achievements of the peace process, and that the programme is contributing effectively to an atmosphere conducive to dialogue and supportive of the peace process;

3. *Requests* the Department of Public Information, in full cooperation and coordination with the Committee on the Exercise of the Inalienable Rights of the Palestinian People, to continue, with the necessary flexibility as may be required by developments affecting the question of Palestine, its special information programme on the question of Palestine for the biennium 1996-1997, with particular emphasis on public opinion in Europe and North America and, in particular:

(*a*) To disseminate information on all the activities of the United Nations system relating to the question of Palestine, including reports on the work carried out by the relevant United Nations organizations;

(*b*) To continue to issue and update publications on the various aspects of the question of Palestine in all fields, including materials concerning the recent developments in that regard, and, in particular, the achievements of the peace process;

(*c*) To expand its audiovisual material on the question of Palestine, including the production of such material;

(*d*) To organize and promote fact-finding news missions for journalists to the area, including the territories under the jurisdiction of the Palestinian Authority and the occupied territories;

(*e*) To organize international, regional and national encounters for journalists;

(*f*) To provide, in cooperation with specialized agencies of the United Nations system, particularly the United Nations Educational, Scientific and Cultural Organization, assistance to the Palestinian people in the field of media development.

D

Peaceful settlement of the question of Palestine

The General Assembly,

Recalling its relevant resolutions,

Recalling also the relevant Security Council resolutions, including resolutions 242 (1967) of 22 November 1967 and 338 (1973) of 22 October 1973,

Having considered the report of the Secretary-General of 7 November 1995, submitted pursuant to the request made in resolution 49/62 D of 14 December 1994,[3]

Convinced that achieving a final and peaceful settlement of the question of Palestine, the core of the Arab-Israeli conflict, is imperative for the attainment of a comprehensive and lasting peace in the Middle East,

Aware that the principle of equal rights and self-determination of peoples is among the purposes and principles of the Charter of the United Nations,

Affirming the principle of the inadmissibility of the acquisition of territory by war,

Affirming also the illegality of the Israeli settlements in the territory occupied since 1967 and of Israeli actions aimed at changing the status of Jerusalem,

Affirming once more the right of all States in the region to live in peace within secure and internationally recognized borders,

Aware of the mutual recognition between the Government of the State of Israel and the Palestine Liberation Organization, the representative of the Palestinian people, and the signing by the two parties of the Declaration of Principles on Interim Self-Government Arrangements[4] at Washington on 13 September 1993, as well as the subsequent implementation agreements, including the Interim Agreement on the West Bank and the Gaza Strip of 28 September 1995,

Noting with satisfaction the withdrawal of the Israeli army, which took place in the Gaza Strip and the Jericho area in accordance with the agreements reached by the parties, and the initiation of the Palestinian Authority in those areas, as well as the beginning of the redeployment of the Israeli army in the rest of the West Bank,

Aware that the United Nations has participated as a full, extraregional participant in the work of the multilateral working groups of the Middle East peace process,

Noting the appointment by the Secretary-General of a "Special Coordinator in the occupied territories", and the positive contribution in this regard,

Welcoming the convening of the Conference to Support Middle East Peace at Washington on 1 October 1993, and all follow-up meetings,

1. *Reaffirms* the necessity of achieving a peaceful settlement of the question of Palestine, the core of the Arab-Israeli conflict, in all its aspects;

2. *Expresses its full support* of the ongoing peace process which began in Madrid and the Declaration of Principles on Interim Self-Government Arrangements, as well as the subsequent implementation agreements, and expresses the hope that the process will lead to the establishment of a comprehensive, just and lasting peace in the Middle East;

3. *Calls* for the timely and scrupulous implementation of the agreements reached between the parties towards the negotiation of the final settlement;

4. *Stresses* the need for:

(*a*) The realization of the inalienable rights of the Palestinian people, primarily the right to self-determination;

(*b*) The withdrawal of Israel from the Palestinian territory occupied since 1967;

5. *Also stresses* the need for resolving the problem of the Palestine refugees in conformity with its resolution 194 (III) of 11 December 1948;

6. *Urges* Member States to expedite the provision of economic and technical assistance to the Palestinian people during this critical period;

---

1 *Official Records of the General Assembly, Fiftieth Session, Supplement No. 35* (A/50/35).

2 A/48/486-S/26560, annex.

3 A/50/725-S/1995/930.

4 A/48/486-S/26560, annex.

7. *Emphasizes* the importance for the United Nations to play a more active and expanded role in the current peace process and in the implementation of the Declaration of Principles, including the monitoring of the forthcoming Palestinian elections;

8. *Requests* the Secretary-General to continue his efforts with the parties concerned, and in consultation with the Security Council, for the promotion of peace in the region and to submit progress reports on developments in this matter.

93rd plenary meeting
15 December 1995

50/129. Economic and Social Repercussions of the Israeli Settlements on the Palestinian People in the Palestinian Territory, Including Jerusalem, Occupied since 1967, and on the Arab Population of the Occupied Syrian Golan

Committee: 2
Vote: 126 - 2 - 28
Ref.: 49/132, 48/212, 47/172, 46/199

The General Assembly,

Recalling Economic and Social Council resolution 1995/49 of 28 July 1995,

Reaffirming the principle of the permanent sovereignty of people under foreign occupation over their national resources,

Guided by the principles of the Charter of the United Nations, affirming the inadmissibility of the acquisition of territory by force, and recalling Security Council resolutions 242 (1967) of 22 November 1967 and 497 (1981) of 17 December 1981,

Recalling Security Council resolution 465 (1980) of 1 March 1980 and other resolutions affirming the applicability of the Geneva Convention relative to the Protection of Civilian Persons in Time of War, of 12 August 1949,[1] to the occupied Palestinian territory, including Jerusalem, and other Arab territories occupied by Israel since 1967,

Recalling also Security Council resolution 904 (1994) of 18 March 1994, in which, among other things, the Council called upon Israel, the occupying Power, to continue to take and implement measures, including, *inter alia,* confiscation of arms, with the aim of preventing illegal acts of violence by Israeli settlers, and called for measures to be taken to guarantee the safety and protection of the Palestinian civilians in the occupied territory,

Aware of the negative and grave economic and social repercussions of the Israeli settlements on the Palestinian people in the Palestinian territory, occupied since 1967, including Jerusalem, and on the Arab population of the occupied Syrian Golan,

Welcoming the ongoing Middle East peace process started at Madrid, in particular the two implementation agreements embodied in the Agreement on the Gaza Strip and Jericho Area,[2] of 4 May 1994, and the interim agreement on the West Bank and Gaza Strip of 28 September 1995,

1. *Takes note* of the report of the Secretary-General;[3]

2. *Reaffirms* that Israeli settlements in the Palestinian territory, including Jerusalem, and other Arab territories occupied since 1967 are illegal and an obstacle to economic and social development;

3. *Recognizes* the economic and social repercussions of the Israeli settlements on the Palestinian people in the Palestinian territory occupied by Israel since 1967, including Jerusalem, and on the Arab population of the occupied Syrian Golan;

4. *Reaffirms* the inalienable right of the Palestinian people and the population of the occupied Syrian Golan to their natural and all other economic resources, and regards any infringement thereupon as illegal;

5. *Requests* the Secretary-General to submit to the General Assembly at its fifty-first session, through the Economic and Social Council, a report on the progress made in the implementation of the present resolution.

96th plenary meeting
20 December 1995

1 United Nations *Treaty Series,* vol.75, No. 973.

2 A/49/180-S/1994/727, annex.

3 A/50/262-E/1995/59.

04.44 TOGOLAND

750 (VIII). The Togoland Unification Problem

Committee: 4
Vote: A: 46 - 0 - 9; B: 52 - 1 - 4; C: 37 - 3 - 12
Ref.: 652(VII), 555(VI), 441(V)

A

The General Assembly,

Having examined the special report[4] of the Trusteeship Council on the Ewe and Togoland unification problem,

Taking into account the conclusion contained in the special report[5] of the 1952 United Nations Visiting Mission (T/1034) that "the people of the Trust Territories desire in principle unification of the two Trust Territories",

Recalling that the General Assembly based its resolution 652 (VII) of 20 December 1952 upon the consideration, *inter alia,* that the unification of the two parts of Togoland is the manifest aspiration of the majority of the population of the two Trust Territories,

Considering that the best means of achieving a form of unification acceptable to all groups of the population is through direct and continuous interchange of opinions among the representatives of those groups, and that such interchange of opinions could be realized in a reconstituted Joint Council for Togoland Affairs with ample powers to examine all aspects of the problem of unification of both Territories and to formulate pertinent recommendations,

Having heard the declarations[6] of the representatives of the All-Ewe Conference, of the Joint Togoland Congress and of the Parti togolais du progrès,

Having heard also the declarations[7] of the representatives of the Administering Authorities concerned,

1. *Regrets* that the Joint Council for Togoland Affairs has not yet been re-established;

2. *Reaffirms* the principles and aims of its resolutions 555 (VI) and 652 (VII) approved on 18 January and 20 December 1952 respectively;

3. *Recommends* that, in order to ensure that the Joint Council will faithfully reflect the wishes of all sections of the population of the two Trust Territories, its members should be directly elected by universal adult suffrage and secret ballot;

4. *Recommends* that the Administering Authorities establish, in consultation with the representatives of the different political parties, the rules concerning the structure which the Joint Council for Togoland Affairs should assume;

5. *Recommends* that the Administering Authorities assist the representatives of the different political parties to explain freely throughout Togoland their views on the problem of unification and, to this effect, that they take all necessary measures to ensure freedom of speech, movement and assembly in all parts of the Territories;

6. *Recommends* that the Administering Authorities disseminate throughout the two Trust Territories the complete texts of the pertinent resolutions of the General Assembly and of the Trusteeship

4 See document A/2424. Appendix 34, p. 497.

5 See document T/1034, p. 127.

6 See *Official Records of the General Assembly, Eighth Session, Fourth Committee,* 365th, 366th and 367th meetings.

7 *Ibid.*, 365th meeting.

Council in the main vernacular languages as well as in French or in English;

7. *Recommends* to the Administering Authorities the re-establishment of the Joint Council with the power to consider and make recommendations on the question of unification, as well as on all political, economic, social and educational matters affecting the two Trust Territories, and to serve as a means of ascertaining the opinions of the inhabitants of the Territories concerning any proposed changes in the terms of the Trusteeship Agreement for either of the Territories;

8. *Re-emphasizes* its recommendation that, through the Joint Council and in other ways, the Administering Authorities adopt measures to promote common policies on political, economic and social matters of mutual concern to the two Trust Territories, and expresses the opinion that the implementation of this recommendation requires that the Administering Authorities accord to each Territory simultaneously large measure of progress towards the objectives of Article 76 of the Charter and harmonize in all major respects the political, economic, social and educational policies and systems applying in the two Trust Territories;

9. *Invites* the Trusteeship Council to submit to the General Assembly at its ninth session a special report concerning the steps which have been taken towards the implementation of the present resolution;

10. *Expresses the hope* that the different political parties of both Territories will cooperate to achieve a formula acceptable to all which will facilitate the unification of the two Trust Territories.

469th plenary meeting
8 December 1953

B

The General Assembly,

Considering that there is an urgent need to develop fully in the two parts of Togoland a system of universal suffrage and that it is consequently essential to establish effective facilities for electoral registration with a view to the formation of an electoral body truly representative of the population of each Territory as a whole,

Noting paragraph (b) of the text of the announcement[1] made by the two Administering Authorities on 12 June 1953 concerning the re-establishment of the Joint Council for Togoland Affairs,

Noting further the observations made on this matter by the, petitioners heard by the Fourth Committee of the General Assembly, as well as the statements made by the representatives of the Administering Authorities,

1. *Urgently invites* the Administering Authorities to revise the system of electoral qualifications in force in the Territories and to put into effect a method of electoral registration based on personal identification which shall permit all adult persons to qualify for the right to vote and shall ensure that electoral consultations be carried out in accordance with the democratic principles of universal, direct and secret suffrage so as to reflect the opinion of the population as a whole;

2. *Recommends* that the political parties in the two Territories collaborate closely with the respective Administering Authorities with a view to carrying out the identification of the adult persons for electoral purposes.

469th plenary meeting
8 December 1953

C

The General Assembly,

Noting that Togoland under British administration is administered as an integral part of the Gold Coast, the Government of which has published a series of proposals[2] for constitutional changes designed to effect a further transfer of executive and legislative powers from the Administering Authority to the Gold Coast Government and to serve as an interim measure leading towards full self-government for the Gold Coast within the British Commonwealth of Nations,

Noting that in the course of these proposals the Government of the Gold Coast expressed confidence that "the United Nations Organization will not fail to give satisfaction to the frequently reiterated and unanimous demand of the people of the Northern Section for their area to become part of the Northern Territories of the Gold Coast" and stated further that "there is a growing opinion in Southern Togoland in favour of integration with the Gold Coast",

Noting also that, in anticipation of further constitutional changes in the Gold Coast, the 1952 United Nations Visiting Mission, in its report[3] on Togoland under British administration, raised with some urgency the question of the compatibility of the provisions of the Trusteeship Agreement with any further appreciable transfer of executive and legislative authority to the Government of the Gold Coast, and expressed the opinion that the prospect of a further constitutional advance in the Gold Coast may require the position of the Trust Territory to be reviewed with particular care within a relatively short period of time,

Recalling further that the Visiting Missions of 1949 and 1952 and the Trusteeship Council at its eleventh session have recognized that the question of the future constitutional association of Togoland with the Gold Coast depends to a large extent upon the settlement of the unification problem,

1. *Expresses the opinion* that further changes in the Constitution of the Gold Coast, with which Togoland under British administration is administered as an integral part, may, to the extent that they provide for an increased measure of self-government, necessitate revision of the existing Trusteeship Agreement in respect of the Trust Territory in so far as concerns the existing administrative union;

2. *Considers* that, in view of the manifest aspiration of the majority of the population of both the Trust Territories of Togoland for the unification of those Territories, any change in the Trusteeship Agreement for Togoland under British administration will necessarily affect the interests of the inhabitants of Togoland under French administration;

3. *Requests* the Trusteeship Council, at its thirteenth session, to re-examine in all aspects the problem of achieving in the two Trust Territories the basic objectives of the International Trusteeship System as set forth in Article 76 of the Charter and, in particular the progressive development of the inhabitants towards self-government or independence as may be appropriate to the particular circumstances of the Territories and their peoples and their freely expressed wishes, having particular regard to the special circumstances created by the constitutional and political situation in the Gold Coast as it affects both Togoland under British administration and Togoland under French administration;

4. *Requests* the Trusteeship Council to submit to the General Assembly at its ninth session a special report on this problem.

469th plenary meeting
8 December 1953

944 (X). The Togoland Unification Problem and the Future of the Trust Territory of Togoland under British Administration

Committee: 4
Vote: I: 42 - 7 - 11; II: 45 - 6 - 9
Ref.: 1477(XV), 1046(XI), 1044(XI)

The General Assembly,

I. The future of Togoland under British administration:

Recalling its resolution 860 (IX) of 14 December 1954, by which the Trusteeship Council was requested to consider the arrangements to be made to ascertain the wishes of the inhabitants of the Trust Territory of Togoland under British administration as to their future, without prejudice to the eventual solution which they might choose, whether it be independence, unification of an independent Togoland

1 See document T/1067/Rev. 1

2 See document A/C.4/249. Appendix 35, p. 502

3 See document T/1040.

under British administration with an independent Togoland under French administration, unification with an independent Gold Coast or some other self-governing or independent status,

Having received the report[1] of the Trusteeship Council transmitting the special report[2] of the United Nations Visiting Mission to the Trust Territories of Togoland under British Administration and Togoland under French Administration, 1955, the observations[3], of the representative of the United Kingdom of Great Britain and Northern Ireland, and the official records of the relevant meetings of the Council,

Noting the opinion of the Trusteeship Council that the views expressed in the special report of the Visiting Mission provide in general a useful basis for determining the arrangements to be made in pursuance of General Assembly resolution 860 (IX),

Taking note also of the views expressed orally by the various local political groups before the Fourth Committee during its hearings,

Noting further the statement of the Government of the United Kingdom that the Gold Coast will attain independence in the near future and that, in consequence it will be impossible thereafter for Togoland under British administration to be administered as at present,

1. *Accepts* the recommendation of the United Nations Visiting Mission to the Trust Territories of Togoland under British Administration and Togoland under French Administration, 1955, contained in its special report that the wishes of the inhabitants of Togoland under British administration as to their future should be ascertained by plebiscite;

2. *Recommends* that the Administering Authority of Togoland under British administration, in pursuance of Article 76 b of the Charter of the United Nations, take steps, in consultation with a United Nations Plebiscite Commissioner, to organize and conduct without delay, under the supervision of the United Nations, a plebiscite in respect of the Trust Territory in order to ascertain the wishes of the majority of its inhabitants in regard to

(*a*) The union of their Territory with an independent Gold Coast; or

(*b*) Separation of Togoland under British administration from the Gold Coast and its continuance under trusteeship pending the ultimate determination of its political future;

3. *Decides* to appoint a United Nations Plebiscite Commissioner who shall exercise on behalf of the General Assembly the powers and functions of supervision defined by the Visiting Mission in its special report, and who shall be assisted by observers and staff to be appointed by the Secretary-General in consultation with him;

4. *Recommends further* that the plebiscite be organized and conducted on the basis of the arrangements proposed in chapter IV of the special report of the Visiting Mission, subject to such modifications of detail as are agreed upon between the Administering Authority and the United Nations Plebiscite Commissioner, and such additional measures as may be proposed by the Commissioner in order to secure a free and neutral atmosphere for the plebiscite;

5. *Requests* the United Nations Plebiscite Commissioner to submit a report on the organization, conduct and results of the plebiscite to the Trusteeship Council for its consideration, and for transmission to the General Assembly at its eleventh session in order that the latter may, in consultation with the Administering Authority, assess the results and determine the further action to be taken on the attainment of independence by the Gold Coast in the light of all the circumstances and in accordance with the Charter of the United Nations and the Trusteeship Agreement;

6. *Requests* the Trusteeship Council, in virtue of the provisions of the Trusteeship Agreement and of the Charter, to continue to exercise its functions at either its regular or special sessions as may be necessary, and to take into consideration any matter that may arise, or be referred to it, in respect of the Trust Territory;

II. The future of Togoland under French administration:

Noting with regard to Togoland under French administration, the statements made by the Administering Authority, as recorded by the United Nations Visiting Mission to the Trust Territories of Togoland under British Administration and Togoland under French Administration, 1955, in its special report, to the effect that the Authority itself taking into account the views of the Territorial Assembly, contemplates holding in due course consultations with the inhabitants of the Territory to ascertain their wishes in respect of the future of the Territory,

Noting also the statements by the representative of France in both the Fourth Committee and the Trusteeship Council to the effect that his Government supports in principle the proposals made by the Visiting Mission,

Noting also the view expressed by the Visiting Mission that, following the political reforms at present contemplated by the Administering Authority, steps will be taken to ascertain the wishes of the inhabitants of the Territory as to their future,

1. *Endorses* the conclusion of the United Nations Visiting Mission to the Trust Territories of Togoland under British Administration and Togoland under French Administration, 1955, in respect of Togoland under French administration, that the implementation of the contemplated political reforms will play a helpful role in enabling the wishes of the inhabitants of the Territory as to their future to be ascertained at an early date by direct and democratic methods;

2. *Recommends* that this consultation of the population be conducted, as in the case of Togoland under British administration, under the supervision of the United Nations;

3. *Requests* the Trusteeship Council, at its forthcoming regular session, to undertake a special study of this matter, in consultation with the Administering Authority, and to report thereon, if possible, to the General Assembly at its eleventh session.

556th plenary meeting
15 December 1955

1044 (XI). The Future of Togoland under British Administration

Committee: 4
Vote: 64 - 0 - 9
Ref.: 1045(XI), 944(X), 860(IX)

The General Assembly,

Recalling that, by resolution 944 (X) of 15 December 1955, it recommended, in pursuance of Article 76 b of the Charter of the United Nations, that a plebiscite be organized and conducted in the Trust Territory of Togoland under British administration by the Administering Authority in consultation with and under the supervision of a United Nations Plebiscite Commissioner, in order to ascertain the wishes of its inhabitants in regard to the union of their Territory with an independent Gold Coast or otherwise,

Having received the report of the United Nations Plebiscite Commissioner[4] on the organization, conduct and results of the plebiscite, and having noted in particular the conclusion contained in the report that the plebiscite was held in an atmosphere of freedom, impartiality and fairness,

Having also received the report of the United Kingdom Plebiscite Administrator,[5]

Noting that the majority of the inhabitants of the Trust Territory participating in the plebiscite have expressed themselves in favour of the union of the Territory with an independent Gold Coast,

Noting also the recommendation of the Trusteeship Council in its resolution 1496 (XVIII) of 31 July 1956 that appropriate steps be taken, in consultation with the Administering Authority, for the

1 *Official Records of the General Assembly, Tenth Session, Annexes,* agenda item 35, document A/ 3046. Appendix 51, p. 477.

2 *Official Records of the Trusteeship Council, Fifth Special Session, Supplement No. 2* (T/1218), document T/1206 and Add.1.

3 *Ibid.*, document T/1214.

4 *Official Records of the General Assembly, Eleventh Session, Annexes,* agenda item 39, documents A/3173 and Add.1.

5 *Official Records of the Trusteeship Council, Eighteenth Session, Annexes,* agenda item 12, documents T/1269 and Add.1.

termination of the Trusteeship Agreement for the Territory to become effective upon the attainment of independence by the Gold Coast,

Having been informed by the Administering Authority that it is the intention of the Government of the United Kingdom of Great Britain and Northern Ireland that the Gold Coast shall become independent on 6 March 1957,

1. *Expresses its approval* of the union of the Territory of Togoland under British administration with an independent Gold Coast and accordingly invites the Administering Authority to take such steps as are necessary to this end;

2. *Resolves*, with the agreement of the Administering Authority, that, on the date on which the Gold Coast becomes independent and the union with it of the Territory of Togoland under British administration takes place, the Trusteeship Agreement approved by the General Assembly in resolution 63 (I) of 13 December 1946 shall cease to be in force, the objectives of trusteeship having been attained;

3. *Requests* the Government of the United Kingdom of Great Britain and Northern Ireland to notify the Secretary-General as soon as the union of the Territory of Togoland under British administration with an independent Gold Coast has been effected;

4. *Requests* the Secretary-General to communicate to all Member States and to the Trusteeship Council at its nineteenth session the notification by the Government of the United Kingdom of Great Britain and Northern Ireland, referred to in paragraph 3 above.

619th plenary meeting
13 December 1956

1253 (XIII). The Future of Togoland under French Administration

Committee: 4
Vote: unanimous
Ref.: 1417(XIV), 1416(XVI), 1254(XIII), 1182(XII), 1046(XI)

The General Assembly,

Recalling its resolution 1182 (XII) of 29 November 1957,

Taking note of the report of the United Nations Commissioner for the Supervision of the Elections in the Trust Territory of Togoland under French Administration[1] on the organization, conduct and results of the elections which took place on 27 April 1958 in the Territory,

Taking note of Trusteeship Council resolution 1921 (S-VIII) of 17 October 1958,

Taking note of the statements made by the representative of France and the Prime Minister of the Republic of Togoland during the thirteenth session of the General Assembly,[2]

Noting further the resolution adopted by the Chamber of Deputies of the Republic of Togoland on 23 October 1958,[3]

1. *Notes* that the Governments of France and of the Republic of Togoland have decided, by mutual agreement, that Togoland shall attain independence in 1960, in accordance with the wishes of the Chamber of Deputies of Togoland;

2. *Expresses its high appreciation* of the work of the United Nations Commissioner and his staff;

3. *Congratulates* France and the authorities and people of Togoland on their achievements in Togoland, which enable the basic objectives of the International Trusteeship System to be attained;

4. *Resolves accordingly*, in agreement with the Administering Authority, that on the day which will be agreed upon between the Government of France and the Government of Togoland, and on which the Republic of Togoland becomes independent in 1960, the Trusteeship Agreement approved by the General Assembly on 13 December 1946 shall cease to be in force, in accordance with Article 76 b of the Charter of the United Nations.

780th plenary meeting
14 November 1958

1 *Official Records of the General Assembly, Thirteenth Session, Annexes,* agenda item 40, document A/3957.

2 *Ibid., Fourth Committee.* 782nd meeting.

3 *Ibid., Annexes,* agenda item 40, document A/C.4/382. Appendix 12, p. 306.

04.45 SOUTHERN RHODESIA

1747 (XVI). The Question of Southern Rhodesia

Committee: -
Vote: 73 - 1 - 27

The General Assembly,

Recalling its resolution 1514 (XV) of 14 December 1960 containing the Declaration on the granting of independence to colonial countries and peoples,

Having considered the report on the question of Southern Rhodesia[4] submitted by the Special Committee on the Situation with regard to the Implementation of the Declaration on the Granting of Independence to colonial Countries and Peoples,

Considering that the vast majority of the people of Southern Rhodesia have rejected the Constitution of 6 December 1961,

Deploring the denial of equal political rights and liberties to the vast majority of the people of Southern Rhodesia,

Noting with regret that the Government of the United Kingdom of Great Britain and Northern Ireland has not yet taken steps to transfer all powers to the people of Southern Rhodesia, as required under paragraph 5 of resolution 1514 (XV),

Having further considered the evidence submitted by the petitioners before the Special Committee,

1. *Approves* the conclusions of the Special Committee on the Situation with regard to the Implementation of the Declaration on the Granting of Independence to colonial Countries and Peoples on Southern Rhodesia, and affirms that the Territory of Southern Rhodesia is a Non-Self-Governing Territory within the meaning of Chapter XI of the Charter of the United Nations;

2. *Requests* the Administering Authority:

(*a*) To undertake urgently the convening of a constitutional conference, in which there shall be full participation of representatives of all political parties, for the purpose of formulating a constitution for Southern Rhodesia, in place of the Constitution of 6 December 1961, which would ensure the rights of the majority of the people, on the basis of "one man, one vote", in conformity with the principles of the Charter of the United Nations and the Declaration on the granting of independence to colonial countries and peoples, embodied in General Assembly resolution 1514 (XV);

(*b*) To take immediate steps to restore all rights of the non-European population and remove all restraints and restrictions in law and in practice on the exercise of the freedom of political activity including all laws, ordinances and regulations which directly or indirectly sanction any policy or practice based on racial discrimination;

(*c*) To grant amnesty to, and ensure the immediate release of, all political prisoners;

3. *Requests* the Special Committee to continue its constructive efforts towards the earliest implementation of resolution 1514 (XV) with regard to Southern Rhodesia in order to ensure its emergence as an independent African State.

1121st plenary meeting
28 June 1902

4 *Official Records of the General Assembly, Sixteenth Session, Annexes,* agenda item 97, document A/5124. Appendix 41, p. 573.

2012 (XX). Question of Southern Rhodesia

Committee: 4
Vote: 107 - 2 - 1
Ref.: 1889(XVIII), 1883(XVIII), 1760(XVII), 1755(XVII)

The General Assembly,

Deeply concerned at the situation in Southern Rhodesia,

Noting with particular concern the repeated threats of the present authorities in Southern Rhodesia immediately to declare unilaterally the independence of Southern Rhodesia, in order to perpetuate minority rule in Southern Rhodesia,

Noting the attitude of the Government of the United Kingdom of Great Britain and Northern Ireland that a unilateral declaration of independence for Southern Rhodesia would be an act of rebellion and that any measure to give it effect would be an act of treason,

1. *Condemns* any attempt on the part of the Rhodesian authorities to seize independence by illegal means in order to perpetuate minority rule in Southern Rhodesia;

2. *Declares* that the perpetuation of such minority rule would be incompatible with the principle of equal rights and self-determination of peoples proclaimed in the Charter of the United Nations and in the Declaration on the Granting of Independence to Colonial Countries and Peoples contained in General Assembly resolution 1514 (XV) of 14 December 1960;

3. *Requests* the United Kingdom of Great Britain and Northern Ireland and all Member States not to accept a declaration of independence for Southern Rhodesia by the present authorities, which would be in the sole interest of the minority, and not to recognize any authorities purporting to emerge therefrom;

4. *Calls upon* the United Kingdom to take all possible measures to prevent a unilateral declaration of independence and, in the event of such a declaration, to take all steps necessary to put an immediate end to the rebellion, with a view to transferring power to a representative government in keeping with the aspirations of the majority of the people;

5. *Decides* to keep the question of Southern Rhodesia under urgent and continuing review during the twentieth session and to consider what further steps may be necessary.

1357th plenary meeting
12 October 1965

2024 (XX). Question of Southern Rhodesia

Committee: 4
Vote: 107 - 2 - 1
Ref.: 2022(XX)

The General Assembly,

Considering the explosive situation created in Southern Rhodesia following the unilateral declaration of independence,

Noting the measures taken by the Government of the United Kingdom of Great Britain and Northern Ireland,

1. *Condemns* the unilateral declaration of independence made by the racialist minority in Southern Rhodesia;

2. *Invites* the United Kingdom of Great Britain and Northern Ireland to implement immediately the relevant resolutions adopted by the General Assembly and the Security Council in order to put an end to the rebellion by the unlawful authorities in Southern Rhodesia;

3. *Recommends* the Security Council to consider this situation as a matter of urgency.

1375th plenary meeting
1 November 1965

2138 (XXI). Question of Southern Rhodesia

Committee: 4
Vote: 86 - 2 - 18

The General Assembly,

Recalling its resolution 1514 (XV) of 14 December 1960,

Recalling further its resolutions 1747 (XVI) of 28 June 1962, 1760 (XVII) of 31 October 1962, 1883 (XVIII) of 14 October 1963, 1889 (XVIII) of 6 November 1963, 1956 (XVIII) of 11 December 1963, 2012 (XX) of 12 October 1965, 2022 (XX) of 5 November 1965 and 2024 (XX) of 11 November 1965, and Security Council resolutions 202 (1965) of 6 May 1965, 216 (1965) of 12 November 1965, 217 (1965) of 20 November 1965 and 221 (1966) of 9 April 1966, and the resolutions adopted by the Special Committee on the Situation with regard to the Implementation of the Declaration on the Granting of Independence to Colonial Countries and Peoples on 22 April 1965,[1] 28 May 1965,[2] 21 April 1966[3] and 31 May 1966,[4] concerning the Non-Self-Governing Territory of Southern Rhodesia,

Noting with grave concern that the "talks about talks" between the Government of the United Kingdom of Great Britain and Northern Ireland and the illegal racist minority regime further jeopardize the inalienable rights of the African people of Zimbabwe,

1. *Condemns* any arrangement reached between the administering Power and the illegal racist minority regime which will not recognize the inalienable rights of the people of Zimbabwe to self-determination and independence in accordance with General Assembly resolution 1514 (XV);

2. *Reaffirms* the obligation of the administering Power to transfer power to the people of Zimbabwe on the basis of universal adult suffrage, in accordance with the principle of "one man, one vote".

1450th plenary meeting
22 October 1966

2877 (XXVI). Question of Southern Rhodesia

Committee: 4
Vote: 94 - 8 - 22
Ref.: 2796(XXVI), 2769(XXVI), 2765(XXVI), 2652(XXV), 2508(XXIV), 2383(XXIII), 2379(XXIII), 2262(XXII), 2151(XXI)

The General Assembly,

Having heard the statement by the representative of the Government of the United Kingdom of Great Britain and Northern Ireland[5] concerning the "proposals for a settlement" agreed upon between that Government and the racist minority regime in Salisbury,[6]

Recalling its resolution 1514 (XV) of 14 December 1960, containing the Declaration on the Granting of Independence to Colonial Countries and Peoples, and its resolution 2621 (XXV) of 12 October 1970, containing the program of action for the full implementation of the Declaration,

Recalling further all previous resolutions concerning the question of Southern Rhodesia adopted by the General Assembly and the Special Committee on the Situation with regard to the Implementation of the Declaration on the Granting of Independence to Colonial Countries and Peoples,

---

1 *Official Records of the General Assembly, Twentieth Session, Annexes,* addendum to agenda item 23 (A/6000/Rev.1), chapter III, para. 292.

2 *Ibid.*, para. 513.

3 *Ibid., Twenty-first Session, Annexes,* addendum to agenda item 23 (A/6300/Rev.1) chapter III para. 587.

4 *Ibid.*, para. 1097.

5 See *Official Records of the General Assembly, Twenty-sixth Session, Fourth Committee,* 1956th meeting.

6 See *Official Records of the Security Council, Twenty-sixth Year, Supplement for October, November and December 1971,* document S/10405.

Recalling also its resolution 2769 (XXVI) of 22 November 1971, in particular paragraphs 1 and 2 thereof,

Gravely concerned at the "proposals for a settlement" which, if implemented, will entrench the rule of the racist minority regime in Southern Rhodesia and will perpetuate the enslavement of the African people of Zimbabwe,

Deeply conscious that the "proposals for a settlement" were agreed upon without the participation of the representatives of the African people of Zimbabwe,

1. *Rejects* the "proposals for a settlement" agreed upon by the Government of the United Kingdom of Great Britain and Northern Ireland and the racist minority regime in Salisbury as constituting a flagrant violation of the inalienable right of the African people of Zimbabwe to self-determination and independence as provided for in General Assembly resolution 1514 (XV);

2. *Reaffirms* that no settlement which does not conform strictly to the principle of "no independence before majority rule" on the basis of one man, one vote, will be acceptable;

3. *Invites* the Security Council, when examining the question of Southern Rhodesia, to consider taking appropriate measures, in accordance with the relevant provisions of the Charter of the United Nations, in order to enable the people of Zimbabwe to exercise freely and without further delay their inalienable right to self-determination and independence;

4. *Welcomes* the decision by the Security Council on 2 December 1971[1] to invite Mr. Joshua Nkomo and the Reverend Ndabaningi Sithole, the respective leaders of the Zimbabwe African People's Union and the Zimbabwe African National Union, to appear before the Council to express their views concerning the future status of the Territory, and calls upon the Government of the United Kingdom, as the administering Power, to comply with that decision;

5. *Calls upon* all States to adhere strictly to the relevant provisions of the resolutions of the General Assembly and the Security Council on the question of Southern Rhodesia, and in particular to observe the resolutions of the Council imposing sanctions against the racist minority regime.

2028th plenary meeting
20 December 1971

3397 (XXX). Question of Southern Rhodesia

Committee: 4
Vote: 103 - 0 - 6
Ref.: 3298(XXIX), 3116(XXVIII), 2946(XXVII), 2765(XVI)

The General Assembly,

Having adopted resolution 3396 (XXX) of 21 November 1975 on the question of Southern Rhodesia,

Strongly deploring the increasing collaboration which certain States, particularly South Africa, in violation of Article 25 of the Charter of the United Nations and of the relevant decisions of the United Nations, maintain with the illegal racist minority regime, thereby seriously impeding the effective application of the sanctions and other measures taken so far against the illegal regime,

Seriously concerned at the continued importation of chrome and nickel into the United States of America from Southern Rhodesia, in violation of the relevant decisions of the Security Council and in disregard of the related resolutions of the General Assembly,

Deeply disturbed at recent reports of widespread violations of United Nations sanctions, including the operation of Southern Rhodesian aircraft for international passenger and cargo traffic and the participation of "Southern Rhodesian" teams in various sporting events, as well as the continued functioning of information and airlines offices of the illegal regime outside Southern Rhodesia and the resultant influx of foreign tourists into the Territory,

Considering that developments in the area call in particular for positive, concerted international action with a view to imposing maximum isolation on the illegal regime,

Reaffirming its conviction that the sanctions will not put an end to the illegal racist minority regime unless they are comprehensive, mandatory and effectively supervised, enforced and complied with by all States, in particular by South Africa,

1. *Strongly condemns* the policies of the Governments, particularly the Government of South Africa, which, in violation of the relevant resolutions of the United Nations and in open contravention of their specific obligations under Article 25 of the Charter of the United Nations, continue to collaborate with the illegal racist minority regime, and calls upon those Governments to cease forthwith all such collaboration;

2. *Condemns* all violations of the mandatory sanctions imposed by the Security Council, as well as the continued failure of certain Member States to enforce those sanctions strictly, as being contrary to the obligations assumed by them under Article 25 of the Charter;

3. *Condemns* the continued importation of chrome and nickel from Southern Rhodesia (Zimbabwe) into the United States of America, and calls upon the Government of the United States to repeal speedily all legislation permitting such importation;

4. *Calls upon* all Governments which so far have not done so:

(*a*) To take stringent enforcement measures to ensure strict compliance by all individuals, associations and bodies corporate under their jurisdiction with the sanctions imposed by the Security Council and to prohibit any form of collaboration by them with the illegal regime;

(*b*) To take effective steps to prevent or discourage the emigration to Southern Rhodesia (Zimbabwe) of any individuals or groups of individuals under their jurisdiction;

(*c*) To discontinue any action which might confer a semblance of legitimacy on the illegal regime, *inter alia* by forbidding the operation and activities of Air Rhodesia, the Rhodesia National Tourist Board and the Rhodesian Information Office, or any other activities which contravene the aims and purposes of the sanctions:

(*d*) To invalidate passports and other documents for travel to the Territory;

5. *Reiterates* its conviction that the scope of the sanctions against the illegal regime must be widened to include all the measures envisaged under Article 41 of the Charter and requests the Security Council to consider taking the necessary measures in that regard as a matter of urgency;

6. *Requests* the Special Committee on the Situation with regard to the Implementation of the Declaration on the Granting of Independence to Colonial Countries and Peoples to follow the implementation of the present resolution and invites the Security Council Committee established in pursuance of resolution 253 (1968) concerning the question of Southern Rhodesia to continue to cooperate in the related work of the Special Committee.

2414th plenary meeting
21 November 1975

34/192. Question of Southern Rhodesia

Committee: -
Vote: 107 - 16 - 21
Ref.: 33/38, 32/116, 31/154, 3396(XXX), 3297(XXIX), 3115(XXVIII), 2945(XXVII), 2796(XXVI), 2652(XXV), 2508(XXIV), 2379(XXIII), 2383(XXIII), 2262(XXII), 2151(XXI), 2022(XX), 1883(XVIII), 1889(XVIII), 1760(XVII), 1755(XVII)

The General Assembly,

Having considered the question of Southern Rhodesia (Zimbabwe),

Having examined the relevant chapters of the report of the Special Committee on the Situation with regard to the Implementation of the

[1] *Ibid., Twenty-sixth Year,* 1604th meeting.

Declaration on the Granting of Independence to Colonial Countries and Peoples,[1]

Having heard the statements of the representative of the administering Power,[2]

Having heard also the statements of the representatives of the Patriotic Front[3] who participated in an observer capacity in the consideration of the item,

Recalling its resolutions 1514 (XV) of 14 December 1960, containing the Declaration on the Granting of Independence to Colonial Countries and Peoples, and 2621 (XXV) of 12 October 1970, containing the program of action for the full implementation of the Declaration, as well as all other resolutions relating to the question of Southern Rhodesia adopted by the General Assembly, the Security Council and the Special Committee,

Reaffirming the responsibility of the United Nations in support of the struggle of the people of Southern Rhodesia for the exercise of their inalienable right to self-determination and independence,

Bearing in mind that the Government of the United Kingdom of Great Britain and Northern Ireland, as the administering Power, has the primary responsibility for decolonizing Southern Rhodesia (Zimbabwe) in conformity with resolution 1514 (XV) and putting an end to the critical situation which, as repeatedly affirmed by the Security Council, constitutes a threat to international peace and security,

Noting that the Government of the United Kingdom has resumed its responsibility as the administering Power and is committed to decolonize Southern Rhodesia on the basis of free and democratic elections which will lead Southern Rhodesia to genuine independence accepted by the international community,

Bearing in mind the resolution on Zimbabwe adopted by the Council of Ministers of the Organization of African Unity at its thirty-third ordinary session, held at Monrovia from 6 to 20 July 1979,[4] especially its affirmation of the Patriotic Front as the sole, legitimate and authentic representative of the people of Zimbabwe,

Bearing in mind also the relevant provisions of the Political Declaration adopted by the Sixth Conference of Heads of State or Government of Non-Aligned Countries, held at Havana from 3 to 9 September 1979,[5]

Concerned about the threats South Africa poses to the independence, unity and peace of Zimbabwe,

Concerned also about the threat posed by mercenaries to the establishment of genuine independence in Zimbabwe,

Bearing in mind that the negotiations at Lancaster House in London were the direct result of the armed struggle by the people of Zimbabwe led by the Patriotic Front, their sole legitimate representative,

Commending the firm determination of the people of Zimbabwe, under the leadership of the Patriotic Front, to achieve freedom and independence,

Deploring the moves by certain States to lift sanctions unilaterally, in violation of the measures imposed by the Security Council under Chapter VII of the Charter of the United Nations,

1. *Reaffirms* the inalienable right of the people of Zimbabwe to self-determination, freedom and independence and the legitimacy of their struggle to secure by all means at their disposal the enjoyment of that right, as set forth in the Charter of the United Nations and in conformity with the objectives of General Assembly resolution 1514 (XV);

2. *Reaffirms* the principle that there should be no independence before majority rule in Zimbabwe and, in this regard, takes note of the agreements reached at Lancaster House intended to bring about genuine independence on the basis of free and fair elections;

3. *Commends* the Patriotic Front for its decisive contribution in the negotiations and solemnly declares that a just and lasting settlement in Zimbabwe is possible only with the full participation of the Patriotic Front at every stage of implementation of the agreements reached at Lancaster House;

4. *Calls* for the full and faithful implementation of the agreements reached at Lancaster House;

5. *Strongly condemns* the racist regime of South Africa for its intervention in Southern Rhodesia, including the presence in the Territory of its military and security forces;

6. *Strongly condemns also* the presence of mercenaries in Southern Rhodesia;

7. *Calls upon* the administering Power to ensure the immediate and complete withdrawal of South African forces as well as all mercenaries from Southern Rhodesia;

8. *Calls upon* the administering Power also to ensure that South Africa shall not carry out its threats to undermine the implementation of the agreements reached at Lancaster House;

9. *Declares* that Security Council resolution 253 (1968) of 29 May 1968, imposing mandatory sanctions against Southern Rhodesia, can be revoked only by a decision of the Council and that any unilateral action in this regard would be in violation of the obligation assumed by Member States under Article 25 of the Charter;

10. *Calls upon* the Security Council to follow the situation closely until the people of Zimbabwe achieve genuine independence and majority rule;

11. *Requests* all States to give urgently substantial material assistance to the Governments of Angola, Botswana, Mozambique and Zambia to enable them to rebuild their socio-economic infrastructure adversely affected by constant acts of aggression by the illegal racist minority regime in Southern Rhodesia and by the application of the mandatory sanctions imposed by the Security Council;

12. *Requests* the Special Committee on the Situation with regard to the Implementation of the Declaration on the Granting of Independence to Colonial Countries and Peoples to keep the situation in the Territory under review and to report thereon to the General Assembly at its thirty-fifth session.

108th plenary meeting
18 December 1979

04.46 OTHER CASES

289 (IV). Question of the Disposal of the Former Italian Colonies

Committee: 1
Vote: A: 48 - 1 - 9; B: 48 - 5 - 3
Ref.: 617(VII), 392(V), 287(III), 266(III)

A

The General Assembly,

In accordance with Annex XI, paragraph 3, of the Treaty of Peace with Italy, 1947, whereby the Powers concerned have agreed to accept the recommendation of the General Assembly on the disposal of the former Italian colonies and to take appropriate measures for giving effect to it,

1 *Official Records of the General Assembly, Thirty-fourth Session, Supplement No. 23* (A/34/23/Rev.1), chaps. V-VIII.

2 *Ibid., Thirty-fourth Session, Fourth Committee,* 29th meeting, paras. 5-17, and 36th meeting, paras. 29-33, and *Ibid., Fourth Committee, Sessional Fascicle,* corrigendum. For the full text of the statement made at the 29th meeting, see A/C.4/34/L.27.

3 *Ibid.,* 26th meeting, paras. 9-23 and 31st meeting paras. 11-19; and *Ibid., Fourth Committee, Sessional Fascicle,* corrigendum. For the full texts, see A/C.4/34/L.27/L.26 and 28.

4 A/34/552 annex I, resolution CM/Res.719 (XXXIII).

5 See A/34/542, annex, sect. I, paras. 51-60.

Having taken note of the report[1] of the Four Power Commission of Investigation, having heard spokesmen of organizations representing substantial sections of opinion in the territories concerned, and having taken into consideration the wishes and welfare of the inhabitants of the territories, the interests of peace and security, the views of the interested Governments and the relevant provisions of the Charter,

A. With respect to Libya, recommends:

1. That Libya, comprising Cyrenaica, Tripolitania and the Fezzan, shall be constituted an independent and sovereign State;

2. That this independence shall become effective as soon as possible and in any case not later than 1 January 1952;

3. That a constitution for Libya, including the form of the government, shall be determined by representatives of the inhabitants of Cyrenaica Tripolitania and the Fezzan meeting and consulting together in a National Assembly;

4. That, for the purpose of assisting the people of Libya in the formulation of the constitution and the establishment of an independent Government, there shall be a United Nations Commissioner in Libya appointed by the General Assembly and a Council to aid and advise him;

5. That the United Nations Commissioner, in consultation with the Council, shall submit to the Secretary-General an annual report and such other special reports as he may consider necessary. To these reports shall be added any memorandum or document that the United Nations Commissioner or a member of the Council may wish to bring to the attention of the United Nations;

6. That the Council shall consist of ten members, namely:

(*a*) One representative nominated by the Government of each of the following countries: Egypt, France, Italy, Pakistan, the United Kingdom of Great Britain and Northern Ireland and the United States of America;

(*b*) One representative of the people of each of the three regions of Libya and one representative of the minorities in Libya;

7. That the United Nations Commissioner shall appoint the representatives mentioned in paragraph 6 (b), after consultation with the administering Powers, the representatives of the Governments mentioned in paragraph 6 (a), leading personalities and representatives of political parties and organizations in the territories concerned;

8. That, in the discharge of his functions, the United Nations Commissioner shall consult and be guided by the advice of the members of his Council it being understood that he may call upon different members to advise him in respect of different regions or different subjects;

9. That the United Nations Commissioner may offer suggestions to the General Assembly, to the Economic and Social Council and to the Secretary-General as to the measures that the United Nations might adopt during the transitional period regarding the economic and social problems of Libya;

10. That the administering Powers in cooperation with the United Nations Commissioner:

(*a*) Initiate immediately all necessary steps for the transfer of power to a duly constituted independent Government;

(*b*) Administer the territories for the purpose of assisting in the establishment of Libyan unity and independence, cooperate in the formation of governmental institutions and coordinate their activities to this end;

(*c*) Make an annual report to the General Assembly on the steps taken to implement these recommendations;

11. That upon its establishment as an independent State, Libya shall be admitted to the United Nations in accordance with Article 4 of the Charter;

B. With respect to Italian Somaliland, recommends:

1. That Italian Somaliland shall be an independent sovereign State;

2. That this independence shall become effective at the end of ten years from the date of the approval of a Trusteeship Agreement by the General Assembly;

3. That, during the period mentioned in paragraph 2, Italian Somaliland shall be placed under the International Trusteeship System with Italy as the Administering Authority;

4. That the Administering Authority shall be aided and advised by an Advisory Council composed of representatives of the following States: Colombia, Egypt and the Philippines. The headquarters of the Advisory Council shall be Mogadiscio. The precise terms of reference of the Advisory Council shall be determined in the Trusteeship Agreement and shall include a provision whereby the Trusteeship Council shall invite the States members of the Advisory Council, if they are not members of the Trusteeship Council, to participate without vote in the debates of the Trusteeship Council on any question relating to this territory;

5. That the Trusteeship Council shall negotiate with the Administering Authority the draft of a Trusteeship Agreement for submission to the General Assembly if possible during the present session, and in any case not later than the fifth regular session;

6. That the Trusteeship Agreement shall include an annex containing a declaration of constitutional principles guaranteeing the rights of the inhabitants of Somaliland and providing for institutions designed to ensure the inauguration, development and subsequent establishment of full self-government;

7. That in the drafting of this declaration the Trusteeship Council and the Administering Authority shall be guided by the annexed text proposed by the Indian delegation;

8. That Italy shall be invited to undertake provisional administration of the territory:

(*a*) At a time and pursuant to arrangements for the orderly transfer of administration agreed upon between Italy and the United Kingdom, after the Trusteeship Council and Italy have negotiated the Trusteeship Agreement;

(*b*) On condition that Italy gives an undertaking to administer the territory in accordance with the provisions of the Charter relating to the International Trusteeship System and to the Trusteeship Agreement pending approval by the General Assembly of a Trusteeship Agreement for the territory;

9. That the Advisory Council shall commence the discharge of its functions when the Italian Government begins its provisional administration;

C. With respect to Eritrea, recommends:

1. That a Commission consisting of representatives of not more than five Member States, as follows, Burma, Guatemala, Norway, Pakistan and the Union of South Africa, shall be established to ascertain more fully the wishes and the best means of promoting the welfare of the inhabitants of Eritrea, to examine the question of the disposal of Eritrea and to prepare a report for the General Assembly, together with such proposal or proposals as it may deem appropriate for the solution of the problem of Eritrea;

2. That in carrying out its responsibilities the Commission shall ascertain all the relevant facts, including written or oral information from the present administering Power, from representatives of the population of the territory, including minorities, from Governments and from such organizations and individuals as it may deem necessary. In particular, the Commission shall take into account:

(*a*) The wishes and welfare of the inhabitants of Eritrea, including the views of the various racial, religious and political groups of the provinces of the territory and the capacity of the people for self-government;

(*b*) The interests of peace and security in East Africa;

(*c*) The rights and claims of Ethiopia based on geographical, historical, ethnic or economic reasons, including in particular Ethiopia's legitimate need for adequate access to the sea;

3. That in considering its proposals the Commission shall take into account the various suggestions for the disposal of Eritrea submitted during the fourth regular session of the General Assembly;

---

1 See *Four Power Commission of Investigation for the former Italian Colonies*, volumes I-III.

4. That the Commission shall assemble at the Headquarters of the United Nations as soon as possible. It shall travel to Eritrea and may visit such other places as in its judgment may be necessary in carrying out its responsibilities. The Commission shall adopt its own rules of procedure. Its report and proposal or proposals shall be communicated to the Secretary-General not later than 15 June 1950 for distribution to Member States so as to enable final consideration during the fifth regular session of the General Assembly. The Interim Committee of the General Assembly shall consider the report and proposal or proposals of the Commission and report, with conclusions, to the fifth regular session of the General Assembly:

D. With respect to the above provisions:

1. *Invites* the Secretary-General to request the necessary facilities from the competent authorities of each of the States in whose territory it may be necessary for the Commission for Eritrea to meet or travel;

2. *Authorizes* the Secretary-General, in accordance with established practices,

(*a*) To arrange for the payment of an appropriate remuneration to the United Nations Commissioner in Libya;

(*b*) To reimburse the travelling and subsistence expenses of the members of the Council for Libya, of one representative from each Government represented on the Advisory Council for Somaliland, and of one representative and one alternate from each Government represented on the Commission for Eritrea;

(*c*) To assign to the United Nations Commissioner in Libya, to the Advisory Council for Somaliland, and to the United Nations Commission for Eritrea such staff and to provide such facilities as the Secretary-General may consider necessary to carry out the terms of the present resolution.

Annexure

Text Proposed by the Delegation of India

The following constitution shall be annexed to and form part of the Trusteeship Agreement for any of the former Italian colonies that may be placed under the International Trusteeship System:

1. The sovereignty of the Trust Territory shall be vested in its people and shall be exercised on their behalf by the authorities and in the manner prescribed herein.

2. The executive authority of the Trust Territory shall be exercised by an Administrator appointed by the Administering Authority.

3. To assist him in the discharge of his functions the Administrator shall appoint a Council consisting of five representatives of the principal political parties or organizations in the Trust Territory.

4. In matters relating to defence and foreign affairs, the Administrator shall be responsible to and carry out the directions of the United Nations acting through its appropriate organs. In all other matters the Administrator shall consult and be guided by the advice of his Council.

5. The legislative authority of the Trust Territory shall normally be exercised by the Administrator with the consent of his Council enlarged by such additional representatives of the people as the Administrator may summon for the purpose. In exceptional circumstances, the Administrator may, subject to the control of the United Nations acting through its appropriate organs, make and promulgate such ordinances as, in his opinion, the circumstances demand.

6. The judicial authority of the Trust Territory shall be exercised by a Supreme Court and courts subordinate thereto. The judges of the Supreme Court shall be appointed by the Administrator but shall hold office during good behaviour and shall not be removable except with the consent of the United Nations acting through its appropriate organs.

7. All the authorities of the Trust Territory shall in the exercise of their respective functions, respect human rights and fundamental freedoms for all without distinction as to race, sex, language or religion.

8. The United Nations, acting through its appropriate organs may:

(*a*) Make rules to supplement this constitution;

(*b*) Review the administration periodically and amend this constitution so as to establish the Trust Territory as an independent State within a period not exceeding five years.

250th plenary meeting
21 November 1949

B

The General Assembly, to assist it in making the appointment of the United Nations Commissioner in Libya,

Decides that a Committee composed of:

The President of the General Assembly, two of the Vice-Presidents of the General Assembly (Brazil and Pakistan), the Chairman of the First Committee, and the Chairman of the *Ad Hoc* Political Committee shall nominate a candidate or, if no agreement can be reached, three candidates.

250th plenary meeting
21 November 1949

*
* *

The Committee established by the General Assembly under resolution 289 (IV) B above to nominate a candidate for the office of United Nations Commissioner in Libya unanimously agreed[1] *on the nomination of Mr. Adrian Pelt (Netherlands), Assistant Secretary-General in charge of Conference and General Services, and proposed him for appointment by the General Assembly.*

The General Assembly at its 276th plenary meeting on 10 December 1949 voted by secret ballot and elected Mr. Pelt to the office of United Nations Commissioner in Libya.

C

The General Assembly,

Considering its recommendations regarding the disposal of the former Italian colonies,

Calls upon the Interim Committee of the General Assembly to study the procedure to be adopted to delimit the boundaries of the former Italian colonies in so far as they are not already fixed by international agreement, and report with conclusions to the fifth regular session of the General Assembly.

250th plenary meeting
21 November 1949

1573 (XV). Question of Algeria

Committee: 1
Vote: 63 - 8 - 27
Ref.: 1184(XII), 1012(XI), 909(X)

The General Assembly,

Having discussed the question of Algeria,

Recalling its resolution 1012 (XI) of 15 February 1957 by which the General Assembly expressed the hope that a peaceful, democratic and just solution would be found through appropriate means, in conformity with the principles of the Charter of the United Nations,

Recalling further its resolution 1184 (XII) of 10 December 1957 by which the General Assembly expressed the wish that *pourparlers* would be entered into, and other appropriate means utilized, with a view to a solution, in conformity with the purposes and principles of the Charter,

Noting with regret that the *pourparlers* contemplated in resolution 1184 (XII) did not materialize,

Recalling Article 1, paragraph 2, of the Charter,

Deeply concerned with the continuance of hostilities in Algeria,

Considering that the present situation in Algeria also constitutes a threat to international peace and security,

---

1 See document A/1235.

Recalling its resolution 1495 (XV) of 17 October 1900 by which the General Assembly urges that immediate and constructive steps should be adopted in regard to the urgent problems concerning the peace of the world,

Taking note of the fact that the two parties concerned have accepted the right of self-determination as the basis for the solution of the Algerian problem,

Recognizing the passionate yearning for freedom of all dependent peoples and the decisive role of such peoples in the attainment of their independence,

Convinced that all peoples have an inalienable right to complete freedom, the exercise of their sovereignty and the integrity of their national territory,

1. *Recognizes* the right of the Algerian people to self-determination and independence;

2. *Recognizes* the imperative need for adequate and effective guarantees to ensure the successful and just implementation of the right of self-determination on the basis of respect for the unity and territorial integrity of Algeria;

3. *Recognizes further* that the United Nations has a responsibility to contribute towards the successful and just implementation of this right.

956th plenary meeting
19 December 1960

1724 (XVI). Question of Algeria

Committee: 1
Vote: 62 - 0 - 38
Ref.: 1754(XVII), 1650(XVI)

The General Assembly,

Having discussed the question of Algeria,

Recalling its resolution 1514 (XV) of 14 December 1960 in which it proclaimed the necessity of bringing to a speedy and unconditional end colonialism in all its forms and manifestations,

Recalling further its resolution 1573 (XV) of 19 December 1960 by which it recognized the right of the Algerian people to self-determination and independence, the imperative need for adequate and effective guarantees to ensure the successful and just implementation of the right to self-determination on the basis of respect for the unity and territorial integrity of Algeria, and the fact that the United Nations has a responsibility to contribute towards the successful and just implementation of that right,

Deeply concerned about the continuance of the war in Algeria,

Taking note of the fact that the two parties concerned have affirmed their willingness to seek a negotiated and peaceful solution on the basis of the right of the Algerian people to self-determination and independence,

Regretting the suspension of the negotiations entered into by the Government of France and the Provisional Government of the Algerian Republic,

Calls upon the two parties to resume negotiations with a view to implementing the right of the Algerian people to self-determination and independence respecting the unity and territorial integrity of Algeria.

1085th plenary meeting
20 December 1961

1605 (XV). Question of the Future of Ruanda-Urundi

Committee: 4
Vote: 86 - 1 - 4
Ref.: 1606(XV), 1580(XV), 1579(XV), 1419(XIV), 1279(XIII), 63(I)

The General Assembly,

Bearing in mind the provisions of the General Assembly's Declaration on the granting of independence to colonial countries and peoples,[1]

Recalling its resolutions 1579 (XV) and 1580 (XV) of 20 December 1960 concerning the future of the Trust Territory of Ruanda-Urundi,

Having received the interim report of the United Nations Commission for Ruanda-Urundi[2] appointed under resolution 1579 (XV),

Regretting the failure of the Administering Authority to implement fully and effectively the terms of resolution 1579 (XV), the resistance to such implementation by the local representatives of the Administering Authority in Ruanda-Urundi and their failure to cooperate fully and effectively with the United Nations Commission for Ruanda-Urundi,

Regretting the *de facto* recognition by the Administering Authority of governmental bodies in Ruanda which were established by irregular and unlawful means and which cannot be regarded as fully representative of all segments of the population in the absence of free and fair elections on the basis of direct universal adult suffrage, as envisaged in resolution 1579 (XV),

Regretting also the setting up of governmental bodies in Urundi on the basis of communal elections, contrary to the assurances given by the Administering Authority that communal elections were purely administrative and had no political character,

Noting the several statements of the representatives of the Administering Authority conveying assurances that it will cooperate fully with the United Nations in Ruanda-Urundi,

Having heard the views of the petitioners from Ruanda-Urundi,

1. *Expresses its appreciation* to the members of the United Nations Commission for Ruanda-Urundi for their conscientious discharge of the duties entrusted to them under General Assembly resolutions 1579 (XV) and 1580 (XV);

2. *Calls upon* the Government of Belgium as the Administering Authority to ensure that the provisions of resolution 1579 (XV) are fully implemented by its representatives in Ruanda-Urundi before the legislative elections;

3. *Recognizes* that the Government of Belgium is alone responsible for the administration of the Trust Territory of Ruanda-Urundi and accountable to the United Nations, and that its responsibilities as Administering Authority cannot in any way be abdicated to local political bodies and leaders until after appropriate democratic institutions have been set up and the Trusteeship Agreement has been terminated, all with the approval of the United Nations;

4. *Considers* it necessary that, pending the establishment of popular governments on the basis of the legislative elections to be held in 1961, broad-based caretaker governments be constituted immediately in both parts of the Trust Territory to attend to current affairs of administration and to act in strict conformity with the obligations of the Administering Authority for the implementation of the resolutions of the General Assembly;

5. *Declares* that it is clearly the obligation and the responsibility of the Administering Authority to create the necessary conditions and atmosphere for the proper conduct of the national elections and not to permit any local authorities to impede the implementation of the resolutions of the General Assembly;

6. *Decides* that the referendum on the question of the Mwami, contemplated in resolution 1580 (XV), and the legislative elections in Ruanda-Urundi should be held in the month of August 1961 on the basis of direct universal adult suffrage, under the supervision of the

---

1 See resolution 1514(XV).

2 *Official Records of the General Assembly, Fifteenth Session, Annexes,* agenda item 45, addendum, documents A/4706 and Add.1.

United Nations, and that these be organized by the Administering Authority in full consultation with the United Nations Commission for Ruanda-Urundi, the actual dates to be fixed, after mutual consultation, in the light of the prevailing circumstances;

7. *Decides* further that the questions to be put at the referendum on the question of the Mwami in Ruanda should be the following:

"1. Do you wish to retain the institution of the Mwami in Ruanda?

"2. If so, do you wish Kigeli V to continue as the Mwami of Ruanda?";

8. *Requests* the United Nations Commission for Ruanda-Urundi, composed of three members elected by the General Assembly on 20 December 1960, hereafter to be designated United Nations Commissioners, to return to Ruanda-Urundi at the earliest possible time to assist and advise the Administering Authority in the full and proper implementation of resolution 1579 (XV) and the present resolution, and to perform the other tasks entrusted to it;

9. *Notes* the information given by the representative of the Administering Authority concerning measures of amnesty already implemented, and recommends that:

(*a*) Full and unconditional amnesty, as envisaged in resolution 1579 (XV), be immediately granted by the Administering Authority;

(*b*) The few remaining cases which, in the Administering Authority's view, are guilty of "very grave crimes" be examined by a Special Commission composed of the representatives of three Member States to be elected by the General Assembly, with a view to securing their release from prison or return from abroad in the full implementation of the Assembly's recommendation concerning amnesty not later than two months before the national elections;

10. *Notes* the observations contained in paragraphs 199-203 of the interim report of the United Nations Commission for Ruanda-Urundi and calls upon the Administering Authority to observe strictly its international obligations under the Trusteeship Agreement;

11. *Requests* the Administering Authority to ensure that the material conditions essential to the successful discharge by the United Nations Commissioners of the responsibilities, such as housing, office space, travel facilities, information and the free use of official broadcasting facilities are provided, and that the local authorities cooperate fully with them;

12. *Requests* the United Nations Commission for Ruanda-Urundi to submit a report on the implementation of the present resolution to the General Assembly at its sixteenth session;

13. *Decides* to maintain this item on the agenda 4 the present session, without closing the debate thereon and authorizes the United Nations Commission for Ruanda-Urundi, in the event that the performance of its duties is hindered through deliberate obstruction or lack of the requisite cooperation from any quarter, return to United Nations Headquarters and request the President of the General Assembly to reconvene the Assembly immediately to consider further measure essential to the discharge of the United Nations obligations with respect to the Trust Territory of Ruanda-Urundi;

14. *Calls upon* the Administering Authority to rescind Legislative Order No. 221/296 of 25 October 1960, so as to ensure that there is no unwarranted interference with the exercise of public freedom and the no persons may be removed or detained without recourse to due process of law;

15. *Reiterates* its conviction that the best future for Ruanda-Urundi lies in the accession of that Territory to independence as a single, united and composite State;

16. *Considers* that the full implementation of all the provisions of the present resolution will enable the General Assembly at its sixteenth session to consider the termination of the Trusteeship Agreement at the earliest possible date.

994th plenary meeting,
21 April 1961

1746 (XVI). The Future of Ruanda-Urundi

Committee: 4
Vote: 93 - 0 - 10
Ref.: 1836(XVII), 1749(XVII), 1748(XVII), 1744(XVI), 1743(XVI)

The General Assembly,

Recalling its resolution 1743 (XVI) of 23 February 1962 and the other resolutions on the question of the future of Ruanda-Urundi, as well as its resolution 63 (I) of 13 December 1946,

Having considered the report of the United Nations Commission for Ruanda-Urundi[1] appointed under paragraph 2 of resolution 1743 (XVI),

Noting that the efforts to maintain the unity of Ruanda-Urundi did not succeed,

Welcoming the Agreement on Economic Union concluded between the Governments of Rwanda and Burundi at the Conference at Addis Ababa held under the auspices of the Commission,

Taking into account the fact that the bulk of the Administering Authority's forces still remain in the Territory notwithstanding the objective, stated in paragraph 3 (e) of resolution 1743 (XVI), of securing the rapid withdrawal of Belgian military and paramilitary forces before independence,

Expressing its satisfaction at the favourable trends towards reconciliation noted by the Commission in its report, in particular, in Rwanda, the participation in the Government of two members of the Opposition,

Having heard the representatives of the Governments of Rwanda and Burundi and the petitioners,

Recalling the Declaration on the granting of independence to colonial countries and peoples embodied in resolution 1514 (XV) of 14 December 1960,

Taking note of the desire of the Governments of Rwanda and Burundi to attain independence as separate States on 1 July 1962, the date envisaged in paragraph 7 of resolution 1743 (XVI),

Taking into account the declaration by the Government of Burundi that from the date of the proclamation of independence it will not agree to the presence of foreign troops on its soil, and the declaration by the Government of Rwanda that the termination of the Trusteeship Agreement will make illegal the presence of Belgian troops in the territory of the Republic,

Noting the declaration of the Administering Authority that it will withdraw its forces from Rwanda and Burundi in accordance with the wishes of the General Assembly and the Governments concerned,

Recalling that after independence Rwanda and Burundi will enjoy sovereign rights,

Bearing in mind the needs which will confront Rwanda and Burundi in all fields when they accede to independence,

Recalling its resolution 1415 (XIV) of 5 December 1959 on assistance to territories emerging from a trust status and to newly independent States,

1. *Expresses its warm appreciation* to the United Nations Commission for Ruanda-Urundi, 1962, for the way it has performed its tasks;

2. *Decides*, in agreement with the Administering Authority, to terminate the Trusteeship Agreement of 13 December 1946 in respect of Ruanda-Urundi on 1 July 1962, on which date Rwanda and Burundi shall emerge as two independent and sovereign States;

3. *Calls upon* the Government of Belgium to withdraw and evacuate its forces still remaining in Rwanda and Burundi, and that, as of 1 July 1962, the Belgian troops in process of evacuation will no longer have any role to play and that the evacuation must be completed by 1 August 1962, without prejudice to the sovereign rights of Rwanda and Burundi;

4. *Requests* the Secretary-General to send immediately to Rwanda and Burundi a representative together with a team of experts whose

---

[1] *Official Records of the General Assembly, Sixteenth Session, Annexes,* second addendum to agenda item 49 (A/5126 and Add.1).

functions shall be:

(*a*) To supervise the withdrawal and evacuation of Belgian forces in accordance with this resolution;

(*b*) To help the Governments of Rwanda and Burundi to secure the implementation of the Agreement on Economic Union reached between the Governments of Rwanda and Burundi at Addis Ababa on 19 April 1962;

(*c*) To study, in consultation with the Governments concerned and in the light of the recommendations made by the United Nations Commission for Ruanda-Urundi, the need for technical and economic assistance in Rwanda and Burundi, so as to enable the Secretary-General to submit a report thereon. together with his recommendation, to the General Assembly at its seventeenth session;

(*d*) To assist the Governments of Rwanda and Burundi, at their request, in the organization of their administrative cadres and other related matters;

(*e*) To assist the Governments of Rwanda and Burundi, at their request, in the development and training of internal security forces;

5. *Authorizes* the Secretary-General, in accordance with the provisions of paragraph I of General Assembly resolution 1735 (XVI) of 20 December 1961 on unforeseen and extraordinary expenses for the financial year 1962, to enter into commitments not exceeding $2 million for the purpose of such emergency measures as may be required to ensure the continuation of essential services in the two countries, pending the consideration by the General Assembly of the report of the Secretary-General referred to in paragraph 4 (c) above;

6. *Requests* the United Nations Special Fund, the Technical Assistance Board and other United Nations bodies, as well as the specialized agencies, to give special consideration to the needs of Rwanda and Burundi;

7. *Expresses the hope* that all Member States of the United Nations will render such technical and economic assistance as they can to the new States of Rwanda and Burundi;

8. *Requests* the Secretary-General to report to the General Assembly at its seventeenth session on the implementation of this resolution;

9. *Recommends* that, after the proclamation of independence on 1 July 1962, Rwanda and Burundi should be admitted as Members of the United Nations under Article 4 of the Charter.

1118th plenary meeting
27 June 1962

2065 (XX). Question of the Falkland Islands (Malvinas)

Committee: 4
Vote: 94 - 0 - 14

The General Assembly,

Having examined the question of the Falkland Islands (Malvinas),

Taking into account the chapters of the reports of the Special Committee on the Situation with regard to the Implementation of the Declaration on the Granting of Independence to Colonial Countries and Peoples relating to the Falkland Islands (Malvinas),[1] and in particular the conclusions and recommendations adopted by the Committee with reference to that Territory

Considering that its resolution 1514 (XV) of 14 December 1960 was prompted by the cherished aim of bringing to an end everywhere colonialism in all its forms, one of which covers the case of the Falkland Islands (Malvinas),

Noting the existence of a dispute between the Governments of Argentina and the United Kingdom of Great Britain and Northern Ireland concerning sovereignty over the said Islands,

1. *Invites* the Governments of Argentina and the United Kingdom of Great Britain and Northern Ireland to proceed without delay with the negotiations recommended by the Special Committee on the Situation with regard to the Implementation of the Declaration on the Granting of Independence to Colonial Countries and Peoples with a view to finding a peaceful solution to the problem, bearing in mind the provisions and objectives of the Charter of the United Nations and of General Assembly resolution 1514 (XV) and the interests of the population of the Falkland Islands (Malvinas);

2. *Requests* the two Governments to report to the Special Committee and to the General Assembly at its twenty-first session on the results of the negotiations.

1398th plenary meeting
16 December 1965

1 *Official Records of the General Assembly, Nineteenth Session, Annexes,* annex No. 8 (part I) (A/5800/Rev.1), chapter XXIII; *Ibid., Twentieth Session, Annexes,* addendum to agenda item 23 (A/6000/Rev.1), chapter XXII.

3160 (XXVIII). Question of the Falkland Islands (Malvinas)

Committee: 4
Vote: 116 - 0 - 4

The General Assembly,

Having considered the question of the Falkland Islands (Malvinas),

Recalling its resolution 1514 (XV) of 14 December 1960 containing the Declaration on the Granting of Independence to Colonial Countries and Peoples,

Recalling also its resolution 2065 (XX) of 16 December 1965, in which it invited the Governments of Argentina and the United Kingdom of Great Britain and Northern Ireland to proceed without delay with the negotiations recommended by the Special Committee on the Situation with regard to the Implementation of the Declaration on the Granting of Independence to Colonial Countries and Peoples with a view to finding a peaceful solution to the problem of the Falkland Islands (Malvinas), bearing in mind the provisions and objectives of the Charter of the United Nations and of resolution 1514 (XV) and the interests of the population of the Falkland Islands (Malvinas),

Gravely concerned at the fact that eight years have elapsed since the adoption of resolution 2065 (XX) without any substantial progress having been made in the negotiations,

Mindful that resolution 2065 (XX) indicates that the way to put an end to this colonial situation is the peaceful solution of the conflict of sovereignty between the Governments of Argentina and the United Kingdom with regard to the aforementioned islands,

Expressing its gratitude for the continuous efforts made by the Government of Argentina, in accordance with the relevant decisions of the General Assembly, to facilitate the process of decolonization and to promote the well-being of the population of the islands,

1. *Approves* the chapters of the report of the Special Committee on the Situation with regard to the Implementation of the Declaration on the Granting of Independence to Colonial Countries and Peoples relating to the Falkland Islands (Malvinas)[2] and, in particular, the resolution adopted by the Special Committee on 21 August 1973 concerning the Territory;[3]

2. *Declares* the need to accelerate the negotiations between the Governments of Argentina and the United Kingdom of Great Britain and Northern Ireland called for in General Assembly resolution 2065 (XX) in order to arrive at a peaceful solution of the conflict of sovereignty between them concerning the Falkland Islands (Malvinas);

3. *Urges* the Governments of Argentina and the United Kingdom, therefore, to proceed without delay with the negotiations, in accordance with the provisions of the relevant resolutions of the General Assembly, in order to put an end to the colonial situation;

4. *Requests* both Governments to report to the Secretary-General and to the General Assembly as soon as possible, and not later than at its twenty-ninth session, on the results of the recommended negotiations.

2202nd plenary meeting
14 December 1973

2 *Official Records of the General Assembly, Twenty-eigth Session, Supplement No. 23* (A/9023/Rev.1), chaps. III and XXVII.

3 *Ibid.*, chap. XXVII, para. 12.

43/25. Question of the Falkland Islands (Malvinas)

Committee: -
Vote: 109 - 5 - 37
Ref.: 42/19, 41/40, 40/21, 39/6, 38/12, 37/9, 31/49

The General Assembly,

Having considered the question of the Falkland Islands (Malvinas) and having received the report of the Secretary-General,[1]

Aware of the interest of the international community in the peaceful and definitive settlement by the Governments of Argentina and the United Kingdom of Great Britain and Northern Ireland of all their differences, in accordance with the Charter of the United Nations,

Taking note of the interest repeatedly expressed by both parties in normalizing their relations,

Convinced that such purpose would be facilitated by a global negotiation between both Governments that will allow them to rebuild mutual confidence on a solid basis and to resolve the pending problems, including all aspects on the future of the Falkland Islands (Malvinas),

1. *Reiterates its request* to the Governments of Argentina and the United Kingdom of Great Britain and Northern Ireland to initiate negotiations with a view to finding the means to resolve peacefully and definitively the problems pending between both countries, including all aspects on the future of the Falkland Islands (Malvinas), in accordance with the Charter of the United Nations;

2. *Requests* the Secretary-General to continue his renewed mission of good offices in order to assist the parties in complying with the request made in paragraph 1 above, and to take the necessary measures to that end;

3. *Also requests* the Secretary-General to submit to the General Assembly at its forty-fourth session a report on the progress made in the implementation of the present resolution;

4. *Decides* to include in the provisional agenda of its forty-fourth session the item entitled "Question of the Falkland Islands (Malvinas)".

54th plenary meeting
17 November 1988

2347 (XXII). Question of the Trust Territory of Nauru

Committee: 4
Vote: unanimous
Ref.: 2226(XXI), 2111(XX), 140(II)

The General Assembly,

Recalling the Trusteeship Agreement for the Territory of Nauru approved by the General Assembly on 1 November 1947,[2]

Recalling its resolutions 2111 (XX) of 21 December 1965 and 2226 (XXI) of 20 December 1966,

Mindful of the relevant provisions of the Charter of the United Nations and General Assembly resolutions 1514 (XV) of 14 December 1960 containing the Declaration on the Granting of Independence to Colonial Countries and Peoples,

Having considered the special report of the Trusteeship Council on its thirteenth special session,[3]

1. *Notes* the formal announcement by the Administering Authority that, following the resumed talks between representatives of the Nauruan people and of the Administering Authority, it was agreed that Nauru should accede to independence on 31 January 1968;[4]

2. *Welcomes* the statement made in the Fourth Committee by the representatives of the Governments of Australia, New Zealand and the United Kingdom of Great Britain and Northern Ireland as the Administering Authority that the Administering Authority has complied with the request of the representatives of the Nauruan people for full and unqualified independence;

3. *Resolves* accordingly, in agreement with the Administering Authority, that the Trusteeship Agreement for the Territory of Nauru approved by the General Assembly on 1 November 1947 shall cease to be in force upon the accession of Nauru to independence on 31 January 1968;

4. *Calls upon* all States to respect the independence and the territorial integrity of the independent State of Nauru;

5. *Urges* the organs of the United Nations concerned and the specialized agencies to render all possible assistance to the people of Nauru in their endeavour to build a new nation.

1641 plenary meeting
19 December 1967

* * *

Pursuant to Article 86 of the Charter of the United Nations, New Zealand will cease to be a member of the Trusteeship Council on the accession of Nauru to independence on 31 January 1968. As from that date the Council will therefore be composed of the following Member States: Australia, China, France, Liberia, Union of Soviet Socialist Republics, United Kingdom of Great Britain and Northern Ireland and United States of America.

2357 (XXII). Question of American Samoa, Antigua, Bahamas, Bermuda, British Virgin Islands, Cayman Islands, Cocos (Keeling) Islands, Dominica, Gilbert and Ellice Islands, Grenada, Guam, Mauritius, Montserrat, New Hebrides, Niue, Pitcairn, St. Helena, St. Kitts-Nevis-Anguilla, St. Lucia, St. Vincent, Seychelles, Solomon Islands, Swaziland, Tokelau Islands, Turks and Caicos Islands and the United States Virgin Islands

Committee: 4
Vote: 86 - 0 - 2
Ref.: 2134(XXI), 2063(XX), 1954(XVIII), 1817(XVII)

The General Assembly,

Having considered the question of American Samoa, Antigua, Bahamas, Bermuda, British Virgin Islands, Cayman Islands, Cocos (Keeling) Islands, Dominica, Gilbert and Ellice Islands, Grenada, Guam, Mauritius, Montserrat, New Hebrides, Niue, Pitcairn, St. Helena, St. Kitts-Nevis-Anguilla, St. Lucia, St. Vincent, Seychelles, Solomon Islands, Swaziland, Tokelau Islands, Turks and Caicos Islands and the United States Virgin Islands,

Having examined the chapters of the report of the Special Committee on the Situation with regard to the Implementation of the Declaration on the Granting of Independence to Colonial Countries and Peoples relating to these Territories,[5]

Recalling its resolutions 1514 (XV) of 14 December 1960 1654 (XVI) of 27 November 1961, 1810 (XVII) of 17 December 1962, 1956 (XVIII) of 11 December 1963, 2066 (XX) of 16 December 1965, 2069 (XX) of 16 December 1965, 2189 (XXI) of 13 December 1966, 2232 (XXI) of 20 December 1966 and 2288 (XXII) of 7 December 1967,

Noting the constitutional changes that were introduced in February and March 1967 in the Territories of Antigua, Dominica, Grenada, St. Kitts-Nevis-Anguilla and St. Lucia and that are envisaged for the Territory of St. Vincent,

Noting further the decision taken by the Special Committee that General Assembly resolution 1514 (XV) containing the Declaration on the Granting of Independence to Colonial Countries and Peoples and other relevant resolutions continue to apply to these Territories,

---

1 A/43/799.

2 See General Assembly resolution 140 (II).

3 *Official Records of the General Assembly, Twenty-second Session, Annexes*, agenda item 13, document A/6926. Appendix 18, p. 479.

4 *Ibid.*, document A/6903, Appendix 19, p. 483.

5 *Ibid.*, chapters XI, XIV to XVIII, XX and XXIII.

Deeply concerned at the information contained in the report of the Special Committee on the continuation of policies which aim, among other things, at the disruption of the territorial integrity of some of these Territories and at the creation by the administering Powers of military bases and installations in contravention of the relevant General Assembly resolutions,

Deploring the attitude of some administering Powers which continue to refuse to allow United Nations visiting missions to visit these Territories,

Conscious that these situations require the continued attention and assistance of the United Nations in the achievement by the peoples of these Territories of their objectives, as embodied in the Charter of the United Nations and in the Declaration on the Granting of Independence to Colonial Countries and Peoples,

Aware of the special circumstances of geographical location and economic conditions of some of these Territories,

1. *Approves* the chapters of the report of the Special Committee on the Situation with regard to the Implementation of the Declaration on the Granting of Independence to Colonial Countries and Peoples relating to these Territories;[1]

2. *Reaffirms* the inalienable right of the peoples of these Territories to self-determination and independence;

3. *Calls upon* the administering Powers to implement without delay the relevant resolutions of the General Assembly;

4. *Reiterates* its declaration that any attempt aimed at the partial or total disruption of the national unity and the territorial integrity of colonial Territories and the establishment of military bases and installations in these Territories is incompatible with the purposes and principles of the Charter of the United Nations and of General Assembly resolution 1514 (XV);

5. *Urges* the administering Powers to allow United Nations visiting missions to visit the Territories and to extend to them full cooperation and assistance;

6. *Decides* that the United Nations should render all help to the peoples of these Territories in their efforts freely to decide their future status;

7. *Requests* the Special Committee to continue to pay special attention to these Territories and to report to the General Assembly at its twenty-third session on the implementation of the present resolution;

8. *Requests* the Secretary-General to continue to provide all possible assistance in the implementation of the present resolution.

1641st plenary meeting
19 December 1967

1 The President of the General Assembly, before putting the text of the present resolution to the vote, pointed out that in approving chapter XI of the Special Committee's report relating to Swaziland, the Assembly would be deciding that subject to the consent of the donor Governments, the contributions so far made to the Fund for the Economic Development of Basutoland, Bechuanaland and Swaziland, established under General Assembly resolution 2063 (XX) of 16 December 1965, would be transferred to the United Nations Development Programme.

50/38. Questions of American Samoa, Anguilla, Bermuda, the British Virgin Islands, the Cayman Islands, Guam, Montserrat, Pitcairn, St. Helena, Tokelau, the Turks and Caicos Islands and the United States Virgin Islands

Committee: 4
Vote: 146 - 4 - 3
Ref.: 49/46, 48/31, 47/27, 46/68, 45/23-32, 44/90-99, 43/35-44, 42/80-89, 41/17-26, 40/41-49, 39/31-40, 38/41-48, 37/20-28, 36/62, 36/63, 35/21-25, 34/34-36, 34/39, 33/32-35, 32/24, 32/28-31, 31/48, 31/52, 31/54, 31/55, 31/57-58, 3433, 3429, 3428, 3427, 3425(XXX), 3290, 3289(XXIX), 3156, 3155(XXVIII), 2986, 2984(XXVII), 2869, 2868(XXVI), 2704(XXV), 2592(XXIV), 2430(XXIII), 2237(XXI), 2069(XX)

A

General

The General Assembly,

Having considered the questions of the Non-Self-Governing Territories of American Samoa, Anguilla, Bermuda, the British Virgin Islands, the Cayman Islands, Guam, Montserrat, Pitcairn, St. Helena, Tokelau, the Turks and Caicos Islands and the United States Virgin Islands, hereinafter "the Territories",

Having examined the relevant chapter of the report of the Special Committee on the Situation with regard to the Implementation of the Declaration on the Granting of Independence to Colonial Countries and Peoples,[2]

Recognizing that 1995 is the fiftieth anniversary of the United Nations and that decolonization is one of the proudest achievements of the Organization,

Recalling its resolution 1514 (XV) of 14 December 1960, containing the Declaration on the Granting of Independence to Colonial Countries and Peoples, and all resolutions and decisions of the United Nations relating to those Territories, including, in particular, the resolutions adopted by the General Assembly at its forty-ninth session on the individual Territories covered by the present resolution,

Recognizing that the specific characteristics and the sentiments of the people of the Territories require flexible, practical and innovative approaches to the options of self-determination, without any prejudice to territorial size, geographical location, size of population or natural resources,

Recalling its resolution 1541 (XV) of 15 December 1960, containing the principles that should guide Member States in determining whether or not an obligation exists to transmit the information called for under Article 73 *e* of the Charter of the United Nations,

Conscious of the need to ensure the full and speedy implementation of the Declaration in respect of the Territories, in view of the target set by the United Nations to eradicate colonialism by the year 2000,

Noting with appreciation the continuing exemplary cooperation of New Zealand, as administering Power, in the work of the Special Committee, and welcoming its statement that it will abide by the wishes of the population of Tokelau in determining their future political status,

Welcoming the stated position of the Government of the United Kingdom of Great Britain and Northern Ireland that it continues to take seriously its obligations under the Charter of the United Nations to develop self-government in the dependent Territories and, in cooperation with the locally elected Governments, to ensure that their constitutional frameworks continue to meet the wishes of the people, and the emphasis that it is ultimately for the peoples of the Territories to decide their future status,

Aware of the special circumstances of the geographical location and economic conditions of each Territory, and bearing in mind the necessity of promoting economic stability and diversifying and

2 A/50/23 (Part VI), chap. X.

strengthening further the economies of the respective Territories as a matter of priority,

Conscious of the particular vulnerability of the small Territories to natural disasters and environmental degradation,

Aware of the usefulness, both to the Territories and to the Special Committee of the participation of appointed and elected representatives of the Territories in the work of the Special Committee,

Expressing its conviction that referendums and other forms of popular consultation on the future status of the Non-Self-Governing Territories are an appropriate means of ascertaining the wishes of the peoples in those Territories with regard to their future political status,

Mindful that United Nations visiting missions provide one effective means of ascertaining the situation in the Territories, and considering that the possibility of sending further visiting missions to the Territories at an appropriate time and in consultation with the administering Powers should be kept under review,

Mindful also that some Territories have not had any United Nations visiting mission for a long period of time,

Noting with appreciation the contribution to the development of some Territories by specialized agencies and other organizations of the United Nations system, in particular the United Nations Development Programme, as well as regional institutions such as the Caribbean Development Bank,

1. *Approves* the chapter of the report of the Special Committee on the Situation with regard to the Implementation of the Declaration on the Granting of Independence to Colonial Countries and Peoples relating to the Non-Self-Governing Territories of American Samoa, Anguilla, Bermuda, the British Virgin Islands, the Cayman Islands, Guam, Montserrat, Pitcairn, St. Helena, Tokelau, the Turks and Caicos Islands and the United States Virgin Islands, hereinafter "the Territories";[1]

2. *Reaffirms* the inalienable right of the people of the Territories to self-determination, including independence, in conformity with the Charter of the United Nations and General Assembly resolution 1514 (XV), containing the Declaration on the Granting of Independence to Colonial Countries and Peoples;

3. *Reaffirms also* that it is ultimately for the people of the Territories themselves to determine freely their future political status in accordance with the relevant provisions of the Charter, the Declaration and the relevant resolutions of the General Assembly, and in that connection calls upon the administering Powers, in cooperation with the territorial Governments, to facilitate programmes of political education in the Territories in order to foster an awareness among the people of the possibilities open to them in the exercise of their right to self-determination, in conformity with the legitimate political status options clearly defined in resolution 1541 (XV);

4. *Requests* the administering Powers to ascertain expeditiously, by means of popular consultations, the wishes and aspirations of the peoples of Non-Self-Governing Territories regarding their future political status so that the Special Committee can review the status of the Territories in accordance with the expressed wishes of the peoples of the Territories;

5. *Also requests* the administering Powers to facilitate the dispatch of the United Nations visiting missions to the Non-Self-Governing Territories regarding their future political status so that the Special Committee can review the status of the Territories in accordance with the expressed wishes of the peoples of the Territory;

6. *Reaffirms* the responsibility of the administering Powers under the Charter to promote the economic and social development and to preserve the cultural identity of the Territories, and recommends that priority continue to be given, in consultation, with the territorial Governments concerned, to the strengthening and diversification of their respective economies;

7. *Requests* the administering Powers to take all necessary measures to protect and conserve the environment of the Territories under their administration against any environmental degradation, and requests the specialized agencies concerned to continue to monitor environmental conditions in those Territories;

8. *Calls upon* the administering Powers to continue to take all necessary measures, in cooperation with the respective territorial Government, to counter problems related to drug trafficking, money laundering and other offences;

9. *Stresses* that the achievement of the declared goal of eradication of colonialism by the year 2000 requires full and constructive cooperation by all parties concerned, and appeals to the administering Powers to continue to give their full support to the Special Committee;

10. *Urges* Member States to contribute to the efforts of the United Nations to usher in the twenty-first century in a world free of colonialism, and calls upon them to continue to give their full support to the Special Committee in its endeavours towards that noble goal;

11. *Invites* the specialized agencies and other organizations of the United Nations system to initiate or to continue to take all necessary measures to accelerate progress in the social and economic life of the Territories;

12. *Requests* the Special Committee to continue the examination of the question of the small Territories and to recommend to the General Assembly the most suitable steps to be taken to enable the populations of those Territories to exercise their right to self-determination, and to report thereon to the Assembly at its fifty-first session.

B

1. American Samoa

The General Assembly,

Referring to resolution A above,

Noting the fact that a large number of American Samoans have emigrated to the United States of America and are residing there,

Noting also the constitutional developments in the Territory,

Noting further that the Territory, similar to isolated communities with limited funds, continues to experience lack of adequate medical facilities and other infrastructural requirements,

Recalling the dispatch in 1981 of a United Nations visiting mission to the Territory,

1. *Requests* the administering Power to carry out, at the earliest possible date, a democratic exercise to ascertain the wishes of the people of American Samoa regarding the future status of the Territory;

2. *Calls upon* the administering Power to continue to assist the territorial Government in the economic and social development of the Territory and the development of manpower resources.

2. Anguilla

The General Assembly,

Referring to resolution A above,

Noting that general elections were held in March 1994,

Conscious of the commitment of both the Government of Anguilla and the administering Power to a new and closer policy of dialogue and partnership through the Country Policy Plan for 1993-1997,

Aware that the exploitation of deep-sea resources would help reduce the risk of depleting the Territory's own fishing resources as a result of overfishing,

Noting the need for continued cooperation between the administering Power and the territorial Government in tackling the problems of drug trafficking and money laundering,

Recalling the dispatch in 1984 of a United Nations visiting mission to the Territory,

1. *Requests* the administering Power to carry out, at the earliest possible date, an exercise to ascertain the wishes of the people of Anguilla regarding the future status of the Territory;

2. *Requests* all countries, organizations and United Nations agencies with deep-sea fishing experience to assist the Territory in improving its capacity in exploiting deep-sea fishing.

[1] *Ibid.*

3. Bermuda

The General Assembly,

Referring to resolution A above,

Noting the results of the independence referendum held on 16 August 1995,

Conscious of the different viewpoints of the political parties of the Territory on the future status of the Territory,

Noting the measures taken by the Government to combat racism and the plan to set up a Commission for Unity and Racial Equality,

Noting also the closure of the Canadian base in 1994 and the announced plans of the United Kingdom of Great Britain and Northern Ireland and the United States of America to close their respective air and naval bases in Bermuda in 1995,

Calls upon the administering Power to continue its programmes of socio-economic development.

4. British Virgin Islands

The General Assembly,

Referring to resolution A above,

Noting the completion of the constitutional review in the Territory and the coming into force of the amended Constitution, and noting also the results of the general elections held on 20 February 1995,

Noting further the results of the constitutional review of 1993-1994, which made it clear that a prerequisite to independence must be a constitutionally expressed wish by the people as a result of a referendum,

Taking note of the statement by the Chief Minister of the British Virgin Islands that the Territory was ready for constitutional and political advancement towards full internal self-government and that the administering Power should assist through gradual transfer of power to elected territorial representatives,

Noting that the Territory is emerging as one of the world's leading off-shore financial centres,

Noting also the need for continued cooperation between the administering Power and the territorial Government in countering drug trafficking and money laundering,

1. *Requests* the administering Power to continue the process for facilitating the expression of the will of the people regarding the future status of the Territory;

2. *Also requests* the administering Power, specialized agencies and other organizations of the United Nations system and all financial institutions to continue to provide assistance to the Territory for socioeconomic development and development of human resources, bearing in mind the vulnerability of the Territory to external factors.

5. Cayman Islands

The General Assembly,

Referring to resolution A above,

Noting the constitutional review of 1992-1993, according to which the population expressed the sentiment that the existing relations with the United Kingdom of Great Britain and Northern Ireland should be maintained and that the current status of the Territory should not be altered,

Noting also the actions taken by the territorial Government to implement its localization programme to promote increased participation of the local population in the decision-making process in the Cayman Islands,

Noting with concern the vulnerability of the Territory to drug trafficking and related activities, as well as the measures taken by the authorities to deal with those problems,

Noting that the Territory has emerged as one of the world's leading off-shore financial centres,

Recalling the dispatch in 1977 of a United Nations visiting mission to the Territory,

1. *Requests* the administering Power to continue to provide the territorial Government with all required expertise to enable it to achieve its socio-economic aims;

2. *Also requests* the administering Power, in consultation with the territorial Government, to continue to facilitate the expansion of the current programme of securing employment for the local population, in particular at the decision-making level;

3. *Requests* the specialized agencies and other organizations of the United Nations system to continue and increase their programmes of assistance to the Territory with a view to strengthening, developing and diversifying its economy;

4. *Calls upon* the administering Power and the territorial Government to continue to cooperate to counter problems related to money laundering, smuggling of funds and other related crimes, as well as drug trafficking.

6. Guam

The General Assembly,

Referring to resolution A above,

Noting the results of the general elections held in November 1994,

Recalling that, in a referendum held in Guam in 1987, the people of Guam endorsed a draft Commonwealth Act that would establish a new framework for relations between the Territory and the administering Power, providing internal self-government for Guam and recognition of the right of the people of Guam to self-determination for the Territory,

Aware of the continued negotiations between the administering Power and the territorial Government on the draft Guam Commonwealth Act and on the future status of the Territory, with particular emphasis on the question of the evolution of the relationship between the United States of America and Guam,

Recalling the statement by the Special Representative of the United States of America on 12 December 1993 that the Administration hoped to have comments on the Commonwealth Bill before Congress by the end of 1994,

Cognizant that the administering Power continues to implement its programme of transferring surplus federal land to the Government of Guam,

Noting that the people of the Territory have called for reform in the programme of the administering Power with respect to the thorough and expeditious transfer of land property to the people of Guam,

Conscious that immigration into Guam has resulted in the indigenous Chamorros becoming a minority in their homeland,

Aware of the potential for diversifying and developing the economy of Guam through commercial fishing and agriculture and other viable activities,

Recalling the dispatch in 1979 of a United Nations visiting mission to the Territory,

1. *Calls upon* the administering Power and the territorial Government to expedite the early conclusion the negotiations on the draft Guam Commonwealth Act and on the future status of the Territory;

2. *Requests* the administering Power to continue to assist the elected territorial Government in achieving its political, economic and social goals;

3. *Also requests* the administering Power, in cooperation with the territorial Government, to continue the transfer of land to the people of the Territory and to take the necessary steps to safeguard their property rights;

4. *Further requests* the administering Power to continue to recognize and respect the political rights a the cultural and ethnic identity of the Chamorro people and to take all necessary measures to respond to the concerns of the territorial Government with regard to the immigration issue;

5. *Requests* the administering Power to continue to support appropriate measures by the territorial Government aimed at promoting growth in commercial fishing and agriculture and other viable activities.

7. Montserrat

The General Assembly,

Referring to resolution A above,

Noting the functioning of a democratic process in Montserrat,

Taking note of the reported statement of the Chief Minister that his preference was for independence within a political union with the Organization of Eastern Caribbean States and that self-reliance was more of a priority than independence,

Recalling that a United Nations visiting mission to the Territory took place in 1982,

1. *Requests* the administering Power to conduct an appropriate exercise, at the earliest possible date, to ascertain the will of the people regarding the future status of the Territory;

2. *Requests* the specialized agencies and other organizations of the United Nations system, as well as regional and other multilateral financial institutions, to continue their assistance to the Territory in the strengthening, development and diversification of the economy of Montserrat in accordance with its medium and long-term development plans.

8. Pitcairn

The General Assembly,

Referring to resolution A above,

Taking into account the unique nature of the Territory in terms of population and area,

Expressing its satisfaction with the continued economic and social advancement of the Territory, as well as with the improvement of its communications with the outside world and its management plan to address conservation issues,

Requests the administering Power to continue its assistance for improvement of the economic, social, educational and other conditions of the population of the Territory.

9. St. Helena

The General Assembly,

Referring to resolution A above,

Aware of the request by the Legislative Council of St. Helena that the administering Power conduct a constitutional review in the Territory,

Taking into account the unique character of the Territory, its population and its natural resources,

Aware of the efforts of the administering Power and the territorial authorities to improve the socio-economic conditions of the population of St. Helena, in particular in the sphere of food production,

1. *Requests* the administering Power to conduct the constitutional review in the Territory, taking into account the wishes of its population;

2. *Requests* the administering Power and relevant regional and international organizations to continue to support the efforts of the territorial Government to address the socio-economic development of the Territory.

10. Tokelau

The General Assembly,

Referring to resolution A above,

Having heard the statements of the representatives of New Zealand, the administering Power, and the Special Representative of Tokelau, who conveyed a message from the Council of Faipule (joint chairmen of the General *Fono* (Council)) to the Committee,

Recalling the solemn declaration on the future status of Tokelau delivered by the *Ulu o Tokelau* (highest authority of Tokelau) on 30 July 1994, that an act of self-determination in Tokelau is now under active consideration, together with the constitution of a self-governing Tokelau, and that the present preference of Tokelau is for a status of free association with New Zealand,

Noting the emphasis placed in the solemn declaration on the terms of Tokelau's intended free association relationship with New Zealand, including the expectation that the form of help Tokelau could continue to expect from New Zealand in promoting the well-being of its people, besides its external interests, would be clearly established in the framework of that relationship,

Noting also the Territory's concentrated focus in 1995 on strengthening its national institutions and creating a structure of government to meet modern needs, preparatory to the exercise by the people of Tokelau of their right to self-determination,

Acknowledging the endeavours of Tokelau to be self-reliant to the greatest extent possible,

Noting with appreciation the continuing exemplary cooperation of the administering Power with regard to the work of the Special Committee on the Situation with regard to the Implementation of the Declaration on the Granting of Independence to Colonial Countries and Peoples relating to Tokelau and its readiness to permit access by United Nations visiting missions to the Territory,

Recalling the dispatch in 1994 of a United Nations visiting mission to Tokelau,

1. *Notes*, on the basis of statements made by representatives of the administering Power and Tokelau subsequent to the 1994 United Nations visiting mission, that Tokelau is working towards an act of self-determination that would result in Tokelau assuming a status in accordance with the options on future status for Non-Self-Governing Territories contained in principle VI of the annex to General Assembly resolution 1541(XV) of 15 December 1960;

2. *Also notes* the expressed wishes of the people of the Territory indicating a strong preference for a status of free association with New Zealand;

3. *Further notes* the readiness of the people of Tokelau to assume full governmental responsibility and to conduct their own affairs within the framework of a constitution, which is currently being developed;

4. *Welcomes* the assurances of the Government of New Zealand that it will meet its obligations to the United Nations with respect to Tokelau and abide by the freely expressed wishes of the people of Tokelau with regard to their future status;

5. *Invites* the administering Power and United Nations agencies to continue their assistance to the social and economic development of Tokelau.

11. Turks and Caicos Islands

The General Assembly,

Referring to resolution A above,

Noting recent changes to the Constitution of the Territory and the intention of the territorial Government to continue to campaign for further constitutional changes,

Noting also that general elections took place in the Territory on 31 January 1995,

Noting further the policy of the authorities of maintaining a balance between creating a more liberal investment environment and preserving access by the population to economic benefits,

Noting the increase in aid, in particular financial assistance, granted to the territorial Government by the Government of the United Kingdom of Great Britain and Northern Ireland,

1. *Requests* the administering Power to conduct, at the earliest possible date, an appropriate exercise to ascertain the will of the people regarding the future status of the Territory;

2. *Calls upon* the administering Power and the relevant regional and international organizations to continuc to support the efforts of the territorial Government to address the socio-economic development of the Territory.

12. United States Virgin Islands

The General Assembly,

Referring to resolution A above,

Noting that general elections were held in November 1994,

Noting that a majority of those who voted in the referendum on the political status of the Territory on 11 October 1993 supported the existing territorial status arrangement with the United States of America,

Noting further the continuing interest of the territorial Government in seeking associate membership in the Organization of Eastern Caribbean States and observer status in the Caribbean Community,

Noting the necessity of further diversifying the Territory's economy,

Noting also that the question of Water Island is still under consideration,

Noting further that in 1993 the territorial Government purchased the assets of the West Indian Company, which had significant property and development interests in the Charlotte Amalie Harbour,

Recalling the dispatch in 1977 of a United Nations visiting mission to the Territory,

1. *Requests* the administering Power to continue to assist the elected territorial Government in achieving its political, economic and social goals;

2. *Also requests* the administering Power to facilitate the participation of the Territory, as appropriate, in various organizations, in particular the Organization of Eastern Caribbean States and the Caribbean Community;

3. *Welcomes* the negotiations between the administering Power and the territorial Government on the question of Water Island.

82nd plenary meeting
6 December 1995

3458 (XXX). Question of Spanish Sahara

Committee: 4
Vote: 88 - 0 - 41

A

The General Assembly,

Having considered the question of Spanish (Western) Sahara,

Recalling its resolution 1514 (XV) of 14 December 1960 containing the Declaration on the Granting of Independence to Colonial Countries and Peoples,

Recalling also its resolutions 2072 (XX) of 16 December 1965, 2229 (XXI) of 20 December 1966, 2354 (XXII) of 19 December 1967, 2428 (XXIII) of 18 December 1968, 2591 (XXIV) of 16 December 1969, 2711 (XXV) of 14 December 1970, 3162 (XXVIII) of 14 December 1973 and 3292 (XXIX) of 13 December 1974 on the question of Spanish Sahara,

Recalling further its resolution 3292 (XXIX) of 13 December 1974, by which it decided to request an advisory opinion from the International Court of Justice and to invite the Special Committee on the Situation with regard to the Implementation of the Declaration on the Granting of Independence to Colonial Countries and Peoples to keep the situation in the Territory under review, including the sending of a visiting mission to the Territory,

Noting that, in paragraph 3 of resolution 3292 (XXIX), it urged the administering Power to postpone the referendum which it contemplated holding in Spanish Sahara until the General Assembly decided on the policy to be followed in order to accelerate the decolonization process in the Territory in accordance with resolution 1514 (XV), in the best possible conditions, in the light of the advisory opinion to be given by the International Court of Justice,

Having considered the advisory opinion delivered by the International Court of Justice on 16 October 1975[1] in response to the request contained in General Assembly resolution 3292 (XXIX),

Having considered the chapter of the report of the Special Committee relating to the Territory of Spanish Sahara,[2]

Having also considered the report of the United Nations Visiting Mission to Spanish Sahara, which in May and June 1975 went successively to Spain, the Territory, Morocco, Algeria and Mauritania, [3]

Having heard the statements of the administering Power[4] and of the Governments of Morocco,[5] Mauritania[6] and Algeria[7]

Having also heard the statements of the petitioners,[8]

Recalling Security Council resolutions 377 (1975) of 22 October 1975, 379 (1975) of 2 November 1975 and 380 (1975) of 6 November 1975 on the situation concerning Western Sahara,

Considering the reports prepared by the Secretary-General pursuant to Security Council resolutions 377 (1975) and 379 (1975) on the situation concerning Western Sahara,[9]

1. *Reaffirms* the inalienable right of the people of Spanish Sahara to self-determination, in accordance with General Assembly resolution 1514 (XV);

2. *Reaffirms* its attachment to the principle of self-determination of peoples and its concern to see that principle applied to the inhabitants of the Territory of Spanish Sahara within a framework that guarantees and permits them the free and genuine expression of their will, in accordance with the relevant resolutions of the United Nations;

3. *Reaffirms* the responsibility of the administering Power and of the United Nations with regard to the decolonization of the Territory and the guaranteeing of the free expression of the wishes of the people of Spanish Sahara;

4. *Takes note with appreciation* of the advisory opinion of the International Court of Justice concerning Western Sahara;[10]

5. *Takes note with satisfaction* of the report of the United Nations Visiting Mission to Spanish Sahara in 1975[11] and endorses its conclusion that measures should be taken to enable all Saharans originating in the Territory to decide on their future in complete freedom and in an atmosphere of peace and security, in accordance with resolution 1514 (XV);

6. *Expresses* its thanks to the Government of Spain and the Governments of Morocco, Algeria and Mauritania for the cooperation and assistance which they extended to the Visiting Mission;

7. *Requests* the Government of Spain, as the administering Power, in accordance with the observations and conclusions of the Visiting Mission and in accordance with the advisory opinion of the International Court of Justice, to take immediately all necessary measures, in consultation with all the parties concerned and interested, so that all Saharans originating in the Territory may exercise fully and freely, under United Nations supervision, their inalienable right to self-determination;

8. *Requests* the Secretary-General, in consultation with the Government of Spain, as the administering Power, and the Special Committee on the Situation with regard to the Implementation of the Declaration on the Granting of Independence to Colonial Countries and

---

1 *Western Sahara, Advisory Opinion,* I.C.J. Reports 1975, p. 12. For the note of transmittal to the members of the General Assembly, see A/10300.

2 *Official Records of the General Assembly, Thirtieth Session, Supplement No. 23* (A/10023/Rev.1), chap. XIII.

3 *Ibid.*, annex.

4 *Ibid., Thirtieth Session, Fourth Committee,* 2170th, 2171st, 2177th and 2178th meetings.

5 *Ibid.*, 2171st, 2177th and 2181st meetings.

6 *Ibid.*, 2173rd, 2177th and 2180th meetings.

7 *Ibid.*, 2170th, 2173rd, 2177th and 2180th meetings.

8 *Ibid.*, 2170th, 2173rd and 2178th meetings.

9 *Official Records of the Security Council, Thirtieth Year, Supplement for October, November and December 1975,* documents S/11863, S/11874, S/11876 and S/11880.

10 *Western Sahara, Advisory Opinion,* I.C.J. Reports 1975, p. 12. For the note of transmittal to the members of the General Assembly, see A/10300.

11 *Official Records of the General Assembly, Thirtieth Session, Supplement No. 23* (A/10023/Rev.l), chap. XIII, annex.

Peoples, to make the necessary arrangements for the supervision of the act of self-determination referred to in paragraph 7 above;

9. *Urges* all the parties concerned and interested to exercise restraint and to desist from any unilateral or other action outside the decisions of the General Assembly on the Territory;

10. *Requests* the Special Committee to follow the implementation of the present resolution and to report on the question to the General Assembly at its thirty-first session.

2435th plenary meeting
10 December 1975

B

The General Assembly,

Reaffirming its resolution 1514 (XV) of 14 December 1960,

Reaffirming its resolutions 1541 (XV) of 15 December 1960 and 2072 (XX) of 16 December 1965 and all other relevant United Nations resolutions, in particular General Assembly resolution 3292 (XXIX) of 13 December 1974,

Taking note of the report of the United Nations Visiting Mission dispatched to the Territory in 1975,[1]

Taking note of the advisory opinion of the International Court of Justice of 16 October 1975 concerning Western Sahara,[2]

Considering Security Council resolutions 377 (1975) of 22 October 1975, 379 (1975) of 2 November 1975 and 380 (1975) of 6 November 1975,

1. *Takes note* of the tripartite agreement concluded at Madrid on 14 November 1975 by the Governments of Mauritania, Morocco and Spain, the text of which was transmitted to the Secretary-General of the United Nations on 18 November 1975;[3]

2. *Reaffirms* the inalienable right to self-determination, in accordance with General Assembly resolution 1514 (XV), of all the Saharan populations originating in the Territory;

3. *Requests* the parties to the Madrid agreement of 14 November 1975 to ensure respect for the freely expressed aspirations of the Saharan populations;

4. *Requests* the interim administration to take all necessary steps to ensure that all the Saharan populations originating in the Territory will be able to exercise their inalienable right to self-determination through free consultations organized with the assistance of a representative of the United Nations appointed by the Secretary-General.

2435th plenary meeting
10 December 1975

50/36. Question of Western Sahara

Committee: 4
Vote: Adopted without a vote
Ref.: 49/44, 48/49, 47/25, 46/67, 45/21, 44/88, 43/33, 42/78, 41/16, 40/50, 39/40, 38/40, 37/28, 36/46, 35/19, 34/37, 33/31, 32/22, 31/45

The General Assembly,

Having considered in depth the question of Western Sahara,

Reaffirming the inalienable right of all peoples to self-determination and independence, in accordance with the principles set forth in the Charter of the United Nations and in General Assembly resolution 1514 (XV) of 14 December 1960, containing the Declaration on the Granting of Independence to Colonial Countries and Peoples,

Recalling its resolution 49/44 of 9 December 1994,

Recalling also the agreement in principle given on 30 August 1988 by the Kingdom of Morocco and the Frente Popular para la Liberación de Saguia el-Hamra y de Río de Oro to the proposals of the Secretary-General of the United Nations and the current Chairman of the Assembly of Heads of State and Government of the Organization of African Unity in the context of their joint mission of good offices,

Recalling further Security Council resolutions 621 (1988) of 20 September 1988, 658 (1990) of 27 June 1990, 690 (1991) of 29 April 1991, 725 (1991) of 31 December 1991, 809 (1993) of 2 March 1993 and 907 (1994) of 29 March 1994 relating to the question of Western Sahara,

Recalling with satisfaction the entry into force of the cease-fire in Western Sahara on 6 September 1991, in accordance with the proposal of the Secretary-General accepted by the two parties,

Noting the adoption by the Security Council of resolutions 973 (1995) of 13 January 1995, 995 (1995) of 26 May 1995, 1002 (1995) of 30 June 1995 and 1017 (1995) of 22 September 1995,

Welcoming the mission of the Security Council, which visited Western Sahara and the countries of the region from 3 to 9 June 1995,

Welcoming also the appointment of Mr. Erik Jensen as acting Special Representative of the Secretary-General for Western Sahara,

Concerned that the parties' continuing suspicion and lack of trust have contributed to delays in the implementation of the settlement plan,[4]

Noting that, for progress to be achieved, the two parties must have a vision of the post-referendum period,

Expressing the hope for a rapid resolution of the problems causing delays in the completion of the identification process, as well as the code of conduct, the release of political prisoners, the confinement of troops of the Frente Popular para la Liberación de Saguia el-Hamra y de Río de Oro and the arrangements for the reduction of the Moroccan troops in the territory,

Stressing the importance and usefulness of the resumption of direct talks between the two parties mentioned above in order to create a propitious atmosphere conducive to a speedy and effective implementation of the settlement plan,

Having examined the relevant chapter of the report of the Special Committee on the Situation with regard to the Implementation of the Declaration on the Granting of Independence to Colonial Countries and Peoples,[5]

Having also examined the report of the Secretary-General,[6]

1. *Takes note with appreciation* of the report of the Secretary-General;

2. *Pays tribute* to the Secretary-General and the personnel of the United Nations Mission for the Referendum in Western Sahara for their action with a view to settling the question of Western Sahara by the implementation of the settlement plan;

3. *Reiterates its support* for further efforts of the Secretary-General for the organization and supervision by the United Nations, in cooperation with the Organization of African Unity, of a referendum for self-determination of the people of Western Sahara, in conformity with Security Council resolutions 658 (1990) and 690 (1991), by which the Council adopted the settlement plan for Western Sahara;

4. *Reaffirms* that the goal on which all were agreed consists of the holding of a free, fair and impartial referendum for the people of Western Sahara, organized and conducted by the United Nations in cooperation with the Organization of African Unity and without any military or administrative constraints, in conformity with the settlement plan;

5. *Notes with concern* the insufficient progress made towards the fulfilment of the settlement plan, including the identification process, the code of conduct, the release of political prisoners, the confinement of troops of the Frente Popular para la Liberación de Saguia el-

---

1 *Ibid.*

2 *Western Sahara, Advisory Opinion,* I.C.J. Reports 197S, p. 12. For the note of transmittal to the members of the General Assembly, see A/ 10300.

3 *Official Records of the Security Council, Thirtieth Year, Supplement for October November and December 1975,* document S/11880, annex III.

4 S/21360 and S/22464 and Corr.1.

5 A/50/23 (Part V), chap. IX.

6 A/50/504.

Hamra y de Río de Oro and the arrangements for the reduction of the Moroccan troops in the territory;

6. *Calls upon* the Kingdom of Morocco and the Frente Popular para la Liberación de Saguia el-Hamra y de Río de Oro to work with the Secretary-General and the United Nations Mission for the Referendum in Western Sahara in a spirit of genuine cooperation to implement the settlement plan in accordance with the relevant Security Council resolutions;

7. *Takes note* of the decision of the Security Council to review the arrangements for the completion of the identification process on the basis of the report of the Secretary-General requested by the Council in paragraph 4 of its resolution 1017 (1995) and to consider at that time any further necessary measures which might need to be taken to ensure the prompt completion of that process and of all the other aspects relevant to the fulfilment of the settlement plan;

8. *Expresses the hope* that direct talks between the two parties will soon resume in order to create a propitious atmosphere conducive to speedy and effective implementation of the settlement plan;

9. *Requests* the Special Committee on the Situation with regard to the Implementation of the Declaration on the Granting of Independence to Colonial Countries and Peoples to continue to consider the situation in Western Sahara, bearing in mind the ongoing referendum process, and to report thereon to the General Assembly at its fifty-first session;

10. *Invites* the Secretary-General to submit to the General Assembly at its fifty-first session a report on the implementation of the present resolution.

82nd plenary meeting
6 December 1995

31/59. Question of French Somaliland

Committee: 4
Vote: 117 - 0 - 19

The General Assembly,

Having considered the question of so-called French Somaliland (Djibouti),

Having examined the relevant chapter of the report of the Special Committee on the Situation with regard to the Implementation of the Declaration on the Granting of Independence to Colonial Countries and Peoples,[1]

Recalling its resolution 1514 (XV) of 14 December 1960 containing the Declaration on the Granting of Independence to Colonial Countries and Peoples,

Recalling also its resolutions 2228 (XXI) of 20 December 1966. 2356 (XXII) of 19 December 1967 and 3480 (XXX) of 11 December 1975 on so-called French Somaliland (Djibouti),

Having heard the statements of the representatives of the liberation movements, the Front de liberation de la Côte des Somalis[2] and the Movement de liberation de Djibouti,[3]

Having also heard the statements of the President of the Government Council of the Territory,[4] as well as those of the representatives of the political parties, namely, the Ligue populaire africaine pour l'indépendance[5] the Union nationale pour l'indépendance[6] and the Mouvement populaire de libération,[7] and of a petitioner,[8]

Taking note of the solemn declarations of the leaders of the delegations of Ethiopia and Somalia before the Council of Ministers of the Organization of African Unity at its twenty-seventh ordinary session, held at Port Louis from 24 June to 3 July 1976, and before the Fourth Committee of the General Assembly,[9] affirming that their respective Governments would recognize, respect and honour the independence, sovereignty and territorial integrity of so-called French Somaliland (Djibouti) after its accession to independence,

Taking note also of the resolution on the question of so-called French Somaliland (Djibouti) adopted by the Conference of Ministers for Foreign Affairs of Non-Aligned Countries, held at Lima from 95 to 30 August 1975,[10] and of that part of the Political Declaration adopted by the Fifth Conference of Heads of State or Government of Non-Aligned Countries, held at Colombo from 16 to 19 August 1976, regarding the question,[11]

Having heard the statement of the representative of France, as the administering Power,[12] in particular the expressed commitment of his Government to lead the Territory to independence in 1977,

1. *Reaffirms* the inalienable right of the people of so-called French Somaliland (Djibouti) to self-determination and independence;

2. *Reaffirms* also its unqualified support of the right of the people of so-called French Somaliland (Djibouti) to immediate and unconditional independence in accordance with the Declaration on the Granting of Independence to Colonial Countries and Peoples;

3. *Calls upon* the Government of France to implement scrupulously and equitably, under democratic conditions, the program for the independence of so-called French Somaliland (Djibouti), as outlined by the representative of France in his statement before the Fourth Committee of the General Assembly,[13] within the indicated time frame, namely, the summer of 1977;

4. *Urges* the leaders of the Government Council of the Territory, as well as the representatives of the libération movements, the Front de libération de la Côte des Somalis and the Mouvement de libération de Djibouti, and of the political parties and groups to enter into the broadest possible discussions on neutral grounds under the auspices of the Organization of African Unity, with a view to resolving their differences, and to agree on a common political platform before the holding of a referendum, in conformity with the resolution adopted by the Council of Ministers at its twenty-seventh ordinary session[14] and subsequently approved by the Assembly of Heads of State and Government of the Organization of African Unity at its thirteenth ordinary session;

5. *Also calls upon* the Government of France to cooperate fully with the Organization of African Unity in its effort to convene, in accordance with the decision of the Assembly of Heads of State and Government, a round-table conference for the speedy implementation of the request contained in paragraph 4 above;

6. *Requests* the Government of France to consider the result of the referendum in its totality thus respecting the territorial integrity of the future State;

7. *Demands* that the Government of France withdraw its military base from the Territory without delay;

8. *Further calls upon* the Government of France to allow and facilitate the return to the Territory of all refugees who are bona fide citizens of the Territory, in accordance with the Organization of African Unity Convention Governing the Specific Aspects of Refugee Problems in Africa of 10 September 1969 and the Convention relating to the Status of Refugees of 1951;[15]

---

1 *Official Records of the General Assembly, Thirty-first Session, Fourth Committee*, chap. XIV.

2 *Ibid.*, 14th meeting, paras. 60-109, 17th meeting, paras. 44-49, and 21st meeting, paras. 22-34; and *Ibid.*, *Sessional Fascicle*, corrigendum.

3 *Ibid.*, 17th meeting, paras. 18-43.

4 *Ibid.*, 14th meeting, paras. 22-58, and 20th meeting, paras. 5-15.

5 *Ibid.*, 17th meeting, paras. 72-94.

6 *Ibid.*, 20th meeting, paras. 35-60.

7 *Ibid.*, 17th meeting, paras. 52-69.

8 *Ibid.*, 20th meeting, paras. 63, 64, 68-70, 78, 79 and 84-87.

9 *Ibid.*, 20th meeting, paras. 92-146 (Ethiopia); 14th meeting, paras. 110-130, and 17th meeting, paras. 13-17 (Somaliland); and *Ibid.*, *Fourth Committee, Sessional Fascicle,* corrigendum.

10 A/10217 and Corr.1, annex I, resolution I.

11 A/31/197, annex I, para. 37.

12 *Official Records of the General Assembly, Thirty-first Session, Fourth Committee,* 14th meeting, paras. 1-20.

13 *Ibid.*

14 A/31/196 and Corr.1, annex, resolution CM/Res.480 (XXVII).

15 United Nations, *Treaty Series,* vol. 189, No. 2545, p. 137.

9. *Requests* the Government of France, in order to ensure the implementation of the request contained in paragraph 8 above, to set up an *Ad Hoc* committee in accordance with the recommendation of the Fact-Finding Mission of the Organization of African Unity;[1]

10. *Reaffirms* its resolution 3480 (XXX);

11. *Endorses* all resolutions adopted by the Organization of African Unity on the question of so-called French Somaliland (Djibouti), in particular resolutions CM/Res.431/Rev.1 (XXV)[2] and CM/Res.480 (XXVII),[3] as well as the declaration adopted by the Organization of African Unity Coordinating Committee for the Liberation of Africa, as approved by the Council of Ministers at its twenty-seventh ordinary session and the Assembly of Heads of State and Government at its thirteenth ordinary session, and welcomes the solemn declarations by the leaders of the declarations of Ethiopia and Somalia before the Council of Ministers of the Organization of-African Unity and before the Fourth Committee of the General Assembly that their Governments would recognize, respect and honour the independence and sovereignty of so-called French Somaliland (Djibouti) and its territorial integrity after its accession to independence;

12. *Calls upon* all States to refrain from interfering in the internal affairs of the Territory and to abstain from any action likely to impede or adversely affect the current process of the country's accession to independence;

13. *Welcomes* the statements by the representatives of the people of so-called French Somaliland (Djibouti) in which they declared that the Territory would become a member of the United Nations and of the Organization of African Unity immediately after independence;

14. *Endorses* the decisions of the Organization of African Unity and the United Nations to send representatives to observe the referendum and all subsequent stages of the independence process to ensure that the principle of self-determination in the Territory is carried out smoothly and in the most democratic manner;[4]

15. *Urges* all Member States, the specialized agencies and other organizations within the United Nations system, in cooperation with the administering Power, to render all possible moral and material assistance to tile people of the Territory.

85th plenary meeting
1 December 1976

49/18. Question of the Comorian Island of Mayotte

Committee: -
Vote: 87 - 2 - 38

The General Assembly,

Recalling its resolutions 1514 (XV) of 14 December 1960, containing the Declaration on the Granting of Independence to Colonial Countries and Peoples, and 2621 (XXV) of 12 October 1970, containing the programme of action for the full implementation of the Declaration,

Recalling also its previous resolutions, in particular resolutions 3161 (XXVIII) of 14 December 1973, 3291 (XXIX) of 13 December 1974, 31/4 of 21 October 1976, 32/7 of 1 November 1977, 34/69 of 6 December 1979, 35/43 of 28 November 1980, 36/105 of 10 December 1981, 37/65 of 3 December 1982, 38/13 of 21 November 1983, 39/48 of 11 December 1984, 40/62 of 9 December 1985, 41/30 of 3 November 1986, 42/17 of 11 November 1987, 43/14 of 26 October 1988, 44/9 of 18 October 1989, 45/11 of 1 November 1990, 46/9 of 16 October 1991, 47/9 of 27 October 1992 and 48/56 of 13 December 1993, in which, *inter alia*, it affirmed the unity and territorial integrity of the Comoros,

Recalling, in particular, its resolution 3385 (XXX) of 12 November 1975, on the admission of the Comoros to membership in the United Nations, in which it reaffirmed the necessity of respecting the unity and territorial integrity of the Comoro Archipelago, composed of the islands of Anjouan, Grande-Comore, Mayotte and Mohéli,

Recalling further that, in accordance with the agreements between the Comoros and France, signed on 15 June 1973, concerning the accession of the Comoros to independence, the results of the referendum of 22 December 1974 were to be considered on a global basis and not island by island,

Convinced that a just and lasting solution to the question of Mayotte is to be found in respect for the sovereignty, unity and territorial integrity of the Comoro Archipelago,

Convinced also that a speedy solution of the problem is essential for the preservation of the peace and security which prevail in the region,

Bearing in mind the wish expressed by the President of the French Republic to seek actively a just solution to that problem,

Noting the repeated wish of the Government of the Comoros to initiate as soon as possible a frank and serious dialogue with the French Government with a view to accelerating the return of the Comorian island of Mayotte to the Islamic Federal Republic of the Comoros,

Taking note of the report of the Secretary-General of 28 October 1994,[1]

Bearing in mind also the decisions of the Organization of African Unity, the Movement of Non-Aligned Countries and the Organization of the Islamic Conference on this question,

1. *Reaffirms* the sovereignty of the Islamic Federal Republic of the Comoros over the island of Mayotte;

2. *Invites* the Government of France to honour the commitments entered into prior to the referendum on the self-determination of the Comoro Archipelago of 22 December 1974 concerning respect for the unity and territorial integrity of the Comoros;

3. *Calls for* the translation into practice of the wish expressed by the President of the French Republic to seek actively a just solution to the question of Mayotte;

4. *Urges* the Government of France to accelerate the process of negotiations with the Government of the Comoros with a view to ensuring the effective and prompt return of the island of Mayotte to the Comoros;

5. *Requests* the Secretary-General of the United Nations to maintain continuous contact with the Secretary-General of the Organization of African Unity with regard to this problem and to make available his good offices in the search for a peaceful negotiated solution to the problem;

6. *Also requests* the Secretary-General to report on this matter to the General Assembly at its fiftieth session;

7. *Decides* to include in the provisional agenda of its fiftieth session the item entitled "Question of the Comorian island of Mayotte".

69th plenary meeting
28 November 1994

---

1 See *Organization of African Unity* document CM/759 (XXVII), 1976.

2 See A/10297, annex I.

3 See A./31/196 and Corr.l, annex.

4 The Secretary-General subsequently announced (A/32/ 66) that, in accordance with thc understanding reached when resolution 31/59 was adopted, he had carried out the necessary consultations with the parties concerned and had appointed Norway, Sri Lanka and Venezuela as members of the United Nations Mission to Observe the Referendum and Elections in French Somaliland (Djibouti), and that the three Member States concerned had designated the following persons to represent them on the Mission: Mr. Ignatius B. Fonseka (Sri Lanka), Miss Mariá Clemencia j (Venezuela) and Mr. Tom Eric Vraalsen (Norway).

04.50 EFFECTS AND PROBLEMS ARISING FROM THE UNIFICATION AND DISSOLUTION OF STATES

04.51 KOREA

112 (II). The Problem of the Independence of Korea

Committee: 1
Vote: 43 - 0 - 6

A[1]

Inasmuch as the Korean question which is before the General Assembly is primarily a matter for the Korean people itself and concerns its freedom and independence, and

Recognizing that this question cannot be correctly and fairly resolved without the participation of representatives of the indigenous population,

The General Assembly

1. *Resolves* that elected representatives of the Korean people be invited to take part in the consideration of the question;

2. *Further resolves* that in order to facilitate and expedite such participation and to observe that the Korean representatives are in fact duly elected by the Korean people and not mere appointees by military authorities in Korea, there be forthwith established a United Nations Temporary Commission on Korea, to be present in Korea, with right to travel, observe and consult throughout Korea.

B

The General Assembly,

Recognizing the urgent and rightful claims to independence of the people of Korea;

Believing that the national independence of Korea should be re-established and all occupying forces then withdrawn at the earliest practicable date;

Recalling its previous conclusion that the freedom and independence of the Korean people cannot be correctly or fairly resolved without the participation of representatives of the Korean people, and its decision to establish a United Nations Temporary Commission on Korea (hereinafter called the "Commission") for the purpose of facilitating and expediting such participation by elected representatives of the Korean people,

1. *Decides* that the Commission shall consist of representatives of Australia, Canada, China, El Salvador, France, India, Philippines, Syria, Ukrainian Soviet Socialist Republic;

2. *Recommends* that the elections be held not later than 31 March 1948 on the basis of adult suffrage and by secret ballot to choose representatives with whom the Commission may consult regarding the prompt attainment of the freedom and independence of the Korean people and which representatives, constituting a National Assembly, may establish a National Government of Korea. The number of representatives from each voting area or zone should be proportionate to the population, and the elections should be under the observation of the Commission;

3. *Further recommends* that as soon as possible after the elections, the National Assembly should convene and form a National Government and notify the Commission of its formation;

4. *Further recommends* that immediately upon the establishment of a National Government, that Government should, in consultation with the Commission: (*a*) constitute its own national security forces and dissolve all military or semimilitary formations not included therein: (*b*) take over the functions of government from the military commands and civilian authorities of north and south Korea, and (*c*) arrange with the occupying Powers for the complete withdrawal from Korea of their armed forces as early as practicable and if possible within ninety days;

5. *Resolves* that the Commission shall facilitate and expedite the fulfilment of the foregoing programme for the attainment of the national independence of Korea and withdrawal of occupying forces, taking into account its observations and consultations in Korea. The Commission shall report, with its conclusions, to the General Assembly and may consult with the Interim Committee (if one be established) with respect to the application of this resolution in the light of developments;

6. *Calls upon* the Member States concerned to afford every assistance and facility to the Commission in the fulfilment of its responsibilities;

7. *Calls upon* all Members of the United Nations to refrain from interfering in the affairs of the Korean people during the interim period preparatory to the establishment of Korean independence, except in pursuance of the decisions of the General Assembly; and thereafter, to refrain completely from any and all acts derogatory to the independence and sovereignty of Korea.

Hundred and twelfth plenary meeting
14 November 1947

195 (III). The Problem of the Independence of Korea

Committee: 1
Vote: 48 - 6 - 1

The General Assembly,

Having regard to its resolution 112 (II) of 14 November 1947 concerning the problem of the independence of Korea,

Having considered the report[2] of the United Nations Temporary Commission on Korea (hereinafter referred to as the "Temporary Commission"), and the report[3] of the Interim Committee of the General Assembly regarding its consultation with the Temporary Commission,

Mindful of the fact that, due to difficulties referred to in the report of the Temporary Commission, the objectives set forth in the resolution of 14 November 1947 have not been fully accomplished, and in particular that unification of Korea has not yet been achieved,

1. *Approves* the conclusions of the reports of the Temporary Commission;

2. *Declares* that there has been established a lawful government (the Government of the Republic of Korea) having effective control and jurisdiction over that part of Korea where the Temporary Commission was able to observe and consult and in which the great majority of the people of all Korea reside; that this Government is based on elections which were a valid expression of the free will of the electorate of that part of Korea and which were observed by the Temporary Commission; and that this is the only such government in Korea;

3. *Recommends* that the occupying Powers should withdraw their occupation forces from Korea as early as practicable;

4. *Resolves* that, as a means to the full accomplishment of the objectives set forth in the resolution of 14 November 1947, a Commission on Korea consisting of Australia, China, El Salvador, France, India, the Philippines and Syria, shall be established to continue the work of the Temporary Commission and carry out the provisions of the present resolution, having in mind the status of the Government of Korea as herein defined, and in particular to:

(*a*) Lend its good offices to bring about the unification of Korea and the integration of all Korean security forces in accordance with the

---

1 A/49/584.

2 See *Official Records of the third session of the General Assembly, Supplement No. 9.*

3 *Ibid., Supplement No. 10*, pp. 18 to 21.

principles laid down by the General Assembly in the resolution of 14 November 1947;

(*b*) Seek to facilitate the removal of barriers to economic, social and other friendly intercourse caused by the division of Korea;

(*c*) Be available for observation and consultation in the further development of representative government based on the freely-expressed will of the people;

(*d*) Observe the actual withdrawal of the occupying forces and verify the fact of withdrawal when such has occurred; and for this purpose, if it so desires, request the assistance of military experts of the two occupying Powers;

5. *Decides* that the Commission:

(*a*) Shall, within thirty days of the adoption of the present resolution, proceed to Korea, where it shall maintain its seat;

(*b*) Shall be regarded as having superseded the Temporary Commission established by the resolution of 14 November 1947;

(*c*) Is authorized to travel, consult and observe throughout Korea;

(*d*) Shall determine its own procedures;

(*e*) May consult with the Interim Committee with respect to the discharge of its duties in the light of developments, and within the terms of the present resolution;

(*f*) Shall render a report to the next regular session of the General Assembly and to any prior special session which might he called to consider the subject-matter of the present resolution, and shall render such interim reports as it may deem appropriate to the Secretary-General for distribution to Members;

6. *Requests* that the Secretary-General shall provide the Commission with adequate staff and facilities, including technical advisers as required; and authorizes the Secretary-General to pay the expenses and *per diem* of a representative and an alternate from each of the States members of the Commission;

7. *Calls upon* the Member States concerned, the Government of the Republic of Korea, and all Koreans to afford every assistance and facility to the Commission in the fulfilment of its responsibilities;

8. *Calls upon* Member States to refrain from any acts derogatory to the results achieved and to be achieved by the United Nations in bringing about the complete independence and unity of Korea;

9. *Recommends* that Member States and other nations, in establishing their relations with the Government of the Republic of Korea, take into consideration the facts set out in paragraph 2 of the present resolution.

Hundred and eighty-seventh plenary meeting
12 December 1948

376 (V). The Problem of the Independence of Korea

Committee: 1
Vote: 47 - 5 - 7
Ref.: 507(VI), 293(IV)

The General Assembly,

Having regard to its resolutions of 14 November 1947 (112 (II)), of 12 December 1948 (195 (III)) and of 21 October 1949 (293 (IV)),

Having received and considered the report[1] of the United Nations Commission on Korea,

Mindful of the fact that the objectives set forth in the resolutions referred to above have not been fully accomplished and, in particular, that the unification of Korea has not yet been achieved, and that an attempt has been made by an armed attack from North Korea to extinguish by force the Government of the Republic of Korea,

Recalling the General Assembly declaration of 12 December 1948 that there has been established a lawful government (the Government of the Republic of Korea) having effective control and jurisdiction over that part of Korea where the United Nations Temporary Commission on Korea was able to observe and consult and in which the great majority of the people of Korea reside; that this government is based on elections which were a valid expression of the free will of the electorate of that part of Korea and which were observed by the Temporary Commission; and that this is the only such government in Korea,

Having in mind that United Nations armed forces are at present operating in Korea in accordance with the recommendations[2] of the Security Council of 27 June 1950, subsequent to its resolution[3] of 25 June 1950, that Members of the United Nations furnish such assistance to the Republic of Korea as may be necessary to repel the armed attack and to restore international peace and security in the area,

Recalling that the essential objective of the resolutions of the General Assembly referred to above was the establishment of a unified, independent and democratic Government of Korea,

1. *Recommends* that

(*a*) All appropriate steps be taken to ensure conditions of stability throughout Korea;

(*b*) All constituent acts be taken, including the holding of elections, under the auspices of the United Nations, for the establishment of a unified, independent and democratic government in the sovereign State of Korea;

(*c*) All sections and representative bodies of the population of Korea, South and North, be invited to cooperate with the organs of the United Nations in the restoration of peace, in the holding of elections and in the establishment of a unified government;

(*d*) United Nations forces should not remain in any part of Korea otherwise than so far as necessary for achieving the objectives specified in sub-paragraphs (*a*) and (*b*) above;

(*e*) All necessary measures be taken to accomplish the economic rehabilitation of Korea;

2. *Resolves* that

(*a*) A Commission consisting of Australia, Chile, Netherlands, Pakistan, Philippines, Thailand and Turkey, to be known as the United Nations Commission for the Unification and Rehabilitation of Korea, be established to (i) assume the functions hitherto exercised by the present United Nations Commission on Korea; (ii) represent the United Nations in bringing about the establishment of a unified, independent and democratic government of all Korea; (iii) exercise such responsibilities in connexion with relief and rehabilitation in Korea as may be determined by the General Assembly after receiving the recommendations of the Economic and Social Council. The United Nations Commission for the Unification and Rehabilitation of Korea should proceed to Korea and begin to carry out its functions as soon as possible;

(*b*) Pending the arrival in Korea of the United Nations Commission for the Unification and Rehabilitation of Korea, the governments of the States represented on the Commission should form an Interim Committee composed of representatives meeting at the seat of the United Nations to consult with and advise the United Nations Unified Command in the light of the above recommendations; the Interim Committee should begin to function immediately upon the approval of the present resolution by the General Assembly;

(*c*) The Commission shall render a report to the next regular session of the General Assembly and to any prior special session which might be called to consider the subject-matter of the present resolution, and shall render such interim reports as it may deem appropriate to the Secretary-General for transmission to Members;

The General Assembly furthermore,

Mindful of the fact that at the end of the present hostilities the task of rehabilitating the Korean economy will be of great magnitude,

3. *Requests* the Economic and Social Council, in consultation with the specialized agencies, to develop plans for relief and rehabilitation on the termination of hostilities and to report to the General Assem-

1 See *Official Records of the General Assembly, Fifth Session, Supplement No. 16.*

2 See *Official Records of the Security Council, Fifth Year, No. 16.*

3 *Ibid.*, No. 15.

bly within three weeks[1] of the adoption of the present resolution by the General Assembly;

4. *Also recommends* the Economic and Social Council to expedite the study of long-term measures to promote the economic development and social progress of Korea, and meanwhile to draw the attention of the authorities which decide requests for technical assistance to the urgent and special necessity of affording such assistance to Korea;

5. *Expresses its appreciation* of the services rendered by the members of the United Nations Commission on Korea in the performance of their important and difficult task;

6. *Requests* the Secretary-General to provide the United Nations Commission for the Unification and Rehabilitation of Korea with adequate staff and facilities, including technical advisers as required. and authorizes the Secretary-General to pay the expenses and *per diem* of a representative and alternate from each of the States members of the Commission.

294th plenary meeting
7 October 1950

498 (V). Intervention of the Central People's Government of the People's Republic of China in Korea

Committee: 1
Vote: 44 - 7 - 9
Ref.: 384(V)

The General Assembly,

Noting that the Security Council, because of lack of unanimity of the permanent members, has failed to exercise its primary responsibility for the maintenance of international peace and security in regard to Chinese Communist intervention in Korea,

Noting that the Central People's Government of the People's Republic of China has not accepted United Nations proposals[2] to bring about a cessation of hostilities in Korea with a view to peaceful settlement, and that its armed forces continue their invasion of Korea and their large-scale attacks upon United Nations forces there,

1. *Finds* that the Central People's Government of the People's Republic of China, by giving direct aid and assistance to those who were already committing aggression in Korea and by engaging in hostilities against United Nations forces there, has itself engaged in aggression in Korea;

2. *Calls upon* the Central People's Government of the People's Republic of China to cause its forces and nationals in Korea to cease hostilities against the United Nations forces and to withdraw from Korea;

3. *Affirms* the determination of the United Nations to continue its action in Korea to meet the aggression;

4. *Calls upon* all States and authorities to continue to lend every, assistance to the United Nations action in Korea;

5. *Calls upon* all States and authorities to refrain from giving any assistance to the aggressors in Korea;

6. *Requests* a Committee composed of the members of the Collective Measures Committee as a matter of urgency to consider additional measures to be employed to meet this aggression and to report thereon to the General Assembly, it being understood that the Committee is authorized to defer its report if the Good Offices Committee referred to in the following paragraph reports satisfactory progress in its efforts;

7. *Affirms* that it continues to be the policy of the United Nations to bring about a cessation of hostilities in Korea and the achievement of United Nations objectives in Korea by peaceful means, and requests the President of the General Assembly to designate forthwith two persons who would meet with him at any suitable opportunity to use their good offices to this end.

327th plenary meeting
1 February 1951

1 See resolution 410 (V), p. 105.
2 See documents A/C.1/643 and A/C.1/645.

500 (V). Additional Measures to be Employed to Meet the Aggression in Korea

Committee: 1
Vote: 47 - 0 - 8

The General Assembly,

Noting the report[3] of the Additional Measures Committee dated 14 May 1951,

Recalling its resolution 498 (V) of 1 February 1951,

Noting that:

(*a*) The Additional Measures Committee established by that resolution has considered additional measures to be employed to meet the aggression in Korea,

(*b*) The Additional Measures Committee has reported[4] that a number of States have already taken measures designed to deny contributions to the military strength of the forces opposing the United Nations in Korea,

(*c*) The Additional Measures Committee has also reported[5] that certain economic measures designed further to deny such contributions would support and supplement the military action of the United Nations in Korea and would assist in putting an end to the aggression,

1. *Recommends* that every State:

(*a*) Apply an embargo on the shipment to areas under the control of the Central People's Government of the People's Republic of China and of the North Korean authorities of arms, ammunition and implements of war, atomic energy materials, petroleum, transportation materials of strategic value, and items useful in the production of arms, ammunition and implements of war;

(*b*) Determine which commodities exported from its territory fall within the embargo, and apply controls to give effect to the embargo;

(*c*) Prevent by all means within its jurisdiction the circumvention of controls on shipments, applied by other States pursuant to the present resolution;

(*d*) Cooperate with other States in carrying out the purposes of this embargo;

(*e*) Report to the Additional Measures Committee, within thirty days and thereafter at the request of the Committee, on the measures taken in accordance with the present resolution;

2. *Requests* the Additional Measures Committee:

(*a*) To report to the General Assembly, with recommendations as appropriate, on the general effectiveness of the embargo and the desirability of continuing, extending or relaxing it;

(*b*) To continue its consideration of additional measures to be employed to meet the aggression in Korea, and to report thereon further to the General Assembly, it being understood that the Committee is authorized to defer its report if the Good Offices Committee reports satisfactory progress in its efforts;

3. *Reaffirms* that it continues to be the policy of the United Nations to bring about a cessation of hostilities in Korea, and the achievement of United Nations objectives in Korea by peaceful means, and requests the Good Offices Committee to continue its good offices.

330th plenary meeting
18 May 1951

3 See document A/1799. Appendix 11, p. 322.
4 See *Official Records of the General Assembly, Fifth Session, First Committee*, 443rd meeting.
5 *Ibid.*

610 (VII). Korea: Reports of the United Nations Commission for the Unification and Rehabilitation of Korea

Committee: 1
Vote: 54 - 5 - 1
Ref.: 410(V)

The General Assembly,

Having received the special report[1] of the United Nations Command of 18 October 1952 on "the present status of the military action and the armistice negotiations in Korea" and other relevant reports relating to Korea,

Noting with approval the considerable progress towards an armistice made by negotiation at Panmunjom and the tentative agreements to end the fighting in Korea and to reach a settlement of the Korean question,

Noting further that disagreement between the parties on one remaining issue, alone, prevents the conclusion of an armistice and that a considerable measure of agreement already exists on the principles on which this remaining issue can be resolved,

Mindful of the continuing and vast loss of life, devastation and suffering resulting from and accompanying the continuance of the fighting,

Deeply conscious of the need to bring hostilities to a speedy end and of the need for a peaceful settlement of the Korean question,

Anxious to expedite and facilitate the convening of the political conference as provided in article 60 of the draft armistice agreement,[2]

1. *Affirms* that the release and repatriation of prisoners of war shall be effected in accordance with the Geneva Convention relative to the Treatment of Prisoners of War,[3] dated 12 August 1949, the well-established principles and practice of international law and the relevant provisions of the draft armistic agreement;

2. *Affirms* that force shall not be used against prisoners of war to prevent or effect their return to their homelands, and that they shall at all time be treated humanely in accordance with the specific provisions of the Geneva Convention and with the general spirit of the Convention;

3. *Accordingly requests* the President of the General Assembly to communicate the following proposals to the Central People's Government of the People's Republic of China and to the North Korean authorities as forming a just and reasonable basis for an agreement so that an immediate cease-fire would result and be effected; to invite their acceptance of these proposals and to make a report to the General Assembly during its present session and as soon as appropriate:

Proposals

I. In order to facilitate the return to their homelands of all prisoners of war, there shall be established a Repatriation Commission consisting of representatives of Czechoslovakia, Poland, Sweden and Switzerland, that is, the four States agreed to for the constitution of the Neutral Nations supervisory Commission and referred to in paragraph 37 of the draft armistice agreement, or constituted, alternatively, of representatives of four States not participating in hostilities, two nominated by each side, but excluding representatives of States that are permanent members of the Security Council.

II. The release and repatriation of prisoners of war shall be effected in accordance with the Geneva Convention relative to the Treatment of Prisoners of War, dated 12 August 1949, the well-established principles and practice of International Law and the relevant provisions of the draft armistice agreement.

III. Force shall not be used against the prisoners of war to prevent or effect their return to their homelands and no violence to their persons or affront to their dignity or self-respect shall be permitted in any manner or for any purpose whatsoever. This duty is enjoined on and entrusted to the Repatriation Commission and each of its members. Prisoners of war shall at all times be treated humanely in accordance with the specific provisions of the Geneva Convention and with the general spirit of that Convention.

IV. All prisoners of war shall be released to the Repatriation Commission from military control and from the custody of the detaining side in agreed numbers and at agreed exchange points in agreed demilitarized zones.

V. Classification of prisoners of war according to nationality and domicile as proposed in the letter[4] of 16 October 1952 from General Kim Il Sung, Supreme Commander of the Korean People's Army, and General Peng Teh-huai, Commander of the Chinese People's Volunteers to General Mark W. Clark, Commander-in-Chief United Nations Command, shall then be carried out immediately.

VI. After classification, prisoners of war shall be free to return to their homelands forthwith, and their speedy return shall be facilitated by all parties concerned.

VII. In accordance with arrangements prescribed for the purpose by the Repatriation Commission, each party to the conflict shall have freedom and facilities to explain to the prisoners of war "depending upon them" their rights and to inform the prisoners of war on any matter relating to their return to their homelands and particularly their full freedom to return.

VIII. Red Cross teams of both sides shall assist the Repatriation Commission in its work and shall have access, in accordance with the terms of the draft armistice agreement, to prisoners of war while they are under the temporary jurisdiction of the Repatriation Commission.

IX. Prisoners of war shall have freedom and facilities to make representations and communications to the Repatriation Commission and to bodies and agencies working under the Repatriation Commission, and to inform any or all such bodies of their desires on any matter concerning themselves, in accordance with arrangements made for the purpose by the Commission.

X. Notwithstanding the provisions of paragraph III above, nothing in this Repatriation Agreement shall be construed as derogating from the authority of the Repatriation Commission (or its authorized representatives) to exercise its legitimate functions and responsibilities for the control of the prisoners under its temporary jurisdiction.

XI. The terms of this Repatriation Agreement and the arrangements arising therefrom shall be made known to all prisoners of war.

XII. The Repatriation Commission is entitled to call upon parties to the conflict, its own member governments, or the Member States of the United Nations for such legitimate assistance as it may require in the carrying out of its duties and tasks and in accordance with the decisions of the Commission in this respect.

XIII. When the two sides have made an agreement for repatriation based on these proposals, the interpretation of that agreement shall rest with the Repatriation Commission. In the event of disagreement in the Commission, majority decisions shall prevail. When no majority decision is possible, an umpire agreed upon in accordance with the succeeding paragraph and with article 132 of the Geneva Convention of 1949 shall have the deciding vote.

XIV. The Repatriation Commission shall at its first meeting and prior to an armistice proceed to agree upon and appoint the umpire who shall at all times be available to the Commission and shall act as its Chairman unless otherwise agreed. If agreement on the appointment of the umpire cannot be reached by the Commission within the period of three weeks after the date of the first meeting this matter should be referred to the General Assembly.

XV. The Repatriation Commission shall also arrange after the armistice for officials to function as umpires with inspecting teams or other bodies to which functions are delegated or assigned by the Commission or under the provisions of the draft armistice agreement, so that the completion of the return of prisoners of war to their homelands shall he expedited.

---

1 See document A/2228.

2 *Ibid.*, annex A.

3 See *Treaty Series, Treaties and International agreements registered or field and recorded with the Secretariat of the United Nations*, Volume 75, 1950, No. 972, p. 135.

4 See document A/2230, annex 3.

XVI. When the Repatriation Agreement is acceded to by the parties concerned and when an umpire has been appointed under paragraph 14 above, the draft armistice agreement, unless otherwise altered by agreement between the parties, shall be deemed to have been accepted by them. The provisions of the draft armistice agreement shall apply except in so far as they are modified by the Repatriation Agreement. Arrangements for repatriation under this agreement will begin when the armistice agreement is thus concluded.

XVII. At the end of ninety days, after the Armistice Agreement has been signed, the disposition of any prisoners of war whose return to their homelands may not have been effected in accordance with the procedure set out in these proposals or as otherwise agreed, shall be referred with recommendations for their disposition, including a target date for the termination of their detention to the political conference to be called as provided under article 60 of the draft armistice agreement. If at the end of a further thirty days there are any prisoners of war whose return to their homelands has not been effected under the above procedures or whose future has not been provided for by the political conference, the responsibility for their care and maintenance and for their subsequent disposition shall be transferred to the United Nations, which in all matters relating to them shall act strictly in accordance with international law.

399th plenary meeting
3 December 1952

906 (IX). Complaint of Detention and Imprisonment of United Nations Military Personnel in Violation of the Korean Armistice Agreement

Committee: -
Vote: 47 - 5 - 7
Ref.: 804(VIII)

The General Assembly,

Having considered the item proposed by the United States of America as the Unified Command regarding eleven members of the United States armed forces under the United Nations Command captured by Chinese forces when undertaking a mission on 12 January 1953, at the direction of the United Nations Command,

Recalling the provisions of article III of the Korean Armistice Agreement[1] regarding the repatriation of prisoners of war,

1. *Declares* that the detention and imprisonment of the eleven American airmen, members of the United Nations Command, referred to in document A/2830,[2] and the detention of all other captured personnel of the United Nations Command desiring repatriation is violation of the Korean Armistice Agreement;

2. *Condemns*, as contrary to the Korean Armistice Agreement, the trial and conviction of prisoners of war illegally detained after 25 September 1953;

3. *Requests* the Secretary-General, in the name the United Nations, to seek the release, in accordance with the Korean Armistice Agreement, of these eleven United Nations Command personnel, and all other captured personnel of the United Nations Command still detained;

4. *Requests* the Secretary-General to make, by means most appropriate in his judgement, continuing and unremitting efforts to this end and to report progress to all Members on or before 31 December 1954.

509th plenary meeting
10 December 1954

1 See *Official Records of the Security Council, Eighth Year, Supplement for July, August and September 1953*, document S/3079.

2 See *Official Records of the General Assembly, Ninth Session, Annexes*, agenda item 72. Appendix 39, p. 414.

2668 (XXV). Question of Korea

Committee: 1
Vote: 67 - 28 - 22
Ref.: 2516(XXIV), 2466(XXIII), 2269(XXII), 2224(XXI), 2132(XX), 1964(XVIII), 1855(XVII), 1740(XVI), 1455(XIV), 1264(XIII), 1180(XII), 1010(XI), 910(X), 811(IX), 804(VIII), 716(VIII), 712(VII), 711(VII), 705(VII)

The General Assembly,

Having noted the report of the United Nations Commission for the Unification and Rehabilitation of Korea, signed at Seoul, Korea, on 13 August 1970,[3]

Reaffirming its resolution 2516 (XXIV) of 25 November 1969 and its previous resolutions on the question of Korea,

Recognizing that the continued division of Korea does not correspond to the wishes of the Korean people and constitutes a source of tension which prevents the full restoration of international peace and security in the area,

Recalling that the United Nations, under the Charter, is fully and rightfully empowered to take collective action to maintain peace and security and to extend its good offices in seeking a peaceful settlement in Korea in accordance with the purposes and principles of the Charter,

Anxious that progress be made towards creating conditions which would facilitate the reunification of Korea on the basis of the freely expressed will of the Korean people,

Concerned at reports of further events in Korea which, if continued, could hamper efforts to create the peaceful conditions which are one of the prerequisites of the establishment of a unified and independent Korea,

1. *Reaffirms* that the objectives of the United Nations in Korea are to bring about by peaceful means, the establishment of a unified, independent and democratic Korea under a representative form of government, and the full restoration of international peace and security in the area;

2. *Expresses the belief* that arrangements should be made to achieve these objectives through genuinely free elections held in accordance with the relevant resolutions of the General Assembly;

3. *Calls* for cooperation in the easing of tensions in the area and, in particular, for the avoidance of incidents and activities in violation of the Armistice Agreement of 1953;

4. *Notes with approval* the efforts made by the United Nations Commission for the Unification and Rehabilitation of Korea, in pursuit of its mandate, to encourage the exercise of restraint and the easing of tensions in the area and to secure maximum support, assistance and cooperation in the realization of the peaceful reunification of Korea;

5. *Requests* the United Nations Commission for the Unification and Rehabilitation of Korea to pursue these and other efforts to achieve the objectives of the United Nations in Korea, to continue to carry out the tasks previously assigned to it by the General Assembly and to keep members of the Assembly informed on the situation in the area and on the results of these efforts through regular reports submitted to the Secretary-General, and to the General Assembly as appropriate;

6. *Notes* that the United Nations forces which were sent to Korea in accordance with United Nations resolutions have in greater part already been withdrawn, that the sole objective of the United Nations forces at present in Korea is to preserve the peace and security of the area, and that the Governments concerned are prepared to withdraw their remaining forces from Korea whenever such action is requested by the Republic of Korea or whenever the conditions for a lasting settlement formulated by the General Assembly have been fulfilled.

1919th plenary meeting
7 December 1970

3 *Official Records of the General Assembly, Twenty-fifth Session, Supplement No.* 26 (A/8026 and Corr.1).

3390 (XXX). Question of Korea

Committee: 1
Vote: A: 59 - 51 - 29; B: 54 - 43 - 42

A

The General Assembly,

Mindful of the hope expressed by it in resolution 3333 (XXIX) of 17 December 1974,

Desiring that progress be made towards the attainment of the goal of peaceful reunification of Korea on the basis of the freely expressed will of the Korean people,

Recalling its satisfaction with the issuance of the joint communiqué at Seoul and Pyongyang on 4 July 1972 and the declared intention of both the South and the North of Korea to continue the dialogue between them,

Further recalling that, by its resolution 711 A (VII) of 28 August 1953, the General Assembly noted with approval the Armistice Agreement of 27 July 1953,[1] and that, in its resolution 811 (IX) of 11 December 1954, it expressly took note of the provision of the Armistice Agreement which requires that the Agreement shall remain in effect until expressly superseded either by mutually acceptable amendments and additions or by provisions in an appropriate agreement for a peaceful settlement at a political level between both sides,

Aware, however, that tension in Korea has not been totally eliminated and that the Armistice Agreement remains indispensable to the maintenance of peace and security in the area,

Noting the letter of 27 June 1975,[2] addressed to the President of the Security Council by the Government of the United States of America, affirming that it is prepared to terminate the United Nations Command on 1 January 1976, provided that the other parties directly concerned reach agreement on alternative arrangements mutually acceptable to them for maintaining the Armistice Agreement,

Noting the statement of 27 June 1975 by the Government of the Republic of Korea affirming its willingness to enter into arrangements for maintaining the Armistice Agreement,

Recognizing that, in accordance with the purposes and principles of the Charter of the United Nations regarding the maintenance of international peace and security, the United Nations has a continuing responsibility to ensure the attainment of this goal on the Korean peninsula,

1. *Reaffirms* the wishes of its members, as expressed in the consensus statement adopted by the General Assembly on 28 November 1973,[3] and urges both the South and the North of Korea to continue their dialogue to expedite the peaceful reunification of Korea;

2. *Expresses the hope* that all the parties directly concerned will enter into negotiations on new arrangements designed to replace the Armistice Agreement, reduce tensions and ensure lasting peace in the Korean peninsula;

3. *Urges* all the parties directly concerned, as a first step, bearing in mind the need to ensure continued observation of the Armistice Agreement and the full maintenance of peace and security in the region, to embark on talks as soon as possible so that the United Nations Command may be dissolved concurrently with arrangements for maintaining the Agreement;

4. *Expresses the further hope* that these discussions will be completed and alternative arrangements for the maintenance of the Armistice Agreement will be made in order that the United Nations Command may be dissolved on 1 January 1976 so that by that date no armed forces under the United Nations flag will remain in the South of Korea.

2409th plenary meeting
18 November 1975

B

The General Assembly,

Noting that the reunification of Korea has not yet been achieved although thirty years have elapsed since Korea was divided into the North and the South and twenty-two years since the establishment of the armistice in Korea,

Recalling the obligations assumed by States in accordance with the Charter of the United Nations on respect for the principle of equality and self-determination of peoples and on refraining from intervening in matters which are within the domestic jurisdiction of any State,

Considering that it conforms with the principles of the Charter to encourage the Korean people to achieve the independent and peaceful reunification of their country at the earliest possible date on the basis of the three principles of independence, peaceful reunification and great national unity and to create favourable conditions for it,

Hoping that the North and the South of Korea will promote their dialogue to accelerate the reunification of the country in accordance with the spirit of the joint statement of 4 July 1972 and with the decision adopted by the General Assembly at its twenty-eighth session, on 28 November 1973,[4] which welcomed the joint statement,

Considering that a durable peace cannot be expected so long as the present state of armistice is kept as it is in Korea,

Considering that, in order to guarantee a durable peace in Korea and accelerate its independent and peaceful reunification, it is urgently necessary to take new decisive measures for terminating foreign interference in its internal affairs, removing tension and preventing armed conflicts in that region,

1. *Considers* that it is necessary to dissolve the "United Nations Command" and withdraw all the foreign troops stationed in South Korea under the flag of the United Nations;

2. *Calls upon* the real parties to the Armistice Agreement to replace the Korean Military Armistice Agreement with a peace agreement as a measure to ease tension and maintain and consolidate peace in Korea in the context of the dissolution of the "United Nations Command" and the withdrawal of all the foreign troops stationed in South Korea under the flag of the United Nations;

3. *Urges* the North and the South of Korea to observe the principles of the North-South joint statement and take practical measures for ceasing arms reinforcement, reducing the armed forces of both sides drastically to an equal level, preventing armed conflicts and guaranteeing against the use of force against the other side, and thereby remove the military confrontation and maintain a durable peace in Korea, conducive to accelerating the independent and peaceful reunification of the country.

2409th plenary meeting
18 November 1975

---

1 See *Official Records of the Security Council, Eighth Year, Supplement for July, August and September 1953,* document S/3079; transmitted to the members of the General Assembly by a note of the Secretary-General (A/2451).

2 *Ibid, Thirtieth Year, Supplement for April, May and June 1975,* document S/11737.

3 *Official Records of the General Assembly, Twenty-eighth Session, Supplement No. 30* (A/9030), p. 24; item 41.

4 *Ibid.*

04.52 GERMANY

510 (VI). Appointment of an Impartial International Commission under United Nations Supervision to Carry out a Simultaneous Investigation in the Federal Republic of Germany, in Berlin, and in the Soviet Zone of Germany in Order to Determine whether Existing Conditions there Make it Possible to Hold Genuinely Free Elections Throughout these Areas

Committee: P
Vote: 45 - 6 - 8

Whereas the Governments of the United Kingdom of Great Britain and Northern Ireland, the United States of America and France, acting on a proposal made by the German Federal Chancellor, have brought before the General Assembly a request[1] for the appointment of an impartial international commission under United Nations supervision to carry out a simultaneous investigation in the Federal Republic of Germany, in Berlin, and in the Soviet Zone of Germany in order to determine whether existing conditions there make it possible to hold genuinely free elections throughout these areas,

Whereas the statements[2] made by the representatives of the Federal Government of Germany, of Berlin, and of the Soviet Zone of Germany before the *Ad Hoc* Political Committee reveal differences of opinion with regard to the conditions existing in these areas, which make it essential that such an investigation shall be carried out by an impartial body,

The General Assembly,

Having regard to the Purposes and Principles of the United Nations as set out in the Charter, taking due account of the responsibilities of the four Powers regarding Germany, and desiring to make its contribution to the achievement of the unity of Germany in the interests of world peace,

1. *Considers* it desirable to give effect to the above request;

2. *Resolves* to appoint a Commission composed of representatives of Brazil, Iceland, the Netherlands, Pakistan and Poland which shall carry out immediately a simultaneous investigation in the Federal Republic of Germany, in Berlin, and in the Soviet Zone of Germany to ascertain and report whether conditions in these areas are such as to make possible the holding of genuinely free and secret elections throughout the areas. The Commission shall investigate the following matters in so far as they affect the holding of free elections:

(*a*) The constitutional provisions in force in these areas and their application as regards the various aspects of individual freedom, in particular the degree to which, in practice, the individual enjoys freedom of movement, freedom from arbitrary arrest and detention, freedom of association and assembly, freedom of speech, press and broadcasting;

(*b*) Freedom of political parties to organize and carry out their activities;

(*c*) The organization and activities of the judiciary, police and other administrative organs;

3. *Calls upon* all authorities in the Federal Republic, in Berlin, and in the Soviet Zone to enable the Commission to travel freely throughout these areas; and to allow the Commission freedom of access to such persons, places and relevant documents as it considers necessary in the course of executing its task and to allow it to summon any witnesses whom it wishes to examine;

4. (*a*) *Directs* the Commission to report at the earliest practicable date to the Secretary-General, for the consideration of the four Powers and for the information of the other Members of the United Nations, on the results of its efforts to make the necessary arrangements with all the parties concerned to enable it to undertake its work according to the terms of the present resolution;

(*b*) *Directs* the Commission, if it is able to make the necessary arrangements throughout the areas concerned, similarly to report on the findings resulting from its investigation of conditions in these areas, it being understood that such findings may include recommendations regarding further steps which might be taken in order to bring about conditions in Germany necessary for the holding of free elections in these areas;

(*c*) *Directs* the Commission, if it is unable forthwith to make these arrangements, to make a further attempt to carry out its task at such time as it is satisfied that the German authorities in the Federal Republic, in Berlin, and in the Soviet Zone will admit the Commission, as it is desirable to leave the door open for the Commission to carry out its task;

(*d*) *Directs* the Commission in any event to report not later than 1 September 1952, on the results of its activities to the Secretary-General, for the consideration of the four Powers and for the information of the other Members of the United Nations;

5. *Declares* that the United Nations is prepared, after being satisfied that the conditions throughout the areas concerned are such as to make possible the holding of genuinely free and secret elections, to offer its assistance in order to guarantee the freedom of the elections;

6. *Requests* the Secretary-General to furnish the Commission with the necessary staff and facilities.

356th plenary meeting
20 December 1951

991 (X). Application of the Federal Republic of Germany for Membership in the International Civil Aviation Organization

Committee: -
Vote: Adopted without a vote

The General Assembly,

Having considered the application[3] of the Federal Republic of Germany for admission to the International Civil Aviation Organization, transmitted by that organization to the General Assembly in accordance with article II of the agreement between the United Nations and the International Civil Aviation Organization,

Decides to inform the International Civil Aviation Organization that it has no objection to the admission of the Federal Republic of Germany to the organization.

537th plenary meeting
25 October 1955

3050 (XXVIII). Admission of the German Democratic Republic and the Federal Republic of Germany to Membership in the United Nations

Committee: -
Vote: Adopted without a vote

The General Assembly,

Having received the recommendation of the Security Council of 22 June 1973 that the German Democratic Republic and the Federal Republic of Germany should be admitted to membership in the United Nations,[4]

Having considered separately the application for membership of the German Democratic Republic[5] and the application for membership of the Federal Republic of Germany, [6]

---

1 *Official Records of the General Assembly, Sixth Session,* agenda item 65, document A/1938. Appendix 17, p. 332.

2 *Ibid, Ad Hoc* Political Committee, 18th and 20th meetings.

3 *Official Records of the General Assembly, Tenth Session, Annexes,* agenda item 57, document A/2912. Appendix 70, p. 611.

4 *Ibid., Twenty-eighth Session, Annexes,* agenda item 27, document A/9080.

5 A/9069-S/10945. For the printed text, see *Official Records of the Security Council, Twenty-eighth Year, Supplement for April, May and June 1973.*

6 A/9070-S/10949. For the printed text, see *Official Records of the Security Council, Twenty-eighth Year, Supplement for April, May and June 1973.*

1. *Decides* to admit the German Democratic Republic to membership in the United Nations;

2. *Decides* to admit the Federal Republic of Germany to membership in the United Nations.

2117th plenary meeting
18 September 1973

04.53 YEMEN

45/193. The Unification of Yemen: Support of the International Community for its Economic and Social Infrastructure

Committee: 2
Vote: Adopted without a vote

The General Assembly,

Welcoming the merger on 22 May 1990 of the Yemen Arab Republic and the People's Democratic Republic of Yemen to form a single sovereign State called the Republic of Yemen,

Taking into consideration the declaration adopted at the fourteenth annual meeting of the Ministers for Foreign Affairs of the members of the Group of 77, held in New York on 3 October 1990,[1] in which the world community was requested to render support for the economic and social infrastructure of Yemen to assist it in achieving prosperity for its people,

Realizing the difficult economic situation facing Yemen as a result of the merger of the economic and social infrastructures of the Yemen Arab Republic and the People's Democratic Republic of Yemen following their unification, in addition to the new economic and social burden resulting from the situation between Iraq and Kuwait,

1. *Expresses its solidarity* with Yemen in its efforts to overcome these conditions;

2. *Calls upon* States and governmental and international non-governmental organizations to extend their assistance in support of the national efforts to improve the economic and social infrastructure of Yemen;

3. *Requests* the Secretary-General to assist in mobilizing resources and to consider, in accordance with the resolution on assistance for the reconstruction and development of Yemen to be adopted by the General Assembly at the present session,[2] developing a comprehensive programme to assess the needs of Yemen resulting from the unification, in order to enable the international community to extend assistance to meet those needs;

4. *Also requests* the Secretary-General to submit a report on the implementation of the present resolution to the General Assembly at its forty-seventh session, through the Economic and Social Council at its second regular session of 1992.

71st plenary meeting
21 December 1990

1 A/45/584, annex.

2 See resolution 45/222.

04.54 YUGOSLAVIA

47/1. Recommendation of the Security Council of 19 September 1992

Committee: -
Vote: 127 - 6 - 26

The General Assembly,

Having received the recommendation of the Security Council of 19 September 1992 that the Federal Republic of Yugoslavia (Serbia and Montenegro) should apply for membership in the United Nations and that it shall not participate in the work of the General Assembly,[3]

1. *Considers* that the Federal Republic of Yugoslavia (Serbia and Montenegro) cannot continue automatically the membership of the former Socialist Federal Republic of Yugoslavia in the United Nations; and therefore decides that the Federal Republic of Yugoslavia (Serbia and Montenegro) should apply for membership in the United Nations and that it shall not participate in the work of the General Assembly;

2. *Takes note* of the intention of the Security Council to consider the matter again before the end of the main part of the forty-seventh session of the General Assembly.

7th plenary meeting
22 September 1992

47/229. Recommendation of the Security Council of 28 April 1993

Committee: -
Vote: 107 - 0 - 11

The General Assembly,

Recalling its resolution 47/1 of 22 September 1992,

Having received the recommendation made by the Security Council in its resolution 821 (1993) of 28 April 1993 that, further to the decisions taken in resolution 47/1, the Federal Republic of Yugoslavia (Serbia and Montenegro) shall not participate in the work of the Economic and Social Council,

1. *Decides* that the Federal Republic of Yugoslavia (Serbia and Montenegro) shall not participate in the work of the Economic and Social Council;

2. *Takes note* of the intention of the Security Council to consider the matter again before the end of the forty-seventh session of the General Assembly.

101st plenary meeting
29 April 1993

3 A/47/456

05.00 ECONOMY AND DEVELOPMENT

05.10 POLICIES AND PRINCIPLES CONCERNING ECONOMY AND DEVELOPMENT

724 (VIII). Economic Development of Under-developed Countries

Committee: 2
Vote: A: 44 - 0 - 6; B: 46 - 5 - 5; C: 51 - 0 - 5
Ref.: 32/179, 3338(XXIX), 2169(XXI), 1515(XV), 1425(XIV), 1316(XIII), 1034(XI), 1033(XI), 627(VII), 523(VI), 521(VI), 408(V), 407(V), 404(V), 403(V), 307(IV), 306(IV), 266(III), 200(III), 198(III)

A

The General Assembly,

Having noted Economic and Social Council resolution 482 A (XVI) of 4 August 1953,

Desirous of strengthening the United Nations in its mission of guarding the peace and security of all peoples and of promoting higher standards of living and conditions of economic and social progress and development in under-developed countries,

Looking forward to the time when sufficient progress in internationally supervised world-wide disarmament will make it propitious to devote additional resources to assist development and reconstruction, particularly in the under-developed countries,

Adopts the following declaration:

"We, the governments of the States Members of the United Nations, in order to promote higher standards of living and conditions of economic and social progress and development, stand ready to ask our peoples, when sufficient progress has been made in internationally supervised world-wide disarmament, to devote a portion of the savings achieved through such disarmament to an international fund, within the framework of the United Nations, to assist development and reconstruction in underdeveloped countries."

468th plenary meeting
7 December 1953

B

The General Assembly,

Having considered the *Report on a Special United Nations Fund for Economic Development*[1] prepared by the Committee of Nine appointed by the Secretary-General, and submitted in pursuance of Economic and Social Council resolution 416 A (XIV) of 23 June 1952 and General Assembly resolution 622 A (VII) of 21 December 1952,

Mindful of the aim expressed in the preamble of the Charter "to employ international machinery for the promotion of the economic and social advancement of all peoples" and of Articles 55 and 56 of the Charter,

Believing that, especially in the present state of world tension, the social and economic advancement of the under-developed countries can contribute towards the achievement of international peace and security,

Confident that an expanded flow of capital to underdeveloped countries would contribute to the solution of the basic economic problems of our time, both for under-developed and developed countries,

Considering that the use of international machinery for financially assisting the acceleration of the economic development of the under-developed countries contributes to the achievement of an expanding and stable world economy,

Noting that the efforts made and the activities undertaken so far by and under the United Nations for the economic development of the under-developed countries have proved beneficial and represent a marked advance in economic cooperation among nations,

Bearing in mind the recommendations contained in Economic and Social Council resolution 482 A (XVI) of 4 August 1953 relating to a special United Nations fund,

Considering that the General Assembly should keep under review the question of the establishment of a special fund and, in particular, be attentive to any changes either in world conditions or in the attitudes of the governments of Member States, which might be propitious to the establishment of such a fund in the near future,

Hopeful that conditions favourable to the establishment of an international fund will be created in the near future and that savings from internationally supervised world-wide disarmament will provide additional means for financing the economic development of under-developed countries, and will further the aims and objectives of such a fund,

1. *Expresses* its great appreciation of the work of the Committee of Nine;

2. *Invites* governments of States Members of the United Nations and of the specialized agencies in the economic and social field to transmit to the Secretary-General their detailed comments both on the recommendations contained in the report of the Committee of Nine and on the degree of moral and material support which may be expected from them for such a fund;

3. *Decides* to appoint the present President of the Economic and Social Council, Mr. Raymond Scheyven, to examine, with the assistance of the Secretary-General, the comments of governments submitted in response to the invitation contained in the preceding paragraph; to collate and where he judges necessary to request elaboration of such comments, if desirable by direct consultation with governments; and to submit to the Economic and Social Council at its eighteenth session an interim report on his work, and, in any event to submit to the General Assembly at its ninth session, a final report together with his comments, with a view to assisting it to make such recommendations as it would find possible which could facilitate the establishment of such a fund as soon as circumstances permit;

4. *Requests* the Secretary-General to:

(*a*) Provide Mr. Scheyven with all necessary assistance and facilities;

(*b*) Transmit to the governments specified in paragraph 2 above the report of the Committee of Nine, together with the records of the discussion on the subject at the eighth session of the General Assembly;

(*c*) Circulate as soon as possible to the governments specified in paragraph 2 above (i) the comments submitted in response to that paragraph, and (ii) the final report of Mr. Scheyven; and submit a summary of the comments of governments to the General Assembly at its ninth session;

(*d*) Prepare a working paper, for submission to the Economic and Social Council, on the extent and methods of coordination which may be desirable or necessary between the activities of such a fund, of the Technical Assistance Board and of such of the specialized agencies as may be engaged in tasks relating to the economic development of under-developed countries;

5. *Requests* the Economic and Social Council to study at its eighteenth session the working paper referred to in paragraph 4 (d) above and to transmit it, together with its views, to the General Assembly at its ninth session;

6. *Decides* to include in the provisional agenda of the ninth session of the General Assembly a separate item for the consideration of the results of the steps provided for above.

468th plenary meeting
7 December 1953

---

[1] See United Nations Publication, Sales No.: 1953.II.B.1.

C

The General Assembly,

Bearing in mind that the general problem of economic development of the under-developed countries concerns both the under-developed and the more developed countries,

Mindful that the economic development of the underdeveloped countries depends primarily on their own efforts and resources,

Recognizing, however, that financial resources at present available in the under-developed countries are inadequate to finance the desired rate of economic development,

Believing that additional external resources, both private and public, made available, as appropriate, within or without the framework of the United Nations, would greatly aid the under-developed countries in financing their development programmes,

I

Bearing in mind General Assembly resolution 622 B (VII) of 21 December 1952 and Economic and Social Council resolutions 416 C (XIV) and 482 B (XVI) of 23 June 1952 and 4 August 1953 respectively,

Having considered the reports[1] of the International Bank for Reconstruction and Development on the question of creating an international finance corporation,

Bearing in mind that the consultations and study requested below might indicate the practicability of establishing such a finance corporation in the near future,

1. *Expresses its appreciation* of the useful contribution the International Bank for Reconstruction and Development has made to the study of the question;

2. *Emphasizes* the beneficial effects the proposed corporation could have in so far as it would promote the mobilization of additional domestic resources in the under-developed countries and the flow of external capital into these countries, in order to augment the financial resources for their economic development;

3. *Urges* governments which have not done so to give early consideration to the merits of establishing an international finance corporation, and to make known to the International Bank their views on the possibility of supporting such a corporation in time for the Bank to take them into consideration when preparing its report for the eighteenth session of the Economic and Social Council, as foreseen in paragraph 4 below;

4. *Requests* the International Bank to:

(*a*) Analyse in detail the questions raised and the views expressed by governments and non-governmental institutions concerning the methods of furnishing the capital for an international finance corporation, its functions and operations;

(*b*) Conduct its consultations in a more intensive manner on the question of the creation of an international finance corporation and on the prospects of financial support for it;

(*c*) Report to the Economic and Social Council at its eighteenth session on the subjects referred to it in sub-paragraphs (a) and (b) above;

5. *Requests* the Economic and Social Council to review at its eighteenth session the reports of the International Bank on the question of creating an international finance corporation and to report thereon to the General Assembly during its ninth session;

II

Recognizing the importance of finding means to stimulate the flow of external private capital to the under-developed countries in order to accelerate their development,

Mindful of General Assembly resolution 622 C (VII) of 21 December 1952,

Requests that the study which is being prepared by the Secretary-General, pursuant to General Assembly resolution 622 C (VII), on the general role of private external capital be examined by the Economic and Social Council during its seventeenth session, with a view to ascertaining under what conditions the flow into under-developed countries of private capital can effectively contribute to the harmonious and adequate integration of the economies of those countries and to their economic and social development;

III

Recognizing the importance of fluctuations in the terms of trade and the effect of these fluctuations on the financing of the economic development of the under-developed countries,

Requests the Economic and Social Council to consider at its seventeenth session the report prepared by the group of experts appointed pursuant to General Assembly resolution 623 (VII) of 21 December 1952 and to make such recommendations as it may find desirable for consideration by the General Assembly at its ninth session.

468th plenary meeting
7 December 1953

810 (IX). International Cooperation in Developing the Peaceful Uses of Atomic Energy

Committee: 1
Vote: unanimous
Ref.: 35/112, 34/63, 33/4, 32/50, 2829(XXVI), 2665(XXV), 2575(XXIV), 2406(XXIII), 2309(XXII), 2056(XX), 1770(XVII), 1344(XIII), 912(X)

The General Assembly,

Believing that the benefits arising from the momentous discovery of atomic energy should be placed at the service of mankind,

Desiring to promote energetically the use of atomic energy to the end that it will serve only the peaceful pursuits of mankind and ameliorate their living conditions,

Recognizing the importance and the urgency of international cooperation in developing and expanding the peaceful uses of atomic energy to assist in lifting the burdens of hunger, poverty and disease,

Believing also that all nations should cooperate in promoting the dissemination of knowledge in the realm of nuclear technology for peaceful ends,

A

Concerning an International Atomic Agency

Recalling the initiative of the President of the United States of America, embodied in his address[2] of 8 December 1953,

Noting that negotiations are in progress, and the intention that they should continue, for the establishment as quickly as possible of an International Atomic Energy Agency to facilitate the use by the entire world of atomic energy for peaceful purposes, and to encourage international cooperation in the further development and practical application of atomic energy for the benefit of mankind,

1. *Expresses the hope* that the International Atomic Energy Agency will be established without delay;

2. *Suggests* that, once the Agency is established, it negotiate an appropriate form of agreement with the United Nations;

3. *Transmits* to the States participating in the creation of the Agency, for their careful consideration, the record of the discussion of this item at the present session of the General Assembly;

4. *Suggests* that Members of the United Nations be informed as progress is achieved in the establishment of the Agency and that the views of Members which have manifested their interest be fully considered;

---

1 See documents E/2215 and E/2441.

2 *Official Records of the General Assembly, Eighth Session,* 470th plenary meeting.

B

Concerning the International Conference on the Peaceful Uses of Atomic Energy

1. *Declares* the interest and concern of the General Assembly in helping in every feasible way to promote the peaceful applications of atomic energy;

2. *Decides* that an international technical conference of Governments should be held, under the auspices of the United Nations, to explore means of developing the peaceful uses of atomic energy through international cooperation and, in particular, to study the development of atomic power and to consider other technical areas - such as biology, medicine, radiation protection, and fundamental science - in which international cooperation might most effectively be accomplished;

3. *Invites* all States Members of the United Nations or of the specialized agencies to participate in the conference and to include among their representatives individual experts competent in the atomic energy field;

4. *Suggests* that the international conference should be held no later than August 1955 at a place to be determined by the Secretary-General and by the Advisory Committee provided for in paragraph 5 below;

5. *Requests* the Secretary-General, acting upon the advice of a small committee composed of representatives of Brazil, Canada, France, India, the Union of Soviet Socialist Republics, the United Kingdom of Great Britain and Northern Ireland and the United States of America, to issue invitations to this conference, to prepare and circulate to all invitees a detailed agenda, and to provide the necessary staff and services;

6. *Suggests* to the Secretary-General and the above-mentioned Advisory Committee that, in making plans for the international conference, they consult with competent specialized agencies, in particular the Food and Agriculture Organization, the World Health Organization, and the United Nations Educational, Scientific and Cultural Organization;

7. *Invites* the interested specialized agencies to designate persons to represent them at the conference;

8. *Requests* that the Secretary-General circulate for information a report on the conference to all Members of the United Nations, and to other Governments and specialized agencies participating in the conference.

503rd plenary meeting
4 December 1954

1831 (XVII). Economic Development and the Conservation of Nature

Committee: 2
Vote: unanimous

The General Assembly,

Noting the steps taken by the Economic and Social Council in its resolution 810 (XXXI) of 24 April 1961, particularly as they affect national parks and equivalent reserves, and the Council's request, in its resolution 910 (XXXIV) of 2 August 1962, for a study of measures proposed for the conservation and amelioration of natural environments,

Noting with satisfaction the initiative taken by the United Nations Educational, Scientific and Cultural Organization in the field of the conservation of nature in the resolution adopted by its General Conference in 1962, and in particular the opinion expressed by that Organization that, to be effective, measures to preserve natural resources, flora and fauna should be taken at the earliest possible moment simultaneously with economic development, including industrialization and urbanization,

Considering that natural resources, flora and fauna may be of considerable importance to the further economic development of countries and of benefit to their populations,

Conscious of the extent to which the economic development of the developing countries may jeopardize their natural resources and their flora and fauna, which in some cases may be irreplaceable if such development takes place without due attention to their conservation and restoration,

1. *Endorses* the decision taken by the United Nations Educational, Scientific and Cultural Organization in the above-mentioned resolution and expresses the hope that early action will be taken, especially in the developing countries, along the lines set out in that resolution which, in paragraph 1, recommends measures directed towards:

(*a*) Preserving, restoring, enriching and making rational use of natural resources and increasing productivity;

(*b*) Assisting the International Union for the Conservation of Nature and Natural Resources and international organizations with similar aims;

(*c*) Observing existing international conventions and treaties on the preservation of the world's flora and fauna;

(*d*) Facilitating the exchange of information and of scientists and specialists in this field;

(*e*) Introducing effective domestic legislation directed at eliminating the wasteful exploitation of soil, rivers and flora and fauna, while taking appropriate steps to prevent the pollution of natural resources and to protect landscapes, and also devising and implementing a suitable educational programme at all levels;

(*f*) Organizing national campaigns through educational institutions and through the press, radio, television and all other possible media for the dissemination of information, in order to secure the cooperation of the population in the achievement of these aims;

(*g*) Associating all interested ministerial departments in this effort to protect flora and fauna;

2. *Calls upon* the Secretary-General, the specialized agencies and other interested international and national organizations, in support of the above-mentioned resolution of the United Nations Educational, Scientific and Cultural Organization, to continue to give the fullest cooperation and to provide technical assistance to the developing countries, at their request, in the conservation and restoration of their natural resources and their flora and fauna.

1197th plenary meeting
18 December 1962

1838 (XVII). Population Growth and Economic Development

Committee: 2
Vote: 69 - 0 - 27
Ref.: 1719(XVI)

The General Assembly,

Considering that rapid economic and social progress in the developing countries is dependent not least upon the ability of these countries to provide their peoples with education, a fair standard of living and the possibility for productive work,

Considering further that economic development and population growth are closely interrelated,

Recognizing that the health and welfare of the family are of paramount importance, not only for obvious humanitarian reasons, but also with regard to economic development and social progress, and that the health and welfare of the family require special attention in areas with a relatively high rate of population growth,

Recognizing further that it is the responsibility of each Government to decide on its own policies and devise its own programmes of action for dealing with the problems of population and economic and social progress,

Reminding States Members of the United Nations and members of the specialized agencies that, according to recent census results, the effective population increase during the last decade has been particularly great in many of the low-income less developed countries,

Reminding Member States that in formulating their economic and social policies it is useful to take into account the latest relevant facts on the interrelationship of population growth and economic and social development, and that the forthcoming World Population Conference and the Asian Population Conference might throw new light on the importance of this problem, especially for the developing countries,

Recalling its resolution 1217 (XII) of 14 December 1957, in which the General Assembly, *inter alia* invited Member States, particularly the developing countries, to follow as closely as possible the interrelationship of economic changes and population changes, and requested the Secretary-General to ensure the coordination of the activities of the United Nations in the demographic and economic fields,

Recalling economic and Social Council resolution 820 B (XXXI) of 28 April 1961 which contains provisions for intensifying efforts to ensure international cooperation in the evaluation, analysis and utilization of population census results and related data, particularly in the less developed countries, and in which the Council requested the Secretary-General to explore the possibilities of increasing technical assistance funds for assistance to Governments requesting it in preparing permanent programmes of demographic research,

Recognizing that further studies and research are necessary to fill the gaps in the present knowledge of the causes and consequences of demographic trends, particularly in the less developed countries,

Recognizing also that removals of large national groups to other countries may give rise to ethnic, political, emotional and economic difficulties,

1. *Notes with appreciation* the report of the Secretary-General on measures proposed for the United Nations Development Decade[1] in which he refers, *inter alia*, to the interrelationship of population growth and economic and social development;

2. *Expresses its appreciation* of the work on population problems which has up to now been carried out under the guidance of the Population Commission;

3. *Requests* the Secretary-General to conduct an inquiry among the Governments of States Members of the United Nations and members of the specialized agencies concerning the particular problems confronting them as a result of the reciprocal action of economic development and population changes;

4. *Recommends* that the Economic and Social Council, in cooperation with the specialized agencies, the regional economic commissions and the Population Commission, and taking into account the results of the inquiry referred to in paragraph 3 above, should intensify its studies and research on the interrelationship of population growth and economic and social development, with particular reference to the needs of the developing countries for investment in health and educational facilities within the framework of their general development programmes;

5. *Further recommends* that the Economic and Social Council should report on its findings to the General Assembly not later than at its nineteenth session;

6. *Endorses* the view of the Population Commission[2] that the United Nations should encourage and assist Governments, especially those of the less developed countries, in obtaining basic data and in carrying out essential studies of the demographic aspects, as well as other aspects, of their economic and social development problems;

7. *Recommends* that the second World Population Conference should pay special attention to the inter-relationship of population growth and economic and social development, particularly in the less developed countries, and that efforts should be made to obtain the fullest possible participation in the Conference by experts from such countries.

1197th plenary meeting
18 December 1962

1 United Nations publication, Sales No.: 62.II.B.2.

2 *Official Records of the Economic and Social Council, Thirty-first Session, Supplement No. 3* (E/3451), para. 15.

2542 (XXIV). Declaration on Social Progress and Development

Committee: 3
Vote: 119 - 0 - 2
Ref.: 41/142, 34/59, 32/117, 2543(XXIV)

The General Assembly,

Mindful of the pledge of Members of the United Nations under the Charter to take joint and separate action in cooperation with the Organization to promote higher standards of living, full employment and conditions of economic and social progress and development,

Reaffirming faith in human rights and fundamental freedoms and in the principles of peace, of the dignity and worth of the human person, and of social justice proclaimed in the Charter,

Recalling the principles of the Universal Declaration of Human Rights, the International Covenants on Human Rights, the Declaration of the Rights of the Child, the Declaration on the Granting of Independence to Colonial Countries and Peoples, the International Convention on the Elimination of All Forms of Racial Discrimination, the United Nations Declaration on the Elimination of All Forms of Racial Discrimination, the Declaration on the Promotion among Youth of the Ideals of Peace, Mutual Respect and Understanding between Peoples, the Declaration on the Elimination of Discrimination against Women and of resolutions of the United Nations,

Bearing in mind the standards already set for social progress in the constitutions, conventions, recommendations and resolutions of the International Labour Organization, the Food and Agriculture Organization of the United Nations, the United Nations Educational, Scientific and Cultural Organization, the World Health Organization, the United Nations Children's Fund and of other organizations concerned,

Convinced that man can achieve complete of his aspirations only within a just social order and that it is consequently of cardinal importance to accelerate social and economic progress everywhere, thus contributing to international peace and solidarity,

Convinced that international peace and security on the one hand, and social progress and economic development on the other, are closely interdependent and influence each other,

Persuaded that social development can be promoted by peaceful coexistence, friendly relations and cooperation among States with different social, economic or political systems,

Emphasizing the interdependence of economic and social development in the wider process of growth and change, as well as the importance of a strategy of integrated development which takes full account at all stages of its social aspects,

Regretting the inadequate progress achieved in the world social situation despite the efforts of States and the international community,

Recognizing that the primary responsibility for the development of the developing countries rests on those countries themselves and acknowledging the pressing need to narrow and eventually close the gap in the standards of living between economically more advanced and developing countries and, to that end, that Member States shall have the responsibility to pursue internal and external policies designed to promote social development throughout the world, and in particular to assist developing countries to accelerate their economic growth,

Recognizing the urgency of devoting to works of peace and social progress resources being expended on armaments and wasted on conflict and destruction,

Conscious of the contribution that science and technology can render towards meeting the needs common to all humanity,

Believing that the primary task of all States and international organizations is to eliminate from the life of society all evils and obstacles to social progress, particularly such evils as inequality, exploitation, war, colonialism and racism,

Desirous of promoting the progress of all mankind towards these goals and of overcoming all obstacles to their realization,

Solemnly proclaims this Declaration on Social Progress and Development and calls for national and international action for its use as a common basis for social development policies:

Part I

Principles

Article 1

All peoples and all human beings, without distinction as to race, colour, sex, language, religion, nationality, ethnic origin, family or social status, or political or other conviction, shall have the right to live in dignity and freedom and to enjoy the fruits of social progress and should, on their part, contribute to it.

Article 2

Social progress and development shall be founded on respect for the dignity and value of the human person and shall ensure the promotion of human rights and social justice, which requires:

(*a*) The immediate and final elimination of all forms of inequality, exploitation of peoples and individuals, colonialism and racism, including nazism and apartheid and all other policies and ideologies opposed to the purposes and principles of the United Nations;

(*b*) The recognition and effective implementation of civil and political rights as well as of economic, social and cultural rights without any discrimination.

Article 3

The following are considered primary conditions of social progress and development:

(*a*) National independence based on the right of peoples to self-determination;

(*b*) The principle of non-interference in the internal affairs of States;

(*c*) Respect for the sovereignty and territorial integrity of States;

(*d*) Permanent sovereignty of each nation over its natural wealth and resources;

(*e*) The right and responsibility of each State and, as far as they are concerned, each nation and people to determine freely its own objectives of social development to set its own priorities and to decide in conformity with the principles of the Charter of the United Nations the means and methods of their achievement without any external interference;

(*f*) Peaceful coexistence, peace, friendly relations and cooperation among States irrespective of differences in their social, economic or political systems.

Article 4

The family as a basic unit of society and the natural environment for the growth and well-being of all its members, particularly children and youth, should be assisted and protected so that it may fully assume its responsibilities within the community. Parents have the exclusive right to determine freely and responsibly the number and spacing of their children.

Article 5

Social progress and development require the full utilization of human resources, including, in particular:

(*a*) The encouragement of creative initiative under conditions of enlightened public opinion;

(*b*) The dissemination of national and international information for the purpose of making individuals aware of changes occurring in society as a whole;

(*c*) The active participation of all elements of society, individually or through associations, in defining and in achieving the common goals of development with full respect for the fundamental freedoms embodied in the Universal Declaration of Human Rights;

(*d*) The assurance to disadvantaged or marginal sectors of the population of equal opportunities for social and economic advancement in order to achieve an effectively integrated society.

Article 6

Social development requires the assurance to everyone of the right to work and the free choice of employment.

Social progress and development require the participation of all members of society in productive and socially useful labour and the establishment, in conformity with human rights and fundamental freedoms and with the principles of justice and the social function of property of forms of ownership of land and of the means of production which preclude any kind of exploitation of man, ensure equal rights to property for all and create conditions leading to genuine equality among people.

Article 7

The rapid expansion of national income and wealth and their equitable distribution among all members of society are fundamental to all social progress, and they should therefore be in the forefront of the preoccupations of every State and Government.

The improvement in the position of the developing countries in international trade resulting, among other things, from the achievement of favourable terms of trade and of equitable and remunerative prices at which developing countries market their products is necessary in order to make it possible to increase national income and in order to advance social development.

Article 8

Each Government has the primary role and ultimate responsibility of ensuring the social progress and well-being of its people, of planning social development measures as part of comprehensive development plans, of encouraging and coordinating or integrating all national efforts towards this end and of introducing necessary changes in the social structure. In planning social development measures, the diversity of the needs of developing and developed areas, and of urban and rural areas, within each country, shall be taken into due account.

Article 9

Social progress and development are the common concerns of the international community, which shall supplement, by concerted international action, national efforts to raise the living standards of peoples.

Social progress and economic growth require recognition of the common interest of all nations in the exploration, conservation, use and exploitation, exclusively for peaceful purposes and in the interests of all mankind, of those areas of the environment such as outer space and the sea-bed and ocean floor and the subsoil thereof, beyond the limits of national jurisdiction, in accordance with the purposes and principles of the Charter of the United Nations.

Part II

Objectives

Social progress and development shall aim at the continuous raising of the material and spiritual standards of living of all members of society, with respect for and in compliance with human rights and fundamental freedoms, through the attainment of the following main goals:

Article 10

(*a*) The assurance at all levels of the right to work and the right of everyone to form trade unions and workers' associations and to bargain collectively; promotion of full productive employment and elimination of unemployment and under-employment; establishment of equitable and favourable conditions of work for all, including the improvement of health and safety conditions; assurance of just remuneration for labour without any discrimination as well as a sufficiently high minimum wage to ensure a decent standard of living; the protection of the consumer;

(*b*) The elimination of hunger and malnutrition and the guarantee of the right to proper nutrition;

(*c*) The elimination of poverty; the assurance of a steady improvement in levels of living and of a just and equitable distribution of income;

(*d*) The achievement of the highest standards of health and the provision of health protection for the entire population, if possible free of charge;

(*e*) The eradication of illiteracy and the assurance of the right to universal access to culture, to free compulsory education at the elementary level and to free education at all levels; the raising of the general level of life-long education;

(*f*) The provision for all, particularly persons in low in some groups and large families, of adequate housing and community services.

Social progress and development shall aim equally at the progressive attainment of the following main goals:

Article 11

(*a*) The provision of comprehensive social security schemes and social welfare services; the establishment and improvement of social security and insurance schemes for all persons who, because of illness, disability or old age, are temporarily or permanently unable to earn a living, with a view to ensuring a proper standard of living for such persons and for their families and dependants;

(*b*) The protection of the rights of the mother and child; concern for the upbringing and health of children; the provision of measures to safeguard the health and welfare of women and particularly of working mothers during pregnancy and the infancy of their children, as well as of mothers whose earnings are the sole source of livelihood for the family; the granting to women of pregnancy and maternity leave and allowances without loss of employment or wages;

(*c*) The protection of the rights and the assuring of the welfare of children, the aged and the disabled; the provision of protection for the physically or mentally disadvantaged;

(*d*) The education of youth in, and promotion among them of, the ideals of justice and peace, mutual respect and understanding among peoples, the promotion of full participation of youth in the process of national development;

(*e*) The provision of social defence measures and the elimination of conditions leading to crime and delinquency, especially juvenile delinquency;

(*f*) The guarantee that all individuals, without discrimination of any kind, are made aware of their rights and obligations and receive the necessary aid in the exercise and safeguarding of their rights.

Social progress and development shall further aim at achieving the following main objectives:

Article 12

(*a*) The creation of conditions for rapid and sustained social and economic development, particularly in the developing countries; change in international economic relations; new and effective methods of international cooperation in which equality of opportunity should be as much a prerogative of nations as of individuals within a nation;

(*b*) The elimination of all forms of discrimination and exploitation and all other practices and ideologies contrary to the purposes and principles of the Charter of the United Nations;

(*c*) The elimination of all forms of foreign economic exploitation particularly that practiced by international monopolies in order to enable the people of every country to enjoy in full the benefits of their national resources.

Social progress and development shall finally aim at the attainment of the following main goals:

Article 13

(*a*) Equitable sharing of scientific and technological advances by developed and developing countries, and a steady increase in the use of science and technology for the benefit of the social development of society;

(*b*) The establishment of a harmonious balance between scientific technological and material progress and the intellectual, spiritual, cultural and moral advancement of humanity;

(*c*) The protection and improvement of the human environment.

Part III

Means and Methods

On the basis of the principles set forth in this Declaration, the achievement of the objectives of social progress and development requires the mobilization of the necessary resources by national and international action, with particular attention to such means and methods as:

Article 14

(*a*) Planning for social progress and development, as an integrated part of balanced over-all development planning;

(*b*) The establishment, where necessary, of national systems for framing and carrying out social policies and programmes, and the promotion by the countries concerned of planned regional development, taking into account differing regional conditions and needs, particularly the development of regions which are less favoured or under-developed by comparison with the rest of the country;

(*c*) The promotion of basic and applied social research, particularly comparative international research applied to the planning and execution of social development programmes.

Article 15

(*a*) The adoption of measures to ensure the effective participation, as appropriate, of all the elements of society in the preparation and execution of national plans and programmes of economic and social development;

(*b*) The adoption of measures for an increasing rate of popular participation in the economic, social, cultural and political life of countries through national governmental bodies, non-governmental organizations, cooperatives, rural associations, workers, and employers, organizations and women's and youth organizations, by such methods as national and regional plans for social and economic progress and community development, with a view to achieving a fully integrated national society, accelerating the process of social mobility and consolidating the democratic system;

(*c*) Mobilization of public opinion, at both national and international levels, in support of the principles and objectives of social progress and development;

(*d*) The dissemination of social information, at the national and the international level, to make people aware of changing circumstances in society as a whole, and to educate the consumer.

Article 16

(*a*) Maximum mobilization of all national resources and their rational and efficient utilization; promotion of increased and accelerated productive investment in social and economic fields and of employment; orientation of society towards the development process;

(*b*) Progressively increasing provision of the necessary budgetary and other resources required for financing the social aspects of development;

(*c*) Achievement of equitable distribution of national income, utilizing, *inter alia*, the fiscal system and government spending as an instrument for the equitable distribution and redistribution of income in order to promote social progress;

(*d*) The adoption of measures aimed at prevention of such an outflow of capital from developing countries as would be detrimental to their economic and social development.

Article 17

(*a*) The adoption of measures to accelerate the process of industrialization, especially in developing countries, with due regard for its social aspects, in the interests of the entire population; development of an adequate organizational and legal framework conducive to an uninterrupted and diversified growth of the industrial sector; measures to overcome the adverse social effects which may result from urban development and industrialization, including automation; maintenance of a proper balance between rural and urban development, and in particular, measures designed to ensure healthier living conditions, especially in large industrial centres;

(*b*) Integrated planning to meet the problems of urbanization and urban development;

(*c*) Comprehensive rural development schemes to raise the levels of living of the rural populations and to facilitate such urban-rural relationships and population distribution as will promote balanced national development and social progress;

(*d*) Measures for appropriate supervision of the utilization of land in the interests of society.

The achievement of the objectives of social progress and development equally requires the implementation of the following means and methods:

Article 18

(*a*) The adoption of appropriate legislative, administrative and other measures ensuring to everyone not only political and civil rights, but also the full realization of economic, social and cultural rights without any discrimination;

(*b*) The promotion of democratically based social and institutional reforms and motivation for change basic to the elimination of all forms of discrimination and exploitation and conducive to high rates of economic and social progress, to include land reform, in which the ownership and use of land will be made to serve best the objectives of social justice and economic development;

(*c*) The adoption of measures to boost and diversify agricultural production through, *inter alia*, the implementation of democratic agrarian reforms, to ensure an adequate and well-balanced supply of food, its equitable distribution among the whole population and the improvement of nutritional standards;

(*d*) The adoption of measures to introduce, with the participation of the Government, low-cost housing programmes in both rural and urban areas;

(*e*) Development and expansion of the system of transportation and communications, particularly in developing countries.

Article 19

(*a*) The provision of free health services to the whole population and of adequate preventive and curative facilities and welfare medical services accessible to all;

(*b*) The enactment and establishment of legislative measures and administrative regulations with a view to the implementation of comprehensive programmes of social security schemes and social welfare services and to the improvement and coordination of existing services;

(*c*) The adoption of measures and the provision of social welfare services to migrant workers and their families, in conformity with the provisions of Convention No. 97 of the International Labour Organisation[1] and other international instruments relating to migrant workers;

(*d*) The institution of appropriate measures for the rehabilitation of mentally or physically disabled persons, especially children and youth, so as to enable them to the fullest possible extent to be useful members of society - these measures shall include the provision of treatment and technical appliances, education, vocational and social guidance, training and selective placement, and other assistance required - and the creation of social conditions in which the handicapped are not discriminated against because of their disabilities.

Article 20

(*a*) The provision of full democratic freedoms to trade unions; freedom of association for all workers, including the right to bargain collectively and to strike, recognition of the right to form other organizations of working people; the provision for the growing participation of trade unions in economic and social development; effective participation of all members of trade unions in the deciding of economic and social issues which affect their interests;

(*b*) The improvement of health and safety conditions for workers, by means of appropriate technological and legislative measures and the provision of the material prerequisites for the implementation of those measures, including the limitation of working hours;

(*c*) The adoption of appropriate measures for the development of harmonious industrial relations.

Article 21

(*a*) The training of national personnel and cadres, including administrative, executive, professional and technical personnel needed for social development and for over-all development plans and policies;

(*b*) The adoption of measures to accelerate the extension and improvement of general, vocational and technical education and of training and retraining, which should be provided free at all levels;

(*c*) Raising the general level of education; development and expansion of national information media, and their rational and full use towards continuing education of the whole population and towards encouraging its participation in social development activities; the constructive use of leisure, particularly that of children and adolescents;

(*d*) The formulation of national and international policies and measures to avoid the "brain drain" and obviate its adverse effects.

Article 22

(*a*) The development and coordination of policies and measures designed to strengthen the essential functions of the family as a basic unit of society;

(*b*) The formulation and establishment, as needed, of programmes in the field of population, within the framework of national demographic policies and as part of the welfare medical services, including education, training of personnel and the provision to families of the knowledge and means necessary to enable them to exercise their right to determine freely and responsibly the number and spacing of their children;

(*c*) The establishment of appropriate child-care facilities in the interest of children and working parents.

The achievement of the objectives of social progress and development finally requires the implementation of the following means and methods:

Article 23

(*a*) The laying down of economic growth rate targets for the developing countries within the United Nations policy for development, high enough to lead to a substantial acceleration of their rates of growth;

(*b*) The provision of greater assistance on better terms the implementation of the aid volume target of a minimum of 1 per cent of the gross national product at market prices of economically advanced countries; the general easing of the terms of lending to the developing countries through low interest rates on loans and long grace periods for the repayment of loans, and the assurance that the allocation of such loans will be based strictly on socioeconomic criteria free of any political considerations;

(*c*) The provision of technical, financial and material assistance, both bilateral and multilateral, to the fullest possible extent and on favourable terms, and improved coordination of international assistance for the achievement of the social objectives of national development plans;

(*d*) The provision to the developing countries of technical, financial and material assistance and of favourable conditions to facilitate the direct exploitation of their national resources and natural wealth by

1 Convention concerning Migration for Employment (Revised 1949), International Labour Office, *Conventions and Recommendations, 1919-1949* (Geneva, 1949), p. 863.

those countries with a view to enabling the peoples of those countries to benefit fully from their national resources;

(*e*) The expansion of international trade based on principles of equality and non-discrimination, the rectification of the position of developing countries in international trade by equitable terms of trade, a general non-reciprocal and non-discriminatory system of preferences for the exports of developing countries to the developed countries, the establishment and implementation of general and comprehensive commodity agreements, and the financing of reasonable buffer stocks by international institutions.

Article 24

(*a*) Intensification of international cooperation with a view to ensuring the international exchange of information, knowledge and experience concerning social progress and development;

(*b*) The broadest possible international technical, scientific and cultural cooperation and reciprocal utilization of the experience of countries with different economic and social systems and different levels of development, on the basis of mutual advantage and strict observance of and respect for national sovereignity;

(*c*) Increased utilization of science and technology for social and economic development; arrangements for the transfer and exchange of technology, including know-how and patents, to the developing countries.

Article 25

(*a*) The establishment of legal and administrative measures for the protection and improvement of the human environment at both national and international levels;

(*b*) The use and exploitation, in accordance with the appropriate international régimes, of the resources of areas of the environment such as outer space and the sea-bed and ocean floor and the subsoil thereof, beyond the limits of national jurisdiction, in order to supplement national resources available for the achievement of economic and social progress and development in every country, irrespective of its geographical location, special consideration being given to the interests and needs of the developing countries.

Article 26

Compensation for damages, be they social or economic in nature - including restitution and reparations - caused as a result of aggression and of illegal occupation of territory by the aggressor.

Article 27

(*a*) The achievement of general and complete disarmament and the channelling of the progressively released resources to be used for economic and social progress for the welfare of people everywhere and, in particular, for the benefit of developing countries;

(*b*) The adoption of measures contributing to disarmament, including, *inter alia*, the complete prohibition of tests of nuclear weapons, the prohibition of the development production and stockpiling of chemical and bacteriological (biological) weapons and the prevention of the pollution of oceans and inland waters by nuclear wastes.

1829th plenary meeting
11 December 1969

2849 (XXVI). Development and Environment

Committee: 2
Vote: 85 - 2 - 34

The General Assembly,

Recalling its resolutions 2398 (XXIII) of 3 December 1968, 2581 (XXIV) of 15 December 1969 and 2657 of 7 December 1970,

Expressing satisfaction for the efforts made and the results already achieved towards planning action to be taken by the United Nations system in the field of the environment in a manner compatible with the priorities and interests of the developing countries,

Taking note with appreciation in particular, of the work done by the regional seminars on development and environment, held under the auspices of the Economic Commission for Asia and the Far East, the Economic Commission for Africa, the Economic Commission for Latin America and the United Nations Economic and Social Office at Beirut, as well as by the Panel of Experts on Development and the Environment,[1]

Conscious of the significance of the results achieved in the Symposium on Problems relating to Environment convened at Prague by the Economic Commission for Europe, for a better understanding of environmental problems,[2]

Fully conscious of the importance, urgency and universality of environmental problems,

Aware that the rational management of the environment is of fundamental importance for the future of mankind,

Convinced that development plans should be compatible with a sound ecology and that adequate environmental conditions can best be ensured by the promotion of development, both at the national and international levels,

Fully aware that the environmental problems generated by the condition of under-development pose a serious threat to the developing countries,

Cognizant that, aside from environmental disturbances provoked by human settlements and ecological problems related to nature itself, pollution of world-wide impact is being caused primarily by some highly developed countries, as a consequence of their own high level of improperly planned and inadequately coordinated industrial activities, and that, therefore, the main responsibility for the financing of corrective measures falls upon those countries,

Convinced that most of the environmental problems existing in developing countries are caused by their lack of economic resources for dealing with such problems as the improvement of unfavourable natural areas or the rehabilitation of environmental conditions that have deteriorated through the application of improper methods and technologies,

Conscious that the main objective of developing countries is integrated and rational development, including industrial development based on advanced and adequate technologies, and that such development represents at the present stage the best possible solution for most of the environmental problems in the developing countries,

Conscious further that the quality of human life in the developing countries also depends, in large measure, on the solution of environmental problems which have their origin in nature and which are the product of underdevelopment itself, within the general framework of development planning and the rational management of natural resources,

Emphasizing that, notwithstanding the general principles that might be agreed upon by the international community, criteria and minimal standards of preservation of the environment as a general rule will have to be defined at the national level and, in all cases, will have to reflect conditions and systems of values prevailing in each country, avoiding where necessary the use of norms valid in advanced countries, which may prove inadequate and of unwarranted social cost for the developing countries,

Stressing that each country has the right to formulate, in accordance with its own particular situation and in full enjoyment of its national sovereignty, its own national policies on the human environment, including criteria for the evaluation of projects,

Stressing further that in the exercise of such right and in the implementation of such policies due account must be taken of the need to avoid producing harmful effects on other countries,

Recognizing the importance of bilateral and multilateral cooperation in solving environmental problems.

Aware of the fact that a greater amount of scientific and technical knowledge than at present available would provide a more adequate basis for the satisfactory comprehension and evaluation of environ-

1 See A/CONF.48/PC/13 and Corr.1, chap. III.

2 See A/CONF.48/PC/13 and Corr.1, chap. III.

mental problems in general, and that, therefore, international cooperation in this field is of paramount importance,

Convinced that rational planning procedures at both the national and the regional levels constitute an essential tool for an adequate equilibrium between the needs of development and the preservation and enhancement of the environment,

Bearing in mind the need for developed countries to provide additional technical assistance and financing beyond the targets indicated in the International Development Strategy for the Second United Nations Development Decade, contained in General Assembly resolution 2626 (XXV) of 24 October 1970, and without affecting adversely their programmes of assistance in other spheres, to enable developing countries to enforce those new and additional measures that might be envisaged as a means of protecting and enhancing the environment,

Considering that environmental conditions can be adversely affected by activities conducted by States beyond the limits of their national jurisdiction, including the sea, the sea-bed, the ocean floor and the atmosphere particularly by the testing of nuclear weapons, with harmful effects for other States,

Considering further that various aspects of marine pollution and related matters will also be dealt with at the forthcoming United Nations Conference on the Law of the Sea and Inter-Governmental Maritime Consultative Organization Conference on Marine Pollution,

1. *Urges* the international community and the organizations of the United Nations system to strengthen international cooperation in the fields of environment, rational utilization of natural resources and preservation of adequate ecological balance;

2. *Requests* the Secretary-General, the Preparatory Committee for the United Nations Conference on the Human Environment and the other bodies established to advise and assist the Secretary-General in the preparations for the Conference to ensure that in the exercise of their responsibilities the documentation to be submitted to participating States and, in particular, the action plan and the action proposals for each of the main subject areas, as well as the draft Declaration on the Human Environment, be elaborated in such a manner as to take into full account the provisions embodied in the preamble and in the operative paragraphs of the present resolution;

3. *Reaffirms* that it is important for the United Nations Conference on the Human Environment to take fully into account the interests of the developing countries and, in this context, endorses the views expressed in part three, section A.VII, of the Declaration and Principles of the Action Programme adopted at Lima on 7 November 1971 by the Second Ministerial Meeting of the Group of Seventy-seven Developing Countries;[1]

4. *Stresses* that both the action plan and the action proposals to be submitted to the United Nations Conference on the Human Environment must, *inter alia*:

(*a*) Respect fully the exercise of permanent sovereignty over natural resources, as well as the right of each country to exploit its own resources in accordance with its own priorities and needs and in such a manner as to avoid producing harmful effects on other countries;

(*b*) Recognize that no environmental policy should adversely affect the present or future development possibilities of the developing countries;

(*c*) Recognize further that the burden of the environmental policies of the developed countries cannot be transferred, directly or indirectly, to the developing countries;

(*d*) Respect fully the sovereign right of each country to plan its own economy, to define its own priorities, to determine its own environmental standards and criteria, to evaluate its own social costs of production and to formulate its own environmental policies, in the full understanding that environmental action must be defined basically at the national level, in accordance with locally prevailing conditions and in such a manner as to avoid producing harmful effects on other countries;

(*e*) Avoid any adverse effects of environmental policies and measures on the economy of the developing countries in all spheres, including international trade, international development assistance and the transfer of technology;

5. *Further stresses* that the action plan and the action proposals should include measures:

(*a*) To promote programmes of training, applied research and exchange of information with the objective of amplifying and disseminating knowledge of questions pertaining to the preservation and improvement of environmental conditions, to an adequate relationship between environmental policies and development policies, and to the question of comparative costs of different technologies in relation to the environment;

(*b*) To provide additional technical assistance and financial resources, beyond the targets indicated in the International Development Strategy, to enable developing countries to enforce those measures and policies acceptable to them in such a manner as to ensure that no action is defined or proposed without the proper means of implementation;

(*c*) To give special attention to the particular problems and conditions of the environment of the landlocked and least developed among the developing countries;

(*d*) To promote programmes designed to assist developing countries, at their request, in solving environmental problems which have their origin in nature itself which are the direct consequence of underdevelopment and which particularly affect the living conditions of the population of developing countries;

(*e*) To study with special attention the environmental problems and conditions of the countries with coastlines particularly exposed to the risks of marine pollution;

(*f*) To promote international cooperation in order to prevent, eliminate or at least adequately reduce and effectively control adverse ecological effects resulting from activities conducted in all spheres, in such a way that due account will be taken of the interests of all States;

6. *Urges* the States possessing nuclear weapons to put an end to the testing of those weapons in all spheres and, also in the context of measures designed to improve environmental conditions on a worldwide basis, stresses the necessity of prohibiting the production and use of nuclear, chemical and biological weapons, and of ensuring their early destruction;

7. *Further urges* Member States, the United Nations system and other international organizations which deal with ecological problems to plan international cooperation in the field of the environment, taking into particular account the need for increased technical and financial assistance to the developing countries to help them improve their ecological conditions, both in rural and urban areas;

8. *Indicates* the advisability of the international financial institutions being enabled, without affecting adversely their operations in other spheres, to consider favourably the increase in the volume and the softening of the terms of their economic assistance to the developing countries for the planning and implementation of projects which, in the exclusive judgement of those countries, might be desirable and which, in their view, might be justifiable on environmental terms;

9. *Requests* the Secretary-General to submit a report to the United Nations Conference on the Human Environment, after ascertaining the views of Member States, on a scheme of voluntary contributions which would provide additional financing by the developed countries to the developing countries for environmental purposes, beyond the resources already contemplated in the International Development Strategy;

10. *Requests* the Secretary-General of the United Nations Conference on Trade and Development to prepare a comprehensive study, to be submitted to the Conference at its third session, on the effects of environmental policies of developed countries which might adversely affect the present or future development possibilities of developing countries, by means of, *inter alia*:

(*a*) A decrease in the flow of international development assistance and a deterioration of its terms and conditions;

1 See A/C.2 /270 and Corr. 1.

(*b*) A further deterioration in the trading prospects of developing countries by the creation of additional obstacles, such as the new non-tariff measures, which might lead to a new type of protectionism;

11. *Reiterates* the primacy of independent economic and social development as the main and paramount objective of international cooperation, in the interests of the welfare of mankind and of peace and world security.

2026th plenary meeting
20 December 1971

3281 (XXIX). Charter of Economic Rights and Duties of States

Committee: 2
Vote: 120 - 6 - 10
Ref.: 44/170, 40/182, 39/163, 37/204, 35/57, 3486(XXX), 3082(XXVIII), 3037(XXVII)

The General Assembly,

Recalling that the United Nations Conference on Trade and Development, in its resolution 45 (III) of 18 May 1972,[1] stressed the urgency to establish generally accepted norms to govern international economic relations systematically and recognized that it is not feasible to establish a just order and a stable world as long as a charter to protect the rights of all countries, and in particular the developing States, is not formulated,

Recalling further that in the same resolution it was decided to establish a Working Group of governmental representatives to draw up a draft Charter of Economic Rights and Duties of States, which the General Assembly, in its resolution 3037 (XXVII) of 19 December 1972, decided should be composed of forty Member States,

Noting that, in its resolution 3082 (XXVIII) of 6 December 1973, it reaffirmed its conviction of the urgent need to establish or improve norms of universal application for the development of international economic relations on a just and equitable basis and urged the Working Group on the Charter of Economic Rights and Duties of States to complete, as the first step in the codification and development of the matter, the elaboration of a final draft Charter of Economic Rights and Duties of States, to be considered and approved by the General Assembly at its twenty-ninth session,

Bearing in mind the spirit and terms of its resolutions 3201 (S-VI) and 3202 (S-VI) of 1 May 1974, containing, respectively, the Declaration and the Programme of Action on the Establishment of a New International Economic Order, which underlined the vital importance of the Charter to be adopted by the General Assembly at its twenty-ninth session and stressed the fact that the Charter shall constitute an effective instrument towards the establishment of a new system of international economic relations based on equity, sovereign equality and interdependence of the interests of developed and developing countries,

Having examined the report of the Working Group on the Charter of Economic Rights and Duties of States on its fourth session,[2] transmitted to the General Assembly by the Trade and Development Board at its fourteenth session,

Expressing its appreciation to the Working Group on the Charter of Economic Rights and Duties of States which, as a result of the task performed in its four sessions held between February 1973 and June 1974, assembled the elements required for the completion and adoption of the Charter of Economic Rights and Duties of States at the twenty-ninth session of the General Assembly, as previously recommended,

Adopts and solemnly proclaims the following Charter:

[1] See *Proceedings of the United Nations Conference of Trade and Development, Third Session,* vol. I, *Report and Annexes* (United Nations publication, Sales No.: E.73.II.D.4), annex I.A.

[2] TD/B/AC.12/4 and Corr.1.

Charter of Economic Rights and Duties of States

Preamble

The General Assembly,

Reaffirming the fundamental purposes of the United Nations, in particular the maintenance of international peace and security, the development of friendly relations among nations and the achievement of international cooperation in solving international problems in the economic and social fields,

Affirming the need for strengthening international cooperation in these fields,

Reaffirming further the need for strengthening international cooperation for development,

Declaring that it is a fundamental purpose of the present Charter to promote the establishment of the new international economic order, based on equity, sovereign equality, interdependence, common interest and cooperation among all States, irrespective of their economic and social systems,

Desirous of contributing to the creation of conditions for:

(*a*) The attainment of wider prosperity among all countries and of higher standards of living for all peoples,

(*b*) The promotion by the entire international community of the economic and social progress of all countries, especially developing countries,

(*c*) The encouragement of cooperation, on the basis of mutual advantage and equitable benefits for all peace-loving States which are willing to carry out the provisions of the present Charter, in the economic, trade, scientific and technical fields, regardless of political, economic or social systems,

(*d*) The overcoming of main obstacles in the way of the economic development of the developing countries,

(*e*) The acceleration of the economic growth of developing countries with a view to bridging the economic gap between developing and developed countries,

(*f*) The protection, preservation and enhancement of the environment,

Mindful of the need to establish and maintain a just and equitable economic and social order through:

(*a*) The achievement of more rational and equitable international economic relations and the encouragement of structural changes in the world economy,

(*b*) The creation of conditions which permit the further expansion of trade and intensification of economic cooperation among all nations,

(*c*) The strengthening of the economic independence of developing countries,

(*d*) The establishment and promotion of international economic relations, taking into account the agreed differences in development of the developing countries and their specific needs,

Determined to promote collective economic security for development, in particular of the developing countries, with strict respect for the sovereign equality of each State and through the cooperation of the entire international community,

Considering that genuine cooperation among States, based on joint consideration of and concerted action regarding international economic problems, is essential for fulfilling the international community's common desire to achieve a just and rational development of all parts of the world,

Stressing the importance of ensuring appropriate conditions for the conduct of normal economic relations among all States, irrespective of differences in social and economic systems, and for the full respect of the rights of all peoples, as well as strengthening instruments of international economic cooperation as a means for the consolidation of peace for the benefit of all,

Convinced of the need to develop a system of international economic relations on the basis of sovereign equality, mutual and equitable benefit and the close interrelationship of the interests of all States,

Reiterating that the responsibility for the development of every country rests primarily upon itself but that concomitant and effective international cooperation is an essential factor for the full achievement of its own development goals,

Firmly convinced of the urgent need to evolve a substantially improved system of international economic relations,

Solemnly adopts the present Charter of Economic Rights and Duties of States.

Chapter I

Fundamentals of International Economic Relations

Economic as well as political and other relations among States shall be governed, *inter alia*, by the following principles:

(*a*) Sovereignty, territorial integrity and political independence of States;

(*b*) Sovereign equality of all States;

(*c*) Non-aggression;

(*d*) Non-intervention;

(*e*) Mutual and equitable benefit;

(*f*) Peaceful coexistence;

(*g*) Equal rights and self-determination of peoples;

(*h*) Peaceful settlement of disputes;

(*i*) Remedying of injustices which have been brought about by force and which deprive a nation of the natural means necessary for its normal development;

(*j*) Fulfilment in good faith of international obligations;

(*k*) Respect for human rights and fundamental freedoms;

(*l*) No attempt to seek hegemony and spheres of influence;

(*m*) Promotion of international social justice;

(*n*) International cooperation for development;

(*o*) Free access to and from the sea by landlocked countries within the framework of the above principles.

Chapter II

Economic Rights and Duties of States

Article 1

Every State has the sovereign and inalienable right to choose its economic system as well as its political, social and cultural systems in accordance with the will of its people, without outside interference, coercion or threat in any form whatsoever.

Article 2

1. Every State has and shall freely exercise full permanent sovereignty, including possession, use and disposal, over all its wealth, natural resources and economic activities.

2. Each State has the right:

(*a*) To regulate and exercise authority over foreign investment within its national jurisdiction in accordance with its laws and regulations and in conformity with its national objectives and priorities. No State shall be compelled to grant preferential treatment to foreign investment;

(*b*) To regulate and supervise the activities of transnational corporations within its national jurisdiction and take measures to ensure that such activities comply with its laws, rules and regulations and conform with its economic and social policies. Transnational corporations shall not intervene in the internal affairs of a host State. Every State should with full regard for its sovereign rights, cooperate with other States in the exercise of the right set forth in this subparagraph;

(*c*) To nationalize, expropriate or transfer ownership of foreign property, in which case appropriate compensation should be paid by the State adopting such measures, taking into account its relevant laws and regulations and all circumstances that the State considers pertinent. In any case where the question of compensation gives rise to a controversy it shall be settled under the domestic law of the nationalizing State and by its tribunals, unless it is freely and mutually agreed by all States concerned that other peaceful means be sought on the basis of the sovereign equality of States and in accordance with the principle of free choice of means.

Article 3

In the exploitation of natural resources shared by two or more countries, each State must cooperate on the basis of a system of information and prior consultations in order to achieve optimum use of such resources without causing damage to the legitimate interest of others.

Article 4

Every State has the right to engage in international trade and other forms of economic cooperation irrespective of any differences in political, economic and social systems. No State shall be subjected to discrimination of any kind based solely on such differences. In the pursuit of international trade and other forms of economic cooperation, every State is free to choose the forms of organization of its foreign economic relations and to enter into bilateral and multilateral arrangements consistent with its international obligations and with the needs of international economic cooperation.

Article 5

All States have the right to associate in organizations of primary commodity producers in order to develop their national economies, to achieve stable financing for their development and, in pursuance of their aims, to assist in the promotion of sustained growth of the world economy, in particular accelerating the development of developing countries. Correspondingly, all States have the duty to respect that right by refraining from applying economic and political measures that would limit it.

Article 6

It is the duty of States to contribute to the development of international trade of goods, particularly by means of arrangements and by the conclusion of long-term multilateral commodity agreements, where appropriate, and taking into account the interests of producers and consumers. All States share the responsibility to promote the regular flow and access of all commercial goods traded at stable, remunerative and equitable prices, thus contributing to the equitable development of the world economy, taking into account, in particular, the interests of developing countries.

Article 7

Every State has the primary responsibility to promote the economic, social and cultural development of its people. To this end, each State has the right and the responsibility to choose its means and goals of development, fully to mobilize and use its resources, to implement progressive economic and social reforms and to ensure the full participation of its people in the process and benefits of development. All States have the duty, individually and collectively, to cooperate in eliminating obstacles that hinder such mobilization and use.

Article 8

States should cooperate in facilitating more rational and equitable international economic relations and in encouraging structural chances in the context of a balanced world economy in harmony with the needs and interests of all countries, especially developing countries, and should take appropriate measures to this end.

Article 9

All States have the responsibility to cooperate in the economic, social, cultural, scientific and technological fields for the promotion of economic and social progress throughout the world, especially that of the developing countries.

Article 10

All States are juridically equal and, as equal members of the international community, have the right to participate fully and effectively in the international decision-making process in the solution of world economic, financial and monetary problems, *inter alia*, through the appropriate international organizations in accordance with their existing and evolving rules, and to share equitably in the benefits resulting therefrom.

Article 11

All States should cooperate to strengthen and continuously improve the efficiency of international organizations in implementing measures to stimulate the general economic progress of all countries, particularly of developing countries, and therefore should cooperate to adapt them, when appropriate, to the changing needs of international economic cooperation.

Article 12

1. States have the right, in agreement with the parties concerned, to participate in subregional, regional and interregional cooperation in the pursuit of their economic and social development. All States engaged in such cooperation have the duty to ensure that the policies of those groupings to which they belong correspond to the provisions of the present Charter and are outward-looking, consistent with their international obligations and with the needs of international economic cooperation, and have full regard for the legitimate interests of third countries, especially developing countries.

2. In the case of groupings to which the States concerned have transferred or may transfer certain competences as regards matters that come within the scope of the present Charter, its provisions shall also apply to those groupings in regard to such matters, consistent with the responsibilities of such States as members of such groupings. Those States shall cooperate in the observance by the groupings of the provisions of this Charter.

Article 13

1. Every State has the right to benefit from the advances and developments in science and technology for the acceleration of its economic and social development.

2. All States should promote international scientific and technological cooperation and the transfer of technology, with proper regard for all legitimate interests including, *inter alia*, the rights and duties of holders, suppliers and recipients of technology. In particular, all States should facilitate the access of developing countries to the achievements of modern science and technology, the transfer of technology and the creation of indigenous technology for the benefit of the developing countries in forms and in accordance with procedures which are suited to their economies and their needs.

3. Accordingly, developed countries should cooperate with the developing countries in the establishment, strengthening and development of their scientific and technological infrastructures and their scientific research and technological activities so as to help to expand and transform the economies of developing countries.

4. All States should cooperate in research with a view to evolving further internationally accepted guidelines or regulations for the transfer of technology, taking fully into account the interests of developing countries.

Article 14

Every State has the duty to cooperate in promoting a steady and increasing expansion and liberalization of world trade and an improvement in the welfare and living standards of all peoples, in particular those of developing countries. Accordingly, all States should cooperate, *inter alia*, towards the progressive dismantling of obstacles to trade and the improvement of the international framework for the conduct of world trade and, to these ends, coordinated efforts shall be made to solve in an equitable way the trade problems of all countries, taking into account the specific trade problems of the developing countries. In this connexion, States shall take measures aimed at securing additional benefits for the international trade of developing countries so as to achieve a substantial increase in their foreign exchange earnings, the diversification of their exports, the acceleration of the rate of growth of their trade, taking into account their development needs, an improvement in the possibilities for these countries to participate in the expansion of world trade and a balance more favourable to developing counties in the sharing of the advantages resulting from this expansion, through, in the largest possible measure, a substantial improvement in the conditions of access for the products of interest to the developing countries and, wherever appropriate, measures designed to attain stable, equitable and remunerative prices for primary products.

Article 15

All States have the duty to promote the achievement of general and complete disarmament under effective international control and to utilize the resources released by effective disarmament measures for the economic and social development of countries, allocating a substantial portion of such resources as additional means for the development needs of developing countries.

Article 16

1. It is the right and duty of all States, individually and collectively, to eliminate colonialism, apartheid, racial discrimination, neo-colonialism and all forms of foreign aggression, occupation and domination, and the economic and social consequences thereof, as a prerequisite for development. States which practice such coercive policies are economically responsible to the countries, territories and peoples affected for the restitution and full compensation for the exploitation and depletion of, and damages to, the natural and all other resources of those countries, territories and peoples. It is the duty of all States to extend assistance to them.

2. No State has the right to promote or encourage investments that may constitute an obstacle to the liberation of a territory occupied by force.

Article 17

International cooperation for development is the shared goal and common duty of all States. Every State should cooperate with the efforts of developing countries to accelerate their economic and social development by providing favourable external conditions and by extending active assistance to them, consistent with their development needs and objectives, with strict respect for the sovereign equality of States and free of any conditions derogating from their sovereignty.

Article 18

Developed countries should extend, improve and enlarge the system of generalized non-reciprocal and non-discriminatory tariff preferences to the developing countries consistent with the relevant agreed conclusions and relevant decisions as adopted on this subject, in the framework of the competent international organizations. Developed countries should also give serious consideration to the adoption of other differential measures, in areas where this is feasible and appropriate and in ways which will provide special and more favourable treatment, in order to meet the trade and development needs of the developing countries. In the conduct of international economic relations the developed countries should endeavour to avoid measures having a negative effect on the development of the national economies of the developing countries, as promoted by generalized tariff preferences and other generally agreed differential measures in their favour.

Article 19

With a view to accelerating the economic growth of developing countries and bridging the economic gap between developed and developing countries developed countries should grant generalized preferential, non-reciprocal and non-discriminatory treatment to developing countries in those fields of international economic cooperation where it may be feasible.

Article 20

Developing countries should, in their efforts to increase their over-all trade, give due attention to the possibility of expanding their trade with socialist countries, by granting to these countries conditions for trade not inferior to those granted normally to the developed market economy countries.

Article 21

Developing countries should endeavour to promote the expansion of their mutual trade and to this end may, in accordance with the existing and evolving provisions and procedures of international agreements where applicable, grant trade preferences to other developing countries without being obliged to extend such preferences to developed countries, provided these arrangements do not constitute an impediment to general trade liberalization and expansion.

Article 22

1. All States should respond to the generally recognized or mutually agreed development needs and objectives of developing countries by promoting increased net flows of real resources to the developing countries from all sources, taking into account any obligations and commitments undertaken by the States concerned in order to reinforce the efforts of developing countries to accelerate their economic and social development.

2. In this context, consistent with the aims and objectives mentioned above and taking into account any obligations and commitments undertaken in this regard, it should be their endeavour to increase the net amount of financial flows from official sources to developing countries and to improve the terms and conditions thereof.

3. The flow of development assistance resources should include economic and technical assistance.

Article 23

To enhance the effective mobilization of their own resources, the developing countries should strengthen their economic cooperation and expand their mutual trade so as to accelerate their economic and social development. All countries, especially developed countries, individually as well as through the competent international organizations of which they are members, should provide appropriate and effective support and cooperation.

Article 24

All States have the duty to conduct their mutual economic relations in a manner which takes into account the interests of other countries. In particular, all States should avoid prejudicing the interests of developing countries.

Article 25

In furtherance of world economic development, the international community, especially its developed members, shall pay special attention to the particular needs and problems of the least developed among the developing countries, of land-locked developing countries and also island developing countries, with a view to helping them to overcome their particular difficulties and thus contribute to their economic and social development.

Article 26

All States have the duty to coexist in tolerance and live together in peace, irrespective of differences in political, economic, social and cultural systems and to facilitate trade between States having different economic and social systems. International trade should be conducted without prejudice to generalized non-discriminatory and non-reciprocal preferences in favour of developing countries, on the basis of mutual advantage, equitable benefits and the exchange of most-favoured-nation treatment.

Article 27

1. Every State has the right to enjoy fully the benefits of world invisible trade and to engage in the expansion of such trade.

2. World invisible trade, based on efficiency and mutual and equitable benefit, furthering the expansion of the world economy, is the common goal of all States. The role of developing countries in world invisible trade should be enhanced and strengthened consistent with the above objectives, particular attention being paid to the special needs of developing countries.

3. All States should cooperate with developing countries in their endeavours to increase their capacity to earn foreign exchange from invisible transactions, in accordance with the potential and needs of each developing country and consistent with the objectives mentioned above.

Article 28

All States have the duty to cooperate in achieving adjustments in the prices of exports of developing countries in relation to prices of their imports so as to promote just and equitable terms of trade for them, in a manner which is remunerative for producers and equitable for producers and consumers.

Chapter III

Common Responsibilities Towards the International Community

Article 29

The sea-bed and ocean floor and the subsoil thereof, beyond the limits of national jurisdiction as well as the resources of the area, are the common heritage of mankind. On the basis of the principles adopted by the General Assembly in resolution 2749 (XXV) of 17 December 1970, all States shall ensure that the exploration of the area and exploitation of its resources are carried out exclusively for peaceful purposes and that the benefits derived therefrom are shared equitably by all States, taking into account the particular interests and needs of developing countries; an international régime applying to the area and its resources and including appropriate international machinery to give effect to its provisions shall be established by an international treaty of a universal character, generally agreed upon.

Article 30

The protection, preservation and enhancement of the environment for the present and future generations is the responsibility of all States. All States shall endeavour to establish their own environmental and developmental policies in conformity with such responsibility. The environmental policies of all States should enhance and not adversely affect the present and future development potential of developing countries. All States have the responsibility to ensure that activities within their jurisdiction or control do not cause damage to the environment of other States or of areas beyond the limits of national jurisdiction. All States should cooperate in evolving international norms and regulations in the field of the environment.

Chapter IV

Final Provisions

Article 31

All States have the duty to contribute to the balanced expansion of the world economy, taking duly into account the close interrelationship between the well-being of the developed countries and the growth and development of the developing countries, and the fact that the prosperity of the international community as a whole depends upon the prosperity of its constituent parts.

Article 32

No State may use or encourage the use of economic, political or any other type of measures to coerce another State in order to obtain from it the subordination of the exercise of its sovereign rights.

Article 33

1. Nothing in the present Charter shall be construed as impairing or derogating from the provisions of the Charter of the United Nations or actions taken in pursuance thereof.

2. In their interpretation and application, the provisions of the present Charter are interrelated and each provision should be construed in the context of the other provisions.

Article 34

An item on the Charter of Economic Rights and Duties of States shall be included in the agenda of the General Assembly at its thirtieth session, and thereafter on the agenda of every fifth session. In this way a systematic and comprehensive consideration of the implementation of the Charter, covering both progress achieved and any improvements and additions which might become necessary, would be carried out and appropriate measures recommended. Such consideration should take into account the evolution of all the economic, social, legal and other factors related to the principles upon which the present Charter is based and on its purpose.

2315th plenary meeting
12 December 1974

3362 (S-VII). Development and International Economic Cooperation

Committee: Ad hoc
Vote: unanimous
Ref.: 39/218, 33/2, 31/174

The General Assembly,

Determined to eliminate injustice and inequality which afflict vast sections of humanity and to accelerate the development of developing countries,

Recalling the Declaration and the Programme of Action on the Establishment of a New International Economic Order,[1] as well as the Charter of Economic Rights and Duties of States,[2] which lay down the foundations of the new international economic order.

Reaffirming the fundamental purposes of the above-mentioned documents and the rights and duties of all States to seek and participate in the solutions of the problems afflicting the world, in particular the imperative need of redressing the economic imbalance between developed and developing countries,

Recalling further the International Development Strategy for the Second United Nations Development Decade,[3] which should be reviewed in the light of the Programme of Action on the Establishment of a New International Economic Order, and determined to implement the targets and policy measures contained in the International Development Strategy,

Conscious that the accelerated development of developing countries would be a decisive element for the promotion of world peace and security,

Recognizing that greater cooperation among States in the fields of trade, industry, science and technology as well as in other fields of economic activities, based on the principles of the Declaration and the Programme of Action on the Establishment of a New International Economic Order and of the Charter of Economic Rights and Duties of States, would also contribute to strengthening peace and security in the world,

Believing that the over-all objective of the new international economic order is to increase the capacity of developing countries, individually and collectively, to pursue their development,

Decides, to this end and in the context of the foregoing, to set in motion the following measures as the basis and framework for the work of the competent bodies and organizations of the United Nations system:

I. International Trade

1. Concerted efforts should be made in favour of the developing countries towards expanding and diversifying their trade, improving and diversifying their productive capacity, improving their productivity and increasing their export earnings, with a view to counteracting the adverse effects of inflation - thereby sustaining real incomes - and with a view to improving the terms of trade of the developing countries and in order to eliminate the economic imbalance between developed and developing countries.

2. Concerted action should be taken to accelerate the growth and diversification of the export trade of developing countries in manufactures and semi-manufactures and in processed and semi-processed products in order to increase their share in world industrial output and world trade within the framework of an expanding world economy.

3. An important aim of the fourth session of the United Nations Conference on Trade and Development, in addition to work in progress elsewhere should be to reach decisions on the improvement of market structures in the field of raw materials and commodities of export interest to the developing countries, including decisions with respect to an integrated programme and the applicability of elements thereof. In this connexion, taking into account the distinctive features of individual raw materials and commodities, the decisions should bear on the following:

(*a*) Appropriate international stocking and other forms of market arrangements for securing stable, remunerative and equitable prices for commodities of export interest to developing countries and promoting equilibrium between supply and demand, including, where possible, long-term multilateral commitments;

(*b*) Adequate international financing facilities for such stocking and market arrangements;

(*c*) Where possible, promotion of long-term and medium-term contracts;

(*d*) Substantial improvement of facilities for compensatory financing of export revenue fluctuations through the widening and enlarging of the existing facilities. Note has been taken of the various proposals regarding a comprehensive scheme for the stabilization of export earnings of developing countries and for a development security facility as well as specific measures for the benefit of the developing countries most in need;

(*e*) Promotion of processing of raw materials in producing developing countries and expansion and diversification of their exports, particularly to developed countries;

(*f*) Effective opportunities to improve the share of developing countries in transport, marketing and distribution of their primary commodities and to encourage measures of world significance for the evolution of the infrastructure and secondary capacity of developing countries from the production of primary commodities to processing, transport and marketing, and to the production of finished manufactured goods, their transport, distribution and exchange, including advanced financial and exchange institutions for the remunerative management of trade transactions.

4. The Secretary-General of the United Nations Conference on Trade and Development should present a report to the Conference at its fourth session on the impact of an integrated programme on the imports of developing countries which are net importers of raw materials and commodities, including those lacking in natural resources, and recommend any remedial measures that may be necessary.

5. A number of options are open to the international community to preserve the purchasing power of developing countries. These need to be further studied on a priority basis. The Secretary-General of the United Nations Conference on Trade and Development should continue to study direct and indirect indexation schemes and other options with a view to making concrete proposals before the Conference at its fourth session.

6. The Secretary-General of the United Nations Conference on Trade and Development should prepare a preliminary study on the proportion between prices of raw materials and commodities exported by developing countries and the final consumer price particularly in developed countries, and submit it, if possible, to the Conference at its fourth session.

7. Developed countries should fully implement agreed provisions on the principle of standstill as regards imports from developing countries, and any departure should be subjected to such measures as consultations and multilateral surveillance and compensation, in accordance with internationally agreed criteria and procedures.

8. Developed countries should take effective steps within the framework of multilateral trade negotiations for the reduction or removal, where feasible and appropriate, of non-tariff barriers affecting the products of export interest to developing countries on a differential

1 Resolutions 3201 (S-VI) and 3202 (S-VI).

2 Resolution 3281 (XXIX).

3 Resolution 2626 (XXV).

and more favourable basis for developing countries. The generalized schema of preferences should not terminate at the end of the period of ten years originally envisaged and should be continuously improved through wider coverage, deeper cuts and other measures, bearing in mind the interests of those developing countries which enjoy special advantages and the need for finding ways and means for protecting their interests.

9. Countervailing duties should be applied only in conformity with internationally agreed obligations. Developed countries should exercise maximum restraint within the framework of international obligations in the imposition of countervailing duties on the imports of products from developing countries. The multilateral trade negotiations under way should take fully into account the particular interests of developing countries with a view to providing them differential and more favourable treatment in appropriate cases.

10. Restrictive business practices adversely affecting international trade, particularly that of developing countries, should be eliminated and efforts should be made at the national and international levels with the objective of negotiating a set of equitable principles and rules.

11. Special measures should be undertaken by developed countries and by developing countries in a position to do so to assist in the structural transformation of the economy of the least developed, land-locked and island developing countries.

12. Emergency measures as spelled out in section X of General Assembly resolution 3202 (S-VI) should be undertaken on a temporary basis to meet the specific problems of the most seriously affected countries as defined in Assembly resolutions 3201 (S-VI) and 3202 (S-VI) of 1 May 1974, without any detriment to the interests of the developing countries as a whole.

13. Further expansion of trade between the socialist countries of Eastern Europe and the developing countries should be intensified as is provided for in resolutions 15 (II) of 25 March 1968[1] and 53 (III) of 19 May 1972[2] of the United Nations Conference on Trade and Development. Additional measures and appropriate orientation to achieve this end are necessary.

II. Transfer of Real Resources for Financing the Development of Developing Countries and International Monetary Reforms

1. Concessional financial resources to developing countries need to be increased substantially, their terms and conditions ameliorated and their flow made predictable, continuous and increasingly assured so as to facilitate the implementation by developing countries of long-term programmes for economic and social development. Financial assistance should, as a general rule, be untied.

2. Developed countries confirm their continued commitment in respect of the targets relating to the transfer of resources, in particular the official development assistance target of 0.7 per cent of gross national product, as agreed in the International Development Strategy for the Second United Nations Development Decade, and adopt as their common aim an effective increase in official development assistance with a view to achieving these targets by the end of the decade. Developed countries which have not yet made a commitment in respect of these targets undertake to make their best efforts to reach these targets in the remaining part of this decade.

3. The establishment of a link between the special drawing rights and development assistance should form part of the consideration by the International Monetary Fund of the creation of new special drawing rights as and when they are created according to the needs of international liquidity. Agreement should be reached at an early date on the establishment of a trust fund, to be financed partly through the International Monetary Fund gold sales and partly through voluntary contributions and to be governed by an appropriate body, for the benefit of developing countries. Consideration of other means of transfer of real resources which are predictable, assured and continuous should be expedited in appropriate bodies.

4. Developed countries and international organizations should enhance the real value and volume of assistance to developing countries and ensure that the developing countries obtain the largest possible share in the procurement of equipment, consultants and consultancy services. Such assistance should be on softer terms and, as a general rule, untied.

5. In order to enlarge the pool of resources available for financing development, there is an urgent need to increase substantially the capital of the World Bank Group, in particular the resources of the International Development Association, to enable it to make additional capital available to the poorest countries on highly concessional terms.

6. The resources of the development institutions of the United Nations system, in particular the United Nations Development Programme, should also be increased. The funds at the disposal of the regional development banks should be augmented. These increases should be without prejudice to bilateral development assistance flows.

7. To the extent desirable, the World Bank Group is invited to consider new ways of supplementing its financing with private management, skills, technology and capital and also new approaches to increase financing of development in developing countries, in accordance with their national plans and priorities.

8. The burden of debt on developing countries is increasing to a point where the import capacity as well as reserves have come under serious strain. At its fourth session the United Nations Conference on Trade and Development shall consider the need for, and the possibility of, convening as soon as possible a conference of major donor, creditor and debtor countries to devise ways and means to mitigate this burden, taking into account the development needs of developing countries, with special attention to the plight of the most seriously affected countries as defined in General Assembly resolutions 3201 (S-VI) and 3202 (S-VI).

9. Developing countries should be granted increased access on favourable terms to the capital markets of developed countries. To this end, the joint Development Committee of the International Monetary Fund and the International Bank for Reconstruction and Development should progress as rapidly as possible in its work. Appropriate United Nations bodies and other related intergovernmental agencies should be invited to examine ways and means of increasing the flow of public and private resources to developing countries, including proposals made at the current session to provide investment in private and public enterprises in the developing countries. Consideration should be given to the examination of an international investment trust and to the expansion of the International Finance Corporation capital without prejudice to the increase in resources of other intergovernmental financial and development institutions and bilateral assistance flows.

10. Developed and developing countries should further cooperate through investment of financial resources and supply of technology and equipment to developing countries by developed countries and by developing countries in a position to do so.

11. Developed countries, and developing countries in a position to do so, are urged to make adequate contributions to the United Nations Special Fund with a view to an early implementation of a programme of lending, preferably in 1976.

12. Developed countries should improve terms and conditions of their assistance so as to include a preponderant grant element for the least developed, land-locked and island developing countries.

13. In providing additional resources for assisting the most seriously affected countries in helping them to meet their serious balance-of-payments deficits, all developed countries, and developing countries in a position to do so, and international organizations such as the International Bank for Reconstruction and Development and the International Monetary Fund, should undertake specific measures in

1 *Proceedings of the United Nations Conference on Trade and Development, Second Session,* vol. I and Corr.1 and 3 and Add.1 and 2, *Report and Annexes* (United Nations publication, Sales No. E.68.II.D.14), p. 32.

2 See *Proceedings of the United Nations Conference on Trade and Development,* Third Session, vol. I, *Report and Annexes* (United Nations publication, Sales No. E.73.II.D.4), annex I.A.

their favour, including those provided in General Assembly resolutions 3201 (S-VI) and 3202 (S-VI).

14. Special attention should be given by the international community to the phenomena of natural disasters which frequently afflict many parts of the world, with far-reaching devastating economic, social and structural consequences particularly in the least developed countries. To this end, the General Assembly at its thirtieth session, in considering this problem, should examine and adopt appropriate measures.

15. The role of national reserve currencies should be reduced and the special drawing rights should become the central reserve asset of the international monetary system in order to provide for greater international control over the creation and equitable distribution of liquidity and in order to limit potential losses as a consequence of exchange rate fluctuations. Arrangements for gold should be consistent with the agreed objective of reducing the role of gold in the system and with equitable distribution of new international liquidity and should in particular take into consideration the needs of developing countries for increased liquidity.

16. The process of decision-making should be fair and responsive to change and should be most specially responsive to the emergence of a new economic influence on the part of developing countries. The participation of developing countries in the decision-making process in the competent organs of international finance and development institutions should be adequately increased and made more effective without adversely affecting the broad geographic representation of developing countries and in accordance with the existing and evolving rules.

17. The compensatory financing facility now available through the International Monetary Fund should be expanded and liberalized. In this connexion, early consideration should be given by the Fund and other appropriate United Nations bodies to various proposals made at the current session - including the examination of a new development security facility - which would mitigate export earnings shortfalls of developing countries, with special regard to the poorest countries, and thus provide greater assistance to their continued economic development. Early consideration should also be given by the International Monetary Fund to proposals to expand and liberalize its coverage of current transactions to include manufactures and services, to ensure that, whenever possible, compensation for export shortfalls takes place at the same time they occur, to take into account, in determining the quantum of compensation, movements in import prices and to lengthen the repayment period.

18. Drawing under the buffer stock financing facility of the International Monetary Fund should be accorded treatment with respect to floating alongside the gold tranche, similar to that under the compensatory financing facility, and the Fund should expedite its study of the possibility of an amendment of the Articles of Agreement, to be presented to the Interim Committee, if possible at its next meeting, that would permit the Fund to provide assistance directly to international buffer stocks of primary products.

III. Science and Technology

1. Developed and developing countries should cooperate in the establishment, strengthening and development of the scientific and technological infrastructure of developing countries. Developed countries should also take appropriate measures, such as contribution to the establishment of an industrial technological information bank and consideration of the possibility of regional and sectoral banks, in order to make available a greater flow to developing countries of information permitting the selection of technologies, in particular advanced technologies. Consideration should also be given to the establishment of an international centre for the exchange of technological information for the sharing of research findings relevant to developing countries. For the above purposes institutional arrangements within the United Nations system should be examined by the General Assembly at its thirtieth session.

2. Developed countries should significantly expand their assistance to developing countries for direct support to their science and technology programmes, as well as increase substantially the proportion of their research and development devoted to specific problems of primary interest to developing countries, and in the creation of suitable indigenous technology, in accordance with feasible targets to be agreed upon. The General Assembly invites the Secretary-General to carry out a preliminary study and to report to the Assembly at its thirty-first session on the possibility of establishing, within the framework of the United Nations system, an international energy institute to assist all developing countries in energy resources research and development.

3. All States should cooperate in evolving an international code of conduct for the transfer of technology, corresponding, in particular, to the special needs of the developing countries. Work on such a code should therefore be continued within the United Nations Conference on Trade and Development and concluded in time for decisions to be reached at the fourth session of the Conference, including a decision on the legal character of such a code with the objective of the adoption of a code of conduct prior to the end of 1977. International conventions on patents and trade marks should be reviewed and revised to meet, in particular, the special needs of the developing countries, in order that these conventions may become more satisfactory instruments for aiding developing countries in the transfer and development of technology. National patents systems should, without delay, be brought into line with the international patent system in its revised form.

4. Developed countries should facilitate the access of developing countries on favourable terms and conditions, and on an urgent basis, to informatique, to relevant information on advanced and other technologies suited to their specific needs as well as on new uses of existing technology, new developments and possibilities of adapting them to local needs. Inasmuch as in market economies advanced technologies with respect to industrial production are most frequently developed by private institutions, developed countries should facilitate and encourage these institutions in providing effective technologies in support of the priorities of developing countries.

5. Developed countries should give developing countries the freest and fullest possible access to technologies whose transfer is not subject to private decision.

6. Developed countries should improve the transparency of the industrial property market in order to facilitate the technological choices of developing countries. In this respect, relevant organizations of the United Nations system, with the collaboration of developed countries, should undertake projects in the fields of information consultancy and training for the benefit of developing countries.

7. A United Nations Conference on Science and Technology for Development should be held in 1978 or 1979 with the main objectives of strengthening the technological capacity of developing countries to enable them to apply science and technology to their own development; adopting effective means for the utilization of scientific and technological potentials in the solution of development problems of regional and global significance, especially for the benefit of developing countries; and providing instruments of cooperation to developing countries in the utilization of science and technology for solving socioeconomic problems that cannot be solved by individual action, in accordance with national priorities taking into account the recommendations made by the Intergovernmental Working Group of the Committee on Science and Technology for Development.

8. The United Nations system should play a major role, with appropriate financing, in achieving the above-stated objectives and in developing scientific and technological cooperation between all States in order to ensure the application of science and technology to development. The work of the relevant United Nations bodies, in particular that of the United Nations Conference on Trade and Development, the United Nations Industrial Development Organization, the International Labour Organisation the United Nations Educational, Scientific and Cultural Organization, the Food and Agriculture Organization of the United Nations, the World Intellectual Property Organization and the United Nations Development Programme, to facilitate the transfer and diffusion of technology should be given urgent priority. The Secretary-General of the United Nations should take steps to ensure that the technology and experience available

within the United Nations system is widely disseminated and readily available to the developing countries in need of it.

9. The World Health Organization and the competent organs of the United Nations system, in particular the United Nations Children's Fund, should intensify the international effort aimed at improving health conditions in developing countries by giving priority to prevention of disease and malnutrition and by providing primary health services to the communities, including maternal and child health and family welfare.

10. Since the outflow of qualified personnel from developing to developed countries seriously hampers the development of the former, there is an urgent need to formulate national and international policies to avoid the "brain drain" and to obviate its adverse effects.

IV. Industrialization

1. The General Assembly endorses the Lima Declaration and Plan of Action on Industrial Development Cooperation[1] and requests all Governments to take individually and for collectively the necessary measures and decisions required to implement effectively their undertakings in terms of the Lima Declaration and Plan of Action.

2. Developed countries should facilitate the development of new policies and strengthen existing policies, including labour market policies, which would encourage the redeployment of their industries which are less competitive internationally to developing countries, thus leading to structural adjustments in the former and a higher degree of utilization of natural and human resources in the latter. Such policies may take into account the economic structure and the economic, social and security objectives of the developed countries concerned and the need for such industries to move into more viable lines of production or into other sectors of the economy.

3. A system of consultations as provided for by the Lima Plan of Action should be established at the global, regional, interregional and sectoral levels within the United Nations Industrial Development Organization and within other appropriate international bodies, between developed and developing countries and among developing countries themselves, in order to facilitate the achievement of the goals set forth in the field of industrialization, including the redeployment of certain productive capacities existing in developed countries and the creation of new industrial facilities in developing countries. In this context, the United Nations Industrial Development Organization should serve as a forum for negotiation of agreements in the field of industry between developed and developing countries and among developing countries themselves, at the request of the countries concerned.

4. The Executive Director of the United Nations Industrial Development Organization should take immediate action to ensure the readiness of that organization to serve as a forum for consultations and negotiation of agreements in the field of industry. In reporting to the next session of the Industrial Development Board on actions taken in this respect, the Executive Director should also include proposals for the establishment of a system of consultations. The Industrial Development Board is invited to draw up, at an early date, the rules of procedure according to which this system would operate.

5. To promote cooperation between developed and developing countries, both should endeavour to disseminate appropriate information about their priority areas for industrial cooperation and the form they would like such cooperation to take. The efforts undertaken by the United Nations Conference on Trade and Development on tripartite cooperation between countries having different economic and social systems could lead to constructive proposals for the industrialization of developing countries.

6. Developed countries should, whenever possible, encourage their enterprises to participate in investment projects within the framework of the development plans and programmes of the developing countries which so desire; such participation should be carried out in accordance with the laws and regulations of the developing countries concerned.

7. A joint study should be undertaken by all Governments under the auspices of the United Nations Industrial Development Organization in consultation with the Secretary-General of the United Nations Conference on Trade and Development, making full use of the knowledge, experience and capacity existing in the United Nations system of methods and mechanisms for diversified financial and technical cooperation which are geared to the special and changing requirements of international industrial cooperation, as well as of a general set of guidelines for bilateral industrial cooperation. A progress report on this study should be submitted to the General Assembly at its thirty-first session.

8. Special attention should be given to the particular problems in the industrialization of the least developed, land-locked and island developing countries - in order to put at their disposal those technical and financial resources as well as critical goods which need to be provided to them to enable them to overcome their specific problems and to play their due role in the world economy, warranted by their human and material resources.

9. The General Assembly endorses the recommendation of the Second General Conference of the United Nations Industrial Development Organization to convert that organization into a specialized agency and decides to establish a Committee on the Drafting of a Constitution for the United Nations Industrial Development Organization, which shall be an intergovernmental committee of the whole, including States which participated in the Second General Conference, to meet in Vienna to draw up a constitution for the United Nations Industrial Development Organization as a specialized agency, to be submitted to a conference of plenipotentiaries to be convened by the Secretary-General in the last quarter of 1976.

10. In view of the importance of the forthcoming Tripartite World Conference on Employment, Income Distribution, Social Progress and the International Division of Labour, Governments should undertake adequate preparations and consultations.

V. Food and Agriculture

1. The solution to world food problems lies primarily in rapidly increasing food production in the developing countries. To this end, urgent and necessary changes in the pattern of world food production should be introduced and trade policy measures should be implemented, in order to obtain a notable increase in agricultural production and the export earnings of developing countries.

2. To achieve these objectives, it is essential that developed countries, and developing countries in a position to do so, should substantially increase the volume of assistance to developing countries for agriculture and food production, and that developed countries should effectively facilitate access to their markets for food and agricultural products of export interest to developing countries, both in raw and processed form, and adopt adjustment measures, where necessary.

3. Developing countries should accord high priority to agricultural and fisheries development increase investment accordingly and adopt policies which give adequate incentives to agricultural producers. It is a responsibility of each State concerned in accordance with its sovereign judgement and development plans and policies, to promote interaction between expansion of food production and socio-economic reforms with a view to achieving an integrated rural development. The further reduction of post-harvest food losses in developing countries should be undertaken as a matter of priority, with a view to reaching at least a 50 per cent reduction by 1985. All countries and competent international organizations should cooperate financially and technically in the effort to achieve this objective. Particular attention should be given to improvement in the systems of distribution of food-stuffs.

4. The Consultative Group on Food Production and Investment in Developing Countries should quickly identify developing countries having the potential for most rapid and efficient increase of food production, as well as the potential for rapid agricultural expansion in other developing countries, especially the countries with food deficits. Such an assessment would assist developed countries and the competent international organizations to concentrate resources for

1 See A/10112, chap. IV.

the rapid increase of agricultural production in the developing countries.

5. Developed countries should adopt policies aimed at ensuring a stable supply and sufficient quantity of fertilizers and other production inputs to developing countries at reasonable prices. They should also provide assistance to, and promote investments in, developing countries to improve the efficiency of their fertilizer and other agricultural input industries. Advantage should be taken of the mechanism provided by the International Fertilizer Supply Scheme.

6. In order to make additional resources available on concessional terms for agricultural development in developing countries, developed countries and developing countries in a position to do so should pledge, on a voluntary basis, substantial contributions to the proposed International Fund for Agricultural Development so as to enable it to come into being by the end of 1975, with initial resources of SDR 1,000 million. Thereafter, additional resources should be provided to the Fund on a continuing basis.

7. In view of the significant impact of basic and applied agricultural research on increasing the quantity and quality of food production, developed countries should support the expansion of the work of the existing international agricultural research centres. Through their bilateral programmes they should strengthen their links with these international research centres and with the national agricultural research centres in developing countries. With respect to the improvement of the productivity and competitiveness with synthetics of non-food agricultural and forestry products, research and technological assistance should be coordinated and financed through an appropriate mechanism.

8. In view of the importance of food aid as a transitional measure, all countries should accept both the principle of a minimum food aid target and the concept of forward planning of food aid. The target for the 1975-1976 season should be 10 million tons of food gains. They should also accept the principle that food aid should be channelled on the basis of objective assessment of requirements in the recipient countries. In this respect all countries are urged to participate in the Global Information and Early Warning System on Food and Agriculture.

9. Developed countries should increase the grant component of food aid, where food is not at pleasant provided as grants, and should accept multilateral channelling of these resources at an expanding rate. In providing food grains and financing on soft terms to developing countries in need of such assistance developed countries and the World Food Programme should take due account of the interests of the food-exporting developing countries and should answer that such assistance includes, wherever possible, purchases of food from the food-exporting developing countries.

10. Developed countries, and developing countries in a position to do so, should provide food grains and financial assistance on most favourable terms to the most seriously affected countries, to enable them to meet their food and agricultural development requirements within the constraints of their balance-of-payments position. Donor countries should also provide aid on soft terms, in cash and in kind, through bilateral and multilateral channels to enable the most seriously affected countries to obtain their estimated requirements of about 1 million tons of plant nutrients during 1975-1976.

11. Developed countries should carry out both their bilateral and multilateral food aid channelling in accordance with the procedures of the Principles of Surplus Disposal of the Food and Agriculture Organization of the United Nations so as to avoid causing undue fluctuations in market prices or the disruption of commercial markets for exports of interest to exporting developing countries.

12. All countries should subscribe to the International Undertaking on World Food Security. They should build up and maintain world food-grain reserves, to be held nationally or regionally and strategically located in developed and developing, importing and exporting countries, large enough to cover foreseeable major production shortfalls. Intensive work should be continued on a priority basis in the World Food Council and other appropriate forums in order to determine, *inter alia*, the size of the required reserve, taking into account among other things the proposal made at the current session that the components of wheat and rice in the total reserve should be 30 million tons. The World Food Council should report to the General Assembly on this matter at its thirty-first session. Developed countries should assist developing countries in their efforts to build up and maintain their agreed shares of such reserves. Pending the establishment of the world food-grain reserve, developed countries and developing countries in a position to do so should earmark stocks and/or funds to be placed at the disposal of the World Food Programme as an emergency reserve to strengthen the capacity of the Programme to deal with crisis situations in developing countries. The aim should be a target of not less than 500,000 tons.

13. Members of the General Assembly reaffirm their full support for the resolutions of the World Food Conference and call upon the World Food Council to monitor the implementation of the provisions under section V of the present resolution and to report to the General Assembly at its thirty-first session.

VI. Cooperation among Developing Countries

1. Developed countries and the United Nations system are urged to provide, as and when requested, support and assistance to developing countries in strengthening and enlarging their mutual cooperation at subregional, regional and interregional levels. In this regard, suitable institutional arrangements within the United Nations development system should be made and, when appropriate, strengthened, such as those within the United Nations Conference on Trade and Development, the United Nations Industrial Development Organization and the United Nations Development Programme.

2. The Secretary-General, together with the relevant organizations of the United Nations system, is requested to continue to provide support to ongoing projects and activities, and to commission further studies through institutions in developing countries, which would take into account the material already available within the United Nations system, including in particular the regional commissions and the United Nations Conference on Trade and Development, and in accordance with existing subregional and regional arrangements. These further studies which should be submitted to the General Assembly at its thirty-first session, should, as a first step, cover:

(*a*) Utilization of know-how, skills, natural resources, technology and funds available within developing countries for promotion of investments in industry, agriculture, transport and communications;

(*b*) Trade liberalization measures including payments and clearing arrangements, covering primary commodities, manufactured goods and services, such as banking, shipping, insurance and reinsurance;

(*c*) Transfer of technology.

3. These studies on cooperation among developing countries, together with other initiatives, would contribute to the evolution towards a system for the economic development of developing countries.

VII. Restructuring of the Economic and Social Sectors of the United Nations System

1. With a view to initiating the process of restructuring the United Nations system so as to make it more fully capable of dealing with problems of international economic cooperation and development in a comprehensive and effective manner, in pursuance of General Assembly resolutions 3172 (XXVIII) of 17 December 1973 and 3343 (XXIX) of 17 December 1974, and to make it more responsive to the requirements of the provisions of the Declaration and the Programme of Action on the Establishment of a New International Economic Order as well as those of the Charter of Economic Rights and Duties of States, an *Ad Hoc* Committee on the Restructuring of the Economic and Social Sectors of the United Nations System, which shall be a committee of the whole of the General Assembly open to the participation of all States,[1] is hereby established to prepare detailed action proposals. The *Ad hoc* Committee should start its work im-

1 It is the understanding of the General Assembly that the "all States" formula will be applied in accordance with the established practice of the General Assembly.

mediately and inform the General Assembly at its thirtieth session on the progress made, and submit its report to the Assembly at its thirty-first session, through the Economic and Social Council at its resumed session. The *Ad Hoc* Committee should take into account in its work, *inter alia*, the relevant proposals and documentation submitted in preparation for the seventh special session of the General Assembly pursuant to Assembly resolution 3343 (XXIX) and other relevant decisions, including the report of the Group of Experts on the Structure of the United Nations System entitled A New United Nations Structure for Global Economic Cooperation,[1] the records of the relevant deliberations of the Economic and Social Council, the Trade and Development Board, the Governing Council of the United Nations Development Programme and the seventh special session of the General Assembly, as well as the results of the forthcoming deliberations on institutional arrangements of the United Nations Conference on Trade and Development at its fourth session and of the Governing Council of the United Nations Environment Programme at its fourth session. All United Nations organs, including the regional commissions, as well as the specialized agencies and the International Atomic Energy Agency, are invited to participate at the executive level in the work of the *Ad Hoc* Committee and to respond to requests that the Committee may make to them for information, data or views.

2. The Economic and Social Council should meanwhile continue the process of rationalization and reform which it has undertaken in accordance with Council resolution 1768 (LIV) of 18 May 1973 and General Assembly resolution 3341 (XXIX) of 17 December 1974, and should take into full consideration those recommendations of the *Ad Hoc* Committee that fall within the scope of these resolutions, at the latest at its resumed sixty-first session.

2349th plenary meeting
16 September 1975

39/29. Declaration on the Critical Economic Situation in Africa

Committee: -
Vote: Adopted without a vote
Ref.: 40/40, 1718(XVI)

The General Assembly,

Alarmed by the critical economic situation currently prevailing in Africa,

Commending the efforts of the Secretary-General in sensitizing the international community to the plight of Africa,

Noting the increased concern of the international community for the worsening plight of African countries affected by the crisis,

Having considered the critical economic situation in Africa, the note by the Secretary-General[2] and his report on the subject,[3]

Taking note of the Declaration and resolutions adopted by the Assembly of Heads of State and Government of the Organization of African Unity at its twentieth ordinary session, held at Addis Ababa from 12 to 15 November 1984,[4]

Taking note also of the statement of the Committee for Development Planning, at the conclusion of its twenty-first session, held at Geneva from 19 to 21 November 1984, on the critical economic situation in Africa,[5]

Convinced of the need for concerted action by the international community to assist the efforts of the African Governments by providing immediate emergency relief, and medium-term and long-term development aid,

1. *Adopts* the Declaration on the Critical Economic Situation in Africa set forth in the annex to the present resolution;

2. *Requests* the Secretary-General to take all appropriate measures for the full and speedy implementation of the objectives contained in the Declaration;

3. *Also requests* the Secretary-General to bring the Declaration to the attention of all States, and intergovernmental and non-governmental organizations;

4. *Further requests* the Secretary-General to continue to monitor the situation, to assess the needs and the responses thereto, and to report thereon to the General Assembly at its fortieth session through the Economic and Social Council.

83rd plenary meeting
3 December 1984

Annex

Declaration on the Critical Economic Situation in Africa

1. We the States Members of the United Nations express our deep concern at the profound economic and social crisis that Africa is experiencing. Over the last few years the situation has assumed alarming proportions, seriously jeopardizing not only the development process but, more ominously, the very survival of millions of people.

2. We are alarmed by the spectre of widespread famine hanging over many African countries. Over 150 million people are facing hunger and malnutrition. Prolonged unprecedented drought, accelerating desertification and other natural disasters have compounded an already serious situation, dislocating normal life all over the continent. Alarming shortages in food and water supplies and the depletion of livestock have led to the displacement of millions of people within and across borders.

3. All these factors are further straining fragile economies crippled by deep-rooted structural deficiencies, that is to say, weak physical and social infrastructures, lack of trained human resources and dependence on the export of a few primary commodities.

4. Africa, despite its enormous potential, remains the least developed of all continents, lagging far behind by every economic indicator. Economic performance of many African countries is characterized by declining per capita incomes and stagnant or negative rates of growth. Furthermore, food production has not kept pace with population growth. According to all projections, prospects for recovery, growth and development remain very dim unless the efforts currently under way in African countries are fully supported by the international community.

5. Furthermore, the international economic environment continues to affect developing countries adversely and, particularly, it had a devastating impact on the already fragile African economies. This is manifested in deteriorating terms of trade, sharp declines in export earnings, the heavy burden of external debt and stagnating resource flows to African countries.

6. We are aware that African countries recognize they have the primary responsibility for their development and for addressing the present crisis. They have therefore undertaken and continue to undertake painful adjustment measures at very high social and political costs. While recognizing the determined efforts of African countries and the support provided by the international community, much more needs to be done as the situation remains very grave.

7. We recognize that, in dealing with the present crisis, African regional and subregional efforts towards economic cooperation and integration as well as enhanced economic and technical cooperation among developing countries play an important role in the achievement of national and collective self-reliance and sustained development in Africa.

8. We are aware that the maintenance of peace and security and the strengthening of international cooperation are important for meeting the challenge of development.

9. We fully recognize that emergency relief aid on a massive scale is urgently needed in the following areas: additional food aid and other emergency supplies, together with the technical and financial assis-

---

1 E/AC.62/9 (United Nations publication, Sales No. E.75. II.A.7).

2 A/39/627.

3 A/39/594.

4 See A/40/87, annex.

5 See *Official Records of the Economic and Social Council, 1985, Supplement No. 9* (E/1985/29).

tance necessary for their transportation, storage and distribution to the affected populations; improvement of water supplies; improvement of health and nutrition, particularly for vulnerable groups, including refugees and displaced persons; safeguarding national nuclei of herds of livestock; establishment of income-generating projects and promotion of new and renewable energy projects, particularly in rural areas. In addition to the assistance already provided by the international community, further urgent assistance from bilateral and multilateral donors and non-governmental organizations is required to meet the above and other identified emergency needs in a comprehensive manner, as well as to strengthen the emergency prevention and preparedness capacities of African countries.

10. Of particular importance is the need to undertake urgent action to speed up and support the recovery and rehabilitation process in African countries, especially of the agricultural and industrial sectors as well as for physical and social infrastructures. Assistance for increasing the import capacity for vital imports, through adequate balance-of-payments support and other relevant measures, would help to establish a sound basis for the resumption and acceleration of sustained economic and social development in Africa.

11. We agree that in confronting the challenge of development, national policies and measures, such as those outlined in the Lagos Plan of Action for the Implementation of the Monrovia Strategy for the Economic Development of Africa, adopted by the Assembly of Heads of State and Government of the Organization of African Unity[1] and the Special Memorandum on Africa's Economic and Social Crisis adopted by the ECA Conference of Ministers,[2] provide a framework for national and subregional action and international support.

12. We recognize that, in view of the high priority attached by African countries to food and agriculture, the first urgent task is the early attainment of national and collective self-reliance in food production. In this connection, as highlighted in the Harare Declaration adopted by the thirteenth FAO Regional Conference for Africa, national food strategies and integrated rural development plans play an important role, especially in the achievement of food security. Moreover, we recognize the important role of women in rural development, particularly in food production, a role for which greater support is needed. Also important are the provision of appropriate incentives, credit, improvement of storage and transport, reduction of food losses, in particular post-harvest losses, achievement of a better balance between agricultural export commodities and food production, diversification of agricultural production and utilization of irrigation potential, particularly in the drought-prone areas.

13. Urgent action is needed at the international level to support national and regional efforts to implement the Regional Plan of Action to Combat the Effects of Drought in Africa[3] and the Plan of Action to Combat Desertification.[4]

14. Increased resources for rapid implementation of the Industrial Development Decade for Africa and the Transport and Communications Decade in Africa are required. Furthermore, efforts at national, subregional and regional levels to develop the necessary and much needed skilled manpower, and to build technological capacities, require increased international support.

15. We fully acknowledge that, in the light of the worsening economic situation in Africa, the interrelationship between the debt problem, concessional flows and export earnings and their direct impact on recovery, growth and development assume even greater significance. It is vital, therefore, to take urgent and mutually-reinforcing measures in those areas, taking into account the Special Memorandum on Africa's Economic and Social Crisis,[5] the Addis Ababa Declaration on Africa's External Indebtedness adopted by the African Ministers of Finance[6] and the World Bank Special Programme for Sub-Saharan Africa, in order to complement and support domestic adjustment efforts in African countries.

16. Africa is experiencing a very serious debt problem, repayment and servicing of which is taking a very high percentage of already reduced export earnings. The problem is further exacerbated by factors such as deteriorating terms of trade, decline in concessional flows in real terms and increased use of short-term commercial credit. Without an increase in net capital inflows and urgent debt relief measures, prospects for recovery and development in Africa will be undermined.

17. Bilateral and multilateral creditors should take concerted measures to ease the debt burden of African countries. For official and officially-guaranteed debt, total or partial conversion of official development assistance (ODA) debts into grants, longer maturities and grace periods, lower or concessional interest rates and extended multi-year rescheduling are among the measures to be dealt with urgently within the framework of close consultation with each of the debtor countries concerned, as well as any other measures to be agreed upon. It is essential to ensure the full and urgent implementation of Trade and Development Board resolution 165 (S-IX) of 11 March 1978.[7] Multilateral financial institutions should expedite resource disbursement. Reduction in international interest rates would further alleviate the debt burden. Moreover, the full cooperation of commercial banks is indispensable. The capacity of African countries to manage their debt should be improved through the provision of technical assistance, particularly by international agencies.

18. We recognize that African countries, in view of their heavy dependence on concessional financial flows and their limited access to alternative sources of external finance, require a substantial and sustained increase in the volume of these flows through bilateral donors and multilateral channels for development finance and technical cooperation. The international community, in particular the developed countries and the multilateral financial institutions, should endeavour to provide the additional financial resources to maintain and increase a net transfer of resources to African countries. The World Bank is strongly urged to explore with donors possible approaches, including a special facility, in mobilizing the resources required to implement the Bank's Special Programme for Sub-Saharan Africa.

19. The full and speedy implementation of the Substantial New Programme of Action for the 1980s for the Least Developed Countries,[8] particularly with regard to the ODA level, would greatly augment resource flows to many African countries. Supplementary funding for the International Development Association and the early completion of the replenishment of the International Fund for Agricultural Development would ensure at least the maintenance of the real value of resources channelled to Africa.

20. The heavy dependence of African countries on the export of a few primary commodities renders them particularly vulnerable to the sharp price fluctuations that result in drastic shortfalls in export earnings. Urgent action is therefore needed to stabilize commodity prices on long-term trends and to improve and increase the use of compensatory financing arrangements for export earnings shortfalls, such as the Compensatory Financing Facility of the International Monetary Fund. Improved market access for African primary and processed products, efforts of African countries to diversify production, and the early and effective operation of the Common Fund for Commodities require intensified international action.

21. The modalities and quality of ODA flows in terms of a greater grant element, untied resources and simplified procedures for aid delivery should be improved through, *inter alia*, speedier disbursements and greater reliance on more flexible forms of assistance, such

[1] A/S-11/14, annex I.

[2] E/1984/110, annex.

[3] See E/1984/109, annex.

[4] *Report of the United Nations Conference on Desertification, Nairobi, 29 August - 9 September 1977* (A/CONF.74/36), chap. I.

[5] E/1984/110, annex.

[6] E/1984/110/Add.1.

[7] *Official Records of the General Assembly, Thirty-third Session, Supplement No. 15* (A/33/15 and Corr.1), vol. I, part two, annex I.

[8] *Report of the United Nations Conference on the Least Developed Countries, Paris, 1-14 September 1981* (United Nations publication, Sales No. E.82.I.8), part one, sect. A.

as non-project programme and sector aid, including local and recurrent costs.

22. We acknowledge that there is room for further improvement in the coordination of assistance and the efficient and effective use of resources. Coordination of multilateral as well as bilateral assistance is primarily the responsibility of recipient Governments and, in this connection, effective national coordinating mechanisms can play an important role. The United Nations system should extend technical assistance in this field to Governments, upon request, and should pursue its own efforts to enhance coordination at the programme and operational levels, in conformity with relevant General Assembly resolutions.

23. We are convinced that in addressing the critical needs of African countries there are many areas where the United Nations could play an important role both in mobilizing the necessary resources and in carrying out specific activities. In this respect, existing resources allocated for programmes in Africa should, in consultation with African Governments, be refocused to address identified priority areas. There is need for further improvement in the efficiency and programme delivery of United Nations activities in Africa. Furthermore, additional voluntary contributions should be mobilized to ensure the implementation of projects and programmes in priority areas.

24. We urge all organs, organizations and bodies of the United Nations system to give greater attention to Africa and to continue to mobilize resources for assisting African countries in dealing with the current crisis and its longer-term ramifications.

25. We further urge bilateral and multilateral donors, as well as non-governmental organizations, to take all necessary measures to support the efforts of the African countries aimed at alleviating the critical economic situation in Africa.

26. We request the Secretary-General to continue his commendable efforts in alerting and sensitizing the international community to the plight of African countries, in mobilizing additional assistance to Africa, as well as in coordinating the activities of the United Nations system in Africa and in monitoring the situation, and to present periodic reports thereon.

27. We are convinced that unless urgent action is taken the rapidly deteriorating situation in Africa may well lead to disaster. We are therefore fully committed to supporting the efforts of African countries to meet the dual challenge of survival and development by taking concerted and urgent measures commensurate with the needs outlined in the present Declaration.

43/191. Food and Agricultural Problems

Committee: 2
Vote: Adopted without a vote
Ref.: 49/103, 47/149, 45/207, 43/191, 41/191, 40/181, 39/166, 38/158, 38/159, 37/245, 37/247, 36/186, 35/69, 2805(XXVI), 2301(XXII), 1496(XV), 1026(XI), 1025(XI), 827(IX), 628(VII), 525(VI), 202(III)

The General Assembly,

Recalling the Declaration and the Programme of Action on the Establishment of a New International Economic Order, contained in its resolutions 3201 (S-VI) and 3202 (S-VI) of 1 May 1974, the Charter of Economic Rights and Duties of States, contained in its resolution 3281 (XXIX) of 12 December 1974, resolution 3362 (S-VII) of 16 September 1975 on development and international economic cooperation, and the International Development Strategy for the Third United Nations Development Decade, contained in the annex to its resolution 35/56 of 5 December 1980,

Recalling also its resolutions on food and agricultural problems, in particular resolution 41/191 of 8 December 1986,

Reaffirming the Universal Declaration on the Eradication of Hunger and Malnutrition adopted by the World Food Conference,[1]

Stressing the imperative need to keep food and agricultural issues at the centre of global attention,

Reaffirming that food and agricultural problems in developing countries should be considered in a comprehensive manner in their different dimensions and in their immediate, short-term and long-term perspectives,

Emphasizing that the continuing gravity of the economic situation in Africa, including the persistence of negative trends in the food and agricultural sectors, requires urgent and decisive action by the international community to accelerate and ensure the full implementation of the United Nations Programme of Action for African Economic Recovery and Development 1986-1990,[2] as stressed during the mid-term review of the implementation of the Programme of Action,

Welcoming the support given by the international donor community to agricultural development in developing countries and the efforts of these countries in the development of their food and agricultural sectors,

Noting with concern that the tensions concerning trade in agricultural markets remain very serious, notably owing to the persistence and, in some cases, intensification of all forms of agricultural support, including export subsidies and import restrictions, as pointed out by ministers of Governments of States members of the Organisation for Economic Cooperation and Development at their meeting in Paris on 18 and 19 May 1988,

Reaffirming that the right to food is a universal human right that should be guaranteed to all people and, in that context, believing in the general principle that food should not be used as an instrument of political pressure, either at the national or at the international level,

Deeply concerned about the worsening of the locust infestation and its spread to several regions of the developing world, particularly the recent infestation of large regions of Africa, as described in the status reports of the Food and Agriculture Organization of the United Nations, and about the grave consequences of the infestation for agriculture and food production in the countries of the affected regions,

Welcoming the ongoing work of the Global Information and Early Warning System on Food and Agriculture in monitoring the world food situation and in alerting the international community to impending problems,

Concerned that, despite some slight improvements in 1987, the economies of developing countries continue to suffer from depressed international commodity prices, protectionism and worsening terms of trade, growing debt service burden and net outflow of financial resources from developing countries as a whole, which have had a negative effect on international trade and agriculture, particularly for developing countries,

1. *Notes with concern* that hunger and malnutrition have been increasing since the World Food Conference in 1974, that the number of people suffering from hunger and malnutrition has increased in the 1980s and that the central objective of the Conference remains largely unfulfilled;

2. *Welcomes* the conclusions and recommendations contained in the report of the World Food Council on the work of its fourteenth ministerial session held at Nicosia from 23 to 26 May 1988,[3] in particular the Cyprus Initiative against Hunger in the World,[4] and calls upon Governments and international and non-governmental organizations to assist the World Food Council fully in implementing the Initiative;

3. *Takes note with appreciation* of the report of the Secretary-General on trends in international agricultural markets with special reference to the share of developing countries;[5]

4. *Stresses* the urgent need for substantial progress in stimulating food production in developing countries and the importance of increasing domestic food production, thereby stimulating national

---

1 *Report of the World Food Conference, Rome, 5-16 November 1974* (United Nations publication, Sales No. E.75.II.A.3), chap. I.

2 Resolution S-13/2, annex.

3 *Official Records of the General Assembly, Forty-third Session, Supplement No. 19* (A/43/19), part one.

4 *Ibid.*, sect. II.

5 E/1988/70.

economic growth and social progress in those countries, in particular in Africa and the least developed countries, and helping to resolve the problems of hunger and malnutrition in an effective way;

5. *Urges*, in this context, the members of the international community, in particular the donor countries, to take further determined action in support of the efforts of developing countries by increasing the flow of resources, including concessional flows designated for agricultural development, and to increase their contributions to intergovernmental organizations;

6. *Stresses* the need for donor countries to increase aid commitments to food and agriculture in developing countries and the need to channel assistance through existing organizations and programmes;

7. *Also stresses* that the provision of food aid in the context of emergency situations resulting, *inter alia*, from natural disasters should be reinforced through additional rehabilitation and development assistance in order to help restore food production capacity and self-reliance;

8. *Calls* for a joint effort by all States and relevant international and intergovernmental organizations to improve the food situation and protect the nutritional levels of affected groups, in particular low-income groups, especially during the implementation of structural adjustment programmes;

9. *Affirms* that increasing food production in developing countries will significantly contribute to the eradication of poverty and the elimination of malnutrition, and recommends that a higher priority be given to supporting food production in the national development efforts of those countries in order to ensure adequate food supplies and distribution;

10. Stresses that the Uruguay Round of multilateral trade negotiations, launched on the occasion of the special session of the Contracting Parties to the General Agreement on Tariffs and Trade, held at Punta del Este, Uruguay, from 15 to 20 September 1986, presents a unique opportunity to develop a more open, viable and durable trading system, to reverse the disquieting rise in protectionism, and to bring agriculture under the strengthened and operationally effective rules and disciplines of the General Agreement on Tariffs and Trade, in accordance with the relevant provisions of the Ministerial Declaration on the Uruguay Round,[1] and urges that concerted efforts to this end should be made at the forthcoming mid-term review of multilateral trade negotiations at Montreal, Canada, taking into account the need to provide special and differential treatment for developing countries, considering their food security objectives and the need to avoid potentially adverse effects on those countries, especially those that import food, bearing in mind the overall benefits of trade liberalization;

11. *Stresses* the need to implement fully the relevant provisions of the Ministerial Declaration concerning tropical products;

12. *Also stresses* the need to improve global economic conditions in order to establish national, subregional and regional food security in developing countries;

13. *Calls upon* the international community to support scientific and technological training and research in developing countries in order to promote agricultural development in those countries, and emphasizes the urgency of strengthening international cooperation in the field of transfer of agricultural technology and of facilitating the free exchange of information on experience and technology relating to food production, processing and storage;

14. *Also calls upon* the international community, through specific and effective measures, to support and complement the efforts made by African Governments to stimulate agriculture and food production and to implement fully the United Nations Programme of Action for African Economic Recovery and Development 1986-1990;[2]

15. *Urges* all States members of the International Fund for Agricultural Development to take decisive action to ensure the timely conclusion of the negotiations on the third replenishment of the resources of the Fund so as to facilitate its adoption by the Governing Council of the Fund in January 1989, thus enabling the Fund to pursue its mandate of assisting developing countries in increasing their food production and in alleviating rural poverty and, to that end, appeals to all parties to make their best efforts to achieve the overall target fixed for the replenishment;

16. *Takes note with satisfaction* of the fact that the target of the Special Programme for Sub-Saharan African Countries Affected by Drought and Desertification of the Fund has been achieved, and appeals for increased contributions to the Fund;

17. *Appeals* to the international community to contribute generously to the World Food Programme so that the pledging target for the period 1989-1990, as set out in General Assembly resolution 42/164 of 11 December 1987, can be attained and the Programme can continue its activity in support of capital investment and in meeting emergency food needs;

18. *Notes with appreciation* the eighth replenishment of the International Development Association for the period 1 July 1987 to 30 June 1990, which provides for a total of 12.4 billion United States dollars, and stresses the need to draw upon those resources for the development of food and agriculture;

19. *Stresses* the need for coordinated international action to tackle the long-term problems of migratory pest control, particularly in Africa, and, expressing gratitude for the support of donors and recognizing the efforts made by the affected countries in the fight against the grasshopper and locust infestation, calls upon donors to continue to give high priority to the implementation and continued coordination by the Food and Agriculture Organization of the United Nations of emergency control programmes, as well as longer-term measures, against grasshoppers and locusts currently affecting vast areas of Africa, as well as other regions of the developing world, and to remain prepared to provide financial and technical assistance to affected countries at short notice;

20. *Takes note* of the establishment, within the framework of the World Food Council, of the informal *ad hoc* consultative group for the implementation of the Cyprus Initiative against Hunger in the World, and urges all Member States and international organizations to participate actively in the work of the group so as:

(*a*) To review and assess the policies and instruments currently available to combat chronic hunger and malnutrition in developing countries, particularly in low-income food-deficit countries, and to identify the reasons and obstacles that may have reduced their impact;

(*b*) To consider concrete and realistic measures that could make existing policies and instruments more effective;

(*c*) To identify workable initiatives;

(*d*) To recommend a course of action to combat hunger and malnutrition more effectively;

21. *Requests* the President of the World Food Council to present to the Council at its fifteenth ministerial session an action-oriented report on the Cyprus Initiative against Hunger in the World;

22. *Urges* the World Food Council to continue, within its mandate:

(*a*) To assess the overall impact of structural adjustment programmes in developing countries on the nutritional levels of their populations, especially among children and low-income groups, and to suggest remedial measures in that area, including ways of stimulating the provision of resources to eliminate the suffering of those groups;

(*b*) To assess the impact of liberalized international trade in agricultural and tropical products on all countries and especially on the food security and development efforts of developing countries and, in this context, to maintain an active interest in the progress and outcome of the Uruguay Round of multilateral trade negotiations;

(*c*) To promote activities related to food security and agricultural trade, as well as to regional and South-South cooperation in food and agriculture, within the context of economic growth and the development needs of developing countries;

(*d*) To stimulate progress in and contribute more actively to the full implementation of the food policy and programme components of the United Nations Programme of Action for African Economic Recovery and Development 1986-1990;

---

1 See GATT, *Focus Newsletter*, No. 41, October 1986.

2 Resolution S-13/2, annex.

23. *Also urges* the World Food Council to continue to exercise leadership in sensitizing the international community to the nature, extent, causes and consequences of hunger and malnutrition and in recommending appropriate practical policies for remedial action;

24. *Requests* the Secretary-General, in consultation with the World Food Council, the United Nations Conference on Trade and Development and the Food and Agriculture Organization of the United Nations, to submit to the Economic and Social Council, at its second regular session of 1989, an updated comprehensive report on trends in the international market for agricultural and tropical products and on the liberalization of international agricultural trade, together with suggestions on ways and means of increasing the share of developing countries in that trade, while avoiding the potentially adverse short-term effects on developing countries, in particular those that import food.

83rd plenary meeting
20 December 1988

S-18/3. Declaration on International Economic Cooperation, in Particular the Revitalization of Economic Growth and Development of the Developing Countries

Committee: Ad hoc
Vote: Adopted without a vote
Ref.: 49/92, 48/185, 47/152, 46/144, 45/234

The General Assembly

Adopts the Declaration on International Economic Cooperation in particular the Revitalization of Economic Growth and Development of the Developing Countries annexed to the present resolution.

11th plenary meeting
1 May 1990

Annex

Declaration on International Economic Cooperation, in Particular the Revitalization of Economic Growth and Development of the Developing Countries

We, the States Members of the United Nations,

Solemnly proclaim our strong commitment to a global consensus to promote urgently international economic cooperation for sustained growth of the world economy and, in particular, to the revitalization of economic growth and development of the developing countries so as to realize the basic right of all human beings to a life free from hunger, poverty, ignorance, disease and fear. To that end, we adopt the present Declaration.

1. This is a time of positive transformation in international relations. The reduction in international political tensions, the increasing integration of the world economy and the broad movement towards economic and political reform will create an opportunity for strengthening international economic cooperation based on the need to provide just and equal opportunities to all peoples to enable them to develop their full potential.

2. We strongly affirm the need to revitalize growth and development in the developing countries and to address together the problems of abject poverty and hunger that continue to afflict far too many people in the world. The international community has a responsibility to give strong support to the efforts of the developing countries to solve their grave economic and social problems through the creation of a favourable international economic environment.

3. In an increasingly interdependent world, the developing countries should play an important role in the growth and expansion of the world economy for the progress and prosperity of all peoples.

4. Each country is responsible for its own economic policies for development, in accordance with its specific situations and conditions, and for the life and well-being of all its citizens. National policies also need to take fully into account the obligations of all countries to international economic cooperation.

I. Assessment of the 1980s

5. In the 1980s, progress in developed and developing countries was uneven. The decade was marked by a widening gap between those groups of countries as well as by relatively slow growth and large global financial and trade imbalances. Developed market-oriented countries have succeeded to a large extent in controlling initiation and in maintaining sustained, though modest, growth. However, many countries, particularly developing countries, have encountered serious difficulties in their attempt to adapt to structural changes, to benefit from the economic growth of the industrialized countries and to promote the well-being of their citizens.

6. External and fiscal imbalances in some of the countries whose economies have the largest impact on the world economy have contributed to international monetary instability and led to higher interest rates. In the late 1980s, such imbalances started to narrow; none the less, they remain large.

7. For many developing countries, the 1980s have been viewed as a decade lost for development. Living conditions in Africa and Latin America and the Caribbean, and in parts of Asia, deteriorated, and economic and social infrastructure eroded, impairing stability and prospects for growth and development. Other developing countries were able to achieve economic and social progress.

8. The position of developing countries in international trade and finance weakened substantially, further widening the gap between developing and developed countries. External indebtedness emerged as a main factor in the economic stalemate in the developing countries. Their capacity to service debt was seriously weakened as interest rates grew and terms of trade deteriorated. This problem has contributed to the fall in investment and the cessation of new financial flows. A long-term downward trend in the prices of commodities has had devastating effects for commodity-dependent developing countries.

9. As a result, there was a large net transfer of resources from the developing to the developed countries, depriving the former of much needed resources for development. This made the process of adjustment more difficult and complicated the tasks of coping with its social consequences and obtaining the necessary political support for reform.

10. Eastern European countries were not appropriately involved in the world economic system. Their need for comprehensive reform and transformation grew and, in the late 1980s, fundamental political and economic changes began to take place. These countries face problems of adaptation to the scientific, technological and structural changes taking place in the world economy.

11. As the world changes around us, we must respond positively. The 1980s marked the beginning of fundamental rethinking towards the achievement of economic development. A gradual convergence of views on economic policy, including the need for sound macro-economic policies and enhanced competition, is emerging. Flexibility, creativity, innovation and openness must be integral pans of our economic systems.

II. Challenges and opportunities for the 1990s

12. The most important challenge for the 1990s is the revitalization of economic growth and social development in the developing countries, which calls for sustained growth of the world economy and favourable external conditions. This major challenge has to be addressed in the context of increasing interdependence and integration in the world economy.

13. It will be essential to stem the increasing marginalization of the least developed countries and to reactivate their growth and development through comprehensive national action and international support measures.

14. Finding an early and durable solution to the international debt problems, meeting the increasing needs for development finance, creating an open and equitable trading system and facilitating the diversification and modernization of the economies of developing countries, particularly those that are commodity-dependent, are conditions for the revitalization of growth and development in the

developing countries in the 1990s and require continued concerned efforts.

15. There is a pressing need to improve the international economic environment in order to ensure the success of national policies. Countries can then take advantage of the major advances in science and technology and the globalization of markets and thereby enhance their human capital and modernize their economies.

16. Economic development must be environmentally sound and sustainable. The deterioration of the environment is a cause of grave concern for all countries. Growing environmental problems, such as pollution, desertification, deforestation and climate change, increasingly pose a serious threat to the future growth of the world economy.

17. Countries have to adapt their national policies to facilitate open exchange and flexible responses to the changing world economy. Effective national policies have a critical role to play in achieving sustained, non-inflationary economic growth in all countries. Such policies should be supportive of investment as well as of efficient allocation and mobilization of resources in order to achieve durable growth.

18. The eradication of poverty and hunger, greater equity in income distribution and the development of human resources remain major challenges everywhere. Economic and social progress requires that growth be broadly based, offering equal opportunities to all people, both women and men, to participate fully in economic, social and political activities.

19. There is a need to integrate the Eastern European countries into the world economy and the international economic system. This should generate positive impulses for world trade and development.

20. The revitalization of economic growth and development of the developing countries will have to be undertaken against the backdrop of these opportunities and challenges. Our collective efforts will be needed to ensure that the rapidly changing realities result in a positive transformation in favour of the economic development of all countries, particularly the developing countries.

III. Commitments and policies for international development cooperation

21. Reactivation of economic growth and development in the developing countries will require a concerted and committed effort by all countries. The present opportunity to restore a long-term approach to development and move beyond short-term adjustment must be seized. The States Members of the United Nations will endeavour to take all necessary steps to reverse the adverse trends of the 1980s, address the challenges of the 1990s and move into a more productive decade. Such actions should take into account the responsibility of each country for its own development and should be in accordance with its capacity and its impact on the international economy.

22. The major industrialized countries influence world economic growth and the international economic environment profoundly. They should continue their effort to promote sustained growth and to narrow imbalances in a manner that can benefit other countries. The coordination of macro-economic polices should take full account of the interests and concerns of all countries, particularly the developing countries. Efforts should be made to enhance the effectiveness of multilateral surveillance aimed at correcting existing external and fiscal imbalances, promoting non-inflationary sustainable growth, lowering real rates of interest and making exchange rates more stable and markets more accessible.

23. In accordance with their legislation, development objectives and national priorities, developing countries should continue to work towards keeping control over inflationary tendencies, promoting domestic savings, achieving favourable conditions for domestic and foreign investment, modernizing their economies and increasing their international competitiveness.

24. However, economic policies should have as their ultimate objective the betterment of the human condition and the enhancement of the contribution of all persons to development. The full utilization of human resources and the recognition of human rights stimulate creativity, innovation and initiative.

25. A primary objective must be to respond to the needs and maximize the potential of all members of society. Health, nutrition, housing, population policies and other social services are a key to both improving individual welfare and successful development. Education and training, which must be available to all, are essential for improving the quality of human resources and for sustaining economic growth. The international community should support efforts to arrest the current escalation of extreme poverty and hunger. It is essential to reverse the present deterioration of this grave situation.

26. A durable and broad solution of the external debt problems of the developing debtor countries should continue to be given urgent attention, and the serious debt-servicing problems of some other countries should be further addressed with a view to an early solution. Recent initiative and measures to reduce the stock and service of debt or to provide debt relief for developing countries should be broadly implemented. Relief measures should aim at the resumption of vigorous growth and development in these countries and should address all types of bilateral debt of debtor developing countries. Serious consideration should be given to continuing to work towards a growth-oriented solution of the problems of developing countries with serious debt-servicing problems, including those whose debt is mainly to of final creditors or to multilateral institutions.

27. Substantial concessional resources will be called for to enable developing countries, especially the least developed ones, to cope with the challenges of the 1990s. Developed countries should implement the undertakings they have made to attain the agreed international target of devoting 0.7 per cent of gross national product to official development assistance and 0.15 per cent to the least developed countries. Developed countries should enhance the quantity and quality of their aid. Appropriate additional resources for the least developed countries should be considered at the Second United Nations Conference on the Least Developed Countries. The special development problems and needs of the island and land-locked developing countries should also be addressed.

28. Scientific and technological capability is increasingly important in the development of developing countries. Developed countries and international organizations should support the efforts of developing countries to create and develop endogenous capacities in this area.

29. The current threat to the environment is the common concern of all. All countries should take effective actions for the protection and enhancement of the environment in accordance with their respective capacities and responsibilities and taking into account the specific needs of developing countries. As the major sources of pollution, the developed countries have the main responsibility for taking appropriate measures urgently. The economic growth and development of developing countries are essential in order to address problems of the degradation and protection of the environment. New and additional financial resources will have to be channelled to developing countries. Effective modalities for favourable access to, and transfer of, environmentally sound technologies, in particular to developing countries, including on concessional and preferential terms, should be examined.

30. Multilateral financial institutions should be in a position to respond to the increasing development needs of developing countries in the 1990s. They should be provided with adequate resources to support long-term development, to facilitate structural reform and to finance programmes to alleviate the adverse social consequences of adjustment for poor and vulnerable groups.

31. Countries should seek to reduce expenditures for military purposes, thereby opening up the possibility of enhanced spending on social and economic development for the benefit of all countries, in particular the developing countries. In this context, the feasibility of channelling some of these reductions through financial mechanisms for development should be explored.

32. An open and credible multilateral trading system is essential for the promotion of growth and development. Any present or future trends towards unilateralism, bilateralism and the erosion of the multilateral trading system must be arrested. Protectionism should be resisted everywhere; commitments to standstill and roll-back of protectionism should be honoured. It is vitally important that the

Uruguay Round of multilateral trade negotiations result in a balanced outcome, preserving and strengthening the multilateral trading system, enabling trade liberalization and increased market access for the exports of developing countries. The principles underlying the multilateral trading system should be reaffirmed, and international organizations active in multilateral trade should be strengthened as part of the process of attaining these objectives.

33. Commodity exports will continue to play a key role in the economies of most developing countries and to make a crucial contribution to export earnings and investment. There is a need for better functioning of commodity markets and more stable and predictable conditions. Diversification helps the developing countries to increase and stabilize their export earnings. All countries and multilateral institutions should undertake measures to support these endeavours.

34. Regional economic integration is important in expanding trade and investment in developing countries. Developing countries should strive to promote economic integration and strengthen economy and technical cooperation among themselves. These efforts should be encouraged and supported by the developed countries, a well as by the international organizations.

35. Eastern European countries should be supported in their efforts to integrate themselves into the international economy, including, as appropriate, their adhesion to international institutions. This will benefit their own people and the rest of the world; it must not detract from the high priority placed on international development cooperation with the developing countries. Their integration will strengthen the role of Eastern Europe as a dynamic trade partner and as a market and source of technology.

36. The United Nations system has a large role to play in international cooperation for revitalizing development in the 1990s. All its Member States have a responsibility for making it more effective and efficient The United Nations is a unique forum in which the communiqué of nations can address all issues in an integrated manner. Its many specialized agencies make an indispensable contribution to development. They have a major responsibility in the great task of revitalizing growth and development in the 1990s.

37. Member States agree to work for fruitful results at the forthcoming Second United Nations Conference on the Least Developed Countries, in the eloboration of a new international development strategy, the World Summit for Children, the eighth session of the United Nations Conference on Trade and Development in 1991, the United Nations Conference on Environment and Development to be held in Brazil in 1992, and the international meeting on population in 1994.

38. The States Members of the United Nations pledge themselves solemnly to advance the multilateral dialogue, to respond to the challenge and commitments contained in the present Declaration through national policies and enhanced international cooperation and to keep the implementation of the Declaration under political review.

46/202. Impact of the Recent Evolution of East-West Relations on the Growth of the World Economy, in Particular on the Economic Growth and Development of the Developing Countries, as well as on International Economic Cooperation

Committee: 2
Vote: Adopted without a vote

The General Assembly,

Recalling its resolution S-18/3 of 1 May 1990, the annex to which contains the Declaration on International Economic Cooperation, in particular the Revitalization of Economic Growth and Development of the Developing Countries, as well as its resolution 45/199 of 21 December 1990, the annex to which contains the International Development Strategy for the Fourth United Nations Development Decade,

Recalling also its resolution 45/182 of 21 December 1990, on the convening of a special high-level meeting of the Economic and Social Council with ministerial participation, on 4 and 5 July 1991, to discuss the impact of the recent evolution of East-West relations on the growth of the world economy, in particular on the economic growth and development of the developing countries, as well as on international economic cooperation,

Taking note of the Declaration of the Ministers for Foreign Affairs of the States members of the Group of 77 adopted on the occasion of their fifteenth annual meeting, held in New York on 30 September 1991, in which the Ministers welcomed the convening of the Special High-level Meeting,[1]

Taking note also of the debate and the views expressed by Member States at the Special High-level Meeting and of the concluding statement of the Chairman of the Special High-level Meeting,[2]

1. *Notes with satisfaction* the holding of the Special High-level Meeting of the Economic and Social Council with ministerial participation at Geneva on 4 and 5 July 1991;

2. *Takes note* of the report of the Economic and Social Council, in particular as it pertains to the Special High-level Meeting;[3]

3. *Recognizes* the need to enhance the positive aspects of the fundamental transformations in the Central and Eastern European countries and their integration into the world economy;

4. *Notes* the assurances given by the developed countries and multilateral financial institutions that the resources allocated to the Central and Eastern European countries would not reduce or divert official development assistance, including food aid, allocated to the developing countries;

5. *Urges* Member States to continue to consider, where appropriate, triangular arrangements which would also involve or benefit developing countries in the supply of the relevant requirements of the Central and Eastern European countries, taking into account the structural transformation needs and requirements of those countries;

6. *Calls on* the international community to consider assisting developing countries whose economies have been most affected by the recent changes in their economic relations with Central and Eastern European countries to adapt to those changes;

7. *Requests* the Secretary-General, in reviewing the impact of the recent evolution of East-West relations on the growth of the world economy, in particular on the economic growth and development of the developing countries, as well as on international economic cooperation, to submit to the General Assembly at its forty-seventh session a report containing, *inter alia*, an analysis of the impact on developing countries of the measures taken to integrate Central and Eastern European countries into the world economy, and on the full implementation of the present resolution.

79th plenary meeting
20 December 1991

46/206. Report of the Committee for Development Planning: Criteria for Identifying the Least Developed Countries

Committee: 2
Vote: Adopted without a vote
Ref.: 37/133, 3487(XXX), 2768(XXVI), 2724(XXV)

The General Assembly,

Recalling its resolution 45/206 of 21 December 1990, on the implementation of the Programme of Action for the Least Developed Countries for the 1990s,

Recalling also the recommendation of the Second United Nations Conference on the Least Developed Countries on the criteria for identifying the least developed among developing countries,[4]

---

1 A/46/520, annex, para. 4.

2 *Official Records of the General Assembly, Forty-sixth Session, Supplement No. 3 (A/46/3/Rev.1)*, chapt. II.

3 *Ibid.*

4 See *Report of the Second United nations Conference on the Least Developed Countries, Paris, 3 - 14 September 1990*, (A/CONF.147/18).

Taking note of paragraph (b) of Economic and Social Council decision 1991/275 of 26 July 1991, on chapter V of the report of the Committee for Development Planning on its twenty-seventh session,[1]

Recognizing that the decision to include any country in the group of least developed countries should be made with its due consent,

1. *Notes with appreciation* the new criteria for identifying the least developed among the developing countries and the graduation rules recommended by the Committee for Development Planning, and requests the Committee to consider further possible improvements in the criteria and their applications and to report thereon to the General Assembly at its fifty-second session through the Economic and Social Council;

2. *Requests* the Committee for Development Planning to undertake every three years a general review of the list of low-income countries, with a view to identifying which of those countries should qualify for inclusion in, or should be graduated from, the list of least developed countries, and to present this review to the General Assembly through the Economic and Social Council;

3. *Decides* that the General Assembly will act on the recommendations of the Committee for Development Planning for the inclusion of a country in the list of least developed countries, provided the country concerned has signified its consent;

4. *Stresses* that there is need for a smooth transition of the countries graduating out of the group of least developed countries, with a view to avoiding disruption to their development plans, programmes and projects, and invites Governments, international organizations and other concerned parties to take appropriate steps to ensure such a smooth transition;

5. *Decides*, in this context, that the graduation of a country will be completed following a transitional period of three years, which will commence immediately after the General Assembly has taken note of the finding of the Committee for Development Planning to graduate that country;

6. *Endorses* the recommendations of the Committee for Development Planning regarding the inclusion of Cambodia, Madagascar, Solomon Islands, Zaire and Zambia in the list of least developed countries;

7. *Takes note* of the finding of the Committee for Development Planning to graduate Botswana from the list of least developed countries, and decides that its graduation from the list will be completed following a transition period of three years, in accordance with paragraph 5 of the present resolution;

8. *Requests* the Secretary-General of the United Nations Conference on Trade and Development to report to the Conference at its eighth session on the resource and other implications of the application of the new criteria for identifying the least developed countries on the implementation of the Programme of Action for the Least Developed Countries for the 1990s;

9. *Also requests* the Secretary-General of the United Nations Conference on Trade and Development to follow his report to the Conference with a report to the General Assembly at its forty-seventh session, through the Economic and Social Council, on the same subject.

79th plenary meeting
20 December 1991

47/181. An Agenda for Development

Committee: 2
Vote: Adopted without a vote
Ref.: 49/126, 48/166

The General Assembly,

Recalling the Charter of the United Nations, in particular the commitment to employ international machinery for the promotion of the economic and social advancement of all peoples,

Taking note of the report of the Secretary-General on the work of the Organization, in particular the reference to an agenda for development, [2]

Reaffirming the unique position of the United Nations as a forum for the promotion of international cooperation for development,

Emphasizing the need to give due consideration to the broad scope of themes related to international cooperation and international economic relations in order to address effectively the issue of development, particularly of developing countries,

Stressing the importance of continuing to strengthen the capacity of the United Nations to foster international cooperation in order to address fully the wide range of issues pertaining to development, particularly that of developing countries,

Stressing also that the objectives and commitments with regard to development adopted by the General Assembly, especially the Declaration on International Economic Cooperation, in particular the Revitalization of Economic Growth and Development of the Developing Countries, [3] the International Development Strategy for the Fourth United Nations Development Decade,[4] the Cartagena Commitment,[5] the United Nations New Agenda for the Development of Africa in the 1990s,[6] the Programme of Action for the Least Developed Countries for the 1990s,[7] and the various consensus agreements and conventions, especially Agenda 21, adopted by the United Nations Conference on Environment and Development[8] at the level of heads of State or government, which mark the beginning of a new global partnership for sustainable development, all together provide the overall framework of international cooperation for development,

Recalling the restructuring and revitalization process initiated by its resolution 45/264 of 13 May 1991, in particular its commitment to promote the achievement of the objectives and priorities of the United Nations in the economic, social and related fields, as set forth in other relevant resolutions,

Requests the Secretary-General to submit to the General Assembly at its forty-eighth session, in consultation with Member States, a report on an agenda for development, taking fully into consideration the objectives and agreements on development adopted by the Assembly, containing an analysis of and recommendations on ways to enhance the role of the United Nations and the relationship between the United Nations and the Bretton Woods institutions in the promotion of international cooperation for development, within the framework and provisions of the Charter of the United Nations and the articles of agreement of the Bretton Woods institutions, and to include therein, *inter alia*, a comprehensive annotated list of substantive themes and areas to be addressed by the United Nations in the agenda, as well as his views on priorities among them, for the consideration of Member States.

93rd plenary meeting
22 December 1992

---

1 *Official Records of the Economic ans Social Council, 1991, Supplement No. 11*, (E/1991/32).

2 *Official Records of the General Assembly, Forty-seventh Session, Supplement No. 1* (A/47/1), para 1. 105.

3 Resolution S.18/3, annex.

4 Rcsolution 45/199, annex.

5 TD/364, part one, sect. A.

6 Resolution 46/151, annex, sect. II.

7 *Report of the Second United Nations Conference on the Least Developed Countries, Paris 3-14 September 1990* (A/CONF.147/18), part one.

8 See *Report of the United Nations Conference on Environment and Development, Rio de Janeiro, 3-14 June 1992* (A/CONF.151/26).

50/161. Implementation of the Outcome of the World Summit for Social Development

Committee: -
Vote: Adopted without a vote

The General Assembly,

Recalling its resolutions 46/139 of 17 December 1991, 47/92 of 16 December 1992 and 48/100 of 20 December 1993,

Recalling also Economic and Social Council decision 1991/230 of 30 May 1991, resolutions 1992/27 of 30 July 1992, 1995/60 of 28 July 1995, and agreed conclusions 1995/1 of 28 July 1995,[1]

Having considered the report of the World Summit for Social Development, held at Copenhagen from 6 to 12 March 1995,[2]

Expressing its profound gratitude to the Government and people of Denmark for the hospitality extended to all participants at the Summit, and for the facilities, staff and services placed at their disposal,

Expressing its satisfaction that for the first time in history, at the invitation of the United Nations, heads of State and Government gathered at Copenhagen to recognize the significance of social development and human well-being for all and to give to these goals the highest priority both now and into the twenty-first century by reaching a successful conclusion and adopting the Copenhagen Declaration on Social Development and Programme of Action,[3]

Critical importance of national action and international cooperation for social development

1. *Takes note with appreciation* of the report of the World Summit for Social Development;

2. *Also takes note* of the report of the Secretary-General on the implementation of the outcome of the World Summit for Social Development;[4]

3. *Endorses* the Copenhagen Declaration on Social Development and Programme of Action of the World Summit for Social Development, adopted on 12 March 1995;

4. *Reaffirms* the pledge by the heads of State and Government at the Summit to give highest priority to national, regional and international policies and actions for the promotion of social progress, justice and the betterment of human condition, based on full participation by all;

5. *Recognizes* the necessity to create a framework for action to place people at the centre of development and direct economies to meet human needs more effectively;

6. *Stresses* the need for a renewed and massive political will at the national and international levels to invest in people and their well-being to achieve the objectives of social development;

7. *Emphasizes* that economic development, social development and environmental protection are interdependent and mutually reinforcing components of sustainable development;

8. *Recognizes* that social development and the implementation of the Programme of Action are primarily the responsibility of Governments, although international cooperation and assistance are essential for their full implementation;

9. *Reiterates* the call to Governments to define time-bound goals and targets for reducing overall poverty and eradicating absolute poverty, expanding employment and reducing unemployment and enhancing social integration, within each national context;

10. *Emphasizes* that there is a need for promotion of an integrated and multidimensional approach for the implementation of the Declaration and Programme of Action at all levels;

11. *Reiterates* the call for formulating or strengthening by 1996 comprehensive cross-sectoral strategies for implementing the outcome of the Summit and national strategies for social development, including government action, actions by States in cooperation with other Governments, international, regional and subregional organizations, and actions taken in partnership and cooperation with actors of civil society, the private sector and cooperatives, with specific responsibilities to be undertaken by each actor and with agreed priorities and time-frames;

12. *Also reiterates* the call for regularly assessing national progress towards implementing the outcome of the Summit, possibly in the form of periodic national reports, outlining successes, problems and obstacles; such reports could be considered within the framework of an appropriate consolidated reporting system, taking into account the different reporting procedures in the economic, social and environmental fields;

13. *Reaffirms* the need for an effective partnership and cooperation between Governments and the relevant actors of civil society, the social partners, the major groups as defined in Agenda 21,[5] including non-governmental organizations and the private sector, in the implementation of and follow-up to the Declaration and Programme of Action, and ensuring their involvement in the planning, elaboration, implementation and evaluation of social policies at the national level;

14. *Recognizes* that the implementation of the Declaration and Programme of Action will require the mobilization of financial resources at the national and international level, as set out in commitments 8 and 9 of the Declaration[6] and paragraphs 87 to 93 of the Programme of Action;[7]

15. *Also recognizes* that the implementation of the Declaration and Programme of Action in developing countries, in particular in Africa and the least developed countries, will need additional financial resources and more effective development cooperation and assistance;

16. *Concurs* that substantial debt reduction is needed to enable developing countries to implement the Declaration and Programme of Action, as set out in commitment 9 (o) of the Declaration and paragraph 90 of the Programme of Action;

17. *Reaffirms* the importance of agreeing on a mutual commitment between interested developed and developing country partners to allocate, on average, 20 per cent of official development assistance and 20 per cent of the national budget, respectively, to basic social programmes;

18. *Recognizes* the necessity of providing appropriate technical cooperation and other forms of assistance to the countries with economies in transition, as set out in the provisions of the Declaration and Programme of Action;

19. *Urges* the Secretary-General, in cooperation with the World Bank, the International Monetary Fund and other multilateral development institutions, to study the impact of structural adjustment programmes on economic and social development and to assist adjusting countries in creating conditions for economic growth, job creation, poverty eradication and social development;

20. *Encourages* Governments as well as public and private institutions and organizations to take initiatives relevant to the high priority attached by the Summit to social development and to the implementation of the objectives and commitments adopted at the Summit;

The role of the United Nations system

21. *Calls upon* all relevant organs, organizations and bodies of the United Nations system to be involved in the follow-up of the Summit, and invites specialized agencies and related organizations of the United Nations system to strengthen and adjust their activities, pro-

---

1 A/50/3, chap. III, para. 22.

2 A/CONF.166/9.

3 A/CONF.166/9, chap. I, resolution 1.

4 A/50/670.

5 *Report of the United Nations Conference on Environment and Development, Rio de Janeiro, 3-14 June 1992* (A/CONF.151/26/Rev.1 (Vol. I and Vol. I/Corr.1, Vol. II, Vol. III and Vol. III/Corr.1)) (United Nations publication, Sales No. E.93.I.8 and corrigenda), vol. I: Resolutions Adopted by the Conference, resolution 1, annex II.

6 *Ibid.*, annex I.

7 *Ibid.*, annex II.

grammes and medium-term strategies, as appropriate, to take into account the follow-up to the Summit;

22. *Reaffirms* that the follow-up to the Summit will be undertaken on the basis of an integrated approach to social development and within the framework of a coordinated follow-up to and implementation of the results of the major international conferences in the economic, social and related fields;

23. *Decides* that the General Assembly, through its role in policy formulation, the Economic and Social Council, through its role in overall guidance and coordination, in accordance with their respective roles under the Charter of the United Nations and with Assembly resolution 48/162 of 20 December 1993, and a revitalized Commission for Social Development shall constitute a three-tiered intergovernmental process in the follow-up to the implementation of the Declaration and Programme of Action;

24. *Decides* to hold a special session of the General Assembly in the year 2000 for an overall review and appraisal of the implementation of the outcome of the Summit and to consider further actions and initiatives;

25. *Reaffirms* that the Economic and Social Council will provide overall guidance and oversee system-wide coordination in the implementation of the outcome of the Summit and make recommendations in this regard;

26. *Requests* the Economic and Social Council, so that it can review progress made towards implementing the outcome of the Summit as well as improving its own effectiveness, to continue examining ways to strengthen, consistent with the mandates of the Charter and in accordance with General Assembly resolutions 45/264 of 13 May 1991, 46/235 of 13 April 1992 and 48/162, its role, authority, structures, resources and processes, bringing specialized agencies into a closer working relationship with it;

27. *Invites* the Economic and Social Council to review the reporting system in the area of social development with a view to establishing a coherent system that could result in clear policy recommendations for Governments and international actors;

28. *Calls upon* the Commission for Social Development, as a functional commission of the Economic and Social Council, with the primary responsibility for the follow-up to and review of the implementation of the Summit, to develop a multi-year programme of work to the year 2000, selecting specific themes and addressing them from an interrelated and integrated perspective, in a manner consistent with the functions and contributions of other relevant organs, organizations and bodies of the United Nations system and to present its recommendations to the Council, which should ensure harmonization between such a multi-year programme of work and those of other relevant functional commissions of the Council;

29. *Endorses* Economic and Social Council resolution 1995/60, and calls upon the Commission for Social Development, when developing at its next session its multi-year programme of work for the follow-up to the Summit:

(*a*) To adapt its mandate in order to ensure an integrated approach to social development;

(*b*) To integrate the current sectoral issues on its agenda in the multi-year programme;

(*c*) To review and update its methods of work and to make recommendations to ensure an effective follow-up to the Summit;

(*d*) To establish the practice of inviting experts to contribute to its work;

(*e*) To consider integrating into its work high-level representatives on social development issues and policies;

30. *Requests* the Commission for Social Development, in view of the scope of work of the Commission, to consider at its next session the composition of the membership of the Commission and the frequency of its sessions, and to make recommendations thereon to the Economic and Social Council;

31. *Also requests* the Commission for Social Development to establish the practice of involving the relevant actors of civil society in the field of social development to contribute to its work, and requests the Secretary-General to present proposals to the Commission and the Economic and Social Council for consideration at their next sessions, taking into account the experience gained in other functional commissions, the Council, the International Labour Organization and the Summit;

32. *Requests* the Economic and Social Council, without prejudice to the outcome of the review of consultative arrangements by the open-ended Working Group on the review of arrangements for consultation with non-governmental organizations to consider authorizing the participation at the next session of the Commission for Social Development of interested civil society organizations that participated, by accreditation, in the Summit;

33. *Invites* within their mandates, the regional commissions, in cooperation with the regional intergovernmental organizations and banks, to consider convening, on a biennial basis, a meeting at a high political level to review progress made towards implementing the outcome of the Summit, to exchange views on their respective experiences and to adopt the appropriate measures;

34. *Emphasizes* the important role of the Committee on Economic, Social and Cultural Rights in monitoring those aspects of the Declaration and Programme of Action that relate to compliance by States parties with the International Covenant on Economic, Social and Cultural Rights;

35. *Notes* the establishment of task forces for the follow-up to the Summit and other related United Nations conferences and invites the Administrative Committee on Coordination to bring system-wide coordination issues to the attention of the Economic and Social Council, in particular its coordination segment, and to make recommendations thereon;

36. *Reiterates* that United Nations operational activities should be strengthened in order to contribute to the implementation of the outcome of the Summit in accordance with relevant resolutions;

37. *Requests* the United Nations Development Programme to facilitate the efforts of the United Nations system towards capacity-building at the local, national and regional levels, and to support the coordinated implementation of social development programmes through the resident coordinator system;

38. *Invites* the International Labour Organization, which, because of its mandate, tripartite structures and expertise, has a special role to play in the field of employment in social development, to continue to contribute to the implementation of the Programme of Action;

39. *Invites* the Bretton Woods institutions to be actively involved in the implementation and the follow-up to the Summit and to enhance their cooperation with other parts of the United Nations system for this purpose;

40. *Invites* the World Trade Organization to consider how it might contribute to the implementation of the Programme of Action, including activities in cooperation with the United Nations system;

41. *Invites* the Secretary-General, including within the framework of the Administrative Committee on Coordination, to make appropriate arrangements, which may include joint meetings, for consultations with the heads of the International Monetary Fund, the World Bank, the International Labour Organization, the United Nations funds and programmes and other relevant agencies, for the purpose of cooperating in the implementation of the Declaration and the Programme of Action in their respective organizations;

42. *Requests* the Secretary-General to ensure an effectively functioning Secretariat, within which clear responsibility is assigned to assist with the implementation and follow-up to the Summit and servicing the intergovernmental bodies involved;

43. *Also requests* the Secretary-General and the United Nations bodies, in a coordinated manner, to take appropriate measures to strengthen the United Nations capacity for gathering and analysing information and developing indicators of social development, taking into account the work carried out by different countries, in particular by developing countries, as well as providing policy and technical support and advice, upon request, to improve national capacities in this regard;

44. *Decides* that the Trust Fund of the World Summit for Social Development, established in accordance with General Assembly

resolution 47/92 of 16 December 1992 to finance preparatory activities, be continued and renamed "Trust Fund for the Follow-up to the World Summit for Social Development", under the authority of the Secretary-General, with the aim of supporting programmes, seminars and activities in the promotion of social development for the implementation of the Declaration and Programme of Action, which includes activities for the United Nations decade for the eradication of poverty, and invites all States to contribute to it;

45. *Requests* the Economic and Social Council to consider new and innovative ideas for generating funds and to offer for this purpose any useful suggestions;

46. *Calls upon* the Secretary-General to disseminate as widely as possible the Copenhagen Declaration on Social Development and Programme of Action, including to all competent organs of the United Nations and specialized agencies;

47. *Decides* to include in the provisional agenda of its fifty-first session the item entitled "Implementation of the outcome of the World Summit for Social Development", and to consider the implications for a more coherent treatment of related items on its agenda in the appropriate fora.

98th plenary meeting
22 December 1995

05.20 INTERNATIONAL TRADE AND DEVELOPMENT

1027 (XI). Development of International Economic Cooperation and the Expansion of International Trade

Committee: 2
Vote: 55 - 7 - 4
Ref.: 1321(XII), 1157(XII), 1156(XII)

The General Assembly,

Noting the growth in world production and trade since the Second World War.

Recognizing the need for continued efforts to reduce or remove obstacles to international trade and to promote its expansion on a multilateral basis,

Considering that the further development of mutually beneficial international economic cooperation, and particularly a continued expansion of international trade, would contribute to the expansion of the economies of all countries,

Considering in particular that a high and stable level of international trade is indispensable to the economic development of the less developed countries, and especially to those countries which depend for their foreign exchange earnings largely on the export of one commodity or a few commodities,

Recognizing that existing international bodies and agreements concerned with international trade provide a framework for the effective consideration of trade problems, payments arrangements and related economic problems of mutual interest, and are doing valuable work in this field,

Recognizing further the desirability of avoiding the waste of resources and the weakening of existing organizations in the field of international trade through the duplication of their functions and activities,

1. *Urges* the Governments of Member States to continue their efforts to reduce existing barriers to international trade in a mutually satisfactory manner for the purpose of expanding such trade at the fastest feasible rate and, in particular:

(*a*) To continue to work toward this objective through the international organizations which are working successfully for the expansion of world trade, and to continue to avail themselves of services offered in the field of trade by these organizations;

(*b*) To reduce or remove restrictions and/or discrimination with regard to trade and payments as soon as their balance of payments and reserve positions permit, having due regard to the special problems arising from the economic development needs of the less developed countries;

(*c*) To conduct their trade policies with due regard to their possible harmful effects on the economies of other countries, especially countries which are dependent on exports of relatively few commodities;

(*d*) To follow internal economic, monetary and fiscal policies which promote high levels of production, employment and investment, keeping in mind the relationship between such internal policies and the possibilities of expanding world trade;

2. *Endorses* Economic and Social Council resolution 614 (XXII) of 9 August 1956 and requests the Council to continue to give particular attention to developments in the field of international trade;

3. *Looks forward with interest* to the establishment of the Organization for Trade Cooperation and urges States Members of the United Nations and members of the specialized agencies to act with a view to approving the agreement establishing the Organization for Trade Cooperation.

656th plenary meeting
20 February 1957

1318 (XIII). Promotion of the International Flow of Private Capital

Committee: 2
Vote: 69 - 8 - 4
Ref.: 1035(XI), 824(IX)

The General Assembly,

Reaffirming the need for a higher level of capital formation for the economic and social progress of the under-developed countries,

Taking note of the expanding bilateral and multilateral arrangements in the field of capital investment, particularly the establishment of the International Finance Corporation and the prospective increase in the resources of the International Bank for Reconstruction and Development,

Confident that such arrangements contribute to a general improvement in the conditions necessary for an expanding flow of private capital for investment beneficial to under-developed countries,

Taking into account its resolution 824 (IX) of 11 December 1954 on the international flow of private capital for the economic development of under-developed countries, and section B of Economic and Social Council resolution 368 (XIII) of 22 August 1951 concerning the objective of achieving an expansion and steadier flow of private foreign capital,

Welcoming the fact that a growing number of countries have become increasingly conscious of the need to improve the international climate in relation to both existing and prospective private investment,

Stressing the need for increased knowledge and better understanding of the conditions of and opportunities for international investment,

1. *Requests* the Secretary-General to consult as appropriate and obtain the views of qualified persons, drawn from both capital-exporting and capital-importing countries, regarding:

(*a*) The fields of activity in which foreign private investment is needed and sought by under-developed countries and the volume and forms in which such investment would be acceptable;

(*b*) The types of projects - including, where possible, specific examples - which private foreign investors may be interested in financing or undertaking in under-developed countries in suitable circumstances;

2. *Further requests* the Secretary-General, drawing on the views of the qualified persons concerned and taking into account other avail-

able information, to prepare a report concerning measures in operation or contemplated, both in capital-exporting and capital-importing countries, for the channelling of an increasing flow of private capital investment into the development of under-developed countries under mutually satisfactory arrangements;

3. *Invites* the Secretary-General to submit his report to the Economic and Social Council at its twenty-ninth session for transmission, with the Council's recommendations, to the General Assembly for consideration at its fifteenth session.

788th plenary meeting
12 December 1958

1324 (XIII). International Commodity Problems

Committee: 2
Vote: 80 - 1 - 0
Ref.: 1218(XII), 1029(XI), 623(VII)

The General Assembly,

Having in mind the importance of export earnings to the economic development of many countries, in particular the less developed countries, and bearing in mind the fact that changes in the terms of trade have consequences on the economic development of many countries,

Appreciating that a more rapid rate of expansion in the export trade of the less developed countries is of major importance for their soundly based economic development,

Considering the serious problems both of a short-term and a long-term nature which confront many countries, particularly the less developed countries, as a result of excessive fluctuations in the prices of many primary products and of the impact on international trade in such products of protectionism in its varied forms,

Realizing therefore the urgent need for continuing efforts to bring about more assured conditions for commodity trade and a mitigation of the difficulties at present facing many producers of both agricultural and mineral commodities,

Noting Economic and Social Council resolution 691 A (XXVI) of 31 July 1958 reconstituting the Commission on International Commodity Trade,

Recognizing that, as stated in that resolution, the development of specific proposals for possible action by Governments with respect to particular commodities continues to be the responsibility mainly of inter-governmental commodity study groups,

Expressing the hope that the Commission on International Commodity Trade will be able to make a greater contribution to the establishment of more assured conditions for international commodity trade,

Recognizing the increasing attention which Governments are giving to commodity problems as evidenced by the work of the Committee on Commodity Problems of the Food and Agriculture Organization of the United Nations and such developments as the recent establishment of a coffee study group, the meetings on copper, lead and zinc recently convened by the United Nations, the recent renegotiations of the International Sugar Agreement, the discussions taking place toward the renegotiation of the International Wheat Agreement, and the consideration currently being given by the contracting parties to the General Agreement on Tariffs and Trade to the commodity aspects of international trade,

Recognizing further that, for the most part, effective action with respect to given commodities will require the active cooperation of both major producing and major consuming countries in their mutual interests,

Noting with satisfaction the growing tendency of Governments to broaden the scope of international study and discussion of commodity problems to cover not only price instability as such but also its underlying causes economic effects and possible means of dealing with them,

1. *Urges* Governments of Member States to continue to examine, on a commodity-by-commodity basis, the question what measures may be desirable and feasible in offering solutions to particular commodity problems;

2. *Supports* the action taken by the Economic and Social Council under resolution 691 (XXVI) for the purpose of making the Commission on International Commodity Trade more effective, and its decision to convene the Commission early in 1959;

3. *Recommends* that the principal producing and consuming countries give careful consideration to the possibility of becoming parties to or actively cooperating with existing international trading arrangements dealing with the problems of commodity trade;

4. *Expresses the hope* that countries which do not participate in or cooperate with established international trading arrangements will refrain from the use of trade practices generally considered to be unfair which would impede or prevent the satisfactory working of those arrangements;

5. *Appeals* to the Governments of all Member States to increase their efforts to promote conditions favourable to the expansion of international trade and, in relation to their commercial policies and trade practices, to take into account any possible harmful repercussions which they might have, particularly on the trade of under-developed countries.

788th plenary meeting
12 December 1958

1421 (XIV). Strengthening and Development of the World Market and Improvement of the Trade Conditions of the Economically Less Developed Countries

Committee: 2
Vote: 80 - 0 - 1
Ref.: 1519(XV)

The General Assembly,

Guided by the principles set forth in the Charter of the United Nations and wishing to extend international economic cooperation, to bring about full employment and to foster economic and social progress and development,

Considering that world trade is a natural and reliable factor in the development of peaceful relations between States,

Desiring to promote the development and extension of trade, to ease the exchange of goods and to create the stability and welfare essential for peaceful and friendly relations between nations,

I

1. *Recommends* that all Member States should, individually and jointly, continue their efforts to promote and extend mutually beneficial trade between all States, regardless of their economic systems;

2. *Reaffirms its belief* that international organizations concerned with the regulation and development of international trade should continue to contribute to the extension of multilateral world commerce and should facilitate the expansion of trade between States regardless of their economic systems;

3. *Requests* the Secretary-General, taking fully into consideration all the views expressed and proposals submitted on this subject at the present session of the General Assembly, to prepare a report on the ways and means of promoting wider trade cooperation among States, irrespective of their economic systems and stages of development, including, *inter alia*, the consideration of all the arrangements for such cooperation;

4. *Requests* the Secretary-General to submit this report to the Economic and Social Council at its thirtieth session and to the General Assembly at its fifteenth session;

II

1. *Considers* that the United Nations and the specialized agencies concerned should expand the useful work which they are doing in promoting the stabilization of the commodity markets and the development of reciprocally beneficial multilateral trade;

2. *Considers* that it would be desirable to work out, within the United Nations and other appropriate forums, measures to promote the stabilization of the commodity markets and the development of trade between the highly developed and the less developed countries on a reciprocally beneficial and non-discriminatory basis, including, where appropriate, short-, medium- or longterm trade agreements, international commodity agreements and the establishment of international study groups;

3. *Recommends* that the industrially developed and the economically less developed countries should continue to encourage, by means of freely negotiated credit arrangements, the export of machinery and industrial equipment to the less developed countries, without any restriction on the freedom of these countries to buy and sell in the best market.

846th plenary meeting
5 December 1959

1423 (XIV). International Measures to Assist in Offsetting Fluctuations in Commodity Prices

Committee: 2
Vote: 72 - 0 - 9
Ref.: 1829(XVII), 1422(XIV)

The General Assembly,

Recalling its resolution 1324 (XIII) of 12 December 1958 and Economic and Social Council resolution 726 (XXVIII) of 24 July 1959,

Bearing in mind the responsibilities laid upon Member States by the Preamble, by Article 1, paragraph 3, by Article 13, paragraph 1, and by Article 55 of the Charter of the United Nations to promote international cooperation in the economic field, higher standards of living, full employment, and conditions of economic and social progress,

Taking into account the harmful potentialities of the widening gap between the levels of per caput income in developed and under-developed countries,

Having examined the report of the Economic and Social Council on international commodity problems[1] and the report of the Commission on International Commodity Trade on its seventh session,[2] particularly paragraph 62 thereof relating to compensatory financing,

Commending the work programme drawn up by the Commission on International Commodity Trade at its seventh session and approved by the Economic and Social Council,

Considering the necessity of devising means to combat large fluctuations in commodity prices when accompanied by a general fall in the price levels of primary commodities and the rising price levels of manufactured goods, and the resulting decline in the terms of trade against the under-developed countries,

Considering that such fluctuations hamper world trade,

Considering further the repercussions of adverse trade balances on the capacity of the under-developed countries to contribute to their own development,

Recognizing the imperative necessity of urgent and effective measures to enable the under-developed countries to initiate and sustain their development programmes at adequate levels,

1. *Requests* the Secretary-General to appoint a group of not more than seven experts to assist the Commission on International Commodity Trade in its consideration of commodity problems by examining the feasibility of establishing machinery, within the framework of the United Nations, designed to assist in offsetting the effects of large fluctuations in commodity prices on balances of payments, with special reference to compensatory financing, and to submit its report and recommendations to the Commission on International Commodity Trade by its ninth session, and requests the Economic and Social Council to comment on and transmit this report to the General Assembly;

2. *Further requests* the Secretary-General to invite the International Monetary Fund and the Food and Agriculture Organization of the United Nations to participate in the work of the group of experts in a consultative capacity.

846th plenary meeting
5 December 1959

[1] *Official Records of the General Assembly, Fourteenth Session, Supplement No. 3* (A/4143), chapter II, section II.

[2] *Official Records of the Economic and Social Council, Twenty-eighth Session, Supplement No. 6* (E/3225).

1707 (XVI). International Trade as the Primary Instrument for Economic Development

Committee: 2
Vote: 89 - 0
Ref.: 1323(XIII), 830(IX)

The General Assembly,

Recalling its resolutions 623 (VII) of 21 December 1952, 1028 (XI) of 20 February 1957, 1324 (XIII) of 12 December 1958, 1421 (XIV) and 1422 (XIV) of 10 December 1959, and 1519 (XV) and 1520 (XV) of 15 December 1960,

Having considered the report of the Secretary-General entitled "Ways and means of promoting wider trade cooperation among States: trade relations between under-developed and industrially advanced countries"[3] and the comments thereon voiced in the Economic and Social Council,[4] and endorsing Council resolution 846 (XXXII) of 3 August 1961,

Convinced that the economic development of countries must be based primarily on their own efforts through the utilization of all their productive resources,

Affirming that, for these national efforts to achieve their objectives more rapidly, it is essential that countries should ensure the maximum expansion of their trade and an increase in their foreign exchange income as a result of growth in the volume and value of their exports,

Considering that the importance of such an expansion of trade, especially for under-developed countries or for countries which depend on a narrow range of primary commodities, calls for constant attention to protectionist policies which are detrimental to the growth of international trade, with a view to the achievement of an increasing degree of trade liberalization through the modification of those policies and, where surpluses arise, strict adherence to the principles of surplus disposal recommended by the Food and Agriculture Organization of the United Nations[5] in respect of any possible effects on international markets,

Deeming it necessary that the economic policies of regional and sub-regional economic groupings avoid the introduction and facilitate the elimination of obstacles and restrictions which may hamper the necessary expansion of the trade of the developing and under-developed countries or discourage the indispensable growth of their economies,

Observing that the practices of dumping and the unrestricted disposal of accumulated stocks on international markets impede the progress of countries in the process of economic development, distort the most effective structure of their industries, and depress the levels of production and prices of primary commodities and manufactures,

Recognizing that the developing and under-developed countries have in recent years suffered from their unfavourable terms of trade with industrialized countries and that this trend has resulted in a declining share of the developing and under-developed countries in the gains

[3] *Official Records of the Economic and Social Council, Thirty-second Session, Annexes,* agenda items 2 and 5, documents E/3520 and Add.1.

[4] *Official Records of the General Assembly, Sixteenth Session, Supplement No. 3* (A/4820 and Corr.2), paras. 191 and 192.

[5] Food and Agriculture Organization of the United Nations, Commodity Policy Studies, No. 10, *Functions of a World Reserve - Scope and Limitations* (Rome, 1956), appendix III.

from international trade and in a chronic gap between their exports earnings and import requirements for development,

Bearing in mind that the instability in primary commodity trade of the developing and the under-developed countries results in variations in their national incomes, in their export earnings and their foreign exchange earnings, and that this instability may often jeopardize the development plans of many countries, which are designed on a long-term basis;

Noting the efforts made and the progress achieved in the study of systems for compensating for the fluctuations in commodity trade, particularly the report of the Committee of Experts on international compensation for fluctuations in commodity trade and on the establishment of a development insurance fund,[1]

Reaffirming that it is the recognized responsibility of the more highly industrialized countries to make all appropriate efforts to cooperate in accelerating the economic development of the developing and underdeveloped countries,

Considering that a faster rate of economic growth is in the interest of all countries and that the United Nations together with other international bodies, as appropriate, should provide ways and means of finding and furthering effective solutions for achieving this purpose,

1. *Urges* the economically developed Member States to take into due account, when formulating and executing their trade and economic policies, the interests of the developing and under-developed countries by making maximum efforts to create conditions through which they extend to these countries advantages not necessarily requiring full reciprocity to improve their economic situation, and to pursue as a matter of great urgency bilateral, multilateral and/or regional negotiations - including, where appropriate, negotiations conducted under the General Agreement on Tariffs and Trade - to facilitate the necessary expansion of their trade and to attain a satisfactory coordination of efforts in the field of trade towards economic development;

2. *Calls upon* States Members of the United Nations and members of the specialized agencies, and especially upon the more highly industrialized countries and the developed countries belonging to regional and subregional economic groupings:

(*a*) To promote, through individual or collective measures, the expansion of world trade, particularly by avoiding undue protection of their domestic production;

(*b*) To avoid measures detrimental to the prospects of international commodity trade for producers outside their own countries or regions;

(*c*) To make every effort to liberalize the restrictive or discriminatory practices that unnecessarily limit the consumption and importation of commodities, especially those which have undergone maximum processing, from the under-developed and developing countries;

(*d*) To pursue policies which would promote the industrialization of the developing countries and to avoid practices such as dumping and the unrestricted disposal of accumulated stocks that may hamper this process;

3. *Recommends* that the Governments of Member States, in recognition of the profound concern of normal commercial exporters, pursue policies designed to avoid the harmful effects on international markets that may result from the disposal of surpluses and, to this end, strictly adhere to the principles of surplus disposal recommended by the Food and Agriculture Organization of the United Nations;

4. *Commends* the efforts made by the International Monetary Fund to increase its activities with regard to drawings and standby arrangements in helping the less developed countries to meet seasonal and cyclical maladjustments arising from fluctuations in their export earnings, and expresses the hope that such efforts will continue;

5. *Notes with satisfaction* that the Commission on International Commodity Trade, at its tenth session, and, at their joint session, the Commission on International Commodity Trade and the Committee on Commodity Problems of the Food and Agriculture Organization will consider ways and means of solving the problems created by fluctuations in the commodity export earnings of the developing and under-developed countries, and urges the above organs to formulate these sessions specific recommendations in this connexion;

6. *Requests* the Secretary-General to consult Governments of States Members of the United Nations a members of the specialized agencies and ascertain the views on the advisability of holding an international conference on international trade problems relating especially to primary commodity markets and, if they deem such a conference advisable, the topics that might be considered for a provisional agenda;

7. *Further requests* the Secretary-General, on the basis of these consultations, to report to the Economic and Social Council at its thirty-fourth session and to the General Assembly at its seventeenth session.

1084th plenary meeting
19 December 1961

1 *International Compensation for Fluctuations in Commodity Trade* (United Nations publication. Sales No.: 61.II.D.3).

3084 (XXVIII). Reform of the International Monetary System

Committee: 2
Vote: Adopted without a vote
Ref.: 2808(XXVI), 2806(XXVI), 2565(XXIV), 2461(XXIII), 2208(XXI)

The General Assembly,

Recalling its resolution 2806 (XXVI) of 14 December 1971, as well as resolution 84 (III) of 20 May 1972 of the United Nations Conference on Trade and Development,[2]

Noting that the Chairman of the Committee on Reform of the International Monetary System and Related Issues, established by the Board of Governors of the International Monetary Fund, has submitted a report on the present status of the Committee's work and a First Outline of the Reform,

Recognizing that the problems in the monetary, trade and finance fields should be resolved in a coordinated manner, taking into account their interdependence through appropriate consultations as envisaged in the relevant resolutions of the United Nations Conference on Trade and Development, with the full participation of developed and developing countries,

1. *Draws attention* to the danger of harmful disruption of world trade and development, in particular for developing countries, as a result of the continuing uncertainty in the international monetary sphere, and welcomes the intention of the Committee on Reform of the International Monetary System and Related Issues to settle the issues of reform by 31 July 1974;

2. *Stresses* that the reformed monetary system should aim at universality and should take into account the interests of the international community as a whole, thereby assisting in the evolution of a system of world economic relations based on the equality and interest of all countries;

3. *Welcomes* the provisions for full and effective participation of the developing countries in the discussions and in the decision-making process of the reform and emphasizes the role of the Committee on Reform of the International Monetary System and Related Issues as the body fully responsible in all negotiations on the reform;

4. *Recognizes* the need for an appropriate degree of flexibility in the new monetary system to take into account *inter alia*, specifically, the special characteristics and specific structural problems of developing countries;

5. *Invites* the International Monetary Fund to give attention to the concerns of the developing countries, particularly in the forthcoming review of its current quota, and through that, consequentially, voting structure;

6. *Endorses further* examination of proposals for establishing a new fund facility to provide longerterm balance-of-payments finance for developing countries;

2 See *Proceedings of the United Nations Conference on Trade and Development, Third Session,* vol. I, *Report and Annexes* (United Nations publication, Sales No.: E.73.II.D.4), annex I.A.

7. *Recognizes* the need for reviewing the methods of operation of the International Monetary Fund, in particular the terms for both credit repayments and "stand-by" arrangements, the system of compensatory financing, and the terms of the financing of commodity buffer stocks, so as to enable the developing countries to make more effective use of them;

8. *Asserts* the fundamental importance of ensuring that the reformed system should both create conditions and contain arrangements for promoting an increasing flow of real resources from the developed countries to the developing countries;

9. *Recommends* that, within the framework of the reform of the international monetary system, the earliest possible decision should be reached, in accordance with the time-table established by the Committee on Reform of the International Monetary System and Related Issues, on the outstanding issues, including the question of establishing a link between special drawing rights and additional development finance;

10. *Emphasizes* that the additional creation of special drawing rights in an adequate and orderly manner by the International Monetary Fund should be determined on the basis of global liquidity needs;

11. *Agrees* that wherever possible the developing countries will be exempted from import and capital outflow controls for balance-of-payments purposes and that special circumstances of developing countries will be taken into account in assessing controls which these countries feel it necessary to apply;

12. *Welcomes* the decision of the Committee on Reform of the International Monetary System and Related Issues to set up a Technical Group on the Transfer of Real Resources in order to examine in detail specific suggestions for action which could be taken by the Committee in accordance with its mandate so as to promote the flow of real resources from developed to developing countries.

2192nd plenary meeting
6 December 1973

33/196. Protectionism

Committee: 2
Vote: 109 - 1 - 21

The General Assembly,

Recalling its resolutions 3201 (S-VI) and 3202 (S-VI) of 1 May 1974 containing the Declaration and the Programme of Action on the Establishment of the New International Economic Order, 3281 (XXIX) of 12 December 1974 containing the Charter of Economic Rights and Duties of States and 3362 (S-VII) of 16 September 1975 on development and international economic cooperation, as well as the relevant resolutions adopted by the United Nations Conference on Trade and Development at its fourth session, held at Nairobi from 5 to 31 May 1976,[1]

Affirming that the expansion of international trade on an equitable basis should be beneficial to all countries and that trade liberalization in favour of developing countries is an important means of achieving such expansion,

Recognizing the vital importance of export earnings to the economies of the developing countries,

Believing that expansion of the exports of developing countries is an important means of financing their self-sustained growth,

Acknowledging that the accelerated growth of the economies of the developing countries is a key element in the over-all improvement of the world economy,

Noting that increasing projectionist measures aggravate inflation in the developed countries, which is in turn transferred to the developing countries,

Bearing in mind the widespread and growing concern about the growth of protectionism in developed countries against the exports of the developing countries,

1. *Calls upon* the developed countries to adhere strictly to the commitment concerning the standstill on new tariff and non-tariff barriers or intensification of existing ones against the exports of developing countries;

2. *Urges* the developed countries to eliminate speedily all forms of projectionist measures and practices against the exports of developing countries, bearing in mind, *inter alia*, section I.3, paragraph (a) (x), of General Assembly resolution 3202 (S-VI) and section I, paragraph 8, of Assembly resolution 3362 (S-VII);

3. *Calls upon* the developed countries to carry out structural changes with respect to less competitive sectors of their economies with a view to expansion of existing, and creation of new, production capacities in developing countries.

95th plenary meeting
29 January 1979

34/197. Effects of the World Inflationary Phenomenon on the Development Process

Committee: 2
Vote: 112 - 0 - 20
Ref.: 33/155, 32/175, 1830(XVII), 1829(XVII)

The General Assembly,

Recalling its resolutions 2626 (XXV) of 24 October 1970, containing the International Development Strategy for the Second United Nations Development Decade, 3201 (S-VI) and 3202 (S-VI) of 1 May 1974 containing the Declaration and the Programme of Action on the Establishment of a New International Economic Order, 3281 (XXIX) of 12 December 1974 containing the Charter of Economic Rights and Duties of States, and 3362 (S-VII) of 16 September 1975 on development and international economic cooperation,

Recalling its resolutions 34/138 and 34/139 of 14 December 1979 on the global negotiations relating to international economic cooperation for development to deal with raw materials, energy, trade, development and financial and monetary questions,

Recalling its resolution 32/175 of 19 December 1977, in which it requested the Secretary-General of the United Nations Conference on Trade and Development to establish a group of high-level governmental experts to prepare a study of the inflationary phenomenon and to transmit it, together with the comments of the Trade and Development Board, to the General Assembly, so that the Assembly might decide what action should be taken, including the possibility of holding a world conference on inflation,

Recalling its resolution 33/155 of 20 December 1978, in which it, *inter alia*, took note of the report of the Group of High-level Governmental Experts on the Effects of the World Inflationary Phenomenon on the Development Process,[2]

Noting with regret that the United Nations Conference on Trade and Development, at its fifth session did not take a firm decision on international policy measures to combat the world inflationary phenomenon or on the conclusions and recommendations contained in the report of the Group of Experts,

Recalling also Trade and Development Board decision 144 (XVI) of 23 October 1976, entitled "Arrangements to keep under review interrelated problems in the field of international trade and related areas of international economic cooperation, in particular development finance and monetary issues",[3] in which, *inter alia*, the Secretary-General of the United Nations Conference on Trade and Development was requested to keep such problems under continuous review,

---

1 See *Proceedings of the United Nations Conference on Trade and Development, Fourth Session*, vol. I, *Report and Annexes* (United Nations publication, Sales No. E.76.II.D.10 and corrigendum), part one, sect. A.

2 See *Official Records of the Trade and Development Board, Eighteenth Session*, Annexes, document TD/B/764.

3 See *Official Records of the General Assembly, Thirty-first Session, Supplement No. 15* (A/31/15 and Corr.1), vol. II, annex I.

Bearing in mind that deteriorating international economic conditions and the high rates of world inflation are hindering the growth of the economies of all countries, particularly the developing countries,

Bearing in mind also that inflation internationally transmitted to the developing countries is acquiring increasingly alarming proportions,

Recognizing the fundamental interconnexion between inflationary pressures, protectionism, growth, balance-of-payments disequilibrium and the uncontrolled creation of international monetary liquidity,

Taking note of the proposal made by the Government of Iraq concerning the establishment of an international fund to combat the adverse effects of imported inflation on the economies of the developing countries,[1]

1. *Recognizes* that the present world inflationary process seriously affects the economies of the developing countries because, *inter alia*:

(*a*) It has increased the cost of their essential imports, particularly capital goods and manufactures;

(*b*) It has led to instability in the export earnings of their essential commodities;

(*c*) It has caused considerable fluctuations in the exchange rates of the countries with greater trading activity, with resultant adverse effects on world trade, particularly on the exports of the developing countries;

(*d*) It has substantially increased the current account deficit and the debt burden of the developing countries;

(*e*) It has reduced the real value of the flow of official development assistance;

(*f*) It has adversely affected the net flow of real resources, thereby aggravating the trade and development problems of the developing countries;

(*g*) It has reduced the real value of the monetary reserves of the developing countries;

2. *Affirms*, therefore, the urgent need for the implementation of policies, particularly by industrialized countries, to control inflation by, *inter alia*, such measures as elimination of protectionism, fiscal and monetary policies, acceleration of the transfer of real resources to developing countries, structural adjustments and sustained real economic growth;

3. *Requests* the Trade and Development Board, when considering the item entitled "Interdependence of trade problems, development finance and the international monetary system", which it maintains on its agenda by virtue of its decision 144 (XVI), to discuss measures to combat the world inflationary phenomenon with a view to accelerating the real growth of the developing countries and increasing their import capacity in a context of just and stable financial markets;

4. *Requests* the Secretary-General of the United Nations Conference on Trade and Development, with the assistance of experts, if necessary, as envisaged in Trade and Development Board decision 144 (XVI), to prepar a report on this subject for consideration by the Trade and Development Board and subsequently by the General Assembly at its thirty-sixth session.

109th plenary meeting
19 December 1979

46/210. Economic Measures as a Means of Political and Economic Coercion Against Developing Countries

Committee: 2
Vote: 97 - 30 - 9
Ref.: 50/96, 48/168, 44/215, 42/173, 41/165, 40/185, 39/210, 38/197

The General Assembly,

Recalling the relevant principles set forth in the Charter of the United Nations,

Recalling also its resolutions 2625 (XXV) of 24 October 1970, 3201 (S-VI) and 3202 (S-VI) of 1 May 1974, and 3281 (XXIX) of 12 December 1974, containing the Charter of Economic Rights and Duties of States,

Reaffirming article 32 of the Charter of Economic Rights and Duties of States, which declares that no State may use or encourage the use of economic, political or any other type of measures to coerce another State in order to obtain from it the subordination of the exercise of its sovereign rights,

Bearing in mind the general principles governing international trade and trade policies for development contained in the relevant resolutions and rules of the United Nations Conference on Trade and Development and the General Agreement on Tariffs and Trade,

Reaffirming its resolutions 38/197 of 20 December 1983, 39/210 of 18 December 1984, 40/185 of 17 December 1985, 41/165 of 5 December 1986, 42/173 of 11 December 1987 and 44/215 of 22 December 1989, and considering that further work needs to be undertaken in order to implement them,

Gravely concerned that the use of coercive economic measures adversely affects the economy and development efforts of developing countries and has a general negative impact on international economic cooperation and on the world-wide effort to move towards a non-discriminatory, open trading system,

Taking into account the note by the Secretary-General prepared in response to General Assembly resolution 44/215,[2] and his assessment of how to continue his task,

Concerned that the mandate provided in paragraph 6 of resolution 44/215 has not been fully implemented,

1. *Calls upon* the international community to adopt urgent and effective measures to eliminate the use by some developed countries of unilateral economic coercive measures against developing countries with the purpose of exerting, directly or indirectly, coercion on the sovereign decisions of the countries subject to those measures;

2. *Deplores* the fact that some developed countries continue to apply economic measures and, in some cases, have increased their scope and magnitude, as evidenced by trade restrictions, blockades, embargoes, freezing of assets and other economic sanctions incompatible with the Charter of the United Nations;

3. *Calls upon* developed countries to refrain from making use of their predominant position in the international economy to exercise political or economic coercion through the application of economic instruments with the purpose of inducing changes in the economic, political, commercial and social policies of other countries;

4. *Requests* the Secretary-General to pursue fully his mandate as contained in paragraph 6 of resolution 44/215, through the Office of the Director-General for Development and International Economic Cooperation and in close cooperation with the United Nations Conference on Trade and Development;

5. *Also requests* the Secretary-General to report to the General Assembly at its forty-eighth session on the implementation of the present resolution.

79th plenary meeting
20 December 1991

47/171. Privatization in the Context of Economic Restructuring, Economic Growth and Sustainable Development

Committee: 2
Vote: Adopted without a vote
Ref.: 48/180

The General Assembly,

Reaffirming its resolution S-18/3 of 1 May 1990, the annex to which contains the Declaration on International Economic Cooperation, in particular the Revitalization of Economic Growth and Development of the Developing Countries, and its resolution 45/199 of 21 Decem-

---

1 *Ibid., Thirty-fourth Session, Second Committee*, 41st meeting, para 41.

2 A/46/567.

ber 1990, the annex to which contains the International Development Strategy for the Fourth United Nations Development Decade, as well as other relevant United Nations resolutions,

Taking note of the Cartagena Commitment, adopted by the United Nations Conference on Trade and Development at its eighth session,[1] and Trade and Development Board decision 398 (XXXVIII) of 7 May 1992,[2] by which, *inter alia*, the Ad Hoc Working Group on Comparative Experiences with Privatization was established, and looking forward to the contribution of the Ad Hoc Working Group,

Taking note also of Economic and Social Council resolution 1992/36 of 30 July 1992 on privatization and foreign investment in the context of economic restructuring,

Recognizing the sovereign right of each State to decide on the development of its private and public sectors, taking into account the comparative advantages of each sector,

Noting that the private sector plays a positive role in mobilizing resources and promoting economic growth and sustainable development,

Noting also that many countries are attaching growing importance, in the context of their economic restructuring policies, to the privatization of enterprises and the demonopolization and administrative deregulation of economic activities, as well as market-oriented reforms, increased competition, the elimination of price-distorting mechanisms, and open markets, all as a means to increase economic efficiency, growth and sustainable development,

Noting further the difficulties these countries encounter in those policies and that various practical modalities and approaches towards privatization can be considered by them,

1. *Welcomes* the activities being undertaken by relevant organs, organizations and bodies of the United Nations system in supporting national efforts aimed at increasing economic efficiency, growth and sustainable development through privatization, demonopolization, administrative deregulation of economic activities and other relevant policies, and urges them:

(*a*) To support, when requested, the national efforts of countries in implementing privatization, demonopolization, administrative deregulation and other relevant policies in the context of their economic reforms and the opening of their economies;

(*b*) To strengthen their communication and cooperation in supporting the national efforts of countries in privatizing enterprises, demonopolizing and deregulating their economic activities and implementing other relevant policies, and invites the Secretary-General to give due attention to coordination of the United Nations system in this field, through, *inter alia*, the Economic and Social Council and other relevant United Nations bodies;

(*c*) To take into account, in implementing their respective mandates, the work already undertaken by the organs, organizations and bodies of the United Nations system in order to maximize the efficiency of the system, mindful of the ongoing process of restructuring the system;

2. *Calls upon* interested Member States to enhance the exchange of information among themselves and all relevant organs, organizations and bodies of the United Nations system on their activities, programmes and experiences concerning privatization, demonopolization, administrative deregulation and other relevant policies in order to increase the efficiency and coordination of technical cooperation in this field;

3. *Requests* the Secretary-General to improve, within existing resources, research activities on all areas of privatization, demonopolization, administrative deregulation and other relevant policies, to enhance cooperation with national and international research institutions, and to include all pertinent findings in relevant United Nations publications, including the *World Economic Survey*;

4. *Also requests* the Secretary-General to include in his report to the General Assembly at its forty-eighth session, to be submitted pursuant to its resolution 46/166 of 19 December 1991 on entrepreneurship, recommendations for action by the United Nations system in support of the present resolution.

93rd plenary meeting
22 December 1992

1 TD/364, part one, sect. A.

2 See *Official Records of the General Assembly, Forty-seventh Session, Supplement No. 15* (A/47/15), vol. I, sect. II.

47/183. Eighth Session of the United Nations Conference on Trade and Development

Committee: 2
Vote: Adopted without a vote
Ref.: 45/205, 42/175, 41/169, 38/155, 37/208, 36/142, 35/60, 33/154, 32/189, 3216(XXIX), 2904(XXVII), 2820(XXVI), 2725(XXV), 2570(XXIV), 2402(XXII), 2296(XXII), 2206(XXI), 2085(XX), 1995(XIX), 1897(XVII), 1785(XVII)

The General Assembly,

Reaffirming the importance and continued validity of the Declaration on International Economic Cooperation, in particular the Revitalization of Economic Growth and Development of the Developing Countries,[3] the International Development Strategy for the Fourth United Nations Development Decade,[4] the United Nations New Agenda for the Development of Africa in the 1990s,[5] the Programme of Action for the Least Developed Countries for the 1990s,[6] and the various agreements, especially Agenda 21,[7] that were adopted during the process of the United Nations Conference on Environment and Development,

Recalling its resolution 1995 (XIX) of 30 December 1964, as amended,[8] on the establishment of the United Nations Conference on Trade and Development as an organ of the General Assembly, and its resolution 45/261 of 3 May 1991, in which it decided to convene the eighth session of the Conference at Cartegena de Indias, Colombia, from 8 to 25 February 1992,

Having considered the final documents adopted by the United Nations Conference on Trade and Development at its eighth session, in particular the Declaration and the document entitled "A New Partnership for Development: The Cartagena Commitment",[9] and noting with satisfaction the highly successful outcome of the eighth session of the Conference and the spirit of genuine cooperation and solidarity - the Spirit of Cartagena - that emerged therefrom,

Expressing its deep gratitude to the Government and the people of Colombia for the hospitality extended to the participants at the eighth session of the United Nations Conference on Trade and Development and for facilities for holding the session,

Noting the importance of follow-up and of keeping under review the implementation of the policies and measures adopted by the United Nations Conference on Trade and Development at its eighth session,

Emphasizing that the concerns of the international community about the current world economic situation, trade and development issues, and the difficulties of many countries in achieving satisfactory rates of development deserve continuing attention, in particular as far as the developing countries are concerned,

Reaffirming, in this context, the need to give priority to problems facing the least developed countries owing to the fragility of their economies and their particular vulnerability to external shocks and natural calamities,

3 Resolution S-18/3, annex.

4 Resolution 45/199, annex.

5 Resolution 46/151, annex, sect. II.

6 *Report of the Second United Nations Conference on the Least Developed Countries. Paris. 3-14 September 1990* (A/CONF.147/18), part one.

7 *Report of the United Nations Conference on Environment and Development. Rio de Janeiro. 3-14 June 1992* (A/CONF.151/26), chap I, resolution 1, annex II.

8 See resolutions 2904 (XXVII), 31/2 A and B and 34/3.

9 TD/364, part one, sect. A.

Reiterating that the Uruguay Round of multilateral trade negotiations should result in a substantial and balanced outcome in all areas involved, and expressing concern that those negotiations have not yet been completed but hopeful that they will come to a successful conclusion rapidly, taking into account the specific interests of developing countries,

I

1. *Endorses* the outcome of the eighth session of the United Nations Conference on Trade and Development, in particular the commitments agreed upon, and emphasizes the importance of the New Partnership for Development, initiated by the Conference at that session, where countries will join actively in cooperative work to address the development challenges of the 1990s, and expresses its political will and responsibility to implement the agreed commitments;

2. *Welcomes* the far-reaching institutional reform measures adopted by the Conference at its eighth session regarding the functions, intergovernmental machinery, methods of work and substantive orientations of the United Nations Conference on Trade and Development, and agrees that those measures are a valuable contribution to the process of restructuring the economic and social sectors of the United Nations launched by the General Assembly;

3. *Reaffirms* the important role of the United Nations Conference on Trade and Development, as a principal organ of the General Assembly in the field of trade and development and as the most appropriate focal point within the United Nations proper for the integrated treatment of development and interrelated issues in key areas, including trade, commodities, finance, investment, services and technology, in the interests of all countries, particularly those of developing countries;

4. *Welcomes* the agreement by the United Nations Conference on Trade and Development to refocus its substantive work on four areas, namely, a new partnership for development, global interdependence, paths to development and sustainable development, which should serve as orientations for developing both fresh approaches to long-standing issues and insights for pursuing relevant new lines of work, and acknowledges the efforts that have been made in this respect and encourages further efforts in this regard;

5. *Also welcomes* the high priority given by the United Nations Conference on Trade and Development to commodities, poverty alleviation, services development, economic cooperation among developing countries, investment and financial flows, privatization, trading opportunities for developing countries, investment and technology transfers, and trade efficiency;

6. *Stresses* the important contribution that the United Nations Conference on Trade and Development can make to sustainable development in the context of the implementation of Agenda 21, *inter alia*, on trade-related issues, and, in this context, requests the Conference to work closely with the Commission on Sustainable Development;

7. *Invites* all organs, organizations and bodies of the United Nations system to respond positively to the requests addressed to them in the relevant parts of the commitments of the United Nations Conference on Trade and Development at its eighth session;

II

8. *Takes note* of the reports of the Trade and Development Board on the second part of its thirty-eighth session[1] and the first part of its thirty-ninth session[2] and calls upon all States to take appropriate action to implement the outcome of those sessions;

9. *Expresses its satisfaction* with the action initiated by the Trade and Development Board for the implementation of the new institutional arrangements and of the substantive orientations agreed upon by the United Nations Conference on Trade and Development, and welcomes Trade and Development Board decision 398 (XXXVIII) of 7 May 1992 on the follow-up to the recommendations adopted by the Conference at its eighth session;[3]

10. *Takes* note of the agreement by the United Nations Conference on Trade and Development at its eighth session to suspend the existing Committees of the Trade and Development Board, with the exception of the Special Committee on Preferences and the Intergovernmental Group of Experts on Restrictive Business Practices;

11. *Endorses* the establishment and the terms of reference of the new standing committees and of the new *ad hoc* working groups, as contained in the annex to Trade and Development Board decision 398 (XXXVIII), as well as the convening of executive sessions of the Board aimed at strengthening its policy function;

12. *Takes note* of Trade and Development Board decision 399 (XXXIX) of 9 October 1992 on the establishment of an *ad hoc* working group to explore the issue of structural adjustment for the transition to disarmament;[4]

13. *Welcomes* the streamlining and strengthening of the intergovernmental machinery of the United Nations Conference on Trade and Development and the improvement of methods of work aimed at providing an enriched substantive and technical basis for the functions of the Conference, as agreed at its eighth session;

14. *Endorses* the convening in 1994, within existing resources, of a United Nations international symposium of one week's duration on trade efficiency, and requests the Secretary-General of the United Nations Conference on Trade and Development to make all the necessary arrangements for that symposium, taking into account the preparatory work of the Ad Hoc Working Group on Trade Efficiency of the United Nations Conference on Trade and Development;

15. *Takes note* of the valuable contribution made by the Trade and Development Board, underpinned by the Trade and Development Report, 1992,[5] to the understanding of the international implications of macroeconomic policies and issues concerning global interdependence, with particular reference to the recent evolution of development problems and prospects, and welcomes the outcome of the deliberations of the Board on this matter;

16. *Also takes note* of the recognition on the part of the United Nations Conference on Trade and Development at its eighth session and of the Trade and Development Board that Governments should consider, as part of fighting protectionism and as appropriate, the establishment of transparent mechanisms at the national level;

III

17. *Calls upon* the international community to assist in promoting measures necessary for the revitalization of the development process in the developing countries, in pursuit of the objective of revitalizing international trade, sustained economic growth and development;

18. *Urges* all countries to fulfil their commitments to halt and reverse protectionism and to reach a final agreement on the remaining issues of the Uruguay Round, and reaffirms that the balanced and comprehensive conclusion of the multilateral trade negotiations is crucial and is needed in order to strengthen the rules and disciplines of the international trading system and significantly enhance the prospects for trade, economic growth and development of all countries, especially developing countries.

93rd plenary meeting
22 December 1992

---

1 *Official Records of the General Assembly, Forty-seventh Session, Supplement No. 15* (A/47/15), vol. I.

2 *Ibid.*, vol. II.

3 *Ibid.*, vol. I. chap. II.

4 *Ibid.*, vol. II, chap. II, sect. B.8.

5 United Nations publication, Sales No. E.92.II.D.7.

49/104. Commodities

Committee: 2
Vote: Adopted without a vote
Ref.: 48/214, 47/185, 45/200, 44/218, 41/168, 38/156, 37/211, 36/143

The General Assembly,

Reaffirming its resolutions 45/200 of 21 December 1990, 47/185 of 22 December 1992 and 48/214 of 23 December 1993, and stressing the urgent need of their full implementation,

Welcoming the importance attached in Agenda 21,[1] adopted by the United Nations Conference on Environment and Development, to issues related to commodities in the context of sustainable development,

Recalling the commitments on market access made in the Final Act of the Uruguay Round of Multilateral Trade Negotiations[2] and the importance attached therein to increased export opportunities for developing countries,

Recognizing that in many developing countries, in particular African countries and least developed countries, the commodity sector remains the principal source of export revenues, employment, income and savings, an important field for investment and a significant contributor to the reactivation of growth and development,

Noting the recent increase of some commodity prices, recognizing that this may not constitute a long-term trend, and recognizing also the need for a better functioning of commodity markets and the necessity of stable and more predictable commodity prices, including avoiding excessive price fluctuations and searching for long-term solutions to commodity problems,

Concerned about the difficulties experienced by the developing countries in financing and implementing viable diversification programmes,

Mindful of the need for developing countries, especially African countries and least developed countries, to diversify their economies and in particular the commodity sector, with a view to modernizing their production, distribution and marketing systems, enhancing productivity and stabilizing and increasing their export earnings in the context of the general decline of primary commodity prices,

1. *Takes note with interest* of the report of the Secretary-General of the United Nations Conference on Trade and Development on the commodity situation, developmental linkages between the commodity sector and other sectors and actions required to develop such linkages in the context of diversification;[3]

2. *Emphasizes* the need for developing countries that are heavily dependent on primary commodities to continue to promote a domestic policy and an institutional environment that encourage diversification and enhance competitiveness;

3. *Expresses* the urgent need for supportive international policies to improve the functioning of commodity markets through efficient and transparent price formation mechanisms, including commodity exchanges, and through the use of commodity price risk management instruments;

4. *Notes* the need expressed by developing countries, in particular the commodity-dependent developing countries, for stable and more predictable commodity prices;

5. *Stresses* the importance of commodity diversification as a means to increase export revenues of developing countries and to improve their competitiveness in the face of the persistent instability in the prices of some primary commodities and the general deterioration in the terms of trade;

6. *Urges* developed countries to continue to support the commodity diversification efforts of developing countries, especially African countries, *inter alia*, by providing technical and financial assistance for the preparatory phase of their commodity diversification programmes;

7. *Reiterates* the importance of maximizing the contribution of the commodity sector to economic growth and sustainable development in commodity- dependent developing countries, and in this respect stresses, *inter alia*, that:

(*a*) An appropriate domestic environment and favourable international environment are critical for successful diversification and the creation of developmental linkages between the commodity sector and other sectors of the economy, as well as for the availability of market outlets;

(*b*) Trade-distorting policies and practices, including tariff and non-tariff barriers, tariff escalation and obstacles to competition, have a negative effect on the ability of developing countries to diversify their exports and to undertake the requisite restructuring of their commodity sector;

(*c*) Expansion of South-South trade in commodities offers opportunities for intersectoral linkages within and among exporting countries;

(*d*) There is a need to promote research and development, to provide infrastructure and support services and to encourage investment, including joint ventures in developing countries engaged in the commodity and commodity- processing sectors;

8. *Emphasizes* the importance for developing countries to process a significant part of their commodities, and in this regard stresses the need for new market opportunities for their processed and semi-processed commodities;

9. *Expresses* the need for the full implementation of the Uruguay Round agreement,[4] taking into account the special and differential treatment agreed for developing countries, including the provisions envisaged for African countries and the least developed countries;

10. *Welcomes* the work being done by the United Nations Conference on Trade and Development on the impact of the results of the Uruguay Round on individual commodities of particular interest to developing countries and invites the Secretary-General of the United Nations Conference on Trade and Development to intensify this exercise in close collaboration with the executive secretaries of the regional commissions and other concerned organizations;

11. *Notes with appreciation* the work under way by the Food and Agriculture Organization of the United Nations in assessing the impact of the Uruguay Round on agricultural commodity markets, and encourages the Organization to pursue its work and to inform the General Assembly of its findings;

12. *Urges* producers and consumers of individual commodities to intensify their efforts aimed at reinforcing mutual cooperation and assistance;

13. *Welcomes* the assignment to the United Nations Conference on Trade and Development of the United Nations global mandate for mineral resources, and urges that efforts be made to mobilize financial resources to allow the Conference, in close collaboration with the regional commissions, to expand its technical assistance to developing countries in that area;

14. *Also welcomes* the decision of the Standing Committee on Commodities of the Trade and Development Board, urging the secretariat of the United Nations Conference on Trade and Development to continue its work on commodity risk management, particularly in relation to developing countries;

15. *Stresses* the importance of improving the competitiveness of natural products with environmental advantages and the impact that this could have on promoting sustainable consumption and production patterns, and calls for financial and technical assistance to the

---

1 *Report of the United Nations Conference on Environment and Development, Rio de Janeiro, 3-14 June 1992,* (A/CONF.151/26/Rev.1 (Vol. I and Vol. I/Corr.1, Vol. II, Vol. III and Vol. III/Corr.1)) (United Nations publication, Sales No. E.93.I.8 and corrigenda), vol. I, Resolutions Adopted by the Conference, resolution 1, annex II.

2 See *Legal Instruments Embodying the Results of the Uruguay Round of Multilateral Trade Negotiations, done at Marrakesh on 15 April 1994* (GATT secretariat publication, Sales No. GATT/1994-7), vol. 1.

3 A/49/226.

4 *Legal Instruments Embodying the Results of the Uruguay Round of Multilateral Trade Negotiations, done at Marrakesh on 15 April 1994* (GATT secretariat publication, Sales No. GATT/1994-7).

developing countries for research and development of such products;

16. *Notes* the increased number of requests for assistance that the Second Account of the Common Fund for Commodities is receiving, expresses the need for efficient allocation of the existing resources, and also notes the expectations expressed by member countries of the Fund that further voluntary contributions will be forthcoming;

17. *Decides* to include the question of commodities in the provisional agenda of its fifty-first session.

92nd plenary meeting
19 December 1994

49/106. Integration of the Economies in Transition into the World Economy

Committee: 2
Vote: Adopted without a vote
Ref.: 48/181, 47/187

The General Assembly,

Reaffirming its resolutions 47/175 and 47/187 of 22 December 1992 and 48/181 of 21 December 1993 and all its other relevant resolutions,

Taking note of the relevant decisions of the Economic Commission for Europe, namely, decisions B (49) and C (49) of 26 April 1994,[1] and the relevant resolutions of the Economic and Social Commission for Asia and the Pacific, namely, 50/1 and 50/2 of 13 April 1994,[2]

Taking note also of the report of the Secretary-General,[3] the Economic Survey of Europe in 1993-1994,[4] the Economic and Social Survey of Asia and the Pacific, 1993[5] and the World Economic and Social Survey, 1994,[6]

Noting the ongoing efforts of the International Monetary Fund and the World Bank to encourage sound macroeconomic policies,

Reaffirming the need for the full integration of countries in transition from centrally planned to market economies, as well as all other countries, into the world economy, which is essential to sustainable development,

1. *Invites* the United Nations system to continue its support for the efforts of economies in transition as they transform their economies and integrate them into the world economy through, *inter alia*, adoption of the international standards and practices of countries with market economies;

2. *Welcomes* the measures undertaken by the United Nations system to strengthen its abilities in response to resolution 48/181 on the economies in transition, and calls upon the United Nations system to continue to conduct analytical activities and to provide policy advice and technical assistance to the economies in transition, tailored to each country's respective stage of economic transformation;

3. *Calls upon* the United Nations system to continue studying, within the scope of the implementation of the present resolution and while continuing the existing cooperation with relevant international institutions and entities, possible ways of enhancing economic and technical cooperation among countries with economies in transition, as well as with developing countries, identifying how the United Nations system can strengthen cooperation while avoiding duplication, with a view to encouraging greater participation by those countries in the world economy;

4. *Requests* the Secretary-General to submit a report on the implementation of the present resolution to the General Assembly at its fifty-first session.

92nd plenary meeting
19 December 1994

---

1 See *Official Records of the Economic ans Social Council, 1994, Supplement No. 17* (E/1994/37), chap. IV.

2 *Ibid., Supplement No. 16* (E/1994/36), chap. IV.

3 A/49/330.

4 *United Nations publication,* Sales No. E.94.II.E.1.

5 *United Nations publication,* Sales No. E.94.II.F.8.

6 *United Nations publication,* Sales No. E.94.II.C.1 and corrigendum.

50/92. Enhancing International Cooperation Towards a Durable Solution to the External Debt Problem of Developing Countries

Committee: 2
Vote: Adopted without a vote
Ref.: 49/94, 48/182, 47/198, 46/138, 45/214, 44/205, 43/198, 42/198, 41/202, 39/176, 33/159, 32/187, 31/158

The General Assembly,

Recalling its resolutions 41/202 of 8 December 1986, 42/198 of 11 December 1987, 43/198 of 20 December 1988, 44/205 of 22 December 1989, 45/214 of 21 December 1990, 46/148 and 46/151 of 18 December 1991 and 47/198 of 22 December 1992, and reaffirming its resolutions 48/182 of 21 December 1993 and 49/94 of 19 December 1994,

Reaffirming its resolution 48/165 of 21 December 1993 on the renewal of the dialogue on strengthening international economic cooperation for development through partnership and 48/166 of 21 December 1993 on an agenda for development,

Noting the improvement in the debt situation of a number of developing countries since the second half of the 1980s and the contribution that the evolving debt strategy has made to this improvement,

Noting with appreciation the debt-relief measures undertaken by creditor countries both within the framework of the Paris Club and through their cancellation and equivalent relief of bilateral official debt, and welcoming the even more favourable terms of the debt-relief measures recently envisaged by the Paris Club, namely the Naples terms of December 1994, for the poorest and heavily indebted countries, to help them exit from the rescheduling process, thus contributing to the prospects of those countries for resuming growth and development,

Reaffirming the urgent need for effective, equitable, development-oriented and durable solutions to the external debt and debt-servicing problems of developing countries, and to help them exit from the rescheduling process,

Emphasizing the importance for debtor countries of continuing to pursue and intensify their efforts with respect to economic reforms, stabilization and structural adjustment programmes, in order to raise savings and investments, reduce inflation and improve economic efficiency, taking into account the need to address the social aspects of development, including the eradication of poverty, and their individual characteristics, as well as the vulnerability of the poorer strata of their populations,

Stressing the urgent need for further assisting developing countries, in particular the poorest and heavily indebted countries, especially in Africa, in their efforts to improve their debt situation in view of their continued very high level of total debt stock and servicing burdens,

Noting the urgent need for full, constructive and expeditious implementation of various debt-relief measures undertaken by creditor countries both within the framework of the Paris Club and through their cancellations and equivalent relief of bilateral official debt,

Noting also that, owing to uneven developments within the context of the evolving international debt strategy, further progress, including new and concrete measures and innovative approaches, is essential as regards contributing to effective, equitable, development-oriented and durable solutions to the external debt and debt-servicing problems of developing countries, particularly the poorest and heavily indebted countries,

Noting with concern the continuing debt and debt-servicing problems of indebted developing countries as constituting an element adversely affecting their development efforts and economic growth, and stressing the importance of alleviating the onerous debt and debt-service burdens connected with various types of debt of many developing countries, on the basis of an effective, equitable, development-oriented and durable approach and, where appropriate, addressing the full stock of debt of the poorest and most indebted developing countries as a matter of priority,

Noting that multilateral lending operations are excluded from debt restructuring and, in this regard, emphasizing the need for the consideration of comprehensive approaches to assist low-income countries with substantial multilateral debt problems through the flexible implementation of existing instruments and new mechanisms where necessary,

Expressing its concern that, in a number of developing countries that are making continuous and strenuous economic reform efforts, the burden of debt and debt service continues to constitute a major obstacle to the revitalization of the economic growth and development of those countries, in particular the least developed among them,

Noting that those developing countries that have continued, at great cost to themselves, to meet their international debt and debt-service obligations in a timely fashion have done so despite serious external and domestic financial constraints,

Expressing its concern that debt-relief measures taken so far have not yet fully provided effective, equitable, development-oriented and durable solutions to the outstanding debt and debt-servicing problems of a large number of developing countries, in particular the poorest and heavily indebted countries,

Reaffirming the results, as agreed, of all major United Nations conferences and summits held since the beginning of the 1990s on development, relating to effective, equitable, development-oriented and durable solutions to the external debt and debt-servicing problems of developing countries, as well as the consideration of appropriate measures relating to the mobilization of substantial, new and additional resources to enable developing countries to achieve sustained economic growth and sustainable development,

Noting, while addressing the external debt and debt-servicing problems of developing countries, the situation in some creditor countries with economies in transition,

Stressing the need for continuing global economic growth and the necessity for a continuing supportive international economic environment with regard to, *inter alia,* terms of trade, commodity prices, improved market access, trade practices, access to technology, exchange rates and international interest rates, and noting the continued need for resources for sustained economic growth and sustainable development of the developing countries,

Taking note of the results of the Eleventh Conference of Heads of State or Government of the Non-Aligned Countries, held at Cartagena de Indias, Colombia, from 18 to 20 October 1995, in particular, chapter m, entitled "Economic issues", of the Final Document of the Conference,

Taking note also of the communiqué of the Summit of the seven major industrialized countries,[1] held at Halifax, Canada, from 15 to 17 June 1995,

Taking note further of the communiqué of the Interim Committee of the Board of Governors of the International Monetary Fund, held at Washington, D.C., on 8 October 1995,

Taking note further of the Ministerial Declaration of the Group of 77[2] adopted at the nineteenth annual meeting of Ministers for Foreign Affairs of the Group of 77 and China, held in New York on 29 September 1995,

1. *Takes note* of the report of the Secretary-General on the developing country debt situation as of mid-1995;[3]

2. *Recognizes* that effective, equitable, development-oriented and durable solutions to the external debt and debt-servicing problems of developing countries can contribute substantially to the strengthening of the global economy and to the efforts of developing countries to achieve sustained economic growth and sustainable development;

3. *Also recognizes* that the evolving international debt strategy has to be supplemented by appropriate external financial flows to indebted developing countries;

4. *Emphasizes* the importance for developing countries of continuing their efforts to promote a favourable environment for attracting foreign investment, thereby promoting economic growth and sustainable development, and stresses the need for the international community to promote a conducive external economic environment through, *inter alia,* improved market access, stabilization of exchange rates, effective stewardship of international interest rates and increased resource flows, as well as improved access to technology for the developing countries;

5. *Stresses* the need for finding effective, equitable, development-oriented and durable solutions to the continuing debt and debt-servicing problems of the poorest and most indebted developing countries and the importance of a full, constructive and expeditious implementation of the Naples terms, agreed upon in the Paris Club in December 1994, for such countries, with a view to helping them exit from the rescheduling process on the basis of sound economic policies in those countries, thus contributing to the promotion of their prospects for resuming growth and development;

6. *Recognizes* the efforts of indebted developing countries in fulfilling their commitments on debt servicing despite the incurring of a high social cost and, in this regard, encourages private creditors and, in particular, commercial banks to continue their initiatives and efforts to address the commercial debt problems of middle-income developing countries;

7. *Invites* creditor countries, private banks and multilateral financial institutions, within their prerogatives, to consider continuing the initiatives and efforts to address the commercial debt problems of the least developed countries and the requests for continued mobilization of resources through the Debt-reduction Facility of the International Development Association in order to help eligible least developed countries reduce their commercial debt;

8. *Notes* the high proportion of multilateral debt of a number of developing countries and invites international financial institutions to examine proposals to tackle the problems of those countries with regard to multilateral debt, taking into account the specific situation of each country, while preserving the preferred creditor status of the multilateral financial institutions, in order to ensure that they can continue to provide concessional financing to those developing countries to assist their development;

9. *Reaffirms* the mid-term global review of the implementation of the Programme of Action for the Least Developed Countries for the 1990s, in particular the appropriate actions in favour of least developed countries concerning their official bilateral, commercial and multilateral debt;

10. *Notes with concern* the continuing burden of debt and debt-service obligations of middle-income countries, including in particular those in Africa, and encourages creditors, including multilateral financial institutions and commercial banks, to continue to address their obligations effectively;

11. *Stresses* the importance of continued concessional Enhanced Structural Adjustment Facility lending operations for low-income countries;

12. *Also stresses* the need for existing facilities to provide debt-relief measures through various debt conversion programmes, where possible, such as debt-equity swaps, debt-for-nature swaps, debt-for-child-development swaps, and other debt-for-development swaps, to be widely implemented so that the countries concerned may be ably assisted in their development efforts, as well as to support measures in favour of the most vulnerable segments of the societies of those countries and to develop techniques of debt conversion applied to social development programmes and projects, in conformity with the priorities of the World Summit for Social Development, held at Copenhagen in March 1995;

13. *Further stresses* the need for, in addition to debt-relief measures that include debt and debt-service reduction, new financial flows to debtor developing countries, and urges creditor countries and multilateral financial institutions to continue to extend concessional financial assistance, particularly to the least developed countries, in order to support the implementation of economic reforms, stabilization and structural adjustment programmes and the eradication of poverty by the developing countries so as to enable them to extricate themselves from the debt overhang and to assist them in achieving sustained economic growth and sustainable development;

---

1 A/50/254-S/1995/501, annex I.

2 A/50/518, annex.

3 A/50/379 and Corr.1.

14. *Further stresses* the need for the expeditious conclusion of the ongoing work of the International Monetary Fund, in close collaboration with the World Bank, on the steps to address the problems of those low-income countries that are undertaking strong adjustment and reform programmes but whose debt situation, including debt to multilateral institutions, may prove unsustainable, even after debt reduction on the Naples terms, within this context urging donor countries to fulfil promptly their commitments to the tenth replenishment of the International Development Association and to support a significant replenishment through the eleventh replenishment of the Association, and requests the Secretary-General to report to the General Assembly at its fifty-first session on the outcome of the meeting of the Development Committee scheduled for April 1996;

15. *Notes* the initiative to develop new, parallel financing arrangements, complementary to the General Arrangements to Borrow, with the aim of doubling the resources currently available under the General Arrangements to Borrow;

16. *Recognizes* that the evolving debt strategy must be accompanied by a favourable and supportive international environment, including the full implementation of the results of the Uruguay Round of multilateral trade negotiations, and the Marrakesh ministerial decisions in favour of the least developed countries and net food importing developing countries;[1]

17. *Invites* the International Monetary Fund to continue devising concrete policy measures and actions to address the problems faced by indebted developing countries;

18. *Underscores* the need for encouragement of private flows to all countries, in particular developing countries, while reducing the risks of volatility;

19. *Stresses* the urgent need to continue to provide social safety nets to vulnerable groups most adversely affected by the implementation of economic reform programmes in the debtor countries, in particular low-income groups;

20. *Urges* the international community, particularly the creditor countries and multilateral institutions, as well as commercial banks and other lending institutions, when continuing the implementation of various measures aimed at contributing to the effective, equitable, development-oriented and durable solutions to the external debt and debt-servicing problems of developing countries, as well as when exploring the need for additional and innovative measures to alleviate substantially the external debt and debt-service burden of developing countries, to ensure that the debt strategy evolved through the years is fully implemented and taken into account;

21. *Recognizes* the urgent need for the international community to assist developing countries, in particular the poorest and heavily indebted countries, in mobilizing the resources needed for their development efforts, and also recognizes that effective, equitable, development-oriented and durable solutions to the external debt and debt-servicing problems of developing countries could contribute towards releasing domestic resources and sustaining their development efforts, in particular those for social development;

22. *Calls upon* the international community, including the relevant institutions, to build upon the momentum gained from the various meetings that have addressed debt issues and to address the external debt and debt-servicing problems of developing countries, particularly those of the least developed countries, in the elaboration of an agenda for development;

23. *Also calls upon* the international community, including the United Nations system, and invites the Bretton Woods institutions, as well as the private sector, to take urgent measures and action for the implementation of the commitments, agreements and decisions of the major United Nations conferences and summits organized since the beginning of the 1990s on development, addressing, *inter alia*, and where appropriate, the question of external debt;

24. *Requests* the Secretary-General to report to the General Assembly at its fifty-first session on the implementation of the present resolution.

96th plenary meeting
20 December 1995

1 See *Legal Instruments Embodying the Results of the Uruguay Round of Multilateral Trade Negotiations, done at Marrakesh on 15 April 1994* (GATT secretariat publication, Sales No. GATT/1994-7).

50/95. International Trade and Development

Committee: 2
Vote: Adopted without a vote
Ref.: 49/99, 48/055, 46/209, 45/203, 40/189, 39/214, 3459(XXX), 3308(XXIX), 3215(XXIX), 2177(XXI)

The General Assembly,

Reaffirming the Declaration on International Economic Cooperation, in particular the Revitalization of Economic Growth and Development of the Developing Countries,[2] the International Development Strategy for the Fourth United Nations Development Decade,[3] the United Nations New Agenda for the Development of Africa in the 1990s,[4] the Programme of Action for the Least Developed Countries for the 1990s,[5] the Cartagena Commitment,[6] Agenda 21,[7] and the various agreements and conferences that provide an overall policy framework for sustained economic growth and sustainable development to address the challenges of the 1990s,

Recalling its resolutions 1995 (XIX) of 30 December 1964, as amended,[8] on the establishment of the United Nations Conference on Trade and Development as an organ of the General Assembly, 47/183 of 22 December 1992 on the eighth session of the Conference, and 48/55 of 10 December 1993 and 49/99 of 19 December 1994 on international trade and development,

Welcoming the appointment of the Secretary-General of the United Nations Conference on Trade and Development,

Noting the progress made by the United Nations Conference on Trade and Development in the implementation of the outcome of its eighth session, in particular its contribution, within its mandate, to trade and development,

Emphasizing the importance of an open, rule-based, equitable, secure, non-discriminatory, transparent and predictable multilateral trading system,

Emphasizing also that a favourable and conducive international economic and financial environment and a positive investment climate are necessary for the economic growth of the world economy, including the creation of employment, in particular for the sustained economic growth and sustainable development of the developing countries, and emphasizing further that each country is responsible for its own economic policies for development,

Welcoming the successful conclusion of the Uruguay Round of multilateral trade negotiations at the Ministerial Meeting of the Trade Negotiations Committee, held at Marrakesh, Morocco, from 12 to 15 April 1994, and noting that the Uruguay Round agreements[9] represent a historic achievement, which is expected to contribute to strengthening the world economy and to lead to more trade, investment, employment and income growth throughout the world and in

2 Resolution S-18/3, annex.

3 Resolution 45/199, annex.

4 Resolution 46/151, annex, sect. II.

5 *Report of the Second United Nations Conference on the Least Developed Countries, Paris, 3-14 September 1990*(A/CONF.147/18), part one.

6 See *Proceedings of the United Nations Conference on Trade and Development, Eighth Session, Report and Annexes* (United Nations publication, Sales No. E.93.II.D.5),part one, sect. A.

7 *Report of the United Nations Conference on Environment and Development, Rio de Janeiro, 3-14 June 1992. Resolutions Adopted by the Conference* (United Nations publication, Sales No. E.93.I.8 and corrigendum), vol. I, resolution 1, annex II.

8 See resolutions 2904 A (XXVII), 31/2 A and B and 34/3.

9 *Legal Instruments Embodying the Results of the Uruguay Round of Multilateral Trade Negotiations, done at Marrakesh on 15 April 1994* (GATT secretariat publication, Sales No. GATT/1994-7).

particular to the promotion of sustained economic growth and sustainable development, especially in the developing countries,

Emphasizing the importance of strengthening and attaining a greater universality of the international trading system and welcoming the process directed towards the accession to the World Trade Organization of economies in transition and developing countries that are not members of the General Agreement on Tariffs and Trade, thereby contributing to their rapid and full integration into the multilateral trading system,

Noting the assessment and recommendations adopted at the Mid-term Global Review of the Implementation of the Programme of Action for the Least Developed Countries for the 1990s, held in New York from 25 September to 6 October 1995,

Noting also that the Uruguay Round agreements should lead, *inter alia,* to a substantial liberalization of international trade, the strengthening of multilateral rules and disciplines to ensure more stability and predictability in trade relations, and the establishing of rules and disciplines in new areas, and noting further the founding of a new institutional framework in the form of the World Trade Organization, with an integrated dispute settlement mechanism which should prevent the application of unilateral actions against international trade rules,

Recognizing that the developing countries have made a major contribution to the success of the Uruguay Round, in particular by accepting the challenges of trade liberalization reforms and measures, and stressing that there is a need for positive efforts designed to ensure that developing countries, especially the least developed among them, secure a share in the growth in international trade commensurate with their economic development needs,

Recognizing also that the subregional and regional economic integration processes, including those among developing countries, which have intensified in recent years, impart substantial dynamism to global trade and enhance trade and development possibilities for all countries, and stressing that, in order to maintain the positive aspects of such integration arrangements and to assure the prevalence of their dynamic growth effects, Member States and groupings should be outward oriented and supportive of the multilateral trading system,

Expressing concern about possible adverse effects for the least developed countries, particularly those in Africa and net food importing developing countries, arising from the implementation of the Uruguay Round agreements, as agreed in the Final Act Embodying the Results of the Uruguay Round of Multilateral Trade Negotiations,[1] signed at Marrakesh, and recognizing the need to assist those disadvantaged developing countries so that they benefit fully from the implementation of the Uruguay Round,

Welcoming the generous offer of the Government of South Africa to act as host for the ninth session of the United Nations Conference on Trade and Development,

Recognizing the role of the United Nations Conference on Trade and Development in identifying and analysing new and emerging issues in the international trade agenda in accordance with agreed conclusions 410 (XL) of 29 April 1994 of the Trade and Development Board on the Uruguay Round,[2] agreed conclusions 419 (XLI) of 30 September 1994 of the Board on the Uruguay Round,[3] and decision 426 (XLII) of 4 May 1995 of the Board,[4] and with the provisional agenda for the ninth session of the United Nations Conference on Trade and Development,[5]

Noting the importance of the inaugural Ministerial Conference of the World Trade Organization, to be held in Singapore in December 1996,

Stressing the need to promote, facilitate and finance, as appropriate, access to and the transfer of environmentally sound technologies and the corresponding know-how in particular to the developing countries, on favourable terms, including concessional and preferential terms, as mutually agreed, taking into account the need to protect intellectual property rights, as well as the special needs of the developing countries in the implementation of Agenda 21,

Taking note with satisfaction of the recommendation on trade, environment and sustainable development made by the Commission on Sustainable Development at its third session,[6] and recognizing, in the spirit of a new global partnership for sustainable development, the need for a balanced and integrated approach to environment, trade and development issues,

1. *Takes note* of the reports of the Trade and Development Board on the second part of its forty-first session[7] and the first part of its forty-second session,[8] and calls upon all States to take appropriate action to implement the outcome of those sessions;

2. *Also takes* note of the Trade and Development Report 1995,[9] and recognizes the contribution such reports have made to the international trade and development dialogue;

3. *Emphasizes* the importance of follow-up and monitoring of the implementation of the policies and measures contained in the Cartagena Commitment,[10] adopted by the United Nations Conference on Trade and Development at its eighth session, held at Cartagena de Indias, Colombia, from 8 to 25 February 1992;

4. *Stresses* the urgent need to continue trade liberalization, including liberalization through a substantial reduction of tariff and other barriers to trade, in particular non-tariff barriers, and the elimination of discriminatory and protectionist practices in international trade relations, and to improve access to the markets of all countries, in particular those of the developed countries, so as to generate sustained economic growth and sustainable development;

5. *Also stresses* the need for the full integration of the economies in transition, as well as other countries, into the world economy, in particular through improved market access for their exports and elimination of discriminatory tariff and non-tariff measures and further liberalization of their trade regimes, including *vis-à-vis* developing countries, and recognizes in this respect the importance of open regional economic integration of interested economies in transition among themselves as well as with developed and/or developing countries in creating new possibilities for expanding trade and investment;

6. *Further stresses* the importance of the timely and full implementation of the agreements contained in the Final Act Embodying the Results of the Uruguay Round of Multilateral Trade Negotiations and the significance of the entering into force on 1 January 1995 of the Agreement Establishing the World Trade Organization;[11]

7. *Emphasizes* the importance of the full and continuing implementation of the provisions contained in the Final Act that confer special and differential treatment for developing countries, including decisions giving special attention to the situation of the least developed countries and the net food importing developing countries;

8. *Notes* the work that has been undertaken jointly and separately by the United Nations Conference on Trade and Development and the World Trade Organization on the impact of the Uruguay Round on developing countries, and looks forward to the integration of this analysis into discussions, including those at ministerial conferences;

9. *Invites* the United Nations Conference on Trade and Development

---

1 *Ibid.*

2 See *Official Records of the General Assembly, Forty-ninth Session, Supplement No. 15* (A/49/15), vol. I, part one, chap. II, sect. A.

3 *Ibid.*, vol.II, chap. II, sect. A.

4 See A/50/15 (vol. II).

5 See A/50/15 (vol. I), chap. I, sect. A.

6 *Official Records of the Economic and Social Council, 1995, Supplement No. 12* (E/1995/32), chap. I, paras. 47-72.

7 A/50/15 (vol. I).

8 A/50/15 (vol. II).

9 United Nations publication, Sales No. E.95.II.D.16.

10 See *Proceedings of the United Nations Conference on Trade and Development, Eighth Session, Report and Annexes* (United Nations publication, Sales No. E.93.II.D.5),part one, sect. A.

11 See *Legal Instruments Embodying the Results of the Uruguay Round of Multilateral Trade Negotiations, done at Marrakesh on 15 April* 1994 (GATT secretariat publication, Sales No. GATT/1994-7), vols.1 and 27-31.

at its ninth session to transmit its assessment of challenges and opportunities arising from the Uruguay Round agreements from a development perspective to the Ministerial Conference of the World Trade Organization;

10. *Emphasizes* the need for continued review and evaluation of the implementation of the Uruguay Round agreements to ensure that the benefits of the evolving multilateral trade system promote sustained economic growth and sustainable development;

11. *Also emphasizes* the significance of the Ministerial Conference of the World Trade Organization, to be held in Singapore in December 1996, in helping to set the future direction of a rule-based multilateral trading system;

12. *Deplores* any attempt to bypass or undermine multilaterally agreed measures of trade liberalization, through resort to unilateral actions over and above those agreed to in the Uruguay Round, and reaffirms that environmental and social concerns should not be used for protectionist purposes;

13. *Notes* the work of the United Nations Conference on Trade and Development on trade and environment, in particular the outcome of its Ad Hoc Working Group on Trade, Environment and Development, and also notes the work of the Committee on Trade and Environment of the World Trade Organization;

14. *Also notes* the progress achieved by the joint United Nations Environment Programme/United Nations Conference on Trade and Development programme in the consideration of trade and environment issues, and invites the two organizations to continue their work in accordance with paragraph 59 of chapter I of the report of the Commission on Sustainable Development on its third session;[1]

15. *Reaffirms* the need as a matter of priority to implement the Programme of Action for the Least Developed Countries for the 1990s, taking into account the assessment and recommendations adopted at the Mid-term Global Review of the Implementation of the Programme of Action for the Least Developed Countries for the 1990s, held in New York from 25 September to 6 October 1995;

16. *Emphasizes* the urgent need for assistance to African countries, *inter alia,* for evaluation of the impact of the Final Act Embodying the Results of the Uruguay Round of Multilateral Trade Negotiations and to enable them to identify and implement adaptive measures to enhance their competitiveness;

17. *Requests* preference-giving countries to improve their preferential schemes, and invites the 1996 policy review of the generalized system of preferences to examine possible adaptations to the system, taking into account paragraphs 134 to 140 of the Cartagena Commitment,[2] as well as the results of the Uruguay Round;

18. *Reaffirms* the role that the United Nations Conference on Trade and Development has been playing as the focal point within the United Nations for the integrated treatment of development and interrelated issues in the areas of trade, finance, technology, investment, services and sustainable development and, within this context, stresses that there should be constructive and effective cooperation between the Conference and the World Trade Organization, based on the complementarity of their functions;

19. *Decides* to enable the United Nations Conference on Trade and Development to discharge its mandate, thereby making it a more effective and efficient instrument for promoting development;

20. *Recognizes* that the United Nations Conference on Trade and Development at its ninth session will, *inter alia*, consider the future role of the Conference, including its relationship with other international institutions, to generate synergies among them and, on the basis of the mandate of the Conference and with a view to strengthening the United Nations system, the Conference should enable the United Nations Conference on Trade and Development to become a more effective instrument for promoting development;

21. *Invites* the United Nations Conference on Trade and Development to consider, in close cooperation with other competent organizations, new and emerging issues in the international trade agenda, taking into account the new multilateral trade framework, with a view to fostering international consensus building among Member States in such areas as trade and environment and competition policy, and, in this regard, recognizes the role of the Conference in preparing the background work and consensus-building on such issues in accordance with agreed conclusions 410 (XL) and 419 (XLI) and decision 426 (XLII) of the Trade and Development Board;

22. *Also invites* the United Nations Conference on Trade and Development, in close cooperation with other competent organizations, to follow developments in the international trading system, in particular their implications for developing countries, and identify new trading opportunities arising from the implementation of the Uruguay Round agreements so as to provide information and technical support with a view to facilitating the integration of those countries into the system and to assist them in taking full advantage of new trading opportunities, in accordance with agreed conclusions 410 (XL) of the Trade and Development Board;

23. *Requests* the United Nations Conference on Trade and Development to monitor, analyse and review the development of trade between economies in transition and developing countries and to recommend appropriate measures for its revival, thus contributing to the strengthening of the multilateral trading system;

24. *Welcomes* the measures taken by the secretariats of the United Nations Conference on Trade and Development and the World Trade Organization and invites them to continue to develop their working relationship, mutual cooperation and complementarity;

25. *Emphasizes* the importance to the international trading system of the inclusion in multilateral trade agreements of all countries that are not members of the World Trade Organization, and urges the international community to assist appropriately and adequately those countries that are not members of the World Trade Organization in the steps towards acceding to that Organization;

26. *Requests* the United Nations Conference on Trade and Development, and invites the World Trade Organization, in accordance with their respective mandates and competence and in close cooperation with other competent United Nations bodies and the regional commissions, to address trade and environment matters comprehensively and to report, through the Commission on Sustainable Development, to the Economic and Social Council and to the General Assembly at its special session in 1997 on the concrete progress achieved on the issue of trade and environment;

27. *Also requests* the United Nations Conference on Trade and Development to continue its special role in the field of trade and environment, including analytical and empirical work, conceptual and empirical studies, policy analysis, and consensus-building, with a view to ensuring transparency and coherence in making environmental and trade policies mutually supportive, taking into account the need for continuing close cooperation and complementarity in the work of the Conference, the United Nations Environment Programme and the World Trade Organization;

28. *Further requests* the United Nations Conference on Trade and Development to focus and intensify, where necessary, its technical assistance in the light of the Uruguay Round agreements, in cooperation with relevant international organizations, in particular the International Trade Centre and the World Trade Organization, with the aim of increasing the capacities of developing countries, especially the least developed countries, African countries, and small island developing States, so that they may participate effectively in the international trading system;

29. *Requests* the United Nations Conference on Trade and Development to continue to provide technical assistance to economies in transition, bearing in mind the needs of developing countries, in particular with regard to their full integration into the multilateral trading system, so as to contribute to the expansion of their external trade, *inter alia,* with developing countries.

96th plenary meeting
20 December 1995

---

1 *Official Records of the Economic and Social Council, 1995, Supplement No. 12* (E/1995/32).

2 See *Proceedings of the United Nations Conference on Trade and Development, Eighth Session, Report and Annexes* (United Nations publication, Sales No. E.93.II.D.5), part one, sect. A.

05.30 DEVELOPMENT ASSISTANCE

05.31 DEVELOPMENT DECADES

1710 (XVI). United Nations Development Decade: A Programme for International Economic Cooperation (I)

Committee: 2
Vote: unanimous
Ref.: 1715 (XVI)

The General Assembly,

Bearing in mind the solemn undertaking embodied in the Charter of the United Nations to promote social progress and better standards of life in larger freedom and to employ international machinery for the advancement of the economic and social development of all peoples,

Considering that the economic and social development of the economically less developed countries is not only of primary importance to those countries but is also basic to the attainment of international peace and security and to a faster and mutually beneficial increase in world prosperity,

Recognizing that during the decade of the nineteen-fifties considerable efforts to advance economic progress in the less developed countries were made by both the newly developing and the more developed countries,

Noting, however, that in spite of the efforts made in recent years the gap in *per caput* incomes between the economically developed and the less developed countries has increased and the rate of economic and social progress in the developing countries is still far from adequate,

Recalling its resolutions 1421 (XIV) of 5 December 1959, 1514 (XV) of 14 December 1960 and 1515 (XV), 1516 (XV), 1519 (XV) and 1526 (XV) of 15 December 1960,

Convinced of the need for concerted action to demonstrate the determination of Member States to give added impetus to international economic cooperation in the current decade, through the United Nations system and on a bilateral or multilateral basis,

1. *Designates* the current decade as the United Nations Development Decade, in which Member States and their peoples will intensify their efforts to mobilize and to sustain support for the measures required on the part of both developed and developing countries to accelerate progress towards self-sustaining growth of the economy of the individual nations and their social advancement so as to attain in each under-developed country a substantial increase in the rate of growth, with each country setting its own target, taking as the objective a minimum annual rate of growth of aggregate national income of 5 per cent at the end of the Decade;

2. *Calls upon* States Members of the United Nations and members of the specialized agencies:

(*a*) To pursue policies designed to enable the less developed countries and those dependent on the export of a small range of primary commodities to sell more of their products at stable and remunerative prices in expanding markets, and thus to finance increasingly their own economic development from their earnings of foreign exchange and domestic savings;

(*b*) To pursue policies designed to ensure to the developing countries an equitable share of earnings from the extraction and marketing of their natural resources by foreign capital, in accordance with the generally accepted reasonable earnings on invested capital;

(*c*) To pursue policies that will lead to an increase in the flow of development resources, public and private, to developing countries on mutually acceptable terms;

(*d*) To adopt measures which will stimulate the flow of private investment capital for the economic development of the developing countries, on terms that are satisfactory both to the capital-exporting countries and the capital-importing countries;

3. *Requests* the Secretary-General to communicate to the Governments of Member States any documentation useful for the study and application of the present resolution and to invite them to make proposals, if possible, concerning the contents of a United Nations programme for the Decade and the application of such measures in their respective plans;

4. *Requests* the Secretary-General, taking account of the views of Governments and in consultation, as appropriate, with the heads of international agencies with responsibilities in the financial, economic and social fields, the Managing Director of the Special Fund, the Executive Chairman of the Technical Assistance Board and the regional economic commissions, to develop proposals for the intensification of action in the fields of economic and social development by the United Nations system of organizations, with particular reference, *inter alia*, to the following approaches and measures designed to further the objectives of paragraph I above:

(*a*) The achievement and acceleration of sound self-sustaining economic development in the less developed countries through industrialization, diversification and the development of a highly productive agricultural sector;

(*b*) Measures for assisting the developing countries, at their request, to establish well-conceived and integrated country plans - including, where appropriate, land reform - which will serve to mobilize internal resources and to utilize resources offered by foreign sources on both a bilateral and a multilateral basis for progress towards self-sustained growth;

(*c*) Measures to improve the use of international institutions and instrumentalities for furthering economic and social development;

(*d*) Measures to accelerate the elimination of illiteracy, hunger and disease, which seriously affect the productivity of the people of the less developed countries;

(*e*) The need to adopt new measures, and to improve existing measures, for further promoting education in general and vocational and technical training in the developing countries with the cooperation, where appropriate, of the specialized agencies and States which can provide assistance in these fields, and for training competent national personnel in the fields of public administration, education, engineering, health and agronomy;

(*f*) The intensification of research and demonstration as well as other efforts to exploit scientific and technological potentialities of high promise for accelerating economic and social development;

(*g*) Ways and means of finding and furthering effective solutions in the field of trade in manufactures as well as in primary commodities, bearing in mind, in particular, the need to increase the foreign exchange earnings of the under-developed countries;

(*h*) The need to review facilities for the collection, collation, analysis and dissemination of statistical and other information required for charting economic and social development and for providing a constant measurement of progress towards the objectives of the Decade;

(*i*) The utilization of resources released by disarmament for the purpose of economic and social development, in particular of the under-developed countries;

(*j*) The ways in which the United Nations can stimulate and support realization of the objectives of the Decade through the combined efforts of national and international institutions, both public and private;

5. *Further requests* the Secretary-General to consult Member States, at their request, on the application of such measures in their respective development plans;

6. *Invites* the Economic and Social Council to accelerate its examination of, and decision on, principles of international economic cooperation directed towards the improvement of world economic relations and the stimulation of international cooperation;

7. *Requests* the Secretary-General to present his proposals for such a programme to the Economic and Social Council at its thirty-fourth session for its consideration and appropriate action;

8. *Invites* the Economic and Social Council to transmit the Secretary-General's recommendations, together with its views and its report on actions undertaken thereon to States Members of the United Nations and members of the specialized agencies and to the General Assembly at its seventeenth session.

1084th plenary meeting
19 December 1961

1715 (XVI). United Nations Development Decade: A Programme for International Economic Cooperation (II)

Committee: 2
Vote: 89 - 0 - 9

The General Assembly,

Having designated the United Nations Development Decade, in its resolution 1710 (XVI) of 19 December 1961, as a period of intensified cooperation among all peoples on behalf of those living in the less developed countries,

Convinced that the Expanded Programme of Technical Assistance and the Special Fund can play an increasingly important role in this major international effort,

Recognizing the necessity of making the fullest possible use of the available financial resources of the Special Fund,

1. *Calls upon* States Members of the United Nations and members of the specialized agencies to review their contributions to the support of the work of the Expanded Programme of Technical Assistance and the Special Fund so that the combined budgets for these two organs in the year 1962 may reach the target of $150 million;

2. *Requests* the Special Fund, following consultations with participating Governments but not later than June 1962, to consider the desirability of establishing a service to provide developing countries, upon request with information and guidance concerning the policies, rules, regulations and practices of existing and future sources of development capital and assistance necessary to enable the less developed countries to determine for themselves the most appropriate sources to which the may turn for assistance as needed.

1084th plenary meeting
19 December 1961

2626 (XXV). International Development Strategy for the Second United Nations Development Decade

Committee: 2
Vote: Adopted without a vote

The General Assembly

1. *Proclaims* the Second United Nations Development Decade starting from 1 January 1971;

2. *Adopts* the following International Development Strategy for the Decade:

A. Preamble

(1) On the threshold of the 1970s, Governments dedicate themselves anew to the fundamental objectives enshrined in the Charter of the United Nations twenty-five years ago to create conditions of stability and well-being and to ensure a minimum standard of living consistent with human dignity through economic and social progress and development,

(2) The launching in 1961 of the First United Nations Development Decade marked a major world-wide endeavour to give concrete substance to this solemn pledge. Since then attempts have continued to be made to adopt specific measures and to fashion and employ new institutions of international cooperation for this purpose.

(3) However, the level of living of countless millions of people in the developing part of the world is still pitifully low. These people are often still undernourished, uneducated, unemployed and wanting in many other basic amenities of life. While a part of the world lives in great comfort and even affluence, much of the larger part suffers from abject poverty, and in fact the disparity is continuing to widen. This lamentable situation has contributed to the aggravation of world tension.

(4) The current frustrations and disappointments must not be allowed to cloud the vision or stand in the way of the development objectives being really ambitious. Youth everywhere is in ferment, and the 1970s must mark a step forward in securing the well-being and happiness not only of the present generation but also of the generations to come.

(5) The success of international development activities will depend in large measure on improvement in the general international situation, particularly on concrete progress towards general and complete disarmament under effective international control, on the elimination of colonialism, racial discrimination, apartheid and occupation of territories of any State and on the promotion of equal political, economic, social and cultural rights for all members of society. Progress towards general and complete disarmament should release substantial additional resources which could be utilized for the purpose of economic and social development, in particular that of developing countries. There should therefore, be a close link between the Second United Nations Development Decade and the Disarmament Decade.

(6) In the conviction that development is the essential path to peace and justice, Governments reaffirm their common and unswerving resolve to seek a better and more effective system of international cooperation whereby the prevailing disparities in the world may be banished and prosperity secured for all.

(7) The ultimate objective of development must be to bring about sustained improvement in the well-being of the individual and bestow benefits on all. If undue privileges, extremes of wealth and social injustices persist, then development fails in its essential purpose. This calls for a global development strategy based on joint and concentrated action by developing and developed countries in all spheres of economic and social life: in industry and agriculture, in trade and finance, in employment and education, in health and housing, in science and technology.

(8) The international community must rise to the challenge of the present age of unprecedented opportunities offered by science and technology in order that the scientific and technological advances may be equitably shared by developed and developing countries, thus contributing to accelerated economic development throughout the world.

(9) International cooperation for development must be on a scale commensurate with that of the problem itself. Partial, sporadic and half-hearted gestures, howsoever well intentioned, will not suffice.

(10) Economic and social progress is the common and shared responsibility of the entire international community. It is also a process in which the benefits derived by the developing countries from the developed countries are shared by the world as a whole. Every country has the right and duty to develop its human and natural resources, but the full benefit of its efforts can be realized only with concomitant and effective international action.

(11) The primary responsibility for the development of developing countries rests upon themselves, as stressed in the Charter of Algiers[1]; but however great their own efforts, these will not be sufficient to enable them to achieve the desired development goals as expeditiously as they must unless they are assisted through increased financial resources and more favourable economic and commercial policies on the part of developed countries.

(12) Governments designate the 1970s as the Second United Nations Development Decade and pledge themselves, individually and collectively, to pursue policies designed to create a more just and rational world economic and social order in which equality of oppor-

1 *Proceedings of the United Nations Conference on Trade and Development, Second Session,* vol. I and Corr.1 and 3 and Add.1 and 2, *Report and Annexes* (United Nations publication, Sales No.: E.68.II.D.14), p. 431.

tunities should be as much a prerogative of nations as of individuals within a nation. They subscribe to the goals and objectives of the Decade and resolve to take the measures to translate them into reality. These aims and measures are set out in the following paragraphs.

B. Goals and Objectives

(13) The average annual rate of growth in the gross product of the developing countries as a whole during the Second United Nations Development Decade should be at least 6 per cent, with the possibility of attaining a higher rate in the second half of the Decade to be specified on the basis of a comprehensive mid-term review. This target and those derived from it are a broad indication of the scope of convergent efforts to be made during the Decade at the national and international levels; it should be the responsibility of each developing country to set its own target for growth in the light of its own circumstances.

(14) The average annual rate of growth of gross product per head in developing countries as a whole during the Decade should be about 3.5 per cent with the possibility of accelerating it during the second half of the Decade in order at least to make a modest beginning towards narrowing the gap in living standards between developed and developing countries. An average annual growth rate of 3.5 per cent per head will represent a doubling of average income per head in the course of two decades. In countries with very low incomes per head, efforts should be made to double such incomes within a shorter period.

(15) The target for growth in average income per head is calculated on the basis of an average annual increase of 2.5 per cent in the population of developing countries, which is less than the average rate at present forecast for the 1970s. In this context, each developing country should formulate its own demographic objectives within the framework of its national development plan.

(16) An average annual rate of growth of at least 6 per cent in the gross product of developing countries during the Decade will imply an average annual expansion of:

(*a*) 4 per cent in agricultural output;

(*b*) 8 per cent in manufacturing output.

(17) For attaining the over-all growth target of at least 6 per cent *per annum*, there should be an average annual expansion of:

(*a*) 0.5 per cent in the ratio of gross domestic saving to the gross product so that this ratio rises to around 20 per cent by 1980;

(*b*) Somewhat less than 7 per cent in imports and somewhat higher than 7 per cent in exports.

(18) As the ultimate purpose of development is to provide increasing opportunities to all people for a better life, it is essential to bring about a more equitable distribution of income and wealth for promoting both social justice and efficiency of production, to raise substantially the level of employment, to achieve a greater degree of income security, to expand and improve facilities for education, health, nutrition, housing and social welfare, and to safeguard the environment. Thus, qualitative and structural changes in the society must go hand in hand with rapid economic growth, and existing disparities - regional, sectoral and social - should be substantially reduced. These objectives are both determining factors and end-results of development; they should therefore be viewed as integrated parts of the same dynamic process and would require a unified approach:

(*a*) Each developing country should formulate its national employment objectives so as to absorb an increasing proportion of its working population in modern-type activities and to reduce significantly unemployment and underemployment;

(*b*) Particular attention should be paid to achieving enrolment of all children of primary school age, improvement in the quality of education at all levels, a substantial reduction in illiteracy, the reorientation of educational programmes to serve development needs and, as appropriate, the establishment and expansion of scientific and technological institutions;

(*c*) Each developing country should formulate a coherent health programme for the prevention and treatment of diseases and for raising general levels of health and sanitation;

(*d*) Levels of nutrition should be improved in terms of the average caloric intake and the protein content, with special emphasis being placed on the needs of vulnerable groups of population;

(*e*) Housing facilities should be expanded and improved, especially for the low-income groups and with a view to remedying the ills of unplanned urban growth and lagging rural areas;

(*f*) The well-being of children should be fostered;

(*g*) The full participation of youth in the development process should be ensured;

(*h*) The full integration of women in the total development effort should be encouraged.

C. Policy Measures

(19) The above goals and objectives call for a continuing effort by all peoples and Governments to promote economic and social progress in developing countries by the formulation and implementation of a coherent set of policy measures. Animated by a spirit of constructive partnership and cooperation, based on the interdependence of their interests and designed to promote a rational system of international division of labour, and reflecting their political will and collective determination to achieve these goals and objectives, Governments, individually and jointly, solemnly resolve to adopt and implement the policy measures set out below.

(20) The policy measures should be viewed in a dynamic context, involving continuing review to ensure their effective implementation and adaptation in the light of new developments, including the far-reaching impact of rapid advance in technology, and to seek new areas of agreement and the widening of the existing ones. Organizations of the United Nations system will appropriately assist in the implementation of these measures and in the search for new avenues of international cooperation for development.

1. International trade

(21) All efforts will be made to secure international action before 31 December 1972, including, where appropriate, the conclusion of international agreements or arrangements on commodities mentioned in resolution 16 (II) of 26 March 1968,[1] adopted by the United Nations Conference on Trade and Development at its second session, in accordance with the procedure agreed upon at that session, and on the basis of a time-table for the consideration of those matters to be drawn up by the Conference.

(22) Commodities already covered by international agreements or arrangements will be kept under review with a view to strengthening the working of such agreements or arrangements and to renewing, where appropriate, agreements or arrangements due to expire.

(23) All possible resources for the pre-financing of buffer stocks, when necessary, will be considered while concluding or reviewing commodity agreements incorporating buffer stock mechanisms.

(24) Efforts will be made to reach agreement, before the third session of the United Nations Conference on Trade and Development, on a set of general principles on pricing policy to serve as guidelines for consultations and actions on individual commodities. As one of the priority aims of pricing policy, particular attention will be paid to securing stable, remunerative and equitable prices with a view to increasing the foreign exchange earnings from exports of primary products from the developing countries.

(25) No new tariff and non-tariff barriers will be raised nor will the existing ones be increased by developed countries against imports of primary products of particular interest to developing countries.

(26) Developed countries will accord priority to reducing or eliminating duties and other barriers to imports of primary products, including those in processed or semi-processed form, of export interest to developing countries through international joint action or unilateral action with a view to ensuring that developing countries have improved access to world markets and to market growth for products in which they are presently or potentially competitive. Achievement of this objective will be sought through the continuance and intensifica-

1 *Ibid.*, p. 34.

tion of intergovernmental consultations with the aim of reaching concrete and significant results early in the Decade. Efforts will be made with a view to achieving these results before 31 December 1972.

(27) Implementation of the provisions of paragraphs 25 and 26 above should take into account the resolutions, decisions and agreements which have been or may be reached in the United Nations Conference on Trade and Development or in other relevant intergovernmental bodies and organizations of the United Nations system.

(28) Developed countries will give increased attention within the framework of bilateral and multilateral programmes to supplementing the resources of the developing countries in their endeavour to accelerate the diversification of their economies with a view to the expansion of the production and exports of semi-manufactures and manufactures, as well as of semi-processed and processed commodities, broadening the patterns of exports in favour of commodities with relatively dynamic demand conditions and increasing food production in food deficient countries. Specific funds for diversification will be one of the features of commodity arrangements wherever considered necessary.

(29) Appropriate action, including the provision of finance, will be taken, as far as practicable, to initiate intensive research and development efforts designed to improve market conditions and cost efficiency and to diversify the end uses of natural products facing competition from synthetics and substitutes. In their financial and technical assistance programmes, developed countries and the international organizations concerned will give sympathetic consideration to requests for assistance to developing countries producing natural products which suffer serious competition from synthetics and substitutes, in order to help them to diversify into other areas of production including processing of primary products. Where natural products are able to satisfy present and anticipated world market requirements, in the context of national policies no special encouragement will be given to the creation and utilization of new production, particularly in the developed countries, of directly competing synthetics.

(30) The machinery for consultation on surplus disposal which existed during the 1960s will be widened and reinforced in order to avoid or minimize possible adverse effects of disposals of production surpluses or strategic reserves, including those of minerals, on normal commercial trade, and to take account of the interest of both surplus and deficit countries.

(31) Special attention will be given to the expansion and diversification of the export trade of developing countries in manufactures and semi-manufactures, particularly for enabling them to attain increased participation, commensurate with the needs of development, in the growth of international trade in these commodities.

(32) Arrangements concerning the establishment of generalized, non-discriminatory, non-reciprocal preferential treatment to exports of developing countries in the markets of developed countries have been drawn up in the United Nations Conference on Trade and Development and considered mutually acceptable to developed and developing countries. Preference-giving countries are determined to seek as rapidly as possible the necessary legislative or other sanction with the aim of implementing the preferential arrangements as early as possible in 1971. Efforts for further improvements of these preferential arrangements with be pursued in a dynamic context in the light of the objectives of resolution 21 (II) of 26 March 1968,[1] adopted by the Conference at its second session.

(33) Developed countries will not, ordinarily, raise existing tariff or non-tariff barriers to exports from developing countries, nor establish new tariff or non-tariff barriers or any discriminatory measures, where such action has the effect of rendering less favourable the conditions of access to the markets of manufactured and semi-manufactured products of export interest to developing countries.

(34) Intergovernmental consultations will be continued and intensified with a view to giving effect early in the Decade to measures for the relaxation and progressive elimination of non-tariff barriers affecting trade in manufactures and semi-manufactures of interest to developing countries. Efforts will be made with a view to implementing such measures before 31 December 1972. These consultations will take into account all groups of processed and semi-processed products of export interest to developing countries.

(35) Developed countries, having in mind the importance of facilitating the expansion of their imports from developing countries, will consider adopting measures and where possible evolving a programme early in the Decade for assisting the adaptation and adjustment of industries and workers in situations where they are adversely affected or may be threatened to be adversely affected by increased imports of manufactures and semi-manufactures from developing countries.

(36) Developing countries will intensify their efforts to make greater use of trade promotion as an instrument for the expansion of their exports both to developed countries and to other developing countries. For this purpose, effective international assistance will be provided.

(37) Restrictive business practices particularly affecting the trade and development of the developing countries will be identified with a view to the consideration of appropriate remedial measures, the aim being to reach concrete and significant results early in the Decade. Efforts will be made with a view to achieving these results before 31 December 1972.

(38) The socialist countries of Eastern Europe will take duly into consideration the trade needs of the developing countries, and in particular their production and export potential, when quantitative targets are fixed in their long-term economic plans, adopt appropriate measures designed to maximize and diversify imports of primary commodities from developing countries and undertake measures so that imports of manufactures and semi-manufactures from developing countries constitute a growing element in their total imports of manufactures and semi-manufactures. They will promote the diversification of the structure and geographical basis of their trade with developing countries in order that the largest possible number of developing countries derive the maximum benefit from this trade. Socialist countries of Eastern Europe will take the necessary action fully to implement, by the beginning of the Decade, and in any case not later than 1972, recommendations contained in section II of resolution 15 (II) of 25 March 1968,[2] adopted by the United Nations Conference on Trade and Development at its second session. As no uniform method of introducing multilateralism in payments relations between developing countries and socialist countries is practical at this time, it is considered desirable that elements of flexibility and multilateralism be progressively introduced or extended in such payments arrangements by appropriate consultations among the countries concerned, taking into account specific circumstances and patterns of trade.

2. Trade expansion, economic cooperation and regional integration among developing countries

(39) The developing countries will continue their efforts to negotiate and put into effect further commitments for instituting the schemes for regional and subregional integration or measures of trade expansion among themselves. They will, in particular, elaborate mutually beneficial and preferential trade arrangements which foster the rational and outward-looking expansion of production and trade, and avoid undue injury to the trading interests of third parties, including third developing countries.

(40) The developed market economy countries will, through the extension of financial and technical assistance or through action in the field of commercial policy, support initiatives in regional and subregional cooperation of developing countries. In this connexion, they will specifically consider what help can be given to any concrete proposals that may be put forward by developing countries. In the efforts of developing countries to carry out trade expansion economic cooperation and regional integration among themselves, the socialist countries of Eastern Europe will extend their full support within the framework of their socio-economic system.

1 *Ibid.*, p. 38.

2 *Ibid*, p. 32.

3. Financial resources for development

(41) Developing countries must, and do, bear the main responsibility for financing their development. They will, therefore, continue to adopt vigorous measures for a fuller mobilization of the whole range of their domestic financial resources and for ensuring the most effective use of available resources, both internal and external. For this purpose, they will pursue sound fiscal and monetary policies and, as required, remove institutional obstacles through the adoption of appropriate legislative and administrative reforms. They will pay particular attention to taking, as appropriate, the necessary steps to streamline and strengthen their systems of tax administration and undertake the necessary tax reform measures. They will keep the increase in their current public expenditure under close scrutiny with a view to releasing maximum resources for investment. Efforts will be made to improve the efficiency of public enterprises so that they make an increasing contribution to investment resources. Every effort will be made to mobilize private savings through financial institutions, thrift societies, post office savings banks and other savings schemes and through expansion of opportunities for saving for specific purposes, such as education and housing. The available supply of saving will be channelled to investment projects in accordance with their development priorities.

(42) Each economically advanced country should endeavour to provide by 1972 annually to developing countries financial resource transfers of a minimum net amount of 1 per cent of its gross national product at market prices in terms of actual disbursements, having regard to the special position of those countries which are net importers of capital. Those developed countries which have already met this target will endeavour to ensure that their net resource transfers are maintained and envisage, if possible, an increase in them. Those developed countries which are unable to achieve this target by 1972 will endeavour to attain it not later than 1975.

(43) In recognition of the special importance of the role which can be fulfilled only by official development assistance, a major part of financial resource transfers to the developing countries should be provided in the form of official development assistance. Each economically advanced country will progressively increase its official development assistance to the developing countries and will exert its best efforts to reach a minimum net amount of 0.7 per cent of its gross national product at market prices by the middle of the Decade.

(44) Developed countries members of the Development Assistance Committee of the Organisation for Economic Cooperation and Development will exert their best efforts to reach as soon as possible, and in any case before 31 December 1971, the norms set out in the Supplement to the 1965 Recommendation on Financial Terms and Conditions adopted by the Development Assistance Committee on 12 February 1969,[1] designed to soften and harmonize the terms and conditions of assistance to developing countries. Developed countries will consider measures aimed at the further softening of the terms and will endeavour to arrive at a more precise assessment of the circumstances of the individual developing countries and at a greater harmonization of terms given by individual developed countries to individual developing countries. Developed countries will consider, in the further evolution of their assistance policy and with a view to attaining concrete and substantive results by the end of the Decade, the specific suggestions contained in decision 29 (II) of 28 March 1968,[2] adopted by the United Nations Conference on Trade and Development at its second session, and made in other international forums for further softening of the terms and conditions of aid.

(45) In the light of the relevant decision of the Conference at its second session, financial assistance will, in principle, be untied. While it may not be possible to untie assistance in all cases, developed countries will rapidly and progressively take what measures they can in this respect both to reduce the extent of tying of assistance and to mitigate any harmful effects. Where loans are tied essentially to particular sources, developed countries will make, to the greatest extent possible, such loans available for utilization by the recipient countries for the purchase of goods and services from other developing countries.

(46) Financial and technical assistance should be aimed exclusively at promoting the economic and social progress of developing countries and should not in any way be used by the developed countries to the detriment of the national sovereignty of recipient countries.

(47) Developed countries will provide, to the greatest extent possible, an increased flow of aid on a long-term and continuing basis and by simplifying the procedure of the granting and effective and expeditious disbursement of aid.

(48) Arrangements for forecasting and, if possible, forestalling debt crises will be improved. Developed countries will help in preventing such crises by providing assistance on appropriate terms and conditions, and developing countries by undertaking sound policies of debt management. Where difficulties do arise, the countries concerned will stand ready to deal reasonably with them within the framework of an appropriate forum in cooperation with the international institutions concerned, drawing upon the full range of the available methods including, as may be required, measures such as arrangements for rescheduling and refinancing of existing debts on appropriate terms and conditions.

(49) The volume of resources made available through multilateral institutions for financial and technical assistance will be increased to the fullest extent possible and techniques will be evolved to enable them to fulfil their role in the most effective manner.

(50) Developing countries will adopt appropriate measures for inviting, stimulating and making effective use of foreign private capital, taking into account the areas in which such capital should be sought and bearing in mind the importance for its attraction of conditions conducive to sustained investment. Developed countries, on their part, will consider adopting further measures to encourage the flow of private capital to developing countries. Foreign private investment in developing countries should be undertaken in a manner consistent with the development objectives and priorities established in their national plans. Foreign private investors in developing countries should endeavour to provide for an increase m the local share in management and administration, employment and training of local labour, including personnel at the managerial and technical levels, participation of local capital and reinvestment of profits. Efforts will be made to foster better understanding of the rights and obligations of both host and capital-exporting countries, as well as of individual investors.

(51) In the context of the search for appropriate means for dealing with the problem of disruption of development arising from adverse movements in the export proceeds of developing countries, the International Bank for Reconstruction and Development has been requested to pursue its efforts at working out a scheme of supplementary financing. The Bank is invited to give further consideration to the adoption of supplementary financial measures at the earliest practicable opportunity.

(52) As soon as adequate experience is available on the working of the scheme of Special Drawing Rights, serious consideration will be given to the possibility of the establishment of a link between the allocation of new reserve assets under the scheme and the provision of additional development finance for the benefit of all developing countries. The question will, in any case, be examined before the allocation of Special Drawing Rights in 1972.

4. Invisibles, including shipping

(53) The objective is to promote, by national and international action, the earnings of developing countries from invisible trade and to minimize the net outflow of foreign exchange from those countries arising from invisible transactions, including shipping. In pursuance of the objective, action should be taken, *inter alia*, in the following areas by Governments and international organizations and, where

---

1 Organisation for Economic Co-operation and Development, *Development Assistance, 1969 Review*, annex III.

2 *Proceedings of the United Nations Conference on Trade and Development, Second Session*, vol. I and Corr.1 and 3 and Add.1 and 2, *Report and Annexes* (United Nations publication, Sales No. E.68.II.D.14), p. 40.

necessary, appropriately involving liner conferences, shippers, councils and other relevant bodies:

(*a*) The principle that the national shipping lines of developing countries should be admitted as full members of liner conferences operating in their national maritime trade and have an increasing and substantial participation in the carriage of cargoes generated by their foreign trade should be implemented in the Decade.

(*b*) Further, Governments should invite liner conferences to consider favourably, fairly and on equal terms applications of the national shipping lines, in particular of developing countries, for admission as full members to way-port trades related to these countries' own foreign trade, subject to the rights and obligations of conference membership as provided in section II, paragraph 4, of resolution 12 (IV) of 4 May 1970[1] adopted by the Committee on Shipping.

(*c*) In order that the developing countries may have an increasing and substantial participation in the carriage of maritime cargoes, and recognizing the need to reverse the existing trend whereby the share of the developing countries in the world merchant fleet has been declining instead of increasing, developing countries should be enabled to expand their national and multinational merchant marines through the adoption of such measures as may be appropriate to permit their shipowners to compete in the international freight market and thus contribute to a sound development of shipping.

(*d*) It is also necessary that further improvements be made in the liner conference system, and all unfair practices and discrimination where such exist in liner conference practices should be eliminated.

(*e*) In the determination and adjustment of liner freight rates, due consideration should be given, as is commercially possible and/or appropriate, to:

(i) The needs of developing countries, in particular their efforts to promote non-traditional exports;

(ii) The special problems of the least developed among the developing countries, in order to encourage and promote the import and export interests in these countries;

(iii) Port improvements leading to a reduction of the cost of shipping operations in ports;

(iv) Technological developments in maritime transport;

(v) Improvements in the organization of trade.

(*f*) Governments of developed countries members of the United Nations Conference on Trade and Development should, upon request made by developing countries within the framework of their over-all development priorities, duly consider extending, directly or through international institutions, financial and technical assistance, including training, to developing countries to establish and expand their national and multinational merchant marines, including tanker and bulk carrier fleets, and to develop and improve their port facilities. Within assistance programmes, special attention should be paid to projects, including training projects, for developing the shipping and ports of the least developed among the developing countries and for reducing their maritime transport costs.

(*g*) The terms and conditions on which bilateral aid and commercial credit are available for the purchase of ships by developing countries should be kept under review in the light of relevant resolutions of the United Nations Conference on Trade and Development, namely, Conference resolution 12 (II) of 24 March 1968[2] and resolution 9 (IV) of 4 May 1970[3] adopted by the Committee on Shipping.

(*h*) Freight rates, conference practices, adequacy of shipping services and other matters of common interest to shippers and shipowners should be the subject of consultation between liner conferences and shippers' and, where appropriate, shippers, councils or equivalent bodies and interested public authorities. Every effort should be made to encourage the institution and operation of shippers' councils, where appropriate, or equivalent bodies and the establishment of effective consultation machinery. Such machinery should provide for consultation by liner conferences well before publicly announcing changes in freight rates.

(*i*) In view of the common interest of member countries of the United Nations Conference on Trade and Development, shippers and shipowners in improving ports, thus lowering the cost of maritime transport and permitting reductions in freight rates, a concerted national and international effort should be evolved in the course of the Decade to promote the development and improvement of port facilities of developing countries.

(*j*) Maritime transport costs, the level and structure of freight rates, conference practices, adequacy of shipping services and related matters should continue to be kept under review within the United Nations Conference on Trade and Development, and additional measures to attain the objective set out in this field should be considered within the work programme of the permanent machinery of the Conference.

(54) Reduction in the cost of insurance and reinsurance for developing countries, especially the foreign exchange cost, will be brought about by appropriate measures, bearing in mind the risks involved, to encourage and assist the growth of national insurance and reinsurance markets in developing countries and the establishment to this end, where appropriate, of institutions in these countries or at the regional level.

(55) Developing countries will expand their tourist industry through the building of tourist infrastructure, adoption of promotional measures and relaxation of travel restrictions. Developed countries will assist in this endeavour. They will try to avoid exchange restrictions on the travel of their residents to developing countries and, where restrictions do exist, to remove them as soon as practicable and to facilitate such travel in other ways.

5. Special measures in favour of the least developed among the developing countries

(56) While it is the objective of the Decade to achieve the rapid economic and social progress of all developing countries, special measures will be taken to enable the least developed among them to overcome their particular disabilities. Every possible effort will be made to ensure the sustained economic and social progress of these countries and to enhance their capacity to benefit fully and equitably from the policy measures for the Decade. Wherever necessary, supplementary measures will be devised and implemented at the national, subregional, regional and international levels. Organizations and bodies of the United Nations system will consider initiating early in the Decade special programmes to alleviate the critical development problems of the least developed among the developing countries; developed countries will assist in the implementation of these programmes.

(57) Concerted efforts will be made early in the Decade by developed countries and international organizations through their programmes of technical assistance and through financial aid, including grants and/or exceptionally soft loans, to meet the needs of the least developed among the developing countries and designed to enhance their absorptive capacity. In particular, attention will be paid to overcoming their problem of the scarcity of indigenous technical and managerial cadres, to building the economic and social infrastructure, to the exploitation by these countries of their natural resources and to assisting them in the task of formulating and implementing national development plans.

(58) Special measures will be taken early in the Decade by national and international organizations to improve the capacity of the least developed among the developing countries to expand and diversify their production structure so as to enable them to participate fully in international trade. Moreover, in the field of primary commodities, special consideration will be given to commodities of interest to these countries and, in concluding commodity agreements, the inter-

---

1 *Official Records of the Trade and Development Board, Tenth Session, Supplement No. 5* (TD/B/301), annex I.

2 *Proceedings of the United Nations Conference on Trade and Development, Second Session,* vol. I and Corr.1 and 3 and Add.1 and 2, *Report and Annexes* (United Nations publication, Sales No. E.68.II.D.14), p. 49.

3 *Official Records of the Trade and Development Board, Tenth Session, Supplement No. 5* (TD/B/301), annex I.

est of these countries will receive due attention. In the field of manufactures and semi-manufactures, measures in favour of developing countries will be so devised as to allow the least developed among developing countries to be in a position to derive equitable benefits from such measures. Particular consideration will be given to the question of including in the general system of preferences products of export interest to these countries. Special attention will also be paid by developed countries and international organizations to the need of these countries to improve the quality of their production for export as well as of marketing techniques in order to enhance their competitive position in world markets. These countries, in cooperation with other developing countries, will intensify their efforts for subregional and regional cooperation, and the developed countries will facilitate their task through technical assistance and favourable financial and trade policy measures.

6. Special measures in favour of the land-locked developing countries

(59) National and international financial institutions will accord appropriate attention to the special needs of land-locked developing countries in extending adequate financial and technical assistance to projects designed for the development and improvement of the transport and communications infrastructure needed by these countries, in particular of the transport modes and facilities most convenient to them and mutually acceptable to the transit and land-locked developing countries concerned. All States invited to become parties to the Convention on Transit Trade of Land-locked States of 8 July 1965[1] which have not already done so, will investigate the possibility of ratifying or acceding to it at the earliest possible date. Implementation of measures designed to assist the land-locked countries in overcoming the handicaps of their landlocked position should take into account the relevant decisions and resolutions which have been or may be adopted by the United Nations Conference on Trade and Development.

7. Science and technology

(60) Concerted efforts will be made by the developing countries, with appropriate assistance from the rest of the world community, to expand their capability to apply science and technology for development so as to enable the technological gap to be significantly reduced.

(61) Developing countries will continue to increase their expenditure on research and development and will endeavour to attain, by the end of the Decade, a minimum average level equivalent to 0.5 per cent of their gross product. They will endeavour to inculcate, among their people, an appreciation of the scientific approach which will influence all their development policies. The research programme will be oriented to the development of technologies that are in line with the circumstances and requirements of individual countries and regions. They will put particular stress on applied research and seek to develop the basic infrastructure of science and technology.

(62) Full international cooperation will be extended for the establishment, strengthening and promotion of scientific research and technological activities which have a bearing on the expansion and modernization of the economies of developing countries. Particular attention will be devoted to fostering technologies suitable for these countries. Concentrated research efforts will be made in relation to selected problems the solutions to which can have a catalytic effect in accelerating development. Assistance will also be provided for building up and, as appropriate, for expanding and improving research institutions in developing countries, especially on a regional or subregional basis. Efforts will be made to promote close cooperation between the scientific work and staff of the research centres in developing countries and between those in developed and developing countries.

(63) Within the framework of their individual aid and technical assistance programmes, developed countries will substantially increase their aid for the direct support of science and technology in developing countries during the Decade. Consideration will be given to the question of setting a target equivalent to a specified percentage of the gross national product of developed countries at the time of the first biennial review, taking fully into account the relevant factors. Moreover the developed countries will, in their research and development programmes, assist in seeking solutions to the specific problems of developing countries and for this purpose will endeavour to provide adequate resources. Serious consideration will be given during the first biennial review to the question of setting a specified target in this field. Developed countries will make all efforts to incur in developing countries a significant proportion of their research and development expenditure on specific problems of developing countries. In cooperation with the developing countries, developed countries will continue to explore the possibility of locating some of their research and development projects in developing countries. Private foundations, institutions and organizations will be encouraged to provide further assistance for expanding and diversifying research activities of benefit to developing countries. In relation to their aid and investment policies, developed countries will assist developing countries in identifying technologies which are appropriate for their circumstances and in avoiding the utilization of scarce resources for inappropriate technologies.

(64) Developed and developing countries and competent international organizations will draw up and implement a programme for promoting the transfer of technology to developing countries, which will include, *inter alia*, the review of international conventions on patents, the identification and reduction of obstacles to the transfer of technology to developing countries, facilitating access to patented and non-patented technology for developing countries under fair and reasonable terms and conditions facilitating the utilization of technology transferred to developing countries in such a manner as to assist these countries in attaining their trade and development objectives, the development of technology suited to the productive structures of developing countries and measures to accelerate the development of indigenous technology.

8. Human development

(65) Those developing countries which consider that their rate of population growth hampers their development will adopt measures which they deem necessary in accordance with their concept of development. Developed countries, consistent with their national policies, will upon request provide support through the supply of means for family planning and further research. International organizations concerned will continue to provide, when appropriate, the assistance that may be requested by interested Governments. Such support or assistance will not be a substitute for other forms of development assistance.

(66) Developing countries will make vigorous efforts to improve labour force statistics in order to be able to formulate realistic quantitative targets for employment. They will scrutinize their fiscal, monetary trade and other policies with a view to promoting both employment and growth. Moreover, for achieving these objectives they will expand their investment through a fuller mobilization of domestic resources and an increased flow of assistance from abroad. Wherever a choice of technology is available, developing countries will seek to raise the level of employment by ensuring that capital-intensive technology is confined to uses in which it is clearly cheaper in real terms and more efficient. Developed countries will assist in this process by adopting measures to bring about appropriate changes in the structures of international trade. As part of their employment strategy, developing countries will put as much emphasis as possible on rural employment and will also consider undertaking public works that harness manpower which would otherwise remain unutilized. These countries will also strengthen institutions able to contribute to constructive industrial relations policies and appropriate labour standards. Developed countries and international organizations will assist developing countries in attaining their employment objectives.

(67) Developing countries will formulate and implement educational programmes taking into account their development needs. Educational and training programmes will be so designed as to increase productivity substantially in the short run and to reduce waste. Particular emphasis will be placed on teacher-training programmes and

1 United Nations, *Treaty Series,* vol. 597 (1967), No. 8641.

on the development of curriculum materials to be used by teachers. As appropriate, curricula will be revised and new approaches initiated in order to ensure at all levels expansion of skills in line with the rising tempo of activities and the accelerating transformations brought about by technological progress. Increasing use will be made of modern equipment, mass media and new teaching methods to improve the efficiency of education. Particular attention will be devoted to technical training, vocational training and retraining. Necessary facilities will be provided for improving the literacy and technical competence of groups that are already productively engaged as well as for adult education. Developed countries and international institutions will assist in the task of extending and improving the systems of education of developing countries, especially by making available some of the educational inputs in short supply in many developing countries and by providing assistance to facilitate the flow of pedagogic resources among them.

(68) Developing countries will establish at least a minimum programme of health facilities comprising an infrastructure of institutions, including those for medical training and research to bring basic medical services within the reach of a specified proportion of their population by the end of the Decade. These will include basic health services for the prevention and treatment of diseases and for the promotion of health. Each developing country will endeavour to provide an adequate supply of potable water to a specified proportion of its population, both urban and rural, with a view to reaching a minimum target by the end of the Decade. Efforts of the developing countries to raise their levels of health will be supported to the maximum feasible extent by developed countries, particularly through assistance in the planning of health promotion strategy and the implementation of some of its segments, including research, training of personnel at all levels and supply of equipment and medicines. A concerted international effort will be made to mount a world-wide campaign to eradicate by the end of the Decade, from as many countries as possible, one or more diseases that still seriously afflict people in many lands. Developed countries and international organizations will assist the developing countries in their health planning and in the establishment of health institutions.

(69) Developing countries will adopt policies consistent with their agricultural and health programmes in an effort towards meeting their nutritional requirements. These will include development and production of high-protein foods and development and wider use of new forms of edible protein. Financial and technical assistance, including assistance for genetic research, will be extended to them by developed countries and international institutions.

(70) Developing countries will adopt suitable national policies for involving children and youth in the development process and for ensuring that their needs are met in an integrated manner.

(71) Developing countries will take steps to provide improved housing and related community facilities in both urban and rural areas, especially for low-income groups. They will also seek to remedy the ills of unplanned urbanization and to undertake necessary town planning. Particular effort will be made to expand low-cost housing through both public and private programmes and on a self-help basis, and also through cooperatives, utilizing as much as possible local raw materials and labour-intensive techniques. Appropriate international assistance will be provided for this purpose.

(72) Governments will intensify national and international efforts to arrest the deterioration of the human environment and to take measures towards its improvement, and to promote activities that will help to maintain the ecological balance on which human survival depends.

9. Expansion and diversification of production

(73) Developing countries will take specific steps to augment production and improve productivity in order to provide goods and services necessary for raising levels of living and improving economic viability. While this will be primarily their own responsibility, production policies will be carried out in a global context designed to achieve optimum utilization of world resources, benefiting both developed and developing countries. Further research will be undertaken, by the international organizations concerned, in the field of optimal international division of labour to assist individual countries or groups of countries in their choice of production and trading structures. Depending on the social and economic structure and particular characteristics of individual countries, consideration will be given to the role which the public sector and cooperatives might play in augmenting production.

(74) Full exercise by developing countries of permanent sovereignty over their natural resources will play an important role in the achievement of the goals and objectives of the Decade. Developing countries will take steps to develop the full potential of their natural resources. Concerted efforts will be made, particularly through international assistance, to enable them to prepare an inventory of natural resources for their more rational utilization in all productive activities.

(75) Developing countries will formulate, early in the Decade, appropriate strategies for agriculture - including animal husbandry, fisheries and forestry - designed to secure a more adequate food supply from both the quantitative and qualitative viewpoints, to meet their nutritional and industrial requirements, to expand rural employment and to increase export earnings. They will undertake, as appropriate, reform of land tenure systems for promoting both social justice and farm efficiency. They will adopt the necessary measures for providing adequate irrigation, fertilizers, improved varieties of seeds and suitable agricultural implements. They will also take steps to expand the infrastructure of marketing and storage facilities and the network of agricultural extension services. They will make increasing provision for the supply of rural credit to farmers. They will encourage cooperatives for the organization of many of these activities. They will adopt appropriate agricultural pricing policies as a complementary instrument for implementing their agricultural strategies. Developed countries will support this endeavour by providing resources to developing countries for obtaining the essential inputs, through assistance in research and for the building of infrastructure and by taking into account in their trade policies the particular needs of developing countries. International organizations will also provide appropriate support.

(76) Developing countries will take parallel steps to promote industry in order to achieve rapid expansion, modernization and diversification of their economies. They will devise measures to ensure adequate expansion of the industries that utilize domestic raw materials, that supply essential inputs to both agriculture and other industries, and that help to increase export earnings. They will seek to prevent the emergence of unutilized capacity in industries, especially through regional groupings wherever possible. Developed countries and international organizations will assist in the industrialization of developing countries through appropriate means.

(77) Developing countries will ensure adequate expansion of their basic infrastructure by enlarging their transport and communication facilities and their supplies of energy. As appropriate, they will seek to achieve this purpose through regional and subregional groupings. International financial and technical assistance will be extended in support of their endeavour.

10. Plan formulation and implementation

(78) Developing countries will, as appropriate, establish or strengthen their planning mechanisms including statistical services, for formulating and implementing their national development plans during the Decade. They will ensure that their development plans are both realistic and ambitious enough to have an impact on the imagination of the people, internally consistent, and widely understood and accepted. Every effort will be made to secure the active support and participation of all segments of the population in the development process. They will pay special attention to the orientation and organization of their public administration at all levels for both the effective formulation and implementation of their development plans. Where necessary, they will seek international assistance in carrying out their planning tasks.

D. Review and Appraisal of Both Objectives and Policies

(79) Appropriate arrangements are necessary to keep under systematic scrutiny the progress towards achieving the goals and objectives of the Decade - to identify shortfalls in their achievement and the

factors which account for them and to recommend positive measures, including new goals and policies as needed. Such reviews and appraisals will be carried out at various levels, involving both developing and developed countries, keeping in view the need for streamlining the existing machinery and avoiding unnecessary duplication or proliferation of review activities.

(80) At the national level, each developing country will, where appropriate, establish evaluation machinery or strengthen the existing one and, whenever necessary, seek international assistance for this purpose. Particular attention will be devoted to improving and strengthening national programming and statistical services.

(81) For appraisals at the regional level, regional economic commissions and the United Nations Economic and Social Office at Beirut, in cooperation with regional development banks and subregional groupings, and with the assistance of other organizations of the United Nations system, will assume the main responsibility.

(82) The United Nations Conference on Trade and Development, the United Nations Industrial Development Organization and the specialized agencies of the United Nations will continue to review progress in their respective sectors according to the procedures already established and to be adapted as necessary.

(83) An over-all appraisal of the progress in implementing the International Development Strategy will be made by the General Assembly, through the Economic and Social Council, on the basis of the above-mentioned reviews and of comments and recommendations, within the framework of a specific mandate, by the Committee for Development Planning. In order to assist in this task, the Secretary-General will prepare and submit appropriate documentation and reports. The over-all appraisal will be made biennially, the second biennial appraisal being in the nature of a mid-term review.

E. Mobilization of Public Opinion

(84) An essential part of the work during the Decade will consist of the mobilization of public opinion in both developing and developed countries in support of the objectives and policies for the Decade. Governments of the more advanced countries will continue and intensify their endeavours to deepen public understanding of the interdependent nature of the development efforts during the Decade - in particular of the benefits accruing to them from international cooperation for development - and of the need to assist the developing countries in accelerating their economic and social progress. The efforts which developing countries themselves are making to meet the requirements of their economic and social progress need to be more clearly and more generally made known in developed countries. Similarly, Governments of the developing countries will continue to make people at all levels aware of the benefits and sacrifices involved and to enlist their full participation in achieving the objectives of the Decade. The mobilization of public opinion has to be the responsibility mainly of national bodies. Governments may give consideration to the establishment of new national bodies or to strengthening the existing ones designed to mobilize public opinion, and, as a long-term measure, to give increasing development orientation to the educational curricula. Considering that leadership can make a significant contribution to the mobilization of public opinion, the formulation of concrete aims by the competent authorities is indispensable. The role of the organizations of the United Nations system will be to assist the various national information media, in particular by supplying adequate basic information from which these media may draw both substance and inspiration for their work. There is also an urgent need for increasingly coordinating the information activities already being undertaken by many organizations within the United Nations system. The information stemming from international sources will be aimed primarily at strengthening the sense of interdependence and partnership implicit in the concept of the Decade.

1883rd plenary meeting
24 October 1970

35/56. International Development Strategy for the Third United Nations Development Decade

Committee: 2
Vote: Adopted without a vote

The General Assembly

1. *Proclaims* the Third United Nations Development Decade, starting on 1 January 1981;

2. *Adopts* the International Development Strategy for the Third United Nations Development Decade, as set forth in the annex to the present resolution.

83rd plenary meeting
5 December 1980

Annex

International Development Strategy for the Third United Nations Development Decade

I. Preamble

1. In launching the Third United Nations Development Decade, starting on 1 January 1981, Governments rededicate themselves to the fundamental objectives enshrined in the Charter on the United Nations. They reaffirm solemnly their determination to establish a new international economic order. To this end, they recall the Declaration and the Programme of Action on the Establishment on a New International Economic Order[1] of the sixth special session on the General Assembly, the Charter of Economic Rights and Duties of States,[2] and the resolution on development and international economic cooperation[3] adopted by the Assembly at its seventh special session, which laid down the foundations for the establishment of the new international economic order.

2. The adoption of the International Development Strategy for the Second United Nations Development Decade[4] was an important step in the promotion of international economic cooperation for development. However, the limitations of a strategy, when conceived within the framework of the existing system of international economic relations, soon became obvious. Inequities and imbalances in these relations are widening the gap between developed and developing countries, constitute a major obstacle to the development of the developing countries and adversely affect international relations and the promotion of world peace and security. Midway through the Decade, the world community called for a fundamental restructuring of international economic relations and embarked upon its quest for a new international economic order.

3. The goals and objectives of the International Development Strategy for the Second Development Decade remain largely unfulfilled. In addition, the present negative trends in the world economy have adversely affected the situation of developing countries and, as a result, have impaired their growth prospects. Developing countries have been hit particularly hard by the continuing economic crisis owing to the greater vulnerability of their economies to external factors. The present difficult international economic environment has particularly aggravated the special problems facing the least developed countries and other developing countries, particularly those in the special categories, where development needs and problems are greatest, and the poorest sections of the population. The stark reality confronting mankind today is that close to 850 million people in the developing world are living at the margin of existence - enduring hunger, sickness, homelessness and absence of meaningful employment.

4. The international economy remains in a state of structural disequilibrium. It is characterized by a slower growth rate accompanied

1 Resolutions 3201 (S-VI) and 3202 (S-VI).

2 Resolution 3281 (XXIX).

3 Resolution 3362 (S-VII).

4 Resolution 2626 (XXV).

by a continuing trend of high inflation and unemployment, prolonged monetary instability, intensified protectionist pressures, structural problems and maladjustment and uncertain long-term growth prospects. In an interdependent world economy, these problems cannot be solved without resolving the particular problems facing the developing countries. Furthermore, accelerated development of developing countries is of vital importance for the steady growth of the world economy and essential for world peace and stability.

5. The current difficulties should not deter the world community from the imperative to restructure international economic relations. The challenge of development calls for a new era of effective and meaningful international cooperation for development responsive to the needs and problems of the developing countries.

6. The International Development Strategy for the Third United Nations Development Decade is an integral part of the continuing efforts of the international community to accelerate the development of developing countries and to establish a new international economic order and is directed towards the achievement of its objectives. These call, in particular, for equitable, full and effective participation by developing countries in the formulation and application of all decisions in the field of development and international economic cooperation with a view to bringing about far-reaching changes in the structure of the present international economic system on a just and equitable basis and the full and permanent sovereignty of every State over its resources and economic activities.

7. The new International Development Strategy aims at the promotion of the economic and social development of the developing countries with a view to reducing significantly the current disparities between the developed and developing countries, as well as the early eradication of poverty and dependency, which, in turn, would contribute to the solution of international economic problems and sustained global economic development, and would also be supported by such development on the basis of justice, equality and mutual benefit. The International Development Strategy is a vast undertaking, involving the entire international community, for the promotion of international development cooperation.

8. The development process must promote human dignity. The ultimate aim of development is the constant improvement of the well-being of the entire population on the basis of its full participation in the process of development and a fair distribution of the benefits therefrom. In this context, a substantial improvement in the status of women will take place during the Decade. In this perspective, economic growth, productive employment and social equity are fundamental and indivisible elements of development. The International Development Strategy should, therefore, full reflect the need for the adoption of adequate and appropriate policies, to be defined by each country within the framework of its development plans and priorities, for movement towards the realization of this ultimate goal of development. The pace of development in the developing countries as a whole should be accelerated substantially in order to enable them to achieve these objectives.

9. The primary responsibility for the development of developing countries rests upon those countries themselves. Effective action by the international community, however, is indispensable for the creation of an environment that is fully supportive of the national and collective efforts of the developing countries for the realization of their development goals. For their part, the developing countries will continue to place increasing emphasis on collective self-reliance as a means of accelerating their development and contributing to the establishment of a new international economic order.

10. The most pressing problems and deteriorating situations of the least developed countries require particular attention, and special and effective measures will be taken for the elimination of the basic constraints facing these countries and to ensure their accelerated development. Likewise, specific measures and actions will be taken to meet the special and pressing problems of the land-locked, island and most seriously affected developing countries.

11. Specific regional problems of developing countries, where they exist and are included in regional development strategies, such as the Lagos Plan of Action for the Implementation of the Monrovia Strategy for the Economic Development of Africa,[1] will also be taken into account through effective and adequate measures within the framework of the general policy measures adopted in favour of all developing countries.

12. Urgent action should be taken by all the members of the international community to end without delay colonialism, imperialism, neo-colonialism, interference in internal affairs, apartheid, racial discrimination, hegemony, expansionism and all forms of foreign aggression and occupation, which constitute major obstacles to the economic emancipation and development of the developing countries.

13. Full respect for the independence, sovereignty and territorial integrity of every country, abstention from the threat or use of force against any State, non-interference in the internal affairs of other States and the settlement by peaceful means of disputes among States are of the utmost importance for the success of the International Development Strategy. There should be concrete progress towards the goals of general and complete disarmament under effective international control, including the urgent implementation of measures of disarmament, which would release substantial additional resources which could be utilized for social and economic development, particularly for the benefit of the developing countries.

14. It is essential to mobilize public opinion in all countries, particularly the developed countries, in order to obtain their full commitment to the goals and objectives and the implementation of the present Strategy. Recognizing the important role of legislative bodies in contributing to realistic preparation and effective implementation of national economic and social development plans, the support of members of legislative bodies will be essential for the implementation of the International Development Strategy.

15. Organs, organizations and bodies of the United Nations system will assist appropriately in the implementation of the Strategy and in the search for new avenues of international cooperation for development.

16. Governments designate the decade starting on 1 January 1981 as the Third United Nations Development Decade and pledge themselves, individually and collectively, to fulfil their commitment to establish a new international economic order based on justice and equity. They subscribe to the goals and objectives of the Strategy and firmly resolve to translate them into reality by adopting a coherent set of interrelated, concrete and effective policy measures in all sectors of development. These goals and objectives and policy measures are set out below.

II. Goals and Objectives

17. The International Development Strategy for the Third United Nations Development Decade, as an integral part of the efforts of the international community to establish a new international economic order, aims at the accelerated development of the developing countries. In contributing to the solution of international economic problems, it will greatly help sustained global economic development and promote the achievement of the ultimate aim of development - the improvement of the conditions of all. It will involve and require changes in the world economy and in the economies of the developed and developing countries themselves; and it calls for institutional and structural changes in international economic relations. In an interdependent world economy, it is the responsibility of all Governments to contribute to the achievement of the goals and objectives of the Strategy. The experience of the 1970s clearly indicates that the goals and objectives of the world community can only be attained through a substantially greater effort in the 1980s than was made in the Second United Nations Development Decade.

18. Particular attention should be given to the need for accelerated development of the least developed countries and other developing countries, particularly those in the special categories, where the development needs and problems are greatest. Special and effective measures should be taken to alleviate their pressing problems and lessen the basic economic constraints facing them.

---

[1] See A/S-11/14, annex I.

19. Accelerated development calls for a more equitable distribution of economic opportunities among nations. In an interdependent world this will be a source of economic strength. It entails changes in the patterns of global production, consumption and trade arising in particular from the industrialization of developing countries; it requires effective control by those countries over the use of their own resources; and it calls for changes in the framework of international economic relations so as to ensure the equitable, full and effective participation of those countries in the formulation and application of all decisions in the field of international economic cooperation for development.

20. Each developing country will set its own target for growth in the light of its particular circumstances. In order to achieve the goals and objectives of the International Development Strategy, the average annual rate of growth of gross domestic product for the developing countries as a whole during the Decade should be 7 per cent, and in the early part of the Decade, as close as possible to this rate. This target and those derived from it are a broad indication of the scope of concerted efforts to be made during the Decade at the national and international levels. on the basis of regional needs, circumstances and patterns of growth, more specific regional goals may be elaborated in the framework of the regional commissions. Special efforts are required to ensure that the low-income developing countries attain the average rate of 7 per cent.

21. If the average annual rate of growth of population in the developing countries were to remain at about 2.5 per cent, an average annual increase of 7 per cent in gross domestic product would lead to an annual increase of about 4.5 per cent in *per capita* gross domestic product. This would double income *per capita* in developing countries around the middle of the 1990s. Such a growth in income is necessary if real progress is to be made towards raising substantially the share of the developing countries in world production of goods and services and towards eliminating the growing gap between the standards of living of developing and developed countries. Such growth is equally essential if the people of developing countries are to benefit from development through expanding employment opportunities, rising levels of income and consumption, better housing and expanding facilities for health and education. Accelerated growth in the developing countries is also needed in order to support national policies aimed at achieving a more equitable distribution of income and benefits from development. Further, such growth will contribute significantly to a more balanced growth of the world economy.

22. An acceleration in the tempo of production in developing countries will require a rapid expansion and diversification of their international trade. For developing countries in general, exports and imports of goods and services should expand at annual rates of not less than 7.5 per cent and 8 per cent, respectively. The attainment of such rates of growth and the improvement of the terms of trade of developing countries will necessitate equitable participation of developing countries in international trade, *inter alia*, through improved market access for their products, and extending to them special and preferential treatment where feasible and appropriate, in the context of the general effort to liberalize world trade, particularly in their favour, and vigorous efforts to resist protectionism, as steps towards promoting equity in trade relations between the developing and developed countries. The industrialized countries will take fully into account the industrialization and development objectives of the developing countries when shaping their trade policies, in particular by continuing and accelerating the implementation of effective adjustment policies based on mutual benefit and dynamic comparative advantage.

23. The acceleration of production will require that gross investment reaches the level of about 28 per cent of gross domestic product by 1990. The developing countries, therefore, must fully mobilize their domestic financial resources. To this end, for developing countries in general, gross domestic saving should be increased to reach about 24 per cent of gross domestic product by 1990. The developing countries that have a saving ratio of less than 15 per cent should make vigorous efforts to raise it to 20 per cent as early as possible. The countries that have or will soon have a saving ratio of 20 per cent should raise it significantly during the Decade.

24. The rising investments and imports needed for an acceleration of growth commensurate with the attainment of the goals and objectives of the International Development Strategy require a substantially greater flow of financial resources in real terms to developing countries. In this context, recent major proposals made by heads of State and Government, and other important proposals to increase substantially concessional and non-concessional flows in real terms to developing countries, should be given urgent consideration by the international community. A major objective of the Decade must be to make possible in the context of continued changes and improvements in the international financial system an enhanced flow of financial resources on terms and conditions that are better attuned to the development aims and economic circumstances of developing countries. A rapid and substantial increase will be made in official development assistance by all developed countries, with a view to reaching and where possible surpassing the agreed international target of 0.7 per cent of the gross national product of developed countries. To this end, developed countries which have not yet reached the target should make their best efforts to reach it by 1985, and in any case not later than in the second half of the Decade. The target of 1 per cent should be reached as soon as possible thereafter. The efforts of developed countries will be greater, the lower their relative performance. Developing countries in a position to do so should also continue to provide assistance to other developing countries. Within the framework of this general increase to all developing countries, and in order to meet the most pressing problems and correct the deteriorating situation of the least developed countries and developing countries in the other special categories where the development needs and problems are greatest, the flows of official development assistance will increasingly be directed towards those countries.

25. Efforts should be made to encourage an increase in net flows of non-concessional capital which is required for the over-all financing needs of the developing countries, taking into account their national plans and legislations.

26. In order to create conditions more favourable to the development of the developing countries and the growth of the world economy in general, efforts to increase the responsiveness of the international monetary system to the needs and interests of the developing countries should be intensified through further reform of the system to be pursued and carried out expeditiously early in and throughout the Decade to the benefit of the entire international community. To these ends, the international monetary system should provide for the equitable and effective participation of developing countries in decision making, taking into account, *inter alia*, their growing role in the world economy, as well as a symmetrical and efficient adjustment process, stability of exchange rates of international currencies, and further strengthening and expansion of the special drawing rights as the central reserve asset in order to ensure better international control over the creation and equitable distribution of international liquidity. In stipulating the conditions attached to the use of its resources, the International Monetary Fund will pay due regard to the social and political domestic objectives of member countries, to their economic priorities and circumstances, including the causes of their balance-of-payments problems. The international and multilateral financial institutions are urged to continue to expand and improve their lending facilities, and to create new ones where necessary, with a view to assisting their members, including in particular the developing countries which face balance-of-payments difficulties.

27. The persistence of inflation in the world economy, particularly in developed countries, impedes growth and development and renders the situation of developing countries even more precarious. The rate of inflation should he substantially reduced and its adverse effects should be mitigated as far as possible so as to help to ensure a sustained, increased and real economic growth, particularly in the developing countries. Rapid economic growth in developing countries will help rationalize productive structures and decrease intiationary pressures.

28. Hunger and malnutrition must be eliminated as soon as possible and certainly by the end of this century. Substantial progress should be made during the Decade towards food self-sufficiency and food security in developing countries so as to ensure an adequate level of

nutrition for everybody. Agricultural production in developing countries as a whole should expand at an average annual rate of at least 4 per cent so that it will be possible to meet the nutritional needs of the populations, to enlarge the base for industrialization and the diversification of economic structures, and to redress current imbalances in world production. The share of developing countries in world exports of food and agricultural products should increase substantially. To those ends, developing countries should continue to strengthen the formulation and implementation on food and agricultural development plans within the framework of their national development priorities and programmes. These objectives should be supported by additional external resource transfers in the context of over-all greater flows of financial resources to developing countries. An improved international framework for the agricultural development of developing countries is also necessary, including increased marked stability, greater security of agricultural supplies and, in order to enlarge the export potential of developing countries, improved access for their agricultural products to world markets.

29. Developing countries as a whole should expand manufacturing output at an average annual rate of 9 per cent, thereby making a significant contribution during the Decade towards raising the share of developing countries in world manufacturing production and laying the basis for achieving the target of a 25 per cent share of world production by the year 2000 as set out in the Lima Declaration and Plan of Action on Industrial Development and Cooperation.[1] Industrialization should be aimed at meeting in an integrated way the over-all requirements of the development of the national economies of developing countries. Manufacturing activities should be geared towards not only satisfying growing domestic demand and employment requirements but also, as a component of independent national economies, increasing the share of developing countries in world exports of manufactured goods. A fundamental objective of the world community is to achieve a system of trade based on a dynamic pattern of comparative advantage reflecting a more effective international division of labour. Far-reaching changes should, therefore, be brought about in the structure of world production, in the spirit of mutual benefit, so as to increase and diversify the production of the developing countries and create new sources of employment there. In this context, improved access to markets for products of export interest to developing countries and continued attention to the formulation and implementation of positive adjustment policies in the industrialized countries are important objectives of international cooperation.

30. The physical and institutional infrastructure in developing countries should be expanded at rates that fully support the rate of expansion of the economy as a whole, and adequate financial and technical resources should be provided for that purpose. Special attention should be given to overcoming the bottle-necks and constraints of transport and communication facing the developing countries, particularly with a view to strengthening intraregional and interregional links.

31. Due account should be taken of the positive role of the public sector in mobilizing internal resources, formulating and implementing over-all national development plans and establishing national priorities.

32. In a growing world economy and without prejudice to the principle of full and permanent sovereignty of each State over its natural resources, the rational development, management and utilization of natural resources should be encouraged in order, *inter alia*, to prevent early exhaustion of finite resources and overburdening of renewable resources. It will be necessary, particularly for the industrialized countries, which bear the heaviest responsibility for the use of natural resources, to encourage new patterns of consumption and production.

33. In the field of raw materials, the agreed objectives of the integrated Programme for Commodities[2] should be actively pursued. In this context, international commodity agreements should be concluded and a more equitable distribution of activities related to the processing of raw materials should be achieved with the aim of increasing the location of those activities in developing countries. Developing countries should also acquire improved capacity to explore and develop their natural resources and to ensure closer integration of the sector in the over-all development of their economies.

34. In order to create conditions more favourable to the development of the developing countries and the growth of the world economy in general, efforts for the development and expansion of all energy resources of the world should be intensified in search of a long-term solution to the energy problem. The international community will have to make substantial and rapid progress in the transition from the present international economy based primarily on hydrocarbons. It will have to rely increasingly on new and renewable sources of energy, seeking to reserve hydrocarbons for non-energy and non-substitutable uses. In view of the finite supply of fossil fuels in the world economy and the often wasteful and inefficient utilization of those resources, effective measures for their conservation will have to be urgently adopted and/or improved, in particular by developed countries which consume the major share of the world's hydrocarbon production.

35. In view of the increasing energy requirements of the developing countries during the Decade and beyond, which will limit their ability to reduce energy use significantly without hindering their development, concerted and adequate measures commensurate with their development goals and their immediate and longer-term needs will be adopted by the international community. In this context, the exploration, development, expansion and processing of all energy resources of the developing countries will be promoted at a rate commensurate with their development objectives and adequate financial and technical resources will be provided for the purpose. The international community will devote serious attention to the effective implementation of the results of the United Nations Conference on New and Renewable Sources of Energy. Adequate financial and technical resources will be devoted to the development of new and renewable sources, to conventional forms of energy and to the adaptation of technology to the needs of developing countries. Developed countries should give or facilitate, as appropriate, the freest and fullest possible access to all energy technologies, particularly those related to the development of new and renewable forms. The problem of energy will be considered within the global negotiations relating to international economic cooperation for development, as agreed to by the General Assembly at its thirty-fourth session.[3]

36. The strengthening of the scientific and technological capacities of developing countries is essential for their sustained and accelerated development. The international community will implement the Vienna Programme of Action on Science and Technology for Development[4] principally in order to strengthen the scientific and technological capacities of developing countries, to restructure the existing pattern of international scientific and technological relations and to strengthen the role of the United Nations system in science and technology and the provision of increased financial resources. Efforts will be made at national and international levels to enable developing countries to have easier access to the technology - including advanced technology - they require and to facilitate the transfer of such technology on a substantially increased scale.

37. The most pressing problems and the deteriorating situation of the least developed countries must receive special attention. In order to remove the basic constraints to their development and thereby transform their economies, efforts by the least developed countries themselves and by the international community must be immediately and substantially expanded. Measures should be focused on promoting a self-sustained process of development, on accelerating agricultural and industrial progress and on ensuring the development of human

1 See A/10112,chap. IV.

2 See *Proceedings of the United Nations Conference on Trade and Development, Fourth Session,* vol. I, *Report and Annexes* (United Nations publication, Sales No. E.76.II.D.10 and corrigendum), part one, sect. A, resolution 93 (IV).

3 Resolution 34/138, para. 2 (*b*).

4 *Report of the United Nations Conference on Science and Technology for Development, Vienna, 20-31 August 1979* (United Nations publication, Sales No. E.79.I.21 and corrigenda), chap. VII.

resources and broadly-based participation in development. The international community will devote serious attention to the effective preparation and conclusion of and follow-up to the United Nations Conference on the Least Developed Countries.

38. The special and pressing problems of the land-locked, island and most seriously affected developing countries need to be met through specific measures and actions.

39. There is a close relationship between disarmament and development. Progress in the former would help greatly in the realization of the latter. Therefore, resources released as a result of the implementation of disarmament measures should be devoted to the economic and social development of all nations and should contribute to the bridging of the economic gap between developed and developing countries.

40. Economic and technical cooperation among developing countries based on the principle of collective self-reliance constitutes a dynamic and vital component of an effective restructuring of international economic relations. While the main elements of economic and technical cooperation among developing countries will be determined by those countries themselves, the international community should accord high priority and urgency to supporting the efforts of developing countries to strengthen and implement their programmes of mutual economic and technical cooperation. Such programmes will contribute to reducing their external dependence and vulnerability, achieving equitable and balanced international economic relations and strengthening their role in the world economy, their self-reliance and autonomous growth and development.

41. Accelerated development in the developing countries could enhance their capacity to improve their environment. The environmental implications of poverty and under-development and the interrelationships between development, environment, population and resources must be taken into account in the process of development. It is essential to avoid environmental degradation and give future generations the benefit of a sound environment. There is need to ensure an economic development process which is environmentally sustainable over the long run and which protects the ecological balance. Determined efforts must be made to prevent deforestation, erosion, soil degradation and desertification. International cooperation in environmental protection should be increased.

42. Development is an integral process, embodying both economic and social objectives. National development plans and targets of the developing countries should be formulated on the basis of a unified approach to economic and social development, which is essential for balanced development of all sectors of the economy, should provide for both accelerated growth and increased effectiveness of production and should fully take into account not only immediate but also long-term social and economic objectives of development of the developing countries. It is for each country to establish adequate national objectives for the promotion of human and social development within the framework of its development plans, priorities and resources and in accordance with its socio-economic structure and existing circumstances. The final aim of development must be the continuing increase in the well-being of the entire population on the basis of its full participation in the process of development and a fair distribution of the benefits therefrom. As part of the efforts to implement the International Development Strategy, the international community will provide technical and financial support to achieve those goals, in the context of an over-all substantial increase in resources for development, paying due respect to the cultural identities of nations and peoples.

43. The reduction and elimination of poverty and a fair distribution of the benefits of development are primary objectives for the international community during the Decade. Great numbers of workers remain under-employed or unemployed. Many millions are illiterate. High infant mortality rates, poor housing and environmental degradation in urban slums and depressed rural areas continue to afflict the people of the developing countries. More resources for production, higher productivity and accelerated development are essential for progress towards higher and more equitable standards of living. These are continuing challenges to the international community, and Governments accordingly reaffirm their commitment to the broad aim of development.

44. The achievement of full employment by the year 2000 remains a primary objective. Intensive efforts will have to be made to increase the opportunities for productive employment, especially for the new entrants to the labour force, as this is expected to increase by 2.5 per cent per annum, and to reduce and eliminate the present massive unemployment and under-employment.

45. The international community recognizes the need for countries to continue to strengthen their implementation of the recommendations of the World Population Plan of Action.[1] Consistent with the World Population Plan of Action, all countries should respect and ensure the right of parents to determine the number and spacing of their children and should, as a matter of urgency, make universally available advice on and means of achieving the desired family size.

46. The development of human resources provides a broad basis for development; it enhances the capacity of people to participate constructively in the development process. In this context, education is an important element, and the provision of universal education on the broadest possible scale, the eradication or considerable reduction of illiteracy, and the closest possible realization of universal primary enrolment by the year 2000 remain major goals of all countries during the Decade. A parallel and harmonious expansion of all levels and types of education is equally necessary, keeping in view the decisive role of education and training for national development and individual fulfilment.

47. The absence or shortage of trained and qualified national personnel often limits the capacity of developing countries to take full advantage of existing or potential development opportunities. The provision of the required trained and qualified personnel on a scale assuring national self-sufficiency in this respect would constitute an important contribution to the achievement of the development goals of the developing countries. The international community should provide adequate financial and technical resources to support the training of national personnel in all sectors of social and economic activities in the developing countries.

48. The attainment by the year 2000 of a level of health that will permit all peoples of the world to lead a socially and economically productive life is an important objective of the international community. Primary health care is a key measure for the attainment of this objective. All countries will broaden the access of the poorest groups in their populations to health facilities and, with the assistance of the international community, will ensure immunization against major infectious diseases for all children as early as possible during the Decade. Safe water and adequate sanitary facilities should also be made available to all in rural and urban areas by 1990. The reduction on mortality rates will be a major objective. In the poorest countries, infant mortality should be reduced to less than 120 per 1,000 live births. Life expectancy in all countries should reach 60 years as a minimum, and infant mortality rates should reach 50 per 1,000 live births, as a maximum, by the year 2000. Particular efforts should be made to integrate the disabled in the development process. Effective measures of prevention and rehabilitation are therefore essential.

49. The provision of basic shelter and infrastructure for all people, in rural as well as urban areas, is a long-term goal. A balanced network of cities, towns and villages is needed for harmonious development, for the emergence of mutually supportive linkages between industrial and agricultural activities, and for the adequate provision of infrastructure and services. Well-balanced programmes for the development of human settlements are necessary so as to provide greater benefits to low-income groups.

50. In pursuit of the objectives highlighted during the International Year of the Child,[2] the welfare of children will be fostered. The essential role of the family in the balanced development of the child should be stressed. Efforts should be made to improve the living

---

1 *Report of the United Nations World Population Conference, Bucharest, 19-30 August 1974* (United Nations publication, Sales No. E.75.XIII.3), chap. I.

2 See resolution 31/169, para. 2.

conditions of children and to eliminate child labour in conformity with the relevant international labour conventions; special attention should be paid to the large number of children under 15 years of age living in poor rural and urban areas.

51. Full and effective participation by the entire population at all stages of the development process should be ensured. In line with the Programme of Action adopted by the World Conference of the United Nations Decade for Women,[1] women should play an active role in that process. Appropriate measures should be taken for profound social and economic changes and for the elimination of the structural imbalances which compound and perpetuate women's disadvantages. To this end, all countries will pursue the objective of securing women's equal participation both as agents and as beneficiaries in all sectors and at all levels of the development process. This should include women's greater access to nutrition, health services, education and training, employment, and financial resources and their greater participation in the analysis, planning, decision-making, implementation and evaluation on development. Changes that will lead to the sharing of responsibilities by men and women in the family and in the management of the household should be encouraged. Institutional and administrative mechanisms to accomplish these objectives should be strengthened. All countries should give high priority to the objectives of mobilizing and integrating youth in development.

III. Policy Measures

A. International trade

52. All countries commit themselves to an open and expanding trade system to further progress in the liberalization of trade and to the promotion of structural adjustment which will facilitate the realization of the dynamic pattern of comparative advantage. The rules and principles governing the functioning of international trade will be kept under review so as to ensure the steady growth of trade under equitable and secure conditions. To this end. there should be more effective implementation, as far as possible, of the principle of differential and more favourable treatment, on a non-reciprocal basis, of developing countries in order to enhance their market access and to increase their share of world trade, taking into account their trade, development and financial needs.

53. As an immediate measure, the agreements reached in the multilateral trade negotiations will be promptly and fully implemented by the parties to those agreements. Steps will be taken early in the Third United Nations Development Decade to reduce or to eliminate existing restrictions on imports from developing countries. Developed countries will implement fully and adhere strictly to the standstill provisions that they have accepted. Concerted efforts will be made, particularly by developed countries, to reduce non-tariff barriers progressively and even abolish them, especially in the case of products or sectors of export interest to the developing countries.

54. Efforts will be pursued to reach an agreement on a multilateral safeguard system based on and subject to objective internationally agreed criteria relating to, *inter alia*, adequate testing on serious injury in order to provide greater uniformity and certainty in implementation and to ensure that the safeguard clause, if used, is not applied for protectionist reasons or to hinder structural change.

55. The Common Fund, as a new entity serving as a key instrument for the attainment on the agreed objectives of the Integrated Programme for Commodities, will urgently be brought into full and effective operation.

56. International commodity agreements, with initial emphasis on the core commodities included in the indicative list of the Integrated Programme for Commodities, should be concluded.

57. A framework of international cooperation will be established within the over-all context of the Integrated Programme for Commodities for expanding in developing countries the processing of primary commodities and exports on processed goods, as well as for the increased participation of developing countries in the marketing, distribution and transportation of their primary commodities.

58. Additional measures for the improvement and stabilization of commodity export earnings of developing countries should be considered as soon as possible.

59. International organizations and developed countries and others in a position to do so should assist developing countries, in particular the least developed countries, through the provision of capital and technology and of training skills for developing, processing and manufacturing capacities and for setting up and strengthening finance, commerce, transport, various services and other infrastructures in developing countries to facilitate and promote their production and exports of manufactured and semi-manufactured goods.

60. Developed countries should exert their best efforts to improve access to their markets for exports of agricultural products on a stable and predictable basis. They should accord developing countries the opportunity to expand their agricultural exports through a continued and accelerated liberalization on agricultural and trade policies. Urgent action will be taken in relevant negotiating forums to move towards the approval and implementation of proposals to bring about the reduction and elimination of barriers to trade in agricultural products, in particular in relation to those of export interest to developing countries, and thus to facilitate, *inter alia*, more efficient patterns of production. Developed countries will make their best efforts to adjust those sectors of their agricultural and manufacturing economies which require protection against exports from developing countries, thus facilitating access to the markets of food and agricultural products. The developed countries should exert their best efforts to avoid adverse effects on the economies of the developing countries while formulating and implementing their domestic agricultural policies.

61. In the context of the framework for international cooperation, measures should be taken, including internationally agreed programmes for research and development, in order to improve the competitiveness of natural products produced in developing countries with the synthetics and substitutes of developed countries. Furthermore, measures should be considered to harmonize, where appropriate, the production of such synthetics and substitutes with the supply of natural products produced in developing countries.

62. Sectoral agreements which result in hampering the growth in the trade of developing countries should be avoided to the maximum extent. Efforts should be made to avoid extending such existing agreements with a view to their eventual elimination.

63. The generalized system of preferences should be continued as an important long-term instrument for promoting trade and development cooperation and, in particular, for bringing about an increased share of developing countries in world trade. The international community reaffirms the importance of the generalized, non-reciprocal and non-discriminatory system of preferences for expansion and diversification of the export trade of developing countries and for acceleration of the rates of their economic growth. To this end, the preference-giving countries will implement fully the agreement reached by the Special Committee on Preferences of the Trade and Development Board at its ninth session.[2] A comprehensive review of the generalized system of preferences should be held in 1990.

64. Efforts should be pursued and intensified by developed countries to take special unilateral measures further to reduce trade barriers facing developing countries in respect of tropical products, including those products in their processed forms, on a non-reciprocal basis. Those reductions should be urgently considered and carried out.

65. The International Trade Centre should be further supported by technical and financial assistance from donor countries in order to increase and strengthen its technical cooperation programme with

---

1 See *Report of the World Conference of the United Nations Decade for Women: Equality, Development and Peace, Copenhagen, 14-30 July 1980* (United Nations publication, Sales No. E.80.IV.3 and corrigendum), chap. 1, sect. A.

2 See *Official Records of the Trade and Development Board, Twenty-first Session, Supplement No. 3* (TD/B/802), annex 1, resolution 6 (IX).

developing countries in trade promotion and export development activities.

66. Socialist countries of Eastern Europe, in the context of their long-term economic plans, will continue to adopt and implement appropriate measures, in order to increase their trade with developing countries, commensurate with the trade needs of the developing countries, including in particular their production and export potential.

67. Developing countries will promote and expand trade among themselves in accordance with the relevant decisions taken by those countries in the Arusha Programme for Collective Self-Reliance and Framework for Negotiations,[1] adopted by the Fourth Ministerial Meeting of the Group of 77, held at Arusha, United Republic of Tanzania, from 12 to 16 February 1979, and in other international forums. The international community will provide appropriate support and assistance to the efforts of developing countries.

Invisibles

68. Measures will be devised during the Decade to encourage a more balanced international distribution of service industries and to assist developing countries in minimizing as far as possible their net outflow of foreign exchange from invisible transactions, including transport. Developing countries will expand their tourist industry. Developed countries will assist in this endeavour as far as possible.

69. The international community will take appropriate measures to help the establishment and growth of local insurance markets in developing countries where such potential exists. As regards those insurance operations that cannot be carried out without using external insurance services, it is essential that the terms and conditions of international insurance and reinsurance transactions are equitable for, and meet the needs of, all parties concerned, in particular those of the developing countries.

Transnational corporations

70. Negotiations on a United Nations code of conduct on transnational corporations will be concluded in 1981 and the code will be adopted expeditiously by all members of the international community soon afterwards, aimed at preventing - with a view to eliminating - the negative effects of activities of transnational corporations and promoting the positive contribution of transnational corporations to the development efforts of the developing countries, consistent with the national development plans and priorities of those countries. National policies which enable Governments to deal with and regulate effectively the operations of the transnational corporations will also be developed and pursued.

Restrictive business practices

71. The principles and rules for the control of restrictive business practices which adversely affect international trade, particularly that of the developing countries, and their economic development, approved by the United Nations Conference on Restrictive Business Practices,[2] will be actively implemented.

B. Industrialization

72. The rapid industrialization on developing countries constitutes an indispensable element and a dynamic instrument of the sustained self-reliant growth of their economies and of their social transformation. It is for each developing country to determine its own industrial development goals and priorities. The attainment of the targets for the industrialization of the developing countries contained in the present Strategy, aimed at, *inter alia*, raising the share of the developing countries in world industrial production in accordance with the Lima Declaration and Plan of Action, calls for far-reaching changes in the structure of world production. To this end, developing and developed countries will consider and adopt appropriate policies and programmes at the national, regional and international levels for the strengthening and expansion of the developing countries' industrial capacities as an essential element of their development process.

73. These policies and programmes include, as a crucial element, the redeployment of industrial capacities. This redeployment will primarily consist of the creation of new industrial capacities in developing countries, as well as the redeployment of industrial capacities from industrialized to developing countries on the principle on dynamic comparative advantage, in conjunction with structural adjustment, and taking fully into account the over-all national objectives and priorities in particular of developing countries. This involves the transfer of financial, technological, managerial, personnel and other resources to developing countries, including the provision of the necessary training and expert services. While economic, institutional, social and other pertinent factors have an important bearing on this process, Governments, in particular those of the developed countries, should encourage and intensify the process by actively pursuing policies with a view to encouraging the continued reallocation of resources and encouraging domestic factors of production to move from internationally less competitive to more viable lines of production or into other sectors of the economy. These policies should be accompanied, to the maximum extent possible, by increased access to their markets of the manufactured products of developing countries.

74. Attention will be given to strengthening the developing countries' industries as a means of independent and autonomous industrial development, working out long-term industrialization plans and programmes, including plans and programmes for the discovery, exploitation and more complete processing of natural resources; a balanced industrial development with heavy and light industries, basic industries, large-scale, intermediate-scale and small-scale production; and the establishment of agro-industrial complexes. Assistance should be given to the developing countries in forms which suit the interests of their self-sustained development.

75. The system of consultations established in the United Nations Industrial Development Organization as permanent activity will be strengthened, developed and made more effective so that it may make a substantial contribution to the industrialization of developing countries and contribute effectively to the achievement of the objectives and targets set out in the present Strategy as will as in the Lima Declaration and Plan of Action.

76. Both multilatera! and bilateral sources of finance should respond, while taking into account the priorities of developing countries, to the need for a substantial increase in the transfer of financial and other resources, including official development assistance transfers, as appropriate, to developing countries to support and reinforce their industrialization programmes. The arrangements for industrial financing should be reviewed early in the Decade, keeping in mind recent proposals with a view to strengthening existing international financing facilities, including appropriate ways to extend or modify those facilities and other measures required towards this end. The United Nations Industrial Development Fund should be strengthened and enlarged to provide a significant increase in the technical assistance necessary for accelerating the industrialization of developing countries.

77. As part of an integrated industrial structure, it is necessary to encourage, *inter alia*, labour-intensive, medium-scale and small-scale industries which are efficient and generate more employment opportunities. The use of appropriate technology and effective policies to increase investments for the development of human resources should be further strengthened and broadened. Industrialization policies should have as one of their aims productive employment generation and the integration and equal participation of women in industrial development programmes.

78. Industrialization policies in developing countries will require vigorous domestic policies supported by international assistance and investment. Those policies could provide for, *inter alia*, increased domestic investment, taking into account the role of the public sector in this process, measures to encourage domestic savings and mutually beneficial foreign direct investment and other sources of private capital. It is for the developing countries to set their own investment priorities and take appropriate decisions regarding admission of foreign investment and private capital in the light of those priorities.

---

1 *Proceedings of the United Nations Conference on Trade and Development, Fifth Session,* vol. I, *Report and Annexes* (United Nations publication, Sales No. E.79.II.D.14), annex VI.

2 See A/C.2/35/6, annex.

79. Consideration should be given by all countries to environmental aspects of industrialization in the formulation and implementation of their industrial policies and plans. Donor countries, suppliers of technology and the relevant international organizations should assist developing countries, at their request, with a view to enhancing their capacities in this respect.

80. The international community will accord highest priority to measures, including adequate financial provisions, as required, for the effective implementation of the Industrial Development Decade for Africa,[1] to be observed in the 1980s.

C. Food and agriculture

81. Agricultural and rural development and the eradication of hunger and malnutrition are among the essential aims of the Third United Nations Development Decade. Developing countries, in the context of their national development plans and priorities, firmly supported by the international community, will take all necessary measures to accelerate food and agricultural production in order to improve national and collective self-sufficiency in food as early as possible. To this end, effective policies should continue to be pursued and invigorated in relation to the provision of appropriate price incentives, distribution of credit, the improvement of storage and transport and reduction of food losses, in particular post-harvest losses. In the efforts to achieve the 4 per cent average annual growth in agricultural production, particular attention should be paid to low-income, food-deficit countries so as to allow them to attain this level of growth as early as possible. The implementation of national policies should take into account the need to mobilize fully the domestic resources of developing countries. Adequate consideration should be given to the implementation of agrarian reforms as one of the important factors for promoting increased agricultural production and rural development in conformity with the national plans and priorities of each developing country. In accordance with their national plans, they will give priority to programmes for adaptation of institutional frameworks so as to allow wider and more equitable access to land and water resources, as well as effective management of forests, pastures, water and other natural resources in their national interests, with wider dissemination and use of new and Improved technology, including greater use of fertilizers, improved seeds and pesticides, utilization of irrigation potential and the development of forests and fisheries. They will make the necessary efforts to develop and promote social and economic services and adequate public utilities in rural areas. They will expand non-agricultural employment opportunities in rural areas, particularly in industries related to agriculture. All countries will take appropriate measures, on a priority basis, to restore and improve water resources and the capacity of the land to produce necessary agricultural products. Extensive reforestation programmes will be carried out to prevent soil erosion, as well as to satisfy local needs for wood as a raw material and source of energy.

82. All countries will take appropriate measures, on a priority basis, to implement the conclusions and recommendations set forth in the Declaration of Principles and the Programme of Action adopted by the World Conference on Agrarian Reform and Rural Development,[2] as well as taking fully into account the conclusions and recommendations made by the relevant United Nations bodies and organizations concerned.

83. In support of measures in developing countries to increase substantially investment in agriculture, donor countries and international financial institutions will take all possible steps to increase the flow of financial resources to the developing countries. The resources of the International Fund for Agricultural Development should be replenished on a continuing basis at a level sufficient to attain its objectives as and when recommended by its Governing Council, taking into consideration the increasing needs on developing countries for external resources, with consultations relating to the first replenishment to be concluded, on a priority basis, before the end of 1980. Furthermore, donors should commit adequate funds for local costs and should meet requests wherever possible for financial participation in recurrent costs of the implementation of development projects in the agricultural sector.

84. Additional resources should be provided for the adaptation and dissemination of agricultural technologies and for the intensification of research into techniques that rely less on costly inputs and to an increasing extent on renewable inputs. High priority will be accorded to strengthening the network of international and regional research, including research training institutions, agricultural extension services and the exchange of information and experience, and to improving their relationship with national research systems. Special attention will be given to the implementation of the results of research at the level of the people concerned.

85. The international community will support measures to provide agricultural inputs, especially fertilizers, improved seeds and pesticides, and efforts directed towards the prevention of food losses, control of the desert locust and control of African trypanosomiasis.

86. Urgent measures will be taken early in the Decade to establish effective world food security. To this end, world cereal stocks should be maintained at an adequate level, which has been estimated at from 17 to 18 per cent of annual world consumption.[3] It is essential that concerted efforts be made to conclude a new international grain agreement aimed at evolving an internationally coordinated system of nationally held food reserves. As an interim measure, early steps will be taken by countries to implement, on a voluntary basis, the Five-Point Plan of Action on World Food Security of the Food and Agriculture Organization of the United Nations, and the resources of the Food Security Assistance Scheme of that Organization will be expanded. Bilateral assistance will be coordinated with the Scheme where appropriate.

87. Long-term measures are needed to step up food production in the developing countries, which is the only lasting way to obtain food security. At the national level and, in appropriate cases, at the regional level, developing countries should set up, as a complement to production policies, the facilities necessary for stocking, conservation, transport and distribution of food, to enable them to meet emergency situations, to reinforce the stability of their markets and to reduce avoidable post-harvest losses. In doing so, they should be supported by the international community by financial and technical assistance, as well as by food aid.

88. Since the Food Aid Convention agreed upon recently for 7.6 million tons falls considerably short of the target of 10 million tons, every effort should be made both to enlist new contributors and to increase the commitments of existing ones so that the new Convention can be renewed by mid-1981 with a firm assurance that the target will be the absolute minimum flow of assistance, even in times of high prices and food shortage. Urgent consideration will be given to a revision of the target, taking into account the estimated requirements of 17 to 18.5 million tons of cereals which provide a useful indicator of the over-all requirement of food aid by 1985. This estimate will be reviewed periodically. In order to ensure continuity, the Food Aid Convention should be extended to three years, if possible, and should provide for a revision of the minimum target to meet growing food aid requirements. Efforts should be made by donor countries and international organizations to meet food aid requirements, especially in the low-income, food-deficit countries.

89. While considering annual requirements of food aid by 1985, estimates of 300,000 tons of dairy products and 350,000 tons of vegetable oil, which also provide useful indicators of annual requirements, should be taken into account.

90. Resources of the World Food Programme will be augmented and every effort will be made to reach the current minimum agreed target

---

1 Proclaimed by the General Assembly in its resolution 35/66 B.

2 See Food and Agriculture Organization of the United Nations, *Report of the World Conference on Agrarian Reform and Rural Development, Rome, 12-20 July 1979* (WCARRD/REP), part one.

3 See Food and Agriculture Organization of the United Nations, *Committee on Commodity Problems, Intergovernmental Group on Grains, Nineteenth Session,* "World food security" (CCP:GR 75/9), August 1975; and *Committee on World Food Security,* "Report on the fifth session" (CL 78/10), April 1980.

of $1 billion for 1981/82 and the target agreed upon for each subsequent biennium during the Decade for this programme.

91. The International Monetary Fund should consider urgently, within the context of its financing facilities, the feasibility of providing additional balance-of-payments support for meeting the rise in food imports bills of low-income, food-deficit countries.

92. The target of 500,000 tons of cereals for the International Emergency Food Reserve should be realized immediately. All countries, particularly those which are not yet contributing to it, should make or increase their contributions to the Reserve. The Reserve should be maintained at 500,000 tons. Early consideration should be given to proposals for strengthening the Reserve, including the possibility of making a legally binding convention. Any proposals agreed upon should, *inter alia,* make provision for increasing the size on the Reserve so as to meet future emergency needs.

93. The eradication of hunger and malnutrition calls for concerted efforts, national food policies, plans and commitments by Governments, as well as appropriate programmes on the part of the United Nations system during the Decade and beyond. A positive commitment to nutrition policies will require efforts at the production and distribution levels to ensure that requisite food supplies are available for those whose consumption of food is inadequate. A special national commitment to the nutritional needs of children should be undertaken. Donor countries are strongly called upon to do their utmost to ensure a high nutritional value of their food aid.

94. Special attention will continue to be given to the impact of food trade on the level of food production in the world, in particular with reference to the economies of the developing countries.

95. In the context of integrated rural development, Governments will encourage rural industrialization, the establishment and strengthening of agro-industrial complexes, the modernization of agriculture, better integration of women in all stages of the production process and the ensuring thereby of increased production of food and other agricultural products, and employment for the rural population. Governments should encourage and support the establishment of agricultural cooperatives.

D. Financial resources for development

96. Developing countries will continue to bear the main responsibility for financing their development and will adopt vigorous measures for a fuller mobilization of their domestic financial resources. External financial resources, particularly official development assistance, constitute an indispensable element of support for the developing countries' own efforts. International financial flows, particularly public flows, should be improved and adapted consistent with the needs of developing countries as regards volume, composition, quality, forms and distribution of flows.

97. Bilateral and multilateral flows will be made on an increasingly assured, continuous and predictable basis.

98. A rapid and substantial increase will be made in official development assistance by all developed countries, with a view to reaching and, where possible, surpassing the agreed international target of 0.7 per cent of the gross national product of developed countries. To this end, developed countries which have not yet reached the target should exert their best efforts to reach it by 1985, and in any case not later than in the second half of the Decade. The target of 1 per cent should be reached as soon as possible thereafter. The efforts of developed countries will be greater, the lower their relative performance. Developing countries in a position to do so should also continue to provide assistance to other developing countries. In the context of this general increase and in order to meet the most pressing problems and the deteriorating situation of the least developed countries and developing countries in the other special categories where the development needs and problems are greatest, the flows of official development assistance will increasingly be directed towards those countries.

99. All developed donor countries should announce annually their plans or intentions, in the light of measures outlined in resolution 129 (V) of 3 June 1979 of the United Nations Conference on Trade and Development,[1] as regards an increase in official development assistance for the longest period ahead and, where possible, nor a minimum period of three years. They should provide full information on their official development assistance flows.

100. The international community will give priority consideration to the immediate and urgent needs of poorer developing countries, in particular the least developed countries, and in this context urgent consideration should be given to establishing emergency programmes of assistance to those countries. The measures on assistance and volume of the programmes will be determined, taking into account their present economic difficulties and longer-term development needs.

101. In the context of the general increase of official development assistance, equitable efforts will be made by donor countries with a view to doubling as soon as possible the flow of official development assistance to the least developed countries, taking into account the relative performance of the donor countries. All donor countries will give all due consideration, not later than at the United Nations Conference on the Least Developed Countries, to be held in 1981, to the proposals for further measures to provide an adequate minimum flow of official development assistance, including those proposals for tripling the net disbursement of concessional assistance by 1984 and quadrupling it by 1990 at 1977 prices.

102. Within the context of this general increase to developing countries as a whole, specific efforts should be undertaken to meet the needs of other special categories of developing countries. To this end, official development assistance to these categories of countries will be increased substantially during the Decade, as appropriate.

103. The terms and conditions of official development assistance should be significantly improved. In particular:

(*a*) The current over-all average rate of concessionality of official development assistance should be further increased. Official development assistance to least developed countries should, as a general rule, be in the form on grants and at high concessionality to other developing countries, particularly those in the special categories, which depend primarily on concessional flows;

(*b*) The official development assistance should, as a general rule, be untied. The share of programme assistance and local and recurrent cost financing in official development assistance should be increased substantially when necessary.

104. Furthermore, sudden and important deterioration in the external conditions of developing countries, beyond their control, will be appropriately taken into account in determining the concessionality and grant element of official development assistance.

105. All developed donor countries will continue to improve their aid-giving procedures, in consultation with the beneficiary countries, so as to reduce obstacles to rapid aid disbursements and effective aid uses, without any discrimination.

106. In the field of export credits, the needs of the developing countries should be recognized by developed countries. To this end, the export credit guarantee agencies of the developed countries should, as appropriate, improve the guarantee conditions, including in particular increasing the guarantee periods granted, within the relevant international arrangements.

107. Flows from international and regional development finance institutions should be increased significantly in response to the growing needs of developing countries, in particular of those eligible for concessional lending from those institutions. The policies as well as the resource base of the multilateral institutions should be reviewed in a regular, timely and coordinated fashion and modified, where necessary, so as to avoid any interruption in their activities and to ensure the expansion of their resources in real terms to adequate levels. In particular, the agreements reached with regard to the increase in the capital of the World Bank and the sixth replenishment of the International Development Association will be speedily im-

[1] See *Proceedings of the United Nations Conference on Trade and Development, Fifth Session,* vol. I, *Report and Annexes* (United Nations publication, Sales No. E.79.II.D.14), part one, sect. A.

plemented. Ways and means should also be considered to achieve long-term financing, including multiyear pledges of programmes of United Nations development assistance organizations. Special attention will be paid by all donors to timely and substantial increases in soft resources through multilateral institutions. The policies of those institutions should further evolve so as to be more responsive to the changing needs and socio-economic objectives of recipient countries, in particular as far as programme assistance, including sectoral assistance, and local cost and recurrent cost financing are concerned.

108. Consideration should be given by the World Bank and regional development banks to ways and means of strengthening their lending capacities. taking into account, *inter alia*, the proposals to raise the lending-capital ratio of those institutions.

109. The World Bank should consider steps in establishment on a long-term financing facility to finance the purchase of capital goods by developing countries, taking into account the related proposal for a subsidy account for the poorer developing countries.

110. Non-concessional flows will continue to be an important source of development finance for many developing countries. Substantially increased transfer of resources largely raised on the financial markets and, without prejudice to official development assistance, through new and innovative means will be further explored in depth to allow action-oriented decisions. In this context, several approaches, including co-financing with private resources and other existing and possible new mechanisms, will be taken into account. Attention should be given, *inter alia*, to multilateral guarantees for borrowing on international financial markets and borrowing in significant measure under the guarantee of members of the international community, taking into account the possibilities of interest-subsidy mechanisms. The appropriate international financial institutions, in their consideration of new forms of lending as a means of channelling external resources to developing countries, should also consider greater reliance on programme or non-project loans. Direct private investments that are compatible with the national priorities and legislation of developing countries will be encouraged. Developing countries interested in foreign direct investments should make efforts to create and maintain a favourable investment climate in the framework of their national plans and policies. The access of developing countries to private capital markets should be improved, further facilitated and encouraged. New ways and forms of lending should be compatible with the development priorities of developing countries and should take due account of their debt-servicing capacity over the longer term. New approaches should be considered to ensure the growth and stability of new types of flows, including available funds in financial and capital markets. New ways and forms of lending should reflect the principles of universality and equity in decision making. The proposal for a world development fund should be examined by the Secretary-General so that a report can be made available as soon as possible and submitted to the General Assembly at the latest at its thirty-sixth session for its consideration and appropriate action.

111. Negotiations regarding internationally agreed features for future operations related to debt problems of interested developing countries should be brought to an early conclusion in the light of the general principles adopted by the Trade and Development Board in section B of its resolution 165(S-IX) of 11 March 1978.[1]

112. Governments should seek to adopt the following debt-relief actions or equivalent measures:

(*a*) Commitments undertaken in pursuance of section A of Trade and Development Board resolution 165 (S-IX) should be fully implemented as quickly as possible;

(*b*) Retroactive adjustment of terms should be continued in accordance with Trade and Development Board resolution 165 (S-IX), so that the improvement in current terms can be applied to outstanding official development assistance debt, and the United Nations Conference on Trade and Development should review the progress made in that regard.

113. In order to alleviate the financial burden of developing countries resulting from price rises in their vital imports, urgent consideration should be given by the international community, through the International Monetary Fund and other relevant international financial institutions, to special and favourable criteria relating to the level of dependence of, and financial burden on, developing countries when they receive balance-of-payments supports from those institutions.

114. There is a close relationship between disarmament and development. Progress in the former would help greatly in the realization of the latter. Taking into consideration the recommendations of the tenth special session of the General Assembly devoted to disarmament, relating to the relationship between disarmament and development,[2] effective measures should be taken, following disarmament measures, to use resources thus released for economic and social development, particularly for the benefit of the developing countries.

E. International monetary and financial issues

115. The international community should work for stable international monetary conditions supportive of a balanced and equitable development of the world economy and the accelerated development of developing countries. In order to create conditions more favourable to the development of the developing countries and the growth of the world economy in general, efforts to increase the responsiveness of the international monetary system to the needs and interests of the developing countries should be intensified through further reform on the system to be pursued and carried out expeditiously early in and throughout the Decade to the benefit of the entire international community. The principal features of a stable, effective and equitable international monetary and financial system should include:

(*a*) An effective, symmetrical and equitable adjustment process consistent with high sustainable employment and growth, price stability and the dynamic expansion of world trade. An effective adjustment process, both cyclical and structural, must be accompanied by access to official credit facilities on terms and conditions adapted to the nature of the balance-of-payments problems of the countries concerned, taking into account their social and political domestic objectives, and their economic priorities and circumstances, including the causes of their balance-of-payments problems;

(*b*) The terms and conditions of existing International Monetary Fund facilities, including the compensatory financing facility, to be reviewed periodically to ensure that these facilities are adequate and adapted to the needs of member countries, taking fully into account the interests of the developing countries, in coping adequately with changing world economic conditions. In this connexion, the Fund should give due consideration to such characteristics as the setting of conditionality associated with the use of its resources, taking into account the causes of deficits, the lengthening of repayment periods, where appropriate, adequate level of assistance and its increase when appropriate and the need to maintain an adequate level of Fund liquidity. The Fund should conclude at an early date its consideration of mechanisms to reduce the cost of using the supplementary financing facility;

(*c*) Assistance to countries, particularly developing countries, with structural imbalance in their external accounts and consequent balance-of-payments difficulties, including immediate action to be taken to improve and expand collaboration between the International Monetary Fund and the World Bank, particularly as regards medium-term balance-of-payments financing. Such action should improve the effectiveness and enhance the level of their support over the medium term for countries facing external cyclical as well as structural disequilibria and consequent international difficulties and lay the foundations for the achievement of high levels of sustainable growth and price stability. In this context, consideration should be given to the need for additional resources, the conditionality attached to those resources and the maturity periods involved. Consideration should also be given to measures to reduce the cost of borrowing for the low-income developing countries to improve their access to the

1 See *Official Records of the General Assembly, Thirty-third Session, Supplement No. 15* (A/33/15 and Corr.1), vol. 1, part two, annex I.

2 See resolution S-10/2.

balance-of-payments financing programmes of the International Monetary Fund;

(*d*) Over the Decade, a more stable, equitable and effective international monetary system, which should be sustained by and promote:

(i) The restoration of high sustainable growth with price stability;

(ii) The reduction of inflation, which imposes a substantial, real and financial cost on all countries, and a particular burden on developing countries, which have vulnerable economies; effective action at both the national and international levels should, therefore, be taken to bring inflation under control;

(iii) A stable, yet sufficiently flexible, exchange-rate régime;

(iv) Equitable and symmetrical treatment by the International Monetary Fund of surplus and deficit countries in exercising its surveillance over exchange rates and balance-of-payments policies;

(v) Arrangements for the creation of international liquidity through collective international action in line with the liquidity requirements of an expanding world economy;

(vi) The development of the special drawing rights as the principal reserve asset of the system; to this end, consideration will be given periodically by the International Monetary Fund to the allocation of new special drawing rights;

(*e*) The establishment of a link between the special drawing rights and development assistance which should form part of the consideration by the International Monetary Fund of the creation of new special drawing rights as and when they are created according to the needs of international liquidity;

(*f*) Provision by the international monetary system for equitable and effective participation of developing countries in decision making, taking into account, *inter alia*, their growing role in the world economy;

F. Technical cooperation

116. In the implementation of the International Development Strategy, intensified emphasis must be accorded to the important role of technical cooperation in the development process. Technical cooperation makes an essential contribution to the efforts of developing countries to achieve self-reliance through its bread role of facilitating and supporting, *inter alia*, investment, research, training and development. Realization of the goals and objectives of the new International Development Strategy will therefore require a renewed emphasis upon technical cooperation and a significant increase in the resources provided for this purpose.

G. Science and technology for development

117. Access to and mastery of modern scientific and technological knowledge are essential for the economic and social progress of developing countries. Accordingly, high priority must be given to increasing the developing countries' scientific and technological capacities. The transfer of technology, which is of the utmost importance in this respect, must be encouraged and improved. International cooperation in those fields must be broadened and intensified. Special attention must be given to the development of technologies adapted to the specific conditions of developing countries.

118. Action will be taken by the international community to restructure the existing patterns of international scientific and technological relations affecting the transfer and development of technology. Developed countries should take adequate specific measures to give or facilitate as appropriate to the developing countries the freest and fullest possible access to technologies. To this end, all countries should take steps for the early finalization, adoption and effective implementation of the international code of conduct on the transfer of technology. Efforts should also be made to bring the negotiations on the revision on the Paris Convention for the Protection of Industrial Property to a successful conclusion as early as possible. The international community should continue to review the ways in which the industrial property system can become a more effective instrument for the economic and technological development of all countries, particularly developing countries.

119. In technology planning and policies, special attention should be given to sectors of critical importance to developing countries. They should also take into account the need to arrive at a reasonable balance between labour-intensive and capital-intensive technologies with a view to achieving the fundamental aim of maximizing growth and employment and satisfying special needs of developing countries.

120. To assist developing countries and to contribute to reducing the imbalances between developed and developing countries in research and development, developed countries and international financial institutions should support these efforts. Developed countries should increase substantially and progressively during the course of the Decade the proportion of their research and development expenditure and efforts to be devoted to the solution of jointly identified specific problems of prime importance to developing countries with the active participation of researchers and institutions of developing countries. Technologically more advanced countries should facilitate the acquisition by developing countries of skills, especially high-level skills, through international exchanges. Developed countries should intensify their support of developing countries' efforts towards greater self-reliance in the field of technological development by taking other specific measures recommended, particularly those in resolution 112(V) of 3 June 1979 of the United Nations Conference on Trade and Development[1] on strengthening the technological capacity of developing countries including accelerating their technological transformation.

121. In accordance with the Vienna Programme of Action on Science and Technology for Development,[2] developing countries, with the necessary support on developed countries and international financial institutions, will intensify their efforts to strengthen their scientific and technological infrastructure and develop their endogenous technological and inventive capacities, in order to enhance their capacity to design and generate new technologies as well as to select, acquire, apply and adapt existing technology, *inter alia*, through:

(*a*) Substantially increasing the resources devoted to education and training in technical, managerial and inventive skills, as well as to research and development, and directing those efforts towards the solution of problems in the areas and sectors of critical concern to those countries;

(*b*) Taking measures aimed at the efficient acquisition and optimum utilization on technology by establishing close and effective linkages between the generators of technology, productive sectors and technology users;

(*c*) Supplementing their efforts at the national level by initiating or strengthening such cooperative measures among themselves as exchanges of skilled personnel, information and experience through the establishment of regional, subregional and national centres for the transfer and development of technology.

122. All countries should seek to ensure that scientific and technological development will involve and benefit men and women equally and measures should be taken to facilitate equal access for men and women to scientific and technological training and to the respective professional careers.

123. Concerned efforts will be made by the international community early in the Decade to take comprehensive and effective action, as recommended by the United Nations Conference on Trade and Development at its fifth session, at the national, regional and international levels, aimed at minimizing the negative impact of the migration of skilled personnel so that such migration from developing countries will constitute an exchange in which the interests of all parties concerned are adequately protected. The international community should consider examining, early in the Decade, in the light of relevant United Nations decisions, arrangements whereby develop-

---

1 See *Proceedings of the United Nations Conference on Trade and Development, Fifth Session, vol. I, Report and Annexes* (United Nations Publication, Sales No. E.79.II.14), part one, sect. A.

2 *Report of the United Nations Conference on Science and Technology for Development, Vienna, 20-31 August 1979* (United Nations publication, Sales No. E.79.I.21 and corrigenda), chap. VII.

ing countries experiencing large-scale outflows of their skilled nationals, which cause economic disruption, could secure assistance in dealing with the adjustment problems arising therefrom.

124. Substantial resources should be mobilized for the United Nations Financing System for Science and Technology for Development, established by the General Assembly in section VI of its resolution 34/218 of 19 December 1979, to support actions needed for the development of science and technology in developing countries. In determining the nature and level of the resources of the Financing System, the following considerations should, *inter alia*, be taken into account:

(*a*) The need for a predictable and continuous flow of resources;

(*b*) The need for substantial resources in addition to those that exist within the United Nations system;

(*c*) The need for untied external resources for the scientific and technological development of the developing countries.

The long-term arrangements of the Financing System will be brought into operation in January 1982, as agreed by the General Assembly at its thirty-fourth session. To this end, the study of the long-term arrangements of the Financing System should proceed expeditiously.

125. As provided for in the Vienna Programme of Action on Science and Technology for Development, the development of the global and international information network should be expedited and, in this context, the Intergovernmental Committee on Science and Technology for Development should consider urgently the establishment of such a system. The existing information systems within the United Nations and other international bodies set up for the exchange of scientific and technological information, which are also serving as industrial technology data banks, should form an integral part of the proposed global network. The network should be designed to meet the urgent needs of the developing countries. Priority should be given to covering alternative sources of technology and scientific, technical, socio-economic, legal and other aspects needed for decision making in the selection and transfer of technology.

H. Energy

126. Effective and urgent measures will be taken by the international community for the attainment of the goals and objectives in the field of energy, as spelt out in paragraph 34 of the present Strategy. These measures will include, *inter alia*, the following:

(*a*) All countries, in particular the developed countries, will undertake immediate measures to rationalize their energy consumption through, *inter alia*, conservation, improved efficiency of their energy systems, especially of hydrocarbons, improved energy management and increased technical manpower training;

(*b*) In conformity with the principle of the full and permanent sovereignty of each country over its natural resources, the exploration and rational exploitation of energy resources, both conventional and non-conventional, should be promoted in accordance with the national plans and priorities of each country. The international community should support and facilitate the effective participation of developing countries in the production, processing, marketing and distribution of those resources;

(*c*) To advance towards the development of indigenous energy resources of developing countries and the satisfaction of their energy needs, developed countries should facilitate the fullest possible access by developing countries to scientific and technological processes to enable them to develop energy sources, including nuclear technology for the production of energy in accordance with the principles set forth in General Assembly resolution 32/50 of 8 December 1977. In this context, developed countries and others with a capacity to do so, as well as international institutions, should assist developing countries in preparing comprehensive assessments of energy needs, uses and resources and facilitating their planning and review of the energy needs implicit in their development goals;

(*d*) The establishment and strengthening of medium-term and long-term national action programmes on new and renewable sources of energy. For this purpose, programmes of development, testing and training cooperation between developed and developing countries with testing centres in similar geophysical and climatic conditions will be established and supported;

(*e*) Much greater participation by the international, national and regional financial institutions in the financing of energy projects, in particular those sited in the least developed countries, so as to bring about an increase in the flow of different types of resources;

(*f*) The improvement of the investment climate in interested developing countries so as to stimulate flows of foreign investment in the framework of their national plans and policies in the field of energy;

(*g*) Meeting the needs of energy-deficient developing countries through cooperation, assistance and investment in relation to conventional as well as new and renewable sources of energy. The United Nations system should strengthen its information services in the field of natural resources.

127. The question of cooperation in the field of energy will be dealt with within the over-all framework of international economic cooperation for development so as to encourage and accelerate energy conservation and the development of world energy resources by, *inter alia*, facilitating and improving access to energy-related technologies, expanded energy research and development and increased investment flows into energy exploration and development.

I. Transport

128. In the transport sector, national and international action will promote the development of world sea-borne trade and other transportation systems and the increase in the participation by developing countries in world transport of international trade and, to this end, appropriate structural changes will be carried out where necessary. The international community will continue to take the necessary steps to enable developing countries to compete more effectively and to expand their national and multinational merchant fleets so as to increase their share substantially with a view to reaching as close as possible to 20 per cent of the dead-weight tonnage of the world merchant fleet by 1990. The Convention on a Code of Conduct for Liner Conferences will be implemented by its signatories. Early in the Decade, the Convention on International Multimodal Transport will come into force, which will facilitate the development of multimodal transport operations by developing countries.

129. The international community will assist the developing countries in their efforts to expand their capabilities in ports and related inland transport facilities and infrastructure in the training of maritime personnel. It should also, where appropriate, assist in the development of their shipbuilding and ship-repairing capacities.

130. Developing countries will be enabled to make major advancements in air transport, particularly in air cargo transport, *inter alia*, through the increase of the air transport fleets and the development of suitable airports and related infrastructures. Particular attention will be given at the international level to the elimination of discriminatory and unfair practices, where they exist, in civil aviation which are detrimental to the growth of the air sector in developing countries.

131. The road and railway transport sectors, which are recognized as important parts of the physical infrastructure in developing countries, will receive considerable support from the international community in order substantially to increase and improve the road and railway networks of the developing countries.

132. The international community will give adequate support, to the extent possible, to regional cooperation in the transport and communication sector, especially to the implementation of the Transport and Communications Decade in Africa, 1978-1988.

133. The international community will explore ways and means of increasing the availability of financing for the development of the transport sector.

J. Economic and technical cooperation among developing countries

134. Developing countries will pursue actively the promotion of economic and technical cooperation among themselves as a basic component of the efforts towards the establishment of the new international economic order which, as such, is based on cooperation among all States. In this context, they are committed to the effective implementation of the Arusha Programme for Collective Self-

reliance as well as to the programmes in those fields agreed at Mexico City, Havana and Buenos Aires and regional programmes, including the Lagos Plan of Action for the implementation of the Monrovia Strategy for the Economic Development of Africa, which was adopted at the second extraordinary session of the Assembly of Heads of State and Government of the organization of African Unity, held at Lagos, on 28 and 29 April 1980.[1] The implementation of these programmes in the 1980s would first of all help the developing countries, through their own efforts, to strengthen their economic potential, accelerate their economic growth and improve their position in the system of international economic relations.

135. On the basis of the proposals of developing countries in competent bodies, the international community will take measures to provide, as appropriate, support and assistance to developing countries in strengthening and enlarging their mutual cooperation, at the subregional, regional and interregional levels, including additional technical support, as well as conference and secretariat services for the holding of meetings in accordance with the established procedures and practices of the United Nations.

K. Least developed countries, most seriously affected countries, developing island countries and land-locked developing countries

1. *Least developed countries*

136. As an essential priority within the International Development Strategy for the Third United Nations Development Decade, the least developed countries - the economically weakest and poorest countries with the most formidable structural problems - require a special programme of sufficient size and intensity consistent with their national plans and priorities to make a decisive break from their past and present situation and their bleak prospects. Efforts must therefore be immediately and substantially expanded in order to transform their economies, to promote a self-sustained process of development, to accelerate agricultural and industrial progress and to ensure development of human resources and broadly based participation in the development process concurrent and consistent with equitable distribution of the gains of socio-economic development. Therefore, the international community will take urgently the necessary steps to finalize and implement the Substantial New Programme of Action for the 1980s for the least developed countries, which was launched by the United Nations Conference on Trade and Development at its fifth session in its resolution 122 (V) of 3 June 1979.[2] The Programme is to be finalized, adopted and supported by the United Nations Conference on the Least Developed Countries, to be convened in 1981.

137. To meet the objectives of the Substantial New Programme of Action for the 1980s, national plans will identify and cost major priority projects and programmes. The details for each country in terms of structural change in agriculture and industry, improved physical, social and institutional infrastructure, and improved performance in connexion with, *inter alia*, nutrition, literacy, health, employment and the development of human resources will be clearly specified. The goals to be achieved will require greater efforts by the least developed countries themselves, together with a substantial expansion of support from the international community.

138. Every possible effort will be made to develop programmes that will enable each least developed country to increase its national income substantially - even doubling it in appropriate cases - by 1990.

139. To help the least developed land-locked countries to alleviate their geographical handicap, specific assistance will be provided for the development and improvement of a transit transport infrastructure, both administrative and physical. Similar specific assistance will be provided to least developed island countries for the development of their transport infrastructure.

140. The expanded planning efforts at the national, subregional and regional levels will be strongly backed by firm international commitments to expand resource flows to the least developed countries by substantial amounts. Commitments already undertaken[3] will be implemented effectively, within the framework of an equitable sharing of effort, taking into account the relative performance of donor countries. The United Nations Conference on the Least Developed Countries will take note of those measures which have already been taken, and consider necessary further measures to ensure an adequate minimum flow of external assistance to each least developed country.

141. To meet the pressing problems of the least developed countries, the modalities by which concessional aid is provided to them will become much more flexible and responsive to their special needs.

142. In national development efforts, high priority will be given to increasing production and export earnings as rapidly as is feasible. The aim should be to make progress towards self-reliance and self-sustained growth by reducing significantly the degree of dependence on foreign assistance flows during the 1990s. The international community will strongly support such efforts through financial and technical assistance and through commercial policy measures.

143. To meet the special needs of the least developed countries, the international community will support efforts towards strengthening the technological and productive capacity of those countries, increasing their absorptive capacity by building up their infrastructure, particularly in transportation, communication and electrification and assistance in the establishment of comprehensive inventories of their resources and preparation of industrial surveys, supporting their full industrialization and full participation in the processes of redeployment and in the international consultations on industrial growth, including the system of consultations, strengthening their import-substitution processes and their manufactures-export performance, setting up joint enterprises under regional cooperation and preferential treatment of the least developed countries within international agreements for industrial products and processed commodities. Financial flows to the least developed countries will be substantially increased on highly concessional terms, *inter alia*, with a view to implementing these measures.

144. To bring about an increase in agricultural production and the structural transformation of agriculture in the least developed countries, the level of annual investments in land development, including flood control, soil and water conservation measures and the establishment of permanent crops, in irrigation, machinery and equipment, livestock development, storage and marketing, transport and first-stage processing of primary agricultural production will be substantially increased. Commitments of external resources to agriculture in the least developed countries will be raised substantially and in real terms. The agreed recommendations of the United Nations Conference on the Least Developed Countries in this regard will be fully implemented.

145. It will also be especially important, in elaborating the Substantial New Programme of Action for the 1980s for the least developed countries, to make maximum use of cooperation arrangements among developing countries, particularly at the regional and subregional levels. In elaborating their programme for greater collective self-reliance and economic and technical cooperation among themselves, the developing countries will pay particular attention to the special difficulties of the least developed countries and to expanding substantially support for the least developed countries as a further important contribution to the above-mentioned programmes.

146. Serious consideration will be given by developed countries to increasing substantially and in real terms official development assistance to the least developed countries during the Decade. The proposals made by the Group of High-Level Experts on the least developed countries for the allocation by developed countries to the least developed countries of a minimum of 0.15 per cent of their gross

---

1 See A/S-11/14, annex 1.

2 See *Proceedings of the United Nations Conference on Trade and Development, Fifth Session,* vol. I, *Report and Annexes* (United Nations publication, Sales No. E.79.II.D.14), part one, sect. A.

3 See *Proceedings of the United Nations Conference on Trade and Development, Fifth Session,* vol. I, *Report and Annexes* (United Nations publication, Sales No. E.79.II.D.14), part one, sect. A, resolution 122 (V).

national product as official development assistance by the first half of the 1980s, rising to 0.20 per cent during the second half of the 1980s, will be appropriately considered by the United Nations Conference on the Least Developed Countries in 1981 within the context of an overall increase in official development assistance with a view to achieving the internationally accepted targets.

2. *Most seriously affected countries*

147. The current world economic situation has given rise to deep concern at the deterioration of the economic and financial situation of those developing countries whose relatively weak economies make them particularly vulnerable to economic crises caused by sharp increases in the prices of their essential imports. The international community will consider extending relief and assistance to those countries which may be most seriously affected by the current economic crisis, bearing in mind immediate balance-of-payments and development needs. To this end, urgent consideration should be given to immediate relief measures in favour of those countries. Concrete measures will need to be urgently considered by the international community with a view to the implementation of recommendations agreed by the General Assembly on the basis of the Secretary-General's report. In the meantime, urgent consideration should be given to the implementation of the measures set out in General Assembly resolution 34/217 of 19 December 1979.

3. *Developing island countries*

148. During the Decade, further specific action will be taken to assist developing island countries in offsetting major handicaps due to geographical and other constraints. In order to lower their vulnerability to economic instability, every effort will be made by the international community to assist them in diversifying their economies, taking into account over-all prospects for, as well as existing levels of, development.

149. Efforts of developing island countries in actively seeking foreign investment will be supported by the international community, including investment in their infrastructural projects, especially in the sectors of water, electricity, industrial estates and transport. The establishment of joint ventures and assistance in strengthening the capacity of developing island countries to negotiate with foreign investors should also be explored during the Decade. Their access to foreign markets will be facilitated by assistance, both technical and financial, in their trade promotion efforts and by the simplification of preference procedures, where appropriate, so that small administrations and enterprises can take full advantage of preferential access to markets where it is in principle available. Assistance will be given in the establishment of appropriate technical education and training programmes, including the areas of marketing and management.

150. Financial and other assistance to developing island countries by multilateral and bilateral institutions will be augmented as appropriate. Assistance procedures should be simplified to the extent possible.

151. The developed countries and international organizations should be ready to take action to ensure that the full benefit of general measures in favour of developing countries is shared by developing island countries.

4. *Land-locked developing countries*

152. An integrated planning approach for the improvement and development of transit transport facilities and services will be encouraged, particularly through more effective cooperation between land-locked countries and the transit countries. Such cooperation will involve the harmonization of transport planning and the promotion of joint ventures in the field of transport at regional, subregional and bilateral levels.

153. The international community will give, in accordance with the priorities of the land-locked countries and accepted development criteria, strong financial and technical assistance support, through specific actions, in accordance with resolution 123 (V) of 3 June 1979 of the United Nations Conference on Trade and Development.

154. In addition, multilateral and bilateral financial institutions will further intensify their efforts to raise the flow of resources to the land-locked developing countries to alleviate their geographical handicaps through diversification of their economies, giving particular priority to the establishment of industries and the development of natural resources.

155. In order to implement the above-mentioned measures, the international community, in particular the developed countries, is invited to contribute significantly and generously to the United Nations Special Fund for Land-locked Developing Countries. Those donor countries which have not yet contributed to the Fund should urgently consider reviewing their positions with a view to extending their full support to the Fund.

L. Environment

156. Because health, nutrition and general well-being depend upon the integrity and productivity of the environment and resources, measures should continue to be developed and carried out to promote the environmental and ecological soundness of developmental activities. Methods will be devised to assist interested developing countries in environmental management and in the evaluation of the costs and benefits, quantitative and qualitative, of environment protection measures with a view to dealing more adequately with the environmental aspects of development activities. This method will be developed taking fully into account the existing knowledge of interrelationships between development, environment, population and resources. To that end, research on these interrelationships will be intensified. The capacity of the developing countries will be strengthened to facilitate their making appropriate scientific and technical choices relating to environment in their development process.

157. Bilateral and multilateral donors will consider, within the overall financing of projects in developing countries, at their request, meeting the costs of taking environmental aspects into account in the design and completion of such projects. They will furthermore provide assistance, including in the field of training, to develop the endogenous capacity of developing countries to follow the methods enumerated in paragraph 156 above, thereby also facilitating technical cooperation among developing countries.

158. The international community, in particular the developed countries, will substantially increase its financial and technical support to drought-stricken countries suffering from desertification. In this context, support to the Plan of Action to Combat Desertification[1] will be augmented.

M. Human settlements

159. The quality of life and the environment should be improved through, *inter alia*, the formulation and implementation of appropriate planning and development policies designed to ensure a better interregional balance between rural and urban development, as well as through the strengthening, in the context of human settlements planning, of measures to improve housing conditions for the most disadvantaged regions and communities - access to services, land and employment - and, in particular, through housing rehabilitation programmes.

160. Developing countries will formulate policies for the provision of basic shelter and infrastructure. To this end, and so as to benefit from the multiplying effect of investment in the field of human settlements, countries will develop their construction industry, particularly for low-cost housing, support relevant financing institutions, stimulate research and disseminate findings on efficient methods of construction, low-cost design and technology for infrastructure, indigenous building materials and environmental protection.

N. Disaster relief

161. Recognizing the detrimental effects of disasters on the development of developing countries, the international community will take measures to improve and strengthen arrangements to provide developing countries with adequate and timely assistance in matters of disaster relief, prevention and preparedness.

---

1 A/CONF.74/36, chap. 1.

O. Social development

162. Each country will freely determine and implement appropriate policies for social development within the framework of its development plans and priorities and in accordance with its cultural identity, socio-economic structure and stage of development. The necessary financial and technical assistance will be provided by the international community through, *inter alia*, specific international programmes to support the national endeavours of the developing countries in key areas of social policy. To this end, an important role should be played by the United Nations system. Each country shall intensify measures for the full utilization of human resources, especially for the training of national personnel, within the framework of its national plans and its present and long-term requirements for qualified national personnel at all levels and in all important sectors of socio-economic activity.

163. Countries will pursue the objectives of the reduction of poverty, promotion of employment opportunities and the provision of the right to work through enhanced economic growth and measures to ensure a fair distribution of the benefits of development and institutional reforms. As development requires productive and adequately remunerative employment, development planning will pay due attention to this aspect. Countries will seek policies to reconcile gains in productivity with increase of employment in the industrial, agricultural, service and other sectors of their economies as well as policies to promote improved working and living conditions in these sectors. Measures to that effect include access to land, credit and know-how, as well as an increase in training facilities adapted to the needs of the various sectors. The creation of producer cooperatives, including credit, marketing and processing, as well as consumer cooperatives will be encouraged. Countries will adopt effective measures to enhance the involvement of women in the development process. Likewise, measures for the benefit of youth will be formulated and adopted. Prompt measures will be taken to eliminate child labour in conformity with relevant international labour conventions and to promote the general welfare of children. In this regard, national development efforts, including policies, programmes and services that affect children, should be reviewed regularly with a view to extending and strengthening the basic services benefiting children, including water and sanitation, health, nutrition and education. International cooperation in support of these measures should be enhanced and strengthened.

164. Countries will formulate and implement education policies appropriate to their economic and social requirements. Each country will determine the balance between the necessary efforts and resources required to promote universal education, including the goal of free education at all levels, non-formal education of adults, cultural development and scientific and technological ability. Increased and equitable access to educational and training facilities will help to reduce income inequalities and to enhance the capability of the society for economic and social progress. Particular attention will be devoted to the transmission by the educational system of the cultural heritage and of universal values of mankind.

165. To attain an acceptable level of health for all by the year 2000, countries will establish an adequate and comprehensive system of primary health care as an integral part of a more general health system and as a part of a general improvement in nutrition and living standards and basic infrastructure for supplying such needs as safe water and basic sanitation. The development of appropriate health technologies, the provision of essential drugs, the prevention of the introduction of dangerous and hazardous drugs, the promotion of health-related research and the training of qualified health personnel at all levels, including highly qualified physicians, will complement the results expected from a multiplication of primary health care centres. Measures to reduce infant and general levels of mortality will include proper nutrition, education of parents, immunization of children and better environment health. Countries will establish the requisite infrastructure and also introduce, expand and improve access to health care services and will strive to achieve the goal of providing health protection to the entire population, if possible free of charge.

166. Population policies will be considered as an integral part of over-all development policies. All countries will continue to integrate their population measures and programmes into their social and economic goals and strategies. Within the framework of national demographic policies, countries will take the measures they deem necessary concerning fertility levels in full respect of the right of parents to determine in a free, informed and responsible manner the number and spacing of their children. The international community will increase the level of population assistance in support of those measures. In addition, due consideration should be given to the need for increased biomedical and social science research into safer, more efficient and more widely acceptable techniques of fertility regulation.

167. It is for each developing country to decide, within the framework of a unified approach to development, the possible content of a national programme for the development of its human resources. Such a programme would include the improvement of primary and secondary education for the entire population, which provide a broad manpower basis for future development, acceleration of community activities and the development of skilled personnel. On the other hand, the developed countries should place increased emphasis on cooperation for the development of human resources in the developing countries. They should explore the most effective means of extending assistance in response to the development needs in specific areas as requested. In this context, the use of the mass media, which will reach a broader section of society, can be an effective measure for the development of human resources. Assistance in the areas of extension services and teacher training will also eventually affect a large part of the population.

168. The important set of measures to improve the status of women contained in the World Plan of Action for the Implementation of the Objectives of the International Women's Year,[1] adopted at Mexico City in 1975, and the important agreed measures relating to the sectors of the International Development Strategy in the Programme of Action for the Second Half of the United Nations Decade for Women,[2] adopted at Copenhagen in 1980, should be implemented.

IV. Review and Appraisal of the Implementation of the new International Development Strategy

169. The process of review and appraisal forms an integral part of the International Development Strategy. Its aim will be to ensure the effective implementation of the International Development Strategy for the Third United Nations Development Decade and to strengthen it as an instrument of policy. The process will be undertaken within the United Nations system at the global, sectoral and regional levels, and at the national level by the respective Governments, making full use of existing mechanisms and facilities and avoiding as far as possible duplication or proliferation of review activities.

170. The process will consist of systematic scrutiny, within the context of an over-all review of the international economic situation, of the progress made towards achieving the goals and objectives of the Strategy and the identification and appraisal of the factors which account for shortfalls that may be encountered.

171. This process should provide an occasion, in the light of this over-all review, to see how the implementation of the Strategy can be strengthened and the necessary political impulses given and to carry out, if necessary, the adjustment, intensification or reformulation of the policy measures in the light of evolving needs and developments.

172. At the national level, Governments will, in accordance with their national priorities and plans, appropriately reflect the goals and objectives and the policy measures of the International Development Strategy in their policy formulation. Where necessary, the evaluation

---

1 See *Report of the World Conference of the International Women's Year, Mexico City, 19 June-21 July 1975* (United Nations publication, Sales No. E.76.IV.1), chap. II, sect. A.

2 See *Report of the World Conference of the United Nations Decade for Women: Equality, Development and Peace, Copenhagen, 14-30 July 1980* (United Nations publication, Sales No. E.80.IV.3 and corrigendum), chap. I, sect. A.

capacity, comprising also the statistical capability, of the countries concerned should be strengthened, including through assistance, upon their request, from appropriate multilateral and bilateral sources.

173. At the regional level, the review and appraisal will be conducted by the respective regional commissions. Development banks, regional and subregional groups and organizations could collaborate with the regional commissions for this purpose. Furthermore, the regional commissions should carry out, as part of their regular activity of preparing economic surveys of the region, periodic reviews of major aspects of development in the evolving development experiences in their regions.

174. The regional commissions should consider the feasibility of preparing action programmes to support the efforts of developing countries in the implementation of the International Development Strategy in their respective areas. Furthermore, the regional commissions, in conjunction with relevant United Nations specialized agencies and multilateral development institutions, might suggest ways of improving United Nations assistance efforts and enhancing their coordination in the context of the particular economic and social development needs of each region.

175. At the sectoral level, the relevant specialized agencies, organs and organizations of the United Nations will contribute from the experience of their respective sectors to the process of review and appraisal at both the global and regional levels.

176. At the global level, review and appraisal will be carried out by the General Assembly, with the assistance, as appropriate, of a body of universal membership, which would report through the Economic and Social Council. The process will take into account the results achieved at the sectoral, regional and national levels. The Committee for Development Planning will be invited to submit its observations and recommendations. The Secretary-General will prepare and submit a comprehensive report and other appropriate documentation in order to assist the process of review and appraisal.

177. Developed countries, individually or through their relevant organizations, are invited to transmit reports of their development assistance efforts in the light of the commitments undertaken by them in the international Development Strategy and in relevant international forums.

178. The process of review and appraisal should, based on an assessment as provided for in General Assembly resolution 33/201 of 29 January 1979, ensure that the operational activities of the United Nations system contribute effectively to the implementation of the International Development Strategy.

179. The review and appraisal will, at all levels, take into account the results of the global negotiations relating to international economic cooperation for development, the United Nations Conference on the Least Developed Countries, the United Nations Conference on New and Renewable Sources of Energy, the International Conference for the Promotion of International Cooperation in the Peaceful Uses of Nuclear Energy, and of such United Nations conferences as effectively contribute to the implementation of the Strategy, as well as the results of relevant regional and interregional meetings. The agreed results will be incorporated in the Strategy by the General Assembly when and as appropriate, with a view to contributing to its effective implementation.

180. The first review and appraisal will be carried out by the General Assembly in 1984, on which occasion a decision as to the timing of a subsequent review or reviews will be taken.

45/199. International Development Strategy for the Fourth United Nations Development Decade

Committee: 2
Vote: Adopted without a vote
Ref.: 44/169

The General Assembly

1. *Proclaims* the Fourth United Nations Development Decade, starting on 1 January 1991;

2. *Adopts* the International Development Strategy for the Fourth United Nations Development Decade, as set forth in the annex to the present resolution.

71st plenary meeting
21 December 1990

Annex

International Development Strategy for the Fourth United Nations Development Decade

I. Preamble

1. We, the States Members of the United Nations, adopt the following International Development Strategy and designate 1 January 1991 to 31 December 2000 as the Fourth United Nations Development Decade. The global consensus reached in the Declaration on International Economic Cooperation, in particular the Revitalization of Economic Growth and Development of the Developing Countries, contained in the annex to General Assembly resolution S-18/3, provides the basis for this Strategy. We pledge ourselves individually and collectively to undertake the measures necessary to implement the Strategy.

2. The goals and objectives of the International Development Strategy for the Third United Nations Development Decade were for the most part unattained. Adverse and unanticipated developments in the world economy wiped out the premises on which growth had been expected. The early years of the 1980s witnessed a recession in the developed, market economy countries. Although growth in these countries resumed in 1983 and was sustained at a moderate tempo virtually without inflation over the remainder of the decade, the period was one of marked imbalances, external as well as fiscal, and of relatively high unemployment. Growth rates slowed down in the countries of Eastern Europe, where the need for structural transformation became increasingly manifest, resulting, by the end of the decade, in sweeping economic and political changes. World trade returned to a path of relatively rapid growth in the second half of the 1980s. But, for the developing countries, the external economic environment over the decade was generally characterized by shrinking resource flows, declining commodity prices, rising interest rates and increasing barriers to market access. During the 1980s, overall growth in the developing countries averaged 3 per cent annually and per capita growth 1 per cent. Over the 1960s and 1970s, by comparison, overall growth in these countries averaged 5.5 per cent and per capita growth 3 per cent.

3. Despite this background, some developing countries, among them some of the biggest and the poorest, succeeded in maintaining a relatively fast tempo of growth and transformation. For most others, however, the decade was one of falling growth rates, declining living standards and deepening poverty. The debt crisis that erupted in 1982 led to the virtual cessation of net commercial bank lending. There was a negative transfer of net financial resources to the indebted countries, whose debt-servicing capacity was further weakened as interest rates grew and terms of trade deteriorated. As a result, the overall growth of developing countries with debt-servicing difficulties was only 1.5 per cent during the period 1981-1990. The decade of the 1980s saw a widening of the gap between the rich and the poor countries. It also witnessed political tensions and conflicts, as well as natural and man-made disasters that were costly and disruptive.

4. If the 1990s are to be a decade of development, this record of unsatisfactory progress and performance needs to be changed. Projections by the organizations of the United Nations system unanimously suggest, however, that in the absence of major changes in policies, the coming decade will be much like the previous one. While relatively rapid growth is foreseen for some countries of Asia, the prospect is one of continued stagnation for others, particularly in Africa and Latin America.

5. Such a prospect is fraught with danger. Growing populations and young and expanding work forces, as well as rising aspirations associated with the spread of education and the impact of communications, are imposing intense pressures on the political and social fabric

of developing countries. Unless these pressures are relieved by decisive improvements in the pace and character of development, economic distress and political and social instability may spread, not only within national boundaries but beyond them as well, and may affect the peace and stability of the world as a whole. In the many developing countries where economic conditions stagnated or declined in the 1980s, absolute poverty became more widespread and conditions deteriorated with regard to nutrition and food security, job creation and education, health care and infant mortality, housing and sanitation. The erosion of living standards and social services brought mounting political unrest to many countries.

6. The interdependence of nations is rapidly becoming far more than a matter of trade and finance links alone. There are strong trends towards greater openness in the movement of funds, people and ideas around the world. Over the past decade, violence, social disorder and terrorism have become more common. Conflicts and upheavals lead to the movement of refugees and international migrants and give rise to problems of border control, admission and assimilation in receiving countries. The illicit traffic in narcotics links the poverty and social problems of the rich countries to those of producers whose traditional crops no longer ensure them a living. Environmental threats and epidemics are often themselves of global scope. These and other related problems can only be aggravated by economic stresses and strains and by the failure of the development process in the developing countries. The entire international community, rich and poor countries alike, has thus a vital stake in ensuring that the decade of the 1990s is truly one of economic and social progress throughout the world.

7. The prospects for the 1990s, assessed on the basis of the continuation of present policies, can and must be changed. The reactivation and acceleration of the development process is in the interest of all countries. The developing countries can provide a strong stimulus to world trade and investment and can contribute to the strength and stability of the world economy. They already account for a significant share of the markets of the developed countries. Far-reaching developments have taken place on the international scene that provide new opportunities for reversing the trends of the 1980s. The relaxation of international tensions offers an opportunity for reducing military spending worldwide, for a reduction of the strains on national economies and for the application of larger resources to the fight against world poverty. The waning of ideological conflicts is improving the climate of cooperation at all levels. There is no universal prescription for successful development, but a growing convergence of views is emerging with respect to effective approaches to economic and social development and with regard to the potential contributions to the development process of the private and public sectors, of individuals and enterprises and of democratic rights and freedoms.

8. A strong stimulus to global cooperation is provided by the consciousness of the global consequences of environmental problems and their interaction with both development and the lack of development and by a growing awareness of the threats to the security of nations that could arise from frustrations and tensions in developing countries. Closer integration, in both Europe and North America, in prospect of the 1990s, has the potential to strengthen major economies and their capacity to support global economic growth if accompanied by openness to the outside world. The reform and restructuring of the economies of Eastern Europe and their integration into the world economy can contribute to the strength and dynamism of world trade. Closer cooperation and integration among the developing countries themselves also offer an opportunity to enhance the vigour of the development process. No less important, the rapid advances in science and technology and in global communications are opening up new vistas for improvement of productivity, structural change and accelerated development.

9. These changes do not by themselves guarantee a reversal of the present trends or ensure that the development experience in the new decade will differ markedly from that of the 1980s. There are dangers, if the opportunities are not grasped, of increasing marginalization of many developing countries in the world economy and of a weakening of the focus on development as an objective of international economic cooperation. But the changes offer a new context for decision-making and policy formulation and for approaches that could reverse the experience of the 1980s. They provide an opportunity for the formulation and implementation of an International Development Strategy that is aimed at releasing the great potential for development that exists in the developing countries and in the world economy.

10. The Declaration on International Economic Cooperation, in particular the Revitalization of Economic Growth and Development of the Developing Countries, contained in the annex to General Assembly resolution S-18/3, contains a pledge that Member States will endeavour to take all necessary steps to reverse the adverse trends of the 1980s, address the challenges of the 1990s and move into a more productive decade, recognizing that such actions should take into account the responsibility of each country for its own development and should be in accordance with its capacity and its impact on the international economy. As in the 1980s, events now unforeseen will undoubtedly put their stamp on the coming decade. This Strategy is flexible. It seeks above all to spell out an agreed understanding on the issues and challenges, the actions and the commitments, on the basis of principles for national and international action that will remain valid.

11. Countries have to adapt their national policies to facilitate open exchange and flexible responses to the changing world economy. Effective national policies have a critical role to play in achieving sustained, non-inflationary economic growth in all countries. Such policies should be supportive of investment, as well as of efficient mobilization and allocation of resources in order to achieve durable growth.

12. It is against this background that Member States agree on the goals and objectives for the Fourth United Nations Development Decade as set out below.

II. Goals and Objectives

13. The principal aim of the Strategy is to ensure that the 1990s are a decade of accelerated development in the developing countries and strengthened international cooperation. The decade should witness a significant improvement in the human condition in the developing countries and a reduction in the gap between rich and poor countries. It should be one in which ways are found for the world community to meet its needs without degrading the environment. The Strategy also has important social and political objectives. Development over the decade should enhance the participation of all men and women in economic and political life, protect cultural identities and assure to all the necessary means of survival. Each country is responsible for its own economic policies for development, in accordance with its specific situation and conditions, and for the life and well-being of all its citizens. The Strategy should help provide an environment that supports the evolution everywhere of political systems based on consent and respect for human rights, as well as social and economic rights, and of systems of justice that protect all citizens.

14. To achieve these fundamental aims six interrelated goals must be met. They are:

(*a*) A surge in the pace of economic growth in the developing countries;

(*b*) A development process that is responsive to social needs, seeks a significant reduction in extreme poverty, promotes the development and utilization of human resources and skills and is environmentally sound and sustainable;

(*c*) An improvement of the international systems of money, finance and trade so as to support the development process;

(*d*) A setting of strength and stability in the world economy and sound macro-economic management, nationally and internationally;

(*e*) A decisive strengthening of international development cooperation;

(*f*) A special effort to deal with the problems of the least developed countries, the weakest among the developing countries.

15. These goals and objectives pose a big challenge. They call for serious and committed efforts by all countries. The developing coun-

tries themselves have the responsibility for the great effort needed to mobilize the potential of their people, to modernize and diversify their economies and to set themselves ambitious targets to build the foundation on which development rests: technical and managerial skills, industrial and agricultural capability and effective government services. Human resources development, entrepreneurship and innovation, and the energetic application of science and technology, in a context of political freedom, respect for human rights, justice and equity, are all essential and relevant to growth and development. The Strategy has singled out a number of areas of special priority: the eradication of poverty and hunger, human resources and institutional development, population, the environment and food and agriculture. The pursuit of goals in these areas calls for resolute and vigorous action and for styles of development that establish a mutually reinforcing relationship between rapid economic growth and social objectives.

16. The efforts of the developing countries will, however, be easily thwarted by an unsupportive external environment. They will be thwarted if sudden external shocks decimate their national product and external revenues, as happened to many of them in the 1980s. All countries live in the international economic environment, but most developing countries remain imperfectly integrated into it and excessively vulnerable to its instability. Many are captives of external debt problems, of reduction in external resource flows, of sharply declining terms of trade and of mounting barriers to market access. Great obligations fall on the industrialized countries, which influence the international economic environment and the functioning of the international economy and are partners in international cooperation for development. Great obligations fall also on the system of international organizations to extend and fulfil their role in the promotion of development. Developing countries can prosper only in a stable and progressive world economy and, conversely, the world community can have a safe and prosperous future only if economic, social and political progress in the developing countries is assured.

17. The attainment of the aims of the Strategy calls for more than marginal increases in growth rates. The developing countries must be enabled to generate progressively the resources needed to ensure productive employment for a fast-growing labour force, to overcome hunger, disease and ignorance and to raise living standards. The negative trends of the 1980s need to be reversed and conditions created for a kind of development that signifies a genuine transformation and does more than keep a growing population from the brink of famine. The time has come to move beyond adjusting to the shocks of the 1980s and to lay the foundations for a new wave of development. For most developing countries, growth rates must accelerate significantly during the decade. Growth objectives will vary from country to country. For the relatively few countries where growth in the 1980s was satisfactory, the aim would be to consolidate progress and ensure that it is sustained. In the many countries where growth was interrupted, the first requirement is a return to a path of expansion where economic growth does not merely keep pace with, but well exceeds, the growth of population. In the second half of the decade, the foundations for higher rates of growth should have been established. On the basis of the experience of some countries, it is considered that sustained growth at a rate of the order of 7 per cent would provide the necessary conditions for a genuine transformation of the economy, with rapid increases in productive employment and poverty eradication, and would generate the resources needed for the protection of the environment.

18. Higher rates of growth in developing countries will reflect progress in several sectors of the economy and in the pursuit of social and other goals. Although the Strategy does not seek to establish comprehensive and interrelated sectoral targets to be attained by the developing countries as a whole, many of its elements have been addressed in the various parts of the United Nations system. They cover such areas, among others, as employment and health, women and children, industry and technology, agriculture and food, population, education and culture, shelter and settlements, telecommunications, transportation, including shipping, and the environment. Sectoral strategies and plans for significant achievements have been agreed upon by Governments. Translated into goals and objectives for both national and international efforts, ambitious and feasible targets of this kind have proved valuable in focusing policies and in monitoring progress. They also serve as reminders of the progress that can be achieved within a decade, with strong political commitment and dedicated efforts.

19. The Strategy must look beyond the constraints of the moment. A decade is not enough to work miracles, but a true decade of development would make a great difference to the world situation on the eve of the next century. Serious development problems would still persist, but the debilitating deadlock of the recent past would have been broken for many developing countries. Their living standards would be rising instead of falling, the younger generation would find employment instead of being condemned to a desperate scurry for survival, and poverty and hunger would be pushed back instead of advancing. Revived investment would lay the foundation for growth in the next century and the energies and talents of the people in the developing countries would be harnessed for building their own future. The world as a whole would be safer and more prosperous than it will if present trends continue. A continued development failure in the next decade would be an invitation to world-wide disorder.

III. Policies and Measures

20. The policies and measures needed to support and realize the Strategy must reflect the urgency of its goals and objectives. They must aim at the acceleration of growth and give attention to issues of special priority in the development process and must respond to special situations, including those of the least developed countries. In each area, there are important policies and measures that need to be adopted in a national context by the developing countries themselves. There are equally important policies and measures that have to be adopted by the developed countries in the context of international cooperation for development. The international community as a whole must also strengthen the systems that support the sound workings of the world economy and the development process. The Strategy is thus of relevance to all countries, which must commit their best efforts to pursuing its goals within the limits of their abilities and responsibilities. The Strategy does not require unrequited sacrifices on the part of any countries. To the extent that public resources must be used in the pursuit of its goals, they represent investments in a better future world, investments that are strikingly modest by the standard of present defence budgets.

A. The Reactivation of Development

1. Economic policy frameworks, external debt, development finance, international trade, commodities

21. The reactivation and acceleration of development requires both a dynamic and supportive international economic environment and determined policies at the national level. It will be frustrated in the absence of either of these requirements. The policies and measures needed for the 1990s must therefore cover both aspects. A supportive external economic environment is crucial. The development process will not gather momentum if the global economy lacks dynamism and stability and is beset with uncertainties. Neither will it gather momentum if the developing countries are weighed down by external indebtedness, if development finance is inadequate, if barriers restrict access to markets and if commodity prices and the terms of trade of developing countries remain depressed. The record of the 1980s was essentially negative on each of these counts and needs to be reversed. The policies and measures needed to create an international environment that is strongly supportive of national development efforts in the 1990s are thus a vital part of the Strategy. So too are national policies for development. Their main elements are set out below.

The economic policy framework

22. A surge in development during the decade of the 1990s can take place only within supportive frameworks of overall economic policy, both national and international. The sound macro-economic management of the world economy is of paramount importance. The major industrialized countries, which broadly determine the international economic environment by their policies, have a special re-

sponsibility to bring about a stable and predictable international economic environment in which development can succeed. The adverse development environment of the 1980s was in part a consequence of restrictive policies of the earlier years of the decade aimed at combating inflation at the expense of growth. The major industrialized countries influence world economic growth and the international economic environment profoundly. They should continue their efforts to promote sustained growth and to narrow imbalances in a manner that can benefit other countries. The coordination of macro-economic policies should take full account of the interests and concerns of all countries, particularly the developing countries. Efforts should be made to enhance the effectiveness of multilateral surveillance aimed at correcting existing external and fiscal imbalances, promoting non-inflationary sustainable growth, lowering real rates of interest and making exchange rates more stable and markets more accessible.

23. The macro-economic policies of the developed countries should take account of the interests and concerns of the developing countries. During the 1980s, the developing countries were seriously affected by increases in real rates of interest and by frequent fluctuations in key exchange rates.

24. The economic policy framework of developing countries helps to shape the national environment for development and will need to take account of the objectives, priorities and particular circumstances of each country. But the acceleration of development will require strenuous efforts on a number of fronts. There is a need for determined policies that aim at increasing domestic savings and raising investments, as well as at improving the returns to investment. National policies must succeed in containing inflationary pressures, which often have adverse economic and social consequences that prove disruptive of development. This calls for monetary and fiscal discipline to promote price stability and external balance and the maintenance of realistic exchange rates without the need for repeated currency depreciations that have often had adverse consequences on social stability and the terms of trade of developing countries.

25. National policies must also be directed at mobilizing all the latent energies and impulses for development within the developing countries, at promoting efficiency in the allocation of resources and at taking advantage of the opportunities for trade, investment and scientific and technological progress provided by a changing global economic environment. The role of the public sector in the development process is essential. Impediments to progress caused by bureaucratic inefficiencies, strains on administration, excessive controls and neglect of market conditions by public enterprises need to be removed. The policy environment should, within the context of national goals, encourage a creative contribution by the private sector, stimulate entrepreneurship and innovation and promote the participation of the people at all levels in the development process. It should provide scope for the operation of market forces and for realistic pricing as a means to greater efficiency and soundness in the allocation of resources. The national policy framework should also enable developing countries to take full advantage of the opportunities of international trade and foreign investment, as well as promote cooperation among themselves. The effectiveness and flexibility of national policy frameworks would be enhanced in a setting of improving political institutions and legal systems. This would be reinforced by conditions that would permit declining military expenditures and thus the channelling of resources released to social and economic development.

External debt

26. For many developing countries, the reactivation of development will not take place without an early and durable solution to the problems of external indebtedness, taking into account the fact that, for many developing countries, external debt burdens are a significant problem. The burden of debt-service payments on those countries has imposed severe constraints on their ability to accelerate growth and eradicate poverty and has led to a contraction in imports, investment and consumption. External indebtedness has emerged as a main factor in the economic stalemate in the developing countries; there has been a large net transfer of resources from the developing to the developed countries, depriving the former of much-needed resources for development. Development during the decade of the 1990s should not be hampered by prolonged failure to resolve the international debt problems. Accordingly, a durable and broad solution to these problems should continue to be given urgent attention as we begin the decade of the 1990s. Innovative solutions need to be found and relief obtained in the initial years of the decade.

27. Recent initiatives and measures to reduce the stock and service of debt or to provide debt relief for developing countries should be broadly implemented. Relief measures should aim at the resumption of vigorous growth and development in these countries and should address all types of bilateral debt of debtor developing countries. Serious consideration should be given to continuing to work towards a growth-oriented solution of the problems of developing countries with serious debt-servicing problems, including those whose debt is mainly to official creditors or to multilateral institutions.

28. Finding a solution to the debt problems is the joint responsibility of debtor and creditor countries, commercial banks and multilateral financial institutions. Debtor countries should continue their efforts to attain efficiency and return to a path of sustained growth by adopting appropriate national economic policies. The creditor countries are encouraged to continue reviewing their tax policies and regulatory and accounting practices in order to facilitate commercial debt and debt-service reduction operations. The multilateral financial institutions should continue to provide support for debt and debt-service reduction packages, with the necessary flexibility, under their established guidelines. Creditor countries should support growth-oriented policies of debtor countries in order to facilitate the resumption of growth and development, as well as the prompt restoration of credit-worthiness of the debtor countries.

29. The measures agreed upon in the Paris Declaration and the Programme of Action for the Least Developed Countries for the 1990s adopted by the Second United Nations Conference on the Least Developed Countries, held in Paris from 3 to 14 September 1990, on the external debt problems of the least developed countries should be urgently and vigorously implemented.

30. The Paris Club is invited to consider increasing the flexibility of its negotiating mechanism and examining the current criteria of eligibility for debt relief, as well as the scope of the initiative taken at the Toronto Economic Summit, held in June 1988,[1] for dealing with the debt problem, taking into account, *inter alia*, the Economic Declaration adopted at the Houston Economic Summit, held in July 1990. Measures must continue to be taken to relieve the external debt burden of low-income and lower-middle-income countries whose debts are mainly to official creditors. Measures to address the external official debt problems of middle-income countries should also be seriously considered.

31. The external debt of the developing countries includes debts to multilateral financial institutions. These institutions must continue to find means to relieve the burdens that arise out of such debt in ways that safeguard the high standing of the institutions in financial markets, such as the World Bank Debt Reduction Facility of the International Development Association established in 1989 to provide debt relief to severely indebted low-income developing countries.

32. There is a close interrelationship between the external debt problem of the developing countries and the global economic environment. The debt-service burden is aggravated by rising interest rates, declining terms of trade, shrinking flows of external resources, protectionist barriers to trade and slow growth in the world economy, and would be lessened by an improvement in these factors. A marked improvement in the international economic environment, combined with appropriate national policies that take advantage of this improvement, is essential in order to solve these debt problems and avoid their proliferation among countries that have hitherto avoided their disruptive consequences.

1 See A/43/435-S/19974.

External development finance

33. Adequate resources, both domestic and external, are an essential condition for the reactivation of development. The developing countries need to mobilize domestic resources to the greatest extent possible and implement determined policies and measures to this end. In the case of most developing countries, domestic savings contribute by far the larger part of the resources utilized for investment.

34. However, the essence of the development problem is that countries that are poor have limited scope for increasing savings by restraining levels of consumption that are already low. The savings efforts of the developing countries need therefore to be supplemented by external resources so as to raise investment to the levels needed for adequate economic growth.

35. Furthermore, the development process is generally dependent on the flow of imported goods and services that are needed for the growth of the economy. Where export earnings fall short of import needs, the development process would be frustrated in the absence of supplementary flows of external resources.

36. The external economic environment of the 1980s did not favour the flow of external resources to developing countries. Falling commodity prices and protectionist trends weakened the export earnings of many countries, while the flow of development finance was impeded by constraints on aid budgets in the donor countries and, after the debt crisis of 1982, the end of net lending by commercial banks to developing countries. Because of this, developing countries became less attractive for foreign investors. By the middle of the 1980s, the net transfer of resources to developing countries on the aggregate turned negative because of the burden of debt-service payments. This trend was further compounded by losses incurred by developing countries on account of the deterioration in their terms of trade.

37. These trends have to be reversed in the 1990s if development is to be accelerated. A surge in the tempo of development is virtually unimaginable if the flow of external resources is from the poorer to the richer countries rather than vice versa. This would make meaningless the concept of a decade of development endorsed by the international community. The new consensus on the need for a reactivating of development and on the priorities of development policies calls for a new commitment on the part of the international community to augment the flow of development finance to the levels needed to attain these agreed goals.

38. A reduction in the burden of debt-service payments, as discussed earlier, is an essential requirement for reversing the negative trends relating to the flow of external resources to developing countries. But there must also be significant improvements in the flow of finance for development from the major sources of such finance, that is, official bilateral assistance, lending by commercial banks, direct private investment and multilateral financial institutions. Such improvements, when taken as a whole, should be adequate for the requirements of development finance in the 1990s. In order merely to restore a positive net transfer to the developing countries in a foreseeable future, during which no substantial flows of commercial credits can be expected, net official flows of loans and grants from all sources, which remained virtually constant at $35 billion in the 1980s, would have to grow substantially in the first half of the 1990s.

39. Economic reforms and the integration of Eastern Europe into the world market will generate substantial new demands for resources. This enlargement of the international division of labour will be to the benefit of all, but such needs should be met without diversion of the flows needed by developing countries.

40. Official development assistance must remain an essential source of concessional aid to the developing countries, particularly to the poorest and the least developed. Aid programmes of donor countries have in many cases remained at low levels and need to be substantially improved in the 1990s. Official development assistance has, on average, remained at only half of the internationally agreed target of 0.7 per cent of their gross national product. Donor countries should, in the 1990s, implement such undertakings as they have made to reach or surpass this target, as well as the targets for the least developed countries as adopted by the Second United Nations Conference on the Least Developed Countries. There should also be continued improvements in the quality of aid as well as in its utilization. The release of resources from any reductions in military spending and the recovery in the industrial countries should ease the budgetary constraints of donor countries, and rising concern about the environment and world poverty should provide new opportunities for development cooperation.

41. New possibilities for increasing the flow of development finance in the 1990s should also be explored. These include proposals for devoting part of the resources that may be released by the disarmament process and reduced military spending to development and for recycling to the developing countries, through suitable mechanisms and modalities, a part of the payment surpluses of major developed countries.

42. Lending by commercial banks, in the aftermath of the debt crisis, has ceased to be a major source of development finance. However, a resumption of such lending is relevant in the context both of solutions to the debt problem and of the needs of the developing countries, particularly those which are not recipients of significant concessional aid. The reactivation and acceleration of growth and an improvement in the global economic environment will help restore confidence in the creditworthiness of borrowing countries and facilitate the return of flight capital. None the less, innovative changes will also be needed to evolve instruments of lending that help cushion borrowing countries against a recurrence of debt-service problems.

43. Foreign direct investment, which is not generally debt creating, could play an increasingly important role as a source of development finance, particularly when international trade is growing, markets are expanding and new opportunities are opening up through scientific and technological developments. Transnational corporations are already channels for technology transfer, world trade and marketing. Many developing countries are seeking, to the extent compatible with national objectives, to establish a positive investment climate and to adopt appropriate investment codes.

44. The need for development finance is unlikely to be met exclusively through channels of official development assistance, lending by commercial banks and direct private foreign investment. The multilateral financial institutions could and should play a major role in the 1990s in development financing. Despite the efforts that have been made to enlarge the resources of the institutions in order to meet new needs, they will have to be considerably expanded in the 1990s. Their resources have been falling behind the growth of the world economy and especially behind that of the world capital markets. The net lending of the World Bank and regional development banks was, by the late 1980s, negligible or negative for a large number of developing countries. These institutions should be enabled to serve the role of intermediation between developing countries and the international capital market, for which they were designed. The conditionality associated with the use of resources should be realistic and in accordance with the need to ensure effective utilization by recipient countries.

45. The international monetary and financial system must evolve in the 1990s and respond to the needs of a changing world, which now calls for universal cooperation. It should become an increasingly important source of both development finance and international liquidity. It should provide greater stability and predictability in exchange rates. Developing countries should have greater influence in decisions that affect them vitally.

International trade

46. The goal of reactivating development requires a strongly supportive environment for international trade in general and for trade of the developing countries in particular over the decade of the 1990s. The international trading system is the pillar of an interdependent world economy and should establish conditions of openness and fairness in the interest of all countries. Growth and development and the solution of the pressing problems facing the developing countries are dependent on an open and credible multilateral trading system based on the principles of non-discrimination and transparency. Outward-looking development policies and export-based industrialization will not succeed if export markets are limited by restrictive barriers. The international trading system will function best in an

environment of growth and dynamism in the world economy, an environment to which the system itself will contribute, but it needs to be strengthened further in the 1990s by specific actions and measures.

47. Policies and measures in the area of international trade must be directed, in the first place, at arresting and reversing trends, particularly apparent during the 1980s, towards the erosion of the multilateral trading system as a result of unilateralism, bilateralism and protectionism. The international organizations in the field of trade should be strengthened to play their part in the achievement of this objective. Many new issues that reflect the changing nature of the world economy are pertinent to the evolution of the international trading system. But the strengthening of the trading system also requires the resolution of a number of ongoing issues, some of which are of special interest to developing countries and are crucial to the development process.

48. The acceleration of development in the decade of the 1990s should, *inter alia*, be supported by the following actions and measures in the field of international trade:

(*a*) Full and effective implementation of the commitment to halt and reverse protectionism, as undertaken in the Ministerial Declaration on the Uruguay Round of multilateral trade negotiations.[1] Protectionist trends of the 1980s have an adverse impact on the world economy and on the development process and performance of the developing countries and should not continue in the 1990s. Recourse to non-tariff barriers of various kinds, which has tended to increase in recent years, has affected the exports of developing countries;

(*b*) Trade liberalization and a sustained improvement in the access of developing country exports to the markets of both developing and developed countries through the reduction and removal of tariff and non-tariff barriers. Rapid structural adjustment in the developed countries in line with shifting comparative advantages will facilitate market access for the growing export capabilities of developing countries that arise in the course of their economic transformation. The rules of the international trading system recognize the need for differential and favourable treatment of developing countries in the contest of the other principles set out in the Ministerial Declaration on the Uruguay Round. This need should be reflected in the functioning of the system;

(*c*) Liberalization of trade in tropical products and natural resource-based products. This should include ending the escalation in tariffs on processed primary products;

(*d*) Bringing trade in textiles under the normal rules of the General Agreement on Tariffs and Trade;

(*e*) Progressive and substantial reduction of support and protection in the field of agriculture;

(*f*) Effective implementation and appropriate improvement of the generalized system of preferences, expansion of product coverage, duty-free treatment and adherence to the principles of non-reciprocity and non-discrimination in its application;

(*g*) Measures to ensure that regional economic integration and the formation of trade blocs will not impede the growth of world trade and are in conformity with the rules of the General Agreement on Tariffs and Trade. In particular, it is necessary to ensure that such developments do not result in additional barriers to developing country exports;

(*h*) Strict adherence to the rules and principles of the General Agreement on Tariffs and Trade by all contracting parties.

49. Developing countries should endeavour to liberalize their trade régimes in ways consistent with their development objectives so as to improve the efficiency and flexibility of their economies and their participation in the world economy. They should create trade opportunities among themselves and promote more rapid industrialization, in particular through the effective implementation of the Global System of Trade Preferences. There is great potential for economic integration among developing countries, and new efforts should be made during the 1990s to establish effective subregional and regional market arrangements among them.

50. The successful and balanced conclusion of the Uruguay Round of multilateral trade negotiations, which aims at strengthening the international trading system, is crucial for progress in the 1990s. The treatment of new issues, hitherto outside the scope of the rules of the system, should take account of the development dimension and of the need for developing countries to build up their own capabilities. The dialogue and negotiations about required improvements in the international trading system should be continued and expanded in the 1990s. The dialogue should focus, *inter alia*, on an equitable balance of interest between developed and developing countries, the adaptation and reform of the system to ensure its relevance to the changing patterns of international trade, and the need to ensure greater coordination between international trade and financial policies.

Commodities

51. The terms of trade of the developing countries are an important aspect of the international economic environment for development. The depressed levels of commodity prices and earnings of developing countries from commodity exports were an important element in the slowing down of the development process in many developing countries in the 1980s. Technological change played some part in depressing the long-term trend of demand for certain commodities. But slow growth and instability in the world economy and persistently high supplies were factors of critical importance. Commodity exports will continue to play a key role during the 1990s in the economies of most developing countries and will remain crucial to their export earnings and livelihood. For these countries, the reactivation of development during the decade will prove difficult in the face of continued weakness in their commodity sectors and terms of trade and will require a flexible response on the supply side to changing market conditions. The Strategy must aim at better functioning of commodity markets with greater transparency and more stable and predictable conditions. There is scope for improving international commodity policies in a number of ways.

52. The Integrated Programme for Commodities sought to improve the functioning of commodity markets through commodity agreements between producers and consumers, with support from the Common Fund for Commodities. The negotiation and renegotiation of such agreements proved difficult in the rapidly changing world economy of the 1980s, and a number of existing agreements broke down. There has been hardly any lasting improvement in most commodity markets since then, and the need for remedial action remains urgent. Commodity agreements between producers and consumers that improve the stability, transparency and functioning of markets and reflect long-term market trends benefit both producers and consumers, and efforts should be made to negotiate or renegotiate agreements of this type in the 1990s. The first window of the Common Fund was established for the specific purpose of supporting such international commodity agreements.

53. The diversification of the economies of developing countries and their increased participation in the processing, marketing and distribution of their commodities is of the utmost importance. The second window of the Common Fund for Commodities should be effectively used in this regard, particularly for technical assistance and for commodity-specific programmes for horizontal and vertical diversification, especially for the least developed countries. The diversification process should also be supported through the provision of improved market access for primary and processed commodities. Cooperation among developing countries could also play a significant role in the processing, transportation and marketing of commodities.

54. Compensatory financing is an important means of cushioning developing countries, in particular the least developed countries, against commodity-related shortfalls in export earnings. Existing compensatory financing schemes, particularly the Compensatory and Contingency Financing Facility of the International Monetary Fund, should be strengthened as appropriate.

1 See GATT, *Focus Newsletter, No. 41*, October 1986.

2. Science and technology, industrial policies and measures, agriculture

55. A solution to the debt problem, adequate resource flows and a supportive environment in the areas of international trade and commodity markets are among the prerequisites for the reactivation of development during the 1990s. But a sustained acceleration of the development process will not take place unless developing countries modernize and transform their industrial and agricultural sectors and participate in the progress made possible by advances in science and technology. National policies in these areas must reflect the particular situations. But many issues have strategic aspects that are widely relevant. These are set out in the paragraphs that follow, as a guide both to national efforts and to the support that is possible and needed through international development cooperation. In virtually all areas of effort, there is scope and need for supportive financial and technical assistance from donor Governments, multilateral lending institutions and international agencies. There are also possibilities and requirements for cooperation among developing countries.

Science and technology

56. The reactivation of development in the decade of the 1990s on a sustained basis will be linked to the ability of the developing countries to participate in the rapid advances in science and technology that have characterized the global economy in recent years and will continue in the future. Knowledge is today a crucial determinant of economic progress. The knowledge gap between the developed and the developing countries has been widening, and policies and measures are needed to help narrow it over the coming decade. High priority must therefore be given by the developing countries to raising their endogenous capacities and capabilities in this area.

57. Development and modernization in a setting of rapid advances in science and technology call for the establishment and strengthening of scientific cadres and for upgrading the skills of the work force. Developing countries, in their plans and policies, should emphasize policies and measures that enhance their scientific and technological capability and should devote adequate resources to that end. Such policies must range from the expansion and adaptation of their educational systems, including vocational education, to the building up of scientific and technological research and development capabilities.

58. Policies and measures in this field should seek to enhance the capacity of developing countries to utilize scientific and technological developments from abroad, as well as to modify and adapt them to suit local conditions. Such policies should also aim at traditional technologies that are capable of being developed as a means of raising productivity.

59. Building the scientific and technological capability of developing countries calls for external assistance in research and development, in the establishment and strengthening of institutions in the area of science and technology, in the diffusion of new technologies and in the training of scientific cadres. Developing countries should not be discriminated against with regard to commercial access to science and technology for development purposes. Commercial channels for the import of technology, including direct foreign investment, are especially relevant and should be utilized on suitable terms and conditions. In addition, with respect to access to and transfer of technology on concessional and preferential terms, in particular to developing countries, effective modalities should be examined with a view to implementing and enhancing such access and transfer as much as possible.

60. The international community should also review ways in which the intellectual property system can promote more effectively the economic and technological development of all countries, particularly the developing countries, and in which intellectual property can be effectively protected. Work on the international code of conduct on the transfer of technology should also be completed.

61. There is considerable scope for cooperation among developing countries in the development of science and technology. The developing countries could help each other through the establishment of common institutions and centres for research and training, the pursuit of joint projects for technological research and development, the offer of facilities for education in science and technology among themselves and the exchange of information. Science and technology must be given a prominent place in schemes for cooperation among developing countries at the global as well as at the regional and subregional levels.

Industrial policies and measures

62. An acceleration in the process of industrialization must be a central element in the economic transformation of most developing countries and in the reactivation of development in the 1990s. Given the limits to agriculture as a means of providing increased employment and additional external earnings, industrialization becomes indispensable for sustained economic growth and social development. It is also through industrialization that developing countries could make use of many of the opportunities provided by advances in science and technology and by international markets. Policies and measures to promote industrialization must thus be a major plank in the Strategy.

63. Some notable exceptions apart, manufacturing industry stagnated in many developing countries during the 1980s. These countries experienced a chronic underutilization of existing industrial capacity, a lack of maintenance, import constraints and technological obsolescence. These problems were at times compounded by mismanagement. For these countries, the rehabilitation of their industrial sectors and an end to the underutilization of capacities must be objectives of priority. The rate of industrialization will obviously vary among countries, but for many countries, especially for those where manufacturing industry was set back in the 1980s, historical experience suggests that the objective should be to raise it significantly, say, to 8 to 10 per cent.

64. Industrial progress requires investments directly related to increasing manufacturing capacity. It is also dependent on an improved and modernized infrastructure in such areas as communications and transport, power and banking and finance. It is dependent, too, on a supportive policy framework in the fiscal and monetary fields. Not least, it is crucially dependent on managerial and technical skills and on a trained and efficient work-force. Industrial development must also make use of linkages with other sectors of the economy, particularly the rural sector, which could supply both materials and markets for industrial growth. These subjects must form an integral part of the policies and measures that developing countries need to take for industrial progress during the decade. But there are also certain other major issues of policy that are central to faster progress in industrialization and that may call for new orientations. These are outlined below.

65. One such issue concerns the relative roles of the public and private sectors. In the past, many developing countries, anxious to speed up industrialization and faced with a weak and inexperienced private sector, sought to establish manufacturing enterprises owned and run by governmental entities and enjoying a high degree of protection. Experience has shown that there can be limitations to such an approach, particularly when administrative capacities are strained. State-run enterprises can be hampered by bureaucratic rigidity and inefficiency, and lack flexibility, competitiveness and innovative power. The capabilities of the private sector have grown in many countries and there is considerable scope for enhancing the contribution that private enterprise can make to a dynamic process of industrialization. Entrepreneurship should be encouraged at all levels for the setting up of industries. There is usually a strong potential for the development of medium- and small-scale industries that could also contribute to enlarging both urban and rural employment opportunities. Where industries are under public ownership, efficiency should be improved through measures that increase their flexibility and their ability to respond to changing conditions.

66. Another issue is that of industrial production for exports as against production for the domestic market and import substitution. The establishment of industries supplying domestic markets is desirable because of market proximity, linkages with other sectors and reduced dependence. But there are often limits to the scope for import-substituting industries, particularly where markets are small. In these cases, policies based excessively on import substitution supported by highly protective barriers result in high cost and ineffi-

ciency. Production for export is a means of overcoming these limitations. It becomes a virtual imperative where the scope for additional agricultural exports is limited. It is also a means of keeping step with technological progress and of closer integration with global markets, since exports call for efficiency and competitiveness.

67. The goal of industrialization calls for the building up of domestic ownership and national managerial and technological capabilities. But direct foreign investment can make an important contribution to industrialization. Such investment not only provides additional resources, but is also a means of having access to modern technologies, skills and markets. The rules and regulations of developing countries should encourage direct foreign investment in wars in which mutual interests are furthered. The constraints to the flow of external resources from other sources give added importance to direct foreign investment as a means of augmenting this flow.

68. The progress of industrialization in developing countries, and of outward-looking development in general, is closely related to openness and non-discrimination in international markets. The implementation of the measures needed in this area, as set out in the section on international trade, such as the lowering of tariff and non-tariff barriers and measures to further structural adjustment in the developed countries, form an important part of the strategy for industrialization.

69. Industrial progress in developing countries can also be significantly enhanced through cooperation among such countries at the global, regional and subregional levels. The integration of markets of developing countries, the setting up of joint ventures and programmes for training and upgrading skills must be among the objectives of policies and measures to promote industrialization during the 1990s.

Agriculture

70. For many countries, agriculture, with its large contribution to the national economy, will remain the principal means for the revitalization of economic growth during the 1990s. To the extent that countries depend on the export of agricultural commodities to world markets, progress will be closely related to the implementation of the measures outlined earlier for strengthening international trade in commodities. But agricultural production is the developing countries also meets the production requirements for the domestic market for food and other products of both the farming and the non-farming population. The acceleration of development calls, therefore, for a special focus on policies and measures aimed at raising agricultural output and at strengthening food security and self-reliance in food.

71. The transition from a traditional system of cultivation, sometimes at a subsistence level, to modernized agriculture should be the underlying aim of agricultural policy. In many developing countries, the pressures on available land are already high and there are limits to what can be achieved through an extension of the area under cultivation. Where such possibilities remain, measures could be taken to bring new land under cultivation through programmes of irrigation and land settlement, provided that adverse environmental consequences, such as could arise from excessive forest clearing, are avoided. In great part, however, progress in agriculture is heavily dependent on raising productivity on lands already under cultivation. The scope for this could be large given the gap, often wide, between current productivity and technical potential.

72. There are several important components of the policies and measures needed for raising agricultural production and productivity. An annual rate of growth of the order of 4 per cent on average in food production would make a major contribution to food security and support agro-industrial development. But the great diversity of country situations means that there is no single set of policies of general applicability. Success will often depend on the removal of key constraints, which vary greatly from country to country. However, policies and measures based on the considerations set out below will be broad applicability.

73. Success in reaching the potential for raising agricultural productivity requires a farming population possessed of the knowledge, the incentives and the means required for this purpose. Improving the knowledge and skills of farmers calls for the diffusion of technology relating to agricultural practices and the use of improved varieties, as well as for the continued development and adaption of technology through research. This underlines the importance both of effective extension efforts and services and of measures to enhance the capabilities of research institutions. The successful adoption of better methods and technologies is crucially for farmers to improve their standard of living. The price incentive is especially important, particularly in the context of the transition from subsistence farming to modernized agriculture. Policies that depress the prices of farm output in order to protect or subsidize living costs for the population at large are often counter-productive. A policy framework that permits more realistic prices that better reflect market situations often yields better results. Such a framework must also remove the shortcomings in marketing, distribution and storage that lead to an excessive gap between retail and farm prices.

74. Farmers must also have access to the means of raising agricultural productivity. Economic units of land secure systems of tenure are often prerequisites for agricultural progress. Facilities for irrigation and a strong infrastructure of transport, communications and power, as well as other services that overcome the remoteness of rural areas, are among the others. A strong network of rural banking and credits is also vital to help farmers procure inputs and make the investments needed for raising production.

75. Policies and measures aimed at raising agricultural production need to take account of the linkages between agriculture and other sectors of the economy. The link with the industrial sector is especially important, since industry is a source of farm inputs and of consumer goods for the rural population, as well as source of demand for agricultural products. Agro-industries located in rural areas can provide both a stimulus to agriculture and a source of employment for under-utilized labour. In a more general sense, there is also a close link between the productivity of farmers and the extent and quality of educational and health services and a housing available to the rural population.

76. There is often considerable potential for improving the contribution of women to agricultural progress. In most developing countries, women form an important part of the active farming population and of the agricultural labour force. Policies and measures to increase their productivity and involve them more in key decisions should raise their contribution to output and their incomes. Schemes for rural self-help and for the mobilization of labour for community development and for the upgrading and maintenance of the rural infrastructure can also play an important part in the drive for agricultural progress.

77. A number of steps are also needed at the international level. Finance for investments in the agricultural sector and technical assistance should form part of programmes for development cooperation, both bilateral and multilateral. Developing countries should have assured access to advances in such fields as biotechnology and genetic engineering, at appropriate costs. The removal of existing distortions in international trade in agriculture is also essential. In particular, the achievement of this objective requires that there be substantial and progressive reduction in support and protection of agriculture - covering internal régimes, market access and export subsidies - in order to avoid inflicting large losses on the more efficient producers, especially in developing countries. Special importance is attached to the successful outcome and effective follow-up of the Uruguay Round in the areas of agriculture, tropical products and natural resource-based products, taking into account of the needs of the net food-importing developing countries.

B. Priority Aspects of Development

78. An acceleration in the rate of economic growth is an essential objective for the 1990s. It is a condition for expanding the resource base of the developing countries and hence for economic, technological and social transformation. But economic growth by itself does not ensure that its benefits will be equalitably distributed or that the physical environment will be protected and improved. Yet, if poverty persists or increases and there is neglect of the human condition, political and social strains will grow and endanger stability in the 1990s and beyond. Similiary, if environmental damage and degradation increases, the natural resource base of the developing countries

and the welfare of populations will be harmed and progress in development itself will become unsustainable. The Strategy must therefore give special attention to the policies and measures needed in the areas of poverty alleviation, human resource development and the environment. It must also pay special attention to the related areas of population growth and the elimination of hunger. The decade of the 1990s must witness a significant improvement in the human condition everywhere and establish a mutually reinforcing relationship between economic growth and human welfare. The need to strengthen this relationship is, in fact, a principal theme of the present Strategy: It has not only to be reflected in national efforts but must also be promoted by the international community through financial and technical support.

1. Eradiction of poverty and hunger

79. The international community, noting the severity of problems related to poverty in developing countries, agrees that the objective of eradicating poverty is of the highest priority. It is encouraging that a broad consensus is emerging on strategies to be pursued towards the achievement of this goal.

80. The goal of eradicating poverty calls for policies and measures on two broad fronts. It calls, in the first place, for a style of development in which economic progress is distributed as widely as possible and not concentrated excessively on a few localities and sectors or limited groups of the population. It also requires, to the extent that poor and vulnerable sections of the population are not reached by this process, special and supplementary programmes and actions that are directly targeted to bring benefits to these groups.

81. The generation of employment and income through productive occupation is a major means of eradicating poverty since the absence of adequate income owing to landlessness or the lack of opportunities for work is a prime cause of poverty. Development programmes and processes that provide employment on a large scale are thus an essential need. The sectors and regions in which development takes place and the technologies adopted must be such as to have a significant impact on employment. This must be an important consideration in establishing the balance between growth in the agricultural, industrial, construction and service sectors. The creation of employment and income through the activation of the informal sector of the economy and through the expansion of self-employment activities should also be an important part of policies to improve income and eradicate poverty.

82. Progress in development, even when occurring on a broad front, might still bypass significantly large sections of the population, particularly the poorest and most vulnerable. Special programmes and measures that are aimed directly at increasing their real income are thus likely to prove necessary. These could include the provision of cheap and subsidised food and other essentials, as well as income support for the poorest and the destitute. They could also include programmes of training and of mobilization of labour for local self-help and community development as well as for production. Such programmes establish a link between activities aimed at the eradication of poverty and productive activities. The provision of facilities at low cost in such areas as health, education and transport is also a means of raising the real income of the poor. Measures to relieve homelessness or poor housing should be another major aspect of poverty eradication programmes. The increase in the number of homeless people in many developing countries has been one of the serious manifestations of the deteriorating human condition, and the improvement of human settlements as agreed in the Global Strategy for Shelter to the Year 2000[1] should be part of the crucial effort in this field.

83. Women and children are a particularly vulnerable group in situations of poverty. Policies and measures for poverty eradication should have a particular focus on their needs and give special attention to maternal and child health care and to nutrition. Food security is also a major aspect of the fight against hunger and poverty and calls for an integrated approach to food production and consumption.

84. Policies and measures that are specifically directed at poverty eradication must carefully target that part of the population which is in need. Subsidized facilities and services that are general in scope and bring benefits to groups that are not in need are normally costly and impose excessive strains on the limited resources available to developing countries. Subsidies of a general nature could also contribute towards distorting prices and may, as in the case of food, have adverse effects on incentives for domestic production.

85. Developing countries need not await the transformation in per capita income to do away with the extremes of poverty, particularly hunger and destitution. Some developing countries with low per capita incomes have succeeded in obtaining relatively good results in the social field. In the long run, however, economic growth is needed to raise living standards and eliminate poverty. Long periods of stagnation or low growth might make unsustainable the initial gains in the social area.

86. The struggle against poverty is the shared responsibility of all countries. The eradication of poverty, as well as broad humanitarian and social goals, such as advancement in the quality of development, broad participation, larger choice and better opportunities for all men and women, need and should have the full support of the international community. A substantial reduction in hunger and malnutrition is within reach. There is considerable scope for international food aid going beyond emergency situations. Member States must give effect to agreements already reached to make all efforts to meet four goals during the decade:

(*a*) The elimination of starvation and death caused by famine;

(*b*) A substantial reduction in malnutrition and mortality among children;

(*c*) A tangible reduction of chronic hunger;

(*d*) The elimination of major nutritional diseases.

2. Human resource and institutional development

87. Human resource development has the closest of interactions with the process of economic and technological transformation. In a broad sense, it covers a wide range of activities that release the creative potential of the individual and determine the style of development. Each country has to choose its approach to human resource and institutional development in accordance with its national priorities, values, traditions and cultures and stage of development. Education and health are, however, essential aspects of human resource development and must receive special attention.

88. Education is both a basic human need and a prerequisite for the achievement of the other objectives of development. The educational skills of the labour force determine to a large extent a country's competitive strength and its capacity to adjust to new and sophisticated technologies. In a number of developing countries, expenditure on education declined in absolute or relative terms during the 1980s against the background of a worsening economic situation, and there was a resulting deterioration in the quality of education. Attention needs to be given, in the light of country situations, to each of the aspects of the educational system. The eradication of illiteracy needs special emphasis, including its eradication among women. A target of reducing adult illiteracy by at least one half during the decade has already been set by the international community. But a sound base of primary and secondary education is a basic requirement. Policies and measures in this area must provide for the relatively rapid increase in the school-age population that accompanies the growth of population common to most developing countries. In fact, the goals for the decade of providing universal access to basic education and of the completion of primary education by at least 80 per cent of the school-age group have been internationally accepted. This calls for adequate resources, both financial and administrative, capital and current, for the provision of facilities and materials and for the recruitment of teachers. At the same time there is a need to ensure that the expansion of the educational base does not result in a deterioration of quality and is supported by policies to train and retain teachers. The content of education at the primary and secondary level must also be relevant to a country's need for economic, social and political progress. In the framework of action to meet basic learning needs, it is

---

1 *Official Records of the General Assembly, Forty-third Session, Supplement No. 8,* addendum (A/43/8/add.1).

important to ensure the speedy implementation of the World Declaration on Education for All, adopted by the World Conference on Education for All.[1]

89. The increasingly important role that knowledge plays in determining economic progress in a rapidly changing global environment of science and technology gives a new urgency to upgrading and transforming the scientific, technological, entrepreneurial and managerial aptitudes of the population. This calls for an emphasis on higher education and on the development of the institutional base for the training of skilled cadres as well as for vocational training. It also calls for policies and incentives that are conducive to retaining skilled personnel in their countries on a voluntary basis. The skills of the work force at all levels may well be the key to progress in the 1990s and beyond.

90. In the field of health services, special attention needs to be given to primary health care and the prevention of chronic diseases, as well as to general development objectives such as sanitation, safe drinking-water and nutrition. This will help relieve the strains on the curative medial system to which increasing numbers tend to have recourse as a result of population growth, education and social change. Policies and measures in the field of health need to give special attention to women and children. Several targets for the decade have already been agreed upon by the international community. These include the reduction of under-five mortality rates by one third or 70 per 1,000 live births (whichever saves more lives); the reduction of malnutrition among children under five by one half; and the halving of maternal mortality rates. The participatory and environmental aspects of health care should be emphasised in the design of programmes. There should also be a special focus on preventing the spread of epidemics and other diseases that are endemic in many developing countries. Urgent steps also need to be taken for the control and prevention of acquired immunodeficiency syndrome (AIDS).

91. As in the field of education, policies and measures for health must give increased attention to institution-building and the training of skilled health personnel at all levels. Here again, conditions have to be created that encourage the retention of skilled cadres.

92. Human resource development could also be promoted by cooperation among developing countries. Developing countries could benefit by opening to each other their centres of quality for higher education and training. They could benefit by the exchange of teachers and of personnel in the field of health and by the sharing of experiences. They could also profit from the joint operation and management of institutions for human resource development, particularly at the regional and subregional levels.

93. The developed countries have an important role to play in promoting human resource and institutional development. Apart from investment support and technical assistance for the supply and use of equipment and for curriculum development, a major contribution can be made by the developed countries through the provision of facilities for the training of skilled cadres. Education abroad has always played an important part in training in developing countries. But in the 1990s and thereafter, its role can be vastly enhanced because of rapid developments in the field of knowledge and the urgent need of the developing countries for larger cadres of skilled personnel. At the same time, the developing countries should be assisted in building up their own institutions for training and higher education. As development progresses, there is need for them to enhance their self-reliance in this field.

94. Human rights and human development are ends in themselves. All human resource activities are mutually reinforcing. Careful analysis, policy design and effective management in education and health programmes will be required, and the support of agencies of the United Nations system should play a vital role. Given the interrelated nature of human resource development activities, inter-agency coordination in education, health, nutrition, housing, employment, child welfare and the advancement of women requires close attention. There should be programmes to integrate the elderly in development.

3. Population

95. Population programmes should be integrated with economic goals and strategies. The 1990s will see the largest increase in the population of developing countries of any decade in history, an increase of well over 20 per cent. The decade will also witness the aging of the world population. The demographic situation varies among countries, but in most developing countries a lowering of the rate of population growth will relieve the strains on the social situation, economic growth, the environment and natural resources. Population growth rates are in fact beginning to decline in a number of developing countries. Over half of the developing countries are pursuing active policies to reduce the rate of population growth and important lessons have been learned from this experience. The education of women, improved maternity and child care and family planning services suited to the socio-cultural environment of individual countries have proved to be effective and successful instruments of population programmes and should be further pursued and strengthened. Assistance to developing countries in the area of population should be substantially increased during the 1990s. Developing countries should also intensify their efforts to allocate adequate resources to population programmes.

4. Environment

96. The current threat to the environment is the common concern of all. All countries should take effective action for the protection and enhancement of the environment in accordance with their respective capacities and responsibilities and taking into account the specific needs of developing countries. As the major sources of pollution, the developed countries have the main responsibility for taking appropriate measures urgently. The economic growth and development of developing countries are essential in order to address problems of the degradation and protection of the environment. New and additional financial resources will have to be channelled to developing countries. Effective modalities for favourable access to, and transfer of, environmentally sound technologies, in particular to developing countries, including on concessional and preferential terms, should be examined.

97. The General Assembly, in its resolution 44/228 of 22 December 1989, has set important goals for the United Nations Conference on Environment and Development in 1992. These goals need to be realized.

IV. Special Situations, Including those of the Least Developed Countries

98. Over two decades ago, the United Nations adopted criteria to identify the countries that were economically the weakest among the developing countries and that faced the most recalcitrant structural problems. It was recognized that those countries, designated the least developed countries, needed special support measures from the international community in their efforts to transform their economies and to improve their prospects for sustained development. In 1981, the United Nations Conference on the Least Developed Countries adopted the Substantial New Programme of Action for the 1980s for the Least Developed Countries,[2] in which a number of measures to support the development process in those countries were agreed upon. The measures included the setting of a target of 0.15 per cent of the gross national product of the developed countries for concessional aid to the least developed countries.

99. However, those very countries, and others that were among the poorest and the weakest, were the hardest hit by the difficulties that arose in the 1980s on the world economic scene. In terms of the

---

1 *Final Report of the World Conference on Education for All: Meeting Basic Learning Needs, Jomtien, Thailand, 5-9 March 1990*, Inter-Agency Commission (UNDP, UNESCO, UNICEF, World Bank) for the World Conference on Education for All, New York, 1990, appendix 1.

2 *Report of the United Nations Conference on the Least Developed Countries, Paris, 1-14 September 1981* (United Nations publication, Sales No. E.82.I.8), part one, sect. A.

criteria initially adopted, the number of countries falling into the category of least developed countries - instead of declining as a result of successful development - actually increased from 24 in 1972 to 41 in 1990. The measures taken by the international community to support the least developed countries did not suffice to offset the adverse factors that affected their development experience in the 1980s. In the light of developments in the world economy there is a risk that those countries will become increasingly marginalized; this risk needs urgently to be avoided.

100. The Second United Nations Conference on the Least Developed Countries was held in Paris in September 1990. It underscored the principle of shared responsibility and strengthened partnership for the growth and development of the least developed countries and called for mutual commitments and strengthened joint efforts on the part of both the least developed countries and their development partners. The programme of action adopted at the Conference needs to be fully implemented. Broad requirements have been set out. The present official development assistance targets, as agreed on at the Conference, should, in the first instance, be met. Special attention is needed to facilitate increased access of exports of the least developed countries to major markets. Enhanced compensatory financing for export earnings shortfalls should be considered. Donors should take the necessary steps to provide further bilateral concessional debt forgiveness to the least developed countries. All donors are urged to implement Trade and Development Board resolution 165 (S-IX) of 11 March 1978[1] as a matter of priority in such a way that the net flows of official development assistance should be improved for the recipient. The Paris Club should consider the application of the terms agreed upon at the Toronto Economic Summit to all the least developed countries in accordance with established procedures and criteria; the Toronto options should be reviewed, taking into account the communiqué of the Houston Economic Summit; and proposals for further debt relief should be examined urgently. Financial institutions, particularly those providing non-concessional credits, are invited to give serious attention to measures to alleviate the burden of the debt that least developed countries owe to them.

101. The special development problems of the land-locked developing countries and of the island developing countries also call for special attention. Measures are needed to lift the constraints on their development arising from the special transportation and communications problems they face, from their limited internal markets and from their high degree of vulnerability to environmental damage and natural disasters.

102. These measures should aim at reducing the cost to those countries of access to and from the sea and world markets, improving the quality, efficiency and reliability of transit-transport facilities and diversifying their economies.

V. Role of the United Nations System

103. The organs, organizations and bodies of the United Nations system have a special responsibility for the pursuit of the goals and objectives of the present Strategy. The system has played a unique role in bringing the development issue to the attention of the international community. Through its studies on the several aspects of the development problem, both national and international, through the international conferences it has convened on major issues, through the understandings, conventions and agreements it has helped to negotiate - some of them of a legal or quasi-legal character - and not least through the technical assistance it has provided to developing countries, it has made an invaluable contribution to ideas, policies and actions in the realm of development. This role must not only continue but must be strengthened and expanded in the 1990s with the support and encouragement of Member States.

104. Virtually every aspect of the Strategy falls within the areas of concern of the various parts of the United Nations system. In many such areas and sectors, goals and targets for the coming decade and the actions needed for realizing them have already been agreed upon by Member States and are crucial to the implementation of the Strategy. The Strategy also provides guidelines for further work on the evolution of policies and programmes and on seeking agreements for new actions. Major conferences of the United Nations system are already scheduled for the initial years and there will be others in the period beyond. These will be important occasions for reaching agreements that give more specific content to the actions and commitments needed to realize the goals of the Strategy.

105. The organs, organizations and bodies of the United Nations system thus have a vital role to play in furthering the analytical work of relevance to the elaboration and implementation of the Strategy, in promoting and securing the international cooperation needed and in providing technical assistance. The work of the international system should be given greater coherence by closer inter-agency cooperation and coordination and by organizational measures that strengthen the contribution of the system to development. The Strategy provides an initial framework for these objectives. The review of the functioning of the United Nations system should continue to be pursued with this aim in view; all of its Member States have a responsibility for making it more effective and efficient.

106. The Secretary-General is encouraged to continue, by such means as he deems appropriate, his efforts to facilitate the solution to the debt problems of developing countries, taking into account all relevant proposals. In addition, the relevant organs and bodies of the United Nations system should undertake follow-up measures pertaining to the Uruguay Round of multilateral trade negotiations.

107. The growing interdependence in the world economy and the increasing linkages between various issues, such as money and finance, trade and development, give a new urgency to the coordination of macro-economic policies and management at the international level. The United Nations should play its role in this area as envisaged in the provisions of the Charter relating to the functions of the Economic and Social Council.

VI. Review and Appraisal

108. A process of review and appraisal should be an integral part of the Strategy so as to ensure its effective implementation. This process should be undertaken at the national level by the respective Member States. But it needs also to be undertaken within the United Nations system at the global, sectoral and regional levels. It should provide an opportunity to give the necessary political stimulus, in the light of evolving needs and developments. It must be expected that conditions in the course of the decade will change in ways that cannot now be foreseen, and there is thus a case for permanent monitoring and periodic review, allowing, when necessary, for amendments and revisions to the Strategy.

109. The recent events in the Gulf region are having repercussions on the immediate economic outlook of many countries, particularly in energy and trade balances. While it is not possible, in view of the uncertainties, to take account of them at present, it is important to keep the situation under review to determine whether in the context of the Strategy additional measures are required.

110. The organs, organizations and bodies of the United Nations system will play an important catalytic role in the implementation of the goals and objectives of the present Strategy in their respective areas of competence.

111. The machinery for continued monitoring exists: the various agencies of the United Nations system and the regional commissions issue annual reports, which, in effect, monitor the state of progress in virtually every area of international development. Governments participate in numerous debates in the specialized agencies, the Economic and Social Council and the General Assembly, in which the state of progress in international development is a major theme. In this sense, review and appraisal is already built into the procedures of the United Nations system.

112. Nevertheless, review and appraisal relating directly to the progress of the Strategy as a whole is also needed on a periodic basis. This should be carried out biennially by the General Assembly through the Economic and Social Council, with an item on the implementation of the Strategy included in their agendas. The Secre-

1 *Official Records of the General Assembly, Thirty-third Session, Supplement No. 15* (A/33/15) vol. I and corrigendum, annex I.

tary-General should submit appropriate recommendations in order to assist in this process of review and appraisal.

05.32 DEVELOPMENT PROGRAMMES

519 (VI). Expanded Programme of Technical Assistance for the Economic Development of Under-developed Countries

Committee: 2
Vote: 51 - 0 - 5
Ref.: 1946(XVIII), 1533(XV), 1432(XIV), 1383(XIV), 1305(XIII), 1216(XII), 1214(XII), 1037(XI), 1022(XI), 1019(XI), 994(X), 831(IX), 722(VIII), 621(VII), 518(VI), 399(V), 305(IV), 304(IV), 200(III)

A

The General Assembly,

Believing that the continuation and extension of the technical assistance programmes of the United Nations and of the specialized agencies are of basic importance to economic development and to effective international cooperation to raise standards of living in underdeveloped countries,

Recognizing that governments requesting technical assistance under the Expanded Programme have the primary responsibility for planning and carrying out, within the framework of available resources, their own programmes of economic and social development,

Recognizing the great importance of close collaboration between agencies giving technical and financial assistance,

1. *Notes with satisfaction* the action taken by the Economic and Social Council in resolution 400 (XIII) of 30 August 1951, the progress already achieved in putting the Expanded Programme of Technical Assistance into operation, and the collaboration which has been developing between agencies giving technical and financial assistance with regard to particular projects;

2. *Welcomes* the action[1] taken by the Technical Assistance Committee of the Economic and Social Council during the latter's thirteenth session recommending that the Secretary-General and the participating organizations should interpret the rules regarding the provision of supplies and equipment more generously than has been done in the past within the framework of Council resolution 222 A (IX) of 15 August 1949 and requesting the Technical Assistance Board:

(*a*) To study the practicability of meeting the needs for supplies and equipment designed to increase the effectiveness of certain economic and social services in the under-developed countries, especially in respect of the establishment of training and research centres;

(*b*) To place greater emphasis on the establishment of training and demonstration projects in the under-developed countries and on the provision of pilot plants and similar facilities;

3. *Requests* that negotiations regarding contributions for the second financial period of the Expanded Programme of Technical Assistance be carried out by any negotiating committee[2] for extra-budgetary funds established during the present session of the General Assembly;

4. *Requests* the Secretary-General:

(*a*) Subject to the provisions of any other resolution adopted by the General Assembly at its sixth regular session concerning the pledging of extra-budgetary funds, to convene a conference for the purpose of ascertaining approximately the total amount of contributions for the second financial period available from the participating governments, subject to the approval of their respective legislative authorities, for the execution of the technical assistance programmes of the United Nations and of the specialized agencies;

(*b*) To invite to the conference with the right to vote all Members of the United Nations and all other States which are members of the specialized agencies participating in the programme; and likewise to invite, without the right to vote, representatives of the specialized agencies;

5. *Approves* the financial arrangements set forth in the annex hereto for the administration of the funds contributed, as agreed by the Economic and Social Council in paragraph 7 of its resolution 400 (XIII) of 30 August 1951;

6. *Urges* the participating organizations, through the Technical Assistance Board, to make such arrangements with governments contributing to the Expanded Programme of Technical Assistance as would ensure the most effective utilization of all currencies, including particularly the contributions in currencies of limited convertibility, contributed to the Special Account;

7. *Calls on* the specialized agencies participating in the Expanded Programme of Technical Assistance to provide, in their regular budget documents, information concerning their estimates for the expenditure of technical assistance funds; and to transmit to the General Assembly, for examination and approval, the audit reports relating to expenditure of technical assistance funds allocated from the Special Account after approval of the appropriate audit reports by the general conferences of their agencies or by such other authorities of the agencies as are constitutionally authorized to approve them;

8. *Expresses the hope* that governments of States which are not Members of the United Nations but are members of participating specialized agencies will attend the conference mentioned in paragraph 4 (a) above, and that they will associate themselves with the financial and other arrangements mentioned above;

9. *Urges* all governments to make contributions to the programme for the year 1952 at least equal to the contributions which they had pledged for the first financial period;

10. *Requests* the Secretary-General, the Economic and Social Council and the specialized agencies to take all possible measures to ensure that technical assistance rendered is consistent with, and makes the maximum contribution to, integrated plans of economic and social development;

11. *Further requests* the Secretary-General, in view of the fact that certain private non-profit organizations are engaged in rendering technical assistance to several under-developed areas, to study the possibility of coordinating their policies and activities with those of the United Nations and the specialized agencies;

12. *Looks forward* to increased collaboration between the agencies furnishing technical assistance and financing agencies so that maximum coordination between technical and financial assistance can be obtained;

13. *Recommends*:

(*a*) That governments requesting technical assistance under the Expanded Programme continue to strengthen their internal machinery for the coordinated planning and implementation of development measures, for the formulation of integrated programmes of development, including priorities, and, in general, for the utilization of technical assistance in as effective a manner as possible, including the possibilities of financing such development projects as may be recommended by technical assistance missions;

(*b*) That governments requested to make available experts and facilities for the Expanded Programme take all possible steps to facilitate the availability of such technical assistance to under-developed countries through the United Nations and the participating specialized agencies, and further that these governments continue to improve their coordinating facilities in order to help accelerate the flow of technical knowledge in the under-developed countries.

360th plenary meeting
12 January 1952

[1] See *Official Records of the Economic and Social Council, Thirteenth Session, Annexes*, agenda item 33, document E/2102.

[2] See resolution 571 B (VI).

Annex

Financial Arrangements

[Agreed by the Economic and Social Council in paragraph 7 of its resolution 400 (XIII)]

(*a*) The amounts allocated for the participating organizations for the first financial period shall remain available for the purpose of assuming obligations or commitments during the second financial period, subject to necessary adjustments for the establishment of the Special Reserve Fund provided for in paragraph (*b*);

(*b*) There shall be established a Special Reserve Fund equivalent to US $3,000,000 for the purpose of assuring the completion of projects which extend beyond the end of the financial period for which funds are available, and of providing funds pending receipt of contributions at the beginning of a financial year. The Special Reserve Fund shall be created from unobligated funds remaining from the first financial period and shall be maintained principally in convertible currencies. The size of the Special Reserve Fund may be changed by the Technical Assistance Committee. Withdrawals from the Special Reserve Fund may be made by the Technical Assistance Board for the purposes described above and shall be replaced as soon as contributions become available;

(*c*) The Secretary-General shall allot contributions received for the second financial period as follows:

(i) $10,000,000 out of contributions received for the second financial period shall be automatically available for allocation to the participating organizations in accordance with paragraph 9 (c) of Council resolution 222 A (IX);

(ii) The balance of contributions received shall be retained in the Special Account for further allocation, as provided in paragraph (*d*) below;

(*d*) Contributions retained under paragraph (c) (ii) above shall be allotted in accordance with decisions of the Technical Assistance Board in such manner and at such time as it may guide, with a view to ensuring the development of well-balanced and Coordinated country and regional technical assistance programmes, taking into consideration all relevant factors, in particular, the amounts and kinds of resources on hand and receivable, the technical assistance requests received which fall within the field of the several participating organizations, the uncommitted balances held by them, and the need for the retention of any reserves to meet unforeseen requests from governments;

(*e*) Unallocated funds remaining in the Special Account from the first financial period after establishment of the Special Reserve Fund shall be available for allocation by the Technical Assistance Board in the second financial period.

B

The General Assembly,

Considering that improvement in the production techniques in industry, agriculture and other branches of the economies of under-developed countries can be greatly advanced by the training of groups of their workers, foremen and technicians in countries which are more developed in certain fields of their economy,

Considering that a valuable method of training such workers, foremen and technicians is by actual employment in appropriate enterprises abroad,

Taking into account, further, that the experience gained by such teams of workers, foremen and technicians has proved useful under various bilateral arrangements in the past,

Recommends that the organizations participating in the Expanded Programme of Technical Assistance give, among other forms of technical assistance, sympathetic consideration to requests for the placement of teams of workers, foremen and technicians from under-developed territories in appropriate enterprises in other countries for such periods as may be necessary for such teams to acquire the technical proficiency necessary for effective use in their country of origin, and also to enable them to train other workers in those techniques or to adapt such techniques to the conditions in their country.

360th plenary meeting
12 January 1952

2029 (XX). Consolidation of the Special Fund and the Expanded Programme of Technical Assistance in a United Nations Development Programme

Committee: 2
Vote: 98 - 0 - 9
Ref.: 36/200, 35/83, 34/106, 32/114, 3252(XXIX), 3126(XXVIII), 2972(XXVII), 2963(XXVII), 2813(XXVI), 2811(XXVI), 2809(XXVI), 2730(XXV), 2689(XXV), 2579(XXIV), 2513(XXIV), 2512(XXIV), 2408(XXIII), 2280(XXII), 2279(XXII), 2278(XXII), 2180(XXI), 2093(XX)

The General Assembly,

Having considered the recommendation of the Economic and Social Council, in its resolution 1020 (XXXVII) of 11 August 1964, to combine the Special Fund and the Expanded Programme of Technical Assistance in a United Nations Development Programme,

Being convinced that such a consolidation would go a long way in streamlining the activities carried on separately and jointly by the Expanded Programme of Technical Assistance and the Special Fund, would simplify organizational arrangements and procedures, would facilitate over-all planning and needed coordination of the several types of technical cooperation programmes carried on within the United Nations system of organizations and would increase their effectiveness,

Recognizing that requests for assistance on the part of the developing countries are steadily increasing in volume and in scope,

Believing that a reorganization is necessary to provide a more solid basis for the future growth and evolution of the assistance programmes of the United Nations system of organizations financed from voluntary contributions,

Being convinced that the United Nations assistance programmes are designed to support and supplement the national efforts of developing countries in solving the most important problems of their economic development, including industrial development,

Recalling and reaffirming section III of its resolution 1219 (XII) of 14 December 1957 and part C of its resolution 1240 (XIII) of 14 October 1958 concerning the decision and the conditions under which the General Assembly shall review the scope and future activities of the Special Fund and take such action as it may deem appropriate,

Reaffirming that the proposed consolidation would be without prejudice to consideration of the study which the General Assembly, in its resolution 1936 (XVIII) of 11 December 1963, requested the Secretary-General to prepare on the practical steps to transform the Special Fund into a capital development fund in such a way as to include both pre-investment and investment activities, and without prejudice to the recommendation of the United Nations Conference on Trade and Development on the gradual transformation of the Special Fund, so as to include not only pre-investment but also investment proper,[1] or to the recommendation of the Economic and Social Council and of the General Assembly thereon,

Taking note of the message of the Secretary-General in which he stated, *inter alia*, that, far from limiting the possibilities of a United Nations capital investment programme, the proposals should enhance those possibilities,[2]

---

1 See *Proceeding of the United Nations Conference on Trade and Development*, vol. I, *Final Act and Report* (United Nations publication, Sales No. 64.II.B.11), annex A.IV.8, p. 47.

2 See *Official Records of the Economic and Social Council, Thirty-seventh Session, Annexes*, agenda item 19, document E/3933, annex VI.

Recognizing that the effective working of a United Nations Development Programme depends upon the full and active participation and the technical contribution of all the organizations concerned,

1. *Decides* to combine the Expanded Programme of Technical Assistance and the Special Fund in a programme to be known as the United Nations Development Programme, it being understood that the special characteristics and operations of the two programmes, as well as two separate funds, will be maintained and that, as hitherto, contributions may be pledged to the two programmes separately;

2. *Reaffirms* the principles, procedures and provisions governing the Expanded Programme of Technical Assistance and the Special Fund not inconsistent with the present resolution and declares that they shall continue to apply to relevant activities within the United Nations Development Programme;

3. *Urges* the Governing Council referred to in paragraph 4 below to consider conditions for an effective implementation of the provisions of section III of General Assembly resolution 1219 (XII) and part C of its resolution 1240 (XIII);

4. *Resolves* that a single inter-governmental Committee of thirty-seven members, to be known as the Governing Council of the United Nations Development Programme, shall be established to perform the functions previously exercised by the Governing Council of the Special Fund and the Technical Assistance Committee, including the consideration and approval of projects and programmes and the allocation of funds: in addition, it shall provide general policy guidance and direction for the United Nations Development Programme as a whole, as well as for the United Nations regular programmes of technical assistance, it shall meet twice a year and shall submit reports and recommendations thereon to the Economic and Social Council for consideration by the Council at its summer session: decisions of the Governing Council shall be made by a majority of the members present and voting;

5. *Requests* the Economic and Social Council to elect the members of the Governing Council from among States Members of the United Nations or members of the specialized agencies or of the International Atomic Energy Agency, providing for equitable and balanced representation of the economically more developed countries, on the one hand, having due regard to their contribution to the United Nations Development Programme, and of the developing countries, on the other hand, taking into account the need for suitable regional representation among the latter members and in accordance with the provisions of the annex to the present resolution, the first election to take place at the first meeting of the Economic and Social Council after the adoption of this resolution;

6. *Decides* to establish, in place of the Technical Assistance Board and the Consultative Board of the Special Fund, an advisory committee, to be known as the Inter-Agency Consultative Board of the United Nations Development Programme, to meet under the chairmanship of the Administrator or Co-Administrator referred to in paragraph 7 below and to include the Secretary-General of the United Nations and the executive heads of the specialized agencies and of the International Atomic Energy Agency or their representatives; the Executive Directors of the United Nations Children's Fund and the World Food Programme should be invited to participate as appropriate; in order that the participating organizations may be provided with the opportunity to take part fully in the process of decision- and policy-making in a consultative capacity, the Inter-Agency Consultative Board shall be consulted on all significant aspects of the United Nations Development Programme and in particular it shall:

(*a*) Advise the management on the programmes and projects submitted by Governments, through the Resident Representative, prior to their submission to the Governing Council for approval, taking into account the programmes of technical assistance being carried out under the regular programmes of the organisations represented on the Consultative Board, with a view to ensuring more effective coordination; the views of the Consultative Board, when it so requests, shall be conveyed by the Administrator to the Governing Council, together with any comments he may wish to make, when recommending for approval general policies for the Programme as a whole or for programmes and projects requested by Governments;

(*b*) Be consulted in the selection of agencies for the execution of specific projects, as appropriate;

(*c*) Be consulted on the appointment of the Resident Representatives and review annual reports submitted by them;

the Inter-Agency Consultative Board shall meet as often and for such periods as may be necessary for the performance of the foregoing functions;

7. *Decides* that, as a transitional measure, the present Managing Director of the Special Fund shall become the Administrator of the United Nations Development Programme and the present Executive Chairman of the Technical Assistance Board shall become the Co-Administrator of the Programme, each to serve until 31 December 1966 or, pending a further review of arrangements at the management level, until such later date as may be determined by the Secretary-General after consultation with the Governing Council;

8. *Decides* that the present resolution shall come into effect on 1 January 1966 and that such action as may be required in terms of this resolution shall be taken prior to that date.

1383rd plenary meeting
22 November 1965

Annex

1. Nineteen seats on the Governing Council of the United Nations Development Programme shall be filled by developing countries and seventeen seats by economically more developed countries, subject to the following conditions:

(*a*) The nineteen seats allocated to developing countries of Africa, Asia and Latin America and to Yugoslavia shall be filled in the following manner: seven seats for African countries, six seats for Asian countries and six seats for Latin American countries, it being understood that agreement has been reached among the developing countries to accommodate Yugoslavia;

(*b*) Of the seventeen seats allocated to the economically more developed countries, fourteen shall be filled by Western European and other countries and three by Eastern European countries;

(*c*) Elections to these thirty-six seats shall be for a term of three years provided, however, that of the members elected at the first election the terms of twelve members shall expire at the end of the year and the terms of twelve other members at the end of two years.

2. The thirty-seventh seat shall rotate among the groups of countries mentioned in paragraph 1 above in accordance with the following nine-year cycle:

First and second years: Western European and other countries;

Third, fourth and fifth years: Eastern European countries;

Sixth year: African countries;

Seventh year: Asian countries;

Eighth year: Latin American countries;

Ninth year: Western European and other countries.

3. Retiring members shall be eligible for re-election.

1714 (XVI). World Food Programme

Committee: 2
Vote: 89 - 0 - 9
Ref.: 2805(XXVI), 2301(XXII), 2095(XX), 1825(XVII)

The General Assembly,

Recalling its resolution 1496 (XV) of 27 October 1960 and Economic and Social Council resolution 832 (XXXII) of 2 August 1960 on the provision of Food surpluses to food-deficient peoples through the United Nations system,

Having considered the report of the Director-General of the Food and Agriculture Organization of the United Nations entitled *Development*

through Food - A Strategy for Surplus Utilization,[1] the report of the Secretary-General entitled "The role of the United Nations and the appropriate specialized agencies in facilitating the best possible use of food surpluses for the economic development of the less developed countries",[2] and the joint proposal by the United Nations and the Food and Agriculture Organization of the United Nations regarding procedures and arrangements for multilateral utilization of surplus food,[3]

Having reviewed the action taken at the eleventh session of the Conference of the Food and Agriculture Organization on the utilization of food surpluses and, specifically, its resolution of 24 November 1961 stating that, subject to the concurrence of the General Assembly of the United Nations, an initial experimental programme for three years, to be known as the World Food Programme should be undertaken, having also noted in particular the reference to safeguards contained in paragraph 13 of the above-mentioned resolution,

Recognizing the existing facilities for consultation provided by the Food and Agriculture Organization through its Consultative Sub-Committee on Surplus Disposals,

Bearing in mind its resolution 1710 (XVI) of 19 December 1961 on the United Nations Development Decade, and in particular the reference in paragraph 4 (*d*) to the elimination of illiteracy, hunger and disease,

I

1. *Approves* the establishment of an experimental World Food Programme to be undertaken jointly by the United Nations and the Food and Agriculture Organization of the United Nations, in cooperation with other interested United Nations agencies and appropriate intergovernmental bodies, bearing in mind that the establishment of such a programme in no way prejudices the bilateral agreements between developed and developing countries, and accepts and endorses the purposes, principles and procedures formulated in the first part of the resolution approved by the Conference of the Food and Agriculture Organization on 24 November 1961, the text of which is annexed to the present resolution, including the safeguards mentioned in that resolution and General Assembly resolution 1496 (XV), especially in paragraph 9 thereof;

2. *Approves* specifically the establishment of a United Nations/FAO Inter-Governmental Committee of twenty States Members of the United Nations and members of the Food and Agriculture Organization to provide guidance on policy, administration and operations, and of a joint United Nations/FAO administrative unit reporting to the Secretary-General of the United Nations and the Director-General of the Food and Agriculture Organization;

3. *Requests* the Economic and Social Council at its resumed thirty-second session to elect, subject to the provisions of paragraph 9 below, ten States Members of the United Nations and members of the Food and Agriculture Organization to the United Nations/FAO Inter-Governmental Committee, taking into account:

(*a*) The representation provided by the ten States that were elected to serve on the United Nations/FAO Inter-Governmental Committee by the Council of the Food and Agriculture Organization;

(*b*) The need for balanced representation of economically developed and developing countries, and other relevant factors such as the representation of potential participating countries, both contributing and recipient, equitable geographical distribution and the representation of both developed and less developed countries having commercial interests in international trade in foodstuffs, especially those highly dependent on such trade;

4. *Calls upon* the Economic and Social Council at its thirty-third session, in cooperation with the Council of the Food and Agriculture Organization, to review and to take appropriate action on the procedures and arrangements for the World Food Programme recommended by the United Nations/FAO Inter-Governmental Committee;

5. *Decides* that pilot projects to be undertaken by the joint United Nations/FAO administrative unit, under the guidance of the United Nations/FAO Inter-Governmental Committee, involving the use of food as an aid to economic and social development, shall be undertaken in agreement between the Secretary-General, acting on behalf of the United Nations, and the Director-General, acting on behalf of the Food and Agriculture Organization;

6. *Concurs* in the calling of a conference where States Members of the United Nations and members of the Food and Agriculture Organization will be invited to pledge contributions;

7. *Requests* the Secretary-General, in cooperation with the Director-General of the Food and Agriculture Organization, to convene such a conference at United Nations Headquarters as soon as feasible after the concurrent sessions of the Economic and Social Council and the Council of the Food and Agriculture Organization;

8. *Urges* States Members of the United Nations and members of the Food and Agriculture Organization, in considering their contributions, to make every effort to assure the early attainment, on a voluntary basis, of the $100 million programme;

9. *Further requests* the Economic and Social Council, in cooperation with the Council of the Food and Agriculture Organization, at its next regular session following the pledging conference, to review the composition of the United Nations/FAO Inter-Governmental Committee and to make, by election for the balance of the three-year programme, any adjustments of membership that might be deemed desirable in the light of the considerations outlined in paragraph 3 above;

10. *Instructs* the United Nations/FAO Inter-Governmental Committee, in preparing recommendations on the conditions and procedures for the establishment and operation of the programme for the review and approval by the Economic and Social Council and the Council of the Food and Agriculture Organization, to proceed on the basis of the present resolution and the resolution of the Conference of the Food and Agriculture Organization of 24 November 1961, taking into account the joint proposal by the United Nations and the Food and Agriculture Organization regarding procedures and arrangements for the multilateral utilization of surplus food,[4] statements made during the debates in the General Assembly and in the Conference of the Food and Agriculture Organization and such other conditions and procedures as may seem to it appropriate;

11. *Recommends* that Governments requesting assistance under this programme, the United Nations/ FAO Inter-Governmental Committee, and the joint United Nations/FAO administrative unit responsible for the administration of the program, keep the resident representatives fully informed about, and, within their field of competence, associated with, activities undertaken under the programme;

12. *Invites* the Secretary-General of the United Nations and the Director-General of the Food and Agriculture Organization to ensure that, in carrying out the programme, the joint United Nations/FAO administrative unit rely to the fullest extent possible on the existing staff and facilities of the United Nations and the Food and Agriculture Organization, as well as other appropriate inter-governmental agencies;

13. *Requests* the United Nations/FAO Inter-Governmental Committee to report annually to the Economic and Social Council and to the Council of the Food and Agriculture Organization on the progress made in the development of the programme and on its administration and operation;

14. *Decides* to undertake, not later than at its nineteenth session, a general review of the programme, taking into account the objectives of its resolution 1496 (XV);

1 Food and Agriculture Organization of the United Nations, Rome, 1961.

2 *Official Records of the Economic and Social Council, Thirty-second Session, Annexes,* agenda item 8, document E/3509.

3 *Official Records of the General Assembly, Sixteenth Session, Annexes,* agenda item 28, document A/4907.

4 *Ibid.*

II

Recognizing that the experimental programme outlined above constitutes a step towards the broader objectives outlined in its resolution 1496 (XV),

Recognizing further that the ultimate solution to this problem of food deficiency lies in self-sustaining economic growth of the economies of the less developed countries to the point where they find it possible to meet their food requirements from their food-producing industries or from the proceeds of their expanding export trade,

Recognizing that the effective utilization of available surplus foodstuffs, in ways compatible with the principles of surplus disposal recommended by the Food and Agriculture Organization of the United Nations, provides an important transitional means of relieving the hunger and malnutrition of food-deficient peoples, particularly in the less developed countries, and for assisting these countries in their economic development,

Recognizing further that food aid is not a substitute for other types of assistance, in particular for capital goods,

1. *Recognizes* that food aid to be provided under this programme should take into account other forms of assistance and country plans for economic and social development;

2. *Requests* the Secretary-General of the United Nations, in close cooperation with the Director-General of the Food and Agriculture Organization of the United Nations and with interested groups or agencies, and jointly where appropriate, to undertake, as soon as feasible, expert studies which would aid in the consideration of the future development of multilateral food programmes;

3. *Expresses the hope* that in the light of these studies and of the experience gained, the progress of the experimental programme will be such as to permit the United Nations and the Food and Agriculture Organization to consider the possibility and advisability of increasing the programme, taking into account the advantages to developing countries, the interests of the contributing States, the interests of the food-exporting countries, the effectiveness of the programme and its contribution to the objectives of General Assembly resolution 1496 (XV);

4. *Endorses again* the Freedom from Hunger Campaign launched by the Food and Agriculture Organization, and requests the Secretary-General of the United Nations and the Director-General of the Food and Agriculture Organization, simultaneously with the implementation of the present resolution, to pay particular attention to the necessity of improving and increasing local food production and to include, where appropriate reference to this subject in the reports mentioned above and requests the United Nations/FAO Inter-Governmental Committee to consider the possibility of applying to this purpose a reasonable proportion of resources resulting from the World Food Programme.

1084th plenary meeting
19 December 1961

Annex

Part I of the Resolution on the Utilization of Food Surpluses Adopted by the Conference of the Food and Agricultural Organization of the United Nations on 24 November 1961

The Conference,

...

I

Resolves, subject to the Concurrence of the General Assembly of the United Nations, that:

1. An initial experimental programme for three years of approximately $100 million with contributions on a voluntary basis be undertaken jointly by the Food and Agriculture Organization and the United Nations, in cooperation with other United Nations agencies, and appropriate inter-governmental bodies;

2. Contributions to the programme, to be known as the World Food Programme, may be pledged by countries in the form of appropriate commodities, acceptable services, and cash aiming in the aggregate at a cash component of at least one-third of the total contributions, and countries should give due regard to the importance of achieving this over-all objective when determining the cash element in their contribution;

3. An Inter-Governmental Committee of twenty nations which are members of FAO or the United Nations be established to provide guidance on policy, administration and operations, as outlined in paragraphs 11 and 12 of part III of the joint report of the Secretary-General and the Director-General;

4. The Committee be elected half by the FAO Council and half by the United Nations, taking into account the need for balanced representation of economically developed countries and of less developed countries and other relevant factors. In appointing its representative each Government should pay due regard to the complexities of the executive and operational planning required for the proposed programme;

5. The Inter-Governmental Committee meet in Rome early in 1962 to develop detailed procedures and arrangements for the Programme on the basis of this resolution, taking due account of the joint report of the Secretary-General and the Director-General and giving consideration to the views expressed in reports of meetings related to this subject held under the auspices of FAO and the United Nations;

6. The procedures and arrangements drawn up by the Inter-Governmental Committee be reviewed and approved in concurrent sessions of the Council of FAO and the Economic and Social Council in New York in April 1962;

7. A conference for contributing countries to pledge their contributions in accordance with paragraph 2 above be convened by the Secretary-General and the Director-General after the concurrent sessions of the FAO Council and the Economic and Social Council;

8. The FAO Council and the Economic and Social Council at their next regular meetings following the pledging conference, should make any adjustment of country composition on the Inter-Governmental Committee (of twenty) that might be deemed desirable in view of the considerations mentioned in paragraph 4 above;

9. Subject to the guidance of the Inter-Governmental Committee, the Programme will be carried on by a joint FAO/United Nations administrative unit located at FAO Headquarters in Rome and reporting to both the Director-General and the Secretary-General, with the costs of administration and operation under this resolution to be met from contributions to the programme;

10. In the administration of the Programme attention should be paid to:

(*a*) Establishing adequate and orderly procedures on a world basis for meeting emergency food needs and emergencies inherent in chronic malnutrition (this could include the establishment of food reserves);

(*b*) Assisting in pre-school and school feeding; and

(*c*) Implementing pilot projects, with the multilateral use of food as an aid to economic and social development, particularly when related to labour-intensive projects and rural welfare;

11. Projects should be undertaken only in response to requests from the recipient country or countries concerned;

12. The administration of the proposed Programme will require close cooperation, particularly on development projects, between FAO and the United Nations, as well as with appropriate United Nations agencies, and other appropriate inter-governmental bodies;

13. The Inter-Governmental Committee shall ensure that:

(i) In accordance with the FAO principles of surplus disposal and with the consultative procedures established by the Committee on Commodity Problems, and in conformity with the United Nations General Assembly resolution 1496 (XV), particularly paragraph 9, commercial markets and normal and developing trade are neither interfered with nor disrupted;

(ii) The agricultural economy in recipient countries is adequately safeguarded with respect both to its domestic markets and the effective development of food production;

(iii) Due consideration is given to safeguarding normal commercial practices in respect to acceptable services.

50/8. Revision of the General Regulations of the World Food Programme and Reconstitution of the Committee on Food Aid Policies and Programmes as the Executive Board of the World Food Programme

Committee: -
Vote: Adopted without a vote

The General Assembly,

Recalling its resolutions 1714 (XVI) of 19 December 1961, 2095 (XX) of 20 December 1965 and 3404 (XXX) of 28 November 1975, concerning the establishment and continuation of the United Nations/Food and Agriculture Organization of the United Nations World Food Programme, and its resolution 46/22 of 5 December 1991 on the revision of the General Regulations of the World Food Programme and enlargement of the Committee on Food Aid Policies and Programmes of the World Food Programme,

Recalling also its resolution 48/162 of 20 December 1993, on further measures for the restructuring and revitalization of the United Nations in the economic, social and related fields,

Having considered Economic and Social Council decision 1995/227 of 6 June 1995 adopted on the recommendation of the Committee on Food Aid Policies and Programmes of the World Food Programme concerning the governance of the Programme, the revision of the General Regulations of the World Food Programme, and the reconstitution of the Committee on Food Aid Policies and Programmes as the Executive Board of the World Food Programme,

1. *Decides*, subject to the concurrence of the Conference of the Food and Agriculture Organization of the United Nations, that the Committee on Food Aid Policies and Programmes shall be reconstituted as the Executive Board of the World Food Programme, with 36 members elected from among the States Members of the United Nations or the States members of the Food and Agriculture Organization of the United Nations, and that the Economic and Social Council and the Council of the Food and Agriculture Organization of the United Nations shall elect 18 members each, as set forth in paragraph 2 below;

2. *Decides* also that the members of the Executive Board of the World Food Programme shall be elected on an interim basis for four years from among the States included in the lists[1] set out in the Basic Texts of the World Food Programme, in accordance with the following distribution of seats, it being understood that this allocation of seats creates no precedent for the composition of other United Nations bodies of a limited membership:

(*a*) Nine members from the States included in list A, five members to be elected by the Economic and Social Council and four by the Council of the Food and Agriculture Organization of the United Nations;

(*b*) Seven members from the States included in list B, four members to be elected by the Economic and Social Council and three by the Council of the Food and Agriculture Organization of the United Nations;

(*c*) Five members from the States included in list C, two members to be elected by the Economic and Social Council and three by the Council of the Food and Agriculture Organization of the United Nations;

(*d*) Twelve members from the States included in list D, six members to be elected by the Economic and Social Council and six by the Council of the Food and Agriculture Organization of the United Nations;

(*e*) Two members from the States included in list E, one member to be elected by the Economic a Social Council and one by the Council of the Food and Agriculture Organization of the United Nations;

(*f*) One additional member alternating between the States included in lists B and C, starting with list C, to be elected by the Council of the Food and Agriculture Organization of the United Nations;

3. *Decides further* that the above-mentioned distribution of seats shall be reviewed within two years after the establishment of the Executive Board with a view to achieving its final outcome in accordance with paragraphs 25 and 30 and other relevant provisions of General Assembly resolution 48/162; that the review shall be conducted in parallel by the Assembly and the Conference of the Food and Agriculture Organization of the United Nations, taking into account the relevant inputs of the Economic and Social Council and the Council of the Food and Agriculture Organization of the United Nations; and that its results shall enter into force on I January 2000;

4. *Requests* the Economic and Social Council, at its resumed substantive session of 1995, to elect 18 members of the Executive Board for a term beginning on 1 January 1996 in accordance with the following distribution and terms of office:

(*a*) Five members from the States included in list A, two for a term of three years, one for a term of two years and two for a term of one year;

(*b*) Pour members from the States included in list B, one for a term of three years, two for a term of two years and one for a term of one year;

(*c*) Two members from the States included in list C, one for a term of three years and one for a term of one year;

(*d*) Six members from the States included in list D, two for a period of three years, two for a period of two years and two for a period of one year;

(*e*) One member from the States included in list E, for a period of two years;

5. *Decides* that thereafter all members of the Executive Board shall be elected for a term of three years and requests the Economic and Social Council to make such provisions as ensure that the terms of office of six members elected by each of the two Councils shall expire in each calendar year;

6. *Decides* to approve the revised General Regulations of the World Food Programme contained in annex I of the note by the Secretary-General on the transformation of the Committee on Food Aid Policies and Programmes of the World Food Programme into an executive board,[2] as endorsed by the Economic and Social Council in its decision 1995/227 and by the Council of the Food and Agriculture Organization of the United Nations at its 108th session, on 12 June 1995.

7. *Decides*, subject to the concurrence of the Conference of the Food and Agriculture Organization of the United Nations, that the revised General Regulations shall enter into force on 1 January 1996.

46th plenary meeting
1 November 1995

2688 (XXV). The Capacity of the United Nations Development System

Committee: 2
Vote: Adopted without a vote
Ref.: 2814(XXVI)

The General Assembly,

Having considered the parts of the reports of the Governing Council of the United Nations Development Programme on its ninth[3] and tenth[4] sessions and of the Economic and Social Council[5] concerning the capacity of the United Nations development system,

---

1 Reproduced in E/1995/L.11, annex II.

2 E/1995/14.

3 *Official Records of the Economic and Social Council, Forty-ninth Session, Supplement No. 6* (E/4782), chapter VI.

4 *Ibid., Supplement No. 6A* (E/4884/Rev.1), chapter V.

Taking note of the observations and reservations made in the Governing Council of the United Nations Development Programme at its tenth session[1] and in the Economic and Social Council at its forty-ninth session,[2]

Noting that some questions remain to be settled within the framework of the examination of this subject,

1. *Approves* the provisions concerning the United Nations Development Programme contained in the annex to the present resolution and declares that such provisions shall apply to activities of the Programme commencing on 1 January 1971, taking into account the transitional measures in those provisions;

2. *Requests* the Governing Council of the United Nations Development Programme to prepare for consideration by the General Assembly at its twenty-sixth session, if possible, a draft omnibus statute for the Programme, incorporating the provisions contained in the annex to the present resolution and appropriate provisions from past resolutions relating to the Programme.

1925th plenary meeting
11 December 1970

Annex

I. The United Nations Development Cooperation Cycle

1. The formulation of the United Nations Development Programme country programme is the first phase of a process which may be called the United Nations Development Cooperation Cycle. The other phases are project formulation, appraisal and approval, implementation, evaluation and follow-up. The Cycle will also include periodic reviews. The scope of the Cycle might expand as envisaged in paragraph 9 below.

II. United Nations Development Programme Country Programming

A. General principles

2. United Nations Development Programme country programming means the programming of its assistance at the country level. It involves the identification of the role of Programme inputs in specified areas within the country's development objectives.

3. Country programming will be used as a means of achieving the most rational and efficient utilization of resources at the disposal of the Programme for its activities in order to have the maximum impact on the economic and social development of the developing country concerned.

4. Country programming will be based on individual national development plans or, where these do not exist, on national development priorities or objectives.

5. It is recognized that the Government of the country concerned has the exclusive responsibility for formulating its national development plan or priorities and objectives. Individual developing countries should be given, at their request, assistance from the United Nations, including the regional economic commissions and the United Nations Economic and Social Office at Beirut, in the general field of planning and from the specialized agencies in sectoral planning.

6. The programming of Programme assistance will be carried out in each country within the framework of indicative planning figures constituting an order of magnitude of the resources expected to be available from the Programme during the country programme period.

7. The country programme, based on national development plans, priorities or objectives and on the indicative planning figures, will be formulated by the Government of the recipient country in cooperation, at an appropriate stage, with representatives of the United Nations system, the latter under the leadership of the resident representative of the Programme; it should coincide, where appropriate, with the period of the country's national development plan. The formulation of the country programme should involve:

(*a*) A broad identification of the needs which arise out of the country's objectives in particular sectors, within the framework of its overall development objectives, and which might appropriately be met by Programme assistance;

(*b*) As precise an indication as possible of the internal inputs, Programme inputs and, wherever possible, other United Nations inputs to meet these needs;

(*c*) A preliminary list of project to be subsequently worked out for financing by the Programme to implement the country programme.

8. The country programme of assistance should support activities which are meaningfully related to the country's development objectives. This implies that the assistance provided constitutes a programme which receives its coherence and balance from its relationship to these national objectives.

9. In the process of country programming, efforts should be made at all levels to coordinate all sources of assistance in the United Nations system, with a view to achieving integration of the assistance at the country level.

10. It will be for the Government to take into account, while preparing the country programme, other external inputs, both multilateral and bilateral.

11. The resident representative will transmit the country programme to the Administrator of the Programme who, in turn, will submit it, with his recommendations, to the Governing Council for its consideration and approval. Approval will cover the entire period of the programme, with provision for periodic reviews aimed at possible adjustments. With the agreement of the country concerned, the Administrator, in submitting the country programme for consideration and approval, will invite the attention of the Governing Council to details of any other related programme of United Nations assistance.

12. The assistance of the Programme must be sufficiently flexible to meet unforeseen needs of recipient countries or exceptional situations, which country programmes could not take into account.

B. Indicative planning figures

13. For the purpose, among others, of establishing the indicative planning figures, any distinctions between the Technical Assistance and Special Fund components will be eliminated. The resources to be devoted to country programming will be a specified percentage of the total resources for the current year, projected over a given period of time and including a rate of growth *per annum* over that period, one of the assumptions being that the resources of the Programme will increase at least at the same rate as the average of the last few years.

14. The indicative country-planning figures should not be construed as representing a commitment, but as a reasonably firm indication for the purpose of forward programming.

15. The indicative planning figures will be proposed by the Administrator to Governments on the basis of the criteria and guidelines established from time to time by the Governing Council. There should be some flexibility in determining the level of resources available for indicative planning figures. After taking into account any comments which Governments may wish to make in regard to the figures, the Administrator will submit his final indicative planning figures for each country for approval by the Governing Council; wherever possible, the country programme concerned will be approved at the same time.

16. As an experimental basis for the first series of indicative planning figures, the Administrator will calculate the percentage devoted to each country of the total earmarkings of programmed resources (that is, Technical Assistance country targets plus Special Fund project earmarkings) during the five-year period from 1966 to 1970, including projects approved by the Governing Council at its eleventh session. He will apply this percentage in each case to resources estimated, in accordance with the procedure laid down in paragraph 13 above, to be available for country programming for a period of from three to five years, consistent with the period of the country's devel-

---

5 *Official Records of the General Assembly, Twenty-fifth Session, Supplement No. 3* (A/8003 and Corr.1), chapter X, section A.

1 *Official Records of the Economic and Social Council, Forty-ninth Session, Supplement No. 6A* (E/4884/Rev.1), chapter V, paras. 95-106.

2 *Ibid., Forty-ninth Session,* 1712th to 1714th meetings.

opment plan or development programme, in order to obtain a preliminary indicative planning figure for each country for that period. He will scrutinize these figures in the light of existing criteria for the allocation of resources and adjust them where necessary to avoid arbitrarily projecting any exceptional present country situations, to correct any inequities due to historical circumstances and, in particular, to ensure that special consideration is given to the situation of the least developed countries and of newly independent countries whose lack of an adequate administrative infrastructure has prevented them from taking proper advantage of programme assistance.

17. The figures will be reviewed periodically by the Administrator and the Governing Council, in consultation with the Government concerned, in the light of progress in the implementation of the country programme.

C. Formulation, appraisal and approval of projects

18. Project formulation will be an on-going process and need not await the approval of the country programme. To ensure the soundness of project formulation, it will be carried out at the country level. Association of various kinds of expertise with the formulation of a particular project will be only at the specific request of the Government which, in the light of the expertise available locally, is in the best position to know the type of expertise required.

19. The appraisal of each project will be, to the fullest extent possible, an integral part of the process of formulation of the project. Thus smaller projects, up to a specified cost limit, will be appraised on behalf of the Programme by the resident representative with the assistance of competent technical expertise whenever necessary. Responsibility for the appraisal of larger projects will rest with the Administrator.

20. The Governing Council alone is empowered to approve projects submitted by countries to the Programme for consideration. The Governing Council, while retaining this authority, delegates to the Administrator for three years the authority to approve projects within country programmes. Nevertheless the Council and the requesting Government reserve the right to request the Administrator to submit particular projects of whatever magnitude to the Council for its consideration and approval. The Administrator may also bring to the Council any project which, because of its policy implications or the magnitude of its impact on the country programme as a whole, deserves the consideration and approval of the Council. The Administrator will, to the maximum extent feasible, which will be determined and indicated by him to the Governing Council in due course, delegate the authority to approve projects to the resident representatives. The Governing Council will be informed as soon as possible of all project decisions completed under its delegation of authority.

III. Intercountry Programming

21. Intercountry programming is the programming of assistance for groups of countries on a subregional, regional, interregional or global basis. Such assistance will be provided through subregional, regional, interregional and global projects at the request of at least two Governments, taking into account the equitable distribution of resources among regions.

22. The programming of such assistance will be based broadly on the same general principles as set out above for country programming, particularly in that it will be systematically related to the development priorities of the countries concerned and, as far as possible, planned in advance over a period of years.

23. The procedures for the formulation, appraisal and approval of intercountry projects will follow, in their relevant aspects, the same general lines as for projects within country programmes, and will be subject to criteria and guidelines established from time to time by the Governing Council. All global projects, however, will require specific approval by the Governing Council.

IV. Over-All Disposition and Management of United Nations Development Programme Resources

A. Over-all disposition of resources

24. The total resources available for programming will be divided between country programming on the one hand and, on the other, intercountry programming consisting of subregional, regional, interregional and global projects.

25. Initially, and until further review by the Governing Council, at least 82 per cent of the net resources available each year, after deduction of programme support costs and administrative costs, as well as resources to meet the requirements set out in paragraph 27 below, will be set aside for country programming and, at most, 18 per cent for intercountry programming, it being understood that these proportions are intended as a planning guide.

26. Subregional, regional and interregional projects, particularly those designed by interested countries to accelerate the process of economic and social integration and to promote other forms of regional and subregional cooperation, will have the first claim on the resources for intercountry programming. Global projects will come next in the order of priority. Subject to review by the Governing Council from time to time, the amount to be allocated for global projects should not exceed 1 per cent of the net resources available for programming.

27. It will be necessary to make provision to meet unforeseen needs, to meet special needs of the least developed of the developing countries, and to finance unanticipated projects or phases of projects, particularly projects of the Special Industrial Services type, which could have a catalytic role in the economic development of the country concerned. At the eleventh session of the Governing Council, the Administrator will make proposals on the manner in which resources to meet such requirements, as well as to maintain under present arrangements the programme of Special Industrial Services at least at the present level, will be made available.

B. Full utilization of resources and financial control

28. All financial resources of the Programme are to be available at all times to the maximum possible extent for programme purposes, subject only to the maintenance on a continuous basis of an operational reserve. After provision has been made annually for programme support and administrative costs; and for replenishment of the operational reserve, all resources not otherwise committed will be utilized for project activities.

29. The purpose of the operational reserve is to guarantee in all circumstances the financial liquidity and integrity of the Programme, to compensate for uneven cash inflows and to meet such other requirements as may be decided upon by the Governing Council at a subsequent stage. The Council will keep under constant review the size and composition of the reserve, basing itself on the planning of payment authorizations and expenditures for the following financial year, At the outset, and pending receipt of a more detailed analysis from the Administrator of the financial position of the Programme up to the end of 1970, the Council, as an interim measure, authorizes the establishment of an operational reserve of $150 million in all categories of resources, the composition of which is to be determined and maintained by the Administrator in accordance with sound principles of financial management, this level to be reviewed by the Council at its twelfth session in the context of the financial review referred to above.

30. Full responsibility for proper utilization of funds of the Programme and for the exercise of financial and accounting controls will be borne by the Administrator. The Secretary-General will continue as custodian of Programme funds, but decisions regarding the Programme investment portfolio and currency management will be reached in agreement with the Administrator, subject to a full report on this arrangement and review by the Governing Council at its twelfth session.

31. In presenting forecasts of expenditure and requests for earmarkings to the Governing Council, the Administrator will distinguish clearly among the following types of expense: (*a*) project costs; (*b*)

programme supports costs, including overhead and consultative services costs, and (*c*) administrative service costs.

C. Assessment of local costs

32. Specific recommendations will be made by the Administrator to the Governing Council at its eleventh session on the formula to be followed for the assessment of local costs, which should make provision for simplified application of full or partial waivers of local costs, taking into account those cases where undue burdens would otherwise be placed on the recipient Government.

D. Agency overhead costs

33. The Administrator will consult with the participating and executing agencies and the Advisory Committee on Administrative and Budgetary Questions with a view to arriving at new methods for calculating appropriate reimbursement for project implementation and for advisory services involving programming, project formulation and policy development. The prospect of entering into general compensatory arrangements for advisory services and separate specific arrangements for the reimbursement of costs in connexion with project execution will be explored. The solution worked out should not be considered as binding until it has been submitted to the Council for consideration and approval, accompanied by a report on the kinds of services to be reimbursed.

34. The Administrator will cooperate to the fullest degree in efforts to achieve common budgeting policies and accounting systems throughout the United Nations family of organizations.

V. Implementation of United Nations Development Programme Assistance

A. Responsibility of the Governing Council

35. The Governing Council has over-all responsibility for ensuring that the resources of the Programme are employed with maximum efficiency and effectiveness in assisting the development of the developing countries.

36. To this end, the principal responsibilities of the Governing Council remain as stated in the relevant resolutions of the General Assembly. In the context of the principles of country and intercountry programming set out above and of the implementation of assistance so provided, the Governing Council will consider and approve country programmes, including indicative country-planning figures, approve certain projects included in the programmes in accordance with the provisions mentioned in paragraphs 20 and 23 above, exercise effective operational control, including periodic reviews of the country programmes, and make broad allocations of resources and control their use.

B. Responsibility of the Administrator

37. In addition to the responsibilities to be delegated to him by the Governing Council, the Administrator will be fully responsible and accountable to the Governing Council for all phases and aspects of the implementation of the Programme.

C. Role of United Nations organizations in implementation of country programmes

38. The role of the organizations of the United Nations system in the implementation of country programmes should be that of partners, under the leadership of the Programme, in a common endeavour of the entire United Nations system. Their advice should be available to the Administrator in the implementation of all projects, as appropriate, whether executed by them or not.

D. Selection and accountability of executing agents

39. The Administrator will consult the Government in each case on the selection of the agent by which Programme assistance to each project will be implemented.

40. The appropriate organizations of the United Nations system will, subject to this procedure, have first consideration as executing agents.

41. When necessary to ensure the maximum effectiveness of Programme assistance or to increase its capacity, and with due regard to the cost factor, increased use may appropriately be made of suitable services obtained from governmental and non-governmental institutions and firms, in agreement with the recipient Government concerned and in accordance with the principles of international competitive bidding. Maximum use should be made of national institutions and firms, if available, within the recipient countries.

42. In cases where expertise or services are required which are not adequately available in kind, quantity and quality within the United Nations system, the Administrator will, in agreement with the Government concerned, exercise his authority to obtain them, while inviting, in appropriate cases, the relevant United Nations organization to provide complementary support.

43. Every executing agent will be accountable to the Administrator for the implementation of Programme assistance to projects.

44. In the selection of individual experts, institutions or firms, in the procurement of equipment and supplies and in the provision of training facilities, the principle of equitable geographical distribution consistent with maximum effectiveness will be observed.

E. Availability and quality of international and national project personnel

45. The Administrator should intensify efforts in coordination with the appropriate organs of the system and should develop suitable proposals for consideration by the Governing Council, to improve the availability, briefing, refresher training and procedures for the punctual recruitment of well-qualified international project personnel. These proposals should particularly take into account the desirability of increasing the number of personnel recruited from the developing countries. The Administrator should also pay particular attention to such factors as the personal suitability of candidates, including their motivation and adaptability; the need for realistic job descriptions and reporting dates; prompt decisions on candidates by the agencies and requesting Governments; and conditions of service that will attract and retain candidates for whose services there is world-wide demand.

46. In suitable cases, qualified nationals may be designated as project managers, assisted by international specialists.

47. Where necessary, and upon the request of the recipient Government, consideration should be given by the Programme to training suitable counterpart personnel as an integral part of a Programme-assisted project, including its planning phase, so that they will be qualified to participate in and ensure effective execution of the project.

48. Since there is no set formula for the proportions of international personnel, fellowships and equipment for a particular project and no ceiling on the ratio of the value of the equipment in relation to the total cost of a project, Programme pre-investment assistance should be sufficiently flexible so that in appropriate cases it may consist of the supply of equipment alone as part of an integrated pre-investment project. In the latter case, particular attention should be given to the availability of personnel qualified to use the equipment or to train personnel in its use in recipient countries.

F. Operational control and assessment of results

49. The monitoring of project assistance, in so far as it is required for the discharge by the Administrator of his responsibility for operational control, will normally be carried out at the country level by the resident representative.

50. Evaluation carried out within the United Nations system of Programme-assisted activities will only be made with the agreement of the Government concerned. This will be carried out jointly by the Government, the Programme, the United Nations agency concerned and, where appropriate, the executing agent outside the United Nations system.

51. Such evaluation shall be on a selective basis and restricted to the minimum essential for the improvement or follow-up of the projects concerned, for the needs of Governments and for the improvement of the Programme. With the agreement of the Government concerned,

the results will be communicated to the Governing Council for its information.

G. Investment and other terms of follow-up

52. Provision for investment and other forms of follow-up to Programme-assisted projects will, when necessary, be an integral part of the programming process and of the formulation, implementation and evaluation of the projects.

53. The Government in each case will be primarily responsible for all measures which should be taken at all stages of a project to ensure effective follow-up, including follow-up investment. It will be open to the Government to seek investment assistance from all available sources. No one source of follow-up investment financing should be regarded as the only acceptable source or as a source enjoying preference over others. The Administrator will assume full responsibility within the United Nations system, as its major source of pre-investment financing, for providing assistance and advice on behalf of the United Nations system on follow-up investment, with the agreement of the Government. The Programme will develop its expertise in this matter to ensure, in consultation with the Government, early coordination, from the planning stage onwards, with potential bilateral and/or multilateral sources of finance for projects requiring follow-up investment.

VI. Timing and Transitional Measures

54. The principles set out above, and the procedures to give effect to them, will be progressively applied from the date of their approval by the competent legislative organs of the United Nations. The Administrator will undertake as soon as possible the necessary measures so that, if possible, some country programmes will be submitted in time for consideration by the Governing Council at its twelfth session in June 1971.

55. In the transitional period, to ensure continuity of action by the Programme in meeting Governments' requests for assistance, the appraisal and approval of projects will be carried out in accordance with existing procedures. These transitional measures may be extended in cases where the Government wishes to start its country programme later than 1972, on the understanding, however, that the total amount of assistance to be provided from 1 January 1972 will be consistent with the indicative planning figures and that the existing distinctions between the two components of the Programme will have been eliminated.

VII. Organization of the United Nations Development Programme

56. The Governing Council recognizes its responsibility for policy formulation, the determination of programme priorities, and the review of implementation in both planning and practice. The decisions of the Council on country programming and its implementation have important organizational implications. The country-programming approach implies that the Administrator will be fully accountable for the management of all aspects of the programme. At the same time, it will be necessary to bring about, within the Programme, greater decentralization of responsibility for programming and implementation from the headquarters to the country level. The application of the twin principle of the Administrator's full accountability for the Programme and the decentralization to the country level will require certain modifications in the existing structure and procedures of the Programme. A clear definition of functions and responsibilities at all levels of the administration will therefore be necessary.

57. At the headquarters level regional bureaux should be established to provide a direct link between the Administrator and the resident representative in all matters concerning field activities. In order to streamline channels of communication and expedite the decision-making process, the heads of these bureaux should have direct access to the Administrator. To achieve the required degree of effectiveness of management of the bureaux, they should be headed by persons with the high qualifications and rank commensurate with their important responsibilities.

58. The country-programming approach also implies that the Programme should not only concern itself with current policy formulation, but should also be able constantly to analyse the main trends in the evolution of the Programme in order to give it new directions and to explore new possibilities for making it more effective. To meet this need, a small but highly competent long-term planning staff should be established at the headquarters level under the direction of a senior official.

59. The country-programming approach also envisages more rational and effective procedures for evaluation and follow-up. This, as well as the need to maintain close relations with other collaborating organizations of the United Nations system, must be fully reflected in the organizational restructuring at the headquarters level. The Administrator is invited to take the necessary steps in this direction and to submit further proposals to the Council.

60. The strengthening of the management of the Programme at the headquarters level, in view of the reform of the system and the expectation of a growing Programme, should be achieved by securing the services of highly qualified and experienced staff with due regard to the principle of equitable geographical distribution and to the need for economy.

61. The Administrator should continue to have the authority to appoint and administer the staff of the Programme. For this purpose, he should have authority, in consultation with the Secretary-General, to frame such staff rules, consistent with the relevant principles laid down by the General Assembly, as he considers necessary to meet the special problems which arise in the service of the Programme.

62. With respect to the organization of the Programme at the country level, the resident representative will be redesignated resident director of the Programme. His appointment by the Administrator will be subject to the prior approval of the Government concerned.

63. There should be the maximum possible delegation of authority to the resident director. His role therefore needs to be greatly strengthened. In this context, his relations with the representatives of other United Nations organizations in the field are of crucial importance. The resident director should be recognized as having full over-all responsibility for the programme in the country concerned and his role in relation to the representatives of the other United Nations organizations, where they are posted with the prior approval of the Government concerned, should be that of the leader of the team, taking into account the professional competence of these United Nations organizations and their relations with appropriate organs of the Government. This role of leadership and over-all responsibility should extend to all contacts with the governmental authorities concerned in connexion with the programme, in regard to which he will be the principal channel of communization between the Programme and the Government. The resident director should have ultimate authority on behalf of the Administrator for all aspects of the programme at the country level and should, subject to the agreement of the organizations concerned, be the central coordinating authority on their behalf for the other development assistance programmes of the United Nations system. In this connexion, the organizations in the United Nations system are requested to ensure that the resident directors of the Programme are consulted on the planning and formulation of development projects with which those organizations are concerned and that they are supplied with reports on the execution of those projects, as requested by the Economic and Social Council in resolution 1453 (XLVII) of 8 August 1969,

64. The creation of new field offices or the enlargement of the existing ones should depend on the volume of Programme operations in the particular country and should be undertaken with due regard to the need for economy. In the strengthening of field offices, priority should be given to effective redeployment of existing staff.

65. The Inter-Agency Consultative Board should continue to be the forum for interagency consultation and coordination relating to the Programme. However, the Board should undertake a thorough review of its basic functions and methods of work and its relations with the Governing Council in the light of the new system of country programming on Programme assistance and the need for the efficient implementation of the country programmes.

S-11/4. Measures to Meet the Critical Situation in the Least Developed Countries

Committee: Ad hoc
Vote: Adopted without a vote
Ref.: 34/210, 33/149, 32/190, 3214(XXIX), 3174(XXVIII), 3036(XXVII), 2971(XXVII), 2569(XXIV), 2564(XXIV)

The General Assembly,

Deeply concerned at the gravity of the deteriorating economic and social situation of the least developed countries and the dismal development record of those countries during the past two decades, as well as at their bleak development prospects for the 1980s,

Also deeply concerned at the continued critical lack of basic infrastructure in the least developed countries,

Recalling resolutions 62 (III) of 19 May 1972[1] and 98 (IV) of 31 May 1976[2] of the United Nations Conference on Trade and Development, as well as other relevant resolutions and decisions of the United Nations system which have remained largely unimplemented,

Recalling also resolution 122 (V) of 3 June 1979[3] of the United Nations Conference on Trade and Development, by which it adopted, as one of its major priorities, a Comprehensive New Programme of Action for the Least Developed Countries in two phases, an Immediate Action Programme, for 1979-1981, and a Substantial New Programme of Action for the 1980s,

Recognizing that primary responsibility for their development rests with the least developed countries themselves,

Recalling its resolution 34/210 of 19 December 1979, in which it endorsed the Comprehensive New Programme of Action for the Least Developed Countries,

Recalling further its resolution 34/203 of 19 December 1979, in which it decided to convene the United Nations Conference on the Least Developed Countries in 1981,

Noting the concern expressed by the international community at the desperate plight of the least developed countries,

Noting with appreciation that some developed countries have taken positive steps towards the implementation of resolution 122 (V) of the United Nations Conference on Trade and Development,

Regretting that, even more than one year after the adoption of the Immediate Action Programme for 1979-1981 contained in resolution 122 (V) of the United Nations Conference on Trade and Development, very limited progress has been made towards its implementation,

Emphasizing the particular importance of the contribution that economic cooperation among developing countries can make, *inter alia*, to the development of the least developed among them,

Reaffirming that there is an immediate need for a greatly expanded increase in the transfer of resources to meet the critical needs of the least developed countries and to help promote their rapid and self-sustained socio-economic development,

1. *Urges* all developed countries, developing countries in a position to do so, multilateral development institutions and other sources to take urgent steps to implement without any further delay, on a priority basis, the commitments undertaken in the Immediate Action Programme for 1979-1981 contained in resolution 122 (V) of the United Nations Conference on Trade and Development;

2. *Also urges* donor countries to make equitable and all possible efforts with a view to doubling, at the earliest possible time within the first half of the 1980s, the flow of official development assistance to the least developed countries, in accordance with the commitments undertaken in paragraph 13 of resolution 122 (V) of the United Nations Conference on Trade and Development, and to give serious consideration to this end to the proposal that such a doubling should be in real terms, taking into account the relative performance of donor countries;

3. *Further urges* donor countries, in the context of the over-all increase of official development assistance, to give serious consideration, not later than at the United Nations Conference on the Least Developed Countries to be held in 1981, to the proposals for further measures to provide an adequate minimum flow of official development assistance, including, *inter alia*, those proposals for tripling the net disbursement of concessional assistance by 1984 and quadrupling it by 1990 at 1977 prices on a predictable, continuous and assured basis;

4. *Urges* all developed countries to provide official development assistance to the least developed countries as a general rule in the form of grants, which should normally be untied;

5. *Calls upon* the international community and the organs, organizations and bodies of the XE "Development System of the UN" to take all necessary measures to ensure the success of the United Nations Conference on the Least Developed Countries, which will, *inter alia*, finalize, adopt and launch the Substantial New Programme of Action for the 1980s, as called for in resolution 122 (V) of the United Nations Conference on Trade and Development;

6. *Requests* multilateral development agencies, including international, interregional, regional and intergovernmental funds, to accord priority to the least developed countries in the programming and allocation of their resources;

7. *Urges* all developed countries, developing countries in a position to do so, multilateral development institutions and other sources to extend substantial assistance to the least developed countries for the development of their energy resources;

8. *Requests* the Secretary-General to monitor implementation of the measures adopted in favour of the least developed countries, including those of the Immediate Action Programme for 1979-1981, and to report thereon to the Economic and Social Council at its second regular session of 1981 and to the General Assembly at its thirty-sixth session.

21st plenary meeting
15 September 1980

S-13/2. United Nations Programme of Action for African Economic Recovery and Development 1986-1990

Committee: Ad hoc
Vote: Adopted without a vote
Ref.: 46/151, 43/027

The General Assembly,

Recalling its resolution 39/29 of 3 December 1984 and the Declaration on the Critical Economic Situation in Africa annexed thereto, as well as its resolution 40/40 of 2 December 1985, in which it decided to convene a special session to focus, in a comprehensive and integrated manner, on the rehabilitation and medium-term and long-term development problems and challenges facing African countries,

Welcoming the efforts of African countries towards their economic recovery and development, as evidenced in Africa's Priority Programme for Economic Recovery 1986-1990[4] adopted by the Assembly of Heads of State and Government of the Organization of African Unity at its twenty-first ordinary session, held at Addis Ababa from l8 to 20 July 1985, in which the Governments of Africa reaffirmed their primary responsibility for the economic and social development of their countries, identified areas for priority action, and undertook to mobilize and utilize domestic resources for the achievement of these priorities,

1 See *Proceedings of the United Nations Conference on Trade and Development, Third Session*, vol. I, *Report and Annexes* (United Nations publication, Sales No. E.73.II.D.4), annex I.A.

2 *Ibid., Fourth Session*, vol. I, *Report and Annexes* (United Nations publication, Sales No. E.76.II.D.10 and corrigendum), part I one, sect. A.

3 *Ibid., Fifth Session*, vol. I, *Report and Annexes* (United Nations publication, Sales No. E.79.II.D.14), part one, sect. A.

4 A/40/666, annex 1, declaration AHG/Decl. 1 (XXI), annex.

Convinced of the need for concerted action by the international community in support of the efforts of African Governments to achieve economic recovery and development,

Emphasizing that the African development crisis is one that concerns the international community as a whole and that greater realization of the rich physical and human potential of the continent is an integral part of a common strategy to promote the economic and social advancement of all people,

Noting with appreciation the strong expression of support and commitment made by the international community during the thirteenth special session of the General Assembly,

1. *Adopts* the United Nations Programme of Action for African Economic Recovery and Development 1986-1990 set forth in the annex to the present resolution;

2. *Emphasizes* the need to intensify economic and technical cooperation with African countries during and beyond the period of the Programme of Action;

3. *Urges* all Governments to take effective action for the rapid and full implementation of the Programme of Action;

4. *Requests* the organs, organizations and bodies of the United Nations system to participate fully in and support the implementation of the Programme of Action;

5. *Calls upon* all concerned intergovernmental and non-governmental organizations, in view of their significant contribution to economic and social development in Africa, to support and contribute to the implementation of the Programme of Action;

6. *Decides* to conduct a review and appraisal of the implementation of the Programme of Action at its forty-third session, in accordance with paragraph 24 (*a*) of the Programme of Action;

7. *Requests* the Secretary-General to monitor the process of implementation of the Programme of Action and to report thereon to the General Assembly at its forty-second and forty-third sessions, as outlined in paragraph 24 (c) of the Programme of Action.

8th plenary meeting
1 June 1986

Annex

United Nations Programme of Action for African Economic Recovery and Development 1986-1990

I

Analysis of Africa's Critical Economic Situation

1. Africa's economic and social crisis has been a cause of grave concern to Africa and the international community alike. The crisis has not only jeopardized the development process of the African economies, but has also threatened the very survival of millions of Africans. The persistent economic crisis in Africa, exacerbated by drought and desertification, and the more recent tragic famine and hunger have strengthened the resolve of the African countries, individually and collectively, to take immediate and concerted actions to achieve sustained economic and social development of their countries in the medium-term and long-term.

2. The international community fully recognizes the pervasive and structural economic problems of the African continent. Some of these lie in the colonial past; some of these flow from the post-independence era; others are a combination of economic, political and endemic factors. The vulnerability and the fragile nature of the African socio-economic structures have now become fully apparent as a consequence of the dramatic effects of drought. The African Governments have initiated actions aiming at long-term structural transformation of their economies which is vital for breaking the vicious cycle of poverty and underdevelopment and for paving the way for self-reliant economic development. Notwithstanding past efforts, it is imperative that the international community intensify its cooperation and substantially increase its support for the African efforts.

3. The persistent economic crisis in Africa has been aggravated by a combination of exogenous and endogenous factors. The endogenous aggravating factors include deficiencies in institutional and physical infrastructures, economic strategies and policies that have fallen short, in some cases, of achieving their objectives, disparities in urban and rural development and income distribution, insufficient managerial/administrative capacities, inadequate human resource development, and lack of financial resources, the demographic factors and political instability manifested, *inter alia*, in a large and growing population of refugees. In addition to these factors, many African countries have to contend with severely adverse consequences of the policy of economic destabilization perpetrated by the racist minority régime in South Africa and by its illegal occupation of Namibia. The serious aggravating exogenous factors include the recent international economic recession, the decline in commodity prices, adverse terms of trade, the decline in financial flows, increased protectionism and high interest rates. The heavy burden of debt and debt-serving obligations also constrains Africa's prospects for economic growth.

4. Urgent, far-reaching and imaginative economic policies are required to avert further deterioration in the economic conditions in Africa and to launch the continent on the path of dynamic self-reliant and self-sustained economic development in a favourable external environment. One immediate task of such efforts should be to increase substantially productivity in all sectors particularly in the central sectors of food and agriculture. Achieving such a task would be extremely difficult without the amelioration of the external and internal factors that have aggravated the structural crisis and without simultaneously enhanced supportive measures by the international community.

5. Africa has taken the main responsibility for its own development. It has organized itself to undertake the necessary measures to overcome the current economic crisis on the basis of Africa's Priority Programme for Economic Recovery 1986-1990,[1] adopted by the Assembly of Heads of State and Government of the Organization of African Unity at its twenty-first ordinary session, held at Addis Ababa from 18 to 20 July 1985. The Programme aims at identifying areas for priority action for the rehabilitation and recovery of the African economies and mobilizing and fully utilizing domestic resources for the achievement of those priorities. However, given the dimensions of internal and external problems now facing the continent, it is obvious that in order to accomplish this complex task Africa must receive the full support of the international community.

6. The African development crisis is not an exclusive African problem but one that concerns mankind as a whole. Interdependence is today a living reality. A stagnant or perpetually economically backward Africa is not in the interest of the world community. Without durable and sustained economic development in the world's poor regions, of which Africa is a notable example, there is a real danger to international peace and security and an impediment to world economic growth and development. The international community recognizes the importance of genuine peace and security, as well as the strengthening of international cooperation, to African economic development.

7. It is consequently essential urgently to develop and implement an international strategy to complement the exceptional efforts that the African countries have themselves initiated to put their economies on course. In developing such a strategy, it is necessary to take full cognizance of the special problems and needs not only those common to Africa as a whole, but also those of subregions and individual African countries in order to ensure balanced and equitable development. The international community must respond positively to the African call for a new era of cooperation based on a spirit of genuine and equal partnership, which is an essential element for harmonious and mutually beneficial economic cooperation in an interdependent world. Africa is convinced that, given the necessary support from the international community, it will be capable, in the not to distant future, of establishing national, subregional and regional structures which would ensure self-reliant sustainable economic development.

---

1 *Ibid.*

II

United Nations Programme of Action for African Economic Recovery and Development 1986-1990

8. The United Nations Programme of Action for African Economic Recovery and Development 1986-1990, based on mutual commitment and cooperation, consists of two central elements:

(*a*) The determination and commitment of the African countries to launch both national and regional programmes of economic development as reflected in Africa's Priority Programme for Economic Recovery 1986-1990, adopted by the African Heads of State and Government in July 1985;

(*b*) The response of the international community and its commitment to support and complement the African development efforts.

A. Africa's Priority Programme for Economic Recovery 1986-1990

9. The African countries have fully committed themselves to the implementation of a sharply focused, practical and operational set of activities, priorities and policies, as elaborated in Africa's Priority Programme for Economic Recovery 1986-1990. The successful implementation of the Priority Programme will lay the foundation for durable structural changes, improve levels of productivity and ensure the rapid recovery of the African economies while at the same time enhancing long-term development prospects.

10. The implementation of the Priority Programme should contribute to the realization of the Lagos Plan of Action for the Implementation of the Monrovia Strategy for the Economic Development of Africa,[1] the Industrial Development Decade for Africa, proclaimed by the General Assembly in its resolution 35/66 B of 5 December 1980, the Transport and Communications Decade in Africa, proclaimed by the Assembly in its resolution 32/160 of 19 December 1977, and the Harare Declaration on the food crisis in Africa, adopted on 25 July 1984 by the Thirteenth FAO Regional Conference for Africa.

11. The Priority Programme stipulates the following priorities at the national, subregional and regional levels:

1. At the National Level

(a) Agricultural development

The Priority Programme lays considerable emphasis on the food and agricultural sector. The Priority Programme seeks to revitalize the more dynamic and internally generated forces for growth and development. Primary focus will be on women farmers who contribute significantly to agricultural production.

(i) *Immediate measures to combat food emergencies*

The immediate objective will be to cope with future emergencies and catastrophes through the following measures:

- To create and sustain national emergency preparedness;
- To institute effective early-warning systems;
- To establish flexible and efficient regional networks of crop protection agencies;
- To establish national food security arrangements.

(ii) *Medium-term measures*

The main objective will be to give a new impetus to agricultural development in order to achieve increasing levels of productivity and production through:

- Raising substantially the level of investment in agriculture;
- Increased food production;
- Restoring, protecting and developing arable land and rendering it more productive;
- Establishment of remunerative produce pricing policies, establishment and strengthening of incentive schemes, eliminating pricing policies that have tended to discourage production and providing effective agriculture credit programmes;
- Development of livestock and livestock products through the utilization of agricultural by-products, improved management, and attention to animal diseases;
- Development of mechanization and the use of modern farm and processing machinery; increased use of fertilizers, improved seeds and pesticides;
- Improving and expanding the storage capacity, distribution and the marketing system;
- Development of agricultural research and extension through the creation of a network of agronomical research stations and extension for the design and diffusion of appropriate agricultural technologies;
- Placing at the disposal of small farmers necessary inputs for increased yields; better utilization and improvement in management of water resources and the establishment of low-cost irrigation schemes;
- Establishment of reforestation, drought and desertification control programmes, including firewood schemes; and improvement of agricultural implement maintenance capacity;
- Establishment of assistance programmes for small farmers, especially women food producers and rural youth;
- Improvement of the distribution of agricultural products.

The above measures should be applied in a suitable combination to achieve the expected results, taking into account the particular situation in each country. Other subregional and regional measures are also envisaged in the Priority Programme to complement national measures.

The total investment required for the implementation of this programme is estimated at $US 57.4 billion which is 44.8 per cent of the total cost of implementing the Priority Programme.

(b) Other sectors in support of agriculture

The success of Africa's effort in achieving the stated objectives for the development and growth of the agricultural sector will depend on the parallel development of the following agriculture support sectors:

(i) *Rehabilitation and development of agro-related industries*

Given the high dependency of Africa on imports of almost all industrial goods in general and agriculture related goods in particular and the urgent need to increase Africa's capacity to increase food production, the following specific measures are to be taken, among others:

- Development of industries for production of agricultural tools and equipment, small-scale irrigation equipment and agricultural inputs;
- Processing of raw materials and intermediate inputs;
- Rehabilitation and upgrading of existing plants;
- Development of capacity for utilization of renewable sources of energy, especially bio-mass and solar energy;
- Establishment of engineering capacity for the production of spare parts and components;
- Provision of training in the above areas and the development of local capacity for project design and preparation.

(ii) *Development of transport and communications*

In this field the objectives are to improve access to production areas, facilitate the development of intra-African trade in agriculture, industrial raw materials and other goods and services in a complementary manner.

Action in this area will consist of:

- Maintenance and development of feeder, access and service roads, small bridges and desert roads;
- Identification of obstacles and rehabilitation and maintenance of existing modes of transport and communication;
- Utilization of labour-intensive techniques in the construction and maintenance of transport infrastructure;
- Production of spare parts for the overhaul repair and maintenance of public vehicles, machinery and equipment;

---

1 A/S-11/14, annex I.

- Participation in the development of multinational and intermodal transport networks.

Africa, in cooperation with the international community, will intensify its efforts in financing and implementing the Transport and Communication Decade in Africa.

(iii) *Trade and finance*

In the field of trade the objective is to improve the distribution channels for domestic trade, by improving market arrangements and reversing the present consumption pattern in favour of domestically produced goods through:

- Adoption of price incentives for agricultural products;
- Improvement of internal distribution channels;
- Identification and elimination of obstacles hindering trade expansion.

In the field of financial cooperation the following measures are envisaged:

- Increased utilization of existing clearing arrangements;
- Adoption of coordinated measures to establish financial markets at the national, subregional and regional levels;
- Intensification of efforts for the establishment of an African Monetary Fund.

The total cost for the implementation of the measures envisaged under the other sectors in support of agriculture is estimated at $60.1 billion.

(c) Drought and desertification

Although drought and desertification require a long-term approach, there is need for immediate action by the African countries at national, subregional and regional levels to implement a comprehensive programme for drought and desertification and to stem and control the effects of drought and desertification on both the ecological environment and the development process. African Governments are, therefore, committed to undertaking as soon as possible the following measures:

- Massive afforestation and reafforestation;
- Better management of water resources, including river basins and irrigation;
- Protection of common eco-systems;
- Development of alternative sources of energy to replace wood fuel;
- Stabilization of sand dunes;
- Measures to stop soil erosion;
- Measures against salination;
- Improvement of drainage in irrigated areas;
- Integrating measures for the protection of the environment in national development programmes and according them high priority;
- Full implementation of the Plan of Action to Combat Desertification[1] approved by the General Assembly in its resolution 32/172 of 19 December 1977.

The total cost of measures envisaged for the implementation of the programme to combat drought and desertification is estimated at $3.41 billion.

(d) Human resources development, planning and utilization

African Governments fully recognize that central to the successful implementation of the proposed actions is the efficient development, planning and utilization of human resources and the full and effective participation of the people in the development process. In this regard, African Governments are adopting the following comprehensive policies for human resource planning, development and utilization with a view to integrating them in their overall national development policies and plans:

- Radically changing the educational systems at all levels to ensure that the skills, knowledge and attitudes that are relevant to Africa's developmental needs are generated;
- Intensifying efforts to promote mass literacy and adult learning programmes;
- Efficiently utilizing manpower resources, including measures to reverse the brain drain and ensure the guarantee of human rights;
- Reducing the present high level of dependence of most African countries on foreign experts to reduce foreign exchange leakage;
- Ensuring good working conditions;
- Encouraging the role and participation of women and youth, particularly those living in the rural areas, in the development process.

The total cost of measures envisaged in the human resources development sector is estimated at $7 billion.

(e) Policy reforms

In order to achieve the objectives of the Priority Programme, African Governments are undertaking a number of major policy measures while focusing attention on the need for policy reonentation. African countries are determined to undertake, individually and collectively, all measures and policy reforms that are necessary for the recovery of their economies and the revitalization of genuine development, particularly in the following areas at the national level:

(i) *Improving management of the economy*

African Governments recognize that genuine efforts must be made to improve the management of the African economies and to rationalize public investment policies, particularly since the public sector will have to continue to play an important role in the development of the region. Such efforts would require, *inter alia*, improvement of public management systems, institutions and practices; improvement of the performance of public enterprises; reforming the public services to make them more development-oriented services; greater mobilization of domestic savings; improvement of financial management, including debt and development aid, fiscal administration and control of public expenditure with a view to promoting the efficient use of resources and cutting wastage and resource misallocation; reduction of foreign exchange leakages. The positive role of the private sector is also to be encouraged through well-defined and consistent policies.

(ii) *Other policy measures*

In accordance with their respective policies and priorities, African Governments have demonstrated their determination to tackle their social and economic problems through, among others, appropriate adjustment measures that have been undertaken when needed. These measures have involved, *inter alia*, exchange rate adjustments, debt-relief arrangements, wage and salary reduction and public employment freeze. Though the tasks involved have often been difficult and painful, African countries have recognized the need to bear the burden and have made the necessary sacrifices to the extent possible. In the coming years short-term adjustment measures should give way to the medium-term and long-term structural transformation. Restructuring measures will be continued with prudence through appropriate monetary and fiscal reforms.

(iii) *Population policy*

Special importance will need to be accorded by each African country to a population policy that, on the basis of the Kilimanjaro Programme of Action for African Population and Self-Reliant Development,[2] adopted by the Second African Population Conference held at Arusha, United Republic of Tanzania, from 9 to 13 January 1984, will, *inter alia*, address issues of high fertility and mortality, rapid urbanization, rural-urban and rural-rural migration, the problems of children and youth and the protection of the environment in a manner that would ensure compatibility between demographic trends, appropriate land utilization and settlement patterns and the desired pace of

1 *Report of the United Nations Conference on Desertification, Nairobi, 29 August-9 September 1977* (A/CONF.74/36), chap. I.

2 See E/ECA/CM.10/14, annex II.

economic growth and development. African countries should also push for the attainment, within the shortest possible time, of an agro-food production growth rate at least equal to the population growth rate.

(iv) *Participation of the people in development*

Special attention will be accorded to the role played by human resources. Policies will need to be pursued to ensure the effective development and utilization of human resources in all fields and sectors through:

- Ensuring the effective participation of the people in all dimensions of development;
- Developing indigenous entrepreneurial capabilities, both private and public;
- Establishing sound bases for political, economic and social justice.

In the food and agricultural sector, the focus of attention must be the peasant farmer with special reference to female farmers who dominate food production in most countries.

(v) *Women and development*

The role of women in development must be taken seriously into account in development planning and in the disbursement of resources, both as contributors to and beneficiaries of development efforts as recommended by the Arusha Forward-looking Strategies for the Advancement of African Women Beyond the United Nations Decade for Women,[1] adopted by the regional intergovernmental preparatory meeting organized by the Economic Commission for Africa and held at Arusha, United Republic of Tanzania, from 8 to 12 October 1984.

In view of the importance accorded to food self-sufficiency and the acknowledged role of women in food production in the continent, the pivotal role of women in this sector must be recognized and encouraged.

2. Subregional Concerns

In order to deal with the divergence and differentiations among African subregions and countries the following actions are necessary, bearing in mind the unique problems which the groups of countries concerned face in their efforts to accelerate their economic growth rates:

(*a*) The areas most seriously affected by drought and desertification have diminishing opportunities of raising domestic resources for implementation of the Priority Programme. They also face problems in instituting recovery programmes because of the limited economic options available in the wake of severe climatic conditions. In fact, for some of these countries, especially those in the Sahel and the members of the Intergovernmental Authority for Drought and Development and the Southern African Development Coordination Conference, the road to self-sufficiency in food production is paved with particular difficulties especially as they are not in a position to mobilize from domestic resources more than 4.21 per cent of their requirements, depending on external sources for the balance. Therefore, in order to tackle the environmental, development and human problems, in these countries, programmes for afforestation and reafforestation, as well as for the development and utilization of water resources will have to be put in place while special investments should be made to develop alternative sources of energy to wood fuel and charcoal in order to protect the ecology This should include research and development of small gas, coal or oil stoves suitable for rural communities. In addition, drought resistant crop varieties will have to be developed.

(*b*) With regard to the African island nations, these countries are visually isolated from the mainland both in terms of transport and communications as well as trade and other factors, unlike their counterparts in the Caribbean which have access to the strong economies of North America. A special programme will need to be devised for these countries to develop trade and transport linkages with the African mainland as well as with the rest of the world. Additional resources are needed for programmes aimed at protecting them against the devastating effects of cyclones, typhoons and floods.

(*c*) Many countries in Africa are faced, *inter alia*, with the serious problems of being land-locked or semi-land-locked, and among the least developed countries; furthermore, countries in southern Africa are subjected to externally-engineered destabilization. These countries require special assistance in tropical and sub-tropical agriculture research. Hitherto, limited locally based agricultural research has been conducted in crop diversification, high-yield seeds and the control of pests. These countries also urgently need intensive research in methods to combat widespread animal and livestock diseases such as rinderpest, foot-and-mouth discase as well as to control the tsetse fly. At the same time, the problems of storage, transport and transit, equally acute, also require large investments.

(*d*) Some of the countries of the North African subregion face substantial balance-of-payments deficits demonstrated by increasing debt-service burden. Agricultural development in some countries of the subregion has been slowing down owing to drought, water shortage, mounting desertification and soil erosion. The widening food gap in the subregion is among the highest gaps in Africa.

(f) Refugees and displaced persons

(i) The plight of 5 million refugees and returnees together with the adverse effects which the refugee burden continues to have on the frail economies of host countries are matters of high priority for many African States.

(ii) The Second International Conference of Assistance to Refugees in Africa, in its Declaration and Programme of Action,[2] has confirmed the spirit of burden-sharing on a strategy for solving the problems of refugees in Africa, that the refugee problem in Africa is a matter of global responsibility, and that refugee aid and development aid must be regarded as complementary for any realistic solution to Africa's refugee problem. On their part, African Governments have clearly reaffirmed their commitment to do everything within their power to promote lasting solutions to the problem. The international community, for its part, has undertaken to join hands with African countries in the support of such lasting solutions and in meeting and promoting technical and capital assistance designed to strengthen the social and economic infrastructure of the affected countries.

(iii) Concrete measures should be undertaken at national, regional and international levels with a view to preventing a new massive population exodus. In this connection, there is a need to accelerate implementation of the recommendations of the Second International Conference on Assistance to Refugees in Africa.

3. At the Regional Level

(a) Strengthening the institutional framework

Proper social and economic management will only materialize if African countries urgently strengthen their social and economic institutions at all levels. To this end, African national and multinational institutions will be made more responsive to the challenges of development through the improvement of their management systems, rationalization of their activities and elimination of duplication of efforts.

(b) Consolidating African cooperation

Existing subregional organizations should be strengthened with a view to consolidating African cooperation in accordance with the objectives of the Lagos Plan of Action. Likewise, the establishment, whenever deemed necessary, of subregional organizations based on economic criteria, including natural resource criteria, should be encouraged with a view to attaining the above objectives.

---

[1] See A/CONF.116/9 and Corr. 1, sect. IV.

[2] See A/39/402, annex.

4. Financial Estimates for Africa's Priority Programme for Economic Recovery 1986- 1990

12. The full implementation of Africa's Priority Programme for Economic Recovery 1986-1990 would require $US 128.1 billion during the period. In spite of severe constraints, the African countries commit themselves to provide $82.5 billion or 64.4 per cent of the total cost of financing the Priority Programme through the mobilization of domestic resources. There is a difference of approximately $46 billion between the total financial requirements for the implementation of the Priority Programme and the resources to be made available through domestic efforts. Accordingly, effective implementation of the Priority Programme will require $9 billion annually, on the average, through external resources.

* * *

Commitment to a common point of reference

13. Africa is committed to providing the necessary framework to launch long-term programmes for self-sustaining socio-economic development and growth. The international community is committed to assist Africa in achieving this objective. Such a framework of understanding will include, *inter alia*:

(*a*) Necessary economic reform and structural adjustment as mentioned in Africa's Priority Programme for Economic Recovery 1986-1990 as a basis the broad-based, sustained economic development.

(*b*) Priority attention and increased resources commitment to the rehabilitation and development of agriculture based on durable structural changes as indicated in the Priority Programme;

(*c*) Appropriate policies that promote development of sectors supportive of agriculture and rural development, namely, agro-related industry as well as essential consumption products, trade, transposition, health, education, environment and other social and commercial services;

(*d*) Fundamental measures to address the problems of drought and desertification as an integral part of agriculture and rural development, with the active involvement of village and community groups, wherever applicable;

(*e*) Efficient development and utilization of human resources with particular reference to the full and equal participation of women in order to maximize the benefit for and the contribution to national development;

(*f*) Undertaking reforms in such a manner as to encourage the broadest possible participation in development and the productive use of scarce resources.

* * *

B. Response and Commitment of the International Community

14. The international community has noted with admiration, the comprehensive and dynamic resolve of the African countries that are embarking upon an unparalleled action to break away from the clutches of underdevelopment and poverty as is reflected in Africa's Priority Programme for Economic Recovery 1986-1990. It notes with particular appreciation that in the face of enormous difficulties the African countries, reaffirming their primary responsibility for the development of their continent, are fully mobilizing their domestic resources in order to implement successfully all measures and policy reforms required for the continent's economic rehabilitation, recovery and long-term development.

15. The international community is aware that the process of development being initiated by the African countries, as reflected in the Priority Programme, has to be supplemented by complementary actions of the international community through intensified cooperation and substantially increased support. In this context, it is also realized that lasting solutions to the serious exogenous constraints, over which Africa has no control, will have to be found since their persistence will impede the efforts of the African countries.

16. The African countries estimate that the full implementation of the Priority Programme would require total financial resources of $128.1 billion, of which the African countries intend to provide $82.5 billion through the mobilization of domestic resources, leaving the approximately $46 billion remaining to be met through external resources. The international community recognizes that the African countries need additional external resources. In this context, it commits itself to making every effort to provide sufficient resources to support and supplement the African development effort; it also appreciates that the realization of Africa's development efforts would be greatly facilitated if the flows of external resources were predictable and assured.

17. The international community recognizes the magnitude of Africa's debt and the severe and restrictive burden which this has placed on many African countries. It realizes that measures have to be taken to alleviate this burden and to enable those countries to concentrate on the full implementation of priorities. In addressing problems arising from such debt, existing mechanisms should respond flexibly and be improved as appropriate.

(a) Improving the quality and modality of external assistance and cooperation

While it is recognized that each bilateral or multilateral donor as well as recipient has its own rules and procedures, there are some general areas in which changes can be usefully made. For an effective support of Africa's efforts, it is realized that the quality and modality of external assistance and cooperation need to be improved along the following lines:

(i) Greater emphasis on programme support in the priority areas of the recipient African countries, with a view to giving an indication of medium-term support;

(ii) Evolution of procurement policies and administrative procedures which would improve delivery of production inputs;

(iii) Speedier disbursement of funds;

(iv) Increase the concessionality, particularly the grant element of development assistance to African countries, with the purpose of improving the quality of aid to those countries;

(v) In planning and implementing programmes of assistance, special consideration shall be given to the indigenous competence, expertise, experience, local conditions, particularly local techniques and equipment as well as to the training of qualified national personnel;

(vi) Develop more effective and efficient coordination methods in order to ensure a greater impact of aid policies;

(vii) Improve the effectiveness of technical assistance and make it more responsive to the needs and priorities of the African countries;

(viii) Donor countries and agencies should consider, as appropriate, measures to assist African countries in meeting recurrent and local costs of programmes and projects;

(ix) Donor countries, international institutions and recipients should take into account the recurrent and local costs of new programmes and projects to ensure their viability

(b) Improvement in the external environment

Many of the issues concerning the external factors that aggravate the African situation need to be addressed and examined in the competent forums. In the present context, there is a need for the international community:

(i) To evolve and implement policies conducive to sustained, equitable and non-flationary growth, including the expansion of trade through, *inter alia*, the elimination of protectionism, particularly non-tariff barriers, in accordance with existing commitments, the adoption of measures which encourage African exports and diversification programmes, and improved market access, especially for tropical products, within the framework of the General Agreement on Tariffs and Trade;

(ii) To deal urgently with commodity issues, taking into account the special interests of the African countries, in the framework of an overall approach, embracing commodity agreements/arrangements and adequate compensatory financing, and also to increase the capacity of African countries to process, market, distribute and transport their exports; and in this context to stress the importance of sufficient ratifications of the *Agreement Establishing the Common Fund for Commodities*,[1] for it quickly to become operational.

(c) Supporting Africa's policy reform

There is need for extensive international support for the priorities and policies that Africa has identified as necessary and on which many African countries have already embarked. African countries need assistance to enable them to achieve a speedier recovery and long-term development. In this regard, the international community, particularly the donor countries, keeping in mind the interests of all developing countries, agree on the importance of increasing official development assistance to Africa, its improved quality and effectiveness. They also agree to:

(i) Placing greater emphasis on non-project aid, including balance-of-payments support, to African countries during the period 1986-1990;

(ii) Evolving aid policies based on technical considerations and specific aid requirements of recipient countries;

(iii) Enabling multilateral development institutions to increase their concessional assistance to African countries;

(iv) In the case of countries concerned, work towards the rapid implementation of the International Monetary Fund Structural Adjustment Facility which provides longer term concessional resources in support of adjustment efforts, including overall development objectives at the national level;

(v) Urge the speedy eighth replenishment of the International Development Association and the fifth African Development Fund at levels which should take into account the need to support fully African recovery and development;

(vi) Strive to ensure that no individual bilateral donor, during the period 1986-1990, becomes a net recipient of official capital flows from African countries that undertake adjustment programmes;

(vii) Increase support, whenever possible, to the International Fund for Agricultural Development Special Programme for Sub-Saharan African Countries Affected by Drought and Desertification;

(viii) Give special attention to financial and technical assistance requirements of countries affected by drought and desertification and in this context utilize the existing subregional organizations such as the Permanent Interstate Committee for Drought Control in the Sahel, the Intergovernmental Authority for Drought and Development and the Southern African Development Coordination Conference;

(ix) Special efforts need also be made to increase resource flows to the least developed countries with a view to enabling them to achieve the objectives of their country programmes within the framework of the Substantial New Programme of Action for the 1980s for the Least Developed Countries[2] and also to allow the African countries to solve the critical problems arising from negative or insufficient flows of resources;

(x) Firmly invite those countries that have not done so to give priority consideration to the implementation of Trade and Development Board resolution 165 (S-IX) of 11 March 1978[3] and note with satisfaction that a number of donor countries have responded favourably to that resolution.

(d) Economic recovery and debt constraints

The international community recognizes that the continued improvement of the external environment and a strong economic adjustment effort may not be sufficient to allow many African States to service their debt while establishing the basis for sustainable economic growth. In these cases, the international community is determined to assist African countries in their efforts to deal with their financial constraints.

South-South cooperation

18. The international community reaffirms its belief in the strategy for collective self-reliance among developing countries and reiterates its conviction that economic and technical cooperation among these countries should constitute a key element in the economic recovery of Africa and be of mutual benefit to developing countries, with due regard to the Caracas Programme of Action on economic cooperation among developing countries[4] and to the Plan of Action to meet the critical economic situation in Africa, adopted by the Movement of Non-Aligned Countries.[5]

19. In this connection, there is an urgent need for African countries, together with other developing countries, to strengthen more vigorously than ever before South-South cooperation and make greater efforts, through action-oriented measures, particularly in the priority areas of food and agricultural production. Technical cooperation at the bilateral, subregional and interregional levels in the following specific areas could contribute towards helping Africa tackle its food production, storage and marketing problems:

(*a*) Water management and small-scale irrigation technology;

(*b*) Dry-land farming;

(*c*) Training in agricultural support services, including extension services for animal husbandry;

(*d*) Institution building, development and management in the area of farm cooperatives;

(*e*) Small-scale rural industrial development;

(*f*) Rural energy production, including the development of new and renewable sources of energy;

(*g*) Agricultural research;

(*h*) Exchange of seed germplasm and assistance in seed production technology and in the production of fertilizers, pesticides and farm equipment;

(*i*) Development of poultry, fisheries and other non-farm produce;

(*j*) Exchange of information and experience on appropriate agricultural policies and strategies.

20. In addition to the above, South-South cooperation should focus on other development priorities, with particular reference to the following areas mentioned in Africa's Priority Programme for Economic Recovery 1986- 1990:

(*a*) Exchange of information, technology and techniques for combating drought and desertification and protecting the environment;

(*b*) Exchange of information on and cooperation in the production of equipment and other inputs for agriculture, industry and transport and communication;

(*c*) Cooperation in the development of human resources;

(*d*) Joint participation in the implementation of self-sustaining, self-generating and self-financing development projects;

(*e*) Trade expansion.

III

Follow Up and Evaluation Machinery

21. The effective implementation of the United Nations Programme of Action for African Economic Recovery and Development 1986-1990 will require a continuous process of follow-up, evaluation and coordination at the national, subregional regional and international levels. Such a process, based on joint efforts and cooperation, would enable the follow-up, evaluation and coordination of the actions of both the national Governments and the international donor commu-

1 United Nations publication, Sales No. E.81.II.D.8 and corrigendum.

2 *Report of the United Nations Conference on the Least Developed Countries, Paris, 1-14 September 1981* (United Nations publication, Sales No. E.82.I.8), part one, sect. A.

3 *Official Records of the General Assembly, Thirty-third Session, Supplement No. 15* (A/33/15), vol. I, part two, annex 1.

4 See A/36/333 and Corr. 1, annex.

5 See A/40/854 and Corr. I, annex II, sect. XXIII.B.

nity. The general principles underlying the establishment of any follow-up and evaluation mechanism are:

(*a*) The sovereign right of each Government to formulate and implement its own programmes and development plans, and to determine appropriate follow-up mechanisms best suited to implementing the Programme of Action;

(*b*) The need for such mechanisms to be simple, operational and not involving substantial additional expenditure;

(*c*) The need for emphasis, as far as possible, on the utilization of existing mechanisms;

(*d*) The need for donor countries and international organizations to enhance coordination of their activities and assistance with the recipient countries.

National Level

22. Governments would, as appropriate, establish follow-up mechanisms, involving joint action with their development partners, within the framework of existing aid coordination machinery, such as round tables and consultative group meetings, as well as within the framework of intergovernmental agreements for economic cooperation. The terms of reference and other details pertaining to such mechanisms, which could take the form of Joint Committees or joint bilateral commissions, would be to be agreed upon among the parties concerned, keeping in mind the following elements:

(i) Comprehensive and simultaneous consideration of all issues, pertaining to the implementation of the United Nations Programme of Action for American Economic Recovery and Development 1986- 1990;

(ii) Review and evaluation of the process of implementation of the jointly agreed upon commitments, on the part of both national Governments and their development partners in the context of the Programme of Action;

(iii) Implementation of the Programme of Action in the context of the long-term development needs and policies of African countries.

Regional Level

23. For a cohesive and balanced implementation of the United Nations Programme of Action for African Economic Recovery and Development 1986- 1990, systematic follow-up action is necessary at the subregional and regional levels. This process, which could be facilitated by the existing mechanisms at the regional level, would assist the African Governments in evaluating and assessing the progress made in the implementation of the Programme of Action, at the subregional and continental levels, and in taking appropriate action.

Global Level

24. At the global level, the following actions are envisaged:

(*a*) A review and appraisal of the implementation of the United Nations Programme of Action for African Economic Recovery and Development 1986-1990 by the General Assembly at its forty-third session in 1988. For that purpose, the General Assembly, at its forty-second session in 1987, shall consider and establish such preparatory mechanisms as may be necessary;

(*b*) The Secretary-General shall coordinate the assistance and support of the organizations and agencies of the United Nations system for the effective implementation of the United Nations Programme of Action for African Economic Recovery and Development 1986-1990;

(*c*) The Secretary-General shall monitor the process of the implementation of the United Nations Programme of Action for African Economic Recovery and Development 1986-1990 and report thereon to the General Assembly at its forty-second and forty-third sessions.

46/151. Final Review and Appraisal of the Implementation of the United Nations Programme of Action for African Economic Recovery and Development 1986-1990

Vote: Adopted without a vote
Ref.: 50/160, 49/142, 48/214

The General Assembly,

Recalling its resolutions S-13/2 of 1 June 1986, the annex to which contains the United Nations Programme of Action for African Economic Recovery and Development 1986-1990, 42/163 of 8 December 1987, in which, *inter alia*, it decided to establish an A*d Hoc* Committee of the Whole for the mid-term review and appraisal of the Programme of Action, and 43/27 of 18 November 1988 on the mid- term review and appraisal of the implementation of the Programme of Action,

Recalling also Economic and Social Council resolution 1990/75 of 27 July 1990 on the final review and appraisal of the Programme of Action,

Recalling further its resolution 45/178 A of 19 December 1990 on the final review and appraisal of the implementation of the Programme of Action,

Noting that the final review and appraisal of the implementation of the Programme of Action by the General Assembly has been an occasion for an in-depth assessment of the actions taken in the implementation of the Programme of Action and of the measures that are needed to sustain accelerated growth and development in Africa beyond 1991,

Taking note of the report of the Secretary-General on the critical economic situation in Africa: final review and appraisal of the implementation of the United Nations Programme of Action for African Economic Recovery and Development 1986-1990,[1]

Taking note of the memorandum prepared by the Conference of Ministers of the Economic Commission for Africa to the A*d Hoc* Committee of the Whole of the General Assembly on the final review and appraisal of the implementation of the United Nations Programme of Action for African Economic Recovery and Development 1986-1990,[2]

Taking note also of Africa's submission on the final review and appraisal of the implementation of the Programme of Action to the General Assembly at its forty-sixth session,[3]

Taking note further of the contribution made by individual Governments, intergovernmental organizations and non-governmental organizations to the work of the A*d Hoc* Committee of the Whole,

1. *Takes note* of the report of the A*d Hoc* Committee of the Whole of the General Assembly on the final review and appraisal of the implementation of the Programme of Action for African Economic Recovery and Development 1986-1990;[4]

2. *Adopts* the conclusions of the final review and appraisal of the implementation of the Programme of Action for African Economic Recovery and Development 1986-1990, consisting of the assessment of the implementation of the Programme of Action and the United Nations New Agenda for the Development of Africa in the 1990s, as set forth in the annex to the present resolution;

3. *Requests* Governments, organs, organizations and bodies of the United Nations system and intergovernmental and non-governmental organizations to take appropriate measures in order to implement the commitments contained in the New Agenda;

4. *Requests* the Secretary-General to report to the General Assembly at its forty-eighth session on the implementation of the New Agenda.

77th plenary meeting
18 December 1991

---

1 A/46/324 and Add.1.

2 A/46/280, annex.

3 A/46/387, annex.

4 Official Records of the General Assembly, Forty Sixth Session, Supplement No. 41 (A/46/41).

Annex

I. Assessment of the Implementation of the United Nations Programme of Action for African Economic Recovery and Development 1986-1990

A. Preamble

1. The United Nations Programme of Action for African Economic Recovery and Development 1986-1990 did not quite become a focal point for economic policy or for resource mobilization on behalf of Africa.

2. Furthermore, the Programme of Action proved to be too optimistic in two basic senses. First, the concept of a global compact at the continental level was difficult to achieve. Specific arrangements, such as World Bank consultative groups and United Nations Development Programme round-table discussions for individual nations, were not always directly related to the goals and targets of the Programme of Action. Second, hopes for a favourable external economic environment for Africa during the period 1986-1990 were not fulfilled. Sharp export price falls, real interest rate increases, and declines in private sector investment and loans all severely limited the positive effects of efforts made by Africa and its development partners. The Programme of Action itself was silent regarding who was to act if unforeseen exogenous contingencies threw the Programme of Action off course; also, its review machinery did not clearly address this issue.

3. In most African States, it is recognized that revised economic reforms and good governance are a key to economic development. It is also accepted that recovery and renewed development will take longer to achieve than was hoped and projected in 1986 by Africa, as well as by donor States and international financial institutions.

4. Bilateral cooperating partners have recognized that speedy, low-cost turn-arounds are the exception, not the rule, or as several have explicitly noted, the time-frame for economic transformation and for agreed agendas for action should be seen in terms of decades, not years. In addition, perception has come much closer to African warnings of the damage done by the debt overhang and worsening terms of trade. Substantial action to overcome these obstacles to African recovery is now agreed to be urgent.

5. The World Bank recognizes that sustained structural adjustment without rapid return to positive real per capita growth rates is difficult, especially in a context of broadening participation and political liberalization. The World Bank also views increased spending on human investment, infrastructure and reduction of absolute poverty as a central priority now that structural adjustment is placed in a ten- to fifteen-year time perspective, gradually phasing into structural transformation. These views are also widely shared by the donor communities and by African Governments. In general, the results achieved by those countries that have embarked on structural transformation have been better than those of countries that have not.

6. The reworking of United Nations system programmes in Africa around the goals of the Programme of Action was real and sustained but, by itself, was by no means large enough to place those goals at the centre of policy dialogue or resource mobilization.

7. Over the period 1986-1990 there developed broad agreement on the lines of short- and medium-term policy and on the need for that policy to lay the foundations for long-term sustainable growth and transformation. The African Alternative Framework to Structural Adjustment Programmes for Socio-economic Recovery and Transformation,[1] adopted by the Conference of Ministers of the Economic Commission for Africa on 10 April 1989, and the World Bank long-term perspective study[2] illustrate this in their very broad range of agreement on goals and instruments. The remaining divergence, while substantial, is largely on issues of timing, sequencing, contexts and balance of instruments. A reduction of the external debt burden of most African States and an enabling environment would make a valuable contribution to sustained development. A consensus needs to develop on how this can be achieved.

8. At some point in the 1990s, a legitimate post-apartheid Government will emerge in South Africa, whose changing role in the economy of Africa will be significant but cannot yet be defined. Because a high rate of absolute poverty and very low human investment in a majority of its people will be the heritage of apartheid, post-apartheid South Africa may require external resource inflows, including official development assistance, although these inflows cannot yet be quantified and are not included in the total targets presented for Africa and its development partners in the 1990s.

9. Many of the African States have made progress in meeting their policy restructuring and resource reallocation commitments. However, none of the goals of the Programme of Action were fully realized. Targets for growth, food security, human investment and debt reduction were missed, so declines rather than hoped-for increases have been recorded by many States and for Africa as a whole.

10. One of the principal causes of this decline was that only two thirds of the countries pursued sustained economic reform. Those that did received increased donor assistance and achieved modest gains in per capita gross domestic product, agricultural production and exports. Other countries continued to decline in these indices, causing negative performance for Africa as a whole.

11. The reasons for this record of non-success are clear. The bilateral and multilateral achievements with respect to net real resource transfers and debt burden reduction were below expectations. A number of African States did not, in fact, fully achieve policy and resource allocation adjustment and transformation. Africa suffered from a serious fall in commodity earnings. War and certain exogenous events, such as drought and collapse in the terms of trade, imposed devastating costs. Another reason for this record of non-success may have been inadequate United Nations and Government debate or dialogue on the experience gained in the implementation of the Programme of Action.

12. However, the Programme of Action was far from being a failure. It assisted in focusing the attention of African and other Governments on the basic economic, human and governance problems of Africa. By doing so, it did achieve policy and efficiency gains and averted a more severe decline in net resource inflows. As a result, the economic decline afflicting Africa from 1981 to 1985 was slowed and, in many countries, halted. Furthermore, the process of African policy restructuring and its interaction with the analyses of external partners have led to substantial lessons of experience for all concerned.

B. Some Aspects of the Performance of the African Economy, 1986-1990

13. Taken as a whole, the performance of the African economies from 1986 to 1990, the period of the Programme of Action, was not satisfactory, with overall growth averaging less than 2.5 per cent a year. The economic performance of the African economy was, it is true, somewhat better than during the period 1980-1985. But output, in per capita terms, continued to fall.

14. The decrease in overall performance was in part accounted for by the unsatisfactory export situation. While 1986-1990 export volume increased an average of 10 per cent a year above that of the period 1981-1985, representing an annual growth of almost 4 per cent, earnings from exports were 18 per cent lower, which represented an annual average decline of 6 per cent. Trade gains fell below expectations by an amount exceeding 50 billion United States dollars. Furthermore, in many key commodity areas, Africa suffered a decline in market share.

15. The benefits of reform in the vital agricultural sector, though often positive, were limited in certain countries by such factors as natural disasters, war or civil strife and a fall in prices from export crops. The human condition of many millions of Africans continued to worsen. Absolute poverty rose in Africa. If present trends hold, Africa risks becoming, by 1995, in terms of human deprivation, the most afflicted region in the world. African Governments made efforts

1 A/44/315, annex.

2 World Bank, Sub Saharan Africa: From Crisis to Sustainable Growth (Washington, D.C., 1989).

to improve public services. Some progress was recorded in certain areas, as was indicated by the United Nations Development Programme in the *Human Development Report 1990*[1], but taken as a whole, the results were insufficient.

16. It would, however, be wrong to paint a totally sombre picture of the economic results of the 1986-1990 period. Growth of output in the majority of African economies had begun, by 1989-1990, to equal or exceed population growth. Important policy reforms had been undertaken and priority given to the restoration of infrastructure and human investment together with measures to encourage enterprise. The quantitative decline of export volumes that was typical of the 1970s and the deterioration of basic public services that characterized the 1981-1985 period have, in a majority of cases, been halted or partially reversed. Requirements for good governance, human investment, an enabling environment and the reduction of absolute poverty are being articulated and brought into operation. A sounder basis for greater production and for improvement in the human condition now exist in many African countries. Recent developments in the world political situation and on the continent give hope for drastic cuts in military expenditures. There is broad agreement everywhere that people are both the objective of and the most important means to the development and improvement of their living standards. The convictions of Africans on this are reflected in the Khartoum Declaration: Towards A Human-focused Approach to Socio-economic Recovery and Development,[2] adopted in 1988, the African Alternative Framework to Structural Adjustment Programmes for Socio-economic Recovery and Transformation,[3] adopted in 1989, and the African Charter for Popular Participation in Development and Transformation,[4] adopted in 1990.

C. Actions of the African Countries

Policy reforms

17. A majority of the African countries initiated and carried out substantial policy transformations during the 1986-1990 period. These have emphasized rationalization and liberalization of prices, especially exchange rates, food price structures and interest rates; prioritization of public expenditure towards human investment and infrastructure; and, where practicable, reduction of military expenditure. These policy reforms also aim at more efficient public sector management, enabling measures to facilitate enterprise and production and the broadening of access to economic and political participation (especially for women and poor rural households), and they include measures to reduce poverty, especially absolute poverty.

18. These policy steps were considered necessary, though generally risky and costly in social and political terms. For most countries undertaking and persisting in them, they have halted declines in per capita production. However, when such policies require extended periods of constant or lowered consumption, they face rising domestic opposition. Their continuation is frequently dependent on being able to show enhanced positive results. In a minority of cases, policy transformations have not been attempted or have been abandoned in the face of high initial costs and apparently low positive results in the Programme of Action period. While understandable, in most cases this has led directly to continued decline of the economies and of the conditions of the peoples concerned, while also hampering increased participation and improved governance. While the efforts of the African Governments are key to economic progress, the donor community has a role in supporting these efforts.

Agricultural development and other sectors in support of agriculture

19. In general, agricultural policies and resource allocations have been prioritized. These have included price and marketing structure reforms, restoration of infrastructure, redesigned research and extension services. They also include programmes to increase the resilience of small farmers to adverse economic circumstances. The results have been positive but inadequate - a 4 per cent annual agricultural output growth rate is widely recognized as essential (for example, in the World Bank long-term perspective study[5]) but only 2 per cent has been attained to date. The southern African subregion has reached a 3 per cent trend equal to population growth. Constraints include inadequate technical knowledge; inefficient research and extension; falling world prices; inadequate access to inputs, despite services prioritization to domestic capacity rehabilitation; limited effective access of the poor, especially access by women farmers to agriculture services and markets; inadequate financial resource availability at both national and farm-household level; and high-cost public and private sector marketing systems.

Drought, desertification and environment

20. Drought, desertification and environmental degradation have received attention based on fuller recognition that Africa is more threatened by them than is any other region. However, improved water conservation and use, afforestation and family forestry as part of mixed farming, crop pattern alteration to lower vulnerability to drought, and other measures have had limited results. This is partly a factor of limited knowledge and experience and the short time since priorities were changed; but it also reflects the lack of resources to implement policies and the impact of pressure to export. Often, the result has been further soil impoverishment.

Human resources and human conditions

21. The rise in the proportion of people in absolute poverty to 30 per cent in Africa and 60 per cent in the worst afflicted countries demonstrates the impact of war, drought and resource shortages. In countries ravaged by war and natural calamities, in spite of efforts by the donor community to provide improved early warning systems and increased emergency assistance, the scarcity of food supplies led to famine. In some countries, emergency relief assistance could not be provided quickly enough to avert the displacement of large numbers of persons and prevent casualties. Food for work (paid in cash or food) programmes have been devised and implemented at the micro-level, as well as more generally in some States, to help rehabilitate drought, flood and war victims.

22. Priority attention to human development - both in resource allocations and in restructuring to improve efficiency and access to basic services - has been a central theme in over half the African States. It has halted the rapid decline in access to basic services and the deterioration in their quality that occurred during the period 1981-1985, but has achieved clear improvements in only a minority of cases. In many cases, efficiency-improving policies were only partially employed, partly because they required resources that were not available.

23. Human-centred concerns, such as those expressed during the United Nations Decade for Women: Equality, Development and Peace and in the adoption of the Convention on the Rights of the Child, have deeply influenced African thinking. Appropriate programmes are now emerging and policy rethinking is more generally in process. However, the results to date are limited, partly because of brief experience and partly because integrating new elements into mainline programmes - especially in agriculture, education and employment - has proven difficult. In the context of limited increase in resources for all programmes, difficult choices must be made in allocating available resources, often resulting in cuts in existing activities. Only in health services has reorientation to support the needs of women and children made sustained progress over the 1986-1990 period, notably in mother and child health care and immunization.

24. Population policies have been adopted by most African Governments. However, it is unclear how much impact they have had to date. The link between the provision of educational and technical services, on the one hand, and other key elements such as reduced

1 UNDP, Human Development Report 1990 (Oxford and New York, Oxford University Press, 1990).

2 A/43/430, annex I.

3 A/44/315, annex.

4 A/45/427, annex, appendix II.

5 World Bank, Sub Saharan Africa: From Crisis to Sustainable Growth (Washington D.C., 1989).

infant mortality, enhanced food security, reduced malnutrition and enhanced female education, on the other hand, remains to be adequately worked out in a majority of cases. In cases where the link has been articulated and applied, there is evidence of a rapidly increasing use of services and declining family size. It is generally realized in Africa and by Africa's development partners that Africa's rapid rate of population growth, averaging over 3 per cent per year, slows the rate of Africa's recovery and development, thus constituting a development issue to be dealt with seriously. During the period of the Programme of Action, there has been a clear downward trend in per capita health spending in real dollar terms, despite gains made in such areas as mother and child health care and immunization. Some diseases made a resurgence in Africa in the 1980s as health expenditures declined, with roughly two out of every three Africans now suffering from one or more debilitating diseases. The problem of declining health services is exacerbated by the continuing phenomenon of the "brain drain" with respect to trained personnel in the health field.

25. Over the 1986-1990 period, war imposed heavy human as well as financial costs on Africa (45 billion dollars in southern Africa alone, according to United Nations estimates). As of 1990, efforts to achieve peace have made substantial progress in southern Africa and other parts of the continent. The consolidation of survival policies and infrastructural safeguards is crucial in those areas, as is their more effective pursuit in the remaining war-ravaged States.

Trade and commodities

26. African States have given priority to policies to restore export growth. The quantitative rise in export growth to 4 per cent indicates considerable success. Unfortunately, declines in terms of trade have more than cancelled out this achievement in real export-value terms. African States have sought to act on the Programme of Action priority focus of commodity market improvement. Market prices for basic commodities, in general, continued to fall. Compensation or stabilization schemes were unable to compensate for declining commodity revenues during the period of the Programme of Action. African Governments were unable to move rapidly towards structural diversification and transformation of export patterns. Furthermore, Africa has in many cases lost market share in the face of new sources of competition, although some countries have adopted policies to regain it.

Debt service

27. African States have developed a common set of guidelines for agreed debt and debt-service reduction (African Common Position on Africa's External Debt Crisis (1987)),[1] which was updated in 1989 and discussed at the forty-fourth session of the General Assembly, and they have devoted on average 30 per cent of export earnings to debt service. The 30 per cent of export earnings paid out covered only about 60 per cent of the debt service payable. The balance was largely rescheduled in ways that stretched out the repayments of the obligations without reducing them or it was added onto rising arrears balances. The Programme of Action goal of resolving the African external debt crisis remains largely unmet. External debt (largely from increased arrears, rescheduled amounts and accrued interest) rose 35 per cent between 1986 and 1990. Although many donor countries cancelled or rescheduled debt on concessional terms, both before and during the Programme of Action period - for example, at the Third Francophone Conference of Heads of State and Government, held at Dakar in May 1989 - in accordance, *inter alia*, with relevant United Nations resolutions, a substantial portion of that external debt remains extremely difficult to service. The debt burden complicated Africa's task of increasing investment and rational planning with respect to fiscal and external accounts. A number of creditor countries and institutions have recently put forward proposals involving greater debt and debt-service reduction for low-income countries, many of which are located in Africa. Since 1985, the Paris Club has eased the terms on which official bilateral debt is rescheduled for the severely indebted low-income countries, many of which are located in Africa. In June 1988, at the Toronto Economic Summit, the group of seven major industrialized countries reached an agreement consisting of options to be chosen by creditor countries, which include partial write-offs, longer repayment periods and concessional interest rates.[2] At the Second United Nations Conference on the Least Developed Countries, in September 1990, there was a call for the cancellation of all official bilateral debt owed by least developed countries and other low-income countries that faced severe debt problems and were implementing sound economic policies in the context of International Monetary Fund programmes.[3] Another proposal was made to modify the Toronto terms of rescheduling by Paris Club creditors in a number of ways. In 1991, the group of seven major industrialized countries agreed on the need for additional debt-relief measures, going well beyond the relief already granted under the Toronto terms. The Trinidad and Tobago terms,[4] proposed in September 1990, as well as other proposals, are now under consideration in the Paris Club. An early agreement on these proposals, combined with appropriate adjustment actions by the African countries themselves, would make a genuine contribution to improving the economic prospects of the countries concerned. More recently, bolder initiatives, such as the recent debt-reduction agreements, have aroused high expectations among debt-distressed countries in Africa. The Personal Representative of the Secretary-General on debt proposed the cancellation of 90 per cent of the bilateral debt service of poor countries and the conversion of the remainder to highly concessional long-term loans. He also proposed that Toronto-type debt relief should be extended to African middle-income countries, as well as more concessional development financing.

Social and political stability

28. Problems associated with governance, accountability and the international economic environment have constrained African growth and development. These problems have hampered domestic savings and private investment flows, which are critical for increased productivity and growth. There is recognition within Africa of the link between improved governance and accountability, a favourable international economic environment and successful long-term development. There has been progress in improving participation and stability in Africa during the period of the Programme of Action. The number of States severely affected by war has been reduced. The freedom of people to pursue their daily lives and livelihood without fear of violence or arbitrary intervention by any person or institution has risen. Participation and human rights have been endorsed in the African Charter for Popular Participation in Development and Transformation.[5] Progress in policies and practices to promote participation and make rights more secure is visible in many States. The enjoyment of human rights under the rule of law is becoming more strongly enshrined.

Implementation at the regional and subregional levels

29. Subregional and regional implementation have received significant attention, especially in eastern and southern Africa. The small size of virtually all African States means that many common goals can be pursued more efficiently in common, or on a coordinated basis, than separately. The Preferential Trade Area for Eastern and Southern African States has made significant progress towards enabling trade expansion via tariff preference, commercial clearing facilitation and documentary plus procedural harmonization. The Southern African Development Coordination Conference has coordinated transport and communications rehabilitation and development, knowledge creation (especially in agriculture and food security), production expansion and the mobilization of domestic and external finance for regionally identified priority projects, with substantial positive results. Other groupings - the Economic Community of West African States, the Arab Maghreb Union, the Union of Central African States and the Economic Community of Central African States -

1 A/42/874, annex II:

2 See A/43/435-S/19974.

3 See A/CONF.147/18, part one, sect.III.C.

4 See A/45/803.

5 A/45/427, annex, appendix II.

have had important results. The Organization of African Unity has increased its economic policy analysis and coordination capacity, leading to the African Common Position on Africa's External Debt Crisis (1987)[1] and to the adoption on 3 June 1991 at Abuja, Nigeria, of the Treaty establishing the African Economic Community.

D. Actions of the International Community

Governments of resource-transferring countries

Resource flows

30. Donor Governments understood the need in the Programme of Action for complementary resources to support the reforms and transformations to which the African States have committed themselves. A significant number have sought to act accordingly and have maintained or increased real resource transfers via official development assistance since 1985, despite, in several cases, significant budgetary constraints of their own. They have remained committed to Africa in the context of new needs in western Asia, as well as in central and eastern Europe. However, despite the fact that sub-Saharan African countries received, on a per capita basis, significantly larger official development assistance than other low- and middle-income countries and despite a 50 per cent current price increase in official development assistance to sub-Saharan Africa, the effects of this assistance have not met expectations.

31. Bilateral official development assistance, broadly defined, rose in current prices from 10.6 to 16.8 billion dollars. However, in constant 1986 prices, the change was from 13.1 to 13.9 billion dollars, only marginally over 1 per cent per year. Meanwhile, net export credits fell 50 per cent even in current terms, from over 2 billion dollars in 1985 to 1 billion dollars in 1990. Net private flows other than from non-governmental organizations fell from 1.8 billion dollars to 1.4 billion dollars in current prices. Non-governmental organization flows rose in current terms from 1 billion to 1.6 billion dollars, or about 1 per cent per year in constant price terms.

Trade and commodities

32. Action to enhance African market access and diversification of exports and to reduce instability and catastrophic falls in commodity prices, as well as to provide compensatory finance for declines, was featured prominently in the Programme of Action. Protectionist barriers persist. African economies still depend on commodity exports, and diversification represents one of the highest priorities. The Stabex[2] and Sysmin[3] systems and the Swiss Compensatory Financing Programme already exist. Various constraints, including conditionality and interest rates, restrict access to International Monetary Fund compensatory facilities. After having reached a peak in the 1970s, commodity prices have collapsed to unprecedentedly low levels. Although exports grew in volume by 10 per cent during the 1986-1990 period over the 1981-1985 period, the share of African exports in world trade was dropping dramatically during the 1986-1990 period.

Debt obligations

33. Debt discussion has continued, and in the past two years creditor country positions have altered significantly. In order to strengthen efforts to relieve the debt burden, creditor countries have presented a number of proposals for further debt alleviation. The proposed Trinidad and Tobago terms[4] would provide for a 50 per cent debt-burden reduction - by write-offs, interest-rate cuts or repayment spread-out - on official debt, including guaranteed export credits for low-income debt-distressed countries pursuing serious policy reforms and transformations. Recent debt-reduction agreements take similar approaches to debt-distressed middle- and low-income countries. Some donor countries have proposed cuts of up to 80 per cent for the most severely debt-distressed low-income sub-Saharan African economies. The Trinidad and Tobago terms envisage similar cuts in commercial external debt, with the present secondary market price (usually under 25 per cent of face value for debt-distressed countries and under 10 per cent for several African ones) as the starting point. Some buy-ups, by individual donors or under World Bank auspices, have taken place.

34. These shifts have been too resent to have a major impact to date. However, they do augur well for the 1990s. About 3 per cent of Africa's debt burden was cancelled or rescheduled at concessional interest rates over the 1986-1990 period. Because this was largely on concessional loans, debt service due was reduced by under 2 per cent and debt service actually being paid was reduced by only 1 per cent. Other rescheduling did not reduce the total burden of payment (indeed by lengthening the period over which interest was payable, the rescheduling often raised it) but simply shifted it forward, providing some relief from arrears build-up for a year or two at a time.

Technical and other external assistance

35. Technical assistance was approximately 25 per cent of official development assistance throughout the period. Problems remained, such as inadequate recipient participation in the selection of experts and the accountability of technical assistance personnel to national institutions and in the decision-making processes in Africa. The enhanced number of donor-paid and other technical-assistance personnel and the increased hiring of African nationals for such posts did increase short-term capability but at the price of fragmenting national policy formulation and implementation and of threatening longer-term African institutional and public service capacity-building. More positively, joint ventures with African training institutions and the creation, by the African Development Bank, the United Nations Development Programme and the World Bank, of the African Capacity Building Foundation were encouraging developments.

United Nations system

36. The United Nations system - including the World Bank and the International Monetary Fund - sought to influence and to support African efforts to regain development through structural adjustment and transformation of policies and resource allocations. Multilateral official development finance rose from 5.3 billion dollars in 1985 to 8.5 billion dollars in 1990 or from 5.8 billion dollars to 6.5 billion dollars in 1986 constant prices.

37. A substantial portion of the increase was centred on the World Bank, whose lending increased from an overall average of about 1.8 billion dollars during the 1981-1985 fiscal period to around 3 billion dollars during the 1986-1991 fiscal period. With respect to International Development Association replenishments eight and nine, sub-Saharan Africa's share of a sustained constant total was raised from 33 per cent to 50 per cent. In addition, the World Bank spearheaded a Special Programme of Assistance for Africa to mobilize and coordinate bilateral funds, which provided 18 billion dollars in adjustment assistance and debt relief to twenty-three eligible African countries between 1988 and 1990. The World Bank also helped fund the African Capacity Building Foundation to assist in developing the central economic analysis and management units in African Governments.

38. The International Monetary Fund reduced net drawings by African States by 2 billion dollars during the 1985-1990 period. While 8-9 per cent short-term drawings were unsuitable for African requirements, the Structural Adjustment Facility and its extended version, which are long-term low-interest facilities, remain less than half-utilized and did not fully offset reduction in standard terms drawings.

39. Other United Nations agencies raised disbursements on behalf of Africa to about 1.5 billion dollars and to 50 per cent of all resources provided globally, in particular through special programmes for African countries affected by drought and desertifisation. While their programmes were focused mainly on and tested against the Programme of Action goals, they were limited in constant-price terms. This limitation flowed from the financial stringency confronting most United Nations agencies, and the United Nations Development Programme in particular, during the period 1986-1990.

---

1 A/42/874, annex II.

2 System of stabilization of export earnings.

3 System for stabilizing export earnings in the mining sector.

4 See A/45/803.

South-South cooperation

40. Global South-South cooperation with Africa was enhanced during the 1986-1990 period. The focus was primarily on southern African economic and human survival in the fase of destabilization. The Action for Resisting Invasion, Colonialism and Apartheid Fund[1] established by the Movement of Non-Aligned Countries raised and disbursed not insignificant resources in this respect. Bilaterally, several South economies provided substantial technical and financial support to Africa.

Non-governmental organizations

41. Non-governmental organizations, as noted, increased resource transfers to Africa. In some cases these transfers assisted the strengthening of African non-governmental organizations and worked in partnership with or through them. In the North, the non-governmental organizations were among the most effective publicists and resource mobilizers for Africa in general and the Programme of Action in particular. The International Conference on Popular Participation in the Recovery and Development Process in Africa, held at Arusha in February 1990, marked the recognition by both African and cooperating States that African non-governmental organizations and similar groupings had a crucial role in transforming human-centred development and good governance from goals into realities.[2]

Structural adjustment programmes

42. Structural adjustment describes a set of actions by African Governments responding to their perseptions of the policy requirements needed to restore economic balance and to mobilize external resources for recovery and structural transformation. Likewise, structural adjustment programmes incorporated the views of the World Bank and bilateral resource donors of the macroeconomic policy weaknesses that hampered effective response to economic shocks in many African States.

43. Prior to 1985, structural adjustment programmes, as the World Bank acknowledged in the long-term perspective study, were often too short term in approach and, as a result, depended too heavily on demand reduction. Since 1985 there has been a shift towards supply expansion, initially underwritten largely by external resource flows but, subsequently, partly by renewed growth of domestic output. Human investment and poverty reduction have emerged as major themes in structural adjustment and increased effort is being devoted to integrating them with the other macroeconomic policy goals.

44. Structural adjustment programmes, when also oriented towards the medium and long-term development needs of the countries that have been implementing them and when persisted in, have, on average, resulted in output growth equal to or above population growth and also in significant increases in external resource inflows. Equally, most have resulted in a halting of previous declines in human investment and basic services spending. But their record on reduction of inflation, reduction of trade deficits and a reduction in numbers of people living in absolute poverty is much more uneven and not yet satisfactory, as the World Bank long-term perspective study notes. How to resolve these problems and to ensure that new rounds of African-owned country programmes achieve both sustainable growth and a substantial improvement in the human condition is a crucial question for the 1990s, which the African Governments, the World Bank, the United Nations Development Programme, and other resource providers are focusing on in national consultative groups, round-table discussions and other forums.

II. United Nations New Agenda for the Development of Africa in the 1990s

A. Preamble

1. The final review and appraisal of the implementation of the United Nations Programme of Action for African Economic Recovery and Development 1986-1990 offers yet another opportunity for renewing the commitment of the international community to support Africa's own efforts to achieve self-sustaining socio-economic growth and development. It is also an occasion to refocus world attention on the socio-economic difficulties which continue to face the African countries. Africa's development is primarily the responsibility of Africans. The international community accepts the principle of shared responsibility and full partnership with Africa and therefore commits itself to giving full and tangible support to the African efforts.

2. The circumstances which led to the adoption of the Programme of Action are as valid today as they were in 1986. Assessments made by African countries themselves or by the Secretary-General and many other organizations and independent observers point to the fact that Africa's socio-economic conditions actually worsened overall over the past five years of the Programme of Action period.

3. The current critical economic situation in Africa calls for solidarity among States Members to act in concert to address the problem. The international community renews its efforts to assist Africa, as enunciated under the Programme of Action and in General Assembly resolution 43/27 of 18 November 1988, in which the Assembly stated, *inter alia*, that "the African economic crisis is one that concerns the international community as a whole" and that "the Programme of Action provides an important framework for cooperation between Africa and the international community", which needs to be renewed in the 1990s.

4. That is why the international community and the countries of Africa should renew their commitment to an agenda of cooperation for sustainable social and economic development of Africa in the 1990s. The agenda is specific and clearly focused on goals and targets to be achieved within that time-frame.

5. A desirable objective should be an average real growth rate of at least 6 per cent per annum of gross national product throughout the period of the New Agenda in order for the continent to achieve sustained and sustainable economic growth and equitable development, increase income and eradicate poverty.

6. The New Agenda has as its priority objectives the accelerated transformation, integration, diversification and growth of the African economies, in order to strengthen them within the world economy, reduce their vulnerability to external shocks and increase their dynamism, internalize the process of development and enhance self-reliance.

7. The New Agenda also accords special attention to human development and increased productive employment, and promotes rapid progress towards the achievement of human-oriented goals by the year 2000 in the areas of life expectancy, integration of women in development, child and maternal mortality, nutrition, health, water and sanitation, basic education and shelter.

8. Peace is an indispensable prerequisite for development. The end of the cold war has opened up opportunities for the peaceful resolution of conflicts and for the intensification of international cooperation for development, particularly with Africa. Peace initiatives by African countries should be encouraged and pursued in order to bring an end to war, destabilization and internal conflicts so as to facilitate the creation of optimal conditions for development. The international community as a whole should endeavour to cooperate with and support the efforts of African countries for a rapid restoration of peace, normalization of life for uprooted populations and national socio-economic reconstruction. Resources freed from military expenditures in all countries can be redirected to socio-economic growth and development.

9. In order to achieve these broad objectives, it is necessary for the international community to enter into a new and stronger accord with Africa, which would spell out clearly the firm commitment of the international community to support and assist Africa in its efforts to implement successfully its development agenda and to reduce, if not entirely eliminate, external impediments and obstacles to Africa's accelerated socio-economic transformation. This New Agenda reflects a mutuality of commitments and accountability and is in two parts: what Africa commits itself to do and what the international community commits itself to do.

---
1 Also called the Africa Fund.

2 A/45/427, annex, appendix II.

B. International Agenda

1. Africa's responsibility and commitment

(a) *Achievement of sustained and sustainable growth and development*

10. Africa is committed to the implementation of policies for the transformation of the structure of its economies in order to achieve growth and development on a sustained and sustainable basis. African countries will persist with necessary reforms and pursue improvement of domestic economic management, including effective mobilization and utilization of domestic resources.

(b) *Promotion of regional and subregional economic cooperation and integration*

11. Africa is resolved to pursue with vigour the policy of achieving effective regional and subregional economic cooperation and integration and is thus committed to the establishment of the African Economic Community - the treaty of which was signed by African leaders on 3 June 1991 at Abuja, Nigeria - and to the effective functioning of its subregional organizations - namely, the Preferential Trade Area of Eastern and Southern African States, the Economic Community of West African States, the Arab Maghreb Union and the Southern African Development Coordination Conference. Africa believes that regional and subregional cooperation and integration will bring about effective transformation of its economies.

12. Africa is committed to the promotion of the sectorial integration of its economies and to ensuring the development and maintenance of reliable networks of agricultural, physical, industrial and institutional infrastructures on the continent. Africa will focus its efforts on the implementation of programmes for the Second Transport and Communications Decade in Africa and the Second Industrial Development Decade for Africa.

(c) *Intensification of the democratization process*

13. Africa is determined to press ahead with the democratization of development and the full implementation of the African Charter on Human and Peoples' Rights, the African Charter for Popular Participation in Development and Transformation,[1] and the Declaration of the Assembly of Heads of State and Government of the Organization of African Unity on the Political and Socio-economic Situation in Africa and the Fundamental Changes Taking Place in the World, adopted on 11 July 1990. Africa is convinced that growth and development on a sustained and sustainable basis can come about only as a result of the full participation of the people in the development process, and to this end continues to be committed to pursuing the process of democratization.

(d) *Investment promotion*

14. Africa is also committed to the creation of an enabling environment that attracts foreign and domestic direct investment, encourages savings, induces the return of flight capital and promotes the full participation by the private sector, including non-governmental organizations, in the growth and development process. Farmers - in particular, small farmers - informal-sector traders and crafts people, and entrepreneurs constitute important elements in the productive base of the economy.

(e) *Human dimension*

15. Africa is equally committed to improving the human rights and the living standards of its people, including the reduction of poverty. Africa is further committed to ensuring equality of opportunity for women at all levels and giving adequate attention to the needs of children.

16. African countries are committed to the intensification of their efforts in human resource development and capacity-building, especially in science, technology and management, and to taking measures to arrest and reverse the brain drain.

(f) *Environment and development*

17. Africa is fully committed to the promotion of sustainable development at all levels of socio-economic activity. Through the Bamako Convention, adopted on 30 January 1991 at Bamako, Africa took the decisive step of banning the import of toxic waste into Africa. Moreover, the Plan of Action to Combat Desertifisation[2] remains a viable framework for cooperation in the field of desertifisation. The international community is called upon to contribute more effectively to the implementation of the Plan. The programme of relevant subregional organizations should continue to receive the full support of Africa and the international community. Africa is keenly participating in international negotiations on climate change, bio-diversity and the preparatory process of the United Nations Conference on Environment and Development, to be held in 1992. In all these negotiations, Africa is fully convinced that the problems of environment and development should be tackled in an integrated and balanced manner, fully taking into account the "polluter pays" principle.

(g) *Population and development*

18. Africa is committed to the deliberate and systematic integration of population factors into the development process in order, *inter alia*, to contain the tremendous strain and stress that a rapid rate of population growth puts on development. To that end, Africa will continue the efforts initiated in 1984 under the Kilimanjaro Programme of Action for African Population and Self-Reliant Development,[3] which currently constitutes Africa's framework for devising and implementing national population policies in all their interrelated aspects, including a reduction in maternal and child mortality and provisions for family planning and female education and the achievement of substantial and sustained increases in the quality of life and standard of living of the entire population. In this regard, reference is also made to the Amsterdam Declaration on a Better Life for Future Generations, adopted by the International Forum on Population in the Twenty-first Century, held at Amsterdam from 6 to 9 November 1989.[4]

(h) *Agriculture, rural development and food security*

19. Africa is committed to the continued pursuit of policies and strategies in the agricultural and rural development sectors in order fully to integrate rural economies into their national contexts and to achieve food security and strengthen self-reliance in food. Africa is committed to the improvement of agricultural policies, the enhancement of agricultural productivity, the improvement of distribution mechanisms, and the establishment of reliable market schemes, credit systems and adequate storage facilities. Efforts will be made to provide food producers - particularly women - with the necessary resources.

(i) *South-South cooperation*

20. Africa is determined to intensify South-South cooperation which Africa is convinced is an indispensable element for the success of the New Agenda for international cooperation.

(j) *Role of non-governmental organizations*

21. The focus of the International Agenda on popular participation, human resource development and capacity-building calls for an increased role for non-governmental organizations (African and non-African) in various areas, including the promotion of indigenous small-scale businesses, especially in the rural sector, community development projects, training etc. African non-governmental organizations should particularly be involved, without any administrative impediment, in the mobilization and efficient utilization of domestic resources.

2. Responsibility and commitment of the international community

22. The international community commits itself to assisting Africa in its efforts to achieve accelerated growth and human-centred devel-

1 A/45/427, annex, appendix II.

2 *Report of the United nations Conference on Desertification, Nairobi, 29 August - 9 September 1977* (A/CONF.74/36), chap. I.

3 E/CONF.76/6, annex V.

4 A/C.2/44/6, annex.

opment on a sustained and sustainable basis. Such support will cover the areas discussed below.

(a) *Solution of Africa's debt problem*

23. Africa's debt burden constitutes a critical bottleneck constraining the recovery and development of the continent. Therefore, a major priority is to tackle Africa's external debt problem which is a serious threat to the continent's recovery and long-term development prospects. In spite of the implementation of several international initiatives, the situation has not significantly improved. Africa's external debt exceeded 270 billion dollars in 1990, with the ratio of external debt to gross domestic product and to exports amounting to over 90 per cent and 334 per cent, respectively. The servicing of this debt accounts for over 30 per cent of the continent's exports.

24. This situation calls for innovative and bold measures to solve Africa's debt problems and the intensification of efforts in the context of the evolving international debt strategy on the part of all concerned. The international community, therefore, in support of Africa's economic reform efforts, undertakes to seek to find durable solutions to the African debt crisis.

25. At the London Economic Summit in July 1991,[1] the group of seven major industrialized countries agreed that Africa deserved special attention. Participants called for additional debt relief measures in favour of the poorest, most indebted countries, that go well beyond the Toronto terms. It called on the Paris Club to continue its discussion on how these measures can best be implemented promptly.

26. Recognizing the magnitude of Africa's debt problem, the measures envisioned by this New Agenda include:

(*a*) A further cancellation or reduction of official development assistance debt and debt service;

(*b*) Additional relief for official bilateral debt or debt service;

(*c*) Encouragement of the write-off of private commercial debt and the use of such techniques as debt-equity swaps, the use of debt where appropriate for the establishment of export-oriented joint ventures, debt buy-backs, debt for environment schemes and debt for poverty alleviation through greater use of the appropriate facilities;

(*d*) Serious consideration to continuing to work towards a growth-oriented solution of the problems of African developing countries with serious debt-servicing problems, including those whose debt is mainly to official creditors or to multilateral institutions;

(*e*) Early implementation of the International Monetary Fund quota increase under the Ninth General Review and the associated Third Amendment to the Articles of Agreement.

27. Additional measures should take into account the need for Africa to benefit from new financial flows, particularly official development assistance.

28. The international community should continue to give serious consideration to the proposal calling for the organization of an international conference on Africa's external indebtedness.

(b) *Resource flows*

29. A critical element of the support from the international community is the provision of adequate resource flows to Africa. These resources are needed to contribute to achieving sustained real growth in gross national product per capita. To achieve an average annual growth rate of real gross national product of at least 6 per cent by African countries over the course of the 1990s the Secretary-General has estimated that a minimum of 30 billion dollars in net official development assistance is required in 1992, after which the real net official development assistance would need to grow at an average rate of 4 per cent per annum. The international community undertakes to pursue its efforts to provide additional resource flows to Africa which will complement domestic efforts and financial resources, bearing in mind these targets. The international community also reaffirms its commitment to work in order to attain the accepted United Nations targets of devoting 0.7 per cent of gross national product to official development assistance as well as the agreed targets established at the Second United Nations Conference on the Least Developed Countries.[2]

30. The international community would introduce measures and devise programmes to encourage direct foreign investment in African countries and support the policy changes undertaken by African countries to attract foreign investment.

(c) *Commodities*

31. Diversification is a strategic short- and long-term solution to the severe commodity problem in Africa which has impeded its economic recovery and development. In order to support effectively efforts to diversify commodity exports and boost earnings, the international community, particularly the major trading partners, commit themselves to grant improved market access to Africa's exports through substantial reduction in or removal of trade barriers. To this end, the international community should ensure an early balanced and successful conclusion of the Uruguay Round. The international community commits itself to correct imperfections in commodity markets.

32. In the short term, the international community recognizes the importance of compensatory financing through such schemes as the Compensatory and Contingency Financing Facility of the International Monetary Fund, Stabex,[3] Sysmin[4] and the Swiss Compensatory Financing Programme and, where appropriate, will examine the means of improving the scope and operations of these schemes. Efforts at international cooperation among producers and consumers of commodities of particular importance to Africa should be renewed, with a view to increasing export earnings of Africa from such commodities through processing and technical assistance.

(d) *Support for the diversification of the African economies*

33. Diversification of the African economies provides a major way out of commodity export dependence and its related problems and contributes to the achievement of more dynamic and resilient economies. While such diversification is primarily the responsibility of African countries, the international community recognizes that additional resources will be required to support Africa's diversification programmes, including development of specific infrastructural and support services and the development of information networks and related services for diversification programmes and projects.

34. The international community notes the proposal that an African diversification fund should be established to provide an essential focal point to galvanize the technical assistance that is required and to provide additional finance for the development and implementation of diversification programmes and projects.

35. A study on the need for and the feasibility of the establishment of a diversification fund for Africa's commodities should urgently be undertaken by the Secretary-General for presentation in 1993 to the General Assembly together with the comments and observations of Member States. The international community will continue to support Africa's effort.

(e) *Trade*

36. In order to support effectively efforts to diversify Africa's economies and to boost export earnings, the international community commits itself to a substantial reduction in or removal of tariff and non-tariff barriers affecting African exports, particularly of processed, semi-processed and manufactured products, and to ensure continued preferential arrangements currently enjoyed by African exports. To this end, the international community should ensure an early balanced and successful conclusion of the Uruguay Round.

(f) *Support for regional economic integration: environment, science and technology*

37. The international community intends to support African countries in their efforts to establish the African Economic Community,

1 See A/46/309-S/22807, annex I.

2 See A/CONF.147/18.

3 System for stabilization of export earnings.

4 System of stabilizing export earning in the mining sector.

strengthen the functioning of the existing subregional intergovernmental organizations and implement joint programmes and projects.

38. Support will also be given to arresting environmental degradation and to enhancing the scientific and technological capacities of African countries.

(g) *Role of the United Nations system*

39. The United Nations system should play a major role in the implementation of the International Agenda. First and foremost, the various United Nations organizations and specialized agencies, in their respective areas and sectors, should devise specific programmes for Africa which are consistent with the elements of the Agenda, and devote adequate resources for their implementation. In this regard, special consideration should be given to programmes that are essential in fostering the economic integration of the African region, such as those related to the Second Industrial Development Decade for Africa and the Second Transport and Communications Decade in Africa, as well as other relevant programmes submitted by regional and subregional organizations.

40. The United Nations system should also contribute to ensuring an efficient follow-up and monitoring of the implementation of the International Agenda. Specifically, a continuous assessment of Africa's performance in the areas outlined in the Agenda would have a great impact in maintaining the momentum within and outside Africa and, eventually, for renewed commitments to the agreed objectives and targets.

(h) *Role of non-African non-governmental organizations*

41. Non-African non-governmental organizations should be given every encouragement to assist in the formulation and implementation of development assistance projects in the context of the International Agenda. They should also assist in promoting non-governmental organizations at the national, subregional and regional levels in Africa.

C. Follow-Up, Monitoring and Evaluation Machinery

42. The follow-up, monitoring and evaluation of the implementation of the New Agenda will require the full involvement of Governments, organizations and programmes of the United Nations system as well as the participation of intergovernmental and non-governmental organizations.

43. To that end the following arrangements for the evaluation, assessment and monitoring of the New Agenda are adopted:

(*a*) In 1993 the General Assembly will conduct a preliminary consideration of the implementation of the New Agenda;

(*b*) In 1995 the Economic and Social Council will devote part of its high-level segment to the consideration of the implementation of the New Agenda;

(*c*) In 1996 the General Assembly will conduct a mid-term review of the implementation of the New Agenda;

(*d*) In 1998 the Economic and Social Council will devote part of its high-level segment to the implementation of the New Agenda;

(*e*) In the year 2000 the General Assembly will conduct the final review and assessment of the implementation of the New Agenda.

44. For the mid-term review in 1996 and the final review and assessment in the year 2000, the General Assembly will take the necessary measures, including, if required, the establishment of an *Ad hoc* committee for the preparation of these reviews.

45. The Secretary-General, taking into account the relevant inputs from relevant organs, organizations and programmes of the United Nations system and other competent bodies, will provide an analytical assessment of the implementation of the New Agenda and make concrete recommendations thereon to the General Assembly and the Economic and Social Council, according to the arrangements outlined in paragraph 43 above.

46. The assessment and recommendations of the Organization of African Unity on the implementation of the New Agenda will also be submitted to the General Assembly and the Economic and Social Council.

47. The Secretary-General will ensure appropriate and adequate support for the follow-up process, including the continuation of the effective public information activities and mobilization of efforts to raise international awareness of the economic crisis in Africa.

48. The ongoing initiatives aimed at assisting Africa in its development efforts should be encouraged. In this regard, consultative groups such as the Global Coalition for Africa should assist in rallying international support for the implementation of the New Agenda. The Global Coalition for Africa may be invited to attend the meetings of the General Assembly and the Economic and Social Council devoted to the New Agenda for Africa.

43/181. Global Strategy for Shelter to the Year 2000

Committee: 2
Vote: Adopted without a vote
Ref.: 48/178, 46/163, 44/173, 42/191, 41/190, 40/203, 39/171, 38/168, 37/221, 36/71

The General Assembly,

Bearing in mind the Vancouver Declaration on Human Settlements, 1976[1] and the recommendations for national action[2] adopted at Habitat: United Nations Conference on Human Settlements,

Recalling its resolution 35/56 of 5 December 1980, the annex to which contains the International Development Strategy for the Third United Nations Development Decade, in which, *inter alia*, the importance of the provision of basic shelter and infrastructure was stressed,

Recalling also its resolution 37/221 of 20 December 1982, by which it proclaimed the year 1987 International Year of Shelter for the Homeless,

Recalling further its resolution 42/191 of 11 December 1987, in which it decided that there should be a Global Strategy for Shelter to the Year 2000,

Recalling the Nairobi Forward-looking Strategies for the Advancement of Women,[3]

Recalling Commission on Human Settlements resolutions 9/9 of 16 May 1986[4] and 10/17 of 16 April 1987[5] on the participation of women in the solution of human settlements problems,

Recalling also Commission on Human Settlements resolution 10/16 of 16 April 1987[6] on the effect of the external debt of the developing countries and their ability to raise the funds needed to solve the housing problems of the homeless up to the year 2000,

Taking note of Commission on Human Settlements resolution 11/7 of 11 April 1988[7] entitled "Coordination and cooperation with agencies and organizations within the United Nations system",

Convinced that the continuous, coordinated and widely based efforts of Governments, organizations of the United Nations system, other intergovernmental and non-governmental organizations and individuals, when guided by an appropriate strategy, will reverse the alarming trends in the field of human settlements and produce clear and visible improvements in the shelter and neighbourhoods of the

---

1 *Report of Habitat: United Nations Conference on Human Settlements, Vancouver, 31 May - 11 June 1976* (United Nations publication, Sales No. E.76.IV.7 and corrigendum), chap. I.

2 *Ibid.*, chap. II.

3 *Report of the World Conference to Review and Appraise the Achievements of the United Nations Decade for Women: Equality, Development and Peace, Nairobi, 15 - 26 July 1985* (United Nations publication, Sales No. E.85.IV.10), chap. I, sect. A.

4 See *Official Records of the General Assembly, Forty-first Session, Supplement No. 8* (A/41/8), annex I, sect. A.

5 *Ibid., Forty-second Session, Supplement No. 8* and corrigendum (A/42/8 and Corr. 1), annex I, sect. A.

6 *Ibid.*

7 *Ibid., Forty-third Session, Supplement No. 8* (A/43/8), annex I, sect. A.

poor and disadvantaged by the year 2000, and that this should be a global responsibility,

Encouraged by action already taken or being taken in many countries to prepare national shelter strategies and to adopt other measures that will promote achievement of the goal of shelter for all,

Recognizing that, despite such efforts, more than one billion people have shelter unfit for human habitation, that this number will increase dramatically, partly as a result of population and urbanization trends, and that determined measures must be taken aimed at profiting from these trends, rather than being penalized by them,

Also recognizing that the International Year of Shelter for the Homeless has confirmed the need to intensify national and international efforts to produce, deliver and improve shelter for all, with specific emphasis on the poor and disadvantaged,

Convinced that shelter problems are universal, that no country has yet completely met its shelter needs, and that every country can profit from the experience of others,

Also convinced that shelter problems are a global concern requiring solutions that relate to other global problems and also requiring the efforts of all countries to reach such solutions, that the demand for shelter in each country can be met by applying a set of common principles, but that goals can only be met by the individual efforts of each Government acting in its own political, economic, social and cultural context,

Recognizing that the core of the Global Strategy for Shelter to the Year 2000[1] consists of integrated national shelter strategies that need to be based on a full understanding of the scale and nature of the problem and the national resource base available to address the problem,

Recognizing also that national shelter strategies need to contain four complementary parts: clear and measurable objectives; national mobilization and distribution of financial resources; promotion of shelter production and improvement with special reference to the management of land, the provision of infrastructure and encouragement of the use of appropriate building materials and technology; and the gradual reorganization of the shelter sector,

1. *Adopts* the Global Strategy for Shelter to the Year 2000;

2. *Decides* that the main objective of the Strategy is to facilitate adequate shelter for all by the year 2000, that the main focus should therefore be on improving the situation of the disadvantaged and the poor, and that the following fundamental objectives and principles should form the basis of the Strategy:

(*a*) Enabling policies, whereby the full potential and resources of all governmental and non-governmental actors in the field of human settlements are utilized, must be at the heart of national and international efforts;

(*b*) Women, as income-earners, home-makers and heads of households, and women's organizations fulfil a crucial role as contributors to the solution of human settlements problems, which should be fully recognized and reflected in equal participation of women in the elaboration of housing policies, programmes and projects, and the specific interests and capabilities of women should be adequately represented in human settlements policy formulation and in government mechanisms employed at all levels for the implementation of housing policies, programmes and projects;

(*c*) Shelter and development are mutually supportive and interdependent, and policies must be developed in full recognition of the important links between shelter and economic development;

(*d*) The concept of sustainable development implies that the provision of shelter and urban development must be reconcilable with a sustainable management of the environment;

3. *Designates* the Commission on Human Settlements as the United Nations intergovernmental body responsible for coordinating, evaluating and monitoring the Strategy and the United Nations Centre for Human Settlements (Habitat) as the secretariat for the Strategy and the lead agency for coordinating and monitoring the relevant programmes and activities of other United Nations organizations and agencies concerned;

4. *Urges* Governments to develop appropriate national and subnational strategies for shelter in the light of the guidelines provided in the report of the Executive Director of the United Nations Centre for Human Settlements (Habitat) entitled "Global Strategy for Shelter to the Year 2000"[2] and to report regularly to the Commission on Human Settlements, beginning at its twelfth session, on their relevant experience and on progress achieved in implementing those strategies;

5. *Requests* the Executive Director to monitor the relevant global experience and progress of all countries in implementing the Strategy and to report thereon to the Commission, beginning at its thirteenth session;

6. *Decides* to review and clarify the Strategy on a biennial basis, within regular budgetary resources, with the assistance of experts selected on the basis of equitable geographic representation, and to revise the Strategy in the light of global and national experience from all regions and subregions;

7. *Requests* the Commission on Human Settlements, as the body designated to coordinate implementation of the Strategy, to report biennially to the General Assembly on progress made in its implementation;

8. *Also requests* the Commission to strengthen, within existing resources, its role in regard to the promotion of innovative measures by which bilateral and multilateral financial institutions may support the shelter strategies of developing countries, for example, by way of suitably devised loan agreements that would lead to the building up of national revolving funds for shelter;

9. *Requests* financial institutions and creditor countries to consider, as one of the conditions for the success of the Strategy, immediate measures to reduce the external debts by their conversion into long-term loans;

10. *Adopts* the guidelines for steps to be taken at the national and international levels, as set out in the annex to the present resolution, in support of the guidelines for national and international action contained in the Global Strategy for Shelter to the Year 2000,[3] prepared pursuant to its resolution 42/191;

11. *Calls upon* all States and others in a position to do so to make generous contributions to the United Nations Habitat and Human Settlements Foundation to facilitate implementation of the Strategy.

83rd plenary meeting
20 December 1988

Annex

I. Guidelines for steps to be taken at the national level

A. Consideration for Governments when Formulating a National Shelter Strategy

1. A national shelter strategy must spell out clear operational objectives for the development of shelter conditions both in terms of the construction of new housing and the upgrading and maintenance of existing housing stock and infrastructure and services.

2. In the definition of those objectives, development of shelter should be seen as a process whereby conditions are gradually improved for both men and women. The objectives need to address the scale of the problem, while the "adequate" standard aimed at should be identified on the basis of an analysis of the standards and options affordable to the target population and society at large. The objectives should be based on a comprehensive view of the magnitude and nature of the problem and of the available resource base, including the potential contribution of men and women. In addition to finance, land, manpower and institutions, building materials and technology also have

---

1 *Official Records of the General Assembly, Forty-third Session, Supplement No. 8*, addendum (A/43/8/Add.1).

2 HS/C/11/3. See also *Official Records of the General Assembly, Forty-third Session, Supplement No. 8*, addendum (A/43/8/Add.1).

3 *Ibid.*

to be considered irrespective of whether they are held by the public or private, formal or informal sector.

3. The objectives of the shelter sector need to be linked to the goals of overall economic policy, social policy, settlement policy and environmental policy.

4. The strategy needs to outline the action through which the objectives can be met. In an enabling strategy, actions such as the provision of infrastructure may mean the direct involvement of the public sector in shelter construction. The objective of "facilitating adequate shelter for all" also implies that direct government support should mainly be allocated to the most needy population groups.

5. The public sector is responsible for developing and implementing measures for national shelter policies and for the adoption of measures to stimulate the desired action by other sectors. This can be done through measures in areas such as the locally based small-scale building-materials industry, appropriate financial schemes or training programmes.

6. Another important component is the development of administrative, institutional and legislative tasks that are the direct responsibility of the Government, for example, land registration and regulation of construction.

7. An analysis of affordability will provide the criteria for defining the right priorities and appropriate approaches and standards for public sector involvement. Likewise, such an analysis gives the criteria for planning the indirect involvement of the public sector, that is, the type of activities to be promoted and the appropriate way of going about it.

8. The appropriate institutional framework for the implementation of a strategy must be identified, which may require much institutional reorganization. Each agency involved must have a clear understanding of its role within the overall organizational framework and of the tasks expected of it. Mechanisms for the coordination of inter- and intra-agency activities need to be developed. Mechanisms such as shelter coalitions are recommended and may be developed in partnership with the private and non-governmental sectors. Finally, arrangements for the continuous monitoring, review and revision of the strategy must be developed.

B. Steps to be Taken by Governments when Implementing a National Strategy

9. Work for the preparation of the strategy must be organized. For instance, a task force may be appointed for the actual work and a steering committee ensuring high-level political commitment set up to guide its work. Alternatively it may be possible to use existing mechanisms. Equal participation of women should be ensured at all levels.

10. Needs and resources must be assessed. Estimates are required of the needs in housing construction and in upgrading and maintenance, including housing-related infrastructure, as well as of the resources that can be mobilized during the period to the year 2000 to cover those needs.

11. Shelter options and standards that are affordable by the target groups and society at large must be analysed, taking into account both the scale of need and all the resources available - finance, land, manpower and institutions, building materials and technology.

12. Objectives must be set for the construction of new housing and for the upgrading and maintenance of the existing housing stock in terms both of the scale of the activities and of the housing standards to be met.

13. Action must be identified through which those objectives can be realistically met. The estimated required resources for this action must not exceed those that can be made available by society. The action includes both direct government involvement and measures needed to encourage, facilitate and integrate active participation of other sectors in shelter delivery.

14. A plan of action must be prepared in consultation and partnership with non-governmental organizations, people and their representatives, which:

(*a*) Lists the activities that are the direct responsibility of the public sector;

(*b*) Lists the activities to be taken to facilitate and encourage the other actors to carry out their part of the task;

(*c*) Outlines resource allocation to the aforementioned activities;

(*d*) Outlines the institutional arrangements for the implementation, coordination, monitoring and review of the strategy;

(*e*) Outlines a schedule for the activities of the various agencies.

II. Guidelines for steps to be taken at the international level

15. International action will be necessary to support the activities of countries in their endeavour to improve the housing situation of their poor and disadvantaged inhabitants. Such assistance should support national programmes and use know-how available locally and within the international community.

16. The goal of external assistance should be to enhance and support national capabilities to develop and implement national action components of the Global Strategy for Shelter to the Year 2000.

17. Mutual cooperation and exchange of information and expertise between developing countries in human settlement work stimulate and enrich national human settlement work.

18. The United Nations Centre for Human Settlements (Habitat) will act as the coordinating agency in the implementation of the Global Strategy for Shelter to the Year 2000, on the basis of biennial plans to be drawn up with the involvement of experts working with Governments and the Centre at the regional and subregional levels.

19. As the coordinating agency for the Strategy, the United Nations Centre for Human Settlements (Habitat) will stimulate international and national action by incorporating the Strategy in its future medium-term plans and biennial work programmes.

20. An inter-agency-level working arrangement will be made within the existing budget to provide continuous coordination of the Strategy.

21. The United Nations Centre for Human Settlements (Habitat) will prepare a reporting format to facilitate monitoring by the Commission on Human Settlements of progress achieved in the implementation of the Global Strategy.

50/103. Implementation of the Programme of Action for the Least Developed Countries for the 1990s

Committee: 2
Vote: Adopted without a vote
Ref.: 49/98, 48/171, 47/173, 46/156, 45/206, 40/205, 39/174, 38/195, 37/224, 36/194, 35/205, 34/203

The General Assembly,

Recalling its resolutions 45/206 of 21 December 1990, in which it endorsed the Paris Declaration and the Programme of Action for the Least Developed Countries for the 1990s[1] and 49/98 of 19 December 1994, in which it decided to convene the High-level Intergovernmental Meeting of the Mid-term Global Review of the Implementation of the Programme of Action for the Least Developed Countries for the 1990s,

Reaffirming the Paris Declaration and the Programme of Action, the prime objective of which is to arrest the further deterioration in the socio-economic situation of the least developed countries, to reactivate and accelerate growth and development in those countries and, in the process, to set them on the path of sustained economic growth and sustainable development,

Expressing serious concern that the least developed countries as a group have not been able to achieve many of the objectives of the Programme of Action and that their overall socio-economic situation has continued to deteriorate,

---

1 *Report of the Second United Nations Conference on the Least Developed Countries, Paris, 3-14 September 1990* (A/CONF.147/18), part one.

Noting with concern the reduced flow of development resources to the least developed countries, the resulting need to accord them priority in the allocation of concessional resources and their continued marginalization in world trade, as well as the fact that many least developed countries face serious debt problems and more than half are considered debt-distressed,

Taking note of agreed conclusions 423 (XLI) of 31 March 1995 of the Trade and Development Board[1] on the annual review of progress in the implementation of the Programme of Action for the Least Developed Countries for the 1990s, which was underpinned by The Least Developed Countries 1995 Report,[2]

Taking note of the note by the Secretary-General[3] transmitting the report of the High-level Intergovernmental Meeting on the Mid-term Global Review of the Implementation of the Programme of Action for the Least Developed Countries for the 1990s,

1. *Reaffirms* the Programme of Action for the Least Developed Countries for the 1990s[4] as the basis for continuing cooperation between the least developed countries, which have the responsibility for their own development, and their development partners, based on shared responsibility and strengthened partnership, as well as its commitment to the full and effective implementation of the Programme of Action;

2. *Endorses* the measures and recommendations contained in the note by the Secretary-General transmitting the report of the High-level Intergovernmental Meeting on the Mid-term Global Review of the Implementation of the Programme of Action for the Least Developed Countries for the 1990s, as annexed hereto,[5] which are designed to ensure the full implementation of the Programme of Action over the second half of the decade;

3. *Calls upon* all Governments, international and multilateral organizations, financial institutions and development funds, the organs, organizations and programmes of the United Nations system, and all other organizations concerned to take immediate, concrete and adequate steps to implement the Programme of Action, taking full account of the measures and recommendations of the mid-term global review so as to ensure sustained economic growth and sustainable development in the least developed countries and to enable them to participate in and benefit from the process of globalization and liberalization;

4. *Notes* that many least developed countries, for their part, have been implementing courageous and far-reaching policy reforms and adjustment measures in line with the Programme of Action, and in that regard emphasizes the need for national policies and measures aimed at establishing macroeconomic stability by rationalizing public expenditure and adopting sound monetary and fiscal policies so as to ensure a dynamic private sector by such means as providing a sound legal framework and improving human resources development, living standards, health and the status of women, and calls upon the international community to provide adequate support thereto;

5. *Strongly urges* all donor countries to implement fully and expeditiously their commitments in all relevant areas, including the agreed menu of aid targets and commitments as set out in the Programme of Action and support to reinforce structural adjustment reform, as well as the measures agreed upon at the midterm global review so as to provide a significant and substantial increase in the aggregate level of external support for the least developed countries, keeping in mind the increased needs of those countries as well as the requirements of the countries added to the list of the least developed countries following the Second United Nations Conference on the Least Developed Countries;

6. *Stresses* the critical importance of providing multilateral assistance for the least developed countries, in the form of grant-based multilateral programmes, and in that regard calls attention to the need to ensure adequate replenishment of the International Development Association and the soft-term windows of the regional development banks;

7. *Emphasizes* the serious debt problems of the least developed countries, which necessitate strengthened efforts to formulate an international debt strategy that should include concrete measures to alleviate the debt burden and increased concessional financing in support of appropriate economic policy measures, which will be critical to the revitalization of the growth and development of the least developed countries, and encourages the Bretton Woods institutions to expedite the ongoing consideration of ways to address the issue of multilateral debt, including those concerning the least developed countries;

8. *Reiterates* that increased opportunities for trade can help reactivate economic growth in the least developed countries, calls for significantly improved market access for their products and emphasizes the importance of applying effectively the provisions of the Final Act Embodying the Results of the Uruguay Round of Multilateral Trade Negotiations,[6] and further emphasizes in that context the importance of taking concrete action, as appropriate, to fully and expeditiously implement the Marrakesh Declaration[7] as it relates to the least developed countries and the ministerial decision on measures in favour of the least developed countries, as well as the measures agreed to at the mid-term global review, with a view to enabling the least developed countries to maximize their benefit from the Final Act and to cope with any adverse effects arising therefrom;

9. *Also reiterates* the importance attached to the implementation of the ministerial decision on measures concerning possible negative effects of reform programmes on the least developed countries and net food-importing developing countries;

10. *Reaffirms* the importance of the follow-up and monitoring mechanisms for implementation of the Programme of Action at the national, regional and global levels as crucial to the implementation of the Programme of Action;

11. *Recalls* that in its resolution 49/98, it invited the Secretary-General to make recommendations to the General Assembly at its fiftieth session, with a view to ensuring that the secretariat of the United Nations Conference on Trade and Development had sufficient capacity to undertake an effective follow-up of the outcome of the mid-term global review and to follow up the conclusions and recommendations relating to the least developed countries adopted by major United Nations conferences, and in this regard takes note of the relevant proposals of the Secretary-General related to the programme budget for the biennium 1996-1997;

12. *Emphasizes* the importance of the annual reviews by the Trade and Development Board of progress in the implementation of the Programme of Action and the pressing need for enabling representatives of the least developed countries to participate in such annual reviews, and to that end requests the Secretary-General to defray the cost of participation of representatives of least developed countries by mobilizing extrabudgetary resources for that purpose and by reallocating existing resources of the regular budget, if required;

13. *Recalls* that at the end of the decade, a global review and appraisal of the implementation of the Programme of Action will be carried out, in accordance with paragraph 140 of the Programme of Action and operative paragraph 7 (c) of General Assembly resolution 45/206 regarding the consideration by the Assembly at its fifty-second session of the holding of a third United Nations conference on the least developed countries;

14. *Calls upon* the United Nations Conference on Trade and Development at its ninth session to take into account the outcome of the

---

1 A/50/15 (vol. I), chap. I, sect. B.

2 United Nations publication, Sales No. E.95.II.D.2.

3 A/50/745.

4 *Report of the Second United Nations Conference on the Least Developed Countries, Paris, 3-14 September 1990* (A/CONF. 147/18), part one.

5 A/50/745, parts one to three, which will be annexed to the final text of the present draft resolution.

6 See *Legal Instruments Embodying the Results of the Uruguay Round of Multilateral Trade Negotiations, done at Marrakesh on 15 April 1994* (GATT secretariat publication, Sales No. GATT/1994-7).

7 *Ibid.*

High-level Intergovernmental Meeting on the Mid-term Global Review of the Programme of Action for the Least Developed Countries for the 1990s;

15. *Requests* the Secretary-General to submit to the General Assembly at its fifty-second session a report on the implementation of the present resolution.

96th plenary meeting
20 December 1995

05.40 SCIENTIFIC AND TECHNICAL COOPERATION FOR DEVELOPMENT

3405 (XXX). New Dimensions in Technical Cooperation

Committee: 2
Vote: Adopted without a vote

The General Assembly,

Bearing in mind its resolutions 3201 (S-VI) and 3202 (S-VI) of 1 May 1974 containing the Declaration and the Programme of Action on the Establishment of a New International Economic Order,

Recalling the consensus, annexed to its resolution 2688 (XXV) of 11 December 1970, as the comprehensive framework for the activities of the United Nations Development Programme, as well as the voluntary and universal character of the Programme,

Recalling its resolution 3362 (S-VII) of 16 September 1975, in particular section II, paragraph 6, thereof,

1. *Endorses* the decision adopted by the Governing Council of the United Nations Development Programme at its twentieth session on new dimensions in technical cooperation, which is set forth in the annex to the present resolution;

2. *Stresses* the importance of applying the general guidelines contained in that decision for the future orientation of the United Nations Development Programme;

3. *Requests* the Governing Council of the United Nations Development Programme to review periodically the progress in the application of these guidelines;

4. *Requests* the Economic and Social Council to give continuing attention to the assessment of the progress in the application of these guidelines and to report thereon on a regular basis to the General Assembly.

2420th plenary meeting
28 November 1975

Annex

Decision of the Governing Council of the United Nations Development Programme[1]

At its 487th meeting, on 25 June 1975, the Governing Council of the United Nations Development Programme:

(*a*) Reaffirmed the consensus of 1970[2] as the comprehensive framework for the activities of the United Nations Development Programme and also reaffirmed the voluntary and universal character of the Programme;

(*b*) Recalled the relevant provisions of General Assembly resolutions 3201 (S-VI) and 3202 (S-VI) of I May 1974 pertaining to the Declaration and the Programme of Action on the Establishment of a New International Economic Order;

(*c*) Took note with appreciation of the documentation submitted by the Administrator, particularly the report of the Administrator on new dimensions in technical cooperation;[3]

(*d*) Requested the Administrator:

(i) To take all necessary measures to introduce more flexibility in the United Nations Development Programme, to enhance its dynamism and effectiveness and make the scope of activities and working methods of the Programme more responsive to the changing needs and priorities emerging from new economic conditions;

(ii) To base those measures on the proposals favourable to developing countries contained in the report of the Administrator on new dimensions in technical cooperation, taking into account the observations made thereon in the Governing Council during its twentieth session;

(*e*) Adopted, in particular, the following general guidelines for the future orientation of the United Nations Development Programme, and requested the Administrator to ensure that the guidelines were reflected to the maximum extent possible in the execution of the Programme:

(i) The basic purpose of technical cooperation should be the promotion of self-reliance in developing countries by building up, *inter alia*, their productive capability and their indigenous resources and by increasing the availability of the managerial, technical, administrative and research capabilities required in the development process;

(ii) The selection of priority areas in which to seek the assistance of the United Nations Development Programme should remain the exclusive responsibility of the Governments of the recipient countries; in that context, the Programme should respond favourably to requests for meeting the most urgent and critical needs of each developing country, taking into account the importance of reaching the poorest and most vulnerable sections of their societies and enhancing the quality of their life;

(iii) Technical cooperation should be seen in terms of output or the results to be achieved, rather than in terms of input;

(iv) So long as projects are for the basic purpose of technical cooperation, the United Nations Development Programme should provide, where appropriate, equipment and material resources, adopt a more liberal policy towards local cost financing and be flexible in requirements for counterpart personnel;

(v) The United Nations Development Programme should diversify the sources of its supply from countries to enable it to mobilize in a prompt and efficient manner all available human and material resources for technical cooperation, including particularly those from developing countries;

(vi) The United Nations Development Programme should give increased support to programmes of technical cooperation among developing countries and should procure as much equipment and as many services as possible on a preferential basis, in accordance with United Nations practice, from local sources or from other developing countries;

(vii) Governments and institutions in recipient countries should be increasingly entrusted with the responsibility for executing projects assisted by the United Nations Development Programme;

(viii) Technical cooperation should be provided at any of the levels and stages of the development process, including assistance for project planning, pre-feasibility, feasibility, detailed engineering design and, where appropriate, construction and initial operations and management;

1 *Official Records of the Economic and Social Council, Fifthy-ninth Session, Supplement No. 2A* (E/5703/Rev.1), para. 54.

2 Resolution 2688 (XXV), annex.

3 DP/ 114.

(ix) In accordance with the consensus, the United Nations Development Programme should more often enter into partnership with capital assistance sources, in the terms expressed in paragraph 53 of the report of the Administrator on new dimensions in technical cooperation, with a view to financing the technical assistance components of projects and programmes, taking into account the close relationship between technical cooperation and capital formation;

(x) In the context of new dimensions of technical cooperation, special attention should be paid to the requirements of the least developed among the developing countries;

(*f*) Decided to undertake periodic reviews of progress in the application of the above guidelines, as part of the continuing and over-all efforts to improve the quality and efficiency of the United Nations Development Programme;

(*g*) Invited the Economic and Social Council to bring this decision, together with the report of the Administrator on new dimensions in technical cooperation and the respective part of the Governing Council's report on its twentieth session,[1] to the attention of the General Assembly as the contribution of the United Nations Development Programme to the preparations for the seventh special session of the Assembly.

34/218. United Nations Conference on Science and Technology for Development

Committee: 2
Vote: Adopted without a vote
Ref.: 33/192, 32/184, 31/184

The General Assembly,

Recalling its resolutions 3201 (S-VI) and 3202 (S-VI) of 1 May 1974, containing the Declaration and the Programme of Action on the Establishment of a New International Economic Order, which give prominence to the role of science and technology in promoting the development of developing countries,

Recalling also its resolutions 3362 (S-VII) of 16 September 1975, 31/184 of 21 December 1976, 32/115 of 15 December 1977 and 33/192 of 29 January 1979 and Economic and Social Council resolutions 1897 (LVII) of 1 August 1974, 2028 (LXI) of 4 August 1976, 2123 (LXIII) of 4 August 1977 and 1978/70 of 4 August 1978, concerning the convening and preparation of the United Nations Conference on Science and Technology for Development,

Recalling further its resolutions 32/197 of 20 December 1977 and 33/202 of 29 January 1979 on the restructuring of the economic and social sectors of the United Nations system,

Convinced of the paramount need for and importance of the application of science and technology to development in establishing a new international economic order,

Recognizing that peace, security and national independence are important factors for ensuring the effective utilization and further development of science and technology for all countries in particular for the developing countries, and that effective measures in the field of real disarmament would increase the possibilities of reallocation of resources now being used for military purposes to economic and social development, particularly for the benefit of the developing countries,

Emphasizing the urgent need to develop and strengthen the scientific and technological capacities of the developing countries in order to enable them to apply science and technology to their own development, with a view to the elimination of existing inequalities between developing and developed countries in science and technology,

Recognizing that concerted and sustained efforts must be made by all sections of the international community in order to achieve the goal of strengthening the endogenous scientific and technological capacities of the developing countries,

Further recognizing the role of the intergovernmental organizations and non-governmental organizations in the implementation of scientific and technological development programmes,

Conscious that deliberate and urgent steps are needed in order to achieve the target of reconstructing the existing pattern of international scientific and technological relations,

Affirming the central role of the United Nations in the promotion of science and technology for development and the need to strengthen that role through, *inter alia*, new institutional arrangements and additional and substantially increased financial resources,

Reaffirming the need to strengthen the role of the United Nations system in the field of science and technology through, *inter alia*, new institutional arrangements and new substantial resources in addition to those which currently exist,

Recognizing the need for adopting effective means of utilizing new science and technology for overcoming obstacles to development and also the role to be played by science and technology in the development strategies for the future,

Taking note of the report adopted by the United Nations Conference on Science and Technology for Development on 31 August 1979,[2]

Noting with satisfaction the agreements reached at the United Nations Conference on Science and Technology for Development as contained in the report adopted by the Conference,[3]

Recognizing the important role of Governments in the execution of the Vienna Programme of Action on Science and Technology for Development,[4] adopted by the Conference, and in the implementation of scientific and technological programmes within the framework of national development programmes,

Expressing regret that no decisions were taken on certain important questions,

Taking note of the report of the Secretary-General on the United Nations Conference on Science and Technology for Development,[5]

I

Vienna Programme of Action on Science and Technology for Development

1. *Expresses its appreciation and thanks* to the Government and people of Austria for the excellent facilities and generous hospitality provided for the United Nations Conference on Science and Technology for Development, held at Vienna from 20 to 31 August 1979;

2. *Endorses* the Vienna Programme of Action on Science and Technology for Development;[6]

3. *Urges* all Governments to take effective action for the implementation of the Vienna Programme of Action;

4. *Requests* organs, organizations and bodies of the United Nations system and other intergovernmental organizations to comply with the recommendations set forth in the Vienna Programme of Action;

5. *Invites* all concerned scientific and technical organizations to be guided by the provisions of the Vienna Programme of Action;

6. *Fully supports* resolution 2, entitled "Women, science and technology", adopted by the Conference on 31 August 1979;[7]

---

1 *Official Records of the Economic and Social Council, Fifty-ninth Session, Supplement No. 2A* (E/5703/Rev.1), chap. II.

2 *Report of the United Nations Conference on Science and Technology for Development, Vienna, 20-31 August 1979* (United Nations publication, Sales No. E.79.I.21 and corrigenda).

3 *Ibid.*

4 *Ibid.*, chap. VII.

5 A/34/587 and Add.1 and 2.

6 *Report of the United Nations Conference on Science and Technology for Development, Vienna, 20-31 August 1979* (United Nations publication, Sales No. E.79.I.21 and corrigenda), chap. VII.

7 *Ibid.*, chap. VI, sect. A.

II

Intergovernmental Committee on Science and Technology for Development

1. *Decides* to establish an Intergovernmental Committee on Science and Technology for Development;[1]

2. *Endorses* the recommendation of the Conference that representation of Member States in the Committee should be at a high level;

3. *Decides* that the Committee shall be open to the participation of all States as full members, shall meet once a year and shall submit its reports and recommendations to the General Assembly through the Economic and Social Council, which may transmit to the Assembly such comments on the report as it may deem necessary, particularly with regard to coordination;

4. *Invites* all States to participate actively in the Committee and to make an effective contribution to its work;

5. *Decides* that the Committee shall assist the General Assembly, *inter alia*, in the following functions:

(*a*) Formulating policy guidelines for the harmonization of policies of the organs, organizations and bodies of the United Nations system in regard to scientific and technological activities, on the basis of the Vienna Programme of Action and with a view to contributing to the establishment of a new international economic order;

(*b*) Promoting the improvement of linkages between the organs, organizations and bodies of the United Nations system, with a view to ensuring the coordinated implementation of the Vienna Programme of Action;[2]

(*c*) Identifying priorities for activities within the Vienna Programme of Action with a view to facilitating operational planning at the national, subregional, regional, interregional and international levels;

(*d*) Preparing an operational plan for carrying out the Vienna Programme of Action;

(*e*) Monitoring the activities and programmes related to science and technology within the organs, organizations and bodies of the United Nations system;

(*f*) Promoting the optimum mobilization of resources in order to enable the organs, organizations and bodies of the United Nations system to carry out the activities of the Vienna Programme of Action;

(*g*) Initiating arrangements for the early identification and assessment of new scientific and technological developments which may adversely affect the development process as well as those which may have specific and potential importance for that process and for strengthening the scientific and technological capacities of the developing countries;

(*h*) Providing directives and policy-making guidance to the United Nations Financing System for Science and Technology for Development, as described in section VI below;

6. *Decides* that the Committee shall, as an exception, hold a one-week additional session early in 1980 to consider, *inter alia*, organizational matters and other issues of a particularly urgent nature and shall hold its regular session in the second quarter of 1980;

7. *Requests* the Committee to establish working procedures and mechanisms necessary for the effective discharge of its responsibilities and to report thereon to the General Assembly at its thirty-fifth session through the Economic and Social Council;

8. *Decides* that the Committee shall establish procedures and mechanisms which will ensure it adequate and effective provision of scientific and technical expert advice, shall consider in this connexion modifying the terms of reference of the Advisory Committee on the Application of Science and Technology to Development so that the latter will be able to provide, upon the request of the Committee, all necessary assistance and advice, and shall report thereon to the General Assembly through the Economic and Social Council;

9. *Invites* the Economic and Social Council to take the necessary action, in the light of recommendations that may be made by the Committee, regarding the Advisory Committee on the Application of Science and Technology to Development;

10. *Decides* to refer those issues on which agreement was not reached at the Conference to the Committee, so that it may decide, at its earliest convenience, what further action, including procedural action, may be required, taking into account the relevant decision of the Conference;

11. *Invites* all organs, organizations and bodies of the United Nations system, including the regional commissions, the specialized agencies and the International Atomic Energy Agency, in accordance with practices established in the light of the relevant resolutions of the General Assembly and the relationship agreements, to participate actively in the work of the Committee at a high level, preferably at the level of heads of secretariat;

12. *Invites* all appropriate intergovernmental organizations, non-governmental organizations and other concerned organizations to participate in the work of the Committee according to procedures established by the Committee;

III

Centre for Science and Technology for Development

1. *Requests* the Secretary-General to establish, as a new, organizationally distinct entity, a Centre for Science and Technology for Development within the United Nations Secretariat;

2. *Decides* that the Centre will be located at United Nations Headquarters and will be headed by an Assistant Secretary-General, who shall be responsible to and report directly to the Director-General for Development and International Economic Cooperation as envisaged in paragraph 64 (*b*) of the annex to General Assembly resolution 32/197 and paragraph 5 (*c*) of section IV of Assembly resolution 33/202;

3. *Decides also* that the Centre shall assist the Director-General in fulfilling the responsibilities assigned to him in the Vienna Programme of Action, particularly in providing the necessary substantive support to the Intergovernmental Committee on Science and Technology for Development and in coordinating activities at the secretariat level related to science and technology within the United Nations system;

4. *Decides further* that in the performance of those responsibilities the Centre should maintain close cooperation with all the relevant entities of the United Nations;[3]

5. *Decides* to allocate all the necessary resources from the United Nations regular budget to the Centre, drawing to the fullest extent possible on resources already existing within the United Nations, and to abolish the Office for Science and Technology, redeploying immediately most of its posts and budgetary resources to the Centre, and decides further that the Committee should determine at the earliest possible time whether such resources should be strengthened;

6. *Agrees* to review the above arrangements, including the level of the head of the Centre, at its thirty-sixth session;

IV

Coordination within the United Nations System

1. *Decides* that the Director-General for Development and International Economic Cooperation shall be responsible for exercising over-all coordination in science and technology, at the secretariat level, within the United Nations system;

2. *Requests* the organizations of the United Nations system, through, *inter alia*, the mechanisms of the Administrative Committee on

---

1 At the same time, the General Assembly recommends to the Economic and Social Council that its Committee on Science and Technology for Development should cease to exist.

2 The Committee for Programme and Co-ordination and the Administrative Committee on Co-ordination should assist the Intergovernmental Committee, at its request, in accordance with their terms of reference.

3 These are, *inter alia*, the United Nations Development Programme, the Department of International Economic and Social Affairs and the Department of Technical Co-operation for Development.

Coordination, to offer their full and effective cooperation and assistance to the Director-General in discharging his responsibilities in this field;

3. *Further decides* to entrust to the Director-General the responsibility of coordinating the contributions of the organs, organizations and bodies of the United Nations, as well as of the specialized agencies and the International Atomic Energy Agency, to the work of the Intergovernmental Committee on Science and Technology for Development;

4. *Calls upon* all organs, organizations and bodies of the United Nations system to cooperate with the Director-General in the accomplishment of his over-all coordination tasks;

5. *Requests* all organs, organizations and bodies of the United Nations system to take the necessary steps to implement the recommendations addressed to them in paragraphs 90 to 99 and 104 to 108 of the Vienna Programme of Action;[1]

V

Study of System-Wide Efficiency

Requests the Secretary-General to prepare a basic study of the activities, mandates and working methods of all the various organs, organizations and bodies of the United Nations system in the field of science and technology for development and to examine the possibilities of improving the efficiency of the system in that field; a preliminary report on this study should be submitted to the Intergovernmental Committee on Science and Technology for Development at its first substantive session in 1980, and a final study, including proposals, should be submitted to it at its 1981 session; the Committee should make preliminary recommendations to the General Assembly at its thirty-fifth session and final proposals to the Assembly at its thirty-sixth session;

VI

Global Financial Arrangements

1. *Decides* to establish a United Nations Financing System for Science and Technology for Development (hereinafter referred to as the Financing System);

A. Objectives

2. *Decides* that the Financing System shall finance a broad range of activities intended to strengthen the endogenous scientific and technological capacities of the developing countries, in particular to assist in the implementation of the measures envisaged in the Vienna Programme of Action, those activities to be complementary to bilateral and multilateral programmes for science and technology and supportive of the national efforts of the developing countries in the field of science and technology, and decides that the Financing System shall be a vehicle for the mobilization, coordination, channelling and disbursement of financial resources;

B. Resources of the Financing System

3. *Agrees* that, in determining the nature and level of the resources of the Financing System, the following considerations should be taken into account:

(*a*) Asymmetry of the technological capacity between developed and developing countries;

(*b*) Need for predictability and continuous flow of financial resources;

(*c*) Need for substantial resources in addition to those which currently exist within the United Nations system;

(*d*) Need for untied external resources for the scientific and technological development of the developing countries;

1 *Report of the United Nations Conference on Science and Technology for Development, Vienna, 20-31 August 1979* (United Nations publication, Sales No. E.79.I.21 and corrigenda), chap. VII.

C. Other financial resources

4. *Decides* that the Financing System may enter into arrangements with international, regional and other public and private financial institutions with a view to the generation and channelling of additional resources to the developing countries for scientific and technological activities, including research and development, and the commercialization and acquisition of technology;

5. *Decides also* that the resources to be derived from those arrangements should be supplementary to the Financing System's own resources; such resources could be provided by:

(*a*) International and regional financial institutions;

(*b*) Public and private banks of national, regional and international types;

(*c*) Public and private corporations;

(*d*) Other public and private financial institutions;

6. *Decides* that, in addition, the Financing System may use other resources, such as:

(*a*) Resources that may accrue from concrete progress on all measures towards general and complete disarmament, including the urgent implementation of the already agreed disarmament measures;

(*b*) Resources that may accrue from the proposed "international labour compensatory facility" related to the reverse transfer of technology;[2]

D. Allocation of resources for the interim and long-term arrangements of the Financing System

7. *Decides further* that the resources available shall be allocated to the various activities identified in the Vienna Programme of Action, including national, subregional, regional and interregional activities; in the context of the decisions on interim arrangements adopted by the General Assembly at its thirty-fourth session and those on long-term arrangements to be adopted at the thirty-sixth session, the Intergovernmental Committee on Science and Technology for Development shall establish guidelines for the allocation and distribution of resources for building up the endogenous scientific and technological capacities of the developing countries; those guidelines should be within the framework of the priorities of the developing countries, at the national, subregional, regional and international levels, for implementing in particular different types of projects and programmes of direct relevance to the developing countries, taking into account, *inter alia*, the need to take special measures to meet the urgent and specific problems of the least developed, land-locked, island and most seriously affected developing countries and the need to overcome poverty and to accelerate the development of the developing countries as well as other criteria to be adopted by the Committee; additional criteria for the allocation of resources should provide, *inter alia*, for a part of the resources to be applied to high-risk research and development projects in science and technology at the national, subregional, regional and interregional levels and to provide support for the developing countries in obtaining financial resources from other sources;

8. *Decides*, in view of the above considerations, as follows:

Long-term arrangements of the Financing System to start in January 1982

(*a*) The directing and policy-making body of the Financing System shall be the Intergovernmental Committee on Science and Technology for Development, which shall, taking into consideration the results of the study described in subparagraph (*b*) below, define the guiding principles, general economic provisions, forms of operation and general procedures for the formulation, submission, consideration and approval of programmes and projects, and shall submit to the General Assembly recommendations regarding the appropriate structure for the executive body of the Financing System;

(*b*) An intergovernmental group of experts, composed of twenty-seven members, shall be elected, on the basis of equitable geographical distribution and the need for an appropriate range of expertise, by

2 See E/1978/92, paras. 100-104.

the Committee at its first substantive session in 1980, which will be held at United Nations Headquarters; with the support of the Director-General for Development and International Economic Cooperation, the group of experts shall undertake a prompt and thorough study of all relevant arrangements for the operation of the Financing System; the terms of reference shall be as follows:

(i) The study will make an assessment of the requirements for additional funding for scientific and technological activities in developing countries and of potential sources of funding;

(ii) The study will include an inventory of existing multilateral and bilateral programmes for providing financial support for such activities;

(iii) The study will review alternative proposals, including all the proposals put to the United Nations Conference on Science and Technology for Development by the Group of Seventy-seven[1] for generating requisite additional funds for scientific and technological development activities on a long-term basis and for the disbursement and control of those funds, as well as those for institutional arrangements, and make recommendations thereon;

(*c*) The intergovernmental group of experts shall submit its final report to the Committee for its consideration so that the latter may, through the Economic and Social Council, make appropriate recommendations to the General Assembly at its thirty-sixth session;

Interim arrangements of the Financing System

(*d*) Pending the establishment of the long-term arrangements for the Financing System, a United Nations Interim Fund for Science and Technology for Development is hereby created, which will be sustained by voluntary contributions; the General Assembly agrees that the target for voluntary contributions for the two-year period 1980-1981 should be no less than $250 million; during the interim period, to the extent that such funds are fully committed and taking fully into account the needs of the developing countries, the $250 million figure will be reviewed by the Committee with the aim of raising additional resources for the Interim Fund;

(*e*) The Interim Fund, which shall have an identifiable and separate basis, shall be administered by the United Nations Development Programme under the policy guidelines established in the annex to the present resolution and also under the guidelines established by the Committee when it starts its meetings; the Secretary-General is requested to convene a pledging conference not later than March 1980; the General Assembly shall provide the Administrator of the United Nations Development Programme with the necessary resources for the initial preparatory responsibility until the Interim Fund is in operation;

9. *Decides* that the establishment of interim arrangements should not prejudice the ultimate decisions with regard to long-term arrangements;

10. *Decides also* that the Interim Fund shall be administered and managed in accordance with the provisions of the annex to the present resolution, and urges that the necessary arrangements be made to ensure that it becomes operational at the earliest possible time;

11. *Urges* all Member States, in particular the developed countries, to contribute generously so that the agreed upon target of $250 million for the Interim Fund may be met.

110th plenary meeting
19 December 1979

Annex

Initial Prospectus for the United Nations Interim Fund for Science and Technology for Development

Contents

I. Interim Fund

1. The United Nations Interim Fund for Science and Technology for Development (hereinafter referred to as the Interim Fund), established by the General Assembly under resolution 34/218 of 19 December 1979, shall operate as an identifiable and separate fund and as an organ of the Assembly in accordance with the provisions set forth below.

II. Purpose of the Interim Fund

2. Subject to the provisions of paragraphs 32 to 52 below, the aims and objectives of the Interim Fund and the purposes for which its resources shall be used are to provide technical and capital assistance to Governments and organizations in accordance with the provisions of paragraph 8 below, for activities intended to promote the objectives of and implement the measures recommended in the Vienna Programme of Action on Science and Technology for Development,[2] as set out in section I thereof, entitled "Strengthening the scientific and technological capacities of the developing countries", and section II entitled "Restructuring the existing pattern of international scientific and technological relations", as endorsed by the General Assembly and as an integral part of the establishment of the new international economic order, *inter alia*:

(*a*) To strengthen the endogenous scientific and technological capacities of the developing countries;

(*b*) To promote the strengthening of international cooperation in the field of science and technology for development by, *inter alia*:

(i) Promoting cooperative arrangements through which developed countries may more effectively support and facilitate the internal efforts of developing countries to achieve development through the establishment and strengthening of their scientific and technological capacities;

(ii) Supporting cooperation among developing countries at the subregional, regional and interregional levels;

(*c*) Pending the coming into operation of the United Nations Financing System for Science and Technology for Development, to support, promote and initiate if appropriate during the interim period the activities necessary to prepare for future efforts to strengthen the scientific and technological capacities of the developing countries.

III. General Principles

3. The Interim Fund shall operate in accordance with the following principles:

(*a*) The provision of assistance shall be in conformity with the purposes and principles of the Charter of the United Nations and within the framework of the priorities of the recipient developing countries;

(*b*) The assistance furnished by the Interim Fund shall not be a means of foreign economic and political interference in the internal affairs of the country or countries concerned and shall not be accompanied by any conditions of a political nature;

(*c*) The resources available to the Interim Fund shall be used to support projects and programmes of the developing countries at the national, subregional, regional and interregional levels, taking due account of the need to ensure adequate linkages between institutions at the national, subregional, regional and interregional levels and between the latter and the productive sectors of the country or region concerned, and taking into account, *inter alia*, the need to take special measures to meet the urgent and specific . problems of the least developed, landlocked, island and most seriously affected de-

1 A/CONF.81/L.1, paras. A.22, A.38, A.50, A.59, B.26 and C.20-C.27.

2 See *Report of the United Nations Conference on Science and Technology for Development, Vienna, 20-31 August 1979* (United Nations publication, Sales No. E.79.I.21 and corrigenda), chap. VII.

veloping countries and the need to overcome poverty and to accelerate the development of the developing countries as well as other criteria to be adopted by the Intergovernmental Committee on Science and Technology for Development;

(*d*) Due account shall be taken, in the use of the resources of the Interim Fund, of the need for an appropriate balance between activities to meet the urgent needs of the developing countries for assistance in the field of science and technology and activities to lay the basis for a sustained effort, over the next decade, to build up and strengthen the scientific and technological capacities of the developing countries, including cooperative undertakings in the field of science and technology for development;

(*e*) The assistance furnished by the Interim Fund to individual countries shall be provided in response to the requests of the Governments concerned;

(*f*) For intercountry projects and programmes, the assistance furnished by the Interim Fund shall be provided in response to requirements as defined by the countries concerned, taking due account of paragraphs 80 and 81 of the Vienna Programme of Action;

(*g*) Subject to the provisions of subparagraphs (*e*) and (*f*) above, the activities supported by the Interim Fund shall be coordinated with, and should not duplicate activities of, bilateral and multilateral programmes for science and technology, including those of the entities of the United Nations system;

(*h*) Assistance from the Interim Fund shall be provided in a flexible manner, and due account shall be taken, in the management of the Interim Fund, of the need to promote innovative approaches and accelerated procedures so as to be fully responsive to the Vienna Programme of Action over the interim period;

(*i*) The resources of the Interim Fund may be used to provide assistance, capital and technical, to promote international collaboration in the field of science and technology;

(*j*) The Interim Fund shall actively promote effective investment and other follow-up to its activities, and shall assist the developing countries in obtaining financial resources for scientific and technological activities from other sources;

(*k*) Measures shall be taken to ensure that the relevant expertise existing in the United Nations system and in the developed and developing countries should be made available in the identification, formulation, appraisal, execution and evaluation of the projects and programmes supported by the Interim Fund.

IV. Basic Activities

4. Within the limits of the resources prospectively available and of the interim period envisaged, the assistance furnished by the Interim Fund in accordance with the provisions of paragraph 8 below shall support a broad range of activities envisaged in the Vienna Programme of Action to strengthen the scientific and technological capacities of the developing countries and likely to contribute to the restructuring of the existing pattern of international scientific and technological relations, including, *inter alia*, the creation and/or strengthening of policy-making capacity for scientific and technological matters; the review of, and international exchange of experience and information on, issues related to science and technology for development; the establishment of appropriate legal, administrative, fiscal and institutional machinery and the services required to carry out the process of scientific and technological development, the establishment and strengthening of national capacities for the assessment, selection, acquisition and adaptation of foreign technology and expertise; the monitoring of future scientific and technological activities to assess their impact, including negative impact, on the developing countries; the preparation of action programmes to strengthen the scientific and technological capacities of developing countries both individually and on a cooperative basis- the establishment and improvement of national, subregional, regional and global information centres networks and systems to meet, particularly, the needs of developing countries; the establishment of global and interregional projects in science and technology for development; the education and training of the human resources required at all levels to generate and implement scientific and technological development policies, plans, programmes and projects; the promotion of basic and applied research; application and pilot testing and the diffusion of innovative technology; the promotion, through the application of science and technology, of the use of natural resources for national, subregional and regional development; the facilitation of the transfer of technology from developed to developing countries; the promotion of activities related to the socio-cultural implications of science and technology for development; the undertaking of a limited number of high-risk, highpotential, research and development projects; the undertaking of international cooperation projects in research development and application, and in training in relation to problems of particular importance to developing countries in the field of science and technology.

V. Participation in the Interim Fund

5. Participation in the Interim Fund shall be open to all States.

VI. General Operational Provisions

A. Forms of cooperation

6. In pursuance of its objectives, the Interim Fund may provide assistance, as appropriate, to projects or programmes in fields such as those mentioned in paragraph 4 above, at the country and intercountry level, through, *inter alia*, one or a combination of several of the following:

(*a*) Services of experts and consultants, including operational personnel;

(*b*) Provision of equipment or supplies;

(*c*) Scholarships and fellowships or other arrangements under which candidates from developing countries may study or receive training within other developing countries or in developed countries;

(*d*) Assistance for research, development and the testing of products and processes and for pilot production;

(*e*) Support for basic and applied research, including support for the creation, adaptation or application of technology in developing countries;

(*f*) Support for the strengthening of existing and the creation of new research institutes;

(*g*) Support for activities conducive to the acquisition of scientific potential and of operative technology and know-how;

(*h*) Survey pilot projects, technical tests, experiments and research;

(*i*) Support for the dissemination of the results of research and development and pilot projects both within and among developing countries;

(*j*) Support to improve both the access of the developing countries to scientific and technical information and their ability to use it in the process of development;

(*k*) Mobilization of additional resources of all kinds to support or follow up the activities of developing countries in the field of science and technology for development;

(*l*) Such other and further assistance as may, in the opinion of the Intergovernmental Committee on Science and Technology for Development, be considered consistent with the objectives of the Interim Fund, taking into account the form of assistance requested by Governments.

7. The assistance referred to in paragraph 6 above to be furnished by the Interim Fund from its resources shall be on a grant basis. In the light of experience of the operations of the Interim Fund, the Committee shall provide policy guidelines on whether any capital assistance extended by the Fund shall be on a loan or a refundable basis.

B. Eligibility

8. Assistance from the Interim Fund may be furnished:

(*a*) To the Governments of all States or groups of States;

(*b*) To organizations eligible for assistance from the United Nations Development Programme, in accordance with the objectives of the Vienna Programme of Action;

(*c*) To other organizations which may be deemed by the Committee to be eligible for assistance in accordance with the objectives of the Vienna Programme of Action;

(*d*) At the request of a Government or Governments of such States:

(i) To an entity having public or private juridical personality within the territory of such States, including, *inter alia*, existing or new research institutes which are engaged in basic or applied scientific and technological research for development;

(ii) To regional or subregional governmental organizations having juridical personalities.

C. General responsibilities of recipients

9. The recipient Governments, organizations and institutions referred to in paragraph 8 above should ensure that the assistance furnished by the Interim Fund is used in an effective manner and in accordance with the purposes for which it is approved.

10. Recipient Governments, organizations and institutions shall maintain the records required by the Interim Fund in connexion with the administration of its assistance.

VII. Resources of the Interim Fund

11. The resources of the Interim Fund shall consist of voluntary contributions from Governments. The Interim Fund shall also be empowered to receive contributions from international organizations, both governmental and non-governmental, and from other private sources. No limitation may be imposed by such donors on the use of donations in a specific recipient country, by a specific agency or for a specific project. Furthermore, while contributions may be accepted on an annual basis, it is desirable, in view of the two years' duration of the Interim Fund, that contributions should be pledged or indicated for two years. Contributions in kind may be accepted by the Interim Fund where the Administrator considers it appropriate to accept them.

12. Contributions pledged to the Interim Fund shall be payable as early as possible; every effort should be made to pay within six months following the pledge.

13. Cash contributions shall be made in convertible currencies or in currency readily usable by the Interim Fund.

14. To ensure that the multilateral character of the Interim Fund shall be strictly respected, no contributing country shall receive special treatment with respect to its contribution nor shall negotiations for the use of its currency take place between contributing and receiving countries.

15. Taking into account the financial situation of the country concerned, recipient Governments shall normally be expected to finance a considerable part of the local currency cost of projects.

16. Trust funds may be established for specific purposes consistent with the policies, aims and activities of the Interim Fund.

17. Assistance provided by the Interim Fund will be intended, *inter alia*, to broaden the financial means available to strengthen the scientific and technological capacities of the developing countries. For this purpose, the Interim Fund may enter into joint financing arrangements with multilateral, bilateral, public or private sources to support projects approved by it.

VIII. Organization and Management

18. The organization and management of the Interim Fund are designed to ensure maximum efficiency in the use of its resources.

A. Intergovernmental arrangements

19. The policy guidelines for the Interim Fund were established by the General Assembly at its thirty-fourth session; guidelines will also be established by the Intergovernmental Committee on Science and Technology for Development when it starts its meetings. The Committee will review, as a separate item of its agenda, the policies and progress of the Interim Fund and will provide the necessary directives and guidance. In this connexion, the Administrator, in consultation with the Director-General for Development and International Economic Cooperation, shall, during the interim period, submit to the Committee annual reports on the implementation of those policies. He shall also report annually to the Committee on the progress of the operations of the Interim Fund.

20. The Administrator shall submit, during the interim period, annual reports to the Governing Council of the United Nations Development Programme on the operations and management of the Interim Fund.

21. The Committee shall, in turn, review the reports referred to above on the progress and performance of the Interim Fund and shall make its report to the General Assembly through the Economic and Social Council.

B. Administrator

22. The Interim Fund shall be administered by the Administrator of the United Nations Development Programme, who shall exercise his functions under the policy guidance of the General Assembly and the Committee and under the operational management of the Governing Council of the United Nations Development Programme. The Administrator shall have over-all responsibility and be accountable for all phases and aspects of the operations of the Interim Fund. He shall establish clear lines of responsibility for the direction of the Interim Fund. The Administrator shall appoint the staff for the Interim Fund, on the delegation of authority by the Secretary-General and in accordance with the Staff Regulations of the United Nations adopted by the Assembly. The selection of the staff and consultants shall be made in accordance with the relevant provisions of the Charter of the United Nations. The Administrator shall have authority on behalf of the Interim Fund to enter into contracts and agreements with Governments organizations and persons.

C. Staff and other administrative matters

23. The General Assembly shall provide the Administrator with the necessary resources for the initial preparatory responsibility until the Interim Fund is in operation.

24. The administrative expenses of the Interim Fund, once it becomes operational, will be met from its own resources.

25. The Interim Fund will operate with the minimum staff required to perform the functions assigned to it by the General Assembly. Its staff shall be assembled as expeditiously as possible and commensurate with its resources and volume of operations for the interim period.

26. In the operations of the Interim Fund, the Administrator will use, to the extent feasible, the capacities, including human resources, available within the United Nations Development Programme and in other entities of the United Nations system.

D. Cooperation with organizations of the United Nations system

27. The Interim Fund shall establish and maintain close and continuous working relationships with the organizations of the United Nations system, in particular the Centre for Science and Technology for Development, the specialized agencies and other United Nations entities concerned, including the regional commissions, in order to give full expression to the Vienna Programme of Action.

28. The Administrator shall take measures to ensure the involvement, as appropriate, of the specialized agencies and United Nations entities concerned in the identification, formulation, appraisal, execution and evaluation of projects.

E. Use of consultants

29. The Administrator should use the expertise available in the United Nations system, in so far as that would minimize consultancy expenses. The Administrator may also obtain the services of expert consultants and consulting organizations to advise him on the activities of the Interim Fund, the cost to be charged to the Fund. It should be ensured to the maximum extent practicable that those services would be obtained from the developing countries.

30. Subject to the provisions of subsection D above, the Administrator, within the limits of the resources available from the Programme Reserve described in paragraph 52 below, may finance, upon the request of Governments, the provision of expert advice and support for the examination and preparation of projects at the formulation

stage. Such resources should be recouped by the Programme Reserve as part of the costs of the project or projects which may result from that preparation.

IX. Procedures

A. Formulation of requests

31. The Administrator shall prescribe the form, content and procedures for requests for assistance from the Interim Fund.

32. Requests shall include all relevant information on the intended use of and benefits expected to be derived from the assistance of the Interim Fund together with statements of the part of the costs which the Governments themselves would be ready to bear.

33. In the formulation and appraisal of projects, the resident representative of the United Nations Development Programme will provide coordination at the field level, until such time as the United Nations resident coordinator has been appointed, taking into account the provisions of paragraph 28 above.

B. Methodology for the formulation and implementation of projects

34. The formulation and implementation of projects at the country level should be done with the full participation of the authorities of the country concerned and in accordance with the relevant recommendation of the Vienna Programme of Action.

35. The formulation and implementation of projects at the intercountry level should be guided by the principles set forth in paragraphs 80 and 81 of the Vienna Programme of Action.

C. Appraisal and approval of requests

36. In considering requests for assistance, pending the guidelines and/or principles to be established by the Intergovernmental Committee on Science and Technology for Development, the Administrator shall be guided by the general principles set out in section III above.

37. The Administrator shall submit for approval to the Governing Council of the United Nations Development Programme projects to be supported by the Interim Fund resources in the amount of $2 million or above on the basis of policy guidelines established by the Committee. Until such time as the Committee adopts additional policy guidelines, the Administrator should follow the policy guidelines set forth in General Assembly resolution 34/218 and the annex thereto.

38. The Administrator shall submit to the Committee at its first regular session proposals on methods for the approval of projects to be adopted by the Governing Council of the United Nations Development Programme.

39. Subject to the provisions of paragraph 8 above, the Administrator shall be authorized to approve projects to be supported by the Interim Fund below the amount of $2 million and shall report in each case to the Governing Council of the United Nations Development Programme.

40. The Governing Council of the United Nations Development Programme shall take final decisions on the projects and programmes recommended by the Administrator in accordance with the provisions of paragraph 37 above, in the light of the guidelines established by the General Assembly and the Committee and of the directives which will be established by the Committee, and shall authorize the Administrator to conclude the appropriate agreements.

D. Execution of projects

41. Projects shall be executed through the channels and arrangements already established for the execution of projects by the United Nations system. Special attention shall be paid to the need to make maximum use of government executing arrangements and national expertise.

42. The Administrator shall apply the existing basic agreements between the United Nations Development Programme and the participating and executing agencies, in those cases where they have been so designated, as the basis for carrying out projects and programmes, subject to whatever modifications may be mutually agreed upon in the light of the special characteristics of the Interim Fund.

43. Bearing in mind the provisions of paragraph 28 above and, when necessary, in order to ensure the maximum effectiveness of the assistance furnished by the Interim Fund or to increase its capacity, and with due regard to the cost factor increased use may appropriately be made of suitable services obtained from governmental and non-governmental institutions and firms, in agreement with the recipient Government concerned and in accordance with the applicable financial rules and regulations. Maximum use should be made of national institutions and firms within the recipient countries.

44. With the approval of the Government or Governments concerned in each case, non-governmental institutions and organizations within the recipient countries may execute projects supported by the Interim Fund.

45. Arrangements for the execution of projects shall be subject to the approval of the requesting Government or Governments and shall be specified in the project document. Such arrangements shall contain provisions regarding costs which the requesting Government will assume and those facilities and services which it will provide.

46. Emphasis shall be placed, in the execution of projects on technical cooperation among developing countries.

47. The Administrator shall make appropriate arrangements to monitor and evaluate the progress and results of projects and programmes supported by the resources of the Interim Fund and shall report to the Governing Council of the United Nations Development Programme and to the Committee on their status.

E. Relations between Governments and the Interim Fund

48. Each Government shall designate to the Administrator an appropriate channel for its relations with the Interim Fund. The Interim Fund shall use only the official channel designated by each Government for the submission of requests.

49. In regard to the operations of the Interim Fund, the existing basic agreements between Governments and the United Nations Development Programme shall apply, subject to such modifications as may be called for having regard to the special characteristics of the Interim Fund and subject to the concurrence of the Governments concerned. In particular the privileges and immunities accorded to the staff of the Interim Fund shall be identical to those accorded to the staff of the United Nations Development Programme.

F. Financial arrangements

50. The financial rules and regulations governing the Interim Fund shall be those of the Financial Regulations and Rules of the United Nations Development Programme. Any amendments which may be necessary to take account of the special requirements of the Interim Fund's operation shall be drafted by the Administrator and submitted for consideration to the Governing Council of the United Nations Development Programme which shall report accordingly to the Committee and the General Assembly.

51. The Administrator will take such steps as are necessary to ensure separate accounting and financial management of the operations of the Interim Fund, while using the existing services of the United Nations Development Programme to the maximum possible extent.

52. The Interim Fund shall be authorized to establish a Programme Reserve by earmarking 2 per cent of the total annual contributions. Such a Programme Reserve shall be used by the Administrator at his discretion for purposes consistent with the Vienna Programme of Action and with the guidelines established by the General Assembly and the Committee, to ensure the flexibility and innovative capacity of the Interim Fund and its ability to provide catalytic support. The Administrator shall ensure the utilization of such a reserve fund and shall report to the Governing Council of the United Nations Development Programme and to the Committee on his decisions and on the results achieved.

53. The Administrator shall not at any time enter into commitments which shall exceed the usable resources of the Interim Fund. Nor shall he incur any liabilities on behalf of the Interim Fund which shall result in a charge against the general resources of the United Nations Development Programme.

G. Period of the Interim Fund

54. In accordance with the decisions adopted by the General Assembly in its resolution 34/218 and the outcome of the Pledging Conference, the Administrator shall determine the date at which the Interim Fund becomes operational and shall report accordingly to the Committee.

55. Time being of the essence, given the limited period of the Interim Fund, the Administrator submitted to the General Assembly at its thirty-fourth session for approval proposals for staffing and other administrative resources required both for the preparatory period and for the full period to the end of 1981.[1]

56. Taking into account the interim nature of the Fund, the General Assembly shall decide at its thirty-sixth session, on the recommendation of the Committee, on the arrangements to be made for an effective transition between the operations of the Interim Fund and the long-term arrangements for the United Nations Financing System for Science and Technology for Development to be determined by the Assembly.

05.50 NEW INTERNATIONAL ECONOMIC ORDER

3201 (S-VI). Declaration on the Establishment of a New International Economic Order

Committee: Ad hoc
Vote: Adopted without a vote
Ref.: 46/52, 44/30, 43/162, 42/149, 41/73, 40/67, 39/75, 38/128, 37/103, 36/107, 35/166, 34/150, 3171(XXVIII)

The General Assembly [1]

Adopts the following Declaration:

Declaration on the Establishment of a New International Economic Order

We, the Members of the United Nations,

Having convened a special session of the General Assembly to study for the first time the problems of raw materials and development, devoted to the consideration of the most important economic problems facing the world community,

Bearing in mind the spirit purposes and principles of the Charter of the United Nations to promote the economic advancement and social progress of all peoples,

Solemnly proclaim our united determination to work urgently for the establishment of a new international economic order based on equity, sovereign equality, interdependence, common interest and cooperation among all States, irrespective of their economic and social systems which shall correct inequalities and redress existing injustices, make it possible to eliminate the widening gap between the developed and the developing countries and ensure steadily accelerating economic and social development and peace and justice for present and future generations, and, to that end, declare:

1. The greatest and most significant achievement during the last decades has been the independence from colonial and alien domination of a large number of peoples and nations which has enabled them to become members of the community of free peoples. Technological progress has also been made in all spheres of economic activities in the last three decades, thus providing a solid potential for improving the well-being of all peoples. However, the remaining vestiges of alien and colonial domination, foreign occupation, racial discrimination, apartheid and neo-colonialism in all its forms continue to be among the greatest obstacles to the full emancipation and progress of the developing countries and all the peoples involved. The benefits of technological progress are not shared equitably by all members of the international community. The developing countries, which constitute 70 per cent of the world's population, account for only 30 per cent of the world's income. It has proved impossible to achieve an even and balanced development of the international community under the existing international economic order. The gap between the developed and the developing countries continues to widen in a system which was established at a time when most of the developing countries did not even exist as independent States and which perpetuates inequality.

2. The present international economic order is in direct conduct with current developments in international political and economic relations. Since 1970 the world economy has experienced a series of grave crises which have had severe repercussions, especially on the developing countries because of their generally greater vulnerability to external economic impulses. The developing world has become a powerful factor that makes its influence felt in all fields of international activity. These irreversible changes in the relationship of forces in the world necessitate the active, full and equal participation of the developing countries in the formulation and application of all decisions that concern the international community.

3. All these changes have thrust into prominence the reality of interdependence of all the members of the world community. Current events have brought into sharp focus the realization that the interests of the developed countries and those of the developing countries can no longer be isolated from each other that there is a close interrelationship between the prosperity of the developed countries and the growth and development of the developing countries, and that the prosperity of the international community as a whole depends upon the prosperity of its constituent parts. International cooperation for development is the shared goal and common duty of all countries. Thus the political, economic and social well-being of present and future generations depends more than ever on cooperation between all the members of the international community on the basis of sovereign equality and the removal of the disequilibrium that exists between them.

4. The new international economic order should be founded on full respect for the following principles:

(*a*) Sovereign equality of States, self-determination of all peoples, inadmissibility of the acquisition of territories by force, territorial integrity and non-interference in the internal affairs of other States;

(*b*) The broadest cooperation of all the States members of the international community, based on equity, whereby the prevailing disparities in the world may be banished and prosperity secured for all;

(*c*) Full and effective participation on the basis of equality of all countries in the solving of world economic problems in the common interest of all countries, bearing in mind the necessity to ensure the accelerated development of all the developing countries, while devoting particular attention to the adoption of special measures in favour of the least developed, land-locked and island developing countries as well as those developing countries most seriously affected by economic crises and natural calamities, without losing sight of the interests of other developing countries;

(*d*) The right of every country to adopt the economic and social system that it deems the most appropriate for its own development and not to be subjected to discrimination of any kind as a result;

(*e*) Full permanent sovereignty of every State over its natural resources and all economic activities. In order to safeguard these resources, each State is entitled to exercise effective control over them and their exploitation with means suitable to its own situation, including the right to nationalization or transfer of ownership to its nationals, this right being an expression of the full permanent sovereignty of the State. No State may be subjected to economic, political or any other type of coercion to prevent the free and full exercise of this inalienable right;

1 See A/34/587/Add.2.

(*f*) The right of all States, territories and peoples under foreign occupation, alien and colonial domination or apartheid to restitution and full compensation for the exploitation and depletion of, and damages to, the natural resources and all other resources of those States, territories and peoples;

(*g*) Regulation and supervision of the activities of transnational corporations by taking measures in the interest of the national economies of the countries where such transnational corporations operate on the basis of the full sovereignty of those countries;

(*h*) The right of the developing countries and the peoples of territories under colonial and racial domination and foreign occupation to achieve their liberation and to regain effective control over their natural resources and economic activities;

(*i*) The extending of assistance to developing countries, peoples and territories which are under colonial and alien domination, foreign occupation, racial discrimination or apartheid or are subjected to economic, political or any other type of coercive measures to obtain from them the subordination of the exercise of their sovereign rights and to secure from them advantages of any kind, and to neocolonialism in all its forms, and which have established or are endeavouring to establish effective control over their natural resources and economic activities that have been or are still under foreign control;

(*j*) Just and equitable relationship between the prices of raw materials, primary commodities, manufactured and semi-manufactured goods exported by developing countries and the prices of raw materials, primary commodities, manufactures, capital goods and equipment imported by them with the aim of bringing about sustained improvement in their unsatisfactory terms of trade and the expansion of the world economy;

(*k*) Extension of active assistance to developing countries by the whole international community free of any political or military conditions;

(*l*) Ensuring that one of the main aims of the reformed international monetary system shall be the promotion of the development of the developing countries and the adequate flow of real resources to them;

(*m*) Improving the competitiveness of natural materials facing competition from synthetic substitutes;

(*n*) Preferential and non-reciprocal treatment for developing countries, wherever feasible, in all fields of international economic cooperation whenever possible;

(*o*) Securing favourable conditions for the transfer of financial resources to developing countries;

(*p*) Giving to the developing countries access to the achievements of modern science and technology and promoting the transfer of technology and the creation of indigenous technology for the benefit of the developing countries in forms and in accordance with procedures which are suited to their economies;

(*q*) The need for all States to put an end to the waste of natural resources, including food products;

(*r*) The need for developing countries to concentrate all their resources for the cause of development;

(*s*) The strengthening, through individual and collective actions, of mutual economic, trade, financial and technical cooperation among the developing countries, mainly on a preferential basis;

(*t*) Facilitating the role which producers, associations may play within the framework of international cooperation and, in pursuance of their aims *inter alia* assisting in the promotion of sustained growth of the world economy and accelerating the development of developing countries.

5. The unanimous adoption of the International Development Strategy for the Second United Nations Development Decade[1] was an important step in the promotion of international economic cooperation on a just and equitable basis. The accelerated implementation of obligations and commitments assumed by the international community within the framework of the Strategy, particularly those concerning imperative development needs of developing countries, would contribute significantly to the fulfilment of the aims and objectives of the present Declaration.

6. The United Nations as a universal organization should be capable of dealing with problems of international economic cooperation in a comprehensive manner and ensuring equally the interests of all countries. It must have an even greater role in the establishment of a new international economic order. The Charter of Economic Rights and Duties of States, for the preparation of which the present Declaration will provide an additional source of inspiration, will constitute a significant contribution in this respect. All the States Members of the United Nations are therefore called upon to exert maximum efforts with a view to securing the implementation of the present Declaration, which is one of the principal guarantees for the creation of better conditions for all peoples to reach a life worthly of human dignity.

7. The present Declaration on the Establishment of a New International Economic Order shall be one of the most important bases of economic relations between all peoples and all nations.

2229th plenary meeting
1 May 1974

3202 (S-VI). Programme of Action on the Establishment of a New International Economic Order

Committee: Ad hoc
Vote: Adopted without a vote

The General Assembly,

Adopts the following Programme of Action:

Programme of Action on the Establishment of a new International Economic Order

Contents

Introduction

1. In view of the continuing severe economic imbalance in the relations between developed and developing countries, and in the context of the constant and continuing aggravation of the imbalance of the economies of the developing countries and the consequent need for the mitigation of their current economic difficulties, urgent and effective measures need to be taken by the international community to assist the developing countries, while devoting particular attention to the least developed, land-locked and island developing countries and those developing countries most seriously affected by economic crises and natural calamities leading to serious retardation of development processes.

---

1 Resolution 2626 (XXV).

2. With a view to ensuring the application of the Declaration on the Establishment of a New International Economic Order,[1] it will be necessary to adopt and implement within a specified period a programme of action of unprecedented scope and to bring about maximum economic cooperation and understanding among all States, particularly between developed and developing countries, based on the principles of dignity and sovereign equality.

I. Fundamental Problems of Raw Materials and Primary Commodities as Related to Trade and Development

1. Raw materials

All efforts should be made:

(*a*) To put an end to all forms of foreign occupation, racial discrimination, apartheid, colonial, neocolonial and alien domination and exploitation through the exercise of permanent sovereignty over natural resources;

(*b*) To take measures for the recovery, exploitation development, marketing and distribution of natural resources, particularly of developing countries, to serve their national interests, to promote collective self-reliance among them and to strengthen mutually beneficial international economic cooperation with a view to bringing about the accelerated development of developing countries;

(*c*) To facilitate the functioning and to further the aims of producers' associations, including their joint marketing arrangements, orderly commodity trading improvement in the export income of producing developing countries and in their terms of trade, and sustained growth of the world economy for the benefit of all;

(*d*) To evolve a just and equitable relationship between the prices of raw materials, primary commodities, manufactured and semi-manufactured goods exported by developing countries and the prices of raw materials, primary commodities, food, manufactured and semi-manufactured goods and capital equipment imported by them, and to work for a link between the prices of exports of developing countries and the prices of their imports from developed countries;

(*e*) To take measures to reverse the continued trend of stagnation or decline in the real price of several commodities exported by developing countries despite a general rise in commodity prices, resulting in a decline in the export earnings of these developing countries;

(*f*) To take measures to expand the markets for natural products in relation to synthetics, taking into account the interests of the developing countries, and to utilize fully the ecological advantages of these products;

(*g*) To take measures to promote the processing of raw materials in the producer developing countries.

2. Food

All efforts should be made:

(*a*) To take full account of specific problems of developing countries, particularly in times of food shortages, in the international efforts connected with the food problem;

(*b*) To take into account that, owing to lack of means, some developing countries have vast potentialities of unexploited or underexploited land which, if reclaimed and put into practical use, would contribute considerably to the solution of the food crisis;

(*c*) By the international community to undertake concrete and speedy measures with a view to arresting desertification, salination and damage by locusts or any other similar phenomenon involving several developing countries, particularly in Africa, and gravely affecting the agricultural production capacity of these countries, and also to assist the developing countries affected by any such phenomenon to develop the affected zones with a view to contributing to the solution of their food problems;

(*d*) To refrain from damaging or deteriorating natural resources and food resources, especially those derived from the sea, by preventing pollution and taking appropriate steps to protect and reconstitute those resources;

(*e*) By developed countries, in evolving their policies relating to production, stocks, imports and exports of food, to take full account of the interests of:

(i) Developing importing countries which cannot afford high prices for their imports;

(ii) Developing exporting countries which need increased market opportunities for their exports;

(*f*) To ensure that developing countries can import the necessary quantity of food without undue strain on their foreign exchange resources and without unpredictable deterioration in their balance of payments, and, in this context, that special measures are taken in respect of the least developed, land-locked and island developing countries as well as those developing countries most seriously affected by economic crises and natural calamities;

(*g*) To ensure that concrete measures to increase food production and storage facilities in developing countries are introduced, *inter alia*, by ensuring an increase in all available essential inputs, including fertilizers, from developed countries on favourable terms;

(*h*) To promote exports of food products of developing countries through just and equitable arrangements, *inter alia*, by the progressive elimination of such protective and other measures as constitute unfair competition.

3. General trade

All efforts should be made:

(*a*) To take the following measures for the amelioration of terms of trade of developing countries and concrete steps to eliminate chronic trade deficits of developing countries:

(i) Fulfilment of relevant commitments already undertaken in the United Nations Conference on Trade and Development and in the International Development Strategy for the Second United Nations Development Decade;[2]

(ii) Improved access to markets in developed countries through the progressive removal of tariff and non-tariff barriers and of restrictive business practices;

(iii) Expeditious formulation of commodity agreements where appropriate, in order to regulate as necessary and to stabilize the world markets for raw materials and primary commodities;

(iv) Preparation of an over-all integrated programme, setting out guidelines and taking into account the current work in this field for a comprehensive range of commodities of export interest to developing countries;

(v) Where products of developing countries compete with the domestic production in developed countries, each developed country should facilitate the expansion of imports from developing countries and provide a fair and reasonable opportunity to the developing countries to share in the growth of the market;

(vi) When the importing developed countries derive receipts from customs duties, taxes and other protective measures applied to imports of these products, consideration should be given to the claim of the developing countries that these receipts should be reimbursed in full to the exporting developing countries or devoted to providing additional resources to meet their development needs;

(vii) Developed countries should make appropriate adjustments in their economies so as to facilitate the expansion and diversification of imports from developing countries and thereby permit a rational, just and equitable international division of labour;

(viii) Setting up general principles for pricing policy for exports of commodities of developing countries, with a view to rectifying and achieving satisfactory terms of trade for them;

---

1 Resolution 3201 (S-VI).

2 Resolution 2626 (XXV).

(ix) Until satisfactory terms of trade are achieved for all developing countries, consideration should be given to alternative means, including improved compensatory financing schemes for meeting the development needs of the developing countries concerned;

(x) Implementation, improvement and enlargement of the generalized system of preferences for exports of agricultural primary commodities, manufactures and semi-manufactures from developing to developed countries and consideration of its extension to commodities including those which are processed or semiprocessed, developing countries which are or will be sharing their existing tariff advantages in some developed countries as the result of the introduction and eventual enlargement of the generalized system of preferences should, as a matter of urgency, be granted new openings in the markets of other developed countries which should offer them export opportunities that at least compensate for the sharing of those advantages;

(xi) The setting up of buffer stocks within the framework of commodity arrangements and their financing by international financial institutions wherever necessary, by the developed countries and, when they are able to do so, by the developing countries, with the aim of favouring the producer developing and consumer developing countries and of contributing to the expansion of world trade as a whole;

(xii) In cases where natural materials can satisfy the requirements of the market, new investment for the expansion of the capacity to produce synthetic materials and substitutes should not be made;

(*b*) To be guided by the principles of non-reciprocity and preferential treatment of developing countries in multilateral trade negotiations between developed and developing countries, and to seek sustained and additional benefits for the international trade of developing countries, so as to achieve a substantial increase in their foreign exchange earnings, diversification of their exports and acceleration of the rate of their economic growth.

4. Transportation and insurance

All efforts should be made:

(*a*) To promote an increasing and equitable participation of developing countries in the world shipping tonnage;

(*b*) To arrest and reduce the ever-increasing freight rates in order to reduce the costs of imports to, and exports from, the developing countries;

(*c*) To minimize the cost of insurance and reinsurance for developing countries and to assist the growth of domestic insurance and reinsurance markets in developing countries and the establishment to this end, where appropriate, of institutions in these countries or at the regional level;

(*d*) To ensure the early implementation of the code of conduct for liner conferences;

(*e*) To take urgent measures to increase the import and export capability of the least developed countries and to offset the disadvantages of the adverse geographic situation of land-locked countries, particularly with regard to their transportation and transit costs, as well as developing island countries in order to increase their trading ability;

(*f*) By the developed countries to refrain from imposing measures or implementing policies designed to prevent the importation, at equitable prices, of commodities from the developing countries or from frustrating the implementation of legitimate measures and policies adopted by the developing countries in order to improve prices and encourage the export of such commodities.

II. International Monetary System and Financing of the Development of Developing Countries

1. Objectives

All efforts should be made to reform the international monetary system with, *inter alia*, the following objectives:

(*a*) Measures to check the inflation already experienced by the developed countries, to prevent it from being transferred to developing countries and to study and devise possible arrangements within the International Monetary Fund to mitigate the effects of inflation in developed countries on the economies of developing countries;

(*b*) Measures to eliminate the instability of the international monetary system, in particular the uncertainty of the exchange rates, especially as it affects adversely the trade in commodities;

(*c*) Maintenance of the real value of the currency reserves of the developing countries by preventing their crosion from inflation and exchange rate depreciation of reserve currencies;

(*d*) Full and effective participation of developing countries in all phases of decision-making for the formulation of an equitable and durable monetary system and adequate participation of developing countries in all bodies entrusted with this reform and, particularly, in the proposed Council of Governors of the International Monetary Fund;

(*e*) Adequate and orderly creation of additional liquidity with particular regard to the needs of the developing countries through the additional allocation of special drawing rights based on the concept of world liquidity needs to be appropriately revised in the light of the new international environment; any creation of international liquidity should be made through international multilateral mechanisms;

(*f*) Early establishment of a link between special drawing rights and additional development financing in the interest of developing countries, consistent with the monetary characteristics of special drawing rights;

(*g*) Review by the International Monetary Fund of the relevant provisions in order to ensure effective participation by developing countries in the decisionmaking process;

(*h*) Arrangements to promote an increasing net transfer of real resources from the developed to the developing countries;

(*i*) Review of the methods of operation of the International Monetary Fund, in particular the terms for both credit repayments and "stand-by" arrangements, the system of compensatory financing, and the terms of the financing of commodity buffer stocks, so as to enable the developing countries to make more effective use of them.

2. Measures

All efforts should be made to take the following urgent measures to finance the development of developing countries and to meet the balance-of-payment crises in the developing world:

(*a*) Implementation at an accelerated pace by the developed countries of the time-bound programme, as already laid down in the International Development Strategy for the Second United Nations Development Decade, for the net amount of financial resource transfers to developing countries; increase in the official component of the net amount of financial resource transfers to developing countries so as to meet and even to exceed the target of the Strategy;

(*b*) International financing institutions should effectively play their role as development financing banks without discrimination on account of the political or economic system of any member country, assistance being untied;

(*c*) More effective participation by developing countries, whether recipients or contributors, in the decision-making process in the competent organs of the International Bank for Reconstruction and Development and the International Development Association, through the establishment of a more equitable pattern of voting rights;

(*d*) Exemption, wherever possible, of the developing countries from, all import and capital outflow controls imposed by the developed countries;

(*e*) Promotion of foreign investment, both public and private, from developed to developing countries in accordance with the needs and requirements in sectors of their economies as determined by the recipient countries;

(*f*) Appropriate urgent measures, including international action, should be taken to mitigate adverse consequences for the current and future development of developing countries arising from the burden of external debt contracted on hard terms;

(*g*) Debt renegotiation on a case-by-case basis with a view to concluding agreements on debt cancellation, moratorium, rescheduling or interest subsidization;

(*h*) International financial institutions should take into account the special situation of each developing country in reorienting their lending policies to suit these urgent needs, there is also need for improvement in practices of international financial institutions in regard to, *inter alia*, development financing and international monetary problems;

(*i*) Appropriate steps should be taken to give priority to the least developed, land-locked and island developing countries and to the countries most seriously affected by economic crises and natural calamities, in the availability of loans for development purposes which should include more favourable terms and conditions.

III. Industrialization

All efforts should be made by the international community to take measures to encourage the industrialization of the developing countries, and to this end:

(*a*) The developed countries should respond favourably, within the framework of their official aid as well as international financial institutions, to the requests of developing countries for the financing of industrial projects;

(*b*) The developed countries should encourage investors to finance industrial production projects particularly export-oriented production, in developing countries, in agreement with the latter and within the context of their laws and regulations;

(*c*) With a view to bringing about a new international economic structure which should increase the share of the developing countries in world industrial production, the developed countries and the agencies of the United Nations system, in cooperation with the developing countries, should contribute to setting up new industrial capacities including raw materials and commodity-transforming facilities as a matter of priority in the developing countries that produce those raw materials and commodities;

(*d*) The international community should continue and expand, with the aid of the developed countries and the international institutions, the operational and instruction-oriented technical assistance programmes including vocational training and management development of national personnel of the developing countries, in the light of their special development requirements.

IV. Transfer of Technology

All efforts should be made:

(*a*) To formulate an international code of conduct for the transfer of technology corresponding to needs and conditions prevalent in developing countries;

(*b*) To give access on improved terms to modern technology and to adapt that technology, as appropriate, to specific economic, social and ecological conditions and varying stages of development in developing countries;

(*c*) To expand significantly the assistance from developed to developing countries in research and development programmes and in the creation of suitable indigenous technology;

(*d*) To adapt commercial practices governing transfer of technology to the requirements of the developing countries and to prevent abuse of the rights of sellers;

(*e*) To promote international cooperation in research and development in exploration and exploitation, conservation and the legitimate utilization of natural resources and all sources of energy.

In taking the above measures, the special needs of the least developed and land-locked countries should be borne in mind.

V. Regulation and Control over the Activities of Corporations

All efforts should be made to formulate, adopt and implement an international code of conduct for transnational corporations:

(*a*) To prevent interference in the internal affairs of the countries where they operate and their collaboration with racist régimes and colonial administrations;

(*b*) To regulate their activities in host countries, to eliminate restrictive business practices and to conform to the national development plans and objectives of developing countries, and in this context facilitate, as necessary, the review and revision of previously concluded arrangements;

(*c*) To bring about assistance, transfer of technology and management skills to developing countries on equitable and favourable terms;

(*d*) To regulate the repatriation of the profits accruing from their operations, taking into account the legitimate interests of all parties concerned;

(*e*) To promote reinvestment of their profits in developing countries.

VI. Charter of Economic Rights and Duties of States

The Charter of Economic Rights and Duties of States, the draft of which is being prepared by a working group of the United Nations and which the General Assembly has already expressed the intention of adopting at its twenty-ninth regular session, shall constitute an effective instrument towards the establishment of a new system of international economic relations based on equity, sovereign equality, and interdependence of the interests of developed and developing countries. It is therefore of vital importance that the aforementioned Charter be adopted by the General Assembly at its twenty-ninth session.

VII. Promotion of Cooperation among Developing Countries

1. Collective self-reliance and growing cooperation among developing countries will further strengthen their role in the new international economic order. Developing countries, with a view to expanding cooperation at the regional, subregional and interregional levels, should take further steps, *inter alia*:

(*a*) To support the establishment and/or improvement of an appropriate mechanism to defend the prices of their exportable commodities and to improve access to and stabilize markets for them. In this context the increasingly effective mobilization by the whole group of oil-exporting countries of their natural resources for the benefit of their economic development is to be welcomed. At the same time there is the paramount need for cooperation among the developing countries in evolving urgently and in a spirit of solidarity all possible means to assist developing countries to cope with the immediate problems resulting from this legitimate and perfectly justified action. The measures already taken in this regard are a positive indication of the evolving cooperation between developing countries;

(*b*) To protect their inalienable right to permanent sovereignty over their natural resources;

(*c*) To promote, establish or strengthen economic integration at the regional and subregional levels;

(*d*) To increase considerably their imports from other developing countries;

(*e*) To ensure that no developing country accords to imports from developed countries more favourable treatment than that accorded to imports from developing countries. Taking into account the existing international agreements, current limitations and possibilities and also their future evolution, preferential treatment should be given to the procurement of import requirements from other developing countries. Wherever possible, preferential treatment should be given to imports from developing countries and the exports of those countries;

(*f*) To promote close cooperation in the fields of finance, credit relations and monetary issues, including the development of credit relations on a preferential basis and on favourable terms;

(*g*) To strengthen efforts which are already being made by developing countries to utilize available financial resources for financing development in the developing countries through investment, financing of exportoriented and emergency projects and other long-term assistance;

(*h*) To promote and establish effective instruments of cooperation in the fields of industry, science and technology, transport, shipping and mass communication media.

2. Developed countries should support initiatives in the regional, subregional and interregional cooperation of developing countries through the extension of financial and technical assistance by more effective and concrete actions, particularly in the field of commercial policy.

VIII. Assistance in the Exercise of Permanent Sovereignty of States over Natural Resources

All efforts should be made:

(*a*) To defeat attempts to prevent the free and effective exercise of the rights of every State to full and permanent sovereignty over its natural resources;

(*b*) To ensure that competent agencies of the United Nations system meet requests for assistance from developing countries in connexion with the operation of nationalized means of production.

IX. Strengthening the Role of the United Nations System in the Field of International Economic Cooperation

1. In furtherance of the objectives of the International Development Strategy for the Second United Nations Development Decade and in accordance with the aims and objectives of the Declaration on the Establishment of a New International Economic Order, all Member States pledge to make full use of the United Nations system in the implementation of the present Programme of Action, jointly adopted by them, in working for the establishment of a new international economic order and thereby strengthening the role of the United Nations in the field of world-wide cooperation for economic and social development.

2. The General Assembly of the United Nations shall conduct an over-all review of the implementation of the Programme of Action as a priority item. All the activities of the United Nations system to be undertaken under the Programme of Action as well as those already planned, such as the World Population Conference, 1974, the World Food Conference, the Second General Conference of the United Nations Industrial Development Organization and the mid-term review and appraisal of the International Development Strategy for the Second United Nations Development Decade should be so directed as to enable the special session of the General Assembly on development called for under Assembly resolution 3172 (XXVIII) of 17 December 1973, to make its full contribution to the establishment of the new international economic order. All Member States are urged, jointly and individually, to direct their efforts and policies towards the success of that special session.

3. The Economic and Social Council shall define the policy framework and coordinate the activities of all organizations, institutions and subsidiary bodies within the United Nations system which shall be entrusted with the task of implementing the present Programme of Action. In order to enable the Economic and Social Council to carry out its tasks effectively:

(*a*) All organizations, institutions and subsidiary bodies concerned within the United Nations system shall submit to the Economic and Social Council progress reports on the implementation of the Programme of Action within their respective fields of competence as often as necessary, but not less than once a year;

(*b*) The Economic and Social Council shall examine the progress reports as a matter of urgency, to which end it may be convened, as necessary, in special session or, if need be, may function continuously. It shall draw the attention of the General Assembly to the problems and difficulties arising in connexion with the implementation of the Programme of Action.

4. All organizations, institutions, subsidiary bodies and conferences of the United Nations system are entrusted with the implementation of the Programme of Action reactivities of the United Nations Conference on Trade and Development, as set forth in General Assembly resolution 1995 (XIX) of 30 December 1964, should be strengthened for the purpose of following in collaboration with other competent organizations the development of international trade in raw materials throughout the world.

5. Urgent and effective measures should be taken to review the lending policies of international financial institutions, taking into account the special situation of each developing country, to suit urgent needs, to improve the practices of these institutions in regard to, *inter alia*, development financing and international monetary problems, and to ensure more effective participation by developing countries - whether recipients or contributors - in the decision-making process through appropriate revision of the pattern of voting rights.

6. The developed countries and others in a position to do so should contribute substantially to the various organizations, programmes and funds established within the United Nations system for the purpose of accelerating economic and social development in developing countries.

7. The present Programme of Action complements and strengthens the goals and objectives embodied in the International Development Strategy for the Second United Nations Development Decade as well as the new measures formulated by the General Assembly at its twenty-eighth session to offset the shortfalls in achieving those goals and objectives.

8. The implementation of the Programme of Action should be taken into account at the time of the midterm review and appraisal of the International Development Strategy for the Second United Nations Development Decade. New commitments, changes additions and adaptations in the Strategy should be made, as appropriate taking into account the Declaration on the Establishment of a New International Economic Order and the present Programme of Action.

X. Special Programme

The General Assembly adopts the following Special Programme, including particularly emergency measures to mitigate the difficulties of the developing countries most seriously affected by economic crisis bearing in mind the particular problem of the least developed and land-locked countries:

The General Assembly,

Taking into account the following considerations:

(*a*) The sharp increase in the prices of their essential imports such as food, fertilizers, energy products, capital goods, equipment and services, including transportation and transit costs, has gravely exacerbated the increasingly adverse terms of trade of a number of developing countries, added to the burden of their foreign debt and cumulatively, created a situation which, if left untended, will make it impossible for them to finance their essential imports and development and result in a further deterioration in the levels and conditions of life in these countries. The present crisis is the outcome of all the problems that have accumulated over the years: in the field of trade, in monetary reform, the world-wide inflationary situation, inadequacy and delay in provision of financial assistance and many other similar problems in the economic and developmental fields. In facing the crisis, this complex situation must be borne in mind so as to ensure that the Special Programme adopted by the international community provides emergency relief and timely assistance to the most seriously affected countries. Simultaneously, steps are being taken to resolve these outstanding problems through a fundamental restructuring of the world economic system, in order to allow these countries while solving the present difficulties to reach an acceptable level of development.

(*b*) The special measures adopted to assist the most seriously affected countries must encompass not only the relief which they require on an emergency basis to maintain their import requirements, but also, beyond that, steps to consciously promote the capacity of these countries to produce and earn more. Unless such a comprehensive approach is adopted, there is every likelihood that the difficulties of the most seriously affected countries may be perpetuated. Nevertheless, the first and most pressing task of the international community is to enable these countries to meet the shortfall in their balance-of-payments positions. But this must be simultaneously supplemented by additional development assistance to maintain and thereafter accelerate their rate of economic development.

(*c*) The countries which have been most seriously affected are precisely those which are at the greatest disadvantage in the world economy: the least developed, the land-locked and other low-income developing countries as well as other developing countries whose economies have been seriously dislocated as a result of the present economic crisis, natural calamities, and foreign aggression and occupation. An indication of the countries thus affected, the level of the impact on their economies and the kind of relief and assistance they require can be assessed on the basis, *inter alia* of the following criteria:

(i) Low per capita income as a reflection of relative poverty, low productivity, low level of technology and development;

(ii) Sharp increase in their import cost of essentials relative to export earnings;

(iii) High ratio of debt servicing to export earnings;

(iv) Insufficiency in export earnings, comparative inelasticity of export incomes and unavailability of exportable surplus;

(v) Low level of foreign exchange reserves or their inadequacy for requirements;

(vi) Adverse impact of higher transportation and transit costs;

(vii) Relative importance of foreign trade in the development process.

(*d*) The assessment of the extent and nature of the impact on the economies of the most seriously affected countries must be made flexible, keeping in mind the present uncertainty in the world economy, the adjustment policies that may be adopted by the developed countries and the flow of capital and investment. Estimates of the payments situation and needs of these countries can be assessed and projected reliably only on the basis of their average performance over a number of years. Long-term projections, at this time, cannot but be uncertain.

(*e*) It is important that in the special measures to mitigate the difficulties of the most seriously affected countries, all the developed countries as well as the developing countries should contribute according to their level of development and the capacity and strength of their economies. It is notable that some developing countries, despite their own difficulties and development needs have shown a willingness to play a concrete and helpful role in ameliorating the difficulties faced by the poorer developing countries. The various initiatives and measures taken recently by certain developing countries with adequate resources on a bilateral and multilateral basis to contribute to alleviating the difficulties of other developing countries are a reflection of their commitment to the principle of effective economic cooperation among developing countries.

(*f*) The response of the developed countries which have by far the greater capacity to assist the affected countries in overcoming their present difficulties must be commensurate with their responsibilities. Their assistance should be in addition to the presently available levels of aid. They should fulfil and if possible exceed the targets of the International Development Strategy for the Second United Nations Development Decade on financial assistance to the developing countries, especially that relating to official development assistance. They should also give serious consideration to the cancellation of the external debts of the most seriously affected countries. This would provide the simplest and quickest relief to the affected countries. Favourable consideration should also be given to debt moratorium and rescheduling. The current situation should not lead the industrialized countries to adopt what will ultimately prove to be a self-defeating policy aggravating the present crisis.

Recalling the constructive proposals made by His Imperial Majesty the Shahanshah of Iran[1] and His Excellency Mr. Houari Boumediène. President of the People's Democratic Republic of Algeria,[2]

1. *Decides* to launch a Special Programme to provide emergency relief and development assistance to the developing countries most seriously affected as a matter of urgency, and for the period of time necessary, at least until the end of the Second United Nations Development Decade, to help them overcome their present difficulties and to achieve self-sustaining economic development;

2. *Decides* as a first step in the Special Programme to request the Secretary-General to launch an emergency operation to provide timely relief to the most seriously affected developing countries, as defined in subparagraph (*c*) above, with the aim of maintaining unimpaired essential imports for the duration of the coming twelve months and to invite the industrialized countries and other potential contributors to announce their contributions for emergency assistance, or intimate their intention to do so, by 15 June 1974 to be provided through bilateral or multilateral channels, taking into account the commitments and measures of assistance announced or already taken by some countries, and further requests the Secretary-General to report the progress of the emergency operation to the General Assembly at its twenty-ninth session, through the Economic and Social Council at its fifty-seventh session;

3. *Calls upon* the industrialized countries and other potential contributors to extend to the most seriously affected countries immediate relief and assistance which must be of an order of magnitude that is commensurate with the needs of these countries. Such assistance should be in addition to the existing level of aid and provided at a very early date to the maximum possible extent on a grant basis and, where not possible, on soft terms. The disbursement and relevant operational procedures and terms must reflect this exceptional situation. The assistance could be provided either through bilateral or multilateral channels, including such new institutions and facilities that have been or are to be set up. The special measures may include the following:

(*a*) Special arrangements on particularly favour able terms and conditions including possible subsidies for and assured supplies of essential commodities and goods;

(*b*) Deferred payments for all or part of imports of essential commodities and goods;

(*c*) Commodity assistance, including food aid, on a grant basis or deferred payments in local currencies, bearing in mind that this should not adversely affect the exports of developing countries;

(*d*) Long-term suppliers, credits on easy terms;

(*e*) Long-term financial assistance on concessionary terms;

(*f*) Drawings from special International Monetary Fund facilities on concessional terms;

(*g*) Establishment of a link between the creation of special drawing rights and development assistance taking into account the additional financial requirements of the most seriously affected countries;

(*h*) Subsidies, provided bilaterally or multilaterally, for interest on funds available on commercial terms borrowed by the most seriously affected countries;

(*i*) Debt renegotiation on a case-by-case basis with a view to concluding agreements on debt cancellation, moratorium or rescheduling:

(*j*) Provision on more favourable terms of capital goods and technical assistance to accelerate the industrialization of the affected countries;

(*k*) Investment in industrial and development projects on favourable terms;

(*l*) Subsidizing the additional transit and transport costs, especially of the land-locked countries;

4. *Appeals* to the developed countries to consider favourably the cancellation. moratorium or rescheduling of the debts of the most seriously affected developing countries, on their request, as an important contribution to mitigating the grave and urgent difficulties of these countries;

5. *Decides* to establish a Special Fund under the auspices of the United Nations, through voluntary contributions from industrialized countries and other potential contributors, as a part of the Special Programme, to provide emergency relief and development assistance, which will commence its operations at the latest by 1 January 1975;

6. *Establishes* an *Ad Hoc* Committee on the Special Programme, composed of thirty-six Member States appointed by the President of the General Assembly, after appropriate consultations, bearing in mind the purposes of the Special Fund and its terms of reference:

---

1 A/9548, annex.

2 *Official Records of the General Assembly, Sixth Special Session,* Plenary Meetings, 2208th meeting, paras. 3-152.

(*a*) To make recommendations, *inter alia*, on the scope, machinery and modes of operation of the Special Fund, taking into account the need for:

(i) Equitable representation on its governing body;

(ii) Equitable distribution of its resources;

(iii) Full utilization of the services and facilities of existing international organizations;

(iv) The possibility of merging the United Nations Capital Development Fund with the operations of the Special Fund;

(v) A central monitoring body to oversee the various measures being taken both bilaterally and multilaterally;

and, to this end, bearing in mind the different ideas and proposals submitted at the sixth special session including those put forward by Iran[1] and those made at the 2208th plenary meeting, and the comments thereon, and the possibility of utilizing the Special Fund to provide an alternative channel for normal development assistance after the emergency period;

(*b*) To monitor, pending commencement of the operations of the Special Fund, the various measures being taken both bilaterally and multilaterally to assist the most seriously affected countries;

(*c*) To prepare, on the basis of information provided by the countries concerned and by appropriate agencies of the United Nations system, a broad assessment of:

(i) The magnitude of the difficulties facing the most seriously affected countries;

(ii) The kind and quantities of the commodities and goods essentially required by them;

(iii) Their need for financial assistance;

(iv) Their technical assistance requirements, including especially access to technology;

7. *Requests* the Secretary-General of the United Nations, the Secretary-General of the United Nations Conference on Trade and Development, the President of the International Bank for Reconstruction and Development, the Managing Director of the International Monetary Fund, the Administrator of the United Nations Development Programme and the heads of the other competent international organizations to assist the *Ad Hoc* Committee on the Special Programme in performing the functions assigned to it under paragraph 6 above, and to help, as appropriate, in the operations of the Special Fund;

8. *Requests* the International Monetary Fund to expedite decisions on:

(*a*) The establishment of an extended special facility with a view to enabling the most seriously affected developing countries to participate in it on favourable terms;

(*b*) The creation of special drawing rights and the early establishment of the link between their allocation and development financing;

(*c*) The establishment and operation of the proposed new special facility to extend credits and subsidize interest charges on commercial funds borrowed by Member States, bearing in mind the interests of the developing countries and especially the additional financial requirements of the most seriously affected countries;

9. *Requests* the World Bank Group and the International Monetary Fund to place their managerial, financial and technical services at the disposal of Governments contributing to emergency financial relief so as to enable them to assist without delay in channelling funds to the recipients, making such institutional and procedural changes as may be required;

10. *Invites* the United Nations Development Programme to take the necessary steps, particularly at the country level, to respond on an emergency basis to requests for additional assistance which it may be called upon to render within the framework of the Special Programme;

11. *Requests* the A*d Hoc* Committee on the Special Programme to submit its report and recommendations to the Economic and Social Council at its fifty-seventh session and invites the Council, on the basis of its consideration of that report, to submit suitable recommendations to the General Assembly at its twenty-ninth session;

12. *Decides* to consider as a matter of high priority at its twenty-ninth session, within the framework of a new international economic order, the question of special measures for the most seriously affected countries.

2229th plenary meeting
1 May 1974

05.60 PERMANENT SOVEREIGNTY OVER NATURAL RESOURCES

626 (VII). Right to Exploit Freely Natural Wealth and Resources

Committee: 2
Vote: 36 - 4 - 20

The General Assembly,

Bearing in mind the need for encouraging the underdeveloped countries in the proper use and exploitation of their natural wealth and resources,

Considering that the economic development of the under-developed countries is one of the fundamental requisites for the strengthening of universal peace,

Remembering that the right of peoples freely to use and exploit their natural wealth and resources is inherent in their sovereignty and is in accordance with the Purposes and Principles of the Charter of the United Nations,

1. *Recommends* all Member States, in the exercise of their right freely to use and exploit their natural wealth and resources wherever deemed desirable by them for their own progress and economic development, to have due regard, consistently with their sovereignty, to the need for maintaining the flow of capital in conditions of security, mutual confidence and economic cooperation among nations;

2. *Further recommends* all Member States to refrain from acts, direct or indirect, designed to impede the exercise of the sovereignty of any State over its natural resources.

411th plenary meeting
21 December 1952

1803 (XVII). Permanent Sovereignty over Natural Resources

Committee: 2
Vote: 87 - 2 - 12
Ref.: 1720(XVI)

The General Assembly,

Recalling its resolutions 523 (VI) of 12 January 1952 and 626 (VII) of 21 December 1952,

Bearing in mind its resolution 1314 (XIII) of 12 December 1958, by which it established the Commission on Permanent Sovereignty over Natural Resources and instructed it to conduct a full survey of the status of permanent sovereignty over natural wealth and resources as a basic constituent of the right to self-determination, with recommendations, where necessary, for its strengthening, and decided further that, in the conduct of the full survey of the status of the permanent sovereignty of peoples and nations over their natural wealth and resources, due regard should be paid to the rights and duties of States under international law and to the importance of encouraging inter-

1 A/AC.166/L.15; see also A/9548, annex.

national cooperation in the economic development of developing countries,

Bearing in mind its resolution 1515 (XV) of 15 December 1960, in which it recommended that the sovereign right of every State to dispose of its wealth and its natural resources should be respected,

Considering that any measure in this respect must be based on the recognition of the inalienable right of all States freely to dispose of their natural wealth and resources in accordance with their national interests, and on respect for the economic independence of States,

Considering that nothing in paragraph 4 below in any way prejudices the position of any Member State on any aspect of the question of the rights and obligations of successor States and Governments in respect of property acquired before the accession to complete sovereignty of countries formerly under colonial rule,

Noting that the subject of succession of States and Governments is being examined as a matter of priority by the International Law Commission,

Considering that it is desirable to promote international cooperation for the economic development of developing countries, and that economic and financial agreements between the developed and the developing countries must be based on the principles of equality and of the right of peoples and nations to self-determination,

Considering that the provision of economic and technical assistance, loans and increased foreign investment must not be subject to conditions which conflict with the interests of the recipient State,

Considering the benefits to be derived from exchanges of technical and scientific information likely to promote the development and use of such resources and wealth, and the important part which the United Nations and other international organizations are called upon to play in that connexion,

Attaching particular importance to the question of promoting the economic development of developing countries and securing their economic independence,

Noting that the creation and strengthening of the inalienable sovereignty of States over their natural wealth and resources reinforces their economic independence,

Desiring that there should be further consideration by the United Nations of the subject of permanent sovereignty over natural resources in the spirit of international cooperation in the field of economic development, particularly that of the developing countries,

I

Declares that:

1. The right of peoples and nations to permanent sovereignty over their natural wealth and resources must be exercised in the interest of their national development and of the well-being of the people of the State concerned.

2. The exploration, development and disposition of such resources, as well as the import of the foreign capital required for these purposes, should be in conformity with the rules and conditions which the peoples and nations freely consider to be necessary or desirable with regard to the authorization, restriction or prohibition of such activities.

3. In cases where authorization is granted, the capital imported and the earnings on that capital shall be governed by the terms thereof, by the national legislation in force, and by international law. The profits derived must be shared in the proportions freely agreed upon, in each case, between the investors and the recipient State, due care being taken to ensure that there is no impairment, for any reason, of that State's sovereignty over its natural wealth and resources.

4. Nationalization, expropriation or requisitioning shall be based on grounds or reasons of public utility, security or the national interest which are recognized as overriding purely individual or private interests, both domestic and foreign. In such cases the owner shall be paid appropriate compensation, in accordance with the rules in force in the State taking such measures in the exercise of its sovereignty and in accordance with international law. In any case where the question of compensation gives rise to a controversy, the national jurisdiction of the State taking such measures shall be exhausted. However, upon agreement by sovereign States and other parties concerned, settlement of the dispute should be made through arbitration or international adjudication.

5. The free and beneficial exercise of the sovereignty of peoples and nations over their natural resources must be furthered by the mutual respect of States based on their sovereign equality.

6. International cooperation for the economic development of developing countries, whether in the form of public or private capital investments, exchange of goods and services technical assistance, or exchange of scientific information shall be such as to further their independent national development and shall be based upon respect for their sovereignty over their natural wealth and resources.

7. Violation of the rights of peoples and nations to sovereignty over their natural wealth and resources is contrary to the spirit and principles of the Charter of the United Nations and hinders the development of international cooperation and the maintenance of peace.

8. Foreign investment agreements freely entered into by or between sovereign States shall be observed in good faith; States and international organizations shall strictly and conscientiously respect the sovereignty of peoples and nations over their natural wealth and resources in accordance with the Charter and the principles set forth in the present resolution.

II

Welcomes the decision of the International Law Commission to speed up its work on the codification of the topic of responsibility of States for the consideration of the General Assembly.[1]

III

Requests the Secretary-General to continue the study of the various aspects of permanent sovereignty over natural resources, taking into account the desire of Member States to ensure the protection of their sovereign rights while encouraging international cooperation in the field of economic development, and to report to the Economic and Social Council and to the General Assembly, if possible at its eighteenth session.

1194th plenary meeting
14 December 1962

3171 (XXVIII). Permanent Sovereignty over Natural Resources

Committee: 2
Vote: 108 - 1 - 16

The General Assembly,

Reiterating that the inalienable right of each State to the full exercise of national sovereignty over its natural resources has been repeatedly recognized by the international community in numerous resolutions of various organs of the United Nations,

Reiterating also that an intrinsic condition of the exercise of the sovereignty of every State is that it be exercised fully and effectively over all the natural resources of the State, whether found on land or in the sea,

Reaffirming the inviolable principle that every country has the right to adopt the economic and social system which it deems most favourable to its development,

Recalling its resolutions 1803 (XVII) of 14 December 1962, 2158 (XXI) of 25 November 1966, 2386 (XXIII) of 19 November 1968, 2625 (XXV) of 24 October 1970, 2692 (XXV) of 11 December 1970 and 3016 (XXVII) of 18 December 1972, and Security Council resolution 330 (1973) of 21 March 1973 which relate to permanent sovereignty over natural resources,

Recalling, in particular, the Declaration on Principles of International Law concerning Friendly Relations and Cooperation among States in

---

1 *Official Records of the General Assembly, Seventeenth Session, Supplement No. 9* (A/5209), paras. 67-69.

accordance with the Charter of the United Nations,[1] which proclaims that no State may use or encourage the use of economic political or any other type of measures to coerce another State in order to obtain from it the subordination of the exercise of its sovereign rights and to secure from it advantages of any kind,

Considering that the full exercise by each State of sovereignty over its natural resources is an essential condition for achieving the objectives and targets of the Second United Nations Development Decade, and that this exercise requires that action by States aimed at achieving a better utilization and use of those resources must cover all stages, from exploration to marketing,

Taking note of section VII of the Economic Declaration adopted by the Fourth Conference of Heads of State or Government of Non-Aligned Countries, held at Algiers from 5 to 9 September 1973,[2]

Taking note also of the report of the Secretary-General on permanent sovereignty over natural resources,[3]

1. *Strongly reaffirms* the inalienable rights of States to permanent sovereignty over all their natural resources, on land within their international boundaries as well as those in the sea-bed and the subsoil thereof within their national jurisdiction and in the superjacent waters;

2. *Supports resolutely* the efforts of the developing countries and of the peoples of the territories under colonial and racial domination and foreign occupation in their struggle to regain effective control over their natural resources;

3. *Affirms* that the application of the principle of nationalization carried out by States, as an expression of their sovereignty in order to safeguard their natural resources, implies that each State is entitled to determine the amount of possible compensation and the mode of payment, and that any disputes which might arise should be settled in accordance with the national legislation of each State carrying out such measures;

4. *Deplores* acts of States which use force, armed aggression, economic coercion or any other illegal or improper means in resolving disputes concerning the exercise of the sovereign rights mentioned in paragraphs 1 to 3 above;

5. *Re-emphasizes* that actions, measures or legislative regulations by States aimed at coercing, directly or indirectly, other States or peoples engaged in the reorganization of their internal structure or in the exercise of their sovereign rights over their natural resources, both on land and in their coastal waters, are in violation of the Charter of the United Nations and of the Declaration contained in General Assembly resolution 2625 (XXV) and contradict the targets, objectives and policy measures of the International Development Strategy for the Second United Nations Development Decade,[4] and that to persist therein could constitute a threat to international peace and security;

6. *Emphasizes* the duty of all States to refrain in their international relations from military, political economic or any other form of coercion aimed against the territorial integrity of any State and the exercise of its national jurisdiction;

7. *Recognizes* that, as stressed in Economic and Social Council resolution 1737 (LIV) of 4 May 1973 one of the most effective ways in which the developing countries can protect their natural resources is to establish, promote or strengthen machinery for cooperation among them which has as its main purpose to concert pricing policies, to improve conditions of access to markets, to coordinate production policies and thus, to guarantee the full exercise of sovereignty by developing countries over their natural resources;

8. *Requests* the Economic and Social Council, at its fifty-sixth session, to consider the report of the Secretary-General mentioned in the last preambular paragraph above and requests the Secretary-General to prepare a supplement to that report, in the light of the discussions that are to take place at the fifty-sixth session of the Council and of any other relevant developments, and to submit that supplementary report to the General Assembly at its twenty-ninth session.

2203rd plenary meeting
17 December 1973

---

1 Resolution 2625 (XXV), annex.

2 A/9330 and Corr.1. p. 66.

3 E/5425 and Corr.1, E/5425/Add.1.

4 Resolution 2626 (XXV).

06.00 HUMAN RIGHTS

06.10 GENERAL MATTERS

217 (III). International Bill of Human Rights

Committee: 3
Vote: A: 48 - 0 - 8; B: 40 - 0 - 8; C: 46 - 6 - 2; D: 44 - 0 - 8; E: 44 - 0 - 8
Ref.: 43(I)

A

Universal Declaration of Human Rights

Preamble

Whereas recognition of the inherent dignity and of the equal and inalienable rights of all members of the human family is the foundation of freedom, justice and peace in the world,

Whereas disregard and contempt for human rights have resulted in barbarous acts which have outraged the conscience of mankind, and the advent of a world in which human beings shall enjoy freedom of speech and belief and freedom from fear and want has been proclaimed as the highest aspiration of the common people,

Whereas it is essential, if man is not to be compelled to have recourse, as a last resort, to rebellion against tyranny and oppression, that human rights should be protected by the rule of law,

Whereas it is essential to promote the development of friendly relations between nations,

Whereas the peoples of the United Nations have in the Charter reaffirmed their faith in fundamental human rights, in the dignity and worth of the human person and in the equal rights of men and women and have determined to promote social progress and better standards of life in larger freedom,

Whereas Member States have pledged themselves to achieve, in cooperation with the United Nations, the promotion of universal respect for and observance of human rights and fundamental freedoms,

Whereas a common understanding of these rights and freedoms is of the greatest importance for the full realization of this pledge,

Now, therefore,

The General Assembly

Proclaims this Universal Declaration of Human Rights as a common standard of achievement for all peoples and all nations, to the end that every individual and every organ of society, keeping this Declaration constantly in mind, shall strive by teaching and education to promote respect for these rights and freedoms and by progressive measures, national and international, to secure their universal and effective recognition and observance, both among the peoples of Member States themselves and among the peoples of territories under their jurisdiction.

Article 1

All human beings are born free and equal in dignity and rights. They are endowed with reason and conscience and should act towards one another in a spirit of brotherhood.

Article 2

Everyone is entitled to all the rights and freedoms set forth in this Declaration, without distinction of any kind, such as race, colour, sex, language, religion, political or other opinion, national or social origin, property, birth or other status.

Furthermore, no distinction shall be made on the basis of the political, jurisdictional or international status of the country or territory to which a person belongs, whether it be independent, trust, non-self-governing or under any other limitation of sovereignty.

Article 3

Everyone has the right to life, liberty and security of person.

Article 4

No one shall be held in slavery or servitude; slavery and the slave trade shall be prohibited in all their forms.

Article 5

No one shall be subjected to torture or to cruel, inhuman or degrading treatment or punishment.

Article 6

Everyone has the right to recognition everywhere as a person before the law.

Article 7

All are equal before the law and are entitled without any discrimination to equal protection of the law. All are entitled to equal protection against any discrimination in violation of this Declaration and against any incitement to such discrimination.

Article 8

Everyone has the right to an effective remedy by the competent national tribunals for acts violating the fundamental rights granted him by the constitution or by law.

Article 9

No one shall be subjected to arbitrary arrest, detention or exile.

Article 10

Everyone is entitled in full equality to a fair and public hearing by an independent and impartial tribunal, in the determination of his rights and obligations and of any criminal charge against him.

Article 11

1. Everyone charged with a penal offence has the right to be presumed innocent until proved guilty according to law in a public trial at which he has had all the guarantees necessary for his defence.

2. No one shall be held guilty of any penal offence on account of any act or omission which did not constitute a penal offence, under national or international law, at the time when it was committed. Nor shall a heavier penalty be imposed than the one that was applicable at the time the penal offence was committed.

Article 12

No one shall be subjected to arbitrary interference with his privacy, family, home or correspondence, nor to attacks upon his honour and reputation. Everyone has the right to the protection of the law against such interference or attacks.

Article 13

1. Everyone has the right to freedom of movement and residence within the borders of each State.

2. Everyone has the right to leave any country, including his own, and to return to his country.

Article 14

1. Everyone has the right to seek and to enjoy in other countries asylum from persecution.

2. This right may not be invoked in the case of prosecutions genuinely arising from non-political crimes or from acts contrary to the purposes and principles of the United Nations.

Article 15

1. Everyone has the right to a nationality.

2. No one shall be arbitrarily deprived of his nationality nor denied the right to change his nationality.

Article 16

1. Men and women of full age, without any limitation due to race, nationality or religion, have the right to marry and to found a family. They are entitled to equal rights as to marriage, during marriage and at its dissolution.

2. Marriage shall be entered into only with the free and full consent of the intending spouses.

3. The family is the natural and fundamental group unit of society and is entitled to protection by society and the State.

Article 17

1. Everyone has the right to own property alone as well as in association with others.

2. No one shall be arbitrarily deprived of his property.

Article 18

Everyone has the right to freedom of thought, conscience and religion; this right includes freedom to change his religion or belief, and freedom, either alone or in community with others and in public or private, to manifest his religion or belief in teaching, practice, worship and observance.

Article 19

Everyone has the right to freedom of opinion and expression; this right includes freedom to hold opinions without interference and to seek, receive and impart information and ideas through any media and regardless of frontiers.

Article 20

1. Everyone has the right to freedom of peaceful assembly and association.

2. No one may be compelled to belong to an association.

Article 21

1. Everyone has the right to take part in the government of his country, directly or through freely chosen representatives.

2. Everyone has the right of equal access to public service in his country.

3. The will of the people shall be the basis of the authority of government; this will shall be expressed in periodic and genuine elections which shall be by universal and equal suffrage and shall be held by secret vote or by equivalent free voting procedures.

Article 22

Everyone, as a member of society, has the right to social security and is entitled to realization, through national effort and international cooperation and in accordance with the organization and resources of each State, of the economic, social and cultural rights indispensable for his dignity and the free development of his personality.

Article 23

1. Everyone has the right to work, to free choice of employment, to just and favourable conditions of work and to protection against unemployment.

2. Everyone, without any discrimination, has the right to equal pay for equal work.

3. Everyone who works has the right to just and favourable remuneration ensuring for himself and his family an existence worthy of human dignity, and supplemented, if necessary, by other means of social protection.

4. Everyone has the right to form and to join trade unions for the protection of his interests.

Article 24

Everyone has the right to rest and leisure, including reasonable limitation of working hours and periodic holidays with pay.

Article 25

1. Everyone has the right to a standard of living adequate for the health and well-being of himself and of his family including food, clothing, housing and medical care and necessary social services, and the right to security in the event of unemployment, sickness, disability, widowhood, old age or other lack of livelihood in circumstances beyond his control.

2. Motherhood and childhood are entitled to special care and assistance. All children, whether born in or out of wedlock, shall enjoy the same social protection.

Article 26

1. Everyone has the right to education. Education shall be free, at least in the elementary and fundamental stages. Elementary education shall be compulsory. Technical and professional education shall be made generally available and higher education shall be equally accessible to all on the basis of merit.

2. Education shall be directed to the full development of the human personality and to the strengthening of respect for human rights and fundamental freedoms. It shall promote understanding, tolerance and friendship among all nations, racial or religious group, and shall further the activities of the United Nations for the maintenance of peace.

3. Parents have a prior right to choose the kind of education that shall be given to their children.

Article 27

1. Everyone has the right freely to participate in the cultural life of the community, to enjoy the arts and to share in scientific advancement and its benefits.

2. Everyone has the right to the protection of the moral and material interests resulting from any scientific, literary or artistic production of which he is the author.

Article 28

Everyone is entitled to a social and international order in which the rights and freedoms set forth in this Declaration can be fully realized.

Article 29

1. Everyone has duties to the community in which alone the free and full development of his personality is possible.

2. In the exercise of his rights and freedoms, everyone shall be subject only to such limitations as are determined by law solely for the purpose of securing due recognition and respect for the rights and freedoms of others and of meeting the just requirements of morality, public order and the general welfare in a democratic society.

3. These rights and freedoms may in no case be exercised contrary to the purposes and principles of the United Nations.

Article 30

Nothing in this Declaration may be interpreted as implying for any State, group or person any right to engage in any activity or to perform any act aimed at the destruction of any of the rights and freedoms set forth herein.

Hundred and eighty-third plenary meeting
10 December 1948

B

Right of Petition

The General Assembly,

Considering that the right of petition is an essential human right, as is recognized in the Constitutions of a great number of countries,

Having considered the draft article on petitions in document A/C.3/306 and the amendments offered thereto by Cuba and France,

Decides not to take any action on this matter at the present session;

Requests the Economic and Social Council to ask the Commission on Human Rights to give further examination to the problem of petitions when studying the draft covenant on human rights and measures of implementation, in order to enable the General Assembly to consider what further action, if any, should be taken at its next regular session regarding the problem of petitions.

Hundred and eighty-third plenary meeting
10 December 1948

C

Fate of Minorities

The General Assembly,

Considering that the United Nations cannot remain indifferent to the fate of minorities,

Considering that it is difficult to adopt a uniform solution of this complex and delicate question, which has special aspects in each State in which it arises,

Considering the universal character of the Declaration of Human Rights,

Decides not to deal in a specific provision with the question of minorities in the text of this Declaration;

Refers to the Economic and Social Council the texts submitted by the delegations of the Union of Soviet Socialist Republics, Yugoslavia and Denmark on this subject contained in document A/C. 3/307/Rev. 2, and requests the Council to ask the Commission on Human Rights and the Sub-Commission on the Prevention of Discrimination and the Protection of Minorities to make a thorough study of the problem of minorities, in order that the United Nations may be able to take effective measures for the protection of racial, national, religious or linguistic minorities.

Hundred and eighty-third plenary meeting
10 December 1948

D

Publicity to be Given to the Universal Declaration of Human Rights

The General Assembly,

Considering that the adoption of the Universal Declaration of Human Rights is an historic act, destined to consolidate world peace through the contribution of the United Nations towards the liberation of individuals from the unjustified oppression and constraint to which they are too often subjected,

Considering that the text of the Declaration should be disseminated among all peoples throughout the world,

1. *Recommends* Governments of Member States to show their adherence to Article 56 of the Charter by using every means within their power solemnly to publicize the test of the Declaration and to cause it to be disseminated, displayed, read and expounded principally in schools and other educational institutions, without distinction based on the political status of countries or territories;

2. *Requests* the Secretary-General to have this Declaration widely disseminated and, to that end, to publish and distribute texts, not only in the official languages, but also, using every means at his disposal, in all languages possible;

3. *Invites* the specialized agencies and non-governmental organizations of the world to do their utmost to bring this Declaration to the attention of their members.

Hundred and eighty-third plenary meeting
10 December 1948

F

Preparation of a Draft Covenant on Human Rights and Draft Measures of Implementation

The General Assembly,

Considering that the plan of work of the Commission on Human Rights provides for an International Bill of Human Rights, to include a Declaration, a Covenant on Human Rights and measures of implementation,

Requests the Economic and Social Council to ask the Commission on Human Rights to continue to give priority in its work to the preparation of a draft Covenant on Human Rights and draft measures of implementation.

Hundred and eighty-third plenary meeting
10 December 1948

2393 (XXIII). Capital Punishment

Committee: 3
Vote: 94 - 0 - 3
Ref.: 37/192, 36/59, 32/61, 3011(XXVII), 2857(XXVI), 2394(XXIII), 2334(XXII), 1918(XVIII), 1396(XIV)

The General Assembly,

Recalling that article 3 of the Universal Declaration of Human Rights provides that everyone has the right to life, liberty and security of person,

Recalling further that article 5 of the Universal Declaration of Human Rights provides that no one shall be subjected to torture or to cruel, inhuman or degrading treatment or punishment,

Having considered the report entitled *Capital Punishment*[1] in the light of the comments[2] thereon of the *Ad Hoc* Advisory Committee of Experts on the Prevention of Crime and the Treatment of Offenders,[3] and the report entitled *Capital Punishment—Developments 1961 to 1965*,[4]

Taking note of the conclusion drawn by the Advisory Committee from the report entitled Capital Punishment that, if one looked at the whole problem of capital punishment in a historical perspective, it became clear that there was a world-wide tendency towards a considerable reduction in the number and categories of offences for which capital punishment might be imposed,

Taking note also of the view expressed in the report entitled *Capital Punishment—Developments 1961 to 1965* that there is an over-all tendency in the world towards fewer executions,

Taking note of the report of the meeting of the Consultative Group on the Prevention of Crime and the Treatment of offenders held in August 1968, in so far as it relates to the question of capital punishment,[5] and of the view of the Group that there is a strong trend in most countries towards the abolition of capital punishment or at least towards fewer executions,

Desiring to promote further the dignity of man and thus to contribute to the International Year for Human Rights,

---

1 United Nations publication, Sales No.: E.67.IV.15, part I.

2 *Official Records of the Economic and Social Council, Thirty-fifth Session, Annexes,* agenda item 11, document E/3724, section III.

3 In accordance with Economic and Social Council resolution 1086 B (XXXIX) of 30 July 1965, the ad hoc Committee was established on a permanent basis as the Advisory Committee of Experts on the Prevention of Crime and the Treatment of Offenders.

4 United Nations publication, Sales No.: E.67.IV.15, part II.

5 *Official Records of the General Assembly, Twenty-third Session, Annexes,* agenda item 59, document A/7243, annex.

1. *Invites* Governments of Member States:

(*a*) To ensure the most careful legal procedures and the greatest possible safeguards for the accused in capital cases in countries where the death penalty obtains, *inter alia*, by providing that:

(i) A person condemned to death shall not be deprived of the right to appeal to a higher judicial authority or, as the case may be, to petition for pardon or reprieve;

(ii) A death sentence shall not be carried out until the procedures of appeal or, as the case may be, of petition for pardon or reprieve have been terminated;

(iii) Special attention be given in the case of indigent persons by the provision of adequate legal assistance at all stages of the proceedings;

(*b*) To consider whether the careful legal procedures and safeguards referred to in sub-paragraph (a) above may not be further strengthened by the fixing of a time-limit or time-limits before the expiry of which no death sentence shall be carried out, as has already been recognized in certain international conventions dealing with specific situations;

(c) To inform the Secretary-General not later than 10 December 1970 of actions which may have been taken in accordance with sub-paragraph (a) above and of the results to which their consideration in accordance with sub-paragraph (b) above may have led;

2. *Requests* the Secretary-General to invite Governments of Member States to inform him of their present attitude to possible further restriction of the use of the death penalty or to its total abolition, and to state whether they are contemplating restriction or abolition and also to indicate whether changes in this respect have taken place since 1965;

3. *Further requests* the Secretary-General to submit a report on the matter dealt with in paragraphs 1 (c) and 2 above to the Economic and Social Council at one of its sessions to be held in 1971.

1727th plenary meeting
26 November 1968

3452 (XXX). Declaration on the Protection of All Persons from Being Subjected to Torture and other Cruel, Inhuman or Degrading Treatment or Punishment

Committee: 3
Vote: Adopted without a vote
Ref.: 38/119, 37/193, 36/60, 35/178, 34/167, 33/178, 32/64, 32/63, 31/85, 3453(XXX), 3218(XXIX), 3059(XXVIII)

The General Assembly,

Considering that, in accordance with the principles proclaimed in the Charter of the United Nations, recognition of the inherent dignity and of the equal and inalienable rights of all members of the human family is the foundation of freedom, justice and peace in the world,

Considering that these rights derive from the inherent dignity of the human person,

Considering also the obligation of States under the Charter, in particular Article 55, to promote universal respect for, and observance of, human rights and fundamental freedoms,

Having regard to article 5 of the Universal Declaration of Human Rights[1] and article 7 of the International Covenant on Civil and Political Rights,[2] both of which provide that no one may be subjected to torture or to cruel, inhuman or degrading treatment or punishment,

Adopts the Declaration on the Protection of All Persons from Being Subjected to Torture and Other Cruel, Inhuman or Degrading Treatment or Punishment, the text of which is annexed to the present resolution, as a guideline for all States and other entities exercising effective power.

2433rd plenary meeting
9 December 1975

Annex

Declaration on the Protection of All Persons from Being Subjected to Torture and other Cruel, Inhuman or Degrading Treatment or Punishment

Article 1

1. For the purpose of this Declaration, torture means any act by which severe pain or suffering, whether physical or mental, is intentionally inflicted by or at the instigation of a public official on a person for such purposes as obtaining from him or a third person information or confession, punishing him for an act he has committed or is suspected of having committed, or intimidating him or other persons. It does not include pain or suffering arising only from, inherent in or incidental to, lawful sanctions to the extent consistent with the Standard Minimum Rules for the Treatment of Prisoners.[3]

2. Torture constitutes an aggravated and deliberate form of cruel, inhuman or degrading treatment or punishment.

Article 2

Any act of torture or other cruel, inhuman or degrading treatment or punishment is an offence to human dignity and shall be condemned as a denial of the purposes of the Charter of the United Nations and as a violation of the human rights and fundamental freedoms proclaimed in the Universal Declaration of Human Rights.

Article 3

No State may permit or tolerate torture or other cruel, inhuman or degrading treatment or punishment. Exceptional circumstances such as a state of war or a threat of war, internal political instability or any other public emergency may not be invoked as a justification of torture or other cruel, inhuman or degrading treatment or punishment.

Article 4

Each State shall, in accordance with the provisions of this Declaration, take effective measures to prevent torture and other cruel, inhuman or degrading treatment or punishment from being practised within its jurisdiction.

Article 5

The training of law enforcement personnel and of other pubic officials who may be responsible for persons deprived of their liberty shall ensure that full account is taken of the prohibition against torture and other cruel, inhuman or degrading treatment or punishment. This prohibition shall also, where appropriate, be included in such general rules or instructions as are issued in regard to the duties and functions of anyone who may be involved in the custody or treatment of such persons.

Article 6

Each State shall keep under systematic review interrogation methods and practices as well as arrangements for the custody and treatment of persons deprived of their liberty in its territory, with a view to preventing any cases of torture or other cruel, inhuman or degrading treatment or punishment

Article 7

Each State shall ensure that all acts of torture as defined in article 1 are offences under its criminal law. The same shall apply in regard to acts which constitute participation in, complicity in, incitement to or an attempt to commit torture.

Article 8

Any person who alleges that he has been subjected to torture or other cruel, inhuman or degrading treatment or punishment by or at the instigation of a public official shall have the right to complain to, and

---

1 Resolution 217 A (III).

2 Resolution 2200 A (XXI), annex.

3 *First United Nations Congress on the Prevention of Crime and the Treatment of Offenders: report by the Secretariat* (United Nations publication, Sales No. 1956.IV.4), annex I.A.

to have his case impartially examined by, the competent authorities of the State concerned.

Article 9

Wherever there is reasonable ground to believe that an act of torture as defined in article 1 has been committed, the competent authorities of the State concerned shall promptly proceed to an impartial investigation even if there has been no formal complaint.

Article 10

If an investigation under article 8 or article 9 establishes that an act of torture as defined in article 1 appears to have been committed, criminal proceedings shall be instituted against the alleged offender or offenders in accordance with national law. If an allegation of other forms of cruel, inhuman or degrading treatment or punishment is considered to be well founded, the alleged offender or offenders shall be subject to criminal, disciplinary or other appropriate proceedings.

Article 11

Where it is proved that an act of torture or other cruel, inhuman or degrading treatment or punishment has been committed by or at the instigation of a public official, the victim shall be afforded redress and compensation in accordance with national law.

Article 12

Any statement which is established to have been made as a result of torture or other cruel, inhuman or degrading treatment or punishment may not be invoked as evidence against the person concerned or against any other person in any proceedings.

34/169. Code of Conduct for Law Enforcement Officials

Committee: 3
Vote: Adopted without a vote
Ref.: 35/170, 33/179

The General Assembly,

Considering that the purposes proclaimed in the Charter of the United Nations include the achievement of international cooperation in promoting and encouraging respect for human rights and for fundamental freedoms for all without distinction as to race, sex, language or religion,

Recalling, in particular, the Universal Declaration of Human Rights[1] and the International Covenants on Human Rights,[2]

Recalling also the Declaration on the Protection of All Persons from Being Subjected to Torture and Other Cruel, Inhuman or Degrading Treatment or Punishment, adopted by the General Assembly in its resolution 3452 (XXX) of 9 December 1975,

Mindful that the nature of the functions of law enforcement in the defence of public order and the manner in which those functions are exercised have a direct impact on the quality of life of individuals as well as of society as a whole,

Conscious of the important task which law enforcement officials are performing diligently and with dignity in compliance with the principles of human rights,

Aware, nevertheless, of the potential for abuse which the exercise of such duties entails,

Recognizing that the establishment of a code of conduct for law enforcement officials is only one of several important measures for providing the citizenry served by law enforcement officials with protection of all their rights and interests,

Aware that there are additional important principles and prerequisites for the humane performance of law enforcement functions, namely:

(*a*) That, like all agencies of the criminal justice system, every law enforcement agency should be representative of and responsive and accountable to the community as a whole,

(*b*) That the effective maintenance of ethical standards among law enforcement officials depends on the existence of a well-conceived, popularly accepted and humane system of laws,

(*c*) That every law enforcement official is part of the criminal justice system, the aim of which is to prevent and control crime, and that the conduct of every functionary within the system has an impact on the entire system,

(*d*) That every law enforcement agency, in fulfilment of the first premise of every profession, should be held to the duty of disciplining itself in complete conformity with the principles and standards herein provided and that the actions of law enforcement officials should be responsive to public scrutiny, whether exercised by a review board, a ministry, a procuracy, the judiciary, an ombudsman, a citizens' committee or arty combination thereof, or any other reviewing agency,

(*e*) That standards as such lack practical value unless their content and meaning, through education and training and through monitoring, become part of the creed of every law enforcement official,

Adopts the Code of Conduct for Law Enforcement Officials set forth in the annex to the present resolution and decides to transmit it to Governments with the recommendation that favourable consideration should be given to its use within the framework of national legislation or practice as a body of principles for observance by law enforcement officials.

106th plenary meeting
17 December 1979

Annex

Code of Conduct for Law Enforcement Officials

Article 1

Law enforcement officials shall at all times fulfil the duty imposed upon them by law, by serving the community and by protecting all persons against illegal acts, consistent with the high degree of responsibility required by their profession.

Commentary:[3]

(*a*) The term "law enforcement officials" includes all officers of the law, whether appointed or elected, who exercise police powers, especially the powers of arrest or detention.

(*b*) In countries where police powers are exercised by military authorities, whether uniformed or not, or by state security forces, the definition of law enforcement officials shall be regarded as including officers of such services.

(*c*) Service to the community is intended to include particularly the rendition of services of assistance to those members of the community who by reason of personal, economic, social or other emergencies are in need of immediate aid.

(*d*) This provision is intended to cover not only all violent, predatory and harmful acts, but extends to the full range of prohibitions under penal statutes. It extends to contact by persons not capable of incurring criminal liability.

Article 2

In the performance of their duty, law enforcement officials shall respect and protect human dignity and maintain and uphold the human rights of all persons.

Commentary:

(*a*) The human rights in question are identified and protected by national and international law. Among the relevant international

1 Resolution 217 A (III).

2 Resolution 2200 A (XXI), annex.

3 The commentaries provide information to facilitate the use of the Code within the framework of national legislation or practice. In addition, national or regional commentaries could identify specific features of the legal systems and practices of different States or regional intergovernmental organizations which would promote the application of the Code.

instruments are the Universal Declaration of Human Rights, the International Covenant on Civil and Political Rights, the Declaration on the Protection of All Persons from Being Subjected to Torture and Other Cruel, Inhuman or Degrading Treatment or Punishment, the United Nations Declaration on the Elimination of All Forms of Racial Discrimination, the International Convention on the Elimination of All Forms of Racial Discrimination, the International Convention on the Suppression and Punishment of the Crime of Apartheid, the Convention on the Prevention and Punishment of the Crime of Genocide, the Standard Minimum Rules for the Treatment of Prisoners and the Vienna Convention on Consular Relations.

(*b*) National commentaries to this provision should indicate regional or national provisions identifying and protecting these rights.

Article 3

Law enforcement officials may use force only when strictly necessary and to the extent required for the performance of their duty.

Commentary:

(*a*) This provision emphasizes that the use of force by law enforcement officials should be exceptional; while it implies that law enforcement officials may be authorized to use force as is reasonably necessary under the circumstances for the prevention of crime or in effecting or assisting in the lawful arrest of offenders or suspected offenders, no force going beyond that may be used.

(*b*) National law ordinarily restricts the use of force by law enforcement officials in accordance with a principle of proportionality. It is to be understood that such national principles of proportionality are to be respected in the interpretation of this provision. In no case should this provision be interpreted to authorize the use of force which is disproportionate to the legitimate objective to be achieved.

(*c*) The use of firearms is considered an extreme measure. Every effort should be made to exclude the use of firearms especially against children. In general, firearms should not be used except when a suspected offender offers armed resistance or otherwise jeopardizes the lives of others and less extreme measures are not sufficient to restrain or apprehend the suspected offender. In every instance in which a firearm is discharged, a report should be made promptly to the competent authorities.

Article 4

Matters of a confidential nature in the possession of law enforcement officials shall be kept confidential, unless the performance of duty or the needs of justice strictly require otherwise.

Commentary:

By the nature of their duties, law enforcement officials obtain information which may relate to private lives or be potentially harmful to the interests, and especially the reputation, of others. Great care should be exercised in safeguarding and using such information, which should be disclosed only in the performance of duty or to serve the needs of justice. Any disclosure of such information for other purposes is wholly improper.

Article 5

No law enforcement official may inflict, instigate or tolerate any act of torture or other cruel, inhuman or degrading treatment or punishment, nor may any law enforcement official invoke superior orders or exceptional circumstances such as a state of war or a threat of war, a threat to national security, internal political instability or any other public emergency as a justification of torture or other cruel, inhuman or degrading treatment or punishment.

Commentary:

(*a*) This prohibition derives from the Declaration on the Protection of All Persons from Being Subjected to Torture and Other Cruel, Inhuman or Degrading Treatment or Punishment, adopted by the General Assembly, according to which:

> "[Such an act is] an offence to human dignity and shall be condemned as a denial of the purposes of the Charter of the United Nations and as a violation of the human rights and fundamental freedoms proclaimed in the Universal Declaration of Human Rights [and other international human rights instruments]."

(*b*) The Declaration defines torture as follows:

> "... torture means any act by which severe pain or suffering, whether physical or mental, is intentionally inflicted by or at the instigation of a public official on a person for such purposes as obtaining from him or a third person information or confession, punishing him for an act he has committed or is suspected of having committed or intimidating him or other persons. It does not include pain or suffering arising only from inherent in or incidental to, lawful sanctions to the extent consistent with the Standard Minimum Rules for the Treatment of Prisoners."[1]

(*c*) The term "cruel, inhuman or degrading treatment or punishment" has not been defined by the General Assembly but should be interpreted so as to extend the widest possible protection against abuses, whether physical or mental.

Article 6

Law enforcement officials shall ensure the full protection of the health of persons in their custody and, in particular, shall take immediate action to secure medical attention whenever required.

Commentary:

(*a*) "Medical attention", which refers to services rendered by any medical personnel, including certified medical practitioners and paramedics, shall be secured when needed or requested.

(*b*) While the medical personnel are likely to be attached to the law enforcement operation, law enforcement officials must take into account the judgement of such personnel when they recommend providing the person in custody with appropriate treatment through, or in consultation with, medical personnel from outside the law enforcement operation.

(*c*) It is understood that law enforcement officials shall also secure medical attention for victims of violations of law or of accidents occurring in the course of violations of law.

Article 7

Law enforcement officials shall not commit any act of corruption. They shall also rigorously oppose and combat all such act.

Commentary:

(*a*) Any act of corruption, in the same way as any other abuse of authority, is incompatible with the profession of law enforcement officials. The law must be enforced fully with respect to any law enforcement official who commits an act of corruption, as Governments cannot expect to enforce the law among their citizens if they cannot, or will not, enforce the law against their own agents and within their own agencies.

(*b*) While the definition of corruption must be subject to national law, it should be understood to encompass the commission or omission of an act in the performance of or in connexion with one's duties, in response to gifts, promises or incentives demanded or accepted, or the wrongful receipt of these once the act has been committed or omitted.

(*c*) The expression "act of corruption" referred to above should be understood to encompass attempted corruption.

Article 8

Law enforcement officials shall respect the law and the present Code. They shall also, to the best of their capability, prevent and rigorously oppose any violations of them.

Law enforcement officials who have reason to believe that a violation of the present Code has occurred or is about to occur shall report the matter to their superior authorities and, where necessary, to other appropriate authorities or organs vested with reviewing or remedial power.

---

1 *First United Nations Congress on the Prevention of Crime and the Treatment of Offenders: report prepared by the Secretariat* (United Nations publication, Sales No. 1956.IV.4), annex I.A.

Commentary:

(*a*) This Code shall be observed whenever it has been incorporated into national legislation or practice. If legislation or practice contains stricter provisions than those of the present Code, those stricter provisions shall be observed.

(*b*) The article seeks to preserve the balance between the need for internal discipline of the agency on which public safety is largely dependent, on the one hand, and the need for dealing with violations of basic human rights, on the other. Law enforcement officials shall report violations within the chain of command and take other lawful action outside the chain of command only when no other remedies are available or effective. It is understood that law enforcement officials shall not suffer administrative or other penalties because they have reported that a violation of this Code has occurred or is about to occur.

(*c*) The term "appropriate authorities or organs vested with reviewing or remedial power" refers to any authority or organ existing under national law, whether internal to the law enforcement agency or independent thereof, with statutory, customary or other power to review grievances and complaints arising out of violations within the purview of this Code.

(*d*) In some countries, the mass media may be regarded as performing complaint review functions similar to those described in subparagraph (c) above. Law enforcement officials may, therefore, be justified if, as a last resort and in accordance with the laws and customs of their own countries and with the provisions of article 4 of the present Code, they bring violations to the attention of public opinion through the mass media.

(*e*) Law enforcement officials who comply with the provisions of this Code deserve the respect, the full support and the cooperation of the community and of the law enforcement agency in which they serve, as well as the law enforcement profession.

34/178. The Right of Amparo, Habeas Corpus or Other Legal Remedies to the Same Effect

Committee: 3
Vote: Adopted without a vote

The General Assembly,

Bearing in mind the provisions of the Universal Declaration of Human Rights,[1] of the Declaration on the Protection of All Persons from Being Subjected to Torture and Other Cruel, Inhuman or Degrading Treatment or Punishment[2] and of the International Covenant on Civil and Political Rights,[3]

Mindful, in particular, of article 9, paragraph 4, of the said Covenant, which stipulates that anyone who is deprived of his liberty by arrest or detention shall be entitled to take proceedings before a court, in order that that court may decide without delay on the lawfulness of his detention and order his release if the detention is not lawful,

Recalling its resolution 32/121 of 16 December 1977, concerning the protection of the human rights of persons who are detained in respect of offences which they have committed, or are suspected of having committed, by reason of their political opinions or convictions,

Recalling also its resolutions 33/169 of 20 December 1978, concerning persons arrested or detained for trade union activities, and 33/173 of 20 December 1978 on disappeared persons,

Noting that the year 1979 marks the three hundredth anniversary of the act which in 1679 gave statutory force to the remedy of habeas corpus,

Recalling that, from 15 to 28 August 1961, a seminar on *amparo, habeas corpus* and other similar remedies was organized by the United Nations at Mexico City,[4] under the programme of advisory services in the field of human rights,

1. *Expresses its conviction* that the application within the legal system of States of *amparo, habeas corpus* or other legal remedies to the same effect is of fundamental importance for:

(*a*) Protecting persons against arbitrary arrest and unlawful detention;

(*b*) Effecting the release of persons who are detained by reason of their political opinions or convictions, including in pursuance of trade union activities;

(*c*) Clarifying the whereabouts and fate of missing and disappeared persons;

2. *Considers* that the use of those remedies may also forestall opportunities for persons exercising power over detainees to engage in torture or other cruel, inhuman or degrading treatment or punishment;

3. *Calls upon* all Governments to guarantee to persons within their jurisdiction the full enjoyment of the right of *amparo, habeas corpus* or other legal remedies to the same effect, as may be applicable in their legal system;

4. *Decides* that, in order to extend the global understanding and larger applications of institutions such as amparo, habeas corpus or other legal remedies to the same effect, an international seminar on the matter would be timely and useful;

5. *Decides further* to consider this question again at its thirty-fifth session.

106th plenary meeting
17 December 1979

37/178. The Right to Education

Committee: 3
Vote: Adopted without a vote

The General Assembly,

Recalling its resolutions 34/170 of 17 December 1979, 35/191 of 15 December 1980 and 36/152 of 16 December 1981 on the right to education,

Recalling the International Covenant on Economic, Social and Cultural Rights, adopted by its resolution 2200 A (XXI) of 16 December 1966, which recognizes the right of everyone to education,

Bearing in mind the importance of the Convention against Discrimination in Education,[5] adopted on 14 December 1960 by the General Conference of the United Nations Educational, Scientific and Cultural Organization,

Reaffirming the paramount importance of the implementation of the right to education for the full development of the human personality and for the enjoyment of other fundamental human rights and freedoms,

Recognizing that for the effective implementation of the right to education the eradication of illiteracy has a particular priority and urgency,

Convinced that the educational process could bring a substantial contribution to social progress, national development, mutual understanding and cooperation among peoples and to strengthening peace and international security,

Recalling that the establishment of the new international economic order requires effective support for the improvement and expansion of educational systems and for the training of specialized personnel and qualified cadres for the economic development of developing countries,

Convinced of the topicality and urgency of provisions on cducation contained in the International Development Strategy for the Third United Nations Development Decade,[6]

---

1 Resolution 217 A (III).

2 Resolution 3452 (XXX), annex.

3 Resolution 2200 A (XXI), annex.

4 The report of the seminar was issued as document ST/TAO/HR/ 12.

5 United Nations, *Treaty Series,* vol. 429, No. 6193, p. 93.

6 See resolution 35/36, annex, sect. O.

Recalling that, since its establishment, the United Nations Educational, Scientific and Cultural Organization has constantly striven for effective realization of the right to education and equality of educational opportunities for all, without distinction as to race, colour, sex, language, religion, political or other opinion, national or social origin, economic status or birth and that, for many years past, activities directed to securing the right to education and the extension and improvement of educational and training systems in Member States, more particularly in the developing countries, have occupied a central place in that organization's programme,

Aware of the important contribution of the United Nations Educational, Scientific and Cultural Organization to the implementation of the International Development Strategy for the Third United Nations Development Decade with a view to fostering the full implementation of the right to education,

Taking note with satisfaction of the interest shown by the Executive Board of the United Nations Educational, Scientific and Cultural Organization for the implementation of General Assembly resolutions 34/170, 35/191 and 36/152,

1. *Takes note* of the conclusions contained in the report of the Director-General of the United Nations Educational, Scientific and Cultural Organization on the right to education;[1]

2. *Commends* the United Nations Educational, Scientific and Cultural Organization for including on a permanent basis, in its medium-term plan, the issue of the implementation of the right to education;

3. *Again invites* all States to consider the adoption of appropriate legislative, administrative and other measures, including material guarantees, in order to ensure full implementation of the right to universal education through, *inter alia*, free and compulsory primary education, universal and gradually free-of-charge secondary education, equal access to all educational facilities and the access of the young generation to science and culture;

4. *Invites* all States to give all necessary attention to defining and determining in a more precise manner the means for implementing the provisions concerning the role of education in the International Development Strategy for the Third United Nations Development Decade;

5. *Invites* all specialized agencies to cooperate with the United Nations Educational, Scientific and Cultural Organization to ensure education a high priority in the implementation of various programmes and projects within the framework of the International Development Strategy for the Third United Nations Development Decade;

6. *Appeals once again* to all States, in particular the developed countries, to support actively, through fellowships and other means, including the general increasing of resources for education and training, the efforts of the developing countries in the education and training of national personnel needed in industry, agriculture and other economic and social sectors;

7. *Expresses its thanks* to the Director-General of the United Nations Educational, Scientific and Cultural Organization for his report on the right to education, submitted in accordance with General Assembly resolution 36/152;

8. *Invites* the United Nations Educational, Scientific and Cultural Organization to continue its intensive efforts for the promotion at the universal level of the right to education and to inform the General Assembly, in appropriate forms, of the progress achieved in this field.

110th plenary meeting
17 December 1982

[1] See A/37/521, annex.

37/194. Principles of Medical Ethics

Committee: 3
Vote: Adopted without a vote
Ref.: 38/118, 36/61, 35/179, 34/168

The General Assembly,

Recalling its resolution 31/85 of 13 December 1976, in which it invited the World Health Organization to prepare a draft code of medical ethics relevant to the protection of persons subjected to any form of detention or imprisonment against torture and other cruel, inhuman or degrading treatment or punishment,

Expressing once again its appreciation to the Executive Board of the World Health Organization which, at its sixty-third session, in January 1979, decided to endorse the principles set forth in a report entitled "Development of codes of medical ethics" containing, in an annex, a draft body of principles prepared by the Council for International Organizations of Medical Sciences and entitled "Principles of medical ethics relevant to the role of health personnel in the protection of persons against torture and other cruel, inhuman or degrading treatment or punishment",

Bearing in mind Economic and Social Council resolution 1981/27 of 6 May 1981, in which the Council recommended that the General Assembly should take measures to finalize the draft Principles of Medical Ethics at its thirty-sixth session,

Recalling its resolution 36/61 of 25 November 1981, in which it decided to consider the draft Principles of Medical Ethics at its thirty-seventh session with a view to adopting them,

Alarmed that not infrequently members of the medical profession or other health personnel are engaged in activities which are difficult to reconcile with medical ethics,

Recognizing that throughout the world significant medical activities are increasingly being performed by health personnel not licensed or trained as physicians, such as physician-assistants, paramedics, physical therapists and nurse practitioners,

Recalling with appreciation the Declaration of Tokyo of the World Medical Association, containing the Guidelines for Medical Doctors concerning Torture and Other Cruel, Inhuman or Degrading Treatment or Punishment in relation to Detention and Imprisonment, adopted by the twenty-ninth World Medical Assembly, held at Tokyo in October 1975,

Noting that in accordance with the Declaration of Tokyo measures should be taken by States and by professional associations and other bodies, as appropriate, against any attempt to subject health personnel or members of their families to threats or reprisals resulting from a refusal by such personnel to condone the use of torture or other forms of cruel, inhuman or degrading treatment,

Reaffirming the Declaration on the Protection of All Persons from Being Subjected to Torture and Other Cruel, Inhuman or Degrading Treatment or Punishment, unanimously adopted by the General Assembly in its resolution 3452 (XXX) of 9 December 1975, in which it declared any act of torture or other cruel, inhuman or degrading treatment or punishment an offence to human dignity, a denial of the purposes of the Charter of the United Nations and a violation of the Universal Declaration of Human Rights,

Recalling that, in accordance with article 7 of the Declaration adopted in resolution 3452 (XXX), each State shall ensure that the commission of all acts of torture, as defined in article 1 of that Declaration, or participation in, complicity in, incitement to or attempt to commit torture are offences under its criminal law,

Convinced that under no circumstances should a person be punished for carrying out medical activities compatible with medical ethics, regardless of the person benefiting therefrom, or be compelled to perform acts or to carry out work in contravention of medical ethics, but that, at the same time, contravention of medical ethics for which health personnel, particularly physicians, can be held responsible should entail accountability,

Desirous of setting further standards in this field which ought to be implemented by health personnel, particularly physicians, and by Government officials,

1. *Adopts* the Principles of Medical Ethics relevant to the role of health personnel, particularly physicians, in the protection of prisoners and detainees against torture and other cruel, inhuman or degrading treatment or punishment, set forth in the annex to the present resolution;

2. *Calls upon* all Governments to give the Principles of Medical Ethics, together with the present resolution, the widest possible distribution, in particular among medical and paramedical associations and institutions of detention or imprisonment, in an official language of the State;

3. *Invites* all relevant intergovernmental organizations, in particular the World Health Organization, and non-governmental organizations concerned to bring the Principles of Medical Ethics to the attention of the widest possible group of individuals, especially those active in the medical and paramedical field.

111th plenary meeting
18 December 1982

Annex

Principles of Medical Ethics Relevant to the Role of Health Personnel, Particularly Physicians, in the Protection of Prisoners and Detainees Against Torture and Other Cruel, Inhuman or Degrading Treatment or Punishment

Principle 1

Health personnel, particularly physicians, charged with the medical care of prisoners and detainees have a duty to provide them with protection of their physical and mental health and treatment of disease of the same quality and standard as is afforded to those who are not imprisoned or detained.

Principle 2

It is a gross contravention of medical ethics, as well as an offence under applicable international instruments, for health personnel, particularly physicians, to engage, actively or passively, in acts which constitute participation in, complicity in, incitement to or attempts to commit torture or other cruel, inhuman or degrading treatment or punishment.[1]

Principle 3

It is a contravention of medical ethics for health personnel, particularly physicians, to be involved in any professional relationship with prisoners or detainees the purpose of which is not solely to evaluate, protect or improve their physical and mental health.

Principle 4

It is a contravention of medical ethics for health personnel, particularly physicians:

(*a*) To apply their knowledge and skills in order to assist in the interrogation of prisoners and detainees in a manner that may adversely affect the physical or mental health or condition of such prisoners or detainees and which is not in accordance with the relevant international instruments;[2]

(*b*) To certify, or to participate in the certification of, the fitness of prisoners or detainees for any form of treatment or punishment that may adversely affect their physical or mental health and which is not in accordance with the relevant international instruments, or to participate in any way in the infliction of any such treatment or punishment which is not in accordance with the relevant international instruments.

Principle 5

It is a contravention of medical ethics for health personnel, particularly physicians, to participate in any procedure for restraining a prisoner or detainee unless such a procedure is determined in accordance with purely medical criteria as being necessary for the protection of the physical or mental health or the safety of the prisoner or detainee himself, of his fellow prisoners or detainees, or of his guardians, and presents no hazard to his physical or mental health.

Principle 6

There may be no derogation from the foregoing principles on any ground whatsoever, including public emergency.

39/11. Declaration of the Right of Peoples to Peace

Committee: -
Vote: 92 - 0 - 34
Ref.: 43/22, 41/10, 40/11

The General Assembly,

Having considered the item entitled "Right of Peoples to peace"

Convinced that a proclamation of the right of peoples to peace would contribute to the efforts aimed at the strengthening of international peace and security,

1. *Approves* the Declaration on the Right of Peoples to Peace, the text of which is annexed to the present resolution;

2. *Requests* the Secretary-General to ensure the widest dissemination of the Declaration to States, intergovernmental and non-governmental organizations as well as other appropriate organizations.

57th plenary meeting
12 November 1984

Annex

Declaration on the Right of Peoples to Peace

The General Assembly,

Reaffirming that the principal aim of the United Nations is the maintenance of international peace and security,

Bearing in mind the fundamental principles of international law set forth in the Charter of the United Nations,

Expressing the will and the aspirations of all peoples to eradicate war from the life of mankind and, above all, to avert a world-wide nuclear catastrophe,

---

1 See the *Declaration on the Protection of All Persons from Being Subjected to Torture and other Cruel, Inhuman or Degrading Treatment or Punishment* (resolution 3452 (XXX), annex), article 1 of which states:

"1. For the purpose of this Declaration, torture means any act by which severe pain or suffering, whether physical or mental, is intentionally inflicted by or at the instigation of a public official on a person for such purposes as obtaining from him or a third person information or confession, punishing him for an act he has committed or is suspected of having committed, or intimidating him or other persons. It does not include pain or suffering arising only from, inherent in or incidental to, lawful sanctions to the extent consistent with the Standard Minimum Rules for the Treatment of Prisoners.

"2. Torture constitutes an aggravated and deliberate form of cruel, inhuman or degrading treatment or punishment." \b

Article 7 of the Declaration states:

"Each State shall ensure that all acts of torture as defined in article 1 are offences under its criminal law. The same shall apply in regard to acts which constitute participation in, complicity in, incitement to or an attempt to commit torture."

2 Particularly the Universal Declaration of Human Rights (resolution 217 A (III)), the International Covenants on Human Rights (resolution 2200 A (XXI), annex), the Declaration on the Protection of All Persons from Being Subjected to Torture and other Cruel, Inhuman or Degrading Treatment or Punishment (resolution 3452 (XXX), annex), and the Standard Minimum Rules for the Treatment of Prisoners *(First United Nations Congress on the Prevention of Crime and the Treatment of Offenders: report by the Secretariat* (United Nations publication, Sales No. 1956.IV.4), annex I.A.).

Convinced that life without war serves as the primary international prerequisite for the material well-being, development and progress of countries, and for the full implementation of the rights and fundamental human freedoms proclaimed by the United Nations,

Aware that in the nuclear age the establishment of a lasting peace on Earth represents the primary condition for the preservation of human civilization and the survival of mankind,

Recognizing that the maintenance of a peaceful life for peoples is the sacred duty of each State,

1. *Solemnly proclaims* that the peoples of our planet have a sacred right to peace;

2. *Solemnly declares* that the preservation of the right of peoples to peace and the promotion of its implementation constitute a fundamental obligation of each State;

3. *Emphasizes* that ensuring the exercise of the right of peoples to peace demands that the policies of States be directed towards the renunciation of the use of force in international relations and the settlement of international disputes by peaceful means on the basis of the Charter of the United Nations;

4. *Appeals* to all States and international organizations to do their utmost to assist in implementing the right of peoples to peace through the adoption of appropriate measures at both the national and the international level.

40/34. Declaration of Basic Principles of Justice for Victims of Crime and Abuse of Power

Committee: 3
Vote: Adopted without a vote

The General Assembly,

Recalling that the Sixth United Nations Congress on the Prevention of Crime and the Treatment of Offenders recommended that the United Nations should continue its present work on the development of guidelines and standards regarding abuse of economic and political power,

Cognizant that millions of people throughout the world suffer harm as a result of crime and the abuse of power and that the rights of these victims have not been adequately recognized,

Recognizing that the victims of crime and the victims of abuse of power, and also frequently their families, witnesses and others who aid them, are unjustly subjected to loss, damage or injury and that they may, in addition, suffer hardship when assisting in the prosecution of offenders,

1. *Affirms* the necessity of adopting national and international measures in order to secure the universal and effective recognition of, and respect for, the rights of victims of crime and of abuse of power;

2. *Stresses* the need to promote progress by all States in their efforts to that end, without prejudice to the rights of suspects or offenders;

3. *Adopts* the Declaration of Basic Principles of Justice for Victims of Crime and Abuse of Power, annexed to the present resolution, which is designed to assist Governments and the international community in their efforts to secure justice and assistance for victims of crime and victims of abuse of power;

4. *Calls upon* Member States to take the necessary steps to give effect to the provisions contained in the Declaration and, in order to curtail victimization as referred to hereinafter, endeavour:

(*a*) To implement social, health, including mental health, educational, economic and specific crime prevention policies to reduce victimization and encourage assistance to victims in distress;

(*b*) To promote community efforts and public participation in crime prevention;

(*c*) To review periodically their existing legislation and practices in order to ensure responsiveness to changing circumstances, and to enact and enforce legislation proscribing acts that violate internationally recognized norms relating to human rights, corporate conduct, and other abuses of power;

(*d*) To establish and strengthen the means of detecting, prosecuting and sentencing those guilty of crimes;

(*e*) To promote disclosure of relevant information to expose official and corporate conduct to public scrutiny, and other ways of increasing responsiveness to public concerns;

(*f*) To promote the observance of codes of conduct and ethical norms, in particular international standards, by public servants, including law enforcement, correctional, medical, social service and military personnel, as well as the staff of economic enterprises;

(*g*) To prohibit practices and procedures conducive to abuse, such as secret places of detention and incommunicado detention;

(*h*) To cooperate with other States, through mutual judicial and administrative assistance, in such matters as the detection and pursuit of offenders, their extradition and the seizure of their assets, to be used for restitution to the victims;

5. *Recommends* that, at the international and regional levels, all appropriate measures should be taken:

(*a*) To promote training activities designed to foster adherence to United Nations standards and norms and to curtail possible abuses;

(*b*) To sponsor collaborative action-research on ways in which victimization can be reduced and victims aided, and to promote information exchanges on the most effective means of so doing;

(*c*) To render direct aid to requesting Governments designed to help them curtail victimization and alleviate the plight of victims;

(*d*) To develop ways and means of providing recourse for victims where national channels may be insufficient;

6. *Requests* the Secretary-General to invite Member States to report periodically to the General Assembly on the implementation of the Declaration, as well as on measures taken by them to this effect;

7. *Also requests* the Secretary-General to make use of the opportunities, which all relevant bodies and organizations within the United Nations system offer, to assist Member States, whenever necessary, in improving ways and means of protecting victims both at the national level and through international cooperation;

8. *Further requests* the Secretary-General to promote the objectives of the Declaration, in particular by ensuring its widest possible dissemination;

9. *Urges* the specialized agencies and other entities and bodies of the United Nations system, other relevant intergovernmental and non-governmental organizations and the public to cooperate in the implementation of the provisions of the Declaration.

96th plenary meeting
29 November 1985

Annex

Declaration of Basic Principles of Justice for Victims of Crime and Abuse of Power

A. Victims of Crime

1. "Victims" means persons who, individually or collectively, have suffered harm, including physical or mental injury, emotional suffering, economic loss or substantial impairment of their fundamental rights, through acts or omissions that are in violation of criminal laws operative within Member States, including those laws proscribing criminal abuse of power.

2. A person may be considered a victim, under this Declaration, regardless of whether the perpetrator is identified, apprehended, prosecuted or convicted and regardless of the familial relationship between the perpetrator and the victim. The term "victim" also includes, where appropriate, the immediate family or dependants of the direct victim and persons who have suffered harm in intervening to assist victims in distress or to prevent victimization.

3. The provisions contained herein shall be applicable to all, without distinction of any kind, such as race, colour, sex, age, language, religion, nationality, political or other opinion, cultural beliefs or

practices, property, birth or family status, ethnic or social origin, and disability.

Access to justice and fair treatment

4. Victims should be treated with compassion and respect for their dignity. They are entitled to access to the mechanisms of justice and to prompt redress, as provided for by national legislation, for the harm that they have suffered.

5. Judicial and administrative mechanisms should be established and strengthened where necessary to enable victims to obtain redress through formal or informal procedures that are expeditious, fair, inexpensive and accessible. Victims should be informed of their rights in seeking redress through such mechanisms.

6. The responsiveness of judicial and administrative processes to the needs of victims should be facilitated by:

(*a*) Informing victims of their role and the scope, timing and progress of the proceedings and of the disposition of their cases, especially where serious crimes are involved and where they have requested such information;

(*b*) Allowing the views and concerns of victims to be presented and considered at appropriate stages of the proceedings where their personal interests are affected, without prejudice to the accused and consistent with the relevant national criminal justice system;

(*c*) Providing proper assistance to victims throughout the legal process;

(*d*) Taking measures to minimize inconvenience to victims, protect their privacy, when necessary, and ensure their safety, as well as that of their families and witnesses on their behalf, from intimidation and retaliation;

(*e*) Avoiding unnecessary delay in the disposition of cases and the execution of orders or decrees granting awards to victims.

7. Informal mechanisms for the resolution of disputes, including mediation, arbitration and customary justice or indigenous practices, should be utilized where appropriate to facilitate conciliation and redress for victims.

Restitution

8. Offenders or third parties responsible for their behaviour should, where appropriate, make fair restitution to victims, their families or dependants. Such restitution should include the return of property or payment for the harm or loss suffered, reimbursement of expenses incurred as a result of the victimization, the provision of services and the restoration of rights.

9. Governments should review their practices, regulations and laws to consider restitution as an available sentencing option in criminal cases, in addition to other criminal sanctions.

10. In cases of substantial harm to the environment, restitution, if ordered, should include, as far as possible, restoration of the environment, reconstruction of the infrastructure, replacement of community facilities and reimbursement of the expenses of relocation, whenever such harm results in the dislocation of a community.

11. Where public officials or other agents acting in an official or quasi-official capacity have violated national criminal laws, the victims should receive restitution from the State whose officials or agents were responsible for the harm inflicted. In cases where the Government under whose authority the victimizing act or omission occurred is no longer in existence, the State or Government successor in title should provide restitution to the victims.

Compensation

12. When compensation is not fully available from the offender or other sources, States should endeavour to provide financial compensation to:

(*a*) Victims who have sustained significant bodily injury or impairment of physical or mental health as a result of serious crimes;

(*b*) The family, in particular dependants of persons who have died or become physically or mentally incapacitated as a result of such victimization.

13. The establishment, strengthening and expansion of national funds for compensation to victims should be encouraged. Where appropriate, other funds may also be established for this purpose, including those cases where the State of which the victim is a national is not in a position to compensate the victim for the harm.

Assistance

14. Victims should receive the necessary material, medical, psychological and social assistance through governmental, voluntary, community-based and indigenous means.

15. Victims should be informed of the availability of health and social services and other relevant assistance and be readily afforded access to them.

16. Police, justice, health, social service and other personnel concerned should receive training to sensitize them to the needs of victims, and guidelines to ensure proper and prompt aid.

17. In providing services and assistance to victims, attention should be given to those who have special needs because of the nature of the harm inflicted or because of factors such as those mentioned in paragraph 3 above.

B. Victims of abuse of power

18. "Victims" means persons who, individually or collectively, have suffered harm, including physical or mental injury, emotional suffering, economic loss or substantial impairment of their fundamental rights, through acts or omissions that do not yet constitute violations of national criminal laws but of internationally recognized norms relating to human rights.

19. States should consider incorporating into the national law norms proscribing abuses of power and providing remedies to victims of such abuses. In particular, such remedies should include restitution and/or compensation, and necessary material, medical, psychological and social assistance and support.

20. States should consider negotiating multilateral international treaties relating to victims, as defined in paragraph 18.

21. States should periodically review existing legislation and practices to ensure their responsiveness to changing circumstances, should enact and enforce, if necessary, legislation proscribing acts that constitute serious abuses of political or economic power, as well as promoting policies and mechanisms for the prevention of such acts, and should develop and make readily available appropriate rights and remedies for victims of such acts.

40/144. Declaration on the Human Rights of Individuals Who Are Not Nationals of the Country in which they Live

Committee: 3
Vote: Adopted without a vote
Ref.: 39/103, 38/87, 37/169, 36/165, 35/199

The General Assembly,

Having considered the question of the human rights of individuals who are not nationals of the country in which they live,

Decides to adopt the Declaration on the Human Rights of Individuals Who are not Nationals of the Country in which They Live, which is annexed to the present resolution.

116th plenary meeting
13 December 1985

Annex

Declaration on the Human Rights of Individuals Who Are Not Nationals of the Country in which they Live

The General Assembly,

Considering that the Charter of the United Nations encourages universal respect for and observance of the human rights and fundamental freedoms of all human beings, without distinction as to race, sex, language or religion,

Considering that the Universal Declaration of Human Rights proclaims that all human beings are born free and equal in dignity and rights and that everyone is entitled to all the rights and freedoms set forth in that Declaration, without distinction of any kind, such as race, colour, sex, language, religion, political or other opinion, national or social origin, property, birth or other status,

Considering that the Universal Declaration of Human Rights proclaims further that everyone has the right to recognition everywhere as a person before the law, that all are equal before the law and entitled without any discrimination to equal protection of the law, and that all are entitled to equal protection against any discrimination in violation of that Declaration and against any incitement to such discrimination,

Being aware that the States parties to the International Covenants on Human Rights undertake to guarantee that the rights enunciated in these Covenants will be exercised without discrimination of any kind as to race, colour, sex, language, religion, political or other opinion, national or social origin, property, birth or other status,

Conscious that, with improving communications and the development of peaceful and friendly relations among countries, individuals increasingly live in countries of which they are not nationals,

Reaffirming the purposes and principles of the Charter of the United Nations,

Recognizing that the protection of human rights and fundamental freedoms provided for in international instruments should also be ensured for individuals who are not nationals of the country in which they live,

Proclaims this Declaration:

Article 1

For the purposes of this Declaration, the term "alien" shall apply, with due regard to qualifications made in subsequent articles, to any individual who is not a national of the State in which he or she is present.

Article 2

1. Nothing in this Declaration shall be interpreted as legitimizing the illegal entry into and presence in a State of any alien, nor shall any provision be interpreted as restricting the right of any State to promulgate laws and regulations concerning the entry of aliens and the terms and conditions of their stay or to establish differences between nationals and aliens. However, such laws and regulations shall not be incompatible with the international legal obligations of that State, including those in the field of human rights.

2. This Declaration shall not prejudice the enjoyment of the rights accorded by domestic law and of the rights which under international law a State is obliged to accord to aliens, even where this Declaration does not recognize such rights or recognizes them to a lesser extent.

Article 3

Every State shall make public its national legislation or regulations affecting aliens.

Article 4

Aliens shall observe the laws of the State in which they reside or are present and regard with respect the custom and traditions of the people of that State.

Article 5

1. Aliens shall enjoy, in accordance with domestic law and subject to the relevant international obligations of the State in which they are present, in particular the following rights:

(*a*) The right to life and security of person; no alien shall be subjected to arbitrary arrest or detention; no alien shall be deprived of his or her liberty except on such grounds and in accordance with such procedures as are established by law;

(*b*) The right to protection against arbitrary or unlawful interference with privacy, family, home or correspondence;

(*c*) The right to be equal before the courts, tribunals and all other organs and authorities administering justice and, when necessary, to free assistance of an interpreter in criminal proceedings and, when prescribed by law, other proceedings;

(*d*) The right to choose a spouse, to marry, to found a family;

(*e*) The right to freedom of thought, opinion, conscience and religion; the right to manifest their religion or beliefs, subject only to such limitations as are prescribed by law and are necessary to protect public safety, order, health or morals or the fundamental rights and freedoms of others;

(*f*) The right to retain their own language, culture and tradition;

(*g*) The right to transfer abroad earnings, savings or other personal monetary assets, subject to domestic currency regulations.

2. Subject to such restrictions as are prescribed by law and which are necessary in a democratic society to protect national security, public safety, public order, public health or morals or the rights and freedoms of others, and which are consistent with the other rights recognized in the relevant international instruments and those set forth in this Declaration, aliens shall enjoy the following rights:

(*a*) The right to leave the country;

(*b*) The right to freedom of expression;

(*c*) The right to peaceful assembly;

(*d*) The right to own property alone as well as in association with others, subject to domestic law.

3. Subject to the provisions referred to in paragraph 2, aliens lawfully in the territory of a State shall enjoy the right to liberty of movement and freedom to choose their residence within the borders of the State.

4. Subject to national legislation and due authorization, the spouse and minor or dependent children of an alien lawfully residing in the territory of a State shall be admitted to accompany, join and stay with the alien.

Article 6

No alien shall be subjected to torture or to cruel, inhuman or degrading treatment or punishment and, in particular, no alien shall be subjected without his or her free consent to medical or scientific experimentation.

Article 7

An alien lawfully in the territory of a State may be expelled therefrom only in pursuance of a decision reached in accordance with law and shall, except where compelling reasons of national security otherwise require, be allowed to submit the reasons why he or she should not be expelled and to have the case reviewed by, and be represented for the purpose before, the competent authority or a person or persons specially designated by the competent authority. Individual or collective expulsion of such aliens on grounds of race, colour, religion, culture, descent or national or ethnic origin is prohibited.

Article 8

1. Aliens lawfully residing in the territory of a State shall also enjoy, in accordance with the national laws, the following rights, subject to their obligations under article 4:

(*a*) The right to safe and healthy working conditions, to fair wages and equal remuneration for work of equal value without distinction of any kind, in particular, women being guaranteed conditions of work not inferior to those enjoyed by men, with equal pay for equal work;

(*b*) The right to join trade unions and other organizations or associations of their choice and to participate in their activities. No restrictions may be placed on the exercise of this right other than those prescribed by law and which are necessary, in a democratic society, in the interests of national security or public order or for the protection of the rights and freedoms of others;

(*c*) The right to health protection, medical care, social security, social services, education, rest and leisure, provided that they fulfil the requirements under the relevant regulations for participation and that undue strain is not placed on the resources of the State.

2. With a view to protecting the rights of aliens carrying on lawful paid activities in the country in which they are present, such rights may be specified by the Governments concerned in multilateral or bilateral conventions.

Article 9

No alien shall be arbitrarily deprived of his or her lawfully acquired assets.

Article 10

Any alien shall be free at any time to communicate with the consulate or diplomatic mission of the State of which he or she is a national or, in the absence, thereof, with the consulate or diplomatic mission of any other State entrusted with the protection of the interests of the State of which he or she is a national in the State where he or she resides.

41/120. Setting International Standards in the Field of Human Rights

Committee: 3
Vote: Adopted without a vote

The General Assembly,

Recalling the extensive network of international standards in the field of human rights, which it and other United Nations bodies, including the specialized agencies, have established,

Emphasizing the primacy of the Universal Declaration of Human Rights, the International Covenant on Civil and Political Rights and the International Covenant on Economic, Social and Cultural Rights in this network,

Reaffirming that effective implementation of these international standards is of fundamental importance,

Recognizing the value of continuing efforts to identify specific areas where further international action is required to develop the existing international legal framework in the field of human rights pursuant to Article 13, paragraph 1 a, of the Charter of the United Nations,

Recognizing also that standard setting should proceed with adequate preparation,

Emphasizing that the standard setting activities of the United Nations should be as effective and efficient as possible,

1. *Calls upon* Member States and United Nations bodies to accord priority to the implementation of existing international standards in the field of human rights and urges broad ratification of, or accession to, existing treaties in this field;

2. *Urges* Member States and United Nations bodies engaged in developing new international human rights standards to give due consideration in this work to the established international legal framework;

3. *Reaffirms* the important role of the Commission on Human Rights, among other appropriate United Nations bodies, in the development of international instruments in the field of human rights;

4. *Invites* Member States and United Nations bodies to bear in mind the following guidelines in developing international instruments in the field of human rights; such instruments should, *inter alia*:

(*a*) Be consistent with the existing body of international human rights law;

(*b*) Be of fundamental character and derive from the inherent dignity and worth of the human person;

(*c*) Be sufficiently precise to give rise to identifiable and practicable rights and obligations;

(*d*) Provide, where appropriate, realistic and effective implementation machinery, including reporting systems;

(*e*) Attract broad international support;

5. *Requests* the Secretary-General to provide appropriate specialized support to United Nations bodies working on standard setting in the field of human rights.

97th plenary meeting
4 December 1986

41/128. Declaration on the Right to Development

Committee: 3
Vote: 146 - 1 - 18
Ref.: 50/184, 49/183, 48/130, 47/123, 46/123, 45/97, 44/62, 43/127, 42/117, 41/133

The General Assembly,

Having considered the question of the right to development,

Decides to adopt the Declaration on the Right to Development, the text of which is annexed to the present resolution.

97th plenary meeting
4 December 1986

Annex

Declaration on the Right to Development

The General Assembly,

Bearing in mind the purposes and principles of the Charter of the United Nations relating to the achievement of international cooperation in solving international problems of an economic, social, cultural or humanitarian nature, and in promoting and encouraging respect for human rights and fundamental freedoms for all without distinction as to race, sex, language or religion,

Recognizing that development is a comprehensive economic, social, cultural and political process, which aims at the constant improvement of the well-being of the entire population and of all individuals on the basis of their active, free and meaningful participation in development and in the fair distribution of benefits resulting therefrom,

Considering that under the provisions of the Universal Declaration of Human Rights everyone is entitled to a social and international order in which the rights and freedoms set forth in that Declaration can be fully realized,

Recalling the provisions of the International Covenant on Economic, Social and Cultural Rights and of the International Covenant on Civil and Political Rights,

Recalling further the relevant agreements, conventions, resolutions, recommendations and other instruments of the United Nations and its specialized agencies concerning the integral development of the human being, economic and social progress and development of all peoples, including those instruments concerning decolonization, the prevention of discrimination, respect for and observance of human rights and fundamental freedoms, the maintenance of international peace and security and the further promotion of friendly relations and cooperation among States in accordance with the Charter,

Recalling the right of peoples to self-determination, by virtue of which they have the right freely to determine their political status and to pursue their economic, social and cultural development,

Recalling also the right of peoples to exercise, subject to the relevant provisions of both International Covenants on Human Rights, full and complete sovereignty over all their natural wealth and resources,

Mindful of the obligation of States under the Charter to promote universal respect for and observance of human rights and fundamental freedoms for all without distinction of any kind such as race, colour, sex, language, religion, political or other opinion, national or social origin, property, birth or other status,

Considering that the elimination of the massive and flagrant violations of the human rights of the peoples and individuals affected by situations such as those resulting from colonialism, neo-colonialism, apartheid, all forms of racism and racial discrimination, foreign domination and occupation, aggression and threats against national sovereignty, national unity and territorial integrity and threats of war would contribute to the establishment of circumstances propitious to the development of a great part of mankind,

Concerned at the existence of serious obstacles to development, as well as to the complete fulfilment of human beings and of peoples, constituted, *inter alia*, by the denial of civil, political, economic, social and cultural rights, and considering that all human rights and fundamental freedoms are indivisible and interdependent and that, in order to promote development, equal attention and urgent consideration should be given to the implementation, promotion and protection of civil, political, economic, social and cultural rights and that, accordingly, the promotion of, respect for and enjoyment of certain human rights and fundamental freedoms cannot justify the denial of other human rights and fundamental freedoms,

Considering that international peace and security are essential elements for the realization of the right to development,

Reaffirming that there is a close relationship between disarmament and development and that progress in the field of disarmament would considerably promote progress in the field of development and that resources released through disarmament measures should be devoted to the economic and social development and well-being of all peoples and, in particular, those of the developing countries,

Recognizing that the human person is the central subject of the development process and that development policy should therefore make the human being the main participant and beneficiary of development,

Recognizing that the creation of conditions favourable to the development of peoples and individuals is the primary responsibility of their States,

Aware that efforts at the international level to promote and protect human rights should be accompanied by efforts to establish a new international economic order,

Confirming that the right to development is an inalienable human right and that equality of opportunity for development is a prerogative both of nations and of individuals who make up nations,

Proclaims the following Declaration on the Right to Development:

Article 1

1. The right to development is an inalienable human right by virtue of which every human person and all peoples are entitled to participate in, contribute to, and enjoy economic, social, cultural and political development, in which all human rights and fundamental freedoms can be fully realized.

2. The human right to development also implies the full realization of the right of peoples to self-determination, which includes, subject to the relevant provisions of both International Covenants on Human Rights, the exercise of their inalienable right to full sovereignty over all their natural wealth and resources.

Article 2

1. The human person is the central subject of development and should be the active participant and beneficiary of the right to development.

2. All human beings have a responsibility for development, individually and collectively, taking into account the need for full respect for their human rights and fundamental freedoms as well as their duties to the community, which alone can ensure the free and complete fulfilment of the human being, and they should therefore promote and protect an appropriate political, social and economic order for development.

3. States have the right and the duty to formulate appropriate national development policies that aim at the constant improvement of the well-being of the entire population and of all individuals, on the basis of their active, free and meaningful participation in development and in the fair distribution of the benefits resulting therefrom.

Article 3

1. States have the primary responsibility for the creation of national and international conditions favourable to the realization of the right to development.

2. The realization of the right to development requires full respect for the principles of international law concerning friendly relations and cooperation among States in accordance with the Charter of the United Nations.

3. States have the duty to cooperate with each other in ensuring development and eliminating obstacles to development. States should realize their rights and fulfil their duties in such a manner as to promote a new international economic order based on sovereign equality, mutual interest and cooperation among all States, as well as to encourage the observance and realization of human rights.

Article 4

1. States have the duty to take steps, individually and collectively, to formulate international development policies with a view to facilitating the full realization of the right to development.

2. Sustained action is required to promote more rapid development of developing countries. As a complement to the efforts of developing countries, effective international cooperation is essential in providing these countries with appropriate means and facilities to foster their comprehensive development.

Article 5

States shall take resolute steps to eliminate the massive and flagrant violations of the human rights of peoples and human beings affected by situations such as those resulting from apartheid, all forms of racism and racial discrimination, colonialism, foreign domination and occupation, aggression, foreign interference and threats against national sovereignty, national unity and territorial integrity, threats of war and refusal to recognize the fundamental right of peoples to self-determination.

Article 6

1. All States should cooperate with a view to promoting, encouraging and strengthening universal respect for and observance of all human rights and fundamental freedoms for all without any distinction as to race, sex, language or religion.

2. All human rights and fundamental freedoms are indivisible and interdependent; equal attention and urgent consideration should be given to the implementation, promotion and protection of civil, political, economic, social and cultural rights.

3. States should take steps to eliminate obstacles to development resulting from failure to observe civil and political rights, as well as economic, social and cultural rights.

Article 7

All States should promote the establishment, maintenance and strengthening of international peace and security and, to that end, should do their utmost to achieve general and complete disarmament under effective international control, as well as to ensure that the resources released by effective disarmament measures are used for comprehensive development, in particular that of the developing countries.

Article 8

1. States should undertake, at the national level, all necessary measures for the realization of the right to development and shall ensure, *inter alia*, equality of opportunity for all in their access to basic resources, education, health services, food, housing, employment and the fair distribution of income. Effective measures should be undertaken to ensure that women have an active role in the development process. Appropriate economic and social reforms should be carried out with a view to eradicating all social injustices.

2. States should encourage popular participation in all spheres as an important factor in development and in the full realization of all human rights.

Article 9

1. All the aspects of the right to development set forth in the present Declaration are indivisible and interdependent and each of them should be considered in the context of the whole.

2. Nothing in the present Declaration shall be construed as being contrary to the purposes and principles of the United Nations, or as

implying that any State, group or person has a right to engage in any activity or to perform any act aimed at the violation of the rights set forth in the Universal Declaration of Human Rights and in the International Covenants on Human Rights.

Article 10

Steps should be taken to ensure the full exercise and progressive enhancement of the right to development, including the formulation, adoption and implementation of policy, legislative and other measures at the national and international levels.

45/98. Respect for the Right of Everyone to Own Property alone as well as in Association with others and its Contribution to the Economic and Social Development of Member States

Committee: 3
Vote: Adopted without a vote
Ref.: 43/123, 42/114, 41/132

The General Assembly,

Recalling its resolutions 41/132 of 4 December 1986 and 43/123 of 8 December 1988,

Reaffirming the right of States and their peoples freely to choose and develop their political, social, economic and cultural systems and to determine their laws and regulations,

Recognizing the value of constructive dialogue in the national context on the ways and means by which States can promote the full enjoyment of the right of everyone to own property alone as well as in association with others,

Recognizing also in this context the importance of enabling everyone to acquire property, alone or in association with others, by taking practical actions that assist the economic development of developing countries,

Convinced that the right of everyone to own property alone as well as in association with others, as set forth in article 17 of the Universal Declaration of Human Rights and as reaffirmed in paragraph 4 of the Declaration on the Rights of Disabled Persons and in article 16, paragraph 1 (*h*), of the Convention on the Elimination of All Forms of Discrimination against Women,[1] is of particular significance in fostering widespread enjoyment of other basic human rights and contributes to securing the goals of economic and social development enshrined in the Charter of the United Nations,

Reaffirming, in accordance with article 29 of the Universal Declaration of Human Rights, that, in the exercise of his or her rights and freedoms, everyone shall be subject only to such limitations as are determined by law solely for the purpose of securing due recognition of and respect for the rights and freedoms of others and of meeting the just requirements of morality, public order and the general welfare in a democratic society,

Taking note of the report of the Secretary-General on respect for the right of everyone to own property alone as well as in association with others and its contribution to the economic and social development of Member States,[2]

1. *Recognizes* that there exist in Member States many forms of legal property ownership, including private, communal, social and state forms, each of which should contribute to ensuring effective development and utilization of human resources by establishing sound bases for political, economic and social justice;

2. *Affirms*, in accordance with article 30 of the Universal Declaration of Human Rights, that nothing in the Declaration, including the right of everyone to own property alone as well as in association with others, may be interpreted as implying for any State, group or person any right to engage in any activity or to perform any act aimed at the destruction of any of the rights and freedoms proclaimed therein;

3. *Considers* that further measures may be appropriate at the national level, consistent with national policies, to ensure respect for the right of everyone to own property alone as well as in association with others and the right not to be arbitrarily deprived of one's property, as set forth in article 17 of the Universal Declaration of Human Rights, so as to protect and preserve these rights in relation to the following types of property:

(*a*) Personal property, including the residence of one's self and family;

(*b*) Economically productive property, including property associated with agriculture, commerce and industry;

4. *Urges* States, therefore, in accordance with their respective constitutional systems and the Universal Declaration of Human Rights, to provide, where they have not done so, adequate constitutional and legal provisions to protect the right of everyone to own property alone as well as in association with others and the right not to be arbitrarily deprived of one's property;

5. *Requests* the Commission on Human Rights, while addressing the question of the realization in all countries of the economic, social and cultural rights contained in the Universal Declaration of Human Rights and in the International Covenant on Economic, Social and Cultural Rights, to consider the means whereby and the degree to which respect for the right to own property alone as well as in association with others contributes to the development of individual liberty and initiative, which serve to foster, strengthen and enhance the exercise of other human rights and fundamental freedoms;

6. *Decides* to consider this question at its forty-seventh session under the item entitled "Alternative approaches and ways and means within the United Nations system for improving the effective enjoyment of human rights and fundamental freedoms".

68th plenary meeting
14 December 1990

46/89. Use of Mercenaries as a Means to Violate Human Rights and to Impede the Exercise of the Right of Peoples to Self-Determination

Committee: 3
Vote: 122 - 11 - 28
Ref.: 50/138, 49/150, 48/92, 47/82, 45/132, 44/81, 43/107, 42/96, 41/102

The General Assembly,

Recalling its resolutions 44/34 of 4 December 1989 on the International Convention against the Recruitment, Use, Financing and Training of Mercenaries and 45/132 of 14 December 1990 on the use of mercenaries as a means to violate human rights and to impede the exercise of the right of peoples to self-determination,

Reaffirming the purposes and principles enshrined in the Charter of the United Nations concerning the strict observance of the principles of sovereign equality, political independence, territorial integrity of States and self-determination of peoples,

Urging strict respect for the principle of the non-use or threat of the use of force in international relations, as developed in the Declaration on Principles of International Law concerning Friendly Relations and Cooperation among States in accordance with the Charter of the United Nations,

Reaffirming the legitimacy of the struggle of peoples and their liberation movements for their independence, territorial integrity, national unity and liberation from colonial domination, apartheid and foreign intervention and occupation, and that their legitimate struggle can in no way be considered as or equated to mercenary activity,

Convinced that the use of mercenaries is a threat to international peace and security,

Deeply concerned about the menace that the activities of mercenaries represent for all States, particularly African and other developing States,

Profoundly alarmed at the continued international criminal activities of mercenaries in collusion with drug traffickers,

---

1 Resolution 34/180, annex.

2 A/45/523.

Recognizing that the activities of mercenaries are contrary to the fundamental principles of international law, such as non-interference in the internal affairs of States, territorial integrity and independence, and impede the process of the self-determination of peoples struggling against colonialism, racism and apartheid and all forms of foreign domination,

Recalling all of its relevant resolutions, in which, *inter alia*, it condemned any State that permitted or tolerated the recruitment, financing, training, assembly, transit and use of mercenaries with the objective of overthrowing the Governments of States Members of the United Nations, especially those of developing countries, or of fighting against national liberation movements, and recalling also the relevant resolutions of the Security Council and the Economic and Social Council, as well as of the Organization of African Unity,

Deeply concerned about the loss of life, the substantial damage to property and the short-term and long-term negative effects on the economy of southern African countries resulting from mercenary aggression,

Convinced that it is necessary to develop international cooperation among States for the prevention, prosecution and punishment of such offences,

Recalling with satisfaction the adoption of the International Convention against the Recruitment, Use, Financing and Training of Mercenaries, and the welcoming fulfilment of the provisions of paragraph 2 of Commission on Human Rights resolution 1991/29 of 5 March 1991, as reflected in the report of the Special Rapporteur of the Commission,

1. *Takes note with appreciation* of the report of the Special Rapporteur of the Commission on Human Rights;

2. *Condemns* the continued recruitment, financing, training, assembly, transit and use of mercenaries, as well as all other forms of support to mercenaries, for the purpose of destabilizing and overthrowing the Governments of African States and of other developing States and fighting against the national liberation movements of peoples struggling for the exercise of their right to self-determination;

3. *Reaffirms* that the use of mercenaries and their recruitment, financing and training, are offences of grave concern to all States and violate the purposes and principles enshrined in the Charter of the United Nations;

4. *Notes with serious concern* the use by the racist South African regime of groups of armed mercenaries against national liberation movements and for the destabilization of the Governments of southern African States;

5. *Denounces* any State that persists in the recruitment, or permits or tolerates the recruitment, of mercenaries and provides facilities to them for launching armed aggression against other States;

6. *Urges* all States to take the necessary steps and to exercise the utmost vigilance against the menace posed by the activities of mercenaries and to ensure, by both administrative and legislative measures, that the territory of those States and other territories under their control, as well as their nationals, are not used for the recruitment, assembly, financing, training and transit of mercenaries, or for the planning of activities designed to destabilize or overthrow the Government of any State and to fight the national liberation movements struggling against racism, apartheid, colonial domination and foreign intervention or occupation;

7. *Calls upon* all States to extend humanitarian assistance to victims of situations resulting from the use of mercenaries, as well as from colonial or alien domination or foreign occupation;

8. *Reaffirms* that to use channels of humanitarian and other assistance to finance, train and arm mercenaries is inadmissible;

9. *Calls upon* all States which have not yet done so to consider taking early action to accede to or to ratify the International Convention against the Recruitment, Use, Financing and Training of Mercenaries;

10. *Requests* the Special Rapporteur of the Commission on Human Rights to report to the General Assembly at its forty-seventh session on the use of mercenaries, especially in view of the additional elements highlighted in his report.

74th plenary meeting
16 December 1991

46/126. Human Rights and Scientific and Technological Progress

Committee: 3
Vote: Adopted without a vote
Ref.: 45/93, 44/133, 43/111, 42/99, 41/113, 40/112, 40/111, 39/134, 39/133, 38/113, 38/112, 37/189, 36/56, 35/130, 33/53, 31/128, 3268(XXIX), 3149(XXVIII), 3026(XXVII), 2721(XXV), 2450(XXIII)

The General Assembly,

Noting that scientific and technological progress is one of the decisive factors in the development of human society,

Bearing in mind the relevant provisions of the Universal Declaration of Human Rights, the International Covenant on Economic, Social and Cultural Rights, the International Covenant on Civil and Political Rights and the Declaration on Social Progress and Development,

Recalling the relevant provisions of the Declaration on the Use of Scientific and Technological Progress in the Interests of Peace and for the Benefit of Mankind,

Reaffirming the need to respect human rights and fundamental freedoms and the dignity of the human person in the conditions of scientific and technological progress,

Bearing in mind that the main and decisive factor in the acceleration of the social and economic development of society is the development of the human being,

Conscious that modern science and technology give the possibility to create material conditions for the prosperity of society and for the thorough development of the human person,

Being convinced that today the resources of mankind and the activities of scientists should be used for the peaceful social, economic and cultural development of all countries, raising the standard of living of all peoples and for better assurance of human rights and fundamental freedoms,

Recognizing the need to broaden the access of developing countries to the achievements of scientific and technological progress,

Recognizing also the important contribution of science and technology to the economic and social progress of mankind,

Aware that the exchange of scientific and technological knowledge is one of the important ways to accelerate the social and economic development of all countries, especially of developing countries,

1. *Underlines* the importance of the implementation by all States of the provisions and principles contained in the Universal Declaration of Human Rights and the International Covenants on Human Rights and the relevant provisions of the Declaration on the Use of Scientific and Technological Progress in the Interests of Peace and for the Benefit of Mankind for the promotion of the realization of human rights and fundamental freedoms;

2. *Calls upon* all Member States to ensure that the achievements of scientific and technological progress and the intellectual potential of mankind are used for promoting and encouraging universal respect for human rights and fundamental freedoms;

3. *Also calls upon* Member States to take the necessary measures to ensure that the results of science and technology are used only for the benefit of the human being and do not lead to the disturbance of the ecological environment;

4. *Emphasizes* that scientific knowledge and technology in health, education, housing and other social spheres should be readily available to the population as the heritage of humanity;

5. *Requests* the specialized agencies and other United Nations bodies to take into consideration the relevant provisions of the international instruments listed above in their programmes and activities;

6. *Decides* to consider the question of human rights and scientific and technological progress at its forty-eighth session under the item entitled "Human rights questions".

75th plenary meeting
17 December 1991

46/127. Human Rights and Mass Exoduses

Committee: 3
Vote: Adopted without a vote
Ref.: 50/182, 48/139, 45/153, 44/164, 43/154, 42/144, 41/148, 40/149, 39/117, 38/103, 37/186, 35/196

The General Assembly,

Mindful of its general humanitarian mandate under the Charter of the United Nations to promote and encourage respect for human rights and fundamental freedoms,

Deeply disturbed by the increasing scale and magnitude of exoduses of refugees and displacements of population in many regions of the world and by the suffering of millions of refugees and displaced persons,

Conscious of the fact that human rights violations are one of the multiple and complex factors causing mass exoduses of refugees and displaced persons, as indicated in the study of the Special Rapporteur of the Commission on Human Rights on this subject and also in the report of the Group of Governmental Experts on International Cooperation to Avert New Flows of Refugees,

Aware of the recommendations concerning mass exoduses made by the Commission on Human Rights to its Subcommission on Prevention of Discrimination and Protection of Minorities and to special rapporteurs to be taken into account when studying violations of human rights in any part of the world,

Deeply preoccupied by the increasingly heavy burden being imposed, particularly upon developing countries with limited resources of their own and upon the international community as a whole, by these sudden mass exoduses and displacements of population,

Stressing the need for international cooperation aimed at averting new massive flows of refugees while providing durable solutions to actual refugee situations,

Reaffirming its resolution 41/70 of 3 December 1986, in which it endorsed the conclusions and recommendations contained in the report of the Group of Governmental Experts on International Cooperation to Avert New Flows of Refugees,

Bearing in mind its resolution 45/153 of 18 December 1990 and Commission on Human Rights resolution 1991/73 of 6 March 1991, as well as all previous relevant resolutions of the General Assembly and the Commission on Human Rights,

Welcoming the steps taken so far by the United Nations to examine the problem of massive outflows of refugees and displaced persons in all its aspects, including its root causes,

Noting that the Executive Committee of the Programme of the United Nations High Commissioner for Refugees has specifically acknowledged the direct relationship between observance of human rights standards, refugee movements and problems of protection,

1. *Reaffirms* its support for the recommendation of the Group of Governmental Experts on International Cooperation to Avert New Flows of Refugees that the principal organs of the United Nations should make fuller use of their respective competencies under the Charter of the United Nations for the prevention of new massive flows of refugees and displaced persons;

2. *Again invites* all Governments and intergovernmental and humanitarian organizations concerned to intensify their cooperation with and assistance to world-wide efforts to address the serious problems resulting from mass exoduses of refugees and displaced persons, and also the causes of such exoduses;

3. *Requests* all Governments to ensure the effective implementation of the relevant international instruments, in particular in the field of human rights, as this would contribute to averting new massive flows of refugees and displaced persons;

4. *Invites* the Commission on Human Rights to keep the question of human rights and mass exoduses under review with a view to supporting the early-warning arrangement instituted by the Secretary-General to avert new massive flows of refugees and displaced persons;

5. *Notes with appreciation* the emphasis placed by the Secretary-General in his annual report on the work of the Organization, on the need to develop the capacity of the United Nations for early warning and preventive diplomacy to help deter humanitarian crises;

6. *Reiterates*, in this regard, its previous resolutions on the question of human rights and mass exoduses and requests the Secretary-General, in the further development of the capacity of the Secretariat for early warning and preventive diplomacy, to pay particular attention to international cooperation to avert new flows of refugees;

7. *Notes* in this connection that mass movements of populations are caused by multiple and complex factors, either man-made or natural, ranging from wars and armed conflicts, invasions and aggressions, violations of human rights, forcible expulsions, economic and social factors, natural disasters, to degradation in the environment, which indicates that early warning requires an intersectoral and multidisciplinary approach;

8. *Takes note* of the report of the Secretary-General on human rights and mass exoduses, and reiterates its request that future reports include information concerning the modalities and operations of early-warning activities to avert new and massive flows of refugees;

9. *Specially encourages* the Secretary-General to continue to discharge the task described in the report of the Group of Governmental Experts on International Cooperation to Avert New Flows of Refugees, including the continuous monitoring of all potential outflows, and to implement the recommendations of the Joint Inspection Unit contained in its report entitled "The coordination of activities related to early warning of possible refugee flows";

10. *Requests* the Secretary-General to intensify his efforts to develop the role of the Office for Research and the Collection of Information of the Secretariat as a focal point for the operation of an effective early-warning system and the strengthening of coordination of information-gathering and analysis among United Nations agencies with a view to preventing new massive flows of refugees and displaced persons;

11. *Reiterates* the importance of the early-warning function of the Office for Research and the Collection of Information;

12. *Urges* the Secretary-General to allocate the necessary resources to consolidate and strengthen the system for undertaking early-warning activities in the humanitarian area by, *inter alia*, the computerization of the Office for Research and the Collection of Information and strengthened coordination among the relevant parts of the United Nations system, especially the Office for Research and the Collection of Information, the Office of the United Nations High Commissioner for Refugees, the Centre for Human Rights of the Secretariat and the relevant specialized agencies;

13. *Welcomes* the information in the report of the Secretary-General that a temporary post is expected to become available in the biennium 1992-1993 in order that a computer specialist can be recruited to further the development of the data system of the Office for Research and the Collection of Information;

14. *Requests* the Secretary-General to make the necessary information available to the competent United Nations organs, bearing in mind the recommendations of the Joint Inspection Unit on coordination;

15. *Invites* bodies of the United Nations system to consider the most expedient ways and means of following up the recommendations of the Joint Inspection Unit on coordination;

16. *Welcomes* the initiation of close contacts between the Office for Research and the Collection of Information and a large number of United Nations agencies and offices in pursuit of a system-wide network for early warning of potential mass exoduses;

17. *Welcomes also* the establishment by the Administrative Committee on Coordination of the Ad Hoc Working Group on Early Warning regarding New Flows of Refugees and Displaced Persons with a

mandate to develop an effective early-warning system related to possible flows of refugees and displaced persons, including practical measures of cooperation and procedures for gathering, analysing and disseminating information in a timely manner to all concerned, and to make recommendations on the need for an inter-agency consultative mechanism;

18. *Urges* the Ad Hoc Working Group to carry out its mandate and submit to the Administrative Committee on Coordination in 1992 its report on the early-warning mechanism to be established;

19. *Emphasizes* the significance of this task of the Ad Hoc Working Group in view of the continuing situation with regard to mass exoduses;

20. *Requests* the Secretary-General to report to the General Assembly at its forty-seventh session on the strengthened role that he is playing in undertaking early-warning activities, especially in the humanitarian area, as well as on any further developments relating to the recommendations contained in the report of the Group of Governmental Experts on International Cooperation to Avert New Flows of Refugees;

21. *Invites* the Secretary-General to keep the General Assembly informed of the efforts to follow up recommendations of the Joint Inspection Unit;

22. *Also invites* the Secretary-General to include in his report to the General Assembly at its forty-seventh session detailed information on the programmatic, institutional, administrative, financial, and managerial efforts instituted to enhance the capacity of the United Nations to avert new flows of refugees and to tackle the root causes of such outflows;

23. *Decides* to continue consideration of the question of human rights and mass exoduses at its forty-seventh session.

75th plenary meeting
17 December 1991

47/133. Declaration on the Protection of all Persons from Enforced Disappearance

Committee: 3
Vote: Adopted without a vote
Ref.: 49/193, 47/132, 46/125, 45/165, 40/147, 39/111, 36/163, 35/193, 33/173

The General Assembly,

Considering that, in accordance with the principles proclaimed in the Charter of the United Nations and other international instruments, recognition of the inherent dignity and of the equal and inalienable rights of all members of the human family is the foundation of freedom, justice and peace in the world,

Bearing in mind the obligation of States under the Charter, in particular Article 55, to promote universal respect for, and observance of, human rights and fundamental freedoms,

Deeply concerned that in many countries, often in a persistent manner, enforced disappearances occur, in the sense that persons are arrested, detained or abducted against their will or otherwise deprived of their liberty by officials of different branches or levels of Government, or by organized groups or private individuals acting on behalf of, or with the support, direct or indirect, consent or acquiescence of the Government, followed by a refusal to disclose the fate or whereabouts of the persons concerned or a refusal to acknowledge the deprivation of their liberty, which places such persons outside the protection of the law,

Considering that enforced disappearance undermines the deepest values of any society committed to respect for the rule of law, human rights and fundamental freedoms, and that the systematic practice of such acts is of the nature of a crime against humanity,

Recalling its resolution 33/173 of 20 December 1978, in which it expressed concern about the reports from various parts of the world relating to enforced or involuntary disappearances, as well as about the anguish and sorrow caused by those disappearances, and called upon Governments to hold law enforcement and security forces legally responsible for excesses which might lead to enforced or involuntary disappearances of persons,

Recalling also the protection afforded to victims of armed conflicts by the Geneva Conventions of 12 August 1949[1] and the Additional Protocols thereto, of 1977,[2]

Having regard in particular to the relevant articles of the Universal Declaration of Human Rights[3] and the International Covenant on Civil and Political Rights,[4] which protect the right to life, the right to liberty and security of the person, the right not to be subjected to torture and the right to recognition as a person before the law,

Having regard also to the Convention against Torture and Other Cruel, Inhuman or Degrading Treatment or Punishment,[5] which provides that States parties shall take effective measures to prevent and punish acts of torture,

Bearing in mind the Code of Conduct for Law Enforcement Officials,[6] the Basic Principles on the Use of Force and Firearms by Law Enforcement Officials,[7] the Declaration of Basic Principles of Justice for Victims of Crime and Abuse of Power[8] and the Standard Minimum Rules for the Treatment of Prisoners,[9]

Affirming that, in order to prevent enforced disappearances, it is necessary to ensure strict compliance with the Body of Principles for the Protection of All Persons under Any Form of Detention or Imprisonment contained in the annex to its resolution 43/173 of 9 December 1988, and with the Principles on the Effective Prevention and Investigation of Extra-legal, Arbitrary and Summary Executions, set forth in the annex to Economic and Social Council resolution 1989/65 of 24 May 1989 and endorsed by the General Assembly in its resolution 44/162 of 15 December 1989,

Bearing in mind that, while the acts which comprise enforced disappearance constitute a violation of the prohibitions found in the aforementioned international instruments, it is none the less important to devise an instrument which characterizes all acts of enforced disappearance of persons as very serious offences and sets forth standards designed to punish and prevent their commission,

1. *Proclaims* the present Declaration on the Protection of All Persons from Enforced Disappearance, as a body of principles for all States;

2. *Urges* that all efforts be made so that the Declaration becomes generally known and respected;

Article 1

1. Any act of enforced disappearance is an offence to human dignity. It is condemned as a denial of the purposes of the Charter of the United Nations and as a grave and flagrant violation of the human rights and fundamental freedoms proclaimed in the Universal Declaration of Human Rights[10] and reaffirmed and developed in international instruments in this field.

2. Any act of enforced disappearance places the persons subjected thereto outside the protection of the law and inflicts severe suffering on them and their families. It constitutes a violation of the rules of international law guaranteeing, *inter alia*, the right to recognition as a person before the law, the right to liberty and security of the person and the right not to be subjected to torture and other cruel, inhuman

---

1 United nations, *Treaty Series*, vol. 75, Nos. 970-973.

2 *Ibid.*, vol. 1125, nos. 17512 and 17513.

3 Resolution 217 A (III).

4 See resolution 2200 a (XXI), annex.

5 Resolution 39/46, annex.

6 Resolution 34/169, annex.

7 See *Eigth United nations Congress on the Prevention of Crime and the Treatment of Offenders, Havana, 27 August - 7 September 1990: report prepared by the Secretariat* (United Nations publications, Sales No. E.91.IV.2), chap. I, sect. B.

8 Resolution 40/34, annex.

9 See *Human Rights: A Compilation of International Instruments* (United nations publication, Sales No. E.88.XIV.1).

10 Resolution 217 A (III).

or degrading treatment or punishment. It also violates or constitutes a grave threat to the right to life.

Article 2

1. No State shall practise, permit or tolerate enforced disappearances.

2. States shall act at the national and regional levels and in cooperation with the United Nations to contribute by all means to the prevention and eradication of enforced disappearance.

Article 3

Each State shall take effective legislative, administrative, judicial or other measures to prevent and terminate acts of enforced disappearance in any territory under its jurisdiction.

Article 4

1. All acts of enforced disappearance shall be offences under criminal law punishable by appropriate penalties which shall take into account their extreme seriousness.

2. Mitigating circumstances may be established in national legislation for persons who, having participated in enforced disappearances, are instrumental in bringing the victims forward alive or in providing voluntarily information which would contribute to clarifying cases of enforced disappearance.

Article 5

In addition to such criminal penalties as are applicable, enforced disappearances render their perpetrators and the State or State authorities which organize, acquiesce in or tolerate such disappearances liable under civil law, without prejudice to the international responsibility of the State concerned in accordance with the principles of international law.

Article 6

1. No order or instruction of any public authority, civilian, military or other, may be invoked to justify an enforced disappearance. Any person receiving such an order or instruction shall have the right and duty not to obey it.

2. Each State shall ensure that orders or instructions directing, authorizing or encouraging any enforced disappearance are prohibited.

3. Training of law enforcement officials shall emphasize the provisions in paragraphs 1 and 2 of the present article.

Article 7

No circumstances whatsoever, whether a threat of war, a state of war, internal political instability or any other public emergency, may be invoked to justify enforced disappearances.

Article 8

1. No State shall expel, return (*refouler*) or extradite a person to another State where there are substantial grounds to believe that he would be in danger of enforced disappearance.

2. For the purpose of determining whether there are such grounds, the competent authorities shall take into account all relevant considerations including, where applicable, the existence in the State concerned of a consistent pattern of gross, flagrant or mass violations of human rights.

Article 9

1. The right to a prompt and effective judicial remedy as a means of determining the whereabouts or state of health of persons deprived of their liberty and/or identifying the authority ordering or carrying out the deprivation of liberty is required to prevent enforced disappearances under all circumstances, including those referred to in article 7 above.

2. In such proceedings, competent national authorities shall have access to all places where persons deprived of their liberty are being held and to each part of those places, as well as to any place in which there are grounds to believe that such persons may be found.

3. Any other competent authority entitled under the law of the State or by any international legal instrument to which the State is a party may also have access to such places.

Article 10

1. Any person deprived of liberty shall be held in an officially recognized place of detention and, in conformity with national law, be brought before a judicial authority promptly after detention.

2. Accurate information on the detention of such persons and their place or places of detention, including transfers, shall be made promptly available to their family members, their counsel or to any other persons having a legitimate interest in the information unless a wish to the contrary has been manifested by the persons concerned.

3. An official up-to-date register of all persons deprived of their liberty shall be maintained in every place of detention. Additionally, each State shall take steps to maintain similar centralized registers. The information contained in these registers shall be made available to the persons mentioned in the preceding paragraph, to any judicial or other competent and independent national authority and to any other competent authority entitled under the law of the State concerned or any international legal instrument to which a State concerned is a party, seeking to trace the whereabouts of a detained person.

Article 11

All persons deprived of liberty must be released in a manner permitting reliable verification that they have actually been released and, further, have been released in conditions in which their physical integrity and ability fully to exercise their rights are assured.

Article 12

1. Each State shall establish rules under its national law indicating those officials authorized to order deprivation of liberty, establishing the conditions under which such orders may be given, and stipulating penalties for officials who, without legal justification, refuse to provide information on any detention.

2. Each State shall likewise ensure strict supervision, including a clear chain of command, of all law enforcement officials responsible for apprehensions, arrests, detentions, custody, transfers and imprisonment, and of other officials authorized by law to use force and firearms.

Article 13

1. Each State shall ensure that any person having knowledge or a legitimate interest who alleges that a person has been subjected to enforced disappearance has the right to complain to a competent and independent State authority and to have that complaint promptly, thoroughly and impartially investigated by that authority. Whenever there are reasonable grounds to believe that an enforced disappearance has been committed, the State shall promptly refer the matter to that authority for such an investigation, even if there has been no formal complaint. No measure shall be taken to curtail or impede the investigation.

2. Each State shall ensure that the competent authority shall have the necessary powers and resources to conduct the investigation effectively, including powers to compel attendance of witnesses and production of relevant documents and to make immediate on-site visits.

3. Steps shall be taken to ensure that all involved in the investigation, including the complainant, counsel, witnesses and those conducting the investigation, are protected against ill-treatment, intimidation or reprisal.

4. The findings of such an investigation shall be made available upon request to all persons concerned, unless doing so would jeopardize an ongoing criminal investigation.

5. Steps shall be taken to ensure that any ill-treatment, intimidation or reprisal or any other form of interference on the occasion of the lodging of a complaint or during the investigation procedure is appropriately punished.

6. An investigation, in accordance with the procedures described above, should be able to be conducted for as long as the fate of the victim of enforced disappearance remains unclarified.

Article 14

Any person alleged to have perpetrated an act of enforced disappearance in a particular State shall, when the facts disclosed by an official investigation so warrant, be brought before the competent civil authorities of that State for the purpose of prosecution and trial unless he has been extradited to another State wishing to exercise jurisdiction in accordance with the relevant international agreements in force. All States should take any lawful and appropriate action available to them to bring to justice all persons presumed responsible for an act of enforced disappearance, who are found to be within their jurisdiction or under their control.

Article 15

The fact that there are grounds to believe that a person has participated in acts of an extremely serious nature such as those referred to in article 4, paragraph 1, above, regardless of the motives, shall be taken into account when the competent authorities of the State decide whether or not to grant asylum.

Article 16

1. Persons alleged to have committed any of the acts referred to in article 4, paragraph 1, above, shall be suspended from any official duties during the investigation referred to in article 13 above.

2. They shall be tried only by the competent ordinary courts in each State, and not by any other special tribunal, in particular military courts.

3. No privileges, immunities or special exemptions shall be admitted in such trials, without prejudice to the provisions contained in the Vienna Convention on Diplomatic Relations.[1]

4. The persons presumed responsible for such acts shall be guaranteed fair treatment in accordance with the relevant provisions of the Universal Declaration of Human Rights and other relevant international agreements in force at all stages of the investigation and eventual prosecution and trial.

Article 17

1. Acts constituting enforced disappearance shall be considered a continuing offence as long as the perpetrators continue to conceal the fate and the whereabouts of persons who have disappeared and these facts remain unclarified.

2. When the remedies provided for in article 2 of the International Covenant on Civil and Political Rights[2] are no longer effective, the statute of limitations relating to acts of enforced disappearance shall be suspended until these remedies are re-established.

3. Statutes of limitations, where they exist, relating to acts of enforced disappearance shall be substantial and commensurate with the extreme seriousness of the offence.

Article 18

1. Persons who have or are alleged to have committed offences referred to in article 4, paragraph 1, above, shall not benefit from any special amnesty law or similar measures that might have the effect of exempting them from any criminal proceedings or sanction.

2. In the exercise of the right of pardon, the extreme seriousness of acts of enforced disappearance shall be taken into account.

Article 19

The victims of acts of enforced disappearance and their family shall obtain redress and shall have the right to adequate compensation, including the means for as complete a rehabilitation as possible. In the event of the death of the victim as a result of an act of enforced disappearance, their dependants shall also be entitled to compensation.

Article 20

1. States shall prevent and suppress the abduction of children of parents subjected to enforced disappearance and of children born during their mother's enforced disappearance, and shall devote their efforts to the search for and identification of such children and to the restitution of the children to their families of origin.

2. Considering the need to protect the best interests of children referred to in the preceding paragraph, there shall be an opportunity, in States which recognize a system of adoption, for a review of the adoption of such children and, in particular, for annulment of any adoption which originated in enforced disappearance. Such adoption should, however, continue to be in force if consent is given, at the time of the review, by the child's closest relatives.

3. The abduction of children of parents subjected to enforced disappearance or of children born during their mother's enforced disappearance, and the act of altering or suppressing documents attesting to their true identity, shall constitute an extremely serious offence, which shall be punished as such.

4. For these purposes, States shall, where appropriate, conclude bilateral and multilateral agreements.

Article 21

The provisions of the present Declaration are without prejudice to the provisions enunciated in the Universal Declaration of Human Rights or in any other international instrument, and shall not be construed as restricting or derogating from any of those provisions.

92nd plenary meeting
18 December 1992

47/134. Human Rights and Extreme Poverty

Committee: 3
Vote: Adopted without a vote
Ref.: 49/179, 46/121

The General Assembly,

Reaffirming the Universal Declaration of Human Rights, the International Covenant on Civil and Political Rights, the International Covenant on Economic, Social and Cultural Rights and other human rights instruments adopted by the United Nations,

Recalling its resolutions 44/148 of 15 December 1989 and 44/212 of 22 December 1989, and other relevant resolutions,

Bearing in mind Commission on Human Rights resolution 1991/14 of 22 February 1991, in which the Commission drew the attention of the General Assembly to the contradiction between the existence of situations of extreme poverty and exclusion from society, which must be overcome, and the duty to guarantee the full enjoyment of human rights,

Recalling its resolution 45/199 of 21 December 1990, in which it proclaimed the Fourth United Nations Development Decade, the main concerns of which are the search for a significant reduction of extreme poverty and the joint responsibility of all countries,

Recognizing that extreme poverty is a violation of human dignity and might, in some situations, constitute a threat to the right to life,

Deeply concerned that extreme poverty continues to spread in all countries of the world, regardless of their economic, social and cultural situation, and seriously affects the most vulnerable and disadvantaged individuals, families and groups, who are thus hindered in the exercise of their human rights and their fundamental freedoms,

Stressing the need for a complete and in-depth study of extreme poverty, based on the experience and the thoughts of the poorest,

Taking note with satisfaction, in that regard, of Commission on Human Rights resolution 1992/11 of 21 February 1992 and resolution 1992/27 of 27 August 1992 of the Subcommission on Prevention of Discrimination and Protection of Minorities, in which the Subcommission designated Mr. Leandro Despouy as Special Rapporteur on this question,

---

1 United Nations, Treaty Series, vol. 500, No. 7310.

2 See resolution 2200 A (XXI), annex.

Recognizing that the elimination of widespread poverty and the full enjoyment of economic, social and cultural rights are interrelated goals,

Recognizing also that the grave suffering of the vast majority of human beings who live in conditions of extreme poverty requires the immediate attention of the international community and the adoption of specific measures to eliminate extreme poverty and exclusion from society,

1. *Reaffirms* that extreme poverty and exclusion from society constitute a violation of human dignity and that urgent national and international action is therefore required to eliminate them;

2. *Expresses its satisfaction* that the Commission on Human Rights, in its resolution 1992/11, requested the Sub-Commission on Prevention of Discrimination and Protection of Minorities to undertake a study of extreme poverty and, in particular, of the following aspects: the effects of extreme poverty on the enjoyment and exercise of all human rights and fundamental freedoms of those experiencing it; the efforts of the poorest to achieve the exercise of those rights and to participate fully in the development of the society in which they live; the conditions in which the poorest may effectively convey their experience and their thoughts and become partners in the realization of human rights; and the means of ensuring a better understanding of the experience and thoughts of the poorest and of the persons working with them;

3. *Again calls upon* States, the specialized agencies, United Nations bodies and other international organizations, including intergovernmental organizations, to give the necessary attention to this problem;

4. *Notes with appreciation* the specific measures taken by the United Nations Children's Fund to mitigate the effects of extreme poverty on children and the efforts of the United Nations Development Programme to give priority to the search for some means of alleviating poverty within the framework of the relevant resolutions;

5. *Decides* to consider this question further at its forty-ninth session under the sub-item entitled "Human rights questions, including alternative approaches for improving the effective enjoyment of human rights and fundamental freedoms".

92nd plenary meeting
18 December 1992

48/132. Strengthening of the Rule of Law

Committee: 3
Vote: Adopted without a vote
Ref.: 50/179, 49/194

The General Assembly,

Recalling that the achievement of international cooperation in promoting and encouraging respect for human rights and fundamental freedoms for all without distinction as to race, sex, language and religion is one of the purposes of the United Nations,

Recalling also that, by adopting the Universal Declaration of Human Rights, Member States have pledged themselves to achieve, in cooperation with the United Nations, the promotion of universal respect for and observance of human rights and fundamental freedoms,

Firmly convinced that, as stressed in the Universal Declaration of Human Rights, the rule of law is an essential factor in the protection of human rights,

Convinced that through their own national legal and judicial systems States must provide appropriate civil, criminal and administrative remedies for violations of human rights,

Aware of the need for the implementation of strengthened advisory services and technical assistance activities in the field of human rights,

Mindful of the significant role played by national institutions in the promotion and protection of universally recognized human rights and fundamental freedoms in their respective countries,

Convinced that the Centre for Human Rights of the Secretariat should play an important role in coordinating system-wide attention for human rights,

Recalling Commission on Human Rights resolution 1992/51 of 3 March 1992, and taking note of Commission resolution 1993/50 of 9 March 1993, both entitled "Strengthening of the rule of law",

Noting with appreciation that in the Vienna Declaration and Programme of Action, adopted by the World Conference on Human Rights on 25 June 1993, the Conference recommended that priority be given to national and international action to promote democracy, development and human rights,

1. *Endorses* the recommendation of the World Conference on Human Rights that a comprehensive programme be established within the United Nations and under the coordination of the Centre for Human Rights of the Secretariat, with a view to helping States in the task of building and strengthening adequate national structures which have a direct impact on the overall observance of human rights and the maintenance of the rule of law;

2. *Expresses its conviction* that such a programme should be able to provide, upon the request of the interested Government, technical and financial assistance for the implementation of national plans of action as well as specific projects for the reform of penal and correctional establishments and the education and training of lawyers, judges and security forces in human rights, and in any other sphere of activity relevant to the good functioning of the rule of law;

3. *Requests* the Secretary-General, in accordance with the request contained in section II, paragraph 70, of the Vienna Declaration and Programme of Action, to submit concrete proposals to the General Assembly at its forty-ninth session containing alternatives for the establishment, structure, operational modalities and funding of the proposed programme, taking into account existing programmes and activities already undertaken by the Centre for Human Rights;

4. *Requests* the Commission on Human Rights to remain actively seized of this question, with a view to further elaborating the outline of the proposed programme;

5. *Decides* to continue its consideration of this question at its forty-ninth session in the light of the proposals of the Secretary-General.

85th plenary meeting
20 December 1993

50/181. Human Rights in the Administration of Justice

Committee: 3
Vote: Adopted without a vote
Ref.: 48/137, 46/120, 45/166, 44/162, 43/153, 42/143, 41/149, 40/146, 39/118, 3144(XXVIII), 2858(XXVI)

The General Assembly,

Recalling its resolution 48/137 of 20 December 1993, and taking note of Commission on Human Rights resolution 1995/41 of 3 March 1995 on human rights in the administration of justice, in particular of children and juveniles in detention,[1]

Bearing in mind the principles embodied in articles 3, 5, 9, 10 and 11 of the Universal Declaration of Human Rights[2] and the relevant provisions of the International Covenant on Civil and Political Rights and the Optional Protocols thereto,[3] in particular article 6 of the Covenant, which explicitly states that no one shall be arbitrarily deprived of his life and prohibits the imposition of the death penalty for crimes committed by persons below eighteen years of age,

Bearing in mind also the relevant principles embodied in the Convention against Torture and Other Cruel, Inhuman or Degrading Treatment or Punishment,[4] the International Convention on the

---

1 *Official Records of the Economic and Social Council, 1995, Supplement No. 3* and corrigenda (E/1995/23 and Corr. 1 and 2), chap. II, sect. A.

2 Resolution 217 A (III).

3 See resolution 2200A (XXI), annex, and resolution 44/128, annex.

4 Resolution 39/46, annex.

Elimination of All Forms of Racial Discrimination[1] and the Convention on the Rights of the Child,[2]

Mindful of the Convention on the Elimination of All Forms of Discrimination against Women,[3] in particular of the obligation of States to treat men and women equally in all stages of procedures in courts and tribunals,

Calling attention to the numerous international standards in the field of the administration of justice,

Recognizing that the rule of law and the proper administration of justice are important elements for sustainable economic and social development and play a central role in the promotion and protection of human rights,

Welcoming the important work of the Commission on Human Rights and of the Subcommission on Prevention of Discrimination and Protection of Minorities in the field of human rights in the administration of justice, in particular regarding the independence of the judiciary, the independence of judges and lawyers, the right to a fair trial, habeas corpus, human rights and states of emergency, the question of arbitrary detention, the human rights of juveniles in detention, the privatization of prisons and the question of the impunity of perpetrators of violations of human rights,

Welcoming also Commission on Human Rights resolution 1995/36 of 3 March 1995 on the independence and impartiality of the judiciary, jurors and assessors and the independence of lawyers,[4]

Welcoming further the important work of the Commission on Crime Prevention and Criminal Justice in the field of human rights in the administration of justice, as reflected, *inter alia,* in Economic and Social Council resolutions 1995/13 of 24 July 1995 on United Nations standards and norms in crime prevention and criminal justice, and 1995/15 of the same date on technical cooperation and interregional advisory services in crime prevention and criminal justice,

Emphasizing the importance of coordinating the activities in this field carried out under the responsibility of the Commission on Human Rights with those under the responsibility of the Commission on Crime Prevention and Criminal Justice,

Noting that many human rights violations in the administration of justice are specifically or primarily directed against women and that the identification and reporting of those violations demand special vigilance,

Aware of the specific situation of children and juveniles in detention and their special needs while deprived of their liberty, in particular their vulnerability to various forms of abuse, injustice and humiliation,

1. *Reaffirms* the importance of the full and effective implementation of all United Nations standards on human rights in the administration of justice;

2. *Acknowledges* that the administration of justice, including law enforcement and prosecutorial agencies and, especially, an independent judiciary and legal profession in full conformity with applicable standards contained in international human rights instruments, are essential to the full and non-discriminatory realization of human rights and indispensable to democratization processes and sustainable development;

3. *Reiterates once again* its call on all Member States to spare no effort in providing for effective legislative and other mechanisms and procedures, as well as adequate resources, to ensure full implementation of those standards;

4. *Appeals* to Governments to include in their national development plans the administration of justice as an integral part of the development process and to allocate adequate resources for the provision of legal-aid services with a view to the promotion and protection of human rights;

5. *Invites* Governments to provide training in human rights in the administration of justice, including juvenile justice, to all judges, lawyers, prosecutors, social workers and other professionals concerned, including police and immigration offices;

6. *Encourages* States to make use of technical assistance offered by the United Nations programmes of advisory services and technical assistance, in order to strengthen national capacities and infrastructures in the field of administration of justice;

7. *Urges* the Secretary-General to consider favourably requests by States for assistance in the field of the administration of justice and to strengthen system-wide coordination in this field, in particular between the United Nations programme of advisory services and technical assistance in the field of human rights and the technical cooperation and advisory services of the United Nations crime prevention and criminal justice programme;

8. *Invites* the international community to respond favourably to requests for financial and technical assistance for the enhancement and strengthening of the administration of justice, with a view to ensuring the promotion and protection of human rights in the administration of justice;

9. *Calls upon* special rapporteurs, special representatives and working groups of the Commission on Human Rights to continue to give special attention to questions relating to the effective protection of human rights in the administration of justice and to provide, wherever appropriate, specific recommendations in this regard, including proposals for concrete measures of advisory services and technical assistance;

10. *Acknowledges* the important role of the regional commissions, specialized agencies and United Nations institutes in the area of human rights and crime prevention and criminal justice, and of other organizations of the United Nations system, as well as intergovernmental and non-governmental organizations, including national professional associations concerned with promoting United Nations standards in this field;

11. *Invites* the Commission on Human Rights and the Commission on Crime Prevention and Criminal Justice to coordinate closely their activities relating to the administration of justice;

12. *Decides* to consider the question of human rights in the administration of justice at its fifty-second session under the item entitled "Human rights questions".

99th plenary meeting
22 December 1995

50/186. Human Rights and Terrorism

Committee: 3
Vote: Adopted without a vote
Ref.: 49/185, 48/122

The General Assembly,

Guided by the Charter of the United Nations, the Universal Declaration of Human Rights,[5] the Declaration on Principles of International Law concerning Friendly Relations and Cooperation among States in accordance with the Charter of the United Nations[6] and the International Covenants on Human Rights,[7]

Recalling the Declaration on the Occasion of the Fiftieth Anniversary of the United Nations,[8]

Taking into account that acts of terrorism in all its forms and manifestations aimed at the destruction of human rights have continued despite national and international efforts,

1 Resolution 2106 A (XX), annex.

2 Resolution 44/25, annex.

3 Resolution 34/180, annex.

4 *Official Records of the Economic and Social Council, 1995, Supplement No. 3* and corrigenda (E/1995/23 AND Corr. 1 and 2), chap. II, sect. A.

5 Resolution 217 A (III).

6 Resolution 2625 (XXV), annex.

7 Resolution 2200 A (XXI), annex.

8 Resolution 50/6 of 24 October 1995.

Bearing in mind that the most essential and basic human right is the right to life,

Bearing in mind also that terrorism creates an environment that destroys the freedom from fear of the people,

Recalling the Vienna Declaration and Programme of Action, adopted by the World Conference on Human Rights, held at Vienna from 14 to 25 June 1993,[1]

Recalling also its resolutions 48/122 of 20 December 1993 and 49/185 of 23 December 1994,

Taking note of Commission on Human Rights resolution 1995/43 of 3 March 1995,[2]

Reiterating that all States have an obligation to promote and protect human rights and fundamental freedoms, and also that every individual should strive to secure their universal and effective recognition and observance,

Seriously concerned at the gross violations of human rights perpetrated by terrorist groups,

Profoundly deploring the increasing number of innocent persons, including women, children and the elderly, killed, massacred and maimed by terrorists in indiscriminate and random acts of violence and terror, which cannot be justified under any circumstances,

Noting with great concern the growing connection between the terrorist groups and other criminal organizations engaged in the illegal traffic in arms and drugs at the national and international levels, as well as the consequent commission of serious crimes such as murder, extortion, kidnapping, assault, taking of hostages and robbery,

Mindful of the need to protect human rights of and guarantees for the individual in accordance with the relevant international human rights principles and instruments, particularly the right to life,

Reaffirming that all measures to counter terrorism must be in strict conformity with international human rights standards,

1. *Expresses its solidarity* with the victims of terrorism;

2. *Reiterates its unequivocal condemnation* of the acts, methods and practices of terrorism as activities aimed at the destruction of human rights, fundamental freedoms and democracy, threatening the territorial integrity and security of States, destabilizing legitimately constituted Governments, undermining pluralistic civil society and having adverse consequences on the economic and social development of States;

3. *Calls upon* States to take all necessary and effective measures in accordance with international standards of human rights to prevent, combat and eliminate all acts of terrorism wherever and by whomever committed;

4. *Urges* the international community to enhance cooperation at regional and international levels in the fight against terrorism in accordance with relevant international instruments, including those relating to human rights, with the aim of its eradication;

5. *Condemns* incitement of ethnic hatred, violence and terrorism;

6. *Requests* the Secretary-General to continue to seek the views of Member States on the possible establishment of a United Nations voluntary fund for victims of terrorism, as well as ways and means to rehabilitate the victims of terrorism and to reintegrate them into society, and to submit to the General Assembly at its fifty-second session, for its consideration, a report containing comments made by Member States on the subject;

7. *Also requests* the Secretary-General to transmit the text of the present resolution to all Member States and to competent specialized agencies and intergovernmental organizations for their consideration;

8. *Encourages* special rapporteurs, special representatives and working groups of the Commission on Human Rights, as well as treaty bodies, to pay appropriate attention, within their mandates, to the consequences of the acts, methods and practices of terrorist groups;

9. *Decides* to consider this question at its fifty-second session under the item entitled "Human rights questions".

99th plenary meeting
22 December 1995

06.20 RACIAL DISCRIMINATION AND APARTHEID

1904 (XVIII). United Nations Declaration on the Elimination of all Forms of Racial Discrimination

Committee: 3
Vote: unanimous
Ref.: 2017(XX), 1905(XVIII), 1906(XVIII), 1780(XVII), 1779(XVII), 1684(XVI)

The General Assembly,

Considering that the Charter of the United Nations is based on the principles of the dignity and equality of all human beings and seeks, among other basic objectives, to achieve international cooperation in promoting and encouraging respect for human rights and fundamental freedoms for all without distinction as to race, sex, language or religion,

Considering that the Universal Declaration of Human Rights proclaims that all human beings are born free and equal in dignity and rights and that everyone is entitled to all the rights and freedoms set out in the Declaration, without distinction of any kind, in particular as to race, colour or national origin,

Considering that the Universal Declaration of Human Rights proclaims further that all are equal before the law and are entitled without any discrimination to equal protection of the law and that all are entitled to equal protection against any discrimination and against any incitement to such discrimination,

Considering that the United Nations has condemned colonialism and all practices of segregation and discrimination associated therewith, and that the Declaration on the granting of independence to colonial countries and peoples proclaims in particular the necessity of bringing colonialism to a speedy and unconditional end,

Considering that any doctrine of racial differentiation or superiority is scientifically false, morally condemnable, socially unjust and dangerous, and that there is no justification for racial discrimination either in theory or in practice,

Taking into account the other resolutions adopted by the General Assembly and the international instruments adopted by the specialized agencies, in particular the International Labour Organization and the United Nations Educational, Scientific and Cultural Organization, in the field of discrimination,

Taking into account the fact that, although international action and efforts in a number of countries have made it possible to achieve progress in that field, discrimination based on race, colour or ethnic origin in certain areas of the world continues none the less to give cause for serious concern,

Alarmed by the manifestations of racial discrimination still in evidence in some areas of the world, some of which are imposed by certain Governments by means of legislative, administrative or other measures, in the form, *inter alia*, of apartheid, segregation and separation as well as by the promotion and dissemination of doctrines of racial superiority and expansionism in certain areas,

Convinced that all forms of racial discrimination and still more so, governmental policies based on the prejudice of racial superiority or

1 *Report of the World Conference on Human Rights, Vienna, 14-25 June 1993*(A/CONF.157/24 (Part 1)), chap. III.

2 *Official Records of the Economic and Social Council, 1995, Supplement No. 3* and corrigenda (E/1995/23 and Corr.1 and 2), chap. II, sect. A.

on racial hatred, besides constituting a violation of fundamental human rights, tend to jeopardize friendly relations among peoples, cooperation between nations and international peace and security,

Convinced also that racial discrimination harms not only those who are its objects but also those who practise it,

Convinced further that the building of a world society free from all forms of racial segregation and discrimination, factors which create hatred and division among men, is one of the fundamental objectives of the United Nations,

1. *Solemnly affirms* the necessity of speedily eliminating racial discrimination throughout the world, in all its forms and manifestations, and of securing understanding of and respect for the dignity of the human person;

2. *Solemnly affirms* the necessity of adopting national and international measures to that end, including teaching, education and information, in order to secure the universal and effective recognition and observance of the principles set forth below;

3. *Proclaims* this Declaration:

Article 1

Discrimination between human beings on the ground of race, colour or ethnic origin is an offence to human dignity and shall be condemned as a denial of the principles of the Charter of the United Nations, as a violation of the human rights and fundamental freedoms proclaimed in the Universal Declaration of Human Rights, as an obstacle to friendly and peaceful relations among nations and as a fact capable of disturbing peace and security among peoples.

Article 2

1. No State, institution, group or individual shall make any discrimination whatsoever in matters of human rights and fundamental freedoms in the treatment of persons, groups of persons or institutions on the ground of race, colour or ethnic origin.

2. No State shall encourage, advocate or lend its support, through police action or otherwise, to any discrimination based on race, colour or ethnic origin by any group, institution or individual.

3. Special concrete measures shall be taken in appropriate circumstances in order to secure adequate development or protection of individuals belonging to certain racial groups with the object of ensuring the full enjoyment by such individuals of human rights and fundamental freedoms. These measures shall in no circumstances have as a consequence the maintenance of unequal or separate rights for different racial groups.

Article 3

1. Particular efforts shall be made to prevent discrimination based on race, colour or ethnic origin, especially in the fields of civil rights, access to citizenship, education, religion, employment, occupation and housing.

2. Everyone shall have equal access to any place or facility intended for use by the general public, without distinction as to race, colour or ethnic origin.

Article 4

All States shall take effective measures to revise governmental and other public policies and to rescind laws and regulations which have the effect of creating and perpetuating racial discrimination wherever it still exists. They should pass legislation for prohibiting such discrimination and should take all appropriate measures to combat those prejudices which lead to racial discrimination.

Article 5

An end shall be put without delay to governmental and other public policies of racial segregation and especially policies of apartheid, as well as all forms of racial discrimination and separation resulting from such policies.

Article 6

No discrimination by reason of race, colour or ethnic origin shall be admitted in the enjoyment by any person of political and citizenship rights in his country, in particular the right to participate in elections through universal and equal suffrage and to take part in the government. Everyone has the right of equal access to public service in his country.

Article 7

1. Everyone has the right to equality before the law and to equal justice under the law. Everyone, without distinction as to race, colour or ethnic origin, has the right to security of person and protection by the State against violence or bodily harm, whether inflicted by government officials or by any individual, group or institution.

2. Everyone shall have the right to an effective remedy and protection against any discrimination he may suffer on the ground of race, colour or ethnic origin with respect to his fundamental rights and freedoms through independent national tribunals competent to deal with such matters.

Article 8

All effective steps shall be taken immediately in the fields of teaching, education and information, with a view to eliminating racial discrimination and prejudice and promoting understanding, tolerance and friendship among nations and racial groups, as well as to propagating the purposes and principles of the Charter of the United Nations, of the Universal Declaration of Human Rights, and of the Declaration on the granting of independence to colonial countries and peoples.

Article 9

1. All propaganda and organizations based on ideas or theories of the superiority of one race or group of persons of one colour or ethnic origin with a view to justifying or promoting racial discrimination in any form shall be severely condemned.

2. All incitement to or acts of violence, whether by individuals or organizations, against any race or group of persons of another colour or ethnic origin shall be considered an offence against society and punishable under law.

3. In order to put into effect the purposes and principles of the present Declaration, all States shall take immediate and positive measures, including legislative and other measures, to prosecute and/or outlaw organizations which promote or incite to racial discrimination, or incite to or use violence for purposes of discrimination based on race, colour or ethnic origin.

Article 10

The United Nations, the specialized agencies, States and non-governmental organizations shall do all in their power to promote energetic action which, by combining legal and other practical measures, will make possible the abolition of all forms of racial discrimination. They shall, in particular, study the causes of such discrimination with a view to recommending appropriate and effective measures to combat and eliminate it.

Article 11

Every State shall promote respect for and observance of human rights and fundamental freedoms in accordance with the Charter of the United Nations and shall fully and faithfully observe the provisions of the present Declaration, the Universal Declaration of Human Rights and the Declaration on the granting of independence to colonial countries and peoples.

1261 plenary meeting
20 November 1963

2784 (XXVI). Elimination of all Forms of Racial Discrimination

Committee: 3
Vote: 93 - 5 - 15
Ref.: 3379(XXX), 2714(XXV), 2646(XXV), 2647(XXV), 2142(XXI), 2106(XX)

The General Assembly,

Firmly convinced that all forms of racial discrimination are a total negation of the purposes and principles of the Charter of the United Nations and that they militate against human progress, peace and justice,

Fully aware that apartheid and all other forms of racial discrimination are instruments of colonialism and imperialism as well as of economic exploitation,

Reiterating its conviction that any doctrine of exclusiveness based on racial differentiation or ethnic or religious superiority is scientifically false, morally condemnable and socially unjust,

Reiterating also its firm determination to bring about the total and unconditional elimination of racial discrimination in all its forms,

Having designated the year 1971 as the International Year for Action to Combat Racism and Racial Discrimination,

Convinced that the International Year for Action to Combat Racism and Racial Discrimination should be observed as the opening year of an ever-growing struggle against racial discrimination in all its forms and manifestations and for the purpose of promoting international solidarity with all those struggling against racism,

Considering that by arousing world public opinion and promoting action against racism the International Year for Action to Combat Racism and Racial Discrimination would contribute to the expansion of national and international efforts towards ensuring the rapid and total eradication of racial discrimination in all its forms,

Believing in the urgent need for eliminating racial discrimination through continuous and vigorous national action and collective international measures in order to alleviate the suffering of millions of people the world over and to ensure them the dignity and equality inherent in all human beings,

I

1. *Requests* the President of the General Assembly to forward the message annexed to the present resolution directly to the heads of State or Government of each State;

2. *Requests* the Secretary-General to submit a report based on the information and comments received from Governments, in accordance with the message sent to heads of State or Government, to the Commission on Human Rights at its twenty-eighth session;

3. *Invites* the Economic and Social Council to request the Commission on Human Rights, bearing in mind the provisions of paragraph 2 above, to submit suggestions with a view to launching continued international action to combat racism on the basis of a "Decade for vigorous and continued mobilization against racism and racial discrimination in all its forms";

II

1. *Reaffirms* that apartheid is a crime against humanity;

2. *Declares* that racial discrimination in all its forms is a criminal affront to the conscience and dignity of mankind;

3. *Emphatically reaffirms* its recognition and vigorous support of the legitimacy of the struggles of all oppressed peoples everywhere, and in particular in southern Africa, against colonial, racial and alien domination or foreign occupation towards the achievement of their inalienable rights to equality and freedom, in accordance with the purposes and principles of the Charter of the United Nations, and calls for increased and continued moral and material support to all peoples struggling for their liberation, self-determination and the elimination of all forms of racial discrimination;

4. *Invites* the Economic and Social Council to request the Commission on Human Rights to study and make recommendations for the further elaboration of international instruments to deal with crimes against humanity, particularly those arising from the policies of apartheid;

5. *Condemns* those countries which, by their political, economic and military collaboration with the Government of South Africa, encourage and incite that Government to persist in its racist policy;

6. *Strongly condemns* all Governments that continue to supply arms to the Pretoria régime in violation of the relevant resolutions of the General Assembly and the Security Council;

III

1. *Takes note with appreciation* of the report of the Committee on the Elimination of Racial Discrimination,[1] established under article 8 of the International Convention on the Elimination of All Forms of Racial Discrimination;

2. *Endorses* the opinions and recommendations submitted by the Committee on the Elimination of Racial Discrimination in its decisions 3 (IV), 4 (IV) and S (IV);[2]

3. *Calls upon* all the trading partners of South Africa to abstain from any action that constitutes an encouragement to the continued violation of the principles and objectives of the International Convention on the Elimination of All Forms of Racial Discrimination by South Africa and the illegal régime in Southern Rhodesia, and to use their influence with a view to ensuring the eradication of the policies of apartheid and racial discrimination in the international territory of Namibia and Southern Rhodesia;

4. *Also calls upon* the United Kingdom of Great Britain and Northern Ireland, the administering Power for Southern Rhodesia, to adopt all the necessary measures, including the use of force, with a view to ending the racist and illegal régime of Ian Smith;

5. *Condemns* the Government of Portugal for persisting in its colonialist policies in Africa and for continuing its war against the peoples of these Territories under its domination;

6. *Invites* the Economic and Social Council to request the Commission on Human Rights to continue its comprehensive studies of policies and practices of racial discrimination, taking into account in particular discrimination against peoples of African origin in all countries, and to submit a report to the General Assembly as soon as possible, but not later that at its twenty-eighth session, together with recommendations for action to combat such policies and practices;

IV

Decides to consider this item again at its twenty-seventh session.

2001st plenary meeting
6 December 1971

Annex

Message from the President of the General Assembly to the Heads of State or Government

I

1. The General Assembly at its twenty-sixth session on the occasion of celebrating the International Year for Action to Combat Racism and Racial Discrimination has requested me, as a matter of urgency, to put before you the following facts concerning the United Nations campaign against racial discrimination:

(*a*) The racist Government of South Africa and the illegal régime in Southern Rhodesia have blatantly continued to pursue policies of racial discrimination and apartheid in flagrant violation of the purposes and principles of the Charter of the United Nations and of those enshrined in the Universal Declaration of Human Rights.

(*b*) The racist Government of South Africa continues to effect an extensive arms build-up, thus posing a serious threat to the security

1 *Ibid., Official Records of the General Assembly, Twenty-sixth Session, Supplement No. 18* (A/8418).

2 *Ibid.*, chap. VII, sect. B.

and sovereignty of independent African States opposed to its racist policies, as well as to all those peoples struggling against the racial and inhuman policies in southern Africa.

(*c*) The racist policies in southern Africa have been permitted, even encouraged, to expand through:

(i) The continued existence and operation of the white racist minority régime in Southern Rhodesia through the deliberate ineffectiveness of measures so far taken by the Government of the United Kingdom of Great Britain and Northern Ireland, the administering Power;

(ii) The illegal occupation of the Territory of Namibia by the racist Government of South Africa.

(*d*) The racist Governments in southern Africa have been further strengthened through:

(i) The maintenance by many States of political, commercial military economic, social and other relations with the racist Governments in southern Africa in utter disregard of United Nations resolutions and of the purposes and principles of the Charter;

(ii) An unholy alliance between South Africa, Portugal and Southern Rhodesia, established in order to suppress the struggle of the peoples of that region and to silence the cry of Africa against racism, apartheid, economic exploitation and colonial domination.

(*e*) The United Nations has vigorously opposed all policies based on racial discrimination and, consequently, has:

(i) Declared that any State whose official policy or practice is based on racial discrimination contravenes the purposes and principles of the Charter, and called upon those Governments to desist forthwith from pursuing such policies;

(ii) Condemned the policies of States which, by political, economic or military collaboration with the racist regimes in southern Africa, enable and encourage those regimes to enforce and perpetuate their racist policies, and called upon those States to desist forthwith from extending such collaboration;

(iii) Reaffirmed time and again the legitimacy of the struggle of all oppressed peoples, in particular in the territories under racial, alien domination or foreign occupation, to obtain liberation and racial equality, and called for increased and continued moral and material support to these struggling peoples.

(*f*) However, the numerous resolutions that have been adopted by the various organs of the United Nations still have little or no effect owing to the arrogant, flagrant and stubborn disregard on the part of South Africa and its racist allies, transplanted to the soil of Africa, and to the continued political, economic and military aid coming from some States.

II

2. The General Assembly, therefore, is as convinced as ever that the continuation of national and international action against racial discrimination in all its forms, old and contemporary alike, is a matter of cardinal importance if the world is to live in peace and justice, the two interdependent and indispensable components of a better future for all mankind.

3. The General Assembly is also convinced that the primary aim of the United Nations and, therefore, of all its Member States in the sphere of human rights is the achievement by each individual of the maximum freedom and dignity and that, for the realization of this objective, the laws of every country should grant each individual, irrespective of race, sex, language, religion or political belief, all the rights inherent in all human beings on the basis of equality and that the people of every country must be made fully aware of the evils of the policies of racial discrimination and of the ideologies based on racial supremacy and must join in condemning, resisting and combating them.

4. The General Assembly is further convinced that the continuation of racism and colonialism cannot but seriously hamper the efforts of the international community to achieve peace, justice and progress.

III

5. The General Assembly, in view of the aforementioned facts and convictions, has authorized me to request you to transmit the present text to the legislative, administrative judicial, educational and trade union bodies of your country, as well as to the mass media of information, in order to ensure the continuation of the world campaign against racial discrimination, bearing in mind that the International Year for Action to Combat Racism and Racial Discrimination should be considered as the opening year for a full decade of vigorous struggle against this evil, until the achievement of its total elimination. To that end, the General Assembly recommends, *inter alia*:

(*a*) The discussion of this problem in all national and international conferences, especially in the fields of education information, trade unions, etc.;

(*b*) The inculcation through education of children and youth in the spirit of human rights by the inclusion in the curricula of special and yearly programmes on the evils of racism and racial discrimination;

(*c*) The continuation of the programmes designated to be carried out during 1971, the International Year for Action to Combat Racism and Racial Discrimination, and their development and updating, in order to intensify the efforts to combat racial discrimination;

(*d*) The continuation of open moral support and the increasing of material aid to the peoples struggling against racial discrimination and apartheid;

(*e*) The termination of all relations with the Government of South Africa and all other racist regimes;

(*f*) Exerting every effort to bring about the full implementation of all Security Council and General Assembly resolutions that reflect the world's resolve to end each and every case of discrimination and foreign exploitation;

(*g*) The repeal of all laws and regulations which contribute to the maintenance and propagation of racial discrimination.

IV

6. The General Assembly has requested the Secretary-General to submit a report on this subject to the Assembly at its twenty-seventh session, in which would be included reports of Governments on the above message.

43/150. Measures to Be Taken Against Nazi, Fascist and Neo-Fascist Activities and all other Forms of Totalitarian Ideologies and Practices Based on Apartheid, Racial Discrimination and Racism, and the Systematic Denial of Human Rights and Fundamental Freedoms

Committee: 3
Vote: Adopted without a vote

The General Assembly,

Recalling that the United Nations emerged from the struggle against nazism, fascism, totalitarian ideologies and regimes, aggression and foreign occupation, and that the peoples expressed their resolve in the Charter of the United Nations to save succeeding generations from the scourge of war,

Aware of the determination proclaimed by the peoples of the world in the Charter to reaffirm faith in fundamental human rights, in the dignity and worth of the human person, in the equal rights of men and women and of nations large and small and to promote social progress and better standards of life in larger freedom,

Noting with regret that in the contemporary world there continue to exist various forms of totalitarian ideologies and practices which entail contempt for the individual or a denial of the intrinsic dignity and equality of all human beings and of equality of opportunity in the civil, political, economic, social and cultural spheres, including the practices of apartheid, racial discrimination and racism,

Emphasizing that the doctrines of political, racial or ethnic superiority on which the totalitarian entities and regimes are based contradict the spirit and principles of the United Nations and that the application of such doctrines in practice leads to wars, mass and flagrant violations of human rights and crimes against humanity, such as genocide, and creates serious obstacles to friendly relations among nations and the development of all countries,

Acknowledging with satisfaction the fact that many States have established legal provisions designed to prevent the revival of Nazi, Fascist and neo-Fascist groups and organizations and are extraditing war criminals and persons having committed crimes against mankind,

Mindful of the principles of international cooperation in the detection, arrest, extradition and punishment of persons guilty of war crimes and crimes against humanity, set forth in its resolution 3074 (XXVIII) of 3 December 1973,

Reaffirming that the prosecution and punishment of war crimes and crimes against peace and humanity, as laid down in its resolutions 3 (I) of 13 February 1946 and 95 (I) of 11 December 1946, constitute a universal commitment for all States,

Recalling its resolutions 2331 (XXII) of 18 December 1967, 2438 (XXIII) of 19 December 1968, 2545 (XXIV) of 11 December 1969, 2713 (XXV) of 15 December 1970, 2839 (XXVI) of 18 December 1971, 34/24 of 15 November 1979, 35/200 of 15 December 1980, 36/162 of 16 December 1981, 37/179 of 17 December 1982, 38/99 of 16 December 1983, 39/114 of 14 December 1984, 40/148 of 13 December 1985 and 41/160 of 4 December 1986,

1. *Again resolutely condemns* all totalitarian or other ideologies and practices, including the Nazi, Fascist and neo-Fascist, that are based on apartheid, racial discrimination and racism, and the systematic denial of human rights and fundamental freedoms, or which have such consequences;

2. *Expresses its determination* to resist all totalitarian ideologies, and especially their practices, which deprive people of basic human rights and fundamental freedoms and of equality of opportunity;

3. *Calls upon* all States to take the necessary measures to ensure the thorough investigation, detection, arrest, extradition and punishment of all war criminals and persons guilty of crimes against humanity who have not yet been brought before a court and appropriately punished;

4. *Also calls upon* all Governments to pay constant attention to educating the young in the spirit of respect for international law and fundamental human rights and freedoms and against Fascist, neo-Fascist and other totalitarian ideologies and practices based on terror, hatred and violence;

5. *Further calls upon* all States, in accordance with the basic principles of international law, to refrain from practices aimed at the violation of basic human rights, particularly the right to self-determination;

6. *Appeals* to States that have not yet done so to consider becoming parties to the International Covenants on Human Rights, the Convention on the Prevention and Punishment of the Crime of Genocide,[1] the International Convention on the Elimination of All Forms of Racial Discrimination, the Convention on the Non-Applicability of Statutory Limitations to War Crimes and Crimes against Humanity[2] and the International Convention on the Suppression and Punishment of the Crime of Apartheid;

7. *Invites* all States and international organizations to submit to the Secretary-General their comments and information on the implementation of the present resolution;

8. *Requests* the Secretary-General to submit a report, through the Economic and Social Council, to the General Assembly at its forty-fifth session in the light of the discussion that will take place in the Commission on Human Rights and on the basis of comments provided by States and international organizations.

75th plenary meeting
8 December 1988

1 Resolution 260 A (III), annex.

2 Resolution 2391 (XXIII), annex.

50/135. Measures to Combat Contemporary Forms of Racism, Racial Discrimination, Xenophobia and Related Intolerance

Committee: 3
Vote: Adopted without a vote
Ref.: 49/147

The General Assembly,

Recalling its resolution 49/147 of 23 December 1994 and Commission on Human Rights resolution 1995/12 of 24 February 1995,

Bearing in mind the outcome of the World Conference on Human Rights, held at Vienna from 14 to 25 June 1993, and, in particular, the attention given in the Vienna Declaration and Programme of Action to the elimination of racism, racial discrimination, xenophobia and other forms of intolerance,

Aware that racism, being one of the exclusionist phenomena plaguing many societies, requires resolute action and cooperation for its eradication,

Having examined the report of the Special Rapporteur of the Commission on Human Rights on contemporary forms of racism, racial discrimination, xenophobia and related intolerance, including its conclusions and recommendations,

Deeply concerned that, despite continued efforts, racism, racial discrimination, xenophobia and related intolerance, as well as acts of racial violence, continue to persist and even grow in magnitude, incessantly adopting new forms, including tendencies to establish policies based on racial, religious, ethnic, cultural and national superiority or exclusivity,

Conscious of the fundamental difference between, on the one hand, racism and racial discrimination as governmental policy or resulting from official doctrines of racial superiority or exclusivity and, on the other hand, other manifestations of racism, racial discrimination, xenophobia and related intolerance taking place in segments of many societies and perpetrated by individuals or groups, some of which are directed against migrant workers and members of their families,

Underlining the importance of creating conditions to foster greater harmony and tolerance within societies,

1. *Welcomes* the report of the Special Rapporteur of the Commission on Human Rights on contemporary forms of racism, racial discrimination, xenophobia and related intolerance;

2. *Expresses its full support* for the work of the Special Rapporteur, and requests him to continue his exchange of views with relevant mechanisms, related United Nations organs and specialized agencies in order to further their effectiveness and mutual cooperation;

3. *Expresses its profound concern at and unequivocal condemnation of* all forms of racism and all racist violence, including related acts of random and indiscriminate violence;

4. *Expresses its deep concern at and condemnation of* manifestations of racism, racial discrimination, xenophobia and related intolerance against migrant workers and members of their families and other vulnerable groups in many societies;

5. *Encourages* all States, in accordance with the conclusions and recommendations of the Special Rapporteur in his most recent report, to include in their educational curricula and social programmes, at all levels as appropriate, knowledge, tolerance and respect for foreign cultures, peoples and countries;

6. *Supports* the efforts of Governments in taking measures aimed at the eradication of all forms of racism, racial discrimination, xenophobia and related intolerance;

7. *Recognizes* that Governments should implement and enforce legislation to prevent acts of racism and racial discrimination;

3 *Official Records of the Economic and Social Council, 1995, Supplement No. 3* (E/1995/23 and Corr.1 and 2), chap. II, sect. A.

4 *Report of the World Conference on Human Rights, Vienna, 14-25 June 1993* (A/CONF.157/24 (Part I)), chap. III.

5 See A/50/476.

6 *Ibid.*

8. *Calls upon* all Governments and intergovernmental organizations, with the assistance of non-governmental organizations, as appropriate, to continue to cooperate with and to supply relevant information to the Special Rapporteur;

9. *Urges* all Governments to cooperate fully with the Special Rapporteur, with a view to enabling him to fulfil his mandate;

10. *Requests, once again,* the Secretary-General promptly to provide the Special Rapporteur with all the necessary human and financial assistance in carrying out his mandate and enabling him to submit, in a timely manner, a preliminary report to the General Assembly at its fifty-first session on this question.

97th plenary meeting
21 December 1995

06.30 RELIGIOUS DISCRIMINATION

103 (I). Persecution and Discrimination

Committee: -
Vote: unanimous

The General Assembly declares that it is in the higher interests of humanity to put an immediate end to religious and so-called racial persecution and discrimination, and calls on the Governments and responsible authorities to conform both to the letter and to the spirit of the Charter of the United Nations, and to take the most prompt and energetic steps to that end.

Forty-eighth plenary meeting
19 November 1946

36/55. Declaration on the Elimination of all Forms of Intolerance and of Discrimination Based on Religion or Belief

Committee: 3
Vote: Adopted without a vote
Ref.: 35/125, 34/43, 33/106, 32/143, 31/138, 3267(XXIX), 3069(XXVIII), 3027(XXVII), 2295(XXII), 2020(XX), 1781(XVII), 1779(XVII), 1684(XVI)

The General Assembly,

Considering that one of the basic principles of the Charter of the United Nations is that of the dignity and equality inherent in all human beings, and that all Member States have pledged themselves to take joint and separate action in cooperation with the United Nations to promote and encourage universal respect for and observance of human rights and fundamental freedoms for all, without distinction as to race, sex, language or religion,

Considering that the Universal Declaration of Human Rights[1] and the International Covenants on Human Rights[2] proclaim the principles of non-discrimination and equality before the law and the right to freedom of thought, conscience, religion and belief,

Considering that the disregard and infringement of human rights and fundamental freedoms, in particular of the right to freedom of thought, conscience, religion or whatever belief, have brought, directly or indirectly, wars and great suffering to mankind, especially where they serve as a means of foreign interference in the internal affairs of other States and amount to kindling hatred between peoples and nations,

Considering that religion or belief, for anyone who professes either, is one of the fundamental elements in his conception of life and that freedom of religion or belief should be fully respected and guaranteed,

Considering that it is essential to promote understanding, tolerance and respect in matters relating to freedom of religion or belief and to ensure that the use of religion or belief for ends inconsistent with the Charter, other relevant instruments of the United Nations and the purposes and principles of the present Declaration is inadmissible,

Convinced that freedom of religion or belief should also contribute to the attainment of the goals of world peace, social justice and friendship among peoples and to the elimination of ideologies or practices of colonialism and racial discrimination,

Noting with satisfaction the adoption of several, and the coming into force of some, conventions, under the aegis of the United Nations and of the specialized agencies, for the elimination of various forms of discrimination,

Concerned by manifestations of intolerance and by the existence of discrimination in matters of religion or belief still in evidence in some areas of the world,

Resolved to adopt all necessary measures for the speedy elimination of such intolerance in all its forms and manifestations and to prevent and combat discrimination on the grounds of religion or belief,

Proclaims this Declaration on the Elimination of All Forms of Intolerance and of Discrimination Based on Religion or Belief:

Article 1

1. Everyone shall have the right to freedom of thought, conscience and religion. This right shall include freedom to have a religion or whatever belief of his choice, and freedom, either individually or in community with others and in public or private, to manifest his religion or belief in worship, observance, practice and teaching.

2. No one shall be subject to coercion which would impair his freedom to have a religion or belief of his choice.

3. Freedom to manifest one's religion or belief may be subject only to such limitations as are prescribed by law and are necessary to protect public safety, order, health or morals or the fundamental rights and freedoms of others.

Article 2

1. No one shall be subject to discrimination by any State, institution, group of persons, or person on grounds of religion or belief.

2. For the purposes of the present Declaration, the expression "intolerance and discrimination based on religion or belief" means any distinction, exclusion, restriction or preference based on religion or belief and having as its purpose or as its effect nullification or impairment of the recognition, enjoyment or exercise of human rights and fundamental freedoms on an equal basis.

Article 3

Discrimination between human beings on grounds of religion or belief constitutes an affront to human dignity and a disavowal of the principles of the Charter of the United Nations, and shall be condemned as a violation of the human rights and fundamental freedoms proclaimed in the Universal Declaration of Human Rights and enunciated in detail in the International Covenants on Human Rights, and as an obstacle to friendly and peaceful relations between nations.

Article 4

1. All States shall take effective measures to prevent and eliminate discrimination on the grounds of religion or belief in the recognition, exercise and enjoyment of human rights and fundamental freedoms in all fields of civil, economic, political, social and cultural life.

2. All States shall make all efforts to enact or rescind legislation where necessary to prohibit any such discrimination, and to take all appropriate measures to combat intolerance on the grounds of religion or belief in this matter.

---

[1] Resolution 217 A (III).

[2] Resolution 2200 A (XXI), annex.

Article 5

1. The parents or, as the case may be, the legal guardians of the child have the right to organize the life within the family in accordance with their religion or belief and bearing in mind the moral education in which they believe the child should be brought up.

2. Every child shall enjoy the right to have access to education in the matter of religion or belief in accordance with the wishes of his parents or, as the case may be, legal guardians, and shall not be compelled to receive teaching on religion or belief against the wishes of his parents or legal guardians, the best interests of the child being the guiding principle.

3. The child shall be protected from any form of discrimination on the ground of religion or belief. He shall be brought up in a spirit of understanding, tolerance, friendship among peoples, peace and universal brotherhood, respect for freedom of religion or belief of others, and in full consciousness that his energy and talents should be devoted to the service of his fellow men.

4. In the case of a child who is not under the care either of his parents or of legal guardians, due account shall be taken of their expressed wishes or of any other proof of their wishes in the matter of religion or belief, the best interests of the child being the guiding principle.

5. Practices of a religion or beliefs in which a child is brought up must not be injurious to his physical or mental health or to his full development, taking into account article 1, paragraph 3, of the present Declaration.

Article 6

In accordance with article 1 of the present Declaration, and subject to the provisions of article 1, paragraph 3, the right to freedom of thought, conscience, religion or belief shall include, *inter alia*, the following freedoms:

(*a*) To worship or assemble in connection with a religion or belief, and to establish and maintain places for these purposes;

(*b*) To establish and maintain appropriate charitable or humanitarian institutions;

(*c*) To make, acquire and use to an adequate extent the necessary articles and materials related to the rites or customs of a religion or belief;

(*d*) To write, issue and disseminate relevant publications in these areas;

(*e*) To teach a religion or belief in places suitable for these purposes;

(*f*) To solicit and receive voluntary financial and other contributions from individuals and institutions;

(*g*) To train, appoint, elect or designate by succession appropriate leaders called for by the requirements and standards of any religion or belief;

(*h*) To observe days of rest and to celebrate holidays and ceremonies in accordance with the precepts of one's religion or belief;

(*i*) To establish and maintain communications with individuals and communities in matters of religion or belief at the national and international levels.

Article 7

The rights and freedoms set forth in the present Declaration shall be accorded in national legislations in such a manner that everyone shall be able to avail himself of such rights and freedoms in practice.

Article 8

Nothing in the present Declaration shall be construed as restricting or derogating from any right defined in the Universal Declaration of Human Rights and the International Covenants on Human Rights.

73rd plenary meeting
25 November 1981

50/183. Elimination of all Forms of Religious Intolerance

Committee: 3
Vote: Adopted without a vote
Ref.: 49/188, 48/128, 47/129, 46/131, 45/136, 44/131, 43/108, 42/97, 41/112, 40/109, 39/131, 38/110, 37/187, 35/125, 34/43, 32/143, 3267(XXIX), 3069(XXVIII)

The General Assembly,

Recalling that all States have pledged themselves, under the Charter of the United Nations, to promote and encourage universal respect for and observance of human rights and fundamental freedoms for all without distinction as to race, sex, language or religion,

Recognizing that these rights derive from the inherent dignity of the human person,

Emphasizing that the right to freedom of thought, conscience, religion and belief is far-reaching and profound and that it encompasses freedom of thought on all matters, personal conviction and the commitment to religion or belief, whether manifested individually or in community with others,

Recalling article 18 of the International Covenant on Civil and Political Rights,[1]

Reaffirming that discrimination against human beings on the grounds of religion or belief constitutes an affront to human dignity and a disavowal of the principles of the Charter,

Reaffirming its resolution 36/55 of 25 November 1981, by which it proclaimed the Declaration on the Elimination of All Forms of Intolerance and of Discrimination Based on Religion or Belief,

Reaffirming the call of the World Conference on Human Rights for all Governments to take all appropriate measures in compliance with their international obligations and with due regard to their respective legal systems to counter intolerance and related violence based on religion or belief, including practices of discrimination against women and the desecration of religious sites, recognizing that every individual has the right to freedom of thought, conscience, expression and religion,

Recalling that the World Conference on Human Rights recognized that the process of promoting and protecting human rights should be conducted in conformity with the purposes and principles of the Charter of the United Nations and international law,

Calling upon all Governments to cooperate with the Special Rapporteur of the Commission on Human Rights on religious intolerance to enable him to carry out his mandate fully,

Recognizing that it is desirable to enhance the promotional and public information activities of the United Nations in matters relating to freedom of religion or belief and that both Governments and non-governmental organizations have an important role to play in this domain,

Emphasizing that non-governmental organizations and religious bodies and groups at every level have an important role to play in the promotion of tolerance and the protection of freedom of religion or belief,

Conscious of the importance of education in ensuring tolerance of religion and belief,

Welcoming the inclusion of events relating to tolerance and religious diversity among the activities undertaken during the United Nations Year for Tolerance,

Alarmed that serious instances of intolerance and discrimination on the grounds of religion or belief, including acts of violence, intimidation and coercion motivated by religious extremism, occur in many parts of the world and threaten the enjoyment of human rights and fundamental freedoms,

Deeply concerned that, as reported by the Special Rapporteur, the rights violated on religious grounds include the right to life, the right to physical integrity and to liberty and security of person, the right to freedom of expression, the right not to be subjected to torture or

1 See resolution 2200 A (XXI), annex.

other cruel, inhuman or degrading treatment or punishment, and the right not to be arbitrarily arrested or detained,

Believing that further efforts are therefore required to promote and protect the right to freedom of thought, conscience, religion and belief and to eliminate all forms of hatred, intolerance and discrimination based on religion or belief,

1. *Reaffirms* that freedom of thought, conscience, religion and belief is a human right derived from the inherent dignity of the human person and guaranteed to all without discrimination;

2. *Urges* States to ensure that their constitutional and legal systems provide adequate and effective guarantees of freedom of thought, conscience, religion and belief to all without discrimination, including the provision of effective remedies in cases where the right to freedom of religion or belief is violated;

3. *Also urges* States to ensure, in particular, that no one within their jurisdiction is, because of their religion or belief, deprived of the right to life or the right to liberty and security of person, or is subjected to torture or arbitrary arrest or detention;

4. *Condemns* all instances of hatred, intolerance and acts of violence, intimidation and coercion motivated by religious extremism and intolerance of religion or belief;

5. *Urges* States, in conformity with international standards of human rights, to take all necessary action to prevent such instances, to take all appropriate measures to combat hatred, intolerance and acts of violence, intimidation and coercion motivated by religious extremism and to encourage understanding, tolerance and respect in matters relating to freedom of religion or belief;

6. *Recognizes* that legislation alone is not enough to prevent violations of human rights, including the right to freedom of religion or belief;

7. *Emphasizes* that, as underlined by the Human Rights Committee, restrictions on the freedom to manifest religion or belief are permitted only if limitations are prescribed by law, are necessary to protect public safety, order, health or morals, or the fundamental rights and freedoms of others, and are applied in a manner that does not vitiate the right to freedom of thought, conscience and religion;

8. *Urges* States to ensure that, in the course of their official duties, members of law enforcement bodies, civil servants, educators and other public officials respect different religions and beliefs and do not discriminate against persons professing other religions or beliefs;

9. *Calls upon* all States to recognize, as provided in the Declaration on the Elimination of All Forms of Intolerance and of Discrimination Based on Religion or Belief, the right of all persons to worship or assemble in connection with a religion or belief, and to establish and maintain places for those purposes;

10. *Expresses its grave concern* at any attack upon religious places, sites and shrines, and calls upon all States, in accordance with their national legislation and in conformity with international human rights standards, to exert utmost efforts to ensure that such places, sites and shrines are fully respected and protected;

11. *Recognizes* that the exercise of tolerance and non-discrimination by persons and groups is necessary for the full realization of the aims of the Declaration;

12. *Considers it desirable* to enhance the promotional and public information activities of the United Nations in matters relating to freedom of religion or belief and to ensure that appropriate measures are taken to this end, including the dissemination, as a matter of high priority, of the text of the Declaration by United Nations information centres, as well as by other interested bodies;

13. *Encourages* the continued efforts on the part of the Special Rapporteur appointed to examine incidents and governmental actions in all parts of the world that are incompatible with the provisions of the Declaration and to recommend remedial measures as appropriate;

14. *Invites* the Special Rapporteur, within the terms of his mandate and in the context of recommending remedial measures, to take into account the experiences of various States as to which measures are most effective in promoting freedom of religion and belief and countering all forms of intolerance;

15. *Encourages* Governments to give serious consideration to inviting the Special Rapporteur to visit their countries so as to enable him to fulfil his mandate even more effectively;

16. *Recommends* that the promotion and protection of the right to freedom of thought, conscience, religion and belief be given appropriate priority in the work of the United Nations programme of advisory services in the field of human rights, including with regard to the drafting of legal texts in conformity with international instruments on human rights and taking into account the provisions of the Declaration;

17. *Welcomes* and encourages the efforts of non-governmental organizations to promote the implementation of the Declaration, and invites them to consider what further contribution they could make to its implementation and dissemination in all parts of the world;

18. *Requests* the Commission on Human Rights to continue its consideration of measures to implement the Declaration;

19. *Requests* the Special Rapporteur of the Commission on Human Rights to submit an interim report to the General Assembly at its fifty-first session;

20. *Requests* the Secretary-General to ensure that the Special Rapporteur receives the necessary staffing and financial and material resources to enable him to discharge his mandate;

21. *Decides* to consider the question of the elimination of all forms of religion intolerance at its fifty-first session under the item entitled "Human rights questions".

99th plenary meeting
22 December 1995

06.40 GROUPS REQUIRING SPECIAL PROTECTION

06.41 WOMEN

2263 (XXII). Declaration on the Elimination of Discrimination Against Women

Committee: 3
Vote: 111 - 0 - 0
Ref.: 2199(XXII), 1921(XVIII)

The General Assembly,

Considering that the peoples of the United Nations have, in the Charter, reaffirmed their faith in fundamental human rights, in the dignity and worth of the human person and in the equal rights of men and women,

Considering that the Universal Declaration on Human Rights asserts the principle of non-discrimination and proclaims that all human beings are born free and equal in dignity and rights and that everyone is entitled to all the rights and freedoms set forth therein, without distinction of any kind, including any distinction as to sex,

Taking into account the resolutions, declarations, conventions and recommendations of the United Nations and the specialized agencies designed to eliminate all forms of discrimination and to promote equal rights for men and women,

Concerned that, despite the Charter of the United Nations, the Universal Declaration of Human Rights, the International Covenants on Human Rights and other instruments of the United Nations and the specialized agencies and despite the progress made in the matter of equality of rights, there continues to exist considerable discrimination against women,

Considering that discrimination against women is incompatible with human dignity and with the welfare of the family and of society, prevents their participation, on equal terms with men, in the political, social, economic and cultural life of their countries and is an obstacle to the full development of the potentialities of women in the service of their countries and of humanity,

Bearing in mind the great contribution made by women to social, political, economic and cultural life and the part they play in the family and particularly in the rearing of children,

Convinced that the full and complete development of a country, the welfare of the world and the cause of peace require the maximum participation of women as well as men in all fields,

Considering that it is necessary to ensure the universal recognition in law and in fact of the principle of equality of men and women,

Solemnly proclaims this Declaration:

Article 1

Discrimination against women, denying or limiting as it does their equality of rights with men, is fundamentally unjust and constitutes an offence against human dignity.

Article 2

All appropriate measures shall be taken to abolish existing laws, customs, regulations and practices which are discriminatory against women, and to establish adequate legal protection for equal rights of men and women, in particular:

(*a*) The principle of equality of rights shall be embodied in the constitution or otherwise guaranteed by law;

(*b*) The international instruments of the United Nations and the specialized agencies relating to the elimination of discrimination against women shall be ratified or acceded to and fully implemented as soon as practicable.

Article 3

All appropriate measures shall be taken to educate public opinion and to direct national aspirations towards the eradication of prejudice and the abolition of customary and all other practices which are based on the idea of the inferiority of women.

Article 4

All appropriate measures shall be taken to ensure to women on equal terms with men, without any discrimination:

(*a*) The right to vote in all elections and be eligible for election to all publicly elected bodies;

(*b*) The right to vote in all public referenda;

(*c*) The right to hold public office and to exercise all public functions.

Such rights shall be guaranteed by legislation.

Article 5

Women shall have the same rights as men to acquire, change or retain their nationality. Marriage to an alien shall not automatically affect the nationality of the wife either by rendering her stateless or by forcing upon her the nationality of her husband.

Article 6

1. Without prejudice to the safeguarding of the unity and the harmony of the family, which remains the basic unit of any society, all appropriate measures, particularly legislative measures, shall be taken to ensure to women, married or unmarried, equal rights with men in the field of civil law, and in particular:

(*a*) The right to acquire, administer, enjoy, dispose of and inherit property, including property acquired during marriage;

(*b*) The right to equality in legal capacity and the exercise thereof;

(*c*) The same rights as men with regard to the law on the movement of persons.

2. All appropriate measures shall be taken to ensure the principle of equality of status of the husband and wife, and in particular:

(*a*) Women shall have the same right as men to free choice of a spouse and to enter into marriage only with their free and full consent;

(*b*) Women shall have equal rights with men during marriage and at its dissolution. In all cases the interest of the children shall be paramount;

(*c*) Parents shall have equal rights and duties in matters relating to their children. In all cases the interest of the children shall be paramount.

3. Child marriage and the betrothal of young girls before puberty shall be prohibited, and effective action including legislation, shall be taken to specify a minimum age for marriage and to make the registration of marriages in an official registry compulsory.

Article 7

All provisions of penal codes which constitute discrimination against women shall be repealed.

Article 8

All appropriate measures, including legislation, shall be taken to combat all forms of traffic in women and exploitation of prostitution of women.

Article 9

All appropriate measures shall be taken to ensure to girls and women, married or unmarried, equal rights with men in education at all levels, and in particular:

(*a*) Equal conditions of access to, and study in, educational institutions of all types, including universities and vocational, technical and professional schools;

(*b*) The same choice of curricula, the same examinations, teaching staff with qualifications of the same standard, and school premises and equipment of the same quality, whether the institutions are co-educational or not;

(*c*) Equal opportunities to benefit from scholarships and other study grants;

(*d*) Equal opportunities for access to programmes of continuing education, including adult literacy programmes;

(*e*) Access to educational information to help in ensuring the health and well-being of families.

Article 10

1. All appropriate measures shall be taken to ensure to women, married or unmarried, equal rights with men in the field of economic and social life, and in particular:

(*a*) The right, without discrimination on grounds of marital status or any other grounds, to receive vocational training, to work, to free choice of profession and employment, and to professional and vocational advancement;

(*b*) The right to equal remuneration with men and to equality of treatment in respect of work of equal value;

(*c*) The right to leave with pay, retirement privileges and provision for security in respect of unemployment, sickness, old age or other incapacity to work;

(*d*) The right to receive family allowances on equal terms with men.

2. In order to prevent discrimination against women on account of marriage or maternity and to ensure their effective right to work, measures shall be taken to prevent their dismissal in the event of marriage or maternity and to provide paid maternity leave, with the guarantee of returning to former employment, and to provide the necessary social services, including child-care facilities.

3. Measures taken to protect women in certain types of work, for reasons inherent in their physical nature shall not be regarded as discriminatory.

Article 11

1. The principle of equality of rights of men and women demands implementation in all States in accordance with the principles of the

Charter of the United Nations and of the Universal Declaration of Human Rights.

2. Governments, non-governmental organizations and individuals are urged, therefore, to do all in their power to promote the implementation of the principles contained in this Declaration.

1597th plenary meeting
7 November 1967

2716 (XXV). Programme of Concerted International Action for the Advancement of Women

Committee: 3
Vote: 114 - 0 - 0
Ref.: 2059(XX), 1777(XVII), 1509(XV), 731(VIII), 729(VIII)

The General Assembly,

Recalling its resolution 1777 (XVII) of 7 December 1962 initiating the study of a unified, long-term United Nations programme for the advancement of women,

Recalling also the Declaration on the Elimination of Discrimination against Women, adopted on 7 November 1967, and the Declaration on Social Progress and Development, adopted on 11 December 1969,

Noting resolution IX of the International Conference on Human Rights held at Teheran in 1968,[1] on measures to promote women's rights in the modern world, including a united, long-term United Nations programme for the advancement of women, which established guidelines for such a programme,

Noting also that, in accordance with General Assembly resolution 2571 (XXIV) of 13 December 1969 and with paragraph 79 of Assembly resolution 2626 (XXV) of 24 October 1970, concerning the International Development Strategy for the Second United Nations Development Decade, arrangements should be made to keep under systematic scrutiny the progress towards achieving the goals and objectives of the Decade, to identify shortfalls in their achievement and the policies that are not consistent with the attainment of those objectives and to recommend positive measures, including new goals and policies as needed,

Expressing the hope that general and complete disarmament under effective international control will allow for the use of the resources released progressively for purposes of economic and social progress of all peoples, including the elaboration of programmes designed to advance the status of women,

Believing that a programme of concerted international action, planned on a long-term basis, will advance the status of women and increase their effective participation in all sectors,

Considering that the success of such a programme will require intensified action on the part of Member States, at the national and regional levels, as well as maximum use of the methods and techniques available through the United Nations system of organizations,

Believing that an important step in the further development of such a programme would be the establishment of concrete objectives and minimum targets,

1. *Recommends* that the objectives and targets set forth in the annex to the present resolution should be achieved as widely as possible during the Second United Nations Development Decade;

2. *Invites* States Members of the United Nations or members of specialized agencies and all organs and agencies within the United Nations system to cooperate in achieving these objectives and targets, and hopes that adequate staff and resources will be made available for this purpose;

3. *Recommends* that concerted efforts should be made to increase the resources available for technical cooperation projects which advance the status of women and that consideration be given to allocating a specific percentage of the available funds for this purpose;

4. *Requests* the Secretary-General to make available to the Commission on the Status of Women, if possible at its twenty-fourth session, information on the extent to which women are participating in, and benefiting from, technical cooperation projects,

5. *Recommends* that conferences, seminars and similar meetings at the regional and international levels should be organized with the participation, wherever possible, of ministers, high government officials and specialists concerted with problems of development, and of representatives of non-governmental organizations concerned with this problem, to consider ways and means of promoting the status of women within the framework of over-all development;

6. *Draws attention* to the important role that may also be played in this respect by the regional training and research centres for social development to be established pursuant to Economic and Social Council resolution 1406 (XLVI) of 5 June 1969;

7. *Suggests* that the continuous education of adults be encouraged with a view to changing in particular their attitude of mind towards the roles to be played by men and women in order to help them to assume their responsibilities in society;

8. *Notes*, notwithstanding the provisions of all the preceding paragraphs, that the family, as the cornerstone of society, must be protected.

1930th plenary meeting
15 December 1970

Annex

I. General Objectives

1. The ratification of, or accession to, the relevant international conventions relating to the status of women.

2. The enactment of legislation to bring national laws into conformity with international instruments relating to the status of women, including in particular the Declaration on the Elimination of Discrimination against Women.

3. The taking of effective legal and other measures to ensure the full implementation of these instruments.

4. The development of effective large-scale educational and informational programmes using all mass media and other available means to make all sectors of the population in rural as well as urban areas fully aware of the norms established by the United Nations and the specialized agencies in the conventions, recommendations, declarations and resolutions adopted under their auspices, and to educate public opinion and enlist its support for all measures aimed at achieving the realization of the standards set forth.

5. The assessment and evaluation of the contribution of women to the various economic and social sectors in relation to the country's over-all development plans and programmes, with a view to establishing specific objectives and minimum targets which might realistically be achieved by 1980 to increase the effective contribution of women to the various sectors.

6. The study of the positive and negative effects of scientific and technological change on the status of women with a view to ensuring continuous progress, especially as regards the education and training as well as the living conditions and employment of women.

7. The elaboration of short-term and long-term programmes to achieve these specific objectives and minimum targets, where possible within the framework of over-all national development plans or programmes, and the provision of adequate funds for programmes which advance the status of women.

8. The establishment of machinery and procedures to make possible the continuous review and evaluation of women's integration into all sectors of economic and social life and their contribution to development.

9. The full utilization of the desire and readiness of women to devote their energies, talents and abilities to the benefit of society.

---

1 *Final Act of the International Conference on Human Rights* (United Nations publication, Sales No.: E.68.XIV.2), p. 10.

II. Minimum Targets to Be Achieved During the Second United Nations Development Decade

A. Education

1. The progressive elimination of illiteracy, ensuring equality in literacy between the sexes, especially among the younger generation.

2. Equal access of boys and girls to education at the primary and secondary levels and at educational institutions of all types, including universities and vocational, technical and profession schools.

3. Decisive progress in achieving free and compulsory education at the primary level and in achieving free education at all levels.

4. The establishment of the same choice of curricula for boys and girls, the same examinations, equally qualified teaching staff, and the same quality of school premises and equipment, whether the institutions are co-educational or not, and equal opportunities to receive scholarships and grants.

5. The achievement of equality in the percentage of boys and girls receiving primary education and of a substantial increase in the number of girls at all educational levels, in particular in the field of technical and professional education.

6. The establishment of educational policies that take account of employment needs and opportunities and of scientific and technological change.

B. Training and employment

1. Provision of the same vocational advice and guidance to members of both sexes.

2. Equal access of girls and women to vocational training and retraining at all levels, with a view to achieving their full participation in the economic and social life of their countries.

3. Universal acceptance of the principle of equal pay for equal work and the adoption of effective measures to implement it.

4. Full acceptance of the policy of non-discrimination in relation to the employment and treatment of women, and measures to give effect to that policy on a progressive basis.

5. A substantial increase in the numbers of qualified women employed in skilled and technical work, and at all higher levels of economic life and in posts of responsibility.

6. A substantial increase in the opportunities for involvement of women in all facets of agricultural development and agricultural services.

C. Health and maternity protection

1. The progressive extension of measures to ensure maternity protection, with a view to ensuring paid maternity leave with the guarantee of returning to former or equivalent employment.

2. The development and extension of adequate child care and other facilities to assist parents with family responsibilities.

3. The adoption of measures for the creation and development of a wide network of special medical establishments for the protection of the health of the mother and child.

4. Making available to all persons who so desire the necessary information and advice to enable them to decide freely and responsibly on the number and spacing of their children and to prepare them for responsible parenthood, including information on the ways in which women can benefit from family planning. Such information and advice should be based on valid and proven scientific expertise, with due regard to the risks that may be involved.

D. Administration and public life

1. A substantial increase in the number of women participating in public and government life at the local, national and international levels. Special attention might be paid to training women for such participation, especially in middle-level and higher posts.

2. A substantial increase in the number of qualified women holding responsible posts at the executive and policy-making levels, including those related to over-all development planning.

46/98. Implementation of the Nairobi Forward-Looking Strategies for the Advancement of Women

Committee: 3
Vote: Adopted without a vote
Ref.: 50/203, 49/161, 48/108, 47/95, 45/129, 44/77, 43/101, 42/62, 41/111, 40/108, 39/129, 38/108, 37/60, 37/58, 36/126, 35/136, 34/162, 34/158, 34/155, 33/190, 33/189, 33/185, 32/140, 31/137, 31/136

The General Assembly,

Recalling all its relevant resolutions, in particular resolution 44/77 of 8 December 1989, in which, *inter alia*, it endorsed and reaffirmed the importance of the Nairobi Forward-looking Strategies for the Advancement of Women for the period up to the year 2000 and set out measures for their immediate implementation and for the overall achievement of the interrelated goals and objectives of the United Nations Decade for Women: Equality, Development and Peace,

Recalling also its resolution 45/129 of 14 December 1990,

Taking into consideration the resolutions adopted by the Economic and Social Council on issues relating to women since its resolution 1987/18 of 26 May 1987,

Reaffirming its resolution 40/30 of 29 November 1985, in which it emphasized that the elderly must be considered an important and necessary element in the development process at all levels within a given society and that, consequently, elderly women should be considered contributors to as well as beneficiaries of development,

Reaffirming also its determination to encourage the full participation of women in economic, social, cultural, civil and political affairs and to promote development, cooperation and international peace,

Conscious of the important and constructive contribution to the improvement of the status of women made by the Commission on the Status of Women, the specialized agencies, the regional commissions and other organizations and bodies of the United Nations system and non-governmental organizations concerned,

Concerned that the resources available to the programme on the advancement of women of the Secretariat are insufficient to ensure adequate support to the Committee on the Elimination of Discrimination against Women and effective implementation of other aspects of the programme, especially the preparations for the Fourth World Conference on Women, to be held in 1995,

Regretting that the high-level inter-regional consultation on women in public life did not take place in 1991 as scheduled,

Recognizing the advancement of women as one of the priorities of the Organization for the biennium 1990-1991,

1. *Takes note* of the report of the Secretary-General;

2. *Reaffirms* paragraph 2 of section I of the recommendations and conclusions arising from the first review and appraisal of the implementation of the Nairobi Forward-looking Strategies for the Advancement of Women, contained in the annex to Economic and Social Council resolution 1990/15 of 24 May 1990, which called for an improved pace in the implementation of the Strategies in the crucial last decade of the twentieth century, since the cost to societies of failing to implement the Strategies would be high in terms of slowed economic and social development, misuse of human resources and reduced progress for society as a whole;

3. *Urges* Governments, international organizations and non-governmental organizations to implement the recommendations;

4. *Calls again upon* Member States to give priority to policies and programmes relating to the subtheme "Employment, health and education", in particular to literacy, for the empowerment of women, especially those in the rural areas, to meet their own needs through self-reliance and the mobilization of indigenous resources, as well as to issues relating to the role of women in economic and political decision-making, population, the environment and information;

5. *Reaffirms* the central role of the Commission on the Status of Women in matters related to the advancement of women, and calls upon it to continue promoting the implementation of the Forward-looking Strategies to the year 2000, based on the goals of the United

Nations Decade for Women: Equality, Development and Peace and the subtheme "Employment, health and education", and urges all organizations of the United Nations system to cooperate effectively with the Commission in this task;

6. *Requests* the Commission, when considering the priority theme relating to development during its thirty-sixth and subsequent sessions, to ensure its early contribution to the work of forthcoming major international conferences such as the United Nations Conference on Environment and Development, to be held in 1992, the World Conference on Human Rights, to be held in 1993, and the International Conference on Population and Development, to be held in 1994, and to address the impact of technologies on women;

7. *Also requests* the Commission to give special attention to women in developing countries, particularly in Africa and the least developed countries, who suffer disproportionately from the effects of the global economic crisis and the heavy external debt burden, and to recommend further measures for the equalization of opportunity and for integration of these women into the development process when considering the priority theme relating to development;

8. *Requests* the Secretary-General to ensure that appropriate staff from the secretariats of the Committee on the Elimination of Discrimination Against Women and the Commission on the Status of Women participate in the preparatory process for the World Conference on Human Rights, as well as in the Conference itself, in accordance with General Assembly resolution 40/108 of 13 December 1985;

9. *Endorses anew* Economic and Social Council resolution 1990/12 of 24 May 1990, in which the Council recommended that a world conference on women should be held in 1995 and requested that the Commission act as the preparatory body for the world conference;

10. *Requests* the Commission to decide on the venue of the Fourth World Conference on Women not later than at its thirty-sixth session, in accordance with Commission decision 35/102 of 8 March 1991, bearing in mind that preference should be given to the region that has not yet hosted a world conference on women;

11. *Requests* the Secretary-General to appoint not later than 1992 the Secretary-General of the Conference;

12. *Requests* the relevant United Nations bodies to continue to provide action-oriented input when reporting to the Commission on the priority theme relating to development;

13. *Notes with satisfaction* the publication of *The World's Women 1970-1990* through the cooperative efforts of various United Nations organizations;

14. *Recommends* the further development of methods of compilation and data collection in areas of concern identified by the Commission, with a view to preparing in all official languages, as a background document for the Fourth World Conference on Women, an updated edition of the publication mentioned in paragraph 13 above;

15. *Emphasizes*, in the framework of the Forward-looking Strategies, the importance of the total integration of women in the development process, bearing in mind the specific and urgent needs of the developing countries, and calls upon Member States to establish specific targets at each level in order to increase the participation of women in professional, management and decision-making positions in their countries;

16. *Emphasizes once again* the need to give urgent attention to redressing socio-economic inequities at the national and international levels as a necessary step towards the full realization of the goals and objectives of the Forward-looking Strategies;

17. *Welcomes* the creation of the *ad hoc* open-ended working group to elaborate standard rules on the equalization of opportunities for persons with disabilities;

18. *Urges* that particular attention be given by the United Nations and Governments to the situation of women with disabilities and that Governments take steps to ensure the equalization of opportunities for these women in the economic, social and political fields;

19. *Takes note* of the Guidelines on the Protection of Refugee Women prepared by the Office of the United Nations High Commissioner for Refugees, which provide practical means of ensuring the protection of refugee women, and which are in keeping with decisions of the Economic and Social Council and the Commission on the Status of Women on this issue;

20. *Recommends* that all organizations of the United Nations system include in the policy analyses of development issues, as well as in proposals for major international conferences and in development projects, the potential contribution of ageing and elderly women, as relevant;

21. *Notes* the relevance of the interregional consultation on women in public life to the preparation for the Fourth World Conference on Women, and requests that the Commission at its thirty-sixth session make recommendations to the General Assembly through the Economic and Social Council for the convening of the consultation not later than 1993;

22. *Urges* the Commission, the relevant organizations of the United Nations system and Governments to give particular attention to refugee women and children and migrant women, taking into account their contribution in the social, economic and political fields and the urgent need to avoid any kind of discrimination against them;

23. *Requests* the Secretary-General, in formulating the system-wide medium-term plan for the advancement of women for the period 1996-2001 and in integrating the Forward-looking Strategies into activities mandated by the General Assembly, to pay particular attention to the strengthening of national machineries for the advancement of women and to specific sectoral themes that cut across the three objectives, equality, development and peace, and include, in particular, literacy, education, health, population, the impact of technology on the environment and its effect on women and the full participation of women in decision-making;

24. *Also requests* the Secretary-General to continue updating the *World Survey on the Role of Women in Development*, bearing in mind its importance, placing particular emphasis on the adverse impact of the difficult economic situation affecting the majority of developing countries, in particular on the condition of women, and giving special attention to worsening conditions for the incorporation of women into the labour force, as well as the impact of reduced expenditures for social services on women's opportunities for education, health and child care, and to submit a preliminary version of the updated *World Survey on the Role of Women in Development* to the Economic and Social Council, through the Commission, in 1993 and a final version in 1994;

25. *Requests* Governments, when presenting candidatures for vacancies in the Secretariat, in particular at the decision-making level, to give priority to women's candidatures, and requests the Secretary-General in reviewing these candidatures to give special consideration to female candidates from underrepresented and unrepresented developing countries and to assist those countries in identifying suitable women candidates to fill vacancies at the decision-making level;

26. *Requests* the Secretary-General to invite Governments, organizations of the United Nations system, including the regional commissions and the specialized agencies, and intergovernmental and non-governmental organizations to report periodically to the Economic and Social Council, through the Commission, on activities undertaken at all levels to implement the Forward-looking Strategies;

27. *Also requests* the Secretary-General to continue to provide for the existing weekly radio programmes on women in the regular budget of the United Nations, making adequate provisions for broadcasts in different languages, and to develop the focal point for issues relating to women in the Department of Public Information of the Secretariat, which, in concert with the Centre for Social Development and Humanitarian Affairs of the Secretariat, should provide a more effective public information programme relating to the advancement of women;

28. *Further requests* the Secretary-General to include in his report on the implementation of the Forward-looking Strategies, to be submitted to the General Assembly at its forty-seventh session, an assessment of recent developments that are relevant to the priority themes to be considered at the subsequent session of the Commission and to transmit to the Commission a summary of relevant views expressed by delegations during the debate in the Assembly;

29. *Requests* the Fifth Committee, in reviewing the programme on the advancement of women contained in the proposed programme budget for the biennium 1992-1993, to ensure that established staffing levels, temporary assistance and other objects of expenditure are sufficient to ensure adequate support to the Committee on the Elimination of Discrimination against Women and effective implementation of other aspects of the programme, especially the preparations for the Fourth World Conference on Women, and, if proposed resources are found to be insufficient, to determine the appropriate resource levels;

30. *Requests* the Secretary-General to report to the General Assembly at its forty-seventh session on measures taken to implement the present resolution;

31. *Decides* to consider the question of the forward-looking strategies for the advancement of women to the year 2000 at its forty-seventh session under the item entitled "Advancement of women".

74th plenary meeting
16 December 1991

48/104. Declaration on the Elimination of Violence Against Women

Committee: 3
Vote: Adopted without a vote

The General Assembly,

Recognizing the urgent need for the universal application to women of the rights and principles with regard to equality, security, liberty, integrity and dignity of all human beings,

Noting that those rights and principles are enshrined in international instruments, including the Universal Declaration of Human Rights, the International Covenant on Civil and Political Rights, the International Covenant on Economic, Social and Cultural Rights, the Convention on the Elimination of All Forms of Discrimination against Women and the Convention against Torture and Other Cruel, Inhuman or Degrading Treatment or Punishment,

Recognizing that effective implementation of the Convention on the Elimination of All Forms of Discrimination against Women would contribute to the elimination of violence against women and that the Declaration on the Elimination of Violence against Women, set forth in the present resolution, will strengthen and complement that process,

Concerned that violence against women is an obstacle to the achievement of equality, development and peace, as recognized in the Nairobi Forward-looking Strategies for the Advancement of Women, in which a set of measures to combat violence against women was recommended, and to the full implementation of the Convention on the Elimination of All Forms of Discrimination against Women,

Affirming that violence against women constitutes a violation of the rights and fundamental freedoms of women and impairs or nullifies their enjoyment of those rights and freedoms, and concerned about the long-standing failure to protect and promote those rights and freedoms in the case of violence against women,

Recognizing that violence against women is a manifestation of historically unequal power relations between men and women, which have led to domination over and discrimination against women by men and to the prevention of the full advancement of women, and that violence against women is one of the crucial social mechanisms by which women are forced into a subordinate position compared with men,

Concerned that some groups of women, such as women belonging to minority groups, indigenous women, refugee women, migrant women, women living in rural or remote communities, destitute women, women in institutions or in detention, female children, women with disabilities, elderly women and women in situations of armed conflict, are especially vulnerable to violence,

Recalling the conclusion in paragraph 23 of the annex to Economic and Social Council resolution 1990/15 of 24 May 1990 that the recognition that violence against women in the family and society was pervasive and cut across lines of income, class and culture had to be matched by urgent and effective steps to eliminate its incidence,

Recalling also Economic and Social Council resolution 1991/18 of 30 May 1991, in which the Council recommended the development of a framework for an international instrument that would address explicitly the issue of violence against women,

Welcoming the role that women's movements are playing in drawing increasing attention to the nature, severity and magnitude of the problem of violence against women,

Alarmed that opportunities for women to achieve legal, social, political and economic equality in society are limited, *inter alia*, by continuing and endemic violence,

Convinced that in the light of the above there is a need for a clear and comprehensive definition of violence against women, a clear statement of the rights to be applied to ensure the elimination of violence against women in all its forms, a commitment by States in respect of their responsibilities, and a commitment by the international community at large to the elimination of violence against women,

Solemnly proclaims the following Declaration on the Elimination of Violence against Women and urges that every effort be made so that it becomes generally known and respected:

Article 1

For the purposes of this Declaration, the term "violence against women" means any act of gender-based violence that results in, or is likely to result in, physical, sexual or psychological harm or suffering to women, including threats of such acts, coercion or arbitrary deprivation of liberty, whether occurring in public or in private life.

Article 2

Violence against women shall be understood to encompass, but not be limited to, the following:

(*a*) Physical, sexual and psychological violence occurring in the family, including battering, sexual abuse of female children in the household, dowry-related violence, marital rape, female genital mutilation and other traditional practices harmful to women, non-spousal violence and violence related to exploitation;

(*b*) Physical, sexual and psychological violence occurring within the general community, including rape, sexual abuse, sexual harassment and intimidation at work, in educational institutions and elsewhere; trafficking in women and forced prostitution;

(*c*) Physical, sexual and psychological violence perpetrated or condoned by the State, wherever it occurs.

Article 3

Women are entitled to the equal enjoyment and protection of all human rights and fundamental freedoms in the political, economic, social, cultural, civil or any other field. These rights include, *inter alia*:

(*a*) The right to life;

(*b*) The right to equality;

(*c*) The right to liberty and security of person;

(*d*) The right to equal protection under the law;

(*e*) The right to be free from all forms of discrimination;

(*f*) The right to the highest standard attainable of physical and mental health;

(*g*) The right to just and favourable conditions of work;

(*h*) The right not to be subjected to torture, or other cruel inhuman or degrading treatment or punishment.

Article 4

States should condemn violence against women and should not invoke any custom, tradition or religious consideration to avoid their obligations with respect to its elimination. States should pursue by all appropriate means and without delay a policy of eliminating violence against women and, to this end, should:

(*a*) Consider, where they have not yet done so, ratifying or acceding to the Convention on the Elimination of All Forms of Discrimination against Women or withdrawing reservations to that Convention;

(*b*) Refrain from engaging in violence against women;

(*c*) Exercise due diligence to prevent, investigate and, in accordance with national legislation, punish acts of violence against women, whether those acts are perpetrated by the State or by private persons;

(*d*) Develop penal, civil, labour and administrative sanctions in domestic legislation to punish and redress the wrongs caused to women who are subjected to violence; women who are subjected to violence should be provided with access to the mechanisms of justice and, as provided for by national legislation, to just and effective remedies for the harm that they have suffered; States should also inform women of their rights in seeking redress through such mechanisms;

(*e*) Consider the possibility of developing national plans of action to promote the protection of women against any form of violence or to include provisions for that purpose in plans already existing, taking into account, as appropriate, such cooperation as can be provided by non-governmental organizations, particularly those concerned with the issue of violence against women;

(*f*) Develop, in a comprehensive way, preventive approaches and all those measures of a legal, political, administrative and cultural nature that promote the protection of women against any form of violence, and ensure that the re-victimization of women does not occur because of laws insensitive to gender considerations, enforcement practices or other interventions;

(*g*) Work to ensure, to the maximum extent feasible in the light of their available resources and, where needed, within the framework of international cooperation, that women subjected to violence and, where appropriate, their children have specialized assistance, such as rehabilitation, assistance in child care and maintenance, treatment, counselling, and health and social services, facilities and programmes as well as support structures, and should take all other appropriate measures to promote their safety and physical and psychological rehabilitation;

(*h*) Include in government budgets adequate resources for their activities related to the elimination of violence against women;

(*i*) Take measures to ensure that law enforcement officers and public officials responsible for implementing policies to prevent investigate and punish violence against women receive training to sensitize them to the needs of women;

(*j*) Adopt all appropriate measures, especially in the field of education, to modify the social and cultural patterns of conduct of men and women and to eliminate prejudices, customary practices and all other practices based on the idea of the inferiority or superiority of either of the sexes and on stereotyped roles for men and women;

(*k*) Promote research, collect data and compile statistics, especially concerning domestic violence, relating to the prevalence of different forms of violence against women and encourage research on the causes, nature, seriousness and consequences of violence against women and on the effectiveness of measures implemented to prevent and redress violence against women; those statistics and findings of the research will be made public;

(*l*) Adopt measures directed towards the elimination of violence against women who are especially vulnerable to violence;

(*m*) Include, in submitting reports as required under relevant human rights instruments of the United Nations, information pertaining to violence against women and measures taken to implement the present Declaration;

(*n*) Encourage the development of appropriate guidelines to assist in the implementation of the principles set forth in the present Declaration;

(*o*) Recognize the important role of the women's movement and non-governmental organizations world wide in raising awareness and alleviating the problem of violence against women;

(*p*) Facilitate and enhance the work of the women's movement and non-governmental organizations and cooperate with them at local national and regional levels;

(*q*) Encourage intergovernmental regional organizations of which they are members to include the elimination of violence against women in their programmes, as appropriate.

Article 5

The organs and specialized agencies of the United Nations system should, within their respective fields of competence, contribute to the recognition and realization of the rights and the principles set forth in the present Declaration and, to this end, should, *inter alia*:

(*a*) Foster international and regional cooperation with a view to defining regional strategies for combating violence, exchanging experiences and financing programmes relating to the elimination of violence against women;

(*b*) Promote meetings and seminars with the aim of creating and raising awareness among all persons of the issue of the elimination of violence against women;

(*c*) Foster coordination and exchange within the United Nations system between human rights treaty bodies to address the issue of violence against women effectively;

(*d*) Include in analyses prepared by organizations and bodies of the United Nations system of social trends and problems, such as the periodic reports on the world social situation, examination of trends in violence against women;

(*e*) Encourage coordination between organizations and bodies of the United Nations system to incorporate the issue of violence against women into ongoing programmes, especially with reference to groups of women particularly vulnerable to violence;

(*f*) Promote the formulation of guidelines or manuals relating to violence against women, taking into account the measures referred to in the present Declaration;

(*g*) Consider the issue of the elimination of violence against women, as appropriate, in fulfilling their mandates with respect to the implementation of human rights instruments;

(*h*) Cooperate with non-governmental organizations in addressing the issue of violence against women.

Article 6

Nothing in the present Declaration shall affect any provision that is more conducive to the elimination of violence against women that may be contained in the legislation of a State or in any international convention, treaty or other instrument in force in a State.

85th plenary meeting
20 December 1993

50/167. Traffic in Women and Girls

Committee: 3
Vote: Adopted without a vote
Ref.: 49/166

The General Assembly,

Reaffirming the principles set forth in the Universal Declaration of Human Rights,[1] the Convention on the Elimination of All Forms of Discrimination against Women,[2] the International Covenants on Human Rights,[3] the Convention against Torture and Other Cruel, Inhuman or Degrading Treatment or Punishment,[4] the Convention on the Rights of the Child[5] and the Declaration on the Elimination of Violence against Women,[6]

Recalling that the Vienna Declaration and Programme of Action, adopted by the World Conference on Human Rights on 25 June

---

1 Resolution 217 A (III).
2 Resolution 34/180, annex.
3 Resolution 2200 A (XXI), annex.
4 Resolution 39/46, annex.
5 Resolution 44/25.
6 Resolution 48/104.

1993,[1] affirmed the human rights of women and the girl child as an inalienable, integral and indivisible part of universal human rights,

Welcoming the Programme of Action of the International Conference on Population and Development, held at Cairo from 5 to 13 September 1994,[2] which, *inter alia,* called upon all Governments to prevent all international trafficking in migrants, especially for the purpose of prostitution, and for the adoption by Governments of both receiving countries and countries of origin of effective sanctions against those who organize undocumented migration, exploit undocumented migrants or engage in trafficking in undocumented migrants, especially those who engage in any form of international traffic of women and children,

Recalling also the recognition by the World Summit for Social Development, held at Copenhagen from 6 to 12 March 1995,[3] of the danger to society of the trafficking in women and children,

Welcoming also the initiatives taken by the Commission on Crime Prevention and Criminal Justice[4] and the Ninth Congress on the Prevention of Crime and the Treatment of Offenders, held at Cairo from 29 April to 10 May 1995,[5] towards criminalizing clandestine traffic in illegal migrants,

Concurring with the conclusion in the Platform for Action of the Fourth World Conference on Women, held at Beijing from 4 to 15 September 1995,[6] that the effective suppression of trafficking in women and girls for the sex trade is a matter of pressing international concern,

Recalling its resolution 49/166 of 23 December 1994 and Commission on the Status of Women resolution 39/6 of 29 March 1995,[7]

Acknowledging the work done by intergovernmental and non-governmental organizations in compiling information on the scale and complexity of the problem of trafficking, in providing shelters for trafficked women and children and in effecting their voluntary repatriation to their countries of origin,

Noting with concern the increasing number of women and girl children from developing countries and from some countries with economies in transition who are being victimized by traffickers, and acknowledging that the problem of trafficking also victimizes young boys,

Convinced of the need to eliminate all forms of sexual violence and sexual trafficking, including for prostitution and other forms of commercial sex, which are violations of the human rights of women and girl children and are incompatible with the dignity and worth of the human person,

Realizing the urgent need for the adoption of effective measures nationally, regionally and internationally to protect women and girl children from this nefarious traffic,

1. *Notes with appreciation* the report of the Secretary-General on the traffic in women and girls;[8]

2. *Appeals* to Governments to take appropriate measures to address the root factors, including external factors, that encourage trafficking in women and girls for prostitution and other forms of commercialized sex, forced marriages and forced labour, so as to eliminate trafficking in women, including by strengthening existing legislation with a view to providing better protection of the rights of women and girls and to punishing perpetrators, through both criminal and civil measures;

3. *Invites* Governments to combat trafficking in women and children through nationally and internationally coordinated measures, at the same time establishing or strengthening institutions for the protection of the victims of trafficking of women and children, and to ensure for victims the necessary assistance, including legal support services that are linguistically and culturally accessible, for their full protection, treatment and rehabilitation;

4. *Also invites* Governments to consider the development of standard minimum rules for the humanitarian treatment of trafficked persons, consistent with human rights standards;

5. *Urges* concerned Governments to support comprehensive, practical approaches by the international community to assist women and children victims of transnational trafficking to return home and be reintegrated into their home societies;

6. *Encourages* Member States to consider signing and ratifying or acceding to the Convention for the Suppression of the Traffic in Persons and the Exploitation of the Prostitution of Others,[9] international agreements on the suppression of slavery and other relevant international instruments;

7. *Invites* the United Nations High Commissioner for Human Rights, in addressing the obstacles to the realization of the human rights of women, in particular, through his contacts with the Special Rapporteur of the Commission on Human Rights on violence against women and the Special Rapporteur of the Commission on Human Rights on the sale of children, child prostitution and child pornography, to include the traffic in women and girls among his priority concerns;

8. *Also encourages* the Centre for Human Rights of the Secretariat to include the traffic in women and girls in its programme of work under its advisory, training and information services, with a view to providing assistance to member Governments, upon their request, in instituting preventive measures against trafficking through education and appropriate information campaigns;

9. *Requests* the Commission on Human Rights to encourage the Working Group on Contemporary Forms of Slavery of the Subcommission on Prevention of Discrimination and Protection of Minorities to continue to address the issue of the traffic in women and girls under its draft programme of action on the traffic in persons and the exploitation of the prostitution of others;

10. *Requests* the Commission on Crime Prevention and Criminal Justice to consider appropriate follow-up to the Ninth Congress on the Prevention of Crime and the Treatment of Offenders on measures to address the problem of trafficking in women and children and to submit a report thereon to the Secretary-General, through the usual channels, for inclusion in his report to the General Assembly;

11. *Invites* relevant intergovernmental and non-governmental organizations to provide advisory services to Governments, upon their request, in planning and setting up rehabilitation programmes for victims of trafficking and in training personnel who will be directly involved in the implementation of these programmes;

12. *Decides* to focus the International Day for the Abolition of Slavery, 2 December 1996, on the problem of trafficking in human persons, especially women and children, and to devote one meeting of the fifty-first session of the General Assembly to the discussion of this problem;

13. *Requests* the Secretary-General to submit to the General Assembly at its fifty-first session, under the item entitled "Advancement of women", a comprehensive report on the implementation of the present resolution, with due regard for possible measures to improve the reporting procedure.

99th plenary meeting
22 December 1995

1 *Report of the World Conference on Human Rights, Vienna, 14-25 June 1993* (A/CONF.157/24 (Part I)), chap. III.

2 *Report of the International Conference on Population and Development, Cairo, 5-13 September 1994* (United Nations publication, Sales No. E.95.XIII.8), chap. I, resolution 1, annex, chap. X.

3 See *Report of the World Summit for Social Development, Copenhagen, 6-12 March 1995* (A/CONF.166/9), chap. I, resolution 1.

4 See *Official Records of the Economic and Social Council, 1995, Supplement No. 10* (E/1995/30), chap. I, sect. B.III.

5 See A/CONF.169/16.

6 *Report of the Fourth World Conference on Women,, Beijing, 4-15 September 1995* (A/CONF.177/20), chap. I, resolution 1, annex II.

7 *Official Records of the Economic and Social Council, 1995, Supplement No. 6* (E/1995/26), chap. I, sect. C.

8 A/50/369.

9 Resolution 317 (IV), annex.

06.42 CHILDREN AND YOUTH

1386 (XIV). Declaration of the Rights of the Child

Committee: 3
Vote: 78 - 0
Ref.: 1387(XIV)

Preamble

Whereas the peoples of the United Nations have, in the Charter, reaffirmed their faith in fundamental human rights and in the dignity and worth of the human person, and have determined to promote social progress and better standards of life in larger freedom,

Whereas the United Nations has, in the Universal Declaration of Human Rights, proclaimed that everyone is entitled to all the rights and freedoms set forth therein, without distinction of any kind, such as race colour, sex, language, religion, political or other opinion, national or social origin, property, birth or other status,

Whereas the child, by reason of his physical and mental immaturity, needs special safeguards and care, including appropriate legal protection, before as well as after birth,

Whereas the need for such special safeguards has been stated in the Geneva Declaration of the Rights of the Child of 1924, and recognized in the Universal Declaration of Human Rights and in the statutes of specialized agencies and international organizations concerned with the welfare of children,

Whereas mankind owes to the child the best it has to give,

Now therefore,

The General Assembly

Proclaims this Declaration of the Rights of the Child to the end that he may have a happy childhood and enjoy for his own good and for the good of society the rights and freedoms herein set forth, and calls upon parents, upon men and women as individuals, and upon voluntary organizations, local authorities and national Governments to recognize these rights and strive for their observance by legislative and other measures progressively taken in accordance with the following principles:

Principle 1

The child shall enjoy all the rights set forth in this Declaration. Every child, without any exception whatsoever, shall be entitled to these rights, without distinction or discrimination on account of race, colour, sex, language, religion, political or other opinion, national or social origin, property, birth or other status, whether of himself or of his family.

Principle 2

The child shall enjoy special protection, and shall be given opportunities and facilities, by law and by other means, to enable him to develop physically, mentally morally, spiritually and socially in a healthy and normal manner and in conditions of freedom and dignity. In the enactment of laws for this purpose, the best interests of the child shall be the paramount consideration.

Principle 3

The child shall be entitled from his birth to a name and a nationality.

Principle 4

The child shall enjoy the benefits of social security. He shall be entitled to grow and develop in health; to this end, special care and protection shall be provided both to him and to his mother, including adequate pre-natal and post-natal care. The child shall have the right to adequate nutrition, housing, recreation and medical services.

Principle 5

The child who is physically, mentally or socially handicapped shall be given the special treatment, education and care required by his particular condition.

Principle 6

The child, for the full and harmonious development of his personality, needs love and understanding. He shall, wherever possible, grow up in the care and under the responsibility of his parents, and, in any case, in an atmosphere of affection and of moral and material security; a child of tender years shall not, save in exceptional circumstances, be separated from his mother. Society and the public authorities shall have the duty to extend particular care to children without a family and to those without adequate means of support. Payment of State and other assistance towards the maintenance of children of large families is desirable.

Principle 7

The child is entitled to receive education, which shall be free and compulsory, at least in the elementary stages. He shall be given an education which will promote his general culture, and enable him, on a basis of equal opportunity, to develop his abilities, his individual judgement, and his sense of moral and social responsibility, and to become a useful member of society.

The best interests of the child shall be the guiding principle of those responsible for his education and guidance; that responsibility lies in the first place with his parents.

The child shall have full opportunity for play and recreation, which should be directed to the same purposes as education; society and the public authorities shall endeavour to promote the enjoyment of this right.

Principle 8

The child shall in all circumstances be among the first to receive protection and relief.

Principle 9

The child shall be protected against all forms of neglect, cruelty and exploitation. He shall not be the subject of traffic, in any form.

The child shall not be admitted to employment before an appropriate minimum age; he shall in no case be caused or permitted to engage in any occupation or employment which would prejudice his health or education, or interfere with his physical, mental or moral development.

Principle 10

The child shall be protected from practices which may foster racial, religious and any other form of discrimination. He shall be brought up in a spirit of understanding, tolerance, friendship among peoples, peace and universal brotherhood, and in full consciousness that his energy and talents should be devoted to the service of his fellow men.

841st plenary meeting
20 November 1959

2018 (XX). Recommendation on Consent to Marriage, Minimum Age for Marriage and Registration of Marriages

Committee: 3
Vote: 95 - 0 - 2
Ref.: 1763(XVII), 1680(XVI)

The General Assembly,

Recognizing that the family group should be strengthened because it is the basic unit of every society, and that men and women of full age have the right to marry and to found a family, that they are entitled to equal rights as to marriage and that marriage shall be entered into only with the free and full consent of the intending spouses, in accordance with the provisions of article 16 of the Universal Declaration of Human Rights,

Recalling its resolution 843 (IX) of 17 December 1954,

Recalling further article 2 of the Supplementary Convention on the Abolition of Slavery, the Slave Trade, and Institutions and Practices Similar to Slavery of 1956,[1] which makes certain provisions con-

1 United Nations publication, Sales No.: 57.XIV.2.

cerning the age of marriage, consent to marriage and registration of marriages,

Recalling also that Article 13, paragraph 1 b, of the Charter of the United Nations provides that the General Assembly shall make recommendations for the purpose of assisting in the realization of human rights and fundamental freedoms for all without distinction as to race, sex, language or religion,

Recalling likewise that, under Article 64 of the Charter, the Economic and Social Council may make arrangements with the Members of the United Nations to obtain reports on the steps taken to give effect to its own recommendations and to recommendations on matters falling within its competence made by the General Assembly,

1. *Recommends* that, where not already provided by existing legislative or other measures, each Member State should take the necessary steps, in accordance with its constitutional processes and its traditional and religious practices, to adopt such legislative or other measures as may be appropriate to give effect to the following principles:

Principle I

(*a*) No marriage shall be legally entered into without the full and free consent of both parties, such consent to be expressed by them in person, after due publicity and in the presence of the authority competent to solemnize the marriage and of witnesses, as prescribed by law.

(*b*) Marriage by proxy shall be permitted only when the competent authorities are satisfied that each party has, before a competent authority and in such manner as may be prescribed by law, fully and freely expressed consent before witnesses and not withdrawn such consent.

Principle II

Member States shall take legislative action to specify a minimum age for marriage, which in any case shall not be less than fifteen years of age; no marriage shall be legally entered into by any person under this age, except where a competent authority has granted a dispensation as to age, for serious reasons, in the interest of the intending spouses.

Principle III

All marriages shall be registered in an appropriate official register by the competent authority.

2. *Recommends* that each Member State should bring the Recommendation on Consent to Marriage, Minimum Age for Marriage and Registration of Marriages contained in the present resolution before the authorities competent to enact legislation or to take other action at the earliest practicable moment and, if possible, no later than eighteen months after the adoption of the Recommendation;

3. *Recommends* that Member States should inform the Secretary-General, as soon as possible after the action referred to in paragraph 2 above, of the measures taken under the present Recommendation to bring it before the competent authority or authorities, with particulars regarding the authority or authorities considered as competent;

4. *Recommends further* that Member States should report to the Secretary-General at the end of three years, and thereafter at intervals of five years, on their law and practice with regard to the matters dealt with in the present Recommendation, showing the extent to which effect has been given or is proposed to be given to the provisions of the Recommendation and such modifications as have been found or may be found necessary in adapting or applying it;

5. *Requests* the Secretary-General to prepare for the Commission on the Status of Women a document containing the reports received from Governments concerning methods of implementing the three basic principles of the present Recommendation;

6. *Invites* the Commission on the Status of Women to examine the reports received from Member States pursuant to the present Recommendation and to report thereon to the Economic and Social Council with such recommendations as it may deem fitting.

1366th plenary meeting
1 November 1965

40/33. United Nations Standard Minimum Rules for the Administration of Juvenile Justice (The Beijing Rules)

Committee: 3
Vote: Adopted without a vote

The General Assembly,

Bearing in mind the Universal Declaration of Human Rights, the International Covenant on Civil and Political Rights and the International Covenant on Economic, Social and Cultural Rights, as well as other international human rights instruments pertaining to the rights of young persons,

Also bearing in mind that 1985 was designated the International Youth Year: Participation, Development, Peace and that the international community has placed importance on the protection and promotion of the rights of the young, as witnessed by the significance attached to the Declaration of the Rights of the Child,[1]

Recalling resolution 4 adopted by the Sixth United Nations Congress on the Prevention of Crime and the Treatment of Offenders,[2] held at Caracas from 25 August to 5 September 1980, which called for the development of standard minimum rules for the administration of juvenile justice and the care of juveniles, which could serve as a model for Member States,

Recalling also Economic and Social Council decision 1984/153 of 25 May 1984, by which the draft rules were forwarded to the Seventh United Nations Congress on the Prevention of Crime and the Treatment of Offenders, through the Interregional Preparatory Meeting, held at Beijing from 14 to 18 May 1984,[3]

Recognizing that the young, owing to their early stage of human development, require particular care and assistance with regard to physical, mental and social development, and require legal protection in conditions of peace, freedom, dignity and security,

Considering that existing national legislation, policies and practices may well require review and amendment in view of the standards contained in the rules,

Considering further that, although such standards may seem difficult to achieve at present in view of existing social, economic, cultural, political and legal conditions, they are nevertheless intended to be attainable as a policy minimum,

1. *Notes with appreciation* the work carried out by the Committee on Crime Prevention and Control, the Secretary-General, the United Nations Asia and Far East Institute for the Prevention of Crime and the Treatment of Offenders and other United Nations institutes in the development of the Standard Minimum Rules for the Administration of Juvenile Justice;

2. *Takes note with appreciation* of the report of the Secretary-General on the draft Standard Minimum Rules for the Administration of Juvenile Justice;[4]

3. *Commends* the Interregional Preparatory Meeting held at Beijing for having finalized the text of the rules submitted to the Seventh United Nations Congress on the Prevention of Crime and the Treatment of Offenders for consideration and final action;

4. *Adopts* the United Nations Standard Minimum Rules for the Administration of Juvenile Justice recommended by the Seventh Congress, contained in the annex to the present resolution, and approves the recommendation of the Seventh Congress that the Rules should be known as "the Beijing Rules";

---

1 Resolution 1386 (XIV).

2 See *Sixth United Nations Congress on the Prevention of Crime and the Treatment of Offenders, Caracas, 25 August - 5 September 1980: report prepared by the Secretariat* (United Nations publication, Sales No. E.81.IV.4), chap. I, sect. B.

3 See *"Report of the International Preparatory Meeting for the Seventh United Nations Congress on the Prevention of Crime and the Treatment of Offenders on topic IV: youth, crime and justice"* \b(A/CONF.121./IPM/1).

4 A/CONF.121/14 and Corr. 1.

5. *Invites* Member States to adapt, wherever this is necessary, their national legislation, policies and practices, particularly in training juvenile justice personnel, to the Beijing Rules and to bring the Rules to the attention of relevant authorities and the public in general;

6. *Calls upon* the Committee on Crime Prevention and Control to formulate measures for the effective implementation of the Beijing Rules, with the assistance of the United Nations institutes on the prevention of crime and the treatment of offenders;

7. *Invites* Member States to inform the Secretary-General on the implementation of the Beijing Rules and to report regularly to the Committee on Crime Prevention and Control on the results achieved;

8. *Requests* Member States and the Secretary-General to undertake research and to develop a data base with respect to effective policies and practices in the administration of juvenile justice;

9. *Requests* the Secretary-General and invites Member States to ensure the widest possible dissemination of the text of the Beijing Rules in all of the official languages of the United Nations, including the intensification of information activities in the field of juvenile justice;

10. *Requests* the Secretary-General to develop pilot projects on the implementation of the Beijing Rules;

11. *Requests* the Secretary-General and Member States to provide the necessary resources to ensure the successful implementation of the Beijing Rules, in particular in the areas of recruitment, training and exchange of personnel, research and evaluation, and the development of new alternatives to institutionalization;

12. *Requests* the Eighth United Nations Congress on the Prevention of Crime and the Treatment of Offenders to review the progress made in the implementation of the Beijing Rules and of the recommendations contained in the present resolution, under a separate agenda item on juvenile justice;

13. *Urges* all relevant organs of the United Nations system, in particular the regional commissions and specialized agencies, the United Nations institutes for the prevention of crime and the treatment of offenders, other intergovernmental organizations and non-governmental organizations to collaborate with the Secretariat and to take the necessary measures to ensure a concerted and sustained effort, within their respective fields of technical competence, to implement the principles contained in the Beijing Rules.

96th plenary meeting
29 November 1985

Annex

United Nations Standard Minimum Rules for the Administration of Juvenile Justice (Beijing Rules)

Part one. General principles

1. Fundamental perspectives

1.1 Member States shall seek, in conformity with their respective general interests, to further the well-being of the juvenile and her or his family.

1.2 Member States shall endeavour to develop conditions that will ensure for the juvenile a meaningful life in the community, which, during that period in life when she or he is most susceptible to deviant behaviour, will foster a process of personal development and education that is as free from crime and delinquency as possible.

1.3 Sufficient attention shall be given to positive measures that involve the full mobilization of all possible resources, including the family, volunteers and other community groups, as well as schools and other community institutions, for the purpose of promoting the well-being of the juvenile, with a view to reducing the need for intervention under the law, and of effectively, fairly and humanely dealing with the juvenile in conflict with the law.

1.4 Juvenile justice shall be conceived as an integral part of the national development process of each country, within a comprehensive framework of social justice for all juveniles, thus, at the same time, contributing to the protection of the young and the maintenance of a peaceful order in society.

1.5 These Rules shall be implemented in the context of economic, social and cultural conditions prevailing in each Member State.

1.6 Juvenile justice services shall be systematically developed and coordinated with a view to improving and sustaining the competence of personnel involved in the services, including their methods, approaches and attitudes.

Commentary

These broad fundamental perspectives refer to comprehensive social policy in general and aim at promoting juvenile welfare to the greatest possible extent, which will minimize the necessity of intervention by the juvenile justice system, and in turn, will reduce the harm that may be caused by any intervention. Such care measures for the young, before the onset of delinquency, are basic policy requisites designed to obviate the need for the application of the Rules.

Rules 1.1 to 1.3 point to the important role that a constructive social policy for juveniles will play, *inter alia*, in the prevention of juvenile crime and delinquency. Rule 1.4 defines juvenile justice as an integral part of social justice for juveniles, while rule 1.6 refers to the necessity of constantly improving juvenile justice, without falling behind the development of progressive social policy for juveniles in general and bearing in mind the need for consistent improvement of staff services.

Rule 1.5 seeks to take account of existing conditions in Member States which would cause the manner of implementation of particular rules necessarily to be different from the manner adopted in other States.

2. Scope of the Rules and definitions used

2.1 The following Standard Minimum Rules shall be applied to juvenile offenders impartially, without distinction of any kind, for example as to race, colour, sex, language, religion, political or other opinions, national or social origin, property, birth or other status.

2.2 For purposes of these Rules, the following definitions shall be applied by Member States in a manner which is compatible with their respective legal systems and concepts:

(a) A juvenile is a child or young person who, under the respective legal systems, may be dealt with for an offence in a manner which is different from an adult;

(b) An offence is any behaviour (act or omission) that is punishable by law under the respective legal systems;

(c) A juvenile offender is a child or young person who is alleged to have committed or who has been found to have committed an offence.

2.3 Efforts shall be made to establish, in each national jurisdiction, a set of laws, rules and provisions specifically applicable to juvenile offenders and institutions and bodies entrusted with the functions of the administration of juvenile justice and designed:

(a) To meet the varying needs of juvenile offenders, while protecting their basic rights;

(b) To meet the needs of society;

(c) To implement the following rules thoroughly and fairly.

Commentary

The Standard Minimum Rules are deliberately formulated so as to be applicable within different legal systems and, at the same time, to set some minimum standards for the handling of juvenile offenders under any definition of a juvenile and under any system of dealing with juvenile offenders. The Rules are always to be applied impartially and without distinction of any kind.

Rule 2.1 therefore stresses the importance of the Rules always being applied impartially and without distinction of any kind. The rule follows the formulation of principle 2 of the Declaration of the Rights of the Child.[1]

Rule 2.2 defines "juvenile" and "offence" as the components of the notion of the "juvenile offender", who is the main subject of these Standard Minimum Rules (see, however, also rules 3 and 4). It should be noted that age limits will depend on, and are explicitly made dependent on, each respective legal system, thus fully respecting the economic, social, political, cultural and legal systems of Member States. This makes for a wide variety of ages coming under the definition of "juvenile", ranging from 7 years to 18 years or above. Such a variety seems inevitable in view of the different national legal systems and does not diminish the impact of these Standard Minimum Rules.

Rule 2.3 is addressed to the necessity of specific national legislation for the optimal implementation of these Standard Minimum Rules, both legally and practically.

3. Extension of the Rules

3.1 The relevant provisions of the Rules shall be applied not only to juvenile offenders but also to juveniles who may be proceeded against for any specific behaviour that would not be punishable if committed by an adult.

3.2 Efforts shall be made to extend the principles embodied in the Rules to all juveniles who are dealt with in welfare and care proceedings.

3.3 Efforts shall also be made to extend the principles embodied in the Rules to young adult offenders.

Commentary

Rule 3 extends the protection afforded by the Standard Minimum Rules for the Administration of Juvenile Justice to cover:

(a) The so-called "status offences" prescribed in various national legal systems where the range of behaviour considered to be an offence is wider for juveniles than it is for adults (for example, truancy, school and family disobedience, public drunkenness, etc.) (rule 3.1);

(b) Juvenile welfare and care proceedings (rule 3.2);

(c) Proceedings dealing with young adult offenders, depending of course on each given age limit (rule 3.3).

The extension of the Rules to cover these three areas seems to be justified. Rule 3.1 provides minimum guarantees in those fields, and rule 3.2 is considered a desirable step in the direction of more fair, equitable and humane justice for all juveniles in conflict with the law.

4. Age of criminal responsibility

4.1 In those legal systems recognizing the concept of the age of criminal responsibility for juveniles, the beginning of that age shall not be fixed at too low an age level, bearing in mind the facts of emotional, mental and intellectual maturity.

Commentary

The minimum age of criminal responsibility differs widely owing to history and culture. The modern approach would be to consider whether a child can live up to the moral and psychological components of criminal responsibility; that is, whether a child, by virtue of her or his individual discernment and understanding, can be held responsible for essentially anti-social behaviour. If the age of criminal responsibility is fixed too low or if there is no lower age limit at all, the notion of responsibility would become meaningless. In general, there is a close relationship between the notion of responsibility for delinquent or criminal behaviour and other social rights and responsibilities (such as marital status, civil majority, etc.).

Efforts should therefore be made to agree on a reasonable lowest age limit that is applicable internationally.

5. Aims of juvenile justice

5.1 The juvenile justice system shall emphasize the well-being of the juvenile and shall ensure that any reaction to juvenile offenders shall always be in proportion to the circumstances of both the offenders and the offence.

Commentary

Rule 5 refers to two of the most important objectives of juvenile justice. The first objective is the promotion of the well-being of the juvenile. This is the main focus of those legal systems in which juvenile offenders are dealt with by family courts or administrative authorities, but the well-being of the juvenile should also be emphasized in legal systems that follow the criminal court model, thus contributing to the avoidance of merely punitive sanctions. (See also rule 14.)

The second objective is "the principle of proportionality". This principle is well-known as an instrument for curbing punitive sanctions, mostly expressed in terms of just desert in relation to the gravity of the offence. The response to young offenders should be based on the consideration not only of the gravity of the offence but also of personal circumstances. The individual circumstances of the offender (for example social status, family situation, the harm caused by the offence or other factors affecting personal circumstances) should influence the proportionality of the reaction (for example by having regard to the offender's endeavour to indemnify the victim or to her or his willingness to turn to a wholesome and useful life).

By the same token, reactions aiming to ensure the welfare of the young offender may go beyond necessity and therefore infringe upon the fundamental rights of the young individual, as has been observed in some juvenile justice systems. Here, too, the proportionality of the reaction to the circumstances of both the offender and the offence, including the victim, should be safeguarded.

In essence, rule 5 calls for no less and no more than a fair reaction in any given case of juvenile delinquency and crime. The issues combined in the rule may help to stimulate development in both regards: new and innovative types of reactions are as desirable as precautions against any undue widening of the net of formal social control over juveniles.

6. Scope of discretion

6.1 In view of the varying special needs of juveniles as well as the variety of measures available, appropriate scope for discretion shall be allowed at all stages of proceedings and at the different levels of juvenile justice administration, including investigation, prosecution, adjudication and the follow-up of dispositions.

6.2 Efforts shall be made, however, to ensure sufficient accountability at all stages and levels in the exercise of any such discretion.

6.3 Those who exercise discretion shall be specially qualified or trained to exercise it judiciously and in accordance with their functions and mandates.

Commentary

Rules 6.1, 6.2 and 6.3 combine several important features of effective, fair and humane juvenile justice administration: the need to permit the exercise of discretionary power at all significant levels of processing so that those who make determinations can take the actions deemed to be most appropriate in each individual case; and the need to provide checks and balances in order to curb any abuses of discretionary power and to safeguard the rights of the young of-

1 Resolution 1386 (XIV). See also the Convention on the Elimination of All Forms of Discrimination against Women (resolution 34/180, annex); the Declaration of the World Conference to Combat Racism and Racial Discrimination (*Report of the World Conference to Combat Racism and Racial Discrimination, Geneva, 14-25 August 1978* (United Nations publication, Sales No. E.79.XIV.2), chap. II); the Declaration on the Elimination of All Forms of Intolerance and of Discrimination Based on Religion or Belief (resolution 36/55); the Standard Minimum Rules for the Treatment of Prisoners (see *Human Rights: A Compilation of International Instruments* (United Nations publication, Sales No. E.83.XIV.1)); the Caracas Declaration (resolution 35/171, annex); and rule 9.

fender. Accountability and professionalism are instruments best apt to curb broad discretion. Thus, professional qualifications and expert training are emphasized here as a valuable means of ensuring the judicious exercise of discretion in matters of juvenile offenders. (See also rules 1.6 and 2.2.) The formulation of specific guidelines on the exercise of discretion and the provision of systems of review, appeal and the like in order to permit scrutiny of decisions and accountability are emphasized in this context. Such mechanisms are not specified here, as they do not easily lend themselves to incorporation into international standard minimum rules, which cannot possibly cover all differences in justice systems.

7. Rights of juveniles

7.1 Basic procedural safeguards such as the presumption of innocence, the right to be notified of the charges, the right to remain silent, the right to counsel, the right to the presence of a parent or guardian, the right to confront and cross-examine witnesses and the right to appeal to a higher authority shall be guaranteed at all stages of proceedings.

Commentary

Rule 7.1 emphasizes some important points that represent essential elements for a fair and just trial and that are internationally recognized in existing human rights instruments. (See also rule 14.) The presumption of innocence, for instance, is also to be found in article 11 of the Universal Declaration of Human Rights and in article 14, paragraph 2, of the International Covenant on Civil and Political Rights.

Rules 14 *seq.* of these Standard Minimum Rules specify issues that are important for proceedings in juvenile cases, in particular, while rule 7.1 affirms the most basic procedural safeguards in a general way.

8. Protection of privacy

8.1 The juvenile's right to privacy shall be respected at all stages in order to avoid harm being caused to her or him by undue publicity or by the process of labelling.

8.2 In principle, no information that may lead to the identification of a juvenile offender shall be published.

Commentary

Rule 8 stresses the importance of the protection of the juvenile's right to privacy. Young persons are particularly susceptible to stigmatization. Criminological research into labelling processes has provided evidence of the detrimental effects (of different kinds) resulting from the permanent identification of young persons as "delinquent" or "criminal".

Rule 8 also stresses the importance of protecting the juvenile from the adverse effects that may result from the publication in the mass media of information about the case (for example the names of young offenders, alleged or convicted). The interest of the individual should be protected and upheld, at least in principle. (The general contents of rule 8 are further specified in rule 21.)

9. Saving clause

9.1 Nothing in these Rules shall be interpreted as precluding the application of the Standard Minimum Rules for the Treatment of Prisoners[1] adopted by the United Nations and other human rights instruments and standards recognized by the international community that relate to the care and protection of the young.

Commentary

Rule 9 is meant to avoid any misunderstanding in interpreting and implementing the present Rules in conformity with principles contained in relevant existing or emerging international human rights instruments and standards - such as the Universal Declaration of Human Rights;[2] the International Covenant on Economic, Social and Cultural Rights[3] and the International Covenant on Civil and Political Rights;[4] and the Declaration of the Rights of the Child[5] and the draft convention on the rights of the child.[6] It should be understood that the application of the present Rules is without prejudice to any such international instruments which may contain provisions of wider application.[7] (See also rule 27.)

Part two. Investigation and prosecution

10. Initial contact

10.1 Upon the apprehension of a juvenile, her or his parents or guardian shall be immediately notified of such apprehension, and, where such immediate notification is not possible, the parents or guardian shall be notified within the shortest possible time thereafter.

10.2 A judge or other competent official or body shall, without delay, consider the issue of release.

10.3 Contacts between the law enforcement agencies and a juvenile offender shall be managed in such a way as to respect the legal status of the juvenile, promote the well-being of the juvenile and avoid harm to her or him, with due regard to the circumstances of the case.

Commentary

Rule 10.1 is in principle contained in rule 92 of the Standard Minimum Rules for the Treatment of Prisoners.[8]

The question of release (rule 10.2) shall be considered without delay by a judge or other competent official. The latter refers to any person or institution in the broadest sense of the term, including community boards or police authorities having power to release an arrested person. (See also the International Covenant on Civil and Political Rights, article 9, paragraph 3.)

Rule 10.3 deals with some fundamental aspects of the procedures and behaviour on the part of the police and other law enforcement offi-

1 See *Human Rights: A Compilation of International Instruments* (United Nations publication, Sales No. E.83.XIV.1).

2 Resolution 217 A(III).

3 See resolution 2200 A(XXI), annex.

4 *Ibid.*

5 Resolution 1386 (XIV). See also the Convention on the Elimination of All Forms of Discrimination against Women (resolution 34/180, annex); the Declaration of the World Conference to Combat Racism and Racial Discrimination (*Report of the World Conference to Combat Racism and Racial Discrimination, Geneva, 14-25 August 1978* (United Nations publication, Sales No. E.79.XIV.2), chap. II); the Declaration on the Elimination of All Forms of Intolerance and of Discrimination Based on Religion or Belief (resolution 36/55); the Standard Minimum Rules for the Treatment of Prisoners (see *Human Rights: A Compilation of International Instruments* (United Nations publication, Sales No. E.83.XIV.1)); the Caracas Declaration (resolution 35/171, annex); and rule 9.

6 See Economic and Social Council resolution 1985/42.

7 See *Human Rights: A Compilation of International Instruments* (United Nations publication, Sales No. E.83.XIV.1).

8 The Standard Minimum Rules for the Treatment of Prisoners and related recommendations were adopted in 1955 (see *First United Nations Congress on the Prevention of Crime and the Treatment of Offenders, Geneva, 22 August - 3 September 1955: report prepared by the Secretariat* (United Nations publication, Sales No. 1956.IV.4). In its resolution 663 C (XXIV) of 31 July 1957, the Economic and Social Council approved the Standard Minimum Rules and endorsed, *inter alia*, the recommendations on the selection and training of personnel for penal and correctional institutions and on open penal and correctional institutions. The Council recommended that Governments should give favourable consideration to the adoption and application of the Standard Minimum Rules and should take the other two groups of recommendations as fully as possible into account in the administration of penal and correctional institutions. The inclusion of a new rule, rule 95, was authorized by the Economic and Social Council in its resolution 2076 (LXII) of 13 May 1977. The complete text of the Standard Minimum Rules for the Treatment of Prisoners is contained in *Human Rights: A Compilation of International Instruments*.

cials in cases of juvenile crime. To "avoid harm" admittedly is flexible wording and covers many features of possible interaction (for example the use of harsh language, physical violence or exposure to the environment). Involvement in juvenile justice processes in itself can be "harmful" to juveniles; the term "avoid harm" should be broadly interpreted, therefore, as doing the least harm possible to the juvenile in the first instance, as well as any additional or undue harm. This is especially important in the initial contact with law enforcement agencies, which might profoundly influence the juvenile's attitude towards the State and society. Moreover, the success of any further intervention is largely dependent on such initial contacts. Compassion and kind firmness are important in these situations.

11. Diversion

11.1 Consideration shall be given, wherever appropriate, to dealing with juvenile offenders without resorting to formal trial by the competent authority, referred to in rule 14.1 below.

11.2 The police, the prosecution or other agencies dealing with juvenile cases shall be empowered to dispose of such cases, at their discretion, without recourse to formal hearings, in accordance with the criteria laid down for that purpose in the respective legal system and also in accordance with the principles contained in these Rules.

11.3 Any diversion involving referral to appropriate community or other services shall require the consent of the juvenile, or her or his parents or guardian, provided that such decision to refer a case shall be subject to review by a competent authority, upon application.

11.4 In order to facilitate the discretionary disposition of juvenile cases, efforts shall be made to provide for community programmes, such as temporary supervision and guidance, restitution, and compensation of victims.

Commentary

Diversion, involving removal from criminal justice processing and, frequently, redirection to community support services, is commonly practised on a formal and informal basis in many legal systems. This practice serves to hinder the negative effects of subsequent proceedings in juvenile justice administration (for example the stigma of conviction and sentence). In many cases, non-intervention would be the best response. Thus, diversion at the outset and without referral to alternative (social) services may be the optimal response. This is especially the case where the offence is of a non-serious nature and where the family, the school or other informal social control institutions have already reacted, or are likely to react, in an appropriate and constructive manner.

As stated in rule 11.2, diversion may be used at any point of decision-making - by the police, the prosecution or other agencies such as the courts, tribunals, boards or councils. It may be exercised by one authority or several or all authorities, according to the rules and policies of the respective systems and in line with the present Rules. It need not necessarily be limited to petty cases, thus rendering diversion an important instrument.

Rule 11.3 stresses the important requirement of securing the consent of the young offender (or the parent or guardian) to the recommended diversionary measure(s). (Diversion to community service without such consent would contradict the Convention concerning the Abolition of Forced Labour.[1]) However, this consent should not be left unchallengeable, since it might sometimes be given out of sheer desperation on the part of the juvenile. The rule underlines that care should be taken to minimize the potential for coercion and intimidation at all levels in the diversion process. Juveniles should not feel pressured (for example in order to avoid court appearance) or be pressured into consenting to diversion programmes. Thus, it is advocated that provision should be made for an objective appraisal of the appropriateness of dispositions involving young offenders by a "competent authority upon application". (The "competent authority" may be different from that referred to in rule 14.)

Rule 11.4 recommends the provision of viable alternatives to juvenile justice processing in the form of community-based diversion. Programmes that involve settlement by victim restitution and those that seek to avoid future conflict with the law through temporary supervision and guidance are especially commended. The merits of individual cases would make diversion appropriate, even when more serious offences have been committed (for example first offence, the act having been committed under peer pressure etc.).

12. Specialization within the police

12.1 In order to best fulfil their functions, police officers who frequently or exclusively deal with juveniles or who are primarily engaged in the prevention of juvenile crime shall be specially instructed and trained. In large cities, special police units should be established for that purpose.

Commentary

Rule 12 draws attention to the need for specialized training for all law enforcement officials who are involved in the administration of juvenile justice. As police are the first point of contact with the juvenile justice system, it is most important that they act in an informed and appropriate manner.

While the relationship between urbanization and crime is clearly complex, an increase in juvenile crime has been associated with the growth of large cities, particularly with rapid and unplanned growth. Specialized police units would therefore be indispensable, not only in the interest of implementing specific principles contained in the present instrument (such as rule 1.6) but more generally for improving the prevention and control of juvenile crime and the handling of juvenile offenders.

13. Detention pending trial

13.1 Detention pending trial shall be used only as a measure of last resort and for the shortest possible period of time.

13.2 Whenever possible, detention pending trial shall be replaced by alternative measures, such as close supervision, intensive care or placement with a family or in an educational setting or home.

13.3 Juveniles under detention pending trial shall be entitled to all rights and guarantees of the Standard Minimum Rules for the Treatment of Prisoners[2] adopted by the United Nations.

13.4 Juveniles under detention pending trial shall be kept separate from adults and shall be detained in a separate institution or in a separate part of an institution also holding adults.

13.5 While in custody, juveniles shall receive care, protection and all necessary individual assistance - social, educational, vocational, psychological, medical and physical - that they may require in view of their age, sex and personality.

Commentary

The danger to juveniles of "criminal contamination" while in detention pending trial must not be underestimated. It is therefore important to stress the need for alternative measures. By doing so, rule 13.1 encourages the devising of new and innovative measures to avoid such detention in the interest of the well-being of the juvenile.

Juveniles under detention pending trial are entitled to all the rights and guarantees of the Standard Minimum Rules for the Treatment of Prisoners as well the International Covenant on Civil and Political Rights, especially article 9 and article 10, paragraphs 2 (b) and 3.

Rule 13.4 does not prevent States from taking other measures against the negative influences of adult offenders which are at least as effective as the measures mentioned in the rule.

---

1 Convention No. 105, adopted on 25 June 1957 by the General Conference of the International Labour Organisation at its fortieth session. With regard to the text of the Convention, see footnote above.

2 See *Human Rights: A Compilation of International Instruments* (United Nations publication, Sales No. E.83.XIV.1).

Different forms of assistance that may become necessary have been enumerated to draw attention to the broad range of particular needs of young detainees to be addressed (for example females or males, drug addicts, alcoholics, mentally ill juveniles, young persons suffering from the trauma of arrest for example, etc.).

Varying physical and psychological characteristics of young detainees may warrant classification measures by which some are kept separate while in detention pending trial, thus contributing to the avoidance of victimization and rendering more appropriate assistance.

The Sixth United Nations Congress on the Prevention of Crime and the Treatment of Offenders, in its resolution 4[1] on juvenile justice standards specified that the Rules, *inter alia*, should reflect the basic principle that pre-trial detention should be used only as a last resort, that no minors should be held in a facility where they are vulnerable to the negative influences of adult detainees and that account should always be taken of the needs particular to their stage of development.

Part three. Adjudication and disposition

14. Competent authority to adjudicate

14.1 Where the case of a juvenile offender has not been diverted (under rule 11), she or he shall be dealt with by the competent authority (court, tribunal, board, council, etc.) according to the principles of a fair and just trial.

14.2 The proceedings shall be conducive to the best interests of the juvenile and shall be conducted in an atmosphere of understanding, which shall allow the juvenile to participate therein and to express herself or himself freely.

Commentary

It is difficult to formulate a definition of the competent body or person that would universally describe an adjudicating authority. "Competent authority" is meant to include those who preside over courts or tribunals (composed of a single judge or of several members), including professional and lay magistrates as well as administrative boards (for example the Scottish and Scandinavian systems) or other more informal community and conflict resolution agencies of an adjudicatory nature.

The procedure for dealing with juvenile offenders shall in any case follow the minimum standards that are applied almost universally for any criminal defendant under the procedure known as "due process of law". In accordance with due process, a "fair and just trial" includes such basic safeguards as the presumption of innocence, the presentation and examination of witnesses, the common legal defences, the right to remain silent, the right to have the last word in a hearing, the right to appeal, etc. (See also rule 7.1).

15. Legal counsel, parents and guardians

15.1 Throughout the proceedings the juvenile shall have the right to be represented by a legal adviser or to apply for free legal aid where there is provision for such aid in the country.

15.2 The parents or the guardian shall be entitled to participate in the proceedings and may be required by the competent authority to attend them in the interest of the juvenile. They may, however, be denied participation by the competent authority if there are reasons to assume that such exclusion is necessary in the interest of the juvenile.

Commentary

Rule 15.1 uses terminology similar to that found in rule 93 of the Standard Minimum Rules for the Treatment of Prisoners.[2] Whereas legal counsel and free legal aid are needed to assure the juvenile legal assistance, the right of the parents or guardian to participate as stated in rule 15.2 should be viewed as general psychological and emotional assistance to the juvenile - a function extending throughout the procedure.

The competent authority's search for an adequate disposition of the case may profit, in particular, from the cooperation of the legal representatives of the juvenile (or, for that matter, some other personal assistant who the juvenile can and does really trust). Such concern can be thwarted if the presence of parents or guardians at the hearings plays a negative role, for instance, if they display a hostile attitude towards the juvenile; hence, the possibility of their exclusion must be provided for.

16. Social inquiry reports

16.1 In all cases except those involving minor offences, before the competent authority renders a final disposition prior to sentencing, the background and circumstances in which the juvenile is living or the conditions under which the offence has been committed shall be properly investigated so as to facilitate judicious adjudication of the case by the competent authority.

Commentary

Social inquiry reports (social reports or pre-sentence reports) are an indispensable aid in most legal proceedings involving juveniles. The competent authority should be informed of relevant facts about the juvenile, such as social and family background, school career, educational experiences, etc. For this purpose, some jurisdictions use special social services or personnel attached to the court or board. Other personnel, including probation officers, may serve the same function. The rule therefore requires that adequate social services should be available to deliver social inquiry reports of a qualified nature.

17. Guiding principles in adjudication and disposition

17.1 The disposition of the competent authority shall be guided by the following principles:

(a) The reaction taken shall always be in proportion not only to the circumstances and the gravity of the offence but also to the circumstances and the needs of the juvenile as well as to the needs of the society;

(b) Restrictions on the personal liberty of the juvenile shall be imposed only after careful consideration and shall be limited to the possible minimum;

(c) Deprivation of personal liberty shall not be imposed unless the juvenile is adjudicated of a serious act involving violence against another person or of persistence in committing other serious offences and unless there is no other appropriate response;

(d) The well-being of the juvenile shall be the guiding factor in the consideration of her or his case.

17.2 Capital punishment shall not be imposed for any crime committed by juveniles.

17.3 Juveniles shall not be subject to corporal punishment.

17.4 The competent authority shall have the power to discontinue the proceedings at any time.

Commentary

The main difficulty in formulating guidelines for the adjudication of young persons stems from the fact that there are unresolved conflicts of a philosophical nature, such as the following:

(a) Rehabilitation versus just desert;

(b) Assistance versus repression and punishment;

(c) Reaction according to the singular merits of an individual case versus reaction according to the protection of society in general;

(d) General deterrence versus individual incapacitation.

The conflict between these approaches is more pronounced in juvenile cases than in adult cases. With the variety of causes and reactions characterizing juvenile cases, these alternatives become intricately interwoven.

---

1 See *Sixth United Nations Congress on the Prevention of Crime and the Treatment of Offenders, Caracas, 25 August - 5 September 1980: report prepared by the Secretariat* (United Nations publication, Sales No. E.81.IV.4), chap. I, sect. B.

2 See *Human Rights: A Compilation of International Instruments* (United Nations publication, Sales No. E.83.XIV.1).

It is not the function of Standard Minimum Rules for the Administration of Juvenile Justice to prescribe which approach is to be followed but rather to identify one that is most closely in consonance with internationally accepted principles. Therefore the essential elements as laid down in rule 17.1, in particular in subparagraphs (a) and (c), are mainly to be understood as practical guidelines that should ensure a common starting point; if heeded by the concerned authorities (See also rule 5), they could contribute considerably to ensuring that the fundamental rights of juvenile offenders are protected, especially the fundamental rights of personal development and education.

Rule 17.1 (b) implies that strictly punitive approaches are not appropriate. Whereas in adult cases, and possibly also in cases of severe offences by juveniles, just desert and retributive sanctions might be considered to have some merit, in juvenile cases such considerations should always be outweighed by the interest of safeguarding the well-being and the future of the young person.

In line with resolution 8 of the Sixth United Nations Congress,[1] it encourages the use of alternatives to institutionalization to the maximum extent possible, bearing in mind the need to respond to the specific requirements of the young. Thus, full use should be made of the range of existing alternative sanctions and new alternative sanctions should be developed, bearing the public safety in mind. Probation should be granted to the greatest possible extent via suspended sentences, conditional sentences, board orders and other dispositions.

Rule 17.1 (c) corresponds to one of the guiding principles in resolution 4 of the Sixth Congress[2] which aims at avoiding incarceration in the case of juveniles unless there is no other appropriate response that will protect the public safety.

The provision prohibiting capital punishment in rule 17.2 is in accordance with article 6, paragraph 5, of the International Covenant on Civil and Political Rights.

The provision against corporal punishment is in line with article 7 of the International Covenant on Civil and Political Rights and the Declaration on the Protection of All Persons from Being Subjected to Torture and Other Cruel, Inhuman or Degrading Treatment or Punishment[3] as well as the Convention against Torture and other Cruel, Inhuman or Degrading Treatment or Punishment[4] and the draft convention on the rights of the child.[5]

The power to discontinue the proceedings at any time (rule 17.4) is a characteristic inherent in the handling of juvenile offenders as opposed to adults. At any time, circumstances may become known to the competent authority which would make a complete cessation of the intervention appear to be the best disposition of the case.

18. Various disposition measures

18.1 A large variety of disposition measures shall be made available to the competent authority, allowing for flexibility so as to avoid institutionalization to the greatest extent possible. Such measures, some of which may be combined, include:

(a) Care, guidance and supervision orders;

(b) Probation;

(c) Community service orders;

(d) Financial penalties, compensation and restitution;

(e) Intermediate treatment and other treatment orders;

(f) Orders to participate in group counselling and similar activities;

(g) Orders concerning foster care, living communities or other educational settings;

(h) Other relevant orders.

18.2 No juvenile shall be removed from parental supervision, whether partly or entirely, unless the circumstances of her or his case make this necessary.

Commentary

Rule 18.1 attempts to enumerate some of the important reactions and sanctions that have been practised and proved successful thus far, in different legal systems. On the whole they represent promising options that deserve replication and further development. The rule does not enumerate staffing requirements because of possible shortages of adequate staff in some regions; in those regions measures requiring less staff may be tried or developed.

The examples given in rule 18.1 have in common, above all, a reliance on and an appeal to the community for the effective implementation of alternative dispositions. Community-based correction is a traditional measure that has taken on many aspects. On that basis, relevant authorities should be encouraged to offer community-based services.

Rule 18.2 points to the importance of the family which, according to article 10, paragraph 1, of the International Covenant on Economic, Social and Cultural Rights, is "the natural and fundamental group unit of society". Within the family, the parents have not only the right but also the responsibility to care for and supervise their children. Rule 18.2, therefore, requires that the separation of children from their parents is a measure of last resort. It may be resorted to only when the facts of the case clearly warrant this grave step (for example child abuse).

19. Least possible use of institutionalization

19.1 The placement of a juvenile in an institution shall always be a disposition of last resort and for the minimum necessary period.

Commentary

Progressive criminology advocates the use of non-institutional over institutional treatment. Little or no difference has been found in terms of the success of institutionalization as compared to non-institutionalization. The many adverse influences on an individual that seem unavoidable within any institutional setting evidently cannot be outbalanced by treatment efforts. This is especially the case for juveniles, who are vulnerable to negative influences. Moreover, the negative effects, not only of loss of liberty but also of separation from the usual social environment, are certainly more acute for juveniles than for adults because of their early stage of development.

Rule 19 aims at restricting institutionalization in two regards: in quantity ("last resort") and in time ("minimum necessary period"). Rule 19 reflects one of the basic guiding principles of resolution 4 of the Sixth United Nations Congress:[6] a juvenile offender should not be incarcerated unless there is no other appropriate response. The rule, therefore, makes the appeal that if a juvenile must be institutionalized, the loss of liberty should be restricted to the least possible degree, with special institutional arrangements for confinement and bearing in mind the differences in kinds of offenders, offences and institutions. In fact, priority should be given to "open" over "closed" institutions. Furthermore, any facility should be of a correctional or educational rather than of a prison type.

20. Avoidance of unnecessary delay

20.1 Each case shall from the outset be handled expeditiously, without any unnecessary delay.

Commentary

The speedy conduct of formal procedures in juvenile cases is a paramount concern. Otherwise whatever good may be achieved by the procedure and the disposition is at risk. As time passes, the juvenile will find it increasingly difficult, if not impossible, to relate the

---

1 See *Sixth United Nations Congress on the Prevention of Crime and the Treatment of Offenders, Caracas, 25 August - 5 September 1980: report prepared by the Secretariat* (United Nations publication, Sales No. E.81.IV.4), chap. I, sect. B.

2 *Ibid.*

3 Resolution 3452 (XXX), annex.

4 Resolution 39/46, annex.

5 See Economic and Social Council resolution 1985/42.

6 See *Sixth United Nations Congress on the Prevention of Crime and the Treatment of Offenders, Caracas, 25 August - 5 September 1980: report prepared by the Secretariat* (United Nations publication, Sales No. E.81.IV.4), chap. I, sect. B.

procedure and disposition to the offence, both intellectually and psychologically.

21. Records

21.1 Records of juvenile offenders shall be kept strictly confidential and closed to third parties. Access to such records shall be limited to persons directly concerned with the disposition of the case at hand or other duly authorized persons.

21.2 Records of juvenile offenders shall not be used in adult proceedings in subsequent cases involving the same offender.

Commentary

The rule attempts to achieve a balance between conflicting interests connected with records or files: those of the police, prosecution and other authorities in improving control versus the interests of the juvenile offender. (See also rule 8.) "Other duly authorized persons" would generally include, among others, researchers.

22. Need for professionalism and training

22.1 Professional education, in-service training, refresher courses and other appropriate modes of instruction shall be utilized to establish and maintain the necessary professional competence of all personnel dealing with juvenile cases.

22.2 Juvenile justice personnel shall reflect the diversity of juveniles who come into contact with the juvenile justice system. Efforts shall be made to ensure the fair representation of women and minorities in juvenile justice agencies.

Commentary

The authorities competent for disposition may be persons with very different backgrounds (magistrates in the United Kingdom of Great Britain and Northern Ireland and in regions influenced by the common law system; legally trained judges in countries using Roman law and in regions influenced by them; and elsewhere elected or appointed laymen or jurists, members of community-based boards etc.). For all these authorities, a minimum training in law, sociology, psychology, criminology and behavioural sciences would be required. This is considered as important as the organizational specialization and independence of the competent authority.

For social workers and probation officers, it might not be feasible to require professional specialization as a prerequisite for taking over any function dealing with juvenile offenders. Thus, professional on-the-job instruction would be minimum qualifications.

Professional qualifications are an essential element in ensuring the impartial and effective administration of juvenile justice. Accordingly, it is necessary to improve the recruitment, advancement and professional training of personnel and to provide them with the necessary means to enable them to properly fulfil their functions.

All political, social, sexual, racial, religious, cultural or any other kind of discrimination in the selection, appointment and advancement of juvenile justice personnel should be avoided in order to achieve impartiality in the administration of juvenile justice. This was recommended by the Sixth United Nations Congress. Furthermore, the Sixth Congress called on Member States to ensure the fair and usual treatment of women as criminal justice personnel and recommended that special measures should be taken to recruit, train and facilitate the advancement of female personnel in juvenile justice administration.[1]

Part four. Non-institutional treatment

23. Effective implementation of disposition

23.1 Appropriate provisions shall be made for the implementation of orders of the competent authority, as referred to in rule 14.1 above, by that authority itself or by some other authority as circumstances may require.

23.2 Such provisions shall include the power to modify the orders as the competent authority may deem necessary from time to time, provided that such modification shall be determined in accordance with the principles contained in these Rules.

Commentary

Disposition in juvenile cases, more so than in adult cases, tends to influence the offender's life for a long period of time. Thus, it is important that the competent authority or an independent body (parole board, probation office, youth welfare institutions or others) with qualifications equal to those of the competent authority that originally disposed of the case should monitor the implementation of the disposition. In some countries a *juge de l'exécution des peines* has been installed for this purpose.

The composition, powers and functions of the authority must be flexible; they are described in general terms in rule 23 in order to ensure wide acceptability.

24. Provision of needed assistance

24.1 Efforts shall be made to provide juveniles, at all stages of the proceedings, with necessary assistance such as lodging, education or vocational training, employment or any other assistance, helpful and practical, in order to facilitate the rehabilitative process.

Commentary

The promotion of the well-being of the juvenile is of paramount consideration. Thus, rule 24 emphasizes the importance of providing requisite facilities, services and other necessary assistance as may further the best interests of the juvenile throughout the rehabilitative process.

25. Mobilization of volunteers and other community services

25.1 Volunteers, voluntary organizations, local institutions and other community resources shall be called upon to contribute effectively to the rehabilitation of the juvenile in a community setting and, as far as possible, within the family unit.

Commentary

This rule reflects the need for a rehabilitative orientation of all juvenile offenders. Cooperation with the community is indispensable if the directives of the competent authority are to be carried out effectively. Volunteers and voluntary services, in particular, have proved to be valuable work with resources but are at present underutilized. In some instances, the cooperation of ex-offenders (including ex-addicts) can be of considerable assistance.

Rule 25 emanates from the principles laid down in rules 1.1 to 1.6 and follows the relevant provisions of the International Covenant on Civil and Political Rights.

Part five. Institutional treatment

26. Objectives of institutional treatment

26.1 The objective of training and treatment of juveniles placed in institutions is to provide care, protection, education and vocational skills, with a view to assisting them to assume socially constructive and productive roles in society.

26.2 Juveniles in institutions shall receive care, protection and all necessary assistance - social, educational, vocational, psychological, medical and physical - that they may require because of their age, sex and personality and in the interest of their wholesome development.

26.3 Juveniles in institutions shall be kept separate from adults and shall be detained in a separate institution or in a separate part of an institution also holding adults.

26.4 Young female offenders placed in an institution deserve special attention as to their personal needs and problems. They shall by no means receive less care, protection, assistance, treatment and training than young male offenders. Their fair treatment shall be ensured.

26.5 In the interest and well-being of the institutionalized juvenile, the parents or guardians shall have a right of access.

---

[1] *Ibid.*

26.6 Inter-ministerial and inter-departmental cooperation shall be fostered for the purpose of providing adequate academic or, as appropriate, vocational training to institutionalized juveniles, with a view to ensuring that they do not leave the institution at an educational disadvantage.

Commentary

The objectives of institutional treatment as stipulated in rules 26.1 and 26.2 would be acceptable to any system and culture. However, they have not yet been attained everywhere, and much more has to be done in this respect.

Medical and psychological assistance, in particular, are extremely important for institutionalized drug addicts, violent and mentally ill young persons.

The avoidance of negative influences through adult offenders and the safe-guarding of the well-being of juveniles in an institutional setting, as stipulated in rule 26.3, are in line with one of the basic guiding principles of the Rules, as set out by the Sixth Congress in its resolution 4.[1] The rule does not prevent States from taking other measures against the negative influences of adult offenders, which are at least as effective as the measures mentioned in the rule. (See also rule 13.4.)

Rule 26.4 addresses the fact that female offenders normally receive less attention than their male counterparts, as pointed out by the Sixth Congress. In particular, resolution 9 of the Sixth Congress[2] calls for the fair treatment of female offenders at every stage of criminal justice processes and for special attention to their particular problems and needs while in custody. Moreover, this rule should also be considered in the light of the Caracas Declaration of the Sixth Congress, which, *inter alia*, calls for equal treatment in criminal justice administration,[3] and against the background of the Declaration on the Elimination of Discrimination against Women[4] and the Convention on the Elimination of All Forms of Discrimination against Women.[5]

The right of access (rule 26.5) follows from the provisions of rules 7.1, 10.1, 15.2 and 18.2. Inter-ministerial and inter-departmental cooperation (rule 26.6) are of particular importance in the interest of generally enhancing the quality of institutional treatment and training.

27. Application of the Standard Minimum Rules for the Treatment of Prisoners adopted by the United Nations

27.1 The Standard Minimum Rules for the Treatment of Prisoners and related recommendations shall be applicable as far as relevant to the treatment of juvenile offenders in institutions, including those in detention pending adjudication.

27.2 Efforts shall be made to implement the relevant principles laid down in the Standard Minimum Rules for the Treatment of Prisoners to the largest possible extent so as to meet the varying needs of juveniles specific to their age, sex and personality.

Commentary

The Standard Minimum Rules for the Treatment of Prisoners were among the first instruments of this kind to be promulgated by the United Nations. It is generally agreed that they have had a worldwide impact. Although there are still countries where implementation is more an aspiration than a fact, those Standard Minimum Rules continue to be an important influence in the humane and equitable administration of correctional institutions.

Some essential protections covering juvenile offenders in institutions are contained in the Standard Minimum Rules for the Treatment of Prisoners (accommodation, architecture, bedding, clothing, complaints and requests, contact with the outside world, food, medical care, religious service, separation of ages, staffing, work, etc.) as are provisions concerning punishment and discipline, and restraint for dangerous offenders. It would not be appropriate to modify those Standard Minimum Rules according to the particular characteristics of institutions for juvenile offenders within the scope of the Standard Minimum Rules for the Administration of Juvenile Justice.

Rule 27 focuses on the necessary requirements for juveniles in institutions (rule 27.1) as well as on the varying needs specific to their age, sex and personality (rule 27.2). Thus, the objectives and content of the rule interrelates to the relevant provisions of the Standard Minimum Rules for the Treatment of Prisoners.

28. Frequent and early recourse to conditional release

28.1 Conditional release from an institution shall be used by the appropriate authority to the greatest possible extent, and shall be granted at the earliest possible time.

28.2 Juveniles released conditionally from an institution shall be assisted and supervised by an appropriate authority and shall receive full support by the community.

Commentary

The power to order conditional release may rest with the competent authority, as mentioned in rule 14.1, or with some other authority. In view of this, it is adequate to refer here to the "appropriate" rather than to the "competent" authority.

Circumstances permitting, conditional release shall be preferred to serving a full sentence. Upon evidence of satisfactory progress towards rehabilitation, even offenders who had been deemed dangerous at the time of their institutionalization can be conditionally released whenever feasible. Like probation, such release may be conditional on the satisfactory fulfilment of the requirements specified by the relevant authorities for a period of time established in the decision, for example relating to "good behaviour" of the offender, attendance in community programmes, residence in half-way houses, etc.

In the case of offenders conditionally released from an institution, assistance and supervision by a probation or other officer (particularly where probation has not yet been adopted) should be Provided and community support should be encouraged.

29. Semi-institutional arrangements

29.1 Efforts shall be made to provide semi-institutional arrangements, such as half-way houses, educational homes, day-time training centres and other such appropriate arrangements that may assist juveniles in their proper reintegration into society.

Commentary

The importance of care following a period of institutionalization should not be underestimated. This rule emphasizes the necessity of forming a net of semi-institutional arrangements.

This rule also emphasizes the need for a diverse range of facilities and services designed to meet the different needs of young offenders re-entering the community and to provide guidance and structural support as an important step towards successful reintegration into society.

Part six. Research, planning, policy formulation and evaluation

30. Research as a basis for Planning, policy formulation and evaluation

30.1 Efforts shall be made to organize and promote necessary research as a basis for effective planning and policy formulation.

30.2 Efforts shall be made to review and appraise periodically the trends, problems and causes of juvenile delinquency and crime as well as the varying particular needs of juveniles in custody.

30.3 Efforts shall be made to establish a regular evaluative research mechanism built into the system of juvenile justice administration and to collect and analyse relevant data and information for appropriate assessment and future improvement and reform of the administration.

30.4 The delivery of services in juvenile justice administration shall be systematically planned and implemented as an integral part of national development efforts.

1 *Ibid.*

2 *Ibid.*

3 See resolution 35/171, annex, para. 1.6.

4 Resolution 2263 (XXII).

5 Resolution 34/180, annex.

Commentary

The utilization of research as a basis for an informed juvenile justice policy is widely acknowledged as an important mechanism for keeping practices abreast of advances in knowledge and the continuing development and improvement of the juvenile justice system. The mutual feedback between research and policy is especially important in juvenile justice. With rapid and often drastic changes in the life-styles of the young and in the forms and dimensions of juvenile crime, the societal and justice responses to juvenile crime and delinquency quickly become outmoded and inadequate.

Rule 30 thus establishes standards for integrating research into the process of policy formulation and application in juvenile justice administration. The rule draws particular attention to the need for regular review and evaluation of existing programmes and measures and for planning within the broader context of overall development objectives.

A constant appraisal of the needs of juveniles, as well as the trends and problems of delinquency, is a prerequisite for improving the methods of formulating appropriate policies and establishing adequate interventions, at both formal and informal levels. In this context, research by independent persons and bodies should be facilitated by responsible agencies, and it may be valuable to obtain and to take into account the views of juveniles themselves, not only those who come into contact with the system.

The process of planning must particularly emphasize a more effective and equitable system for the delivery of necessary Services. Towards that end, there should be a comprehensive and regular assessment of the wide-ranging, particular needs and problems of juveniles and an identification of clear-cut priorities. In that connection, there should also be a coordination in the use of existing resources, including alternatives and community support that would be suitable in setting up specific procedures designed to implement and monitor established programmes.

41/85. Declaration on Social and Legal Principles Relating to the Protection and Welfare of Children, with Special Reference to Foster Placement and Adoption Nationally and Internationally

Committee: 6
Vote: Adopted without a vote

The General Assembly,

Recalling its resolutions 36/167 of 16 December 1981, 37/115 of 16 December 1982, 38/142 of 19 December 1983 and 39/89 of 13 December 1984, and its decision 40/422 of 11 December 1985,

Taking note of the draft Declaration on Social and Legal Principles relating to the Protection and Welfare of Children, with Special Reference to Foster Placement and Adoption Nationally and Internationally, as submitted by the Economic and Social Council by its resolution 1979/28 of 9 May 1979,

Taking note with appreciation of the work done on this question in the Third and Sixth Committees, as well as the efforts made by Member States representing different legal systems, during the consultations held at Headquarters from 16 to 27 September 1985 and early in the forty-first session, to join in the common endeavour of completing the work on the draft Declaration,

Adopts the Declaration on Social and Legal Principles relating to the Protection and Welfare of Children, with Special Reference to Foster Placement and Adoption Nationally and Internationally, the text of which is annexed to the present resolution.

95th plenary meeting
3 December 1986

Annex

Declaration on Social and Legal Principles Relating to the Protection and Welfare of Children, with Special Reference to Foster Placement and Adoption Nationally and Internationally

The General Assembly,

Recalling the Universal Declaration of Human Rights,[1] the International Covenant on Economic, Social and Cultural Rights,[2] the International Covenant on Civil and Political Rights,[3] the International Convention on the Elimination of All Forms of Racial Discrimination[4] and the Convention on the Elimination of All Forms of Discrimination against Women,[5]

Recalling also the Declaration of the Rights of the Child, which it proclaimed by its resolution 1386 (XIV) of 20 November 1959,

Reaffirming principle 6 of that Declaration, which states that the child shall, wherever possible, grow up in the care and under the responsibility of his parents and, in any case, in an atmosphere of affection and of moral and material security,

Concerned at the large number of children who are abandoned or become orphans owing to violence, internal disturbance, armed conflicts, natural disasters, economic crises or social problems,

Bearing in mind that in all foster placement and adoption procedures the best interests of the child should be the paramount consideration,

Recognizing that under the principal legal systems of the world, various valuable alternative institutions exist, such as the Kafala of Islamic Law, which provide substitute care to children who cannot be cared for by their own parents,

Recognizing further that only where a particular institution is recognized and regulated by the domestic law of a State would the provisions of this Declaration relating to that institution be relevant and that such provisions would in no way affect the existing alternative institutions in other legal systems,

Conscious of the need to proclaim universal principles to be taken into account in cases where procedures are instituted relating to foster placement or adoption of a child, either nationally or internationally,

Bearing in mind, however, that the principles set forth hereunder do not impose on States such legal institutions as foster placement or adoption,

Proclaims the following principles:

A. General Family and Child Welfare

Article 1

Every State should give a high priority to family and child welfare.

Article 2

Child welfare depends upon good family welfare.

Article 3

The first priority for a child is to be cared for by his or her own parents.

Article 4

When care by the child's own parents is unavailable or inappropriate, care by relatives of the child's parents, by another substitute - foster or adoptive - family or, if necessary, by an appropriate institution should be considered.

---

1 Resolution 217 A (III).
2 See resolution 2200 A (XXI), annex.
3 See resolution 2200 A (XXI), annex.
4 Resolution 2106 A (XX), annex.
5 Resolution 34/180, annex.

Article 5

In all matters relating to the placement of a child outside the care of the child's own parents, the best interests of the child, particularly his or her need for affection and right to security and continuing care, should be the paramount consideration.

Article 6

Persons responsible for foster placement or adoption procedures should have professional or other appropriate training.

Article 7

Governments should determine the adequacy of their national child welfare-services and consider appropriate actions.

Article 8

The child should at all times have a name, a nationality and a legal representative. The child should not, as a result of foster placement, adoption or any alternative régime, be deprived of his or her name, nationality or legal representative unless the child thereby acquires a new name, nationality or legal representative.

Article 9

The need of a foster or an adopted child to know about his or her background should be recognized by persons responsible for the child's care, unless this is contrary to the child's best interests.

B. Foster Placement

Article 10

Foster placement of children should be regulated by law.

Article 11

Foster family care, though temporary in nature, may continue, if necessary, until adulthood but should not preclude either prior return to the child's own parents or adoption.

Article 12

In all matters of foster family care, the prospective foster parents and, as appropriate, the child and his or her own parents should be properly involved. A competent authority or agency should be responsible for supervision to ensure the welfare of the child.

C. Adoption

Article 13

The primary aim of adoption is to provide the child who cannot be cared for by his or her own parents with a permanent family.

Article 14

In considering possible adoption placements, persons responsible for them should select the most appropriate environment for the child.

Article 15

Sufficient time and adequate counselling should be given to the child's own parents, the prospective adoptive parents and, as appropriate, the child in order to reach a decision on the child's future as early as possible.

Article 16

The relationship between the child to be adopted and the prospective adoptive parents should be observed by child welfare agencies or services prior to the adoption. Legislation should ensure that the child is recognized in law as a member of the adoptive family and enjoys all the rights pertinent thereto.

Article 17

If a child cannot be placed in a foster or an adoptive family or cannot in any suitable manner be cared for in the country of origin, intercountry adoption may be considered as an alternative means of providing the child with a family.

Article 18

Governments should establish policy, legislation and effective supervision for the protection of children involved in intercountry adoption. Intercountry adoption should, wherever possible, only be undertaken when such measures have been established in the States concerned.

Article 19

Policies should be established and laws enacted, where necessary, for the prohibition of abduction and of any other act for illicit placement of children.

Article 20

In intercountry adoption, placements should, as a rule, be made through competent authorities or agencies with application of safeguards and standards equivalent to those existing in respect of national adoption. In no case should the placement result in improper financial gain for those involved in it.

Article 21

In intercountry adoption through persons acting as agents for prospective adoptive parents, special precautions should be taken in order to protect the child's legal and social interests.

Article 22

No intercountry adoption should be considered before it has been established that the child is legally free for adoption and that any pertinent documents necessary to complete the adoption, such as the consent of competent authorities, will become available. It must also be established that the child will be able to migrate and to join the prospective adoptive parents and may obtain their nationality.

Article 23

In intercountry adoption, as a rule, the legal validity of the adoption should be assured in each of the countries involved.

Article 24

Where the nationality of the child differs from that of the prospective adoptive parents, all due weight shall be given to both the law of the State of which the child is a national and the law of the State of which the prospective adoptive parents are nationals. In this connection due regard shall be given to the child's cultural and religious background and interests.

45/112. United Nations Guidelines for the Prevention of Juvenile Delinquency (The Riyadh Guidelines)

Committee: 3
Vote: Adopted without a vote

The General Assembly,

Bearing in mind the Universal Declaration of Human Rights, the International Covenant on Economic, Social and Cultural Rights and the International Covenant on Civil and Political Rights, as well as other international instruments pertaining to the rights and well-being of young persons, including relevant standards established by the International Labour Organisation,

Bearing in mind also the Declaration of the Rights of the Child,[1] the Convention on the Rights of the Child, and the United Nations Standard Minimum Rules for the Administration of Juvenile Justice (The Beijing Rules),

Recalling General Assembly resolution 40/33 of 29 November 1985, by which the Assembly adopted the Beijing Rules recommended by the Seventh United Nations Congress on the Prevention of Crime and the Treatment of Offenders,

Recalling that the General Assembly, in its resolution 40/35 of 29 November 1985, called for the development of standards for the

1 Resolution 1386 (XIV).

prevention of juvenile delinquency which would assist Member States in formulating and implementing specialized programmes and policies, emphasizing assistance, care and community involvement, and called upon the Economic and Social Council to report to the Eighth United Nations Congress on the Prevention of Crime and the Treatment of Offenders on the progress achieved with respect to these standards, for review and action,

Recalling also that the Economic and Social Council, in section II of its resolution 1986/10 of 21 May 1986, requested the Eighth Congress to consider the draft standards for the prevention of juvenile delinquency, with a view to their adoption,

Recognizing the need to develop national, regional and international approaches and strategies for the prevention of juvenile delinquency,

Affirming that every child has basic human rights, including, in particular, access to free education,

Mindful of the large number of young persons who may or may not be in conflict with the law but who are abandoned, neglected, abused, exposed to drug abuse, and are in marginal circumstances and in general at social risk,

Taking into account the benefits of progressive policies for the prevention of delinquency and for the welfare of the community,

1. *Notes with satisfaction* the substantive work accomplished by the Committee on Crime Prevention and Control and the Secretary-General in the formulation of the guidelines for the prevention of juvenile delinquency;

2. *Expresses appreciation* for the valuable collaboration of the Arab Security Studies and Training Centre at Riyadh, in hosting the International Meeting of Experts on the Development of the United Nations Draft Guidelines for the Prevention of Juvenile Delinquency, held at Riyadh from 28 February to 1 March 1988, in cooperation with the United Nations Office at Vienna;

3. *Adopts* the United Nations Guidelines for the Prevention of Juvenile Delinquency contained in the annex to the present resolution, to be designated "the Riyadh Guidelines";

4. *Calls upon* Member States, in their comprehensive crime prevention plans, to apply the Riyadh Guidelines in national law, policy and practice and to bring them to the attention of relevant authorities, including policy makers, juvenile justice personnel, educators, the mass media, practitioners and scholars;

5. *Requests* the Secretary-General and invites Member States to ensure the widest possible dissemination of the text of the Riyadh Guidelines in all of the official languages of the United Nations;

6. *Requests* the Secretary-General and invites all relevant United Nations offices and interested institutions, in particular, the United Nations Children's Fund, as well as individual experts, to make a concerted effort to promote the application of the Riyadh Guidelines;

7. *Also requests* the Secretary-General to intensify research on particular situations of social risk and on the exploitation of children, including the use of children as instruments of criminality, with a view to developing comprehensive countermeasures and to report thereon to the Ninth United Nations Congress on the Prevention of Crime and the Treatment of Offenders;

8. *Further requests* the Secretary-General to issue a composite manual on juvenile justice standards, containing the United Nations Standard Minimum Rules for the Administration of Juvenile Justice (The Beijing Rules), the United Nations Guidelines on the Prevention of Juvenile Delinquency (The Riyadh Guidelines), and the United Nations Rules for the Protection of Juveniles Deprived of their Liberty,[1] and a set of full commentaries on their provisions;

9. *Urges* all relevant bodies within the United Nations system to collaborate with the Secretary-General in taking appropriate measures to ensure the implementation of the present resolution;

10. *Invites* the Sub-Commission on Prevention of Discrimination and Protection of Minorities of the Commission on Human Rights to consider this new international instrument with a view to promoting the application of its provisions;

11. *Invites* Member States to support strongly the organization of technical and scientific workshops, and pilot and demonstration projects on practical issues and policy matters relating to the application of the provisions of the Riyadh Guidelines and to the establishment of concrete measures for community-based services designed to respond to the special needs, problems and concerns of young persons, and requests the Secretary-General to coordinate efforts in this respect;

12. *Also invites* Member States to inform the Secretary-General on the implementation of the Riyadh Guidelines and to report regularly to the Committee on Crime Prevention and Control on the results achieved;

13. *Recommends* that the Committee on Crime Prevention and Control request the Ninth Congress to review the progress made in the promotion and application of the Riyadh Guidelines and the recommendations contained in the present resolution, under a separate agenda item on juvenile justice and keep the matter under constant review.

68th plenary meeting
14 December 1990

Annex

United Nations Guidelines for the Prevention of Juvenile Delinquency (The Riyadh Guidelines)

I. Fundamental Principles

1. The prevention of juvenile delinquency is an essential part of crime prevention in society. By engaging in lawful, socially useful activities and adopting a humanistic orientation towards society and outlook on life, young persons can develop non-criminogenic attitudes.

2. The successful prevention of juvenile delinquency requires efforts on the part of the entire society to ensure the harmonious development of adolescents, with respect for and promotion of their personality from early childhood.

3. For the purposes of the interpretation of the present Guidelines, a child-centred orientation should be pursued. Young persons should have an active role and partnership within society and should not be considered as mere objects of socialization or control.

4. In the implementation of the present Guidelines, in accordance with national legal systems, the well-being of young persons from their early childhood should be the focus of any preventive programme.

5. The need for and importance of progressive delinquency prevention policies and the systematic study and the elaboration of measures should be recognized. These should avoid criminalizing and penalizing a child for behaviour that does not cause serious damage to the development of the child or harm to others. Such policies and measures should involve:

(a) The provision of opportunities, in particular educational opportunities, to meet the varying needs of young persons and to serve as a supportive framework for safeguarding the personal development of all young persons, particularly those who are demonstrably endangered or at social risk and are in need of special care and protection;

(b) Specialized philosophies and approaches for delinquency prevention, on the basis of laws, processes, institutions, facilities and a service delivery network aimed at reducing the motivation, need and opportunity for, or conditions giving rise to, the commission of infractions;

(c) Official intervention to be pursued primarily in the overall interest of the young person and guided by fairness and equity;

(d) Safeguarding the well-being, development, rights and interests of all young persons;

(e) Consideration that youthful behaviour or conduct that does not conform to overall social norms and values is often part of the maturation and growth process and tends to disappear spontaneously in most individuals with the transition to adulthood;

---

1 Resolution 45/113, annex.

(f) Awareness that, in the predominant opinion of experts, labelling a young person as "deviant", "delinquent" or "pre-delinquent" often contributes to the development of a consistent pattern of undesirable behaviour by young persons.

6. Community-based services and programmes should be developed for the prevention of juvenile delinquency, particularly where no agencies have yet been established. Formal agencies of social control should only be utilized as a means of last resort.

II. Scope of the Guidelines

7. The present Guidelines should be interpreted and implemented within the broad framework of the Universal Declaration of Human Rights, the International Covenant on Economic, Social and Cultural Rights, the International Covenant on Civil and Political Rights, the Declaration of the Rights of the Child and the Convention on the Rights of the Child, and in the context of the United Nations Standard Minimum Rules for the Administration of Juvenile Justice (The Beijing Rules), as well as other instruments and norms relating to the rights, interests and well-being of all children and young persons.

8. The present Guidelines should also be implemented in the context of the economic, social and cultural conditions prevailing in each Member State.

III. General Prevention

9. Comprehensive prevention plans should be instituted at every level of government and include the following:

(a) In-depth analyses of the problem and inventories of programmes, services, facilities and resources available;

(b) Well-defined responsibilities for the qualified agencies, institutions and personnel involved in preventive efforts;

(c) Mechanisms for the appropriate coordination of prevention efforts between governmental and non-governmental agencies;

(d) Policies, programmes and strategies based on prognostic studies to be continuously monitored and carefully evaluated in the course of implementation;

(e) Methods for effectively reducing the opportunity to commit delinquent acts;

(f) Community involvement through a wide range of services and programmes;

(g) Close interdisciplinary cooperation between national, state, provincial and local governments, with the involvement of the private sector, representative citizens of the community to be served, and labour, child-care, health education, social, law enforcement and judicial agencies in taking concerted action to prevent juvenile delinquency and youth crime;

(h) Youth participation in delinquency prevention policies and processes, including recourse to community resources, youth self-help, and victim compensation and assistance programmes;

(i) Specialized personnel at all levels.

IV. Socialization Processes

10. Emphasis should be placed on preventive policies facilitating the successful socialization and integration of all children and young persons, in particular through the family, the community, peer groups, schools, vocational training and the world of work, as well as through voluntary organizations. Due respect should be given to the proper personal development of children and young persons, and they should be accepted as full and equal partners in socialization and integration processes.

A. Family

11. Every society should place a high priority on the needs and well-being of the family and of all its members.

12. Since the family is the central unit responsible for the primary socialization of children, governmental and social efforts to preserve the integrity of the family, including the extended family, should be pursued. The society has a responsibility to assist the family in providing care and protection and in ensuring the physical and mental well-being of children. Adequate arrangements including day-care should be provided.

13. Governments should establish policies that are conducive to the bringing up of children in stable and settled family environments. Families in need of assistance in the resolution of conditions of instability or conflict should be provided with requisite services.

14. Where a stable and settled family environment is lacking and when community efforts to assist parents in this regard have failed and the extended family cannot fulfil this role, alternative placements, including foster care and adoption, should be considered. Such placements should replicate, to the extent possible, a stable and settled family environment, while, at the same time, establishing a sense of permanency for children, thus avoiding problems associated with "foster drift".

15. Special attention should be given to children of families affected by problems brought about by rapid and uneven economic, social and cultural change, in particular the children of indigenous, migrant and refugee families. As such changes may disrupt the social capacity of the family to secure the traditional rearing and nurturing of children, often as a result of role and culture conflict, innovative and socially constructive modalities for the socialization of children have to be designed.

16. Measures should be taken and programmes developed to provide families with the opportunity to learn about parental roles and obligations as regards child development and child care, promoting positive parent-child relationships, sensitizing parents to the problems of children and young persons and encouraging their involvement in family and community-based activities.

17. Governments should take measures to promote family cohesion and harmony and to discourage the separation of children from their parents, unless circumstances affecting the welfare and future of the child leave no viable alternative.

18. It is important to emphasize the socialization function of the family and extended family; it is also equally important to recognize the future role, responsibilities, participation and partnership of young persons in society.

19. In ensuring the right of the child to proper socialization, Governments and other agencies should rely on existing social and legal agencies, but, whenever traditional institutions and customs are no longer effective, they should also provide and allow for innovative measures.

B. Education

20. Governments are under an obligation to make public education accessible to all young persons.

21. Education systems should, in addition to their academic and vocational training activities, devote particular attention to the following:

(a) Teaching of basic values and developing respect for the child's own cultural identity and patterns, for the social values of the country in which the child is living, for civilizations different from the child's own and for human rights and fundamental freedoms;

(b) Promotion and development of the personality, talents and mental and physical abilities of young people to their fullest potential;

(c) Involvement of young persons as active and effective participants in, rather than mere objects of, the educational process;

(d) Undertaking activities that foster a sense of identity with and of belonging to the school and the community;

(e) Encouragement of young persons to understand and respect diverse views and opinions, as well as cultural and other differences;

(f) Provision of information and guidance regarding vocational training, employment opportunities and career development;

(g) Provision of positive emotional support to young persons and the avoidance of psychological maltreatment;

(h) Avoidance of harsh disciplinary measures, particularly corporal punishment.

22. Educational systems should seek to work together with parents, community organizations and agencies concerned with the activities of young persons.

23. Young persons and their families should be informed about the law and their rights and responsibilities under the law, as well as the universal value system, including United Nations instruments.

24. Educational systems should extend particular care and attention to young persons who are at social risk. Specialized prevention programmes and educational materials, curricula, approaches and tools should be developed and fully utilized.

25. Special attention should be given to comprehensive policies and strategies for the prevention of alcohol, drug and other substance abuse by young persons. Teachers and other professionals should be equipped and trained to prevent and deal with these problems. Information on the use and abuse of drugs, including alcohol, should be made available to the student body.

26. Schools should serve as resource and referral centres for the provision of medical, counselling and other services to young persons, particularly those with special needs and suffering from abuse, neglect, victimization and exploitation.

27. Through a variety of educational programmes, teachers and other adults and the student body should be sensitized to the problems, needs and perceptions of young persons, particularly those belonging to underprivileged, disadvantaged, ethnic or other minority and low-income groups.

28. School systems should attempt to meet and promote the highest professional and educational standards with respect to curricula, teaching and learning methods and approaches, and the recruitment and training of qualified teachers. Regular monitoring and assessment of performance by the appropriate professional organizations and authorities should be ensured.

29. School systems should plan, develop and implement extra-curricular activities of interest to young persons, in cooperation with community groups.

30. Special assistance should be given to children and young persons who find it difficult to comply with attendance codes, and to "drop-outs".

31. Schools should promote policies and rules that are fair and just; students should be represented in bodies formulating school policy, including policy on discipline, and decision-making.

C. Community

32. Community-based services and programmes which respond to the special needs, problems, interests and concerns of young persons and which offer appropriate counselling and guidance to young persons and their families should be developed, or strengthened where they exist.

33. Communities should provide, or strengthen where they exist, a wide range of community-based support measures for young persons, including community development centres, recreational facilities and services to respond to the special problems of children who are at social risk. In providing these helping measures, respect for individual rights should be ensured.

34. Special facilities should be set up to provide adequate shelter for young persons who are no longer able to live at home or who do not have homes to live in.

35. A range of services and helping measures should be provided to deal with the difficulties experienced by young persons in the transition to adulthood. Such services should include special programmes for young drug abusers which emphasize care, counselling, assistance and therapy-oriented interventions.

36. Voluntary organizations providing services for young persons should be given financial and other support by Governments and other institutions.

37. Youth organizations should be created or strengthened at the local level and given full participatory status in the management of community affairs. These organizations should encourage youth to organize collective and voluntary projects, particularly projects aimed at helping young persons in need of assistance.

38. Government agencies should take special responsibility and provide necessary services for homeless or street children; information about local facilities, accommodation, employment and other forms and sources of help should be made readily available to young persons.

39. A wide range of recreational facilities and services of particular interest to young persons should be established and made easily accessible to them.

D. Mass media

40. The mass media should be encouraged to ensure that young persons have access to information and material from a diversity of national and international sources.

41. The mass media should be encouraged to portray the positive contribution of young persons to society.

42. The mass media should be encouraged to disseminate information on the existence of services, facilities and opportunities for young persons in society.

43. The mass media generally, and the television and film media in particular, should be encouraged to minimize the level of pornography, drugs and violence portrayed and to display violence and exploitation disfavourably, as well as to avoid demeaning and degrading presentations, especially of children, women and interpersonal relations, and to promote egalitarian principles and roles.

44. The mass media should be aware of its extensive social role and responsibility, as well as its influence, in communications relating to youthful drug and alcohol abuse. It should use its power for drug abuse prevention by relaying consistent messages through a balanced approach. Effective drug awareness campaigns at all levels should be promoted.

V. Social Policy

45. Government agencies should give high priority to plans and programmes for young persons and should provide sufficient funds and other resources for the effective delivery of services, facilities and staff for adequate medical and mental health care, nutrition, housing and other relevant services, including drug and alcohol abuse prevention and treatment, ensuring that such resources reach and actually benefit young persons.

46. The institutionalization of young persons should be a measure of last resort and for the minimum necessary period, and the best interests of the young person should be of paramount importance. Criteria authorizing formal intervention of this type should be strictly defined and limited to the following situations: (a) where the child or young person has suffered harm that has been inflicted by the parents or guardians; (b) where the child or young person has been sexually, physically or emotionally abused by the parents or guardians; (c) where the child or young person has been neglected, abandoned or exploited by the parents or guardians; (d) where the child or young person is threatened by physical or moral danger due to the behaviour of the parents or guardians; and (e) where a serious physical or psychological danger to the child or young person has manifested itself in his or her own behaviour and neither the parents, the guardians, the juvenile himself or herself nor non-residential community services can meet the danger by means other than institutionalization.

47. Government agencies should provide young persons with the opportunity of continuing in full-time education, funded by the State where parents or guardians are unable to support the young persons, and of receiving work experience.

48. Programmes to prevent delinquency should be planned and developed on the basis of reliable, scientific research findings, and periodically monitored, evaluated and adjusted accordingly.

49. Scientific information should be disseminated to the professional community and to the public at large about the sort of behaviour or situation which indicates or may result in physical and psychological victimization, harm and abuse, as well as exploitation, of young persons.

50. Generally, participation in plans and programmes should be voluntary. Young persons themselves should be involved in their formulation, development and implementation.

51. Governments should begin or continue to explore, develop and implement policies, measures and strategies within and outside the criminal justice system to prevent domestic violence against and affecting young persons and to ensure fair treatment to these victims of domestic violence.

VI. Legislation and Juvenile Justice Administration

52. Governments should enact and enforce specific laws and procedures to promote and protect the rights and well-being of all young persons.

53. Legislation preventing the victimization, abuse, exploitation and the use for criminal activities of children and young persons should be enacted and enforced.

54. No child or young person should be subjected to harsh or degrading correction or punishment measures at home, in schools or in any other institutions.

55. Legislation and enforcement aimed at restricting and controlling accessibility of weapons of any sort to children and young persons should be pursued.

56. In order to prevent further stigmatization, victimization and criminalization of young persons, legislation should be enacted to ensure that any conduct not considered an offence or not penalized if committed by an adult is not considered an offence and not penalized if committed by a young person.

57. Consideration should be given to the establishment of an office of ombudsman or similar independent organ, which would ensure that the status, rights and interests of young persons are upheld and that proper referral to available services is made. The ombudsman or other organ designated would also supervise the implementation of the Riyadh Guidelines, the Beijing Rules and the Rules for the Protection of Juveniles Deprived of their Liberty. The ombudsman or other organ would, at regular intervals, publish a report on the progress made and on the difficulties encountered in the implementation of the instrument. Child advocacy services should also be established.

58. Law enforcement and other relevant personnel, of both sexes, should be trained to respond to the special needs of young persons and should be familiar with and use, to the maximum extent possible, programmes and referral possibilities for the diversion of young persons from the justice system.

59. Legislation should be enacted and strictly enforced to protect children and young persons from drug abuse and drug traffickers.

VII. Research, Policy Development and Coordination

60. Efforts should be made and appropriate mechanisms established to promote, on both a multidisciplinary and an intradisciplinary basis, interaction and coordination between economic, social, educational and health agencies and services, the justice system, youth, community and development agencies and other relevant institutions.

61. The exchange of information, experience and expertise gained through projects, programmes, practices and initiatives relating to youth crime, delinquency prevention and juvenile justice should be intensified at the national, regional and international levels.

62. Regional and international cooperation on matters of youth crime, delinquency prevention and juvenile justice involving practitioners, experts and decision makers should be further developed and strengthened.

63. Technical and scientific cooperation on practical and policy-related matters, particularly in training, pilot and demonstration projects, and on specific issues concerning the prevention of youth crime and juvenile delinquency should be strongly supported by all Governments, the United Nations system and other concerned organizations.

64. Collaboration should be encouraged in undertaking scientific research with respect to effective modalities for youth crime and juvenile delinquency prevention and the findings of such research should be widely disseminated and evaluated.

65. Appropriate United Nations bodies, institutes, agencies and offices should pursue close collaboration and coordination on various questions related to children, juvenile justice and youth crime and juvenile delinquency prevention.

66. On the basis of the present Guidelines, the United Nations Secretariat, in cooperation with interested institutions, should play an active role in the conduct of research, scientific collaboration, the formulation of policy options and the review and monitoring of their implementation, and should serve as a source of reliable information on effective modalities for delinquency prevention.

45/113. United Nations Rules for the Protection of Juveniles Deprived of their Liberty

Committee: 3
Vote: Adopted without a vote

The General Assembly,

Bearing in mind the Universal Declaration of Human Rights, the International Covenant on Civil and Political Rights, the Convention against Torture and Other Cruel, Inhuman or Degrading Treatment or Punishment[1] and the Convention on the Rights of the Child, as well as other international instruments relating to the protection of the rights and well-being of young persons,

Bearing in mind also the Standard Minimum Rules for the Treatment of Prisoners adopted by the First United Nations Congress on the Prevention of Crime and the Treatment of Offenders,

Bearing in mind further the Body of Principles for the Protection of All Persons under Any Form of Detention or Imprisonment, approved by the General Assembly by its resolution 43/173 of 9 December 1988 and contained in the annex thereto,

Recalling the United Nations Standard Minimum Rules for the Administration of Juvenile Justice (The Beijing Rules),

Recalling also resolution 21 of the Seventh United Nations Congress on the Prevention of Crime and the Treatment of Offenders, in which the Congress called for the development of rules for the protection of juveniles deprived of their liberty,

Recalling further that the Economic and Social Council, in section II of its resolution 1986/10 of 21 May 1986, requested the Secretary-General to report on progress achieved in the development of the rules to the Committee on Crime Prevention and Control at its tenth session and requested the Eighth United Nations Congress on the Prevention of Crime and the Treatment of Offenders to consider the proposed rules with a view to their adoption,

Alarmed at the conditions and circumstances under which juveniles are being deprived of their liberty world wide,

Aware that juveniles deprived of their liberty are highly vulnerable to abuse, victimization and the violation of their rights,

Concerned that many systems do not differentiate between adults and juveniles at various stages of the administration of justice and that juveniles are therefore being held in goals and facilities with adults,

1. *Affirms* that the placement of a juvenile in an institution should always be a disposition of last resort and for the minimum necessary period;

2. *Recognizes* that, because of their high vulnerability, juveniles deprived of their liberty require special attention and protection and that their rights and well-being should be guaranteed during and after the period when they are deprived of their liberty;

3. *Notes with appreciation* the valuable work of the Secretariat and the collaboration which has been established between the Secretariat and experts, practitioners, intergovernmental organizations, the non-governmental community, particularly Amnesty International, Defence for Children International and Rädda Barnen International (Swedish Save the Children Federation), and scientific institutions concerned with the rights of children and juvenile justice in the development of the United Nations draft Rules for the Protection of Juveniles Deprived of their Liberty;

---

1 Resolution 39/46, annex.

4. *Adopts* the United Nations Rules for the Protection of Juveniles Deprived of their Liberty contained in the annex to the present resolution;

5. *Calls upon* the Committee on Crime Prevention and Control to formulate measures for the effective implementation of the Rules, with the assistance of the United Nations institutes on the prevention of crime and the treatment of offenders;

6. *Invites* Member States to adapt, wherever necessary, their national legislation, policies and practices, particularly in the training of all categories of juvenile justice personnel, to the spirit of the Rules, and to bring them to the attention of relevant authorities and the public in general;

7. *Also invites* Member States to inform the Secretary-General of their efforts to apply the Rules in law, policy and practice and to report regularly to the Committee on Crime Prevention and Control on the results achieved in their implementation;

8. *Requests* the Secretary-General and invites Member States to ensure the widest possible dissemination of the text of the Rules in all of the official languages of the United Nations;

9. *Requests* the Secretary-General to conduct comparative research, pursue the requisite collaboration and devise strategies to deal with the different categories of serious and persistent young offenders, and to prepare a policy-oriented report thereon for submission to the Ninth United Nations Congress on the Prevention of Crime and the Treatment of Offenders;

10. *Also requests* the Secretary-General and urges Member States to allocate the necessary resources to ensure the successful application and implementation of the Rules, in particular in the areas of recruitment, training and exchange of all categories of juvenile justice personnel;

11. *Urges* all relevant bodies of the United Nations system, in particular the United Nations Children's Fund, the regional commissions and specialized agencies, the United Nations institutes for the prevention of crime and the treatment of offenders and all concerned intergovernmental and non-governmental organizations, to collaborate with the Secretary-General and to take the necessary measures to ensure a concerted and sustained effort within their respective fields of technical competence to promote the application of the Rules;

12. *Invites* the Sub-Commission on Prevention of Discrimination and Protection of Minorities of the Commission on Human Rights to consider this new international instrument, with a view to promoting the application of its provisions;

13. *Requests* the Ninth Congress to review the progress made on the promotion and application of the Rules and on the recommendations contained in the present resolution, under a separate agenda item on juvenile justice.

68th plenary meeting
14 December 1990

Annex

United Nations Rules for the Protection of Juveniles Deprived of their Liberty

I. Fundamental Perspectives

1. The juvenile justice system should uphold the rights and safety and promote the physical and mental well-being of juveniles. Imprisonment should be used as a last resort.

2. Juveniles should only be deprived of their liberty in accordance with the principles and procedures set forth in these Rules and in the United Nations Standard Minimum Rules for the Administration of Juvenile Justice (The Beijing Rules). Deprivation of the liberty of a juvenile should be a disposition of last resort and for the minimum necessary period and should be limited to exceptional cases. The length of the sanction should be determined by the judicial authority, without precluding the possibility of his or her early release.

3. The Rules are intended to establish minimum standards accepted by the United Nations for the protection of juveniles deprived of their liberty in all forms, consistent with human rights and fundamental freedoms, with a view to counteracting the detrimental effects of all types of detention and to fostering integration in society.

4. The Rules should be applied impartially, without discrimination of any kind as to race, colour, sex, age, language, religion, nationality, political or other opinion, cultural beliefs or practices, property, birth or family status, ethnic or social origin, and disability. The religious and cultural beliefs, practices and moral concepts of the juvenile should be respected.

5. The Rules are designed to serve as convenient standards of reference and to provide encouragement and guidance to professionals involved in the management of the juvenile justice system.

6. The Rules should be made readily available to juvenile justice personnel in their national languages. Juveniles who are not fluent in the language spoken by the personnel of the detention facility should have the right to the services of an interpreter free of charge whenever necessary, in particular during medical examinations and disciplinary proceedings.

7. Where appropriate, States should incorporate the Rules into their legislation or amend it accordingly and provide effective remedies for their breach, including compensation when injuries are inflicted on juveniles. States should also monitor the application of the Rules.

8. The competent authorities should constantly seek to increase the awareness of the public that the care of detained juveniles and preparation for their return to society is a social service of great importance, and to this end active steps should be taken to foster open contacts between the juveniles and the local community.

9. Nothing in the Rules should be interpreted as precluding the application of the relevant United Nations and human rights instruments and standards, recognized by the international community, that are more conducive to ensuring the rights, care and protection of juveniles, children and all young persons.

10. In the event that the practical application of particular Rules contained in sections II to V, inclusive, presents any conflict with the Rules contained in the present section, compliance with the latter shall be regarded as the predominant requirement.

II. Scope and Application of the Rules

11. For the purposes of the Rules, the following definitions should apply:

(a) A juvenile is every person under the age of 18. The age limit below which it should not be permitted to deprive a child of his or her liberty should be determined by law;

(b) The deprivation of liberty means any form of detention or imprisonment or the placement of a person in a public or private custodial setting, from which this person is not permitted to leave at will, by order of any judicial, administrative or other public authority.

12. The deprivation of liberty should be effected in conditions and circumstances which ensure respect for the human rights of juveniles. Juveniles detained in facilities should be guaranteed the benefit of meaningful activities and programmes which would serve to promote and sustain their health and self-respect, to foster their sense of responsibility and encourage those attitudes and skills that will assist them in developing their potential as members of society.

13. Juveniles deprived of their liberty shall not for any reason related to their status be denied the civil, economic, political, social or cultural rights to which they are entitled under national or international law, and which are compatible with the deprivation of liberty.

14. The protection of the individual rights of juveniles with special regard to the legality of the execution of the detention measures shall be ensured by the competent authority, while the objectives of social integration should be secured by regular inspections and other means of control carried out, according to international standards, national laws and regulations, by a duly constituted body authorized to visit the juveniles and not belonging to the detention facility.

15. The Rules apply to all types and forms of detention facilities in which juveniles are deprived of their liberty. Sections I, II, IV and V of the Rules apply to all detention facilities and institutional settings

in which juveniles are detained, and section III applies specifically to juveniles under arrest or awaiting trial.

16. The Rules shall be implemented in the context of the economic, social and cultural conditions prevailing in each Member State.

III. Juveniles under Arrest or Awaiting Trial

17. Juveniles who are detained under arrest or awaiting trial ("untried") are presumed innocent and shall be treated as such. Detention before trial shall be avoided to the extent possible and limited to exceptional circumstances. Therefore, all efforts shall be made to apply alternative measures. When preventive detention is nevertheless used, juvenile courts and investigative bodies shall give the highest priority to the most expeditious processing of such cases to ensure the shortest possible duration of detention. Untried detainees should be separated from convicted juveniles.

18. The conditions under which an untried juvenile is detained should be consistent with the rules set out below, with additional specific provisions as are necessary and appropriate, given the requirements of the presumption of innocence, the duration of the detention and the legal status and circumstances of the juvenile. These provisions would include, but not necessarily be restricted to, the following:

(a) Juveniles should have the right of legal counsel and be enabled to apply for free legal aid, where such aid is available, and to communicate regularly with their legal advisers. Privacy and confidentiality shall be ensured for such communications;

(b) Juveniles should be provided, where possible, with opportunities to pursue work, with remuneration, and continue education or training, but should not be required to do so. Work, education or training should not cause the continuation of the detention;

(c) Juveniles should receive and retain materials for their leisure and recreation as are compatible with the interests of the administration of justice.

IV. The Management of Juvenile Facilities

A. Records

19. All reports, including legal records, medical records and records of disciplinary proceedings, and all other documents relating to the form, content and details of treatment, should be placed in a confidential individual file, which should be kept up to date, accessible only to authorized persons and classified in such a way as to be easily understood. Where possible, every juvenile should have the right to contest any fact or opinion contained in his or her file so as to permit rectification of inaccurate, unfounded or unfair statements. In order to exercise this right, there should be procedures that allow an appropriate third party to have access to and to consult the file on request. Upon release, the records of juveniles shall be sealed, and, at an appropriate time, expunged.

20. No juvenile should be received in any detention facility without a valid commitment order of a judicial, administrative or other public authority. The details of this order should be immediately entered in the register. No juvenile should be detained in any facility where there is no such register.

B. Admission, registration, movement and transfer

21. In every place where juveniles are detained, a complete and secure record of the following information should be kept concerning each juvenile received:

(a) Information on the identity of the juvenile;

(b) The fact of and reasons for commitment and the authority therefor;

(c) The day and hour of admission, transfer and release;

(d) Details of the notifications to parents and guardians on every admission, transfer or release of the juvenile in their care at the time of commitment;

(e) Details of known physical and mental health problems, including drug and alcohol abuse.

22. The information on admission, place, transfer and release should be provided without delay to the parents and guardians or closest relative of the juvenile concerned.

23. As soon as possible after reception, full reports and relevant information on the personal situation and circumstances of each juvenile should be drawn up and submitted to the administration.

24. On admission, all juveniles shall be given a copy of the rules governing the detention facility and a written description of their rights and obligations in a language they can understand, together with the address of the authorities competent to receive complaints, as well as the address of public or private agencies and organizations which provide legal assistance. For those juveniles who are illiterate or who cannot understand the language in the written form, the information should be conveyed in a manner enabling full comprehension.

25. All juveniles should be helped to understand the regulations governing the internal organization of the facility, the goals and methodology of the care provided, the disciplinary requirements and procedures, other authorized methods of seeking information and of making complaints, and all such other matters as are necessary to enable them to understand fully their rights and obligations during detention.

26. The transport of juveniles should be carried out at the expense of the administration in conveyances with adequate ventilation and light, in conditions that should in no way subject them to hardship or indignity. Juveniles should not be transferred from one facility to another arbitrarily.

C. Classification and placement

27. As soon as possible after the moment of admission, each juvenile should be interviewed, and a psychological and social report identifying any factors relevant to the specific type and level of care and programme required by the juvenile should be prepared. This report, together with the report prepared by a medical officer who has examined the juvenile upon admission, should be forwarded to the director for purposes of determining the most appropriate placement for the juvenile within the facility and the specific type and level of care and programme required and to be pursued. When special rehabilitative treatment is required, and the length of stay in the facility permits, trained personnel of the facility should prepare a written, individualized treatment plan specifying treatment objectives and time-frame and the means, stages and delays with which the objectives should be approached.

28. The detention of juveniles should only take place under conditions that take full account of their particular needs, status and special requirements according to their age, personality, sex and type of offence, as well as mental and physical health, and which ensure their protection from harmful influences and risk situations. The principal criterion for the separation of different categories of juveniles deprived of their liberty should be the provision of the type of care best suited to the particular needs of the individuals concerned and the protection of their physical, mental and moral integrity and well-being.

29. In all detention facilities juveniles should be separated from adults, unless they are members of the same family. Under controlled conditions, juveniles may be brought together with carefully selected adults as part of a special programme that has been shown to be beneficial for the juveniles concerned.

30. Open detention facilities for juveniles should be established. Open detention facilities are those with no or minimal security measures. The population in such detention facilities should be as small as possible. The number of juveniles detained in closed facilities should be small enough to enable individualized treatment. Detention facilities for juveniles should be decentralized and of such size as to facilitate access and contact between the juveniles and their families. Small-scale detention facilities should be established and integrated into the social, economic and cultural environment of the community.

D. Physical environment and accommodation

31. Juveniles deprived of their liberty have the right to facilities and services that meet all the requirements of health and human dignity.

32. The design of detention facilities for juveniles and the physical environment should be in keeping with the rehabilitative aim of residential treatment, with due regard to the need of the juvenile for privacy, sensory stimuli, opportunities for association with peers and participation in sports, physical exercise and leisure-time activities. The design and structure of juvenile detention facilities should be such as to minimize the risk of fire and to ensure safe evacuation from the premises. There should be an effective alarm system in case of fire, as well as formal and drilled procedures to ensure the safety of the juveniles. Detention facilities should not be located in areas where there are known health or other hazards or risks.

33. Sleeping accommodation should normally consist of small group dormitories or individual bedrooms, account being taken of local standards. During sleeping hours there should be regular, unobtrusive supervision of all sleeping areas, including individual rooms and group dormitories, in order to ensure the protection of each juvenile. Every juvenile should, in accordance with local or national standards, be provided with separate and sufficient bedding, which should be clean when issued, kept in good order and changed often enough to ensure cleanliness.

34. Sanitary installations should be so located and of a sufficient standard to enable every juvenile to comply, as required, with their physical needs in privacy and in a clean and decent manner.

35. The possession of personal effects is a basic element of the right to privacy and essential to the psychological well-being of the juvenile. The right of every juvenile to possess personal effects and to have adequate storage facilities for them should be fully recognized and respected. Personal effects that the juvenile does not choose to retain or that are confiscated should be placed in safe custody. An inventory thereof should be signed by the juvenile. Steps should be taken to keep them in good condition. All such articles and money should be returned to the juvenile on release, except in so far as he or she has been authorized to spend money or send such property out of the facility. If a juvenile receives or is found in possession of any medicine, the medical officer should decide what use should be made of it.

36. To the extent possible juveniles should have the right to use their own clothing. Detention facilities should ensure that each juvenile has personal clothing suitable for the climate and adequate to ensure good health, and which should in no manner be degrading or humiliating. Juveniles removed from or leaving a facility for any purpose should be allowed to wear their own clothing.

37. Every detention facility shall ensure that every juvenile receives food that is suitably prepared and presented at normal meal times and of a quality and quantity to satisfy the standards of dietetics, hygiene and health and, as far as possible, religious and cultural requirements. Clean drinking water should be available to every juvenile at any time.

E. Education, vocational training and work

38. Every juvenile of compulsory school age has the right to education suited to his or her needs and abilities and designed to prepare him or her for return to society. Such education should be provided outside the detention facility in community schools wherever possible and, in any case, by qualified teachers through programmes integrated with the education system of the country so that, after release, juveniles may continue their education without difficulty. Special attention should be given by the administration of the detention facilities to the education of juveniles of foreign origin or with particular cultural or ethnic needs. Juveniles who are illiterate or have cognitive or learning difficulties should have the right to special education.

39. Juveniles above compulsory school age who wish to continue their education should be permitted and encouraged to do so, and every effort should be made to provide them with access to appropriate educational programmes.

40. Diplomas or educational certificates awarded to juveniles while in detention should not indicate in any way that the juvenile has been institutionalized.

41. Every detention facility should provide access to a library that is adequately stocked with both instructional and recreational books and periodicals suitable for the juveniles, who should be encouraged and enabled to make full use of it.

42. Every juvenile should have the right to receive vocational training in occupations likely to prepare him or her for future employment.

43. With due regard to proper vocational selection and to the requirements of institutional administration, juveniles should be able to choose the type of work they wish to perform.

44. All protective national and international standards applicable to child labour and young workers should apply to juveniles deprived of their liberty.

45. Wherever possible, juveniles should be provided with the opportunity to perform remunerated labour, if possible within the local community, as a complement to the vocational training provided in order to enhance the possibility of finding suitable employment when they return to their communities. The type of work should be such as to provide appropriate training that will be of benefit to the juveniles following release. The organization and methods of work offered in detention facilities should resemble as closely as possible those of similar work in the community, so as to prepare juveniles for the conditions of normal occupational life.

46. Every juvenile who performs work should have the right to an equitable remuneration. The interests of the juveniles and of their vocational training should not be subordinated to the purpose of making a profit for the detention facility or a third party. Part of the earnings of a juvenile should normally be set aside to constitute a savings fund to be handed over to the juvenile on release. The juvenile should have the right to use the remainder of those earnings to purchase articles for his or her own use or to indemnify the victim injured by his or her offence or to send it to his or her family or other persons outside the detention facility.

F. Recreation

47. Every juvenile should have the right to a suitable amount of time for daily free exercise, in the open air whenever weather permits, during which time appropriate recreational and physical training should normally be provided. Adequate space, installations and equipment should be provided for these activities. Every juvenile should have additional time for daily leisure activities, part of which should be devoted, if the juvenile so wishes, to arts and crafts skill development. The detention facility should ensure that each juvenile is physically able to participate in the available programmes of physical education. Remedial physical education and therapy should be offered, under medical supervision, to juveniles needing it.

G. Religion

48. Every juvenile should be allowed to satisfy the needs of his or her religious and spiritual life, in particular by attending the services or meetings provided in the detention facility or by conducting his or her own services and having possession of the necessary books or items of religious observance and instruction of his or her denomination. If a detention facility contains a sufficient number of juveniles of a given religion, one or more qualified representatives of that religion should be appointed or approved and allowed to hold regular services and to pay pastoral visits in private to juveniles at their request. Every juvenile should have the right to receive visits from a qualified representative of any religion of his or her choice, as well as the right not to participate in religious services and freely to decline religious education, counselling or indoctrination.

H. Medical Care

49. Every juvenile shall receive adequate medical care, both preventive and remedial, including dental, ophthalmological and mental health care, as well as pharmaceutical products and special diets as medically indicated. All such medical care should, where possible, be

provided to detained juveniles through the appropriate health facilities and services of the community in which the detention facility is located, in order to prevent stigmatization of the juvenile and promote self-respect and integration into the community.

50. Every juvenile has a right to be examined by a physician immediately upon admission to a detention facility, for the purpose of recording any evidence of prior ill-treatment and identifying any physical or mental condition requiring medical attention.

51. The medical services provided to juveniles should seek to detect and should treat any physical or mental illness, substance abuse or other condition that may hinder the integration of the juvenile into society. Every detention facility for juveniles should have immediate access to adequate medical facilities and equipment appropriate to the number and requirements of its residents and staff trained in preventive health care and the handling of medical emergencies. Every juvenile who is ill, who complains of illness or who demonstrates symptoms of physical or mental difficulties, should be examined promptly by a medical officer.

52. Any medical officer who has reason to believe that the physical or mental health of a juvenile has been or will be injuriously affected by continued detention, a hunger strike or any condition of detention should report this fact immediately to the director of the detention facility in question and to the independent authority responsible for safeguarding the well-being of the juvenile.

53. A juvenile who is suffering from mental illness should be treated in a specialized institution under independent medical management. Steps should be taken, by arrangement with appropriate agencies, to ensure any necessary continuation of mental health care after release.

54. Juvenile detention facilities should adopt specialized drug abuse prevention and rehabilitation programmes administered by qualified personnel. These programmes should be adapted to the age, sex and other requirements of the juveniles concerned, and detoxification facilities and services staffed by trained personnel should be available to drug- or alcohol-dependent juveniles.

55. Medicines should be administered only for necessary treatment on medical grounds and, when possible, after having obtained the informed consent of the juvenile concerned. In particular, they must not be administered with a view to eliciting information or a confession, as a punishment or as a means of restraint. Juveniles shall never be testees in the experimental use of drugs and treatment. The administration of any drug should always be authorized and carried out by qualified medical personnel.

I. Notification of illness, injury and death

56. The family or guardian of a juvenile and any other person designated by the juvenile have the right to be informed of the state of health of the juvenile on request and in the event of any important changes in the health of the juvenile. The director of the detention facility should notify immediately the family or guardian of the juvenile concerned, or other designated person, in case of death, illness requiring transfer of the juvenile to an outside medical facility, or a condition requiring clinical care within the detention facility for more than 48 hours. Notification should also be given to the consular authorities of the State of which a foreign juvenile is a citizen.

57. Upon the death of a juvenile during the period of deprivation of liberty, the nearest relative should have the right to inspect the death certificate, see the body and determine the method of disposal of the body. Upon the death of a juvenile in detention, there should be an independent inquiry into the causes of death, the report of which should be made accessible to the nearest relative. This inquiry should also be made when the death of a juvenile occurs within six months from the date of his or her release from the detention facility and there is reason to believe that the death is related to the period of detention.

58. A juvenile should be informed at the earliest possible time of the death, serious illness or injury of any immediate family member and should be provided with the opportunity to attend the funeral of the deceased or go to the bedside of a critically ill relative.

J. Contacts with the wider community

59. Every means should be provided to ensure that juveniles have adequate communication with the outside world, which is an integral part of the right to fair and humane treatment and is essential to the preparation of juveniles for their return to society. Juveniles should be allowed to communicate with their families, friends and other persons or representatives of reputable outside organizations, to leave detention facilities for a visit to their home and family and to receive special permission to leave the detention facility for educational, vocational or other important reasons. Should the juvenile be serving a sentence, the time spent outside a detention facility should be counted as part of the period of sentence.

60. Every juvenile should have the right to receive regular and frequent visits, in principle once a week and not less than once a month, in circumstances that respect the need of the juvenile for privacy, contact and unrestricted communication with the family and the defence counsel.

61. Every juvenile should have the right to communicate in writing or by telephone at least twice a week with the person of his or her choice, unless legally restricted, and should be assisted as necessary in order effectively to enjoy this right. Every juvenile should have the right to receive correspondence.

62. Juveniles should have the opportunity to keep themselves informed regularly of the news by reading newspapers, periodicals and other publications, through access to radio and television programmes and motion pictures, and through the visits of the representatives of any lawful club or organization in which the juvenile is interested.

K. Limitations of physical restraint and the use of force

63. Recourse to instruments of restraint and to force for any purpose should be prohibited, except as set forth in rule 64 below.

64. Instruments of restraint and force can only be used in exceptional cases, where all other control methods have been exhausted and failed, and only as explicitly authorized and specified by law and regulation. They should not cause humiliation or degradation, and should be used restrictively and only for the shortest possible period of time. By order of the director of the administration, such instruments might be resorted to in order to prevent the juvenile from inflicting self-injury, injuries to others or serious destruction of property. In such instances, the director should at once consult medical and other relevant personnel and report to the higher administrative authority.

65. The carrying and use of weapons by personnel should be prohibited in any facility where juveniles are detained.

L. Disciplinary procedures

66. Any disciplinary measures and procedures should maintain the interest of safety and an ordered community life and should be consistent with the upholding of the inherent dignity of the juvenile and the fundamental objective of institutional care, namely, instilling a sense of justice, self-respect and respect for the basic rights of every person.

67. All disciplinary measures constituting cruel, inhuman or degrading treatment shall be strictly prohibited, including corporal punishment, placement in a dark cell, closed or solitary confinement or any other punishment that may compromise the physical or mental health of the juvenile concerned. The reduction of diet and the restriction or denial of contact with family members should be prohibited for any purpose. Labour should always be viewed as an educational tool and a means of promoting the self-respect of the juvenile in preparing him or her for return to the community and should not be imposed as a disciplinary sanction. No juvenile should be sanctioned more than once for the same disciplinary infraction. Collective sanctions should be prohibited.

68. Legislation or regulations adopted by the competent administrative authority should establish norms concerning the following, taking full account of the fundamental characteristics, needs and rights of juveniles:

(a) Conduct constituting a disciplinary offence;

(b) Type and duration of disciplinary sanctions that may be inflicted;

(c) The authority competent to impose such sanctions;

(d) The authority competent to consider appeals.

69. A report of misconduct should be presented promptly to the competent authority, which should decide on it without undue delay. The competent authority should conduct a thorough examination of the case.

70. No juvenile should be disciplinarily sanctioned except in strict accordance with the terms of the law and regulations in force. No juvenile should be sanctioned unless he or she has been informed of the alleged infraction in a manner appropriate to the full understanding of the juvenile, and given a proper opportunity of presenting his or her defence, including the right of appeal to a competent impartial authority. Complete records should be kept of all disciplinary proceedings.

71. No juveniles should be responsible for disciplinary functions except in the supervision of specified social, educational or sports activities or in self-government programmes.

M. Inspection and complaint

72. Qualified inspectors or an equivalent duly constituted authority not belonging to the administration of the facility should be empowered to conduct inspections on a regular basis and to undertake unannounced inspections on their own initiative, and should enjoy full guarantees of independence in the exercise of this function. Inspectors should have unrestricted access to all persons employed by or working in any facility where juveniles are or may be deprived of their liberty, to all juveniles and to all records of such facilities.

73. Qualified medical officers attached to the inspecting authority or the public health service should participate in the inspections, evaluating compliance with the rules concerning the physical environment, hygiene, accommodation, food, exercise and medical services, as well as any other aspect or conditions of institutional life that affect the physical and mental health of juveniles. Every juvenile should have the right to talk in confidence to any inspecting officer.

74. After completing the inspection, the inspector should be required to submit a report on the findings. The report should include an evaluation of the compliance of the detention facilities with the present rules and relevant provisions of national law, and recommendations regarding any steps considered necessary to ensure compliance with them. Any facts discovered by an inspector that appear to indicate that a violation of legal provisions concerning the rights of juveniles or the operation of a juvenile detention facility has occurred should be communicated to the competent authorities for investigation and prosecution.

75. Every juvenile should have the opportunity of making requests or complaints to the director of the detention facility and to his or her authorized representative.

76. Every juvenile should have the right to make a request or complaint, without censorship as to substance, to the central administration, the judicial authority or other proper authorities through approved channels, and to be informed of the response without delay.

77. Efforts should be made to establish an independent office (ombudsman) to receive and investigate complaints made by juveniles deprived of their liberty and to assist in the achievement of equitable settlements.

78. Every juvenile should have the right to request assistance from family members, legal counsellors, humanitarian groups or others where possible, in order to make a complaint. Illiterate juveniles should be provided with assistance should they need to use the services of public or private agencies and organizations which provide legal counsel or which are competent to receive complaints.

N. Return to the community

79. All juveniles should benefit from arrangements designed to assist them in returning to society, family life, education or employment after release. Procedures, including early release, and special courses should be devised to this end.

80. Competent authorities should provide or ensure services to assist juveniles in re-establishing themselves in society and to lessen prejudice against such juveniles. These services should ensure, to the extent possible, that the juvenile is provided with suitable residence, employment, clothing, and sufficient means to maintain himself or herself upon release in order to facilitate successful reintegration. The representatives of agencies providing such services should be consulted and should have access to juveniles while detained, with a view to assisting them in their return to the community.

V. Personnel

81. Personnel should be qualified and include a sufficient number of specialists such as educators, vocational instructors, counsellors, social workers, psychiatrists and psychologists. These and other specialist staff should normally be employed on a permanent basis. This should not preclude part-time or volunteer workers when the level of support and training they can provide is appropriate and beneficial. Detention facilities should make use of all remedial, educational, moral, spiritual, and other resources and forms of assistance that are appropriate and available in the community, according to the individual needs and problems of detained juveniles.

82. The administration should provide for the careful selection and recruitment of every grade and type of personnel, since the proper management of detention facilities depends on their integrity, humanity, ability and professional capacity to deal with juveniles, as well as personal suitability for the work.

83. To secure the foregoing ends, personnel should be appointed as professional officers with adequate remuneration to attract and retain suitable women and men. The personnel of juvenile detention facilities should be continually encouraged to fulfil their duties and obligations in a humane, committed, professional, fair and efficient manner, to conduct themselves at all times in such a way as to deserve and gain the respect of the juveniles, and to provide juveniles with a positive role model and perspective.

84. The administration should introduce forms of organization and management that facilitate communications between different categories of staff in each detention facility so as to enhance cooperation between the various services engaged in the care of juveniles, as well as between staff and the administration, with a view to ensuring that staff directly in contact with juveniles are able to function in conditions favourable to the efficient fulfilment of their duties.

85. The personnel should receive such training as will enable them to carry out their responsibilities effectively, in particular training in child psychology, child welfare and international standards and norms of human rights and the rights of the child, including the present rules. The personnel should maintain and improve their knowledge and professional capacity by attending courses of in-service training, to be organized at suitable intervals throughout their career.

86. The director of a facility should be adequately qualified for his or her task, with administrative ability and suitable training and experience, and should carry out his or her duties on a full-time basis.

87. In the performance of their duties, personnel of detention facilities should respect and protect the human dignity and fundamental human rights of all juveniles, in particular, as follows:

(a) No member of the detention facility or institutional personnel may inflict, instigate or tolerate any act of torture or any form of harsh, cruel, inhuman or degrading treatment, punishment, correction or discipline under any pretext or circumstance whatsoever;

(b) All personnel should rigorously oppose and combat any act of corruption, reporting it without delay to the competent authorities;

(c) All personnel should respect the present Rules. Personnel who have reason to believe that a serious violation of the present Rules has occurred or is about to occur should report the matter to their superior authorities or organs vested with reviewing or remedial power;

(d) All personnel should ensure the full protection of the physical and mental health of juveniles, including protection from physical, sexual and emotional abuse and exploitation, and should take immediate action to secure medical attention whenever required;

(e) All personnel should respect the right of the juvenile to privacy, and in particular should safeguard all confidential matters concerning juveniles or their families learned as a result of their professional capacity;

(f) All personnel should seek to minimize any differences between life inside and outside the detention facility which tend to lessen due respect for the dignity of juveniles as human beings.

06.43 ELDERLY PERSONS

46/91. Implementation of the International Plan of Action on Ageing and Related Activities

Committee: 3
Vote: Adopted without a vote
Ref.: 48/98, 47/86, 45/106, 44/67, 43/93, 42/51, 40/30

The General Assembly,

Recalling Economic and Social Council resolution 1989/50 of 24 May 1989, in which the Council endorsed a draft programme of United Nations activities relating to the tenth anniversary of the adoption of the International Plan of Action on Ageing, in 1992,

Pursuant to its resolution 45/106 of 14 December 1990, in which it endorsed the action programme on ageing for 1992 and beyond as outlined in the report of the Secretary-General on the question of ageing, invited Member States, the United Nations and non-governmental organizations to consider innovative and effective ways of cooperating on the selection of targets in the field of ageing during 1991 and 1992, and urged Member States, the organs, organizations and bodies of the United Nations system and intergovernmental and non-governmental organizations concerned to participate in the action programme on ageing for 1992 and beyond, especially in selecting targets in the field of ageing, in organizing community-wide activities and in launching an information and fund-raising campaign to celebrate the tenth anniversary of the adoption of the International Plan of Action on Ageing at the local, national, regional and global levels,

Recalling that in resolution 45/106 it endorsed also the convening of an *ad hoc* working group of the Commission for Social Development at its thirty-second session to monitor the activities for the tenth anniversary, especially the launching of a global information campaign, and the selection of targets that might form the basis of the third review and appraisal of the International Plan of Action on Ageing to be made by the Commission at its thirty-third session, in 1993, and recommended that the Commission should give consideration to the desirability of convening, subject to the availability of funds, regional and sectoral meetings on the selection of targets in the field of ageing during 1991 and 1992 and global consultations in 1993 and 1997,

Recalling also that in resolution 45/106, it recognized the complexity and rapidity of the ageing of the world's population and the need to have a common basis and frame of reference for the protection and promotion of the rights of the elderly, including the contribution that the elderly can and should make to society,

Aware of the plight of the elderly in developing countries, particularly the least developed among them, as well as those in difficult circumstances, such as refugees, migrant workers and victims of conflict,

Recalling Economic and Social Council resolution 1751 (LIV) of 16 May 1973 on the aged and social security,

1. *Recommends* that the United Nations define, on the basis of the recommendations of a small expert group meeting to be held in 1992 within existing resources, targets on ageing to provide a pragmatic focus for the broad and ideal goals of the International Plan of Action on Ageing, and issue them as "Targets on ageing: programme recommendations at the national level for the year 2001";

2. *Urges* Member States to identify their specific national targets on ageing for the year 2001, on the basis of the proposed targets on ageing;

3. *Invites* the Centre for Social Development and Humanitarian Affairs of the Secretariat to develop, in consultation with United Nations organizations and bodies and international non-governmental organizations, a set of suggested global targets designed to support implementation of the national targets on ageing;

4. *Decides* to devote four plenary meetings, that is, two working days, at its forty-seventh session to an international conference on ageing to consolidate a set of targets on ageing for the year 2001 and to celebrate on an appropriate global scale the tenth anniversary of the adoption of the International Plan of Action on Ageing;

5. *Urges* the United Nations to give special attention to implementing the action programme on ageing for 1992 and beyond;

6. *Calls upon* the Secretary-General to give all possible support, in the form of both regular and extrabudgetary resources, to the Ageing Unit of the Centre for Social Development and Humanitarian Affairs, to enable it to fulfil its mandate as lead agency for the action programme on ageing;

7. *Requests* the Secretary-General to designate the Director-General of the United Nations Office at Vienna as coordinator for the preparations for the tenth anniversary of the adoption of the International Plan of Action on Ageing and for the implementation of the action programme on ageing for 1992 and beyond;

8. *Invites* the Secretary-General to explore the feasibility of appointing an interregional adviser on ageing to assist developing countries in expanding their ability to respond effectively to the ageing of their populations;

9. *Invites* the United Nations to examine the feasibility of launching a service composed of experts who are elderly, modelled on the United Nations Volunteers;

10. *Urges* the United Nations Postal Administration, as called upon in General Assembly resolution 44/67 of 8 December 1989, to issue a stamp to mark the tenth anniversary of the adoption of the International Plan of Action on Ageing;

11. *Also urges* the United Nations Postal Administration to consider, on an exceptional basis, issuing a medal on ageing bearing the emblem of the World Assembly on Ageing to mark activities planned for the decade 1992-2001;

12. *Decides* to launch a global information campaign on the action programme on ageing for 1992 and beyond, and welcomes the cooperation of the Department of Public Information of the Secretariat and the Centre for Social Development and Humanitarian Affairs and other United Nations bodies, specialized agencies and non-governmental organizations in this endeavour;

13. *Recommends* that the United Nations provide further advisory services to countries in the process of development, change and transition, at their request, to ensure that the issue of ageing remains an important part of their social development programmes;

14. *Adopts* the United Nations Principles for Older Persons, based on the International Plan of Action on Ageing, annexed to the present resolution.

74th plenary meeting
16 December 1991

Annex

United Nations Principles for Older Persons[1]
To Add Life to the Years that Have Been Added to Life

The General Assembly,

Appreciating the contribution that older persons make to their societies,

Recognizing that, in the Charter of the United Nations, the peoples of the United Nations declare, *inter alia*, their determination to reaffirm

1 Based on the *International Plan of Action on Aging;* see *Report of the World Assembly on Aging, Vienna, 26 July - 6 August 1982* (United Nations Publications, Sales No.E.82.I.16), chap. VI, sect. A.

faith in fundamental human rights, in the dignity and worth of the human person, in the equal rights of men and women and of nations large and small and to promote social progress and better standards of life in larger freedom,

Noting the elaboration of those rights in the Universal Declaration of Human Rights, the International Covenant on Economic, Social and Cultural Rights and the International Covenant on Civil and Political Rights and other declarations to ensure the application of universal standards to particular groups,

In pursuance of the International Plan of Action on Ageing, adopted by the World Assembly on Ageing and endorsed by the General Assembly in its resolution 37/51 of 3 December 1982,

Appreciating the tremendous diversity in the situation of older persons, not only between countries but within countries and between individuals, which requires a variety of policy responses,

Aware that in all countries, individuals are reaching an advanced age in greater numbers and in better health than ever before,

Aware of the scientific research disproving many stereotypes about inevitable and irreversible declines with age,

Convinced that in a world characterized by an increasing number and proportion of older persons, opportunities must be provided for willing and capable older persons to participate in and contribute to the ongoing activities of society,

Mindful that the strains on family life in both developed and developing countries require support for those providing care to frail older persons,

Bearing in mind the standards already set by the International Plan of Action on Ageing and the conventions, recommendations and resolutions of the International Labour Organisation, the World Health Organization and other United Nations entities,

Encourages Governments to incorporate the following principles into their national programmes whenever possible:

Independence

1. Older persons should have access to adequate food, water, shelter, clothing and health care through the provision of income, family and community support and self-help.

2. Older persons should have the opportunity to work or to have access to other income-generating opportunities.

3. Older persons should be able to participate in determining when and at what pace withdrawal from the labour force takes place.

4. Older persons should have access to appropriate educational and training programmes.

5. Older persons should be able to live in environments that are safe and adaptable to personal preferences and changing capacities.

6. Older persons should be able to reside at home for as long as possible.

Participation

7. Older persons should remain integrated in society, participate actively in the formulation and implementation of policies that directly affect their well-being and share their knowledge and skills with younger generations.

8. Older persons should be able to seek and develop opportunities for service to the community and to serve as volunteers in positions appropriate to their interests and capabilities.

9. Older persons should be able to form movements or associations of older persons.

Care

10. Older persons should benefit from family and community care and protection in accordance with each society's system of cultural values.

11. Older persons should have access to health care to help them to maintain or regain the optimum level of physical, mental and emotional well-being and to prevent or delay the onset of illness.

12. Older persons should have access to social and legal services to enhance their autonomy, protection and care.

13. Older persons should be able to utilize appropriate levels of institutional care providing protection, rehabilitation and social and mental stimulation in a humane and secure environment.

14. Older persons should be able to enjoy human rights and fundamental freedoms when residing in any shelter, care or treatment facility, including full respect for their dignity, beliefs, needs and privacy and for the right to make decisions about their care and the quality of their lives.

Self-fulfilment

15. Older persons should be able to pursue opportunities for the full development of their potential.

16. Older persons should have access to the educational, cultural, spiritual and recreational resources of society.

Dignity

17. Older persons should be able to live in dignity and security and be free of exploitation and physical or mental abuse.

18. Older persons should be treated fairly regardless of age, gender, racial or ethnic background, disability or other status, and be valued independently of their economic contribution.

06.44 DISABLED PERSONS

2856 (XXVI). Declaration on the Rights of Mentally Retarded Persons

Committee: 3
Vote: 110 - 0 - 9

The General Assembly,

Mindful of the pledge of the States Members of the United Nations under the Charter to take joint and separate action in cooperation with the Organization to promote higher standards of living, full employment and conditions of economic and social progress and development,

Reaffirming faith in human rights and fundamental freedoms and in the principles of peace, of the dignity and worth of the human person and of social justice proclaimed in the Charter,

Recalling the principles of the Universal Declaration of Human Rights, the International Covenants on Human Rights, the Declaration of the Rights of the Child and the standards already set for social progress in the constitutions, conventions, recommendations and resolutions of the International Labour Organisation, the United Nations Educational, Scientific and Cultural Organization, the World Health Organization, the United Nations Children's Fund and other organizations concerned,

Emphasizing that the Declaration on Social Progress and Development has proclaimed the necessity of protecting the rights and assuring the welfare and rehabilitation of the physically and mentally disadvantaged,

Bearing in mind the necessity of assisting mentally retarded persons to develop their abilities in various fields of activities and of promoting their integration as far as possible in normal life,

Aware that certain countries, at their present stage of development, can devote only limited efforts to this end,

Proclaims this Declaration on the Rights of Mentally Retarded Persons and calls for national and international action to ensure that it will be used as a common basis and frame of reference for the protection of these rights:

1. The mentally retarded person has, to the maximum degree of feasibility, the same rights as other human beings.

2. The mentally retarded person has a right to proper medical care and physical therapy and to such education, training, rehabilitation and guidance as will enable him to develop his ability and maximum potential.

3. The mentally retarded person has a right to economic security and to a decent standard of living. He has a right to perform pro-

ductive work or to engage in any other meaningful occupation to the fullest possible extent of his capabilities.

4. Whenever possible, the mentally retarded person should live with his own family or with foster parents and participate in different forms of community life. The family with which he lives should receive assistance. If care in an institution becomes necessary, it should be provided in surroundings and other circumstances as close as possible to those of normal life.

5. The mentally retarded person has a right to a qualified guardian when this is required to protect his personal well-being and interests.

6. The mentally retarded person has a right to protection from exploitation, abuse and degrading treatment. If prosecuted for any offence, he shall have a right to due process of law with full recognition being given to his degree of mental responsibility.

7. Whenever mentally retarded persons are unable, because of the severity of their handicap, to exercise all their rights in a meaningful way or it should become necessary to restrict or deny some or all of these rights, the procedure used for that restriction or denial of rights must contain proper legal safeguards against every form of abuse. This procedure must be based on an evaluation of the social capability of the mentally retarded person by qualified experts and must be subject to periodic review and to the right of appeal to higher authorities.

2027th plenary meeting
20 December 1971

3447 (XXX). Declaration on the Rights of Disabled Persons

Committee: 3
Vote: Adopted without a vote
Ref.: 31/82

The General Assembly,

Mindful of the pledge made by Member States, under the Charter of the United Nations, to take joint and separate action in cooperation with the Organization to promote higher standards of living, full employment and conditions of economic and social progress and development,

Reaffirming its faith in human rights and fundamental freedoms and in the principles of peace, of the dignity and worth of the human person and of social justice proclaimed in the Charter,

Recalling the principles of the Universal Declaration of Human Rights,[1] the International Covenants on Human Rights,[2] the Declaration of the Rights of the Child[3] and the Declaration on the Rights of Mentally Retarded Persons,[4] as well as the standards already set for social progress in the constitutions, conventions, recommendations and resolutions of the International Labour Organisation, the United Nations Educational, Scientific and Cultural Organization, the World Health Organization, the United Nations Children's Fund and other organizations concerned,

Recalling also Economic and Social Council resolution 1921 (LVIII) of 6 May 1975 on the prevention of disability and the rehabilitation of disabled persons,

Emphasizing that the Declaration on Social Progress and Development[5] has proclaimed the necessity of protecting the rights and assuring the welfare and rehabilitation of the physically and mentally disadvantaged,

Bearing in mind the necessity of preventing physical and mental disabilities and of assisting disabled persons to develop their abilities in the most varied fields of activities and of promoting their integration as far as possible in normal life,

Aware that certain countries, at their present stage of development, can devote only limited efforts to this end,

Proclaims this Declaration on the Rights of Disabled Persons and calls for national and international action to ensure that it will be used as a common basis and frame of reference for the protection of these rights:

1. The term "disabled person" means any person unable to ensure by himself or herself, wholly or partly, the necessities of a normal individual and/or social life, as a result of a deficiency, either congenital or not, in his or her physical or mental capabilities.

2. Disabled persons shall enjoy all the rights set forth in this Declaration. These rights shall be granted to all disabled persons without any exception whatsoever and without distinction or discrimination on the basis of race, colour, sex, language, religion, political or other opinions, national or social origin state of wealth, birth or any other situation applying either to the disabled person himself or herself or to his or her family.

3. Disabled persons have the inherent right to respect for their human dignity. Disabled persons, whatever the origin, nature and seriousness of their handicaps and disabilities, have the same fundamental rights as their fellow-citizens of the same age, which implies first and foremost the right to enjoy a decent life, as normal and full as possible.

4. Disabled persons have the same civil and political rights as other human beings; paragraph 7 of the Declaration on the Rights of Mentally Retarded Persons applies to any possible limitation or suppression of those rights for mentally disabled persons.

5. Disabled persons are entitled to the measures designed to enable them to become as self-reliant as possible.

6. Disabled persons have the right to medical, psychological and functional treatment, including prosthetic and orthetic appliances, to medical and social rehabilitation, education, vocational training and rehabilitation, aid, counselling, placement services and other services which will enable them to develop their capabilities and skills to the maximum and will hasten the process of their social integration or reintegration.

7. Disabled persons have the right to economic and social security and to a decent level of living. They have the right, according to their capabilities, to secure and retain employment or to engage in a useful, productive and remunerative occupation and to join trade unions.

8. Disabled persons are entitled to have their special needs taken into consideration at all stages of economic and social planning.

9. Disabled persons have the right to live with their families or with foster parents and to participate in all social, creative or recreational activities. No disabled person shall be subjected, as far as his or her residence is concerned, to differential treatment other than that required by his or her condition or by the improvement which he or she may derive therefrom. If the stay of a disabled person in a specialized establishment is indispensable, the environment and living conditions therein shall be as close as possible to those of the normal life of a person of his or her age.

10. Disabled persons shall be protected against all exploitation, all regulations and all treatment of a discriminatory, abusive or degrading nature.

11. Disabled persons shall be able to avail themselves of qualified legal aid when such aid proves indispensable for the protection of their persons and property. If judicial proceedings are instituted against them, the legal procedure applied shall take their physical and mental condition fully into account.

12. Organizations of disabled persons may be usefully consulted in all matters regarding the rights of disabled persons.

13. Disabled persons, their families and communities shall be fully informed, by all appropriate means, of the rights contained in this Declaration.

2433rd plenary meeting
9 December 1975

---

1 Resolution 217 A (III).
2 Resolution 2200 A (XXI), annex.
3 Resolution 1386 (XIV).
4 Resolution 2856 (XXVI).
5 Resolution 2542 (XXIV).

37/52. World Programme of Action Concerning Disabled Persons

Committee: 3
Ref.: 50/144, 48/99, 47/88, 46/96, 45/91, 44/70, 43/98, 42/58, 41/106, 40/31, 38/28, 37/53

The General Assembly,

Recalling its resolutions 31/123 of 16 December 1976 by which it proclaimed the year 1981 International Year of Disabled Persons, 32/133 of 16 December 1977 by which it established the Advisory Committee for the International Year of Disabled Persons, 33/170 of 20 December 1978, 34/154 of 17 December 1979, in which it, *inter alia*, decided to expand the theme of the International Year of Disabled Persons to "full participation and equality", 35/133 of 11 December 1980 and 36/77 of 8 December 1981,

Deeply concerned that no less than five hundred million persons are estimated to suffer from disability of one form or another, of whom four hundred million are estimated to be in developing countries,

Reiterating the continuing need to promote the realization of the right of disabled persons to participate fully in the social life and development of their societies and to enjoy living conditions equal to those of other citizens, as well as to share equally in improvements in living conditions resulting from social and economic development,

Recognizing that the International Year of Disabled Persons contributed to the acceptance by the community of the right of disabled persons to participate fully in the social life and development of their societies and to enjoy living conditions equal to those of their fellow citizens,

Convinced that the International Year of Disabled Persons gave a genuine and meaningful impetus to activities related to equalization of opportunities for disabled persons, as well as prevention and rehabilitation at all levels,

Expressing its satisfaction with the efforts of Member States during the International Year of Disabled Persons to improve the conditions and well-being of disabled persons and their willingness to involve disabled persons and their organizations in all matters of concern to them,

Also expressing its satisfaction with the initiatives taken by the specialized agencies and other organizations of the United Nations system, non-governmental organizations and, in particular, organizations of disabled persons,

Taking note of the emergence of organizations of disabled persons in all parts of the world and their positive influence on the image and condition of persons with a disability,

Having considered the Vienna Affirmative Action Plan adopted by the World Symposium of Experts on Technical Cooperation among Developing Countries and Technical Assistance in Disability Prevention and Rehabilitation,[1]

Expressing its appreciation to the Advisory Committee for the International Year of Disabled Persons for the work it has done,

Having considered the report of the Advisory Committee for the International Year of Disabled Persons on its fourth session and its proposal for a World Programme of Action concerning Disabled Persons,[2]

Desirous of ensuring an effective follow-up to the International Year of Disabled Persons and aware that if this is to be achieved Member States, organs, organizations and agencies of the United Nations system, non-governmental organizations and organizations of disabled persons must therefore be encouraged to continue the activities already undertaken and to initiate new programmes and activities,

Stressing that the primary responsibility for promoting effective measures for prevention of disability, rehabilitation and the realization of the goals of "full participation" of disabled persons in social life and development and of "equality" rests with individual countries and that international action should be directed to assist and support national efforts in this regard,

1. *Adopts* the World Programme of Action concerning Disabled Persons, as set forth in recommendation 1 (IV) of the Advisory Committee for the International Year of Disabled Persons;[3]

2. *Calls upon* all Member States, all non-governmental organizations concerned and organizations of disabled persons and, through a reallocation of existing resources, calls also upon all organs, organizations and agencies of the United Nations system to ensure early implementation of the World Programme of Action concerning Disabled persons;

3. *Decides* to evaluate at its forty-second session, with the help of the Secretary-General, the implementation of the World Programme of Action concerning Disabled Persons.

90th plenary meeting
3 December 1982

[1] IYDP/SYMP/L.2/Rev.1.

[2] A/37/351/Add.1 and Add.1/Corr.1, annex.

[3] *Ibid.*, sect. VII.

46/119. The Protection of Persons with Mental Illness and the Improvement of Mental Health Care

Committee: 3
Vote: Adopted without a vote

The General Assembly,

Mindful of the provisions of the Universal Declaration of Human Rights, the International Covenant on Civil and Political Rights, the International Covenant on Economic, Social and Cultural Rights and other relevant instruments, such as the Declaration on the Rights of Disabled Persons and the Body of Principles for the Protection of All Persons under Any Form of Detention or Imprisonment,

Recalling its resolution 33/53 of 14 December 1978, in which it requested the Commission on Human Rights to urge the Subcommission on Prevention of Discrimination and Protection of Minorities to undertake, as a matter of priority, a study of the question of the protection of those detained on the grounds of mental ill-health, with a view to formulating guidelines,

Recalling also its resolution 45/92 of 14 December 1990, in which it welcomed the progress made by the working group of the Commission on Human Rights in elaborating a draft body of principles for the protection of persons with mental illness and for the improvement of mental health care on the basis of a draft submitted to the Commission by the Subcommission on Prevention of Discrimination and Protection of Minorities,

Taking note of Commission on Human Rights resolution 1991/46 of 5 March 1991, in which the Commission endorsed the draft body of principles that had been submitted to it by the working group and decided to transmit it, as well as the report of the working group, to the General Assembly, through the Economic and Social Council,

Taking note also of Economic and Social Council resolution 1991/29 of 31 May 1991, in which the Council decided to submit the draft body of principles and the report of the working group to the General Assembly,

Taking note further of the recommendations of the Commission on Human Rights in its resolution 1991/46 and of the Economic and Social Council in its resolution 1991/29 that, on the adoption by the General Assembly of the draft body of principles, the full text thereof should be given the widest possible dissemination and that the introduction to the body of principles should at the same time be published as an accompanying document for the benefit of Governments and the public at large,

Taking note of the note by the Secretary-General, the annex to which contains the draft body of principles and the introduction to the body of principles,

1. *Adopts* the Principles for the Protection of Persons with Mental Illness and for the Improvement of Mental Health Care, the text of which is contained in the annex to the present resolution;

2. *Requests* the Secretary-General to include the text of the Principles, together with the introduction, in the next edition of the publication entitled *Human Rights: A Compilation of International Instruments*;

3. *Requests* the Secretary-General to give the Principles the widest possible dissemination and to ensure that the introduction is published at the same time as an accompanying document for the benefit of Governments and the public at large.

75th plenary meeting
17 December 1991

Annex

Principles for the Protection of Persons with Mental Illness and for the Improvement of Mental Health Care

Application

The present Principles shall be applied without discrimination on any grounds, such as disability, race, colour, sex, language, religion, political or other opinion, national, ethnic or social origin, legal or social status, age, property or birth.

Definitions

In the present Principles:

(*a*) "Counsel" means a legal or other qualified representative;

(*b*) "Independent authority" means a competent and independent authority prescribed by domestic law;

(*c*) "Mental health care" includes analysis and diagnosis of a person's mental condition, and treatment, care and rehabilitation for a mental illness or suspected mental illness;

(*d*) "Mental health facility" means any establishment, or any unit of an establishment, which as its primary function provides mental health care;

(*e*) "Mental health practitioner" means a medical doctor, clinical psychologist, nurse, social worker or other appropriately trained and qualified person with specific skills relevant to mental health care;

(*f*) "Patient" means a person receiving mental health care and includes all persons who are admitted to a mental health facility;

(*g*) "Personal representative" means a person charged by law with the duty of representing a patient's interests in any specified respect or of exercising specified rights on the patient's behalf, and includes the parent or legal guardian of a minor unless otherwise provided by domestic law;

(*h*) "The review body" means the body established in accordance with principle 17 to review the involuntary admission or retention of a patient in a mental health facility.

General limitation clause

The exercise of the rights set forth in the present Principles may be subject only to such limitations as are prescribed by law and are necessary to protect the health or safety of the person concerned or of others, or otherwise to protect public safety, order, health or morals or the fundamental rights and freedoms of others.

Principle 1

Fundamental freedoms and basic rights

1. All persons have the right to the best available mental health care, which shall be part of the health and social care system.

2. All persons with a mental illness, or who are being treated as such persons, shall be treated with humanity and respect for the inherent dignity of the human person.

3. All persons with a mental illness, or who are being treated as such persons, have the right to protection from economic, sexual and other forms of exploitation, physical or other abuse and degrading treatment.

4. There shall be no discrimination on the grounds of mental illness. "Discrimination" means any distinction, exclusion or preference that has the effect of nullifying or impairing equal enjoyment of rights. Special measures solely to protect the rights, or secure the advancement, of persons with mental illness shall not be deemed to be discriminatory. Discrimination does not include any distinction, exclusion or preference undertaken in accordance with the provisions of the present Principles and necessary to protect the human rights of a person with a mental illness or of other individuals.

5. Every person with a mental illness shall have the right to exercise all civil, political, economic, social and cultural rights as recognized in the Universal Declaration of Human Rights, the International Covenant on Economic, Social and Cultural Rights, the International Covenant on Civil and Political Rights and in other relevant instruments, such as the Declaration on the Rights of Disabled Persons and the Body of Principles for the Protection of All Persons under Any Form of Detention or Imprisonment.

6. Any decision that, by reason of his or her mental illness, a person lacks legal capacity, and any decision that, in consequence of such incapacity, a personal representative shall be appointed, shall be made only after a fair hearing by an independent and impartial tribunal established by domestic law. The person whose capacity is at issue shall be entitled to be represented by a counsel. If the person whose capacity is at issue does not himself or herself secure such representation, it shall be made available without payment by that person to the extent that he or she does not have sufficient means to pay for it. The counsel shall not in the same proceedings represent a mental health facility or its personnel and shall not also represent a member of the family of the person whose capacity is at issue unless the tribunal is satisfied that there is no conflict of interest. Decisions regarding capacity and the need for a personal representative shall be reviewed at reasonable intervals prescribed by domestic law. The person whose capacity is at issue, his or her personal representative, if any, and any other interested person shall have the right to appeal to a higher court against any such decision.

7. Where a court or other competent tribunal finds that a person with mental illness is unable to manage his or her own affairs, measures shall be taken, so far as is necessary and appropriate to that person's condition, to ensure the protection of his or her interests.

Principle 2

Protection of minors

Special care should be given within the purposes of the Principles and within the context of domestic law relating to the protection of minors to protect the rights of minors, including, if necessary, the appointment of a personal representative other than a family member.

Principle 3

Life in the community

Every person with a mental illness shall have the right to live and work, to the extent possible, in the community.

Principle 4

Determination of mental illness

1. A determination that a person has a mental illness shall be made in accordance with internationally accepted medical standards.

2. A determination of mental illness shall never be made on the basis of political, economic or social status, or membership in a cultural, racial or religious group, or for any other reason not directly relevant to mental health status.

3. Family or professional conflict, or non-conformity with moral, social, cultural or political values or religious beliefs prevailing in a person's community, shall never be a determining factor in the diagnosis of mental illness.

4. A background of past treatment or hospitalization as a patient shall not of itself justify any present or future determination of mental illness.

5. No person or authority shall classify a person as having, or otherwise indicate that a person has, a mental illness except for purposes directly relating to mental illness or the consequences of mental illness.

Principle 5

Medical examination

No person shall be compelled to undergo medical examination with a view to determining whether or not he or she has a mental illness except in accordance with a procedure authorized by domestic law.

Principle 6

Confidentiality

The right of confidentiality of information concerning all persons to whom the present Principles apply shall be respected.

Principle 7

Role of community and culture

1. Every patient shall have the right to be treated and cared for, as far as possible, in the community in which he or she lives.

2. Where treatment takes place in a mental health facility, a patient shall have the right, whenever possible, to be treated near his or her home or the home of his or her relatives or friends and shall have the right to return to the community as soon as possible.

3. Every patient shall have the right to treatment suited to his or her cultural background.

Principle 8

Standards of care

1. Every patient shall have the right to receive such health and social care as is appropriate to his or her health needs, and is entitled to care and treatment in accordance with the same standards as other ill persons.

2. Every patient shall be protected from harm, including unjustified medication, abuse by other patients, staff or others or other acts causing mental distress or physical discomfort.

Principle 9

Treatment

1. Every patient shall have the right to be treated in the least restrictive environment and with the least restrictive or intrusive treatment appropriate to the patient's health needs and the need to protect the physical safety of others.

2. The treatment and care of every patient shall be based on an individually prescribed plan, discussed with the patient, reviewed regularly, revised as necessary and provided by qualified professional staff.

3. Mental health care shall always be provided in accordance with applicable standards of ethics for mental health practitioners, including internationally accepted standards such as the Principles of Medical Ethics relevant to the role of health personnel, particularly physicians, in the protection of prisoners and detainees against torture and other cruel, inhuman or degrading treatment or punishment, adopted by the United Nations General Assembly. Mental health knowledge and skills shall never be abused.

4. The treatment of every patient shall be directed towards preserving and enhancing personal autonomy.

Principle 10

Medication

1. Medication shall meet the best health needs of the patient, shall be given to a patient only for therapeutic or diagnostic purposes and shall never be administered as a punishment or for the convenience of others. Subject to the provisions of paragraph 15 of principle 11 below, mental health practitioners shall only administer medication of known or demonstrated efficacy.

2. All medication shall be prescribed by a mental health practitioner authorized by law and shall be recorded in the patient's records.

Principle 11

Consent to treatment

1. No treatment shall be given to a patient without his or her informed consent, except as provided for in paragraphs 6, 7, 8, 13 and 15 of the present principle.

2. Informed consent is consent obtained freely, without threats or improper inducements, after appropriate disclosure to the patient of adequate and understandable information in a form and language understood by the patient on:

(a) The diagnostic assessment;

(b) The purpose, method, likely duration and expected benefit of the proposed treatment;

(c) Alternative modes of treatment, including those less intrusive;

(d) Possible pain or discomfort, risks and side-effects of the proposed treatment.

3. A patient may request the presence of a person or persons of the patient's choosing during the procedure for granting consent.

4. A patient has the right to refuse or stop treatment, except as provided for in paragraphs 6, 7, 8, 13 and 15 of the present principle. The consequences of refusing or stopping treatment must be explained to the patient.

5. A patient shall never be invited or induced to waive the right to informed consent. If the patient should seek to do so, it shall be explained to the patient that the treatment cannot be given without informed consent.

6. Except as provided in paragraphs 7, 8, 12, 13, 14 and 15 of the present principle, a proposed plan of treatment may be given to a patient without a patient's informed consent if the following conditions are satisfied:

(a) The patient is, at the relevant time, held as an involuntary patient;

(b) An independent authority, having in its possession all relevant information, including the information specified in paragraph 2 of the present principle, is satisfied that, at the relevant time, the patient lacks the capacity to give or withhold informed consent to the proposed plan of treatment or, if domestic legislation so provides, that, having regard to the patient's own safety or the safety of others, the patient unreasonably withholds such consent;

(c) The independent authority is satisfied that the proposed plan of treatment is in the best interest of the patient's health needs.

7. Paragraph 6 above does not apply to a patient with a personal representative empowered by law to consent to treatment for the patient; but, except as provided in paragraphs 12, 13, 14 and 15 of the present principle, treatment may be given to such a patient without his or her informed consent if the personal representative, having been given the information described in paragraph 2 of the present principle, consents on the patient's behalf.

8. Except as provided in paragraphs 12, 13, 14 and 15 of the present principle, treatment may also be given to any patient without the patient's informed consent if a qualified mental health practitioner authorized by law determines that it is urgently necessary in order to prevent immediate or imminent harm to the patient or to other persons. Such treatment shall not be prolonged beyond the period that is strictly necessary for this purpose.

9. Where any treatment is authorized without the patient's informed consent, every effort shall nevertheless be made to inform the patient about the nature of the treatment and any possible alternatives and to involve the patient as far as practicable in the development of the treatment plan.

10. All treatment shall be immediately recorded in the patient's medical records, with an indication of whether involuntary or voluntary.

11. Physical restraint or involuntary seclusion of a patient shall not be employed except in accordance with the officially approved pro-

cedures of the mental health facility and only when it is the only means available to prevent immediate or imminent harm to the patient or others. It shall not be prolonged beyond the period which is strictly necessary for this purpose. All instances of physical restraint or involuntary seclusion, the reasons for them and their nature and extent shall be recorded in the patient's medical record. A patient who is restrained or secluded shall be kept under humane conditions and be under the care and close and regular supervision of qualified members of the staff. A personal representative, if any and if relevant, shall be given prompt notice of any physical restraint or involuntary seclusion of the patient.

12. Sterilization shall never be carried out as a treatment for mental illness.

13. A major medical or surgical procedure may be carried out on a person with mental illness only where it is permitted by domestic law, where it is considered that it would best serve the health needs of the patient and where the patient gives informed consent, except that, where the patient is unable to give informed consent, the procedure shall be authorized only after independent review.

14. Psychosurgery and other intrusive and irreversible treatments for mental illness shall never be carried out on a patient who is an involuntary patient in a mental health facility and, to the extent that domestic law permits them to be carried out, they may be carried out on any other patient only where the patient has given informed consent and an independent external body has satisfied itself that there is genuine informed consent and that the treatment best serves the health needs of the patient.

15. Clinical trials and experimental treatment shall never be carried out on any patient without informed consent, except that a patient who is unable to give informed consent may be admitted to a clinical trial or given experimental treatment, but only with the approval of a competent, independent review body specifically constituted for this purpose.

16. In the cases specified in paragraphs 6, 7, 8, 13, 14 and 15 of the present principle, the patient or his or her personal representative, or any interested person, shall have the right to appeal to a judicial or other independent authority concerning any treatment given to him or her.

Principle 12

Notice of rights

1. A patient in a mental health facility shall be informed as soon as possible after admission, in a form and a language which the patient understands, of all his or her rights in accordance with the present Principles and under domestic law, and the information shall include an explanation of those rights and how to exercise them.

2. If and for so long as a patient is unable to understand such information, the rights of the patient shall be communicated to the personal representative, if any and if appropriate, and to the person or persons best able to represent the patient's interests and willing to do so.

3. A patient who has the necessary capacity has the right to nominate a person who should be informed on his or her behalf, as well as a person to represent his or her interests to the authorities of the facility.

Principle 13

Rights and conditions in mental health facilities

1. Every patient in a mental health facility shall, in particular, have the right to full respect for his or her:

(a) Recognition everywhere as a person before the law;

(b) Privacy;

(c) Freedom of communication, which includes freedom to communicate with other persons in the facility; freedom to send and receive uncensored private communications; freedom to receive, in private, visits from a counsel or personal representative and, at all reasonable times, from other visitors; and freedom of access to postal and telephone services and to newspapers, radio and television;

(d) Freedom of religion or belief.

2. The environment and living conditions in mental health facilities shall be as close as possible to those of the normal life of persons of similar age and in particular shall include:

(a) Facilities for recreational and leisure activities;

(b) Facilities for education;

(c) Facilities to purchase or receive items for daily living, recreation and communication;

(d) Facilities, and encouragement to use such facilities, for a patient's engagement in active occupation suited to his or her social and cultural background, and for appropriate vocational rehabilitation measures to promote reintegration in the community. These measures should include vocational guidance, vocational training and placement services to enable patients to secure or retain employment in the community.

3. In no circumstances shall a patient be subject to forced labour. Within the limits compatible with the needs of the patient and with the requirements of institutional administration, a patient shall be able to choose the type of work he or she wishes to perform.

4. The labour of a patient in a mental health facility shall not be exploited. Every such patient shall have the right to receive the same remuneration for any work which he or she does as would, according to domestic law or custom, be paid for such work to a non-patient. Every such patient shall, in any event, have the right to receive a fair share of any remuneration which is paid to the mental health facility for his or her work.

Principle 14

Resources for mental health facilities

1. A mental health facility shall have access to the same level of resources as any other health establishment, and in particular:

(a) Qualified medical and other appropriate professional staff in sufficient numbers and with adequate space to provide each patient with privacy and a programme of appropriate and active therapy;

(b) Diagnostic and therapeutic equipment for the patient;

(c) Appropriate professional care;

(d) Adequate, regular and comprehensive treatment, including supplies of medication.

2. Every mental health facility shall be inspected by the competent authorities with sufficient frequency to ensure that the conditions, treatment and care of patients comply with the present Principles.

Principle 15

Admission principles

1. Where a person needs treatment in a mental health facility, every effort shall be made to avoid involuntary admission.

2. Access to a mental health facility shall be administered in the same way as access to any other facility for any other illness.

3. Every patient not admitted involuntarily shall have the right to leave the mental health facility at any time unless the criteria for his or her retention as an involuntary patient, as set forth in principle 16 below, apply, and he or she shall be informed of that right.

Principle 16

Involuntary admission

1. A person may be admitted involuntarily to a mental health facility as a patient or, having already been admitted voluntarily as a patient, be retained as an involuntary patient in the mental health facility if, and only if, a qualified mental health practitioner authorized by law for that purpose determines, in accordance with principle 4 above, that that person has a mental illness and considers:

(*a*) That, because of that mental illness, there is a serious likelihood of immediate or imminent harm to that person or to other persons; or

(*b*) That, in the case of a person whose mental illness is severe and whose judgement is impaired, failure to admit or retain that person is likely to lead to a serious deterioration in his or her condition or will prevent the giving of appropriate treatment that can only be given by admission to a mental health facility in accordance with the principle of the least restrictive alternative.

In the case referred to in subparagraph (b), a second such mental health practitioner, independent of the first, should be consulted where possible. If such consultation takes place, the involuntary admission or retention may not take place unless the second mental health practitioner concurs.

2. Involuntary admission or retention shall initially be for a short period as specified by domestic law for observation and preliminary treatment pending review of the admission or retention by the review body. The grounds of the admission shall be communicated to the patient without delay and the fact of the admission and the grounds for it shall also be communicated promptly and in detail to the review body, to the patient's personal representative, if any, and, unless the patient objects, to the patient's family.

3. A mental health facility may receive involuntarily admitted patients only if the facility has been designated to do so by a competent authority prescribed by domestic law.

Principle 17

Review body

1. The review body shall be a judicial or other independent and impartial body established by domestic law and functioning in accordance with procedures laid down by domestic law. It shall, in formulating its decisions, have the assistance of one or more qualified and independent mental health practitioners and take their advice into account.

2. The initial review of the review body, as required by paragraph 2 of principle 16 above, of a decision to admit or retain a person as an involuntary patient shall take place as soon as possible after that decision and shall be conducted in accordance with simple and expeditious procedures as specified by domestic law.

3. The review body shall periodically review the cases of involuntary patients at reasonable intervals as specified by domestic law.

4. An involuntary patient may apply to the review body for release or voluntary status, at reasonable intervals as specified by domestic law.

5. At each review, the review body shall consider whether the criteria for involuntary admission set out in paragraph 1 of principle 16 above are still satisfied, and, if not, the patient shall be discharged as an involuntary patient.

6. If at any time the mental health practitioner responsible for the case is satisfied that the conditions for the retention of a person as an involuntary patient are no longer satisfied, he or she shall order the discharge of that person as such a patient.

7. A patient or his personal representative or any interested person shall have the right to appeal to a higher court against a decision that the patient be admitted to, or be retained in, a mental health facility.

Principle 18

Procedural safeguards

1. The patient shall be entitled to choose and appoint a counsel to represent the patient as such, including representation in any complaint procedure or appeal. If the patient does not secure such services, a counsel shall be made available without payment by the patient to the extent that the patient lacks sufficient means to pay.

2. The patient shall also be entitled to the assistance, if necessary, of the services of an interpreter. Where such services are necessary and the patient does not secure them, they shall be made available without payment by the patient to the extent that the patient lacks sufficient means to pay.

3. The patient and the patient's counsel may request and produce at any hearing an independent mental health report and any other reports and oral, written and other evidence that are relevant and admissible.

4. Copies of the patient's records and any reports and documents to be submitted shall be given to the patient and to the patient's counsel, except in special cases where it is determined that a specific disclosure to the patient would cause serious harm to the patient's health or put at risk the safety of others. As domestic law may provide, any document not given to the patient should, when this can be done in confidence, be given to the patient's personal representative and counsel. When any part of a document is withheld from a patient, the patient or the patient's counsel, if any, shall receive notice of the withholding and the reasons for it and it shall be subject to judicial review.

5. The patient and the patient's personal representative and counsel shall be entitled to attend, participate and be heard personally in any hearing.

6. If the patient or the patient's personal representative or counsel requests that a particular person be present at a hearing, that person shall be admitted unless it is determined that the person's presence could cause serious harm to the patient's health or put at risk the safety of others.

7. Any decision on whether the hearing or any part of it shall be in public or in private and may be publicly reported shall give full consideration to the patient's own wishes, to the need to respect the privacy of the patient and of other persons and to the need to prevent serious harm to the patient's health or to avoid putting at risk the safety of others.

8. The decision arising out of the hearing and the reasons for it shall be expressed in writing. Copies shall be given to the patient and his or her personal representative and counsel. In deciding whether the decision shall be published in whole or in part, full consideration shall be given to the patient's own wishes, to the need to respect his or her privacy and that of other persons, to the public interest in the open administration of justice and to the need to prevent serious harm to the patient's health or to avoid putting at risk the safety of others.

Principle 19

Access to information

1. A patient (which term in the present principle includes a former patient) shall be entitled to have access to the information concerning the patient in his or her health and personal records maintained by a mental health facility. This right may be subject to restrictions in order to prevent serious harm to the patient's health and avoid putting at risk the safety of others. As domestic law may provide, any such information not given to the patient should, when this can be done in confidence, be given to the patient's personal representative and counsel. When any of the information is withheld from a patient, the patient or the patient's counsel, if any, shall receive notice of the withholding and the reasons for it and it shall be subject to judicial review.

2. Any written comments by the patient or the patient's personal representative or counsel shall, on request, be inserted in the patient's file.

Principle 20

Criminal offenders

1. The present Principle applies to persons serving sentences of imprisonment for criminal offences, or who are otherwise detained in the course of criminal proceedings or investigations against them, and who are determined to have a mental illness or who it is believed may have such an illness.

2. All such persons should receive the best available mental health care as provided in principle 1 above. The present Principles shall apply to them to the fullest extent possible, with only such limited modifications and exceptions as are necessary in the circumstances. No such modifications and exceptions shall prejudice the persons' rights under the instruments noted in paragraph 5 of principle 1 above.

3. Domestic law may authorize a court or other competent authority, acting on the basis of competent and independent medical advice, to order that such persons be admitted to a mental health facility.

4. Treatment of persons determined to have a mental illness shall in all circumstances be consistent with principle 11 above.

Principle 21

Complaints

Every patient and former patient shall have the right to make a complaint through procedures as specified by domestic law.

Principle 22

Monitoring and remedies

States shall ensure that appropriate mechanisms are in force to promote compliance with the present Principles, for the inspection of mental health facilities, for the submission, investigation and resolution of complaints and for the institution of appropriate disciplinary or judicial proceedings for professional misconduct or violation of the rights of a patient.

Principle 23

Implementation

1. States should implement the present Principles through appropriate legislative, judicial, administrative, educational and other measures, which they shall review periodically.

2. States shall make the present Principles widely known by appropriate and active means.

Principle 24

Scope of principles relating to mental health facilities

The present Principles apply to all persons who are admitted to a mental health facility.

Principle 25

Saving of existing rights

There shall be no restriction upon or derogation from any existing rights of patients, including rights recognized in applicable international or domestic law, on the pretext that the present Principles do not recognize such rights or that they recognize them to a lesser extent.

48/96. Standard Rules on the Equalization of Opportunities for Persons with Disabilities

Committee: 3
Vote: Adopted without a vote
Ref.: 50/144, 49/153

The General Assembly,

Recalling Economic and Social Council resolution 1990/26 of 24 May 1990, in which the Council authorized the Commission for Social Development to consider, at its thirty-second session, the establishment of an *ad hoc* open-ended working group of government experts, funded by voluntary contributions, to elaborate standard rules on the equalization of opportunities for disabled children, youth and adults, in close collaboration with the specialized agencies, other intergovernmental bodies and non-governmental organizations, especially organizations of disabled persons, and requested the Commission, should it establish such a working group, to finalize the text of those rules for consideration by the Council in 1993 and for submission to the General Assembly at its forty-eighth session,

Also recalling that the Commission for Social Development, in its resolution 32/2 of 20 February 1991,[1] decided to establish an *ad hoc* open-ended working group of government experts in accordance with Economic and Social Council resolution 1990/26,

Noting with appreciation the participation of many States, specialized agencies, intergovernmental bodies and non-governmental organizations, especially organizations of disabled persons, in the deliberations of the working group,

Also noting with appreciation the generous financial contributions of Member States to the working group,

Welcoming the fact that the working group was able to fulfil its mandate within three sessions of five working days each,

Acknowledging with appreciation the report of the *ad hoc* open-ended working group to elaborate standard rules on the equalization of opportunities for persons with disabilities,[2]

Noting the discussion in the Commission for Social Development at its thirty-third session[3] on the draft standard rules contained in the report of the working group,

1. *Adopts* the Standard Rules on the Equalization of Opportunities for Persons with Disabilities, set forth in the annex to the present resolution;

2. *Requests* Member States to apply the Rules in developing national disability programmes;

3. *Urges* Member States to meet the requests of the Special Rapporteur[4] for information on the implementation of the Rules;

4. *Requests* the Secretary-General to promote the implementation of the Rules and to report thereon to the General Assembly at its fiftieth session;

5. *Urges* Member States to support, financially and otherwise, the implementation of the Rules.

Annex

Standard Rules on the Equalization of Opportunities for Persons with Disabilities

Introduction

Background and current needs

1. There are persons with disabilities in all parts of the world and at all levels in every society. The number of persons with disabilities in the world is large and is growing.

2. Both the causes and the consequences of disability vary throughout the world. Those variations are the result of different socio-economic circumstances and of the different provisions that States make for the well-being of their citizens.

3. Present disability policy is the result of developments over the past 200 years. In many ways it reflects the general living conditions and social and economic policies of different times. In the disability field, however, there are also many specific circumstances that have influenced the living conditions of persons with disabilities. Ignorance, neglect, superstition and fear are social factors that throughout the history of disability have isolated persons with disabilities and delayed their development.

4. Over the years disability policy developed from elementary care at institutions to education for children with disabilities and rehabilitation for persons who became disabled during adult life. Through education and rehabilitation, persons with disabilities became more active and a driving force in the further development of disability policy. Organizations of persons with disabilities, their families and

1 *Official Records of the Economic and Social Counicl, 1991, Supplement No. 6* (E/1991/26), chap. I, sect. D.

2 E/CN.5/1993/5, annex.

3 See *Official Records of the Economic and Social Counicl, 1993, Supplement No. 4* (E/1993/24), chap. III, sect. E.

4 See sect. IV, para.2, of the annex to the present resolution.

advocates were formed, which advocated better conditions for persons with disabilities. After the Second World War the concepts of integration and normalization were introduced, which reflected a growing awareness of the capabilities of persons with disabilities.

5. Towards the end of the 1960s organizations of persons with disabilities in some countries started to formulate a new concept of disability. That new concept indicated the close connection between the limitation experienced by individuals with disabilities, the design and structure of their environments and the attitude of the general population. At the same time the problems of disability in developing countries were more and more highlighted. In some of those countries the percentage of the population with disabilities was estimated to be very high and, for the most part, persons with disabilities were extremely poor.

Previous international action

6. The rights of persons with disabilities have been the subject of much attention in the United Nations and other international organizations over a long period of time. The most important outcome of the International Year of Disabled Persons, 1981, was the World Programme of Action concerning Disabled Persons,[1] adopted by the General Assembly by its resolution 37/52 of 3 December 1982. The Year and the World Programme of Action provided a strong impetus for progress in the field. They both emphasized the right of persons with disabilities to the same opportunities as other citizens and to an equal share in the improvements in living conditions resulting from economic and social development. There also, for the first time, handicap was defined as a function of the relationship between persons with disabilities and their environment.

7. The Global Meeting of Experts to Review the Implementation of the World Programme of Action concerning Disabled Persons at the Mid-Point of the United Nations Decade of Disabled Persons was held at Stockholm in 1987. It was suggested at the Meeting that a guiding philosophy should be developed to indicate the priorities for action in the years ahead. The basis of that philosophy should be the recognition of the rights of persons with disabilities.

8. Consequently, the Meeting recommended that the General Assembly convene a special conference to draft an international convention on the elimination of all forms of discrimination against persons with disabilities, to be ratified by States by the end of the Decade.

9. A draft outline of the convention was prepared by Italy and presented to the General Assembly at its forty-second session. Further presentations concerning a draft convention were made by Sweden at the forty-fourth session of the Assembly. However, on both occasions, no consensus could be reached on the suitability of such a convention. In the opinion of many representatives, existing human rights documents seemed to guarantee persons with disabilities the same rights as other persons.

Towards standard rules

10. Guided by the deliberations in the General Assembly, the Economic and Social Council, at its first regular session of 1990, finally agreed to concentrate on the elaboration of an international instrument of a different kind. By its resolution 1990/26 of 24 May 1990, the Council authorized the Commission for Social Development to consider, at its thirty-second session, the establishment of an *ad hoc* open-ended working group of government experts, funded by voluntary contributions, to elaborate standard rules on the equalization of opportunities for disabled children, youth and adults, in close collaboration with the specialized agencies, other intergovernmental bodies and non-governmental organizations, especially organizations of disabled persons. The Council also requested the Commission to finalize the text of those rules for consideration in 1993 and for submission to the General Assembly at its forty-eighth session.

11. The subsequent discussions in the Third Committee of the General Assembly at the forty-fifth session showed that there was wide support for the new initiative to elaborate standard rules on the equalization of opportunities for persons with disabilities.

12. At the thirty-second session of the Commission for Social Development, the initiative for standard rules received the support of a large number of representatives and discussions led to the adoption of resolution 32/2 of 20 February 1991, in which the Commission decided to establish an *ad hoc* open-ended working group in accordance with Economic and Social Council resolution 1990/26.

Purpose and content of the Standard Rules on the Equalization of Opportunities for Persons with Disabilities

13. The Standard Rules on the Equalization of Opportunities for Persons with Disabilities have been developed on the basis of the experience gained during the United Nations Decade of Disabled Persons (1983-1992).[2] The International Bill of Human Rights, comprising the Universal Declaration of Human Rights,[3] the International Covenant on Economic, Social and Cultural Rights[4] and the International Covenant on Civil and Political Rights,[5] the Convention on the Rights of the Child[6] and the Convention on the Elimination of All Forms of Discrimination against Women,[7] as well as the World Programme of Action concerning Disabled Persons, constitute the political and moral foundation for the Rules.

14. Although the Rules are not compulsory, they can become international customary rules when they are applied by a great number of States with the intention of respecting a rule in international law. They imply a strong moral and political commitment on behalf of States to take action for the equalization of opportunities for persons with disabilities. Important principles for responsibility, action and cooperation are indicated. Areas of decisive importance for the quality of life and for the achievement of full participation and equality are pointed out. The Rules offer an instrument for policy-making and action to persons with disabilities and their organizations. They provide a basis for technical and economic cooperation among States, the United Nations and other international organizations.

15. The purpose of the Rules is to ensure that girls, boys, women and men with disabilities, as members of their societies, may exercise the same rights and obligations as others. In all societies of the world there are still obstacles preventing persons with disabilities from exercising their rights and freedoms and making it difficult for them to participate fully in the activities of their societies. It is the responsibility of States to take appropriate action to remove such obstacles. Persons with disabilities and their organizations should play an active role as partners in this process. The equalization of opportunities for persons with disabilities is an essential contribution in the general and worldwide effort to mobilize human resources. Special attention may need to be directed towards groups such as women, children, the elderly, the poor, migrant workers, persons with dual or multiple disabilities, indigenous people and ethnic minorities. In addition, there are a large number of refugees with disabilities who have special needs requiring attention.

Fundamental concepts in disability policy

16. The concepts set out below appear throughout the Rules. They are essentially built on the concepts in the World Programme of Action concerning Disabled Persons. In some cases they reflect the development that has taken place during the United Nations Decade of Disabled Persons.

1 A/37/351/Add.1 and Add.1/Corr.1, annex, sect. VIII, recommendation 1 (IV).

2 Proclaimed by the General Assembly in its resolution 37/53.

3 Resolution 217 A (III).

4 See resolution 2200 A (XXI), annex.

5 See resolution 2200 A (XXI), annex.

6 Resolution 44/25, annex.

7 Resolution 34/180, annex.

Disability and handicap

17. The term "disability" summarizes a great number of different functional limitations occurring in any population in any country of the world. People may be disabled by physical, intellectual or sensory impairment, medical conditions or mental illness. Such impairments, conditions or illnesses may be permanent or transitory in nature.

18. The term "handicap" means the loss or limitation of opportunities to take part in the life of the community on an equal level with others. It describes the encounter between the person with a disability and the environment. The purpose of this term is to emphasize the focus on the shortcomings in the environment and in many organized activities in society, for example, information, communication and education, which prevent persons with disabilities from participating on equal terms.

19. The use of the two terms "disability" and "handicap", as defined in paragraphs 17 and 18 above, should be seen in the light of modern disability history. During the 1970s there was a strong reaction among representatives of organizations of persons with disabilities and professionals in the field of disability against the terminology of the time. The terms "disability" and "handicap" were often used in an unclear and confusing way, which gave poor guidance for policy-making and for political action. The terminology reflected a medical and diagnostic approach, which ignored the imperfections and deficiencies of the surrounding society.

20. In 1980, the World Health Organization adopted an international classification of impairments, disabilities and handicaps, which suggested a more precise and at the same time relativistic approach. The International Classification of Impairments, Disabilities, and Handicaps[1] makes a clear distinction between "impairment", "disability" and "handicap". It has been extensively used in areas such as rehabilitation, education, statistics, policy, legislation, demography, sociology, economics and anthropology. Some users have expressed concern that the Classification, in its definition of the term "handicap", may still be considered too medical and too centred on the individual, and may not adequately clarify the interaction between societal conditions or expectations and the abilities of the individual. Those concerns, and others expressed by users during the 12 years since its publication, will be addressed in forthcoming revisions of the Classification.

21. As a result of experience gained in the implementation of the World Programme of Action and of the general discussion that took place during the United Nations Decade of Disabled Persons, there was a deepening of knowledge and extension of understanding concerning disability issues and the terminology used. Current terminology recognizes the necessity of addressing both the individual needs (such as rehabilitation and technical aids) and the shortcomings of the society (various obstacles for participation).

Prevention

22. The term "prevention" means action aimed at preventing the occurrence of physical, intellectual, psychiatric or sensory impairments (primary prevention) or at preventing impairments from causing a permanent functional limitation or disability (secondary prevention). Prevention may include many different types of action, such as primary health care, prenatal and postnatal care, education in nutrition, immunization campaigns against communicable diseases, measures to control endemic diseases, safety regulations, programmes for the prevention of accidents in different environments, including adaptation of workplaces to prevent occupational disabilities and diseases, and prevention of disability resulting from pollution of the environment or armed conflict.

Rehabilitation

23. The term "rehabilitation" refers to a process aimed at enabling persons with disabilities to reach and maintain their optimal physical, sensory, intellectual, psychiatric and/or social functional levels, thus providing them with the tools to change their lives towards a higher level of independence. Rehabilitation may include measures to provide and/or restore functions, or compensate for the loss or absence of a function or for a functional limitation. The rehabilitation process does not involve initial medical care. It includes a wide range of measures and activities from more basic and general rehabilitation to goal-oriented activities, for instance vocational rehabilitation.

Equalization of opportunities

24. The term "equalization of opportunities" means the process through which the various systems of society and the environment, such as services, activities, information and documentation, are made available to all, particularly to persons with disabilities.

25. The principle of equal rights implies that the needs of each and every individual are of equal importance, that those needs must be made the basis for the planning of societies and that all resources must be employed in such a way as to ensure that every individual has equal opportunity for participation.

26. Persons with disabilities are members of society and have the right to remain within their local communities. They should receive the support they need within the ordinary structures of education, health, employment and social services.

27. As persons with disabilities achieve equal rights, they should also have equal obligations. As those rights are being achieved, societies should raise their expectations of persons with disabilities. As part of the process of equal opportunities, provision should be made to assist persons with disabilities to assume their full responsibility as members of society.

Preamble

States,

Mindful of the pledge made, under the Charter of the United Nations, to take joint and separate action in cooperation with the Organization to promote higher standards of living, full employment, and conditions of economic and social progress and development,

Reaffirming the commitment to human rights and fundamental freedoms, social justice and the dignity and worth of the human person proclaimed in the Charter,

Recalling in particular the international standards on human rights, which have been laid down in the Universal Declaration of Human Rights,[2] the International Covenant on Economic, Social and Cultural Rights[3] and the International Covenant on Civil and Political Rights,[4]

Underlining that those instruments proclaim that the rights recognized therein should be ensured equally to all individuals without discrimination,

Recalling the Convention on the Rights of the Child,[5] which prohibits discrimination on the basis of disability and requires special measures to ensure the rights of children with disabilities, and the International Convention on the Protection of the Rights of All Migrant Workers and Members of Their Families,[6] which provides for some protective measures against disability,

Recalling also the provisions in the Convention on the Elimination of All Forms of Discrimination against Women[7] to ensure the rights of girls and women with disabilities,

Having regard to the Declaration on the Rights of Disabled Persons,[8] the Declaration on the Rights of Mentally Retarded Persons,[9] the

1 Proclaimed by the General Assembly in its resolution 37/53.

2 Resolution 217 A (III).

3 See resolution 2200 A (XXI), annex.

4 See resolution 2200 A (XXI), annex.

5 Resolution 44/25, annex.

6 Resolution 45/158, annex.

7 Resolution 34/180, annex.

8 Resolution 3447 (XXX).

9 Resolution 2856 (XXVI).

Declaration on Social Progress and Development,[1] the Principles for the Protection of Persons with Mental Illness and for the Improvement of Mental Health Care[2] and other relevant instruments adopted by the General Assembly,

Also having regard to the relevant conventions and recommendations adopted by the International Labour Organisation, with particular reference to participation in employment without discrimination for persons with disabilities,

Mindful of the relevant recommendations and work of the United Nations Educational, Scientific and Cultural Organization, in particular the World Declaration on Education for All, the World Health Organization, the United Nations Children's Fund and other concerned organizations,

Having regard to the commitment made by States concerning the protection of the environment,

Mindful of the devastation caused by armed conflict and deploring the use of scarce resources in the production of weapons,

Recognizing that the World Programme of Action concerning Disabled Persons and the definition therein of equalization of opportunities represent earnest ambitions on the part of the international community to render those various international instruments and recommendations of practical and concrete significance,

Acknowledging that the objective of the United Nations Decade of Disabled Persons (1983-1992) to implement the World Programme of Action is still valid and requires urgent and continued action,

Recalling that the World Programme of Action is based on concepts that are equally valid in developing and industrialized countries,

Convinced that intensified efforts are needed to achieve the full and equal enjoyment of human rights and participation in society by persons with disabilities,

Re-emphasizing that persons with disabilities, and their parents, guardians, advocates and organizations, must be active partners with States in the planning and implementation of all measures affecting their civil, political, economic, social and cultural rights,

In pursuance of Economic and Social Council resolution 1990/26, and basing themselves on the specific measures required for the attainment by persons with disabilities of equality with others, enumerated in detail in the World Programme of Action,

Have adopted the Standard Rules on the Equalization of Opportunities for Persons with Disabilities outlined below, in order:

(*a*) To stress that all action in the field of disability presupposes adequate knowledge and experience of the conditions and special needs of persons with disabilities;

(*b*) To emphasize that the process through which every aspect of societal organization is made accessible to all is a basic objective of socio-economic development;

(*c*) To outline crucial aspects of social policies in the field of disability, including, as appropriate, the active encouragement of technical and economic cooperation;

(*d*) To provide models for the political decision-making process required for the attainment of equal opportunities, bearing in mind the widely differing technical and economic levels, the fact that the process must reflect keen understanding of the cultural context within which it takes place and the crucial role of persons with disabilities in it;

(*e*) To propose national mechanisms for close collaboration among States, the organs of the United Nations system, other intergovernmental bodies and organizations of persons with disabilities;

(*f*) To propose an effective machinery for monitoring the process by which States seek to attain the equalization of opportunities for persons with disabilities.

[1] Resolution 2542 (XXVI).

[2] Resolution 46/119, annex.

I. Preconditions for Equal Participation

Rule 1. Awareness-Raising

States should take action to raise awareness in society about persons with disabilities, their rights, their needs, their potential and their contribution.

1. States should ensure that responsible authorities distribute up-to-date information on available programmes and services to persons with disabilities, their families, professionals in the field and the general public. Information to persons with disabilities should be presented in accessible form.

2. States should initiate and support information campaigns concerning persons with disabilities and disability policies, conveying the message that persons with disabilities are citizens with the same rights and obligations as others, thus justifying measures to remove all obstacles to full participation.

3. States should encourage the portrayal of persons with disabilities by the mass media in a positive way; organizations of persons with disabilities should be consulted on this matter.

4. States should ensure that public education programmes reflect in all their aspects the principle of full participation and equality.

5. States should invite persons with disabilities and their families and organizations to participate in public education programmes concerning disability matters.

6. States should encourage enterprises in the private sector to include disability issues in all aspects of their activity.

7. States should initiate and promote programmes aimed at raising the level of awareness of persons with disabilities concerning their rights and potential. Increased self-reliance and empowerment will assist persons with disabilities to take advantage of the opportunities available to them.

8. Awareness-raising should be an important part of the education of children with disabilities and in rehabilitation programmes. Persons with disabilities could also assist one another in awareness-raising through the activities of their own organizations.

9. Awareness-raising should be part of the education of all children and should be a component of teacher-training courses and training of all professionals.

Rule 2. Medical Care

States should ensure the provision of effective medical care to persons with disabilities.

1. States should work towards the provision of programmes run by multidisciplinary teams of professionals for early detection, assessment and treatment of impairment. This could prevent, reduce or eliminate disabling effects. Such programmes should ensure the full participation of persons with disabilities and their families at the individual level, and of organizations of persons with disabilities at the planning and evaluation level.

2. Local community workers should be trained to participate in areas such as early detection of impairments, the provision of primary assistance and referral to appropriate services.

3. States should ensure that persons with disabilities, particularly infants and children, are provided with the same level of medical care within the same system as other members of society.

4. States should ensure that all medical and paramedical personnel are adequately trained and equipped to give medical care to persons with disabilities and that they have access to relevant treatment methods and technology.

5. States should ensure that medical, paramedical and related personnel are adequately trained so that they do not give inappropriate advice to parents, thus restricting options for their children. This training should be an ongoing process and should be based on the latest information available.

6. States should ensure that persons with disabilities are provided with any regular treatment and medicines they may need to preserve or improve their level of functioning.

Rule 3. Rehabilitation[1]

States should ensure the provision of rehabilitation services to persons with disabilities in order for them to reach and sustain their optimum level of independence and functioning.

1. States should develop national rehabilitation programmes for all groups of persons with disabilities. Such programmes should be based on the actual individual needs of persons with disabilities and on the principles of full participation and equality.

2. Such programmes should include a wide range of activities, such as basic skills training to improve or compensate for an affected function, counselling of persons with disabilities and their families, developing self-reliance, and occasional services such as assessment and guidance.

3. All persons with disabilities, including persons with severe and/or multiple disabilities, who require rehabilitation should have access to it.

4. Persons with disabilities and their families should be able to participate in the design and organization of rehabilitation services concerning themselves.

5. All rehabilitation services should be available in the local community where the person with disabilities lives. However, in some instances, in order to attain a certain training objective, special time-limited rehabilitation courses may be organized, where appropriate, in residential form.

6. Persons with disabilities and their families should be encouraged to involve themselves in rehabilitation, for instance as trained teachers, instructors or counsellors.

7. States should draw upon the expertise of organizations of persons with disabilities when formulating or evaluating rehabilitation programmes.

Rule 4. Support Services

States should ensure the development and supply of support services, including assistive devices for persons with disabilities, to assist them to increase their level of independence in their daily living and to exercise their rights.

1. States should ensure the provision of assistive devices and equipment, personal assistance and interpreter services, according to the needs of persons with disabilities, as important measures to achieve the equalization of opportunities.

2. States should support the development, production, distribution and servicing of assistive devices and equipment and the dissemination of knowledge about them.

3. To achieve this, generally available technical know-how should be utilized. In States where high-technology industry is available, it should be fully utilized to improve the standard and effectiveness of assistive devices and equipment. It is important to stimulate the development and production of simple and inexpensive devices, using local material and local production facilities when possible. Persons with disabilities themselves could be involved in the production of those devices.

4. States should recognize that all persons with disabilities who need assistive devices should have access to them as appropriate, including financial accessibility. This may mean that assistive devices and equipment should be provided free of charge or at such a low price that persons with disabilities or their families can afford to buy them.

5. In rehabilitation programmes for the provision of assistive devices and equipment, States should consider the special requirements of girls and boys with disabilities concerning the design, durability and age-appropriateness of assistive devices and equipment.

6. States should support the development and provision of personal assistance programmes and interpretation services, especially for persons with severe and/or multiple disabilities. Such programmes would increase the level of participation of persons with disabilities in everyday life at home, at work, in school and during leisure-time activities.

7. Personal assistance programmes should be designed in such a way that the persons with disabilities using the programmes have a decisive influence on the way in which the programmes are delivered.

II. Target Areas for Equal Participation

Rule 5. Accessibility

States should recognize the overall importance of accessibility in the process of the equalization of opportunities in all spheres of society. For persons with disabilities of any kind, States should (a) introduce programmes of action to make the physical environment accessible; and (b) undertake measures to provide access to information and communication.

(a) Access to the physical environment

1. States should initiate measures to remove the obstacles to participation in the physical environment. Such measures should be to develop standards and guidelines and to consider enacting legislation to ensure accessibility to various areas in society, such as housing, buildings, public transport services and other means of transportation, streets and other outdoor environments.

2. States should ensure that architects, construction engineers and others who are professionally involved in the design and construction of the physical environment have access to adequate information on disability policy and measures to achieve accessibility.

3. Accessibility requirements should be included in the design and construction of the physical environment from the beginning of the designing process.

4. Organizations of persons with disabilities should be consulted when standards and norms for accessibility are being developed. They should also be involved locally from the initial planning stage when public construction projects are being designed, thus ensuring maximum accessibility.

(b) Access to information and communication

5. Persons with disabilities and, where appropriate, their families and advocates should have access to full information on diagnosis, rights and available services and programmes, at all stages. Such information should be presented in forms accessible to persons with disabilities.

6. States should develop strategies to make information services and documentation accessible for different groups of persons with disabilities. Braille, tape services, large print and other appropriate technologies should be used to provide access to written information and documentation for persons with visual impairments. Similarly, appropriate technologies should be used to provide access to spoken information for persons with auditory impairments or comprehension difficulties.

7. Consideration should be given to the use of sign language in the education of deaf children, in their families and communities. Sign language interpretation services should also be provided to facilitate the communication between deaf persons and others.

8. Consideration should also be given to the needs of people with other communication disabilities.

9. States should encourage the media, especially television, radio and newspapers, to make their services accessible.

10. States should ensure that new computerized information and service systems offered to the general public are either made initially accessible or are adapted to be made accessible to persons with disabilities.

11. Organizations of persons with disabilities should be consulted when measures to make information services accessible are being developed.

[1] Rehabilitation is a fundamental concept in disability policy and is defined above in paragraph 23 of the introduction.

Rule 6. Education

States should recognize the principle of equal primary, secondary and tertiary educational opportunities for children, youth and adults with disabilities, in integrated settings. They should ensure that the education of persons with disabilities is an integral part of the educational system.

1. General educational authorities are responsible for the education of persons with disabilities in integrated settings. Education for persons with disabilities should form an integral part of national educational planning, curriculum development and school organization.

2. Education in mainstream schools presupposes the provision of interpreter and other appropriate support services. Adequate accessibility and support services, designed to meet the needs of persons with different disabilities, should be provided.

3. Parent groups and organizations of persons with disabilities should be involved in the education process at all levels.

4. In States where education is compulsory it should be provided to girls and boys with all kinds and all levels of disabilities, including the most severe.

5. Special attention should be given in the following areas:

(*a*) Very young children with disabilities;

(*b*) Pre-school children with disabilities;

(*c*) Adults with disabilities, particularly women.

6. To accommodate educational provisions for persons with disabilities in the mainstream, States should:

(*a*) Have a clearly stated policy, understood and accepted at the school level and by the wider community;

(*b*) Allow for curriculum flexibility, addition and adaptation;

(*c*) Provide for quality materials, ongoing teacher training and support teachers.

7. Integrated education and community-based programmes should be seen as complementary approaches in providing cost-effective education and training for persons with disabilities. National community-based programmes should encourage communities to use and develop their resources to provide local education to persons with disabilities.

8. In situations where the general school system does not yet adequately meet the needs of all persons with disabilities, special education may be considered. It should be aimed at preparing students for education in the general school system. The quality of such education should reflect the same standards and ambitions as general education and should be closely linked to it. At a minimum, students with disabilities should be afforded the same portion of educational resources as students without disabilities. States should aim for the gradual integration of special education services into mainstream education. It is acknowledged that in some instances special education may currently be considered to be the most appropriate form of education for some students with disabilities.

9. Owing to the particular communication needs of deaf and deaf/blind persons, their education may be more suitably provided in schools for such persons or special classes and units in mainstream schools. At the initial stage, in particular, special attention needs to be focused on culturally sensitive instruction that will result in effective communication skills and maximum independence for people who are deaf or deaf/blind.

Rule 7. Employment

States should recognize the principle that persons with disabilities must be empowered to exercise their human rights, particularly in the field of employment. In both rural and urban areas they must have equal opportunities for productive and gainful employment in the labour market.

1. Laws and regulations in the employment field must not discriminate against persons with disabilities and must not raise obstacles to their employment.

2. States should actively support the integration of persons with disabilities into open employment. This active support could occur through a variety of measures, such as vocational training, incentive-oriented quota schemes, reserved or designated employment, loans or grants for small business, exclusive contracts or priority production rights, tax concessions, contract compliance or other technical or financial assistance to enterprises employing workers with disabilities. States should also encourage employers to make reasonable adjustments to accommodate persons with disabilities.

3. States' action programmes should include:

(*a*) Measures to design and adapt workplaces and work premises in such a way that they become accessible to persons with different disabilities;

(*b*) Support for the use of new technologies and the development and production of assistive devices, tools and equipment and measures to facilitate access to such devices and equipment for persons with disabilities to enable them to gain and maintain employment;

(*c*) Provision of appropriate training and placement and ongoing support such as personal assistance and interpreter services.

4. States should initiate and support public awareness-raising campaigns designed to overcome negative attitudes and prejudices concerning workers with disabilities.

5. In their capacity as employers, States should create favourable conditions for the employment of persons with disabilities in the public sector.

6. States, workers' organizations and employers should cooperate to ensure equitable recruitment and promotion policies, employment conditions, rates of pay, measures to improve the work environment in order to prevent injuries and impairments and measures for the rehabilitation of employees who have sustained employment-related injuries.

7. The aim should always be for persons with disabilities to obtain employment in the open labour market. For persons with disabilities whose needs cannot be met in open employment, small units of sheltered or supported employment may be an alternative. It is important that the quality of such programmes be assessed in terms of their relevance and sufficiency in providing opportunities for persons with disabilities to gain employment in the labour market.

8. Measures should be taken to include persons with disabilities in training and employment programmes in the private and informal sectors.

9. States, workers' organizations and employers should cooperate with organizations of persons with disabilities concerning all measures to create training and employment opportunities, including flexible hours, part-time work, job-sharing, self-employment and attendant care for persons with disabilities.

Rule 8. Income maintenance and social security

States are responsible for the provision of social security and income maintenance for persons with disabilities.

1. States should ensure the provision of adequate income support to persons with disabilities who, owing to disability or disability-related factors, have temporarily lost or received a reduction in their income or have been denied employment opportunities. States should ensure that the provision of support takes into account the costs frequently incurred by persons with disabilities and their families as a result of the disability.

2. In countries where social security, social insurance or other social welfare schemes exist or are being developed for the general population, States should ensure that such systems do not exclude or discriminate against persons with disabilities.

3. States should also ensure the provision of income support and social security protection to individuals who undertake the care of a person with a disability.

4. Social security systems should include incentives to restore the income-earning capacity of persons with disabilities. Such systems should provide or contribute to the organization, development and financing of vocational training. They should also assist with placement services.

5. Social security programmes should also provide incentives for persons with disabilities to seek employment in order to establish or re-establish their income-earning capacity.

6. Income support should be maintained as long as the disabling conditions remain in a manner that does not discourage persons with disabilities from seeking employment. It should only be reduced or terminated when persons with disabilities achieve adequate and secure income.

7. States, in countries where social security is to a large extent provided by the private sector, should encourage local communities, welfare organizations and families to develop self-help measures and incentives for employment or employment-related activities for persons with disabilities.

Rule 9. Family life and personal integrity

States should promote the full participation of persons with disabilities in family life. They should promote their right to personal integrity and ensure that laws do not discriminate against persons with disabilities with respect to sexual relationships, marriage and parenthood.

1. Persons with disabilities should be enabled to live with their families. States should encourage the inclusion in family counselling of appropriate modules regarding disability and its effects on family life. Respite-care and attendant-care services should be made available to families which include a person with disabilities. States should remove all unnecessary obstacles to persons who want to foster or adopt a child or adult with disabilities.

2. Persons with disabilities must not be denied the opportunity to experience their sexuality, have sexual relationships and experience parenthood. Taking into account that persons with disabilities may experience difficulties in getting married and setting up a family, States should encourage the availability of appropriate counselling. Persons with disabilities must have the same access as others to family-planning methods, as well as to information in accessible form on the sexual functioning of their bodies.

3. States should promote measures to change negative attitudes towards marriage, sexuality and parenthood of persons with disabilities, especially of girls and women with disabilities, which still prevail in society. The media should be encouraged to play an important role in removing such negative attitudes.

4. Persons with disabilities and their families need to be fully informed about taking precautions against sexual and other forms of abuse. Persons with disabilities are particularly vulnerable to abuse in the family, community or institutions and need to be educated on how to avoid the occurrence of abuse, recognize when abuse has occurred and report on such acts.

Rule 10. Culture

States will ensure that persons with disabilities are integrated into and can participate in cultural activities on an equal basis.

1. States should ensure that persons with disabilities have the opportunity to utilize their creative, artistic and intellectual potential, not only for their own benefit, but also for the enrichment of their community, be they in urban or rural areas. Examples of such activities are dance, music, literature, theatre, plastic arts, painting and sculpture. Particularly in developing countries, emphasis should be placed on traditional and contemporary art forms, such as puppetry, recitation and story-telling.

2. States should promote the accessibility to and availability of places for cultural performances and services, such as theatres, museums, cinemas and libraries, to persons with disabilities.

3. States should initiate the development and use of special technical arrangements to make literature, films and theatre accessible to persons with disabilities.

Rule 11. Recreation and sports

States will take measures to ensure that persons with disabilities have equal opportunities for recreation and sports.

1. States should initiate measures to make places for recreation and sports, hotels, beaches, sports arenas, gym halls, etc., accessible to persons with disabilities. Such measures should encompass support for staff in recreation and sports programmes, including projects to develop methods of accessibility, and participation, information and training programmes.

2. Tourist authorities, travel agencies, hotels, voluntary organizations and others involved in organizing recreational activities or travel opportunities should offer their services to all, taking into account the special needs of persons with disabilities. Suitable training should be provided to assist that process.

3. Sports organizations should be encouraged to develop opportunities for participation by persons with disabilities in sports activities. In some cases, accessibility measures could be enough to open up opportunities for participation. In other cases, special arrangements or special games would be needed. States should support the participation of persons with disabilities in national and international events.

4. Persons with disabilities participating in sports activities should have access to instruction and training of the same quality as other participants.

5. Organizers of sports and recreation should consult with organizations of persons with disabilities when developing their services for persons with disabilities.

Rule 12. Religion

States will encourage measures for equal participation by persons with disabilities in the religious life of their communities.

1. States should encourage, in consultation with religious authorities, measures to eliminate discrimination and make religious activities accessible to persons with disabilities.

2. States should encourage the distribution of information on disability matters to religious institutions and organizations. States should also encourage religious authorities to include information on disability policies in the training for religious professions, as well as in religious education programmes.

3. They should also encourage the accessibility of religious literature to persons with sensory impairments.

4. States and/or religious organizations should consult with organizations of persons with disabilities when developing measures for equal participation in religious activities.

III. Implementation Measures

Rule 13. Information and research

States assume the ultimate responsibility for the collection and dissemination of information on the living conditions of persons with disabilities and promote comprehensive research on all aspects, including obstacles that affect the lives of persons with disabilities.

1. States should, at regular intervals, collect gender-specific statistics and other information concerning the living conditions of persons with disabilities. Such data collection could be conducted in conjunction with national censuses and household surveys and could be undertaken in close collaboration, *inter alia*, with universities, research institutes and organizations of persons with disabilities. The data collection should include questions on programmes and services and their use.

2. States should consider establishing a data bank on disability, which would include statistics on available services and programmes as well as on the different groups of persons with disabilities. They should bear in mind the need to protect individual privacy and personal integrity.

3. States should initiate and support programmes of research on social, economic and participation issues that affect the lives of persons with disabilities and their families. Such research should include studies on the causes, types and frequencies of disabilities, the availability and efficacy of existing programmes and the need for development and evaluation of services and support measures.

4. States should develop and adopt terminology and criteria for the conduct of national surveys, in cooperation with organizations of persons with disabilities.

5. States should facilitate the participation of persons with disabilities in data collection and research. To undertake such research States should particularly encourage the recruitment of qualified persons with disabilities.

6. States should support the exchange of research findings and experiences.

7. States should take measures to disseminate information and knowledge on disability to all political and administration levels within national, regional and local spheres.

Rule 14. Policy-making and planning

States will ensure that disability aspects are included in all relevant policy-making and national planning.

1. States should initiate and plan adequate policies for persons with disabilities at the national level, and stimulate and support action at regional and local levels.

2. States should involve organizations of persons with disabilities in all decision-making relating to plans and programmes concerning persons with disabilities or affecting their economic and social status.

3. The needs and concerns of persons with disabilities should be incorporated into general development plans and not be treated separately.

4. The ultimate responsibility of States for the situation of persons with disabilities does not relieve others of their responsibility. Anyone in charge of services, activities or the provision of information in society should be encouraged to accept responsibility for making such programmes available to persons with disabilities.

5. States should facilitate the development by local communities of programmes and measures for persons with disabilities. One way of doing this could be to develop manuals or check-lists and provide training programmes for local staff.

Rule 15. Legislation

States have a responsibility to create the legal bases for measures to achieve the objectives of full participation and equality for persons with disabilities.

1. National legislation, embodying the rights and obligations of citizens, should include the rights and obligations of persons with disabilities. States are under an obligation to enable persons with disabilities to exercise their rights, including their human, civil and political rights, on an equal basis with other citizens. States must ensure that organizations of persons with disabilities are involved in the development of national legislation concerning the rights of persons with disabilities, as well as in the ongoing evaluation of that legislation.

2. Legislative action may be needed to remove conditions that may adversely affect the lives of persons with disabilities, including harassment and victimization. Any discriminatory provisions against persons with disabilities must be eliminated. National legislation should provide for appropriate sanctions in case of violations of the principles of non-discrimination.

3. National legislation concerning persons with disabilities may appear in two different forms. The rights and obligations may be incorporated in general legislation or contained in special legislation. Special legislation for persons with disabilities may be established in several ways:

(a) By enacting separate legislation, dealing exclusively with disability matters;

(b) By including disability matters within legislation on particular topics;

(c) By mentioning persons with disabilities specifically in the texts that serve to interpret existing legislation.

A combination of those different approaches might be desirable. Affirmative action provisions may also be considered.

4. States may consider establishing formal statutory complaints mechanisms in order to protect the interests of persons with disabilities.

Rule 16. Economic policies

States have the financial responsibility for national programmes and measures to create equal opportunities for persons with disabilities.

1. States should include disability matters in the regular budgets of all national, regional and local government bodies.

2. States, non-governmental organizations and other interested bodies should interact to determine the most effective ways of supporting projects and measures relevant to persons with disabilities.

3. States should consider the use of economic measures (loans, tax exemptions, earmarked grants, special funds, and so on) to stimulate and support equal participation by persons with disabilities in society.

4. In many States it may be advisable to establish a disability development fund, which could support various pilot projects and self-help programmes at the grass-roots level.

Rule 17. Coordination of work

States are responsible for the establishment and strengthening of national coordinating committees, or similar bodies, to serve as a national focal point on disability matters.

1. The national coordinating committee or similar bodies should be permanent and based on legal as well as appropriate administrative regulation.

2. A combination of representatives of private and public organizations is most likely to achieve an intersectoral and multidisciplinary composition. Representatives could be drawn from concerned government ministries, organizations of persons with disabilities and non-governmental organizations.

3. Organizations of persons with disabilities should have considerable influence in the national coordinating committee in order to ensure proper feedback of their concerns.

4. The national coordinating committee should be provided with sufficient autonomy and resources to fulfil its responsibilities in relation to its decision-making capacities. It should report to the highest governmental level.

Rule 18. Organizations of persons with disabilities

States should recognize the right of the organizations of persons with disabilities to represent persons with disabilities at national, regional and local levels. States should also recognize the advisory role of organizations of persons with disabilities in decision-making on disability matters.

1. States should encourage and support economically and in other ways the formation and strengthening of organizations of persons with disabilities, family members and/or advocates. States should recognize that those organizations have a role to play in the development of disability policy.

2. States should establish ongoing communication with organizations of persons with disabilities and ensure their participation in the development of government policies.

3. The role of organizations of persons with disabilities could be to identify needs and priorities, to participate in the planning, implementation and evaluation of services and measures concerning the lives of persons with disabilities, and to contribute to public awareness and to advocate change.

4. As instruments of self-help, organizations of persons with disabilities provide and promote opportunities for the development of skills in various fields, mutual support among members and information sharing.

5. Organizations of persons with disabilities could perform their advisory role in many different ways such as having permanent representation on boards of government-funded agencies, serving on

public commissions and providing expert knowledge on different projects.

6. The advisory role of organizations of persons with disabilities should be ongoing in order to develop and deepen the exchange of views and information between the State and the organizations.

7. Organizations should be permanently represented on the national coordinating committee or similar bodies.

8. The role of local organizations of persons with disabilities should be developed and strengthened to ensure that they influence matters at the community level.

Rule 19. Personnel training

States are responsible for ensuring the adequate training of personnel, at all levels, involved in the planning and provision of programmes and services concerning persons with disabilities.

1. States should ensure that all authorities providing services in the disability field give adequate training to their personnel.

2. In the training of professionals in the disability field, as well as in the provision of information on disability in general training programmes, the principle of full participation and equality should be appropriately reflected.

3. States should develop training programmes in consultation with organizations of persons with disabilities, and persons with disabilities should be involved as teachers, instructors or advisers in staff training programmes.

4. The training of community workers is of great strategic importance, particularly in developing countries. It should involve persons with disabilities and include the development of appropriate values, competence and technologies as well as skills which can be practised by persons with disabilities, their parents, families and members of the community.

Rule 20. National monitoring and evaluation of disability programmes in the implementation of the Rules

States are responsible for the continuous monitoring and evaluation of the implementation of national programmes and services concerning the equalization of opportunities for persons with disabilities.

1. States should periodically and systematically evaluate national disability programmes and disseminate both the bases and the results of the evaluations.

2. States should develop and adopt terminology and criteria for the evaluation of disability-related programmes and services.

3. Such criteria and terminology should be developed in close cooperation with organizations of persons with disabilities from the earliest conceptual and planning stages.

4. States should participate in international cooperation in order to develop common standards for national evaluation in the disability field. States should encourage national coordinating committees to participate also.

5. The evaluation of various programmes in the disability field should be built in at the planning stage, so that the overall efficacy in fulfilling their policy objectives can be evaluated.

Rule 21. Technical and economic cooperation

States, both industrialized and developing, have the responsibility to cooperate in and take measures for the improvement of the living conditions of persons with disabilities in developing countries.

1. Measures to achieve the equalization of opportunities of persons with disabilities, including refugees with disabilities, should be integrated into general development programmes.

2. Such measures must be integrated into all forms of technical and economic cooperation, bilateral and multilateral, governmental and non-governmental. States should bring up disability issues in discussions on such cooperation with their counterparts.

3. When planning and reviewing programmes of technical and economic cooperation, special attention should be given to the effects of such programmes on the situation of persons with disabilities. It is of the utmost importance that persons with disabilities and their organizations are consulted on any development projects designed for persons with disabilities. They should be directly involved in the development, implementation and evaluation of such projects.

4. Priority areas for technical and economic cooperation should include:

(a) The development of human resources through the development of skills, abilities and potentials of persons with disabilities and the initiation of employment-generating activities for and of persons with disabilities;

(b) The development and dissemination of appropriate disability-related technologies and know-how.

5. States are also encouraged to support the formation and strengthening of organizations of persons with disabilities.

6. States should take measures to improve the knowledge of disability issues among staff involved at all levels in the administration of technical and economic cooperation programmes.

Rule 22. International cooperation

States will participate actively in international cooperation concerning policies for the equalization of opportunities for persons with disabilities.

1. Within the United Nations, the specialized agencies and other concerned intergovernmental organizations, States should participate in the development of disability policy.

2. Whenever appropriate, States should introduce disability aspects in general negotiations concerning standards, information exchange, development programmes, etc.

3. States should encourage and support the exchange of knowledge and experience among:

(*a*) Non-governmental organizations concerned with disability issues;

(*b*) Research institutions and individual researchers involved in disability issues;

(*c*) Representatives of field programmes and of professional groups in the disability field;

(*d*) Organizations of persons with disabilities;

(*e*) National coordinating committees.

4. States should ensure that the United Nations and the specialized agencies, as well as all intergovernmental and interparliamentary bodies, at global and regional levels, include in their work the global and regional organizations of persons with disabilities.

IV. Monitoring Mechanism

1. The purpose of a monitoring mechanism is to further the effective implementation of the Rules. It will assist each State in assessing its level of implementation of the Rules and in measuring its progress. The monitoring should identify obstacles and suggest suitable measures that would contribute to the successful implementation of the Rules. The monitoring mechanism will recognize the economic, social and cultural features existing in individual States. An important element should also be the provision of advisory services and the exchange of experience and information between States.

2. The Rules shall be monitored within the framework of the sessions of the Commission for Social Development. A Special Rapporteur with relevant and extensive experience in disability issues and international organizations shall be appointed, if necessary, funded by extrabudgetary resources, for three years to monitor the implementation of the Rules.

3. International organizations of persons with disabilities having consultative status with the Economic and Social Council and organizations representing persons with disabilities who have not yet formed their own organizations should be invited to create among themselves a panel of experts, on which organizations of persons with disabilities shall have a majority, taking into account the different kinds of disabilities and necessary equitable geographical distri-

bution, to be consulted by the Special Rapporteur and, when appropriate, by the Secretariat.

4. The panel of experts will be encouraged by the Special Rapporteur to review, advise and provide feedback and suggestions on the promotion, implementation and monitoring of the Rules.

5. The Special Rapporteur shall send a set of questions to States, entities within the United Nations system, and intergovernmental and non-governmental organizations, including organizations of persons with disabilities. The set of questions should address implementation plans for the Rules in States. The questions should be selective in nature and cover a number of specific rules for in-depth evaluation. In preparing the questions the Special Rapporteur should consult with the panel of experts and the Secretariat.

6. The Special Rapporteur shall seek to establish a direct dialogue not only with States but also with local non-governmental organizations, seeking their views and comments on any information intended to be included in the reports. The Special Rapporteur shall provide advisory services on the implementation and monitoring of the Rules and assistance in the preparation of replies to the sets of questions.

7. The Department for Policy Coordination and Sustainable Development of the Secretariat, as the United Nations focal point on disability issues, the United Nations Development Programme and other entities and mechanisms within the United Nations system, such as the regional commissions and specialized agencies and inter-agency meetings, shall cooperate with the Special Rapporteur in the implementation and monitoring of the Rules at the national level.

8. The Special Rapporteur, assisted by the Secretariat, shall prepare reports for submission to the Commission for Social Development at its thirty-fourth and thirty-fifth sessions. In preparing such reports, the Rapporteur should consult with the panel of experts.

9. States should encourage national coordinating committees or similar bodies to participate in implementation and monitoring. As the focal points on disability matters at the national level, they should be encouraged to establish procedures to coordinate the monitoring of the Rules. Organizations of persons with disabilities should be encouraged to be actively involved in the monitoring of the process at all levels.

10. Should extrabudgetary resources be identified, one or more positions of interregional adviser on the Rules should be created to provide direct services to States, including:

(*a*) The organization of national and regional training seminars on the content of the Rules;

(*b*) The development of guidelines to assist in strategies for implementation of the Rules;

(*c*) Dissemination of information about best practices concerning implementation of the Rules.

11. At its thirty-fourth session, the Commission for Social Development should establish an open-ended working group to examine the Special Rapporteur's report and make recommendations on how to improve the application of the Rules. In examining the Special Rapporteur's report, the Commission, through its open-ended working group, shall consult international organizations of persons with disabilities and specialized agencies, in accordance with rules 71 and 76 of the rules of procedure of the functional commissions of the Economic and Social Council.

12. At its session following the end of the Special Rapporteur's mandate, the Commission should examine the possibility of either renewing that mandate, appointing a new Special Rapporteur or considering another monitoring mechanism, and should make appropriate recommendations to the Economic and Social Council.

13. States should be encouraged to contribute to the United Nations Voluntary Fund on Disability in order to further the implementation of the Rules.

06.45 PERSONS IN DETENTION AND IMPRISONMENT

32/121. Protection of the Human Rights of Certain Categories of Prisoners

Committee: 3
Vote: Adopted without a vote
Ref.: 35/189, 32/122

The General Assembly,

Bearing in mind the provisions of the Universal Declaration of Human Rights,[1] in particular its articles 5, 10 and 19,

Recalling article 19 of the International Covenant on Civil and Political Rights,[2] which guarantees to everyone the right to hold opinions and to freedom of expression, subject only to such restrictions as are provided by law and are necessary for the respect of the rights or reputation of others or for the protection of national security or of public order, or of public health or morals,

Recalling also the prohibition against torture and other cruel, inhuman or degrading treatment or punishment which is laid down in article 7 of the International Covenant on Civil and Political Rights,

Noting, in this connexion, further efforts to eliminate torture which have been made in the United Nations and which have been reflected in the Declaration on the Protection of All Persons from Being Subjected to Torture and Other Cruel, Inhuman or Degrading Treatment or Punishment, adopted by the General Assembly in its resolution 3452 (XXX) of 9 December 1975,

Further recalling article 14 of the International Covenant on Civil and Political Rights, which provides that all persons, in the determination of any criminal charge against them, are entitled to a fair hearing by a competent, independent and impartial tribunal established by law,

Recognizing the importance of full respect for the human rights and fundamental freedoms of all persons detained or imprisoned as a result of their struggle against colonialism, aggression and foreign occupation and for self-determination, independence, the elimination of apartheid and all forms of racial discrimination and racism, and the termination of all these violations of human rights,

Aware of the fact that in many parts of the world numerous persons are detained in respect of offences which they committed, or are suspected of having committed, by reason of their political opinions or convictions,

Noting that these persons are often exposed to special dangers as regards the protection of their human rights and fundamental freedoms,

Realizing, therefore, that special attention should be given to the full respect of the human rights and fundamental freedoms of these persons,

1. *Requests* Member States:

(*a*) To take effective measures to safeguard the human rights and fundamental freedoms of the above-mentioned persons;

(*b*) To ensure, in particular, that such persons are not subjected to torture or other cruel, inhuman or degrading treatment or punishment;

(*c*) Also to ensure that such persons, in the determination of any criminal charge against them, receive a fair hearing by a competent, independent and impartial tribunal established by law;

2. *Calls upon* Member States to examine periodically the possibility of releasing such persons as an act of clemency or by way of conditional release or otherwise.

105th plenary meeting
16 December 1977

---

1 Resolution 217 A (III).

2 Resolution 2200 A (XXI), annex.

43/173. Body of Principles for the Protection of all Persons under any Form of Detention or Imprisonment

Committee: 6
Vote: Adopted without a vote

The General Assembly,

Recalling its resolution 35/177 of 15 December 1980, in which it referred the task of elaborating the draft Body of Principles for the Protection of All Persons under Any Form of Detention or Imprisonment to the Sixth Committee and decided to establish an open-ended working group for that purpose,

Taking note of the report of the Working Group on the Draft Body of Principles for the Protection of All Persons under Any Form of Detention or Imprisonment,[1] which met during the forty-third session of the General Assembly and completed the elaboration of the draft Body of Principles,

Considering that the Working Group decided to submit the text of the draft Body of Principles to the Sixth Committee for its consideration and adoption,[2]

Convinced that the adoption of the draft Body of Principles would make an important contribution to the protection of human rights,

Considering the need to ensure the wide dissemination of the text of the Body of Principles,

1. *Approves* the Body of Principles for the Protection of All Persons under Any Form of Detention or Imprisonment, the text of which is annexed to the present resolution;

2. *Expresses its appreciation* to the Working Group on the Draft Body of Principles for the Protection of All Persons under Any Form of Detention or Imprisonment for its important contribution to the elaboration of the Body of Principles;

3. *Requests* the Secretary-General to inform the States Members of the United Nations or members of specialized agencies of the adoption of the Body of Principles;

4. *Urges* that every effort be made so that the Body of Principles becomes generally known and respected.

76th plenary meeting
9 December 1988

Annex

Body of Principles for the Protection of all Persons under any Form of Detention or Imprisonment

Scope of the Body of Principles

These principles apply for the protection of all persons under any form of detention or imprisonment.

Use of terms

For the purposes of the Body of Principles:

(*a*) "Arrest" means the act of apprehending a person for the alleged commission of an offence or by the action of an authority;

(*b*) "Detained person" means any person deprived of personal liberty except as a result of conviction for an offence;

(*c*) "Imprisoned person" means any person deprived of personal liberty as a result of conviction for an offence;

(*d*) "Detention" means the condition of detained persons as defined above;

(*e*) "Imprisonment" means the condition of imprisoned persons as defined above;

(*f*) The words "a judicial or other authority" mean a judicial or other authority under the law whose status and tenure should afford the strongest possible guarantees of competence, impartiality and independence.

1 A/C.6/43/L.9.

2 *Ibid.*, para. 4.

Principle 1

All persons under any form of detention or imprisonment shall be treated in a humane manner and with respect for the inherent dignity of the human person.

Principle 2

Arrest, detention or imprisonment shall only be carried out strictly in accordance with the provisions of the law and by competent officials or persons authorized for that purpose.

Principle 3

There shall be no restriction upon or derogation from any of the human rights of persons under any form of detention or imprisonment recognized or existing in any State pursuant to law, conventions, regulations or custom on the pretext that this Body of Principles does not recognize such rights or that it recognizes them to a lesser extent.

Principle 4

Any form of detention or imprisonment and all measures affecting the human rights of a person under any form of detention or imprisonment shall be ordered by, or be subject to the effective control of, a judicial or other authority.

Principle 5

1. These principles shall be applied to all persons within the territory of any given State, without distinction of any kind, such as race, colour, sex, language, religion or religious belief, political or other opinion, national, ethnic or social origin, property, birth or other status.

2. Measures applied under the law and designed solely to protect the rights and special status of women, especially pregnant women and nursing mothers, children and juveniles, aged, sick or handicapped persons shall not be deemed to be discriminatory. The need for, and the application of, such measures shall always be subject to review by a judicial or other authority.

Principle 6

No person under any form of detention or imprisonment shall be subjected to torture or to cruel, inhuman or degrading treatment or punishment.[3] No circumstance whatever may be invoked as a justification for torture or other cruel, inhuman or degrading treatment or punishment.

Principle 7

1. States should prohibit by law any act contrary to the rights and duties contained in these principles, make any such act subject to appropriate sanctions and conduct impartial investigations upon complaints.

2. Officials who have reason to believe that a violation of this Body of Principles has occurred or is about to occur shall report the matter to their superior authorities and, where necessary, to other appropriate authorities or organs vested with reviewing or remedial powers.

3. Any other person who has ground to believe that a violation of this Body of Principles has occurred or is about to occur shall have the right to report the matter to the superiors of the officials involved as well as to other appropriate authorities or organs vested with reviewing or remedial powers.

3 The term "cruel, inhuman or degrading treatment or punishment" should be interpreted so as to extend the widest possible protection against abuses, whether physical or mental, including the holding of a detained or imprisoned person in conditions which deprive him, temporarily or permanently, of the use of any of his natural senses, such as sight or hearing, or of his awareness of place and the passing of time.

Principle 8

Persons in detention shall be subject to treatment appropriate to their unconvicted status. Accordingly, they shall, whenever possible, be kept separate from imprisoned persons.

Principle 9

The authorities which arrest a person, keep him under detention or investigate the case shall exercise only the powers granted to them under the law and the exercise of these powers shall be subject to recourse to a judicial or other authority.

Principle 10

Anyone who is arrested shall be informed at the time of his arrest of the reason for his arrest and shall be promptly informed of any charges against him.

Principle 11

1. A person shall not be kept in detention without being given an effective opportunity to be heard promptly by a judicial or other authority. A detained person shall have the right to defend himself or to be assisted by counsel as prescribed by law.

2. A detained person and his counsel, if any, shall receive prompt and full communication of any order of detention, together with the reasons therefor.

3. A judicial or other authority shall be empowered to review as appropriate the continuance of detention.

Principle 12

1. There shall be duly recorded:

(*a*) The reasons for the arrest;

(*b*) The time of the arrest and the taking of the arrested person to a place of custody as well as that of his first appearance before a judicial or other authority;

(*c*) The identity of the law enforcement officials concerned;

(*d*) Precise information concerning the place of custody.

2. Such records shall be communicated to the detained person, or his counsel, if any, in the form prescribed by law.

Principle 13

Any person shall, at the moment of arrest and at the commencement of detention or imprisonment, or promptly thereafter, be provided by the authority responsible for his arrest, detention or imprisonment, respectively, with information on and an explanation of his rights and how to avail himself of such rights.

Principle 14

A person who does not adequately understand or speak the language used by the authorities responsible for his arrest, detention or imprisonment is entitled to receive promptly in a language which he understands the information referred to in principle 10, principle 11, paragraph 2, principle 12, paragraph 1, and principle 13 and to have the assistance, free of charge, if necessary, of an interpreter in connection with legal proceedings subsequent to his arrest.

Principle 15

Notwithstanding the exceptions contained in principle 16, paragraph 4, and principle 18, paragraph 3, communication of the detained or imprisoned person with the outside world, and in particular his family or counsel, shall not be denied for more than a matter of days.

Principle 16

1. Promptly after arrest and after each transfer from one place of detention or imprisonment to another, a detained or imprisoned person shall be entitled to notify or to require the competent authority to notify members of his family or other appropriate persons of his choice of his arrest, detention or imprisonment or of the transfer and of the place where he is kept in custody.

2. If a detained or imprisoned person is a foreigner, he shall also be promptly informed of his right to communicate by appropriate means with a consular post or the diplomatic mission of the State of which he is a national or which is otherwise entitled to receive such communication in accordance with international law or with the representative of the competent international organization, if he is a refugee or is otherwise under the protection of an intergovernmental organization.

3. If a detained or imprisoned person is a juvenile or is incapable of understanding his entitlement, the competent authority shall on its own initiative undertake the notification referred to in the present principle. Special attention shall be given to notifying parents or guardians.

4. Any notification referred to in the present principle shall be made or permitted to be made without delay. The competent authority may however delay a notification for a reasonable period where exceptional needs of the investigation so require.

Principle 17

1. A detained person shall be entitled to have the assistance of a legal counsel. He shall be informed of his right by the competent authority promptly after arrest and shall be provided with reasonable facilities for exercising it.

2. If a detained person does not have a legal counsel of his own choice, he shall be entitled to have a legal counsel assigned to him by a judicial or other authority in all cases where the interests of justice so require and without payment by him if he does not have sufficient means to pay.

Principle 18

1. A detained or imprisoned person shall be entitled to communicate and consult with his legal counsel.

2. A detained or imprisoned person shall be allowed adequate time and facilities for consultations with his legal counsel.

3. The right of a detained or imprisoned person to be visited by and to consult and communicate, without delay or censorship and in full confidentiality, with his legal counsel may not be suspended or restricted save in exceptional circumstances, to be specified by law or lawful regulations, when it is considered indispensable by a judicial or other authority in order to maintain security and good order.

4. Interviews between a detained or imprisoned person and his legal counsel may be within sight, but not within the hearing, of a law enforcement official.

5. Communications between a detained or imprisoned person and his legal counsel mentioned in the present principle shall be inadmissible as evidence against the detained or imprisoned person unless they are connected with a continuing or contemplated crime.

Principle 19

A detained or imprisoned person shall have the right to be visited by and to correspond with, in particular, members of his family and shall be given adequate opportunity to communicate with the outside world, subject to reasonable conditions and restrictions as specified by law or lawful regulations.

Principle 20

If a detained or imprisoned person so requests, he shall if possible be kept in a place of detention or imprisonment reasonably near his usual place of residence.

Principle 21

1. It shall be prohibited to take undue advantage of the situation of a detained or imprisoned person for the purpose of compelling him to confess, to incriminate himself otherwise or to testify against any other person.

2. No detained person while being interrogated shall be subject to violence, threats or methods of interrogation which impair his capacity of decision or his judgement.

Principle 22

No detained or imprisoned person shall, even with his consent, be subjected to any medical or scientific experimentation which may be detrimental to his health.

Principle 23

1. The duration of any interrogation of a detained or imprisoned person and of the intervals between interrogations as well as the identity of the officials who conducted the interrogations and other persons present shall be recorded and certified in such form as may be prescribed by law.

2. A detained or imprisoned person, or his counsel when provided by law, shall have access to the information described in paragraph 1 of the present principle.

Principle 24

A proper medical examination shall be offered to a detained or imprisoned person as promptly as possible after his admission to the place of detention or imprisonment, and thereafter medical care and treatment shall be provided whenever necessary. This care and treatment shall be provided free of charge.

Principle 25

A detained or imprisoned person or his counsel shall, subject only to reasonable conditions to ensure security and good order in the place of detention or imprisonment, have the right to request or petition a judicial or other authority for a second medical examination or opinion.

Principle 26

The fact that a detained or imprisoned person underwent a medical examination, the name of the physician and the results of such an examination shall be duly recorded. Access to such records shall be ensured. Modalities therefore shall be in accordance with relevant rules of domestic law.

Principle 27

Non-compliance with these principles in obtaining evidence shall be taken into account in determining the admissibility of such evidence against a detained or imprisoned person.

Principle 28

A detained or imprisoned person shall have the right to obtain within the limits of available resources, if from public sources, reasonable quantities of educational, cultural and informational material, subject to reasonable conditions to ensure security and good order in the place of detention or imprisonment.

Principle 29

1. In order to supervise the strict observance of relevant laws and regulations, places of detention shall be visited regularly by qualified and experienced persons appointed by, and responsible to, a competent authority distinct from the authority directly in charge of the administration of the place of detention or imprisonment.

2. A detained or imprisoned person shall have the right to communicate freely and in full confidentiality with the persons who visit the places of detention or imprisonment in accordance with paragraph 1 of the present principle, subject to reasonable conditions to ensure security and good order in such places.

Principle 30

1. The types of conduct of the detained or imprisoned person that constitute disciplinary offences during detention or imprisonment, the description and duration of disciplinary punishment that may be inflicted and the authorities competent to impose such punishment shall be specified by law or lawful regulations and duly published.

2. A detained or imprisoned person shall have the right to be heard before disciplinary action is taken. He shall have the right to bring such action to higher authorities for review.

Principle 31

The appropriate authorities shall endeavour to ensure, according to domestic law, assistance when needed to dependent and, in particular, minor members of the families of detained or imprisoned persons and shall devote a particular measure of care to the appropriate custody of children left without supervision.

Principle 32

1. A detained person or his counsel shall be entitled at any time to take proceedings according to domestic law before a judicial or other authority to challenge the lawfulness of his detention in order to obtain his release without delay, if it is unlawful.

2. The proceedings referred to in paragraph 1 of the present principle shall be simple and expeditious and at no cost for detained persons without adequate means. The detaining authority shall produce without unreasonable delay the detained person before the reviewing authority.

Principle 33

1. A detained or imprisoned person or his counsel shall have the right to make a request or complaint regarding his treatment, in particular in case of torture or other cruel, inhuman or degrading treatment, to the authorities responsible for the administration of the place of detention and to higher authorities and, when necessary, to appropriate authorities vested with reviewing or remedial powers.

2. In those cases where neither the detained or imprisoned person nor his counsel has the possibility to exercise his rights under paragraph 1 of the present principle, a member of the family of the detained or imprisoned person or any other person who has knowledge of the case may exercise such rights.

3. Confidentiality concerning the request or complaint shall be maintained if so requested by the complainant.

4. Every request or complaint shall be promptly dealt with and replied to without undue delay. If the request or complaint is rejected or, in case of inordinate delay, the complainant shall be entitled to bring it before a judicial or other authority. Neither the detained or imprisoned person nor any complainant under paragraph 1 of the present principle shall suffer prejudice for making a request or complaint.

Principle 34

Whenever the death or disappearance of a detained or imprisoned person occurs during his detention or imprisonment, an inquiry into the cause of death or disappearance shall be held by a judicial or other authority, either on its own motion or at the instance of a member of the family of such a person or any person who has knowledge of the case. When circumstances so warrant, such an inquiry shall be held on the same procedural basis whenever the death or disappearance occurs shortly after the termination of the detention or imprisonment. The findings of such inquiry or a report thereon shall be made available upon request, unless doing so would jeopardize an ongoing criminal investigation.

Principle 35

1. Damage incurred because of acts or omissions by a public official contrary to the rights contained in these principles shall be compensated according to the applicable rules on liability provided by domestic law.

2. Information required to be recorded under these principles shall be available in accordance with procedures provided by domestic law for use in claiming compensation under the present principle.

Principle 36

1. A detained person suspected of or charged with a criminal offence shall be presumed innocent and shall be treated as such until proved guilty according to law in a public trial at which he has had all the guarantees necessary for his defence.

2. The arrest or detention of such a person pending investigation and trial shall be carried out only for the purposes of the administration of

justice on grounds and under conditions and procedures specified by law. The imposition of restrictions upon such a person which are not strictly required for the purpose of the detention or to prevent hindrance to the process of investigation or the administration of justice, or for the maintenance of security and good order in the place of detention shall be forbidden.

Principle 37

A person detained on a criminal charge shall be brought before a judicial or other authority provided by law promptly after his arrest. Such authority shall decide without delay upon the lawfulness and necessity of detention. No person may be kept under detention pending investigation or trial except upon the written order of such an authority. A detained person shall, when brought before such an authority, have the right to make a statement on the treatment received by him while in custody.

Principle 38

A person detained on a criminal charge shall be entitled to trial within a reasonable time or to release pending trial.

Principle 39

Except in special cases provided for by law, a person detained on a criminal charge shall be entitled, unless a judicial or other authority decides otherwise in the interest of the administration of justice, to release pending trial subject to the conditions that may be imposed in accordance with the law. Such authority shall keep the necessity of detention under review.

General clause

Nothing in this Body of Principles shall be construed as restricting or derogating from any right defined in the International Covenant on Civil and Political Rights.[1]

45/111. Basic Principles for the Treatment of Prisoners

Committee: 3
Vote: Adopted without a vote

The General Assembly,

Bearing in mind the long-standing concern of the United Nations for the humanization of criminal justice and the protection of human rights,

Bearing in mind also that sound policies of crime prevention and control are essential to viable planning for economic and social development,

Recognizing that the Standard Minimum Rules for the Treatment of Prisoners, adopted by the First United Nations Congress on the Prevention of Crime and the Treatment of Offenders, are of great value and influence in the development of penal policy and practice,

Considering the concern of previous United Nations congresses on the prevention of crime and the treatment of offenders, regarding the obstacles of various kinds that prevent the full implementation of the Standard Minimum Rules,

Believing that the full implementation of the Standard Minimum Rules would be facilitated by the articulation of the basic principles underlying them,

Recalling resolution 10 on the status of prisoners and resolution 17 on the human rights of prisoners, adopted by the Seventh United Nations Congress on the Prevention of Crime and the Treatment of Offenders,

Recalling also the statement submitted at the tenth session of the Committee on Crime Prevention and Control by Caritas Internationalis, the Commission of the Churches on International Affairs of the World Council of Churches, the International Association of Educators for World Peace, the International Council for Adult Education, the International Federation of Human Rights, the International Prisoners' Aid Association, the International Union of Students, the World Alliance of Young Men's Christian Associations and the World Council of Indigenous Peoples,[2] which are non-governmental organizations in consultative status with the Economic and Social Council, category II,

Recalling further the relevant recommendations contained in the report of the Interregional Preparatory Meeting for the Eighth United Nations Congress on the Prevention of Crime and the Treatment of Offenders on topic II, "Criminal justice policies in relation to problems of imprisonment, other penal sanctions and alternative measures",

Aware that the Eighth Congress coincided with International Literacy Year, proclaimed by the General Assembly in its resolution 42/104 of 7 December 1987,

Desiring to reflect the perspective noted by the Seventh Congress, namely, that the function of the criminal justice system is to contribute to safeguarding the basic values and norms of society,

Recognizing the usefulness of drafting a declaration on the human rights of prisoners,

Affirms the Basic Principles for the Treatment of Prisoners, contained in the annex to the present resolution, and requests the Secretary-General to bring it to the attention of Member States.

68th plenary meeting
14 December 1990

Annex

Basic Principles for the Treatment of Prisoners

1. All prisoners shall be treated with the respect due to their inherent dignity and value as human beings.

2. There shall be no discrimination on the grounds of race, colour, sex, language, religion, political or other opinion, national or social origin, property, birth or other status.

3. It is, however, desirable to respect the religious beliefs and cultural precepts of the group to which prisoners belong, whenever local conditions so require.

4. The responsibility of prisons for the custody of prisoners and for the protection of society against crime shall be discharged in keeping with a State's other social objectives and its fundamental responsibilities for promoting the well-being and development of all members of society.

5. Except for those limitations that are demonstrably necessitated by the fact of incarceration, all prisoners shall retain the human rights and fundamental freedoms set out in the Universal Declaration of Human Rights, and, where the State concerned is a party, the International Covenant on Economic, Social and Cultural Rights, and the International Covenant on Civil and Political Rights and the Optional Protocol thereto, as well as such other rights as are set out in other United Nations covenants.

6. All prisoners shall have the right to take part in cultural activities and education aimed at the full development of the human personality.

7. Efforts addressed to the abolition of solitary confinement as a punishment, or to the restriction of its use, should be undertaken and encouraged.

8. Conditions shall be created enabling prisoners to undertake meaningful remunerated employment which will facilitate their reintegration into the country's labour market and permit them to contribute to their own financial support and to that of their families.

9. Prisoners shall have access to the health services available in the country without discrimination on the grounds of their legal situation.

10. With the participation and help of the community and social institution, and with due regard to the interests of victims, favourable conditions shall be created for the reintegration of the ex-prisoner into society under the best possible conditions.

11. The above Principles shall be applied impartially.

---

1 See resolution 2200 A (XXI), annex.

2 See E/AC.57/1988/NGO/3.

06.46 MINORITIES AND INDIGENOUS PEOPLE

47/135. Declaration on the Rights of Persons Belonging to National or Ethnic, Religious and Linguistic Minorities

Committee: 3
Vote: Adopted without a vote
Ref.: 50/180, 49/192, 48/138, 46/115

The General Assembly,

Reaffirming that one of the main purposes of the United Nations, as proclaimed in the Charter of the United Nations, is to achieve international cooperation in promoting and encouraging respect for human rights and for fundamental freedoms for all without distinction as to race, sex, language or religion,

Noting the importance of the even more effective implementation of international human rights instruments with regard to the rights of persons belonging to national or ethnic, religious and linguistic minorities,

Welcoming the increased attention given by human rights treaty bodies to the non-discrimination and protection of minorities,

Aware of the provisions of article 27 of the International Covenant on Civil and Political Rights concerning the rights of persons belonging to ethnic, religious or linguistic minorities,

Considering that the United Nations has an increasingly important role to play regarding the protection of minorities,

Bearing in mind the work done so far within the United Nations system, in particular through the relevant mechanisms of the Commission on Human Rights and the Subcommission on Prevention of Discrimination and Protection of Minorities, in promoting and protecting the rights of persons belonging to national or ethnic, religious and linguistic minorities,

Recognizing the important achievements in this regard in regional, subregional and bilateral frameworks, which can provide a useful source of inspiration for future United Nations activities,

Stressing the need to ensure for all, without discrimination of any kind, full enjoyment and exercise of human rights and fundamental freedoms, and emphasizing the importance of the draft Declaration on the Rights of Persons Belonging to National or Ethnic, Religious and Linguistic Minorities in that regard,

Recalling its resolution 46/115 of 17 December 1991 and taking note of Commission on Human Rights resolution 1992/16 of 21 February 1992, by which the Commission approved the text of the draft declaration on the rights of persons belonging to national or ethnic, religious and linguistic minorities, and Economic and Social Council resolution 1992/4 of 20 July 1992, in which the Council recommended it to the General Assembly for adoption and further action,

Having considered the note by the Secretary-General,

1. *Adopts* the Declaration on the Rights of Persons Belonging to National or Ethnic, Religious and Linguistic Minorities, the text of which is annexed to the present resolution;

2. *Requests* the Secretary-General to ensure the distribution of the Declaration as widely as possible and to include the text of the Declaration in the next edition of Human Rights: A Compilation of International Instruments;

3. *Invites* United Nations agencies and organizations and intergovernmental and non-governmental organizations to intensify their efforts with a view to disseminating information on the Declaration and to promoting understanding thereof;

4. *Invites* the relevant organs and bodies of the United Nations, including treaty bodies, as well as representatives of the Commission on Human Rights and the Subcommission on Prevention of Discrimination and Protection of Minorities, to give due regard to the Declaration within their mandates;

5. *Requests* the Secretary-General to consider appropriate ways for the effective promotion of the Declaration and to make proposals thereon;

6. *Also requests* the Secretary-General to report to the General Assembly at its forty-eighth session on the implementation of the present resolution under the item entitled "Human rights questions".

Annex

Declaration on the Rights of Persons Belonging to National or Ethnic, Religious and Linguistic Minorities

The General Assembly,

Reaffirming that one of the basic aims of the United Nations, as proclaimed in the Charter, is to promote and encourage respect for human rights and for fundamental freedoms for all, without distinction as to race, sex, language or religion,

Reaffirming faith in fundamental human rights, in the dignity and worth of the human person, in the equal rights of men and women and of nations large and small,

Desiring to promote the realization of the principles contained in the Charter, the Universal Declaration of Human Rights, the Convention on the Prevention and Punishment of the Crime of Genocide, the International Convention on the Elimination of All Forms of Racial Discrimination, the International Covenant on Civil and Political Rights, the International Covenant on Economic, Social and Cultural Rights, the Declaration on the Elimination of All Forms of Intolerance and of Discrimination Based on Religion or Belief, and the Convention on the Rights of the Child, as well as other relevant international instruments that have been adopted at the universal or regional level and those concluded between individual States Members of the United Nations,

Inspired by the provisions of article 27 of the International Covenant on Civil and Political Rights concerning the rights of persons belonging to ethnic, religious or linguistic minorities,

Considering that the promotion and protection of the rights of persons belonging to national or ethnic, religious and linguistic minorities contribute to the political and social stability of States in which they live,

Emphasizing that the constant promotion and realization of the rights of persons belonging to national or ethnic, religious and linguistic minorities, as an integral part of the development of society as a whole and within a democratic framework based on the rule of law, would contribute to the strengthening of friendship and cooperation among peoples and States,

Considering that the United Nations has an important role to play regarding the protection of minorities,

Bearing in mind the work done so far within the United Nations system, in particular by the Commission on Human Rights, the Subcommission on Prevention of Discrimination and Protection of Minorities and the bodies established pursuant to the International Covenants on Human Rights and other relevant international human rights instruments in promoting and protecting the rights of persons belonging to national or ethnic, religious and linguistic minorities,

Taking into account the important work which is done by intergovernmental and non-governmental organizations in protecting minorities and in promoting and protecting the rights of persons belonging to national or ethnic, religious and linguistic minorities,

Recognizing the need to ensure even more effective implementation of international human rights instruments with regard to the rights of persons belonging to national or ethnic, religious and linguistic minorities,

Proclaims this Declaration on the Rights of Persons Belonging to National or Ethnic, Religious and Linguistic Minorities:

Article 1

1. States shall protect the existence and the national or ethnic, cultural, religious and linguistic identity of minorities within their respective territories and shall encourage conditions for the promotion of that identity.

2. States shall adopt appropriate legislative and other measures to achieve those ends.

Article 2

1. Persons belonging to national or ethnic, religious and linguistic minorities (hereinafter referred to as persons belonging to minorities) have the right to enjoy their own culture, to profess and practise their own religion, and to use their own language, in private and in public, freely and without interference or any form of discrimination.

2. Persons belonging to minorities have the right to participate effectively in cultural, religious, social, economic and public life.

3. Persons belonging to minorities have the right to participate effectively in decisions on the national and, where appropriate, regional level concerning the minority to which they belong or the regions in which they live, in a manner not incompatible with national legislation.

4. Persons belonging to minorities have the right to establish and maintain their own associations.

5. Persons belonging to minorities have the right to establish and maintain, without any discrimination, free and peaceful contacts with other members of their group and with persons belonging to other minorities, as well as contacts across frontiers with citizens of other States to whom they are related by national or ethnic, religious or linguistic ties.

Article 3

1. Persons belonging to minorities may exercise their rights, including those set forth in the present Declaration, individually as well as in community with other members of their group, without any discrimination.

2. No disadvantage shall result for any person belonging to a minority as the consequence of the exercise or non-exercise of the rights set forth in the present Declaration.

Article 4

1. States shall take measures where required to ensure that persons belonging to minorities may exercise fully and effectively all their human rights and fundamental freedoms without any discrimination and in full equality before the law.

2. States shall take measures to create favourable conditions to enable persons belonging to minorities to express their characteristics and to develop their culture, language, religion, traditions and customs, except where specific practices are in violation of national law and contrary to international standards.

3. States should take appropriate measures so that, wherever possible, persons belonging to minorities may have adequate opportunities to learn their mother tongue or to have instruction in their mother tongue.

4. States should, where appropriate, take measures in the field of education, in order to encourage knowledge of the history, traditions, language and culture of the minorities existing within their territory. Persons belonging to minorities should have adequate opportunities to gain knowledge of the society as a whole.

5. States should consider appropriate measures so that persons belonging to minorities may participate fully in the economic progress and development in their country.

Article 5

1. National policies and programmes shall be planned and implemented with due regard for the legitimate interests of persons belonging to minorities.

2. Programmes of cooperation and assistance among States should be planned and implemented with due regard for the legitimate interests of persons belonging to minorities.

Article 6

States should cooperate on questions relating to persons belonging to minorities, *inter alia*, exchanging information and experiences, in order to promote mutual understanding and confidence.

Article 7

States should cooperate in order to promote respect for the rights set forth in the present Declaration.

Article 8

1. Nothing in the present Declaration shall prevent the fulfilment of international obligations of States in relation to persons belonging to minorities. In particular, States shall fulfil in good faith the obligations and commitments they have assumed under international treaties and agreements to which they are parties.

2. The exercise of the rights set forth in the present Declaration shall not prejudice the enjoyment by all persons of universally recognized human rights and fundamental freedoms.

3. Measures taken by States to ensure the effective enjoyment o f the rights set forth in the present Declaration shall not prima facie be considered contrary to the principle of equality contained in the Universal Declaration of Human Rights.

4. Nothing in the present Declaration may be construed as permitting any activity contrary to the purposes and principles of the United Nations, including sovereign equality, territorial integrity and political independence of States.

Article 9

The specialized agencies and other organizations of the United Nations system shall contribute to the full realization of the rights and principles set forth in the present Declaration, within their respective fields of competence.

92nd plenary meeting
18 December 1992

50/157. Programme of Activities for the International Decade of the World's Indigenous People

Committee: 3
Vote: Adopted without a vote
Ref.: 49/180, 48/124, 47/130, 46/128, 45/151, 44/147

The General Assembly,

Bearing in mind that one of the purposes of the United Nations, as set forth in the Charter, is the achievement of international cooperation in solving international problems of an economic, social, cultural or humanitarian character and in promoting and encouraging respect for human rights and fundamental freedoms for all without distinction as to race, sex, language or religion,

Recalling its resolutions 48/163 of 21 December 1993 and 49/214 of 23 December 1994 on the International Decade of the World's Indigenous People, and Commission on Human Rights resolution 1995/28 of 3 March 1995,[1]

Recalling also that the goal of the Decade is to strengthen international cooperation for the solution of problems faced by indigenous people in such areas as human rights, the environment, development, education and health, and that the theme of the Decade is "Indigenous people: partnership in action",

Recognizing the importance of consultation and cooperation with indigenous people in planning and implementing the programme of activities for the Decade, the need for adequate financial support from the international community, including support from within the United Nations and the specialized agencies, and the need for adequate coordination and communication channels,

Recalling its invitation to organizations of indigenous people and other non-governmental organizations concerned to consider the contributions they can make to the success of the Decade, with a view to presenting them to the Working Group on Indigenous Populations,

---

1 *Official Records of the Economic and Social Council, 1995, Supplement No. 3* and corrigenda (E/1995/23 and Corr.1 and 2), chap. II, sect. A.

Taking note of Economic and Social Council decision 1992/255 of 20 July 1992, in which the Council requested United Nations bodies and specialized agencies to ensure that all technical assistance financed or provided by them was compatible with international instruments and standards, and encouraged efforts to promote coordination in this field and greater participation of indigenous people in the planning and implementation of projects affecting them,

Mindful of the relevant recommendations of the World Conference on Human Rights, the United Nations Conference on Environment and Development, the International Conference on Population and Development, the Fourth World Conference on Women and the World Summit on Social Development, and of the Declaration on the Occasion of the Fiftieth Anniversary of the United Nations,[1]

Recognizing the value and diversity of the cultures and forms of social organization of indigenous people, and convinced that the development of indigenous people within their countries will contribute to the socio-economic, cultural and environmental advancement of all the countries of the world,

1. *Takes note* of the final report of the Secretary-General on a comprehensive programme of action for the International Decade of the World's Indigenous People and the annexes to that report;[2]

2. *Decides* to adopt the programme of activities for the Decade contained in the annex to the present resolution;

3. *Also decides* that the programme of activities for the Decade may be reviewed and updated throughout the Decade and that at the midpoint of the Decade the Economic and Social Council and the General Assembly should review the results of the activities to identify obstacles to achievement of the goals of the Decade and to recommend solutions for overcoming those obstacles;

4. *Affirms* as a major objective of the Decade the adoption by the General Assembly of a declaration on the rights of indigenous people;

5. *Welcomes* the establishment of an open-ended inter-sessional Working Group of the Commission on Human Rights with the sole purpose of elaborating a draft declaration, considering the draft contained in the annex to resolution 1994/45 of 26 August 1994 of the Subcommission on Prevention of Discrimination and Protection of Minorities, entitled "Draft United Nations declaration on the rights of indigenous peoples", for consideration and adoption by the General Assembly within the Decade;

6. *Also welcomes* the decisions of the Economic and Social Council to approve the participation of some organizations of indigenous people in the open-ended inter-sessional Working Group, and encourages the continuing cooperation of the Economic and Social Council, the Committee on Non-governmental Organizations and the Centre for Human Rights of the Secretariat in processing further applications as a matter of priority in accord with the relevant resolutions of the Commission on Human Rights and the Economic and Social Council;

7. *Recognizes* among the important objectives of the Decade the consideration of the possible establishment of a permanent forum for indigenous people within the United Nations, as recommended in the Vienna Declaration and Programme of Action, adopted by the World Conference on Human Rights, held at Vienna from 14 to 25 June 1993,[3] and welcomes the report of the workshop on the possible establishment of a permanent forum for indigenous people held at Copenhagen from 26 to 28 June 1995[4] and the ongoing dialogue on this subject;

8. *Recommends* that the Secretary-General, drawing on the expertise of the Commission on Human Rights as well as the Commission for Sustainable Development and other relevant bodies, undertake a review, in close consultation with Governments and taking into account the views of indigenous people, of the existing mechanisms, procedures and programmes within the United Nations concerning indigenous people, and report to the General Assembly at its fifty-first session;

9. *Also recommends* that the Commission on Human Rights, drawing on the results of the review and the Copenhagen workshop, consider the convening of a second workshop on the possible establishment of a permanent forum for indigenous people with the participation of independent experts as well as representatives of Governments, organizations of indigenous people and other non-governmental organizations concerned and United Nations bodies and specialized agencies;

10. *Recognizes* the importance of strengthening the human and institutional capacity of indigenous people to develop their own solutions to their problems and, for these purposes, recommends that the United Nations University consider the possibility of sponsoring, in each region, one or more institutions of higher education as centres of excellence and the diffusion of expertise, and invites the Commission on Human Rights to recommend appropriate means of implementation;

11. *Recommends* that special attention be given to improving the extent and effectiveness of the participation of indigenous people in planning and implementing the activities for the Decade, including through the recruitment, where appropriate, by relevant United Nations bodies and specialized agencies of staff from among indigenous nationals of Member States, consistent with Article 101 of the Charter of the United Nations and within existing resources and staff levels;

12. *Recommends* that the Secretary-General:

(*a*) Request United Nations representatives in countries where there are indigenous people to promote, through the appropriate channels, greater participation of indigenous people in the planning and implementation of projects affecting them;

(*b*) Ensure coordinated follow-up to the recommendations concerning indigenous people of relevant world conferences, namely the World Conference on Human Rights, the United Nations Conference on Environment and Development, the International Conference on Population and Development, the Fourth World Conference on Women and the World Summit for Social Development;

(*c*) Urge relevant United Nations conferences to promote and facilitate to the extent possible and as appropriate the effective input of the views of indigenous people;

(*d*) Ensure that information about the programme of activities for the Decade, and opportunities for indigenous people to participate in those activities, is disseminated in all countries and to the greatest possible extent in indigenous languages, to be financed from within existing budgetary resources;

(*e*) Report on progress made at the national, regional and international levels in accomplishing these objectives to the General Assembly at its fifty-first session;

13. *Requests* the United Nations High Commissioner for Human Rights to promote the objectives of the Decade, taking into account the special concerns of indigenous people, in the fulfilment of his functions;

14. *Requests* the Assistant Secretary-General for Human Rights, in his capacity as Coordinator of the Decade, bearing in mind the contribution that indigenous people have the capacity to make, to establish, within existing resources, a unit within the Centre for Human Rights, including indigenous persons, to support its activities related to indigenous people, in particular to plan, coordinate and implement activities for the Decade;

15. *Invites* the Assistant Secretary-General for Human Rights to consider the appointment of a fund-raiser who could develop new sources of funding for the Decade;

16. *Requests* the Administrative Committee on Coordination, through its inter-agency process, to consult and coordinate on the Decade, with a view to assisting the Coordinator of the Decade to fulfil his function, and to report on activities of the United Nations system in relation to the Decade to the General Assembly in each year of the Decade;

---

1 Resolution 50/6.

2 A/50/511.

3 A/CONF.157/24 (Part I), chap. III.

4 E/CN.4/Sub.2/AC.4/1995/7 and Add.1-3.

17. *Invites* the United Nations financial and development institutions, operational programmes and specialized agencies, in accordance with the existing procedures of their governing bodies:

(*a*) To give increased priority and resources to improving the conditions of indigenous people, with particular emphasis on the needs of those people in developing countries, including by the preparation of specific programmes of action for the implementation of the goals of the Decade, within their areas of competence;

(*b*) To launch special projects, through appropriate channels and in collaboration with indigenous people, for strengthening their community-level initiatives, and to facilitate the exchange of information and expertise among indigenous people and other relevant experts;

(*c*) To designate focal points for coordination with the Centre for Human Rights of activities related to the Decade;

18. *Emphasizes* the important role of international cooperation in promoting the goals and activities of the Decade and the rights, well-being and sustainable development of indigenous people;

19. *Also emphasizes* the importance of action at the national level to the implementation of the goals and activities of the Decade;

20. *Encourages* Governments to support the Decade by:

(*a*) Contributing to the United Nations Trust Fund for the Decade;

(*b*) Preparing relevant programmes, plans and reports in relation to the Decade, in consultation with indigenous people;

(*c*) Seeking means, in consultation with indigenous people, of giving indigenous people greater responsibility for their own affairs and an effective voice in decisions on matters which affect them;

(*d*) Establishing national committees or other mechanisms involving indigenous people to ensure that the objectives and activities of the Decade are planned and implemented on the basis of full partnership with indigenous people;

21. *Also encourages* Governments to consider contributing, as appropriate, to the Fund for the Development of Indigenous Peoples of Latin America and the Caribbean, in support of the achievement of the goals of the Decade;

22. *Appeals* to Governments and intergovernmental and non-governmental organizations to support the Decade by identifying resources for activities designed to implement the goals of the Decade, in cooperation with indigenous people;

23. *Decides* to include in the provisional agenda of its fifty-first session the item entitled "Programme of activities of the International Decade of the World's Indigenous People".

Annex

Programme of Activities for the International Decade of the World's Indigenous People

A. Objectives

1. Taking into account General Assembly resolution 48/163 of 21 December 1993, the main objective of the International Decade of the World's Indigenous People is the strengthening of international cooperation for the solution of problems faced by indigenous people in such areas as human rights, the environment, development, health, culture and education.

2. The specialized agencies of the United Nations system and other international and national agencies, as well as communities and private enterprises, should devote special attention to development activities of benefit to indigenous communities.

3. A major objective of the Decade is education of indigenous and non-indigenous societies concerning the situation, cultures, languages, rights and aspirations of indigenous people. In particular, efforts should be made to cooperate with the United Nations Decade for Human Rights Education.

4. An objective of the Decade is the promotion and protection of the rights of indigenous people, and their empowerment to make choices that enable them to retain their cultural identity while participating in political, economic and social life, with full respect for their cultural values, languages, traditions and forms of social organization.

5. An objective of the Decade is to further the implementation of the recommendations pertaining to indigenous people of all high-level international conferences, including the United Nations Conference on Environment and Development, the World Conference on Human Rights, in particular its recommendation that consideration be given to the establishment of a permanent forum for indigenous people in the United Nations system, the United Nations Conference on Population and Development and the World Summit for Social Development as well as all future high-level meetings.

6. An objective of the Decade is the adoption of the draft "United Nations declaration on the rights of indigenous peoples" and the further development of international standards as well as national legislation for the protection and promotion of the human rights of indigenous people, including effective means of monitoring and guaranteeing those rights.

7. The objectives of the Decade should be assessed by quantifiable outcomes that will improve the lives of indigenous people and that can be evaluated halfway through the Decade and at its end.

B. Activities to be undertaken by the major actors

1. United Nations observances

8. A formal observance each year on the International Day of the World's Indigenous People, in New York, Geneva and other offices of the United Nations.

9. Official observance of the Decade as part of the Fourth World Conference on Women, the United Nations Conference on Human Settlements (Habitat II) and other international conferences related to the aims and themes of the Decade.

10. Issuance of a special series of stamps by the United Nations Postal Administration highlighting the goals and themes of the Decade.

2. Activities of the Coordinator and the Centre for Human Rights

11. Establish, as a matter of urgency, an adequately staffed and resourced indigenous people's unit.

12. Request Governments to second qualified indigenous people, in consultation with interested national indigenous organizations, to assist in the administration of the Decade.

13. Create a fellowship programme, in collaboration with the Advisory Services of the Centre for Human Rights of the Secretariat and Governments, to assist indigenous people wishing to gain experience in the different branches of the Centre, and in other parts of the United Nations system. Such fellowships might be available for indigenous research and other similar activities.

14. Open a roster of indigenous experts in various fields who might be available to assist United Nations agencies, in collaboration with Governments as appropriate, as partners or consultants.

15. Create an advisory group of persons with relevant knowledge of indigenous issues, acting in their personal capacity, to advise the Coordinator for the Decade and United Nations organizations, at their request. The members of this advisory group could include eminent indigenous persons, governmental representatives, independent experts and officials of the specialized agencies.

16. Consider the need to hold coordination meetings of Governments, organizations of the United Nations system and indigenous and non-governmental organizations, as necessary, to consider, examine and evaluate Decade activities and to develop an integrated, action-oriented strategy to advance the interests of indigenous people. The Economic and Social Council should hold mid-term and end-term reviews of the Decade in accordance with its resolution 1988/63 of 27 July 1988. The Working Group on Indigenous Populations should review international activities undertaken during the Decade and receive information from Governments on the implementation of the goals of the Decade in their respective countries.

17. Compile, on the basis of communications of the focal points in the United Nations system, a regular news-sheet containing information about meetings of interest, major or innovatory projects, new sources of funding, policy developments and other news to be widely distributed.

18. Encourage the development of partnership projects in association with Governments to address specific regional or thematic issues bringing together Governments, indigenous people and appropriate United Nations agencies.

19. Establish an information programme linking the Coordinator to focal points of the United Nations system, national committees for the Decade and, through appropriate channels, indigenous networks; also develop a database of indigenous organizations and other relevant information, in cooperation with indigenous people, Governments, academic institutions and other relevant bodies.

20. Organize meetings on relevant themes of concern to indigenous people with indigenous participation.

21. Launch a series of publications on indigenous issues to inform policy makers, opinion-formers, students and other interested people.

22. Develop, in collaboration with Governments, training programmes on human rights for indigenous people, including the preparation of relevant training materials, when possible in indigenous languages.

23. Establish a board of trustees or advisory group, including indigenous people, to assist the Coordinator of the Voluntary Fund for the International Decade.

24. Encourage the development of projects and programmes, in collaboration with Governments, and taking into account the views of indigenous people and the appropriate United Nations agencies, for support by the Voluntary Fund for the Decade.

25. Ensure, in coordination with Governments and indigenous organizations, the necessary measures to guarantee financing of the objectives of the Decade.

3. United Nations public information activities

26. Produce and disseminate a series of posters on the Decade using designs by indigenous artists.

27. Organize a lecture series at United Nations information centres and campuses linked to the United Nations University, using indigenous speakers.

28. Publish in indigenous languages the Universal Declaration of Human Rights, international human rights conventions and, upon its adoption, the United Nations declaration on the rights of indigenous people. Consider the use of audiovisual material for this purpose. Consider also the involvement of indigenous experts and their own information networks to disseminate information about the Decade.

29. Prepare, in collaboration with the Centre for Human Rights, information about indigenous people for distribution to the general public.

4. Operational activities of the United Nations system

30. Establish focal points for indigenous issues in all appropriate organisations of the United Nations system.

31. Adopt programmes of action for the Decade in the governing bodies of specialized agencies of the United Nations system in their own fields of competence, in close cooperation with indigenous people.

32. Urge Governments to ensure that the programmes and budgets of relevant intergovernmental organizations give priority and devote sufficient resources for furthering the aims of the Decade, and request that regular reports on the action taken be submitted to the governing body or executive council of each organization.

33. Prepare, publish and disseminate a manual containing practical information for indigenous people on the operations and procedures of United Nations agencies.

34. Develop research on the socio-economic conditions of indigenous people, in collaboration with indigenous organizations and other appropriate partners, with a view to publishing regular reports in order to contribute to the solution of problems faced by indigenous people, taking into account paragraph 6.26 of the Programme of Action of the International Conference on Population and Development, held at Cairo from 5 to 13 September 1994.[1]

35. Encourage Governments to establish appropriate mechanisms and practices to ensure the participation of indigenous people in the design and implementation of national and regional programmes of concern to them.

36. Hold regular inter-agency consultations, in collaboration with Governments and indigenous people, to exchange views and develop strategies on the programme of action for the Decade.

37. Hold consultations with Governments to examine, with national committees and development agencies, possibilities of cooperation in the activities of the Decade.

38. Develop training materials for indigenous people on human rights, including the translation of the main international instruments into different indigenous languages, and give them wide distribution. Consider the possibility of using radio programmes in order to gain access to indigenous communities not having written languages.

39. Prepare a database on national legislation on matters of particular relevance to indigenous people.

40. Hold consultations of all interested parties on the themes of human rights, development, the environment, health and education, and culture, with a view to elaborating programmes in these areas.

5. Activities of regional organizations

41. Implement existing and develop new regional programmes of action to promote and support the objectives of the Decade.

42. Hold regional meetings on indigenous issues with existing regional organizations with a view to strengthening coordination, taking advantage of the machinery of the United Nations system and promoting the direct and active participation of indigenous people of the different regions in collaboration with Governments. The Working Group on Indigenous Populations could consider the possibility of holding its sessions in conjunction with these meetings.

43. Develop training courses and technical assistance programmes for indigenous people in areas such as project design and management, environment, health and education, and promote the exchange of skills and experiences of indigenous people from different regions.

44. Make funds available at the regional level to activities benefiting indigenous people.

45. Encourage regional organizations to draw up regional instruments for the promotion and protection of indigenous people in the framework of their own structures, and promote existing regional instruments.

6. Activities of Member States

46. Establish national committees for the Decade or similar mechanisms, to include indigenous people, all relevant departments and other interested parties duly convened by Governments, to mobilize public support for the various activities connected with the Decade.

47. Intensify coordination and communication at the national level between relevant ministries, agencies and regional and local authorities by establishing focal points or other mechanisms for coordination and dissemination of information.

48. Use part of the resources of existing programmes and of international assistance for activities of direct benefit to indigenous people and, where possible, provide additional funds for specific activities.

49. Develop, in collaboration with indigenous communities, national plans for the Decade, including main objectives and targets, fixing quantitative outcomes and taking into account the need for resources and possible sources of financing.

50. Provide appropriate resources for indigenous institutions, organizations and communities to develop their own plans and actions according to their own priorities.

51. Adopt measures, in cooperation with indigenous people, to increase knowledge, starting at the elementary-school level and in accord with the age and development of schoolchildren, concerning

1 A/CONF.171/13, chap.I, resolution 1, annex.

the history, traditions, culture and rights of indigenous people, with special emphasis on the education of teachers at all levels, and adopt measures to restore indigenous place names.

52. Consider ratification and implementation of the International Labour Organization Convention (No. 169) on Indigenous and Tribal Peoples and other international and regional instruments in close consultation with the indigenous organizations of each country.

53. Recognize the existence, identity and rights of indigenous people through constitutional reforms or the adoption of new laws, when appropriate, to improve their legal status and guarantee their economic, social, cultural, political and civil rights.

54. Implement chapter 26 of Agenda 21,[1] adopted by the United Nations Conference on Environment and Development, and the relevant provisions of the Convention on Biological Diversity,[2] the Vienna Declaration and Programme of Action,[3] the Programme of Action of the International Conference on Population and Development,[4] the Programme of Action of the World Summit for Social Development,[5] as well as the relevant provisions of future high-level conferences.

7. Activities of organizations of indigenous people

55. Establish an information network which can be linked to the Coordinator and facilitate communications between the United Nations system, relevant governmental departments and indigenous communities.

56. Indigenous organizations and international indigenous networks should develop information for local communities concerning the goals of the Decade and the activities of the United Nations.

57. Establish and support indigenous schools and university-level institutions and collaborate with the relevant United Nations agencies; participate in the revision of school texts and the contents of programmes of study in order to eliminate discriminatory content and promote the development of indigenous cultures and, where appropriate, in indigenous languages and scripts; develop indigenous curricula for schools and research institutions.

58. Create documentation centres, archives and *in situ* museums concerning indigenous people, their cultures, laws, beliefs and values, with material that could be used to inform and educate non-indigenous people on these matters. Indigenous people should participate on a preferential basis in the administration of these centres.

59. Establish and promote networks of indigenous journalists and launch indigenous periodicals at the regional and international levels.

60. Indigenous people may transmit to Governments, the United Nations and the specialized agencies and regional organizations their views on the programmes concerning their priority rights.

8. Activities of non-governmental organizations and other interested parties, including education establishments, the media and business

61. Cooperate with indigenous organizations, communities and people in the planning of activities for the Decade.

62. Non-governmental organizations working with indigenous people should involve indigenous people in their activities.

63. Create radio and television centres in indigenous regions when appropriate and in accordance with national legislation to provide information on the problems and proposals of indigenous people and to improve communications between indigenous communities.

64. Promote indigenous cultures with due respect for intellectual property rights through the publication of books, the production of compact discs, and the organization of various artistic and cultural events which enhance knowledge of and serve to develop indigenous cultures and establish indigenous cultural and documentation centres.

65. Involve different social and cultural groups in the activities planned for the Decade.

97th plenary meeting
Date: 21 December 1995

06.50 HUMAN RIGHTS SITUATION IN PARTICULAR COUNTRIES

385 (V). Observance in Bulgaria, Hungary and Romania of Human Rights and Fundamental Freedoms

Committee: P
Vote: 40 - 5 - 12

The General Assembly,

Considering that one of the purposes of the United Nations is to achieve international cooperation in promoting and encouraging respect for human rights and fundamental freedoms for all without distinction as to race, sex, language or religion,

Having regard to General Assembly resolutions 272 (III) and 294 (IV) concerning the question of the observance in Bulgaria, Hungary and Romania of human rights and fundamental freedoms, and to its decision in the latter resolution to submit certain questions to the International Court of Justice for an advisory opinion,

1. *Takes note* of the advisory opinions[6] delivered by the International Court of Justice on 30 March 1950 and 18 July 1950 to the effect that:

(*a*) The diplomatic exchanges between Bulgaria, Hungary and Romania on the one hand, and certain Allied and Associated Powers signatories to the Treaties of Peace on the other, concerning the implementation of article 2 of the Treaties with Bulgaria and Hungary and article 3 of the Treaty with Romania, disclose disputes to the provisions for the settlement of disputes contained in article 36 of the Treaty of Peace with Bulgaria, article 40 of the Treaty of Peace with Hungary, and article 38 of the Treaty of Peace with Romania;

(*b*) The Governments of Bulgaria, Hungary and Romania are obligated to carry out the provisions of those articles of the Treaties of Peace which relate to the settlement of disputes, including the provisions for the appointment of their representatives to the Treaty Commissions;

(*c*) If one party fails to appoint a representative to a Treaty Commission under the Treaties of Peace with Bulgaria, Hungary and Romania where that party is obligated to appoint a representative to the Treaty Commission, the Secretary-General of the United Nations is not authorized to appoint the third member of the Commission upon the request of the other party to a dispute;

---

1 *Report of the United Nations Conference on Environment and Development. Rio de Janeiro. 3-14 June 1992* (United Nations publication, Sales No. E.93.I.8 and corrigenda), vol. I: Resolutions adopted by the Conference, resolution 1, annex II.

2 See *United Nations Environment Programme, Convention on Biological Diversity* (Environmental Law and Institutions Programme Activity Centre), June 1992.

3 A/CONF.157/24 (Part I), chap. III.

4 A/CONF.171/13, chap. I, resolution 1, annex.

5 A/CONF.166/9, chap. I, resolution I, annex II.

6 See *Interpretation of Peace Treaties, Advisory Opinion:* I.C.J. Reports 1950, p. 65 and *Interpretation of Peace Treaties (second phase), Advisory Opinion:* I.C.J. Reports 1950, p. 221.

2. *Condemns* the wilful refusal of the Governments of Bulgaria, Hungary and Romania to fulfil their obligation under the provisions of the Treaties of Peace to appoint representatives to the Treaty Commissions, which obligation has been confirmed by the International Court of Justice;

3. *Is of the opinion* that the conduct of the Governments of Bulgaria, Hungary and Romania in this matter is such as to indicate that they are aware of breaches being committed of those articles of the Treaties of Peace under which they are obligated to secure the enjoyment of human rights and fundamental freedoms in their countries; and that they are callously indifferent to the sentiments of the world community;

4. *Notes* with anxiety the continuance of serious accusations on these matters against the Governments of Bulgaria, Hungary and Romania, and that the three Governments have made no satisfactory refutation of these accusations;

5. *Invites* Members of the United Nations, and in particular those which are parties to the Treaties of Peace with Bulgaria, Hungary and Romania, to submit to the Secretary-General all evidence which they now hold or which may become available in future in relation to this question;

6. *Likewise invites* the Secretary-General to notify the Members of the United Nations of any information he may receive in connexion with this question.

303rd plenary meeting
3 November 1950

2079 (XX). Question of Tibet

Committee: -
Vote: 43 - 26 - 22
Ref.: 1723(XVI), 1353(XIV)

The General Assembly,

Bearing in mind the principles relating to human rights and fundamental freedoms set forth in the Charter of the United Nations and proclaimed in the Universal Declaration of Human Rights,

Reaffirming its resolutions 1353 (XIV) of 21 October 1959 and 1723 (XVI) of 20 December 1961 on the question of Tibet,

Gravely concerned at the continued violation of the fundamental rights and freedoms of the people of Tibet and the continued suppression of their distinctive cultural and religious life, as evidenced by the exodus of refugees to the neighbouring countries,

1. *Deplores* the continued violation of the fundamental rights and freedoms of the people of Tibet;

2. *Reaffirms* that respect for the principles of the Charter of the United Nations and of the Universal Declaration of Human Rights is essential for the evolution of a peaceful world order based on the rule of law;

3. *Declares* its conviction that the violation of human rights and fundamental freedoms in Tibet and the suppression of the distinctive cultural and religious life of its people increase international tension and embitter relations between peoples;

4. *Solemnly renews* its call for the cessation of all practices which deprive the Tibetan people of the human rights and fundamental freedoms which they have always enjoyed;

5. *Appeals* to all States to use their best endeavours to achieve the purposes of the present resolution.

1403rd plenary meeting
18 December 1965

33/162. Migratory Labour in Southern Africa

Committee: 3
Vote: Adopted without a vote
Ref.: 38/11

The General Assembly,

Recalling its resolutions 32/105 A to N of 14 December 1977 and 32/105 O of 16 December 1977 relating to the policies of apartheid of the Government of South Africa,

Recalling further Economic and Social Council resolution 2082 B (LXII) of 13 May 1977, in which the Council recommended that the General Assembly should declare 1978 the International Anti-Apartheid Year,

Noting with satisfaction the proclamation of the year beginning on 21 March 1978 and ending on 20 March 1979 as International Anti-Apartheid Year,

Bearing in mind the Programme for the International Anti-Apartheid Year,[1]

Recalling also the resolutions on accelerated economic development and international action and on the promotion of development strategies with a view to reducing economic dependence on South Africa and the Charter of Rights for Migrant Workers in Southern Africa which were adopted by the Conference on Migratory Labour in Southern Africa,[2] held at Lusaka from 4 to 8 April 1978, and organized by the Economic Commission for Africa and the International Labour Organisation, in cooperation with the Government of Zambia and the liberation movements of southern Africa that are recognized by the Organization of African Unity,

Aware of the heavy dependence of Botswana, Lesotho, Malawi, Mozambique, Namibia and Swaziland on their supply of migrant labour to South Africa and of the need to eliminate such undesirable dependence,

Convinced that the continuance of the system of migrant labour to South Africa both perpetuates the evils of apartheid and retards the social and economic advancement of the States supplying migrant labour,

Convinced also that the removal of this evil system of migrant labour would facilitate the elimination of apartheid and accelerate the socio-economic development and transformation of the supplier States,

Realizing that the weak position of the supplier States to take action individually with a view to extricating their dependent economies and their migrant nationals from the stranglehold of apartheid and the economy of South Africa calls for urgent concerted action and cooperation among the affected Member States as well as assistance from other African States, international organizations, non-African Governments and other organizations,

1. *Endorses* the Charter of Rights for Migrant Workers in Southern Africa as adopted by the Lusaka Conference on Migratory Labour in Southern Africa on 7 April 1978 and annexed to the present resolution;

2. *Urges* all Member States and all organizations of the United Nations system and other international organizations, pursuant to the Lagos Declaration for Action against Apartheid[3] adopted by the World Conference for Action against Apartheid, to extend to the African States affected by the migration of labour to South Africa all material, financial, technical and political support for the initiation and implementation of specific development programmes and projects aimed at enabling those States to utilize fully their available labour force for the development of their own economies and thereby eliminate the necessity to

---

1 Resolution 32/105 B, annex.

2 E/CN. 14/ECO/ 142, part two.

3 *Report of the World Conference for Action against* Apartheid, *Lagos, 22-26 August 1977* (United Nations publication Sales No. E.77.XIV.2 and corrigendum) sect. X.

export such labour to the apartheid economy of South Africa.

90th plenary meeting
20 December 1978

Annex

Charter of Rights for Migrant Workers in Southern Africa Adopted on 7 April 1978 by the Conference on Migratory Labour in Southern Africa

We, the representatives of the States and peoples of southern Africa,

Noting that apartheid has been declared a crime against humanity by the General Assembly of the United Nations,

Noting the work done by the International Labour Organisation on the problems of migratory labour in southern Africa and recalling International Labour Organisation Conventions No. 87 of 9 July 1948 and Nos. 97 and 98 of 1 July 1949[1] concerning, respectively, the freedom of association and protection of the right to organize, migration for employment and the application of the principles of the right to organize and to bargain collectively,

Recognizing that the migratory labour system is one of the major instruments of apartheid,

Mindful of the gross indignities it inflicts on workers, who are denied many of their basic human rights,

Noting that it undermines family life and disrupts agrarian economies,

Hereby pledge ourselves to strive for the abolition of the migratory labour system practised in South Africa and, pending its elimination agree to the present Charter of Rights for Migrant Workers in Southern Africa.

Chapter I

Rights of Association, Movement and Residence

Article 1

All workers shall have the right to:

(a) Form and join trade unions of their own choice;

(b) Participate in collective bargaining on equal terms with all other workers regardless of race, sex, political affiliation or religion;

(c) Withhold their labour by strike action in support of their demands.

Article 2

All workers shall have the right to freedom of movement and shall not be required to carry a pass or similar document.

Article 3

All workers shall have the right to be accommodated near their place of work with their families in suitable houses under home ownership schemes or to reside elsewhere if they choose so to do.

Article 4

All workers shall have the right of occupation free from colour bar, job reservation and all other forms of discrimination.

Article 5

Every worker, regardless of race or sex, shall have the right to work, choose his occupation and change from one employer to another without loss of accrued benefits and claim to promotion.

Article 6

All workers, without exception, shall have the right to equal pay for equal work.

Article 7

All workers shall have equal rights to vocational training and adult education for the purpose of acquiring skills and increasing their awareness.

Chapter II

Right to a Decent Standard of Living

Article 8

Every worker is entitled to a minimum basic wage sufficient for the maintenance of the health and well-being of his family.

Article 9

All workers shall have the right to adequate protection against occupational accidents and diseases by means of approved safeguards and close supervision by an independent industrial and farming inspectorate operating in conjunction with workers' representatives.

Article 10

All workers and their families shall have an equal and absolute right to adequate, immediate and effective compensation for death or disability arising out of occupational diseases and accidents.

Article 11

All workers shall have a right to:

(a) Free medical services for themselves and their families;

(b) Sick leave and, where applicable, maternity leave with full pay;

(c) Annual paid holidays.

Article 12

All workers shall be entitled to retire on full pension or with a gratuity proportionate to their period of service.

Article 13

All workers shall have a right to determine their terms and conditions of employment through collective bargaining.

Article 14

All workers shall have a right to unemployment benefits.

Article 15

All women workers shall have the right to participate in all sectors of the economy without discrimination in respect of wages, training, job allocation or pension benefits.

43/92. Adverse Consequences for the Enjoyment of Human Rights of Political, Military, Economic and other Forms of Assistance Given to the Racist and Colonialist Régime of South Africa

Committee: 3
Vote: 129 - 10 - 27
Ref.: 45/84, 31/33

The General Assembly,

Recalling its resolutions 3382 (XXX) and 3383 (XXX) of 10 November 1975, 33/23 of 29 November 1978, 35/32 of 14 November 1980, 37/39 of 3 December 1982, 39/15 of 23 November 1984 and 41/95 of 4 December 1986,

Recalling also its resolutions 3201 (S-VI) and 3202 (S-VI) of 1 May 1974, containing the Declaration and the Programme of Action on the Establishment of a New Interna-

1 See International Labour Organisation, *Conventions and Recommendations adopted by the International Labour Conference, 1919-1966* (Geneva, International Labour Office, 1966).

tional Economic Order, and 3281 (XXIX) of 12 December 1974, containing the Charter of Economic Rights and Duties of States,

Mindful of its resolution 3171 (XXVIII) of 17 December 1973 relating to permanent sovereignty over natural resources of both developing countries and territories under colonial and foreign domination or subjected to the apartheid régime,

Recalling its resolutions on military collaboration with South Africa, as well as Security Council resolutions 418 (1977) of 4 November 1977, 421 (1977) of 9 December 1977, 558 (1984) of 13 December 1984 and 569 (1985) of 26 July 1985,

Taking into account, in particular, the relevant decisions adopted by the Assembly of Heads of State and Government of the Organization of African Unity at its twenty-fourth ordinary session, held at Addis Ababa from 25 to 28 May 1988,[1] and by the Council of Ministers of that organization at its forty-eighth ordinary session, held at Addis Ababa from 19 to 23 May 1988,[2]

Taking note with satisfaction of the updated report prepared by the Special Rapporteur of the Sub-Commission on Prevention of Discrimination and Protection of Minorities on the adverse consequences for the enjoyment of human rights of political, military, economic and other forms of assistance given to the racist and colonialist régime of South Africa,[3]

Noting with regret that the request contained in its resolution 41/95 with regard to making available to the Special Rapporteur two economists was not implemented,

Reaffirming that any collaboration with the racist régime of South Africa constitutes a hostile act against the oppressed peoples of southern Africa in their struggle for freedom and independence and a contemptuous defiance of the United Nations and of the international community,

Considering that such collaboration enables South Africa to acquire the means necessary to carry out acts of aggression and blackmail against independent African States,

Deeply concerned that the major Western and other trading partners of South Africa continue to collaborate with that racist régime and that their collaboration constitutes the main obstacle to the liquidation of that racist régime and the elimination of the inhuman and criminal system of apartheid,

Alarmed at the continued collaboration of certain Western States and Israel with the racist régime of South Africa in the nuclear field,

Regretting that the Security Council has not been in a position to take binding decisions to prevent any collaboration in the nuclear field with South Africa,

Affirming that the highest priority must be accorded to international action to secure the full implementation of the resolutions of the United Nations for the eradication of apartheid and the liberation of the peoples of southern Africa,

Conscious of the continuing need to mobilize world public opinion against the political, military, economic and other forms of assistance given to the racist and colonialist régime of South Africa,

1. *Reaffirms* the inalienable right of the oppressed peoples of southern Africa to self-determination, independence and the enjoyment of the natural resources of their territories;

2. *Again reaffirms* the right of those same peoples to dispose of those resources for their greater well-being and to obtain just reparation for the exploitation, depletion, loss or depreciation of those natural resources, including reparation for the exploitation and abuse of their human resources;

3. *Vigorously condemns* the collaboration of certain Western States, Israel and other States, as well as the transnational corporations and other organizations, which maintain or continue to increase their collaboration with the racist and colonialist régime of South Africa, especially in the political, economic, military and nuclear fields, thus encouraging that régime to persist in its inhuman and criminal policy of brutal oppression of the peoples of southern Africa and denial of their human rights;

4. *Reaffirms once again* that States and organizations that give assistance to the racist régime of South Africa become accomplices in the inhuman practices of racial discrimination, colonialism and apartheid perpetrated by that régime, as well as in the acts of aggression against the liberation movements and neighbouring States;

5. *Requests* the Security Council once again urgently to consider the imposition of comprehensive and mandatory sanctions under Chapter VII of the Charter of the United Nations against the racist régime of South Africa, in pa·ticular:

(*a*) The prohibition of all technological assistance or collaboration in the manufacture of arms and military supplies in South Africa;

(*b*) The cessation of all collaboration with South Africa in the nuclear field;

(*c*) The prohibition of all loans to, and all investments in, South Africa and the cessation of any trade with South Africa;

(*d*) An embargo on the supply of petroleum, petroleum products and other strategic goods to South Africa;

6. *Appeals* to all States, specialized agencies and non-governmental organizations to extend all possible cooperation to the liberation movements of southern Africa recognized by the United Nations and the Organization of African Unity;

7. *Expresses its appreciation* to the Special Rapporteur of the Sub-Commission on Prevention of Discrimination and Protection of Minorities for his updated report;

8. *Reaffirms* that the updating of the report on the adverse consequences for the enjoyment of human rights of political, military, economic and other forms of assistance given to the racist and colonialist régime of South Africa is of the greatest importance to the cause of fighting apartheid and other violations of human rights in South Africa and Namibia;

9. *Invites* the Special Rapporteur:

(*a*) To continue to update, subject to annual review, the list of banks, transnational corporations and other organizations assisting the racist and colonialist régime of South Africa, giving such details regarding enterprises listed as the Rapporteur may consider necessary and appropriate, including explanations of responses, if any, and to submit the updated report to the General Assembly at its forty-fifth session;

(*b*) To use all available material from other United Nations organs, Member States, national liberation movements recognized by the Organization of African Unity, specialized agencies and other intergovernmental and non-governmental organizations, as well as other relevant sources, in order to indicate the volume, nature and adverse human consequences of the assistance given to the racist régime of South Africa;

(*c*) To intensify direct contacts with the United Nations Centre on Transnational Corporations, the Centre against Apartheid of the Secretariat and the United Nations Council for Namibia, with a view to consolidating mutual cooperation in updating his report;

10. *Requests* the Secretary-General to give the Special Rapporteur all the assistance, including adequate travel funds, that he may require in the exercise of his mandate, with a view, in particular, to intensifying direct contacts with the United Nations Centre on Transnational Corporations, the Centre against Apartheid and the United Nations

---

1 See A/43/398, annex II.

2 *Ibid.*, annex I.

3 E/CN.4/Sub.2/1988/6 and Add.1.

Council for Namibia, to expanding his work on the annotation of certain selected cases as reflected in the list contained in his report and to continuing the computerization of future updated lists;

11. *Demands* that the Secretary-General, in accordance with Economic and Social Council decision 1986/145 of 23 May 1986, make available to the Special Rapporteur two economists to help him to develop his work of analysis and documentation of some special cases mentioned in his report;

12. *Notes with satisfaction* the disinvestment measures, trade restrictions and other positive measures taken by some countries and transnational corporations, and encourages them to continue in this direction;

13. *Requests* the Special Rapporteur to include in his updated report a list of partial disinvestment of foreign enterprises from South Africa, enumerating various techniques employed to avoid total withdrawal from participation in the South African economy;

14. *Calls upon* the Governments of the countries where the banks, transnational corporations and other organizations named and listed in the updated report are based to take effective action to put a stop to their trading, manufacturing and investing activities in the territory of South Africa as well as in the Territory of Namibia illegally occupied by the racist Pretoria régime;

15. *Urgently requests* all specialized agencies, particularly the International Monetary Fund and the World Bank, to refrain from granting loans or financial assistance of any type to the racist régime of South Africa;

16. *Requests* the Secretary-General to transmit the updated report to the Special Committee against Apartheid, the United Nations Council for Namibia, other bodies concerned within the United Nations system and regional international organizations;

17. *Invites* the Secretary-General to give the updated report the widest dissemination, to issue it as a United Nations publication and to make it available to learned societies, research centres, universities, political and humanitarian organizations and other interested groups;

18. *Calls upon* all Governments to cooperate with the Special Rapporteur in making the report even more accurate and informative;

19. *Calls upon* all States, specialized agencies and regional, intergovernmental and other organizations concerned to give wide publicity to the updated report;

20. *Invites* the Commission on Human Rights to give high priority at its forty-fifth session to the consideration of the updated report;

21. *Decides* to consider at its forty-fifth session, as a matter of high priority, the item entitled "Adverse consequences for the enjoyment of human rights of political, military, economic and other forms of assistance given to the racist and colonialist régime of South Africa", in the light of any recommendations which the Sub-Commission on Prevention of Discrimination and Protection of Minorities, the Commission on Human Rights, the Economic and Social Council and the Special Committee against Apartheid may wish to submit to it.

S-16/1. Declaration on Apartheid and its Destructive Consequences in Southern Africa

Committee: Ad hoc
Vote: Adopted without a vote

The General Assembly,

Adopts the Declaration on Apartheid and its Destructive Consequences in Southern Africa, annexed to the present resolution

6th plenary meeting
14 December 1989

Annex

Declaration on Apartheid and its Destructive Consequences

We, the State Members of the United Nations,

Assembled at the sixteenth special session of the General Assembly, a special session on apartheid and its destructive consequences in southern Africa, guided by the fundamental and universal principles enshrined in the Charter of the United Nations and the Universal Declaration of Human Rights,[1] in the context of our efforts to establish peace throughout the world by ending all conflicts through negotiations, and desirous of making serious efforts to bring an end to the unacceptable situation prevailing in southern Africa, which is a result of the polices and practices of apartheid, through negotiations based on the principle of justice and peace for all:

Reaffirming our conviction, which history confirms, that where colonial and racial domination or apartheid exist, there can be neither peace nor justice,

Reiterating, accordingly, that while the apartheid system in South Africa persists, the peoples of Africa as a whole cannot achieve the fundamental objectives of justice, human dignity and peace which are both crucial in themselves and fundamental to the stability and development of the continent,

Recognizing that, with regard to southern Africa, the entire world is vitally interested that the processes in which that region is involved, leading to the genuine national independence of Namibia and peace in Angola and Mozambique, should succeed in the shortest possible time, and equally recognizing that the world is deeply concerned that destabilization by South Africa of the countries of the region, whether through direct aggression, sponsorship of surrogates, economic subversion or other means, is unacceptable in all its forms and must not occur,

Also recognizing the reality that permanent peace and stability in southern Africa can only be achieved when the system of apartheid in South Africa has been eradicated and South Africa has been transformed into a united, democratic and non-racial country, and therefore reiterating that all the necessary measures should be adopted now to bring a speedy end to the apartheid system in the interest of all the people of southern Africa, the continent and the world at large,

Believing that, as a result of the legitimate struggle of the South African people for the elimination of apartheid, and of international pressure against that system, as well as global efforts to resolve regional conflicts, possibilities exist for further movement towards the resolution of the problems facing the people of South Africa,

Reaffirming the right of all peoples, including the people of South Africa, to determine their own destiny and to work out for themselves the institutions and the system of government under which they will, by general consent, live and work together to build a harmonious society, and remaining committed to doing everything possible and necessary to assist the people of South Africa, in such ways as they may, through their genuine representatives, determine to achieve this objective,

Making these commitments because we believe that all people are equal and have equal rights to human dignity and respect, regardless of colour, race, sex or creed, that all men and women have the right and duty to participate in their own government, as equal members of society, and that no individual or group of individuals has any right to govern others without their democratic consent, and reiterating that the apartheid system violate violates all these fundamental and universal principles,

[1] Resolution 217 A (III).

Affirming that apartheid, characterized as a crime against the conscience and dignity of mankind, is responsible for the death of countless number of people in South Africa, has sought to dehumanize entire peoples and has imposed a brutal war on the region of southern Africa, which has resulted in untold loss of life, destruction of property and massive displacement of innocent men, women and children and which is a scourge and affront to humanity that must be fought and eradicated in its totality,

Therefore we support and continue to support all those in South Africa who pursue this noble objective. We believe this to be our duty, carried out in the interest of all humanity,

While extending this support to those who strive for a non-racial and democratic society in South Africa, a point on which no compromise is possible, we have repeatedly expressed our objective of a solution arrived at by peaceful means; we note that the people of South Africa, and their liberation movements who felt compelled to take up arms, have also upheld their preference for this position for many decades and continue to do so,

Welcoming the Declaration of the A*d Hoc* Committee of the Organization of African Unity on Southern Africa on the question of South Africa, adopted at Harare on 21 August 1989,[1] and subsequently endorsed by the Heads of State or Government of Non-Aligned Country at their Ninth Conference, held at Belgrade from 4 to 7 September 1989,[2] as a reaffirmation of readiness to resolve the problems of South Africa through negotiations. The Declaration is consistent with the positions contained in the Lusaka Manifesto[3] of two decades ago, in particular regarding the preference of the African people for peaceful change, and takes into account the changes that have taken place in southern Africa since then. The Declaration constitutes a new challenge to the Pretoria régime to join in the noble efforts to end the apartheid system, an objective to which the United Nations has always been committed,

Noting with appreciation that the Commonwealth Heads of Government, at their meeting held at Kuala Lumpur from 18 to 24 October 1989, noted with satisfaction the strong preference for the path of negotiated and peaceful settlement inherent in the Declaration adopted at Harare on 21 August 1989, and considered what further steps they might take to advance the prospects for negotiations,[4]

Also noting with appreciation that the Third Francophone Conference of Heads of State and Government, held at Dakar from 24 to 26 May 1989, likewise called for negotiations between Pretoria and representatives of the majority of the people with a view to the establishment of a democratic and egalitarian system in South Africa,

Consequently, we shall continue to do everything in our power to increase support for the legitimate struggle of the South African people, including maintaining international pressure against the system of apartheid until that system is ended and South Africa is transformed into a united, democratic and non-racial country, with justice and security for all its citizens,

In keeping with this solemn resolve, and responding directly to the wishes of the majority of the people of South Africa, we publicly pledge ourselves to the positions contained hereunder, convinced that their implementation will lead to a speedy end of the apartheid system and herald the dawn of a new era of peace for all the peoples of Africa, in a continent finally free from racism, white minority rule and colonial domination,

Declare as follows:

1. A conjuncture of circumstances exists, which, if there is a demonstrable readiness on the part of the South African régime to engage in negotiations genuinely and seriously, given the repeated expression of the majority of the people of South Africa of their long-standing preference to arrive at a political settlement, could create the possibility to end apartheid through negotiations.

2. We would therefore encourage the people of South Africa, as part of their legitimate struggle, to join together to negotiate an end to the apartheid system and agree on all the measures that are necessary to transform their country into a non-racial democracy. We support the position held by the majority of the people of South Africa that these objectives, and not the amendment or reform of the apartheid system, should be the goals of the negotiations.

3. We are at one with the people of South Africa that the outcome of such a process should be a new constitutional order determined by them and based on the Charter of the United Nations and the Universal Declaration of Human Rights. We therefore hold the following fundamental principles to be of importance:

(*a*) South Africa shall become a united, non-racial and democratic State;

(*b*) All its people shall enjoy common and equal citizenship and nationality, regardless of race, colour, sex or creed;

(*c*) All its people shall have the right to participate in the government and administration of the country on the basis of universal, equal suffrage, under a non-racial voters' roll, and by secret ballot, in a united and non-fragmented South Africa;

(*d*) All shall have the right to form and join any political party of their choice, provided that this is not in furtherance of racism;

(*e*) All shall enjoy universally recognized human rights, freedoms and civil liberties, protected under an entrenched bill of rights;

(*f*) South Africa shall have a legal system that will guarantee equality of all before the law;

(*g*) South Africa shall have an independent and non-racial judiciary;

(*h*) There shall be created an economic order that will promote and advance the well-being of all South Africans;

(*i*) A democratic South Africa shall respect the rights, sovereignty and territorial integrity of all countries and pursue a policy of peace, friendship and mutually beneficial cooperation with all peoples.

4. We believe that acceptance of these fundamental principles could constitute the basis for an internationally acceptable solution that will enable South Africa to take its rightful place as an equal partner among the world community of nations.

A. Climate for Negotiations

5. We believe that it is essential that the necessary climate be created for negotiations. There is an urgent need to respond positively to this universally acclaimed demand and thus create this climate.

6. Accordingly, the present South African regime should, at the least:

(*a*) Release all political prisoners and detainees unconditionally and refrain from imposing any restrictions on them;

(*b*) Lift all bans and restrictions on all proscribed and restricted organizations and persons;

(*c*) Remove all troops from the townships;

(*d*) End the state of emergency and repeal all legislation, such as the Internal Security Act, designed to circumscribe political activity;

(*e*) Cease all political trials and political executions.

7. These measures would help create the necessary climate in which free political discussion can take place - an essen-

---

1 A/44/697, annex.

2 See A/44/551-S/20870, annex.

3 See *Official Records of the General Assembly, Twenty-fourth Session, Annexes*, agenda item 106, document A/7754.

4 See A/44/672-S/20914.

tial condition to ensure that the people themselves participate in the process of remaking their country.

B. Guidelines to the Process of Negotiations

8. We are of the view that the parties concerned should, in the context of the necessary climate, negotiate the future of their country and its people in good faith and in an atmosphere which, by mutual agreement between the liberation movements and the South African regime, would be free of violence. The process could commence along the following guidelines:

(*a*) Agreement on the mechanism for the drawing up of a new constitution, based on, among others, the principles enunciated above, and the basis for its adoption;

(*b*) Agreement on the role to be played by the international community in ensuring a successful transition to a democratic order,

(*c*) Agreed transitional arrangements and modalities for the process of the drawing up and adoption of a new constitution, and for the transition to a democratic order, including the holding of elections.

C. Programme of Action

9. In pursuance of the objectives stated in this Declaration, we hereby decide:

(*a*) To remain seized of the issue of a political resolution of the South African question;

(*b*) To step up all-round support for the opponents of apartheid and to campaign internationally in pursuance of this objective;

(*c*) To use concerted and effective measures, including the full observance by all countries of the mandatory arms embargo, aimed at applying pressure to ensure a speedy end to apartheid;

(*d*) To ensure that the international community does not relax existing measures aimed at encouraging the South African régime to eradicate apartheid until there is dear evidence of profound and irreversible changes, bearing in mind the objectives of this Declaration;

(*e*) To render all possible assistance to the front-line and neighbouring States to enable them: to rebuild their economies, which have been adversely affected by South Africa's acts of aggression and destabilization; to withstand any further such acts; and to continue to support the peoples of Namibia and South Africa;

(*f*) To extend such assistance to the Governments of Angola and Mozambique as they may request in order to secure peace for their peoples, and to encourage and support peace initiatives undertaken by the Governments of Angola and Mozambique aimed at bringing about peace and normalization of life in their countries;

(*g*) The new South Africa shall, upon adoption of the new constitution, participate fully in relevant organs and specialized agencies of the United Nations.

10. We request the Secretary-General to transmit copies of the present Declaration to the South African Government and the representatives of the oppressed people of South Africa and also request the Secretary-General to prepare a report and submit it to the General Assembly by 1 July 1990 on the progress made in the implementation of the present Declaration.

46/79. Policies of Apartheid of the Government of South Africa

Committee: -
Vote: A: adopted without a vote; B: 143 - 0 - 16; C: 121 - 2 - 34; D: 93 - 31 - 30; E: 127 - 3 - 28; F: Adopted without a vote
Ref.: 45/176, 44/27, 43/50, 42/23, 41/35, 40/64, 39/72, 38/39, 37/69, 36/172, 35/206, 34/93, 33/183, 32/105, 31/6, 3411(XXX), 3324(XXIX), 3151(XXVIII), 2923(XXVII), 2764(XXVI), 2775(XXVI), 2671(XXV), 2642(XXV), 2506(XXIV), 2396(XXIII), 2307(XXII), 2202(XXI), 2054(XX), 1881(XV), 1978(XVIII), 1761(XVII), 1663(XVI), 1598(XV), 1375(XIV), 1248(XIII), 1178(XII), 1016(XI), 917(X), 820(IX), 721(VIII), 616(VII)

A

International Efforts Towards the Total Eradication of Apartheid and Support for the Establishment of a United, Non-Racial and Democratic South Africa

The General Assembly,

Recalling the Declaration on Apartheid and its Destructive Consequences in Southern Africa, contained in the annex to its resolution S-16/1 of 14 December 1989, its resolution 45/176 A of 19 December 1990 and its decision 45/457 B of 13 September 1991,

Taking note of the report of the Special Committee against Apartheid and the second progress report of the Secretary-General on the implementation of the Declaration, as well as the reports of the Secretary-General on the coordinated approach by the United Nations system on questions relating to South Africa and on the concerted and effective measures aimed at eradicating apartheid,

Convinced that broad-based negotiations leading to a new constitutional order providing for universal, equal suffrage under a non-racial voters' roll will lead to the total eradication of apartheid through peaceful means and the establishment of a non-racial democracy in South Africa,

Welcoming the signing on 14 September 1991 of the National Peace Accord and expressing the hope that this will finally end the tragic bloodshed in South Africa,

Welcoming the efforts of all parties, including ongoing talks among them, such as the recently held Patriotic/United Front conference, aimed at facilitating the commencement of substantive broad-based negotiations towards a new constitution and arrangements on the transition to a democratic order,

Welcoming the accession of South Africa on 10 July 1991 to the Treaty on the Non-Proliferation of Nuclear Weapons and subsequent conclusion and ratification of a related safeguards agreement,

Noting with satisfaction that fundamental principles for a new constitutional order, as set out in the Declaration, are receiving broad acceptance in South Africa,

Welcoming the convening of the preparatory meeting for the Convention for a Democratic South Africa,

Noting that while positive measures have been undertaken by the South African authorities, including the repeal and revision of the major apartheid and security laws, further efforts are needed to enhance the climate for free political activity and to address the inequities resulting from the legacy of these laws,

Gravely concerned that the persistence of violence, resulting largely from apartheid, including actions by those opposed to the democratic transformation of the country, poses a threat to the negotiating process and to the vital interests of all people of South Africa,

Concerned about any remaining obstacles to free political activity, as identified in the Declaration, including the delay in the full implementation of agreements regarding the release of any remaining political prisoners and the return of refugees and exiles, the use of repressive legislation still in place as well as other attempts aimed at undermining the democratic forces,

Noting with serious concern the remaining effects of the acts of aggression and destabilization that were committed by South Africa against neighbouring independent African States,

Convinced that international pressure, both that exerted by Governments and by individual citizens and organizations, has had and continues to have a significant impact on developments in South Africa,

Recognizing the responsibility of the United Nations and the international community, as envisaged in the Declaration, to continue to take all necessary measures aimed at the eradication of apartheid through peaceful means, in particular by adhering to the programme of action contained in the Declaration,

1. *Reaffirms* its support for the legitimate struggle of the South African people for the total eradication of apartheid through peaceful means and the establishment of a united, non-racial and democratic South Africa in which all its people, irrespective of race, colour, sex or creed, will enjoy the same fundamental freedoms and human rights;

2. *Reaffirms* the Declaration on Apartheid and its Destructive Consequences in Southern Africa and the need for the full and immediate implementation of the provisions not yet fulfilled;

3. *Calls* for an immediate end to violence and the removal of any remaining obstacles to free political activity;

4. *Urges* the South African authorities to take immediate further action to end the recurring violence and acts of terrorism, including actions by those opposed to the democratic transformation of the country, by ensuring that all competent authorities act effectively and impartially;

5. *Calls upon* all signatories of the National Peace Accord to manifest their commitment to peace by fully implementing its provisions, and calls upon all other parties to contribute to the attainment of its objectives;

6. *Calls upon* the South African authorities to enhance the climate conducive to negotiations by ensuring the immediate release of any remaining political prisoners, the unhindered return of refugees and exiles and the repeal of repressive and discriminatory legislation still in place, and to address the glaring inequalities created by apartheid;

7. *Calls upon* the representatives of the people of South Africa to commence in good faith, urgently, broad-based substantive negotiations towards an agreement on the basic principles of a new constitution, taking into account the fundamental principles in the Declaration and its suggested guidelines on the modalities for the elaboration of a new constitution, on transitional arrangements inspiring general confidence in the administration of the country until the new constitution takes effect, and on the role to be played by the international community in ensuring the successful transition to a democratic order;

8. *Appeals* to the international community to give its full and concerted support to the vulnerable and critical process now under way in South Africa through a phased application of appropriate pressure on the South African authorities, as warranted by developments, and to provide assistance to the opponents of apartheid and the disadvantaged sectors of society in order to ensure the rapid and peaceful attainment of the objectives of the Declaration;

9. *Calls upon* the international community, in view of progress made in overcoming obstacles to negotiations, to resume academic, scientific and cultural links with democratic anti-apartheid organizations and the individuals in these fields, to resume sports links with unified non-racial sporting organizations of South Africa which have received endorsement by appropriate non-racial sporting organizations within South Africa and to assist disadvantaged athletes in that country;

10. *Also calls upon* the international community, within the context of the need to respond appropriately to ongoing developments in South Africa, to review existing restrictive measures as warranted by positive developments, such as agreement by the parties on transitional arrangements, and agreement on a new, non-racial democratic constitution;

11. *Calls upon* all Governments to observe fully the mandatory arms embargo, requests the Security Council to continue to monitor effectively its strict implementation and urges States to adhere to the provisions of other Security Council resolutions on the import of arms from South Africa and the export of equipment and technology destined for military or police purposes in that country;

12. *Appeals* to the international community to increase humanitarian and legal assistance to the victims of apartheid, returning refugees and exiles and released political prisoners;

13. *Also appeals* to the international community to increase its material, financial and other contributions to the victims and opponents of apartheid to help them address the glaring socio-economic inequalities, particularly in the areas of education, health, housing and social welfare;

14. *Further appeals* to the international community to render all possible assistance to the front-line and neighbouring States to enable their economies to recover from the effects of years of destabilization and to support the current efforts to achieve a durable peace in Angola and Mozambique, which would contribute to the stability and prosperity of the region;

15. *Welcomes* the agreement reached on 4 September 1991 by the United Nations High Commissioner for Refugees with the South African authorities concerning the voluntary repatriation of South African refugees and exiles, and appeals to the international community to provide and urges the Secretary-General to facilitate, through the relevant United Nations agencies and offices in cooperation with the High Commissioner, all necessary humanitarian assistance to ensure the successful implementation of the repatriation programme;

16. *Urges* the Secretary-General to facilitate, through the relevant United Nations agencies and offices and in a concerted manner, humanitarian and educational assistance inside South Africa for the reintegration of political exiles and released political prisoners and to the disadvantaged sectors of South African society;

17. *Also urges* the Secretary-General, at the appropriate time, in the light of positive developments such as agreement on transitional arrangements, to expand, in a concerted manner, through the relevant United Nations offices and in collaboration with the specialized agencies, the scope of assistance provided inside South Africa aimed at addressing socio-economic issues, particularly in the areas of education, health, housing and social welfare, which may entail the physical presence of the United Nations system in that country;

18. *Requests* the Secretary-General to continue to ensure the coordination of activities of the United Nations system in the implementation of the Declaration and of the present resolution and to report thereon to the General Assembly at its forty-seventh session, and to continue monitoring the implementation of the Declaration as well as pursuing appropriate initiatives to facilitate all efforts leading to the peaceful eradication of apartheid.

72nd plenary meeting
13 December 1991

B

Programme of Work of the Special Committee Against Apartheid

The General Assembly,

Having considered the report of the Special Committee against Apartheid,

1. *Commends* the Special Committee against Apartheid for the diligent manner in which it has discharged its responsibilities in monitoring the situation in South Africa and in promoting concerted international support for the process towards the early establishment of a democratic, non-racial society;

2. *Takes note* of the report of the Special Committee and endorses its recommendations relating to its programme of work;

3. *Authorizes* the Special Committee, in accordance with its mandate as the focal point for the international campaign against apartheid and for the promotion of the implementation of the Declaration on Apartheid and its Destructive Consequences in Southern Africa and acting with the support services of the Centre against Apartheid:

(*a*) To continue monitoring closely developments in South Africa and the actions of the international community, particularly regarding appropriate pressure on South Africa and timely assistance to the victims and opponents of apartheid;

(*b*) To continue mobilizing international action in support of the early establishment of a democratic, non-racial South Africa, *inter alia*, through collection, analysis and dissemination of information, through liaison and consultations with Governments, intergovernmental and non-governmental organizations and relevant individuals and groups, both inside and outside South Africa, able to influence public opinion and decision-making, and through missions, hearings, conferences, publicity and other pertinent activities, and to continue undertaking activities aimed at supporting the political process towards the establishment of a non-racial, democratic South Africa;

4. *Appeals* to all Governments, intergovernmental and non-governmental organizations to increase their cooperation with the Special Committee and the Centre in the discharge of their mandates;

5. *Requests* all components of the United Nations system to cooperate further with the Special Committee and the Centre in their activities in order to ensure consistency, improve coordination and efficient use of available resources and avoid duplication of efforts in the implementation of the relevant resolutions of the General Assembly and the Security Council;

6. *Appeals* to all Governments, intergovernmental and non-governmental organizations, information media and individuals to cooperate with the Centre and the Department of Public Information of the Secretariat in their activities relating to South Africa and, in particular, in disseminating information on the evolving situation in South Africa and on the considerable assistance needs of the opponents of apartheid and the disadvantaged sectors of South African society in rectifying the glaring socio-economic inequalities in their country, and further appeals to them to make generous contributions to the Trust Fund for Publicity against Apartheid;

7. *Decides* to continue the authorization of adequate financial provision in the regular budget of the United Nations to enable the African National Congress of South Africa and the Pan Africanist Congress of Azania to maintain offices in New York in order to participate effectively in the deliberations of the Special Committee and other appropriate bodies;

8. *Also decides* that the special allocation of 480,000 United States dollars to the Special Committee for 1992 from the regular budget of the United Nations should be used towards the cost of special projects aimed at promoting the process towards the elimination of apartheid and the democratization of South Africa, with particular emphasis on the issues of constitution building, human rights, domestic peace, education and training and ways to help address the serious socio-economic inequalities in the country.

72nd plenary meeting
13 December 1991

C

Military and Other Collaboration with South Africa

The General Assembly,

Recalling the Declaration on Apartheid and its Destructive Consequences in Southern Africa, its resolutions 45/176 B and C of 19 December 1990, as well as the resolutions of the Security Council on the arms embargo and military collaboration with South Africa,

Taking note of the report of the Special Committee against Apartheid and the report of the Security Council Committee established by Council resolution 421 (1977) of 9 December 1977 concerning the question of South Africa on its activities during the period 1980-1989,

Noting with appreciation the resolve and effectiveness of the Security Council in its handling of questions relating to the preservation of international peace and security,

Noting that the monitoring and enforcement mechanism of the mandatory sanctions imposed by the Security Council on South Africa in its resolution 418 (1977) of 4 November 1977 would benefit from further strengthening,

Reiterating that the full implementation of the mandatory arms embargo against South Africa is an essential element of international action towards the eradication of apartheid,

Convinced that sanctions and other restrictive measures have had a significant impact on recent developments in South Africa and that the phased application of appropriate pressure remains an effective and necessary instrument in the process towards the peaceful end to apartheid,

Taking note of the accession of South Africa on 10 July 1991 to the Treaty on the Non-Proliferation of Nuclear Weapons and subsequent conclusion and ratification of a related safeguards agreement,

Expressing serious concern about the continued violations of the mandatory arms embargo, particularly by those countries which surreptitiously trade in arms with South Africa,

Expressing concern that South Africa's external military relations, especially in the area of military technology and, in particular, in the production and testing of missiles, continue unabated, as mentioned in paragraphs 100 to 102 of the report of the Special Committee,

Gravely concerned about the practice carried out by certain oil-producing States whereby oil is exchanged for South African arms,

1. *Deplores* the actions of those States which, directly or indirectly, continue to violate the mandatory arms embargo and collaborate with South Africa in the military, nuclear, intelligence and technology fields, and calls upon those States to terminate forthwith any illegal acts and honour their obligations under Security Council resolution 418 (1977);

2. *Urges* all States to adopt strict legislation relating to the implementation of the arms embargo and prohibit the supply to South Africa of nuclear and military products, as well as computer and communications equipment, technological skills and services, including military intelligence, destined for use by the military, police and security agencies of that country, until free and fair elections have been held and a democratic government has been established;

3. *Calls* for the early and full disclosure by South Africa of its nuclear installations and materials in conformity with its treaty obligations as an essential element to the peace and security of the southern African region;

4. *Urges* the Security Council to consider immediate steps to ensure the full implementation and the effective monitoring of the arms embargo imposed by the Council in its resolutions 418 (1977) and 558 (1984) of 13 December 1984, to implement the recommendations of the Committee established under Council resolution 421 (1977) concerning appropriate measures in response to violations of the mandatory arms embargo and to provide information on a regular basis to the Secretary-General for general distribution to Member States;

5. *Calls upon* all States to maintain existing financial measures, and, in particular, urges Governments and private financial institutions, as well as the International Monetary Fund and the World Bank, not to extend new loans and credits to South Africa, whether to the public or private

sector, until agreement has been reached on a non-racial democratic constitution or until specific recommendations are made on this matter by the transitional authorities to be established by the Convention for a Democratic South Africa;

6. *Requests* the Special Committee against Apartheid to keep the issue of military and nuclear collaboration with South Africa under constant review and to report thereon to the General Assembly and the Security Council as appropriate.

72nd plenary meeting
13 December 1991

D

Relations Between South Africa and Israel

The General Assembly,

Recalling its previous resolutions concerning the relations between South Africa and Israel and, in particular, its resolution 45/176 D of 19 December 1990,

Having considered the report of the Special Committee against Apartheid on recent developments concerning relations between South Africa and Israel, and the report of the Secretary-General on South Africa's nuclear-tipped ballistic missile capability,

Noting with concern that the military relations between South Africa and Israel, especially in the area of military technology and in particular the collaboration in the production and testing of nuclear missiles, continue unabated,

1. *Strongly deplores* the collaboration of Israel with the South African régime in the military and nuclear fields;

2. *Reiterates its demand* that Israel desist from and terminate forthwith all forms of collaboration with South Africa, particularly in the military and nuclear fields;

3. *Urges* the Security Council to consider taking appropriate measures against Israel for its violation of the mandatory arms embargo against South Africa;

4. *Requests* the Special Committee against Apartheid to continue to monitor the relations between South Africa and Israel and keep them under constant review and report to the General Assembly and the Security Council as appropriate.

72nd plenary meeting
13 December 1991

E

Oil Embargo Against South Africa

The General Assembly,

Having considered the report of the Intergovernmental Group to Monitor the Supply and Shipping of Oil and Petroleum Products to South Africa,

Recalling its resolutions on the oil embargo against South Africa, in particular resolution 45/176 F of 19 December 1990,

Recognizing the importance of the oil embargo as a major contribution to the pressure exerted on South Africa towards the eradication of apartheid through negotiations, as well as the importance of maintaining pressure until there is clear evidence of profound and irreversible changes, bearing in mind the objectives of the Declaration on Apartheid and its Destructive Consequences in Southern Africa, such as the adoption of a non-racial and democratic constitution for a free South Africa,

Noting that the most effective way to enforce the oil embargo against South Africa remains the adoption by the Security Council of a mandatory embargo under Chapter VII of the Charter of the United Nations,

Concerned that the oil embargo against South Africa is still being violated and that South Africa, because of loopholes in the embargo, such as lack of effective legislation, has been able to acquire oil and petroleum products,

Convinced that an effective oil embargo against South Africa would contribute to the efforts of the international community to bring about a negotiated settlement and the establishment of a united, non-racial and democratic South Africa,

1. *Takes note* of the report of the Intergovernmental Group to Monitor the Supply and Shipping of Oil and Petroleum Products to South Africa and endorses its recommendations;

2. *Requests* all States to adopt, if they have not already done so, and otherwise to maintain and enforce effective measures prohibiting the supply and shipping of oil and petroleum products to South Africa, whether directly or indirectly, and in particular:

(*a*) To apply strictly the "end users" clause and other conditions concerning restriction on destination to ensure compliance with the embargo;

(*b*) To compel the companies originally selling or purchasing oil or petroleum products, as appropriate to each nation, to desist from selling, reselling or otherwise transferring oil and petroleum products to South Africa, whether directly or indirectly;

(*c*) To establish strict control over the supply of oil and petroleum products to South Africa by intermediaries, oil companies and traders by placing responsibilities for the fulfilment of the contract on the first buyer or seller of oil and petroleum products who would, therefore, be liable for the actions of these parties;

(*d*) To prevent South African companies from acquiring holdings in oil companies outside South Africa;

(*e*) To prohibit all assistance to South Africa in the oil sector, including finance, technology, equipment or personnel;

(*f*) To prohibit the transport of oil and petroleum products to South Africa by ships flying their flags, or by ships that are ultimately owned, managed or chartered by their nationals or by companies within their jurisdiction;

(*g*) To develop a system for registration of ships, registered in their territory or owned by their nationals, that have violated the oil embargo, and to discourage such ships from calling at South African ports;

(*h*) To impose penal action against companies and individuals that have been involved in violating the oil embargo, and to publicize cases of successful prosecutions in conformity with their national laws;

(*i*) To gather, exchange and disseminate information regarding violations of the oil embargo, including ways and means to prevent such violations, and to take concerted measures against violators;

(*j*) To discourage ships within their jurisdiction from engaging in activities that give rise to violation of the oil embargo against South Africa, taking into account legislative and other measures already adopted;

3. *Commends* to Member States for their consideration the draft model law annexed to the report of the Intergovernmental Group and recommends that they strive for an effective oil embargo by adopting the general principles of the model law within the framework of their own legal practices;

4. *Authorizes* the Intergovernmental Group to take action to promote public awareness of the oil embargo against South Africa, including, when necessary, sending missions and participating in relevant conferences and meetings;

5. *Requests* the Intergovernmental Group to submit to the General Assembly at its forty-seventh session a report on the implementation of the present resolution;

6. *Requests* all States to extend their cooperation to the Intergovernmental Group with all necessary assistance for the implementation of the present resolution.

72nd plenary meeting
13 December 1991

F

United Nations Trust Fund for South Africa

The General Assembly,

Recalling its resolutions on the United Nations Trust Fund for South Africa, in particular resolution 45/176 H of 19 December 1990,

Having considered the report of the Secretary-General on the United Nations Trust Fund for South Africa, to which is annexed the report of the Committee of Trustees of the Trust Fund,

Taking note of its resolution 45/176 A adopted without a vote on 19 December 1990, and in particular of paragraph 16, relating to the reintegration of released political prisoners into South African society,

Welcoming the repeal and revision of the major apartheid and security laws and a number of discriminatory and repressive laws, rules and regulations,

Welcoming also the release of a large number of political prisoners and the agreement reached between the South African authorities and the United Nations High Commissioner for Refugees allowing for the voluntary repatriation of political exiles and refugees,

Further welcoming the National Peace Accord signed on 14 September 1991 as a significant initiative towards addressing the critical issue of violence in the country and providing a framework within which substantive and broad-based discussions can take place,

Remaining concerned about the continued existence of a number of discriminatory and repressive laws, rules and regulations in South Africa,

Concerned about the delay in the full implementation of agreements regarding the release of any remaining political prisoners and the return of refugees and exiles and about reports that trials of politically motivated cases were carried out in 1991,

Recognizing the work carried out by the International Defence and Aid Fund for Southern Africa over the years in providing legal and humanitarian assistance to the victims of apartheid and their families and noting with satisfaction the transfer of programmes of the Fund to broad-based, impartial organizations inside South Africa,

Strongly convinced that continued, direct and substantial contributions to the Trust Fund and to the voluntary agencies concerned are necessary to enable them to meet the extensive needs for humanitarian, legal and relief assistance during the critical transition to a non-racial and democratic South Africa,

1. *Endorses* the report of the Secretary-General on the United Nations Trust Fund for South Africa;

2. *Supports* continued and substantial humanitarian, legal and educational assistance by the international community in order to alleviate the plight of those persecuted under discriminatory legislation in South Africa and their families, and to facilitate the reintegration of released political prisoners and returning exiles into South African society;

3. *Supports* assistance by the Trust Fund for work in the legal field aimed at ensuring effective implementation of legislation repealing major apartheid laws, redressing continuing adverse effects of these laws and encouraging increased confidence in the rule of law;

4. *Expresses its appreciation* to the Governments, organizations and individuals that have contributed to the Trust Fund and to the voluntary agencies engaged in rendering humanitarian and legal assistance to the victims of apartheid in South Africa;

5. *Appeals* for generous contributions to the Trust Fund;

6. *Also appeals* for direct contributions to the voluntary agencies engaged in rendering assistance to the victims of apartheid and racial discrimination in South Africa;

7. *Commends* the Secretary-General and the Committee of Trustees of the Trust Fund for their persistent efforts to promote humanitarian and legal assistance to persons persecuted under repressive and discriminatory legislation in South Africa, as well as assistance to their families and to refugees from South Africa.

72nd plenary meeting
13 December 1991

44/166. Situation of Human Rights in Chile

Committee: 3
Vote: 84 - 2 - 60
Ref.: 43/158, 42/147, 41/161, 40/145, 39/121, 38/102, 37/183, 36/157, 35/188, 34/179, 33/175, 32/118, 31/124, 3448(XXX), 3219(XXIX)

The General Assembly,

Guided by the purposes and principles of the Charter of the United Nations and bearing in mind the Universal Declaration of Human Rights, the International Covenant on Economic, Social and Cultural Rights, and the International Covenant on Civil and Political Rights,

Aware of its responsibility to promote and encourage respect for human rights and fundamental freedoms, and determined to remain vigilant with regard to violations of human rights wherever they occur,

Reiterating that the Government of Chile has the obligation to respect and protect human rights in accordance with the international instruments to which Chile is a party,

Bearing in mind that the concern of the international community about the situation of human rights in Chile has been expressed by the General Assembly in a number of resolutions, particularly resolution 33/173 of 20 December 1978 on disappeared persons and resolution 43/158 of 8 December 1988,

Bearing in mind the pertinent resolutions of the Commission on Human Rights, particularly resolution 1989/62 of 8 March 1989, in which the Commission decided, *inter alia*, to extend the mandate of the Special Rapporteur for one year, to consider the question as a matter of high priority in view of the persistence of serious violations of human rights in Chile and to determine how the item was to be dealt with on the agenda of its forty-sixth session in the light of developments in the situation,

Regretting the decision of the Government of Chile to discontinue its cooperation with the Special Rapporteur,

Regretting also that the process of restoration of civil and political rights in Chile does not yet include the amendment of numerous laws that constitute an institutional and legal framework that makes violations of human rights possible,

1. *Takes note with appreciation* of the report of the Special Rapporteur submitted in accordance with Commission on Human Rights resolution 1989/62;

2. *Congratulates* the Chilean people on their peaceful progress towards the re-establishment of a representative and pluralist democracy based on respect for human rights and fundamental freedoms, and for reaffirming their will to achieve peace and national reconciliation through the restoration of justice;

3. *Expresses its satisfaction* at the progress of the Chilean electoral process which it considers an important step towards the rapid return of democracy in that country;

4. *Welcomes*, as a positive development, the decision by the Government of Chile to heed the demands of democratic sectors of the country and of the international community with regard to reforming certain aspects of the institutional and legal framework harmful to civil and political rights;

5. *Takes note with satisfaction* of the decision by the Government of Chile to incorporate the International Covenant on Civil and Political Rights and the International Covenant on Economic, Social and Cultural Rights into domestic law;

6. *Welcomes* the improvement of the situation of human rights in Chile noted by the Special Rapporteur during the six months covered by his report;

7. *Regrets*, nevertheless, the decision of the Government of Chile to discontinue its cooperation with the Special Rapporteur in the fulfilment of his mandate, and urges it to resume such cooperation in compliance with the resolutions of the General Assembly and the Commission on Human Rights;

8. *Urges* the Government of Chile to continue to make progress regarding respect for human rights and fundamental freedoms for all the Chilean people, including the indigenous peoples, especially by adapting the legal system to the relevant principles and provisions, and refraining from making any more changes in national institutions without duly consulting the people, and to be guided by those principles and provisions in the exercise of its powers in the same way as the judiciary;

9. *Also urges* the Government of Chile for that purpose to ensure the independence of the judiciary and the effectiveness of judicial remedies, by respecting procedural guarantees, equality before the law and the right to defence in all cases;

10. *Expresses its concern* at acts of violence of any origin that continue to occur in Chile, thereby aggravating the climate of insecurity and rendering the return to democracy more difficult;

11. *Again expresses* its serious concern at the persistence of violations of human rights and fundamental freedoms in Chile involving, *inter alia*, cases of death, torture and ill-treatment, and at the Colonia Dignidad case, as described by the Special Rapporteur in his report;

12. *Urges* the Government of Chile to investigate all cases of serious violations of human rights that occurred in the past, bearing in mind the reports of special rapporteurs;

13. *Invites* the Commission on Human Rights to evaluate at its forty-sixth session the situation of human rights in Chile, bearing in mind the reports presented by special rapporteurs, to consider the mandate of the Special Rapporteur and also how the item is to be dealt with on the agenda in the light of developments in the situation, and to report to the General Assembly at its forty-fifth session.

82nd plenary meeting
15 December 1989

46/7. The Situation of Democracy and Human Rights in Haiti

Committee: -
Vote: Adopted without a vote
Ref.: 50/196, 50/86, 49/201, 49/27, 48/151, 48/27, 47/143, 47/20, 46/138

The General Assembly,

Having considered the item entitled "The situation of democracy and human rights in Haiti",

Bearing in mind that, on the basis of its resolution 45/2 of 10 October 1990, the United Nations system, at the request of the lawful authorities of that country and in cooperation with the Organization of American States, supported the efforts of the people of Haiti to consolidate their democratic institutions and also supported the holding of free elections on 16 December 1990,

Concerned about the critical events occurring in Haiti since 29 September 1991, which have brought about a sudden and violent interruption of the democratic process in that country, entailing human rights abuses and the loss of human lives,

Bearing in mind the presentation made by the President of Haiti, Mr. Jean-Bertrand Aristide, to the Security Council on 3 October 1991,

Given the importance of support from the international community for the development of democracy in Haiti by strengthening its institutions and giving high priority to the serious social and economic problems that it faces,

Aware that, in accordance with the Charter of the United Nations, the Organization promotes and encourages respect for human rights and fundamental freedoms for all, and that the Universal Declaration of Human Rights states that "the will of the people shall be the basis of the authority of government",

Welcoming resolutions MRE/RES.1/91 and MRE/RES.2/91 adopted on 3 and 8 October 1991, respectively, by the Ministers for Foreign Affairs of the member countries of the Organization of American States,

1. *Strongly condemns* the attempted illegal replacement of the constitutional President of Haiti, the use of violence and military coercion and the violation of human rights in that country;

2. *Affirms* as unacceptable any entity resulting from that illegal situation and demands the immediate restoration of the legitimate Government of President Jean-Bertrand Aristide, together with the full application of the National Constitution and hence the full observance of human rights in Haiti;

3. *Requests* the Secretary-General of the United Nations, in accordance with his functions, to consider providing support sought by the Secretary-General of the Organization of American States in implementing the mandates arising from resolutions MRE/RES.1/91 and MRE/RES.2/91 adopted by that organization;

4. *Appeals* to the States Members of the United Nations to take measures in support of the resolutions of the Organization of American States referred to in paragraph 3 above;

5. *Emphasizes* that an increase in technical, economic and financial cooperation, when constitutional order is restored in Haiti, is necessary to support its economic and social development efforts in order to strengthen its democratic institutions;

6. *Requests* the Secretary-General to submit a report as soon as possible on the implementation of the present resolution;

7. *Decides* to keep open the consideration of this item until a solution to the situation is found.

31st plenary meeting
11 October 1991

50/188. Situation of Human Rights in the Islamic Republic of Iran

Committee: 3
Vote: 78 - 27 - 58
Ref.: 49/202, 48/145, 47/146, 45/173, 44/163, 43/137, 42/136, 41/159, 40/141

The General Assembly,

Guided by the Charter of the United Nations, the Universal Declaration of Human Rights[1] and the International Covenants on Human Rights,[2]

Recalling the Vienna Declaration and Programme of Action,[3] as endorsed by the General Assembly in its resolution 48/121 of 20 December 1993, in particular part I, paragraph 1, in which the World Conference on Human Rights reaffirmed, *inter alia*, that human rights and fundamental freedoms were the birthright of all human beings and that their protection and promotion was the first responsibility of Governments,

---

1 Resolution 217 A (p).

2 Resolution 2200 A (XXI), annex.

3 *Report of the World Conference on Human Rights, Vienna, 14-25 June 1993* (A/CONF.157/24 (Part I)), chap. III.

Reaffirming that all Member States have a duty to fulfil the obligations they have undertaken under the various international instruments in this field,

Mindful that the Islamic Republic of Iran is a party to the International Covenants on Human Rights,

Recalling Commission on Human Rights resolution 1984/54 of 14 March 1984,[1] in which the Commission requested its Chairman to appoint a special representative to make a thorough study of the human rights situation in the Islamic Republic of Iran, based on such information as the Special Representative might deem relevant, including comments and material provided by the Government of the Islamic Republic of Iran,

Noting the appointment by the Chairman of the Commission on Human Rights of Professor Maurice Danby Copithorne as Special Representative of the Commission on the situation of human rights in the Islamic Republic of Iran, and paying tribute to his predecessor Professor Reinaldo Galindo Pohl,

Recalling its previous resolutions expressing concern at the violations of human rights by the Government of the Islamic Republic of Iran, including the most recent, resolution 49/202 of 23 December 1994, and the resolutions of the Commission on Human Rights, including the most recent, resolution 1995/68 of 8 March 1995,[2] and of the Subcommission on Prevention of Discrimination and Protection of Minorities, including the most recent, resolution 1995/18 of 24 August 1995,[3]

Reaffirming that Governments are accountable for assassinations and attacks by their agents against persons in the territory of another State, as well as for the incitement, approval or wilful condoning of such acts,

Noting the Special Representative's view that the significant number of communications received by the Centre for Human Rights of the Secretariat for the attention of the Special Representative and the important concerns reflected therein will need careful scrutiny,

Welcoming the announcement by the Special Representative that he has been invited to visit the Islamic Republic of Iran and the high priority given by the Special Representative to visiting the country,

Noting the stated readiness of the Government of the Islamic Republic of Iran to invite the Special Rapporteur of the Commission on Human Rights on religious intolerance and the Special Rapporteur of the Commission on freedom of expression to visit the Islamic Republic of Iran,

Noting also the concluding observations of the Committee on the Elimination of Racial Discrimination, the Human Rights Committee and the Committee on Economic, Social and Cultural Rights on the human rights situation in the Islamic Republic of Iran,

Noting further that the Subcommission on Prevention of Discrimination and Protection of Minorities, in its resolution 1995/18, condemned the flagrant violations of human rights in the Islamic Republic of Iran,

Taking note of the interim report of the Special Representative of 20 October 1995,[4] and his intention to present a substantive report to the Commission on Human Rights,

Taking into account the reports of the former Special Representative, including his report of 16 January 1995,[5]

Considering that continued international scrutiny of human rights and fundamental freedoms in the Islamic Republic of Iran is warranted and that the subject should remain on the agenda of the General Assembly,

1. *Expresses its concern* at violations of human rights in the Islamic Republic of Iran, in particular the high number of executions, cases of torture and cruel, inhuman or degrading treatment or punishment, the failure to meet international standards with regard to the administration of justice, the absence of guarantees of due process of law, the discriminatory treatment of minorities by reason of their religious beliefs, notably the Baha'is, whose existence as a viable religious community in the Islamic Republic of Iran is threatened, lack of adequate protection for the Christian minorities, some members of which have been the target of intimidation and assassinations, excessive force in suppressing demonstrations, restrictions on the freedom of expression, thought, opinion and the press and widespread discrimination against women;

2. *Urges* the Government of the Islamic Republic of Iran, as a State party to the International Covenants on Human Rights, to abide by its freely undertaken obligations under the Covenants and under other international instruments on human rights, and to ensure that all individuals within its territory and subject to its jurisdiction, including religious groups, enjoy the rights recognized in those instruments;

3. *Calls upon* the Government of the Islamic Republic of Iran to implement existing agreements with international humanitarian organizations;

4. *Also calls upon* the Government of the Islamic Republic of Iran to take the necessary steps so that the visit of the Special Representative of the Commission on Human Rights on the situation of human rights in the Islamic Republic of Iran can take place as soon as possible and without conditions;

5. *Expresses its grave concern* that there are continuing threats to the life of Mr. Salman Rushdie, as well as to individuals associated with his work, which appear to have the support of the Government of the Islamic Republic of Iran;

6. *Urges* the Government of the Islamic Republic of Iran to refrain from activities against members of the Iranian opposition living abroad and to cooperate wholeheartedly with the authorities of other countries in investigating and punishing offences reported by them;

7. *Requests* the Secretary-General to give all necessary assistance to the Special Representative to enable him to discharge his mandate fully;

8. *Decides* to continue the examination of the situation of human rights in the Islamic Republic of Iran, including the situation of minority groups such as the Baha'is, during its fifty-first session under the item entitled "Human rights questions", on the basis of the report of the Special Representative and in the light of additional elements provided by the Commission on Human Rights and the Economic and Social Council.

99th plenary meeting
22 December 1995

50/193. Situation of Human Rights in the Republic of Bosnia and Herzegovina, the Republic of Croatia and the Federal Republic of Yugoslavia (Serbia and Montenegro)

Committee: 3
Vote: 144 - 1 - 20
Ref.: 49/196, 48/153, 47/147

The General Assembly,

Guided by the purposes and principles of the Charter of the United Nations, the Universal Declaration of Human Rights,[6] the International Covenants on Human Rights,[7]

---

1 *Official Records of the Economic and Social Council, 1984, Supplement No. 4* (E/1984/14 and Corr.1), chap. II, sect. A.

2 *Ibid., 1995, Supplement No. 3* and corrigenda (E/1995/23 and Corr.1 and 2), chap. II, sect. A.

3 See E/CN.4/1996/2.

4 A/50/661.

5 E/CN.4/1995/55.

6 Resolution 217 A (III).

7 Resolution 2200 A (XXI), annex.

the International Convention on the Elimination of All Forms of Racial Discrimination,[1] the Convention on the Rights of the Child,[2] the Convention on the Prevention and Punishment of the Crime of Genocide,[3] the Convention against Torture and Other Cruel, Inhuman or Degrading Treatment or Punishment,[4] the Convention on the Elimination of All Forms of Discrimination against Women[5] and instruments of international humanitarian law, including the Geneva Conventions of 12 August 1949 for the protection of victims of war[6] and the Additional Protocols thereto, of 1971[7] as well as the principles and commitments undertaken by States members of the Organization for Security and Cooperation in Europe,

Reaffirming that all Member States have an obligation to promote and protect human rights and fundamental freedoms and to fulfil the obligations they have under the human rights instruments to which they are party, and reaffirming also the obligation of all to respect international humanitarian law,

Welcoming the General Framework Agreement for Peace in Bosnia and Herzegovina[8] initialled by the Republic of Bosnia and Herzegovina, the Republic of Croatia and the Federal Republic of Yugoslavia (Serbia and Montenegro), representing also the Bosnian Serb party, at Dayton, Ohio, on 21 November 1995 which commits the parties to the conflict to ending the war and starting to build peace with justice; enables Bosnia and Herzegovina to continue its legal existence as a single State within its internationally recognized borders with full respect for its sovereignty, territorial integrity and political independence by its neighbours; and commits the parties in Bosnia and Herzegovina to respect fully human rights,

Welcoming also the basic agreement on the region of Eastern Slavonia, Baranja and Western Sirmium,[9] signed on 12 November 1995 by the Government of the Republic of Croatia and the local Serb representatives,

None the less gravely concerned at the human tragedy that has occurred in the territories of the Republic of Bosnia and Herzegovina, the Republic of Croatia and the Federal Republic of Yugoslavia (Serbia and Montenegro) and at the massive and systematic violations of human rights and international humanitarian law,

Recalling its resolution 49/196 of 23 December 1994, Commission on Human Rights resolution 1995/89 of 8 March 1995,[10] and all relevant resolutions of the Security Council,

Recalling specifically the relevant Security Council resolutions in which the Council demanded, *inter alia,* that all parties and others concerned in the former Yugoslavia immediately cease and desist from all breaches of international humanitarian law, requested the Secretary-General to establish a commission of experts to examine and analyse information relating to serious violations of such law being committed in the territory of the former Yugoslavia, established an international tribunal for the prosecution of persons responsible for such violations and condemned in particular the unacceptable practice of ethnic cleansing perpetrated in areas of the Republic of Bosnia and Herzegovina under the control of Bosnian Serb forces,

Recalling additional relevant Security Council resolutions, in particular resolutions 824 (1993) of 6 March 1993 and 836 (1993) of 4 June 1993, in which the Council declared that Sarajevo, Tuzla, Zepa, Gorazde, Bihac, Srebrenica and their surroundings should be treated as safe areas, that international humanitarian agencies should be given free and unimpeded access to those areas and that there should be freedom of movement for the civilian population and humanitarian goods to, from and within the areas,

Recalling also Security Council resolution 1019 (1995) of 9 November 1995, in which the Council demanded that the Bosnian Serb party give immediate and unimpeded access to representatives of the United Nations High Commissioner for Refugees, the International Committee of the Red Cross and other international agencies to persons displaced and to persons detained or reported missing from Srebrenica, Zepa and the regions of Banja Luka and Sanski Most,

Gravely concerned at attacks and capture by the Bosnian Serbs and Croatian Serb forces of safe areas, in violation of the relevant Security Council resolutions,

Recalling Security Council resolution 1009 (1995) of 10 August 1995, in which the Council demanded that the Government of the Republic of Croatia respect fully the rights of the local Serb population, including their rights to remain, leave or return in safety, allow access to this population by international humanitarian organizations and create conditions conducive to the return of those persons who have left their homes,

Noting with appreciation the efforts of the United Nations Peace Forces to help to create the conditions for the peaceful settlement of the conflicts in the Republic of Bosnia and Herzegovina and the Republic of Croatia and to provide protection for the delivery of humanitarian aid and the protection of human rights, and also noting the obstacles faced by those forces in the performance of their mandates,

Acknowledging the progress made by the Bosnian Federation as a model for ethnic reconciliation in the region,

Encouraging the international community, acting through the United Nations and other international organizations as well as bilaterally, to enhance significantly humanitarian support for the people of the region and promote human rights, economic reconstruction, the repatriation of refugees and the holding of free elections in the Republic of Bosnia and Herzegovina,

Welcoming the efforts of the European Union to promote respect for human rights and fundamental freedoms, and endorsing the Special Rapporteur's recommendation that economic and other aid must be made conditional on meaningful progress on human rights,

Gravely concerned at the human rights violations in the Republic of Bosnia and Herzegovina, the Republic of Croatia and the Federal Republic of Yugoslavia (Serbia and Montenegro), in particular at those committed in the context of the odious practice of ethnic cleansing, which has been the direct cause of the vast majority of human rights violations there and whose principal victims have been the Muslim population, as well as the Croats and others,

Also gravely concerned at reports, including by the Representative of the Secretary-General, of grave violations of international humanitarian law and of human rights in and around Srebrenica, and in the areas of Banja Luka and Sanski Most, including reports of mass murder, unlawful detention and forced labour, rape and deportation of civilians,

Dismayed by the huge number of missing persons still unaccounted for, particularly in Bosnia and Herzegovina and in Croatia,

Deeply concerned by the situations reflected in the report of the Secretary-General on rape and abuse of women in the areas of armed conflict in the former Yugoslavia,[11] and

---

1 Resolution 2106 A (XX), annex.

2 Resolution 44/25, annex.

3 Resolution 260 A (III).

4 Resolution 39/46, annex.

5 Resolution 34/180, annex.

6 United Nations, *Treaty Series,* vol.75, Nos. 970-973.

7 Ibid., vol. 1 125, Nos. 17512 and 17513.

8 See A/50/790-S/1995/999.

9 A/50/757-S/1995/951, annex.

10 See *Official Records of the Economic and Social Council, 1995, Supplement No.3* and corrigenda (E/1995/23 and Corr.1 and 2), chap. II, sect. A.

11 A/50/205.

stressing the need for detailed reporting on this subject,

Alarmed that the conflict in the Republic of Bosnia and Herzegovina and in the Republic of Croatia has also been characterized by the systematic destruction and profanation of mosques, churches and other places of worship, religious buildings and sites of cultural heritage,

Expressing its particular concern for the situation of the children and the elderly as well as other vulnerable groups in the area,

Calling attention to the reports and recommendations of the Special Rapporteur of the Commission on Human Rights on the situation of human rights in the territories of the Republic of Bosnia and Herzegovina, the Republic of Croatia and the Federal Republic of Yugoslavia (Serbia and Montenegro), including the most recent report[1] by the newly appointed Special Rapporteur, Mrs. Elisabeth Rehn,

Expressing its deep appreciation for the activity and efforts of the previous Special Rapporteur, Mr. Tadeusz Mazowiecki, in the discharge of his mandate,

Noting the recommendations of the Special Rapporteur that respect for human rights should be given priority during and after the peace negotiations and that, without genuine improvements in the human rights situation in the area, any peace agreement will not have a solid foundation,

1. *Commends* both the former and the current Special Rapporteurs of the Commission on Human Rights on the situation of human rights in the territories of the Republic of Bosnia and Herzegovina, the Republic of Croatia, and the Federal Republic of Yugoslavia (Serbia and Montenegro) for their efforts, and notes that the presence of the Rapporteur can be a positive factor towards reducing the instances of all human rights violations in the region;

2. *Expresses its outrage* at the instances of massive and systematic violations of human rights and humanitarian law as described in the reports of the Special Rapporteur, including ethnic cleansing, killings, disappearances, torture, rape, detentions, beatings, arbitrary searches, destruction of houses, illegal evictions and other acts of violence aimed at forcing individuals from their homes;

3. *Condemns in the strongest terms* all violations of human rights and international humanitarian law by the parties to the conflict, recognizing that the leadership in territories under the control of Serbs in the Republic of Bosnia and Herzegovina and formerly Serb-held areas of the Republic of Croatia, the commanders of Serb paramilitary forces and political and military leaders in the Federal Republic of Yugoslavia (Serbia and Montenegro) bear primary responsibility for most of those violations, and that persons who commit such acts will be held personally responsible and accountable;

4. *Condemns* the attacks on the safe areas of Srebrenica and Zepa by Bosnian Serb forces, which led to gross abuses of human rights and grave breaches of international humanitarian law and the disappearance of thousands of persons, as detailed in the reports of the former and the current Special Rapporteurs;

5. *Also condemns* the indiscriminate shelling of civilians in the safe areas of Sarajevo, Tuszla, Bihac and Gorazde and the use of cluster bombs on civilian targets by Bosnian Serb and Croatian Serb forces;

6. *Further condemns* violations of human rights and international humanitarian law, including killings, the burning and looting of houses, the shelling of residential areas, harassment of and attacks on refugees, the elderly and the infirm perpetrated by members of the Croatian armed forces and civilians in the formerly Serb-controlled regions of Croatia during and subsequent to the military operations there in August 1995;

7. *Welcomes* the withdrawal of the heavy weapons surrounding Sarajevo following the decision to implement Security Council resolution 836 (1993), reinforced by the London Conference, to respond to attacks on safe areas, and notes that this opened Sarajevo to badly needed humanitarian relief;

8. *Notes with appreciation* the efforts of the International Tribunal for the Prosecution of Persons Responsible for Serious Violations of International Humanitarian Law Committed in the Territory of the Former Yugoslavia since 1991, established pursuant to Security Council resolutions 806 (1993) of 5 February 1993 and 827 (1993) of 25 May 1993, notes the issuance of indictments against individuals, and urges that the Tribunal be given the resources it needs;

9. *Requests* States, as a matter of urgency, to continue to make available to the Tribunal expert personnel, adequate resources and services to aid in the investigation and prosecution of persons accused having committed serious violations of international humanitarian law;

10. *Reminds* all States of their obligation under Security Council resolution 827 (1993) to cooperate with the Tribunal, including through compliance with requests for assistance and orders issued by a trial chamber of the Tribunal, and, in this regard, urges the parties to allow the establishment of offices of the Tribunal in their territories and draws the attention of the Federal Republic of Yugoslavia (Serbia and Montenegro), the Republic of Croatia and the Republic of Bosnia and Herzegovina to their obligation to cooperate with the Tribunal, in particular to arrest, detain and facilitate the transfer to the custody of the Tribunal any and all indicted war criminals who reside in or transit through or are otherwise present in their respective territories;

11. *Demands* that all parties refrain from any action intended to destroy, alter, conceal or damage any evidence of violations of human rights and international humanitarian law and that they preserve such evidence;

12. *Expresses its complete support* for the victims of violations of human rights and international humanitarian law, recognizes the right of refugees and displaced persons freely to return to their homes of origin in safety and dignity, to have restored to them property of which they were deprived in the course of hostilities since 1991 and to be compensated for any such property that cannot be restored to them, considers null any commitments made under duress, and urges all parties to fulfil their agreements to this end;

13. *Condemns all* deliberate obstruction of the delivery of food and medical and other supplies essential for the civilian population, which constitutes a serious violation of international humanitarian law and international human rights law, and of medical evacuations, and demands that all parties ensure that all persons under their control cease such acts;

14. *Also condemns* all attacks on the United Nations Peace Forces and on personnel working with the Office of the United Nations High Commissioner for Refugees and other humanitarian organizations by parties to the conflict;

15. *Expresses its outrage* that the systematic practice of rape has been used as a weapon of war against women and children and as an instrument of ethnic cleansing, and recognizes that rape in this context constitutes a war crime;

16. *Condemns* police violence against the non-Serb populations in Kosovo, the Sandjak, Vojvodina and other areas of the Federal Republic of Yugoslavia (Serbia and Montenegro), particularly the systematic acts of harassment, beatings, torture, warrantless searches, arbitrary detention and unfair trials, including those directed mainly against members of the Muslim population;

17. *Strongly urges* the authorities of the Federal Republic of Yugoslavia (Serbia and Montenegro) to take appropriate measures to respect fully all human rights and fundamental freedoms and to take urgent action to ensure the rule of law in order to prevent arbitrary evictions and dismissals and discrimination against any ethnic or national, religious and

[1] A/30/727-S/1995/933.

linguistic group, including in the fields of education and information;

18. *Cautions* against any attempts to use Serb refugees to alter the population balance in Kosovo, the Sandjak, Vojvodina and any other part of the country, thus further suppressing the enjoyment of human rights in those areas;

19. *Strongly encourages* all parties to fulfil the commitments made at Dayton, Ohio, to release without delay all civilians and combatants held in prison or detention in relation to the conflict, in conformity with international humanitarian law and the provisions of the General Framework Agreement for Peace in Bosnia and Herzegovina, and demands that the parties cooperate fully with the International Committee of the Red Cross, the Special Rapporteur and her staff, the United Nations High Commissioner for Refugees, the United Nations High Commissioner for Human Rights, and the monitoring and other missions of the European Union and the Organization for Security and Cooperation in Europe;

20. *Urges* Member States to consider positively the Special Rapporteur's recommendation that economic and other aid must be made conditional on meaningful progress on human rights;

21. *Recognizes* that the Bosnian Federation should be further developed to serve as a model for ethnic reconciliation in the region;

22. *Urges* all parties, in particular the Government of the Federal Republic of Yugoslavia (Serbia and Montenegro), to cooperate with the "Special Process" on missing persons in the territory of the former Yugoslavia established pursuant to paragraph 24 of Commission on Human Rights resolution 1994/72,[1] and reiterated in resolution 1995/35, by disclosing information and documentation on inmates in prisons, camps and other places of detention;

23. *Also urges* all parties to provide full access for monitoring the human rights situation, including by allowing access to the missions of the Organization for Security and Cooperation in Europe, including in Kosovo, as called for by the General Assembly in its resolution 49/196 and by the Security Council in its resolution 855 (1993) of 9 August 1993, and in the Sandjak, Vojvodina and other affected areas, and requests that the Federal Republic of Yugoslavia (Serbia and Montenegro) permit the opening of a field office of the Centre for Human Rights as called for by the General Assembly in resolution 49/196;

24. *Urges* the Secretary-General to take all necessary steps to ensure the full and effective coordination of the activities of all United Nations bodies in implementing the present resolution, and urges those bodies concerned with the situation in the territories of Bosnia and Herzegovina, Croatia and the Federal Republic of Yugoslavia (Serbia and Montenegro) to coordinate closely with the United Nations High Commissioner for Human Rights, the Special Rapporteur and the Tribunal, and to provide to the Special Rapporteur on a continuing basis all relevant and accurate information in their possession on the situation of human rights in Bosnia and Herzegovina, Croatia and the Federal Republic of Yugoslavia (Serbia and Montenegro);

25. *Draws attention* to the need for an immediate and urgent investigation by qualified experts of several mass grave sites near Srebrenica and Vukovar and other mass grave sites and places where mass killings are reported to have taken place, and requests the Secretary-General, within existing resources, to make available the necessary means for this undertaking;

26. *Urges* the Secretary-General, within existing resources, to make all necessary resources available for the Special Rapporteur to carry out her mandate and in particular to provide her with adequate staff based in the territories of Bosnia and Herzegovina, Croatia and the Federal Republic of Yugoslavia (Serbia and Montenegro) to ensure effective continuous monitoring of the human rights situation there and coordination with other United Nations bodies involved, including the United Nations Peace Forces;

27. *Welcomes* the effort by the Government of Bosnia and Herzegovia to uphold human rights in its territory, and urges it to fulfil the human rights commitments it has made;

28. *Notes with concern* that many of the past recommendations of the Special Rapporteur have not been fully implemented, in some cases because of resistance by the parties on the ground, and urges the parties, all States and relevant organizations to give immediate consideration to them, in particular the calls of the former and the current Special Rapporteurs:

(a) For the de facto Bosnian Serb authorities to provide prompt access to humanitarian monitors to territories controlled by them, in particular to the Banja Luka region and to Srebrenica, emphasizing that the fate of thousands of missing persons from Srebrenica requires immediate clarification;

(b) For the Government of Croatia to fulfil its responsibilities to secure the human rights of the remaining ethnic Serb population in all recently retaken territories and to remove all legal and administrative hurdles which are preventing the return of refugees and displaced persons;

(c) For greater cooperation between Governments and non-governmental organizations, recognizing that the work and role of non-governmental organizations is vital to the promotion and protection of the rights of the individual and respect and protection of human rights in the region;

(d) For the Federal Republic of Yugoslavia (Serbia and Montenegro) to undertake measures to respect fully the rights of persons belonging to national or ethnic, religious and linguistic minorities;

29. Invites the Commission on Human Rights at its fifty-second session to request the Special Rapporteur to report to the General Assembly at its fifty-first session;

30. Decides to continue its examination of this question at its fifty-first session under the item entitled "Human rights questions".

99th plenary meeting
22 December 1995

50/200. Situation of Human Rights in Rwanda

Committee: 3
Vote: Adopted without a vote
Ref.: 49/206

The General Assembly,

Guided by the Charter of the United Nations, the Universal Declaration of Human Rights,[2] the International Covenants on Human Rights,[3] the Convention on the Prevention and the Punishment of the Crime of Genocide[4] and other applicable human rights and humanitarian law standards,

Recalling its resolution 49/206 of 23 December 1994 and Commission on Human Rights resolution 1995/91 of 8 March 1995,[5] in which the Commission renewed the mandate of the Special Rapporteur to investigate the human rights situation in Rwanda,

Welcoming the commitments of the Government of Rwanda to protect and promote respect for human rights and fundamental freedoms and to eliminate impunity, recalling the efforts to restore the rule of law and reconstruct the civil administration and the social, legal and human rights infrastructure, and noting that these efforts are hampered by a

1 See *Official Records of the Economic and Social Council, 1994, Supplement No. 4* and corrigendum (E/1994/24 and Corr.1), chap. II, sect. A.

2 Resolution 217 A (III).

3 Resolution 2200 A (XXI), annex.

4 Resolution 260 A (III).

5 *Official Records of the Economic and Social Council, 1995, Supplement No. 3* and corrigenda (E/1995/23 and Corr.1 and 2), chap. II, sect. A.

lack of resources,

Noting the concerns of the Special Rapporteur, as set out in his report of 28 June 1995,[1] that the human rights situation is exacerbated by the insufficient system for the administration of justice, characterized by a shortage of both human and material means, and that there are threats and violence against the physical integrity of individuals, arrest, detention and treatment and conditions of detention, which do not conform to international standards,

Expressing its grave concern at the tragedy of Kibeho in April 1995, and recalling the conclusions of the International Commission of Inquiry in its report of 18 May 1995,

Recalling the obligations of all States to punish all persons who commit or authorize genocide or other grave violations of international humanitarian law or those who are responsible for grave violations of human rights and, pursuant to Security Council resolution 978 (1995) of 27 February 1995, to exert every effort, without delay, to bring those responsible to justice in accordance with international principles of due process, and to honour their obligations under international law in this regard, particularly under the Convention on the Prevention and Punishment of the Crime of Genocide,

Welcoming the measures taken by the United Nations High Commissioner for Human Rights to put in place the human rights field operation in Rwanda and to coordinate its activities with those of the Special Representative of the Secretary-General, the United Nations High Commissioner for Refugees, the United Nations Development Programme, the United Nations Assistance Mission for Rwanda, the International Criminal Tribunal for the Prosecution of Persons Responsible for Genocide and Other Serious Violations of International Humanitarian Law Committed in the Territory of Rwanda and Rwandan Citizens Responsible for Genocide and Other Such Violations Committed in the Territory of Neighbouring States between 1 January and 31 December 1994, the Department of Humanitarian Affairs of the Secretariat, and other United Nations agencies and intergovernmental and non-governmental organizations, and the International Committee of the Red Cross,

Recognizing the valuable contribution that the human rights officers deployed by the United Nations High Commissioner for Human Rights to Rwanda have made towards the improvement of the overall situation.

Deeply concerned by the reports of the Special Rapporteur and the United Nations High Commissioner for Human Rights, according to which genocide and systematic, widespread and flagrant violations of international humanitarian law, including crimes against humanity and grave violations and abuses of human rights, were committed in Rwanda,

Welcoming the policy of the Government of Rwanda to facilitate the process of voluntary and safe return, resettlement and reintegration of refugees, as reaffirmed in the Cairo Declaration on the Great Lakes Region of 29 November 1995,[2]

Noting the United Nations support for all efforts to reduce tension and restore stability in the Great Lake region, and supporting initiatives of the Secretary-General in this regard, particularly implementing the Cairo Declaration on the Great Lakes Region, and continuing consultations with the aim of convening a conference on security, stability and development in the Great Lakes region, as appropriate,

Recalling Security Council resolution 1029 (1995) of 12 December 1995, in which the Council renewed the mandate of the United Nations Assistance Mission for Rwanda to exercise its good offices to assist in achieving the voluntary and safe repatriation of Rwandan refugees within the frame of reference of the recommendations of the Bujumbura Conference and the Cairo Summit of the Heads of State of the Great Lakes Region, and in promoting genuine national reconciliation, to assist the Office of the United Nations High Commissioner for Refugees and other international agencies in the provision of logistical support for the repatriation of refugees, to contribute, with the agreement of the Government of Rwanda, to the protection of the International Tribunal for Rwanda as an interim measure until alternative arrangements agreed with the Government of Rwanda can be put in place,

Acknowledging the responsibility of the Government of Rwanda for the safety and security of all personnel attached to the United Nations Assistance Mission for Rwanda, United Nations agencies and humanitarian organizations and other international staff operating in the country,

Recognizing the important role played by non-governmental organizations in providing humanitarian assistance and contributing to the reconstruction and rehabilitation of Rwanda,

Recognizing also that effective action must be taken to ensure that the perpetrators of genocide and crimes against humanity are promptly brought to justice,

Recognizing further that effective action to prevent further violations of human rights and fundamental freedoms must be a central and integral element of the overall Rwandan and United Nations responses to the situation in Rwanda and that a strong human rights component is indispensable to the political peace process and the post-conflict reconstruction of Rwanda,

1. *Welcomes* the report of the United Nations High Commissioner for Human Rights on the human rights field operation in Rwanda,[3] and recalls the reports of the Special Rapporteur of the Commission on Human Rights on violations committed during the tragedy in Rwanda and on the current situation of human rights in Rwanda;[4]

2. *Condemns in the strongest terms* the acts of genocide, violations of international humanitarian law and all violations and abuses of human rights that occurred during the tragedy in Rwanda, especially following the events of 6 April 1994, and which resulted in a massive loss of human life, up to one million people;

3. *Expresses its deep concern* at the intense suffering of the victims of genocide and crimes against humanity, recognizes the ongoing suffering of their survivors, particularly the extremely high number of traumatized children and women victims of rape and sexual violence, and urges the international community to provide adequate assistance to them;

4. *Condemns* the killing of personnel attached to the United Nations Assistance Mission for Rwanda, United Nations agencies and humanitarian organizations operating in the country, including Rwandan personnel working with them;

5. *Calls upon* the Government of Rwanda to take all necessary measures to ensure the safety and security of all personnel attached to the United Nations Assistance Mission for Rwanda, United Nations agencies and humanitarian organizations and other international staff operating in the country;

6. *Reaffirms* that all persons who commit or authorize genocide or other grave violations of international humanitarian law or those who are responsible for grave violations of human rights are individually responsible and accountable for those violations;

7. *Urges* all States, pursuant to Security Council resolution 978 (1995), to exert, without delay, every effort, including arrest and detention, in order to bring those responsible to justice in accordance with international principles of due process, and also urges States to honour their obligations under international law in this regard, particularly under the Convention on the Prevention and Punishment of the Crime of Genocide;

---

1 A/50/709-S/1995/915, annex III.

2 S/1995/1001, annex.

3 A/50/743, annex.

4 A/50/709-S/1995/915, annexes I-III.

8. *Recognizes* that effective action must be taken by all States concerned to ensure that the perpetrators of genocide and crimes against humanity are promptly brought to justice, and urges all States concerned to cooperate fully with the International Criminal Tribunal for the Prosecution of Persons Responsible for Genocide and Other Serious Violations of International Humanitarian Law Committed in the Territory of Rwanda and Rwandan Citizens Responsible for Genocide and Other Such Violations Committed in the Territory of Neighbouring States between 1 January and 31 December 1994, taking into account the obligations contained in Security Council resolutions 955 (1994) of 8 November 1994 and 978 (1995), and to intensify efforts for the effective functioning of the Tribunal without delay;

9. *Commends* the efforts of the United Nations High Commissioner for Human Rights, working in cooperation with and assisting the Government of Rwanda, to ensure that human rights monitoring, a comprehensive programme of human rights assistance and confidence-building measures form integral parts of Rwandan and United Nations efforts aimed at conflict prevention and peace-building in Rwanda, drawing as appropriate on the expertise and capacities of all parts of the United Nations system, thus contributing to the promotion and protection of human rights in Rwanda;

10. *Encourages* the Government of Rwanda, in a spirit of national reconciliation, to intensify efforts to protect and promote respect for human rights and fundamental freedoms and to create an environment conducive to the realization of civil, political, economic, social and cultural rights, and the voluntary and safe return of refugees to their homes;

11. *Takes note with concern* of the findings of the Special Rapporteur as set out in his report of 28 June 1995, and of the Human Rights Field Operation in Rwanda, that the human rights situation is exacerbated by the insufficient system for the administration of justice, characterized by a shortage of both human and material means;

12. *Notes with concern* the arrest, detention and treatment and conditions of detention that do not conform to international standards, as set out in the report of the Special Rapporteur;

13. *Also notes with concern* that a situation still exists, evidenced by reports of threats and violence against the physical integrity of individuals, which is sometimes exacerbated by incursions;

14. *Urges* Governments in the region to take measures to prevent their territory from being used to pursue a strategy of destabilization of Rwanda, and, in this regard, urges all States concerned to cooperate fully with the International Commission of Inquiry on arms flows in the Great Lakes region, established in pursuance of Security Council resolution 1013 (1995) of 7 September 1995;

15. *Condemns* the mass killings of civilians at Kibeho in April 1995, recalls the conclusions of the International Commission of Inquiry in its report of 18 May 1995, and expresses its grave concern at the events in Kanama in September 1995;

16. *Welcomes* the efforts of the Government of Rwanda to reconstruct the civil administration and the social, legal, economic and human rights infrastructure of Rwanda, encourages the Government to intensify its efforts, with the assistance of the international community, the Human Rights Field Operation in Rwanda and other United Nations bodies, to expedite the processing of cases, to ensure conditions and treatment in detention in conformity with international standards, and to train civilian police in the legal procedures governing arrest and detention, and notes that efforts in this regard are hampered by a lack of human and financial resources;

17. *Invites* Member States, the organizations and bodies of the United Nations system and intergovernmental and non-governmental organizations to continue and intensify their efforts to contribute financial and technical support to the efforts of the Government of Rwanda to reconstruct the civil administration and the social, legal, economic and human rights infrastructure of Rwanda, particularly in the areas of the administration of justice, and welcomes the contributions made, including those at the Round Table Conference at Geneva and its mid-term review, and urges States and donor agencies to fulfil their earlier commitments;

18. *Condemns* all violence and intimidation against persons in the refugee camps in neighbouring countries, calls upon the appropriate authorities to ensure security in such camps, and welcomes the commitments undertaken by the Governments in the region in the Cairo Declaration on the Great Lakes Region of 29 November 1995;

19. *Welcomes* the joint efforts of the Government of Rwanda, neighbouring countries and the United Nations High Commissioner for Refugees to assist the voluntary and safe return of refugees through, *inter alia,* the work of the Tripartite Commission and the agreements reached at Nairobi in January 1995, Bujumbura in February 1995 and Cairo in November 1995, and welcomes also the efforts of the United Nations High Commissioner for Refugees, the United Nations High Commissioner for Human Rights, the United Nations Assistance Mission for Rwanda and the United Nations Development Programme to coordinate their efforts to ensure protection of the human rights of refugees during their return, resettlement and reintegration;

20. *Also welcomes* the measures taken by the United Nations High Commissioner for Human Rights, working in cooperation with and assisting the Government of Rwanda, to put in place the Human Rights Field Operation in Rwanda, which has as its objective:

(*a*) The investigation of violations of human rights and humanitarian law, including acts of genocide and crimes against humanity;

(*b*) The monitoring of the human rights situation and the prevention of future violations;

(*c*) Cooperation with other international agencies in re-establishing confidence and thus facilitating the voluntary return and resettlement of refugees and displaced persons;

(*d*) The rebuilding of civil society, through programmes of human rights education and technical cooperation, particularly in the areas of the administration of justice and conditions of arrest, detention and treatment in detention, and through programmes of cooperation with Rwandan human rights organizations;

and requests the High Commissioner to report regularly on all of these activities of the Field Operation and to cooperate and share information with the Special Rapporteur in order to assist him in fulfilling his mandate;

21. *Further welcomes* the cooperation the Government of Rwanda has extended to the United Nations High Commissioner for Human Rights, the Human Rights Field Operation in Rwanda and the Special Rapporteur and the acceptance by the Government of Rwanda of the deployment of human rights field officers throughout the country;

22. *Requests* the Secretary-General to take appropriate steps to ensure adequate financial and human resources and logistical support for the Human Rights Field Operation in Rwanda, taking into account the need to deploy a sufficient number of human rights field officers and the need for programmes of technical assistance and advisory services for the Government of Rwanda and Rwandan human rights organizations, especially in the field of the administration of justice;

23. *Requests* the United Nations High Commissioner for Human Rights to report on the activities of the Human Rights Field Operation in Rwanda to the Commission on Human Rights at its fifty-second session and to the General Assembly at its fifty-first session.

99th plenary meeting
22 December 1995

07.00 HUMANITARIAN LAW

07.10 ARMED CONFLICTS

427 (V). Measures for the Peaceful Solution of the Problem of Prisoners of War

Committee: 3
Vote: 43 - 5 - 6
Ref.: 741(VIII)

The General Assembly,

Mindful that one of the principal Purposes of the United Nations is to achieve international cooperation in solving international problems of a humanitarian character and in promoting and encouraging respect for human rights and fundamental freedoms for all,

Considering that the General Assembly may recommend measures for the peaceful adjustment of any situation, regardless of origin, which it deems likely to impair the general welfare or friendly relations among nations,

Believing that all prisoners having originally come within the control of the Allied Powers as a consequence of the Second World War should either have been repatriated long since or have been otherwise accounted for,

Recalling that this is required both by recognized standards of international conduct and the Geneva Convention of 1949[1] for the protection of war victims, and by specific agreements between the Allied Powers,

1. *Expresses its concern* at the information presented to it tending to show that large numbers of prisoners taken in the course of the Second World War have neither been repatriated nor otherwise accounted for;

2. *Calls upon* all governments still having control of such persons to act in conformity with the recognized standards of international conduct and with the above-mentioned international agreements and conventions which require that, upon the cessation of active hostilities, all prisoners should, with the least possible delay, be given an unrestricted opportunity of repatriation and, to that end, to publish and transmit to the Secretary-General before 30 April 1951:

(*a*) The names of such prisoners still held by them, the reasons for which they are still detained and the places in which they are detained;

(*b*) The names of prisoners who have died while under their control as well as the date and cause of death, and the manner and place of burial in each case;

3. *Requests* the Secretary-General to establish an *Ad Hoc* Commission composed of three qualified and impartial persons chosen by the International Red Cross or, failing that, by the Secretary-General himself, with a view to settling the question of the prisoners of war in a purely humanitarian spirit and on terms acceptable to all the governments concerned. The Commission shall convene at a suitable date after 30 April 1951 to examine and evaluate, in the light of the information made available to the fifth session of the General Assembly, the information furnished by governments in accordance with the terms of the preceding paragraph. In the event that the Commission considers that this information is inadequate or affords reasonable ground for believing that prisoners coming within the custody or control of any foreign government as a consequence of military operations of the Second World War have not been repatriated or otherwise accounted for, the General Assembly:

(*a*) Requests the Commission to seek from the governments or authorities concerned full information regarding such prisoners;

(*b*) Requests the Commission to assist all governments and authorities who so desire in arranging for and facilitating the repatriation of such prisoners;

(*c*) Authorizes the Commission to use the good offices of any qualified and impartial person or organization whom it considers might contribute to the repatriation or accounting for of such prisoners;

(*d*) Urges all governments and authorities concerned to cooperate fully with the Commission, to supply all necessary information and to grant right of access to their respective countries and to areas in which such prisoners are detained;

(*e*) Requests the Secretary-General to furnish the Commission with the staff and facilities necessary for the effective accomplishment of its task;

4. *Urgently requests* all the governments to make the greatest possible efforts, based in particular on the documentation to be provided, to search for prisoners of war whose absence has been reported and who might be in their territories;

5. *Directs* the Commission to report as soon as practicable the results of its work to the Secretary-General for transmission to the Members of the United Nations.

325th plenary meeting
14 December 1950

2675 (XXV). Basic Principles for the Protection of Civilian Populations in Armed Conflicts

Committee: 3
Vote: 109 - 0 - 8

The General Assembly,

Noting that in the present century the international community has accepted an increased role and new responsibilities for the alleviation of human suffering in any form and in particular during armed conflicts,

Recalling that to this end a series of international instruments has been adopted, including the four Geneva Conventions of 1949,[2]

Recalling further its resolution 2444 (XXIII) of 19 December 1968 on respect for human rights in armed conflicts,

Bearing in mind the need for measures to ensure the better protection of human rights in armed conflicts of all types;

Noting with appreciation the work that is being undertaken in this respect by the International Committee of the Red Cross,

Noting with appreciation the reports of the Secretary-General on respect for human rights in armed conflicts,[3]

Convinced that civilian populations are in special need of increased protection in time of armed conflicts,

Recognizing the importance of the strict application of the Geneva Convention relative to the Protection of Civilian Persons in Time of War, of 12 August 1949,[4]

Affirms the following basic principles for the protection of civilian populations in armed conflicts, without prejudice to their future elaboration within the framework of progressive development of the international law of armed conflict:

1. Fundamental human rights, as accepted in international law and laid down in international instruments, continue to apply fully in situations of armed conflict.

---

1 See *Geneva Convention relative to the Treatment of Prisoners of War of August 12, 1949*, International Committee of the Red Cross, Geneva 1949.

2 United Nations, *Treaty Series*, vol. 75 (1950), Nos. 970-973.

3 A/7720 and A/8052.

4 United Nations, *Treaty Series*, vol. 75 (1950), No. 973.

2. In the conduct of military operations during armed conflicts, a distinction must be made at all times between persons actively taking part in the hostilities and civilian populations.

3. In the conduct of military operations, every effort should be made to spare civilian populations from the ravages of war, and all necessary precautions should be taken to avoid injury, loss or damage to civilian populations.

4. Civilian populations as such should not be the object of military operations.

5. Dwellings and other installations that are used only by civilian populations should not be the object of military operations.

6. Places or areas designated for the sole protection of civilians, such as hospital zones or similar refuges, should not be the object of military operations.

7. Civilian populations, or individual members thereof, should not be the object of reprisals, forcible transfers or other assaults on their integrity.

8. The provision of international relief to civilian populations is in conformity with the humanitarian principles of the Charter of the United Nations, the Universal Declaration of Human Rights and other international instruments in the field of human rights. The Declaration of Principles for International Humanitarian Relief to the Civilian Population in Disaster Situations, as laid down in resolution XXVI adopted by the twenty-first International Conference of the Red Cross,[1] shall apply in situations of armed conflict, and all parties to a conflict should make every effort to facilitate this application.

1922nd plenary meeting
9 December 1970.

3102 (XXVIII). Respect for Human Rights in Armed Conflicts

Committee: 6
Vote: 107 - 0 - 6
Ref.: 32/44, 31/19, 3500(XXX), 3319(XXIX), 3032(XXVII), 2854(XXVI), 2853(XXVI), 2852(XXVI), 2677(XXV), 2676(XXV), 2675(XXV), 2674(XXV), 2597(XXIV), 2546(XXIV), 2444(XXIII), 2443(XXIII)

The General Assembly,

Reaffirming that only complete respect for the Charter of the United Nations and general and complete disarmament under effective international control can bring about full guarantees against armed conflicts and the suffering caused by such conflicts, and determined to continue all efforts to these ends,

Conscious of the fact that armed conflicts continue to cause untold human suffering and material devastation,

Convinced that in all such conflicts rules designed to reduce the suffering as much as possible and to increase the protection of noncombatants and civilian objects are needed,

Reaffirming the urgent need to ensure full and effective application by all parties to armed conflicts of existing legal rules relating to such conflicts, in particular the Hague Conventions of 1899 and 1907,[2] the Geneva Protocol of 1925[3] and the Geneva Conventions of 1949,[4] and to supplement these rules by new ones which take into account the modern developments in methods and means of warfare and which are practicable,

Welcoming the convocation by the Swiss Federal Council of the first session of the Diplomatic Conference on the Reaffirmation and Development of International Humanitarian Law Applicable in Armed Conflicts, to be held at Geneva from 20 February to 29 March 1974, with a possible second session in 1975,

Welcoming as an excellent basis for discussion at this Conference the draft Additional Protocols to the Geneva Conventions of 1949 prepared by the International Committee of the Red Cross after thorough consultations with government experts, particularly during conferences held at Geneva in 1971 and 1972,

Recalling the successive resolutions adopted in the preceding years by the United Nations relating to human rights in armed conflicts, in particular General Assembly resolutions 2852 (XXVI) and 2853 (XXVI) of 20 December 1971 and 3032 (XXVII) of 18 December 1972,

Noting resolution XIII adopted by the twenty-first International Conference of the Red Cross, held at Istanbul in 1969[5] and the resolution on the reaffirmation and development of international humanitarian law adopted by the twenty-second International Conference of the Red Cross, held at Teheran in 1973,[6]

Noting with appreciation the report of the Secretary-General on respect for human rights in armed conflicts,[7]

Recalling resolution 3058 (XXVIII) of 2 November 1973 in which the General Assembly invited the Diplomatic Conference to submit its comments and advice regarding the draft articles on the protection of journalists engaged in dangerous missions in areas of armed conflict,

Recalling its resolution 3076 (XXVIII) of 6 December 1973 concerning napalm and other incendiary weapons and all aspects of their possible use as well as the resolution on the prohibition or restriction of use of certain weapons adopted by the twenty-second International Conference of the Red Cross, held at Teheran in 1973,[8] inviting the Diplomatic Conference to take up the question of rules on the prohibition or restriction of use of specific conventional weapons which may cause unnecessary suffering or have indiscriminate effects,

Welcoming, in this regard, the survey prepared by the Secretariat on existing rules of international law concerning the prohibition or restriction of use of specific weapons,[9]

1. *Expresses its appreciation* to the Swiss Federal Council for convoking in 1974 the Diplomatic Conference on the Reaffirmation and Development of International Humanitarian Law Applicable in Armed Conflicts and to the International Committee of the Red Cross for the extensive work it has performed in preparing the draft Additional Protocols to the Geneva Conventions of 1949;

2. *Urges* that the national liberation movements recognized by the various regional intergovernmental organizations concerned be invited to participate in the Diplomatic Conference as observers in accordance with the practice of the United Nations;

3. *Urges* all participants in the Diplomatic Conference to do their utmost to reach agreement on additional rules which may help to alleviate the suffering brought about by armed conflicts and to protect noncombatants and civilian objects in such conflicts;

4. *Calls upon* all parties to armed conflicts to acknowledge and to comply with their obligations under the humanitarian instruments and to observe the international humanitarian rules which are applicable, in particular the Hague Conventions of 1899 and 1907, the Geneva Protocol of 1925 and the Geneva Conventions of 1949;

5. *Urges* that instruction concerning such rules be provided to armed forces and information concerning the same rules be given to civilians everywhere, with a view to securing their strict observance;

6. *Requests again* the Secretary-General to encourage the study and teaching of principles of international humanitarian rules applicable in armed conflicts;

7. *Requests* the Secretary-General to report to the General Assembly at its twenty-ninth session on relevant developments concerning

1 *International Review of the Red Cross,* No. 104 (November 1969), p. 632.

2 Carnegie Endowment for International Peace, *The Hague Conventions and Declarations of 1899 and 1907* (New York, Oxford University Press, 1915).

3 League of Nations, *Treaty Series,* vol. XCIV, No. 2138, p. 65.

4 United Nations, *Treaty Series,* vol. 75, Nos. 970-973.

5 See A/7720, annex I, sect. D.

6 A/9123/Add.2, annex, sect. IV.

7 A/9123 and Corr.1 and Add.1 and 2.

8 A/9123/Add.2, annex, sect. III.

9 A/9215.

human rights in armed conflicts, in particular on the proceedings and results of the 1974 session of the Diplomatic Conference;

8. *Decides* to include in the provisional agenda of its twenty-ninth session the item entitled "Respect for human rights in armed conflicts".

2197th plenary meeting
12 December 1973

3103 (XXVIII). Basic Principles of the Legal Status of the Combatants Struggling Against Colonial and Alien Domination and Racist Régimes

Committee: 6
Vote: 83 - 13 - 19

The General Assembly,

Recalling that the Charter of the United Nations reaffirms faith in the dignity and worth of the human person,

Recalling resolution 2444 (XXIII) of 19 December 1968 in which the General Assembly, *inter alia*, recognized the need for applying basic humanitarian principles in all armed conflicts,

Recognizing further the importance of respecting the Hague Convention of 1907,[1] the Geneva Protocol of 1925[2] the Geneva Conventions of 1949[3] and other universally recognized norms of modern international law for the protection of human rights in armed conflicts,

Reaffirming that the continuation of colonialism in all its forms and manifestations, as noted in General Assembly resolution 2621 (XXV) of 12 October 1970, is a crime and that colonial peoples have the inherent right to struggle by all necessary means at their disposal against colonial Powers and alien domination in exercise of their right of self-determination recognized in the Charter of the United Nations and the Declaration on Principles of International Law concerning Friendly Relations and Cooperation among States in accordance with the Charter of the United Nations,[4]

Stressing that the policy of apartheid and racial oppression has been condemned by all countries and peoples, and that the pursuing of such a policy has been recognized as an international crime,

Reaffirming the declarations made in General Assembly resolutions 2548 (XXIV) of 11 December 1969 and 2708 (XXV) of 14 December 1970 that the practice of using mercenaries against national liberation movements in the colonial Territories constitutes a criminal act,

Recalling the numerous appeals of the General Assembly to the colonial Powers and those occupying foreign territories as well as to the racist régimes set forth, *inter alia*, in resolutions 2383 (XXIII) of 7 November 1968, 2508 (XXIV) of 21 November 1969, 2547 (XXIV) of 11 December 1969, 2652 (XXV) of 3 December 1970, 2678 (XXV) of 9 December 1970, 2707 (XXV) of 14 December 1970, 2795 (XXVI) and 2796 (XXVI) of 10 December 1971 and 2871 (XXVI) of 20 December 1971, to ensure the application to the fighters for freedom and self-determination of the provisions of the Geneva Convention relative to the Treatment of Prisoners of War, of 12 August 1949,[5] and the Geneva Convention relative to the Protection of Civilian Persons in Time of War, of 12 August 1949,[6]

Deeply concerned at the fact that, despite the numerous appeals of the General Assembly, compliance with the provisions of the said Conventions has not yet been ensured,

Noting that the treatment of the combatants struggling against colonial and alien domination and racist régimes captured as prisoners still remains inhuman,

Recalling its resolutions 2674 (XXV) of 9 December 1970 and 2852 (XXVI) of 20 December 1971, in which it pointed out the need for the elaboration of additional international instruments and norms envisaging, *inter alia*, the increase of the protection of persons struggling for freedom against colonial and alien domination and racist régimes,

Solemnly proclaims the following basic principles of the legal status of the combatants struggling against colonial and alien domination and racist régimes without prejudice to their elaboration in future within the framework of the development of international law applying to the protection of human rights in armed conflicts:

1. The struggle of peoples under colonial and alien domination and racist régimes for the implementation of their right to self-determination and independence is legitimate and in full accordance with the principles of international law.

2. Any attempt to suppress the struggle against colonial and alien domination and racist régimes is incompatible with the Charter of the United Nations, the Declaration on Principles of International Law concerning Friendly Relations and Cooperation among States in accordance with the Charter of the United Nations, the Universal Declaration of Human Rights and the Declaration on the Granting of Independence to Colonial Countries and Peoples[7] and constitutes a threat to international peace and security.

3. The armed conflicts involving the struggle of peoples against colonial and alien domination and racist régimes are to be regarded as international armed conflicts in the sense of the 1949 Geneva Conventions, and the legal status envisaged to apply to the combatants in the 1949 Geneva Conventions and other international instruments is to apply to the persons engaged in armed struggle against colonial and alien domination and racist régimes.

4. The combatants struggling against colonial and alien domination and racist régimes captured as prisoners are to be accorded the status of prisoners of war and their treatment should be in accordance with the provisions of the Geneva Convention relative to the Treatment of Prisoners of War, of 12 August 1949.

5. The use of mercenaries by colonial and racist régimes against the national liberation movements struggling for their freedom and independence from the yoke of colonialism and alien domination is considered to be a criminal act and the mercenaries should accordingly be punished as criminals.

6. The violation of the legal status of the combatants struggling against colonial and alien domination and racist régimes in the course of armed conflicts entails full responsibility in accordance with the norms of international law.

2197th plenary meeting
12 December 1973

3318 (XXIX). Declaration on the Protection of Women and Children in Emergency and Armed Conflict

Committee: -
Vote: Adopted without a vote

The General Assembly,

Having considered the recommendation of the Economic and Social Council contained in its resolution 1861 (LVI) of 16 May 1974,

Expressing its deep concern over the sufferings of women and children belonging to the civilian population who in periods of emergency and armed conflict in the struggle for peace, self-determination, national liberation and independence are too often the victims of inhuman acts and consequently suffer serious harm,

Aware of the suffering of women and children in many areas of the world, especially in those areas subject to suppression, aggression, colonialism, racism, alien domination and foreign subjugation,

1 Carnegie Endowment for International Peace, *The Hague Conventions and Declarations of 1899 and 1907* (New York, Oxford University Press, 1915).

2 League of Nations, *Treaty Series,* vol. XCIV, No. 2138, p. 65.

3 United Nations, *Treaty Series,* vol. 75, Nos. 970-973.

4 Resolution 2625 (XXV), annex.

5 United Nations, *Treaty Series,* vol. 75, No. 972, p. 135.

6 *Ibid.*, No.973, p. 287.

7 Resolution 1514 (XV).

Deeply concerned by the fact that, despite general and unequivocal condemnation, colonialism, racism and alien and foreign domination continue to subject many peoples under their yoke, cruelly suppressing the national liberation movements and inflicting heavy losses and incalculable sufferings on the populations under their domination, including women and children,

Deploring the fact that grave attacks are still being made on fundamental freedoms and the dignity of the human person and that colonial and racist foreign domination Powers continue to violate international humanitarian law,

Recalling the relevant provisions contained in the instruments of international humanitarian law relative to the protection of women and children in time of peace and war,

Recalling, among other important documents, its resolutions 2444 (XXIII) of 19 December 1968, 2597 (XXIV) of 16 December 1969 and 2674 (XXV) and 2675 (XXV) of 9 December 1970, on respect for human rights and on basic principles for the protection of civilian populations in armed conflicts, as well as Economic and Social Council resolution 1515 (XLVIII) of 28 May 1970 in which the Council requested the General Assembly to consider the possibility of drafting a declaration on the protection of women and children in emergency or wartime,

Conscious of its responsibility for the destiny of the rising generation and for the destiny of mothers, who play an important role in society, in the family and particularly in the upbringing of children,

Bearing in mind the need to provide special protection of women and children belonging to the civilian population,

Solemnly proclaims this Declaration on the Protection of Women and Children in Emergency and Armed Conflict and calls for the strict observance of the Declaration by all Member States:

1. Attacks and bombings on the civilian population, inflicting incalculable suffering, especially on women and children, who are the most vulnerable members of the population, shall be prohibited, and such acts shall be condemned.

2. The use of chemical and bacteriological weapons in the course of military operations constitutes one of the most flagrant violations of the Geneva Protocol of 1925,[1] the Geneva Conventions of 1949[2] and the principles of international humanitarian law and inflicts heavy losses on civilian populations, including defenceless women and children, and shall be severely condemned.

3. All States shall abide fully by their obligations under the Geneva Protocol of 1925 and the Geneva Conventions of 1949, as well as other instruments of international law relative to respect for human rights in armed conflicts, which offer important guarantees for the protection of women and children.

4. All efforts shall be made by States involved in armed conflicts, military operations in foreign territories or military operations in territories still under colonial domination to spare women and children from the ravages of war. All the necessary steps shall be taken to ensure the prohibition of measures such as persecution, torture, punitive measures, degrading treatment and violence, particularly against that part of the civilian population that consists of women and children.

5. All forms of repression and cruel and inhuman treatment of women and children, including imprisonment, torture, shooting, mass arrests, collective punishment, destruction of dwellings and forcible eviction, committed by belligerents in the course of military operations or in occupied territories shall be considered criminal.

6. Women and children belonging to the civilian population and finding themselves in circumstances of emergency and armed conflict in the struggle for peace, self-determination, national liberation and independence, or who live in occupied territories, shall not be deprived of shelter, food, medical aid or other inalienable rights, in accordance with the provisions of the Universal Declaration of Human Rights, the International Covenant on Civil and Political Rights,[3] the International Covenant on Economic, Social and Cultural Rights, [4] the Declaration of the Rights of the Child[5] or other instruments of international law.

2319th plenary meeting
14 December 1974

1 League of Nations, *Treaty Series*, vol. XCIV, No. 2138, p. 65.

2 United Nations, *Treaty Series*, vol. 75, Nos. 970-973.

46/216. International Cooperation to Mitigate the Environmental Consequences on Kuwait and other Countries in the Region Resulting from the Situation Between Iraq and Kuwait

Committee: 2
Vote: 135 - 0 - 1

The General Assembly,

Aware of the disastrous situation caused in Kuwait and neighbouring areas by the torching and destruction of hundreds of its oil wells and of the other environmental consequences on the atmosphere, land and marine life,

Bearing in mind all relevant Security Council resolutions, in particular section E of resolution 687 (1991) of 3 April 1991,

Having taken note of the report submitted by the Secretary-General to the Security Council describing the nature and extent of the environmental damage suffered by Kuwait,[6]

Having also taken note of decision 16/11 A adopted by the Governing Council of the United Nations Environment Programme on 31 May 1991,[7]

Profoundly concerned at the deterioration in the environment as a consequence of the damage, especially the threat posed to the health and well-being of the people of Kuwait and the people of the region, and the adverse impact on the economic activities of Kuwait and other countries of the region, including the effects on livestock, agriculture and fishing, as well as on wildlife,

Acknowledging the fact that dealing with this catastrophe goes beyond the capabilities of the countries of the region and, in that regard, recognizing the need for strengthened international cooperation to deal with the issue,

Noting with appreciation the appointment by the Secretary-General of an Under-Secretary-General as his Personal Representative to coordinate United Nations efforts in this field,

Also noting with appreciation the efforts already undertaken by the Member States of the region, other States, the organizations of the United Nations system, and governmental and non-governmental organizations to study, mitigate and minimize the consequences of this environmental catastrophe,

Bearing in mind the effective work of the Regional Organization for the Protection of the Marine Environment and the inter-agency task force established under the leadership of the United Nations Environment Programme especially for the environmental situation in the region, and the plan of action,

Expressing its special appreciation to the Governments which have extended financial support to the two trust funds established for the purpose by the Secretary-General of the International Maritime Organization and the Executive Director of the United Nations Environment Programme,

Emphasizing the need to continue to take comprehensive measures to study and mitigate these environmental consequences within a framework of sustained and coordinated international cooperation,

3 Resolution 2200 A (XXI), annex.

4 Resolution 2200 A (XXI), annex.

5 Resolution 1386 (XIV).

6 See S/22535 and Corr. 1 and 2, annex; see *Official Records of the Security Council, Forty-sixth Year, Supplement for April, May and June 1991*, document S/22535

7 See *Official Records of the General Assembly, Forty-sixth Session, Supplement No. 25* (A/46/25), annex.

1. *Urgently appeals* to all States Members of the United Nations, intergovernmental and non-governmental organizations, scientific bodies and individuals to provide assistance for programmes aimed at the study and mitigation of the environmental deterioration of the region and for strengthening the Regional Organization for the Protection of the Marine Environment and its role in coordinating the implementation of these programmes;

2. *Calls upon* the organizations and programmes of the United Nations system, in particular the International Maritime Organization and the United Nations Environment Programme, to pursue their efforts to assess and counteract the short-term as well as long-term impact of the environmental deterioration of the region;

3. *Requests* the Secretary-General, through his Personal Representative, to render assistance to the members of the Regional Organization for the Protection of the Marine Environment in the formulation and implementation of a coordinated and consolidated programme of action comprising costed project profiles, to help identify all possible resources for the programme of action and, *inter alia*, for strengthening the environmental capacities of the members of the Regional Organization for the Protection of the Marine Environment to surmount the problem, and to allocate, within existing resources, the minimum resources required to enable his Personal Representative to continue to help coordinate the activities of the United Nations system to that end;

4. *Also requests* the Secretary-General to submit to the General Assembly at its forty-seventh session, through the Economic and Social Council, a report on the implementation of the present resolution;

5. *Decides* to include in the provisional agenda of its forty-seventh session a sub-item entitled "International cooperation to mitigate the environmental consequences on Kuwait and other countries in the region resulting from the situation between Iraq and Kuwait" under the item entitled "Development and international economic cooperation".

79th plenary meeting
20 December 1991

47/37. Protection of the Environment in Times of Armed Conflict

Committee: 6
Vote: Adopted without a vote

The General Assembly,

Recognizing that the use of certain means and methods of warfare may have dire effects on the environment,

Recognizing also the importance of the provisions of international law applicable to the protection of the environment in times of armed conflict and, in particular, both the rules of universal applicability laid down in the Hague Convention respecting the Laws and Customs of War on Land, of 18 October 1907, with the Regulations annexed thereto,[1] and the Geneva Convention relative to the Protection of Civilian Persons in Time of War, of 12 August 1949,[2] and the applicable rules of the Protocol Additional to the Geneva Conventions of 12 August 1949, and relating to the Protection of Victims of International Armed Conflicts (Protocol I), of 1977,[3] and of the Convention on the Prohibition of Military or Any Other Hostile Use of Environmental Modification Techniques, of 1976,[4]

Expressing its deep concern about environmental damage and depletion of natural resources, including the destruction of hundreds of oil-well heads and the release and waste of crude oil into the sea, during recent conflicts,

Noting that existing provisions of international law prohibit such acts,[5]

Stressing that destruction of the environment, not justified by military necessity and carried out wantonly, is clearly contrary to existing international law,

Concerned that the provisions of international law prohibiting such acts may not be widely disseminated and applied,

Noting the work on environmental protection carried out within the United Nations system and at meetings and symposia on the subject,

Taking note of the Final Declaration of the Second Review Conference of the Parties to the Convention on the Prohibition of Military or Any Other Hostile Use of Environmental Modification Techniques,

Taking note also of the Rio Declaration on Environment and Development,[6] adopted at the United Nations Conference on Environment and Development at Rio de Janeiro on 14 June 1992, in particular principle 24 thereof, and other relevant decisions of the Conference,

Expressing its appreciation for the report of the Secretary-General[7] submitted pursuant to General Assembly decision 46/417 of 9 December 1991,

Welcoming the activities of the International Committee of the Red Cross in this field, including plans to continue its consultation of experts with an enlarged basis of participation and its readiness to prepare a handbook of model guidelines for military manuals,

1. *Urges* States to take all measures to ensure compliance with the existing international law applicable to the protection of the environment in times of armed conflict;

2. *Appeals* to all States that have not yet done so to consider becoming parties to the relevant international conventions;

3. *Urges* States to take steps to incorporate the provisions of international law applicable to the protection of the environment into their military manuals and to ensure that they are effectively disseminated;

4. *Requests* the Secretary-General to invite the International Committee of the Red Cross to report on activities undertaken by the Committee and other relevant bodies with regard to the protection of the environment in times of armed conflict, and to submit to the General Assembly at its forty-eighth session, under the item entitled "United Nations Decade of International Law", a report on activities reported by the Committee.

73rd plenary meeting
25 November 1992

1 See Carnegie Endowment for International Peace, *The Hague Conventions and Declarations of 1899 and 1907* (New York, Oxford University Press, 1915).

2 United Nations, *Treaty Series*, vol. 79, No. 973.

3 *Ibid.*, vol. 1125, No. 17512.

4 *Ibid.*, vol. 1108, No. 17119.

5 EMOD/CONF.II/12, part II.

6 See *Report of the United Nations Conference on Environment and Development, Rio de Janeiro, 3-14 June 1992* (A/CONF.151/26), chap. I, resolution 1, annex I.

7 A/47/328.

07.20 WAR CRIMES AND GENOCIDE

3 (I). Extradition and Punishment of War Criminals

Committee: 1
Vote: unanimous

The General Assembly:
taking note of the Moscow Declaration of 1 November 1943 by President Roosevelt, Marshal Stalin and Prime Minister Churchill concerning enemy atrocities in the course of the war, and of the declaration by certain allied governments of 13 January and 18 December 1942 concerning the same matter;

taking note of the laws and usages of warfare established by the fourth Hague Convention of 1907;

taking note of the definition of war crimes and crimes against peace and against humanity contained in the Charter of the International Military Tribunal dated 8 August 1945;

believing that certain war criminals continue to evade justice in the territories of certain States;

recommends
that Members of the United Nations forthwith take all the necessary measures to cause the arrest of those war criminals who have been responsible for or have taken a consenting part in the above crimes, and to cause them to be sent back to the countries in which their abominable deeds were done, in order that they may be judged and punished according to the laws of those countries;

and calls upon
the governments of States which are not Members of the United Nations also to take all necessary measures for the apprehension of such criminals in their respective territories with a view to their immediate removal to the countries in which the crimes were committed for the purpose of trial and punishment according to the laws of those countries.

Thirty-second plenary meeting
13 February 1946

95 (I). Affirmation of the Principles of International Law Recognized by the Charter of the Nürnberg Tribunal

Committee: 6
Vote: unanimous
Ref.: 488(V), 176(II)

The General Assembly,
Recognizes the obligation laid upon it by Article 13, paragraph 1, sub-paragraph a, of the Charter, to initiate studies and make recommendations for the purpose of encouraging the progressive development of international law and its codification;

Takes note of the Agreement for the establishment of an International Military Tribunal for the prosecution and punishment of the major war criminals of the European Axis signed in London on 8 August 1945, and of the Charter annexed thereto, and of the fact that similar principles have been adopted in the Charter of the International Military Tribunal for the trial of the major war criminals in the Far East, proclaimed at Tokyo on 19 January 1946;

Therefore,
Affirms the principles of international law recognized by the Charter of the Nürnberg Tribunal and the judgment of the Tribunal;

Directs the Committee on the codification of international law established by the resolution of the General Assembly of 11 December 1946,[1] to treat as a matter of primary importance plans for the formulation, in the context of a general codification of offences against the peace and security of mankind, or of an International Criminal Code, of the principles recognized in the Charter of the Nürnberg Tribunal and in the judgment of the Tribunal.

Fifty-fifth plenary meeting
11 December 1946

96 (I). The Crime of Genocide

Committee: 6
Vote: unanimous
Ref.: 795(VIII), 691(VII), 605(VI), 368(IV), 260(III), 180(II)

Genocide is a denial of the right of existence of entire human groups, as homicide is the denial of the right to live of individual human beings; such denial of the right of existence shocks the conscience of mankind, results in great losses to humanity in the form of cultural and other contributions represented by these human groups, and is contrary to moral law and to the spirit and aims of the United Nations.

Many instances of such crimes of genocide have occurred when racial, religious, political and other groups have been destroyed, entirely or in part.

The punishment of the crime of genocide is a matter of international concern.

The General Assembly, therefore,
Affirms that genocide is a crime under international law which the civilized world condemns, and for the commission of which principals and accomplices - whether private individuals, public officials or statesmen, and whether the crime is committed on religious, racial, political or any other grounds - are punishable;

Invites the Member States to enact the necessary legislation for the prevention and punishment of this crime;

Recommends that international cooperation be organized between States with a view to facilitating the speedy prevention and punishment of the crime of genocide, and, to this end,

Requests the Economic and Social Council to undertake the necessary studies, with a view to drawing up a draft convention on the crime of genocide to be submitted to the next regular session of the General Assembly.

Fifty-fifth plenary meeting
11 December 1946

3074 (XXVIII). Principles of International Cooperation in the Detection, Arrest, Extradition and Punishment of Persons Guilty of War Crimes and Crimes Against Humanity

Committee: 3
Vote: 94 - 0 - 29
Ref.: 170(II), 2338(XXII), 2392(XXIII), 2583(XXIV), 2712(XXV), 2840(XXVI), 3020(XXVII)

The General Assembly,
Recalling its resolutions 2583 (XXIV) of 15 December 1969, 2712 (XXV) of 15 December 1970, 2840 (XXVI) of 18 December 1971 and 3020 (XXVII) of 18 December 1972,

Taking into account the special need for international action in order to ensure the prosecution and punishment of persons guilty of war crimes and crimes against humanity,

Having considered the draft principles of international cooperation in the detection, arrest, extradition and punishment of persons guilty of war crimes and crimes against humanity,[2]

---

1 See resolution 94 (I).

2 See A/9136.

Declares that the United Nations, in pursuance of the principles and purposes set forth in the Charter concerning the promotion of cooperation between peoples and the maintenance of international peace and security, proclaims the following principles of international cooperation in the detection, arrest, extradition and punishment of persons guilty of war crimes and crimes against humanity:

1. War crimes and crimes against humanity, wherever they are committed, shall be subject to investigation and the persons against whom there is evidence that they have committed such crimes shall be subject to tracing, arrest, trial and, if found guilty, to punishment.
2. Every State has the right to try its own nationals for war crimes or crimes against humanity.
3. States shall cooperate with each other on a bilateral and multilateral basis with a view to halting and preventing war crimes and crimes against humanity, and shall take the domestic and international measures necessary for that purpose.
4. States shall assist each other in detecting arresting and bringing to trial persons suspected of having committed such crimes and, if they are found guilty, in punishing them.
5. Persons against whom there is evidence that they have committed war crimes and crimes against humanity shall be subject to trial and, if found guilty, to punishment, as a general rule in the countries in which they committed those crimes. In that connexion, States shall cooperate on questions of extraditing such persons.
6. States shall cooperate with each other in the collection of information and evidence which would help to bring to trial the persons indicated in paragraph 5 above and shall exchange such information.
7. In accordance with article 1 of the Declaration on Territorial Asylum of 14 December 1967[1] States shall not grant asylum to any person with respect to whom there are serious reasons for considering that he has committed a crime against peace, a war crime or a crime against humanity.
8. States shall not take any legislative or other measures which may be prejudicial to the international obligations they have assumed in regard to the detection, arrest, extradition and punishment of persons guilty of war crimes and crimes against humanity.
9. In cooperating with a view to the detection arrest and extradition of persons against whom there is evidence that they have committed war crimes and crimes against humanity and, if found guilty, their punishment, States shall act in conformity with the provisions of the Charter of the United Nations and of the Declaration on Principles of International Law concerning Friendly Relations and Cooperation among States in accordance with the Charter of the United Nations.[2]

2187th plenary meeting
3 December 1973

46/242. The Situation in Bosnia and Herzegovina

Committee: -
Vote: Adopted without a vote
Ref.: 47/80, 47/121, 48/88, 49/10, 49/43

The General Assembly,

Having considered the item entitled "The situation in Bosnia and Herzegovina",

Reaffirming the purposes and principles of the Charter of the United Nations and guided by the need to implement them,

Aware of its responsibility to promote and encourage respect for international legitimacy,

Considering that the United Nations, pursuant to the provisions of its Charter, has a major role to play in, and responsibility for, the maintenance of international peace and security,

Recalling the relevant resolutions of the Security Council, the United Nations Educational, Scientific and Cultural Organization and the Commission on Human Rights, as well as Economic and Social Council decision 1992/305 of 18 August 1992,

Noting that a large number of States have reserved their position regarding the succession of the Socialist Federal Republic of Yugoslavia by the Federal Republic of Yugoslavia (Serbia and Montenegro),

Deploring the grave situation in Bosnia and Herzegovina and the serious deterioration of the living conditions of the people there, especially the Muslim and Croat populations, arising from the aggression against the territory of the Republic of Bosnia and Herzegovina, which constitutes a threat to international peace and security,

Alarmed by the prospect of further escalation of the fighting in the region,

Expressing grave alarm at continuing reports of widespread violations of international humanitarian law occurring within the territory of the former Yugoslavia and especially in Bosnia and Herzegovina, including reports of mass forcible expulsion and deportation of civilians, imprisonment and abuse of civilians in detention centres and deliberate attacks on non-combatants, hospitals and ambulances, impeding the delivery of food and medical supplies to the civilian population, as well as wanton devastation and destruction of property,

Strongly condemning the abhorrent practice of "ethnic cleansing", which constitutes a grave and serious violation of international humanitarian law,

Recalling the report of the Secretary-General of 12 May 1992, in which he states that "all international observers agree that what is happening is a concerted effort by the Serbs of Bosnia and Herzegovina, with the acquiescence of, and at least some support from, the Yugoslav People's Army, to create 'ethnically pure' regions in the context of negotiations on the 'cantonization' of the Republic in the Conference of the European Community on Bosnia and Herzegovina",[3]

Expressing grave concern that, despite the relevant resolutions of the Security Council, no effective measure has been implemented to stop the abhorrent practice of "ethnic cleansing", or to reverse and discourage the policies and proposals that might encourage it,

Appalled by the continuing reports of widespread, massive and grave violations of human rights perpetrated within the territory of the former Yugoslavia and especially in Bosnia and Herzegovina, including reports of summary and arbitrary executions, forced disappearances, torture, rape and other cruel, inhuman or degrading treatment, as well as arbitrary arrest and detention,

Expressing grave concern that, despite repeated demands by the Security Council, the cease-fire agreed upon by all parties has not been respected,

Concerned that other demands made by the Security Council in its relevant resolutions, especially resolutions 752 (1992) of 15 May 1992, 757 (1992) of 30 May 1992, 764 (1992) of 13 July 1992 and 770 (1992) and 771 (1992) of 13 August 1992, have not been complied with,

Reaffirming the necessity of respecting the sovereignty, territorial integrity, political independence and national unity of the Republic of Bosnia and Herzegovina and rejecting any attempt to change the boundaries of that Republic,

Reaffirming also the inherent right of the Republic of Bosnia and Herzegovina to individual or collective self-defence in accordance with Article 51 of the Charter,

Underlining the imperative need for an urgent peaceful solution to the situation in Bosnia and Herzegovina, in conformity with the Charter and the principles of international law, in particular the principles of respect for sovereignty and territorial integrity of States, non-recognition of the fruits of aggression and non-recognition of the

---

1 Resolution 2312 (XXII).

2 Resolution 2625 (XXV), annex.

3 See S/23900, para. 5; see *Official Records of the Security Council, Forty-seventh Year, Supplement for April, May and June 1992*, document S/23900.

acquisition of territory by force, and welcoming in this context the International Conference on the Former Yugoslavia, scheduled to be convened in London on 26 August 1992,

Commending the efforts of the Secretary-General, the Security Council, United Nations agencies, including the Office of the United Nations High Commissioner for Refugees, and other international and relief organizations, including the Organization of the Islamic Conference, the European Community, the Conference on Security and Cooperation in Europe and the International Committee of the Red Cross,

Commending also the United Nations Protection Force for its continuing action in support of the relief operation in Sarajevo and other parts of Bosnia and Herzegovina,

Deeply concerned about the safety of the personnel of the United Nations Protection Force and expressing sympathy for the losses suffered by them,

1. *Demands* that all parties to the conflict immediately stop fighting and find a peaceful solution in line with the Charter of the United Nations and the principles of international law, and in particular the principles of respect for sovereignty and territorial integrity of States, non-recognition of the fruits of aggression and non-recognition of the acquisition of territory by force;

2. *Demands also* that all forms of interference from outside the Republic of Bosnia and Herzegovina cease immediately;

3. *Demands further* that those units of the Yugoslav People's Army and elements of the Croatian Army now in Bosnia and Herzegovina must either be withdrawn, or be subject to the authority of the Government of Bosnia and Herzegovina, or be disbanded and disarmed with their weapons placed under and effective international monitoring, and requests the Secretary-General to consider without delay what kind of international assistance could be provided in this connection;

4. *Reaffirms* its support for the Government and people of the Republic of Bosnia and Herzegovina in their just struggle to safeguard their sovereignty, political independence, territorial integrity and unity;

5. *Urges* the Security Council to consider, on an urgent basis, taking further appropriate measures, as provided in Chapter VII of the Charter, to put an end to the fighting and to restore the unity and the territorial integrity of the Republic of Bosnia and Herzegovina;

6. *Condemns* the violation of the sovereignty, territorial integrity and political independence of the Republic of Bosnia and Herzegovina as well as the massive violations of human rights and international humanitarian law, in particular the abhorrent practice of "ethnic cleansing", and demands that this practice be brought to an end immediately and that further steps be taken, on an urgent basis, to stop the massive and forcible displacement of population from and within the Republic of Bosnia and Herzegovina, as well as all other forms of violation of human rights in the former Yugoslavia;

7. *Affirms* that States are to be held accountable for violations of human rights which their agents commit upon the territory of another State;

8. *Calls upon* all States and international organizations not to recognize the consequences of the acquisition of territory by force and of the abhorrent practice of "ethnic cleansing";

9. *Demands* that the International Committee of the Red Cross be granted immediate, unimpeded and continued access to all camps, prisons and other places of detention within the territory of the former Yugoslavia and that all parties ensure complete safety and freedom of movement for the International Committee and otherwise facilitate such access;

10. *Demands also* the safe, unconditional and honourable repatriation of the refugees and deportees to their homes in Bosnia and Herzegovina and recognizes their right to receive reparation for their losses;

11. *Calls upon* organs of the United Nations and all international relief agencies to facilitate the return of the displaced people to their homes in the Republic of Bosnia and Herzegovina, as well as their rehabilitation;

12. *Commends* the untiring efforts and the bravery of the United Nations Protection Force in securing the relief operation in the Republic of Bosnia and Herzegovina, as well as the efforts of the Office of the United Nations High Commissioner for Refugees and other relief agencies;

13. *Urges* all parties and others concerned to take the necessary measures to secure the safety of the United Nations Protection Force and all other United Nations personnel;

14. *Urges* all States to support the ongoing efforts to be taken in accordance with the relevant Security Council resolutions to facilitate the delivery of humanitarian assistance to all parts of the Republic of Bosnia and Herzegovina;

15. *Requests* the Secretary-General to report to the General Assembly at its forty-seventh session on the implementation of the present resolution;

16. *Decides* to remain seized of the matter and to continue its consideration of this item at its forty-seventh session.

91st plenary meeting
25 August 1992

50/192. Rape and Abuse of Women in the Areas of Armed Conflict in the Former Yugoslavia

Committee: 3
Vote: Adopted without a vote
Ref.: 49/205, 48/143

The General Assembly,

Guided by the purposes and principles of the Charter of the United Nations, the Universal Declaration of Human Rights,[1] the International Covenants on Human Rights,[2] the Convention on the Prevention and Punishment of the Crime of Genocide,[3] the Convention against Torture and Other Cruel, Inhuman or Degrading Treatment or Punishment,[4] the Convention on the Elimination of All Forms of Discrimination against Women,[5] the Convention on the Rights of the Child[6] and instruments of human rights and international humanitarian law, including the Geneva Conventions of 12 August 1949[7] and the Additional Protocols thereto, of 1977,[8]

Recalling its resolution 3074(XXVIII) of 3 December 1973, entitled "Principles of international cooperation in the detection, arrest, extradition and punishment of persons guilty of war crimes and crimes against humanity", as well as Commission on Human Rights resolution 1994/77 of 9 March 1993, General Assembly resolutions 48/143 of 20 December 1993 and 49/205 of 23 December 1994, and relevant resolutions of the Commission on the Status of Women,

Reaffirming the relevant Security Council resolutions, in particular resolution 798 (1992) of 18 December 1992, in which, *inter alia*, the Council strongly condemned those acts of unspeakable brutality,

Welcoming the initialling of the General Framework Agreement for Peace in Bosnia and Herzegovina and the annexes thereto[9] by the Republic of Bosnia and Herzegovina, the Republic of Croatia and the Federal Republic of Yugoslavia (Serbia and Montenegro) and other parties thereto at Dayton, Ohio, on 21 November 1995,

Noting with deep concern all reports of the Special Rapporteur on the situation of human rights in the territory of the former Yugoslavia, regarding rape and abuse of women in the territory of the former Yugoslavia, particularly in the Republic of Bosnia and Herzegovina,

---

1 Resolution 217 A (III).
2 Resolution 2200 A (XXI), annex.
3 Resolution 260 A (III).
4 Resolution 39/46, annex.
5 Resolution 34/180, annex.
6 Resolution 44/25, annex.
7 United Nations, *Treaty Series*, vol.75, Nos. 970-973.
8 Ibid., vol. 1125, Nos. 17512 and 17513.
9 See A/50/770-S/1995/999.

Convinced that this heinous practice constitutes a deliberate weapon of war in fulfilling the policy of ethnic cleansing carried out by Serbian forces in the Republic of Bosnia and Herzegovina, and noting General Assembly resolution 47/121 of 18 December 1992, in which the Assembly stated, *inter alia*, that the abhorrent policy of ethnic cleansing was a form of genocide,

Desirous of ensuring that persons accused of authorizing, aiding and perpetrating rape and sexual violence as a weapon of war in the areas of armed conflict in the former Yugoslavia will be brought to justice without further delay by the International Tribunal for the Prosecution of Persons Responsible for Serious Violations of International Humanitarian Law Committed in the Territory of the Former Yugoslavia since 1991, where appropriate,

Underlining, in this context, the need for the protection of the rape victims and the provision of effective guarantees of privacy and confidentiality of the rape victims, and desirous of facilitating their participation in the proceedings of the Tribunal and ensuring that further traumatization will be prevented,

Deeply alarmed at the situation facing victims of rape in armed conflicts in different parts of the world and any use of rape as a weapon of war, in particular in the Republic of Bosnia and Herzegovina,

Noting with appreciation the efforts of Governments and the work of the United Nations High Commissioner for Refugees, the United Nations Educational, Scientific and Cultural Organization, humanitarian organizations, and non-governmental organizations aimed at supporting the victims of rape and abuse and alleviating their suffering,

Welcoming the report of the Secretary-General of 29 August 1995,[1] submitted pursuant to resolution 49/205,

1. *Strongly condemns* the abhorrent practice of rape and abuse of women and children in the areas of armed conflict in the former Yugoslavia, which constitutes a war crime;

2. *Expresses its outrage* that the systematic practice of rape has been used as a weapon of war and an instrument of ethnic cleansing against women and children in the Republic of Bosnia and Herzegovina;

3. *Reaffirms* that rape in the conduct of armed conflict constitutes a war crime and that under certain circumstances it constitutes a crime against humanity and an act of genocide as defined in the Convention on the Prevention and Punishment of the Crime of Genocide, and calls upon States to take all measures required for the protection of women and children from such acts and to strengthen mechanisms to investigate and punish all those responsible and bring the perpetrators to justice;

4. *Also reaffirms* that all persons who perpetrate or authorize crimes against humanity or other violations of international humanitarian law are individually responsible for those violations and that those in positions of authority who have failed to ensure that persons under their control comply with the relevant international instruments are accountable, together with the perpetrators:

5. *Reminds* all States of their obligation to cooperate with the International Tribunal for the Prosecution of Persons Responsible for Serious Violations of International Humanitarian Law Committed in the Territory of the Former Yugoslavia since 1991 and the Office of the Prosecutor also in the investigation and prosecution of persons accused of using rape as a weapon of war;

6. *Calls upon* States to put experts, including experts in the prosecution of crimes of sexual violence, as well as adequate resources and services, at the disposal of the Chief Prosecutor and the Tribunal;

7. *Urges* all States and relevant organizations to continue to give serious consideration to the recommendations in the reports of the Special Rapporteur, in particular the recommendation concerning provision for the continuation of necessary medical and psychological care to victims of rape within the framework of programmes to rehabilitate women and children traumatized by war, as well as the provision of protection, counselling and support to victims and witnesses;

8. *Recognizes* the extraordinary suffering of the victims of rape and sexual violence and the necessity for an appropriate response to provide assistance to those victims, and expresses its concern, in particular, for the welfare of those victims who are currently among the internally displaced or otherwise affected by the war and who have experienced severe trauma and require psychosocial and other assistance;

9. *Urges* all States and all relevant intergovernmental and non-governmental organizations, as well as the United Nations Children's Fund, the Office of the United Nations High Commissioner for Refugees, the United Nations High Commissioner for Human Rights, the United Nations Educational, Scientific and Cultural Organization and the World Health Organization, to continue to provide to the victims of such rape and abuse appropriate assistance for their physical and mental rehabilitation, and to extend their support to the community-based assistance programmes;

10. *Demands* that the parties cooperate fully with the International Committee of the Red Cross, the United Nations High Commissioner for Human Rights, the Special Rapporteur and her staff, as well as other mechanisms of the Commission on Human Rights, the United Nations High Commissioner for Refugees, the monitoring and other missions of the European Union and the Organization for Security and Cooperation in Europe, including by providing full access;

11. *Encourages* the new Special Rapporteur on the situation of human rights in the territory of the former Yugoslavia to continue to pay particular attention to the use of rape as a weapon of war, particularly in the Republic of Bosnia and Herzegovina;

12. *Requests* the Secretary-General to submit a report, as appropriate, to the General Assembly at its fifty-first session on the implementation of the present resolution;

13. *Decides* to continue its consideration of this question at its fifty-first session.

99th plenary meeting
22 December 1995

---

[1] A/50/329.

07.30 REFUGEES, DISPLACED PERSONS AND STATELESS PERSONS

319 (IV). Refugees and Stateless Persons

Committee: 3
Vote: A: 35 - 7 - 13; B: 32 - 6 - 17
Ref.: 1107(XI), 928(X), 896(IX), 638(VII), 629(VII), 539(VI), 538(VI), 430(V), 429(V), 281(III), 62(I), 8(I), 7(I)

A

The General Assembly,

Considering that the problem of refugees is international in scope and nature and that its final solution can only be provided by the voluntary repatriation of the refugees or their assimilation within new national communities,

Recognizing the responsibility of the United Nations for the international protection of refugees,

Having examined resolution 248(IX) A[1] of the Economic and Social Council of 6 August 1949, the report[2] of the Secretary-General of 26 October 1949, and the communications from the General Council of the International Refugee Organization of 11 July 1949[3] and of 20 October 1949,[4]

Considering that in its aforementioned resolution the Economic and Social Council requested the Governments of States Members of the United Nations, and of other States, to provide the necessary legal protection for refugees who have been the concern of the International Refugee Organization and recommended that the General Assembly at its fourth session should decide the functions and organizational arrangements, within the framework of the United Nations, necessary for the international protection of refugees after the International Refugee Organization terminates its activities,

1. *Decides* to establish, as of 1 January 1951, a High Commissioner's Office for Refugees in accordance with the provisions of the annex to the present resolution to discharge the functions enumerated therein and such other functions as the General Assembly may from time to time confer upon it;

2. *Decides* that, unless the General Assembly subsequently decides otherwise, no expenditure other than administrative expenditures relating to the functioning of the High Commissioner's Office should be borne on the budget of the United Nations, and that all other expenditures relating to the activities of the High Commissioner should be financed by voluntary contributions;

3. *Requests* the Secretary-General:

(*a*) To prepare detailed draft provisions for the implementation of the present resolution and the annex attached thereto, to circulate these draft provisions to Governments for comments, and to submit them to the Economic and Social Council at its eleventh session, together with such comments thereon as may have been received from Governments;

(*b*) To prepare, in consultation with the Advisory Committee on Administrative and Budgetary Questions, a draft budget for the operation in 1951 of the High Commissioner's Office for Refugees;

4. *Requests* the Economic and Social Council:

(*a*) To prepare, at its eleventh session, a draft resolution embodying provisions for the functioning of the High Commissioner's Office for Refugees and to submit the draft resolution to the General Assembly for consideration at its fifth regular session;

(*b*) To transmit to the General Assembly at its fifth regular session such recommendations as the Council may deem appropriate regarding the definitions of the term "refugee" to be applied by the High Commissioner;

5. *Decides* to review, not later than at its eighth regular session, the arrangements for the High Commissioner's Office for Refugees with a view to determining whether the Office should be continued beyond 31 December 1953.

265th plenary meeting
3 December 1949

Annex

1. The High Commissioner's Office for Refugees should:

(*a*) Be so organized within the framework of the United Nations as to possess the degree of independence and the prestige required for the effective performance of the High Commissioner's duties;

(*b*) Be financed under the budget of the United Nations; and

(*c*) Receive policy directives from the United Nations according to methods to be determined by the General Assembly.

2. Means should be provided whereby interested Governments, non-members of the United Nations, may be associated with the work of the High Commissioner's Office.

3. Persons falling under the competence of the High Commissioner's Office for Refugees should be, for the time being, refugees and displaced persons defined in annex I of the Constitution of the International Refugee Organization and, thereafter, such persons as the General Assembly may from time to time determine, including any persons brought under the jurisdiction of the High Commissioner's Office under the terms of international conventions or agreements approved by the General Assembly.

4. The High Commissioner, in order to promote, stimulate and facilitate the execution of the most suitable solution to the problem with which he is entrusted, should provide for the protection of refugees and displaced persons falling under the competence of the Office by:

(*a*) Promoting the conclusion and ratification of international conventions providing for the protection of refugees, supervising the application of the provisions of such conventions, and proposing any necessary amendments thereto;

(*b*) Promoting through special agreements with Governments, the execution of any measures calculated to improve the situation of refugees and to reduce the number of refugees requiring protection;

(*c*) Assisting Governments and private organizations in their efforts to promote voluntary repatriation of refugees or their assimilation within new national communities;

(*d*) Facilitating the coordination of the efforts of voluntary agencies concerned with the welfare of refugees.

5. The High Commissioner should distribute among private and, as appropriate, official agencies which he deems best qualified to administer such assistance any funds, public or private, which he may receive for this purpose. He should not, however, appeal to Governments or make a general appeal to non-governmental sources except with the prior approval of the General Assembly. The accounts relating to these funds should be periodically verified by the auditors of the United Nations. For the information of the General Assembly, the High Commissioner should include in his annual report a statement of his activities in this field.

6. The High Commissioner should engage in such additional activities, including repatriation and resettlement activities, as the General Assembly may determine.

7. The High Commissioner should report annually on his work to the General Assembly through the Economic and Social Council.

---

1 See *Official Records of the Economic and Social Council, Fourth Year,* Ninth Session, Resolutions, p. 58.

2 See *Official Records of the fourth session of the General Assembly, Annex to the Third Committee,* document A/C.3/527.

3 See document E/1392.

4 See *Official Records of the fourth session of the General Assembly, Annex to the Third Committee,* document A/C.3/528.

8. The High Commissioner's work should be of an entirely non-political character and relate as a rule to groups and categories of refugees. In the performance of his duties he should:

(*a*) Keep in close touch with the Governments and inter-governmental organizations concerned and invite the assistance of the various specialized agencies;

(*b*) Establish contact in such manner as he may think best with private organizations dealing with refugee questions.

9. The High Commissioner should be elected by the General Assembly, on the nomination of the Secretary-General, for a term of three years from 1 January 1951.

10. The High Commissioner should appoint for a period of three years a deputy High Commissioner, who should not have the same nationality as the High Commissioner. He should also appoint, under the regulations of the United Nations, a small staff of persons devoted to the purposes of the Office to assist him.

11. The High Commissioner should consult the Governments of the countries of residence of refugees as to the need for appointing representatives therein. In any country recognizing such need, he may appoint a representative approved by the Government of that country. Subject to the foregoing, the same representative may serve in more than one country.

12. The High Commissioner's Office for Refugees should be located in Geneva.

B

The General Assembly,

Having taken cognizance of the memorandum addressed to it by the General Council of the International Refugee Organization on 20 October 1949,

Being anxious to give the International Refugee organization the support without which that organization does not feel able to complete its task rapidly and fully,

1. *Decides* to address an urgent appeal to all States, whether or not Members of the United Nations, calling upon them to furnish to the International Refugee Organization the widest possible assistance, particularly in respect of the admission and care of refugees in the most destitute categories;

2. *Decides*, in the absence of definite data, to postpone, until its fifth regular session, the examination of the problems of assistance raised by the above-mentioned memorandum, should these problems still be in existence at that date.

265th plenary meeting
3 December 1949

2312 (XXII). Declaration on Territorial Asylum

Committee: 6
Vote: unanimous
Ref.: 3456(XXX), 2372(XXIX), 2203(XXI), 2100(XX), 1839(XVII)1682(XVI), 1571(XV), 1400(XIV)

The General Assembly,

Recalling its resolutions 1839 (XVII) of 19 December 1962, 2100 (XX) of 20 December 1965 and 2203 (XXI) of 16 December 1966 concerning a declaration on the right of asylum,

Considering the work of codification to be undertaken by the International Law Commission in accordance with General Assembly resolution 1400 (XIV) of 21 November 1959,

Adopts the following Declaration:

Declaration on Territorial Asylum

The General Assembly,

Noting that the purposes proclaimed in the Charter of the United Nations are to maintain international peace and security, to develop friendly relations among all nations and to achieve international cooperation in solving international problems of an economic, social, cultural or humanitarian character and in promoting and encouraging respect for human rights and for fundamental freedoms for all without distinction as to race, sex, language or religion,

Mindful of the Universal Declaration of Human Rights, which declares in article 14 that:

"1. Everyone has the right to seek and to enjoy in other countries asylum from persecution.

"2. This right may not be invoked in the case of prosecutions genuinely arising from non-political crimes or from acts contrary to the purposes and principles of the United Nations",

Recalling also article 13, paragraph 2, of the Universal Declaration of Human Rights, which states:

"Everyone has the right to leave any country, including his own, and to return to his country",

Recognizing that the grant of asylum by a State to persons entitled to invoke article 14 of the Universal Declaration of Human Rights is a peaceful and humanitarian act and that, as such, it cannot be regarded as unfriendly by any other State,

Recommends that, without prejudice to existing instruments dealing with asylum and the status of refugees and stateless persons, States should base themselves in their practices relating to territorial asylum on the following principles:

Article 1

1. Asylum granted by a State, in the exercise of its sovereignty, to persons entitled to invoke article 14 of the Universal Declaration of Human Rights, including persons struggling against colonialism, shall be respected by all other States.

2. The right to seek and to enjoy asylum may not be invoked by any person with respect to whom there are serious reasons for considering that he has committed a crime against peace, a war crime or a crime against humanity, as defined in the international instruments drawn up to make provision in respect of such crimes.

3. It shall rest with the State granting asylum to evaluate the grounds for the grant of asylum.

Article 2

1. The situation of persons referred to in article 1, paragraph 1, is, without prejudice to the sovereignty of States and the purposes and principles of the United Nations, of concern to the international community.

2. Where a State finds difficulty in granting or continuing to grant asylum, States individually or jointly or through the United Nations shall consider, in a spirit of international solidarity, appropriate measures to lighten the burden on that State.

Article 3

1. No person referred to in article 1, paragraph 1, shall be subjected to measures such as rejection at the frontier or, if he has already entered the territory in which he seeks asylum, expulsion or compulsory return to any State where he may be subjected to persecution.

2. Exception may be made to the foregoing principle only for overriding reasons of national security or in order to safeguard the population, as in the case of a mass influx of persons.

3. Should a State decide in any case that exception to the principle stated in paragraph 1 of this article would be justified, it shall consider the possibility of granting to the person concerned, under such conditions as it may deem appropriate, an opportunity, whether by way of provisional asylum or otherwise, of going to another State.

Article 4

States granting asylum shall not permit persons who have received asylum to engage in activities contrary to the purposes and principles of the United Nations.

1631st plenary meeting
14 December 1967

50/195. Protection of and Assistance to Internally Displaced Persons

Committee: 3
Vote: Adopted without a vote

The General Assembly,

Deeply disturbed by the growing number of internally displaced persons throughout the world who receive inadequate protection and assistance, and conscious of the serious problems this is creating for the international community,

Recalling the relevant norms of international human rights instruments and of international humanitarian law,

Bearing in mind the Vienna Declaration and Programme of Action,[1] adopted by the World Conference on Human Rights on 25 June 1993, which calls for a comprehensive approach by the international community with regard to refugees and displaced persons,

Reiterating its call for a more concerted response by the international community to the needs of internally displaced persons, while emphasizing that activities on their behalf must not undermine the institution of asylum,

Conscious of the continuing need for the United Nations system to gather information comprehensively on the issue of the protection of human rights of and assistance to internally displaced persons,

Welcoming the decision of the Commission on Human Rights in its resolution 1995/57 of 3 March 1995,[2] in which it extended the mandate of the representative of the Secretary-General on internally displaced persons for another three years to continue his review of the need for protection of and assistance to internally displaced persons, including his compilation and analysis of legal norms, the root causes of internal displacement, prevention and long-term solutions,

Noting the progress made thus far by the representative of the Secretary-General in developing a legal framework, studying the causes and manifestations of internal displacement, and analysing institutional arrangements, undertaking dialogue with Governments, issuing a series of reports on particular country situations together with proposals for remedial measures, and raising the level of awareness, at both the national and international levels, to the problem of internal displacement,

Welcoming the cooperation already established between the representative of the Secretary-General and the United Nations humanitarian assistance and development organizations engaged in protecting and assisting internally displaced persons, as well as the International Committee of the Red Cross, the International Federation of Red Cross and Red Crescent Societies and other relevant organizations,

Welcoming in particular the decision by the Executive Committee of the Programme of the United Nations High Commissioner for Refugees to promote further consultations with the representative of the Secretary-General on the issue of internally displaced persons, as well as the decision by the Inter-Agency Standing Committee and its working group to invite the representative to participate in relevant meetings and in its Task Force on internally displaced persons,

Recalling the report of the representative of the Secretary-General submitted to the Commission on Human Rights at its fifty-first session,[3] and the conclusions and recommendations contained therein with regard to improving protection of, assistance to and development for internally displaced persons,

1. *Takes note with appreciation* of the report of the representative of the Secretary-General;[4]

2. *Commends* the representative for the catalytic role he is playing to raise the level of consciousness about the plight of internally displaced persons;

3. *Noting* the efforts of the representative to develop a framework and to promote strategies for better protection, assistance and development for internally displaced persons;

4. *Encourages* the representative to continue his analysis of the causes of internal displacement, the needs of those displaced, measures of prevention and ways to increase protection, assistance and solutions for the internally displaced persons;

5. *Also encourages* the representative to continue to pay specific attention in his review to the protection and assistance needs of women and children, bearing in mind the relevant strategic objective in the Beijing Declaration and Platform for Action,[5] adopted by the Fourth World Conference on Women, held at Beijing from 4 to 15 September 1995;

6. *Calls upon* the representative to continue to study the problem of internally displaced persons and to invite, with the approval of Governments, specialists and consultants to contribute expert assistance during missions, and to make use of research facilities;

7. *Invites* the representative to finalize his compilation and analysis of existing legal norms for inclusion in his report to the Commission on Human Rights at its fifty-second session;

8. *Calls upon* the Commission on Human Rights to consider the question of establishing a framework in this regard on the basis of the report of the representative and the recommendations contained therein;

9. *Calls upon* all Governments to continue to facilitate the activities of the representative, encourages them to give serious consideration to inviting the representative to visit their countries so as to enable him to study and analyse more fully the issues involved, and thanks those Governments that have already done so;

10. *Invites* Governments to give due consideration, in dialogue with the representative, to the recommendations and suggestions made to them by him, in accordance with his mandate, and to inform him of measures taken thereon;

11. *Urges* all relevant United Nations humanitarian assistance and development organizations concerned to establish frameworks of cooperation with the representative so as to provide all possible assistance and support to him in the implementation of his programme of activities, and invites the representative to report thereon;

12. *Calls upon* the representative and regional intergovernmental organizations, such as the Organization of African Unity, the Organization of American States and the Organization for Security and Cooperation in Europe, to intensify their cooperation with a view to encouraging their undertaking initiatives to facilitate assistance to and protection of internally displaced persons;

13. *Requests* the Secretary-General to give all necessary assistance to the representative to carry out his mandate effectively;

14. *Decides* to continue its consideration of this question at its fifty-second session.

99th plenary meeting
22 December 1995

---

1 *Report of the World Conference on Human Rights, Vienna, 14-25 June 1993* (A/CONF.157/24 (Part I)), chap. III.

2 *Official Records of the Economic and Social Council, 1995, Supplement No. 3* and corrigenda (E/1995/23 and Corr.1 and 2), chap. II, sect. A.

3 E/CN.4/1995/50 and Add.1 and Add.1/Corr.1, Add.2 and Add.2/Corr.1, Add.3 and Add.4.

4 A/50/558, annex.

5 *Report of the Fourth World Conference on Women, Beijing, 4-15 September 1995* (A/CONF.177/20), chap. I, resolution 1.

08.00 QUESTIONS CONCERNING TERRITORY, SEA AND SPACE

08.10 LAW OF THE SEA

2749 (XXV). Declaration of Principles Governing the Sea-Bed and the Ocean Floor, and the Subsoil Thereof, beyond the Limits of National Jurisdiction

Committee: I
Vote: 108 - 0 - 14

The General Assembly,

Recalling its resolutions 2340 (XXII) of 18 December 1967, 2467 (XXIII) of 21 December 1968 and 2574 (XXIV) of 15 December 1969, concerning the area to which the title of the item refers,

Affirming that there is an area of the sea-bed and the ocean floor, and the subsoil thereof, beyond the limits of national jurisdiction, the precise limits of which are yet to be determined,

Recognizing that the existing legal régime of the high seas does not provide substantive rules for regulating the exploration of the aforesaid area and the exploitation of its resources,

Convinced that the area shall be reserved exclusively for peaceful purposes and that the exploration of the area and the exploitation of its resources shall be carried out for the benefit of mankind as a whole,

Believing it essential that an international régime applying to the area and its resources and including appropriate international machinery should be established as soon as possible,

Bearing in mind that the development and use of the area and its resources shall be undertaken in such a manner as to foster the healthy development of the world economy and balanced growth of international trade, and to minimize any adverse economic effects caused by the fluctuation of prices of raw materials resulting from such activities,

Solemnly declares that:

1. The sea-bed and ocean floor, and the subsoil thereof, beyond the limits of national jurisdiction (hereinafter referred to as the area), as well as the resources of the area, are the common heritage of mankind.

2. The area shall not be subject to appropriation by any means by States or persons, natural or juridical, and no State shall claim or exercise sovereignty or sovereign rights over any part thereof.

3. No State or person, natural or juridical, shall claim, exercise or acquire rights with respect to the area or its resources incompatible with the international régime to be established and the principles of this Declaration.

4. All activities regarding the exploration and exploitation of the resources of the area and other related activities shall be governed by the international régime to be established.

5. The area shall be open to use exclusively for peaceful purposes by all States, whether coastal or land-locked, without discrimination, in accordance with the international régime to be established.

6. States shall act in the area in accordance with the applicable principles and rules of international law, including the Charter of the United Nations and the Declaration on Principles of International Law concerning Friendly Relations and Cooperation among States in accordance with the Charter of the United Nations, adopted by the General Assembly on 24 October 1970,[1] in the interests of maintaining international peace and security and promoting international cooperation and mutual understanding.

7. The exploration of the area and the exploitation of its resources shall be carried out for the benefit of mankind as a whole, irrespective of the geographical location of States, whether land-locked or coastal, and taking into particular consideration the interests and needs of the developing countries.

8. The area shall be reserved exclusively for peaceful purposes, without prejudice to any measures which have been or may be agreed upon in the context of international negotiations undertaken in the field of disarmament and which may be applicable to a broader area. One or more international agreements shall be concluded as soon as possible in order to implement effectively this principle and to constitute a step towards the exclusion of the sea-bed, the ocean floor and the subsoil thereof from the arms race.

9. On the basis of the principles of this Declaration, an international régime applying to the area and its resources and including appropriate international machinery to give effect to its provisions shall be established by an international treaty of a universal character, generally agreed upon. The régime shall, *inter alia*, provide for the orderly and safe development and rational management of the area and its resources and for expanding opportunities in the use thereof, and ensure the equitable sharing by States in the benefits derived therefrom, taking into particular consideration the interests and needs of the developing countries, whether land-locked or coastal.

10. States shall promote international cooperation in scientific research exclusively for peaceful purposes:

(*a*) By participation in international programmes and by encouraging cooperation in scientific research by personnel of different countries;

(*b*) Through effective publication of research programmes and dissemination of the results of research through international channels;

(*c*) By cooperation in measures to strengthen research capabilities of developing countries, including the participation of their nationals in research programmes.

No such activity shall form the legal basis for any claims with respect to any part of the area or its resources.

11. With respect to activities in the area and acting in conformity with the international régime to be established, States shall take appropriate measures for and shall cooperate in the adoption and implementation of international rules, standards and procedures for, *inter alia*:

(*a*) The prevention of pollution and contamination, and other hazards to the marine environment including the coastline, and of interference with the ecological balance of the marine environment;

(*b*) The protection and conservation of the natural resources of the area and the prevention of damage to the flora and fauna of the marine environment.

12. In their activities in the area, including those relating to its resources, States shall pay due regard to the rights and legitimate interests of coastal States in the region of such activities, as well as of all other States, which may be affected by such activities. Consultations shall be maintained with the coastal States concerned with respect to activities relating to the exploration of the area and the exploitation of its resources with a view to avoiding infringement of such rights and interests.

13. Nothing herein shall affect:

(*a*) The legal status of the waters superjacent to the area or that of the air space above those waters;

(*b*) The rights of coastal States with respect to measures to prevent, mitigate or eliminate grave and imminent danger to their coastline or related interests from pollution or threat thereof or from other hazardous occurrences resulting from or caused by any activities in the area, subject to the international régime to be established.

14. Every State shall have the responsibility to ensure that activities in the area, including those relating to its resources, whether under-

1 Resolution 2625 (XXV).

taken by governmental agencies, or non-governmental entities or persons under its jurisdiction, or acting on its behalf shall be carried out in conformity with the international régime to be established. The same responsibility applies to international organizations and their members for activities undertaken by such organizations or on their behalf. Damage caused by such activities shall entail liability.

15. The parties to any dispute relating to activities in the area and its resources shall resolve such dispute by the measures mentioned in Article 33 of the Charter of the United Nations and such procedures for settling disputes as may be agreed upon in the international régime to be established.

1933rd plenary meeting
17 December 1970

46/215. Large-Scale Pelagic Drift-Net Fishing and its Impact on the Living Marine Resources of the World's Oceans and Seas

Committee: 2
Vote: Adopted without a vote
Ref.: 50/25, 49/436, 48/445, 47/443, 45/197, 44/225

The General Assembly,

Recalling its resolutions 44/225 and 45/197, concerning large-scale pelagic drift-net fishing and its impact on the living marine resources of the world's oceans and seas, including enclosed and semi-enclosed seas, which took into account the concerns of the developing countries and were adopted by consensus on 22 December 1989 and 21 December 1990, respectively,

Also recalling, in particular, that the General Assembly recommended that all members of the international community agree to certain measures specified in the operative paragraphs of resolution 44/225,

Further recalling the relevant principles elaborated in the United Nations Convention on the Law of the Sea,[1] which are referred to in the seventh to tenth preambular paragraphs of resolution 44/225,

Expressing deep concern about reports of expansion of large-scale pelagic drift-net fishing activities on the high seas in contravention of resolutions 44/225 and 45/197, including attempts to expand large-scale pelagic drift-net fishing in the high seas areas of the Indian Ocean,

Commending the unilateral, regional and international efforts that have been undertaken by members of the international community and international organizations to implement and support the objectives of resolutions 44/225 and 45/197,

Noting that at the Twenty-second South Pacific Forum, held at Palikir on 29 and 30 July 1991, the heads of Government reaffirmed their opposition to large-scale pelagic drift-net fishing,[2] and in this regard, *inter alia*, welcomed the entry into force on 17 May 1991 of the Convention for the Prohibition of Fishing with Long Drift-nets in the South Pacific,

Recalling the Castries Declaration,[3] in which the Authority of the Organization of Eastern Caribbean States resolved to establish a regional regime for the regulation and management of the pelagic resources in the Lesser Antilles region that would outlaw the use of drift-nets and called upon other States in the region to cooperate in this regard,

Welcoming the actions taken that have resulted in the cessation of all large-scale pelagic drift-net fishing activities in the South Pacific in advance of the date stipulated in paragraph 4 (*b*) of resolution 44/225 for the termination of such activities,

Also welcoming the decision of other members of the international community to cease large-scale pelagic drift-net fishing on the high seas,

Commending the efforts of many members of the international community to compile data on large-scale pelagic drift-net fishing and to submit their findings to the Secretary-General,

Noting the contributions to the report of the Secretary-General made by some members of the international community and by intergovernmental and non-governmental organizations,

Noting also the significant concerns expressed by members of the international community and competent regional fisheries bodies regarding the impact of large-scale pelagic drift-net fishing on the marine environment,

Noting further that, in accordance with paragraph 3 of resolution 44/225, some members of the international community have reviewed the best available scientific data on the impact of large-scale pelagic drift-net fishing and have failed to conclude that this practice has no adverse impact which threatens the conservation and sustainable management of living marine resources,

Noting that the grounds for concerns expressed in resolutions 44/225 and 45/197 about the unacceptable impact of large-scale pelagic drift-net fishing have been confirmed and that evidence has not demonstrated that the impact can be fully prevented,

Recognizing that a moratorium on large-scale pelagic drift-net fishing is required, notwithstanding that it will have adverse socio-economic effects on the communities involved in high seas pelagic drift-net fishing operations,

1. *Recalls* its resolutions 44/225 and 45/197;

2. *Commends* the efforts jointly to collect statistically sound data regarding large-scale pelagic drift-net fishing in the North Pacific Ocean, which were reviewed at the meeting of scientists held at Sidney, Canada, in June 1991, and presented at the symposium on the high seas drift-net fisheries in the North Pacific Ocean, held at Tokyo in November 1991 under the auspices of the International North Pacific Fisheries Commission;

3. *Calls upon* all members of the international community to implement resolutions 44/225 and 45/197 by, *inter alia*, taking the following actions:

(*a*) Beginning on 1 January 1992, reduce fishing effort in existing large-scale pelagic high seas drift-net fisheries by, *inter alia*, reducing the number of vessels involved, the length of the nets and the area of operation, so as to achieve, by 30 June 1992, a 50 per cent reduction in fishing effort;

(*b*) Continue to ensure that the areas of operation of large-scale pelagic high seas drift-net fishing are not expanded and, beginning on 1 January 1992, are further reduced in accordance with paragraph 3 (*a*) of the present resolution;

(*c*) Ensure that a global moratorium on all large-scale pelagic drift-net fishing is fully implemented on the high seas of the world's oceans and seas, including enclosed seas and semi-enclosed seas, by 31 December 1992;

4. *Reaffirms* the importance it attaches to compliance with the present resolution and encourages all members of the international community to take measures, individually and collectively, to prevent large-scale pelagic drift-net fishing operations on the high seas of the world's oceans and seas, including enclosed seas and semi-enclosed seas;

5. *Requests* the Secretary-General to bring the present resolution to the attention of all members of the international community, intergovernmental and non-governmental organizations and well-established scientific institutions with expertise in relation to living marine resources;

6. *Requests* the members and organizations referred to above to submit to the Secretary-General information concerning activities or conduct inconsistent with the terms of the present resolution;

7. *Also requests* the Secretary-General to submit to the General Assembly at its forty-seventh session a report on the implementation of the present resolution.

79th plenary meeting
20 December 1991

---

1 *Official Records of the Third United nations Conference on the Law of the Sea,* vol. XVII (United Nations publications, Sales No. E.84.V.3), document A/CONF. 62/122.

2 See A/46/344, annex.

3 A/45/64, annex.

49/116. Unauthorized Fishing in Zones of National Jurisdiction and its Impact on the Living Marine Resources of the World's Oceans and Seas

Committee: 2
Vote: Adopted without a vote
Ref.: 50/25, 46/215, 45/197, 44/225

The General Assembly,

Inviting all members of the international community, particularly those with fishing interests, to strengthen their cooperation in the conservation and management of living marine resources in accordance with international law as reflected in the United Nations Convention on the Law of the Sea,[1]

Recalling Agenda 21,[2] adopted by the United Nations Conference on Environment and Development, in particular its chapter 17, concerning the sustainable development and conservation of the marine living resources of areas under national jurisdiction,

Recalling also the Programme of Action for the Sustainable Development of Small Island Developing States,[3] adopted by the Global Conference on the Sustainable Development of Small Island Developing States, in particular chapter IV, concerning the sustainable development and conservation of the coastal and marine resources of areas under national jurisdiction,

Noting that, in the Rio Declaration on Environment and Development[4] the international community recognized that the special situation and needs of developing countries, particularly the least developed and those most environmentally vulnerable, should be given special priority,

Expressing deep concern at the detrimental impact of unauthorized fishing in zones under national jurisdiction, where the overwhelming proportion of the global fish catch is harvested, on the sustainable development of the world's fishery resources and on the food security and economies of many States, particularly the developing countries,

Reaffirming the rights and duties of coastal States to ensure proper conservation and management measures with respect to the living resources in zones under their national jurisdiction, in accordance with international law, as reflected in the United Nations Convention on the Law of the Sea,

Taking note of recent discussions, at the international, regional and subregional levels, on fishery conservation and management measures, and on compliance with and enforcement thereof,

1. *Calls upon* States to take the responsibility, consistent with their obligations under international law as reflected in the United Nations Convention on the Law of the Sea, of taking measures to ensure that no fishing vessels entitled to fly their national flag fish in zones under the national jurisdiction of other States unless duly authorized by the competent authorities of the coastal State or States concerned; such authorized fishing operations should be carried out in accordance with the conditions set out in the authorization;

2. *Calls upon* development assistance organizations to make it a high priority to support efforts, including through financial and/or technical assistance, by the developing coastal States, in particular the least developed countries and the small island developing States, to improve the monitoring and control of fishing activities, and the enforcement of fishing regulations;

3. *Requests* the Secretary-General to bring the present resolution to the attention of all members of the international community, relevant intergovernmental organizations, the organizations and bodies of the United Nations system, regional and subregional fisheries bodies, and relevant non-governmental organizations;

4. *Also requests* the Secretary-General to submit to the General Assembly, at its fiftieth session, a report on the steps taken and on problems encountered in the implementation of the present resolution, and thereafter as may be determined by the Assembly.

92nd plenary meeting
19 December 1994

49/118. Fisheries By-Catch and Discards and their Impact on the Sustainable Use of the World's Living Marine Resources

Committee: 2
Vote: Adopted without a vote
Ref.: 50/25, 46/215, 45/197, 44/225

The General Assembly,

Recognizing that in relevant provisions of the United Nations Convention on the Law of the Sea,[5] States are called upon to take into consideration, when establishing conservation and management measures for target fisheries, the effects on associated or dependent species, taking into account the best scientific evidence available,

Recalling that the United Nations Conference on Environment and Development, held at Rio de Janeiro in June 1992,[6] and the International Conference on Responsible Fishing, held at Cancún, Mexico, in May 1992,[7] agreed to promote the development and use of selective fishing gears and practices that minimized waste in the catch of target fish species and minimized by-catch of non-target fish and non-fish species,

Recalling also that the World Fisheries Congress, held at Athens in 1992, discussed various aspects of the fisheries discard issue,

Noting the work of the Food and Agriculture Organization of the United Nations on fisheries by-catch and discards in the development of an international code of conduct for responsible fishing and the fact that the United Nations Conference on Straddling Fish Stocks and Highly Migratory Fish Stocks is considering provisions on fisheries by-catch and discards,

Recognizing the efforts that international organizations and members of the international community have made to reduce by-catch and discards in fishing operations and the need for continued international cooperation in this field,

Recognizing also that improvements in monitoring and assessing by-catch and discards and in by-catch reduction techniques continue to be necessary,

1. *Notes* the important role that fisheries play in contributing to a sustainable food supply and livelihood of present and future generations;

---

1 *Official Records of the Third United Nations Conference on the Law of the Sea,* vol. XVII (United Nations publication, Sales No. E.84.V.3), document A/CONF.62/122.

2 *Report of the United nations Conference on Environment and Development, Rio de Janeiro, 3 - 14 June 1992* (A/CONF.151/26/Rev.1 (Vol. I and Vol. I/Corr.1, Vol. II, Vol. III and Vol. III/Corr.1)) (United Nations publication, Sales No. E.93.I.8 and corrigenda), vol. I: Resolutions Adopted by the Conference, resolution 1, annex II.

3 *Report of the Global Conference on the Sustainable Development of Small Island Developing States, Bridgetown, 25 April - 6 May 1994* (A/CONF.167/9 and Corr.1 and 2) (United Nations publications, Sales No. E.94.I.18 and corrigenda), chap. I, resolution 1, annex II.

4 *Report of the United nations Conference on Environment and Development, Rio de Janeiro, 3 - 14 June 1992* (A/CONF.151/26/Rev.1 (Vol. I and Vol. I/Corr.1, Vol. II, Vol. III and Vol. III/Corr.1)) (United Nations publication, Sales No. E.93.I.8 and corrigenda), vol. I: Resolutions Adopted by the Conference, resolution 1, annex I.

5 *Official Records of the Third United nations Conference on the Law of the Sea,* vol. XVII (United Nations publication, Sales No. E.84.V.3), document A/CONF.62/122.

6 *Report of the United nations Conference on Environment and Development, Rio de Janeiro, 3 - 14 June 1992* (A/CONF.151/26/Rev.1 (Vol. I and Vol. I/Corr.1, Vol. II, Vol. III and Vol. III/Corr.1)) (United Nations publication, Sales No. E.93.I.8 and corrigenda), vol. I: Resolutions Adopted by the Conference, resolution 1, annex II.

7 See A/CONF.164/INF/2, annex 2.

2. *Believes* that the issue of by-catch and discards in fishing operations warrants serious attention by the international community;

3. *Also believes* that a continued and effective response to the issue of addressing fisheries by-catch and discards is necessary so as to ensure the long-term and sustainable development of fisheries, taking into account the relevant principles contained in the Rio Declaration on Environment and Development;[1]

4. *Invites* the Food and Agriculture Organization of the United Nations to formulate fisheries by-catch and discard provisions in its international code of conduct for responsible fishing, taking into account work being done elsewhere;

5. *Invites* the United Nations Conference on Straddling Fish Stocks and Highly Migratory Fish Stocks to elaborate fisheries by-catch and discard provisions, taking into account work being done elsewhere;

6. *Invites* relevant subregional and regional fisheries management organizations and arrangements and the Food and Agriculture Organization of the United Nations to review, within their respective competences, the impact of fisheries by-catch and discards on the sustainable use of living marine resources, taking into account, as appropriate, the relevant deliberations of the Food and Agriculture Organization of the United Nations with respect to the international code of conduct for responsible fishing and the relevant deliberations of the United Nations Conference on Straddling Fish Stocks and Highly Migratory Fish Stocks;

7. *Decides* to consider this question at its fiftieth session, under the item entitled 'Environment and sustainable development'.

92nd plenary meeting
19 December 1994

08.20 LAW OF OUTER SPACE

1348 (XIII). Question of the Peaceful Use of Outer Space

Committee: 1
Vote: 53 - 9 - 19

The General Assembly,

Recognizing the common interest of mankind in outer space and recognizing that it is the common aim that outer space should be used for peaceful purposes only,

Bearing in mind the provision of Article 2, paragraph 1, of the Charter of the United Nations, which states that the Organization is based on the principle of the sovereign equality of all its Members,

Wishing to avoid the extension of present national rivalries into this new field,

Desiring to promote energetically the fullest exploration and exploitation of outer space for the benefit of mankind,

Conscious that recent developments in respect of outer space have added a new dimension to man's existence and opened new possibilities for the increase of his knowledge and the improvement of his life,

Noting the success of the scientific cooperative programme of the International Geophysical Year in the exploration of outer space and the decision to continue and expand this type of cooperation,

Recognizing the great importance of international cooperation in the study and utilization of outer space for peaceful purposes,

Considering that such cooperation will promote mutual understanding and the strengthening of friendly relations among peoples,

Believing that the development of programmes of international and scientific cooperation in the peaceful uses of outer space should be vigorously pursued,

Believing that progress in this field will materially help to achieve the aim that outer space should be used for peaceful purposes only,

Considering that an important contribution can be made by the establishment within the framework of the United Nations of an appropriate international body for cooperation in the study of outer space for peaceful purposes,

Desiring to obtain the fullest information on the many problems relating to the peaceful uses of outer space before recommending specific programmes of international cooperation in this field,

1. *Establishes* an *Ad Hoc* Committee on the Peaceful Uses of Outer Space composed of the representatives of Argentina, Australia, Belgium, Brazil, Canada, Czechoslovakia, France, India, Iran, Italy, Japan, Mexico, Poland, Sweden, the Union of Soviet Socialist Republics, the United Arab Republic, the United Kingdom of Great Britain and Northern Ireland and the United States of America, and requests it to report to the General Assembly at its fourteenth session on the following:

(*a*) The activities and resources of the United Nations, of its specialized agencies and of other international bodies relating to the peaceful uses of outer space;

(*b*) The area of international cooperation and programmes in the peaceful uses of outer space which could appropriately be undertaken under United Nations auspices to the benefit of States irrespective of the state of their economic or scientific development, taking into account the following proposals, *inter alia*:

(i) Continuation on a permanent basis of the outer space research now being carried on within the framework of the International Geophysical Year;

(ii) Organization of the mutual exchange and dissemination of information on outer space research;

(iii) Coordination of national research programmes for the study of outer space, and the rendering of all possible assistance and help towards their realization;

(*c*) The future organizational arrangements to facilitate international cooperation in this field within the framework of the United Nations;

(*d*) The nature of legal problems which may arise in the carrying out of programmes to explore outer space;

2. Requests the Secretary-General to render appropriate assistance to the above-named Committee and to recommend any other steps that might be taken within the existing United Nations framework to encourage the fullest international cooperation for the peaceful uses of outer space.

792nd plenary meeting
13 December 1958

1962 (XVIII). Declaration of Legal Principles Governing the Activities of States in the Exploration and Use of Outer Space

Committee: 1
Vote: unanimous

The General Assembly,

Inspired by the great prospects opening up before mankind as a result of man's entry into outer space,

Recognizing the common interest of all mankind in the progress of the exploration and use of outer space for peaceful purposes,

Believing that the exploration and use of outer space should be carried on for the betterment of mankind and for the benefit of States irrespective of their degree of economic or scientific development,

1 *Report of the United nations Conference on Environment and Development, Rio de Janeiro, 3 - 14 June 1992* (A/CONF.151/26/Rev.1 (Vol. I and Vol. I/Corr.1, Vol. II, Vol. III and Vol. III/Corr.1)) (United Nations publication, Sales No. E.93.I.8 and corrigenda), vol. I: Resolutions Adopted by the Conference, resolution 1, annex I.

Desiring to contribute to broad international cooperation in the scientific as well as in the legal aspects of exploration and use of outer space for peaceful purposes,

Believing that such cooperation will contribute to the development of mutual understanding and to the strengthening of friendly relations between nations and peoples,

Recalling its resolution 110 (II) of 3 November 1947, which condemned propaganda designed or likely to provoke or encourage any threat to the peace, breach of the peace, or act of aggression, and considering that the aforementioned resolution is applicable to outer space,

Taking into consideration its resolutions 1721 (XVI) of 20 December 1961 and 1802 (XVII) of 14 December 1962, adopted unanimously by the States Members of the United Nations,

Solemnly declares that in the exploration and use of outer space States should be guided by the following principles:

1. The exploration and use of outer space shall be carried on for the benefit and in the interests of all mankind.

2. Outer space and celestial bodies are free for exploration and use by all States on a basis of equality and in accordance with international law.

3. Outer space and celestial bodies are not subject to national appropriation by claim of sovereignty, by means of use or occupation, or by any other means.

4. The activities of States in the exploration and use of outer space shall be carried on in accordance with international law, including the Charter of the United Nations, in the interest of maintaining international peace and security and promoting international cooperation and understanding.

5. States bear international responsibility for national activities in outer space, whether carried on by governmental agencies or by non-governmental entities, and for assuring that national activities are carried on in conformity with the principles set forth in the present Declaration. The activities of non-governmental entities in outer space shall require authorization and continuing supervision by the State concerned. When activities are carried on in outer space by an international organization responsibilities for compliance with the principles set forth in this Declaration shall be borne by the international organization and by the States participating in it.

6. In the exploration and use of outer space, States shall be guided by the principle of cooperation and mutual assistance and shall conduct all their activities in outer space with due regard for the corresponding interests of other States. If a State has reason to believe that an outer space activity or experiment planned by it or its nationals would cause potentially harmful interference with activities of other States in the peaceful exploration and use of outer space, it shall undertake appropriate international consultations before proceeding with any such activity or experiment. A State which has reason to believe that an outer space activity or experiment planned by another State would cause potentially harmful interference with activities in the peaceful exploration and use of outer space may request consultation concerning the activity or experiment.

7. The State on whose registry an object launched into outer space is carried shall retain jurisdiction and control over such object, and any personnel thereon, while in outer space. Ownership of objects launched into outer space, and of their component parts, is not affected by their passage through outer space or by their return to the earth. Such objects or component parts found beyond the limits of the State of registry shall be returned to that State, which shall furnish identifying data upon request prior to return.

8. Each State which launches or procures the launching of an object into outer space, and each State from whose territory or facility an object is launched, is internationally liable for damage to a foreign State or to its natural or juridical persons by such object or its component parts on the earth, in air space, or in outer space.

9. States shall regard astronauts as envoys of mankind in outer space, and shall render to them all possible assistance in the event of accident, distress, or emergency landing on the territory of a foreign State or on the high seas. Astronauts who make such a landing shall be safely and promptly returned to the State of registry of their space vehicle.

1280th plenary meeting
13 December 1963

37/92. Principles Governing the Use by States of Artificial Earth Satellites for International Direct Television Broadcasting

Committee: P
Vote: 107 - 13 - 13)

The General Assembly,

Recalling its resolution 2916 (XXVII) of 9 November 1972, in which it stressed the necessity of elaborating principles governing the use by States of artificial earth satellites for international direct television broadcasting, and mindful of the importance of concluding an international agreement or agreements,

Recalling further its resolutions 3182 (XXVIII) of 18 December 1973, 3234 (XXIX) of 12 November 1974, 3388 (XXX) of 18 November 1975, 31/8 of 8 November 1976, 32/196 of 20 December 1977, 33/16 of 10 November 1978, 34/66 of 5 December 1979 and 35/14 of 3 November 1980, and its resolution 36/35 of 18 November 1981 in which it decided to consider at its thirty-seventh session the adoption of a draft set of principles governing the use by States of artificial earth satellites for international direct television broadcasting,

Noting with appreciation the efforts made in the Committee on the Peaceful Uses of Outer Space and its Legal Sub-Committee to comply with the directives issued in the above-mentioned resolutions,

Considering that several experiments of direct broadcasting by satellite have been carried out and that a number of direct broadcasting satellite systems are operational in some countries and may be commercialized in the very near future,

Taking into consideration that the operation of international direct broadcasting satellites will have significant international political, economic, social and cultural implications,

Believing that the establishment of principles for international direct television broadcasting will contribute to the strengthening of international cooperation in this field and further the purposes and principles of the Charter of the United Nations,

Adopts the Principles Governing the Use by States of Artificial Earth Satellites for International Direct Television Broadcasting set forth in the annex to the present resolution.

100th plenary meeting
10 December 1982

Annex

Principles Governing the Use by States of Artificial Earth Satellites for International Direct Television Broadcasting

A. Purposes and objectives

1. Activities in the field of international direct television broadcasting by satellite should be carried out in a manner compatible with the sovereign rights of States, including the principle of non-intervention, as well as with the right of everyone to seek, receive and impart information and ideas as enshrined in the relevant United Nations instruments.

2. Such activities should promote the free dissemination and mutual exchange of information and knowledge in cultural and scientific fields, assist in educational, social and economic development, particularly in the developing countries, enhance the qualities of life of all peoples and provide recreation with due respect to the political and cultural integrity of States.

3. These activities should accordingly be carried out in a manner compatible with the development of mutual understanding and the strengthening of friendly relations and cooperation among all States

and peoples in the interest of maintaining international peace and security.

B. Applicability of international law

4. Activities in the field of international direct television broadcasting by satellite should be conducted in accordance with international law, including the Charter of the United Nations, the Treaty on Principles Governing the Activities of States in the Exploration and Use of Outer Space, including the Moon and Other Celestial Bodies,[1] of 27 January 1967, the relevant provisions of the International Telecommunication Convention and its Radio Regulations and of international instruments relating to friendly relations and cooperation among States and to human rights.

C. Rights and benefits

5. Every State has an equal right to conduct activities in the field of international direct television broadcasting by satellite and to authorize such activities by persons and entities under its jurisdiction. All States and peoples are entitled to and should enjoy the benefits from such activities. Access to the technology in this field should be available to all States without discrimination on terms mutually agreed by all concerned.

D. International cooperation

6. Activities in the field of international direct television broadcasting by satellite should be based upon and encourage international cooperation. Such cooperation should be the subject of appropriate arrangements. Special consideration should be given to the needs of the developing countries in the use of international direct television broadcasting by satellite for the purpose of accelerating their national development.

E. Peaceful settlement of disputes

7. Any international dispute that may arise from activities covered by these principles should be settled through established procedures for the peaceful settlement of disputes agreed upon by the parties to the dispute in accordance with the provisions of the Charter of the United Nations.

F. State responsibility

8. States should bear international responsibility for activities in the field of international direct television broadcasting by satellite carried out by them or under their jurisdiction and for the conformity of any such activities with the principles set forth in this document.

9. When international direct television broadcasting by satellite is carried out by an international intergovernmental organization, the responsibility referred to in paragraph 8 above should be borne both by that organization and by the States participating in it.

G. Duty and right to consult

10. Any broadcasting or receiving State within an international direct television broadcasting satellite service established between them requested to do so by any other broadcasting or receiving State within the same service should promptly enter into consultations with the requesting State regarding its activities in the field of international direct television broadcasting by satellite, without prejudice to other consultations which these States may undertake with any other State on that subject.

H. Copyright and neighbouring rights

11. Without prejudice to the relevant provisions of international law, States should cooperate on a bilateral and multilateral basis for protection of copyright and neighbouring rights by means of appropriate agreements between the interested States or the competent legal entities acting under their jurisdiction. In such cooperation they should give special consideration to the interests of developing countries in the use of direct television broadcasting for the purpose of accelerating their national development.

1 Resolution 2222 (XXI), annex.

I. Notification to the United Nations

12. In order to promote international cooperation in the peaceful exploration and use of outer space, States conducting or authorizing activities in the field of international direct television broadcasting by satellite should inform the Secretary-General of the United Nations, to the greatest extent possible, of the nature of such activities. On receiving this information, the Secretary-General should disseminate it immediately and effectively to the relevant specialized agencies, as well as to the public and the international scientific community.

J. Consultations and agreements between States

13. A State which intends to establish or authorize the establishment of an international direct television broadcasting satellite service shall without delay notify the proposed receiving State or States of such intention and shall promptly enter into consultation with any of those States which so requests.

14. An international direct television broadcasting satellite service shall only be established after the conditions set forth in paragraph 13 above have been met and on the basis of agreements and/or arrangements in conformity with the relevant instruments of the International Telecommunication Union and in accordance with these principles.

15. With respect to the unavoidable overspill of the radiation of the satellite signal, the relevant instruments of the International Telecommunication Union shall be exclusively applicable.

45/55. Prevention of an Arms Race in Outer Space

Committee: 1
Vote: A: 149 - 0 - 1; B: 149 - 0 - 1
Ref.: 49/74, 48/74, 47/51, 46/33, 44/112, 43/70, 42/33, 41/53, 40/87, 39/59, 38/70, 37/83

A

Prevention of an Arms Race in Outer Space

The General Assembly,

Recognizing the common interest of all mankind in the exploration and use of outer space for peaceful purposes,

Reaffirming the will of all States that the exploration and use of outer space, including the Moon and other celestial bodies, shall be for peaceful purposes, shall be carried out for the benefit and in the interest of all countries, irrespective of their degree of economic or scientific development, and shall be the province of all mankind,

Reaffirming also provisions of articles III and IV of the Treaty on Principles Governing the Activities of States in the Exploration and Use of Outer Space, including the Moon and Other Celestial Bodies,[2]

Recalling the obligation of all States to observe the provisions of the Charter of the United Nations regarding the use or threat of use of force in their international relations, including in their space activities,

Reaffirming further paragraph 80 of the Final Document of the Tenth Special Session of the General Assembly,[3] in which it is stated that in order to prevent an arms race in outer space further measures should be taken and appropriate international negotiations held in accordance with the spirit of the Treaty,

Recalling its previous resolutions on this issue and of the Declaration adopted by the Ninth Conference of Heads of State or Government of Non-Aligned Countries, held at Belgrade from 4 to 7 September 1989,[4] and taking note also of the proposals submitted to the General Assembly at its tenth special session and at its regular sessions, and of the recommendations made to the competent organs of the United Nations and to the Conference on Disarmament,

Recognizing the grave danger for international peace and security of an arms race in outer space and of developments contributing to it,

2 Resolution 2222 (XXI), annex.

3 Resolution S-10/2.

4 See A/44/551- S/20870, annex.

Emphasizing the paramount importance of strict compliance with existing arms limitation and disarmament agreements relevant to outer space, including bilateral agreements, and with the existing legal regime concerning the use of outer space,

Noting that bilateral negotiations between the Union of Soviet Socialist Republics and the United States of America have continued since 1985 with the declared objective of working out effective agreements aimed, *inter alia*, at preventing an arms race in outer space,

Welcoming the re-establishment of the *Ad Hoc Committee* on the Prevention of an Arms Race in Outer Space at the 1990 session of the Conference on Disarmament, in the exercise of the negotiating responsibilities of this sole multilateral negotiating body on disarmament, to continue to examine and identify, through substantive and general consideration, issues relevant to the prevention of an arms race in outer space,

Noting also that the *Ad Hoc Committee* on the Prevention of an Arms Race in Outer Space, taking into account its previous efforts since its establishment in 1985, continued the examination and identification of various issues, existing agreements and existing proposals, as well as future initiatives relevant to the prevention of an arms race in outer space,[1] and that this contributed to a better understanding of a number of problems and to a clearer perception of the various positions,

Emphasizing the mutually complementary nature of bilateral and multilateral efforts in the field of preventing an arms race in outer space, and hoping that concrete results will emerge from these efforts as soon as possible,

Convinced that further measures should be examined in the search for effective and verifiable bilateral and multilateral agreements in order to prevent an arms race in outer space,

1. *Reaffirms* the importance and urgency of preventing an arms race in outer space and the readiness of all States to contribute to that common objective, in conformity with the provisions of the Treaty on Principles Governing the Activities of States in the Exploration and Use of Outer Space, including the Moon and Other Celestial Bodies;

2. *Recognizes*, as stated in the report of the *Ad Hoc Committee* on the Prevention of an Arms Race in Outer Space, that the legal régime applicable to outer space by itself does not guarantee the prevention of an arms race in outer space, that this legal régime plays a significant role in the prevention of an arms race in that environment, the need to consolidate and reinforce that régime and enhance its effectiveness, and the importance of the strict compliance with existing agreements, both bilateral and multilateral;[2]

3. *Emphasizes* the necessity of further measures with appropriate and effective provisions for verification to prevent an arms race in outer space;

4. *Calls upon* all States, in particular those with major space capabilities, to contribute actively to the objective of the peaceful use of outer space and of the prevention of an arms race in outer space and to refrain from actions contrary to that objective and to the relevant existing treaties in the interest of maintaining international peace and security and promoting international cooperation;

5. *Reiterates* that the Conference on Disarmament, as the single multilateral disarmament negotiating forum, has the primary role in the negotiation of a multilateral agreement or agreements, as appropriate, on the prevention of an arms race in outer space in all its aspects;

6. *Requests* the Conference on Disarmament to consider as a matter of priority the question of preventing an arms race in outer space;

7. *Also requests* the Conference on Disarmament to intensify its consideration of the question of the prevention of an arms race in outer space in all its aspects, building upon areas of convergence and taking into account relevant proposals and initiatives, including those presented in the *Ad Hoc Committee* at the 1990 session of the Conference and at the forty-fifth session of the General Assembly;

8. *Recognizes*, in this regard, the relevance of considering measures on confidence-building and greater transparency and openness in space as stated in the report of the *Ad Hoc Committee*;

9. *Further requests* the Conference on Disarmament to re-establish an *Ad Hoc* committee with an adequate mandate at the beginning of its 1991 session and to continue building upon areas of convergence with a view to undertaking negotiations for the conclusion of an agreement or agreements, as appropriate, to prevent an arms race in outer space in all its aspects;

10. *Urges* the Union of Soviet Socialist Republics and the United States of America to pursue intensively their bilateral negotiations in a constructive spirit with a view to reaching early agreement for preventing an arms race in outer space, and to advise the Conference on Disarmament periodically of the progress of their bilateral sessions so as to facilitate its work;

11. *Decides* to include in the provisional agenda of its forty-sixth session the item entitled "Prevention of an arms race in outer space".

54th plenary meeting
4 December 1990

B

Confidence-Building Measures in Outer Space

The General Assembly,

Conscious of the importance and urgency of preventing an arms race in outer space,

Recalling that, in accordance with the Treaty on Principles Governing the Activities of States in the Exploration and Use of Outer Space, including the Moon and Other Celestial Bodies,[3] the exploration and use of outer space, including the Moon and other celestial bodies, shall be carried out for the benefit and in the interest of all countries, irrespective of their degree of economic or scientific development, and shall be the province of all mankind,

Aware of the fact that more and more States are taking an active interest in outer space or participating in important space programmes for the exploration and exploitation of that environment,

Recognizing, in this context, the relevancy space has gained as an important factor for the socio-economic development of many States, in addition to its undeniable role in security issues,

Emphasizing that the growing use of outer space has increased the need for more transparency as well as confidence-building measures,

Recalling that the international community has unanimously recognized the importance and usefulness of confidence-building measures, which can significantly contribute to the promotion of peace and security and disarmament, in particular through General Assembly resolutions 43/78 H of 7 December 1988 and 44/116 U of 15 December 1989,

Noting the important work being carried out by the *Ad Hoc Committee* on the Prevention of an Arms Race in Outer Space of the Conference on Disarmament, which contributes to identifying potential areas of confidence-building measures,

Aware of the existence of a number of different proposals and initiatives addressing this subject, which attests to a growing convergence of views,

1. *Reaffirms* the importance of confidence-building measures as means conducive to ensuring the attainment of the objective of the prevention of an arms race in outer space;

2. *Recognizes* their applicability in the space environment under specific criteria yet to be defined;

3. *Requests* the Secretary-General to carry out, with the assistance of government experts, a study on the specific aspects related to the application of different confidence-building measures in outer space, including the different technologies available, possibilities for defining appropriate mechanisms of international cooperation in specific areas of interest and so on, and to report thereon to the General Assembly at its forty-eighth session.

54th plenary meeting
4 December 1990

---

1 See *Official Records of the General Assembly, Forty-fifth Session, Supplement No. 27* (A/45/27), para. 118.

2 *Ibid.*, para. 63 of the quoted text.

3 Resolution 2222 (XXI), annex.

47/68. Principles Relevant to the Use of Nuclear Power Sources in Outer Space

Committee: Special Political Committee
Vote: Adopted without a vote

The General Assembly,

Having considered the report of the Committee on the Peaceful Uses of Outer Space on the work of its thirty-fifth session[1] and the text of the Principles Relevant to the Use of Nuclear Power Sources in Outer Space as approved by the Committee and annexed to its report,[2]

Recognizing that for some missions in outer space nuclear power sources are particularly suited or even essential owing to their compactness, long life and other attributes,

Recognizing also that the use of nuclear power sources in outer space should focus on those applications which take advantage of the particular properties of nuclear power sources,

Recognizing further that the use of nuclear power sources in outer space should be based on a thorough safety assessment, including probabilistic risk analysis, with particular emphasis on reducing the risk of accidental exposure of the public to harmful radiation or radioactive material,

Recognizing the need, in this respect, for a set of principles containing goals and guidelines to ensure the safe use of nuclear power sources in outer space,

Affirming that this set of Principles applies to nuclear power sources in outer space devoted to the generation of electric power on board space objects for non-propulsive purposes, which have characteristics generally comparable to those of systems used and missions performed at the time of the adoption of the Principles,

Recognizing that this set of Principles will require future revision in view of emerging nuclear power applications and of evolving international recommendations on radiological protection,

Adopts the Principles Relevant to the Use of Nuclear Power Sources in Outer Space as set forth below.

Principle 1.

Applicability of international law

Activities involving the use of nuclear power sources in outer space shall be carried out in accordance with international law, including in particular the Charter of the United Nations and the Treaty on Principles Governing the Activities of States in the Exploration and Use of Outer Space, including the Moon and Other Celestial Bodies.[3]

Principle 2.

Use of terms

1. For the purpose of these Principles, the terms "launching State" and "State launching" mean the State which exercises jurisdiction and control over a space object with nuclear power sources on board at a given point in time relevant to the principle concerned.

2. For the purpose of principle 9, the definition of the term "launching State" as contained in that principle is applicable.

3. For the purposes of principle 3, the terms "foreseeable" and "all possible" describe a class of events or circumstances whose overall probability of occurrence is such that it is considered to encompass only credible possibilities for purposes of safety analysis. The term "general concept of defence-in-depth" when applied to nuclear power sources in outer space refers to the use of design features and mission operations in place of or in addition to active systems, to prevent or mitigate the consequences of system malfunctions.

Redundant safety systems are not necessarily required for each individual component to achieve this purpose. Given the special requirements of space use and of varied missions, no particular set of systems or features can be specified as essential to achieve this objective. For the purposes of paragraph 2 (*d*) of principle 3, the term "made critical" does not include actions such as zero-power testing which are fundamental to ensuring system safety.

Principle 3.

Guidelines and criteria for safe use

In order to minimize the quantity of radioactive material in space and the risks involved, the use of nuclear power sources in outer space shall be restricted to those space missions which cannot be operated by non-nuclear energy sources in a reasonable way.

1. General goals for radiation protection and nuclear safety

(*a*) States launching space objects with nuclear power sources on board shall endeavour to protect individuals, populations and the biosphere against radiological hazards. The design and use of space objects with nuclear power sources on board shall ensure, with a high degree of confidence, that the hazards, in foreseeable operational or accidental circumstances, are kept below acceptable levels as defined in paragraphs 1 (*b*) and (*c*). Such design and use shall also ensure with high reliability that radioactive material does not cause a significant contamination of outer space.

(*b*) During the normal operation of space objects with nuclear power sources on board, including re-entry from the sufficiently high orbit as defined in paragraph 2 (*b*), the appropriate radiation protection objective for the public recommended by the International Commission on Radiological Protection shall be observed. During such normal operation there shall be no significant radiation exposure.

(*c*) To limit exposure in accidents, the design and construction of the nuclear power source systems shall take into account relevant and generally accepted international radiological protection guidelines.

Except in cases of low-probability accidents with potentially serious radiological consequences, the design for the nuclear power source systems shall, with a high degree of confidence, restrict radiation exposure to a limited geographical region and to individuals to the principal limit of 1 mSv in a year. It is permissible to use a subsidiary dose limit of 5 mSv in a year for some years, provided that the average annual effective dose equivalent over a lifetime does not exceed the principal limit of 1 mSv in a year.

The probability of accidents with potentially serious radiological consequences referred to above shall be kept extremely small by virtue of the design of the system.

Future modifications of the guidelines referred to in this paragraph shall be applied as soon as practicable.

(*d*) Systems important for safety shall be designed, constructed and operated in accordance with the general concept of defence-in-depth. Pursuant to this concept, foreseeable safety-related failures or malfunctions must be capable of being corrected or counteracted by an action or a procedure, possibly automatic. The reliability of systems important for safety shall be ensured, *inter alia*, by redundancy, physical separation, functional isolation and adequate independence of their components.

Other measures shall also be taken to raise the level of safety.

2. Nuclear reactors

(*a*) Nuclear reactors may be operated:

(i) On interplanetary missions;

(ii) In sufficiently high orbits as defined in paragraph 2 (b);

(iii) In low-Earth orbits if they are stored in sufficiently high orbits after the operational part of their mission.

(*b*) The sufficiently high orbit is one in which the orbital lifetime is long enough to allow for a sufficient decay of the fission products to approximately the activity of the actinides. The sufficiently high orbit must be such that the risks to existing and future outer space missions and of collision with other space objects are kept to a minimum. The necessity for the parts of a destroyed reactor also to attain the required decay time before re-entering the Earth's atmosphere shall be considered in determining the sufficiently high orbit altitude.

---

1 *Official Records of the General Assembly, Forty-seventh session, Supplement No. 20* (A/47/20).

2 *Ibid.*, annex.

3 Resolution 2222 (XXI), annex.

(*c*) Nuclear reactors shall use only highly enriched uranium 235 as fuel. The design shall take into account the radioactive decay of the fission and activation products.

(*d*) Nuclear reactors shall not be made critical before they have reached their operating orbit or interplanetary trajectory.

(*e*) The design and construction of the nuclear reactor shall ensure that it can not become critical before reaching the operating orbit during all possible events, including rocket explosion, re-entry, impact on ground or water, submersion in water or water intruding into the core.

(*f*) In order to reduce significantly the possibility of failures in satellites with nuclear reactors on board during operations in an orbit with a lifetime less than in the sufficiently high orbit (including operations for transfer into the sufficiently high orbit), there shall be a highly reliable operational system to ensure an effective and controlled disposal of the reactor.

3. Radioisotope generators

(*a*) Radioisotope generators may be used for interplanetary missions and other missions leaving the gravity field of the Earth. They may also be used in Earth orbit if, after conclusion of the operational part of their mission, they are stored in a high orbit. In any case ultimate disposal is necessary.

(*b*) Radioisotope generators shall be protected by a containment system that is designed and constructed to withstand the heat and aerodynamic forces of re-entry in the upper atmosphere under foreseeable orbital conditions, including highly elliptical or hyperbolic orbits where relevant. Upon impact, the containment system and the physical form of the isotope shall ensure that no radioactive material is scattered into the environment so that the impact area can be completely cleared of radioactivity by a recovery operation.

Principle 4.

Safety assessment

1. A launching State as defined in principle 2, paragraph 1, at the time of launch shall, prior to the launch, through cooperative arrangements, where relevant, with those which have designed, constructed or manufactured the nuclear power source, or will operate the space object, or from whose territory or facility such an object will be launched, ensure that a thorough and comprehensive safety assessment is conducted. This assessment shall cover as well all relevant phases of the mission and shall deal with all systems involved, including the means of launching, the space platform, the nuclear power source and its equipment and the means of control and communication between ground and space.

2. This assessment shall respect the guidelines and criteria for safe use contained in principle 3.

3. Pursuant to article XI of the Treaty on Principles Governing the Activities of States in the Exploration and Use of Outer Space, including the Moon and Other Celestial Bodies, the results of this safety assessment, together with, to the extent feasible, an indication of the approximate intended time-frame of the launch, shall be made publicly available prior to each launch, and the Secretary-General of the United Nations shall be informed on how States may obtain such results of the safety assessment as soon as possible prior to each launch.

Principle 5.

Notification of re-entry

1. Any State launching a space object with nuclear power sources on board shall in a timely fashion inform States concerned in the event this space object is malfunctioning with a risk of re-entry of radioactive materials to the Earth. The information shall be in accordance with the following format:

(*a*) System parameters:

(i) Name of launching State or States, including the address of the authority which may be contacted for additional information or assistance in case of accident;

(ii) International designation;

(iii) Date and territory or location of launch;

(iv) Information required for best prediction of orbit lifetime, trajectory and impact region;

(v) General function of spacecraft;

(*b*) Information on the radiological risk of nuclear power source(s):

(i) Type of nuclear power source: radioisotopic/reactor;

(ii) The probable physical form, amount and general radiological characteristics of the fuel and contaminated and/or activated components likely to reach the ground. The term "fuel" refers to the nuclear material used as the source of heat or power. This information shall also be transmitted to the Secretary-General of the United Nations.

2. The information, in accordance with the format above, shall be provided by the launching State as soon as the malfunction has become known. It shall be updated as frequently as practicable and the frequency of dissemination of the updated information shall increase as the anticipated time of re-entry into the dense layers of the Earth's atmosphere approaches so that the international community will be informed of the situation and will have sufficient time to plan for any national response activities deemed necessary.

3. The updated information shall also be transmitted to the Secretary-General of the United Nations with the same frequency.

Principle 6.

Consultations

States providing information in accordance with principle 5 shall, as far as reasonably practicable, respond promptly to requests for further information or consultations sought by other States.

Principle 7.

Assistance to States

1. Upon the notification of an expected re-entry into the Earth's atmosphere of a space object containing a nuclear power source on board and its components, all States possessing space monitoring and tracking facilities, in the spirit of international cooperation, shall communicate the relevant information that they may have available on the malfunctioning space object with a nuclear power source on board to the Secretary-General of the United Nations and the State concerned as promptly as possible to allow States that might be affected to assess the situation and take any precautionary measures deemed necessary.

2. After re-entry into the Earth's atmosphere of a space object containing a nuclear power source on board and its components:

(*a*) The launching State shall promptly offer and, if requested by the affected State, provide promptly the necessary assistance to eliminate actual and possible harmful effects, including assistance to identify the location of the area of impact of the nuclear power source on the Earth's surface, to detect the re-entered material and to carry out retrieval or clean-up operations;

(*b*) All States, other than the launching State, with relevant technical capabilities and international organizations with such technical capabilities shall, to the extent possible, provide necessary assistance upon request by an affected State.

In providing the assistance in accordance with subparagraphs (a) and (b) above, the special needs of developing countries shall be taken into account.

Principle 8.

Responsibility

In accordance with article VI of the Treaty on Principles Governing the Activities of States in the Exploration and Use of Outer Space, including the Moon and Other Celestial Bodies, States shall bear international responsibility for national activities involving the use of nuclear power sources in outer space, whether such activities are carried on by governmental agencies or by non-governmental entities, and for assuring that such national activities are carried out in conformity with that Treaty and the recommendations contained in these Principles. When activities in outer space involving the use of nuclear power sources are carried on by an international organization, responsibility for compliance with the aforesaid Treaty and the recommendations contained in these Principles shall be borne both by the international organization and by the States participating in it.

Principle 9.

Liability and compensation

1. In accordance with article VII of the Treaty on Principles Governing the Activities of States in the Exploration and Use of Outer Space, including the Moon and Other Celestial Bodies, and the provisions of the Convention on International Liability for Damage Caused by Space Objects,[1] each State which launches or procures the launching of a space object and each State from whose territory or facility a space object is launched shall be internationally liable for damage caused by such space objects or their component parts. This fully applies to the case of such a space object carrying a nuclear power source on board. Whenever two or more States jointly launch such a space object, they shall be jointly and severally liable for any damage caused, in accordance with article V of the above-mentioned Convention.

2. The compensation that such States shall be liable to pay under the aforesaid Convention for damage shall be determined in accordance with international law and the principles of justice and equity, in order to provide such reparation in respect of the damage as will restore the person, natural or juridical, State or international organization on whose behalf a claim is presented to the condition which would have existed if the damage had not occurred.

3. For the purposes of this principle, compensation shall include reimbursement of the duly substantiated expenses for search, recovery and clean-up operations, including expenses for assistance received from third parties.

Principle 10.

Settlement of disputes

Any dispute resulting from the application of these Principles shall be resolved through negotiations or other established procedures for the peaceful settlement of disputes, in accordance with the Charter of the United Nations.

Principle 11.

Review and revision

These Principles shall be reopened for revision by the Committee on the Peaceful Uses of Outer Space no later than two years after their adoption.

85th plenary meeting
14 December 1992

50/27. International Cooperation in the Peaceful Uses of Outer Space

Committee: 4
Vote: Adopted without a vote
Ref.: 49/34, 48/39, 47/67, 46/45, 45/72, 44/46, 43/56, 42/68, 41/64, 40/162, 39/96, 38/80, 37/89, 36/35, 35/14, 34/66, 33/16, 32/196, 31/8, 3388(XXX), 3234(XXIX), 3182(XXVIII), 2915(XXVII), 2776(XXVI), 2733(XXV), 2600(XXIV), 2601(XXIV), 2453(XXIII), 2130(XX), 1963(XVIII), 1802(XVII), 1721(XVI), 1472(XIV)

The General Assembly,

Recalling its resolution 49/34 of 9 December 1994,

Deeply convinced of the common interest of mankind in promoting the exploration and use of outer space for peaceful purposes and in continuing efforts to extend to all States the benefits derived therefrom, and also of the importance of international cooperation in this field, for which the United Nations should continue to provide a focal point,

Reaffirming the importance of international cooperation in developing the rule of law, including the relevant norms of space law and their important role in international cooperation for the exploration and use of outer space for peaceful purposes,

Concerned about the possibility of an arms race in outer space,

Recognizing that all States, in particular those with major space capabilities, should contribute actively to the goal of preventing an arms race in outer space as an essential condition for the promotion of international cooperation in the exploration and use of outer space for peaceful purposes,

Considering that space debris is an issue of concern to all nations,

Noting the progress achieved in the further development of peaceful space exploration and application as well as in various national and cooperative space projects, which contribute to international cooperation, and the importance of further international cooperation in this field,

Taking note of the report of the Secretary-General[2] on the implementation of recommendations of the Second United Nations Conference on the Exploration and Peaceful Uses of Outer Space,[3]

Having considered the report of the Committee on the Peaceful Uses of Outer Space on the work of its thirty-eighth session,[4]

1. *Endorses* the report of the Committee on the Peaceful Uses of Outer Space;

2. *Invites* States that have not yet become parties to the international treaties governing the uses of outer space[5] to give consideration to ratifying or acceding to those treaties;

3. *Notes* that, at its thirty-fourth session, the Legal Subcommittee of the Committee on the Peaceful Uses of Outer Space, in its working groups, continued its work as mandated by the General Assembly in its resolution 49/34;[6]

4. *Endorses* the recommendations of the Committee that the Legal Subcommittee, at its thirty-fifth session, taking into account the concerns of all countries, particularly those of developing countries, should:

(*a*) Continue its consideration of the question of review and possible revision of the Principles Relevant to the Use of Nuclear Power Sources in Outer Space;[7]

(*b*) Continue, through its working group, its consideration of matters relating to the definition and delimitation of outer space and to the character and utilization of the geostationary orbit, including consideration of ways and means to ensure the rational and equitable use of the geostationary orbit without prejudice to the role of the International Telecommunication Union;

(*c*) Continue, through its working group, its consideration of the legal aspects related to the application of the principle that the exploration

1 Resolution 2777 (XXVI), annex.

2 A/50/384.

3 See *Report of the Second United Nations Conference on the Exploration and Peaceful Uses of Outer Space, Vienna, 9-21 August 1982,* and corrigenda (A/CONF.101/10 and Corr.1 and 2).

4 *Official Records of the General Assembly, Fiftieth Session, Supplement No. 20* (A/50/20).

5 Treaty on Principles Governing the Activities of States in the Exploration and Use of Outer Space, including the Moon and other Celestial Bodies (resolution 2222 (XXI), annex); Agreement on the Rescue of Astronauts, the Return of Astronauts and the Return of Objects Launched into Outer Space (resolution 2345 (XXII), annex); Convention on International Liability for Damage Caused by Space Objects (resolution 2777 (XXVI), annex); Convention on Registration of Objects Launched into Outer Space (resolution 3235 (XXIX), annex); Agreement Governing the Activities of States on the Moon and other Celestial Bodies (resolution 34/68, annex).

6 See *Official Records of the General Assembly, Fiftieth Session, Supplement No. 20* (A/50/20), sect. II.C.

7 See resolution 47/68.

and utilization of outer space should be carried out for the benefit and in the interests of all States, taking into particular account the needs of developing countries;

5. *Also endorses* the recommendation of the Committee that the Legal Subcommittee, at its thirty-fifth session, should suspend consideration in its working group of the Principles Relevant to the Use of Nuclear Power Sources in Outer Space pending the results of the work in the Scientific and Technical Subcommittee, without prejudice to the possibility of reconvening its working group on that item if in the opinion of the Legal Subcommittee sufficient progress was made in the Scientific and Technical Subcommittee at its session in 1996 to warrant the reconvening of the working group;

6. *Notes* that deliberations on the question of the geostationary orbit have been undertaken by the Legal Subcommittee as reflected in its report,[1] on the basis of recent proposals which might provide a new and enhanced basis for future work:

7. *Endorses* the recommendations and agreements concerning the organization of work in the Legal Subcommittee;

8. *Notes* that, in accordance with its recommendation, the Chairman of the Legal Subcommittee, at its thirty-fourth session, conducted extensive, open-ended informal consultations with all members of the Subcommittee on the working methods and agenda of the Legal Subcommittee, including the consideration of possible additional items for inclusion in the agenda as outlined in the report of the Committee,[2] and also notes that, in accordance with the recommendation of the Committee, a Working Group of the Whole was established at its thirty-eighth session to examine the working methods of the Committee and its subsidiary bodies, which took particular account of the results of the informal consultations of the Chairman of the Legal Subcommittee;

9. *Endorses* the recommendations of the Committee as contained in the report of its thirty-eighth session with regard to its working methods and to the reconvening of the Working Group of the Whole at the thirty-ninth session of the Committee;[3]

10. *Notes* that, in accordance with the recommendation contained in resolutions 48/222 B of 23 December 1993 and 49/221 B of 23 December 1994, the Committee reviewed its needs for written records;

11. *Endorses* the recommendation of the Committee that, beginning with its thirty-ninth session, the Committee would be provided with unedited transcripts of its session in lieu of verbatim records, as described in the Secretariat report on this matter;[4]

12. *Requests* the Legal Subcommittee to review, at its thirty-fifth session, its requirement for summary records with a view to determining whether it may be possible to utilize unedited transcripts at its subsequent sessions and to consider under what circumstances there might be a need to revert to summary records should a decision be taken to utilize unedited transcripts;

13. *Notes* that the Scientific and Technical Subcommittee of the Committee on the Peaceful Uses of Outer Space, at its thirty-second session, continued its work as mandated by the General Assembly in its resolution 49/34;[5]

14. *Welcomes* the decision of the Committee to consider the matter of space debris as a matter of priority on the agenda of the Scientific and Technical Subcommittee;

15. *Notes* that under that item the Scientific and Technical Subcommittee continued to consider scientific research relating to space debris, including relevant studies, mathematical modelling and other analytical work on the characterization of the space debris environment;

16. *Agrees* with the endorsement by the Committee of the multi-year plan for consideration of the agenda item on space debris approved by the Scientific and Technical Subcommittee at its thirty-second session,[6] and also agrees that the work plan should be implemented with flexibility;

17. *Also endorses* the recommendations of the Committee that the Scientific and Technical Subcommittee, at its thirty-third session, taking into account the concerns of all countries, particularly those of developing countries, should:

(*a*) Consider the following items on a priority basis:

(i) United Nations Programme on Space Applications and the coordination of space activities within the United Nations system;

(ii) Implementation of the recommendations of the Second United Nations Conference on the Exploration and Peaceful Uses of Outer Space;[7]

(iii) Matters relating to remote sensing of the Earth by satellites, including, *inter alia,* applications for developing countries;

(iv) Use of nuclear power sources in outer space;

(v) Space debris;

(*b*) Consider the following items:

(i) Questions relating to space transportation systems and their implications for future activities in space;

(ii) Examination of the physical nature and technical attributes of the geostationary orbit and of its utilization and applications, including, *inter alia,* in the field of space communications, as well as other questions relating to space communications developments, taking particular account of the needs and interests of developing countries;

(iii) Matters relating to life sciences, including space medicine;

(iv) Progress in national and international space activities related to the Earth's environment, in particular progress in the geosphere-biosphere (global change) programme;

(v) Matters relating to planetary exploration;

(vi) Matters relating to astronomy;

(vii) The theme fixed for special attention at the 1996 session of the Scientific and Technical Subcommittee: "Utilization of micro- and small satellites for the expansion of low-cost space activities, taking into account the special needs of developing countries"; the Committee on Space Research and the International Astronautical Federation, in liaison with Member States, should be invited to arrange a symposium, with as wide a participation as possible, to be held during the first week of the Subcommittee's session, to complement discussions within the Subcommittee on the special theme;

18. *Considers* in the context of paragraph 17 (a) (ii) above, that it is particularly urgent to implement the following recommendations:

(*a*) All countries should have the opportunity to use the techniques resulting from medical studies in space;

(*b*) Data banks at the national and regional levels should be strengthened and expanded and an international space information service should be established to function as a centre of coordination;

(*c*) The United Nations should support the creation of adequate training centres at the regional level, linked, whenever possible, to institutions implementing space programmes; necessary funding for the development of such centres should be made available through financial institutions;

(*d*) The United Nations should organize a fellowship programme through which selected graduates or postgraduates from developing countries should get in-depth, long-term exposure to space technology or applications; it is also desirable to encourage the availability

---

1 See *Official Records of the General Assembly, Fiftieth Session, Supplement No. 20* (A/50/20), sect. II.C.

2 *Ibid.*, (A/50/20), sect. II.E.3.

3 *Ibid.*

4 A/AC.105/L.207.

5 See *Official Records of the General Assembly, Fiftieth Session, Supplement No. 20* (A/50/20), sect. II.B.

6 A/AC.105/605, para. 83.

7 See *Report of the Second United Nations Conference on the Exploration and Peaceful Uses of Outer Space, Vienna, 9-21 August 1982,* and corrigenda (A/CONF.101/10 and Corr. 1 and 2)

of opportunities for such exposure on other bilateral or multilateral bases outside the United Nations system;

19. *Endorses* the recommendation of the Committee that the Scientific and Technical Subcommittee should reconvene, at its thirty-third session, the Working Group of the Whole to Evaluate the Implementation of the Recommendations of the Second United Nations Conference on the Exploration and Peaceful Uses of Outer Space, to continue its work;

20. *Also endorses* the recommendations of the Working Group of the Whole of the Scientific and Technical Subcommittee, as endorsed by the Committee and as contained in the report of the Working Group of the Whole;[1]

21. *Decides* that, during the thirty-third session of the Scientific and Technical Subcommittee, the Working Group on the Use of Nuclear Power Sources in Outer Space should be reconvened, and invites Member States to report to the Secretary-General on a regular basis with regard to national and international research concerning the safety of nuclear-powered satellites;

22. *Endorses* the United Nations Programme on Space Applications for 1996, as proposed to the Committee by the Expert on Space Applications;[2]

23. *Emphasizes* the urgency and importance of implementing fully the recommendations of the Second United Nations Conference on the Exploration and Peaceful Uses of Outer Space;

24. *Reaffirms its approval* of the recommendation of the Conference regarding the establishment and strengthening of regional mechanisms of cooperation and their promotion and creation through the United Nations system;

25. *Expresses its appreciation* to all Governments that have made, or expressed their intention to make, contributions towards carrying out the recommendations of the Conference;

26. *Invites* all Governments to take effective action for the implementation of the recommendations of the Conference;

27. *Requests* all organs, organizations and bodies of the United Nations system and other intergovernmental organizations working in the field of outer space or on space-related matters to cooperate in the implementation of the recommendations of the Conference;

28. *Invites* the Secretary-General to report to the General Assembly at its fifty-first session on the implementation of the recommendations of the Conference;

29. *Notes with satisfaction* that, in the context of paragraph 18 (c) above, significant progress has been achieved in establishing regional centres for space science and technology education in each region covered by the regional commissions;

30. *Endorses* the recommendation of the Committee that these centres be established on the basis of affiliation to the United Nations as early as possible and that such affiliation would provide the centres with the necessary recognition and would strengthen the possibilities of attracting donors and of establishing academic relationships with national and international space-related institutions;

31. *Notes* that, pursuant to its request in paragraph 27 of resolution 49/34, the Scientific and Technical Subcommittee, at its thirty-second session, continued its discussions on the possibility of holding a third United Nations Conference on the Exploration and Peaceful Uses of Outer Space and that the Committee continued these discussions at its thirty-eighth session with a view to promoting an early conclusion on the matter by the Committee;

32. *Agrees* that a third United Nations Conference on the Exploration and Peaceful Uses of Outer Space could be convened before the turn of the present century, and that, prior to recommending a date for the conference, there should be a consensus recommendation on the agenda, venue and funding of the conference;

33. *Recommends* that the Scientific and Technical Subcommittee, at its thirty-third session, continue the work it had conducted at its thirty-second session, taking into particular account the report of its Working Group of the Whole,[3] with the aim being to complete the development and refinement of a framework that would allow an evaluation of proposals by the Committee at its thirty-ninth session, and that this framework should allow for the consideration of all possibilities of achieving the final objectives of such a conference;

34. *Agrees* that, on the basis of the work to be conducted at the thirty-third session of the Scientific and Technical Subcommittee, the Committee, at its thirty-ninth session, should consider all issues related to the possible convening of a third United Nations Conference on the Exploration and Peaceful Uses of Outer Space, including its technical and political objectives, a detailed and sharply focused agenda, funding, timing and other organizational aspects as well as whether the objectives of the conference could be achieved by other means, with a view to making a final recommendation to the General Assembly at that session of the Committee;

35. *Notes with interest* the plans of the Government of Uruguay to host the Third Space Conference of the Americas at Punta del Este in 1996;

36. *Recommends* that more attention be paid to all aspects related to the protection and the preservation of the outer space environment, especially those potentially affecting the Earth's environment;

37. *Considers* that it is essential that Member States pay more attention to the problem of collisions of space objects, including nuclear power sources, with space debris, and other aspects of space debris, calls for the continuation of national research on this question, for the development of improved technology for the monitoring of space debris and for the compilation and dissemination of data on space debris, and also considers that, to the extent possible, information thereon should be provided to the Scientific and Technical Subcommittee;

38. *Urges* all States, in particular those with major space capabilities, to contribute actively to the goal of preventing an arms race in outer space as an essential condition for the promotion of international cooperation in the exploration and uses of outer space for peaceful purposes;

39. *Emphasizes* the need to increase the benefits of space technology and its applications and to contribute to an orderly growth of space activities favourable to the socio-economic advancement of humanity, in particular that of the people of the developing countries;

40. *Takes note* of the views expressed during the thirty-eighth session of the Committee and during the fiftieth session of the General Assembly concerning ways and means of maintaining outer space for peaceful purposes;

41. *Requests* the Committee to continue to consider, as a matter of priority, ways and means of maintaining outer space for peaceful purposes and to report thereon to the General Assembly at its fifty-fifth session;

42. *Also requests* the Committee to continue to consider at its thirty-ninth session its agenda item entitled "Spin-off benefits of space technology: review of current status";

43. *Requests* the specialized agencies and other international organizations to continue and, where appropriate, enhance their cooperation with the Committee and to provide it with progress reports on their work relating to the peaceful uses of outer space;

44. *Requests* the Committee to continue its work, in accordance with the present resolution, to consider, as appropriate, new projects in outer space activities and to submit a report to the General Assembly at its fifty-first session, including its views on which subjects should be studied in the future.

82nd plenary meeting
6 December 1995

1 A/AC.105/605, annex II.

2 A/AC.105/595, sect. I.

3 A/AC.105/605, annex II.

08.30 ANTARCTICA

49/80. Question of Antarctica

Committee: 1
Vote: Adopted without a vote
Ref.: 48/80, 47/57, 46/41, 45/78, 44/124, 43/83, 42/46, 41/88, 40/156, 39/152, 38/77

The General Assembly,

Having considered the item entitled "Question of Antarctica",

Taking into account the debates on this item held since its thirty-eighth session,

Reaffirming the interest of the international community in information on Antarctica,

Welcoming the provision by the Antarctic Treaty Consultative Parties to the Secretary-General of the final report of the Eighteenth Antarctic Treaty Consultative Meeting,[1] held at Kyoto, Japan, from 11 to 22 April 1994,

Conscious of the particular significance of Antarctica to the international community, including for international peace and security, the global and regional environment, its effects on global and regional climate conditions, and scientific research,

Reaffirming that the management and use of Antarctica should be conducted in accordance with the purposes and principles of the Charter of the United Nations and in the interest of maintaining international peace and security and of promoting international cooperation for the benefit of mankind as a whole,

Recognizing that the Antarctic Treaty,[2] which provides, *inter alia*, for the demilitarization of the continent, the prohibition of nuclear explosions and the disposal of nuclear wastes, the freedom of scientific research and the free exchange of scientific information, is in furtherance of the purposes and principles of the Charter,

Conscious also of the interrelationship between Antarctica and the physical, chemical and biological processes that regulate the total Earth system,

Taking into account the Protocol on Environmental Protection to the Antarctic Treaty, adopted by the Antarctic Treaty Parties at Madrid on 4 October 1991,

Welcoming the designation, in the Protocol, of Antarctica as a natural reserve devoted to peace and science and the procedures contained in the Protocol regarding the protection of the Antarctic environment and dependent and associated ecosystems in the planning and conduct of all activities in Antarctica,

Commending the prohibition on mineral resource activities contained in the Protocol,

Welcoming the recognition by the United Nations Conference on Environment and Development of the value of Antarctica as an area for the conduct of scientific research in particular research essential to understanding the global environment,[3]

Welcoming also the continuing cooperation among countries undertaking scientific research activities in Antarctica, which may help to minimize human impacts on the Antarctic environment,

Welcoming further the increasing awareness of an interest in Antarctica shown by the international community, and convinced of the advantages to the whole of mankind of a better knowledge of Antarctica,

Affirming its conviction that, in the interest of all mankind Antarctica should continue forever to be used exclusively for peaceful purposes and that it should not become the scene or object of international discord,

1. *Takes note* of the report of the Secretary-General on Antarctica[4] and of the report of the Eighteenth Antarctic Treaty Consultative Meeting;[5]

2. *Welcomes* the practice whereby the Antarctic Treaty Consultative Parties regularly provide the Secretary-General with information on their consultative meetings and on their activities in Antarctica, encourages the Parties to continue to provide to the Secretary-General and other interested States information on developments in relation to Antarctica, and requests the Secretary-General to submit that information in a report to the General Assembly at its fifty-first session;

3. *Notes* the role accorded by the Secretary-General to the United Nations Environment Programme in relation to Antarctic matters;

4. *Urges* the Antarctic Treaty Parties to extend invitations to the Executive Director of the United Nations Environment Programme to attend future consultative meetings in order to assist them in the substantive work;

5. *Welcomes* the statement under chapter 17 of Agenda 21,[6] adopted by the United Nations Conference on Environment and Development, that States carrying out research activities in Antarctica should, as provided for in article 111 of the Antarctic Treaty, continue to:

(*a*) Ensure that data and information resulting from such research are freely available to the international community;

(*b*) Enhance access of the international scientific community and specialized agencies of the United Nations to such data and information, including the encouragement of periodic seminars and symposia;

6. *Urges* the Antarctic Treaty Consultative Parties to take into account in their deliberations the outcomes of the United Nations Conference on Environment and Development, particularly as noted in paragraph 5 above;

7. *Requests* the Antarctic Treaty Parties to continue to make available information on Antarctica as a means of promoting further public awareness of the importance of Antarctica to the global and regional environment;

8. *Urges* the Antarctic Treaty Parties to consider becoming parties as soon as possible to the Protocol on Environmental Protection to the Antarctic Treaty, and so bring the Protocol into force, in order to ensure the implementation of strengthened measures for the protection of the Antarctic environment and dependent and associated ecosystems;

9. *Urges* countries whose nationals undertake activities in Antarctica to ensure that all such activities are carried out in a manner consistent with the principles of the Protocol;

10. *Decides* to include in the provisional agenda of its fifty-first session the item entitled "Question of Antarctica".

90th plenary meeting
15 December 1994

---

1 See A/49/370.

2 United Nations, *Treaty Series*, vol. 402, No. 5778.

3 See *Report of the United Nations Conference on Environment and Development, Rio de Janeiro, 3-14 June 1992* (A/CONF.151/26/Rev.1 (Vol. I and Vol. I/Corr.1, Vol. II Vol. III and Vol. III/Corr.1))(United Nations publication. Sales No E.93.1.8 and corrigenda), vol. I: Resolutions Adopted by the Conference, resolution 1, annex II, chap. 17, para. 17.104.

4 A/49/370.

5 See A/49/370.

6 See *Report of the United Nations Conference on Environment and Development, Rio de Janeiro, 3-14 June 1992* (A/CONF.151/26/Rev.1 (Vol. I and Vol. I/Corr.1, Vol. II Vol. III and Vol. III/Corr.1))(United Nations publication. Sales No E.93.1.8 and corrigenda), vol. I: Resolutions Adopted by the Conference, resolution 1, annex II, chap. 17, para. 17.104.

09.00 SOCIAL ISSUES

09.10 CULTURE

50/56. Return or Restitution of Cultural Property to the Countries of Origin

Committee: -
Vote: 124 - 0 - 24

The General Assembly,

Recalling its resolutions 3026 A (XXVII) of 18 December 1972, 3148 (XXVIII) of 14 December 1973, 3187 (XXVIII) of 18 December 1973, 3391 (XXX) of 19 November 1975, 31/40 of 30 November 1976, 32/18 of 11 November 1977, 33/50 of 14 December 1978, 34/64 of 29 November 1979, 35/127 and 35/128 of 11 December 1980, 36/64 of 27 November 1981, 38/34 of 25 November 1983, 40/19 of 21 November 1985, 42/7 of 22 October 1987, 44/18 of 6 November 1989, 46/10 of 22 October 1991 and 48/15 of 2 November 1993,

Recalling also the Convention on the Means of Prohibiting and Preventing the Illicit Import, Export and Transfer of Ownership of Cultural Property[1] adopted on 14 November 1970 by the General Conference of the United Nations Educational, Scientific and Cultural Organization,

Taking note with satisfaction of the report of the Secretary-General submitted in cooperation with the Director-General of the United Nations Educational, Scientific and Cultural Organization,[2]

Noting with satisfaction that, following its appeal, other Member States have become parties to the Convention,

Aware of the importance attached by the countries of origin to the return of cultural property which is of fundamental spiritual and cultural value to them, so that they may constitute collections representative of their cultural heritage,

1. *Commends* the United Nations Educational, Scientific and Cultural Organization and the Intergovernmental Committee for Promoting the Return of Cultural Property to Its Countries of Origin or Its Restitution in Case of Illicit Appropriation on the work they have accomplished, in particular through the promotion of bilateral negotiations, for the return or restitution of cultural property, the preparation of inventories of movable cultural property, the reduction of illicit traffic in cultural property and the dissemination of information to the public;

2. *Reaffirms* that the restitution to a country of its objets d'art, monuments, museum pieces, archives, manuscripts, documents and any other cultural or artistic treasures contributes to the strengthening of international cooperation and to the preservation and flowering of universal cultural values through fruitful cooperation between developed and developing countries;

3. *Requests* the Secretary-General, in collaboration with the United Nations Educational, Scientific and Cultural Organization, to continue to develop all possibilities for bringing about the attainment of the objectives of resolution 48/15 of 29 October 1993;

4. *Requests* the Secretary-General, in cooperation with the Director-General of the United Nations Educational, Scientific and Cultural Organization, to submit to the General Assembly at its fifty-second session a report on the implementation of the present resolution;

5. *Decides* to include in the provisional agenda of its fifty-second session the item entitled "Return or restitution of cultural property to the countries of origin".

87th plenary meeting
11 December 1995

09.20 INFORMATION

425 (V). Question of the Freedom of Information and of the Press in Times of Emergency

Committee: 3
Vote: 41 - 5 - 2

The General Assembly,

Considering that freedom of information and of the Press is one of the fundamental freedoms and should be advanced and safeguarded,

Considering that limitations might be placed on this freedom in emergencies or on the pretext of emergencies,

Recommends to all Member States that, when they are compelled to declare a state of emergency, measures to limit freedom of information and of the Press shall be taken only in the most exceptional circumstances and then only to the extent strictly required by the situation.

325th plenary meeting,
14 December 1950.

50/31. Questions Relating to Information

Committee: 4
Vote: Adopted without a vote
Ref.: 49/38, 48/44, 47/73, 46/73, 45/076, 44/50, 43/60, 42/162, 41/68, 40/164, 39/98, 38/82, 37/94, 36/149, 35/201, 34/182, 33/115

A

Information in the Service of Humanity

The General Assembly,

Taking note of the comprehensive and important report of the Committee on Information,[3]

Also taking note of the report of the Secretary-General on questions relating to information,[4]

Urges all countries, organizations of the United Nations system as a whole and all others concerned, reaffirming their commitment to the principles of the Charter of the United Nations and to the principles of freedom of the press and freedom of information, as well as to those of the independence, pluralism and diversity of the media, deeply concerned by the disparities existing between developed and developing countries and the consequences of every kind arising

1 United Nations Educational, Scientific and Cultural Organization, *Records of the General Conference, Sixteenth Session,* vol. 1, *Resolutions,* p. 135.

2 A/50/498.

3 *Official Records of the General Assembly, Fiftieth Session, Supplement No. 21* (A/50/21).

4 A/50/462.

from those disparities that affect the capability of the public, private or other media and individuals in developing countries to disseminate information and communicate their views and their cultural and ethical values through endogenous cultural production, as well as to ensure the diversity of sources and their free access to information, and recognizing the call in this context for what in the United Nations and at various international forums has been termed "a new world information and communication order, seen as an evolving and continuous process":

(*a*) To cooperate and interact with a view to reducing existing disparities in information flows at all levels by increasing assistance for the development of communication infrastructures and capabilities in developing countries, with due regard for their needs and the priorities attached to such areas by those countries, and in order to enable them and the public, private or other media in developing countries to develop their own information and communication policies freely and independently and increase the participation of media and individuals in the communication process, and to ensure a free flow of information at all levels;

(*b*) To ensure for journalists the free and effective performance of their professional tasks and condemn resolutely all attacks against them;

(*c*) To provide support for the continuation and strengthening of practical training programmes for broadcasters and journalists from public, private and other media in developing countries;

(*d*) To enhance regional efforts and cooperation among developing countries, as well as cooperation between developed and developing countries, to strengthen communication capacities and to improve the media infrastructure and communication technology in the developing countries, especially in the areas of training and dissemination of information;

(*e*) To aim, in addition to bilateral cooperation, at providing all possible support and assistance to the developing countries and their media, public, private or other, with due regard to their interests and needs in the field of information and to action already adopted within the United Nations system, including:

(i) The development of the human and technical resources that are indispensable for the improvement of information and communication systems in developing countries and support for the continuation and strengthening of practical training programmes, such as those already operating under both public and private auspices throughout the developing world;

(ii) The creation of conditions that will enable developing countries and their media, public, private or other, to have, by using their national and regional resources, the communication technology suited to their national needs, as well as the necessary programme material, especially for radio and television broadcasting;

(iii) Assistance in establishing and promoting telecommunication links at the subregional, regional and interregional levels, especially among developing countries;

(iv) The facilitation, as appropriate, of access by the developing countries to advanced communication technology available on the open market;

(*f*) To provide full support for the International Programme for the Development of Communication[1] of the United Nations Educational, Scientific and Cultural Organization, which should support both public and private media.

[1] See United Nations Educational, Scientific and Cultural Organization, *Records of the General Conference, Twenty-first Session, Belgrade, 23 September to 28 October 1980,* vol. I, *Resolutions,* sect. III.4, resolution 4/21.

B

United Nations public information policies and activities

The General Assembly,

Reaffirming its primary role in elaborating, coordinating and harmonizing United Nations policies and activities in the field of information,

Also reaffirming that the Secretary-General should ensure that the activities of the Department of Public Information of the Secretariat, as the focal point of the public information tasks of the United Nations, are strengthened and improved, keeping in view the purposes and principles of the Charter of the United Nations, the priority areas defined by the General Assembly and the recommendations of the Committee on Information,

Taking note of all the reports of the Secretary-General submitted to the Committee on Information,

1. *Welcomes* Belize, Croatia, the Czech Republic, Kazakstan, and South Africa following the establishment of a united, non-racial and democratic Government in that country, to membership in the Committee on Information;

2. *Decides* to consolidate the role of the Committee on Information as its main subsidiary body mandated to make recommendations relating to the work of the Department of Public Information of the Secretariat;

3. *Calls upon* the Secretary-General, in respect of the public information policies and activities of the United Nations, to implement fully the recommendations contained in paragraph 2 of resolution 48/44 B of 10 December 1993;

4. *Requests* the Secretary-General, in order to put into practice the need for an effective public information capacity of the Department of Public Information for the formation and day-to-day functioning of the information components of peace-keeping and other field operations of the United Nations, to ensure the involvement of the Department at the planning stage of such future operations through interdepartmental consultations and coordination with the other substantive departments of the Secretariat;

5. *Takes note* of the report of the Secretary-General regarding the continuous and major publications of the Department of Public Information[2] and urges all efforts to ensure timely production and dissemination of its major publications, in particular the UN Chronicle, the Yearbook of the United Nations and Africa Recovery, maintaining consistent editorial independence and accuracy, and taking the necessary measures to ensure that its output contains adequate, objective and equitable information about issues before the Organization, reflecting divergent opinions wherever they occur;

6. *Requests* the Secretary-General to increase his efforts for the early resumption of the publication Development Forum, or an alternative system-wide publication that meets the requirements set out for new publications by the Committee on Information;

7. *Requests* the management of the Department of Public Information to review the Department's publications and proposals for publications to ensure that all publications fulfil an identifiable need, that they do not duplicate other publications inside or outside the United Nations system and that they are produced in a cost-effective manner, and to report to the Committee on Information at its eighteenth session;

8. *Reaffirms* the importance attached by Member States to the role of United Nations information centres in effectively and comprehensively disseminating information, particularly in developing countries and countries in transition, about United Nations activities;

9. *Takes note* of the report of the Secretary-General on the results of the trial of integrating United Nations information centres with field offices of the United Nations Development Programme,[3] and invites the Secretary-General to continue the integration exercise whenever feasible, on a case-by-case basis, while taking into account the views

[2] A/AC. 198/1995/3.

[3] A/AC. 198/1995/5.

of the host country, and ensuring that the information functions and autonomy of the United Nations information centres are not adversely affected, and to report to the Committee on Information;

10. *Reaffirms* the role of the General Assembly in relation to the opening of new United Nations information centres and invites the Secretary-General, as well, to make such recommendations as he may judge necessary regarding the establishment and location of these centres;

11. *Takes note* of the report of the Secretary-General on the allocation of resources to United Nations information centres in 1994[1] and calls upon him to continue to study ways and means to rationalize and effect equitable disbursement of available resources to all United Nations information centres and to report thereon to the Committee on Information at its eighteenth session;

12. *Welcomes* the action by some Member States with regard to financial and material support to United Nations information centres in their respective capitals;

13. *Welcomes* the successful conclusion of the negotiations on the establishment of a United Nations information component at Warsaw;

14. *Notes* the progress made by the Secretary-General and the German authorities towards establishing, within existing resources of the Department of Public Information, a United Nations information centre at Bonn;

15. *Notes with appreciation* the action taken, or being taken, by the Secretary-General regarding the reactivation and enhancement of the United Nations information centres at Bujumbura, Dar es Salaam, Dhaka and Tehran;

16. *Welcomes* the continued enhanced cooperation between the Department of Public Information and the University for Peace in Costa Rica as a focal point for promoting United Nations activities and disseminating United Nations information materials;

17. *Takes note* of the requests of Bulgaria, Gabon, Guinea, Haiti and Slovakia for information centres or information components;

18. *Expresses* its full support for the wide and prompt coverage of United Nations activities through a continuation of United Nations press releases in both working languages of the Secretariat, namely, English and French, and welcomes the improvements in the quality and speedy issue of those press releases in both working languages;

19. *Encourages* the Secretary-General to explore ways and means to improve the access of United Nations radio to airwaves world wide, bearing in mind that radio is one of the most cost-effective and far-reaching media available to the Department of Public Information and is an important instrument in United Nations activities with regard to development and peace-keeping;

20. *Notes with appreciation* the efforts of the Department of Public Information to take advantage of recent developments in information technology in order to improve the dissemination of information on the United Nations, and encourages the Department to continue its efforts in this field;

21. *Notes* the important role the Department of Public Information will have to play in responding to the increased public interest resulting from the fiftieth anniversary of the United Nations, and requests the Department to ensure the greatest possible access for United Nations guided tours, as well as to ensure that displays in public areas are kept as informative, up to date and relevant as possible;

22. *Invites* Member States that wish to do so to submit to the Secretary-General by 15 March 1996 their observations and suggestions on ways and means of furthering the development of communication infrastructures and capabilities in developing countries, with a view to consolidating recent experience in the field of international cooperation aimed at enabling them to develop their own information and communication capacities freely and independently, and requests the Secretary-General to report thereon to the Committee on Information at its eighteenth session;

23. *Recommends* in order to continue to facilitate contact between the Department of Public Information and the Committee on Information between sessions, that the Bureau of the Committee, together with representatives of each regional group, the Group of 77 and China, in close contact with the members of the Committee, should meet on a regular basis and consult at periodic intervals with representatives of the Department;

24. *Takes note* of the request of Belarus, the Russian Federation and Ukraine concerning information activities for the tenth anniversary in 1996 of the Chernobyl disaster and calls upon the Department of Public Information to continue cooperation with the countries concerned, and with the relevant organizations and bodies of the United Nations system, with a view to establishing and implementing such activities as appropriate, and within existing resources;

25. *Requests* the Secretary-General to report to the Committee on Information at its eighteenth session, in 1996, and to the General Assembly at its fifty-first session, in 1996, on the activities of the Department of Public Information and on the implementation of the recommendations contained in the present resolution;

26. *Decides* that the next session of the Committee on Information should last not more than ten working days, and invites the Bureau of the Committee to explore ways and means of making optimum use of the Committee's time;

27. *Requests* the Committee on Information to report to the General Assembly at its fifty-first session;

28. *Decides* to include in the provisional agenda of its fifty-first session the item entitled "Questions relating to information".

82nd plenary meeting
6 December 1995

1 A/AC. 198/1995/2.

09.30 HEALTH

2848 (XXVI). Protein Resources

Committee: 2
Vote: 109 - 0 - 10
Ref.: 2684(XXV), 2416(XXIII), 2319(XXII)

The General Assembly,

Recalling its resolutions 2416 (XXIII) of 17 December 1968 and 2684 (XXV) of 11 December 1970, Economic and Social Council resolution 1640 (LI) of 30 July 1971, World Health Assembly resolution WHA22.56 of 25 July 1969 and resolutions 2/69 and 7/71 adopted by the Conference of the Food and Agriculture Organization of the United Nations on 26 November 1969 and 22 November 1971,

Recalling also paragraphs 18 and 69 of the International Development Strategy for the Second United Nations Development Decade,

Bearing in mind the Declaration on the world food problem adopted on 22 March 1968[2] by the United Nations Conference on Trade and Development at its second session,

Recognizing that the protein problem is part of the general problem of food production and supply, which depends on a great many economic, social, cultural and political factors, including social and economic under-development, which is manifested in unemployment and under-employment, extremely low incomes, poor nutritional habits, poor health and sanitary conditions, low agricultural productivity and serious defects in marketing,

2 *Proceedings of the United Nations Conference on Trade and Development, Second Session*, vol. I and Corr.1 and 3 and Add.1 and 2, *Report and Annexes* (United Nations publication, Sales No.: E.68.11.D.14), p. 28.

Recognizing also that protein-calorie malnutrition is the primary cause of high infant and child mortality, reaching from 25 to 30 per cent in many developing countries, that it increases susceptibility to infection and can permanently impair growth and development in the survivors, to the detriment of their later physical and intellectual performance,

Considering that it is in the interests of developing countries to make increased use of the external - and particularly multilateral - financial and technical assistance available for dealing with problems of food supply and nutrition since the direct and indirect costs of malnutrition to national development are often far more than the amount that would be required for its prevention,

Recognizing that, since the ultimate solution of the protein problem can only be found over the long term while immediate action with respect to vulnerable groups is required if irreversible damage is to be prevented, clear national and international priorities must be set now in taking remedial action, and that consequently external short-term assistance such as emergency food support must be combined with assistance for vital long-range projects,

Acknowledging the programme and assistance activities relating to the protein problem being undertaken by various organizations of the United Nations system and particularly by the Protein Advisory Group and its four sponsoring organizations - the United Nations Children's Fund, the Food and Agriculture Organization of the United Nations, the World Health Organization and the International Bank for Reconstruction and Development - and emphasizing that their efforts must be further integrated to achieve the maximum effectiveness,

Concerned that increasing awareness of the extent and implications of the problem of protein-calorie malnutrion has not led to the type and scope of national or international response required for an effective approach to the solution

1. *Urges* developing countries to establish or emphasize short-term priorities and undertake special action and information programmes with regard to protein malnutrition in accordance with their respective national plans, since the alleviation of the situation in the short-term must be based upon the improved utilization of existing national and international resources;

2. *Urges* the developed countries to reinforce their support for both bilateral and multilateral projects and programmes dealing with the protein problem in a manner compatible with the requests of the developing countries;

3. *Urges* developing countries:

(*a*) To draw up comprehensive statements of national nutrition policy and related food and agricultural policy to be incorporated, under the most appropriate administrative arrangements, in their development plans;

(*b*) To encourage and make the maximum use of surveys and studies of their food and nutrition situations and to encourage the training of the necessary professional personnel in science and technology related to food, agriculture, nutrition and other relevant fields.

4. *Urges* Governments to implement as appropriate, but as soon as possible, the essential elements of the Strategy Statement on Action to Avert the Protein Crisis in the Developing Countries[1] — prepared by the Panel to Assist the Secretary-General in the Formulation of a Strategy Statement on the Protein Problem Confronting the Developing Countries, convened in pursuance of General Assembly resolution 2684 (XXV)—as set forth in the annex to the present resolution;

5. *Requests* appropriate United Nations organs particularly the United Nations Development Programme, the specialized agencies and the International Atomic Energy Agency, to assist the developing countries, at their request, in all possible ways to implement the undertakings set out in paragraphs 1, 3 and 4 above;

6. *Recommends* to the sponsoring agencies that the terms of reference of the Protein Advisory Group should be modified as follows so as to enable the Group to broaden its activities and to play a more active and stimulative role:

(*a*) To advise on the technical, economic, educational, social and other related aspects of all the programmes within the United Nations system related to improving protein nutrition;

(*b*) To advise on current programmes and on new areas of activity;

(*c*) To provide guidelines for the formulation of the broad programmes of the United Nations system of organizations involved in the various aspects of the protein problem;

(*d*) To seek, evaluate and disseminate new information on all aspects of the protein problem;

(*e*) To advise on the improvement of procedures for project evaluation and feasibility studies.

(*f*) To identify, evaluate and advise on problems in protein resource development and protein-calorie malnutrition requiring scientific and technological research;

(*g*) To advise on such other matters as the various United Nations bodies refer to it;

7. *Urges* the United Nations bodies concerned, in particular the World Food Programme, the International Labour Organisation, the United Nations Educational, Scientific and Cultural Organization and the International Atomic Energy Agency, to become full sponsors of the Protein Advisory Group so that it can effectively carry out its terms of reference in support of the United Nations system

8. *Requests*, to this same end, the Secretary-General, in consultation with the Administrator of the United Nations Development Programme, the Secretary-General of the United Nations Conference on Trade and Development and the Executive Director of the United Nations Industrial Development Organization, to study and report to the Economic and Social Council at its fifty-second session on the possible modalities of United Nations sponsorship of the Protein Advisory Group;

9. *Commends* paragraphs 6 and 7 of Economic and Social Council resolution 1640 (LI) of 30 July 1971 relating to further discussion of the protein strategy in other forums and the submission of annual reports by the Protein Advisory Group;

10. *Welcomes* the recent establishment by the Council of the Food and Agriculture Organization of the United Nations, pursuant to resolution 7/71 adopted on 22 November 1971 by the Conference of that organization, of a special seven-member committee to review the work of the organization in the protein field;

11. *Requests* the Economic and Social Council during its discussion of the terms of reference of its Committee on Science and Technology,[2] to give sympathetic consideration to inviting appropriate representation of the Protein Advisory Group to sessions of the Committee held to review and focus attention on the protein problem and to urging Governments, the United Nations and the specialized agencies concerned to assign representatives at a high level to attend such meetings;

12. *Requests* the Secretary-General, in cooperation with the Administrator of the United Nations Development Programme and in consultation with the executive heads of the organizations sponsoring the Protein Advisory Group, to arrange, at the request of Governments, for persons who took part in the Panel convened by the Secretary-General in pursuance of General Assembly resolution 2684 (XXV) to visit the Governments in order to enhance the establishment of national policies and arrangements to deal with the protein problem, and to report as appropriate to the Committee on Science and Technology;

13. *Further requests* the Secretary-General to seek the views of Governments on the recommendation of the Panel and of the Advisory Committee on the Application of Science and Technology to Development for the establishment of a special protein fund under the United Nations Development Programme in order to ascertain the views of Governments on its feasibility and to ascertain whether significant resources would be made available to it without prejudice

---

1 See *Strategy Statement on Action to Avert the Protein Crisis in the Developing Countries* (United Nations publication, Sales No.: E.71.II.A.17), annex.

2 Established under paragraph I of Economic and Social Council resolution 1621 B (LI) of 30 July 1971.

to the increased resources envisaged for the Programme, and to report to the General Assembly at its twenty-seventh session through the Economic and Social Council.

2026th plenary meeting
20 December 1971.

Annex

Essential Elements of the Strategy Statement on Action to Avert the Protein Crisis in the Developing Countries

1. Make every effort to increase the production of food crops, particularly through the exploitation of new high-yield varieties, bearing in mind the special need for an expanded production of protein-rich pulses and oilseeds;

2. Encourage accelerated and expanded research designed to improve the nutritive value of cereal proteins through genetic engineering;

3. Encourage accelerated and expanded research designed to develop high-yielding pulses, legumes and oilseed crops;

4. Encourage the increased production of animal proteins, particularly through research on increasing forage yields and production;

5 Make every effort to prevent an unnecessary loss of protein-containing foods in field, storage, transport and home;

6. Encourage increased production from marine and freshwater fishery resources;

7. Encourage the development, distribution and promotion of formulated protein foods;

8. Facilitate the application of science and technology to the development of new protein sources in order to supplement conventional food resources;

9. Develop and support regional and national centres for research and training in agricultural technology, food science, food technology and nutrition;

10. Conduct informational and educational campaigns related to protein production and consumption;

11. Improve protein utilization through the control and prevention of infectious diseases;

12. Review and improve policies, legislation and regulations regarding all aspects of food and protein production, processing and marketing so as to remove unnecessary obstacles and encourage appropriate activities;

13. Give special attention to the protein needs of vulnerable groups;

14. Initiate intervention programmes aimed at ensuring that vulnerable groups will receive the most appropriate type and a sufficient quantity of food by the most effective means;

15. Recognize the important relationships between family size, population growth and the protein problem;

16. Recognize the role of economic development and social modernization in solving the protein problem.

36/43. Global Strategy for Health for All by the Year 2000

Committee: 2
Vote: Adopted without a vote

The General Assembly,

Recalling its resolution 34/58 of 29 November 1979 concerning health as an integral part of development,

Noting with approval World Health Assembly resolution WHA 34.36 of 22 May 1981 by which the thirty-fourth Assembly unanimously adopted the Global Strategy for Health for All by the Year 2000,

Considering that the Global Strategy fully reflects the spirit of General Assembly resolution 34/58,

Considering that peace and security are important conditions for the preservation and improvement of the health of all people and that cooperation among nations on vital health issues can contribute substantially to peace,

Noting further that the Global Strategy is based upon the principles of the Declaration of Alma-Ata[1] on primary health care, which implies an integrated approach to the solution of health care problems and requires the fullest support and involvement of all economic and social development sectors,

Recognizing that the implementation of the Global Strategy will constitute a valuable contribution to the improvement of over-all socio-economic conditions, and thus to the fulfilment of the International Development Strategy for the Third United Nations Development Decade,[2]

1. *Endorses* the Global Strategy for Health for All by the Year 2000 as a major contribution of Member States to the attainment of the world-wide social goal of health for all by the year 2000 and to the fulfilment of the International Development Strategy for the Third United Nations Development Decade;

2. *Urges* all Member States to ensure the implementation of the Global Strategy as part of their multisectoral efforts to implement the provisions contained in the International Development Strategy;

3. *Also urges* all Member States to cooperate with one another and with the World Health Organization to ensure that the necessary international action is taken to implement the Global Strategy as part of the fulfilment of the International Development Strategy;

4. *Requests* all appropriate organizations and bodies of the United Nations system—including the United Nations Children's Fund, the Food and Agriculture Organization of the United Nations, the International Labour Organisation, the United Nations Development Programme, the United Nations Environment Programme, the United Nations Educational, Scientific and Cultural Organization, the United Nations Fund for Population Activities and the World Bank—to collaborate fully with the World Health Organization in carrying out the Global Strategy;

5. *Requests* the Director-General of the World Health Organization to ensure that measures to implement the Global Strategy are taken into account in the review and appraisal of the implementation of the International Development Strategy.

64th plenary meeting
19 November 1981

36/166. Exchange of Information on Banned Hazardous Chemicals and Unsafe Pharmaceutical Products

Committee: 3
Vote: Adopted without a vote

The General Assembly,

Recalling its resolution 34/173 of 17 December 1979, in which it recognized the urgent need to take concrete measures to prevent adverse effects on health on a world-wide basis,

Recalling also its resolution 35/186 of 15 December 1980, in which it invited Member States to provide information on measures they have taken on exchange of information on hazardous chemicals and unsafe pharmaceutical products that have been banned in their territories and requesting the Secretary-General in cooperation with the United Nations organs, organizations and bodies concerned to submit a report to the General Assembly at its thirty-sixth session on the experience of Member States and the United Nations organs, organizations and bodies concerned,

Conscious of the importance of the information system on transnational corporations for the analysis of the activities in these corporations in certain sectors of special social and humanitarian interest to

---

1 See World Health Organization, *Health Care: Report of the International Conference on Primary Health Care, Alma-Ata, Union of Soviet Socialist Republics, 6-12 September 1978* (Geneva, 1978).

2 Resolution 35/56, annex.

the countries in which operations take place, particularly developing countries,

Taking into account that in resolution 35/186 the General Assembly requested the Commission on Transnational Corporations to study, during its seventh session, ways and means within the information system on transnational corporations to improve the exchange of information on those products with a view to formulating appropriate recommendations,

Bearing in mind the importance of objective information on banned hazardous chemicals and unsafe pharmaceutical products,

Aware that the production and export of banned or severely restricted hazardous substances - including pharmaceuticals, pesticides and industrial chemicals - endanger public health and the environment,

1. *Takes note* of the report of the Secretary-General on the exchange of information on banned hazardous chemicals and unsafe pharmaceutical products;[1]

2. *Takes note also* of the conclusions and recommendations in the report of the United Nations Centre on Transnational Corporations[2] which was submitted to the Commission at its seventh session;

3. *Reiterates* the need to intensify international cooperation in the search for the solution to problems arising from the production and export of banned or severely restricted substances;

4. *Urges* Member States and other interested parties, including transnational corporations to cooperate more fully in providing data on banned or severely restricted substances to the appropriate organs, organizations and bodies of the United Nations system with responsibility for information exchange in regard to such substances;

5. *Calls upon* the organs, organizations and other competent United Nations bodies involved in disseminating information on this subject to ensure that the documentation they prepare is adequately suited to the needs and clearly understood by all those engaged in processing, handling, dispensing or using all banned hazardous chemicals and unsafe pharmaceutical products;

6. *Requests* the Secretary-General, the organs, organizations and other competent United Nations bodies to provide, within available resources, the necessary technical assistance to the developing countries, at their request, to help them establish an adequate system for monitoring the import of unsafe pharmaceutical products of doubtful therapeutic value and banned hazardous chemicals, on the one hand, and to train scientific personnel to handle these problems, on the other;

7. *Invites* Member States to deal with this subject through appropriate means, including possible legislation at national level, where they do not yet exist;

8. *Once again requests* the Secretary-General to consult Member States on the existing information systems on banned hazardous chemicals and unsafe pharmaceutical products and to report to the General Assembly at the thirty-eighth session through the Economic and Social Council.

101st plenary meeting
16 December 1981

39/248. Consumer Protection

Committee: 2
Vote: Adopted without a vote

The General Assembly,

Recalling Economic and Social Council resolution 1981/62 of 23 July 1981, in which the Council requested the Secretary-General to continue consultations on consumer protection with a view to elaborating a set of general guidelines for consumer protection, taking particularly into account the needs of the developing countries,

Recalling further General Assembly resolution 38/147 of 19 December 1983,

Noting Economic and Social Council resolution 1984/63 of 26 July 1984,

1. *Decides* to adopt the guidelines for consumer protection annexed to the present resolution;

2. *Requests* the Secretary-General to disseminate the guidelines to Governments and other interested parties;

3. *Requests* all organizations of the United Nations system that elaborate guidelines and related documents on specific areas relevant to consumer protection to distribute them to the appropriate bodies of individual States.

106th plenary meeting
9 April 1985

Annex

Guidelines for Consumer Protection

I. Objectives

1. Taking into account the interests and needs of consumers in all countries, particularly those in developing countries; recognizing that consumers often face imbalances in economic terms, educational levels, and bargaining power; and bearing in mind that consumers should have the right of access to non-hazardous products, as well as the right to promote just, equitable and sustainable economic and social development, these guidelines for consumer protection have the following objectives:

(*a*) To assist countries in achieving or maintaining adequate protection for their population as consumers;

(*b*) To facilitate production and distribution patterns responsive to the needs and desires of consumers;

(*c*) To encourage high levels of ethical conduct for those engaged in the production and distribution of goods and services to consumers;

(*d*) To assist countries in curbing abusive business practices by all enterprises at the national and international levels which adversely affect consumers;

(*e*) To facilitate the development of independent consumer groups;

(*f*) To further international cooperation in the field of consumer protection;

(*g*) To encourage the development of market conditions which provide consumers with greater choice at lower prices.

II. General principles

2. Governments should develop, strengthen or maintain a strong consumer protection policy, taking into account the guidelines set out below. In so doing, each Government must set its own priorities for the protection of consumers in accordance with the economic and social circumstances of the country, and the needs of its population, and bearing in mind the costs and benefits of proposed measures.

3. The legitimate needs which the guidelines are intended to meet are the following:

(*a*) The protection of consumers from hazards to their health and safety;

(*b*) The promotion and protection of the economic interests of consumers;

(*c*) Access of consumers to adequate information to enable them to make informed choices according to individual wishes and needs;

(*d*) Consumer education;

(*e*) Availability of effective consumer redress;

(*f*) Freedom to form consumer and other relevant groups or organizations and the opportunity of such organizations to present their views in decision-making processes affecting them.

4. Governments should provide or maintain adequate infrastructure to develop, implement and monitor consumer protection policies. Special care should be taken to ensure that measures for consumer protection are implemented for the benefit of all sectors of the population, particularly the rural population.

---

1 A/36/255.

2 E/C.10/90

5. All enterprises should obey the relevant laws and regulations of the countries in which they do business. They should also conform to the appropriate provisions of international standards for consumer protection to which the competent authorities of the country in question have agreed. (Hereinafter references to international standards in the guidelines should be viewed in the context of this paragraph.)

6. The potential positive role of universities and public and private enterprises in research should be considered when developing consumer protection policies.

III. Guidelines

7. The following guidelines should apply both to home-produced goods and services and to imports.

8. In applying any procedures or regulations for consumer protection, due regard should be given to ensuring that they do not become barriers to international trade and that they are consistent with international trade obligations.

A. Physical safety

9. Governments should adopt or encourage the adoption of appropriate measures, including legal systems, safety regulations, national or international standards, voluntary standards and the maintenance of safety records to ensure that products are safe for either intended or normally foreseeable use.

10. Appropriate policies should ensure that goods produced by manufacturers are safe for either intended or normally foreseeable use. Those responsible for bringing goods to the market, in particular suppliers, exporters, importers, retailers and the like (hereinafter referred to as "distributors"), should ensure that while in their care these goods are not rendered unsafe through improper handling or storage and that while in their care they do not become hazardous through improper handling or storage. Consumers should be instructed in the proper use of goods and should be informed of the risks involved in intended or normally foreseeable use. Vital safety information should be conveyed to consumers by internationally understandable symbols wherever possible.

11. Appropriate policies should ensure that if manufacturers or distributors become aware of unforeseen hazards after products are placed on the market, they should notify the relevant authorities and, as appropriate, the public without delay. Governments should also consider ways of ensuring that consumers are properly informed of such hazards.

12. Governments should, where appropriate, adopt policies under which, if a product is found to be seriously defective and/or to constitute a substantial and severe hazard even when properly used, manufacturers and/or distributors should recall it and replace or modify it, or substitute another product for it; if it is not possible to do this within a reasonable period of time, the consumer should be adequately compensated.

B. Promotion and protection of consumers' economic interests

13. Government policies should seek to enable consumers to obtain optimum benefit from their economic resources. They should also seek to achieve the goals of satisfactory production and performance standards, adequate distribution methods, fair business practices, informative marketing and effective protection against practices which could adversely affect the economic interests of consumers and the exercise of choice in the market-place.

14. Governments should intensify their efforts to prevent practices which are damaging to the economic interests of consumers through ensuring that manufacturers, distributors and others involved in the provision of goods and services adhere to established laws and mandatory standards. Consumer organizations should be encouraged to monitor adverse practices, such as the adulteration of foods, false or misleading claims in marketing and service frauds.

15. Governments should develop, strengthen or maintain, as the case may be, measures relating to the control of restrictive and other abusive business practices which may be harmful to consumers, including means for the enforcement of such measures. In this connection, Governments should be guided by their commitment to the Set of Multilaterally Agreed Equitable Principles and Rules for the Control of Restrictive Business Practices adopted by the General Assembly in resolution 35/63 of 5 December 1980.

16. Governments should adopt or maintain policies that make clear the responsibility of the producer to ensure that goods meet reasonable demands of durability, utility and reliability, and are suited to the purpose for which they are intended, and that the seller should see that these requirements are met. Similar policies should apply to the provision of services.

17. Governments should encourage fair and effective competition in order to provide consumers with the greatest range of choice among products and services at the lowest cost.

18. Governments should, where appropriate, see to it that manufacturers and/or retailers ensure adequate availability of reliable after-sales service and spare parts.

19. Consumers should be protected from such contractual abuses as one-sided standard contracts, exclusion of essential rights in contracts, and unconscionable conditions of credit by sellers.

20. Promotional marketing and sales practices should be guided by the principle of fair treatment of consumers and should meet legal requirements. This requires the provision of the information necessary to enable consumers to take informed and independent decisions, as well as measures to ensure that the information provided is accurate.

21. Governments should encourage all concerned to participate in the free flow of accurate information on all aspects of consumer products.

22. Governments should, within their own national context, encourage the formulation and implementation by business, in cooperation with consumer organizations, of codes of marketing and other business practices to ensure adequate consumer protection. Voluntary agreements may also be established jointly by business, consumer organizations and other interested parties. These codes should receive adequate publicity.

23. Governments should regularly review legislation pertaining to weights and measures and assess the adequacy of the machinery for its enforcement.

C. Standards for the safety and quality of consumer goods and services

24. Governments should, as appropriate, formulate or promote the elaboration and implementation of standards, voluntary and other, at the national and international levels for the safety and quality of goods and services and give them appropriate publicity. National standards and regulations for product safety and quality should be reviewed from time to time, in order to ensure that they conform, where possible, to generally accepted international standards.

25. Where a standard lower than the generally accepted international standard is being applied because of local economic conditions, every effort should be made to raise that standard as soon as possible.

26. Governments should encourage and ensure the availability of facilities to test and certify the safety, quality and performance of essential consumer goods and services.

D. Distribution facilities for essential consumer goods and services

27. Governments should, where appropriate, consider:

(*a*) Adopting or maintaining policies to ensure the efficient distribution of goods and services to consumers; where appropriate, specific policies should be considered to ensure the distribution of essential goods and services where this distribution is endangered, as could be the case particularly in rural areas. Such policies could include assistance for the creation of adequate storage and retail facilities in rural centres, incentives for consumer self-help and better control of the conditions under which essential goods and services are provided in rural areas;

(*b*) Encouraging the establishment of consumer cooperatives and related trading activities, as well as information about them, especially in rural areas.

E. Measures enabling consumers to obtain redress

28. Governments should establish or maintain legal and/or administrative measures to enable consumers or, as appropriate, relevant organizations to obtain redress through formal or informal procedures that are expeditious, fair, inexpensive and accessible. Such procedures should take particular account of the needs of low-income consumers.

29. Governments should encourage all enterprises to resolve consumer disputes in a fair, expeditious and informal manner, and to establish voluntary mechanisms, including advisory services and informal complaints procedures, which can provide assistance to consumers.

30. Information on available redress and other dispute-resolving procedures should be made available to consumers.

F. Education and information programmes

31. Governments should develop or encourage the development of general consumer education and information programmes, bearing in mind the cultural traditions of the people concerned. The aim of such programmes should be to enable people to act as discriminating consumers, capable of making an informed choice of goods and services, and conscious of their rights and responsibilities. In developing such programmes, special attention should be given to the needs of disadvantaged consumers, in both rural and urban areas, including low-income consumers and those with low or non-existent literacy levels.

32. Consumer education should, where appropriate, become an integral part of the basic curriculum of the educational system, preferably as a component of existing subjects.

33. Consumer education and information programmes should cover such important aspects of consumer protection as the following:

(*a*) Health, nutrition, prevention of food-borne diseases and food adulteration;

(*b*) Product hazards;

(*c*) Product labelling;

(*d*) Relevant legislation, how to obtain redress, and agencies and organizations for consumer protection;

(*e*) Information on weights and measures, prices, quality, credit conditions and availability of basic necessities; and

(*f*) As appropriate, pollution and environment.

34. Governments should encourage consumer organizations and other interested groups, including the media, to undertake education and information programmes, particularly for the benefit of low-income consumer groups in rural and urban areas.

35. Business should, where appropriate, undertake or participate in factual and relevant consumer education and information programmes.

36. Bearing in mind the need to reach rural consumers and illiterate consumers, Governments should, as appropriate, develop or encourage the development of consumer information programmes in the mass media.

37. Governments should organize or encourage training programmes for educators, mass media professionals and consumer advisers, to enable them to participate in carrying out consumer information and education programmes.

G. Measures relating to specific areas

38. In advancing consumer interests, particularly in developing countries, Governments should, where appropriate, give priority to areas of essential concern for the health of the consumer, such as food, water and pharmaceuticals. Policies should be adopted or maintained for product quality control, adequate and secure distribution facilities, standardized international labelling and information, as well as education and research programmes in these areas. Government guidelines in regard to specific areas should be developed in the context of the provisions of this document.

39. *Food*. When formulating national policies and plans with regard to food, Governments should take into account the need of all consumers for food security and should support and, as far as possible, adopt standards from the Food and Agriculture Organization of the United Nations and the World Health Organization Codex Alimentarius or, in their absence, other generally accepted international food standards. Governments should maintain, develop or improve food safety measures, including, *inter alia*, safety criteria, food standards and dietary requirements and effective monitoring, inspection and evaluation mechanisms.

40. *Water*. Governments should, within the goals and targets set for the International Drinking Water Supply and Sanitation Decade, formulate, maintain or strengthen national policies to improve the supply, distribution and quality of water for drinking. Due regard should be paid to the choice of appropriate levels of service, quality and technology, the need for education programmes and the importance of community participation.

41. *Pharmaceuticals*. Governments should develop or maintain adequate standards, provisions and appropriate regulatory systems for ensuring the quality and appropriate use of pharmaceuticals through integrated national drug policies which could address, *inter alia*, procurement, distribution, production, licensing arrangements, registration systems and the availability of reliable information on pharmaceuticals. In so doing, Governments should take special account of the work and recommendations of the World Health Organization on pharmaceuticals. For relevant products, the use of that organization's Certification Scheme on the Quality of Pharmaceutical Products Moving in International Commerce and other international information systems on pharmaceuticals should be encouraged. Measures should also be taken, as appropriate, to promote the use of international non-proprietary names (INNs) for drugs, drawing on the work done by the World Health Organization.

42. In addition to the priority areas indicated above, Governments should adopt appropriate measures in other areas, such as pesticides and chemicals in regard, where relevant, to their use, production and storage, taking into account such relevant health and environmental information as Governments may require producers to provide and include in the labelling of products.

IV. International cooperation

43. Governments should, especially in a regional or subregional context:

(*a*) Develop, review, maintain or strengthen, as appropriate, mechanisms for the exchange of information on national policies and measures in the field of consumer protection;

(*b*) Cooperate or encourage cooperation in the implementation of consumer protection policies to achieve greater results within existing resources. Examples of such cooperation could be collaboration in the setting up or joint use of testing facilities, common testing procedures, exchange of consumer information and education programmes, joint training programmes and joint elaboration of regulations;

(*c*) Cooperate to improve the conditions under which essential goods are offered to consumers, giving due regard to both price and quality. Such cooperation could include joint procurement of essential goods, exchange of information on different procurement possibilities and agreements on regional product specifications.

44. Governments should develop or strengthen information links regarding products which have been banned, withdrawn or severely restricted in order to enable other importing countries to protect themselves adequately against the harmful effects of such products.

45. Governments should work to ensure that the quality of products, and information relating to such products, does not vary from country to country in a way that would have detrimental effects on consumers.

46. Governments should work to ensure that policies and measures for consumer protection are implemented with due regard to their not becoming barriers to international trade, and that they are consistent with international trade obligations.

46/203. Prevention and Control of Acquired Immunodeficiency Syndrome (AIDS)

Committee: 2
Vote: Adopted without a vote
Ref.: 47/40, 45/187, 44/233, 43/15, 42/8

The General Assembly,

Recalling its resolution 45/187 of 21 December 1990 and World Health Assembly resolutions WHA 41.24 of 13 May 1988,[1] WHA 42.33 and WHA 42.34 of 19 May 1989[2] and WHA 43.10 of 16 May 1990,[3] and taking note of Economic and Social Council resolution 1991/66 of 26 July 1991 and of decision 1991/23 of 3 May 1991 adopted by the Executive Board of the United Nations Children's Fund,[4] as well as other relevant resolutions and decisions adopted by organizations of the United Nations system,

Noting with appreciation the established leadership and coordinating role of the World Health Organization and the efforts of other organizations of the United Nations system, such as the United Nations Development Programme and the United Nations Children's Fund, and of Governments, intergovernmental and non- governmental organizations, and the public and private sectors in combating the spread of AIDS,

Noting that the World Health Organization estimates that nine to eleven million men, women and children are currently infected with the human immunodeficiency virus (HIV), that a further ten to twenty million adults are expected to become infected and that five to ten million children are expected to be born with HIV infection during the 1990s, creating a cumulative total of some thirty to forty million infected persons by the year 2000, 90 per cent of whom will be in developing countries, and that by then ten to fifteen million children will be orphaned by the death of a parent or both parents as a result of AIDS,

Concerned that, although the reported number of HIV cases in some industrial countries is increasing more slowly than projected, there is still a continuous rapid increase in urban areas and that the pandemic is increasing dramatically in developing countries,

Recognizing that the response to the pandemic must be multisectoral in order to mitigate effectively the social and economic consequences of AIDS and that all sectors of society must be mobilized in support of national programmes to provide support, care, education, counselling and resources to combat AIDS,

Emphasizing the need to counter discrimination and to respect the human rights and dignity of all persons, including those affected by HIV and AIDS, their families and those with whom they live, and noting the relevant work carried out by the Sub-Commission on Prevention of Discrimination and Protection of Minorities and the results of the International Consultation on AIDS and Human Rights, organized by the Centre for Human Rights of the Secretariat at Geneva from 26 to 28 July 1989,

Recognizing that discriminatory measures related, *inter alia*, to quarantine, mandatory testing and coercive and/or restrictive policies dealing with travel and freedom of movement, including transfrontier movement, more often drive the disease underground, where it is more difficult to combat, but do not stop its spread,

Stressing the need to promote safer sexual practices, including responsible sexual behaviour, and to detect and treat other sexually transmitted diseases as early as possible,

Stressing, therefore, the importance of information, education and other support particularly targeted to young people to encourage behavioural practices that enable them to remain uninfected,

Also stressing the need to prevent the spread of HIV infection by any and all means of transmission, including intravenous drug use and unsafe medical practices, occurring in both specific and general population groups,

Further stressing the need to continue to address the economic and social status of women in society in order to provide them with the means to protect themselves from infection, particularly through sexual transmission,

Noting that scientific research, including social and behavioural research, is making progress in developing improved diagnostic, therapeutic and preventive technologies and pharmaceuticals, and stressing the importance of making these technologies and pharmaceuticals available as soon as possible and at an affordable price,

1. *Takes note with appreciation* of the report of the Director-General of the World Health Organization[5] on the implementation of the global strategy for the prevention and control of AIDS;

2. *Urges* Member States and, where appropriate, intergovernmental organizations:

(*a*) To continue to give the AIDS pandemic top priority and to speak openly about AIDS and sexual behaviour within the context of their sexual, cultural and religious norms;

(*b*) To continue to develop strong national AIDS programmes with priority placed, in particular, on prevention of sexual transmission through the promotion of safer sexual practices, including responsible sexual behaviour, as well as on measures to prevent transmission through intravenous drug use and unsafe medical practices;

(*c*) To develop services, in particular for the young, in regard to information, sex education and counselling on contraception and sexually transmitted diseases, as well as on other aspects of HIV transmission, within the context of their sexual, cultural and religious norms;

(*d*) To ensure a multisectoral response to the socio-economic consequences of AIDS through the mobilization of all sectors of society;

(*e*) To encourage the private sector, community groups and non-governmental organizations to participate actively in the national response to AIDS and HIV infection by providing, *inter alia*, support, care, education, counselling and resources;

(*f*) To reinforce efforts to combat denial and complacency;

3. *Urges* Member States and, where appropriate, intergovernmental organizations to protect the human rights and dignity of HIV-infected persons, persons with AIDS and members of particular population groups and to avoid discriminatory action against and stigmatization of them in the provision of services and in employment and travel;

4. *Calls upon* the scientific community to continue to undertake the necessary research into social and behavioural aspects of HIV transmission and to develop the vaccines and pharmaceuticals that will provide effective means of prevention or therapy, and encourages it to make its findings available as soon as possible;

5. *Requests* the World Health Organization to explore the possibility of further strengthening the exchange of information among States Members of the United Nations both on the AIDS pandemic and on national AIDS-related policies designed to combat it;

6. *Requests* the Secretary-General to invite the Director-General of the World Health Organization to intensify his efforts within the United Nations system, in collaboration with the Administrator of the United Nations Development Programme and the heads of the World Bank, the United Nations Population Fund and the United Nations Children's Fund, and all other relevant United Nations organizations:

(*a*) To continue to advance coordinated multisectoral implementation of the global strategy for the prevention and control of AIDS;

(*b*) To support and encourage countries in developing plans to meet the economic and social consequences of the AIDS pandemic, paying attention, in particular, to women, uninfected children with HIV-

---

1 See World Health Organization, *Forty-first World Health Assembly, Geneva, 2 - 13 May 1988, Resolutions and Decisions, Annexes* (WHA 41/1988/REC/1).

2 *Ibid., Forty-second World Health Assembly, Geneva, 8 - 19 May 1989, Resolutions and Decisons, Annexes* (WHA 42/1989/REC/1).

3 *Ibid., Forty-third World Health Assembly, Geneva, 7 - 17 May 1990, Resolutions and Decisions, Annexes* (WHA 43/1990/REC/1).

4 See *Official Records of the Economic and Social Council, 1991, Supplement No. 12* (E/1991/33), chap. IV.

5 A/46/171-E/1991/61, annex.

infected parents or orphaned by AIDS, and elderly people left without providers and often responsible for orphaned grandchildren, as well as to those working with persons with AIDS/HIV;

(*c*) To mobilize the necessary resources, both human and financial, in the health and other sectors, particularly for the developing countries, to develop and implement activities and technologies for the prevention of HIV- infection/AIDS and the care of HIV-infected persons;

(*d*) To ensure that, in the search for prevention, cure and palliation, the concerns, needs and experience of persons with AIDS/HIV, as well as the special needs of women and children, are addressed;

7. *Requests* the Secretary-General, in view of the serious socio-economic consequences of the AIDS pandemic and its negative impact on development in many developing countries, in collaboration with the Director-General of the World Health Organization, to utilize fully the research, analytical capacity and experience of the United Nations system in the planning of multisectoral activities and the earmarking of funds for countries requesting assistance for those activities;

8. *Also requests* the Secretary-General, in close cooperation with the Director-General of the World Health Organization, to use fully the information capacity of the United Nations system to intensify public information activities with respect to HIV and AIDS;

9. *Further requests* the Secretary-General to invite the Director-General of the World Health Organization, in close collaboration with all other appropriate bodies, organs and programmes of the United Nations system, to report, through the Secretary-General, to the General Assembly at its forty-seventh session, through the Economic and Social Council, on the implementation of the present resolution, taking into account the health aspects and all other dimensions of the pandemic.

79th plenary meeting
20 December 1991

09.40 CRIME

09.41 TERRORISM AND HIJACKING

2551 (XXIV). Forcible Diversion of Civil Aircraft in Flight

Committee: 6
Vote: 77 - 2 - 17
Ref.: 927(X)

The General Assembly,

Deeply concerned over acts of unlawful interference with international civil aviation,

Considering it necessary to recommend effective measures against hijacking in all its forms, or any other unlawful seizure or exercise of control of aircraft,

Mindful that such acts may endanger the life and health of passengers and crew in disregard of commonly accepted humanitarian considerations,

Aware that international civil aviation can only function properly in conditions guaranteeing the safety of its operations and the due exercise of the freedom of air travel,

1. *Calls upon* States to take every appropriate measure to ensure that their respective national legislations provide an adequate framework for effective legal measures against all kinds of acts of unlawful interference with, seizure of, or other wrongful exercise of control by force or threat thereof over, civil aircraft in flight;

2. *Urges* States in particular to ensure that persons on board who perpetrate such acts are prosecuted;

3. *Urges* full support for the efforts of the International Civil Aviation Organization directed towards the speedy preparation and implementation of a convention providing for appropriate measures, *inter alia*, with respect to making the unlawful seizure of civil aircraft a punishable offence and to the prosecution of persons who commit that offence;

4. *Invites* States to ratify or accede to the Convention on Offences and Certain Other Acts Committed on Board Aircraft, signed at Tokyo on 14 September 1963,[1] in conformity with the Convention.

1831st plenary meeting
12 December 1969.

[1] United Nations, *Treaty Series*, vol. 704 (1969), No. 10106.

2645 (XXV). Aerial Hijacking or Interference with Civil Air Travel

Committee: 6
Vote: 105 - 0 - 8

The General Assembly,

Recognizing that international civil aviation is a vital link in the promotion and preservation of friendly relations among States and that its safe and orderly functioning is in the interest of all peoples,

Gravely concerned over acts of aerial hijacking or other wrongful interference with civil air travel,

Recognizing that such acts jeopardize the lives and safety of the passengers and crew and constitute a violation of their human rights,

Aware that international civil aviation can only function properly in conditions guaranteeing the safety of its operations and the due exercise of the freedom of air travel,

Endorsing the solemn declaration[2] of the extraordinary session of the Assembly of the International Civil Aviation Organization held at Montreal from 16 to 30 June 1970,

Bearing in mind General Assembly resolution 2551 (XXIV) of 12 December 1969 and Security Council resolution 286 (1970) of 9 September 1970 adopted by consensus at the 1552nd meeting of the Council,

1. *Condemns*, without exception whatsoever, all acts of aerial hijacking or other interference with civil air travel, whether originally national or international, through the threat or use of force, and all acts of violence which may be directed against passengers, crew and aircraft engaged in, and air navigation facilities and aeronautical communications used by, civil air transport;

2. *Calls upon* States to take all appropriate measures to deter, prevent or suppress such acts within their jurisdiction, at every stage of the execution of those acts, and to provide for the prosecution and punishment of persons who perpetrate such acts, in a manner commensurate with the gravity of those crimes, or, without prejudice to the rights and obligations of States under existing international instruments relating to the matter, for the extradition of such persons for the purpose of their prosecution and punishment;

3. *Declares* that the exploitation of unlawful seizure of aircraft for the purpose of taking hostages is to be condemned;

4. *Declares further* that the unlawful detention of passengers and crew in transit or otherwise engaged in civil air travel is to be con-

[2] International Civil Aviation Organization, *Resolutions adopted by the Assembly, Seventeenth Session (Extraordinary)* (Montreal, 1970), resolution A17-1.

demned as another form of wrongful interference with free and uninterrupted air travel;

5. *Urges* States to the territory of which a hijacked aircraft is diverted to provide for the care and safety of its passengers and crew and to enable them to continue their journey as soon as practicable, and to return the aircraft and its cargo to the persons lawfully entitled to possession;

6. *Invites* States to ratify or accede to the Convention on Offences and Certain Other Acts Committed on Board Aircraft, signed at Tokyo on 14 September 1963,[1] in conformity with the Convention;

7. *Requests* concerted action on the part of States in accordance with the Charter of the United Nations towards suppressing all acts which jeopardize the safe and orderly development of international civil air transport;

8. *Calls upon* States to take joint and separate action, in accordance with the Charter, in cooperation with the United Nations and the International Civil Aviation Organization to ensure that passengers, crew and aircraft engaged in civil aviation are not used as a means of extorting advantage of any kind;

9. *Urges* full support for the current efforts of the International Civil Aviation Organization towards the development and coordination, in accordance with its competence, of effective measures in respect of interference with civil air travel;

10. *Calls upon* States to make every possible effort to achieve a successful result at the diplomatic conference to convene at The Hague in December 1970 for the purpose of the adoption of a convention on the unlawful seizure of aircraft, so that an effective convention may be brought into force at an early date.

1914th plenary meeting
25 November 1970.

39/159. Inadmissibility of the Policy of State Terrorism and any Actions by States Aimed at Undermining the Socio-Political System in other Sovereign States

Committee: 1
Vote: 117 - 0 - 30

The General Assembly,

Reaffirming the obligation of all States to refrain in their international relations from the threat or use of force against the sovereignty, territorial integrity and political independence of any State, as well as the inalienable right of all peoples to determine their own form of government and to choose their own economic, political and social system free from outside intervention, subversion, coercion and constraint of any kind whatsoever,

Expressing its profound concern that State terrorism has lately been practised ever more frequently in relations between States and that military and other actions are being taken against the sovereignty and political independence of States and the self-determination of peoples,

Noting that all this seriously endangers the independent existence of States and the possibility of ensuring peaceful relations and mutual trust between them and leads to a sharp exacerbation of tensions and a growing threat of war,

Reaffirming the inalienable right of all peoples freely to determine their own destiny and the course of their development,

Convinced that the interests of maintaining peace require that relations between States, regardless of ideologies, should be based on strict observance of the Charter of the United Nations, as well as on generally recognized principles and norms of international relations, *inter alia*, renunciation of the threat or use of force against the territorial integrity or political independence of any State, non-intervention and non-interference in the internal and external affairs of States, permanent sovereignty of States and peoples over their natural resources and self-determination and independence of peoples under colonial domination, foreign occupation or racist régimes,

Categorically rejecting all concepts, doctrines or ideologies intended to justify actions of States aimed at undermining the socio-political system of other States,

1. *Resolutely condemns* policies and practices of terrorism in relations between States as a method of dealing with other States and peoples;

2. *Demands* that all States take no actions aimed at military intervention and occupation, forcible change in or undermining of the socio-political system of States, destabilization and overthrow of their Governments and, in particular, initiate no military action to that end under any pretext whatsoever and cease forthwith any such action already in progress;

3. *Urges* all States to respect and strictly observe, in accordance with the Charter of the United Nations, the sovereignty and political independence of States and the right of peoples to self-determination, as well as their right freely, without outside interference and intervention, to choose their socio-political system and to pursue their political, economic, social and cultural development.

102nd plenary meeting
17 December 1984

49/60. Measures to Eliminate International Terrorism

Committee: 6
Vote: Adopted without a vote
Ref.: 50/53, 48/411, 46/51, 44/29, 42/159, 40/61, 38/130, 36/109, 34/145, 32/147, 31/102, 3034(XXVII)

The General Assembly,

Recalling its resolution 46/51 of 9 December 1991 and its decision 48/411 of 9 December 1993,

Taking note of the report of the Secretary-General,[2]

Having considered in depth the question of measures to eliminate international terrorism,

Convinced that the adoption of the declaration on measures to eliminate international terrorism should contribute to the enhancement of the struggle against international terrorism,

1. *Approves* the Declaration on Measures to Eliminate International Terrorism, the text of which is annexed to the present resolution;

2. *Invites* the Secretary-General to inform all States, the Security Council, the International Court of Justice and the relevant specialized agencies, organizations and organisms of the adoption of the Declaration;

3. *Urges* that every effort be made in order that the Declaration becomes generally known and is observed and implemented in full;

4. *Urges* States, in accordance with the provisions of the Declaration, to take all appropriate measures at the national and international levels to eliminate terrorism;

5. *Invites* the Secretary-General to follow up closely the implementation of the present resolution and the Declaration, and to submit to the General Assembly at its fiftieth session a report thereon, relating, in particular, to the modalities of implementation of paragraph 10 of the Declaration;

6. *Decides* to include in the provisional agenda of its fiftieth session the item entitled "Measures to eliminate international terrorism", in order to examine the report of the Secretary-General requested in paragraph 5 above, without prejudice to the annual or biennial consideration of the item.

84th plenary meeting
9 December 1994

---

[1] United Nations, *Treaty Series*, vol. 704 (1969), No. 10106.

[2] A/49/257 and Add.1-3.

Annex

Declaration on Measures to Eliminate International Terrorism

The General Assembly,

Guided by the purposes and principles of the Charter of the United Nations,

Recalling the Declaration on Principles of International Law concerning Friendly Relations and Cooperation among States in accordance with the Charter of the United Nations,[1] the Declaration on the Strengthening of International Security,[2] the Definition of Aggression,[3] the Declaration on the Enhancement of the Effectiveness of the Principle of Refraining from the Threat or Use of Force in International Relations,[4] the Vienna Declaration and Programme of Action, adopted by the World Conference on Human Rights,[5] the International Covenant on Economic, Social and Cultural Rights[6] and the International Covenant on Civil and Political Rights,[7]

Deeply disturbed by the world-wide persistence of acts of international terrorism in all its forms and manifestations, including those in which States are directly or indirectly involved, which endanger or take innocent lives, have a deleterious effect on international relations and may jeopardize the security of States,

Deeply concerned by the increase, in many regions of the world, of acts of terrorism based on intolerance or extremism,

Concerned at the growing and dangerous links between terrorist groups and drug traffickers and their paramilitary gangs, which have resorted to all types of violence, thus endangering the constitutional order of States and violating basic human rights,

Convinced of the desirability for closer coordination and cooperation among States in combating crimes closely connected with terrorism, including drug trafficking, unlawful arms trade, money laundering and smuggling of nuclear and other potentially deadly materials, and bearing in mind the role that could be played by both the United Nations and regional organizations in this respect,

Firmly determined to eliminate international terrorism in all its forms and manifestations,

Convinced also that the suppression of acts of international terrorism, including those in which States are directly or indirectly involved, is an essential element for the maintenance of international peace and security,

Convinced further that those responsible for acts of international terrorism must be brought to justice,

Stressing the imperative need further to strengthen international cooperation between States in order to take and adopt practical and effective measures to prevent, combat and eliminate all forms of terrorism that affect the international community as a whole,

Conscious of the important role that might be played by the United Nations, the relevant specialized agencies and States in fostering widespread cooperation in preventing and combating international terrorism, *inter alia*, by increasing public awareness of the problem,

Recalling the existing international treaties relating to various aspects of the problem of international terrorism, *inter alia*, the Convention on Offences and Certain Other Acts Committed on Board Aircraft,[8] signed at Tokyo on 14 September 1963, the Convention for the Suppression of Unlawful Seizure of Aircraft,[9] signed at The Hague on 16 December 1970, the Convention for the Suppression of Unlawful Acts against the Safety of Civil Aviation,[10] concluded at Montreal on 23 September 1971, the Convention on the Prevention and Punishment of Crimes against Internationally Protected Persons, including Diplomatic Agents,[11] adopted in New York on 14 December 1973, the International Convention against the Taking of Hostages,[12] adopted in New York on 17 December 1979, the Convention on the Physical Protection of Nuclear Material[13], adopted at Vienna on 3 March 1980, the Protocol for the Suppression of Unlawful Acts of Violence at Airports Serving International Civil Aviation, supplementary to the Convention for the Suppression of Unlawful Acts against the Safety of Civil Aviation,[14] signed at Montreal on 24 February 1988, the Convention for the Suppression of Unlawful Acts against the Safety of Maritime Navigation,[15] done at Rome on 10 March 1988, the Protocol for the Suppression of Unlawful Acts against the Safety of Fixed Platforms located on the Continental Shelf,[16] done at Rome on 10 March 1988, and the Convention on the Marking of Plastic Explosives for the Purpose of Detection,[17] done at Montreal on 1 March 1991,

Welcoming the conclusion of regional agreements and mutually agreed declarations to combat and eliminate terrorism in all its forms and manifestations,

Convinced of the desirability of keeping under review the scope of existing international legal provisions to combat terrorism in all its forms and manifestations, with the aim of ensuring a comprehensive legal framework for the prevention and elimination of terrorism,

Solemnly declares the following:

I

1. The States Members of the United Nations solemnly reaffirm their unequivocal condemnation of all acts, methods and practices of terrorism as criminal and unjustifiable, wherever and by whomever committed, including those which jeopardize the friendly relations among States and peoples and threaten the territorial integrity and security of States;

2. Acts, methods and practices of terrorism constitute a grave violation of the purposes and principles of the United Nations, which may pose a threat to international peace and security, jeopardize friendly relations among States, hinder international cooperation and aim at the destruction of human rights, fundamental freedoms and the democratic bases of society;

3. Criminal acts intended or calculated to provoke a state of terror in the general public, a group of persons or particular persons for political purposes are in any circumstance unjustifiable, whatever the considerations of a political, philosophical, ideological, racial, ethnic, religious or any other nature that may be invoked to justify them;

II

4. States, guided by the purposes and principles of the Charter of the United Nations and other relevant rules of international law, must refrain from organizing, instigating, assisting or participating in terrorist acts in territories of other States, or from acquiescing in or encouraging activities within their territories directed towards the commission of such acts;

5. States must also fulfil their obligations under the Charter of the United Nations and other provisions of international law with respect

---

1 Resolution 2625 (XXV), annex.

2 Resolution 2734 (XXV).

3 Resolution 3314 (XXIX), annex.

4 Resolution 42/22, annex.

5 *Report of the World Conference on Human Rights, Vienna, 14-25 June 1993* (A/CONF.157/24 (Part I)), chap. III.

6 See resolution 2200 A (XXI), annex.

7 *Ibid.*

8 United Nations, *Treaty Series*, vol. 704, No. 10106.

9 *Ibid.*, vol. 860, No. 12325.

10 *Ibid.*, vol. 974, No. 14118.

11 *Ibid.*, vol. 1035, No. 15410.

12 Resolution 34/146, annex.

13 International Atomic Energy Agency, document INFCIRC/225; to be published in United Nations, Treaty Series, vol. 1456, No. 24631.

14 International Civil Aviation Organization, document DOC 9518.

15 International Maritime Organization, document SUA/CONF/15/Rev.1.

16 *Ibid.*, document SUA/CONF/16/Rev.2.

17 S/22393; see *Official Records of the Security Council, Forty-sixth year, Supplement for January, February and March 1991.*

to combating international terrorism and are urged to take effective and resolute measures in accordance with the relevant provisions of international law and international standards of human rights for the speedy and final elimination of international terrorism, in particular:

(*a*) To refrain from organizing, instigating, facilitating, financing, encouraging or tolerating terrorist activities and to take appropriate practical measures to ensure that their respective territories are not used for terrorist installations or training camps, or for the preparation or organization of terrorist acts intended to be committed against other States or their citizens;

(*b*) To ensure the apprehension and prosecution or extradition of perpetrators of terrorist acts, in accordance with the relevant provisions of their national law;

(*c*) To endeavour to conclude special agreements to that effect on a bilateral, regional and multilateral basis, and to prepare, to that effect, model agreements on cooperation;

(*d*) To cooperate with one another in exchanging relevant information concerning the prevention and combating of terrorism;

(*e*) To take promptly all steps necessary to implement the existing international conventions on this subject to which they are parties, including the harmonization of their domestic legislation with those conventions;

(*f*) To take appropriate measures, before granting asylum, for the purpose of ensuring that the asylum seeker has not engaged in terrorist activities and, after granting asylum, for the purpose of ensuring that the refugee status is not used in a manner contrary to the provisions set out in subparagraph (a) above;

6. In order to combat effectively the increase in, and the growing international character and effects of, acts of terrorism, States should enhance their cooperation in this area through, in particular, systematizing the exchange of information concerning the prevention and combating of terrorism, as well as by effective implementation of the relevant international conventions and conclusion of mutual judicial assistance and extradition agreements on a bilateral, regional and multilateral basis;

7. In this context, States are encouraged to review urgently the scope of the existing international legal provisions on the prevention, repression and elimination of terrorism in all its forms and manifestations, with the aim of ensuring that there is a comprehensive legal framework covering all aspects of the matter;

8. Furthermore States that have not yet done so are urged to consider, as a matter of priority, becoming parties to the international conventions and protocols relating to various aspects of international terrorism referred to in the preamble to the present Declaration;

III

9. The United Nations, the relevant specialized agencies and intergovernmental organizations and other relevant bodies must make every effort with a view to promoting measures to combat and eliminate acts of terrorism and to strengthening their role in this field;

10. The Secretary-General should assist in the implementation of the present Declaration by taking, within existing resources, the following practical measures to enhance international cooperation:

(*a*) A collection of data on the status and implementation of existing multilateral, regional and bilateral agreements relating to international terrorism, including information on incidents caused by international terrorism and criminal prosecutions and sentencing, based on information received from the depositaries of those agreements and from Member States;

(*b*) A compendium of national laws and regulations regarding the prevention and suppression of international terrorism in all its forms and manifestations, based on information received from Member States;

(*c*) An analytical review of existing international legal instruments relating to international terrorism, in order to assist States in identifying aspects of this matter that have not been covered by such instruments and could be addressed to develop further a comprehensive legal framework of conventions dealing with international terrorism;

(*d*) A review of existing possibilities within the United Nations system for assisting States in organizing workshops and training courses on combating crimes connected with international terrorism;

IV

11. All States are urged to promote and implement in good faith and effectively the provisions of the present Declaration in all its aspects;

12. Emphasis is placed on the need to pursue efforts aiming at eliminating definitively all acts of terrorism by the strengthening of international cooperation and progressive development of international law and its codification, as well as by enhancement of coordination between, and increase of the efficiency of, the United Nations and the relevant specialized agencies, organizations and bodies.

09.42 DRUG ABUSE AND DRUG TRAFFICKING

39/142. Declaration on the Control of Drug Trafficking and Drug Abuse

Committee: 3
Vote: Adopted without a vote
Ref.: 37/168, 36/168, 35/195, 34/177, 33/168, 31/126, 32/124, 3445(XXX), 3444(XXX), 3443(XXX), 3279(XXIX), 3147(XXVIII), 3146(XXVIII), 3145(XXVIII), 3014(XXVII), 3013(XXVII), 3012(XXVII), 2859(XXVI), 2720(XXV), 2719(XXV), 2434(XXIII), 1774(XVII), 1587(XV), 1395(XIV), 834(IX)774(XVIII), 455(V), 211(III), 135(II), 134(II)

The General Assembly,

Recalling its resolutions 33/168 of 20 December 1978, 35/195 of 15 December 1980, 36/132 of 14 December 1981, 36/168 of 16 December 1981, 37/168 of 17 December 1982, 37/198 of 18 December 1982, 38/93, 38/98 and 38/122 of 16 December 1983 and other relevant provisions,

Recognizing the concern that prevails in the international community about the problem of the illegal production of, illicit trafficking in and abuse of drugs,

Adopts the Declaration set forth in the annex to the present resolution.

101st plenary meeting
14 December 1984

Annex

Declaration on the Control of Drug Trafficking and Drug Abuse

The General Assembly,

Bearing in mind that the purposes and principles of the Charter of the United Nations reaffirm faith in the dignity and worth of the human person and promote social progress and better standards of life in larger freedom and international cooperation in solving problems of an economic, social, cultural or humanitarian character,

Considering that Member States have undertaken in the Universal Declaration of Human Rights[1] to promote social progress and better standards of life for the peoples of the world,

Considering that the international community has expressed grave concern at the fact that trafficking in narcotics and drug abuse constitute an obstacle to the physical and moral well-being of peoples and of youth in particular,

Desiring to heighten the awareness of the international community of the urgency of preventing and punishing the illicit demand for, abuse of and illicit production of and traffic in drugs,

1 Resolution 217 A (III)

Considering that the Quito Declaration against Traffic in Narcotic Drugs of 11 August 1984[1] and the New York Declaration against Drug Trafficking and the Illicit Use of Drugs of 1 October 1984[2] recognize the international nature of this problem and emphasize that it should be solved with the firm support of the entire international community,

Considering that the Commission on Narcotic Drugs, the International Narcotics Control Board and the United Nations Fund for Drug Abuse Control have made valuable contributions to the control and elimination of drug trafficking and drug abuse,

Recognizing that existing international instruments, including the Single Convention on Narcotic Drugs of 1961, as amended by the 1972 Protocol Amending the Single Convention on Narcotic Drugs of 1961,[3] and the Convention on Psychotropic Substances of 1971,[4] have created a legal framework for combating trafficking in narcotic drugs and drug abuse in their specialized fields,

Declares that:

1. Drug trafficking and drug abuse are extremely serious problems which, owing to their magnitude, scope and widespread pernicious effects, have become an international criminal activity demanding urgent attention and maximum priority.

2. The illegal production of, illicit demand for, abuse of and illicit trafficking in drugs impede economic and social progress, constitute a grave threat to the security and development of many countries and peoples and should be combated by all moral, legal and institutional means, at the national, regional and international levels.

3. The eradication of trafficking in narcotic drugs is the collective responsibility of all States, especially those affected by problems relating to illicit production, trafficking or abuse.

4. States Members shall utilize the legal instruments against the illicit production of and demand for, abuse of and illicit traffic in drugs and adopt additional measures to counter new manifestations of this shameful and heinous crime.

5. States Members undertake to intensify efforts and to coordinate strategies aimed at the control and eradication of the complex problem of drug trafficking and drug abuse through programmes including economic, social and cultural alternatives.

44/141. Global Programme of Action Against Illicit Narcotic Drugs

Committee: 3
Vote: Adopted without a vote

The General Assembly,

Alarmed by the dramatic increase in drug abuse and illicit production and trafficking in narcotics, which is threatening the health and well-being of millions of people, in particular youth, in the majority of countries of the world,

Deeply concerned that the evolving drug problem is assuming new dimensions and is threatening the economic, social and political structures of affected countries, through acts of violence perpetrated against their democratic institutions and the extensive economic power of illicit drug organizations,

Commending the determined efforts of the Government of Colombia to stop drug trafficking and recognizing the importance of support for such efforts by the international community,

Welcoming the increasing international attention to these issues and the unflinching commitment demonstrated at the highest levels by heads of Government and State to increase their efforts and resources to achieve coordinated action in the international fight against production, trafficking and abuse of narcotic drugs,

Recognizing that the collective responsibility of States for the campaign against the demand for, production of and trafficking in illicit drugs requires intensified international cooperation and joint action, including the capability to provide, in appropriate forms, necessary support and assistance, if requested by affected States, in order to strengthen their capacity to deal with the problem in all its aspects,

Noting with appreciation the work carried out within the United Nations in the field of drug abuse control and the valuable knowledge and experience represented there,

Recognizing the important contributions made to the international campaign against drug abuse and illicit trafficking by the International Conference on Drug Abuse and Illicit Trafficking, held at Vienna from 17 to 26 June 1987, and, in particular by its adoption of the Declaration[5] and the Comprehensive Multidisciplinary Outline of Future Activities in Drug Abuse Control,[6] as well as by the conference of plenipotentiaries, held at Vienna from 25 November to 20 December 1988, which adopted the United Nations Convention against Illicit Traffic in Narcotic Drugs and Psychotropic Substances,[7]

Deeply concerned that, owing to a lack of resources, it has not been possible for the United Nations organs concerned to execute several of the important steps and measures that were mandated for the biennium 1988-1989,

Acknowledging the recommendations made by the Administrative Committee on Coordination and the Committee for Programme and Coordination at their twenty-fourth series of Joint Meetings,[8] at which they concluded, *inter alia*, that the Administrative Committee on Coordination should prepare a system-wide action plan leading to specific activities to be undertaken by organizations of the United Nations system, individually and collectively, and that consideration could be given to the need for the establishment of additional mechanisms to enhance the effectiveness of the United Nations system in the field of drug abuse control,

Recognizing that the new dimensions taken on by the drug menace will necessitate a more comprehensive approach to international drug control and a more efficient and coordinated structure in this field in order to enable the United Nations to play the central and greatly increased role necessary for countering this threat,

Bearing in mind its decision in resolution 44/16 of 1 November 1989, to hold a special session to consider the question of international cooperation against illicit production, supply, demand, trafficking and distribution of narcotic drugs, with a view to expanding the scope and increasing the effectiveness of such cooperation, and stressing the importance of this special session and of the need for Member States to make the fullest possible contributions to its preparatory work,

1. *Resolves* that action against drug abuse and illicit production and trafficking in narcotics should, as a collective responsibility, be accorded the highest possible priority by the international community and that the United Nations should be the main focus for concerted action against illicit drugs;

2. *Agrees* to strengthen the capability of the United Nations in order to achieve more efficient and coordinated cooperation at the international, regional and national levels against the threats posed by illicit narcotic drugs and psychotropic substances;

3. *Requests* the Secretary-General, in his capacity as Chairman of the Administrative Committee on Coordination, to coordinate at the inter-agency level, the development of a United Nations system-wide action plan on drug abuse control aimed at the full implementation of all existing mandates and subsequent decisions of intergovernmental bodies throughout the United Nations system, using as a guide the Declaration of the International Conference on Drug Abuse and Illicit Trafficking and the recommendations in the Comprehensive Multidisciplinary Outline of Future Activities in Drug Abuse Control, and for the attainment of this purpose:

1 A/39/407, annex.
2 A/39/551 and Corr. 1 and 2, annex.
3 United Nations publication, Sales No. E.77.XI.3, p. 13.
4 United Nations publication, Sales No. E.78.XI.3, p. 7.

5 See *Report of the International Conference on Drug Abuse and Illicit Trafficking, Vienna, 17 - 26 June 1987* (United Nations publication, Sales No. E.87.I.18), chap. I, sect. B.
6 *Ibid.*, sect. A.
7 E/CONF.82/15 and Corr. 2.
8 See E/1990/4, sect. III.

(*a*) Calls upon the Division on Narcotic Drugs of the Secretariat, the International Narcotics Control Board and its secretariat, as well as the United Nations Fund for Drug Abuse Control, to consult closely with and contribute their expertise to the other agencies represented on the Administrative Committee on Coordination in developing the action plan;

(*b*) Requests the Administrative Committee on Coordination to include in the action plan, *inter alia*:

(i) A statement of purposes that defines the overall goal and denotes specific objectives;

(ii) An outline of concrete activities that each agency should undertake, within its mandate, ensuring that there is no duplication or overlap;

(iii) A reasonable time-frame for implementation of each portion of the action plan;

(iv) A realistic cost estimate for implementing the action plan, being mindful that resources are limited and that it would be necessary for agencies to focus priorities, review deployment of resources or obtain, if necessary, from their governing bodies the authority needed to fulfil their part of the plan;

(*c*) Requests the Administrative Committee on Coordination to present the action plan to all Member States no later than 31 March 1990, in order to permit discussion by the Committee for Programme and Coordination at its thirtieth session and by the Economic and Social Council at its next regular session of 1990;

(*d*) Requests that the executive heads of United Nations bodies report annually to the Administrative Committee on Coordination on the progress made in implementing the action plan and that the Administrative Committee include the same information in its annual report, so as to enable the Committee for Programme and Coordination and the Economic and Social Council to consider it, within their respective mandates, and to make appropriate recommendations to the General Assembly;

(*e*) Requests the Administrative Committee on Coordination to make the necessary adjustments to the action plan annually and to ensure that each agency brings up to date and revises its related activities annually in order to meet changing circumstances;

4. *Requests* the Secretary-General to select a limited number of experts from developed and developing countries to advise and assist him for a maximum period of one year, in full cooperation with United Nations officials, in order to enhance the efficiency of the United Nations structure for drug abuse control, taking into account the ability of the United Nations to perform its increasing tasks in the light of existing mandates and of decisions adopted by the General Assembly at its special session, and to report to the Assembly at its forty-fifth session;

5. *Requests* States, without prejudice to the basic criteria that the General Assembly shall adopt at its special session, to consider in the preparatory work for that session, *inter alia*, the following areas, with the purpose of ensuring that all aspects of the problem are adequately addressed in the elaboration of a global programme of action against illicit narcotic drugs for adoption at the special session:

(*a*) Giving increased attention to curbing the rising demand for narcotic drugs by intensified rehabilitative, legal and preventive measures, including public information and education;

(*b*) The possibility of declaring a United Nations decade against drug abuse, with the purpose of raising public awareness through a world-wide campaign against drug abuse;

(*c*) The expansion of the scope of international cooperation in support of rural development programmes and other economic development and technical assistance programmes aimed at reducing illicit production and drug trafficking through the strengthening of economic, judicial and legal systems;

(*d*) The full involvement of international, regional and national financial institutions within their respective areas of competence in the elaboration of measures to counteract the negative economic and social consequences of the drug problem in all its aspects, paying special attention to the characteristics and magnitude of the conversion and transference of drug-related monies in the economic systems of countries;

(*e*) The development of mechanisms to prevent the use of the banking system and other financial institutions for the processing or laundering of drug-related money;

(*f*) An examination of recommendations to enhance the efficiency of the United Nations structure for drug abuse control in the most appropriate way to enable the United Nations to perform its increasing tasks in the most effective and coordinated manner;

(*g*) The development of recommendations for generating increased financial resources to the United Nations drug effort and for ensuring sufficient regular budget resources for the United Nations drug bodies to carry out their mandates;

(*h*) The coordination of an expanded programme of training for national narcotics agents in investigative methods, interdiction and narcotics intelligence;

(*i*) The feasibility of establishing a reserve pool of experienced narcotics agents and experts pledged by other States, whose services States may request for specified periods of time;

(*j*) The establishment under the United Nations of a facility to gather and collate information on the financial flow from drug-related funds, to be made available to States at their request;

(*k*) The feasibility of a United Nations capability that, at the request of States, would provide training and equipment for the anti-drug operations of the States to inhibit the use, interdict the supply and eliminate the illicit trafficking of drugs;

(*l*) The elaboration of any other appropriate measures whereby the United Nations can contribute further to concerted international action against illicit narcotic drugs;

6. *Invites* States, at the special session of the General Assembly, to consider requesting the Secretary-General to appoint a limited number of experts, representing the various aspects of the drug problem with regard to both developed and developing countries, to develop further the global programme of action as adopted at the special session;

7. *Requests* the Secretary-General to give priority to narcotics control activities in his proposals for the medium-term plan for the period beginning in 1992;

8. *Urges* States to contribute to the United Nations Fund for Drug Abuse Control;

9. *Also urges* States to consider giving financial or other support to enhance the efficiency of the United Nations structure for drug abuse control and to assist and promote a truly comprehensive global programme of action;

10. *Requests* the Secretary-General to transmit the present resolution to the Preparatory Committee of the Whole for the Seventeenth Special Session of the General Assembly, which the Assembly established by its decision 44/410 of 14 November 1989.

82nd plenary meeting
15 December 1989

S-17/2. Political Declaration and Global Programme of Action Adopted by the General Assembly at its Seventeenth Special Session, Devoted to the Question of International Cooperation Against Illicit Production, Supply, Demand, Trafficking and Distribution of Narcotic Drugs and Psychotropic Substances

Committee: -
Vote: Adopted without a vote
Ref.: 46/102, 45/148, 44/16

The General Assembly

Adopts the Political Declaration and the Global Programme of Action on international cooperation against illicit production, supply, demand, trafficking and distribution of narcotic drugs and psychotropic substances annexed to the present resolution.

8th plenary meeting
23 February 1990

Annex

Political Declaration

We the States Members of the United Nations,

Assembled at the seventeenth special session of the General Assembly to consider the question of international cooperation against illicit production, supply, demand, trafficking and distribution of narcotic drugs and psychotropic substances,

Deeply alarmed by the magnitude of the rising trend in the illicit demand, production, supply, trafficking and distribution of narcotic drugs and psychotropic substances, which are a grave and persistent threat to the health and well-being of mankind, the stability of nations, the political, economic, social and cultural structures of all societies and the lives and dignity of millions of human beings, most especially of young people,

Aware of the dangers posed for all countries alike by the illicit cultivation, production, supply, demand, trafficking and distribution of narcotic drugs and psychotropic substances, and aware also of the need for a comprehensive approach in combating them,

Conscious that the extraordinarily high levels of illicit consumption, cultivation and production of narcotic drugs and of illicit drug trafficking necessitate a more comprehensive approach to international cooperation in drug abuse control and counter-offensives at the national, regional and international levels,

Reaffirming our determination to combat the scourge of drug abuse and illicit trafficking in narcotic drugs and psychotropic substances in strict conformity with the principles of the Charter of the United Nations, the principles of international law, in particular respect for the sovereignty and territorial integrity of States, the principle of noninterference in the internal affairs of States and non-use of force or the threat of force in international relations, and the provisions of the international drug control conventions,

Reaffirming also the provisions set forth in the Single Convention on Narcotic Drugs of 1961,[1] and in that Convention as amended by the 1972 Protocol Amending the Single Convention on Narcotic Drugs of 1961,[2] the Convention on Psychotropic Substances of 1971[3] and the United Nations Convention against Illicit Traffic in Narcotic Drugs and Psychotropic Substances adopted in 1988,[4]

Reaffirming further the principle of shared responsibility in combating drug abuse and illicit traffic in narcotic drugs and psychotropic substances,

Recognizing the links between the illicit demand, consumption, production, supply, trafficking and distribution of narcotic drugs and psychotropic substances and the economic, social and cultural conditions in the countries affected by them,

Deeply concerned about the violence and corruption generated by the illicit demand, production, trafficking and distribution of narcotic drugs and psychotropic substances and the high human, political, economic and social costs of drug abuse and of the fight against the drug problem, entailing the diversion of scarce resources from other national priorities, which in the case of developing countries includes development activities,

Conscious that international cooperation for the development of the developing countries should be strengthened, allowing all countries to participate more fully in an effective fight against the drug problem,

Recognizing the links between drug abuse and a wide range of adverse health consequences, including the transmission of human immunodeficiency virus (HIV) infection and the spread of acquired immunodeficiency syndrome (AIDS),

Recognizing also that illicit trafficking in narcotic drugs and psychotropic substances is a criminal activity and that its suppression requires a higher priority and concerted action at the national, regional and international levels by all States, including rapid ratification of and accession to the United Nations Convention against Illicit Traffic in Narcotic Drugs and Psychotropic Substances,

Noting that the large financial profits derived from illicit drug trafficking and related criminal activities enable transnational criminal organizations to penetrate, contaminate and corrupt the structure of Governments, legitimate commercial activities and society at all levels, thereby vitiating economic and social development, distorting the process of law and undermining the foundations of States,

Recognizing that a growing number of countries, in particular developing countries, are affected by illicit transit trafficking in narcotic drugs because of their geographical location or economic situation, which imposes serious burdens on the drug law enforcement machinery of those countries and forces diversion of scarce resources from pressing developmental needs and other national priorities,

Convinced that the fight against illicit trafficking in narcotic drugs and psychotropic substances has to comprise effective measures aimed, *inter alia*, at eliminating illicit consumption, cultivation and production of narcotic drugs and psychotropic substances; preventing the diversion from legitimate uses of precursor chemicals, specific substances, materials and equipment frequently used in the illicit manufacture of narcotic drugs and psychotropic substances; and preventing the use of the banking system and other financial institutions for the laundering of proceeds derived from illicit drug trafficking by making such activities criminal offences,

Alarmed at the growing link between illicit trafficking in narcotic drugs and terrorist activities, which is aggravated by insufficient control of commerce in arms and by illicit or covert arms transfers, as well as by illegal activities of mercenaries,

Mindful of the results already achieved by the United Nations in the field of drug abuse control, including the Declaration[5] and the Comprehensive Multidisciplinary Outline of Future Activities in Drug Abuse Control,[6] adopted at the International Conference on Drug Abuse and Illicit Trafficking, as well as the United Nations Convention against Illicit Trafficking in Narcotic Drugs and Psychotropic Substances,

Convinced that action against drug abuse and illicit production of and trafficking in narcotic drugs and psychotropic substances should, as a shared responsibility, be accorded a higher priority by the international community and convinced also that the United Nations should be the main focus for concerted action and should play an enhanced role in that field,

Considering that the goals of intensified international cooperation and increased efforts of States in that direction would be served by the proclamation of a United Nations decade against drug abuse,

Agree on the following:

1. We resolve to protect mankind from the scourge of drug abuse and illicit trafficking in narcotic drugs and psychotropic substances;

2. We affirm that the fight against drug abuse and illicit trafficking in narcotic drugs and psychotropic substances should be accorded high priority by Governments and by all relevant regional and international organizations;

3. We are determined to take the necessary actions to combat the drug problem, taking into account the fundamental responsibility resting with each State in that regard;

4. We shall expand the scope and increase the effectiveness of international cooperation against illicit demand, production, supply, trafficking and distribution of narcotic drugs and psychotropic substances, with strict respect for the sovereignty and territorial integrity of States and the principle of non-interference in their internal affairs;

5. We shall increase our efforts and resources in order to intensify international cooperation and concerted action, based upon the prin-

[1] United Nations, *Treaty Series*, vol. 520, No. 7515.

[2] *Ibid.*, vol. 976, No. 14152.

[3] *Ibid.*, vol. 1019, No. 14956.

[4] E/CONF.82/15 and Corr.2.

[5] *Report of the International Conference on Drug Abuse and Illicit Trafficking, Vienna, 17-26 June 1987* (United Nations publication, Sales No. E.87.1.18), chap. I, sect. B.

[6] *Ibid.*, sect. A.

ciple of shared responsibility, including the necessary cooperation and assistance to affected States, when requested, in the economic, health, social, judicial and law enforcement sectors in order to strengthen the capabilities of States to deal with the problem in all its aspects;

6. We shall pursue strategies that are comprehensive and multidisciplinary in scope and that comprise measures to eliminate illicit demand for narcotic drugs and psychotropic substances, cultivation of illicit crops and illicit drug trafficking, to prevent the misuse of the financial and banking systems and to promote effective treatment, rehabilitation and social reintegration;

7. We commend the efforts made by some States in the fight against illicit drug production, trafficking and consumption and urge that current levels of international cooperation be increased and strengthened;

8. We condemn the crime of illicit drug trafficking in all its forms and reaffirm our political commitment to concerted international action;

9. We are convinced that the international fight against illicit drug trafficking should be pursued in full conformity with the principles of non-interference in internal affairs and respect for the territorial integrity of States and free from unrelated political motivations;

10. We shall continue our national efforts in the simultaneous fight on all levels against the phenomenon of illicit drug trafficking, with special emphasis on the need for stronger measures to eliminate illicit demand for narcotic drugs and psychotropic substances;

11. We shall reinforce our polices aiming at the prevention, reduction and elimination of illicit demand;

12. We shall intensify our efforts in the fields of health, education and public information, including well-targeted campaigns involving the relevant United Nations specialized agendas and non-governmental organizations, as an essential measure to reduce illicit demand;

13. We urge the international community to increase economic and technical cooperation to developing countries and to facilitate trade flows in support of viable alternative income schemes, such as crop-substitution programmes, by means of integrated rural development strategies, including facilitation of appropriate efficient marketing and sound economic policies, so as to eliminate illicit cultivation and production of narcotic drugs;

14. We call for international cooperation to assist and support transit countries, in particular developing transit countries, by implementing appropriate programmes of technical and financial assistance through competent international or regional organizations for the purpose of expanding and strengthening the infrastructure needed for effective control and prevention of illicit drug trafficking;

15. We stress the need for effective action to prevent the diversion for illicit purposes of precursors and other chemicals, materials and equipment frequently used in the illicit manufacture of narcotic drugs and psychotropic substances;

16. We urge the international community to strengthen international cooperation under mutually agreed conditions through bilateral, regional and multilateral mechanisms;

17. We stress that all initiatives undertaken within the United Nations in the field of international drug abuse control shall take into consideration the competence of its organs as defined in the Charter of the United Nations;

18. We shall further develop and utilize, to the maximum extent, existing bilateral and other international instruments or arrangements for enhancing international legal and law enforcement cooperation;

19. We reaffirm the principles set forth in the Declaration of the International Conference on Drug Abuse and Illicit Trafficking[1] and undertake to apply, as appropriate, the recommendations of the Comprehensive Multidisciplinary Outline of Future Activities in Drug Abuse Control;[2]

20. We urge States to ratify or accede to the United Nations conventions in the field of drug abuse control and illicit trafficking and, to the extent they are able to do so, to apply provisionally the terms of the United Nations Convention against Illicit Traffic in Narcotic Drugs and Psychotropic Substances;

21. We commend the important work carried out by the organizations of the United Nations system in the field of international drug abuse control with regard to combating the abuse and production of and trafficking in illicit drugs and psychotropic substances, as well as the work done in other multilateral forums;

22. We commend also the positive action undertaken by the Division of Narcotic Drugs of the Secretariat, the International Narcotics Control Board and its secretariat, and the United Nations Fund for Drug Abuse Control;

23. We call upon the United Nations, the specialized agencies and other organizations of the United Nations system to give higher priority in their programmes of work, in accordance with existing procedures, to international measures to combat illicit production, supply, demand, trafficking and distribution of narcotic drugs and psychotropic substances;

24. We emphasize the importance of the development and implementation of a United Nations system-wide action plan aimed at the fulfilment of all existing mandates for drug abuse control and the implementation of subsequent decisions of intergovernmental bodies throughout the United Nations system;

25. We shall strengthen and enhance the capability of the United Nations to achieve more effective and coordinated cooperation at the international, regional and national levels against the threats posed by illicit production and illicit trafficking and abuse of narcotic drugs and psychotropic substances;

26. We stress the need to reinforce United Nations structures for drug abuse control in order to increase their effectiveness and status;

27. We recognize the need for additional financial and human resources, which shall be made available for United Nations activities in the area of drug abuse control, bearing in mind the Organization's additional responsibilities in that regard;

28. We attach high priority to the speedy and effective implementation of the Global Programme of Action;

29. We proclaim the period from 1991 to 2000 the United Nations Decade against Drug Abuse, to be devoted to effective and sustained national, regional and international actions to promote the implementation of the Global Programme of Action, taking into account and paying due consideration to the guidelines for international decades recommended by the Economic and Social Council in its resolution 1988/63 of 27 July 1988;

30. We resolve to keep under constant review the activities set out in the present Declaration and in the Global Programme of Action.

Global Programme of Action

I. Introduction

1. The international community confronts a dramatic problem of drug abuse and the illicit cultivation, production, processing, distribution and trafficking of narcotic drugs and psychotropic substances, insufficiently effective controls over or monitoring of specific chemical substances and monitoring of the economic benefits of drug trafficking. States are not in a position to deal with this scourge individually. Therefore, international solidarity and the concerted, collective and simultaneous action of the international community are required.

2. An important aspect of the fight against drug abuse has been the elaboration of international legal instruments. The adoption of the Single Convention on Narcotic Drugs of 1961[3] and of that Convention as amended by the 1972 Protocol Amending the Single Conven-

[1] *Report of the International Conference on Drug Abuse and Illicit Trafficking, Vienna, 17-26 June 1987* (United Nations publication, Sales No. E.87.1.18), chap. I, sect. B.

[2] *Ibid.*, sect. A.

[3] United Nations, *Treaty Series,* vol. 520, No. 7515.

tion on Narcotic Drugs of 1961[1] and of the Convention on Psychotropic Substances of 1971[2] were first important steps in that direction.

3. By its resolution 40/122 of 13 December 1985, the General Assembly decided to convene an International Conference on Drug Abuse and Illicit Trafficking. The Conference took place at Vienna from 17 to 26 June 1987 and adopted a Declaration[3] and a Comprehensive Multidisciplinary Outline of Future Activities in Drug Abuse Control.[4]

4. In order to reinforce and supplement the measures provided in existing legal instruments and to counter the new magnitude and extent of illicit drug trafficking and its grave consequences, a United Nations plenipotentiary conference, held at Vienna from 25 November to 20 December 1988, adopted the United Nations Convention against Illicit Traffic in Narcotic Drugs and Psychotropic Substances.[5]

5. The General Assembly, in its resolution 44/16 of 1 November 1989, decided to convene a special session of the Assembly to consider, as a matter of urgency, the question of international cooperation against illicit production, supply, demand, trafficking and distribution of narcotic drugs, with a view to expanding the scope and increasing the effectiveness of such cooperation.

6. Cognizant of the above, and following extensive deliberations at its seventeenth special session, the General Assembly, in order to achieve the goal of an international society free of illicit drugs and drug abuse, adopts the present Global Programme of Action and commits itself to its full and speedy implementation, where necessary following due consideration of the modalities by the competent technical bodies.

7. In adopting the Global Programme of Action, and without prejudice to the existing procedures, the General Assembly also decides to accord, within the United Nations system, a higher priority to the allocation of the necessary financial, personnel and other resources. There is a need for all parts of the United Nations system to galvanize efforts to improve international cooperation to stamp out the scourge of illicit drugs and drug abuse. The requirement for additional resources for that purpose is explicitly recognized, in the full expectation that that will be reflected as a high priority in the medium-term plan for the period 1992-1997 and in the programme budget for the biennium 1992-1993, as well as future medium-term plans and biennial budgets. The General Assembly also recognizes that the effective implementation of the Global Programme of Action will require examination of the structure of the existing drug control units based at the United Nations Office at Vienna with a view to enhancing their effectiveness and status in the system.

II. Activities of the Global Programme of Action

8. The Comprehensive Multidisciplinary Outline of Future Activities in Drug Abuse Control[6] shall be used by national authorities and interested organizations as a basis for developing and translating into action, at the national, regional and international levels, to the widest extent possible, balanced strategies aimed at combating all aspects of drug abuse and illicit trafficking. Those strategies shall include, in particular, the aspects described below.

A. Prevention and reduction of drug abuse with a view to elimination of the illicit demand for narcotic drugs and psychotropic substances

9. States[7] shall give higher priority to prevention and reduction of drug abuse with a view to elimination of the illicit demand for narcotic drugs and psychotropic substances at the national and international levels. National strategies, plans and programmes for combating drug abuse shall be elaborated, adopted and implemented through the necessary policy and legislative adjustments, including the allocation of appropriate resources and services for prevention, treatment, rehabilitation and social reintegration.

10. The causes generating illicit demand for narcotic drugs and psychotropic substances, including its recent increase, shall be analysed and the necessary measures shall be identified in order to combat drug abuse at the root of the problem. In this regard, special attention shall be given to the social causes underlying the drug problem, which should be adequate reflected in national social policies.

11. Information and education programmes shall be used to prevent the abuse of narcotic drugs and psychotropic substances and to increase awareness of their harmful effects. In this context, States, relevant specialized agencies and non-governmental organizations shall coordinate and exchange information with a view to initiating well-targeted campaigns in this field.

12. The role of the United Nations as an advisory centre for collecting, analysing and disseminating information and experience in the field of reduction of illicit demand, for reviewing and evaluating national scientific programmes in the field of combating drug abuse and for coordinating efforts of States concerning those activities shall be further enhanced. Bodies of the United Nations system such as the United Nations Educational, Scientific and Cultural Organization, the United Nations Children's Fund (including its national committees), the United Nations Development Programme, the World Health Organization, the International Labour Organisation and the United Nations information centres shall play a more active role in collecting and disseminating information and exchanging experience.

13. States shall establish and promote national systems to assess the extent of drug abuse and to collect data on trends of abuse. For that purpose, they shall establish data bases that should be based on the international drug abuse assessment system being developed by the Division of Narcotic Drugs of the Secretariat with financial support from the United Nations Fund for Drug Abuse Control. The Division, in collaboration with other United Nations drug control bodies and the World Health Organization, shall assist Governments in establishing such data bases and shall work to establish a data base concerning the nature and extent of drug abuse at the international level.

14. The Division of Narcotic Drugs shall publish and update periodically a digest listing national focal points that deal with various aspects of the drug problem, including information on direct channels of communication.

15. In order to assess the level of national and international progress towards prevention and reduction of the demand for narcotic drugs and psychotropic substances with a view to its elimination, and in implementing the seven targets set out in chapter I of the Comprehensive Multidisciplinary Outline of Future Activities in Drug Abuse Control, the Division of Narcotic Drugs shall submit, by 31 December each year, a succinct questionnaire to all Governments, regional intergovernmental organizations, and non-governmental organizations in consultative status with the Economic and Social Council. The questionnaire shall request details of action taken in this regard at the national and regional levels, the results achieved by the measures taken, and details of any practical difficulties encountered. The Secretary-General is requested to prepare a report, in collaboration with the International Labour Organisation, the United Nations Educational, Scientific and Cultural Organization and the World Health Organization, to be submitted to the Commission on Narcotic Drugs at its regular and special sessions analysing the information submit-

1 *Ibid.*, vol. 976, No. 14152.

2 *Ibid.*, vol. 1019, No. 14956.

3 *Report of the International Conference on Drug Abuse and Illicit Trafficking, Vienna, 17-26 June 1987* (United Nations publication, Sales No. E.87.1.18), chap. I, sect. B.

4 *Ibid.*, sect. A.

5 E/CONF.82/15 and Corr.2.

6 *Report of the International Conference on Drug Abuse and Illicit Trafficking, Vienna, 17-26 June 1987* (United Nations publication, Sales No. E.87.1.18), chap. I, sect. A.

7 References to States in the present Global Programme of Action should be understood to refer also to regional economic integration organizations within the limits of their competence.

ted and assessing, in particular, the best means of providing assistance to States in furthering demand-reduction strategies.

16. States and regional intergovernmental organizations shall cooperate fully in the preparation of that report by providing in good time the information required by the questionnaire.

17. In the light of the experience of operating that questionnaire and reporting system, the Commission on Narcotic Drugs shall consider the necessity and feasibility of elaborating, under the auspices of the United Nations, an international instrument that would deal especially with the reduction of the illicit demand for drugs and that would provide, *inter alia*, comprehensive and specific measures for the control and elimination of illicit demand for narcotic drugs and psychotropic substances, as well as for treatment and rehabilitation of drug addicts.

18. The recommendations of all international high-level meetings aimed at the reduction and eventual elimination of illicit demand for narcotic drugs and psychotropic substances, including those of the World Ministerial Summit to Reduce Demand for Drugs and to Combat the Cocaine Threat, to be held in London from 9 to 11 April 1990, shall be submitted to States for reference, if requested, in order to make it possible for them to consider such recommendations in the elaboration of their national anti-drug campaigns and policies.

19. The United Nations Educational, Scientific and Cultural Organization, in collaboration with the World Health Organization and other appropriate United Nations bodies, shall be encouraged to solicit, compile and analyse information on effective prevention strategies, including public information, education programmes and professional training, and on programme evaluation techniques and to disseminate that material to States upon request.

20. The United Nations Children's Fund shall be encouraged to give financial support to developing countries in order to enhance their campaigns to prevent drug abuse by children and the use of children for the illicit production and traffic in narcotic drugs and psychotropic substances, as well as for implementing programmes to rehabilitate such children.

21. The International Labour Organisation shall be invited to provide, upon request, advice on education programmes to reduce drug abuse in the work-place and monitor their effectiveness.

22. Measures for the prevention of drug abuse shall be developed and included to the extent possible in the curricula of all educational institutions if circumstances so require. The expertise of relevant United Nations bodies should be made available to all countries, in particular developing countries, in order to assist them in elaborating such curricula.

23. Information on the rational prescribing and use of narcotic drugs and psychotropic substances and pharmaceutical preparations containing such substances shall be incorporated into the curricula of training institutions for health-care personnel.

24. The World Health Organization, in collaboration with United Nations drug control bodies, non-governmental organizations and other organizations involved in the rational use of pharmaceutical preparations containing narcotic drugs and psychotropic substances, shall be encouraged to assist national educational authorities in developing training materials and conducting training courses to ensure that medical practitioners and other health personnel are well trained in rational prescribing and use of narcotic drugs and psychotropic substances.

25. The mass media shall be encouraged to publish and disseminate information in support of national and international strategies for the elimination of illicit demand for narcotic drugs and psychotropic substances.

26. The establishment of national committees or other *ad hoc* structures aimed at mobilizing public support and the participation of communities and at cooperating in and implementing the activities emanating from the Global Programme of Action shall be considered.

27. States shall, as appropriate, promote increased cooperation with and involvement of non-governmental organizations in the field of reduction of illicit demand, thus encouraging initiatives and programmes at the grass-roots level.

28. Appropriate United Nations bodies shall be invited to collaborate with non-governmental organizations with special expertise in the field of narcotic drugs and psychotropic substances to identify and make available technical expertise on strategies and methods for reduction of illicit demand.

29. The United Nations shall undertake a review of activities of the United Nations system and the specialized agencies for the reduction of illicit demand in order to identify the needs for intensified action consistent with the principles of the Global Programme of Action.

B. Treatment, rehabilitation and social reintegration of drug addicts

30. National strategies in the health, social, legal and penal fields shall contain programmes for the social reintegration, rehabilitation and treatment of drug abusers and drug-addicted offenders. Such programmes shall be in conformity with national laws and regulations and be based on respect for basic human rights and the dignity of the individual, showing due regard for the diverse needs of individual drug addicts.

31. The United Nations shall act as a clearing-house for information on effective policies and techniques, programme modalities and resource materials for the treatment, rehabilitation and occupational reintegration of former drug addicts. The World Health Organization and the International Labour Organisation, in collaboration with other organizations of the United Nations system and non-governmental organizations, shall be encouraged to contribute to that end.

32. The relevant United Nations bodies should render assistance to interested States, in particular developing countries, in their programmes for treatment and rehabilitation of drug abusers.

33. Training programmes relating to the latest developments and techniques in the field of treatment of drug addiction and rehabilitation and reintegration of former addicts shall be conducted more regularly at the national, regional and international levels. Governments, the relevant United Nations bodies, the specialized agencies, intergovernmental organizations and non-governmental organizations in a position to do so shall, upon request, provide advice, information and proposals on existing training programmes, new methods and techniques and other general guidelines for States wishing to develop their training programmes further.

34. The World Health Organization shall be encouraged to work with Governments with a view to facilitating access to drug-treatment programmes and to strengthening the capacity of primary health care to respond to drug-related health problems.

35. The World Health Organization shall be encouraged to continue to explore with Governments the development of health education programmes and policies for the reduction of risk and harm of drug abuse as a means of preventing the transmission by drug abusers of the human immunodeficiency virus (HIV) and of securing appropriate treatment and counselling for drug abusers who are HIV-positive or who have developed acquired immunodeficiency syndrome (AIDS), and to report thereon.

36. The International Labour Organisation should prepare and publish guidelines for programmes to reintegrate former addicts into occupational activities or vocational training.

37. States shall, as appropriate, facilitate and promote the involvement of non-governmental organizations in all areas of treatment and rehabilitation and intensify their cooperation with the relevant United Nations bodies.

C. Control of supply of narcotic drugs and psychotropic substances

1. *Eradication and substitution of illicit production of narcotic drugs, and eradication of illicit processing of such drugs and of illicit production and diversion of psychotropic substances*

38. States shall consider, at the national and international levels, means by which the internal sector of those economies that are affected by the illicit production and processing of narcotic drugs and psychotropic substances might be strengthened, in order to support and strengthen the implementation, by competent national authori-

ties, of effective anti-drug programmes, including the following measures:

(a) Prompt identification, eradication and substitution of illicit cultivation of narcotic plants, taking into account the need to protect the environment; for the purpose of crop surveys and monitoring efforts, such technologies as high-resolution satellite imagery and aerial photography could be used when agreement has been reached with the Government concerned;

(b) Further development and implementation of comprehensive and well-articulated reduction programmes with a view to eliminating illicit production of narcotic drugs and psychotropic substances in countries affected by illicit production, taking particular account of traditional licit uses of such cultivation;

(c) Identification and provision of further incentives for crop substitution;

(d) Assessment and study, by the United Nations Environment Programme, of effects on the environment of the expanding cultivation and production of narcotic drugs and the use and disposal of chemical substances related to those activities, as well as methods used for the eradication of illicit production of narcotic drugs;

(e) Extension of the scope of economic and technical cooperation in support of crop substitution and integrated rural development programmes and other economic and technical programmes aimed at reducing illicit production and processing of narcotic drugs and psychotropic substances;

(f) Establishment of complementary programmes in the fields of employment, health, housing and education;

(g) Elaboration and implementation of programmes for agroindustrial development;

(h) Elaboration and implementation of programmes for economic recovery of the social and economic sectors in countries that are adversely affected by the diversion for supply-reduction programmes of resources that would otherwise be used for development.

39. The external sectors of those economies that are affected by illicit production and processing of narcotic drugs and psychotropic substances shall be strengthened in order to support and strengthen the implementation by competent national authorities of effective anti-drug programmes by the following means:

(a) Consideration of measures to strengthen international cooperation to facilitate trade flows, in particular measures to create expanded opportunities for trade and investment in order to provide access to international markets for crop-substitution products and other goods produced by countries affected by the illicit production and processing of narcotic drugs;

(b) Consideration by States of entering into multilateral, bilateral or regional agreements with countries affected by illicit drug production and processing, with a view to facilitating access by those countries to international markets and to assisting them in strengthening and adapting their internal capacity to produce exportable goods;

(c) Consideration of economic and other forms of cooperation with developing countries directly affected by the illicit transit of narcotic drugs through their territories, including measures to create expanded opportunities for trade and investment;

(d) Regular submission by States to the relevant United Nations drug control bodies of information on the extent of the manufacture, availability and abuse of illicit synthetic drugs in their territories.

2. *Licit production, manufacture and supply of narcotic drugs and psychotropic substances*

40. A balance shall be maintained between demand and supply of raw materials, intermediates and final products for legitimate uses, including medical and scientific purposes.

41. International cooperation, solidarity and assistance are called for to overcome the problem of excess stock of opiate raw materials in traditional supplier countries. This may include international assistance, particularly to developing countries, to help them establish the necessary opiate drug management régime to enable them to meet their potential legitimate need for opiates.

3. *Cooperation on the multilateral level*

42. The United Nations Fund for Drug Abuse Control, in collaboration, where appropriate, with the United Nations Development Programme and other United Nations bodies, is invited to elaborate for consideration by States a subregional strategy covering all aspects of drug abuse control and concentrating on the most affected areas where the problems are most complex and grave. States shall increase their cooperation with the Fund in support of such a subregional strategy.

43. States should endeavour to obtain the support of international, regional and national financial institutions, within their respective areas of competence, with the goal of identifying alternative development and crop-substitution programmes to support countries so that they can carry out sound economic policies and effective programmes against illicit drugs. States should also encourage those institutions to consider the economic and social consequences of drug trafficking when analysing the economic systems of those countries. In this regard, those institutions should consider availing themselves of assistance from and cooperation with the United Nations Fund for Drug Abuse Control.

44. Specialized agencies and other United Nations bodies such as the United Nations Development Programme and the Food and Agriculture Organization of the United Nations, as well as the international financial institutions, in accordance with their mandates, should consider the possibility of undertaking further activities in the field of prevention and substitution of illicit production of narcotic drugs.

4. *Monitoring and control mechanisms*

45. States shall take all necessary measures, such as the conclusion of bilateral and regional agreements, to establish monitoring and control systems to prevent diversion from legitimate purposes of specific chemical substances, materials and equipment frequently used in the illicit manufacture of narcotic drugs and psychotropic substances, in particular through the application of articles 12 and 13 of the United Nations Convention against Illicit Traffic in Narcotic Drugs and Psychotropic Substances adopted in 1988.[1]

46. Consideration shall be given to the convening of an international conference on the production and distribution of chemical products used in the illicit production of narcotic drugs and psychotropic substances, in order to coordinate efforts for more effective prevention of the diversion of precursor chemicals, specific substances, materials and equipment for illicit purposes. It is desirable that States include representatives of manufacturing and distribution enterprises in their delegations to that conference.

47. The World Health Organization, in collaboration with the Division of Narcotic Drugs and the International Narcotics Control Board, should assist national drug regulatory authorities in developing and strengthening their pharmaceutical administrations and control laboratories in order to enable them to control pharmaceutical preparations containing narcotic drugs and psychotropic substances.

48. Governmental, intergovernmental and non-governmental organizations and the United Nations shall be encouraged to cooperate in measures within the guidelines set out in the Comprehensive Multidisciplinary Outline of Future Activities in Drug Abuse Control[2] to strengthen national and international systems of control of narcotic drugs and psychotropic substances, in particular those established under the Single Convention on Narcotic Drugs of 1961,[3] and that Convention as amended by the 1972 Protocol Amending the Single Convention on Narcotic Drugs of 1961[4] and the Convention on Psychotropic Substances of 1971.[5]

---

1 E/CONF.82/15 and Corr.2.

2 *Report of the International Conference on Drug Abuse and Illicit Trafficking, Vienna, 17-26 June 1987* (United Nations publication, Sales No. E.87.1.18), chap. I, sect. A.

3 *Ibid.*, vol. 520, No. 7515.

4 *Ibid.*, vol. 976, No. 14152.

5 *Ibid.*, vol. 1019, No. 14956.

49. The International Narcotics Control Board is invited to advise States, at their request, and to extend its technical cooperation activities with a view to furthering the aims of the Single Convention on Narcotic Drugs of 1961 and that Convention as amended by the 1972 Protocol Amending the Single Convention on Narcotic Drugs of 1961, the Convention on Psychotropic Substances of 1971 and the United Nations Convention against Illicit Traffic in Narcotic Drugs and Psychotropic Substances adopted in 1988.

50. Special attention shall be paid to cooperation that will enable States to strengthen their drug detection and pharmaceutical control laboratories, as well as their police and customs activities in the field of drug control.

D. Suppression of illicit trafficking in narcotic drugs and psychotropic substances

1. *Traffic*

51. States shall proceed rapidly and make every effort to ratify or accede to the United Nations Convention against Illicit Traffic in Narcotic Drugs and Psychotropic Substances, adopted in 1988, in order to enable the entry into force of the Convention, preferably by the end of 1990.

52. The United Nations, in particular the Division of Narcotic Drugs, the International Narcotics Control Board and the United Nations Fund for Drug Abuse Control, shall provide expertise and assistance to States, at their request, to enable them to establish the legislative and administrative measures for the ratification and effective implementation of the United Nations Convention.

53. States shall, to the extent and where they are able to do so, apply provisionally the measures set forth in the United Nations Convention.

54. Consistent with the United Nations Convention, consideration shall be given to the conclusion of bilateral, regional and multilateral agreements and other arrangements aimed at suppressing illicit trafficking in narcotic drugs and psychotropic substances.

55. States that have not yet done so shall consider ratification of or accession to the Single Convention on Narcotic Drugs of 1961[1] and that Convention as amended by the 1972 Protocol Amending the Single Convention on Narcotic Drugs of 1961[2] and the Convention on Psychotropic Substances of 1971.[3]

56. States in a position to do so and the organizations of the United Nations system, in particular the United Nations Fund for Drug Abuse Control, shall provide appropriate technical and financial support to enable States, at their request, to establish effective mechanisms against illicit trafficking in narcotic drugs and psychotropic substances. Particular attention shall be given, in that regard, to the strengthening of interdiction capabilities of transit States, including control of land, sea and air boundaries. To that end, States should undertake an analysis of the methods and routes used for illicit transit traffic in narcotic drugs and psychotropic substances, and should monitor them in their respective territories on a continuing basis, bearing in mind that the routes and methods used change frequently and affect a growing number of States. States shall consider appropriate information-sharing in this respect on a bilateral, regional or multilateral basis.

57. Interested States may consider, in conformity with international law and the Charter of the United Nations, the possibility of jointly establishing border inspection check-points, with a view to suppressing illicit trans-boundary movement of narcotic drugs and psychotropic substances, without affecting the national sovereignty and territorial integrity of States.

58. Specialized agencies such as the International Civil Aviation Organization and the International Maritime Organization, in collaboration with member States and intergovernmental and non-governmental organizations, shall be invited to expand the development of programmes whereby such organizations and member States work with the transportation industry to suppress illicit trafficking in narcotic drugs and psychotropic substances.

59. States shall make increased use of the meetings of Heads of National Drug Law Enforcement Agencies and other intergovernmental organizations, such as the Customs Cooperation Council and the International Criminal Police Organization (Interpol), regional cooperation arrangements and other relevant institutional frameworks, for the purpose of coordinating cooperation in law enforcement and expanding programmes of training for law enforcement personnel in investigative matters and methods, interdiction and narcotics intelligence.

60. The United Nations, in particular the United Nations Fund for Drug Abuse Control, should assist States, at their request, in equipping and strengthening their law enforcement authorities and criminal justice systems.

2. *Distribution*

61. States shall strengthen their national efforts to curb and eradicate domestic illicit commerce and distribution of narcotic drugs and psychotropic substances.

E. Measures to be taken against the effects of money derived from, used in or intended for use in illicit drug trafficking, illegal financial flows and illegal use of the banking system

62. Priority shall be accorded to the implementation of the United Nations Convention against Illicit Traffic in Narcotic Drugs and Psychotropic Substances, adopted in 1988, and the conclusion of bilateral regional and multilateral agreements on trading, freezing and seizure and forfeiture or confiscation of property and proceeds derived from, used in or intended for use in illicit drug trafficking.

63. Mechanisms shall be developed to prevent the banking system and other financial institutions from being used for the processing and laundering of drug-related money. To this end, consideration should be given by States to entering into bilateral, regional and multilateral agreements and developing mechanisms to trace property and proceeds derived from, used in or intended for use in drug-related activities through the international banking system, facilitate access to banking records and provide for the exchange of information between law enforcement, regulatory or investigative agencies concerning the financial flow of property or proceeds related to illicit drug trafficking.

64. The Division of Narcotic Drugs of the Secretariat, in cooperation with the Customs Cooperation Council and the International Criminal Police Organization (Interpol), should promote bilateral or regional exchanges of information between governmental regulatory or investigative agencies concerning the financial flow of illicit drug proceeds.

65. The Division of Narcotic Drugs and Interpol shall be invited to develop a repository of laws and regulations on money laundering, currency reporting, bank secrecy and forfeiture of property and proceeds, as well as procedures and practices designed to prevent banking systems and other financial institutions from money laundering, and shall make this information available to States, at their request.

66. States shall consider enacting legislation to prevent the use of the banking system for the processing and laundering of drug-related money, *inter alia* through declaring such activities criminal offences.

67. States shall consider enacting legislation to permit the seizure and forfeiture of property and proceeds derived from, used in or intended for use in illicit drug trafficking. To that end, consideration should be given by States to concluding bilateral and multilateral agreements to enhance the effectiveness of international cooperation taking into particular account article 5, paragraph 5, of the United Nations Convention against Illicit Traffic in Narcotic Drugs and Psychotropic Substances.

68. States shall encourage international, regional and national financial associations to develop guidelines to assist their members in cooperating with government authorities in identifying, detecting,

---

1 United Nations, *Treaty Series*, vol. 520, No. 7515.

2 *Ibid.*, vol. 976, No. 14152.

3 *Ibid.*, vol. 1019, No. 14956.

trading freezing and seizing proceeds and property related to illicit trafficking in narcotic drugs and psychotropic substances.

69. The elaboration of international agreements providing for stringent controls on money derived from, used in or intended for use in drug-related activities and penalizing the laundering of such money might be considered. Such instruments might also deal with the forfeiture or confiscation of funds, proceeds and property acquired through revenues deriving from drug-related activities.

70. States shall consider measures on an international level, including the feasibility of a United Nations facility to strengthen the gathering, collation and exchange of information on the financial flow from drug-related funds, giving particular emphasis to principles, rules and national law concerning the protection of ongoing law enforcement investigations and of individuals with regard to automatic processing of personal data.

71. States should encourage international, regional and national financial institutions, within their respective areas of competence, to pay special attention, in their analyses of the economies of States, to the characteristics and magnitude of the conversion and transfer of drug-related monies in order to contribute to international efforts aimed at counteracting the negative economic and social consequences of the drug problem.

72. States shall consider the possibility of using forfeited property and proceeds for activities to combat drug abuse and illicit trafficking. In that context, the possible use of such proceeds and property or their equivalent value for United Nations drug-related activities shall also be taken into consideration.

73. All measures and proposals on possible action to prevent the use of the banking systems and financial institutions for money laundering, such as the conclusions arising from the study undertaken by the Financial Action Task Force, established at the Summit of seven major industrial nations, held in Paris from 14 to 16 July 1989, shall be made available to all States for information.

F. Strengthening of judicial and legal systems, including law enforcement

74. States shall, as soon as possible, ratify or accede to the United Nations conventions in the field of drug abuse control and illicit trafficking.

75. States in a position to do so and the United Nations, strengthening their action in coordination with the regional institutes of the United Nations with mandates in this sphere, shall provide advice and legal and technical assistance to enable States, at their request, to adapt their national legislation to international conventions and decisions dealing with drug abuse and illicit trafficking.

76. States are invited to give consideration to the model treaties on mutual assistance in criminal matters and on extradition, which contain specific provisions related to illicit traffic in narcotic drugs and psychotropic substances and are to be dealt with by the Eighth United Nations Congress on the Prevention of Crime and the Treatment of Offenders.

77. States shall encourage international and regional organizations to elaborate model agreements on cooperation among customs officials, law enforcement agencies and other interested organs in the field of combating drug abuse and illicit trafficking.

78. The scope of international cooperation in support of technical assistance programmes aimed at the strengthening of judicial, legal and law enforcement systems, in particular in the field of the administration of justice, shall be extended. Particular attention shall be given to the training of personnel at all levels.

79. Measures to protect the judiciary from any form of exposure and intimidation threatening its independence and integrity shall be studied and promoted.

80. The United Nations shall act as a clearing-house for information on training programmes in drug law enforcement, including training for national narcotics agents in investigative methods, interdiction and narcotics intelligence.

81. Consideration shall be given to establishing a capability within the United Nations system to coordinate the provision by States of training and equipment to other States, at their request, for their own anti-drug operations, within their territories, to inhibit the use, interdict the supply and eliminate the illicit trafficking of drugs.

82. Since the International Law Commission has been requested to consider the question of establishing an international criminal court or other international trial mechanism with jurisdiction over persons alleged to be engaged in illicit trafficking in narcotic drugs across national frontiers, the Administrative Committee on Coordination shall consider, in its annual adjustments to the United Nations system-wide action plan on drug abuse control requested by the General Assembly in its resolution 44/141 of 15 December 1989, the report of the International Law Commission on the question.

83. States shall consider the appropriateness of establishing arrangements, on the basis of bilateral, regional and multilateral agreements, which would allow them to benefit from one another's criminal justice system in dealing with similar drug-related offences.

84. Consideration shall be given to establishing a register of antidrug expertise and services, under the supervision of the Division of Narcotic Drugs, which could be made available to States, at their request.

85. A review should be undertaken of international and regional law enforcement activities funded or sponsored by the United Nations, as well as those of other intergovernmental organizations and regional arrangements, to ensure a coherent approach to law enforcement activities within the overall context of the Global Programme of Action.

G. Measures to be taken against the diversion of arms and explosives and illicit traffic by vessels, aircraft and vehicles

86. States shall consider the adoption of measures, within their territories, to strengthen arrangements for controlling or monitoring the licit transportation of narcotic drugs and psychotropic substances including the vessels, aircraft and vehicles being used for that purpose so as to prevent their misuse for the illicit transportation of narcotic drugs and psychotropic substances.

87. Effective measures should be taken to prevent illicit and covert transfers of arms and explosives and their diversion to illicit drug traffic-related activities.

88. Alarmed by the growing link between illicit traffic in narcotic drugs, illegal activities of mercenaries and subversive and terrorist activities, States shall take prompt measures on their prevention.

89. States shall take strict measures to prevent private aircraft, vessels and vehicles registered in their territory from engaging in illicit drug trafficking and related activities.

H. Resources and structure

90. There is need both for optimum utilization of existing resources of the United Nations drug-related units and for additional resources to be allocated to those units in order to enable them fully to implement their mandates, bearing in mind their increased responsibilities

91. A higher priority shall be accorded to United Nations drug control activities in the medium-term plan for the period 1992-1997 and in the corresponding biennial budgets, and the General Assembly, at its forty-fifth session, is invited to take appropriate action in this regard, in accordance with existing procedures.

92. Priority shall be given to providing, on both a short-term and long-term basis, extrabudgetary support to enhance the efficiency of the United Nations structure for drug abuse control and to achieve and promote a truly comprehensive global programme of action.

93. Intensification of efforts at the national level and increased intergovernmental cooperation require a commensurate strengthening of the United Nations drug control organs and their secretariats. Against this background, the functioning of the United Nations structure for drug abuse control needs to be reviewed and assessed, in accordance with the mandate given to the Secretary-General by the General Assembly in paragraph 4 of its resolution 44/141, for the purpose of identifying alternative structural possibilities, the end result being the establishment of a stronger, more efficient United Nations drug

control structure with enhanced status, with a report to be made to the General Assembly at its forty-fifth session.

94. Attention shall be given to the need for (a) coherence of actions within the United Nations drug-related units and coordination, complementarity and non-duplication of all drug-related activities across the United Nations system; (b) integration of drug-related information within the United Nations system; (c) integration of the reduction of illicit demand in United Nations programming; (d) integration of law enforcement field expertise in United Nations programmes; (e) compliance with all non-discretionary obligations mandated by the three drug control conventions; and 0 an estimate of resources necessary to carry out these mandates successfully.

95. More States should contribute financial and other resources to the operational activities of the United Nations Fund for Drug Abuse Control in order to enable the Fund to expand its technical cooperation programmes and to develop an operational structure capable of assisting States in joint efforts on the subregional level.

III. Follow-Up Measures

96. States should take the necessary measures to promote and implement the Global Programme of Action and to translate it into practical action to the widest possible extent at the national, regional and international levels. The United Nations and its relevant bodies and specialized agencies, other relevant intergovernmental organizations and non-governmental organizations should extend their cooperation and assistance to States in the promotion and implementation of the Global Programme of Action.

97. The Commission on Narcotic Drugs and the United Nations drug control bodies should continuously monitor the progress on the implementation of the Global Programme of Action, and the Secretary-General should report annually to the General Assembly on all activities relating to the Global Programme of Action and the efforts of Governments.

98. The Secretary-General shall, in consultation with all Member States, identify, whenever necessary, a limited number of experts, from different regions of the world, on various aspects pertaining to the drug problem to advise him and existing United Nations drug control units and other bodies and specialized agencies on specific issues dealt with in the Global Programme of Action that may require further elaboration. These experts shall be funded exclusively from voluntary contributions.

99. The United Nations Decade against Drug Abuse, covering the years 1991 to 2000, as proclaimed by the General Assembly in the Political Declaration adopted at its seventeenth special session, is a period for intensifying and sustaining international, regional and national efforts in the fight against drug abuse on the basis of the measures contained in the Global Programme of Action.

100. The International Day against Drug Abuse and Illicit Trafficking, 26 June, as proclaimed by the General Assembly in its resolution 4V112 of 7 December 1987, shall be observed in the continuing effort to raise public awareness of the fight against drug abuse and illicit trafficking in narcotic drugs and psychotropic substances, as well as to promote preventive measures.

46/104. United Nations International Drug Control Programme

Committee: 3
Vote: Adopted without a vote
Ref.: 47/101, 45/179

The General Assembly,

Recalling its resolution 45/179 of 21 December 1990, by which it requested the Secretary-General to create a single drug control programme to be called the United Nations International Drug Control Programme, based at Vienna, and to integrate fully therein the structures and the functions of the Division of Narcotic Drugs of the Secretariat, the secretariat of the International Narcotics Control Board and the United Nations Fund for Drug Abuse Control with the objective of enhancing the effectiveness and efficiency of the United Nations structure for drug control in keeping with the functions and mandates of the United Nations in this field,

Recalling also the Political Declaration and the Global Programme of Action adopted on 23 February 1990 at its seventeenth special session,[1]

Emphasizing that the problem of drug abuse and illicit trafficking has to be considered within the broader economic and social context,

Reaffirming the importance of the role of the United Nations International Drug Control Programme as the main focus for concerted international action for drug abuse control,

Underlining the role of the Commission on Narcotic Drugs as the principal United Nations policy-making body on drug control issues, and endorsing paragraph 1 (c) of Economic and Social Council resolution 1991/38 of 21 June 1991,

Reaffirming the importance of the full technical independence of the International Narcotics Control Board in accordance with article 9, paragraph 2, of the Single Convention on Narcotic Drugs of 1961,[2] and endorsing Economic and Social Council resolution 1991/48 of 21 June 1991 approving administrative arrangements between the Board and the United Nations International Drug Control Programme to ensure this independence,

Recognizing that international cooperation against illicit trafficking should be pursued in full conformity with the principles enshrined in the Charter of the United Nations and the principles of international law,

Having considered the report of the Secretary-General on the measures taken to implement resolution 45/179 on the enhancement of the United Nations structure for drug abuse control,[3]

Noting that in the consideration of the programme budget proposals submitted by the Secretary-General for the biennium 1992-1993[4] full account should be taken of the measures proposed pursuant to resolution 45/179,

Commending the United Nations International Drug Control Programme for the activities undertaken so far in the performance of the functions entrusted to it,

1. *Takes note with appreciation* of the report of the Secretary-General on the measures taken to implement resolution 45/179 on the enhancement of the United Nations structure for drug abuse control;

2. *Welcomes* the integration of the structures and functions of the Division of Narcotic Drugs, the secretariat of the International Narcotics Control Board and the United Nations Fund for Drug Abuse Control into a single international drug control programme based at Vienna;

3. *Emphasizes* the need for the Executive Director of the United Nations International Drug Control Programme to have the necessary degree of managerial flexibility to discharge effectively and expeditiously the functions of the Programme under the terms of United Nations treaties and resolutions relating to international drug control, while recognizing that the Programme is now a part of the United Nations Secretariat;

4. *Requests* that the restructuring process envisaged in resolution 45/179 and in the present resolution be completed as soon as possible so that the United Nations International Drug Control Programme can fulfil its mandates with enhanced effectiveness and efficiency;

5. *Endorses* Economic and Social Council resolution 1991/38, which calls on the Commission on Narcotic Drugs to give policy guidance to the United Nations International Drug Control Programme and to monitor its activities;

6. *Urges* the United Nations International Drug Control Programme to give special emphasis to the implementation of those issues from the Global Programme of Action identified as priorities by the

---

1 Resolution S-17/2, annex.

2 United Nations, *Treaty Series*, vol. 520, No. 7515.

3 A/46/480.

4 See *Official Records of the General Assembly, Forty-sixth Session, Supplement No. 6* (A/46/6/Rev.1).

Commission on Narcotic Drugs in its resolution 2 (XXXIV) adopted at its thirty-fourth session;[1]

7. *Requests* the Executive Director of the United Nations International Drug Control Programme, in accordance with the authority delegated to him by the Secretary-General, to coordinate and provide effective leadership for all United Nations drug control activities, in order to ensure coherence of actions within the Programme as well as coordination, complementarity and non-duplication of such activities across the United Nations system, and in this context actively to seek cooperation and support for a global approach from other international organizations, non-governmental organizations, bilateral programmes and national institutions;

8. *Strongly urges* all Governments to provide the fullest possible financial and political support to the United Nations International Drug Control Programme, in particular by increasing the extrabudgetary contributions to the Programme, with a view to expanding and strengthening its operational activities and technical cooperation in particular with developing countries;

9. *Endorses* the proposal of the Secretary-General to place the financial resources of the existing United Nations Fund for Drug Abuse Control under the direct responsibility of the Executive Director of the United Nations International Drug Control Programme as a fund for financing operational activities, mainly in developing countries;

10. *Emphasizes* that, in accordance with established United Nations priorities as contained in the medium-term plan for the period 1992-1997[2] adequate resources should be allocated so as to enable the United Nations International Drug Control Programme to carry out its activities and fulfil the functions assigned to it by resolution 45/179 and by other relevant General Assembly and Economic and Social Council resolutions;

11. *Requests* the Secretary-General to report to the General Assembly at its forty-seventh session on measures taken to implement the present resolution.

74th plenary meeting
16 December 1991

50/148. International Action to Combat Drug Abuse and Illicit Production and Drug Trafficking

Committee: 3
Vote: Adopted without a vote
Ref.: 49/168, 48/112, 47/102, 46/103, 45/149, 44/142, 43/122, 42/113, 41/127, 40/121, 39/143, 38/93, 38/122, 37/198, 36/132, 32/126

The General Assembly,

Recalling its resolutions 48/12 of 28 October 1993, 48/112 of 20 December 1993 and 49/168 of 23 December 1994,

Profoundly alarmed by the magnitude of the rising trend in drug abuse, illicit production and trafficking in narcotics and psychotropic substances, including synthetic or designer drugs, that threaten the health and well-being of millions of persons, in particular the youth, in all countries of the world,

Gravely concerned that, despite increased efforts by States and relevant international organizations, the illicit demand for, production of and traffic in narcotic drugs and psychotropic substances, including synthetic and designer drugs, have expanded globally and, therefore, continue to threaten seriously the socio-economic and political systems and the stability, national security and sovereignty of an increasing number of States,

Deeply alarmed by the growing violence and economic power of criminal organizations and terrorist groups that engage in the production of, traffic in and distribution of drugs, arms and precursors and essential chemicals, which at times places them beyond the reach of the law, corrupting institutions, undermining the full exercise of human rights and threatening the stability of many societies in the world,

Deeply alarmed also by the growing links at the transnational level between criminal organizations and terrorist groups engaged in drug trafficking activities and other criminal activities, such as money laundering, and illicit traffic of arms and precursors and essential chemicals,

Fully aware that States, the relevant organizations of the United Nations system and multilateral development banks need to accord a higher priority to dealing with this scourge, which undermines development, economic and political stability and democratic institutions, and the combat against which entails increasing economic costs for Governments and the irreparable loss of human lives,

Convinced of the desirability of closer coordination and cooperation among States in combating drug-related crimes, such as terrorism, illicit arms trade and money laundering, and bearing in mind the role that could be played by both the United Nations and regional organizations in this respect,

Reaffirming that a comprehensive framework for international cooperation in drug control is provided by the existing drug control conventions, the Declaration[3] and the Comprehensive Multidisciplinary Outline of Future Activities in Drug Abuse Control,[4] the Political Declaration and Global Programme of Action adopted by the General Assembly at its seventeenth special session, devoted to the question of international cooperation against illicit production, supply, demand, trafficking and distribution of narcotic and psychotropic substances,[5] the Declaration adopted by the World Ministerial Summit to Reduce the Demand for Drugs and to Combat the Cocaine Threat,[6] the United Nations System-Wide Action Plan on Drug Abuse Control,[7] the Naples Political Declaration and Global Plan of Action against Organized Transnational Crime[8] and other relevant international standards, and stressing the need for increased efforts to implement them,

Recognizing the efforts of countries that produce narcotic drugs for scientific, medicinal and therapeutic uses to prevent the diversion of such substances to illicit markets and to maintain production at a level consistent with licit demand in line with the Single Convention on Narcotic Drugs of 1961,[9]

Acknowledging that there are links, under certain circumstances, between poverty and the increase in the illicit production of and trafficking in narcotic drugs and psychotropic substances and that the promotion of the economic development of countries affected by the illicit drug trade requires appropriate measures, including strengthened international cooperation in support of alternative and sustainable development activities in the affected areas of those countries, which have as their objectives the reduction and elimination of illicit drug production,

Emphasizing the need for an analysis of transit routes used by drug traffickers, which are constantly changing and expanding to include a growing number of countries and regions in all parts of the world,

Underlining the role of the Commission on Narcotic Drugs as the principal United Nations policy-making body on drug control issues,

Reaffirming the leadership role of the United Nations International Drug Control Programme as the main focus for concerted international action for drug abuse control and commending the way in which it has carried out the functions entrusted to it,

1 See *Official Records of the Economic and Social Council, 1991, Supplement No. 4* (E/1991/24), chap. XIV, sect. A

2 *Official Records of the General Assembly, Forty-fifth Session, Supplement No. 6* (A/45/6/Rev.1), vol. II, programme 28.

3 See *Report of the International Conference on Drug Abuse and Illicit Trafficking, Vienna, 17-26 June 1987* (United Nations publication, Sales No. E.87.I.18),chap. I, sect. A.

4 *Ibid.*, sect. B.

5 Resolution S-17/2, annex.

6 A/45/262, annex.

7 See A/49/139-E/1994/57.

8 See A/49/748, annex, sect. I.A.

9 United Nations, *Treaty Series*, vol. 520, No. 7515.

Recognizing that the new forms of criminal activities of international drug trafficking organizations call for enhanced international cooperation as well as a renewal of the international commitment to fight against these menaces, and require the formulation of new strategies, approaches and objectives that, respectful of the sovereignty of States, can deal more effectively with the international operations of those involved in the illegal traffic of drugs and arms, the diversion of precursors and essential chemicals, and money laundering through financial and non-financial operations,

I

Respect for the Principles Enshrined in the Charter of the United Nations and International Law in the Fight Against Drug Abuse and Illicit Production and Trafficking

1. *Reaffirms* that the fight against drug abuse and illicit trafficking should not in any way justify violation of the principles enshrined in the Charter of the United Nations and international law, particularly respect for the sovereignty and territorial integrity of States and non-use of force or the threat of force in international relations;

2. *Calls upon* all States to intensify their actions to promote effective cooperation in the efforts to combat drug abuse and illicit trafficking, so as to contribute to a climate conducive to achieving this end, on the basis of the principles of equal rights and mutual respect;

II

International Action to Combat Drug Abuse and Illicit Production and Trafficking

1. *Renews its commitment* to further strengthening international cooperation and substantially increasing efforts against the illicit production, sale, demand, traffic and distribution of narcotics and psychotropic substances, based on the principle of shared responsibility and taking into account experience gained;

2. *Urges* all States to ratify or accede to and implement all the provisions of the Single Convention on Narcotic Drugs of 1961[1] as amended by the 1972 Protocol,[2] the Convention on Psychotropic Substances of 1971[3] and the United Nations Convention against Illicit Traffic in Narcotic Drugs and Psychotropic Substances of 1988;[4]

3. *Calls upon* all States to adopt adequate national laws and regulations, to strengthen national judicial systems and to carry out effective drug control activities in cooperation with other States in accordance with those international instruments;

4. *Requests* the United Nations International Drug Control Programme to continue to provide legal assistance to Member States that request it in adjusting their national laws, policies and infrastructures to implement the international drug control conventions, as well as assistance in training personnel responsible for applying the new laws;

5. *Supports* the focus on regional, subregional and national strategies for drug abuse control, particularly the master-plan approach, and urges the United Nations International Drug Control Programme to continue to complement those strategies with effective interregional strategies;

6. *Reaffirms* the danger and threat posed to civil society by drug trafficking and its links to terrorism, transnational crime, money laundering and the arms trade, and encourages Governments to deal with this threat and to cooperate to prevent the channelling of funds to and between those engaged in such activities;

7. *Acknowledges* that there are links between the illicit production of, demand for and traffic in narcotic drugs and psychotropic substances and the economic and social conditions in the affected countries, and that there are differences and diversity in the problems of each country;

8. *Calls upon* the international community to provide increased economic and technical support to Governments that request it for programmes of alternative and sustainable development that have as their objectives the reduction and elimination of illicit drug production and take fully into account the cultural traditions of peoples;

9. *Notes* the strong support expressed by members of the Commission on Narcotic Drugs for the initiatives of the United Nations International Drug Control Programme to establish a dialogue with multilateral development banks so that they might undertake lending and programming activities related to drug control in interested and affected countries, and requests the Executive Director of the Programme to inform the Commission of further progress made in this area;

10. *Stresses* the need for effective government action to prevent the diversion to illicit markets of precursors and essential chemicals, materials and equipment used in the illicit manufacture of narcotic drugs and psychotropic substances;

11. *Commends* the International Narcotics Control Board for its valuable work in monitoring the production and distribution of narcotic drugs and psychotropic substances so as to limit their use to medical and scientific purposes, and urges increased efforts to implement its mandate under article 12 of the United Nations Convention against Illicit Traffic in Narcotic Drugs and Psychotropic Substances concerning the monitoring of the movement of precursors and essential chemicals;

12. *Calls upon* the United Nations International Drug Control Programme to continue providing assistance to Member States that request it in establishing or strengthening national drug detection laboratories;

13. *Calls upon* States to increase efforts, with international cooperation, to reduce and eliminate illegal crops from which narcotics are obtained, as well as to prevent and reduce the demand for and the consumption of illicit drugs;

14. *Underlines* the need for Governments, with international cooperation, to increase and implement alternative development programmes with the objective of reducing and eliminating the production of illicit drugs, taking into account the economic, social, cultural, political and environmental aspects of the area concerned;

15. *Emphasizes* the need to maintain the capacity of the International Narcotics Control Board, including through the provision of appropriate means by the Secretary-General, within existing resources, and adequate technical support by the United Nations International Drug Control Programme;

16. *Reaffirms* the importance of achieving the objectives of the United Nations Decade against Drug Abuse 1991-2000, under the theme "A global response to a global challenge", by Member States, the United Nations International Drug Control Programme and the United Nations system;

17. *Takes note* of the provisional report presented to the Commission on Narcotic Drugs at its thirty-eighth session by the Executive Director of the United Nations International Drug Control Programme on the economic and social consequences of drug abuse and illicit trafficking,[5] and invites the Commission to continue considering this issue in the context of the general debate;

18. *Welcomes* resolution 13 (XXXVIII) of the Commission on Narcotic Drugs on the implementation of General Assembly resolution 48/12;[6]

19. *Welcomes* with satisfaction Economic and Social Council resolution 1995/16 of 24 July 1995 on the integration of demand reduction initiatives into a cohesive strategy to combat drug abuse, in which, *inter alia*, the Council requested the Executive Director of the United Nations International Drug Control Programme, in consultation with

1 United Nations, *Treaty Series*, vol. 520, No. 7515.

2 *Ibid.*, vol. 976, No. 14152.

3 *Ibid.*, vol. 1019, No. 14956.

4 United Nations publication, Sales No. E.91.XI.6.

5 E/CN.7/1995/3.

6 *Official Records of the Economic and Social Council, 1995, Supplement No. 9* (E/1995/29), chap. XII, sect. A.

Governments and appropriate agencies and organizations, to define clearly their global strategy for demand reduction and to develop a draft declaration on the guiding principles of demand reduction for submission to the Commission on Narcotic Drugs at its thirty-ninth session;

20. *Welcomes with satisfaction* resolution 5 (XXXVIII) of the Commission on Narcotic Drugs on strategies for illicit supply reduction[1] reaffirming the need to apply effective strategies for supply reduction, based on the implementation of plans and programmes for alternative development, which have as their objectives the reduction and elimination of illicit drug production;

21. *Invites* the Economic and Social Council, while considering the issue of international cooperation against the illicit production, sale, demand, traffic and distribution of narcotics and psychotropic substances at its high-level segment of 1996, to pay special attention to the recommendations on the follow-up to General Assembly resolution 48/12, contained in the report of the Commission on Narcotic Drugs;[2]

22. *Requests* the United Nations International Drug Control Programme, in its report on illicit traffic in drugs, to include an assessment of worldwide trends in illicit traffic and transit in narcotic drugs and psychotropic substances, including methods and routes wed, and to recommend ways and means for improving the capacity of States along those routes to deal with all aspects of the drug problem;

III

Global Programme of Action

1. *Reaffirms* the importance of the Global Programme of Action[3] as a comprehensive framework for national, regional and international action to combat illicit production of, demand for and trafficking in narcotic drugs and psychotropic substances;

2. *Calls upon* States to implement the mandates and recommendations of the Global Programme of Action, with a view to translating it into practical action for drug abuse control at the national, regional and international levels;

3. *Urges* all Governments and competent regional organizations to develop a balanced approach within the framework of comprehensive demand reduction activities, giving adequate priority to prevention, treatment, research, social reintegration and training in the context of national strategic plans to combat drug abuse;

4. *Calls upon* the relevant United Nations bodies, the specialized agencies, the international financial institutions and other concerned intergovernmental and non-governmental organizations to cooperate with and assist States in their efforts to promote and implement the Global Programme of Action;

5. *Welcomes* the efforts made by the Commission on Narcotic Drugs and the United Nations International Drug Control Programme to facilitate reporting by Governments on the implementation of the Global Programme of Action and encourages them to pursue those efforts so as to increase the number of Governments that respond;

6. *Notes* the efforts being made by the United Nations International Drug Control Programme and other United Nations bodies to obtain reliable data on drug abuse and illicit trafficking, including the development of the International Drug Abuse Assessment System, encourages the Programme, in cooperation with other United Nations bodies, to take further steps to facilitate the efficient collection of data so as to avoid duplication of effort, and encourages also the increased and timely provision of updated information by Member States;

7. *Invites* the United Nations International Drug Control Programme to consider ways of providing assistance to Member States that request it in their efforts to establish appropriate mechanisms to collect and analyse data and to seek voluntary resources for this purpose;

IV

Proposal for an International Conference to Combat the Illicit Production, Sale, Demand, Traffic and Distribution of Narcotic Drugs and Psychotropic Substances and Related Activities

1. *Takes note* of the recommendations contained in the report of the Executive Director of the United Nations International Drug Control Programme on the implementation of General Assembly resolution 48/12,[4] including the recommendation regarding the proposal to convene an international conference ten years after the International Conference on Drug Abuse and Illicit Trafficking, to review progress made by Governments and the United Nations system in combating drug abuse and illicit trafficking;[5]

2. *Takes note* of resolution 13 (XXXVIII) of the Commission on Narcotic Drugs,[6] in which the Commission decided to keep under consideration the proposal for the convening of an international conference to review progress made by Governments and the United Nations system in combating drug abuse and illicit trafficking;

3. *Takes note also* of Economic and Social Council resolution 1995/40 of 27 July 1995, in which the Council recommended that the General Assembly and the Commission on Narcotic Drugs give priority consideration to the proposal to convene an international conference for the purpose of evaluating the international situation and the status of international cooperation against the illicit production, sale, demand, traffic and distribution of narcotic drugs and psychotropic substances and related activities;

4. *Takes note* of the proposal to hold a second international conference and requests the Commission on Narcotic Drugs to discuss fully, as a matter of priority, this issue at its thirty-ninth session, and to present its conclusions and suggestions, through the Economic and Social Council, to the General Assembly at its fifty-first session;

5. *Stresses* that, when discussing this issue, the Commission on Narcotic Drugs should take into account that the proposed conference should focus, with a balanced and integral approach, *inter alia*, on the assessment of existing strategies, as well as on the consideration of new strategies, methods, practical measures and concrete actions to strengthen international cooperation to address the problem of illicit drugs, including illicit demand reduction, illicit supply reduction, the promotion of alternative development programmes, the combat against criminal organizations and illicit arms trade related to drug trafficking, money laundering, the diversion of essential chemicals, the control of stimulants and their precursors and the promotion of law enforcement cooperation, on the basis of the principles and guidelines set forth in the present resolution;

6. *Also stresses* that, when considering the proposal for holding such a conference, the Commission on Narcotic Drugs should take into account international drug control priorities and resources, the financial and other implications of holding such a conference, as well as ways and means to increase the implementation of existing international conventions and other international instruments for cooperation on drug control;

V

Implementation of the United Nations System-Wide Action Plan on Drug Abuse Control: Action by Organizations of the United Nations System

1. *Supports* the United Nations System-wide Action Plan on Drug Abuse Control[7] as a vital tool for the coordination and enhancement

---

1 *Ibid.*

2 *Ibid.*, chap. VII.

3 See *Official Records of the Economic and Social Council. 1994, Supplement No. 10* (E/1994/30), chap. XI, resolution 3 (XXXVII).

4 E/CN.7/1995/14.

5 *Ibid.*, para. 50.

6 *Official Records of the Economic and Social Council, 1995, Supplement No. 9* (E/1995/29), chap. XII, sect. A.

7 See A/49/139-E/1994/57.

of drug abuse control activities within the United Nations system and requests that it be updated and reviewed on a biennial basis with a view to continuing efforts to improve its presentation and usefulness as a strategic tool of the United Nations for the drug problem;

2. *Reaffirms* the role of the Executive Director of the United Nations International Drug Control Programme in coordinating and providing effective leadership for all United Nations drug control activities so as to increase cost-effectiveness and ensure coherence of action within the Programme as well as coordination, complementarity and non-duplication of such activities across the United Nations system;

3. *Endorses* the agreed conclusions adopted by the Economic and Social Council at its coordination segment of 1994[1] regarding coordination by the United Nations International Drug Control Programme of drug control-related policies and activities of the United Nations system, including international financial institutions;

4. *Urges* the governing bodies of the United Nations organizations associated with the United Nations System-wide Action Plan on Drug Abuse Control to help ensure effective follow-up by including drug control in their agendas with a view to assessing the activities undertaken in accordance with the Plan and examining how the drug problem is addressed in relevant programmes;

5. *Invites* Member States to inform the Economic and Social Council at its high-level segment of 1996 on progress in international cooperation, especially on specific national efforts to engage the United Nations system and the multilateral development banks in addressing the drug problem;

VI

United Nations International Drug Control Programme

1. *Welcomes* the efforts of the United Nations International Drug Control Programme to implement its mandates within the framework of the international drug control treaties, the Comprehensive Multidisciplinary Outline of Future Activities in Drug Abuse Control, the Global Programme of Action and relevant consensus documents;

2. *Notes with concern* the decline of available resources for the Fund of the United Nations International Drug Control Programme;

3. *Urges* all Governments to provide the fullest possible financial and political support to the United Nations International Drug Control Programme, in particular by increasing voluntary contributions to the Programme, to enable it to continue, expand and strengthen its operational and technical cooperation activities;

4. *Invites* Governments and the United Nations International Drug Control Programme to consider ways and means of improving the coordination of United Nations drug control-related activities;

5. *Welcomes* the work of the Commission on Narcotic Drugs at its thirty-eighth session on the programme budget of the Fund of the United Nations International Drug Control Programme, in accordance with the mandate contained in section XVI, paragraph 2, of General Assembly resolution 46/185 C of 20 December 1991;

6. *Notes with appreciation* the efforts made by the Executive Director of the United Nations International Drug Control Programme to comply with the approved format and methodology of the programme budget of the Fund, in accordance with relevant resolutions of the Commission on Narcotic Drugs and the General Assembly and the recommendations of the Advisory Committee on Administrative and Budgetary Questions, and encourages the Executive Director to continue his efforts to improve the presentation and transparency of the budget;

7. *Stresses* the importance of the meetings of heads of national law enforcement agencies, and encourages them to consider ways to improve their functioning and to strengthen their impact so as to enhance cooperation in the fight against drugs at the regional level;

VII

1. *Takes note* of the reports of the Secretary-General submitted under the item entitled "International drug control";[2]

2. *Requests* the Secretary-General, taking into account the promotion of integrated reporting:

(*a*) To submit to the General Assembly at its fifty-first session an updated report on the status of the United Nations Convention against Illicit Traffic in Narcotic Drugs and Psychotropic Substances;

(*b*) To include in his annual report on the implementation of the Global Programme of Action recommendations on ways and means to improve implementation and provision of information by Member States.

97th plenary meeting
21 December 1995

09.43 PREVENTION AND INTERNATIONAL COOPERATION AGAINST CRIME

45/107. International Cooperation for Crime Prevention and Criminal Justice in the Context of Development

Committee: 3
Vote: Adopted without a vote
Ref.: 44/72, 43/99, 42/59

The General Assembly,

Reaffirming the purposes and principles of the United Nations and the commitment of all States to respect the obligations assumed by them, in accordance with the Charter of the United Nations,

Convinced that crime prevention and criminal justice in the context of development should be oriented towards the observance of the principles contained in the Caracas Declaration,[3] the Milan Plan of Action,[4] the Guiding Principles for Crime Prevention and Criminal Justice in the Context of Development and a New International Economic Order[5] and other relevant resolutions and recommendations of the Seventh United Nations Congress on the Prevention of Crime and the Treatment of Offenders,

Recalling its resolution 43/99 of 8 December 1988, in which it stressed the need for Member States to continue to make concerted and systematic efforts to strengthen international cooperation in crime prevention and criminal justice, as identified in the Milan Plan of Action, and to facilitate the adoption by the Eighth United Nations Congress on the Prevention of Crime and the Treatment of Offenders of viable and constructive action-oriented strategies against crime,

Recalling also its resolution 44/72 of 8 December 1989,

Recalling further Economic and Social Council resolution 1989/68 of 24 May 1989, in which the Council reaffirmed its conviction of the importance of the programme of the United Nations in the field of crime prevention and criminal justice and the necessity of strengthening it in order to make it fully responsive to the needs and expectations of Member States,

Adopts the recommendations on international cooperation for crime prevention and criminal justice in the context of development, as contained in the annex to the present resolution.

68th plenary meeting
14 December 1990

---

1 See *Official Records of the General Assembly, Forty-ninth Session, Supplement No. 3* (A/49/3/Rev.1), chap. III, sect. B.

2 A/50/460 and A/50/461.

3 Resolution 35/171, annex.

4 See *Seventh United Nations Congress on the Prevention of Crime and the Treatment of Offenders, Milan, 26 August-6 September 1985: report prepared by the Secretariat* (United Nations publication, Sales No. E.86.IV.1), chap. I, sect. A.

5 *Ibid.*, sect. B.

Annex

Recommendations on International Cooperation for Crime Prevention and Criminal Justice in the Context of Development

A. Crime Prevention and Criminal Justice in the Context of Development

1. Governments should reaffirm their commitment to respect the existing international treaties and their adherence to principles expressed in the Charter of the United Nations and in other relevant international instruments. Crime can also be prevented by ensuring that those principles are not sacrificed.

2. Member States should intensify the struggle against international crime by respecting and promoting the rule of law and legality in international relations and, for that purpose, they should complete and further develop international criminal law, fully implement the obligations following from international treaties and instruments in this field (*pacta sunt servanda*), and examine their national legislation in order to ensure that it meets the needs of international criminal law.

3. Governments should accord priority attention to the promulgation and implementation of appropriate laws and regulations to control and combat transnational crime and illegal international transactions, especially by the provision of proper collaborative schemes and trained personnel. Also, national laws should be reviewed in order to ensure a more effective and adequate response to the new forms of criminal activity, not only through the application of criminal penalties, but also through civil or administrative measures.

4. The national, regional and international aspects of growing pollution and the exploitation and destruction of the environment should be recognized and controlled as a matter of urgency, in view of the increasing and alarming devastation, deriving from various sources. Besides measures of administrative law and liability under civil law, the role of criminal law as an instrument that can help to achieve such control should be kept under review. The desirability of elaborating guiding principles for the prevention of crimes against the environment should be considered.

5. In view of the fact that advanced technology and specialized technical knowledge are employed in criminal activities pursued in international trade and commerce, including computer fraud, by the misuse of banking facilities and the manipulation of tax laws and customs regulations, law enforcement and criminal justice officials should be properly trained and provided with adequate legal and technical means to be able to detect and investigate such offences. The coordination and cooperation of other relevant agencies at the national level should be ensured and their capacities further improved. The development and strengthening of direct arrangements of international cooperation between the various agencies of national criminal justice systems should also be pursued.

6. Since even legitimate enterprises, organizations and associations may sometimes be involved in transnational criminal activities affecting national economies, Governments should adopt measures for the control of such activities. They should also collect information from various sources so as to have a solid base for the detection and punishment of enterprises, organizations and associations, their officials, or both, if they are involved in such criminal activities, with a view also to preventing similar conduct in the future.

7. Note should be taken of the fact that many countries lack adequate laws to deal with the emerging manifestations of transnational crime, and that the adoption and implementation of appropriate instruments and measures to prevent this type at criminality are urgently needed. In this regard, the exchange of information on existing laws and regulations should be encouraged in order to facilitate the dissemination and adoption of appropriate measures.

8. Because the corrupt activities of public officials can destroy the potential effectiveness of all types of governmental programmes, hinder development, and victimize individuals and groups, it is of crucial importance that all nations should (a) review the adequacy of their criminal laws, including procedural legislation, in order to respond to all forms of corruption and related actions designed to assist or to facilitate corrupt activities, and should have recourse to sanctions that will ensure adequate deterrence; (b) devise administrative and regulatory mechanisms for the prevention of corrupt practices or the abuse of power; (c) adopt procedures for the detection, investigation and conviction of corrupt officials; (d) create legal provisions for the forfeiture of funds and property from corrupt practices; and (e) take appropriate measures against enterprises involved in corruption. The Crime Prevention and Criminal Justice Branch of the Centre for Social Development and Humanitarian Affairs of the Secretariat should coordinate the elaboration of materials to assist countries in these efforts, including the development of a manual to combat corruption, and should provide specialized training to judges and prosecutors that would qualify them to deal with the technical aspects of corruption, as well as with the experiences derived from specialized courts handling such matters.

9. Noting the alarming threat posed by illicit trafficking in narcotic drugs and psychotropic substances, which is among the worst crimes that humanity is facing, and the action taken by United Nations drug control units and bodies in this field, and concerned that, despite all the efforts made at the national, regional and international levels, this phenomenon persists unabated, it is important that efforts to combat this type of criminality be given a central place in all crime prevention and criminal justice plans and programmes. The work of the Crime Prevention and Criminal Justice Branch of the Centre for Social Development and Humanitarian Affairs in this area should be strengthened. Special assistance should be extended to developing countries for the implementation of drug abuse control programmes and the elaboration of collaborative prevention and control strategies.

10. The process of developing comprehensive model codes, especially at the regional and subregional levels, to combat crimes of transnational and international dimensions, should be encouraged. Also, efforts should be made to harmonize national criminal laws, so as to make them fully responsive to the realities and ramifications of such crimes. Practical arrangements, such as extradition, mutual assistance in criminal justice and the sharing and exchange of expertise and information, should be pursued. Adequate attention should be given to effective enforcement mechanisms in order to minimize the consequences of transborder crimes, including their effect on countries not directly involved.

11. Appropriate educational policies should be developed for making the populations of Member States more sensitive to the problem through formal educational systems and general public information programmes, with a view to promoting awareness of the ways and means by which criminal victimization can be avoided, as well as acquainting the public at large with the objectives and processes of the criminal justice system.

12. In recognition of the need for specific preventive measures related to such types of criminality as burglary, violent theft and street crime, an inventory of preventive measures should be prepared by the United Nations on the basis of an in-depth assessment and evaluation of their effectiveness in various cultural, social, economic and political contexts.

13. With respect to the victims of crime and abuse of power, a guide containing an inventory of comprehensive measures for education on the prevention of victimization, and on the protection of, and assistance and compensation to, victims should be prepared. This guide should be applied in accordance with the legal, socio-cultural and economic circumstances of each nation, taking into account the important role of non-governmental organizations in this sphere.

14. In view of its crucial function in crime prevention, the criminal justice system should be developed on the basis of the progressive rationalization and humanization of criminal laws and procedures, sentencing policies and dispositional alternatives, within the overall framework of social justice and societal aspirations.

15. A systematic approach to crime prevention planning should be pursued to provide for the incorporation of crime prevention policies into national development planning, starting from an overall reassessment of substantive criminal and procedural laws whenever appropriate. This approach would include the introduction of the processes of decriminalization, depenalization and diversion, as well

as reforms of procedures that would ensure the support of members of the public and review of existing policies with a view to assessing their impact. It would also include appropriate links to be established between the criminal justice system and other development sectors, including education, employment, health, social policy and other related fields.

16. The trial process should be consonant with the cultural realities and social values of society, in order to make it understood and to permit it to operate effectively within the community it serves. Observance of human rights, equality, fairness and consistency should be ensured at all stages of the process.

B. International, Scientific and Technical Cooperation

17. In order to increase the effectiveness of international cooperation in crime prevention and criminal justice, concerted efforts should be made towards (a) the ratification and implementation of existing international instruments; (b) the development of bilateral and multilateral instruments; and (c) the preparation and elaboration of model instruments and standards for use at the national, bilateral, multilateral, subregional, regional and interregional levels.

18. The formulation of international instruments, standards and norms should include the following specific areas of concern: (a) judicial assistance treaties, in particular between common law and civil law countries, dealing with the means for obtaining evidence conforming to the requirements of the requesting State; (b) development of standardized requests for extradition and mutual assistance; (c) development of the means of providing assistance to victims of crime and abuse of power, with emphasis on the implementation of the Declaration of Basic Principles of Justice for Victims of Crime and Abuse of Power,[1] and of providing adequate protection for witnesses; (d) further consideration of issues of transnational jurisdiction in order to assist in the process of responding to requests for extradition and mutual assistance and in the implementation of international instruments; and (e) elaboration of standards for international assistance in respect of bank secrecy, facilitating the seizure and confiscation of proceeds in bank accounts derived from criminal acts. In particular, banks and other financial institutions should be urged to standardize their reporting requirements and documents so that these can be used more rapidly and effectively as evidence. More effective international standards to inhibit the laundering of money and investment connected with criminal activities, such as narcotics trafficking and terrorism, should also be developed.

19. Member States, intergovernmental and non-governmental organizations and international, national and private funding agencies should assist the United Nations in the establishment and operation of a global crime prevention and criminal justice information network. Member States are urged to contribute to this endeavour by financing equipment and expertise. Consideration should also be given to determining the categories of criminal justice data that can be provided and exchanged on a regular basis.

20. In accordance with the numerous decisions and resolutions of relevant organs of the United Nations, including the quinquennial United Nations congresses on the prevention of crime and the treatment of offenders, measures should be taken to strengthen programmes of international technical and scientific cooperation in the field of crime prevention and criminal justice on a bilateral and multilateral basis, as substantive components of broader development programmes, taking into account the special needs of developing countries and, in particular, the worsening socio-economic situation in many of them, which contributes to the increase of structural inequality and criminality.

21. In order to formulate and develop proper regional and interregional strategies of international, technical and scientific cooperation in combating crime and improving the effectiveness of preventive and criminal justice activities, the programmes of technical and scientific cooperation should be directed especially towards (a) reinforcement of the technical capacities of the criminal justice agencies; (b) an upgrading of the human and technical resources in all sectors of the criminal justice system in order to stimulate technical assistance, model and demonstration projects, research activities and training programmes, in close cooperation with the United Nations regional and interregional institutes for the prevention of crime and the treatment of offenders and competent non-governmental organizations; (c) the further development and improvement, at the national, regional, interregional and international levels, of information bases for the collection, analysis and dissemination of data on crime trends, innovative ways and methods of crime prevention and control, and the operation of criminal justice agencies, in order to provide an appropriate basis for policy-formulation and programme implementation; (d) the promotion, through educational programmes and training activities, of the implementation of United Nations norms, guidelines and standards in crime prevention and criminal justice; and (e) the elaboration and implementation of joint strategies and collaborative arrangements to deal with crime problems of mutual concern.

22. The Crime Prevention and Criminal Justice Branch of the Centre for Social Development and Humanitarian Affairs, as the focal point of United Nations activities in this field, the United Nations institutes for the prevention of crime and the treatment of offenders, the cooperating entities like the Arab Security Studies and Training Centre, the interregional advisory services in crime prevention and criminal justice, and other relevant United Nations bodies, as well as intergovernmental and non-governmental organizations enjoying consultative status with the Economic and Social Council, should be strengthened so as to increase the scope of their operations, improve their coordination and diversify forms and methods of technical and scientific cooperation.

23. The role of the Committee on Crime Prevention and Control as the principal body dealing with crime prevention and criminal justice matters, which is entrusted, *inter alia*, with the preparations for the United Nations congresses on the prevention of crime and the treatment of offenders, should be further enhanced so as to enable it to fulfil its important functions.

24. The capacity of the Crime Prevention and Criminal Justice Branch of the Centre for Social Development and Humanitarian Affairs, as the only professional and specialized entity within the United Nations system with overall responsibility for its crime prevention and criminal justice programme, should be strengthened in terms of both human and financial resources. Prompt implementation of the General Assembly and Economic and Social Council resolutions related thereto is urgently needed. In particular, priority attention should be given to the implementation of paragraphs 4 and 5 of General Assembly resolution 42/59 of 30 November 1987, in which the Assembly approved the recommendations contained in Economic and Social Council resolutions 1986/11 and 1987/53, concerning the review of the functioning and programme of work of the United Nations in the field of crime prevention and criminal justice,[2] and requested the Secretary-General, *inter alia*, to take measures to ensure that the programme of work is supported by adequate resources; and paragraph 3 (a) of Economic and Social Council resolution 1987/53, in which the Council requested the Secretary-General to develop the Crime Prevention and Criminal Justice Branch of the Centre for Social Development and Humanitarian Affairs as a specialized body and facilitating agent in the field of crime prevention and criminal justice. Attention should also be given to other relevant resolutions of the General Assembly and the Economic and Social Council, as well as to the recommendations of the regional preparatory meetings for the Eighth United Nations Congress on the Prevention of Crime and the Treatment of Offenders and of the Committee on Crime Prevention and Control.

25. The United Nations institutes for the prevention of crime and the treatment of offenders should further develop their research, training and technical assistance capacities, and widen their collaborative networks through more extensive reliance on non-governmental organizations and national research and educational institutions, in order to meet the growing requests from developing countries for technical and scientific assistance. The Governments concerned,

1 Resolution 40/34, annex.

2 See E/1987/43.

relevant regional bodies and organizations and United Nations entities should actively assist the United Nations institutes for the prevention of crime and the treatment of offenders, and, in particular, should assist the African Institute for the Prevention of Crime and the Treatment of Offenders, in consolidating its status and further promoting its activities.

26. Governments should be invited to fund regional advisory services in their regions, directly or through the United Nations Development Programme, so as to develop further and complement existing structures and possibilities in this field. The regional commissions should be encouraged to do likewise and should be supported in their efforts to that end.

27. Special attention should be paid to strengthening the collaborative ties in the field of crime prevention and criminal justice between the Centre for Social Development and Humanitarian Affairs and the Department of Technical Cooperation for Development of the Secretariat, the United Nations Development Programme, the World Bank and other relevant entities, with a view to ensuring adequate resources for technical cooperation activities in crime prevention and criminal justice. Interested Governments should give priority to the inclusion of crime prevention and criminal justice projects in the national and regional programmes proposed for the support of the United Nations Development Programme.

28. In order to fully implement the mandates emerging from the crime prevention and criminal justice programme and to provide additional technical and scientific expertise and resources for matters of international cooperation in this field, broader involvement of, and assistance by, non-governmental organizations are required.

29. Governments and other funding agencies should contribute to the United Nations Trust Fund for Social Defence in order to enable the United Nations to implement, in an adequate and effective manner, programmes of technical and scientific cooperation in this field.

45/110. United Nations Standard Minimum Rules for Non-Custodial Measures (The Tokyo Rules)

Committee: 3
Vote: Adopted without a vote

The General Assembly,

Bearing in mind the Universal Declaration of Human Rights[1] and the International Covenant on Civil and Political Rights,[2] as well as other international human rights instruments pertaining to the rights of persons in conflict with the law,

Bearing in mind also the Standard Minimum Rules for the Treatment of Prisoners,[3] adopted by the First United Nations Congress on the Prevention of Crime and the Treatment of Offenders, and the important contribution of those Rules to national policies and practices,

Recalling resolution 8 of the Sixth United Nations Congress on the Prevention of Crime and the Treatment of Offenders[4] on alternatives to imprisonment,

Recalling also resolution 16 of the Seventh United Nations Congress on the Prevention of Crime and the Treatment of Offenders[5] on the reduction of the prison population, alternatives to imprisonment, and social integration of offenders,

Recalling further section XI of Economic and Social Council resolution 1986/10 of 21 May 1986, on alternatives to imprisonment, in which the Secretary-General was requested to prepare a report on alternatives to imprisonment for the Eighth United Nations Congress on the Prevention of Crime and the Treatment of Offenders and to study that question with a view to the formulation of basic principles in that area, with the assistance of the United Nations institutes for the prevention of crime and the treatment of offenders,

Recognizing the need to develop local, national, regional and international approaches and strategies in the field of non-institutional treatment of offenders and the need to formulate standard minimum rules, as emphasized in the section of the report of the Committee on Crime Prevention and Control on its fourth session, concerning the methods and measures likely to be most effective in preventing crime and improving the treatment of offenders,[6]

Convinced that alternatives to imprisonment can be an effective means of treating offenders within the community to the best advantage of both the offenders and society,

Aware that the restriction of liberty is justifiable only from the viewpoints of public safety, crime prevention, just retribution and deterrence and that the ultimate goal of the criminal justice system is the reintegration of the offender into society,

Emphasizing that the increasing prison population and prison overcrowding in many countries constitute factors that create difficulties for the proper implementation of the Standard Minimum Rules for the Treatment of Prisoners,

Noting with appreciation the work accomplished by the Committee on Crime Prevention and Control, as well as by the Interregional Preparatory Meeting for the Eighth United Nations Congress on the Prevention of Crime and the Treatment of Offenders on topic II, "Criminal justice policies in relation to problems of imprisonment, other penal sanctions and alternative measures," and by the regional preparatory meetings for the Eighth Congress,

Expressing its gratitude to the United Nations Asia and Far East Institute for the Prevention of Crime and the Treatment of Offenders for the work accomplished in the development of standard minimum rules for non-custodial measures, as well as to the various intergovernmental and non-governmental organizations involved, in particular, the International Penal and Penitentiary Foundation for its contribution to the preparatory work,

1. *Adopts* the United Nations Standard Minimum Rules for Non-custodial Measures, contained in the annex to the present resolution, and approves the recommendation of the Committee on Crime Prevention and Control that the Rules should be known as "the Tokyo Rules";

2. *Recommends* the Tokyo Rules for implementation at the national, regional and interregional levels, taking into account the political, economic, social and cultural circumstances and traditions of countries;

3. *Calls upon* Member States to apply the Tokyo Rules in their policies and practice;

4. *Invites* Member States to bring the Tokyo Rules to the attention of, in particular, law enforcement officials, prosecutors, judges, probation officers, lawyers, victims, offenders, social services and non-governmental organizations involved in the application of non-custodial measures, as well as members of the executive, the legislature and the general public;

5. *Requests* Member States to report on the implementation of the Tokyo Rules every five years, beginning in 1994;

6. *Urges* the regional commissions, the United Nations institutes for the prevention of crime and the treatment of offenders, specialized agencies and other entities within the United Nations system, other intergovernmental organizations concerned and non-governmental organizations in consultative status with the Economic and Social Council to be actively involved in the implementation of the Tokyo Rules;

7. *Calls upon* the Committee on Crime Prevention and Control to consider, as a matter of priority, the implementation of the present resolution;

8. *Requests* the Secretary-General to take the necessary steps to prepare a commentary to the Tokyo Rules, which is to be submitted

---

1 Resolution 217 A (III).

2 Resolution 2200 A (XXI), annex.

3 See *Human Rights: A Compilation of international Instruments* (United Nations publication, Sales No. E.88.XIV.1), sect. G.

4 See *Sixth United Nations Congress on the Prevention of Crime and the Treatment of Offenders. Caracas, 25 August-5 September 1980: report prepared by the Secretariat* (United Nations publication, Sales No. E.81.IV.4), chap. I, sect. B.

5 *Ibid.*, chap. I, sect. E.

6 E/CN.5/536, annex IV.

to the Committee on Crime Prevention and Control at its twelfth session for approval and further dissemination, paying special attention to the legal safeguards, the implementation of the Rules and the development of similar guidelines at the regional level;

9. *Invites* the United Nations institutes for the prevention of crime and the treatment of offenders to assist the Secretary-General in that task;

10. *Urges* intergovernmental and non-governmental organizations and other entities concerned to remain actively involved in this initiative;

11. *Requests* the Secretary-General to take steps, as appropriate, to ensure the widest possible dissemination of the Tokyo Rules, including their transmission to Governments, interested intergovernmental and non-governmental organizations and other parties concerned;

12. *Also requests* the Secretary-General to prepare every five years, beginning in 1994, a report on the implementation of the Tokyo Rules for submission to the Committee on Crime Prevention and Control;

13. *Further requests* the Secretary-General to assist Member States, at their request, in the implementation of the Tokyo Rules and to report regularly thereon to the Committee on Crime Prevention and Control;

14. *Requests* that the present resolution and the text of the annex be brought to the attention of all United Nations bodies concerned and be included in the next edition of the United Nations publication entitled *Human Rights: A Compilation of International Instruments*.

68th plenary meeting
14 December 1990

Annex

United Nations Standard Minimum Rules for Non-Custodial Measures (The Tokyo Rules)

I. General Principles

1. Fundamental aims

1.1 The present Standard Minimum Rules provide a set of basic principles to promote the use of non-custodial measures, as well as minimum safeguards for persons subject to alternatives to imprisonment.

1.2 The Rules are intended to promote greater community involvement in the management of criminal justice, specifically in the treatment of offenders, as well as to promote among offenders a sense of responsibility towards society.

1.3 The Rules shall be implemented taking into account the political, economic, social and cultural conditions of each country and the aims and objectives of its criminal justice system.

1.4 When implementing the Rules, Member States shall endeavour to ensure a proper balance between the rights of individual offenders, the rights of victims, and the concern of society for public safety and crime prevention.

1.5 Member States shall develop non-custodial measures within their legal systems to provide other options, thus reducing the use of imprisonment, and to rationalize criminal justice policies, taking into account the observance of human rights, the requirements of social justice and the rehabilitation needs of the offender.

2. The scope of non-custodial measures

2.1 The relevant provisions of the present Rules shall be applied to all persons subject to prosecution, trial or the execution of a sentence, at all stages of the administration of criminal justice. For the purposes of the Rules, these persons are referred to as "offenders", irrespective of whether they are suspected, accused or sentenced.

2.2 The Rules shall be applied without any discrimination on the grounds of race, colour, sex, age, language, religion, political or other opinion, national or social origin, property, birth or other status.

2.3 In order to provide greater flexibility consistent with the nature and gravity of the offence, with the personality and background of the offender and with the protection of society and to avoid unnecessary use of imprisonment, the criminal justice system should provide a wide range of non-custodial measures, from pre-trial to post-sentencing dispositions. The number and types of non-custodial measures available should be determined in such a way that consistent sentencing remains possible.

2.4 The development of new non-custodial measures should be encouraged and closely monitored and their use systematically evaluated.

2.5 Consideration shall be given to dealing with offenders in the community, avoiding as far as possible resort to formal proceedings or trial by a court, in accordance with legal safeguards and the rule of law.

2.6 Non-custodial measures should be used in accordance with the principle of minimum intervention.

2.7 The use of non-custodial measures should be part of the movement towards depenalization and decriminalization instead of interfering with or delaying efforts in that direction.

3. Legal safeguards

3.1 The introduction, definition and application of non-custodial measures shall be prescribed by law.

3.2 The selection of a non-custodial measure shall be based on an assessment of established criteria in respect of both the nature and gravity of the offence and the personality, the background of the offender, the purposes of sentencing and the rights of victims.

3.3 Discretion by the judicial or other competent independent authority shall be exercised at all stages of the proceedings by ensuring full accountability and only in accordance with the rule of law.

3.4 Non-custodial measures imposing an obligation on the offender, applied before or instead of formal proceedings or trial, shall require the offender's consent.

3.5 Decisions on the imposition of non-custodial measures shall be subject to review by a judicial or other competent independent authority, upon application by the offender.

3.6 The offender shall be entitled to make a request or complaint to a judicial or other competent independent authority on matters affecting his or her individual rights in the implementation of non-custodial measures.

3.7 Appropriate machinery shall be provided for the recourse and, if possible, redress of any grievance related to non-compliance with internationally recognized human rights.

3.8 Non-custodial measures shall not involve medical or psychological experimentation on, or undue risk of physical or mental injury to, the offender.

3.9 The dignity of the offender subject to non-custodial measures shall be protected at all times.

3.10 In the implementation of non-custodial measures, the offender's rights shall not be restricted further than was authorized by the competent authority that rendered the original decision.

3.11 In the application of non-custodial measures, the offender's right to privacy shall be respected, as shall be the right to privacy of the offender's family.

3.12 The offender's personal records shall be kept strictly confidential and closed to third parties. Access to such records shall be limited to persons directly concerned with the disposition of the offender's case or to other duly authorized persons.

4. Saving clause

4.1 Nothing in the present Rules shall be interpreted as precluding the application of the Standard Minimum Rules for the Treatment of Prisoners,[1] the United Nations Standard Minimum Rules for the Administration of Juvenile Justice (The Beijing Rules),[2] the Body of Principles for the Protection of All Persons under Any Form of Detention or Imprisonment[3] or any other human rights instruments and standards recognized by the international community and relating to the treatment of offenders and the protection of their basic human rights.

II. Pre-Trial Stage

5. Pre-trial dispositions

5.1 Where appropriate and compatible with the legal system, the police, the prosecution service or other agencies dealing with criminal cases should be empowered to discharge the offender if they consider that it is not necessary to proceed with the case for the protection of society, crime prevention or the promotion of respect for the law and the rights of victims. For the purpose of deciding upon the appropriateness of discharge or determination of proceedings, a set of established criteria shall be developed within each legal system. For minor cases the prosecutor may impose suitable non-custodial measures, as appropriate.

6. Avoidance of pre-trial detention

6.1 Pre-trial detention shall be used as a means of last resort in criminal proceedings, with due regard for the investigation of the alleged offence and for the protection of society and the victim.

6.2 Alternatives to pre-trial detention shall be employed at as early a stage as possible. Pre-trial detention shall last no longer than necessary to achieve the objectives stated under rule 5.1 and shall be administered humanely and with respect for the inherent dignity of human beings.

6.3 The offender shall have the right to appeal to a judicial or other competent independent authority in cases where pre-trial detention is employed.

III. Trial and Sentencing Stage

7. Social inquiry reports

7.1 If the possibility of social inquiry reports exists, the judicial authority may avail itself of a report prepared by a competent, authorized official or agency. The report should contain social information on the offender that is relevant to the person's pattern of offending and current offences. It should also contain information and recommendations that are relevant to the sentencing procedure. The report shall be factual, objective and unbiased, with any expression of opinion clearly identified.

8. Sentencing dispositions

8.1 The judicial authority, having at its disposal a range of non-custodial measures, should take into consideration in making its decision the rehabilitative needs of the offender, the protection of society and the interests of the victim, who should be consulted whenever appropriate.

8.2 Sentencing authorities may dispose of cases in the following ways:

(a) Verbal sanctions, such as admonition, reprimand and warnings;

(b) Conditional discharge;

(c) Status penalties;

(d) Economic sanctions and monetary penalties, such as fines and day-fines;

(e) Confiscation or an expropriation order;

(f) Restitution to the victim or a compensation order;

(g) Suspended or deferred sentence;

(h) Probation and judicial supervision;

(i) A community service order;

(j) Referral to an attendance centre;

(k) House arrest;

(l) Any other mode of non-institutional treatment;

(m) Some combination of the measures listed above.

IV. Post-Sentencing Stage

9. Post-sentencing dispositions

9.1 The competent authority shall have at its disposal a wide range of post-sentencing alternatives in order to avoid institutionalization and to assist offenders in their early reintegration into society.

9.2 Post-sentencing dispositions may include:

(a) Furlough and half-way houses;

(b) Work or education release;

(c) Various forms of parole;

(d) Remission;

(e) Pardon.

9.3 The decision on post-sentencing dispositions, except in the case of pardon, shall be subject to review by a judicial or other competent independent authority, upon application of the offender.

9.4 Any form of release from an institution to a non-custodial programme shall be considered at the earliest possible stage.

V. Implementation of Non-Custodial Measures

10. Supervision

10.1 The purpose of supervision is to reduce reoffending and to assist the offender's integration into society in a way which minimizes the likelihood of a return to crime.

10.2 If a non-custodial measure entails supervision, the latter shall be carried out by a competent authority under the specific conditions prescribed by law.

10.3 Within the framework of a given non-custodial measure, the most suitable type of supervision and treatment should be determined for each individual case aimed at assisting the offender to work on his or her offending. Supervision and treatment should be periodically reviewed and adjusted as necessary.

10.4 Offenders should, when needed, be provided with psychological, social and material assistance and with opportunities to strengthen links with the community and facilitate their reintegration into society.

11. Duration

11.1 The duration of a non-custodial measure shall not exceed the period established by the competent authority in accordance with the law.

11.2 Provision may be made for early termination of the measure if the offender has responded favourably to it.

12. Conditions

12.1 If the competent authority shall determine the conditions to be observed by the offender, it should take into account both the needs of society and the needs and rights of the offender and the victim.

12.2 The conditions to be observed shall be practical, precise and as few as possible, and shall be aimed at reducing the likelihood of an offender relapsing into criminal behaviour and at increasing the offender's chances of social integration, taking into account the needs of the victim.

12.3 At the beginning of the application of a non-custodial measure, the offender shall receive an explanation, orally and in writing,

1 See *Human Rights: A Compilation of International Instrumens,* (UN publication, Sales No. E.88.XIV.1), sect. G.

2 Resolution 40/33, annex.

3 Resolution 43/173, annex.

of the conditions governing the application of the measure, including the offender's obligations and rights.

12.4 The conditions may be modified by the competent authority under the established statutory provisions, in accordance with the progress made by the offender.

13. Treatment process

13.1 Within the framework of a given non-custodial measure, in appropriate cases, various schemes, such as case-work, group therapy, residential programmes and the specialized treatment of various categories of offenders, should be developed to meet the needs of offenders more effectively.

13.2 Treatment should be conducted by professionals who have suitable training and practical experience.

13.3 When it is decided that treatment is necessary, efforts should be made to understand the offender's background, personality, aptitude, intelligence, values and, especially, the circumstances leading to the commission of the offence.

13.4 The competent authority may involve the community and social support systems in the application of non-custodial measures.

13.5 Case-load assignments shall be maintained as far as practicable at a manageable level to ensure the effective implementation of treatment programmes.

13.6 For each offender, a case record shall be established and maintained by the competent authority.

14. Discipline and breach of conditions

14.1 A breach of the conditions to be observed by the offender may result in a modification or revocation of the non-custodial measure.

14.2 The modification or revocation of the non-custodial measure shall be made by the competent authority: this shall be done only after a careful examination of the facts adduced by both the supervising officer and the offender.

14.3 The failure of a non-custodial measure should not automatically lead to the imposition of a custodial measure.

14.4 In the event of a modification or revocation of the non-custodial measure, the competent authority shall attempt to establish a suitable alternative non-custodial measure. A sentence of imprisonment may be imposed only in the absence of other suitable alternatives.

14.5 The power to arrest and detain the offender under supervision in cases where there is a breach of the conditions shall be prescribed by law.

14.6 Upon modification or revocation of the non-custodial measure, the offender shall have the right to appeal to a judicial or other competent independent authority.

VI. Staff

15. Recruitment

15.1 There shall be no discrimination in the recruitment of staff on the grounds of race, colour, sex, age, language, religion, political or other opinion, national or social origin, property, birth or other status. The policy regarding staff recruitment should take into consideration national policies of affirmative action and reflect the diversity of the offenders to be supervised.

15.2 Persons appointed to apply non-custodial measures should be personally suitable and, whenever possible, have appropriate professional training and practical experience. Such qualifications shall be clearly specified.

15.3 To secure and retain qualified professional staff, appropriate service status, adequate salary and benefits commensurate with the nature of the work should be ensured and ample opportunities should be provided for professional growth and career development.

16. Staff training

16.1 The objective of training shall be to make clear to staff their responsibilities with regard to rehabilitating the offender, ensuring the offender's rights and protecting society. Training should also give staff understanding of the need to cooperate in and coordinate activities with the agencies concerned.

16.2 Before entering duty, staff shall be given training that includes instruction on the nature of non-custodial measures, the purposes of supervision and the various modalities of the application of non-custodial measures.

16.3 After entering on duty, staff shall maintain and improve their knowledge and professional capacity by attending in-service training and refresher courses. Adequate facilities shall be made available for that purpose.

VII. Volunteers and other Community Resources

17. Public participation

17.1 Public participation should be encouraged as it is a major resource and one of the most important factors in improving ties between offenders undergoing non-custodial measures and the family and community. It should complement the efforts of the criminal justice administration.

17.2 Public participation should be regarded as an opportunity for members of the community to contribute to the protection of their society.

18. Public understanding and cooperation

18.1 Government agencies, the private sector and the general public should be encouraged to support voluntary organizations that promote non-custodial measures.

18.2 Conferences, seminars, symposia and other activities should be regularly organized to stimulate awareness of the need for public participation in the application of non-custodial measures.

18.3 All forms of the mass media should be utilized to help to create a constructive public attitude, leading to activities conducive to a broader application of non-custodial treatment and the social integration of offenders.

18.4 Every effort should be made to inform the public of the importance of its role in the implementation of non-custodial measures.

19. Volunteers

19.1 Volunteers shall be carefully screened and recruited on the basis of their aptitude for and interest in the work involved. They shall be properly trained for the specific responsibilities to be discharged by them and shall have access to support and counselling from, and the opportunity to consult with, the competent authority.

19.2 Volunteers should encourage offenders and their families to develop meaningful ties with the community and a broader sphere of contact by providing counselling and other appropriate forms of assistance according to their capacity and the offenders' needs.

19.3 Volunteers shall be insured against accident, injury and public liability when carrying out their duties. They shall be reimbursed for authorized expenditures incurred in the course of their work. Public recognition should be extended to them for the services they render for the well-being of the community.

VIII. Research, Planning, Policy Formulation and Evaluation

20. Research and planning

20.1 As an essential aspect of the planning process, efforts should be made to involve both public and private bodies in the organization and promotion of research on the non-custodial treatment of offenders.

20.2 Research on the problems that confront clients, practitioners, the community and policy makers should be carried out on a regular basis.

20.3 Research and information mechanisms should be built into the criminal justice system for the collection and analysis of data and statistics on the implementation of non-custodial treatment for offenders.

21. Policy formulation and programme development

21.1 Programmes for non-custodial measures should be systematically planned and implemented as an integral part of the criminal justice system within the national development process.

21.2 Regular evaluations should be carried out with a view to implementing non-custodial measures more effectively.

21.3 Periodic reviews should be conducted to assess the objectives, functioning and effectiveness of non-custodial measures.

22. Linkages with relevant agencies and activities

22.1 Suitable mechanisms should be evolved at various levels to facilitate the establishment of linkages between services responsible for non-custodial measures, other branches of the criminal justice system, social development and welfare agencies, both governmental and non-governmental, in such fields as health, housing, education and labour, and the mass media.

23. International cooperation

23.1 Efforts shall be made to promote scientific cooperation between countries in the field of non-institutional treatment. Research, training, technical assistance and the exchange of information among Member States on non-custodial measures should be strengthened, through the United Nations institutes for the prevention of crime and the treatment of offenders, in close collaboration with the Crime Prevention and Criminal Justice Branch of the Centre for Social Development and Humanitarian Affairs of the United Nations Secretariat.

23.2 Comparative studies and the harmonization of legislative provisions should be furthered to expand the range of non-institutional options and facilitate their application across national frontiers, in accordance with the Model Treaty on the Transfer of Supervision of Offenders Conditionally Sentenced or Conditionally Released.[1]

45/116. Model Treaty on Extradition

Committee: 3
Vote: Adopted without a vote

The General Assembly,

Bearing in mind the Milan Plan of Action,[2] adopted by the Seventh United Nations Congress on the Prevention of Crime and the Treatment of Offenders and approved by the General Assembly in its resolution 40/32 of 29 November 1985,

Bearing in mind also the Guiding Principles for Crime Prevention and Criminal Justice in the Context of Development and a New International Economic Order,[3] principle 37 of which stipulates that the United Nations should prepare model instruments suitable for use as international and regional conventions and as guides for national implementing legislation,

Recalling resolution 1 of the Seventh Congress,[4] on organized crime, in which Member States were urged, *inter alia*, to increase their activity at the international level in order to combat organized crime, including, as appropriate, entering into bilateral treaties on extradition and mutual legal assistance,

Recalling also resolution 23 of the Seventh Congress,[5] on criminal acts of a terrorist character, in which all States were called upon to take steps to strengthen cooperation, *inter alia*, in the area of extradition,

Calling attention to the United Nations Convention against Illicit Traffic in Narcotic Drugs and Psychotropic Substances,[6]

Acknowledging the valuable contributions of Governments, non-governmental organizations and individual experts, in particular the Government of Australia and the International Association of Penal Law,

Gravely concerned by the escalation of crime, both national and transnational,

Convinced that the establishment of bilateral and multilateral arrangements for extradition will greatly contribute to the development of more effective international cooperation for the control of crime,

Conscious of the need to respect human dignity and recalling the rights conferred upon every person involved in criminal proceedings, as embodied in the Universal Declaration of Human Rights[7] and the International Covenant on Civil and Political Rights,[8]

Conscious that in many cases existing bilateral extradition arrangements are outdated and should be replaced by modern arrangements which take into account recent developments in international criminal law,

Recognizing the importance of a model treaty on extradition as an effective way of dealing with the complex aspects and serious consequences of crime, especially in its new forms and dimensions,

1. *Adopts* the Model Treaty on Extradition contained in the annex to the present resolution as a useful framework that could be of assistance to States interested in negotiating and concluding bilateral agreements aimed at improving cooperation in matters of crime prevention and criminal justice;

2. *Invites* Member States, if they have not yet established treaty relations with other States in the area of extradition, or if they wish to revise existing treaty relations, to take into account, whenever doing so, the Model Treaty on Extradition;

3. *Urges* all States to strengthen further international cooperation in criminal justice;

4. *Requests* the Secretary-General to bring the present resolution, with the Model Treaty, to the attention of Member States;

5. *Urges* Member States to inform the Secretary-General periodically of efforts undertaken to establish extradition arrangements;

6. *Requests* the Committee on Crime Prevention and Control to review periodically the progress attained in this field;

7. *Also requests* the Committee on Crime Prevention and Control, where requested, to provide guidance and assistance to Member States in the development of legislation that would enable giving effect to the obligations in such treaties as are to be negotiated on the basis of the Model Treaty on Extradition;

8. *Invites* Member States, on request, to make available to the Secretary-General the provisions of their extradition legislation so that these may be made available to those Member States desiring to enact or further develop legislation in this field.

68th plenary meeting
14 December 1990

Annex

Model Treaty on Extradition

The ... and the ...

Desirous of making more effective the cooperation of the two countries in the control of crime by concluding a treaty on extradition,

---

1 See resolution 45/119, annex.

2 See *Seventh United Nations Congress on the Prevention of Crime and the Treatment of Offenders, Milan, 26 August - 6 September 1985: report prepared by the Secretariat* (United Nations publications, Sales No. E.86.IV.1), chap. I, sect. A.

3 *Ibid.*, sect. B.

4 *Ibid.*, sect. E.

5 *Ibid.*

6 E/CONF.82/15 and Corr.2.

7 Resolution 217 A (III).

8 See resolution 2200 A (XXI), annex.

Have agreed as follows:

Article 1
Obligation to Extradite

Each Party agrees to extradite to the other, upon request and subject to the provisions of the present Treaty, any person who is wanted in the requesting State for prosecution for an extraditable offence or for the imposition or enforcement of a sentence in respect of such an offence.[1]

Article 2
Extraditable Offences

1. For the purposes of the present Treaty, extraditable offences are offences that are punishable under the laws of both Parties by imprisonment or other deprivation of liberty for a maximum period of at least one/two year(s), or by a more severe penalty. Where the request for extradition relates to a person who is wanted for the enforcement of a sentence of imprisonment or other deprivation of liberty imposed for such an offence, extradition shall be granted only if a period of at least four/six months of such sentence remains to be served.

2. In determining whether an offence is an offence punishable under the laws of both Parties, it shall not matter whether:

(a) The laws of the Parties place the acts or omissions constituting the offence within the same category of offence or denominate the offence by the same terminology;

(b) Under the laws of the Parties the constituent elements of the offence differ, it being understood that the totality of the acts or omissions as presented by the requesting State shall be taken into account.

3. Where extradition of a person is sought for an offence against a law relating to taxation, customs duties, exchange control or other revenue matters, extradition may not be refused on the ground that the law of the requested State does not impose the same kind of tax or duty or does not contain a tax, customs duty or exchange regulation of the same kind as the law of the requesting State.[2]

4. If the request for extradition includes several separate offences each of which is punishable under the laws of both Parties, but some of which do not fulfil the other conditions set out in paragraph 1 of the present article, the requested Party may grant extradition for the latter offences provided that the person is to be extradited for at least one extraditable offence.

Article 3
Mandatory Grounds for Refusal

Extradition shall not be granted in any of the following circumstances:

(*a*) If the offence for which extradition is requested is regarded by the requested State as an offence of a political nature;[3]

(*b*) If the requested State has substantial grounds for believing that the request for extradition has been made for the purpose of prosecuting or punishing a person on account of that person's race, religion, nationality, ethnic origin, political opinions, sex or status, or that that person's position may be prejudiced for any of those reasons;

(*c*) If the offence for which extradition is requested is an offence under military law, which is not also an offence under ordinary criminal law;

(*d*) If there has been a final judgement rendered against the person in the requested State in respect of the offence for which the person's extradition is requested;

(*e*) If the person whose extradition is requested has, under the law of either Party, become immune from prosecution or punishment for any reason, including lapse of time or amnesty;[4]

(*f*) If the person whose extradition is requested has been or would be subjected in the requesting State to torture or cruel, inhuman or degrading treatment or punishment or if that person has not received or would not receive the minimum guarantees in criminal proceedings, as contained in the International Covenant on Civil and Political Rights, article 14;[5]

(*g*) If the judgement of the requesting State has been rendered *in absentia*, the convicted person has not had sufficient notice of the trial or the opportunity to arrange for his or her defence and he has not had or will not have the opportunity to have the case retried in his or her presence.[6]

Article 4
Optional Grounds for Refusal

Extradition may be refused in any of the following circumstances:

(a) If the person whose extradition is requested is a national of the requested State. Where extradition is refused on this ground, the requested State shall, if the other State so requests, submit the case to its competent authorities with a view to taking appropriate action against the person in respect of the offence for which extradition had been requested;

(b) If the competent authorities of the requested State have decided either not to institute or to terminate proceedings against the person for the offence in respect of which extradition is requested;

(c) If a prosecution in respect of the offence for which extradition is requested is pending in the requested State against the person whose extradition is requested;

(d) If the offence for which extradition is requested carries the death penalty under the law of the requesting State, unless that State gives such assurance as the requested State considers sufficient that the death penalty will not be imposed or, if imposed, will not be carried out;[7]

(e) If the offence for which extradition is requested has been committed outside the territory of either Party and the law of the requested State does not provide for jurisdiction over such an offence committed outside its territory in comparable circumstances;

(f) If the offence for which extradition is requested is regarded under the law of the requested State as having been committed in whole or in part within that State.[8] Where extradition is refused on this ground, the requested State shall, if the other State so requests, submit the case to its competent authorities with a view to taking appropriate action against the person for the offence for which extradition had been requested;

(g) If the person whose extradition is requested has been sentenced or would be liable to be tried or sentenced in the requesting State by an extraordinary or *ad hoc* court or tribunal;

(h) If the requested State, while also taking into account the nature of the offence and the interests of the requesting State, considers that, in the circumstances of the case, the extradition of that person would be

1 Reference to the imposition of a sentence may not be necessary for all countries.

2 Some countries may wish to omit this paragraph or providc an optional ground for refusal under article 4.

3 Some countries may wish to add the following text: "Reference to an offence of a political nature shall not include any offence in respect of which the Parties have assumed an obligation, pursuant to any multilateral convention, to take prosecutorial action where they do not extradite, or any other offence that the Parties have agreed is not an offence of a political character for the purposes of extradition."

4 Some countries may wish to make this an optional ground for refusal under article 4.

5 See resolution 2200 A (XXI), annex.

6 Some countries may wish to add to article 3 the following ground for refusal: "If there is insufficient proof, according to the evidentiary standards of the requested State, that the person whose extradition is requested is a party to the offence".

7 Some countries may wish to apply the same restriction to the imposition of a life, or indeterminate, sentence.

8 Some countries may wish to make specific reference to a vessel under its flag or an aircraft registered under its law at the time of the commission of the offence.

incompatible with humanitarian considerations in view of age, health or other personal circumstances of that person.

Article 5
Channels of Communication and Required Documents

1. A request for extradition shall be made in writing. The request, supporting documents and subsequent communications shall be transmitted through the diplomatic channel, directly between the ministries of justice or any other authorities designated by the Parties.

2. A request for extradition shall be accompanied by the following:

(*a*) In all cases,

(i) As accurate a description as possible of the person sought, together with any other information that may help to establish that person's identity, nationality and location;

(ii) The text of the relevant provision of the law creating the offence or, where necessary, a statement of the law relevant to the offence and a statement of the penalty that can be imposed for the offence;

(*b*) If the person is accused of an offence, by a warrant issued by a court or other competent judicial authority for the arrest of the person or a certified copy of that warrant, a statement of the offence for which extradition is requested and a description of the acts or omissions constituting the alleged offence, including an indication of the time and place of its commission;[1]

(*c*) If the person has been convicted of an offence, by a statement of the offence for which extradition is requested and a description of the acts or omissions constituting the offence and by the original or certified copy of the judgement or any other document setting out the conviction and the sentence imposed, the fact that the sentence is enforceable, and the extent to which the sentence remains to be served;

(*d*) If the person has been convicted of an offence in his or her absence, in addition to the documents set out in paragraph 2 (c) of the present article, by a statement as to the legal means available to the person to prepare his or her defence or to have the case retried in his or her presence;

(*e*) If the person has been convicted of an offence but no sentence has been imposed, by a statement of the offence for which extradition is requested and a description of the acts or omissions constituting the offence and by a document setting out the conviction and a statement affirming that there is an intention to impose a sentence.

3. The documents submitted in support of a request for extradition shall be accompanied by a translation into the language of the requested State or in another language acceptable to that State.

Article 6
Simplified Extradition Procedure

The requested State, if not precluded by its law, may grant extradition after receipt of a request for provisional arrest, provided that the person sought explicitly consents before a competent authority.

Article 7
Certification and Authentication

Except as provided by the present Treaty, a request for extradition and the documents in support thereof, as well as documents or other material supplied in response to such a request, shall not require certification or authentication.[2]

Article 8
Additional Information

If the requested State considers that the information provided in support of a request for extradition is not sufficient, it may request that additional information be furnished within such reasonable time as it specifies.

Article 9
Provisional Arrest

1. In case of urgency the requesting State may apply for the provisional arrest of the person sought pending the presentation of the request for extradition. The application shall be transmitted by means of the facilities of the International Criminal Police Organization, by post or telegraph or by any other means affording a record in writing.

2. The application shall contain a description of the person sought, a statement that extradition is to be requested, a statement of the existence of one of the documents mentioned in paragraph 2 of article 5 of the present Treaty, authorizing the apprehension of the person, a statement of the punishment that can be or has been imposed for the offence, including the time left to be served and a concise statement of the facts of the case, and a statement of the location, where known, of the person.

3. The requested State shall decide on the application in accordance with its law and communicate its decision to the requesting State without delay.

4. The person arrested upon such an application shall be set at liberty upon the expiration of [40] days from the date of arrest if a request for extradition, supported by the relevant documents specified in paragraph 2 of article 5 of the present Treaty, has not been received. The present paragraph does not preclude the possibility of conditional release of the person prior to the expiration of the [40] days.

5. The release of the person pursuant to paragraph 4 of the present article shall not prevent rearrest and institution of proceedings with a view to extraditing the person sought if the request and supporting documents are subsequently received.

Article 10
Decision on the Request

1. The requested State shall deal with the request for extradition pursuant to procedures provided by its own law, and shall promptly communicate its decision to the requesting State.

2. Reasons shall be given for any complete or partial refusal of the request.

Article 11
Surrender of the Person

1. Upon being informed that extradition has been granted, the Parties shall, without undue delay, arrange for the surrender of the person sought and the requested State shall inform the requesting State of the length of time for which the person sought was detained with a view to surrender.

2. The person shall be removed from the territory of the requested State within such reasonable period as the requested State specifies and, if the person is not removed within that period, the requested State may release the person and may refuse to extradite that person for the same offence.

3. If circumstances beyond its control prevent a Party from surrendering or removing the person to be extradited, it shall notify the other Party. The two Parties shall mutually decide upon a new date of surrender, and the provisions of paragraph 2 of the present article shall apply.

Article 12
Postponed or Conditional Surrender

1. The requested State may, after making its decision on the request for extradition, postpone the surrender of a person sought, in order to proceed against that person, or, if that person has already been convicted, in order to enforce a sentence imposed for an offence other than that for which extradition is sought. In such a case the requested State shall advise the requesting State accordingly.

---

1 Countries that require a judicial assessment of the sufficiency of evidence may wish to add the following clause: "and sufficient proof in a form acceptable under the law of the requested State, establishing, according to the evidentiary standards of that State, that the person is a party to the offence".

2 The laws of some countries require authentication before documents transmitted from other countries can be admitted in their courts and, therefore, would require a clause setting out the authentication required.

2. The requested State may, instead of postponing surrender, temporarily surrender the person sought to the requesting State in accordance with conditions to be determined between the Parties.

Article 13
Surrender of Property

1. To the extent permitted under the law of the requested State and subject to the rights of third parties, which shall be duly respected, all property found in the requested State that has been acquired as a result of the offence or that may be required as evidence shall, if the requesting State so requests, be surrendered if extradition is granted.

2. The said property may, if the requesting State so requests, be surrendered to the requesting State even if the extradition agreed to cannot be carried out.

3. When the said property is liable to seizure or confiscation in the requested State, it may retain it or temporarily hand it over.

4. Where the law of the requested State or the protection of the rights of third parties so require, any property so surrendered shall be returned to the requested State free of charge after the completion of the proceedings, if that State so requests.

Article 14
Rule of Speciality

1. A person extradited under the present Treaty shall not be proceeded against, sentenced, detained, re-extradited to a third State, or subjected to any other restriction of personal liberty in the territory of the requesting State for any offence committed before surrender other than:

(*a*) An offence for which extradition was granted;

(*b*) Any other offence in respect of which the requested State consents.[1] Consent shall be given if the offence for which it is requested is itself subject to extradition in accordance with the present Treaty.[2]

2. A request for the consent of the requested State under the present article shall be accompanied by the documents mentioned in paragraph 2 of article 5 of the present Treaty and a legal record of any statement made by the extradited person with respect to the offence.

3. Paragraph 1 of the present article shall not apply if the person has had an opportunity to leave the requesting State and has not done so within [30/45] days of final discharge in respect of the offence for which that person was extradited or if the person has voluntarily returned to the territory of the requesting State after leaving it.

Article 15
Transit

1. Where a person is to be extradited to a Party from a third State through the territory of the other Party, the Party to which the person is to be extradited shall request the other Party to permit the transit of that person through its territory. This does not apply where air transport is used and no landing in the territory of the other Party is scheduled.

2. Upon receipt of such a request, which shall contain relevant information, the requested State shall deal with this request pursuant to procedures provided by its own law. The requested State shall grant the request expeditiously unless its essential interests would be prejudiced thereby.[3]

3. The State of transit shall ensure that legal provisions exist that would enable detaining the person in custody during transit.

4. In the event of an unscheduled landing, the Party to be requested to permit transit may, at the request of the escorting officer, hold the person in custody for [48] hours, pending receipt of the transit request to be made in accordance with paragraph 1 of the present article.

Article 16
Concurrent Requests

If a Party receives requests for extradition for the same person from both the other Party and a third State it shall, at its discretion, determine to which of those States the person is to be extradited.

Article 17
Costs

1. The requested State shall meet the cost of any proceedings in its jurisdiction arising out of a request for extradition.

2. The requested State shall also bear the costs incurred in its territory in connection with the seizure and handing over of property, or the arrest and detention of the person whose extradition is sought.[4]

3. The requesting State shall bear the costs incurred in conveying the person from the territory of the requested State, including transit costs.

Article 18
Final Provisions

1. The present Treaty is subject to [ratification, acceptance or approval] . The instruments of [ratification, acceptance or approval] shall be exchanged as soon as possible.

2. The present Treaty shall enter into force on the thirtieth day after the day on which the instruments of [ratification, acceptance or approval] are exchanged.

3. The present Treaty shall apply to requests made after its entry into force, even if the relevant acts or omissions occurred prior to that date.

4. Either Contracting Party may denounce the present Treaty by giving notice in writing to the other Party. Such denunciation shall take effect six months following the date on which such notice is received by the other Party.

In witness whereof the undersigned, being duly authorized thereto by their respective Governments, have signed the present Treaty.

DONE at... on ... in the ... and ... languages, [both/all] texts being equally

45/117. Model Treaty on Mutual Assistance in Criminal Matters

Committee: 3
Vote: Adopted without a vote

The General Assembly,

Bearing in mind the Milan Plan of Action,[5] adopted by the Seventh United Nations Congress on the Prevention of Crime and the Treatment of Offenders and approved by the General Assembly in its resolution 40/32 of 29 November 1985,

Bearing in mind also the Guiding Principles for Crime Prevention and Criminal Justice in the Context of Development and a New International Economic Order,[6] principle 37 of which stipulates that the United Nations should prepare model instruments suitable for use as international and regional conventions and as guides for national implementing legislation,

---

1 Some countries may wish to add, as a third case, explicit consent of the person.

2 Some countries may not wish to assume that obligation and may wish to include other grounds in determining whether or not to grant consent.

3 Some countries may wish to agree on other grounds for refusal, which may also warrant refusal for extradition, such as those related to the nature of the offence (e.g. political, fiscal, military) or to the status of the person (e.g. their own nationals.)

4 Some countries may wish to consider reimbursement of costs incurred as a result of withdrawal of a request for extradition or provisional arrest.

5 See *Seventh United Nations Congress on the Prevention of Crime and the Treatment of Offenders, Milan, 26 August - 6 September 1985: report prepared by the Secretariat* (United Nations publications, Sales No. E.86.IV.1), chap. I, sect. A

6 *Ibid.*, sect. B.

Recalling resolution 1 of the Seventh Congress,[1] on organized crime, in which Member States were urged, *inter alia*, to increase their activity at the international level in order to combat organized crime, including, as appropriate, entering into bilateral treaties on extradition and mutual legal assistance,

Recalling also resolution 23 of the Seventh Congress,[2] on criminal acts of a terrorist character, in which all States were called upon to take steps to strengthen cooperation particularly, *inter alia*, in the area of mutual legal assistance,

Recalling further the United Nations Convention against Illicit Traffic in Narcotic Drugs and Psychotropic Substances,[3]

Acknowledging the valuable contributions to the development of a model treaty on mutual assistance in criminal matters that Governments, non-governmental organizations and individual experts have made, in particular the Government of Australia and the International Association of Penal Law,

Gravely concerned about the escalation of crime, both national and transnational,

Convinced that the establishment of bilateral and multilateral arrangements for mutual assistance in criminal matters will greatly contribute to the development of more effective international cooperation for the control of criminality,

Conscious of the need to respect human dignity and recalling the rights conferred upon every person involved in criminal proceedings, as embodied in the Universal Declaration of Human Rights[4] and the International Covenant on Civil and Political Rights,[5]

Recognizing the importance of a model treaty on mutual assistance in criminal matters as an effective way of dealing with the complex aspects and serious consequences of crime, especially in its new forms and dimensions,

1. *Adopts* the Model Treaty on Mutual Assistance in Criminal Matters together with the Optional Protocol thereto, contained in the annex to the present resolution, as a useful framework that could be of assistance to States interested in negotiating and concluding bilateral agreements aimed at improving cooperation in matters of crime prevention and criminal justice;

2. *Invites* Member States, if they have not yet established treaty relations with other States in the matter of mutual assistance in criminal matters, or if they wish to revise existing treaty relations, to take into account, whenever doing so, the Model Treaty;

3. *Urges* all States to strengthen further international cooperation and mutual assistance in criminal justice;

4. *Requests* the Secretary-General to bring the present resolution, with the Model Treaty and the Optional Protocol thereto, to the attention of Governments;

5. *Urges* Member States to inform the Secretary-General periodically of efforts undertaken to establish mutual assistance arrangements in criminal matters;

6. *Requests* the Committee on Crime Prevention and Control to review periodically the progress attained in this field;

7. *Also requests* the Committee on Crime Prevention and Control, where requested, to provide guidance and assistance to Member States in the development of legislation which would enable giving effect to the obligations which will be contained in such treaties as are to be negotiated on the basis of the Model Treaty;

8. *Invites* Member States, on request, to make available to the Secretary-General the provisions of their legislation on mutual assistance in criminal matters so that these may be made available to those Member States desiring to enact or further develop legislation in this field.

68th plenary meeting
14 December 1990

1 *Ibid.*, sect. E.
2 *Ibid.*, sect. E.
3 E/CONF.82/15 and Corr.2.
4 Resolution 217 A (III).
5 See resolution 2200 A (XXI), annex.

Annex

Model Treaty on Mutual Assistance in Criminal Matters

The ... and the ...

Desirous of extending to each other the widest measure of cooperation to combat crime,

Have agreed as follows:

Article 1
Scope of Application[6]

1. The Parties shall, in accordance with the present Treaty, afford to each other the widest possible measure of mutual assistance in investigations or court proceedings in respect of offences the punishment of which, at the time of the request for assistance, falls within the jurisdiction of the judicial authorities of the requesting State.

2. Mutual assistance to be afforded in accordance with the present Treaty may include:

(a) Taking evidence or statements from persons;

(b) Assisting in the availability of detained persons or others to give evidence or assist in investigations;

(c) Effecting service of judicial documents;

(d) Executing searches and seizures;

(e) Examining objects and sites;

(f) Providing information and evidentiary items;

(g) Providing originals or certified copies of relevant documents and records, including bank, financial, corporate or business records.

3. The present Treaty does not apply to:

(a) The arrest or detention of any person with a view to the extradition of that person;

(b) The enforcement in the requested State of criminal judgements imposed in the requesting State except to the extent permitted by the law of the requested State and the Optional Protocol to the present Treaty;

(c) The transfer of persons in custody to serve sentences;

(d) The transfer of proceedings in criminal matters.

Article 2[7]
Other Arrangements

Unless the Parties decide otherwise, the present Treaty shall not affect obligations subsisting between them whether pursuant to other treaties or arrangements or otherwise.

Article 3
Designation of Competent Authorities

Each Party shall designate and indicate to the other Party an authority or authorities by or through which requests for the purpose of the present Treaty should be made or received.

Article 4[8]
Refusal of Assistance

1. Assistance may be refused if:[9]

6 Additions to the scope of assistance to be provided, such as provisions covering information on sentences passed on nationals of the Parties, can be considered bilaterally. Obviously, such assistance must be compatible with the law of the requested State.

7 Article 2 recognizes the continuing role of informal assistance between law enforcement agencies and associated agencies in different countries.

8 Article 4 provides an illustrative list of the grounds for refusal.

9 Some countries may wish to delete or modify some of the provisions or include other grounds for refusal, such as those related to the nature of the offence (e.g. fiscal), the nature of the applicable penalty (e.g. capital punishment), requirements of shared concepts (e.g. double jurisdiction, no lapse of time) or specific kinds of assistance (e.g. interception of telecommunications, performing deoxyribonucleic-acid (DNA) tests). In particular, some countries may wish to include as grounds of refusal the fact that the act on which the request is based would not be an offence if committed in the territory of the requested State (dual criminality).

(*a*) The requested State is of the opinion that the request, if granted, would prejudice its sovereignty, security, public order (*ordre public*) or other essential public interests;

(*b*) The offence is regarded by the requested State as being of a political nature;

(*c*) There are substantial grounds for believing that the request for assistance has been made for the purpose of prosecuting a person on account of that person's race, sex, religion, nationality, ethnic origin or political opinions or that that person's position may be prejudiced for any of those reasons;

(*d*) The request relates to an offence that is subject to investigation or prosecution in the requested State or the prosecution of which in the requesting State would be incompatible with the requested State's law on double jeopardy (*ne bis in idem*);

(*e*) The assistance requested requires the requested State to carry out compulsory measures that would be inconsistent with its law and practice had the offence been the subject of investigation or prosecution under its own jurisdiction;

(*f*) The act is an offence under military law, which is not also an offence under ordinary criminal law.

2. Assistance shall not be refused solely on the ground of secrecy of banks and similar financial institutions.

3. The requested State may postpone the execution of the request if its immediate execution would interfere with an ongoing investigation or prosecution in the requested State.

4. Before refusing a request or postponing its execution, the requested State shall consider whether assistance may be granted subject to certain conditions. If the requesting State accepts assistance subject to these conditions, it shall comply with them.

5. Reasons shall be given for any refusal or postponement of mutual assistance.

Article 5
Contents of Requests

1. Requests for assistance shall include:[1]

(a) The name of the requesting office and the competent authority conducting the investigation or court proceedings to which the request relates;

(b) The purpose of the request and a brief description of the assistance sought;

(c) A description of the facts alleged to constitute the offence and a statement or text of the relevant laws, except in cases of a request for service of documents;

(d) The name and address of the person to be served, where necessary;

(e) The reasons for and details of any particular procedure or requirement that the requesting State wishes to be followed, including a statement as to whether sworn or affirmed evidence or statements are required;

(f) Specification of any time-limit within which compliance with the request is desired;

(g) Such other information as is necessary for the proper execution of the request.

2. Requests, supporting documents and other communications made pursuant to the present Treaty shall be accompanied by a translation into the language of the requested State or another language acceptable to that State.

3. If the requested State considers that the information contained in the request is not sufficient to enable the request to be dealt with, it may request additional information.

1 This list can be reduced or expanded in bilateral negotiations.

Article 6
Execution of Requests[2]

Subject to article 19 of the present Treaty, requests for assistance shall be carried out promptly, in the manner provided for by the law and practice of the requested State. To the extent consistent with its law and practice, the requested State shall carry out the request in the manner specified by the requesting State.

Article 7
Return of Material to the Requested State

Any property, as well as original records or documents, handed over to the requesting State under the present Treaty shall be returned to the requested State as soon as possible unless the latter waives its right of return thereof.

Article 8[3]
Limitation on Use

The requesting State shall not, without the consent of the requested State, use or transfer information or evidence provided by the requested State for investigations or proceedings other than those stated in the request. However, in cases where the charge is altered, the material provided may be used in so far as the offence, as charged, is an offence in respect of which mutual assistance could be provided under the present Treaty.

Article 9
Protection of Confidentiality [4]

Upon request:

(a) The requested State shall use its best endeavours to keep confidential the request for assistance, its contents and its supporting documents as well as the fact of granting of such assistance. If the request cannot be executed without breaching confidentiality, the requested State shall so inform the requesting State, which shall then determine whether the request should nevertheless be executed;

(b) The requesting State shall keep confidential evidence and information provided by the requested State, except to the extent that the evidence and information is needed for the investigation and proceedings described in the request.

Article 10
Service of Documents[5]

1. The requested State shall effect service of documents that are transmitted to it for this purpose by the requesting State.

2. A request to effect service of summonses shall be made to a requested State not less than [...][6] days before the date on which the

2 More detailed provisions may be included concerning the provision of information on the time and place of execution of the request and requiring the requested State to inform promptly the requesting State in cases where significant delay is likely to occur or where a decision is made not to comply with the request and the reasons for refusal.

3 Some countries may wish to omit article 8 or modify it, e.g. restrict it to fiscal offences.

4 Provisions relating to confidentiality will be important for many countries but may present problems to others. The nature of the provisions in individual treaties can be determined in bilateral negotiations.

5 More detailed provisions relating to the service of documents, such as writs and judicial verdicts, can be determined bilaterally. Provisions may be desired for the service of documents by mail or other manner and for the forwarding of proof of service of the documents. For example, proof of service could be given by means of a receipt dated and signed by the person served or by means of a declaration made by the requested State that service has been effected, with an indication of the form and date of such service. One or other of these documents could be sent promptly to the requesting State. The requested State could, if the requesting State so requests, state whether service has been effected in accordance with the law of the requested State. If service could not be effected, the reasons could be communicated promptly by the requested State to the requesting State.

6 Depending on travel distance and related arrangements.

appearance of a person is required. In urgent cases, the requested State may waive the time requirement.

Article 11[1]
Obtaining of evidence

1. The requested State shall, in conformity with its law and upon request, take the sworn or affirmed testimony, or otherwise obtain statements of persons or require them to produce items of evidence for transmission to the requesting State.

2. Upon the request of the requesting State, the parties to the relevant proceedings in the requesting State, their legal representatives and representatives of the requesting State may, subject to the laws and procedures of the requested State, be present at the proceedings.

Article 12
Right or Obligation to Decline to Give Evidence

1. A person who is required to give evidence in the requested or requesting State may decline to give evidence where either:

(*a*) The law of the requested State permits or requires that person to decline to give evidence in similar circumstances in proceedings originating in the requested State; or

(*b*) The law of the requesting State permits or requires that person to decline to give evidence in similar circumstances in proceedings originating in the requesting State.

2. If a person claims that there is a right or obligation to decline to give evidence under the law of the other State, the State where that person is present shall, with respect thereto, rely on a certificate of the competent authority of the other State as evidence of the existence or non-existence of that right or obligation.

Article 13
Availability of Persons in Custody to Give Evidence or to Assist in Investigations[2]

1. Upon the request of the requesting State, and if the requested State agrees and its law so permits, a person in custody in the latter State may, subject to his or her consent, be temporarily transferred to the requesting State to give evidence or to assist in the investigations.

2. While the person transferred is required to be held in custody under the law of the requested State, the requesting State shall hold that person in custody and shall return that person in custody to the requested State at the conclusion of the matter in relation to which transfer was sought or at such earlier time as the person's presence is no longer required.

3. Where the requested State advises the requesting State that the transferred person is no longer required to be held in custody, that person shall be set at liberty and be treated as a person referred to in article 14 of the present Treaty.

Article 14
Availability of Other Persons to Give Evidence or Assist in Investigations[3]

1. The requesting State may request the assistance of the requested State in inviting a person:

(a) To appear in proceedings in relation to a criminal matter in the requesting State unless that person is the person charged; or

(b) To assist in the investigations in relation to a criminal matter in the requesting State.

2. The requested State shall invite the person to appear as a witness or expert in proceedings or to assist in the investigations. Where appropriate, the requested State shall satisfy itself that satisfactory arrangements have been made for the person's safety.

3. The request or the summons shall indicate the approximate allowances and the travel and subsistence expenses payable by the requesting State.

4. Upon request, the requested State may grant the person an advance, which shall be refunded by the requesting State.

Article 15[4]
Safe Conduct

1. Subject to paragraph 2 of the present article, where a person is in the requesting State pursuant to a request made under article 13 or 14 of the present Treaty:

(*a*) That person shall not be detained, prosecuted, punished or subjected to any other restrictions of personal liberty in the requesting State in respect of any acts or omissions or convictions that preceded the person's departure from the requested State;

(*b*) That person shall not, without that person's consent, be required to give evidence in any proceeding or to assist in any investigation other than the proceeding or investigation to which the request relates.

2. Paragraph 1 of the present article shall cease to apply if that person, being free to leave, has not left the requesting State within a period of 15 consecutive days, or any longer period otherwise agreed on by the Parties, after that person has been officially told or notified that his or her presence is no longer required or, having left, has voluntarily returned.

3. A person who does not consent to a request pursuant to article 13 or accept an invitation pursuant to article 14 shall not, by reason thereof, be liable to any penalty or be subjected to any coercive measure, notwithstanding any contrary statement in the request or summons.

Article 16
Provision of Publicly Available Documents and other Records[5]

1. The requested State shall provide copies of documents and records in so far as they are open to public access as part of a public register or otherwise, or in so far as they are available for purchase or inspection by the public.

2. The requested State may provide copies of any other document or record under the same conditions as such document or record may be provided to its own law enforcement and judicial authorities.

Article 17
Search and Seizure[6]

The requested State shall, in so far as its law permits, carry out requests for search and seizure and delivery of any material to the requesting State for evidentiary purposes, provided that the rights of *bona fide* third parties are protected.

Article 18
Certification and Authentication[7]

A request for assistance and the documents in support thereof, as well as documents or other material supplied in response to such a request, shall not require certification or authentication.

---

1 Article 11 is concerned with the obtaining of evidence in judicial proceedings, the taking of a person's statement by a less formal process and the production of items of evidence.

2 In bilateral negotiations, provisions may also be introduced to deal with such matters as the modalities and time of restitution of evidence and the setting of a time-limit for the presence of the person in custody in the requesting State.

3 Provisions relating to the payment of the expenses of the person providing assistance are contained in paragraph 3 of article 14. Additional details, such as provision for the payment of costs in advance, can be subject of bilateral negotiations.

4 The provisions in article 15 may be required as the only way of securing important evidence in proceedings involving serious national and transnational crime. However, as they may raise difficulties for some countries, the precise content of the article, including any additions or modifications, can be determined in bilateral negotiations.

5 The question may arise as the whether this should be discretionary. This provision can be the subject of bilateral negotiations.

6 Bilateral arrangements may cover the provision of information on the results of search and seizure and the observance of conditions imposed in relation to the delivery of seized property.

7 The laws of some countries require authentication before documents transmitted from other countries can be admitted in their courts, and, therefore, would require a clause setting out the authentication required.

Article 19
Costs[1]

The ordinary costs of executing a request shall be borne by the requested State, unless otherwise determined by the Parties. If expenses of a substantial or extraordinary nature are or will be required to execute the request, the Parties shall consult in advance to determine the terms and conditions under which the request shall be executed as well as the manner in which the costs shall be borne.

Article 20
Consultation

The Parties shall consult promptly, at the request of either, concerning the interpretation, the application or the carrying out of the present Treaty either generally or in relation to a particular case.

Article 21
Final Provisions

1. The present Treaty is subject to [ratification, acceptance or approval]. The instruments of [ratification, acceptance or approval] shall be exchanged as soon as possible.

2. The present Treaty shall enter into force on the thirtieth day after the day on which the instruments of [ratification, acceptance or approval] are exchanged.

3. The present Treaty shall apply to requests made after its entry into force, even if the relevant acts or omissions occurred prior to that date.

4. Either Contracting Party may denounce the present Treaty by giving notice in writing to the other Party. Such denunciation shall take effect six months following the date on which it is received by the other Party.

IN WITNESS WHEREOF the undersigned, being duly authorized thereto by their respective Governments, have signed the present Treaty.

DONE at ... on ... in the ... and ... languages, [both/all] texts being equally authentic.

Optional Protocol to the Model Treaty on Mutual Assistance in Criminal Matters concerning the proceeds of crime[2]

1. In the present Protocol "proceeds of crime" means any property suspected, or found by a court, to be property directly or indirectly derived or realized as a result of the commission of an offence or to represent the value of property and other benefits derived from the commission of an offence.

2. The requested State shall, upon request, endeavour to ascertain whether any proceeds of the alleged crime are located within its jurisdiction and shall notify the requesting State of the results of its inquiries. In making the request, the requesting State shall notify the requested State of the basis of its belief that such proceeds may be located within its jurisdiction.

3. In pursuance of a request made under paragraph 2 of the present Protocol, the requested State shall endeavour to trace assets, investigate financial dealings, and obtain other information or evidence that may help to secure the recovery of proceeds of crime.

4. Where, pursuant to paragraph 2 of the present Protocol, suspected proceeds of crime are found, the requested State shall upon request take such measures as are permitted by its law to prevent any dealing in, transfer or disposal of, those suspected proceeds of crime, pending a final determination in respect of those proceeds by a court of the requesting State.

5. The requested State shall, to the extent permitted by its law, give effect to or permit enforcement of a final order forfeiting or confiscating the proceeds of crime made by a court of the requesting State or take other appropriate action to secure the proceeds following a request by the requesting State.[3]

6. The Parties shall ensure that the rights of *bona fide* third parties shall be respected in the application of the present Protocol.

IN WITNESS WHEREOF, the undersigned, being duly authorized thereto by their respective Governments, have signed the present Protocol.

DONE at ... on ... in the ... and ... languages, [both/all] texts being equally authentic.

45/118. Model Treaty on the Transfer of Proceedings in Criminal Matters

Committee: 3
Vote: Adopted without a vote

The General Assembly,

Recalling the Milan Plan of Action,[4] adopted by the Seventh United Nations Congress on the Prevention of Crime and the Treatment of Offenders and approved by the General Assembly in its resolution 40/32 of 29 November 1985,

Recalling also the Guiding Principles for Crime Prevention and Criminal Justice in the Context of Development and a New International Economic Order,[5] principle 37 of which stipulates that the United Nations should prepare model instruments suitable for use as international and regional conventions and as guides for national implementing legislation,

Recalling further resolution 12 of the Seventh Congress,[6] on the transfer of proceedings in criminal matters, in which the Committee on Crime Prevention and Control was requested to study the question and to consider the possibility of formulating a model agreement in this area,

Acknowledging the valuable contributions made by Governments, non-governmental organizations and individual experts to the drafting of a model treaty on the transfer of proceedings in criminal matters, in particular the International Expert Meeting on the United Nations and Law Enforcement, held under the auspices of the United Nations at Baden, Austria, from 16 to 19 November 1987, the Interregional Preparatory Meeting for the Eighth United Nations Congress on the Prevention of Crime and the Treatment of Offenders on topic V, "United Nations norms and guidelines in crime prevention and

---

1 More detailed provisions may be included. For example, the requested State would meet the ordinary cost of fulfilling the request for assistance except that the requesting State would bear (*a*) the exceptional or extraordinary expenses required to fulfil the request, where required by the requested State and subject to previous consultations; (*b*) the expenses associated with conveying any person to or from the territory of the requested State, and any fees, allowances or expenses payable to that person while in the requesting State pursuant to a request under article 11, 13 or 14; (*c*) the expenses associated with conveying custodial or escorting officers; and (*d*) the expenses involved in obtaining reports of experts.

2 The present Optional Protocol is included on the ground that questions of forfeiture are conceptually different from, although closely related to, matters generally accepted as failing within the description of mutual assistance. However, States may wish to include these provisions in the text because of their importance in dealing with organized crime. Moreover, assistance in forfeiting the proceeds of crime has now emerged as a new instrument in international cooperation. Provisions similiar to those outlined in the present Protocol appear in many bilateral assistance treaties. Further details can be provided in bilateral arrangements. One matter that could be considered is the need for other provisions dealing with issues related to bank secrecy. An addition could, for example, be made to paragraph 4 of the present Protocol providing that the requested State shall, upon request, take such measures as are permitted by its law to require compliance with monitoring orders by financial institutions. Provision could be made for the sharing of the proceeds of crime between the Contracting States for consideration of the disposal of the proceeds on a case-by-case basis.

3 The Parties might consider widening the scope of the present Protocol by the inclusion of references to victims' restitutions and the recovery of fines imposed as a sentence in a criminal prosecution.

4 See *Seventh United Nations Congress on the Prevention of Crime and the Treatment of Offenders, Milan, 26 August - 6 September 1985: report prepared by the Secretariat* (United Nations publications, Sales No. E.86.IV.1), chap. I, sect. A.

5 *Ibid.*, sect. B.

6 *Ibid.*, sect. E.

criminal justice: implementation and priorities for further standard setting"[1] and the regional preparatory meetings for the Eighth Congress,

Convinced that the establishment of bilateral and multilateral arrangements for the transfer of proceedings in criminal matters will greatly contribute to the development of more effective international cooperation aimed at controlling crime,

Conscious of the need to respect human dignity and recalling the rights conferred upon every person involved in criminal proceedings, as embodied in the Universal Declaration of Human Rights[2] and the International Covenant on Civil and Political Rights,[3]

Recognizing the importance of a model treaty on the transfer of proceedings in criminal matters as an effective way of dealing with the complex aspects, consequences and modern evolution of transnational crime,

1. *Adopts* the Model Treaty on the Transfer of Proceedings in Criminal Matters, contained in the annex to the present resolution, as a useful framework that could be of assistance to States interested in negotiating and concluding bilateral or multilateral treaties aimed at improving cooperation in matters of crime prevention and criminal justice;

2. *Invites* Member States, if they have not yet established treaty relations with other States in regard to transfer of proceedings in criminal matters, or if they wish to revise existing treaty relations, to take the Model Treaty into account whenever doing so;

3. *Urges* Member States to strengthen international cooperation in criminal justice;

4. *Also urges* Member States to inform the Secretary-General periodically of efforts undertaken to establish arrangements for the transfer of proceedings in criminal matters;

5. *Requests* the Committee on Crime Prevention and Control to conduct periodic reviews of the progress attained in this field;

6. *Requests* the Secretary-General to assist Member States, at their request, in the development of treaties on the transfer of proceedings in criminal matters and to report regularly thereon to the Committee.

68th plenary meeting
14 December 1990

Annex

Model Treaty on the Transfer of Proceedings in Criminal Matters

The ... and the ...

Desirous of further strengthening international cooperation and mutual assistance in criminal justice, on the basis of the principles of respect for national sovereignty and jurisdiction and of non-interference in the internal affairs of States,

Believing that such cooperation should further the ends of justice, the social resettlement of offenders and the interests of the victims of crime,

Bearing in mind that the transfer of proceedings in criminal matters contributes to effective administration of justice and to reducing conflicts of competence,

Aware that the transfer of proceedings in criminal matters can help to avoid pre-trial detention and thus reduce the prison population,

Convinced, therefore, that the transfer of proceedings in criminal matters should be promoted,

Have agreed as follows:

Article 1
Scope of Application

1. When a person is suspected of having committed an offence under the law of a State which is a Contracting Party, that State may, if the interests of the proper administration of justice so require, request another State which is a Contracting Party to take proceedings in respect of this offence.

2. For the purpose of applying the present Treaty, the Contracting Parties shall take the necessary legislative measures to ensure that a request of the requesting State to take proceedings shall allow the requested State to exercise the necessary jurisdiction.

Article 2
Channels of Communications

A request to take proceedings shall be made in writing. The request, supporting documents and subsequent communication shall be transmitted through diplomatic channels, directly between the Ministries of Justice or any other authorities designated by the Parties.

Article 3
Required Documents

1. The request to take proceedings shall contain or be accompanied by the following information:

(*a*) The authority presenting the request;

(*b*) A description of the act for which transfer of proceedings is being requested, including the specific time and place of the offence;

(*c*) A statement on the results of investigations which substantiate the suspicion of an offence;

(*d*) The legal provisions of the requesting State on the basis of which the act is considered to be an offence;

(*e*) A reasonably exact statement on the identity, nationality and residence of the suspected person.

2. The documents submitted in support of a request to take proceedings shall be accompanied by a translation into the language of the requested State or into another language acceptable to that State.

Article 4
Certification and Authentication

Subject to national law and unless the Parties decide otherwise, a request to take proceedings and the documents in support thereof, as well as the documents and other material supplied in response to such a request, shall not require certification or authentication.[4]

Article 5
Decision on the Request

The competent authorities of the requested State shall examine what action to take on the request to take proceedings in order to comply, as fully as possible, with the request under their own law, and shall promptly communicate their decision to the requesting State.

Article 6
Dual Criminality

A request to take proceedings can be complied with only if the act on which the request is based would be an offence if committed in the territory of the requested State.

Article 7
Grounds for Refusal

If the requested State refuses acceptance of a request for transfer of proceedings, it shall communicate the reasons for refusal to the requesting State. Acceptance may be refused if:[5]

(*a*) The suspected person is not a national of or ordinary resident in the requested State:

1 See A/CONF.144/IPM.5 and Corr.1.

2 Resolution 217 A (III).

3 See resolution 2200 A (XXI), annex.

4 The laws of some countries require authentication before documents transmitted from other countries can be admitted in their courts and, therefore, would require a clause setting out the authentication required.

5 When negotiating on the basis of the present Model Treaty, States may wish to add other grounds for refusal or conditions to this list, relating, for example, to the nature or gravity of the offence, to the protection of fundamental human rights, or to considerations of public order.

(*b*) The act is an offence under military law, which is not also an offence under ordinary criminal law;

(*c*) The offence is in connection with taxes, duties, customs or exchange;

(*d*) The offence is regarded by the requested State as being of a political nature.

Article 8
The Rights of the Suspected Person

1. The suspected person may express to either State his or her interest in the transfer of the proceedings. Similarly, such interest may be expressed by the legal representative or close relatives of the suspected person.

2. Before a request for transfer of proceedings is made, the requesting State shall, if practicable, allow the suspected person to present his or her views on the alleged offence and the intended transfer, unless that person has absconded or otherwise obstructed the course of justice.

Article 9
The Rights of the Victim

The requesting and requested States shall ensure in the transfer of proceedings that the rights of the victim of the offence, in particular his or her right to restitution or compensation, shall not be affected as a result of the transfer. If a settlement of the claim of the victim has not been reached before the transfer, the requested State shall permit the representation of the claim in the transferred proceedings, if its law provides for such a possibility. In the event of the death of the victim, these provisions shall apply to his or her dependants accordingly.

Article 10
Effects of the Transfer of Proceedings on the Requesting State
(*Ne Bis In Idem*)

Upon acceptance by the requested State of the request to take proceedings against the suspected person, the requesting State shall provisionally discontinue prosecution, except necessary investigation, including judicial assistance to the requested State, until the requested State informs the requesting State that the case has been finally disposed of. From that date on, the requesting State shall definitely refrain from further prosecution of the same offence.

Article 11
Effects of the Transfer of Proceedings on the Requested State

1. The proceedings transferred upon agreement shall be governed by the law of the requested State. When charging the suspected person under its law, the requested State shall make the necessary adjustment with respect to particular elements in the legal description of the offence. Where the competence of the requested State is based on the provision set forth in paragraph 2 of article 1 of the present Treaty, the sanction pronounced in that State shall not be more severe than that provided by the law of the requesting State.

2. As far as compatible with the law of the requested State, any act with a view to proceedings or procedural requirements performed in the requesting State in accordance with its law shall have the same validity in the requested State as if the act had been performed in or by the authorities of that State.

3. The requested State shall inform the requesting State of the decision taken as a result of the proceedings. To this end a copy of any final decision shall be transmitted to the requesting State upon request.

Article 12
Provisional Measures

When the requesting State announces its intention to transmit a request for transfer of proceedings, the requested State may, upon a specific request made for this purpose by the requesting State, apply all such provisional measures, including provisional detention and seizure, as could be applied under its own law if the offence in respect of which transfer of proceedings is requested had been committed in its territory.

Article 13
The Plurality of Criminal Proceedings

When criminal proceedings are pending in two or more States against the same suspected person in respect of the same offence, the States concerned shall conduct consultations to decide which of them alone should continue the proceedings. An agreement reached thereupon shall have the consequences of a request for transfer of proceedings.

Article 14
Costs

Any costs incurred by a Contracting Party because of a transfer of proceedings shall not be refunded, unless otherwise agreed by both the requesting and requested States.

Article 15
Final Provisions

1. The present Treaty is subject to [ratification, acceptance or approval]. The instruments of [ratification, acceptance or approval] shall be exchanged as soon as possible.

2. The present Treaty shall enter into force on the thirtieth day after the day on which the instruments of [ratification, acceptance or approval] are exchanged.

3. The present Treaty shall apply to requests made after its entry into force, even if the relevant acts or omissions occurred prior to that date.

4. Either Contracting Party may denounce the present Treaty by giving notice in writing to the other Party. Such denunciation shall take effect six months following the date on which it is received by the other Party.

IN WITNESS WHEREOF the undersigned, being duly authorized thereto by their respective Governments, have signed the present Treaty.

DONE at ... on ... in the ... and ... languages, [both/all] texts being equally authentic.

45/119. Model Treaty on the Transfer of Supervision of Offenders Conditionally Sentenced or Conditionally Released

Committee: 3
Vote: Adopted without a vote

The General Assembly,

Bearing in mind the Milan Plan of Action,[1] adopted by the Seventh United Nations Congress on the Prevention of Crime and the Treatment of Offenders and approved by the General Assembly in its resolution 40/32 of 29 November 1985,

Bearing in mind also the Guiding Principles for Crime Prevention and Criminal Justice in the Context of Development and a New International Economic Order,[2] principle 37 of which stipulates that the United Nations should prepare model instruments suitable for use as international and regional conventions and as guides for national implementing legislation,

Recalling resolution 13 of the Seventh Congress,[3] on the transfer of supervision of foreign offenders who have been conditionally sentenced or conditionally released, in which the Committee on Crime Prevention and Control was requested to study this subject and to consider the possibility of formulating a model treaty in this area,

Acknowledging the valuable contributions made by Governments, non-governmental organizations and individual experts to the drafting of a model treaty on the transfer of supervision of offenders conditionally sentenced or conditionally released, in particular the

---

1 See *Seventh United Nations Congress on the Prevention of Crime and the Treatment of Offenders, Milan, 26 August - 6 September 1985: report prepared by the Secretariat* (United Nations publications, Sales No. E.86.IV.1), chap. I, sect. A.

2 *Ibid.*, sect. B.

3 *Ibid.*, sect. E.

International Expert Meeting on the United Nations and Law Enforcement, held under the auspices of the United Nations at Baden, Austria, from 16 to 19 November 1987, the Interregional Preparatory Meeting for the Eighth United Nations Congress on the Prevention of Crime and the Treatment of Offenders on topic V, "United Nations norms and guidelines in crime prevention and criminal justice: implementation and priorities for further standard setting"[1] and the regional preparatory meetings for the Eighth Congress,

Convinced that the establishment of bilateral and multilateral arrangements for transfer of supervision of offenders conditionally sentenced or conditionally released will greatly contribute to the development of more effective international cooperation in penal matters,

Conscious of the need to respect human dignity and recalling the rights conferred upon every person involved in criminal proceedings, as embodied in the Universal Declaration of Human Rights[2] and the International Covenant on Civil and Political Rights,[3]

1. *Adopts* the Model Treaty on the Transfer of Supervision of Offenders Conditionally Sentenced or Conditionally Released, contained in the annex to the present resolution, as a useful framework that could be of assistance to States interested in negotiating and concluding bilateral or multilateral treaties aimed at improving cooperation in matters of crime prevention and criminal justice;

2. *Invites* Member States, if they have not yet established treaty relations with other States in the area of the transfer of supervision of offenders conditionally sentenced or conditionally released, or if they wish to revise existing treaty relations, to take into account the Model Treaty whenever doing so;

3. *Urges* all Member States to strengthen international cooperation in criminal justice;

4. *Also urges* Member States to inform the Secretary-General periodically of efforts undertaken to establish arrangements on the transfer of supervision of offenders conditionally sentenced or conditionally released;

5. *Requests* the Committee on Crime Prevention and Control to conduct periodic reviews of the progress attained in this field;

6. *Requests* the Secretary-General to assist Member States, at their request, in the development of treaties on the transfer of supervision of offenders conditionally sentenced or conditionally released and to report regularly thereon to the Committee.

68th plenary meeting
14 December 1990

Annex

Model Treaty on the Transfer of Supervision of Offenders Conditionally Sentenced or Conditionally Released

The ... and the ...

Desirous of further strengthening international cooperation and mutual assistance in criminal justice, on the basis of the principles of respect for national sovereignty and jurisdiction and of non-interference in the internal affairs of States,

Believing that such cooperation should further the ends of justice, the social resettlement of sentenced persons and the interests of the victims of crime,

Bearing in mind that the transfer of supervision of offenders conditionally sentenced or conditionally released can contribute to an increase in the use of alternatives to imprisonment,

Aware that supervision in the home country of the offender rather than enforcement of the sentence in a country where the offender has no roots also contributes to an earlier and more effective reintegration into society,

Convinced, therefore, that the social rehabilitation of offenders and the increased application of alternatives to imprisonment would be promoted by facilitating the supervision of conditionally sentenced or conditionally released offenders in their State of ordinary residence,

Have agreed as follows:

Article 1
Scope of Application

1. The present Treaty shall be applicable, if, according to a final court decision, a person has been found guilty of an offence and has been:

(*a*) Placed on probation without sentence having been pronounced;

(*b*) Given a suspended sentence involving deprivation of liberty;

(*c*) Given a sentence, the enforcement of which has been modified (parole) or conditionally suspended, in whole or in part, either at the time of the sentence or subsequently.

2. The State where the decision was taken (sentencing State) may request another State (administering State) to take responsibility for applying the terms of the decision (transfer of supervision).

Article 2
Channels of Communication

A request for the transfer of supervision shall be made in writing. The request, supporting documents and subsequent communication shall be transmitted through diplomatic channels, directly between the Ministries of Justice or any other authorities designated by the Parties.

Article 3
Required Documents

1. A request for the transfer of supervision shall contain all necessary information on the identity, nationality and residence of the sentenced person. The request shall be accompanied by the original or a copy of any court decision referred to in article 1 of the present Treaty and a certificate that this decision is final.

2. The documents submitted in support of a request for transfer of supervision shall be accompanied by a translation into the language of the requested State or into another language acceptable to that State.

Article 4
Certification and Authentication

Subject to national law and unless the Parties decide otherwise, a request for transfer of supervision and the documents in support thereof, as well as the documents and other material supplied in response to such a request, shall not require certification or authentication.[4]

Article 5
Decision on the Request

The competent authorities of the administering State shall examine what action to take on the request for supervision in order to comply, as fully as possible, with the request under their own law, and shall promptly communicate their decision to the sentencing State.

Article 6
Dual Criminality[5]

A request for transfer of supervision can be complied with only if the act on which the request is based would constitute an offence if committed in the territory of the administering State.

1 See A/CONF.144/IPM.5 and Corr.1.

2 Resolution 217 A (III).

3 *Ibid.*

4 The laws of some countries require authentication before documents transmitted from other countries can be admitted in their courts and, therefore, would require a clause setting out the authentication required.

5 When negotiating on the basis of the present Model Treaty, States may wish to waive the requirements of dual criminality.

Article 7
Grounds for Refusal[1]

If the administering State refuses acceptance of a request for transfer of supervision, it shall communicate the reasons for refusal to the sentencing State. Acceptance may be refused where:

(*a*) The sentenced person is not an ordinary resident in the administering State;

(*b*) The act is an offence under military law, which is not also an offence under ordinary criminal law;

(*c*) The offence is in connection with taxes, duties, customs or exchange;

(*d*) The offence is regarded by the administering State as being of a political nature;

(*e*) The administering State, under its own law, can no longer carry out the supervision or enforce the sanction in the event of revocation because of lapse of time.

Article 8
The Position of the Sentenced Person

Whether sentenced or standing trial, a person may express to the sentencing State his or her interest in a transfer of supervision and his or her willingness to fulfil any conditions to be imposed. Similarly, such interest may be expressed by his or her legal representative or close relatives. Where appropriate, the Contracting States shall inform the offender or his or her close relatives of the possibilities under the present Treaty.

Article 9
The Rights of the Victim

The sentencing State and the administering State shall ensure in the transfer of supervision that the rights of the victims of the offence, in particular his or her rights to restitution or compensation, shall not be affected as a result of the transfer. In the event of the death of the victim, this provision shall apply to his or her dependants accordingly.

Article 10
The Effects of the Transfer of Supervision on the Sentencing State

The acceptance by the administering State of the responsibility for applying the terms of the decision rendered in the sentencing State shall extinguish the competence of the latter State to enforce the sentence.

Article 11
The Effects of the Transfer of Supervision on the Administering State

1. The supervision transferred upon agreement and the subsequent procedure shall be carried out in accordance with the law of the administering State. That State alone shall have the right of revocation. That State may, to the extent necessary, adapt to its own law the conditions or measures prescribed, provided that such conditions or measures are, in terms of their nature or duration, not more severe than those pronounced in the sentencing State.

2. If the administering State revokes the conditional sentence or conditional release, it shall enforce the sentence in accordance with its own law without, however, going beyond the limits imposed by the sentencing State.

Article 12
Review, Pardon and Amnesty

1. The sentencing State alone shall have the right to decide on any application to reopen the case.

2. Each Party may grant pardon, amnesty or commutation of the sentence in accordance with the provisions of its Constitution or other laws.

[1] When negotiating on the basis of the present Model Treaty, States may wish to add other grounds for refusal or conditions to this list, relating, for example, to the nature or gravity of the offence, to the protection of fundamental human rights, or to considerations of public order.

Article 13
Information

1. The Contracting Parties shall keep each other informed, in so far as it is necessary, of all circumstances likely to affect measures of supervision or enforcement in the administering State. To this end they shall transmit to each other copies of any relevant decisions in this respect.

2. After expiration of the period of supervision, the administering State shall provide to the sentencing State, at its request, a final report concerning the supervised person's conduct and compliance with the measures imposed.

Article 14
Costs

Supervision and enforcement costs incurred in the administering State shall not be refunded, unless otherwise agreed by both the sentencing State and the administering State.

Article 15
Final Provisions

1. The present Treaty is subject to [ratification, acceptance or approval]. The instruments of [ratification, acceptance or approval] shall be exchanged as soon as possible.

2. The present Treaty shall enter into force on the thirtieth day after the day on which the instruments of ratification, acceptance or approval are exchanged.

3. The present Treaty shall apply to requests made after its entry into force, even if the relevant acts or omissions occurred prior to that date.

4. Either Contracting Party may denounce the present Treaty by giving notice in writing to the other Party. Such denunciation shall take effect six months following the date on which it is received by the other Party.

In witness whereof the undersigned, being duly authorized thereto by their respective Governments, have signed the present Treaty.

DONE at ... on ... in the ... and ... languages, [both/all] texts being equally authentic.

45/123. International Cooperation in Combating Organized Crime

Committee: 3
Vote: Adopted without a vote
Ref.: 47/87, 44/71

The General Assembly,

Recalling the responsibility assumed by the United Nations in the field of crime prevention and criminal justice,

Concerned that organized crime has increased in many parts of the world and has become more transnational in character, leading, in particular, to the spread of such negative phenomena as violence, terrorism, corruption and illegal trade in narcotic drugs and, in general, undermining the development process, impairing the quality of life and threatening human rights and fundamental freedoms,

Recalling Economic and Social Council resolution 1989/70 of 24 May 1989 and General Assembly resolution 44/71 of 8 December 1989,

Taking note of resolution 15 entitled "Organized crime" and resolution 24 entitled "Prevention and control of organized crime", adopted by the Eighth United Nations Congress on the Prevention of Crime and the Treatment of Offenders, held at Havana from 27 August to 7 September 1990,[2]

Recalling its resolution S-17/2 of 23 February 1990,

Convinced of the need to strengthen international cooperation in combating organized crime,

[2] See A/CONF.144/28, chap. I, sect. C.

Noting with appreciation that the Eighth Congress explored the possibilities and ways of strengthening further international cooperation in combating organized crime and adopted the Guidelines for the prevention and control of organized crime, as contained in the annex to its resolution 24, as well as model treaties relating to it,[1]

1. *Urges* Member States to give favourable consideration to the implementation of the Guidelines for the prevention and control of organized crime at both national and international levels;

2. *Invites* Member States to make available to the Secretary-General, on request, the provisions of their legislation relating to money laundering, the tracing, monitoring and forfeiture of the proceeds of crime and the monitoring of large-scale cash transactions and other measures so that they may be made available to Member States desiring to enact or further develop legislation in these fields;

3. *Requests* the Committee on Crime Prevention and Control to consider ways of strengthening international cooperation in combating organized crime, taking due account of the opinions of Governments, international organizations and non-governmental organizations, as well as opinions expressed at and decisions taken by the Eighth United Nations Congress on the Prevention of Crime and the Treatment of Offenders, and to submit its views, through the Economic and Social Council, to the General Assembly at its forty-seventh session;

4. *Requests* the Secretary-General to include activities of the United Nations crime prevention and criminal justice programme, related to organized crime, in the United Nations System-Wide Action Plan on Drug Abuse Control;[2]

5. *Calls upon* Member States, international organizations and interested non-governmental organizations to cooperate with the United Nations in organizing the International Seminar on Organized Crime Control, to be held in Moscow in October 1991.

68th plenary meeting
14 December 1990

46/152. Creation of an Effective United Nations Crime Prevention and Criminal Justice Programme

Committee: 3
Vote: Adopted without a vote
Ref.: 50/146, 49/158, 48/103, 47/91, 44/72, 43/99, 42/59, 41/107, 36/21, 35/171, 32/60, 3139(XXVIII), 3021(XXVII)

The General Assembly,

Alarmed by the scope of criminality and by the dangers posed to the welfare of all nations by the rising incidence of crime generally and by the many forms of criminal activity that have international dimensions,

Alarmed also by the high cost of crime in both human and material terms, especially in its new and transnational forms, and aware of the effects of crime both on States and on individual victims,

Recalling that, in its resolution 45/108 of 14 December 1990, it decided to establish an intergovernmental working group to produce a report elaborating proposals for an effective crime prevention and criminal justice programme and suggesting how that programme could most appropriately be implemented,

Acknowledging with appreciation the work of the Intergovernmental Working Group on the Creation of an Effective International Crime and Justice Programme,[3] which met at Vienna from 5 to 9 August 1991,

Acknowledging with appreciation also the work of the Ministerial Meeting on the Creation of an Effective United Nations Crime Prevention and Criminal Justice Programme, held in Paris from 21 to 23 November 1991,[4]

Recognizing that criminality is a major concern of all nations and that it calls for a concerted response from the international community aimed at preventing crime and recidivism, improving the functioning of criminal justice and law enforcement, and increasing respect for individual rights,

Acknowledging that a United Nations programme devoted to crime prevention and criminal justice can only be effective with the direct involvement of Member States,

Convinced that the principal purpose of such a programme should be to provide practical assistance to States in combating both national and transnational crime,

Noting the principles contained in the Milan Plan of Action[5] and the Guiding Principles for Crime Prevention and Criminal Justice in the Context of Development and a New International Economic Order,[6] as well as other pertinent instruments formulated by United Nations congresses on the prevention of crime and the treatment of offenders and approved by the General Assembly,

Recalling its relevant resolutions in which it stressed the importance of the Commission on Human Rights and the Centre for Human Rights of the Secretariat with regard to respect for human rights in the administration of justice,

Recognizing the urgent need to promote and intensify international cooperation in crime prevention and criminal justice, and the fact that this cooperation can be effective only if it is executed with the direct participation of the receiving States, with due respect for their needs and priorities,

1. *Takes note with appreciation* of the report of the Ministerial Meeting on the Creation of an Effective United Nations Crime Prevention and Criminal Justice Programme;[7]

2. *Approves* the statement of principles and programme of action, annexed to the present resolution, recommending the establishment of a United Nations crime prevention and criminal justice programme;

3. *Supports* a clearer definition of the mandate of the programme with regard to crime prevention and criminal justice, under the aegis and guidance of the United Nations, whose aim will be to respond to the most pressing priorities and needs of the international community in the face of both national and transnational criminality;

4. *Requests* the Secretary-General to give a high level of priority within the United Nations framework, and within the overall existing United Nations resources, to the activities of the United Nations crime prevention and criminal justice programme;

5. *Decides* that the United Nations crime prevention and criminal justice programme shall be devoted to providing States with practical assistance, such as data collection, information and experience sharing, and training, in order to achieve the goals of preventing crime within and among States and of improving the response to crime;

6. *Invites* Member States to give their political and financial support and to take measures that will ensure the implementation of the provisions of the statement of principles and programme of action as they relate to the strengthening of the United Nations crime prevention and criminal justice programme in terms of its structure, content and priorities;

7. *Requests* the Secretary-General to take the necessary action within the overall existing United Nations resources in accordance with the financial rules and regulations of the United Nations and to provide appropriate resources for the effective functioning of the United Nations crime prevention and criminal justice programme in accordance with the principles outlined in the statement of principles and programme of action;

8. *Urges* all entities of the United Nations system, including the regional commissions, the United Nations congresses on the preven-

---

1 *Ibid.*, chap. IV, sect. C.1.

2 See E/1990/39 and Corr.1 and 2 and Add.1.

3 See A/CONF. 156/2.

4 See A/46/703 and Corr.1.

5 See *Seventh United Nations Congress on the Prevention of Crime and the Treatment of Offenders, Milan, 26 August-6 September 1985: report prepared by the Secretariat* (United Nations publication, Sales No. E.86.IV.1), chap. I, sect. A.

6 *Ibid.*, sect. B.

7 See A/CONF. 156/2.

tion of crime and the treatment of offenders, the United Nations institutes for the prevention of crime and the treatment of offenders, the specialized agencies and the relevant intergovernmental and non-governmental organizations, to assist the United Nations crime prevention and criminal justice programme in fulfilling its tasks;

9. *Encourages* all developed countries to review their aid programmes in order to ensure that there is a full and proper contribution in the field of criminal justice within the overall context of development priorities;

10. *Decides* to recommend that a commission on crime prevention and criminal justice be established as a functional commission of the Economic and Social Council, which would hold its inaugural meeting during 1992, and recommends that the meeting of the Committee on Crime Prevention and Control scheduled for February 1992 be cancelled and that the funds necessary for the work of the new commission be made available within the programme budget for the biennium 1992-1993;

11. *Requests* the Economic and Social Council at its organizational session for 1992:

(*a*) To dissolve the Committee on Crime Prevention and Control;

(*b*) To establish the commission on crime prevention and criminal justice as a new functional commission of the Economic and Social Council, in accordance with the recommendations contained in the statement of principles and programme of action;

(*c*) To endorse the role and functions of the United Nations congresses on the prevention of crime and the treatment of offenders, in accordance with the recommendations contained in the statement of principles and programme of action;

12. *Decides* that the present members of the Committee on Crime Prevention and Control should be invited to participate during the first two days of the inaugural session of the new commission, at the expense of their respective Governments, except in the case of Committee members from least developed countries, in order to facilitate an orderly transition;

13. *Also decides* to retain for the United Nations crime prevention and criminal justice programme, without prejudice to additional funds that may be made available by the Secretary-General, all funds currently allocated to the programme, as well as any savings realized by restructuring;

14. *Requests* the Secretary-General to report to the General Assembly at its forty-seventh session on measures taken to implement the statement of principles and programme of action.

77th plenary meeting
18 December 1991

Annex

Statement of Principles and Programme of Action of the United Nations Crime Prevention and Criminal Justice Programme

We, Member States of the United Nations,

Assembled in Paris to consider ways and means of promoting international cooperation in crime prevention and criminal justice and of strengthening the United Nations crime prevention and criminal justice programme in order to make it fully effective and responsive to the needs and priorities of Member States,

Considering that one of the purposes of the United Nations, as stated in the Charter of the United Nations, is to achieve international cooperation in solving international problems of an economic, social, cultural or humanitarian character, and in promoting and encouraging respect for human rights and for fundamental freedoms for all without distinction as to race, sex, language, or religion,

Convinced of the urgent need for more efficient international mechanisms to assist States and to facilitate joint strategies in the field of crime prevention and criminal justice, thus consolidating the role of the United Nations as the focal point in that field,

Noting the importance of the principles contained in the Milan Plan of Action[1] and the Guiding Principles for Crime Prevention and Criminal Justice in the Context of Development and a New International Economic Order,[2] as well as other pertinent instruments formulated by United Nations congresses on the prevention of crime and the treatment of offenders and approved by the General Assembly,

Reaffirming the responsibility assumed by the United Nations in crime prevention and criminal justice,

Bearing in mind the goals of the United Nations in the field of crime prevention and criminal justice, specifically the reduction of criminality, more efficient and effective law enforcement and administration of justice, the observance of human rights and the promotion of the highest standards of fairness, humanity and professional conduct,

Recognizing that it is essential to elicit active support for, and to provide the means of assistance for the development of, an effective United Nations crime prevention and criminal justice programme and to devise appropriate implementation mechanisms,

Deeply concerned about the extent and growth of crime, with its financial, economic and social consequences,

Alarmed at the high cost of crime in both human and material terms, as well as in its new national and transnational forms, and aware of the effects of crime both on States and on individual victims,

Recognizing that the primary responsibility for crime prevention and criminal justice rests with Member States,

Emphasizing the need for strengthened regional and international cooperation to combat crime and recidivism, to effect the improved functioning of criminal justice systems, to promote respect for individual rights and to safeguard the rights of victims of crime and the general security of the public,

Aware that there is unanimity about the need to create a new, vigorous United Nations crime prevention and criminal justice programme, as well as agreement on the need to establish an intergovernmental body for policy-making and priority-setting, to strengthen the effectiveness of the Secretariat unit within the Centre for Social Development and Humanitarian Affairs of the United Nations Office at Vienna, and to increase technical cooperation to help countries, particularly developing countries, translate United Nations policy-guidelines into practice, including training,

Determined to translate our political will into concrete action:

(*a*) By creating the essential mechanisms for practical collaboration against common problems;

(*b*) By providing a framework for inter-State cooperation and coordination to respond to the serious new forms and transnational aspects and dimensions of crime;

(*c*) By establishing information exchanges concerning the implementation and effectiveness of the United Nations norms and standards in crime prevention and criminal justice;

(*d*) By providing means of assistance, particularly to developing countries, for more effective crime prevention and more human justice;

(*e*) By establishing an adequate resource base for a truly effective United Nations crime prevention and criminal justice programme,

Proclaim our strong commitment to the above-mentioned goals and agree on the following:

I. Statement of Principles

1. We recognize that the world is experiencing very important changes resulting in a political climate conducive to democracy, to international cooperation, to more widespread enjoyment of basic human rights and fundamental freedoms, and to the realization of the aspirations of all nations to economic development and social welfare. Notwithstanding these developments, the world today is still

---

1 See *Seventh United Nations Congress on the Prevention of Crime and the Treatment of Offenders, Milan. 26 August-6 September 1985: report prepared by the Secretariat* (United Nations publication, Sales No. E.86.IV.1), chap. I, sect. A.

2 *Ibid.*, sect. B.

beset by violence and other forms of serious crime. These phenomena, wherever they occur, constitute a threat to the maintenance of the rule of law.

2. We believe that justice based on the rule of law is the pillar on which civilized society rests. We seek to improve its quality. A humane and efficient criminal justice system can be an instrument of equity, constructive social change and social justice, protecting basic values and peoples' inalienable rights. Every right of the individual should enjoy the protection of the law against violation, a process in which the criminal justice system plays an essential role.

3. We have in mind the fact that the lowering of the world crime rate is related to, among other factors, the improvement of the social conditions of the population. The developed countries and the developing countries are experiencing difficult situations in this respect. Nevertheless, the specific problems encountered by the developing countries justify priority being given to dealing with the situation confronting these countries.

4. We believe that rising crime is impairing the process of development and the general well-being of humanity and is causing general disquiet within our societies. If this situation continues, progress and development will be the ultimate victims of crime.

5. We also believe that the growing internationalization of crime must generate new and commensurate responses. Organized crime is exploiting the relaxation of border controls designed to foster legitimate trade and, hence, development. The incidence and scope of such crimes may increase further in the coming years unless sound preventive measures are taken. It is thus particularly important to anticipate events and to assist Member States in mounting suitable preventive and control strategies.

6. We recognize that many criminal offences have international dimensions. In this context, there is an urgent need for States to address, while respecting the sovereignty of States, problems arising in collecting evidence, extraditing offenders and promoting mutual legal assistance, for example, when such offences are committed across frontiers or when frontiers are used to escape detection or prosecution. Despite differences in legal systems, experience has shown that mutual assistance and cooperation can be effective countermeasures and can help to prevent conflicts of jurisdiction.

7. We also recognize that democracy and a better quality of life can flourish only in a context of peace and security for all. Crime poses a threat to stability and to a safe environment. Crime prevention and criminal justice, with due regard to the observance of human rights, is thus a direct contribution to the maintenance of peace and security.

8. We must ensure that any increases in the capacity and capabilities of perpetrators of crime are matched by similar increases in the capacity and capabilities of law enforcement and criminal justice authorities. By pooling our knowledge and developing suitable countermeasures, success in the prevention of crime and the reduction of victimization can be maximized. We recognize in particular the need to improve and strengthen the means of the crime prevention and control authorities in the developing countries, whose critical economic and social situation is further increasing the difficulties in this area.

9. We call on the international community to increase its support of technical cooperation and assistance activities for the benefit of all countries, including developing and smaller countries, and for the purpose of expanding and strengthening the infrastructure needed for effective crime prevention and viable, fair and humane criminal justice systems.

10. We acknowledge the contribution of the United Nations crime prevention and criminal justice programme to the international community. We note that it is a long-recognized fact that inadequate resources have been devoted to the implementation of the programme, which has in the past been inhibited from achieving its potential. We also note that a strengthening of the resources devoted to the implementation of the programme was called for by the Sixth United Nations Congress for the Prevention of Crime and the Treatment of Offenders,[1] the Seventh United Nations Congress for the Prevention of Crime and the Treatment of Offenders[2] and the Eighth United Nations Congress for the Prevention of Crime and the Treatment of Offenders.[3] We further note that the Committee on Crime Prevention and Control, at its eleventh session, gave priority attention to the conclusions and recommendations of a subcommittee established to provide an overview of the problem of crime and to assess the most efficient means of stimulating practical international action in support of Member States, in pursuance of General Assembly resolution 44/72 of 8 December 1989. The Committee, in its resolution 11/3 of 16 February 1990,[4] unanimously approved a report of the subcommittee on the need for the creation of an effective international crime and justice programme.[5] That report, which was endorsed by the Eighth Congress, was used as an important tool for the establishment of the United Nations crime prevention and criminal justice programme, in line with the provisions of General Assembly resolution 45/108.

11. We accordingly recommend intensified international cooperation in crime prevention and criminal justice, including the creation of an effective United Nations crime prevention and criminal justice programme.

12. We are convinced that there is a need for Governments to define more clearly the role and functions of the United Nations crime prevention and criminal justice programme and the secretariat of the programme and to determine priorities within that programme.

13. We strongly believe that the review of the programme should aim at strengthening its effectiveness, improving its efficiency and establishing an adequate Secretariat support structure.

II. Programme of Action

A. Definition

14. The United Nations crime prevention and criminal justice programme shall bring together the work of the commission on crime prevention and criminal justice, the United Nations institutes for the prevention of crime and the treatment of offenders, the network of government-appointed national correspondents in the field of crime prevention and criminal justice, the Global Crime and Criminal Justice Information Network and the United Nations congresses on the prevention of crime and the treatment of offenders in providing assistance to Member States in their efforts to reduce the incidence and costs of crime and in developing the proper functioning of their criminal justice systems. The establishment of this programme will be effected in accordance with the procedures defined below and within the framework of the total available resources of the United Nations.

B. Goals

15. The programme shall be designed to assist the international community in meeting its pressing needs in the field of crime prevention and criminal justice and to provide countries with timely and practical assistance in dealing with problems of both national and transnational crime.

16. The general goals of the programme shall be to contribute to the following:

---

1 See *Sixth United Nations Congress on the Prevention of Crime and the Treatment of Offenders, Caracas, 25 August - 5 September 1980: report prepared by the Secretariat* (United Nations publication, Sales No. E.81.IV.4).

2 See *Seventh United Nations Congress on the Prevention of Crime and the Treatment of Offenders, Milan, 26 August - 6 September 1985: report prepared by the Secretariat* (United Nations publication, Sales No. E.86.IV.1).

3 See *Eighth United Nations Congress on the Prevention of Crime and the Treatment of Offenders, Havana, 27 August - 7 September 1990: report prepared by the Secretariat* (United Nations publication, Sales No. E.91.IV.2).

4 See *Official Records of the Economic and Social Council, 1990, Supplement No. 10* (E/1990/31), chap. I, sect. D.

5 E/1990/31/Add.1.

(*a*) The prevention of crime within and among States;

(*b*) The control of crime both nationally and internationally;

(*c*) The strengthening of regional and international cooperation in crime prevention, criminal justice and the combating of transnational crime;

(*d*) The integration and consolidation of the efforts of Member States in preventing and combating transnational crime;

(*e*) More efficient and effective administration of justice, with due respect for the human rights of all those affected by crime and all those involved in the criminal justice system;

(*f*) The promotion of the highest standards of fairness, humanity, justice and professional conduct.

C. Scope of the United Nations Crime Prevention and Criminal Justice Programme

17. The programme shall include appropriate forms of cooperation for the purpose of assisting States in dealing with problems of both national and transnational crime. In particular, it may include:

(*a*) Research and studies at the national, regional and global levels on specific prevention issues and criminal justice measures;

(*b*) Regular international surveys to assess trends in crime and developments in the operation of criminal justice systems and in crime prevention strategies;

(*c*) Exchange and dissemination of information among States on crime prevention and criminal justice, particularly with regard to innovative measures and the results achieved in their application;

(*d*) Training and upgrading of the skills of personnel working in the various areas of crime prevention and criminal justice;

(*e*) Technical assistance, including advisory services, particularly in respect of the planning, implementation and evaluation of crime prevention and criminal justice programmes, training and the use of modern communication and information techniques; such assistance may be implemented by means of, for example, fellowships, study tours, consultancies, secondments, courses, seminars and demonstration and pilot projects.

18. Within the framework of the programme, the United Nations should directly carry out the above-mentioned forms of cooperation or should act as a coordinating or facilitating agent. Special attention should be paid to the creation of mechanisms to provide flexible and appropriate assistance and to respond to the needs of Member States at their request, without duplicating the activities of other existing mechanisms.

19. For the purpose of those forms of cooperation, Member States should establish and maintain reliable and effective channels of communication among themselves and with the United Nations.

20. The programme may also include, as appropriate, while respecting the sovereignty of States, a review of the effectiveness and application of and, where necessary, further development and promotion of international instruments on crime prevention and criminal justice.

D. Programme Priorities

21. In developing the programme, areas of priority shall be determined in response to the needs and concerns of Member States, with particular consideration being given to the following:

(*a*) Empirical evidence, including research findings and other information on the nature and extent of crime and on trends in crime;

(*b*) The social, financial and other costs of various forms of crimes and/or crime control to the individual, the local, national and international community, and to the development process;

(*c*) The need of developing or developed countries, which are confronting specific difficulties related to national or international circumstances, to have recourse to experts and other resources necessary for establishing and developing programmes for crime prevention and criminal justice that are appropriate at the national and local levels;

(*d*) The need for a balance within the programme of work between programme development and practical action;

(*e*) The protection of human rights in the administration of justice and the prevention and control of crime;

(*f*) The assessment of areas in which concerted action at the international level and within the framework of the programme would be most effective;

(*g*) Avoidance of overlapping with the activities of other entities of the United Nations system or of other organizations.

22. The commission on crime prevention and criminal justice shall not be bound by mandates conferred prior to its formation, but shall assess them on their merits by applying the principles mentioned in paragraph 21 above.

E. Structure and Management

1. Commission on crime prevention and criminal justice

23. A commission on crime prevention and criminal justice shall be established as a functional commission of the Economic and Social Council. The commission shall have the power to create *ad hoc* working groups and to appoint special rapporteurs, as it deems necessary.

Membership

24. The commission shall consist of forty Member States of the United Nations, elected by the Economic and Social Council on the basis of the principle of equitable geographical distribution. Its members shall serve for a term of three years, except that the terms of one half of the first elected members, whose names shall be chosen by lot, shall expire after two years. Each Member State shall make every effort to ensure that its delegation includes experts and senior officials with special training and practical experience in crime prevention and criminal justice, preferably with policy responsibility in the field. Provisions should be made in the regular budget of the United Nations to defray the travel costs of the representatives of the least developed countries that are members of the Commission.[1]

Sessions

25. The commission shall hold annual sessions of not more than ten working days.

Functions

26. The commission shall have the following functions:

(*a*) To provide policy guidance to the United Nations in the field of crime prevention and criminal justice;

(*b*) To develop, monitor and review the implementation of the programme on the basis of a system of medium-term planning in accordance with the priority principles provided in paragraph 21 above;

(*c*) To facilitate and help to coordinate the activities of the United Nations institutes for the prevention of crime and the treatment of offenders;

(*d*) To mobilize the support of Member States for the programme;

(*e*) To prepare for the United Nations congresses on the prevention of crime and the treatment of offenders and to consider suggestions regarding possible subjects for the programme of work as submitted by the congresses.

2. Committee on crime prevention and control

27. The Committee on Crime Prevention and Control should be dissolved by the Economic and Social Council upon the establishment by the Council of the commission on crime prevention and criminal justice. There will be a basic need for involving independent experts in the area of crime prevention and control.

---

1 In its recommended that in order to commence the work of the commission as soon as possible, the geographical distribution of the commission should be as follows: African States (12), Asian States (9), Latin American and Caribbean States (7), Western European and other States (8), Eastern European States (4). The size and geographical distribution of the commission may be reviewed two years after the first session of the commission.

28. The commission shall, when necessary, use the services of a limited number of qualified and experienced experts, either as individual consultants or in working groups, in order to assist in the preparations for and follow-up work of the commission. Their advice shall be transmitted to the commission for consideration. The commission shall be encouraged to seek such advice whenever it is needed. One of the major tasks of the experts shall be to assist in the preparations for the United Nations congresses on the prevention of crime and the treatment of offenders.[1]

3. United Nations congresses on the prevention of crime and the treatment of offenders

29. The United Nations congresses on the prevention of crime and the treatment of offenders, as a consultative body of the programme, shall provide a forum for:

(*a*) The exchange of views between States, intergovernmental organizations, non-governmental organizations and individual experts representing various professions and disciplines;

(*b*) The exchange of experiences in research, law and policy development;

(*c*) The identification of emerging trends and issues in crime prevention and criminal justice;

(*d*) The provision of advice and comments to the commission on crime prevention and criminal justice on selected matters submitted to it by the commission;

(*e*) The submission of suggestions, for the consideration of the commission, regarding possible subjects for the programme of work.

30. In order to enhance the effectiveness of the programme and to achieve optimal results, the following arrangements should be implemented:

(*a*) The congresses should be held every five years, for a period of between five and ten working days;

(*b*) The commission shall select precisely defined topics for the congresses in order to ensure a focused and productive discussion;

(*c*) Quinquennial regional meetings should be held under the guidance of the commission on issues related to the agenda of the commission or of the congresses, or on any other matters, except when a region does not consider it necessary to hold such a meeting. The United Nations institutes for the prevention of crime and the treatment of offenders should be fully involved, as appropriate, in the organization of those meetings. The commission shall give due consideration to the need to finance such meetings, in particular in developing regions, through the regular budget of the United Nations;

(*d*) Action-oriented research workshops on topics selected by the commission, as part of the programme of a congress, and ancillary meetings associated with the congresses should be encouraged.

4. Organizational structure of the secretariat and of the programme

31. The secretariat of the programme shall be the permanent body responsible for facilitating the implementation of the programme, the priorities of which shall be established by the commission on crime prevention and criminal justice and for assisting the commission in conducting evaluations of the progress made and analyses of the difficulties encountered. For that purpose, the secretariat shall:

(*a*) Mobilize existing resources, including institutes, intergovernmental organizations, non-governmental organizations and other competent authorities for the implementation of the programme;

(*b*) Coordinate research, training and the collection of data on crime and justice, and provide technical assistance and practical information for Member States, particularly through the Global Crime and Criminal Justice Information Network;

(*c*) Assist the commission in the organization of its work and in the preparations, in accordance with the directions of the commission, for the congresses and any other events relating to the programme;

(*d*) Ensure that the potential donors of criminal justice assistance are put in touch with countries needing the help in question;

(*e*) Make the case for assistance in the field of criminal justice to the appropriate funding agencies.

32. It is recommended to the Secretary-General that, in recognition of the high priority that should be accorded to the programme, an upgrading of the Crime Prevention and Criminal Justice Branch of the Centre for Social Development and Humanitarian Affairs of the Secretariat into a division should be effected as soon as possible, under the conditions set out in paragraph 14 above, bearing in mind the structure of the United Nations Office at Vienna.

33. The Professional staff of the secretariat of the programme shall be called "Crime Prevention and Criminal Justice Officers".

34. The secretariat of the programme shall be directed by a senior official responsible for the overall day-to-day management and supervision of the programme, communicating with the relevant government officials, the specialized agencies and intergovernmental organizations whose activities are relevant to the programme.

F. Programme Support

1. United Nations institutes for the prevention of crime and the treatment of offenders

35. The activities of the United Nations institutes for the prevention of crime and the treatment of offenders[2] should be supported by Member States and the United Nations, with particular attention being given to the needs of such institutes located in developing countries. Given the important role of such institutes, their contributions to policy development and implementation, and their resource requirements, especially those of the United Nations African Institute for the Prevention of Crime and the Treatment of Offenders, should be fully integrated into the overall programme.

2. Coordination among the United Nations institutes for the prevention of crime and the treatment of offenders

36. The institutes should keep one another and the commission on crime prevention and criminal justice informed on a regular basis about their programme of work and its implementation.

1 The secretariat of the programme shall keep a list of such experts. The experts shall be selected by the commission in collaboration with the secretariat, the United Nations institutes for the prevention of crime and the treatment of offenders and non-governmental organizations. The commission, in consultation with Member States, shall develop a mechanism for that purpose. Such experts, who may be either government officials or other individuals, shall be chosen on the basis of equitable geographical distribution. They should be available to the programme in their individual independent capacity for at least three years. Expert group meetings shall take place subject to the conditions set out in paragraph 14.

2 The United Nations institutes for the prevention of crime and the treatment of offenders consist of the following:

(*a*) The United Nations Asia and Far East Institute for the Prevention of Crime and the Treatment of Offenders, established in 1961 at Fuchu, Japan;

(*b*) The United Nations Interregional Crime and Justice Research Institute, established in 1968 at Rome;

(*c*) The United Nations Latin American Institute for the Prevention of Crime and Treatment of Offenders, established in 1975 at San José;

(*d*) The Helsinki Institute for Crime Prevention and Control, affiliated with the United Nations, established in 1981 at Helsinki;

(*e*) The United Nations African Institute for the Prevention of Crime and the Treatment of Offenders, established in 1989 at Kampala;

In addition, three other institutes are currently cooperating closely with the United Nations in the field of crime prevention and criminal justice:

(*a*) The Arab Security Studies and Training Centre, at Riyadh;

(*b*) The Australian Institute of Criminology, at Canberra;

(*c*) The International Centre for Criminal Law Reform and Criminal Justice Policy, at Vancouver, Canada.

37. The commission may request the institutes, subject to the availability of resources, to implement select elements of the programme. The commission may also suggest areas for inter-institute activities.

38. The commission shall seek to mobilize extrabudgetary support for the activities of the institutes.

3. Network of government-appointed national correspondents in the field of crime prevention and criminal justice

39. Member States should designate one or more national correspondents in the field of crime prevention and criminal justice as focal points for the purpose of maintaining direct communication with the secretariat of the programme and other elements of the programme.

40. The national correspondents shall facilitate contact with the secretariat on matters of legal, scientific and technical cooperation, training, information on national laws and regulations, legal policy, the organization of the criminal justice system, crime prevention measures and penitentiary matters.

4. Global Crime and Criminal Justice Information Network

41. Member States shall support the United Nations in the development and maintenance of the Global Crime and Criminal Justice Information Network in order to facilitate the collection, analysis, exchange and dissemination, as appropriate, of information and the centralization of inputs from non-governmental organizations and scientific institutions in the field of crime prevention and criminal justice.

42. Member States shall undertake to provide the Secretary-General on a regular basis and upon request with data on the dynamics, structure and extent of crime and on the operation of crime prevention and criminal justice strategies in their respective countries.

5. Intergovernmental and non-governmental organizations

43. Intergovernmental and non-governmental organizations and the scientific community are a valuable source of professional expertise, advocacy and assistance. Their contributions should be fully utilized in programme development and implementation.

G. Funding of the Programme

44. The programme shall be funded from the regular budget of the United Nations. Funds allocated for technical assistance may be supplemented by direct voluntary contributions from Member States and interested funding agencies. Member States are encouraged to make contributions to the United Nations Trust Fund for Social Defence, to be renamed the United Nations Crime Prevention and Criminal Justice Fund. They are also encouraged to contribute in kind for the operational activities of the programme, particularly by seconding staff, organizing training courses and seminars, and providing the requisite equipment and services.

48/102. Prevention of the Smuggling of Aliens

Committee: 3
Vote: Adopted without a vote

The General Assembly,

Concerned that the activities of criminal organizations that profit illicitly by smuggling human beings and preying on the dignity and lives of migrants contribute to the complexity of the phenomenon of increasing international migration,

Recognizing that international criminal groups often convince individuals to migrate illegally by various means for enormous profits and use the proceeds from smuggling human beings to finance other criminal activities, thus bringing great harm to the States concerned,

Aware that such activities endanger the lives of those individuals and impose severe costs on the international community, particularly upon certain States that have been called upon to rescue and to provide medical care, food, housing and transportation for those individuals,

Recognizing that socio-economic factors influence the problem of the smuggling of aliens and also contribute to the complexity of current international migration,

Noting that smugglers, particularly in the State of destination of the smuggling of aliens, often force migrants into forms of debt, bondage or servitude, often involving criminal activities, in order to pay for their passage,

Convinced of the need to provide humane treatment and protect the full human rights of migrants,

Recognizing that this illegal smuggling activity has high social and economic costs, contributes to corruption and burdens law enforcement agencies in all States where illegal aliens transit or are found,

Recalling relevant international agreements and conventions, including the International Convention for the Safety of Life at Sea, 1960,[1] the International Convention for the Safety of Life at Sea, 1974,[2] and the Protocol relating thereto of 1978,[3] by which specific safety standards are established for certain passenger ships, each State party is required to take the necessary steps to ensure that no vessel covered by the Conventions and flying its flag is permitted to carry passengers on international voyages unless it meets the standards established by the Conventions, and each port State party is required to prevent a foreign flag passenger vessel from sailing from its port when the condition of the ship or of its equipment is not in compliance with the Conventions,

Recalling also the undertaking of States parties to the Supplementary Convention on the Abolition of Slavery, the Slave Trade, and Institutions and Practices Similar to Slavery,[4] done at Geneva on 7 September 1956, to take all practicable and necessary legislative and other measures to bring about progressively and as soon as possible the complete abolition or abandonment of the practice of debt bondage,

Reaffirming that the sovereignty and territorial integrity of all States must be respected, including their right to control their own borders,

Concerned that the smuggling of aliens undermines public confidence in policies and procedures for immigration and for the protection of refugees,

Noting that the smuggling of aliens can involve criminal elements in many States, including the State or States where the smuggling scheme was planned, the State of nationality of the aliens, the State where the means of transport was prepared, the flag State of any vessels or aircraft that transport the aliens, States through which the aliens transit to their destination or in order to be repatriated and the State of destination,

Taking into account the efforts of the Office of the United Nations High Commissioner for Refugees, the International Organization for Migration, the International Civil Aviation Organization and the International Maritime Organization in responding to requests from States for assistance in dealing with the smuggling of aliens,

Emphasizing the need for States to cooperate urgently at the bilateral and multilateral levels, as appropriate, to thwart these activities,

1. *Condemns* the practice of smuggling aliens in violation of international and national law and without regard for the safety, well-being and human rights of the migrants;

2. *Commends* those States that have cooperated to combat the smuggling of aliens and to address specific incidents where smuggled aliens have needed to be processed in accordance with international standards and the domestic laws and procedures of the State concerned and returned safely to appropriate destinations;

3. *Urges* States to take appropriate steps to frustrate the objectives and activities of smugglers of aliens and thus to protect would-be migrants from exploitation and loss of life, *inter alia*, by amending criminal laws, if necessary, to encompass the smuggling of aliens and by establishing or improving procedures to permit the ready discovery of false travel documents supplied by smugglers;

---

1 United Nations, *Treaty Series,* vol. 536, No. 7794.

2 *Ibid.*, vol. 1184, No. 18961.

3 *Ibid.*, vol. 1226, No. 18961.

4 *Ibid.*, vol. 266, No. 3822.

4. *Requests* that States cooperate in order to prevent the illegal transport by smugglers of third country nationals through their territory;

5. *Requests* States that have not done so to make special efforts to prevent their airports, means of ground transportation and air carriers from being used by smugglers of aliens;

6. *Also requests* States to cooperate in the interest of safety of life at sea, to increase their efforts to prevent the smuggling of aliens on ships and to ensure that prompt and effective action is taken against the smuggling of aliens by ship;

7. *Calls upon* Member States and relevant specialized agencies and international organizations to take into account socio-economic factors and to cooperate at the bilateral and multilateral levels in addressing all aspects of the problem of the smuggling of aliens;

8. *Reaffirms* the importance of existing international conventions in preventing the economic exploitation and loss of life that can result from smuggling aliens, and calls upon all States to exchange information and to consider ratifying or acceding to such conventions where they have not done so and to implement fully and enforce them;

9. *Emphasizes* that international efforts to prevent the smuggling of aliens should not inhibit legal migration or freedom of travel or undercut the protection provided by international law to refugees;

10. *Reaffirms also* the need to observe fully international and national law in dealing with the smuggling of aliens, including the provision of humane treatment and strict observance of all the human rights of migrants;

11. *Requests* the relevant specialized agencies and intergovernmental organizations, in particular the International Organization for Migration, the International Maritime Organization, the International Criminal Police Organization and the International Civil Aviation Organization, to consider ways and means, within their respective spheres of competence, to enhance international cooperation to combat the smuggling of aliens;

12. *Requests* the Commission on Crime Prevention and Criminal Justice to consider giving special attention to the question of the smuggling of aliens at its third session, to be held in 1994, in order to encourage international cooperation to address this problem within the framework of its mandate;

13. *Requests* the Secretary-General to transmit the text of the present resolution to all Member States and to relevant specialized agencies and intergovernmental organizations;

14. *Invites* Member States and relevant specialized agencies and intergovernmental organizations to report to the Secretary-General on the measures they have taken to combat the smuggling of aliens;

15. *Also requests* the Secretary-General to report to the General Assembly on the measures taken by States, specialized agencies and intergovernmental organizations to combat the smuggling of aliens, and decides to consider this question at its forty-ninth session under the item entitled "Crime prevention and criminal justice".

85th plenary meeting
20 December 1993

49/159. Naples Political Declaration and Global Action Plan Against Organized Transnational Crime

Committee: 3
Vote: Adopted without a vote

The General Assembly,

Alarmed by the rapid growth and geographical extension of organized crime in its various forms, both nationally and internationally, undermining the development process, impairing the quality of life and threatening human rights and fundamental freedoms,

Recognizing that the growing threat of organized crime, with its highly destabilizing and corrupting influence on fundamental social, economic and political institutions, represents a challenge demanding increased and more effective international cooperation,

Recalling its resolutions 44/71 of 8 December 1989, 45/121 and 45/123 of 14 December 1990, 47/87 of 16 December 1992 and 48/103 of 20 December 1993 and Economic and Social Council resolutions 1992/22 and 1992/23 of 30 July 1992 and 1993/29 and 1993/30 of 27 July 1993, and taking note of Council resolutions 1994/12 and 1994/13 of 25 July 1994,

Recalling in particular its resolution 46/152, in which it approved the statement of principles and programme of action on the creation of an effective United Nations crime prevention and criminal justice programme contained in the annex to that resolution,

Acknowledging with appreciation the work of the World Ministerial Conference on Organized Transnational Crime, held at Naples, Italy, from 21 to 23 November 1994,

Also acknowledging with appreciation also the work of the International Conference on Preventing and Controlling Money Laundering and the Use of the Proceeds of Crime: A Global Approach, held at Courmayeur, Italy, from 18 to 20 June 1994, and organized by the International Scientific and Professional Advisory Council of the United Nations crime prevention and criminal justice programme and the Government of Italy, under the auspices of the Crime Prevention and Criminal Justice Branch of the Secretariat,

Noting regional initiatives in this field, such as the Conference on Drugs and Organized Crime, between the countries of the European Union and the countries of Central and Eastern Europe, as reflected in the Berlin Declaration of 8 September 1994, the fifteenth summit of Central American Presidents, held at Guácimo, Costa Rica, from 18 to 20 August 1994, and the South Asian Association for Regional Cooperation Convention on Narcotic Drugs and Psychotropic Substances, as well as the Declaration of the sixteenth plenary session of the Inter-American Drug Abuse Control Commission of the Organization of American States, held at Santiago in October 1994,

Recognizing that organized transnational crime is a major concern of all countries and that it calls for a concerted response from the international community,

Emphasizing the need for strengthened and improved international cooperation at all levels and for more effective technical cooperation to assist States in their fight against organized transnational crime,

1. *Expresses its appreciation* to the Government of Italy for acting as host to the World Ministerial Conference on Organized Transnational Crime;

2. *Takes note with appreciation* of the conclusions and recommendations of the Conference;[1]

3. *Approves* the Political Declaration and Global Action Plan against Organized Transnational Crime,[2] adopted at Naples by the Conference and urges States to implement them as a matter of urgency;

4. *Requests* the Secretary-General to transmit the Naples Political Declaration and Global Action Plan against Organized Transnational Crime to the Commission on Crime Prevention and Criminal Justice for appropriate action, while recommending a higher level of priority for the United Nations crime prevention and criminal justice programme within the framework of the United Nations;

5. *Urges* all entities of the United Nations system, including the regional commissions and the specialized agencies, and the relevant intergovernmental and non-governmental organizations to extend to the United Nations crime prevention and criminal justice programme their full support in the fulfilment of its tasks;

6. *Invites* Governments to contribute to the United Nations Crime Prevention and Criminal Justice Fund in order to enable the programme to respond to the most urgent needs of States in the field of the prevention and control of organized transnational crime;

7. *Resolves* to take decisions at its fiftieth session on the allocation of adequate resources to the Untied Nations crime prevention and criminal justice programme on the basis of proposals for the modification of the programme to be submitted by the Secretary-General, taking into account the responsibilities entrusted to the Untied Nations pursuant to the Naples Political Declaration and Global Action Plan;

---

1 See A/49/748, annex.

2 *Ibid.*, sect. I. A.

8. *Requests* the Commission on Crime Prevention and Criminal Justice to keep the implementation of the Naples Political Declaration and Global Action Plan under regular review;

9. *Requests* the Secretary-General to report to the General Assembly at its fiftieth session on the implementation of the present resolution.

94th plenary meeting
23 December 1994

09.50 EMERGENCY ASSISTANCE

46/182. Strengthening of the Coordination of Humanitarian Emergency Assistance of the United Nations

Committee: -
Vote: Adopted without a vote
Ref.: 50/57, 49/139, 48/57, 47/168

The General Assembly,

Recalling its resolution 2816 (XXVI) of 14 December 1971 and its subsequent resolutions and decisions on humanitarian assistance, including its resolution 45/100 of 14 December 1990,

Recalling also its resolution 44/236 of 22 December 1989, the annex to which contains the International Framework of Action for the International Decade for Natural Disaster Reduction,

Deeply concerned about the suffering of the victims of disasters and emergency situations, the loss in human lives, the flow of refugees, the mass displacement of people and the material destruction,

Mindful of the need to strengthen further and make more effective the collective efforts of the international community, in particular the United Nations system, in providing humanitarian assistance,

Taking note with satisfaction of the report of the Secretary-General on the review of the capacity, experience and coordination arrangements in the United Nations system for humanitarian assistance,

1. *Adopts* the text contained in the annex to the present resolution for the strengthening of the coordination of emergency humanitarian assistance of the United Nations system;

2. *Requests* the Secretary-General to report to the General Assembly at its forty-seventh session on the implementation of the present resolution.

78th plenary meeting
19 December 1991

Annex

I. Guiding Principles

1. Humanitarian assistance is of cardinal importance for the victims of natural disasters and other emergencies.

2. Humanitarian assistance must be provided in accordance with the principles of humanity, neutrality and impartiality.

3. The sovereignty, territorial integrity and national unity of States must be fully respected in accordance with the Charter of the United Nations. In this context, humanitarian assistance should be provided with the consent of the affected country and in principle on the basis of an appeal by the affected country.

4. Each State has the responsibility first and foremost to take care of the victims of natural disasters and other emergencies occurring on its territory. Hence, the affected State has the primary role in the initiation, organization, coordination, and implementation of humanitarian assistance within its territory.

5. The magnitude and duration of many emergencies may be beyond the response capacity of many affected countries. International cooperation to address emergency situations and to strengthen the response capacity of affected countries is thus of great importance. Such cooperation should be provided in accordance with international law and national laws. Intergovernmental and non-governmental organizations working impartially and with strictly humanitarian motives should continue to make a significant contribution in supplementing national efforts.

6. States whose populations are in need of humanitarian assistance are called upon to facilitate the work of these organizations in implementing humanitarian assistance, in particular the supply of food, medicines, shelter and health care, for which access to victims is essential.

7. States in proximity to emergencies are urged to participate closely with the affected countries in international efforts, with a view to facilitating, to the extent possible, the transit of humanitarian assistance.

8. Special attention should be given to disaster prevention and preparedness by the Governments concerned, as well as by the international community.

9. There is a clear relationship between emergency, rehabilitation and development. In order to ensure a smooth transition from relief to rehabilitation and development, emergency assistance should be provided in ways that will be supportive of recovery and long-term development. Thus, emergency measures should be seen as a step towards long-term development.

10. Economic growth and sustainable development are essential for prevention of and preparedness against natural disasters and other emergencies. Many emergencies reflect the underlying crisis in development facing developing countries. Humanitarian assistance should therefore be accompanied by a renewal of commitment to economic growth and sustainable development of developing countries. In this context, adequate resources must be made available to address their development problems.

11. Contributions for humanitarian assistance should be provided in a way which is not to the detriment of resources made available for international cooperation for development.

12. The United Nations has a central and unique role to play in providing leadership and coordinating the efforts of the international community to support the affected countries. The United Nations should ensure the prompt and smooth delivery of relief assistance in full respect of the above-mentioned principles, bearing in mind also relevant General Assembly resolutions, including resolutions 2816 (XXVI) of 14 December 1971 and 45/100 of 14 December 1990. The United Nations system needs to be adapted and strengthened to meet present and future challenges in an effective and coherent manner. It should be provided with resources commensurate with future requirements. The inadequacy of such resources has been one of the major constraints in the effective response of the United Nations to emergencies.

II. Prevention

13. The international community should adequately assist developing countries in strengthening their capacity in disaster prevention and mitigation, both at the national and regional levels, for example, in establishing and enhancing integrated programmes in this regard.

14. In order to reduce the impact of disasters there should be increased awareness of the need for establishing disaster mitigation strategies, particularly in disaster-prone countries. There should be greater exchange and dissemination of existing and new technical information related to the assessment, prediction and mitigation of disasters. As called for in the International Decade for Natural Disaster Reduction, efforts should be intensified to develop measures for prevention and mitigation of natural disasters and similar emergencies through programmes of technical assistance and modalities for favourable access to, and transfer of, relevant technology.

15. The disaster management training programme recently initiated by the Office of the United Nations Disaster Relief Coordinator and

the United Nations Development Programme should be strengthened and broadened.

16. Organizations of the United Nations system involved in the funding and the provision of assistance relevant to the prevention of emergencies should be provided with sufficient and readily available resources.

17. The international community is urged to provide the necessary support and resources to programmes and activities undertaken to further the goals and objectives of the Decade.

III. Preparedness

18. International relief assistance should supplement national efforts to improve the capacities of developing countries to mitigate the effects of natural disasters expeditiously and effectively and to cope efficiently with all emergencies. The United Nations should enhance its efforts to assist developing countries to strengthen their capacity to respond to disasters, at the national and regional levels, as appropriate.

Early warning

19. On the basis of existing mandates and drawing upon monitoring arrangements available within the system, the United Nations should intensify efforts, building upon the existing capacities of relevant organizations and entities of the United Nations, for the systematic pooling, analysis and dissemination of early-warning information on natural disasters and other emergencies. In this context, the United Nations should consider making use as appropriate of the early-warning capacities of Governments and intergovernmental and non-governmental organizations.

20. Early-warning information should be made available in an unrestricted and timely manner to all interested Governments and concerned authorities, in particular of affected or disaster-prone countries. The capacity of disaster-prone countries to receive, use and disseminate this information should be strengthened. In this connection, the international community is urged to assist these countries upon request with the establishment and enhancement of national early-warning systems.

IV. Stand-By Capacity

(a) Contingency funding arrangements

21. Organizations and entities of the United Nations system should continue to respond to requests for emergency assistance within their respective mandates. Reserve and other contingency funding arrangements of these organizations and entities should be examined by their respective governing bodies to strengthen further their operational capacities for rapid and coordinated response to emergencies.

22. In addition, there is a need for a complementary central funding mechanism to ensure the provision of adequate resources for use in the initial phase of emergencies that require a system-wide response.

23. To that end, the Secretary-General should establish under his authority a central emergency revolving fund as a cash-flow mechanism to ensure the rapid and coordinated response of the organizations of the system.

24. This fund should be put into operation with an amount of 50 million United States dollars. The fund should be financed by voluntary contributions. Consultations among potential donors should be held to this end. To achieve this target, the Secretary-General should launch an appeal to potential donors and convene a meeting of those donors in the first quarter of 1992 to secure contributions to the fund on an assured, broad-based and additional basis.

25. Resources should be advanced to the operational organizations of the system on the understanding that they would reimburse the fund in the first instance from the voluntary contributions received in response to consolidated appeals.

26. The operation of the fund should be reviewed after two years.

(b) Additional measures for rapid response

27. The United Nations should, building upon the existing capacities of relevant organizations, establish a central register of all specialized personnel and teams of technical specialists, as well as relief supplies, equipment and services available within the United Nations system and from Governments and intergovernmental and non-governmental organizations, that can be called upon at short notice by the United Nations.

28. The United Nations should continue to make appropriate arrangements with interested Governments and intergovernmental and non-governmental organizations to enable it to have more expeditious access, when necessary, to their emergency relief capacities, including food reserves, emergency stockpiles and personnel, as well as logistic support. In the context of the annual report to the General Assembly mentioned in paragraph 35 (i) below, the Secretary-General is requested to report on progress in this regard.

29. Special emergency rules and procedures should be developed by the United Nations to enable all organizations to disburse quickly emergency funds, and to procure emergency supplies and equipment, as well as to recruit emergency staff.

30. Disaster-prone countries should develop special emergency procedures to expedite the rapid procurement and deployment of equipment and relief supplies.

V. Consolidated Appeals

31. For emergencies requiring a coordinated response, the Secretary-General should ensure that an initial consolidated appeal covering all concerned organizations of the system, prepared in consultation with the affected State, is issued within the shortest possible time and in any event not longer than one week. In the case of prolonged emergencies, this initial appeal should be updated and elaborated within four weeks, as more information becomes available.

32. Potential donors should adopt necessary measures to increase and expedite their contributions, including setting aside, on a stand-by basis, financial and other resources that can be disbursed quickly to the United Nations system in response to the consolidated appeals of the Secretary-General.

VI. Coordination, Cooperation and Leadership

(a) Leadership of the Secretary-General

33. The leadership role of the Secretary-General is critical and must be strengthened to ensure better preparation for, as well as rapid and coherent response to, natural disasters and other emergencies. This should be achieved through coordinated support for prevention and preparedness measures and the optimal utilization of, *inter alia*, an inter-agency standing committee, consolidated appeals, a central emergency revolving fund and a register of stand-by capacities.

34. To this end, and on the understanding that the requisite resources envisaged in paragraph 24 above would be provided, a high-level official (emergency relief coordinator) would be designated by the Secretary-General to work closely with and with direct access to him, in cooperation with the relevant organizations and entities of the system dealing with humanitarian assistance and in full respect of their mandates, without prejudice to any decisions to be taken by the General Assembly on the overall restructuring of the Secretariat of the United Nations. This high-level official should combine the functions at present carried out in the coordination of United Nations response by representatives of the Secretary-General for major and complex emergencies, as well as by the United Nations Disaster Relief Coordinator.

35. Under the aegis of the General Assembly and working under the direction of the Secretary-General, the high-level official would have the following responsibilities:

(*a*) Processing requests from affected Member States for emergency assistance requiring a coordinated response;

(*b*) Maintaining an overview of all emergencies through, *inter alia*, the systematic pooling and analysis of early-warning information as envisaged in paragraph 19 above, with a view to coordinating and facilitating the humanitarian assistance of the United Nations system to those emergencies that require a coordinated response;

(*c*) Organizing, in consultation with the Government of the affected country, a joint inter-agency needs-assessment mission and preparing a consolidated appeal to be issued by the Secretary-General, to be followed by periodic situation reports including information on all sources of external assistance;

(*d*) Actively facilitating, including through negotiation if needed, the access by the operational organizations to emergency areas for the rapid provision of emergency assistance by obtaining the consent of all parties concerned, through modalities such as the establishment of temporary relief corridors where needed, days and zones of tranquility and other forms;

(*e*) Managing, in consultation with the operational organizations concerned, the central emergency revolving fund and assisting in the mobilization of resources;

(*f*) Serving as a central focal point with Governments and intergovernmental and non-governmental organizations concerning United Nations emergency relief operations and, when appropriate and necessary, mobilizing their emergency relief capacities, including through consultations in his capacity as Chairman of the Inter-Agency Standing Committee;

(*g*) Providing consolidated information, including early warning on emergencies, to all interested Governments and concerned authorities, particularly affected and disaster-prone countries, drawing on the capacities of the organizations of the system and other available sources;

(*h*) Actively promoting, in close collaboration with concerned organizations, the smooth transition from relief to rehabilitation and reconstruction as relief operations under his aegis are phased out;

(*i*) Preparing an annual report for the Secretary-General on the coordination of humanitarian emergency assistance, including information on the central emergency revolving fund, to be submitted to the General Assembly through the Economic and Social Council.

36. The high-level official should be supported by a secretariat based on a strengthened Office of the United Nations Disaster Relief Coordinator and the consolidation of existing offices that deal with complex emergencies. This secretariat could be supplemented by staff seconded from concerned organizations of the system. The high-level official should work closely with organizations and entities of the United Nations system, as well as the International Committee of the Red Cross, the League of Red Cross and Red Crescent Societies, the International Organization for Migration and relevant non-governmental organizations. At the country level, the high-level official would maintain close contact with and provide leadership to the resident coordinators on matters relating to humanitarian assistance.

37. The Secretary-General should ensure that arrangements between the high-level official and all relevant organizations are set in place, establishing responsibilities for prompt and coordinated action in the event of emergency.

(b) Inter-Agency Standing Committee

38. An Inter-Agency Standing Committee serviced by a strengthened Office of the United Nations Disaster Relief Coordinator should be established under the chairmanship of the high-level official with the participation of all operational organizations and with a standing invitation to the International Committee of the Red Cross, the League of Red Cross and Red Crescent Societies, and the International Organization for Migration. Relevant non-governmental organizations can be invited to participate on an *ad hoc* basis. The Committee should meet as soon as possible in response to emergencies.

(c) Country-level coordination

39. Within the overall framework described above and in support of the efforts of the affected countries, the resident coordinator should normally coordinate the humanitarian assistance of the United Nations system at the country level. He/She should facilitate the preparedness of the United Nations system and assist in a speedy transition from relief to development. He/She should promote the use of all locally or regionally available relief capacities. The resident coordinator should chair an emergency operations group of field representatives and experts from the system.

VII. Continuum for Relief to Rehabilitation and Development

40. Emergency assistance must be provided in ways that will be supportive of recovery and long-term development. Development assistance organizations of the United Nations system should be involved at an early stage and should collaborate closely with those responsible for emergency relief and recovery, within their existing mandates.

41. International cooperation and support for rehabilitation and reconstruction should continue with sustained intensity after the initial relief stage. The rehabilitation phase should be used as an opportunity to restructure and improve facilities and services destroyed by emergencies in order to enable them to withstand the impact of future emergencies.

42. International cooperation should be accelerated for the development of developing countries, thereby contributing to reducing the occurrence and impact of future disasters and emergencies.

49/170. New International Humanitarian Order

Committee: 3
Vote: Adopted without a vote
Ref.: 47/106, 45/101, 43/129, 42/120, 40/126, 38/125, 37/201, 36/136

The General Assembly,

Recalling its resolution 47/106 of 16 December 1992 and other pertinent resolutions relating to the promotion of a new international humanitarian order and of international cooperation in the humanitarian field,

Taking note of the report of the Secretary-General[1] and the previous reports[2] containing the comments and views of Governments, specialized agencies and non-governmental organizations,

Noting that a number of Governments have not yet submitted their comments in regard to the above-mentioned resolutions,

1. *Expresses its appreciation* to the Secretary-General for his continuing support for the efforts to promote a new international humanitarian order;

2. *Urges* Governments and governmental and non-governmental organizations that have not yet done so to provide their comments and views to the Secretary-General regarding the promotion of the new international humanitarian order;

3. *Requests* Governments to make available to the Secretary-General, on a voluntary basis, information and expertise on humanitarian issues of special concern to them within their own countries, in order to identify opportunities for future action;

4. *Invites* the Independent Bureau for Humanitarian Issues to continue and further strengthen its activities in cooperation with the Governments and the governmental and non-governmental organizations concerned;

5. *Requests* the Secretary-General to remain in contact with Governments and non-governmental organizations and the Independent Bureau for Humanitarian Issues in order to report on the progress made by them to the General Assembly at its fifty-first session;

6. *Decides* to review at its fifty-first session the question of a new international humanitarian order.

9th plenary meeting
23 December 1994

---

1 A/49/577 and Corr. 1.

2 A/37/145, A/38/450, A/40/358 and Add.1 and 2, A/41/472, A/43/734 and Add.1, A/45/524 and A/47/352.

10.00 ENVIRONMENT

2996 (XXVII). International Responsibility of States in Regard to the Environment

Committee: 2
Vote: 112 - 0 - 10
Ref.: 36/7, 35/8

The General Assembly,

Recalling principles 21 and 22 of the Declaration of the United Nations Conference on the Human Environment[1] concerning the international responsibility of States in regard to the environment,

Bearing in mind that those principles lay down the basic rules governing this matter,

Declares that no resolution adopted at the twenty-seventh session of the General Assembly can affect principles 21 and 22 of the Declaration of the United Nations Conference on the Human Environment.

2112th plenary meeting
15 December 1972

2997 (XXVII). Institutional and Financial Arrangements for International Environmental Cooperation

Committee: 2
Vote: 116 - 0 - 10

The General Assembly,

Convinced of the need for prompt and effective implementation by Governments and the international community of measures designed to safeguard and enhance the environment for the benefit of present and future generations of man,

Recognizing that responsibility for action to protect and enhance the environment rests primarily with Governments and, in the first instance, can be exercised more effectively at the national and regional levels,

Recognizing further that environmental problems of broad international significance fall within the competence of the United Nations system,

Bearing in mind that international cooperative programmes in the field of the environment must be undertaken with due respect for the sovereign rights of States and in conformity with the Charter of the United Nations and principles of international law,

Mindful of the sectoral responsibilities of the organizations in the United Nations system,

Conscious of the significance of regional and subregional cooperation in the field of the environment and of the important role of the regional economic commissions and other regional intergovernmental organizations,

Emphasizing that problems of the environment constitute a new and important area for international cooperation and that the complexity and interdependence of such problems require new approaches,

Recognizing that the relevant international scientific and other professional communities can make an important contribution to international cooperation in the field of the environment,

Conscious of the need for processes within the United Nations system which would effectively assist developing countries to implement environmental policies and programmes that are compatible with their development plans and to participate meaningfully in international environmental programmes,

Convinced that, in order to be effective, international cooperation in the field of the environment requires additional financial and technical resources,

Aware of the urgent need for a permanent institutional arrangement within the United Nations system for the protection and improvement of the environment,

Taking note of the report of the Secretary-General on the United Nations Conference on the Human Environment,[2]

I

Governing Council of the United Nations Environment Programme

1. *Decides* to establish a governing Council of the United Nations Environment Programme, composed of fifty-eight members elected by the General Assembly for three-year terms on the following basis:

(*a*) Sixteen seats for African States;

(*b*) Thirteen seats for Asian States;

(*c*) Six seats for Eastern European States;

(*d*) Ten seats for Latin American States;

(*e*) Thirteen seats for Western European and other States;

2. *Decides* that the Governing Council shall have the following main functions and responsibilities:

(*a*) To promote international cooperation in the field of the environment and to recommend, as appropriate, policies to this end;

(*b*) To provide general policy guidance for the direction and coordination of environmental programmes within the United Nations system;

(*c*) To receive and review the periodic reports of the Executive Director of the United Nations Environment Programme, referred to in section II, paragraph 2, below, on the implementation of environmental programmes within the United Nations system;

(*d*) To keep under review the world environmental situation in order to ensure that emerging environmental problems of wide international significance receive appropriate and adequate consideration by Governments;

(*e*) To promote the contribution of the relevant international scientific and other professional communities to the acquisition, assessment and exchange of environmental knowledge and information and, as appropriate, to the technical aspects of the formulation and implementation of environmental programmes within the United Nations system;

(*f*) To maintain under continuing review the impact of national and international environmental policies and measures on developing countries, as well as the problem of additional costs that may be incurred by developing countries in the implementation of environmental programmes and projects, and to ensure that such programmes and projects shall be compatible with the development plans and priorities of those countries;

(*g*) To review and approve annually the programme of utilization of resources of the Environment Fund referred to in section III below;

3. *Decides* that the Governing Council shall report annually to the General Assembly through the Economic and Social Council, which will transmit to the Assembly such comments on the report as it may deem necessary, particularly with regard to questions of coordination and to the relationship of environmental policies and programmes within the United Nations system to overall economic and social policies and priorities;

II

Environment Secretariat

1. *Decides* that a small secretariat shall be established in the United Nations to serve as a focal point for environmental action and coordination within the United Nations system in such a way as to ensure a high degree of effective management;

---

1 A/CONF. 48/14 and Corr.1, chap. I.

2 A/8783 and Add.1, Add.1/Corr.1 and Add.2.

2. *Decides* that the environment secretariat shall be headed by the Executive Director of the United Nations Environment Programme, who shall be elected by the General Assembly on the nomination of the Secretary-General for a term of four years and who shall be entrusted, *inter alia*, with the following responsibilities:

(*a*) To provide substantive support to the Governing Council of the United Nations Environment Programme;

(*b*) To coordinate, under the guidance of the Governing Council, environmental programmes within the United Nations system, to keep their implementation under review and to assess their effectiveness;

(*c*) To advise, as appropriate and under the guidance of the Governing Council, intergovernmental bodies of the United Nations system on the formulation and implementation of environmental programmes;

(*d*) To secure the effective cooperation of, and contribution from, the relevant scientific and other professional communities in all parts of the world;

(*e*) To provide, at the request of all parties concerned, advisory services for the promotion of international cooperation in the field of the environment;

(*f*) To submit to the Governing Council, on his own initiative or upon request, proposals embodying medium-range and long-range planning for United Nations programmes in the field of the environment;

(*g*) To bring to the attention of the Governing Council any matter which he deems to require consideration by it;

(*h*) To administer, under the authority and policy guidance of the Governing Council, the Environment Fund referred to in section III below;

(*i*) To report on environmental matters to the Governing Council;

(*j*) To perform such other functions as may be entrusted to him by the Governing Council;

3. *Decides* that the costs of servicing the Governing Council and providing the small secretariat referred to in paragraph 1 above shall be borne by the regular budget of the United Nations and that operational programme costs, programme support and administrative costs of the Environment Fund established under section III below shall be borne by the Fund;

III

Environment Fund

1. *Decides* that, in order to provide for additional financing for environmental programmes, a voluntary fund shall be established, with effect from 1 January 1973, in accordance with existing United Nations financial procedures;

2. *Decides* that, in order to enable the Governing Council of the United Nations Environment Programme to fulfil its policy-guidance role for the direction and coordination of environmental activities, the Environment Fund shall finance wholly or partly the costs of the new environmental initiatives undertaken within the United Nations system - which will include the initiatives envisaged in the Action Plan for the Human Environment[1] adopted by the United Nations Conference on the Human Environment, with particular attention to integrated projects, and such other environmental activities as may be decided upon by the Governing Council - and that the Governing Council shall review these initiatives with a view to taking appropriate decisions as to their continued financing;

3. *Decides* that the Environment Fund shall be used for financing such programmes of general interest as regional and global monitoring, assessment and data-collecting systems, including, as appropriate, costs for national counterparts; the improvement of environmental quality management; environmental research; information exchange and dissemination; public education and training; assistance for national, regional and global environmental institutions; the promotion of environmental research and studies for the development of industrial and other technologies best suited to a policy of economic growth compatible with adequate environmental safeguards; and such other programmes as the Governing Council may decide upon, and that in the implementation of such programmes due account should be taken of the special needs of the developing countries;

4. *Decides* that, in order to ensure that the development priorities of developing countries shall not be adversely affected, adequate measures shall be taken to provide additional financial resources on terms compatible with the economic situation of the recipient developing country, and that, to this end, the Executive Director, in cooperation with competent organizations, shall keep this problem under continuing review;

5. *Decides* that the Environment Fund, in pursuance of the objectives stated in paragraphs 2 and 3 above, shall be directed to the need for effective coordination in the implementation of international environmental programmes of the organizations in the United Nations system and other international organizations;

6. *Decides* that, in the implementation of programmes to be financed by the Environment Fund, organizations outside the United Nations system, particularly those in the countries and regions concerned, shall also be utilized as appropriate, in accordance with the procedures established by the Governing Council, and that such organizations are invited to support the United Nations environmental programmes by complementary initiatives and contributions;

7. *Decides* that the Governing Council shall formulate such general procedures as are necessary to govern the operations of the Environment Fund;

IV

Environment Coordination Board

1. *Decides* that, in order to provide for the most efficient coordination of United Nations environmental programmes, an Environment Coordination Board, under the chairmanship of the Executive Director of the United Nations Environment Programme, shall be established under the auspices and within the framework of the Administrative Committee on Coordination;

2. *Further decides* that the Environment Coordination Board shall meet periodically for the purpose of ensuring cooperation and coordination among all bodies concerned in the implementation of environmental programmes and that it shall report annually to the Governing Council of the United Nations Environment Programme;

3. *Invites* the organizations of the United Nations system to adopt the measures that may be required to undertake concerted and coordinated programmes with regard to international environmental problems, taking into account existing procedures for prior consultation, particularly on programme and budgetary matters;

4. *Invites* the regional economic commissions and the United Nations Economic and Social Office at Beirut, in cooperation where necessary with other appropriate regional bodies, to intensify further their efforts directed towards contributing to the implementation of environmental programmes in view of the particular need for the rapid development of regional cooperation in this field;

5. *Also invites* other intergovernmental and those non-governmental organizations that have an interest in the field of the environment to lend their full support and collaboration to the United Nations with a view to achieving the largest possible degree of cooperation and coordination;

6. *Calls upon* Governments to ensure that appropriate national institutions shall be entrusted with the task of the coordination of environmental action, both national and international;

7. *Decides* to review as appropriate, at its thirty-first session, the above institutional arrangements, bearing in mind, *inter alia*, the responsibilities of the Economic and Social Council under the Charter of the United Nations.

2112th plenary meeting
15 December 1972

1 A/CONF.48/14 and Corr.1, chap. II.

34/186. Cooperation in the Field of the Environment Concerning Natural Resources Shared by Two or More States

Committee: 2
Vote: Adopted without a vote
Ref.: 33/87, 3129(XXVIII)

The General Assembly,

Recalling the relevant provisions of its resolutions 3201 (S-VI) and 3202 (S-VI) of 1 May 1974, in which it reaffirmed the principle of full permanent sovereignty of every State over its natural resources and the responsibility of States as set out in the Declaration of the United Nations Conference on the Human Environment[1] to ensure that activities within their jurisdiction or control do not cause damage to the environment of other States and to cooperate in developing the international law regarding liability and compensation for such damages,

Recalling its resolution 3129 (XXVIII) of 13 December 1973 on cooperation in the field of the environment concerning natural resources shared by two or more States,

Recalling also the Charter of Economic Rights and Duties of States, contained in its resolution 3281 (XXIX) of 12 December 1974,

Noting that the Governing Council of the United Nations Environment Programme, by its decision 6/14 of 19 May 1978,[2] invited the General Assembly to adopt the draft principles of conduct in the field of the environment for the guidance of States in the conservation and harmonious utilization of natural resources shared by two or more States, including the explanatory note, contained in the report of the Intergovernmental Working Group of Experts on Natural Resources Shared by Two or More States[3] established under Governing Council decision 44 (III) of 25 April 1975,

Taking note of the report of the Secretary-General[4] requested by the General Assembly in its resolution 33/87 of 15 December 1978 and containing summaries of the comments made by Governments regarding the draft principles, as well as other significant information, recommendations and suggestions in connexion therewith,

Desiring to promote effective cooperation among States for the development of international law regarding the conservation and harmonious utilization of natural resources shared by two or more States,

Recognizing the right of States to provide specific solutions on a bilateral or regional basis,

Recalling that the principles have been drawn up for the guidance of States in the conservation and harmonious utilization of natural resources shared by two or more States,

1. *Takes note* of the report as adopted of the Intergovernmental Working Group of Experts on Natural Resources Shared by Two or More States established under decision 44 (III) of the Governing Council of the United Nations Environment Programme in conformity with General Assembly resolution 3129 (XXVIII);

2. *Takes note* of the draft principles as guidelines and recommendations in the conservation and harmonious utilization of natural resources shared by two or more States without prejudice to the binding nature of those rules already recognized as such in international law;

3. *Requests* all States to use the principles as guidelines and recommendations in the formulation of bilateral or multilateral conventions regarding natural resources shared by two or more States, on the basis of the principle of good faith and in the spirit of good neighbourliness and in such a way as to enhance and not adversely affect development and the interests of all countries, in particular the developing countries;

4. *Requests* the Governing Council of the United Nations Environment Programme to submit to the General Assembly at its thirty-sixth session, through the Economic and Social Council, a report on the progress made in the implementation of the present resolution.

107th plenary meeting
18 December 1979

37/7. World Charter for Nature

Committee: -
Vote: 111 - 1 - 18
Ref.: 36/6, 35/7

The General Assembly,

Having considered the report of the Secretary-General on the revised draft World Charter for Nature,[5]

Recalling that, in its resolution 35/7 of 30 October 1980, it expressed its conviction that the benefits which could be obtained from nature depended on the maintenance of natural processes and on the diversity of life forms and that those benefits were jeopardized by the excessive exploitation and the destruction of natural habitats,

Further recalling that, in the same resolution, it recognized the need for appropriate measures at the national and international levels to protect nature and promote international cooperation in that field,

Recalling that, in its resolution 36/6 of 27 October 1981, it again expressed its awareness of the crucial importance attached by the international community to the promotion and development of cooperation aimed at protecting and safeguarding the balance and quality of nature and invited the Secretary-General to transmit to Member States the text of the revised version of the draft World Charter for Nature contained in the report of the *Ad Hoc* Group of Experts on the draft World Charter for Nature,[6] as well as any further observations by States, with a view to appropriate consideration by the General Assembly at its thirty-seventh session,

Conscious of the spirit and terms of its resolutions 35/7 and 36/6, in which it solemnly invited Member States, in the exercise of their permanent sovereignty over their natural resources, to conduct their activities in recognition of the supreme importance of protecting natural systems, maintaining the balance and quality of nature and conserving natural resources, in the interests of present and future generations,

Having considered the supplementary report of the Secretary-General,[7]

Expressing its gratitude to the *Ad Hoc* Group of Experts which, through its work, has assembled the necessary elements for the General Assembly to be able to complete the consideration of and adopt the revised draft World Charter for Nature at its thirty-seventh session, as it had previously recommended,

Adopts and solemnly proclaims the World Charter for Nature contained in the annex to the present resolution.

48th plenary meeting
28 October 1982

Annex

World Charter for Nature

The General Assembly,

Reaffirming the fundamental purposes of the United Nations, in particular the maintenance of international peace and security, the development of friendly relations among nations and the achievement of international cooperation in solving international problems

1 *Report of the United Nations Conference on the Human Environment, Stockholm, 5-16 June 1972* (United Nations publication, Sales No. E.73.II.A.14 and corrigendum), chap 1.

2 See *Official Records of the General Assembly, Thirty-third Session, Supplement No. 25* (A/33/25), annex I.

3 UNEP/GC.6/17.

4 A/34/557 and Corr.1.

5 A/36/539.

6 *Ibid.*, annex I.

7 A/37/398 and Add. 1.

of an economic, social, cultural, technical, intellectual or humanitarian character,

Aware that:

(a) Mankind is a part of nature and life depends on the uninterrupted functioning of natural systems which ensure the supply of energy and nutrients,

(b) Civilization is rooted in nature, which has shaped human culture and influenced all artistic and scientific achievement, and living in harmony with nature gives man the best opportunities for the development of his creativity, and for rest and recreation,

Convinced that:

(a) Every form of life is unique, warranting respect regardless of its worth to man, and, to accord other organisms such recognition, man must be guided by a moral code of action,

(b) Man can alter nature and exhaust natural resources by his action or its consequences and, therefore, must fully recognize the urgency of maintaining the stability and quality of nature and of conserving natural resources,

Persuaded that:

(a) Lasting benefits from nature depend upon the maintenance of essential ecological processes and life support systems, and upon the diversity of life forms, which are jeopardized through excessive exploitation and habitat destruction by man,

(b) The degradation of natural systems owing to excessive consumption and misuse of natural resources, as well as to failure to establish an appropriate economic order among peoples and among States, leads to the breakdown of the economic, social and political framework of civilization,

(c) Competition for scarce resources creates conflicts, whereas the conservation of nature and natural resources contributes to justice and the maintenance of peace and cannot be achieved until mankind learns to live in peace and to forsake war and armaments,

Reaffirming that man must acquire the knowledge to maintain and enhance his ability to use natural resources in a manner which ensures the preservation of the species and ecosystems for the benefit of present and future generations,

Firmly convinced of the need for appropriate measures, at the national and international, individual and collective, and private and public levels, to protect nature and promote international cooperation in this field,

Adopts, to these ends, the present World Charter for Nature, which proclaims the following principles of conservation by which all human conduct affecting nature is to be guided and judged.

I. General Principles

1. Nature shall be respected and its essential processes shall not be impaired.

2. The genetic viability on the earth shall not be compromised; the population levels of all life forms, wild and domesticated, must be at least sufficient for their survival, and to this end necessary habitats shall be safeguarded.

3. All areas of the earth, both land and sea, shall be subject to these principles of conservation; special protection shall be given to unique areas, to representative samples of all the different types of ecosystems and to the habitats of rare or endangered species.

4. Ecosystems and organisms, as well as the land, marine and atmospheric resources that are utilized by man, shall be managed to achieve and maintain optimum sustainable productivity, but not in such a way as to endanger the integrity of those other ecosystems or species with which they coexist.

5. Nature shall be secured against degradation caused by warfare or other hostile activities.

II. Functions

6. In the decision-making process it shall be recognized that man's needs can be met only by ensuring the proper functioning of natural systems and by respecting the principles set forth in the present Charter.

7. In the planning and implementation of social and economic development activities, due account shall be taken of the fact that the conservation of nature is an integral part of those activities.

8. In formulating long-term plans for economic development, population growth and the improvement of standards of living, due account shall be taken of the long-term capacity of natural systems to ensure the subsistence and settlement of the populations concerned, recognizing that this capacity may be enhanced through science and technology.

9. The allocation of areas of the earth to various uses shall be planned and due account shall be taken of the physical constraints, the biological productivity and diversity and the natural beauty of the areas concerned.

10. Natural resources shall not be wasted, but used with a restraint appropriate to the principles set forth in the present Charter, in accordance with the following rules:

(a) Living resources shall not be utilized in excess of their natural capacity for regeneration;

(b) The productivity of soils shall be maintained or enhanced through measures which safeguard their long-term fertility and the process of organic decomposition, and prevent erosion and all other forms of degradation;

(c) Resources, including water, which are not consumed as they are used shall be reused or recycled;

(d) Non-renewable resources which are consumed as they are used shall be exploited with restraint, taking into account their abundance, the rational possibilities of converting them for consumption, and the compatibility of their exploitation with the functioning of natural systems.

11. Activities which might have an impact on nature shall be controlled, and the best available technologies that minimize significant risks to nature or other adverse effects shall be used; in particular:

(a) Activities which are likely to cause irreversible damage to nature shall be avoided;

(b) Activities which are likely to pose a significant risk to nature shall be preceded by an exhaustive examination; their proponents shall demonstrate that expected benefits outweigh potential damage to nature, and where potential adverse effects are not fully understood, the activities should not proceed;

(c) Activities which may disturb nature shall bc prcceded by assessment of their consequences, and environmental impact studies of development projects shall be conducted sufficiently in advance, and if they are to be undertaken, such activities shall be planned and carried out so as to minimize potential adverse effects;

(d) Agriculture, grazing, forestry and fisheries practices shall be adapted to the natural characteristics and constraints of given areas;

(e) Areas degraded by human activities shall be rehabilitated for purposes in accord with their natural potential and compatible with the well-being of affected populations.

12. Discharge of pollutants into natural systems shall be avoided and:

(a) Where this is not feasible, such pollutants shall be treated at the source, using the best practicable means available;

(b) Special precautions shall be taken to prevent discharge of radioactive or toxic wastes.

13. Measures intended to prevent, control or limit natural disasters, infestations and diseases shall be specifically directed to the causes of these scourges and shall avoid adverse side-effects on nature.

III. Implementation

14. The principles set forth in the present Charter shall be reflected in the law and practice of each State, as well as at the international level.

15. Knowledge of nature shall be broadly disseminated by all possible means, particularly by ecological education as an integral part of general education.

16. All planning shall include, among its essential elements, the formulation of strategies for the conservation of nature, the establishment of inventories of ecosystems and assessments of the effects

on nature of proposed policies and activities; all of these elements shall be disclosed to the public by appropriate means in time to permit effective consultation and participation.

17. Funds, programmes and administrative structures necessary to achieve the objective of the conservation of nature shall be provided.

18. Constant efforts shall be made to increase knowledge of nature by scientific research and to disseminate such knowledge unimpeded by restrictions of any kind.

19. The status of natural processes, ecosystems and species shall be closely monitored to enable early detection of degradation or threat, ensure timely intervention and facilitate the evaluation of conservation policies and methods.

20. Military activities damaging to nature shall be avoided.

21. States and, to the extent they are able, other public authorities, international organizations, individuals, groups and corporations shall:

(a) Cooperate in the task of conserving nature through common activities and other relevant actions, including information exchange and consultations;

(b) Establish standards for products and manufacturing processes that may have adverse effects on nature, as well as agreed methodologies for assessing these effects;

(c) Implement the applicable international legal provisions for the conservation of nature and the protection of the environment;

(d) Ensure that activities within their jurisdictions or control do not cause damage to the natural systems located within other States or in the areas beyond the limits of national jurisdiction;

(e) Safeguard and conserve nature in areas beyond national jurisdiction.

22. Taking fully into account the sovereignty of States over their natural resources, each State shall give effect to the provisions of the present Charter through its competent organs and in cooperation with other States.

23. All persons, in accordance with their national legislation, shall have the opportunity to participate, individually or with others, in the formulation of decisions of direct concern to their environment, and shall have access to means of redress when their environment has suffered damage or degradation.

24. Each person has a duty to act in accordance with the provisions of the present Charter; acting individually, in association with others or through participation in the political process, each person shall strive to ensure that the objectives and requirements of the present Charter are met.

42/186. Environmental Perspective to the Year 2000 and Beyond

Committee: 2
Vote: Adopted without a vote

The General Assembly,

Recalling its resolution 38/161 of 19 December 1983 on the process of preparation of the Environmental Perspective to the Year 2000 and Beyond, in which it, *inter alia*, welcomed the desire of the Governing Council of the United Nations Environment Programme to develop the Environmental Perspective and transmit it to the General Assembly for adoption, benefiting in carrying out that function from its consideration of the relevant proposals made by a special commission, which adopted the name World Commission on Environment and Development,

Welcoming the Environmental Perspective to the Year 2000 and Beyond, prepared by the Intergovernmental Inter-sessional Preparatory Committee on the Environmental Perspective to the Year 2000 and Beyond of the United Nations Environment Programme, referred to in General Assembly resolution 38/161, considered further by the Governing Council of the United Nations Environment Programme at its fourteenth session and adopted in its decision 14/13 of 19 June 1987, as a basis for the further elaboration of its programme and operations, while acknowledging that different views exist on some aspects,

Appreciating that concepts, ideas and recommendations contained in the report of the World Commission on Environment and Development have been incorporated into the Environmental Perspective,

1. *Expresses its appreciation* for the efforts of the Governing Council of the United Nations Environment Programme and its Intergovernmental Inter-sessional Preparatory Committee on the Environmental Perspective to the Year 2000 and Beyond in the preparation of the Environmental Perspective to the Year 2000 and Beyond;

2. *Adopts* the Environmental Perspective to the Year 2000 and Beyond, contained in the annex to the present resolution, as a broad framework to guide national action and international cooperation on policies and programmes aimed at achieving environmentally sound development, and specifically as a guide to the preparation of further system-wide medium-term environment programmes and the medium-term programmes of the organizations and bodies of the United Nations system, in the light of Governing Council decision 14/13;

3. *Notes* that the perceptions generally shared by Governments of the nature of environmental problems, and their interrelations with other international problems, and of the efforts to deal with them include the following:

(*a*) An international atmosphere of peace, security and cooperation, free from the presence and the threat of wars of all types, especially nuclear war, in which intellectual and natural resources are not wasted on armaments by any nation, would greatly enhance environmentally sound development;

(*b*) The imbalance of present world economic conditions makes it extremely difficult to bring about sustained improvement in the world's environmental situation; accelerated and balanced world development and lasting improvements in the global environment require improved world economic conditions, especially for the developing countries;

(*c*) Since mass poverty is often at the root of environmental degradation, its elimination and ensuring equitable access of people to environmental resources are essential for sustained environmental improvements;

(*d*) The environment puts constraints on as well as provides opportunities for economic growth and social well-being; environmental degradation, in its various forms, has assumed such proportions as can cause irreversible changes in ecosystems, which threaten to undermine human well-being; environmental constraints, however, are generally relative to the state of technology and socio-economic conditions, which can and should be improved and managed to achieve sustained world economic growth;

(*e*) Environmental issues are closely intertwined with development policies and practices; consequently, environmental goals and actions need to be defined in relation to development objectives and policies;

(*f*) Although it is important to tackle immediate environmental problems, anticipatory and preventive policies are the most effective and economical in achieving environmentally sound development;

(*g*) The environmental impacts of actions in one sector are often felt in other sectors; thus internalization of environmental considerations in sectoral policies and programmes and their coordination are essential for the achievement of sustainable development;

(*h*) Since conflicts of interest among population groups, or among countries, are often inherent in the nature of environmental problems, the participation of the concerned parties is essential in determining effective environmental management practices;

(*i*) Environmental degradation can be controlled and reversed only by ensuring that the parties causing the damage will be accountable for their actions, and that they will participate, on the basis of full access to available knowledge, in improving environmental conditions;

(*j*) Renewable resources, as part of complex and interlinked ecosystems, can have sustainable yields only if used while taking into account system-wide effects of exploitation;

(*k*) The safeguarding of species is a moral obligation of humankind and should improve and sustain human well-being;

(l) Building awareness at various levels of environmental conditions and management, through the provision of information, education and training, is essential for environmental protection and improvement;

(*m*) Strategies to deal with environmental challenges have to be flexible and should allow for adjustments to emerging problems and evolving environmental management technology;

(*n*) International environmental disputes which are growing in number and variety, need to be resolved by peaceful means;

4. *Welcomes* as the overall aspirational goal for the world community the achievement of sustainable development on the basis of prudent management of available global resources and environmental capacities and the rehabilitation of the environment previously subjected to degradation and misuse, and the aspirational goals to the year 2000 and beyond as set out in the Environmental Perspective, namely:

(*a*) The achievement over time of such a balance between population and environmental capacities as would make possible sustainable development, keeping in view the links between population levels, consumption patterns, poverty and the natural resource base;

(*b*) The achievement of food security without resource depletion or environmental degradation and restoration of the resource base where environmental damage has been occurring;

(*c*) The provision of sufficient energy at reasonable cost, notably by increasing access to energy substantially in the developing countries, to meet current and expanding needs in ways which minimize environmental degradation and risks, conserve non-renewable sources of energy and realize the full potential of renewable sources of energy;

(*d*) The sustained improvements in levels of living in all countries, especially the developing countries, through industrial development that prevents or minimizes environmental damage and risks;

(*e*) The provision of improved shelter with access to essential amenities in a clean and secure setting conducive to health and to the prevention of environment-related diseases, which would, at the same time, alleviate serious environmental degradation;

(*f*) The establishment of an equitable system of international economic relations aimed at achieving continuing economic advancement for all States based on principles recognized by the international community, in order to stimulate and sustain environmentally sound development, especially in developing countries;

5. *Agrees* that the recommendations for action contained in the Environmental Perspective should be implemented, as appropriate, through national and international action by Governments, intergovernmental and non-governmental organizations and scientific bodies;

6. *Requests* the Governing Council to keep under review the extent to which the long-term environmental actions recommended in the Environmental Perspective have been implemented and to identify any new environmental concerns that may arise;

7. *Calls* special attention to section IV of the Environmental Perspective, which spells out instruments of environmental action, to be used as support in addressing, as appropriate, problems dealt with in previous sections of the Environmental Perspective;

8. *Stresses* the essential role of the United Nations Environment Programme within the United Nations system in catalyzing environmentally sound and sustainable development, and agrees with the Governing Council that this role should be strengthened and that the resources of the Environment Fund should be substantially increased with greater participation;

9. *Endorses* the priorities and functions for the United Nations Environment Programme set out in paragraph 117 of the Environmental Perspective;

10. *Decides* to transmit the text of the Environmental Perspective to all Governments and to the governing bodies of the organs and organizations of the United Nations system as a broad framework to guide national action and international cooperation on policies and programmes aimed at achieving environmentally sound and sustainable development;

11. *Calls upon* the governing bodies of the organs and organizations of the United Nations system to consider the Environmental Perspective and take it into account in the development of their own medium-term plans and programmes as relevant to their own mandates;

12. *Requests* the governing bodies of relevant United Nations organizations to report regularly to the General Assembly on the progress made in achieving the objectives of environmentally sound and sustainable development in line with paragraph 114 of the Environmental Perspective;

13. *Invites* the Governing Council of the United Nations Environment Programme to report to the General Assembly at its forty-fourth session on the implementation of the present resolution and the relevant provisions of the Environmental Perspective to the Year 200 and Beyond.

96th plenary meeting
11 December 1987

Annex

Environmental Perspective to the Year 2000 and Beyond

Contents

I. Introduction

1. Awareness of environmental issues has been growing during the past decade. This awareness has emerged among and within the Governments as they have addressed environmental problems singly, bilaterally, regionally and globally. The establishment of ministries for environmental conservation and enhancement is but one sign of this growth of common concern. Much of this concern has crystallized in the decisions of the Governing Council of the United Nations Environment Programme. Despite these noteworthy developments, and the emergence in the world community of many shared perceptions regarding environmental problems and actions, environmental degradation has continued unabated, threatening human well-being and, in some instances, the very survival of life on our planet.

2. To meet this challenge, the overall aspirational goal must be sustainable development on the basis of prudent management of available global resources and environmental capacities, and the rehabilitation of the environment previously subjected to degradation and misuse. Development is sustainable when it meets the needs of the present without compromising the ability of future generations to meet theirs.

3. The following are some shared perceptions of Governments of the nature of environmental issues and their interrelations with other international problems and the efforts to deal with them:

(a) An international atmosphere of peace, security and cooperation, free from the presence and the threat of wars of all types, especially nuclear war, in which intellectual and natural resources are not wasted on armaments by any nation, would greatly enhance environmentally sound development;

(b) The imbalance of present world economic conditions makes it extremely difficult to bring about sustained improvement in the world's environmental situation. Accelerated and balanced world development and lasting improvements in the global environment require improved world economic conditions, especially in the developing countries;

(c) Since mass poverty is often at the root of environmental degradation, its elimination and ensuring equitable access of people to environmental resources are essential for sustained environmental improvements;

(d) The environment puts constraints on as well as provides opportunities for economic growth and social well-being. Environmental degradation, in its various forms, has assumed such proportions as can cause irreversible changes in ecosystems which threaten to undermine human well-being. Environmental constraints, however, are generally relative to the state of technology and socio-economic conditions, which can and should be improved and managed to achieve sustained world economic growth;

(e) Environmental issues are closely intertwined with development policies and practices; consequently, environmental goals and actions need to be defined in relation to development objectives and policies;

(f) Although it is important to tackle immediate environmental problems, anticipatory and preventive policies are the most effective and economical in achieving environmentally sound development;

(g) The environmental impacts of actions in one sector are often felt in other sectors; thus, internalization of environmental considerations in sectoral policies and programmes and their coordination are essential for the achievement of sustainable development;

(h) Since conflicts of interest among population groups, or among countries, are often inherent in the nature of environmental problems, participation of the concerned parties is essential in determining effective environmental management practices;

(i) Environmental degradation can be controlled and reversed only by ensuring that the parties causing the damage will be accountable for their actions, and that they will participate, on the basis of full access to available knowledge, in improving environmental conditions;

(j) Renewable resources, as part of complex and interlinked ecosystems, can have sustainable yields only if used while taking into account system-wide effects of exploitation;

(k) The safeguarding of species is a moral obligation of humankind, and should improve and sustain human well-being;

(l) Building awareness at various levels of environmental conditions and management through the provision of information, education and training is essential for environmental protection and improvement;

(m) Strategies to deal with environmental challenges have to be flexible and should allow for adjustments to emerging problems and evolving environmental management technology;

(n) International environmental disputes, which are growing in number and variety, need to be resolved by peaceful means.

4. Environmental problems cut across a range of policy issues and are mostly rooted in inappropriate development patterns. Consequently, environmental issues, goals and actions cannot be framed in isolation from the development and policy sectors from which they emanate. Against this background, and in the light of General Assembly resolution 38/161 of 19 December 1983, the present document reflects an intergovernmental consensus on growing environmental challenges to the year 2000 and beyond, in six main sectors. In addition, the document discusses briefly other issues of global concern which do not fit easily under the sectoral headings and considers instruments for environmental action, including the role of institutions in dealing with environmental issues. Throughout the Environmental Perspective, an attempt has been made to reflect consistently the interdependent and integrated nature of environmental issues. Under each sectoral heading, this document covers: the issue; the outlook; the goal to be aspired to in dealing with the issue; and recommended action. While drawing upon the report of the World Commission on Environment and Development, the Environmental Perspective has sought to delineate, in an organized manner, the elements of shared perceptions, environmental issues, aspirational goals and the agenda for action envisaged for the Environmental Perspective by the Governing Council and the General Assembly.

II. Sectoral Issues

A. Population

1. *Issue and outlook*

5. *Issue*: The optimum contribution of human resources for the achievement of sustainable development has not been realized. Yet population levels, growth and distribution will continue to overload the capacities of the environment in many countries. Rapid population growth, among other factors, has exacerbated poverty. The negative interaction between population and environment has tended to create social tensions.

6. *Outlook*: People are the most valuable asset anywhere for the betterment of economic and social conditions and the quality of life. Yet, in a number of countries, the momentum of population growth today, coupled with poverty, environmental degradation and an unfavourable economic situation, has tended to create serious disequilibria between population and environment and to aggravate the problem of "environmental refugees". Traditions and social attitudes, especially in rural areas, have been a major impediment to population planning.

7. World population may exceed 6 billion by the year 2000. Several countries have achieved population equilibrium as defined by low birth and death rates and high life expectancies. But, for a large part of the developing world, this has not happened because of unfavourable economic conditions. Over 90 per cent of the net addition to the world's population between now and the year 2025, when the world population may exceed 8 billion, will occur in the developing countries. Many of them already suffer from desertification, fuelwood deficits, and loss of forests. Population planning would help, but is not sufficient, to achieve equilibrium between population and environmental capacities. Countries have not yet related population planning to development planning, nor have they linked population and environmental action for mutually reinforcing improvements. Equally, there is the need for more concern for human progress and social justice as factors influencing human resources development and environmental improvement.

2. *Goal and recommended action*

8. *Goal*: The achievement over time of such a balance between population and environmental capacities as would make possible sustainable development, keeping in view the links between population levels, consumption patterns, poverty and the natural resource base.

9. *Recommended action*:

(a) Development planning which takes into account environmental considerations should be an important instrument in achieving population goals. Countries should identify the rural and urban areas with acute population pressures on the environment. The environmental problems of large cities in developing countries should receive special attention. As poverty increases, economic development decreases and population rates grow, development plans should give special attention to population-related programmes aimed at improving environmental conditions at local levels;

(b) Significant changes in natural resources should be monitored and anticipated. This information should be fed back into sub-national and national development plans and related to the planning of spatial distribution of populations;

(c) Land and water use and spatial planning should bring about a balanced distribution of population through, for example, incentives for industrial location, and for resettlement and development of intermediate-sized towns, keeping in view the capacities of the environment;

(d) Public works, including food-for-work programmes, should be designed and implemented in areas of environmental stress and population pressures, with a view to providing employment and simultaneously improving the environment;

(e) Governments and voluntary organizations should increase public understanding, through formal and non-formal education, of the significance of population planning for environmental improvement and the important role of local action. The role of women in improving the environment and in population planning should receive special attention, as social changes that raise the status of women can have a profound effect in bringing down population growth rates;

(f) Private enterprise, and industry in particular, should participate actively in the work of governmental and non-governmental organizations aimed at relieving population and environmental stress;

(g) Education should be geared towards making people more capable of dealing with problems of excessive population density. Such education should help people acquire practical and vocational skills to enable them to become more self-reliant and enhance their participation in the improvement of the environment at the local level;

(h) International agencies, notably, the United Nations Fund for Population Activities, the United Nations Children's Fund, the International Labour Organisation, the World Health Organization and the

World Food Programme, should give priority attention to the geographical areas experiencing acute population pressures on the environment. They should reflect sensitivity to environmental improvement in the design and implementation of their population-related programmes. Multilateral and bilateral development assistance should be increased to finance innovative projects to make population programmes more effective by relating them to environmental improvement;

(i) Population policies must have a broader focus than controlling numbers. Governments should work on several fronts: to achieve and maintain population equilibrium, to expand the carrying capacity of the environment and improve health and sanitation at local levels, to develop human resources through education and training, and to ensure equitable distribution of the benefits of economic growth.

B. Food and agriculture

1. *Issue and outlook*

10. *Issue*: The shortage of food in many developing countries creates insecurity and environmental threats. The quest to meet rapidly growing food needs, combined with insufficient attention to the environmental impact of agricultural policies and practices, has been causing great environmental damage. This includes: degradation and depletion in the form of loss of soil and forests; drought and desertification; loss and deterioration of the quality of surface and ground water; reduction in genetic diversity and of fish stocks; damage to the sea floor; waterlogging, salinization, and siltation; soil, water and air pollution; and eutrophication caused by improper use of fertilizers and pesticides and by industrial effluents.

11. *Outlook*: While food production capabilities have increased greatly over the last three decades, self-reliance in food production has not been achieved in many countries. In the absence of proper environmental management, the conversion of forests and grassland into cropland will increase land degradation. For example, in sub-Saharan Africa desertification and frequent droughts are major concerns causing large-scale migration from rural areas. In most developing countries the pressure on the natural resources, including those in the public domain, is a serious concern. In some developed countries loss of land productivity from excessive use of chemicals and loss of prime quality land to urbanization are major concerns.

12. Soil erosion has increased in all regions: increased intensity of land use has resulted in the reduction of fallowing which, in turn, has undermined soil conservation, management of moisture and control of weeds and diseases in small holder agriculture. The main causes of soil erosion have been deforestation, overgrazing and overworking of farmland. Inappropriate patterns of land use and inadequate access to land are other factors which have been at work. Some off-site impacts have been flooding, reduction in hydro-electric capacity, reduced life of irrigation systems and declines in fish catches. The world's rivers may be carrying 24 billion tons of sediment to the seas annually. Technologies which make optimal use of natural resources, minimum tillage, fallowing and drought-, pest- and disease-resistant varieties, combined with mixed cropping, crop rotation, terracing and agro-forestry, have kept erosion under control in some places.

13. Nearly one third of all land is at risk from desertification. Over the last quarter century the population in arid lands has increased by more than 80 per cent. Since the adoption in 1977 of the Plan of Action to Combat Desertification[1] awareness of the problem has grown and so have organizational efforts to deal with it. But the basic elements of the action needed, namely, to stop the process, to rehabilitate degraded lands, and to ensure their effective management, do not yet receive the attention they urgently need. Although long-term economic returns on investments in the control of dryland degradation are high, insufficient resources are being devoted to it.

14. Forests cover approximately one third of all land. Tropical forests occupy over 1.9 billion hectares, of which 1.2 billion hectares are closed forests, and the remaining open tree formations. Although the rate of tree plantations in the tropics has accelerated recently (about 1.1 million hectares annually), it amounts to only about one tenth of the rate of deforestation. Use of forest land for agriculture through shifting or sedentary cultivation, increasing demand for fuelwood, unmanaged clearance and logging, burning and conversion for pastoral purposes are the main factors behind tropical deforestation. In semi-humid and dry climates fire can be a significant cause as well. Widespread deforestation has brought about far-reaching changes in tropical forest ecosystems, which no longer can perform well their essential functions of water retention, climate control, soil conservation and provision of livelihood.

15. Timber, an increasingly scarce commodity, has become the subject of extensive international negotiations. The International Tropical Timber Agreement, ratified in 1985, aims at promoting international trade in industrial wood and environmental management of tropical forests. The Tropical Forestry Action Plan, prepared under the auspices of the Food and Agriculture Organization of the United Nations, puts forward five priority areas aimed at: forestry land use planning, forestry-based industrial development, fuelwood and energy planning, conservation of tropical forest ecosystems and institutional support for better forestry management.

16. There have been significant changes in weather patterns as a result in part of loss of forests and vegetation cover. This has reduced river flows and lake levels and also lowered agricultural productivity. Irrigation has greatly improved arability in many areas of uncertain, or inadequate, rainfall. It has also been playing a vital role in the Green Revolution. Inappropriate irrigation, however, has wasted water, washed out nutrients and, through salinization and alkalinization, damaged the productivity of millions of hectares. Globally, salinization alone may be removing as much land from production as the land being irrigated, and about half of the land under surface irrigation may be saline or waterlogged. Excessive use of ground water for irrigation has resulted in lower water tables and semi-arid conditions.

17. Fisheries potential has not yet been tapped sufficiently or in such ways as to ensure sustainable yields, particularly in the developing coastal States, which do not possess the necessary infrastructure, technology or trained manpower to develop and manage fisheries in their exclusive economic zones. Excessive fishing activities have led to overexploitation of several important fish stocks and the exhaustion of some. By the year 2000, annual fish supplies may fall short of demand by about 10 to 15 million tons. Regional agreements on coordination of national fishing policies for licensing procedures, catch reporting, monitoring and surveillance have begun to consider sustainability of yields and use of appropriate technology. The World Conference on Fisheries Management and Development[2] established a framework and programmes of action for fisheries management.

18. Freshwater fish farming and aquaculture now produce annually about 8 million tons of fish. In Europe and in South and South-East Asia, aquaculture has made important strides. Whether as part of a traditional way of supplementing farm incomes and protein intake or as an industry, carefully practised aquaculture holds great promise for integrated environmental management and rural development in many countries.

19. The use of high-yielding seed varieties has multiplied agricultural output but has led to a reduction in the genetic diversity of crops and an increase in their vulnerability to diseases and pests. The emerging technology of direct gene transfer, or transfer of the symbiotic nitrogen-fixing capacity of leguminous crops to cereals, can greatly increase production and reduce costs. Also, the spread of gene banks, through the International Board for Plant Genetic Resources, and the work of the International Centre for Genetic Engineering and Biotechnology should improve the prospects for genetic diversity, and thereby enhance agricultural productivity.

20. Overuse of pesticides has polluted water and soil, damaging the ecology of agriculture and creating hazards for human and animal health. Pesticides have to be used to increase agricultural production,

---

1 *Report of the United Nations Conference on Desertification, Nairobi, 29 August - 9 September 1977* (A/CONF.74/36), chap. I.

2 Food and Agriculture Organization of the United Nations, *Report of the FAO World Conference on Fisheries Management and Development, Rome, 27 June - 6 July 1984.*

but their indiscriminate use has destroyed natural predators and other non-target species and increased resistance in target pests. More than 400 insect species are believed to be resistant to pesticides and their number is increasing.

21. Use of chemical fertilizers per capita has increased fivefold between 1950 and 1983. In some countries excessive use of fertilizers, along with household and industrial effluents, has caused eutrophication of lakes, canals, irrigation reservoirs, and even coastal seas through runoffs of nitrogen compounds and phosphates. Ground water has also been polluted by nitrates in many places, and nitrate levels in rivers have risen steadily over the last two decades. Degradation of the quality of surface and ground water, caused by chemicals, including nitrates, has been a significant problem in developed and developing countries alike.

22. In North America, Western Europe and some other areas, food surpluses have accumulated as a result in part of farm price subsidization. The push to produce more in response to incentives, coupled with excessive use of fertilizers and pesticides, has led to degradation and soil erosion in some countries. Similarly, export subsidization of food grains by some countries has undermined agricultural exports of some others, and also led to environmental neglect of farmland. In some countries, however, there is a trend towards reducing the scale of farming, encouraging organic farming, restoring the natural beauty of the countryside and diversifying the rural economy.

23. In the developing countries, farmers receive too little for their produce, and production is thereby discouraged. City dwellers often buy food at subsidized prices, and peasants may receive only a fraction of the market price. In countries where farmers have begun to receive better prices for their produce, agricultural production has increased and soil and water management has improved. When equitable agricultural prices are accompanied by technical assistance for environmental management of farming, they can help improve the quality of life in the countryside as well as in cities, partly by stemming the flow of rural-urban migration. Upward adjustment of food prices is, however, a politically sensitive issue, especially in situations of low resource productivity, low income, large-scale unemployment and slow economic growth.

2. *Goal and recommended action*

24. *Goal*: The achievement of food security without resource depletion or environmental degradation, and restoration of the resource base where environmental damage has been occurring.

25. *Recommended action*:

(a) Policies of Governments for using agricultural land, forests and water resources should take into account degradation trends as well as evaluation of potentials. Agricultural policies should vary from region to region to reflect different regional needs, encouraging farmers to adopt practices that are ecologically sustainable in their own areas and promote national food security. Local communities should be involved in the design and implementation of such policies;

(b) Policy distortions that have caused undue pressures on marginal lands, or taken away prime farmland for urbanization, or led to environmental neglect of natural resources, have to be identified and eliminated;

(c) Governments should design and implement regulatory measures, as well as taxation and price policies and incentives, aimed at ensuring that the right of owning agricultural land carries an obligation to sustain its productivity. Long-term agricultural credits should require farmers to undertake soil conservation practices, including keeping a portion of land fallow, where appropriate;

(d) Governments should promote equity in means for food production and in distribution. Governments should design and implement comprehensive agrarian reforms to improve the levels of living of farm workers who lack land. Governments should take decisive action to turn the terms of trade in favour of farmers, through pricing policy and government expenditure reallocation;

(e) Governments should ascertain direct and indirect environmental impacts of alternative crop, forestry and land use patterns. Fiscal and trade policies should be based on such environmental assessments. Governments should give priority to establishing a national policy and to creating or strengthening institutions to restore areas where natural factors and land use practices have reduced productivity;

(f) In the national development plans and agricultural programmes of countries experiencing desertification, dryland rehabilitation and management have to figure prominently. Better systems of early warning against drought and other dryland disasters have to be developed, with the World Meteorological Organization, the Food and Agriculture Organization of the United Nations, the United Nations Environment Programme and the relevant regional organizations playing appropriate roles;

(g) Sound forest policies should be based on an analysis of the capacity of the forests and the land under them to perform various functions. Programmes to conserve forest resources should start with the local people. Contracts covering forest use will have to be negotiated or renegotiated to ensure sustainability. Clear-cutting of large forest areas should be avoided and replanting of logged forestry areas should be required. Portions of forests should be designated as protected areas to conserve soil, water, wildlife and genetic resources in their natural habitat;

(h) Social and economic costs of deforestation, including clear-cutting, have to be estimated and reported on in relation to the periodic national reporting on the economic performance of forestry. Similarly, the damage costs of waterlogging and salinization have to be reported in conjunction with the reporting on irrigation and agricultural production. The loss of land to deserts and its consequences for food production, trade, employment and income have to be made part of the annual reporting on economic growth. Economic policies and planning have to reflect such environmental accounting;

(i) In areas experiencing deforestation and lack of forest resources, economic and other incentives should be introduced to manage forests and woody vegetation from an environmental standpoint and to promote tree nurseries, tree farming and fuelwood plantations. Local communities should be encouraged to take major responsibility for such undertakings;

(j) Projects should be designed and implemented to promote afforestation, agro-forestry systems, water management and soil conservation measures, such as land contour-levelling and terracing, in areas of environmental stress. Such projects should respond to the needs of the local people for food, fodder and fuel, while increasing the long-term productivity of natural resources. Environmental improvement schemes should become a regular part of national relief, rural employment and incomesupport schemes to sustain development in regions prone to drought or other environmental stress;

(k) Within the framework of a national water policy, which should facilitate an intersectoral and integrated approach to water development and use, technical, economic and organizational means have to be geared to improving efficiency of water use in farming and animal husbandry. Emphasis on ground-water storage in drylands should improve assurance of water availability. Improvements in water application techniques to minimize wastage, coordination of farming patterns with water supply, and such pricing of water as would cover the cost of its collection, storage and supply, should be introduced to conserve water in scarcity areas;

(l) In the choice of technology and the scale of irrigation environmental costs and benefits should be taken into account. Decentralized and small-scale irrigation have to receive special attention. Proper drainage to prevent salinization and waterlogging has to accompany irrigation. Development assistance has to play a vital role in improving productivity of existing irrigation, reducing its environmental damage and adapting it to the needs of small-scale, diversified agriculture;

(m) The traditional rights of subsistence farmers, particularly shifting cultivators, pastoralists, and nomads, must be protected from encroachment. Provision of infrastructure, services and information should help modernize nomadic life-styles without damaging their traditionally harmonious relationships with ecosystems. Programmes of land clearance and resettlement should be based on an assessment of their environmental, along with their social and economic, impacts. Agro-industry, mining and schemes of geographical dispersal of settlements should also aim at improving environmental conditions in rural areas;

(n) Public education, information campaigns, technical assistance, training, legislation, standard setting and incentives should be oriented toward encouraging the use of organic matter in agriculture. The use of fertilizers and pesticides has to be guided, *inter alia*, through training, awareness building and appropriate price policies, so as to establish integrated nutrient supply systems responsive to environmental impacts. Similarly, subsidies, which have led to the overuse or abuse of chemical fertilizers and pesticides, have to be phased out;

(o) Decentralized storage facilities, with the upgrading of traditional methods to ensure protection of stored grains, should receive attention in the planning of support services for rural and agricultural development;

(p) Where the agricultural frontier has extended in an uncontrolled manner, Governments should make special efforts to expand the area under woodland and nature reserves;

(q) Satellite imagery, aerial photography and geographical information systems of assessing and monitoring should be deployed to establish natural resource data bases. Such data should be made available, freely or at a nominal charge, to the countries in need. The United Nations Environment Programme should coordinate international programmes in this field. Such data collection and their socio-economic analyses should facilitate the design and implementation of land use and natural resource development plans, and improve international cooperation in the environmental management of trans-boundary natural resources;

(r) In international cooperation, priority should be given to schemes aimed at strengthening skills and institutional capabilities in the developing countries in fields such as applied genetics, agro-forestry, organic recycling, integrated pest management, crop rotation, drainage, soil-conserving ploughing, sand-dune stabilization, small-scale irrigation and environmentally sound management of fresh-water systems;

(s) Biotechnology, including tissue culture, conversion of biomass into useful produce, micro-electronics and information technology, should be deployed, after assessing carefully their environmental impacts and cost effectiveness, with a view to promoting environmental management of agriculture. Governments should enhance the access of farmers to such technologies through national policies and international cooperation. Research should be intensified on new technologies urgently needed in regions which have unreliable rainfall, uneven topography, and poor soils. Governments should also set up targets for the development of cadres of professionals specializing in environmental management of soil, water and forests and in biotechnology with a multidisciplinary and integrated outlook;

(t) Agriculture should be developed to the fullest, where possible in conjunction with farming, using low-cost, simple, labour-intensive technology. Cooperation for environmental management of marine living resources and fisheries should be intensified, through technical assistance as well as conventions and agreements;

(u) Because of women's important role in agriculture in many developing countries, they should be provided with adequate education and training opportunities. They should also have the necessary power to take decisions regarding agriculture and forestry programmes;

(v) Distortions in the structure of the world food market should be minimized, and the focus of production should be shifted to food deficit countries. In developed countries incentive systems should be changed to discourage overproduction and foster improved soil and water management. Governments must recognize that all parties lose through protectionist barriers, and redesign trade and tax policies using environmental and economic criteria;

(w) International agreements should be concluded in respect of agricultural price policies, with a view to minimizing waste and mismanagement of food and natural resources in agriculture. Such agreements should aim at bringing about an international division of labour in agriculture in conformity with the long-term capabilities of countries in agricultural production. In this context, consideration should be given to strengthening the work of the World Food Programme through the establishment of a world food bank from which countries could draw food supplies in emergency situations;

(x) Special attention should be given to protection and careful development of wetlands, particularly in view of their long-term economic value;

(y) Sustainable exploitation of living wild resources should receive special consideration in the light of its contribution to achieving food security.

C. Energy

1. *Issue and outlook*

26. *Issue*: There are vast disparities in the patterns of energy consumption. Accelerated economic growth and growing populations require a rapid expansion in energy production and consumption. Major problems in this regard include: depletion of the supplies of, and inadequate access to, fuelwood, and environmental impacts of fossil energy production, transmission and use, for example, acidification of the environment, accumulation of greenhouse gases and consequent climatic change. Although energy is crucial to the development process, there has been little concerted action to balance environmental imperatives and energy demands.

27. *Outlook*: About three fourths of the world's energy consumption is in the form of fossil fuels: oil, coal, and natural gas. The remainder is supplied mainly by biomass, hydropower and nuclear power. The main problems caused by fossil fuel use are: air pollution, acidification of soil, fresh water and forests, and climatic change, especially warming of the atmosphere. The costs of controlling these problems and of dealing with their environmental and health impacts have been enormous. New and renewable sources of energy, including solar, wind, ocean and geothermal, are being developed but are unlikely to make a significant contribution during the rest of this century.

28. International oil prices are fluctuating. The immediate economic impact of lower prices has been significant, yet the momentum of efforts to improve energy efficiency and to develop alternatives for fossil fuels, which began in the wake of high oil prices, may decline.

29. Though developing countries account for about one third of the world's energy consumption, many of them do not have adequate access to energy. Most of them depend on oil imports and on biomass and animal energy. Wood, which provides energy to about half of the world's people, is becoming scarce, and overcutting has devastated the environment. Some countries have made progress in developing biogas while improving the environment, but the potential of biogas remains largely untapped. Given the needs of industrialization and the trends of population growth, energy needs will increase tremendously during the coming decades. If energy efficiency measures are not put in place, it will not be possible to meet those needs.

30. Many countries have made efforts to control air pollution by setting standards and introducing appropriate equipment in factories as well as automobiles, and by developing clean technologies for cooking, space heating, industrial processes and power generation. But attempts to deal with urban and industrial air pollution have often effectively transported the problem, for example, in the form of acid deposition, to other areas and countries. At least 5 to 6 per cent of the European forests may have already died because of acidification. As a first step, some European countries have agreed on a technical cooperation programme to monitor and control long-range transmission of some air pollutants. Reducing emissions of sulphur dioxide and nitrogen oxides, however, is rather costly, although effective reduction technologies have been introduced in some countries. On the other hand, no effective technologies exist to control carbon dioxide accumulation which can markedly change climate. Moreover, available technology is not being fully utilized. The difficulty is to determine up to what level the damage costs of polluting fossil fuels should be accepted and how much to invest in scientific research to develop clean technologies.

31. Energy is often used in wasteful ways. The costs of this waste are being borne by all, but mostly by the poor. Moreover, part of these costs are being transferred to children, future generations and other countries. Several countries have experimented successfully over the

last decade with conservation of energy for domestic use, improved efficiency of energy in industry and agriculture and adoption of energy mixes to minimize environmental damage. In some countries the nature of industrial growth has been changing in ways which economize on energy, for example, rapid growth of electronic, recreation and service industries. Consequently, there has been a noticeable delinking of economic growth from increase in energy consumption. Energy savings, renewable sources and new technologies can reduce energy consumption while maintaining the momentum of economic growth.

32. While oil exploration and coal mining have received great attention, the potential of natural gas has not been realized. Considerable quantities are being wasted in the absence of necessary infrastructure and investment. The world also has a relatively untapped capacity to develop hydropower. In the past, environmental planning has not received adequate attention in hydropower development. Decentralized small-scale hydropower schemes are not yet used on a significant scale, although they may be capable of providing economical, efficient and environmentally sound sources of energy.

33. Nuclear energy is widely used as a source of electricity, and the International Atomic Energy Agency has formulated guidelines to ensure that it is developed and used safely. The problems associated with it include the risk of accidental contamination, which can spread quickly over long distances, and the safe handling and disposal of radioactive wastes, including decommissioned nuclear reactors.

2. *Goal and recommended action*

34. *Goal*: The provision of sufficient energy at reasonable cost, notably by increasing access to energy substantially in the developing countries, to meet current and expanding needs in ways that minimize environmental degradation and risks, conserve nonrenewable sources of energy and realize the full potential of renewable sources of energy.

35. *Recommended action*:

(a) Governments' energy plans should systematically take into account environmental requirements. Energy efficiency policies coupled with environmentally sound energy production and appropriate energy mixes should be pursued to achieve sustainable energy consumption patterns. National efforts should be supported by international cooperation, especially scientific research, establishment of standards and transfer of technology and information;

(b) Energy pricing, taxation, trade and other policies should take into account the environmental costs of all forms of energy. Subsidies for fossil fuels should be progressively phased out. Private enterprise, consumers and government institutions should be provided with economic incentives to make greater use of renewable sources of energy. Where needed, international cooperation should facilitate the exploration for and environmentally sound production of energy;

(c) Information should be made available on the harmful environmental impacts of intensive use of fossil fuels. Urban and industrial air pollution, accumulation of greenhouse gases and the attendant climatic change, as well as transfrontier transport of air pollutants in all regions must receive urgent attention, including monitoring by appropriate methods. Standards must be set and enforced within and among countries, and conventions and agreements should be concluded to deal with these problems. In this context, the "polluter pays principle" should be accepted. Governments should ensure that clean technologies are put into practice on a wider scale than in the past at the local level. The United Nations system, in conjunction with other intergovernmental bodies, should improve access to information on renewable sources of energy and on efficient energy use;

(d) In view of the significance of fuelwood, national programmes of afforestation and of environmental management of woodlands should receive increased resources. Agro-forestry programmes, tree plantations and village woodlots should receive special encouragement in countries experiencing fuelwood deficit. Commercial cutting of fuelwood should be subjected to rigorous scrutiny and control, in view of its environmental costs. Application of fuel-efficient stoves and charcoal should be encouraged. Pricing of fuelwood should be guided by the consideration of sustaining supplies consistent with needs;

(e) As biogas can be an important source of energy, the existing technology for the use of agricultural, animal and human wastes should be applied more widely by means of incentives and guidance. Technical cooperation among developing countries should play a vital part in this process, bearing in mind its sanitation and agricultural benefits;

(f) Decisions on large-scale hydropower projects should be guided by analysis of social costs and benefits in the light of likely environmental impacts. Small-scale hydropower schemes should receive particular attention since they could facilitate simultaneous attainment of environmental, economic and social objectives;

(g) Renewable energy sources should receive high priority and should be applied on a wider scale than in the past, giving full consideration to their environmental impacts. Technologies to develop renewable sources of energy, such as wind, geo-thermal and especially solar, should receive particular attention. International cooperation should facilitate this process;

(h) International cooperation should aim at the creation of a régime for the safe production and use of nuclear energy, as well as the safe handling of radioactive waste, taking into account, through appropriate mechanisms including prior consultations, the interests and concerns of countries that have decided not to produce nuclear energy, in particular concerns regarding the siting of nuclear plants close to their borders. This régime should extend globally to encompass observance of comparable standards and procedures on management of reactors and the sharing of information and technology for nuclear safety. The Convention on Early Notification of a Nuclear Accident and the Convention on Assistance in the Case of a Nuclear Accident or Radiological Emergency[1] should be complemented by bilateral and subregional agreements and should also lead to technical cooperation among countries on environmental management of nuclear energy.

D. Industry

1. *Issue and outlook*

36. *Issue*: Industrial development brings obvious benefits, but it frequently entails damage to the environment and to human health. The main negative impacts are: wasteful use and depletion of scarce natural resources; air, water and soil pollution; congestion, noise and squalor; accumulation of hazardous wastes; and accidents with significant environmental consequences. Industrialization patterns and the consequent exploitation of natural resources and environmental degradation have been markedly unbalanced. The prospect for accelerated, yet environmentally sound, world industrial development is slim in the absence of concerted international action.

37. *Outlook*: Although some efforts to deal with environmental problems of industry have been made, negative impacts will grow in magnitude if not addressed methodically now. A promising trend is the steadily growing awareness of industrial environmental risks throughout the world. While this awareness increasingly informs and influences public policy, environmental knowledge remains as yet markedly uneven. In the absence of mechanisms for the unhindered sharing of environmental knowledge, Governments and industry may import hazardous materials and allow establishment of processes discarded elsewhere. Inadequate knowledge at the grassroots level of changes in the environment, and of their causes as well as economic implications, impedes participation of the concerned people in decision-making on siting of industrial plants and choice of industrial technology.

38. Natural resources have been used wastefully in industry. Recently, a number of countries have made significant progress in developing and adopting low-waste and clean industrial technologies and in recovering as well as recycling scarce industrial raw materials.

---

1 See International Atomic Energy Agency, *Final Document, Resolutions and Conventions adopted by the first special session of the General Conference, 24-26 September 1986,* sects. I-IV.

New materials and processing technologies have made it possible to save raw materials and energy resources and to reduce environmental stress. Nevertheless, in many countries resource-intensive processes persist in the absence of suitable policies and access to proper technology.

39. Uncontrolled industrial practices have led to unacceptably high levels of harmful or toxic substances in the air, the pollution of rivers, lakes, coastal waters and soil, the destruction of forests, and the accumulation of carbon dioxide and other greenhouse gases which threaten to cause climatic changes, including a global warming of the atmosphere. Sea levels may rise considerably as a result. Industrial production and emission of chlorofluorocarbons threaten a significant depletion of the ozone layer, leading to increased ultraviolet radiation.

40. Recently, there has been an increase in the seriousness of industrial accidents, particularly in the chemicals industry. Even in the developed countries, the state of preparedness to meet such contingencies has been inadequate. Also, frameworks for international cooperation in such situations have been lacking. A crucial problem has been the lack of timely warning and of full sharing of information on the nature and magnitude of the hazards at local and regional levels.

41. With industrial growth and spread, the transport, storage and disposal of chemical, toxic and radioactive wastes will pose an increasingly serious challenge. The "polluter pays principle" has been applied with good results in some countries, but in many others it is still not applied at all, so that the source of environmental damage often is not held accountable for the harm caused. In the pursuit of rapid industrialization, some polluting industries may be relocated from other countries. As many developing countries do not possess the technical or institutional capability to analyse or monitor environmental implications of industrial processes, products or wastes, they are vulnerable to industrial environmental damage.

42. Many developed countries have successfully applied technology, policies and institutional and legislative frameworks to deal with industrial pollution. Several have succeeded in innovating or applying lowwaste or clean technologies. The Industry and Environment Office of the United Nations Environment Programme has produced publications with extensive and detailed information on environmentally sound technologies in specific industries. Thus, although environmental hazards of industrial processes, products and wastes persist, there is available considerable experience, expertise and technology to prevent industrial accidents and implement environmentally responsible practices.

43. Technical innovation has opened up promising opportunities for achieving mutually supportive economic and environmental objectives. Properly guided technology can transform patterns of industrialization and improve the international division of labour. Innovation in microelectronics and opto-electronics has revolutionized information and communications industries and could lead to geographical dispersal of industry. These innovations hold promise for developing countries suffering from the twin problems of excessive industrial concentration in urban areas and relative neglect of rural areas.

44. In the decades ahead, the developing countries will depend more and more on industry, including processing of their own raw materials, for incomes and employment. In contrast, in some developed countries, the pattern of industry is changing in the direction of knowledge-intensive, energy-saving, and materials-saving activities. Moreover, leisure and service industries have begun to play a significant part in this change.

45. Countries have been coming together to forge agreements on preventive measures to contain global, regional and transfrontier environmental impacts of industrial products and processes. Examples of this encouraging trend include: conventions and protocols for the control of land-based sources of marine pollution within the frameworks of various regional seas programmes; the Vienna Convention for the Protection of the Ozone Layer and the evolving international consensus on the control of emission of chlorofluorocarbons; the Convention on Long-range Transboundary Air Pollution and its Cooperative Programme for the Monitoring and Evaluation of Long-range Transmission of Air Pollutants in Europe; and the Cairo Guidelines and Principles for the Environmentally Sound Management of Hazardous Wastes,[1] sponsored by the United Nations Environment Programme. Such international cooperation can extend into many areas of industrial environmental management and many geographical regions. Moreover, industry itself, following the World Industry Conference on Environmental Management convened in 1984 by the United Nations Environment Programme, is increasingly ready to undertake environmental responsibilities.

2. *Goal and recommended action*

46. *Goal*: Sustained improvements in levels of living in all countries, especially the developing countries, through industrial development that prevents or minimizes environmental damage and risks.

47. *Recommended action*:

(a) Governments should implement policies to assist in the transition of economies characterized by the wasteful use of natural resources and raw materials and dependence on their export, to environmentally sound industrial development. National efforts to plan and implement environmentally sound industrial policies should be intensified. Governments should introduce incentive schemes to help establish facilities for recovery and recycling of scarce raw materials. The transfer of industrial technology and skills from developed to developing countries to arrest environmental degradation associated with industry should be internationally supported. The United Nations Development Programme, the United Nations Environment Programme, the Economic Commission for Europe, and the United Nations Industrial Development Organization should intensify efforts in this direction;

(b) Governments should introduce programmes to monitor air, soil, fresh water and coastal pollution from industrial emissions and effluents, and hazardous industrial activities, where such programmes do not already exist;

(c) Governments should establish and enforce environmental standards, and should provide fiscal and other incentives to industry for the retro-fitting of equipment for pollution control. They should also ensure penalties for non-compliance, in conformity with the "polluter pays principle". International organizations should cooperate with Governments in establishing global or regional standards;

(d) Governments should require periodic reports by industries on measures implemented to protect and improve the environment, especially those industries involving high environmental and health risks;

(e) Industrial enterprises should carry out environmental impact and social cost-benefit analyses prior to the siting and design of industrial plants. Governments should ensure that such analyses are carried out and made public. Governmental policies should facilitate the location of industries in areas which would relieve urban congestion and encourage rural development. Industries which use each other's products and wastes should be located near each other;

(f) Governments and industrial enterprises should be receptive to the views of citizen groups, community associations, labour organizations and professional and scientific bodies in arriving at and implementing decisions on industrial siting, design and technologies to meet the environmental, economic and social needs of the people;

(g) Chambers of commerce and federations of industry should collaborate actively in implementing emissions standards and pollution control measures. They should establish mechanisms to bridge the gap in environmental management knowledge and capabilities among their members. Such cooperation should also be encouraged among smallscale producers;

(h) Transnational corporations should comply with the environmental legislation of the host country, while respecting similar legislation of the home country. Legislation could include requirements for public environmental audits of the activities of transnational corporations and local enterprises. In accordance with proposed international

1 *Official Records of the General Assembly, Forty-second Session, Supplement No. 25* (A/42/25 and Corr. 1), annex II.

codes of conduct, transnational corporations should establish progressively in the host countries the skills and technological capabilities needed for environmentally sound management of industry, even in the absence of legislation on desirable environmental standards;

(i) International industrial collaboration, like national industry, should be subjected to environmental impact assessments;

(j) Countries, especially developing countries, should, as a matter of urgency, design and implement research, training and manpower-planning programmes to strengthen the management of hazardous industrial processes and wastes;

(k) International organizations, including the United Nations Development Programme, the United Nations Industrial Development Organization, the World Health Organization, the Food and Agriculture Organization of the United Nations, the World Meteorological Organization and the International Labour Organisation, and intergovernmental organizations, such as the Organisation for Economic Cooperation and Development, and the Council for Mutual Economic Assistance, should ensure that their programmes will progressively strengthen the capacities of the developing countries for designing and implementing industrial operations along environmentally sound lines. They should also assist in establishing or strengthening information services on environmental and health implications of industrial processes, products and wastes. In addition, access of the developing countries to information and data on environmentally benign technologies should be promoted, including risk management techniques;

(l) International cooperation for the monitoring of the accumulation of carbon dioxide and other greenhouse gases and of their impacts on climate and sea levels must be strengthened to encompass both the conclusion of international agreements and the formulation of industrial strategies to mitigate the environmental, economic, and social impacts of potential changes. Intergovernmental negotiations, based on the Vienna Convention for the Protection of the Ozone Layer, should lead to agreements on the reduction of ozone-depleting substances;

(m) Within the framework of their existing legal and technical activities, United Nations organizations, especially the United Nations Environment Programme, in closer cooperation with regional organizations, should progressively establish international agreements and monitoring mechanisms to deal with spills and other industrial accidents, particularly chemical; to control the transportation, storage, management and disposal of hazardous industrial wastes- and to settle disputes involving damages and claims for compensation. United Nations and regional organizations should encourage Governments to extend the "polluter pays principle" to transboundary problems;

(n) The International Register of Potentially Toxic Chemicals programme of the United Nations Environment Programme should maintain and improve its assistance to Governments in assessing whether producing, marketing, distributing or disposing of any industrial substances, including chemicals and wastes, are potentially damaging to health and environment.

E. Health and human settlements

1. *Issue and outlook*

48. *Issue*: Despite considerable advances in dealing with problems of health and human settlements, the environmental basis for further improving the situation is deteriorating. Inadequate shelter and basic amenities, rural underdevelopment, overcrowded cities and urban decay, lack of access to clean water, poor sanitation and other environmental deficiencies continue to cause widespread disease and death, ill-health and intolerable living conditions in many parts of the world. Poverty, malnutrition and ignorance compound these problems.

49. *Outlook*: Human ability to prevent disease has grown greatly over the last few decades, mainly owing to scientific achievements and better access to sanitation, clean water and safe waste disposal. In many developed countries better living conditions have helped prevent disease and have enhanced average life expectancy. In the developing countries, however, achievements have lagged behind what is technically feasible.

50. More than 4 million children under the age of five die of diarrhoea in the developing countries annually. Even when it does not cause death, diarrhoea saps vitality and stops physical and mental growth. Malaria is another water-borne disease which infects about 100 million annually. Typhoid and cholera are similarly endemic in the developing countries. Bilharzia and river blindness are other common diseases caused by mismanagement of water. Sleeping sickness, caused by the tsetse fly, effectively denies the use of vast tracts of land in Africa for pastoral or settlements development. The burning of coal, oil, wood, dung and agricultural wastes builds up dangerous concentrations of toxic gases in houses and factories, and chronic heart and lung diseases, bronchitis, emphysema and asthma are the result.

51. In warm, humid countries where storage is inadequate, aflatoxins in food cause liver cancer. On the other hand, over-use of fertilizer has caused excessive nitrate levels in ground water, endangering children's health, and nitrate run-offs have led to eutrophication of surface waters and contamination of shellfish. Phosphates in fertilizer have caused high concentrations of cadmium in food. Further, pesticides, herbicides and fungicides pose a direct threat to health in the rural areas when their use is not properly guided. Over-use of pesticides has also led to high levels of pesticide residue in food.

52. About a billion people do not have adequate shelter, and millions practically live on the streets. By the year 2000, about 2 billion people, or 40 per cent of the developing countries' population, will live in cities and towns, thereby putting pressure on city planners and Governments. Most developing countries already do not have the resources required to provide housing and services to the people who need them. The influx of refugees in some developing countries has exacerbated health, shelter and environmental conditions. Also, where rural settlements are widely dispersed, health, housing and infrastructural services become practically unattainable.

53. About one third of all city and town dwellers in the developing countries live in slums and shanties, with no help or infrastructural support whatever, and often under adverse conditions. The inexorable trend towards urbanization will ensure that by the year 2000, 15 of the world's 20 largest urban metropolitan areas will be in the developing countries. Simultaneously, rural environmental degradation reinforces migration to urban areas even when people are unable to earn incomes high enough to ensure decent housing and there is no prospect of meeting their infrastructural needs.

54. There are three main environmental aspects of urbanization: characteristics of the dwelling - living space, ventilation, sanitation, water supply, waste disposal, recreation space, domestic energy; ambient environmental situation - air pollution, water pollution, environmental risks and hazards, noise, stress and crime; and environment of the area surrounding the urban centres - deforestation, soil erosion, changes in micro-climate. Between a quarter and a half of all urban residents in the developing countries live in unhealthy and degraded dwellings. Consequently, diarrhoea, dysentery and typhoid are common, and there are periodic outbreaks of cholera and hepatitis. Tuberculosis and other respiratory diseases spread easily in ill-ventilated, damp and crowded surroundings.

55. Excessive concentrations of industry and commerce in a few urban centres often reflect a dualistic development pattern, implying a relative neglect of rural and agricultural development. Concentrations of people, settlements and income and employment opportunities often become mutually reinforcing in such a situation. People continue to migrate to the urban areas even if their expected incomes are not high enough to ensure decent housing, or there is no prospect of their infrastructural needs being met. Thus, the problems of safe disposal of toxic and hazardous wastes, control of air and water pollution, collection and disposal of domestic wastes and provision of clean drinking water assume gigantic proportions, requiring enormous finance and great organizational and technical capabilities. Photochemical smog, oxides of nitrogen and sulphur, hydrocarbons, lead, mercury, cadmium poisoning, carbon monoxide, polychlonnated biphenyls, asbestos and other particulate matter along with the respiratory and gastroenteritic diseases and malnutrition, cause seri-

ous damage to public health. The consequent stress of living in such conditions contributes to social tensions and outbreaks of violence and unrest. When industrial accidents or natural disasters occur, loss of life and human suffering follow on a large scale because of the congestion, lack of organizational and technical capacities and vulnerability.

56. Heavy urban concentrations have also placed excessive demands on natural resources and polluted and degraded surrounding areas. High land prices have caused good agricultural land to be used for construction and speculation. Urban firewood demand has led to widespread deforestation, soil erosion and even changes in microclimate.

57. The congestion of settlements near factories multiplies the health risks of chemicals production in the developing countries. The accumulation of toxic wastes and their inappropriate disposal similarly endanger the health of millions. Awareness of the risks to human health posed by environmental contamination has increased greatly. Such risks arise partly through an absence of environmental regulation and management capability. Most developed countries have succeeded in reducing environmental pollution and its risks and impacts. International cooperation has also progressed on several fronts: national programmes launched under the International Drinking Water Supply and Sanitation Decade, the World Health Organization/United Nations Children's Fund Programme on Primary Health Care, the Onchocerciasis Control Programme in Africa in the Volta River basin, the United Nations Environment Programme/World Health Organization/International Labour Organisation International Programme on Chemical Safety, the dissemination of information on chemicals of environmental concern through the International Register of Potentially Toxic Chemicals of the United Nations Environment Programme, the International Code of Conduct on the Distribution and Use of Pesticides of the Food and Agriculture Organization of the United Nations and its accompanying technical guidelines, the Food and Agriculture Organization of the United Nations/United Nations Environment Programme Panel of Experts on Integrated Pest Control, the United Nations Development Programme/ World Bank/World Health Organization Special Programme for Research and Training in Tropical Diseases, the World Health Organization/Food and Agriculture Organization of the United Nations/ United Nations Environment Programme Panel of Experts on Environmental Management of Disease Vector Control, the specification of radiation dose limits by the International Commission on Radiological Protection, and the two recent international Conventions adopted under the auspices of the International Atomic Energy Agency on exchange of information and assistance in the event of a nuclear accident,[1] are some examples.

2. *Goal and recommended action*

58. *Goal*: The provision of improved shelter with access to essential amenities in a clean and secure setting conducive to health and to the prevention of environment-related diseases, which would, at the same time, alleviate serious environmental degradation.

59. *Recommended action*:

(a) Governments should make health and settlements development an integral part of environmental management of natural resources and geographically-balanced development. They should address systematically the issue of equity in development to ensure provision of basic health, housing and amenities for their people;

(b) International cooperation should be intensified in the field of scientific research to deal with the environmental conditions underlying tropical diseases;

(c) Rural development, including natural resources management and provision of drinking water and sanitation, should receive systematic attention in public policies. Governments should design and implement, with the participation of the communities concerned, integrated programmes to improve water supply and management, sanitation and waste disposal;

(d) Governments should set targets at national, provincial and district levels for such priority areas as housing, access to clean water and sanitation, and control of air pollution in urban areas;

(e) To reduce adverse environmental impacts of transportation, especially in highly populated areas, Governments should give priority to facilitating commuting between residential and working areas, enforcing emission standards for vehicles, encouraging fuel efficiency and improving traffic management policies and urban planning;

(f) Intermediate-sized towns should receive particular attention in programmes of industrial and settlement development;

(g) Governments should create an "enabling environment", in which the creativity and resources of people are mobilized to improve the health conditions, shelter and environmental information at local levels. This should include collection and disposal of domestic, agricultural and human wastes, land use planning, area development and self-help construction. Efforts should be made to encourage the participation of the private sector and non-governmental organizations;

(h) Industrial, agricultural, energy, irrigation and land development and resettlement projects should include a component which addresses environmental and health impacts, including risk assessment, which, in turn, should be influential in guiding the location, scale and choice of technology for the projects. Regulations should be established to prevent settlements development in high environmental-risk areas, such as those proximate to chemical or nuclear plants. Responsibility for enforcing such regulations should be shared with the private sector;

(i) Primary and occupational education should include information on the environment. The mass media should regularly make available information and know-how to enable people to improve sanitation, waste disposal and drinking water quality. Deterrents and incentives should be introduced at local levels to encourage people to keep their immediate environment healthy;

(j) Scientific research should be geared to the immediate improvement of the health and environmental situation of degraded settlements. Technologies for the safe disposal of wastes with minimum use of water in arid and semi-arid areas, improvement of water quality, reuse of waste water, and harvesting of rain should be developed. The United Nations Centre for Human Settlements (Habitat), the World Health Organization and the United Nations Children's Fund should intensify efforts to promote the application of such technologies in the developing countries;

(k) Urban planning should receive priority attention, together with the rational management of natural resources. Staffing, finance and organizational efforts should reflect the high priority given to this issue. Urban centres should systematically provide areas to meet the needs of various income categories, for industry, business, recreation and open spaces. Technical cooperation in this field has to expand greatly under the leadership of the United Nations Centre for Human Settlements (Habitat);

(l) Countries hosting a large number of refugees should receive more international assistance through the Office of the United Nations High Commissioner for Refugees and other bodies to improve environmental conditions of refugee settlements.

F. International economic relations

1. *Issue and outlook*

60. *Issue*: Inequalities in international economic relations, coupled with inappropriate economic policies in many developed and developing countries alike, continue to affect adversely sustainable development and cause environmental degradation. Deteriorating terms of trade, chronic trade deficits, which are partly caused by growing protectionism, heavy debt-service payments, and inadequate financial flows have made it very difficult to allocate resources to environmental protection and improvement, particularly in developing countries. Specific problems include: insufficient consideration of

[1] See International Atomic Energy Agency, *Final Document, Resolutions and Conventions adopted by the first special session of the General Conference, 24-26 September 1986*, sects. I-IV.

environmental impacts in development cooperation; insufficient control of trade in scarce natural resources and hazardous substances; and transnational investment and transfer of technology without adequate observance of environmental standards or information on environmental management.

61. *Outlook*: Awareness of the environmental aspects of international economic relations has increased, but it has not yet found adequate expression in institutional practices and national policies.

62. Development cooperation projects have not helped build significantly national capabilities to avert environmental disasters. The environmental damage resulting from the execution of some large-scale projects is now better understood than in the past. There is also a growing awareness of the need for additional resources to rehabilitate degraded environments.

63. Long-term declines in commodity prices, coupled with their inequity and instability, have adversely affected environmental management of natural resources. Furthermore, these prices do not fully reflect the environmental costs of depletion of the resource base. Good quality land, fishing areas and other natural resources are being overworked, and tropical forests are being encroached upon in order to achieve additional income. The substitution of export crops in place of subsistence crops has displaced small farmers and pastoralists from good quality land and has led to excessive pressures on marginal land and natural resources.

64. There is a growing awareness of the hazards associated with trade in chemicals, pesticides and some other products, but international practices for controlling the transport of hazardous chemical goods do not yet provide for a systematic consideration of the environment.

65. Mounting debt burdens, repayment obligations, austerity measures and reductions in financial flows to developing countries have endangered and, in some cases, blocked sustainable development, and this has had negative economic, environmental and social impacts.

66. Recent years have seen a sharp worsening of the international economic situation. Its impact has been particularly severe on developing countries. Lack of economic growth in developing countries could have devastating consequences.

2. *Goal and recommended action*

67. *Goal*: The establishment of an equitable system of international economic relations aimed at achieving continuing economic advancement for all States, based on principles recognized by the international community, in order to stimulate and sustain environmentally sound development, especially in developing countries.

68. *Recommended action*:

(a) In the ongoing search for concerted action to deal with international economic problems, the urgent need to improve the world environmental situation and to ensure a solid environmental foundation for sustainable development has to be recognized. Correcting the deteriorating terms of trade and stabilizing international commodity prices at equitable levels, through international commodity agreements such as the Integrated Programme on Commodities, in conjunction with appropriate environmental management practices in the producing countries, should play an important role in this regard;

(b) Especially in situations of environmental stress, development cooperation should aim at long-term improvement of natural resource productivity and environmental health. Projects that focus on the alleviation of poverty and improve the environment should receive greater attention in development cooperation. Such cooperation has to increase substantially, keeping in view the growing need for environmental rehabilitation;

(c) Development cooperation institutions should increase significantly their assistance to the developing countries for environmental restoration, protection and improvement;

(d) Country programmes and policy papers prepared by multilateral and bilateral development cooperation institutions for allocation of aid resources should provide for analyses of the environmental needs of recipient countries, with particular focus on major problems, such as desertification, deforestation and pollution. Developing countries should be assisted where necessary in preparing environmental accounting and relating it to the reporting on national economic well-being;

(e) The system of appraising development cooperation projects should provide for assessments of environmental and socio-economic impacts of alternative designs and locations. Area development programmes, in particular, should seek to establish mutual support between environmental and socio-economic objectives. Development cooperation institutions should train their staff according to these objectives;

(f) Trade in hazardous industrial products, such as toxic chemicals and pesticides, and in some other products, such as pharmaceuticals, should be subjected to regulations to ensure sharing by the contracting parties, Governments and consumers of information on their environmental and health implications and on methods for their safe use and disposal. Labelling of products should be in local languages. Governments of the exporting as well as the importing countries should collaborate in this regard. They should also agree on the selection of chemicals for priority testing;

(g) International trade and commodity agreements should provide environmental safeguards, where applicable. They should also encourage producers to take a long-term view and provide for assistance for diversification programmes, where appropriate. Governments should study the environmental impacts of their trade practices and make the findings available to their agencies responsible for trade negotiations, which should take them into account. The United Nations Conference on Trade and Development and the General Agreement on Tariffs and Trade should develop and apply effective policies and instruments to integrate environment and development considerations in international trade;

(h) Environmentally related regulations and standards should not be used for protectionist purposes. The International Trade Centre should assist countries in meeting such requirements. The United Nations Conference on Trade and Development should make available information on such regulations and standards as they apply to commodities and manufactured products;

(i) Host Governments should institute policies and regulations to ensure sound environmental management of transnational investments. In agreements on transnational, including corporate, investments, Governments, through appropriate controls, should ensure that information and technology on environmental management will be provided specifying the responsibilities of the parties concerned. In accordance with proposed code of conduct on transnational corporations of the Commission on Transnational Corporations, transnational corporations should implement programmes in the host countries to minimize the environmental hazards of their activities. These programmes should include training of personnel. The United Nations Centre on Transnational Corporations should play a role in facilitating this process;

(j) The transfer of clean, low-waste and pollution control technologies should be promoted through international cooperation. The possibility of making such technologies available at concessional prices to the countries in need should be explored. Governments of recipient countries should establish procedures for ascertaining the environmental implications of imported technologies;

(k) International financial institutions, while dealing with questions of structural adjustment in developing countries and world economic reform, should link short-term financial stabilization to sustainable development.

III. Other Issues of Global Concern

69. This section discusses briefly the major environmental issues of global concern that have not been adequately dealt with in previous sections.

A. Oceans and seas

70. Oceans and seas are being polluted extensively. The rising pollution levels and degradation of coastal ecosystems threaten the life-support capacities of oceans and seas and undermine their role in the food chain. Efforts to monitor the state of oceans and seas, including those of the United Nations Environment Programme and other

international organizations, confirm that there is cause for concern. This problem is particularly serious for coastal waters and semi-enclosed seas that border highly populated and industrialized zones. The situation will get much worse unless concerted action is undertaken now. The ongoing monitoring effort is far from comprehensive and, where it has advanced, it has not yet led to adequate change in the practices causing environmental damage.

71. The challenge is to control and decrease marine pollution, and establish or strengthen régimes of environmental management of oceans and seas through international cooperation and national action.

72. A comprehensive data base should be established over time on which action programmes to restore and preserve the environmental balance in the world's oceans and seas can be based. Among others, the Global Environmental Monitoring System, Global Resource Information Data Base and the oceans and coastal areas programmes of the United Nations Environment Programme should intensify efforts towards this end.

73. Conventions and agreements to monitor and manage human activities with a view to ensuring environmental protection of the seas and oceans should be ratified and implemented by all concerned countries. Where such legal instruments do not exist, they should be negotiated. Governments should strengthen or introduce policies and measures aimed at preventing practices harmful to marine ecosystems and ensuring environmentally sound development of inland areas. Such policies and measures should include control of the discharge of industrial effluents and sewage, dumping of wastes, including hazardous and radioactive materials, disposal of hazardous residues and operational wastes from ships, incineration at sea, and oil spills from tankers and off-shore platforms. Environmentally sound land-based technology for the disposal of hazardous wastes should be developed and promoted. The United Nations Environment Programme should continue to collaborate in this work with the Intergovernmental Oceanographic Commission, the International Maritime Organization and other appropriate international organizations.

B. Outer space

74. Outer space has now become a recognized area of human activity. As activity in this area develops over the coming decades, sound management of outer space will become increasingly important. To this end, international cooperation exclusively for the peaceful use of outer space is essential, especially on the part of those countries that now have the capacity to undertake outer space activities.

75. All countries, in particular those with a major capacity to exploit the benefits of outer space, should create conditions, including specifically the maintenance of its non-militarization, for broad international cooperation in the exploration and use of outer space for peaceful purposes. This should include the use of space technology to monitor Earth's environment. The benefits of the peaceful use of outer space, including weather forecasting, remote sensing and medical benefits, should be made readily available to the world community, particularly through assistance to the developing countries.

C. Biological diversity

76. Traditional crop and livestock species are giving way to high-yielding varieties and breeds. As the genetic base of plants, animals and micro-organisms becomes narrower, some genetic material is being irretrievably lost at such a rate that the world could lose one tenth to one fifth of its 5 to 10 million species by the year 2000.

77. Over 100 countries are collaborating in the global programme coordinated by the International Board for Plant Genetic Resources for conserving crop genetic resources, and the global gene banks network contains over 1 million samples of crop germ plasm. Yet, in many countries, national efforts for conservation are still ill-organized and underfinanced, and often do not attend systematically to the components of planning, training, education and research. International cooperation and technical assistance in this field should be further developed.

78. An international network of protected areas for conserving animal and plant genetic resources, encompassing about 10 per cent of the world's land area, should be established to reverse the trend towards depletion of species. Management plans for conserving ecosystems as reservoirs of species diversity have to be prepared.

79. Efforts to conserve crop genetic resources and the global data banks network have to be extended to cover adequately germ plasm with economic potential for providing food, fodder, fibres, waxes, oils, gums, medicines, energy and insecticides. *In situ* and *ex situ* components of conservation have to develop in a complementary manner in the light of the interdependence of nature conservation and genetic diversity.

80. Mechanisms should be established to provide information on rates of exploitation of genetic resources to facilitate selection of those to be conserved.

81. The gap between conservation of species and economic access to them should be bridged through maximum international cooperation. Agreements involving rights of possession of and access to genetic material, including research results, should facilitate such cooperation. Conserved genetic resources should be regarded as a common interest of mankind.

D. Security and environment

82. The accumulation and deployment of weapons of war and destruction present very grave risks to the environment. The use of weapons of mass destruction, including nuclear, chemical and biological weapons, could bring about far-reaching, even irreversible, changes in the global environment.

83. The development and stockpiling of nuclear arms and delivery systems at current levels have made the human race technically capable of putting an end to its own existence. In addition, the growing capacity of some States to undertake deliberate manipulation of the environment represents an immense potential danger. If the material, financial and intellectual resources devoted to armaments were to be used to solve problems such as those of the human environment, food security and shelter, prospects for sustainable development would be considerably enhanced.

84. The World Charter for Nature proclaims that "Nature shall be secured against degradation caused by warfare or other hostile activities".[1] A comprehensive system of international security is essential in order to ensure that this declaration is implemented.

85. Progressive disarmament through détente, negotiation, and avoidance of the use of force as a means of resolving conflicts should be pursued to minimize the environmental risks associated with armed conflicts. Governments should continue to pursue, in relevant negotiating forums, efforts to ban weapons that have the effect of modifying the environment.

86. One of the roles of the United Nations Environment Programme is to promote environmentally sound development in harmony with peace and security, and towards this end, issues of disarmament and security, in so far as they relate to the environment, should continue to receive appropriate attention.

IV. Instruments of Environmental Action

87. Sections I, II and III above largely sought to indicate how to deal effectively with environmental problems by addressing their policy sources. However, such actions need to be reinforced by the performance of certain overarching functions. This section deals with those functions.

A. Assessment

88. Environmental rehabilitation and management depend upon the availability of organized information on the state of the environment, its trends, and their relationship to social and economic factors. Decisions, however, continue to be made in ignorance of the changing state of the environment and its implications for human well-being. It is essential, therefore, that reliable environmental information, obtained and analysed using modern technology, is made avail-

[1] Resolution 37/7, annex, sect. 1, para. 5.

able to planners and managers in a usable form. Most developing countries face the constraint of lack of access to modern technology and to the necessary expertise to collect and interpret environmental data.

89. Environmental and resource data are being collected at global and regional levels by the United Nations and international organizations working with Governments. Additional data also exist at the national level, although often in a fragmented form. The institutional mechanisms needed to relate such data sets to each other and to analyse them in the context of existing practices and policies are often lacking. Governments and intergovernmental organizations at the regional level should intensify efforts to collect and analyse data, especially data relating to common environmental problems.

90. The United Nations Environment Programme, working through the United Nations system, coordinates the collection, monitoring and assessment of selected environmental variables and distributes this information worldwide through: the Global Environmental Monitoring System, encompassing the monitoring and assessment systems relating to climate, health and natural resources and the Global Resource Information Data Base; data bases and systems for the conservation and management of genetic resources; the International Register of Potentially Toxic Chemicals, which operates a global information exchange network to provide information and data on chemicals and their effects on health and environment through a query-response service and evaluations of the effects of chemicals on the environment; INFOTERRA, the International Referral System for sources of environmental information; and the state of the environment reports of the United Nations Environment Programme, which address major issues of topical environmental concern.

91. Through improved collection and analysis of data and its wide distribution to potential users, which should be a service to countries as well as international organizations, the United Nations Environment Programme should become, and come to be accepted as, a leading authority in environmental assessment.

92. Countries, particularly developing countries, should be assisted, through international cooperation on environmental assessment, with the participation of the United Nations system and with the United Nations Environment Programme playing a leading role, in establishing effective national monitoring systems, geographic information systems and assessment capabilities, and improving data compatibility. In order for this to take place, technical cooperation among countries regionally and globally has to increase significantly.

93. Notable environmental assessments have been carried out recently and related to socio-economic factors by non-governmental organizations in some countries. These have helped expand awareness and stimulate action to protect and improve the environment. Governments should encourage such efforts.

B. Planning

94. Environmental planning should provide a conceptual, methodological and institutional framework within which to internalize progressively the consideration of the environment in development decision-making. Every country should define its national environmental objectives and make them part of its plans for socio-economic development. Just as each country sets targets for sectoral growth, it should set time-bound targets in respect of environmental resources and indicators of major concern. Plans and policies at sub-national levels should also provide for the simultaneous pursuit of the specified environmental and development objectives.

95. Governments should establish mechanisms and procedures to facilitate interdepartmental coordination of policies and unified direction for integrating environmental concerns in development planning. Use of analytical methods to ascertain the environmental and socioeconomic implications of alternative courses of action should inform decisions on projects and programmes. It should also help resolve conflicts of interest among departments, among population groups and among regions.

96. The allocation of investment resources of a national plan among regions and sectors has to reflect a sensitivity to environmental constraints and objectives. This should be facilitated by periodic analyses of the socio-economic significance of the changing state of natural resources and the environment at national and provincial levels. Efforts should also be made to prepare an accounting of the use of scarce natural resources, focusing particularly on the country's major environmental problems, for example desertification, and to relate it to the periodic reporting on national income and well-being.

97. Sectoral ministries should be encouraged to apply environmental impact assessments and social cost-benefit analyses in decision-making regarding development projects and programmes. Taxation and economic policies should encourage sectoral decisions that favour environmentally benign technologies and locations, recycling and safe disposal of wastes and conservation of natural resources, and should establish mutual support between environmental and economic objectives. Land and water use plans should be prepared and their implementation monitored. Already some countries have made progress in planning at the district level to reflect environmental needs.

98. There have been advances in the analytical methods of environmental impact and risk assessment, social benefit-cost analyses of environmental measures, physical planning and environmental accounting. Theoretical work on decision models with multiple objectives and constraints has also progressed. The United Nations Environment Programme, the Scientific Committee on Problems of the Environment and the Organisation for Economic Cooperation and Development have played a useful role. This work should be strengthened so that it will have a greater impact on decision-making.

99. Environmental action and economic planning remain insufficiently related to each other in most countries. Efforts must be intensified at national and international levels to promote the application of suitable methods, procedures and institutional arrangements to make economic planning fully responsive to environmental constraints and opportunities. The guiding role of the United Nations Environment Programme in this field should include technical assistance to the developing countries. Collaborative arrangements should be made at the working level between the United Nations Environment Programme, the United Nations Development Programme, the Department of Technical Cooperation for Development of the United Nations Secretariat and the World Bank. They should set up, or strengthen, units to conduct environmental analyses of their projects and programmes and, in collaboration with the United Nations Environment Programme, assist Governments in systematically considering the environment in development planning.

C. Legislation and environmental law

100. Increasingly, environmental legislation has been providing practical frameworks at the national level for implementing environmental standards and regulating the activities of enterprises and people in the light of environmental objectives. At the international level, conventions, protocols and agreements have been providing a basis for cooperation among countries at bilateral, regional and global levels for the management of environmental risks, control of pollution and conservation of natural resources.

101. There is a need to expand the number of accessions to and ratifications of these conventions and to institute mechanisms at the national level to ensure their application. The present momentum should be maintained of concluding conventions on questions such as hazards relating to chemicals, treatment and international transport of hazardous wastes, industrial accidents, climate change, protection of the ozone layer, protection of the marine environment from pollution from land-based sources and protection of biological diversity, in which the United Nations Environment Programme has been playing an active part.

102. Groundwork has been prepared over the last 15 years under the aegis of the United Nations Environment Programme to establish legal frameworks to manage regional seas. Governments should intensify their efforts to implement legislative measures and other policies at national levels so that the policy sources of the environmental problems of the regional seas are effectively tackled. Increasingly, environmental management of rivers, lakes and forests has been posing a challenge to international cooperation. Governments,

with the collaboration of the Programme and concerned international organizations, should accelerate action to establish legal régimes at international and national levels to improve significantly the environmental management of rivers, lakes and forests. The new programme for environmental management of freshwater systems, sponsored by the United Nations Environment Programme, is a promising start.

103. The Montevideo Programme for the Development and Periodic Review of Environmental Law,[1] prepared under the auspices of the United Nations Environment Programme, should be implemented fully. Development of international environmental law should continue, with a view to providing a strong basis for fostering cooperation among countries. The progressive emergence of general environmental norms and principles and the codification of existing agreements could lead to a global convention on protection and enhancement of the environment.

104. Governments should settle their environmental disputes by peaceful means, making use of existing and emerging agreements and conventions. The International Court of Justice, the International Court of Arbitration and regional mechanisms should facilitate peaceful settlement of environmental disputes.

D. Awareness building and training

105. The participation of people in environmental protection and improvement depends upon their being aware of the environmental problems and possibilities, of how the changing state of the environment affects their well-being, and how their lifestyles affect the environment. People's effectiveness in dealing with environmental problems depends upon their technical and organizational capabilities to design and implement the needed measures.

106. Since the United Nations Conference on the Human Environment, held at Stockholm in 1972, awareness of the interrelationship between human activities and the environment has steadily grown. Voluntary action groups at the community level, national and global non-governmental organizations, scientific bodies, schools and universities, mass media and Governments all have played a part in this process. Also the United Nations Environment Programme, through its programme and through its information activities, has helped build environmental awareness.

107. In a large number of developing countries, knowledge of proper environmental management practices still does not reach millions who suffer as a result of environmental degradation. People are the most valuable resource in development, but in order for them to participate constructively in accelerating and sustaining development, environmental information must be made available in languages they understand and in a form that can help them relate it easily to their own situation. Governments should intensify efforts to make this possible. Non-governmental organizations, with appropriate support from the United Nations Environment Programme, should play an increasingly active role in this field, especially by way of provision of requisite materials.

108. The United Nations Educational, Scientific and Cultural Organization, in collaboration with the United Nations Environment Programme should ensure systematic coverage of environmental education needs at all levels of schooling, especially in the developing countries. They should also prepare and promote course materials which would include environmental components in professional training given to selected occupational groups, for example, engineers, builders, foresters, farm extension workers and managers. Training in analysing environmental considerations in relation to economic and other goals also has to receive growing attention. Governments should make environmental education and training an integral part of their education and communication policies and programmes.

109. International support for the training of personnel in environmental assessment and management, especially in the developing countries, has grown steadily. It is essential, however, to ensure that the content and modality of such instruction is relevant to the needs of the countries where it is intended that the skills be applied. International cooperation and governmental efforts should also help ensure a progressive strengthening of institutional capabilities within the developing countries themselves to make available such training.

E. Institutions

110. Consideration of the environment must be internalized in sectoral policies and practices to ensure that environmental objectives are met and sustainable development is achieved. Sectoral bodies should be made accountable for such internalization. Existing environmental problems also have to be dealt with through concerted action and allocation of resources. This is true at both national and international levels.

111. At the national level, the mandates of sectoral ministries and other governmental institutions should explicitly state their responsibility and accountability for sustainable development and environmental protection within their sectors. Their policies, functions, structures and budgetary allocations should be consistent with this. As appropriate, the same should apply at provincial and local levels. Authoritative mechanisms and procedures are needed to oversee and ensure that national environmental objectives are met throughout the Government. Governments should establish or strengthen environmental ministries to stimulate, guide, support and monitor actions to achieve these objectives. To this end, essential functions should include: environmental assessment, planning and incentives, legislative and regulatory advice, awareness-building and training, stimulation of research and application of its results. Environmental ministries should also provide leadership and coordination for direct action to deal with environmental problems, including rehabilitation. Bilateral and multilateral institutions and international organizations should assist developing countries in this regard.

112. International institutions, both inside and outside of the United Nations system, dealing with such areas as food and agriculture, health, industry, energy, science, trade, finance and development assistance, should reorient their policies and programmes to make steady progress towards environmentally sound development.

113. These institutions should be accountable for integrating the objectives of sustainable development into their policies, budgets and staffing strategies. Governments should ensure, through consistent policy guidance to these institutions, that their mandates and programmes meet this objective.

114. The governing bodies of all United Nations organizations should report regularly to the General Assembly on the progress made in achieving the objectives of sustainable development. Such reports should also be submitted to the Governing Council of the United Nations Environment Programme for that body to provide comments on matters within its mandate to the General Assembly. The Administrative Committee on Coordination, under the chairmanship of the Secretary-General, should oversee effectively the inclusion of the concept of sustainable development in all programmes of the United Nations system, by reviewing and coordinating the efforts of all organs, organizations and bodies of the United Nations system in this field, and by including this in its reports to the General Assembly and the Governing Council of the Programme.

115. The inter-agency mechanism of Designated Officials for Environmental Matters should guide, support and monitor more effectively activities within the United Nations system to ensure consistent policy.

116. In parallel with the institutional arrangements at the national level, the United Nations Environment Programme should promote, guide, support and monitor actions to achieve environmentally sound development and stimulate and coordinate action to deal with environmental problems.

117. The major priorities and functions of the United Nations Environment Programme should be:

(a) To provide leadership, advice and guidance in the United Nations system on restoring, protecting, and improving the environmental basis for, and in general act as a catalyst in the promotion of, sustainable development;

---

1 UNEP/GC.10/5/Add.2 and Corr.1 and 2, annex, chap. II.

(b) To monitor, assess and report regularly on the state of the environment and natural resources and emerging environmental issues;

(c) To support priority scientific and technological research on major environmental and natural resource protection issues;

(d) To make available, in cooperation with other agencies where appropriate, guidance for environmental management, including the development of management techniques, criteria and indicators for environmental quality standards and guidelines for the sustainable use and management of natural resources;

(e) To initiate and support the programmes and activities worked out by the developing countries for dealing with their serious environmental problems;

(f) To initiate and facilitate the development and, upon request, the coordination of the implementation of action plans in the developing countries for the management of ecosystems and critical environmental problems. Such plans should be implemented and financed by the Governments concerned with appropriate external assistance;

(g) To encourage and promote international agreements on critical environmental issues and to support and facilitate the development of international laws, conventions and cooperative arrangements for environmental and natural resource conservation and protection;

(h) In cooperation with other concerned institutions, to establish and strengthen the institutional and professional capacity of developing countries, with a view to integrating environmental considerations into their development policy and planning;

(i) To promote awareness of environmental matters through education and the mass media;

(j) To cooperate with the United Nations Development Programme and other United Nations agencies, the World Bank and regional development banks, to strengthen the environmental dimensions of their programmes and technical assistance projects, *inter alia*, through training and personnel secondments.

118. Specialized agencies, organizations and bodies of the United Nations system should more speedily assume full operational and financial responsibility for environmental programmes supported by the United Nations Environment Programme in their sectors included in the system-wide medium-term environment programme and the Environment Fund. The human and financial resources which will become available to the United Nations Environment Programme as a result should be concentrated on the priority areas listed above.

119. Environmentally sound development cannot be assured solely by actions of governmental, intergovernmental or international organizations. It requires the participation of other entities, particularly industry, non-governmental environmental and development organizations and the scientific community. Non-governmental organizations have important contributions to make in various areas, including environmental education and awareness, as well as design and implementation of programmes at the grass-roots levels. The scientific community should continue to play an important role in environmental research and risk assessment and international scientific cooperation.

120. Regional and continental cooperative arrangements are being established to deal with common environmental problems. For example, the first session of the African Ministerial Conference on the Environment, held at Cairo in 1985, adopted the Cairo Programme for African Cooperation and modalities to implement it. Governments and development cooperation agencies should support such institutional arrangements and programmes.

44/172. Plan of Action to Combat Desertification

Committee: 2
Vote: A + B adopted
Ref.: 50/114, 50/112, 49/234, 48, 191, 48/175, 47/188, 46/161, 42/189, 40/198, 39/168, 37/218, 35/73, 34/184, 33/89

A

Implementation of the Plan of Action to Combat Desertification

The General Assembly,

Recalling its resolution 32/172 of 19 December 1977, by which it approved the Plan of Action to Combat Desertification,[1] and all its subsequent resolutions on the subject,

Recalling also its resolution S-13/2 of 1 June 1986, by which it adopted the United Nations Programme of Action for African Economic Recovery and Development 1986-1990, which identified measures to combat desertification as a priority,

Bearing in mind the draft resolution to be adopted at the present session,[2] concerning the United Nations conference on environment and development, to be held in 1992, fifteen years after the adoption of the Plan of Action to Combat Desertification,

Deeply concerned that the problem of desertification, which has a global impact, is still on the fringe of the growing awareness on the part of the international community that it is imperative to combat environmental deterioration effectively within the framework of the interdependence of nations,

Gravely concerned by the continuing spread and intensification of desertification in developing countries, particularly in Africa, and the indescribable human suffering, economic and financial losses and social disruption caused by that scourge,

Aware that drought and desertification place a considerable burden on the economic and financial capacities of the developing countries affected and that the negative effects of the international economic environment impede their efforts to undertake effective and sustained programmes to combat desertification, for which they bear primary responsibility,

1. *Takes note* of the report of the Secretary-General on the implementation of General Assembly resolutions 42/189 A, B and C of 11 December 1987[3] and of the relevant section of the report of the Governing Council of the United Nations Environment Programme;[4]

2. *Expresses its deep concern* about the inadequacy of financial resources for the implementation of the Plan of Action to Combat Desertification;

3. *Urges* Governments, in particular those of the developed countries, United Nations organizations and other intergovernmental bodies to increase and intensify their efforts to combat desertification and to accord the highest priority to the recommendations contained in the Plan of Action;

4. *Invites* the Executive Director of the United Nations Environment Programme to consult the principal international organizations, private foundations, individuals and the major media enterprises that finance or promote environmental protection activities in order to draw their attention to the compelling need to consider desertification control on an equal footing with other current environmental issues;

5. *Invites* the United Nations conference on environment and development, to be held in 1992, to accord high priority to desertification control and to deploy all means necessary, including financial, scientific and technological resources, to halt and reverse the process of desertification with a view to preserving the ecological balance of the planet;

---

1 *Report of the United Nations Conference on Desertification, Nairobi, 29 August - 9 September 1977* (A/CONF.74/36), chap. I.

2 See *Official Records of the General Assembly, Forty-fourth Session, Annexes,* agenda item 82, document A/44/746/Add. 7, para. 55, draft resolution V. The draft was subsequently adopted as resolution 44/228.

3 A/44/351-E/1989/122.

4 *Official Records of the General Assembly, Forty-fourth Session, Supplement No. 25* (A/44/25), chap. VI.

6. *Invites* the Governing Council of the United Nations Environment Programme to contribute substantially to the discussion on desertification at the conference, *inter alia*, by undertaking a general evaluation, sufficiently in advance of the conference, of the progress achieved in implementing the Plan of Action;

7. *Requests* the Secretary-General, in consultation with the Executive Director of the United Nations Environment Programme, to submit to the conference, through its preparatory committee, a report containing relevant expert studies on, *inter alia*, the following:

(*a*) Relevant suggestions and proposals formulated within the United Nations system on the possibility of utilizing new methods to finance the programmes of multilateral organizations at the global level, over and above regular budgets and conventional extrabudgetary resources;

(*b*) The state of implementation of the Plan of Action and objectives and courses of action to further the struggle against desertification, including an evaluation of the additional resources needed in order to attain the minimum objectives of the struggle against desertification;

(*c*) Ways and means of promoting, in particular in the developing countries, research into and development of existing and potential technology to combat desertification and procedures for the transfer of such technology on favourable terms, in particular to developing countries;

(*d*) Possibilities for obtaining loans on concessional terms, from Governments and other sources, to finance the struggle against desertification;

(*e*) Possibilities for reducing the impact of desertification, including reafforestation, with the help of mechanisms involving the cancellation or reduction of external debt;

(*f*) Possibilities for strengthening and coordinating the activities of funds established for that purpose in various international institutions;

(*g*) Ways of encouraging the active participation of non-governmental organizations, foundations and individuals in the financing of training and scientific research programmes to combat desertification, including reafforestation programmes;

8. *Decides* to close the Special Account to finance the implementation of the Plan of Action to Combat Desertification, and requests the Executive Director of the United Nations Environment Programme to take the necessary steps to do so;

9. *Also decides* that the Consultative Group for Desertification Control will meet every year until the conference on environment and development is held in 1992 and every two years thereafter, and reaffirms its mandate as contained in resolutions 32/172 of 19 December 1977 and 39/168 of 17 December 1984;

10. *Calls upon* the Consultative Group, in cooperation with the Executive Director of the United Nations Environment Programme, to contribute to the enhancement of awareness of environmental issues and to intensify its efforts to mobilize additional resources, to exchange information on scientific research, national programmes and the implementation of the Plan of Action and to give its opinions on the actions to be undertaken in the battle against desertification;

11. *Urges* the Governments of countries affected by desertification to accord high priority, in their national development plans, to medium-term and long-term strategies and programmes for desertification control;

12. *Requests* the Secretary-General, together with the Executive Director of the United Nations Environment Programme and the Administrator of the United Nations Development Programme, to submit a report to the General Assembly at its forty-sixth session, through the Economic and Social Council, on the various provisions of the present resolution, and to ensure that it is submitted, immediately after publication, to the preparatory committee for the United Nations conference on environment and development.

83rd plenary meeting
19 December 1989

B

Implementation in the Sudano-Sahelian region of the Plan of Action to Combat Desertification

The General Assembly,

Recalling its resolutions 32/170 of 19 December 1977, 33/88 of 15 December 1978, 34/187 of 18 December 1979, 35/72 of 5 December 1980, 36/190 of 17 December 1981, 37/216 of 20 December 1982, 38/164 of 19 December 1983, 39/168 B and 39/206 of 17 December 1984, 40/198 B of 17 December 1985, S-13/2 of 1 June 1986 and 42/189 B of 11 December 1987,

Bearing in mind the particularly serious nature of the problem of desertification in the Sudano-Sahelian region and of the critical situations it creates, which impede the economic and social development of the region and have tragic implications for the living conditions of the population,

1. *Takes note with appreciation* of the report of the Administrator of the United Nations Development Programme on the activities of the United Nations Sudano-Sahelian Office,[1] as well as the relevant section of the report of the Governing Council of the United Nations Environment Programme;[2]

2. *Stresses with deep concern*:

(*a*) That desertification in the countries of the Sudano-Sahelian region has worsened and that it has spread to other regions of Africa;

(*b*) That the chronic insufficiency of financial resources continues to pose obstacles to desertification control;

(*c*) That the struggle against desertification requires financial and technical resources beyond the means of the affected countries;

3. *Urges* the affected countries that have not yet done so to include projects to combat desertification and drought in their national development plans and to accord high priority to them;

4. *Also urges* the affected countries to use all appropriate mechanisms, including the round-table meetings of the United Nations Development Programme and the consultative groups of the World Bank, to mobilize resources for the implementation of programmes to combat desertification, and appeals to donor countries to provide substantial additional resources for the financing of such programmes;

5. *Notes with satisfaction* that the United Nations Sudano-Sahelian Office has endorsed the concept of sustainable development in adopting a global approach to the question of the management and conservation of natural resources and to environmental issues and in emphasizing the importance of the incorporation of desertification control activities in national development plans;

6. *Urges* the United Nations Sudano-Sahelian Office to assist the countries of the region with their preparations for the United Nations conference on environment and development, to be held in 1992, and with the resulting follow-up activities;

7. *Notes with appreciation* the interest displayed at the Summit of the seven major industrial nations, held in Paris from 14 to 16 July 1989, in aspects of the struggle against desertification and, specifically, in the planned observatory for the Sahara and the Sahel;[3]

8. *Expresses its gratitude* to those Governments which contribute to the United Nations Trust Fund for Sudano-Sahelian Activities, and renews its urgent appeal to all members of the donor community to contribute substantially to the Trust Fund in order to enable the United Nations Sudano-Sahelian Office to respond more effectively to the pressing needs of the African countries stricken by desertification;

9. *Requests* the Executive Director of the United Nations Environment Programme and the Administrator of the United Nations Development Programme to strengthen their common undertaking to support the United Nations Sudano-Sahelian Office;

---

1 DP/1989/50.

2 *Official Records of the General Assembly, Forty-fourth Session, Supplement No. 25* (A/44/25), chap. VI.

3 A/C.2/44/11, para. 51.

10. *Invites* the United Nations Sudano-Sahelian Office:

(*a*) To intensify its efforts to mobilize additional resources to support the efforts of the countries covered under its mandate and of the relevant regional organizations, in particular the Intergovernmental Authority for Drought and Development and the Permanent Inter-State Committee on Drought Control in the Sahel;

(*b*) To continue to support the Ministerial Conference for a joint policy to combat desertification in the countries of the Permanent Inter-State Committee on Drought Control in the Sahel and the Economic Community of West African States, in the Maghreb countries, in Egypt and in the Sudan (COMIDES) and, in this context, to cooperate with the Southern African Development Coordination Conference and with the Arab Maghreb Union.

83rd plenary meeting
19 December 1989

44/226. Traffic in and Disposal, Control and Transboundary Movements of Toxic and Dangerous Products and Wastes

Committee: 2
Vote: Adopted without a vote
Ref.: 47/151

The General Assembly,

Recalling its resolutions 37/137 of 17 December 1982, 38/149 of 19 December 1983 and 39/229 of 18 December 1984, as well as its decision 41/450 of 8 December 1986,

Recalling also its resolution 42/183 of 11 December 1987 on traffic in toxic and dangerous products and wastes,

Recalling further its resolution 43/212 of 20 December 1988, entitled "Responsibility of States for the protection of the environment: prevention of the illegal international traffic in, and the dumping and resulting accumulation of, toxic and dangerous products and wastes affecting the developing countries in particular",

Recalling Economic and Social Council resolutions 1988/70 and 1988/71 of 28 July 1988 and taking note of Council resolution 1989/104 of 27 July 1989,

Taking note of the report of the Secretary-General on products harmful to health and the environment[1] and Economic and Social Council decision 1989/177 of 27 July 1989,

Taking note also of decisions 15/28 and 15/30 of 25 May 1989 of the Governing Council of the United Nations Environment Programme,[2]

Welcoming the report of the Secretary-General on illegal traffic in toxic and dangerous products and wastes,[3]

Taking note of the conclusion of the Basel Convention on the Control of Transboundary Movements of Hazardous Wastes and their Disposal,[4]

Inviting all States to consider signing the Basel Convention without prejudice to the final positions to be taken by regional intergovernmental organizations in this regard,

Mindful of the growing threat to the environment and to human health and safety posed by the improper management and the increased generation, complexity and transboundary movement of hazardous wastes,

Convinced that illegal traffic in toxic and dangerous products and wastes poses a severe threat to the environment and to human health and safety,

Also convinced that these problems cannot be resolved without adequate cooperation among members of the international community,

Deeply concerned by the fact that cases of illegal transboundary movement and dumping of dangerous products and wastes particularly harmful for the environment and human health continue to occur, affecting, in particular, developing countries,

Convinced of the need to assist all countries, particularly developing countries, in obtaining all appropriate information concerning toxic and dangerous products and wastes and in reinforcing their capacity to detect and halt any illegal attempt to introduce toxic and dangerous products and wastes into the territory of any State in contravention of national legislation and relevant international legal instruments, as well as traffic not carried out in compliance with internationally accepted guidelines and principles in this field,

I

Traffic in toxic and dangerous products and wastes

1. *Requests* each regional commission, within existing resources, to contribute to the prevention of the illegal traffic in toxic and dangerous products and wastes by monitoring and making regional assessments of this illegal traffic and its environmental and health implications, on a continuing basis, in each region, and, in this context, in cooperation with and relying upon expert support and advice from the United Nations Environment Programme and other relevant bodies of the United Nations, including the International Register of Potentially Toxic Chemicals, the *Ad Hoc* Working Group of Experts on Prior Informed Consent and Other Modalities to Supplement the London Guidelines for the Exchange of Information on Chemicals in International Trade, and the Interim Secretariat of the Basel Convention on the Control of Transboundary Movements of Hazardous Wastes and their Disposal, without prejudice to the final position to be taken by regional intergovernmental organizations on the Convention, and to report to the Economic and Social Council at its second regular session starting in 1990;

2. *Also requests* the regional commissions to interact among themselves and cooperate with the United Nations Environment Programme, with a view to maintaining efficient and coordinated monitoring and assessment of the illegal traffic in toxic and dangerous products and wastes;

3. *Requests* the Economic and Social Council to submit recommendations to the General Assembly on the findings and conclusions of the regional commissions, in their consideration of environmental issues;

4. *Calls upon* all countries to cooperate with their respective regional commissions with the aim of preventing the illegal traffic in toxic and dangerous products and wastes;

II

Protection against products harmful to health and the environment

1. *Expresses its appreciation* to the Secretary-General for his report on products harmful to health and the environment,[5] which contains a review of the Consolidated List of Products Whose Consumption and/or Sale Have Been Banned, Withdrawn, Severely Restricted or Not Approved by Governments;

2. *Notes with appreciation* the cooperative relationship established between the United Nations, the World Health Organization and the United Nations Environment Programme International Register of Potentially Toxic Chemicals for the preparation of the Consolidated List;

3. *Notes*, in this context, the need to utilize also the work being done by the Working Group on Export of Domestically Prohibited Goods and Other Hazardous Substances established by the General Agreement on Tariffs and Trade and those activities which are currently under way within the framework of the United Nations Environment Programme and the Food and Agriculture Organization of the United Nations in connection with implementation of prior informed consent schemes for chemicals and pesticides in international trade and which implement the system of information exchange envisaged by the developers of the Consolidated List, as well as the work being done under international agreements and conventions in related areas;

---

1 A/44/276-E/1989/78.

2 *Official Records of the General Assembly, Forty-fourth Session, Supplement No. 25* (A/44/25), annex I.

3 A/44/362 and Corr. 1.

4 See UNEP/IG.80/3.

5 A/44/276-E/1989/78.

4. *Expresses its appreciation* for the growing cooperation by Governments in the preparation of the Consolidated List, and urges all Governments that have not yet done so to provide the necessary information for inclusion in updated versions of the Consolidated List;

5. *Requests* the Secretary-General to ensure, within existing resources, publication of the Consolidated List in English, French and Spanish, in accordance with demand, bearing in mind Assembly resolution 39/229;

6. *Also requests* the Secretary-General to undertake a special effort to ensure effective and wider dissemination of the Consolidated List in all appropriate circles;

7. *Further requests* the Secretary-General, in this context, to consider ways and means of ensuring more effective involvement of non-governmental organizations in promoting the dissemination and utilization of the Consolidated List;

8. *Requests* the Secretary-General, in the context of the preparation of his next scheduled report on the question:

(*a*) To make specific suggestions on ways and means of providing technical cooperation, including through appropriate United Nations organizations, to countries, in particular developing countries, to create and strengthen their capacity to utilize the Consolidated List;

(*b*) To study all the pending issues, such as sustainable alternatives to banned and severely restricted products and unregistered pesticides, with a focus on improving the usefulness of the Consolidated List;

III

Control of transboundary movements of hazardous wastes and their disposal

1. *Recognizes* the necessity of developing rules of international law, as early as practicable, on liability and compensation for damage resulting from the transboundary movement and disposal of hazardous wastes;

2. *Requests* the Executive Director of the United Nations Environment Programme, in accordance with the resolutions adopted at the Conference of Plenipotentiaries on the Global Convention on the Control of Transboundary Movements of Hazardous Wastes, held at Basel, Switzerland, from 20 to 22 March 1989, to establish, on the basis of equitable geographical representation and in consultation with Governments, an *Ad Hoc* working group of legal and technical experts to develop, as early as practicable, elements that might be included in a protocol on liability and compensation for damage resulting from the transboundary movement and disposal of hazardous wastes and to report to the preparatory committee of the United Nations conference on environment and development and to the Governing Council of the United Nations Environment Programme, in accordance with its mandate in this regard;

3. *Invites* the Executive Director of the United Nations Environment Programme and the Secretary-General of the International Maritime Organization, in consultation, as appropriate, with other relevant international organizations, to review the existing rules, regulations and practices with respect to the disposal of hazardous wastes at sea, in order to harmonize the provisions of the relevant conventions as adopted in this regard;

4. *Requests* the Secretary-General, in cooperation with the Executive Director of the United Nations Environment Programme, to report to the General Assembly at its forty-sixth session, through the Economic and Social Council, on the progress achieved in the implementation of the provisions of the Basel Convention on the Control of Transboundary Movements of Hazardous Wastes and their Disposal and of the present resolution.

85th plenary meeting
22 December 1989

45/94. Need to Ensure a Healthy Environment for the Well-Being of Individuals

Committee: 3
Vote: Adopted without a vote

The General Assembly,

Recalling that, in accordance with the provisions of the Universal Declaration of Human Rights[1] and the International Covenant on Economic, Social and Cultural Rights,[2] everyone has the right to an adequate standard of living for his or her own health and well-being and that of his or her family and to the continuous improvement of living conditions,

Recognizing the need to promote universal respect for, and observance of, human rights and fundamental freedoms in all their aspects,

Considering that a better and healthier environment can help contribute to the full enjoyment of human rights by all,

Reaffirming that in accordance with the Declaration of the United Nations Conference on the Human Environment,[3] men and women have the fundamental right to freedom, equality and adequate conditions of life in an environment of a quality that permits a life of dignity and well-being, and that they bear a solemn responsibility to protect and improve the environment for present and future generations,

Bearing in mind the fact that increasing environmental degradation could endanger the very basis of life,

Bearing in mind also that the economic growth and development of the developing countries are essential in order to address the problems of the degradation and protection of the environment,

Emphasizing the increasing role of the United Nations in addressing global environmental problems,

Recalling that the United Nations Conference on Environment and Development, to be held in Brazil in 1992, will elaborate strategies and measures to halt and reverse the effects of environmental degradation in the context of strengthened national and international efforts to promote sustainable and environmentally sound development in all countries,

Stressing the importance for all countries to take effective actions for the protection and enhancement of the environment in accordance with their respective capacities and responsibilities and taking into account the specific needs of developing countries and that, as the major sources of pollution, the developed countries have the main responsibility for taking appropriate measures urgently,

Welcoming Commission on Human Rights resolution 1990/41 of 6 March 1990[4] and Sub-Commission on Prevention of Discrimination and Protection of Minorities resolution 1990/7 of 30 August 1990,[5] in which they decided to study the problems of the environment and its relation to human rights,

1. *Recognizes* that all individuals are entitled to live in an environment adequate for their health and well-being;

2. *Calls upon* Member States and intergovernmental and non-governmental organizations dealing with environmental questions to enhance their efforts towards ensuring a better and healthier environment;

3. *Encourages* the Commission on Human Rights, with the assistance of its Sub-Commission on Prevention of Discrimination and Protection of Minorities, to continue studying the problems of the environment and its relation to human rights, with a view to submitting to the Preparatory Committee of the United Nations Conference on Envi-

---

1 Resolution 217 A (III).

2 See resolution 2200 A (XXI), annex.

3 *Report of the United Nations Conference on the Human Environment, Stockholm, 5-16 June 1972* (United Nations publication, Sales No. E.73.II.A.14 and corrigendum), chap. I.

4 See *Official Records of the Economic and Social Council, 1990, Supplement No. 2* and corrigendum (E/1990/22 and Corr. 1), chap. II, sect. A.

5 See E/CN.4/1991/2-E/CN.4/Sub.2/1990/59.

ronment and Development, through the Economic and Social Council, a report on the progress made on the matter;

4. *Believes* that appropriate organs of the United Nations, within their respective competences, should pursue active efforts in seeking to promote a better and healthier environment.

68th plenary meeting
14 December 1990

46/150. Strengthening of International Cooperation and Coordination of Efforts to Study, Mitigate and Minimize the Consequences of the Chernobyl Disaster

Committee: 2
Vote: Adopted without a vote
Ref.: 50/134, 48/206, 47/165, 45/190

The General Assembly,

Reaffirming its resolution 45/190 of 21 December 1990,

Recalling Economic and Social Council resolution 1990/50 of 13 July 1990, and taking note of Council resolution 1991/51 of 26 July 1991,

Taking note with appreciation of the decisions adopted by the organs, organizations and programmes of the United Nations system in the implementation of General Assembly resolution 45/190, and the decisions of other international organs and organizations,

Taking note of International Atomic Energy Agency resolution GC(XXXV)/RES/553 of 20 September 1991,

Expressing continuing concern about the ongoing effects on the lives and health of people, especially children, first and foremost in the affected regions of Belarus, Ukraine and the Russian Soviet Federative Socialist Republic and also in other countries affected by the Chernobyl disaster,

Aware of the need to strengthen further the coordination of active efforts to carefully study, mitigate and minimize the radiological, health, socio-economic, psychological and environmental consequences of that disaster, as well as its possible long-term effects, including those resulting from transboundary contamination,

Stressing the importance of providing extensive information on all aspects of the unprecedented disaster for the purpose of avoiding similar calamities in the future,

Welcoming the growing international solidarity with the victims of Chernobyl and the large-scale efforts made by the United Nations and the organizations of the United Nations system, as well as the contribution made by Member States, intergovernmental and non-governmental organizations, charity foundations, the business community, scientific bodies and individuals, in the development of cooperation to mitigate the consequences of the Chernobyl disaster,

Noting the various assessments of the radiological consequences of the Chernobyl accident, in particular the report of the International Advisory Committee[1] that was presented and discussed at the conference held at Vienna from 21 to 24 May 1991, and recognizing the need for further study,

Stressing that it is essential to achieve and maintain the highest available standards of safety of nuclear power generation, including radiologial protection, and to encourage cooperation to this end throughout the world and, in particular, in Central and Eastern Europe,

Noting with appreciation the activities recently initiated with the purpose of bringing forward the shutting down of the nuclear power plant at Chernobyl, and stressing the need for technical assistance from the international community to that end,

Noting with interest the findings, conclusions and recommendations of the International Conference on the Safety of Nuclear Power, held at Vienna from 2 to 6 September 1991,[2]

1. *Takes note with appreciation* of the report of the Secretary-General on the implementation of General Assembly resolution 45/190;[3]

2. *Welcomes* the practical measures that have been taken by the Secretary-General and the United Nations Coordinator of International Cooperation for Chernobyl to strengthen coordination of international efforts in that area, *inter alia*, in the setting up of the corresponding Inter-Agency Task Force and the preparation of the Joint Plan of international cooperation to mitigate the consequences of the Chernobyl disaster;

3. *Notes with appreciation* the results of the United Nations Pledging Conference to mobilize support for extending international cooperation to mitigate the consequences of the Chernobyl disaster;

4. *Appeals* to all Member States, intergovernmental and non-governmental organizations, charity foundations, the business community, scientific bodies and individuals to provide cooperation in various forms and special and other assistance, taking into account the nature of the radiation and environmental disaster and the emergency situation that has developed in the areas most affected, particularly in Belarus, Ukraine and the Russian Soviet Federative Socialist Republic, as described in the conclusions and recommendations of the International Chernobyl Project[4] in its assessment of radiological consequences and evaluation of protective measures and other relevant studies;

5. *Requests* the organs, specialized agencies and programmes of the United Nations system to continue the consideration of possible technical and other specialized assistance and specific actions in the areas most affected by the accident, particularly in Belarus, Ukraine and the Russian Soviet Federative Socialist Republic, in close cooperation with the United Nations Coordinator, taking into account the Joint Plan, as introduced by the Secretary-General at the Chernobyl Pledging Conference;

6. *Requests* the Secretary-General to continue the activities related to the coordination of efforts to mitigate the consequences of the Chernobyl disaster in accordance with resolution 45/190;

7. *Also requests* the Secretary-General to submit to the General Assembly at its forty-seventh session, through the Economic and Social Council, a report on the implementation of the present resolution;

8. *Decides* to include in the provisional agenda of its forty-seventh session an item entitled "Strengthening of international cooperation and coordination of efforts to study, mitigate and minimize the consequences of the Chernobyl disaster".

77th plenary meeting
18 December 1991

48/192. Strengthening International Cooperation in the Monitoring of Global Environmental Problems

Committee: 2
Vote: Adopted without a vote
Ref.: 46/217, 44/224

The General Assembly,

Reaffirming its resolutions 44/224 of 22 December 1989 and 46/217 of 20 December 1991 on international cooperation in the monitoring, assessment and anticipation of environmental threats and in assistance in cases of environmental emergency,

Reaffirming also the relevant provisions of Agenda 21[5] and the Rio Declaration on Environment and Development, adopted by the

---

1 See *The International Chernobyl Project: An Overview* (Vienna, International Atomic Energy Agency, 1991).

2 See International Atomic Energy Agency, publication STI/PUB/880.

3 A/46/215/Rev.1-E/1991/76/Rev.1

4 See *International Chernobyl Project: An Overview* (Vienna, International Atomic Energy Agency, 1991).

5 *Report of the United Nations Conference on Environment and Development, Rio de Janeiro, 3 - 14 June 1992* (A/CONF:151/26/Rev.1 (Vol. I and Vol. I/Corr.1, Vol. II, Vol. III and Vol. III/Corr.1)) (United Nations publication, Sales No.E.93.I.8 and corrigenda), vol. I: Resolutions adopted by the Conference, resolution 1, annex II.

United Nations Conference on Environment and Development,[1] including principle 2 of the Declaration, which states that States have, in accordance with the Charter of the United Nations and the principles of international law, the sovereign right to exploit their own resources pursuant to their own environmental and developmental policies, and the responsibility to ensure that activities within their jurisdiction or control do not cause damage to the environment of other States or of areas beyond the limits of national jurisdiction,

Recalling decision 16/37 of 31 May 1991 of the Governing Council of the United Nations Environment Programme on early warning and forecasting of environmental emergencies,[2] and taking note of Governing Council decision 17/26 of 21 May 1993 on the United Nations Centre for Urgent Environmental Assistance,[3]

Taking note of the relevant parts of the reports of the Committee on the Peaceful Uses of Outer Space on its thirty-fifth[4] and thirty-sixth[5] sessions in particular, in which the Committee noted the importance of remote sensing by satellites for monitoring the Earth's environment and, in particular, for studying and monitoring global change,

Taking into account the ongoing activities of the Committee on Earth Observation Satellites in support of global environment monitoring and related applications,

Bearing in mind the importance of the participation of relevant organs, specialized agencies and other organizations of the United Nations system, within their respective mandates, in Earthwatch, in particular in its environmental monitoring programmes, and the need for early warning capabilities in those programmes,

Recognizing the need to make Earthwatch a more efficient instrument for environmental sensing and assessment of all elements influencing the global environment in order to ensure a balanced approach in serving, in particular, he needs of developing countries,

Recognizing also the potential and importance of current available methods, technologies and techniques of monitoring, assessment and anticipation of global environmental problems, including remote sensing and monitoring from outer space,

1. *Invites* Governments, relevant organizations of the United Nations system, within their respective mandates, and other relevant entities to review, as appropriate, their contribution to international cooperation in environmental monitoring, including environmentally related remote sensing and data assessment, and to provide appropriate support for such activities within existing resources;

2. *Requests* the Executive Director of the United Nations Environment Programme to prepare and to submit to the Governing Council of the United Nations Environment Programme at its eighteenth session a report on the activities of the Programme in environmental monitoring, containing proposals and recommendations within the context of Agenda 21 and a review of Earthwatch, taking into account the decisions adopted by the Governing Council at its seventeenth session, in cooperation with relevant entities within the United Nations system and, where appropriate, outside the United Nations system;

3. *Invites* the Governing Council of the United Nations Environment Programme to consider the above-mentioned report at its eighteenth session and to submit its conclusions and recommendations to the General Assembly at its fiftieth session, through the Economic and Social Council.

86th plenary meeting
21 December 1993

---

1 *Report of the United Nations Conference on Environment and Development, Rio de Janeiro, 3 - 14 June 1992* (A/CONF:151/26/Rev.1 (Vol. I and Vol. I/Corr.1, Vol. II, Vol. III and Vol. III/Corr.1)) (United nations publication, Sales No.E.93.I.8 and corrigenda), vol. I: Resolutions adopted by the Conference, resolution 1, annex I.

2 *Official Records of the General Assembly, Forty-sixth Session, Supplement No. 25* (A/46/25), annex.

3 *Ibid., Forty-eigth Session, Supplement No. 25* (A/48/25), annex.

4 *Ibid., Forty-seventh Session, Supplement No. 20* (A/47/20).

5 *Ibid., Forty-eigth Session, Supplement No. 20* (A/48/20).

50/115. Protection of Global Climate for Present and Future Generations of Mankind

Committee: 2
Vote Adopted without a vote:
Ref.: 49/120, 48/189, 47/103, 46/169, 45/212, 44/207, 43/53

The General Assembly,

Recalling its resolutions 45/212 of 21 December 1990, 46/169 of 19 December 1991, 47/195 of 22 December 1992, 48/189 of 21 December 1993 and 49/120 of 19 December 1994,

Noting with satisfaction that a large number of States and one regional economic integration organization have ratified the United Nations Framework Convention on Climate Change[6] and calling upon other States to take appropriate action to that end,

Noting that, in accordance with paragraphs 1 and 2 of General Assembly resolution 48/189, the first session of the Conference of the Parties to the United Nations Framework Convention on Climate Change was convened from 28 March to 7 April 1995 in Berlin, and that it was attended by one hundred and sixteen of the then one hundred and eighteen Parties to the Convention, as well as by a large number of governmental, intergovernmental and non-governmental observers,

Expressing its deep appreciation to the Government of Germany for the generous manner in which it hosted the first session of the Conference of the Parties,

Looking forward to the ongoing work of the Conference of the Parties and its subsidiary bodies in addressing climate change within the framework of the United Nations Framework Convention on Climate Change and to the successful conclusion of the Berlin Mandate[7] process at the third session of the Conference of the Parties,

Noting the important scientific contribution of the World Meteorological Organization/United Nations Environment Programme Intergovernmental Panel on Climate Change to the Convention process and looking forward to the completion of its second assessment report,

Recognizing the contribution to the Convention process of the interim secretariat of the Convention, within the framework of the Department for Policy Coordination and Sustainable Development of the Secretariat, as well as the support provided to that secretariat by the World Meteorological Organization, the United Nations Environment Programme, the United Nations Conference on Trade and Development, the United Nations Development Programme and bilateral contributors,

Taking note of the advice of the Secretary-General on an institutional linkage for the secretariat of the Convention with the United Nations, including the procedures indicated therein for the application of the Financial Regulations and the Staff Regulations and Staff Rules of the United Nations and for the appointment and accountability of the head of that secretariat,[8]

Taking note also of the decision of the Conference of the Parties,[9] on the basis of the advice of the Secretary-General, that the Convention secretariat shall be institutionally linked to the United Nations, while not being fully integrated into the work programme and management structure of any particular department or programme,

Taking note further of the financial procedures for the Conference of the Parties to the United Nations Framework Convention on Climate Change, its subsidiary bodies and its permanent secretariat adopted at its first session,[10] whereby, *inter alia*, the Secretary-General is asked to establish trust funds for the purposes of the Convention, to be managed by the head of the Convention secretariat in accordance with duly delegated authority,

---

6 A/AC.237/18 (Part II)/Add.1 and Corr.1, annex I.

7 FCCC/CP/1995/7/Add.1, decision 1/CP.1.

8 See A/AC.237/79/Add.1; FCCC/CP/1995/5/Add.4; and A/50/716, para. 49.

9 FCCC/CP/1995/7/Add.1, decision 14/CP.1.

10 FCCC/CP/1995/7/Add.1, decision 15/CP.1, annex I.

Taking note further of the decision of the Conference of the Parties[1] whereby the General Assembly is requested, bearing in mind the institutional linkage of the Convention secretariat to the United Nations and the large number of States that are Parties to the Convention, to decide to finance from the regular programme budget of the United Nations the conference-servicing costs arising from sessions of the Conference of the Parties and its subsidiary bodies for the duration of the institutional linkage mentioned above,

Having considered the report of the Secretary-General on the implementation of General Assembly resolution 49/120, with particular reference to the implications arising from the report of the Conference of the Parties on its first session,[2]

1. *Takes note with appreciation* of:

(*a*) The report of the Intergovernmental Negotiating Committee on a Framework Convention on Climate Change on its eleventh session;[3]

(*b*) The final report prepared on behalf of the Committee, by its Chairman, on the completion of the Committee's work;[4]

(*c*) The report of the Conference of the Parties to the Convention on its first session[5] and its presentation on behalf of the President of the Conference;

2. *Endorses* the institutional linkage between the Convention secretariat and the United Nations, as advised by the Secretary-General and adopted by the Conference of the Parties;[6]

3. *Requests* the Secretary-General to review the functioning of this institutional linkage not later than 31 December 1999, in consultation with the Conference of the Parties, with a view to making such modifications as may be considered desirable by both parties and to report thereon to the General Assembly;

4. *Notes* that the Conference of the Parties has decided to accept the offer of the Government of Germany to host the Convention secretariat[7] and expresses its appreciation for the support offered by the future host Government for the relocation and effective functioning of the Convention secretariat;

5. *Notes with appreciation contributions* made to the extrabudgetary funds established under paragraphs 10 and 20 of General Assembly resolution 45/212, and maintained in accordance with Assembly resolution 47/195;

6. *Urges* Member States that are Parties to the Convention to pay promptly and in full for each of the years 1996 and 1997, in accordance with the indicative scale adopted by consensus by the Conference of the Parties,[8] the contributions required for the trust fund for the core budget of the Convention envisaged in paragraph 13 of its financial procedures, so as to ensure continuity in the cash flow required to finance the ongoing work of the Conference of the Parties, the subsidiary bodies and the Convention secretariat;

7. *Calls upon* Member States that are Parties to the Convention to also contribute generously to the trust fund for participation in the Convention process envisaged in paragraph 15 of its financial procedures, as well as to the trust funds envisaged for supplementary activities under the Convention;[9]

8. *Decides* to include in the calendar of conferences and meetings for 1996-1997 the sessions of the Conference of the Parties and its subsidiary bodies envisaged for that biennium entailing twelve weeks of conference-servicing facilities;

9. *Requests* the Secretary-General to make the necessary arrangements to include in the calendar of conferences and meetings for the biennium 1998-1999 those sessions of the Conference of the Parties and its subsidiary bodies that the Conference may need to convene in that period;

10. *Takes note* of the transitional arrangement for administrative support to the Convention secretariat, outlined in the report of the Secretary-General on the implementation of General Assembly resolution 49/120, with particular reference to the implications arising from the report of the Conference of the Parties, on its first session,[10] which should facilitate the establishment and relocation of the Convention secretariat and assist it in addressing any initial financial and personnel problems that may be encountered within this context, also takes note of the financing arrangements contained in operative paragraphs 8 and 9 above, and requests the Secretary-General to review these arrangements towards the end of the biennium 1996-1997 and to report upon the results of this review to the Assembly at its fifty-second session;

11. *Notes* that the Secretary-General intends:

(*a*) To transfer the end-1995 balance in the trust fund for the negotiating process established under paragraph 20 of General Assembly resolution 45/212 into the trust fund for the core budget of the Convention envisaged in paragraph 13 of its financial procedures;

(*b*) To transfer the end-1995 balance in the special voluntary fund for participation in the negotiating process established under paragraph 10 of the same resolution into the trust fund for participation in the Convention process envisaged in paragraph 15 of the aforementioned financial procedures;

12. *Requests* the Secretary-General to report to the General Assembly at its fifty-first session on the implementation of the present resolution;

13. *Decides* to include in the provisional agenda of its fifty-first session the item entitled "Protection of global climate for present and future generations of mankind".

96th plenary meeting
20 December 1995

---

1 FCCC/CP/1995/7/Add.1, decision 14/CP.1.

2 A/50/716.

3 A/AC.237/91 and Add.1.

4 A/50/536.

5 FCCC/CP/1995/7 and Add.1.

6 FCCC/CP/1995/7/Add.1, decision 14/CP.1.

7 *Ibid.*, decision 16/CP.1.

8 FCCC/CP/1995/7/Add.1, decision 15/CP.1, annex II.

9 *Ibid.*, decision 15/CP.1, annex I, and decision 18/CP.1.

10 A/50/716, paras. 36-38.

11.00 FUNCTIONING OF THE UNITED NATIONS

11.10 TRANSFER OF FUNCTIONS FROM THE LEAGUE OF NATIONS TO THE UNITED NATIONS

24 (I). Transfer of Certain Functions, Activities and Assets of the League of Nations

Committee: League of Nations Committee
Vote: Adopted without a vote
Ref.: 250(III), 79(I)

I

Functions and Powers Belonging to the League of Nations Under International Agreements

Under various treaties and international conventions, agreements and other instruments, the League of Nations and its organs exercise, or may be requested to exercise, numerous functions or powers for the continuance of which, after the dissolution of the League, it is, or may be, desirable that the United Nations should provide.

Certain Members of the United Nations, which are parties to some of these instruments and are Members of the League of Nations, have informed the General Assembly that, at the forthcoming session of the Assembly of the League, they intend to move a resolution whereby the Members of the League would, so far as this is necessary, assent and give effect to the steps contemplated below.

Therefore:

1. *The General Assembly* reserves the right to decide, after due examination, not to assume any particular function or power, and to determine which organ of the United Nations or which specialized agency brought into relationship with the United Nations should exercise each particular function or power assumed.

2. *The General Assembly* records that those Members of the United Nations which are parties to the instruments referred to above assent by this resolution to the steps contemplated below and express their resolve to use their good offices to secure the cooperation of the other parties to the instruments so far as this may be necessary.

3. *The General Assembly* declares that the United Nations is willing in principle, and subject to the provisions of this resolution and of the Charter of the United Nations, to assume the exercise of certain functions and powers previously entrusted to the League of Nations, and adopts the following decisions, set forth in A, B, and C below.

A. Functions Pertaining to a Secretariat

Under certain of the instruments referred to at the beginning of this resolution, the League of Nations has, for the general convenience of the parties, undertaken to act as custodian of the original signed texts of the instruments, and to perform certain functions, pertaining to a secretariat, which do not affect the operation of the instruments and do not relate to the substantive rights and obligations of the parties. These functions include: The receipt of additional signatures and of instruments of ratification, accession and denunciation; receipt of notice of extension of the instruments to colonies or possessions of a party or to protectorates or territories for which it holds a mandate; notification of such acts to other parties and other interested States; the issue of certified copies; and the circulation of information or documents which the parties have undertaken to communicate to each other. Any interruption in the performance of these functions would be contrary to the interests of all the parties. It would be convenient for the United Nations to have the custody of those instruments which are connected with activities of the League of Nations and which the United Nations is likely to continue.

Therefore:

The General Assembly declares that the United Nations is willing to accept the custody of the instruments and to charge the Secretariat of the United Nations with the task of performing for the parties the functions, pertaining to a secretariat, formerly entrusted to the League of Nations.

B. Functions and Powers of a Technical and Non-Political Character

Among the instruments referred to at the beginning of this resolution are some of a technical and non-political character which contain provisions, relating to the substance of the instruments, whose due execution is dependent on the exercise, by the League of Nations or particular organs of the League, of functions or powers conferred by the instruments. Certain of these instruments are intimately connected with activities which the United Nations will or may continue.

It is necessary, however, to examine carefully which of the organs of the United Nations or which of the specialized agencies brought into relationship with the United Nations should, in the future, exercise the functions and powers in question, in so far as they are maintained.

Therefore:

The General Assembly is willing, subject to these reservations, to take the necessary measures to ensure the continued exercise of these functions and powers, and refers the matter to the Economic and Social Council.

C. Functions and Powers under Treaties, International Conventions, Agreements and Other Instruments Having a Political Character

The General Assembly will itself examine, or will submit to the appropriate organ of the United Nations, any request from the parties that the United Nations should assume the exercise of functions or powers entrusted to the League of Nations by treaties, international conventions, agreements and other instruments having a political character.

II

Non-Political Functions and Activities of the League of Nations other than those Mentioned in Section I

1. *The General Assembly* requests the Economic and Social Council to survey the functions and activities of a non-political character which have hitherto been performed by the League of Nations in order to determine which of them should, with such modifications as are desirable, be assumed by organs of the United Nations or be entrusted to specialized agencies which have been brought into relationship with the United Nations. Pending the adoption of the measures decided upon as the result of this examination, the Council should, on or before the dissolution of the League, assume and continue provisionally the work hitherto done by the following League departments: the Economic, Financial and Transit Department, particularly the research and statistical work; the Health Section, particularly the epidemiological service; the Opium Section and the secretariats of the Permanent Central Opium Board and Supervisory Body.

2. *The General Assembly* requests the Secretary-General to make provision for taking over and maintaining in operation the Library and Archives and for completing the League of Nations treaty series.

3. *The General Assembly* considers that it would also be desirable for the Secretary-General to engage for the work referred to in paragraphs 1 and 2 above, on appropriate terms, such members of the experienced personnel by whom it is at present being performed as the Secretary-General may select.

III

Transfer of the Assets of the League of Nations to the United Nations

The General Assembly, having considered the report of the Committee set up by the Preparatory Commission to discuss and establish with the Supervisory Commission of the League of Nations a common plan for the transfer of the assets of the League of Nations, approves of both the report of the Committee set up by the Preparatory Commission and of the common plan submitted by it (document A/18 and Corr.1, Add. 1 and 2.)

IV

Appointment of a Negotiating Committee

The General Assembly approves of the setting up of a small negotiating committee to assist the Secretary-General in negotiating further agreements in connection with the transfer of certain assets in Geneva, and in connection with the premises in the Peace Palace in The Hague. This committee shall consist of one representative designated by the delegations, if they so desire, of each of the same eight Members as previously constituted the Committee created by the Preparatory Commission: Chile, China, France, Poland, Union of South Africa, Union of Soviet Socialist Republics, United Kingdom and United States of America.

Twenty-ninth plenary meeting
12 February 1946

51 (I). Transfer to the United Nations of Certain Non-Political Functions and Activities of the League of Nations, other than those Pursuant to International Agreements

Committee: Joint Second and Third
Vote: unanimous

In accordance with the resolution adopted by the General Assembly on 12 February 1946 and the resolution adopted by the Economic and Social Council on 16 February 1946, the Secretary-General submitted to the Economic and Social Council, at its third session, a report dated 26 September 1946 concerning the provisional assumption and continuation of certain non-political functions and activities of the League of Nations, other than those exercised pursuant to international agreements.

The Economic and Social Council took note of the Secretary-General's report on 2 October 1946 and has transmitted it to the General Assembly.

The General Assembly recognizes that it is desirable for the United Nations to assume and continue the non-political functions and activities of the League of Nations which are described in the report of the Secretary-General dated 26 September 1946.

The General Assembly, therefore,

Authorizes and requests the Secretary-General to assume and continue the non-political functions and activities of the League of Nations previously performed by the League of Nations Secretariat, with the exception of:

(*a*) Those functions and activities exercised pursuant to international agreements;

(*b*) Those functions and activities entrusted to specialized agencies which have been, or are to be, brought into relationship with the United Nations, under Articles 57 and 63 of the Charter.

The Secretary-General shall exercise the functions and activities authorized by this paragraph, subject to such policies as may be established by the Economic and Social Council.

Authorizes and requests the Economic and Social Council to assume and continue the non-political functions and activities of the League of Nations previously performed by the various committees and commissions of the League with the exception of:

(*a*) Those functions and activities exercised pursuant to international agreements;

(*b*) Those functions and activities entrusted to specialized agencies, which have been, or are to be brought into relationship with the United Nations, under Articles 57 and 63 of the Charter.

This resolution shall not affect any decision of the General Assembly with respect to functions and activities exercised by the League of Nations pursuant to international agreements.

Sixty-fifth plenary meeting
14 December 1946

794 (VIII). Transfer to the United Nations of the Functions Exercised by the League of Nations under the Slavery Convention of 25 September 1926

Committee: 6
Vote: 50 - 0 - 6
Ref.: 255(III), 126(II), 54(I)

The General Assembly,

Considering Economic and Social Council resolution 475 (XV), adopted on 27 April 1953, concerning the transfer to the United Nations of the functions exercised by the League of Nations under the Slavery Convention of 25 September 1926,

Desirous of continuing international cooperation relating to the elimination of slavery,

1. *Approves* the Protocol which accompanies the present resolution;

2. *Urges* all States Parties to the Slavery Convention to sign or accept this Protocol;

3. *Recommends* all other States to accede at their earliest opportunity to the Slavery Convention as amended by the present Protocol.

453rd plenary meeting
23 October 1953

Protocol Amending the Slavery Convention Signed at Geneva on 25 September 1926

The States Parties to the present Protocol,

Considering that under the Slavery Convention signed at Geneva on 25 September 1926 (hereinafter called "the Convention") the League of Nations was invested with certain duties and functions, and

Considering that it is expedient that these duties and functions should be continued by the United Nations,

Have agreed as follows:

Article I

The States Parties to the present Protocol undertake that as between themselves they will, in accordance with the provisions of the Protocol, attribute full legal force and effect to and duly apply the amendments to the Convention set forth in the annex to the Protocol.

Article II

1. The present Protocol shall be open for signature or acceptance by any of the States Parties to the Convention to which the Secretary-General has communicated for this purpose a copy of the Protocol.

2. States may become Parties to the present Protocol by:

(*a*) Signature without reservation as to acceptance;

(*b*) Signature with reservation as to acceptance, followed by acceptance;

(*c*) Acceptance.

3. Acceptance shall be effected by the deposit of a formal instrument with the Secretary-General of the United Nations.

Article III

1. The present Protocol shall come into force on the date on which two States shall have become Parties thereto, and shall thereafter come into force in respect of each State upon the date on which it becomes a Party to the Protocol.

2. The amendments set forth in the annex to the present Protocol shall come into force when twenty-three States shall have become Parties to the Protocol, and consequently any State becoming a Party to the Convention, after the amendments thereto have come into force, shall become a Party to the Convention as so amended.

Article IV

In accordance with paragraph 1 of Article 102 of the Charter of the United Nations and the regulations pursuant thereto adopted by the General Assembly, the Secretary-General of the United Nations is authorized to effect registration of the present Protocol and of the amendments made in the Convention by the Protocol on the respective dates of their entry into force and to publish the Protocol and the amended text of the Convention as soon as possible after registration.

Article V

The present Protocol, of which the Chinese, English, French, Russian and Spanish texts are equally authentic, shall be deposited in the archives of the United Nations Secretariat. The texts of the Convention to be amended in accordance with the annex being authentic in the English and French languages only, the English and French texts of the annex shall be equally authentic, and the Chinese, Russian and Spanish texts shall be translations. The Secretary-General shall prepare certified copies of the Protocol, including the annex, for communication to States Parties to the Convention, as well as to all other States Members of the United Nations. He shall likewise prepare for communication to States, including States not Members of the United Nations, upon the entry into force of the amendments as provided in article III, certified copies of the Convention as so amended.

In witness whereof the undersigned, being duly authorized thereto by their respective Governments, signed the present Protocol on the date appearing opposite their respective signatures.

Done at the Headquarters of the United Nations, New York,

this ... day of ...[1] one thousand nine hundred and fifty-three.

Annex

to the Protocol Amending the Slavery Convention Signed at Geneva on 25 September 1926

In *article 7* "the Secretary-General of the United Nations" shall be substituted for "the Secretary-General of the League of Nations".

In *article 8* "the International Court of Justice" shall be substituted for "the Permanent Court of International Justice", and "the Statute of the International Court of Justice" shall be substituted for "the Protocol of December 16th, 1920, relating to the Permanent Court of International Justice".

In the first and second paragraphs of *article 10* "the United Nations" shall be substituted for "the League of Nations".

The last three paragraphs of *article 11* shall be deleted and the following substituted:

> "The present Convention shall be open to accession by all States, including States which are not Members of the United Nations, to which the Secretary-General of the United Nations shall have communicated a certified copy of the Convention.
>
> "Accession shall be effected by the deposit of a formal instrument with the Secretary-General of the United Nations, who shall give notice thereof to all States Parties to the Convention and to all other States contemplated in the present article, informing them of the date on which each such instrument of accession was received in deposit."

In *article 12* "the United Nations" shall be substituted for "the League of Nations".

11.20 INTERNAL ORGANIZATION AND PRINCIPAL ORGANS

267 (III). The Problem of Voting in the Security Council

Committee: P
Vote: 43 - 6 - 2

The General Assembly,

Having considered the report of its Interim Committee on the problem of voting in the Security Council,[2] and

Exercising the authority conferred upon it by Article 10 of the Charter to discuss any question within the scope of the Charter or relating to the functions of any organ of the United Nations and to make recommendations to the Members of the United Nations and to the Security Council thereon,

1. *Recommends* to the members of the Security Council that, without prejudice to any other decisions which the Security Council may deem procedural, the decisions set forth in the attached annex be deemed procedural and that the members of the Security Council conduct their business accordingly;

2. *Recommends* to the permanent members of the Security Council that they seek agreement among themselves upon what possible decisions by the Security Council they might forbear to exercise their veto, when seven affirmative votes have already been cast in the Council, giving favourable consideration to the list of such decisions contained in conclusion 2 of part IV of the report of the Interim Committee;

3. *Recommends* to the permanent members of the Security Council, in order to avoid impairment of the usefulness and prestige of the Council through excessive use of the veto:

(*a*) To consult together wherever feasible upon important decisions to be taken by the Security Council;

(*b*) To consult together wherever feasible before a vote is taken if their unanimity is essential to effective action by the Security Council;

(*c*) If there is not unanimity, to exercise the veto only when they consider the question of vital importance, taking into account the interest of the United Nations as a whole, and to state upon what ground they consider this condition to be present;

4. *Recommends* to the Members of the United Nations that in agreements conferring functions on the Security Council such conditions of voting within that body be provided as would to the greatest extent feasible exclude the application of the rule of unanimity of the permanent members.

195th plenary meeting
14 April 1949

Annex

Decisions Deemed Procedural

Decision to postpone consideration of or voting on a recommendation of a State for membership until the next occasion for the consideration of applications.

Submission to the General Assembly of any questions relating to the maintenance of international peace and security.

1 The above Protocol was opened for signature or acceptance at United Nations Headquarters on 7 December 1953.

2 See document A/578.

Request to the General Assembly that the General Assembly make a recommendation on a dispute or situation in respect of which the Security Council is exercising the functions assigned to it in the Charter.

Consent to notification by the Secretary-General to the General Assembly or to Members of the United Nations of any matters relative to the maintenance of international peace and security which are being dealt with by the Security Council.

Consent to notification by the Secretary-General to the General Assembly or to Members of the United Nations of any matters relative to the maintenance of international peace and security with which the Security Council ceases to deal.

Request to the Secretary-General for the convocation of a special session of the General Assembly.

Approval of credentials of representatives of members of the Security Council.

Approval of annual reports to the General Assembly.

Submission and approval of special reports to the General Assembly.

Organization of the Security Council in such manner as to enable it to function continuously.

Arrangement of the holding of periodic meetings.

Holding of meetings at places other than the seat of the United Nations.

Establishment of such subsidiary organs as the Security Council deems necessary for the performance of its functions.

Steps incidental to the establishment of a subsidiary organ: appointment of members, terms of reference, interpretation of terms of reference, reference of questions for study, approval of rules of procedure. However, the approval of the terms of reference of such subsidiary organs should require the unanimity of the permanent members if the subsidiary organ were given authority to take steps which, if taken by the Security Council, would be subject to the veto, or if the conferring of such authority would constitute a non-procedural decision.

Adoption of rules of procedure:

Decisions to adopt rules of procedure and decisions in application of the provisional rules of procedure, not contained elsewhere in the list:

(1) Overruling of ruling of the President on a point of order (rule 30).

(2) Order of principal motions and draft resolutions (rule 32).

(3) To suspend the meeting; to adjourn the meeting; to adjourn the meeting to a certain day or hour; to postpone discussion of the question to a certain day or indefinitely (rule 33).

(4) Order in which amendments to motions or draft resolutions are to be voted upon (rule 36).

(5) Request to members of the Secretariat or to other persons for information or for other assistance (rule 39).

(6) Publication of documents in any language other than the official languages (rule 47).

(7) To hold a meeting in private (rule 48).

(8) To determine what records shall be kept of a private meeting (rule 51).

(9) To approve important corrections to the records (rule 52).

(10) To grant access to the records of private meetings to authorized representatives of other Members of the United Nations (rule 56).

(11) To determine which records and documents shall be made available to other Members of the United Nations, which shall be made public, and which shall remain confidential (rule 57).

Adoption of the method of selecting the President.

Participation without vote of Members of the United Nations not members of the Security Council in the discussion of any question brought before the Security Council whenever the Security Council considers that the interests of those Members are specially affected.

Invitation to a Member of the United Nations which is not a member of the Security Council or to any State which is not a Member of the United Nations to participate without vote in the discussion relating to a dispute to which it is a party.

Enunciation of conditions for such participation of a State which is not a Member of the United Nations.

Decision whether a State not a Member of the United Nations has accepted the conditions deemed just by the Security Council for participation under Article 32 of the Charter.

Approval of credentials of representatives of States invited under Articles 31 and 32 of the Charter and rule 39 of the provisional rules of procedure.

Decision to remind Members of their obligations under the Charter.

Establishment of procedures for the hearing of disputes or situations.

Request for information on the progress or the results of resort to peaceful means of settlement.

Deletion of a question from the list of questions of which the Security Council is seized.

Decision to consider and discuss a dispute or a situation brought before the Security Council (adoption of the agenda).

Decision whether a State not a Member of the United Nations has accepted, for the purposes of the dispute which it desires to bring to the attention of the Security Council, the obligations of pacific settlement provided in the Charter.

Invitation to a Member of the United Nations not a member of the Security Council to participate in the decisions of the Security Council concerning the employment of contingents of that Member's armed forces.

Approval of rules of procedure and organization of the Military Staff Committee.

Request for assistance from the Economic and Social Council.

Decision to avail itself of the assistance of the Trusteeship Council to perform those functions of the United Nations under the Trusteeship System relating to political, economic, social and educational matters in the strategic areas.

Decision to dispense, on grounds of security, with the assistance of the Trusteeship Council.

Request of the Security Council for the appointment of a joint conference for the purpose of choosing one name for each vacant seat in the International Court of Justice.

Fixation of a period within which those members of the International Court of Justice who have already been elected shall proceed to fill the vacant seats by selection from among those candidates who have obtained votes either in the General Assembly or in the Security Council.

Fixation of the date of the election to fill vacancies in the International Court of Justice.

1991 (XVIII). Question of Equitable Representation on the Security Council and the Economic and Social Council

Committee: 1 (Special Political)
Vote: A: 97 - 11 - 4; B: 96 - 11 - 5
Ref.: 1404(XIV), 1299(XIII), 1190(XII)

A

The General Assembly,

Considering that the present composition of the Security Council is inequitable and unbalanced,

Recognizing that the increase in the membership of the United Nations makes it necessary to enlarge the membership of the Security Council, thus providing for a more adequate geographical representation of non-permanent members and making it a more effective organ for carrying out its functions under the Charter of the United Nations,

Bearing in mind the conclusions and recommendations of the Committee on arrangements for a conference for the purpose of reviewing the Charter,[1]

1. *Decides* to adopt, in accordance with Article 108 of the Charter of the United Nations, the following amendments to the Charter and to submit them for ratification by the States Members of the United Nations:

(*a*) In Article 23, paragraph 1, the word "eleven" in the first sentence shall be replaced by the word "fifteen", and the word "six" in the third sentence by the word "ten";

(*b*) In Article 23, paragraph 2, the second sentence shall then be reworded as follows:

"In the first election of the non-permanent members after the increase of the membership of the Security Council from eleven to fifteen, two of the four additional members shall be chosen for a term of one year";

(*c*) In Article 27, paragraph 2, the word "seven" shall be replaced by the word "nine";

(*d*) In Article 27, paragraph 3, the word "seven" shall be replaced by the word "nine";

2. *Calls upon* all Member States to ratify the above amendments, in accordance with their respective constitutional processes, by 1 September 1965;

3. *Further decides* that the ten non-permanent members of the Security Council shall be elected according to the following pattern:

(*a*) Five from African and Asian States;

(*b*) One from Eastern European States;

(*c*) Two from Latin American States;

(*d*) Two from Western European and other States.

1285th plenary meeting
17 December 1963

B

The General Assembly,

Recognizing that the increase in the membership of the United Nations makes it necessary to enlarge the membership of the Economic and Social Council, with a view to providing for a more adequate geographical representation therein and making it a more effective organ for carrying out its functions under Chapters IX and X of the Charter of the United Nations,

Recalling Economic and Social Council resolutions 974 B and C (XXXVI) of 22 July 1963,

Bearing in mind the conclusions and recommendations of the Committee on arrangements for a conference for the purpose of reviewing the Charter,[2]

1. *Decides* to adopt, in accordance with Article 108 of the Charter of the United Nations, the following amendment to the Charter and to submit it for ratification by the States Members of the United Nations:

"Article 61

"1. The Economic and Social Council shall consist of twenty-seven Members of the United Nations elected by the General Assembly.

"2. Subject to the provisions of paragraph 3, nine members of the Economic and Social Council shall be elected each year for a term of three years. A retiring member shall be eligible for immediate reelection.

"3. At the first election after the increase in the membership of the Economic and Social Council from eighteen to twenty-seven members, in addition to the members elected in place of the six members whose term of office expires at the end of that year, nine additional members shall be elected. Of these nine additional members, the term of office of three members so elected shall expire at the end of one year, and of three other members at the end of two years, in accordance with arrangements made by the General Assembly.

"4. Each member of the Economic and Social Council shall have one representative.";

2. *Calls upon* all Member States to ratify the above amendment, in accordance with their respective constitutional processes, by 1 September 1965;

3. *Further decides* that, without prejudice to the present distribution of seats in the Economic and Social Council, the nine additional members shall be elected according to the following pattern:

(*a*) Seven from African and Asian States;

(*b*) One from Latin American States;

(*c*) One from Western European and other States.

1285th plenary meeting
17 December 1963

47/62. Question of Equitable Representation on and Increase in the Membership of the Security Council

Committee: -
Vote: Adopted without a vote
Ref.: 48/26, 1991(XVIII), 1404(XIV), 1299(XIII), 1190(XII)

The General Assembly,

Recognizing the increasingly crucial role of the Security Council in maintaining international peace and security,

Recognizing also the changed international situation and the substantial increase in the membership of the United Nations, the total membership having reached one hundred and seventy-nine,

Acting in accordance with the principles and objectives of the Charter of the United Nations,

Reaffirming the principle of sovereign equality of all Members of the United Nations,

Mindful of Article 23 of the Charter of the United Nations,

Realizing the need to continue the process of revitalization and restructuring of certain organs of the United Nations,

Recalling the statements made on the subject at its forty-seventh session,[3] as well as the statement on the same subject contained in the final documents of the Tenth Conference of Heads of State or Government of Non-Aligned Countries, held at Jakarta from 1 to 6 September 1992,[4]

1. *Requests* the Secretary-General to invite Member States to submit, not later than 30 June 1993, written comments on a possible review of the membership of the Security Council;

2. *Also requests* the Secretary-General to submit to the General Assembly at its forty-eighth session, for its consideration, a report containing comments made by Member States on the subject;

3. *Decides* to include in the provisional agenda of its forty-eighth session the item entitled "Question of equitable representation on and increase in the membership of the Security Council".

84th plenary meeting
11 December 1992

---

1 *Official Records of the General Assembly, Eigtheenth Session*, agenda item 21, document A/5487, para. 9. Appendix 43, p. 478.

2 *Ibid.*, agenda item 21, document A/5487, para. 9. Appendix 43, p. 478.

3 See A/47/PV.69.

4 See A/47/675-S/24816, annex, document NAC 10/Doc.1/Rev.2/ sect. C.

Rules of Procedure of the General Assembly

UN Doc.: A/520/Rev.15/Amend.2[1]
Ref.: 102 (I); 173 (II); 116 (II); 262 (III); 271 (III); 362 (IV); 366 (IV); 377A (V); 475 (V); 479 (V); 597 (VI); 684 (VII); 689A (VII); 791 (VIII); 844 (IX); 1104 (XI); 1192 (XII); 1659 (XVI); 1845 (XVII); 1898 (XVIII); 1990 (XVIII); 2046 (XX); 2323 (XXII); 2390 (XXIII); 2479 (XXIII); 2553 (XXIV); 2632 (XXV); 2837 (XXVI); 2798 (XXVI); 2847 (XXVI); 2913 (XXVII); 3189 (XXVIII); 3190 (XXVIII); 31/95; 32/103; 33/12; 33/138; 34/401; 35/219A u. B; 39/88B; 45/45; 47/233

Explanatory note

Rules 49, 82, 83, 85, 144, 146 and 161, which reproduce textually provisions of the Charter, are printed in bold type and are, in addition, provided with a footnote. A footnote has also been added to other rules which, while based directly on provisions of the Charter, do not reproduce those provisions textually. Figures indicated between square brackets in sections dealing with rules for plenary meetings refer to identical or corresponding rules for committee meetings, and vice versa. Attention is drawn to rule 162, which provides that the italicized headings of the rules, which were inserted for reference purposes only, shall be disregarded in the interpretation of the rules.

Rules of Procedure

I. Sessions

Regular Sessions

Opening date

Rule 1[2]

The General Assembly shall meet every year in regular session commencing on the third Tuesday in September.

Closing date

Rule 2

On the recommendation of the General Committee, the General Assembly shall, at the beginning of each session, fix a closing date for the session.

Place of meeting

Rule 3

The General Assembly shall meet at the Headquarters of the United Nations unless convened elsewhere in pursuance of a decision taken at a previous session or at the request of a majority of the Members of the United Nations.

Rule 4

Any Member of the United Nations may, at least one hundred and twenty days before the date fixed for the opening of a regular session, request that the session be held elsewhere than at the Headquarters of the United Nations. The Secretary-General shall immediately communicate the request, together with his recommendations, to the other Members of the United Nations. If within thirty days of the date of this communication a majority of the Members concur in the request, the session shall be held accordingly.

Notification of session

Rule 5

The Secretary-General shall notify the Members of the United Nations, at least sixty days in advance, of the opening of a regular session.

Temporary adjournment of session

Rule 6

The General Assembly may decide at any session to adjourn temporarily and resume its meetings at a later date.

Special Sessions

Summoning by the General Assembly

Rule 7[3]

The General Assembly may fix a date for a special session.

Summoning at the request of the Security Council or Members

Rule 8

(a) Special sessions of the General Assembly shall be convened within fifteen days of the receipt by the Secretary-General of a request for such a session from the Security Council or from a majority of the Members of the United Nations or of the concurrence of a majority of Members as provided in rule 9.

(b) Emergency special sessions pursuant to General Assembly Resolution 377 A (V) shall be convened within twenty-four hours of the receipt by the Secretary-General of a request for such a session from the Security Council, on the vote of any nine members thereof, or of a request from a majority of the Members of the United Nations expressed by vote in the Interim Committee or otherwise, or of the concurrence of a majority of Members as provided in rule 9.

Request by Members

Rule 9

(a) Any Member of the United Nations may request the Secretary-General to convene a special session of the General Assembly. The Secretary-General shall immediately inform the other Members of the request and inquire whether they concur in it. If within thirty days of the date of the communication of the Secretary-General a majority of the Members concur in the request, a special session of the General Assembly shall be convened in accordance with rule 8.

(b) This rule shall apply also to a request by any Member of the United Nations for an emergency special session pursuant to Resolution 377 A (V). In such a case, the Secretary-General shall communicate with the other Members by the most expeditious means of communication available.

Notification of session

Rule 10

The Secretary-General shall notify the Members of the United Nations, at least fourteen days in advance, of the opening of a special session convened at the request of the Security Council, and at least ten days in advance in the case of a session convened at the request of a majority of the Members or upon the concurrence of a majority in the request of any Member. In the case of an emergency special session convened pursuant to rule 8 (b), the Secretary-General shall notify Members at least twelve hours before the opening of the session.

Regular and special Sessions

Notification to other bodies

Rule 11

Copies of the notice convening each session of the General Assembly shall be addressed to all other principal organs of the United Nations and to the specialized agencies referred to in Article 57, paragraph 2, of the Charter.

---

1 The last amendment of resolution 47/233 has been included in the text by the editors.

2 Rule based directly on a provision of the Charter (Art. 20).

3 Rule based directly on a provision of the Charter (Art. 20).

II. Agenda

Regular Sessions

Provisional agenda

Rule 12

The provisional agenda for a regular session shall be drawn up by the Secretary-General and communicated to the Members of the United Nations at least sixty-days before the opening of the session.

Rule 13

The provisional agenda of a regular session shall include:

(a) The report of the Secretary-General on the work of the Organization;

(b) Reports from the Security Council, the Economic and Social Council, the Trusteeship Council, the International Court of Justice, the subsidiary organs of the General Assembly and the specialized agencies (where such reports are called for under agreements entered into);

(c) All items the inclusion of which has been ordered by the General Assembly at a previous session;

(d) All items proposed by the other principal organs of the United Nations;

(e) All items proposed by any Members of the United Nations;

(f) All items pertaining to the budget for the next financial year and the report on the accounts for the last financial year;

(g) All items which the Secretary-General deems it necessary to put before the General Assembly;

(h) All items proposed under Article 35, paragraph 2, of the Charter by States not Members of the United Nations.

Supplementary items

Rule 14

Any Member or principal organ of the United Nations or the Secretary-General may, at least thirty days before the date fixed for the opening of a regular session, request the inclusion of supplementary items in the agenda. Such items shall be placed on a supplementary list, which shall be communicated to members at least twenty days before the opening of the session.

Additional items

Rule 15

Additional items of an important and urgent character, proposed for inclusion in the agenda less than thirty days before the opening of a regular session or during a regular session, may be placed on the agenda if the General Assembly so decides by a majority of the members present and voting. No additional item may, unless the General Assembly decides otherwise by a two-thirds majority of the members present and voting, be considered until seven days have elapsed since it was placed on the agenda and until a committee has reported upon the question concerned.

Special Sessions

Provisional agenda

Rule 16

The provisional agenda of a special session convened at the request of the Security Council shall be communicated to the Members of the United Nations at least fourteen days before the opening of the session. The provisional agenda of a special session convened at the request of a majority of the Members, or upon the concurrence of a majority in the request of any member, shall be communicated at least ten days before the opening of the session. The provisional agenda of an emergency special session shall be communicated to members simultaneously with the communication convening the session.

Rule 17

The provisional agenda for a special session shall consist only of those items proposed for consideration in the request for the holding of the session.

Supplementary items

Rule 18

Any Member or principal organ of the United Nations or the Secretary-General may, at least four days before the date fixed for the opening of a special session, request the inclusion of supplementary items in the agenda. Such items shall be placed on a supplementary list, which shall be communicated to Members as soon as possible.

Additional items

Rule 19

During a special session, items on the supplementary list and additional items may be added to the agenda by a two-thirds majority of the members present and voting. During an emergency special session, additional items concerning the matters dealt with in Resolution 377 A (V) may be added to the agenda by a two-thirds majority of the members present and voting.

Regular and special sessions

Explanatory memorandum

Rule 20

Any item proposed for inclusion in the agenda shall be accompanied by an explanatory memorandum and, if possible, by basic documents or by a draft resolution.

Adoption of the agenda

Rule 21

At each session the provisional agenda and the supplementary list, together with the report of the General Committee thereon, shall be submitted to the General Assembly for approval as soon as possible after the opening of the session.

Amendment and deletion of items

Rule 22

Items on the agenda may be amended or deleted by the General Assembly by a majority of the members present and voting.

Debate on inclusion of items

Rule 23

Debate on the inclusion of an item in the agenda, when that item has been recommended for inclusion by the General Committee, shall be limited to three speakers in favour of, and three against, the inclusion. The President may limit the time to be allowed to speakers under this rule.

Modification of the allocation of expenses

Rule 24

No proposal for a modification of the allocation of expenses for the time being in force shall be placed on the agenda unless it has been communicated to the Members of the United Nations at least ninety days before the opening of the session.

III. Delegations

Composition

Rule 25[1]

The delegation of a Member shall consist of not more than five

[1] Rule based directly on a provision of the Charter (Art. 9 para. 2).

representatives and five alternate representatives and as many advisers, technical advisers, experts and persons of similar status as may be required by the delegation.

Alternatives

Rule 26

An alternative representative may act as a representative upon designation by the chairman of the delegation.

IV. Credentials

Submission of credentials

Rule 27

The credentials of representatives and the names of members of a delegation shall be submitted to the Secretary-General if possible not less than one week before the opening of the session. The credentials shall be issued either by the Head of the State or Government or by the Minister for Foreign Affairs.

Credentials Committee

Rule 28

A Credentials Committee shall be appointed at the beginning of each session. It shall consist of nine members, who shall be appointed by the General Assembly on the proposal of the President. The Committee shall elect its own officers. It shall examine the credentials of representatives and report without delay.

Provisional admission to a session

Rule 29

Any representative to whose admission a Member has made objection shall be seated provisionally with the same rights as other representatives until the Credentials Committee has reported and the General Assembly has given its decision.

V. President and Vice-Presidents

Temporary President

Rule 30

At the opening of each session of the General Assembly, the chairman of that delegation from which the President of the previous session was elected shall preside until the Assembly has elected a President for the session.

Elections

Rule 31

The General Assembly shall elect a President and twenty-one Vice-Presidents,[1] who shall hold office until the close of the session at which they are elected.[2] The Vice-Presidents shall be elected, after the election of the Chairmen of the six Main Committees referred to in rule 98, in such a way as to ensure the representative character of the General Committee.

Acting President

Rule 32 [105]

If the President finds it necessary to be absent during a meeting or any part thereof, he shall designate one of the Vice-Presidents to take his place.

Rule 33 [105]

A Vice-President acting as President shall have the same powers and duties as the President.

Replacement of the President

Rule 34 [105]

If the President is unable to perform his functions, a new President shall be elected for the unexpired term.

General powers of the President

Rule 35 [106]

In addition to exercising the powers conferred upon him elsewhere by these rules, the President shall declare the opening and closing of each plenary meeting of the session, direct the discussions in the plenary meeting, ensure observance of these rules, accord the right to speak, put questions and announce decisions. He shall rule on points of order and, subject to these rules, shall have complete control of the proceedings at any meeting and over the maintenance of order thereat. The President may, in the course of the discussion of an item, propose to the General Assembly the limitation of the time to be allowed to speakers, the limitation of the number of times each representative may speak, the closure of the list of speakers or the closure of the debate. He may also propose the suspension or the adjournment of the meeting or the adjournment of the debate on the item under discussion.

Rule 36 [107]

The President, in the exercise of his functions, remains under the authority of the General Assembly.

The President shall not vote

Rule 37 [104]

The President, or a Vice-President acting as President, shall not vote but shall designate another member of his delegation to vote in his place.

VI. General Committee

Composition

Rule 38

The General Committee shall comprise the President of the General Assembly, who shall preside, the twenty-one Vice-Presidents and the Chairmen of the six Main Committees. No two members of the General Committee shall be members of the same delegation, and it shall

---

1 In the annex to resolution 33/138 of 19 December 1978, the General Assembly decided as follows:

"1. In the election of the President of the General Assembly, regard shall be had for equitable geographical rotation of this office among the regions mentioned in paragraph 4 below.

"2. The twenty-one Vice-Presidents of the General Assembly shall be elected according to the following pattern, subject to paragraph 3 below:

"(a) Six representatives from African States;

"(b) Five representatives from Asian States;

"(c) One representative from an Eastern European State;

"(d) Three representatives from Latin American States;

"(e) Two representatives from Western European and other States;

"(f) Five representatives from the permanent members of the Security Council.

"3. The election of the President of the General Assembly will, however, have the effect of reducing by one the number of vice-presidencies allocated to the region from which the President is elected.

"4. The seven Chairmen of the Main Committees shall be elected according to the following pattern:

"(a) Two representatives from African States;

"(b) One representative from an Asian State;

"(c) One representative from an Eastern European State;

"(d) One representative from a Latin American State;

"(e) One representative from a Western European or other State;

"(f) The seventh chairmanship shall rotate every alternate year among representatives of States mentioned in subparagraphs (b) and (d) above".

2 Rule based directly on a provision of the Charter (Art. 21, second sentence).

be so constituted as to ensure its representative character. Chairmen of other committees upon which all Members have the right to be represented and which are established by the General Assembly to meet during the session shall be entitled to attend meetings of the General Committee and may participate without vote in the discussions.

Substitute members

Rule 39

If a Vice-President of the General Assembly finds it necessary to be absent during a meeting of the General Committee, he may designate a member of his delegation to take his place. The Chairman of a Main Committee shall, in case of absence, designate one of the Vice-Chairmen of the Committee to take his place. A Vice-Chairman shall not have the right to vote if he is of the same delegation as another member of the General Committee.

Functions

Rule 40

The General Committee shall, at the beginning of each session, consider the provisional agenda, together with the supplementary list, and shall make recommendations to the General Assembly, with regard to each item proposed, concerning its inclusion in the agenda, the rejection of the request for inclusion or the inclusion of the item in the provisional agenda of a future session. It shall, in the same manner, examine requests for the inclusion of additional items in the agenda and shall make recommendations thereon to the General Assembly. In considering matters relating to the agenda of the General Assembly, the General Committee shall not discuss the substance of any item except in so far as this bears upon the question whether the General Committee should recommend the inclusion of the item in the agenda, the rejection of the request for inclusion or the inclusion of the item in the provisional agenda of a future session, and what priority should be accorded to an item the inclusion of which has been recommended.

Rule 41

The General Committee shall make recommendations to the General Assembly concerning the closing date of the session. It shall assist the President and the General Assembly in drawing up the agenda for each plenary meeting, in determining the priority of its items and in coordinating the proceedings of all committees of the Assembly. It shall assist the President in the general conduct of the work of the General Assembly which falls within the competence of the President. It shall not, however, decide any political question.

Rule 42

The General Committee shall meet periodically throughout each session to review the progress of the General Assembly and its committees and to make recommendations for furthering such progress. It shall also meet at such other times as the President deems necessary or upon the request of any other of its members.

Participation by members requesting the inclusion of items in the agenda

Rule 43

A member of the General Assembly which has no representative on the General Committee and which has requested the inclusion of an item in the agenda shall be entitled to attend any meeting of the General Committee at which its request is discussed and may participate, without vote, in the discussion of that item.

Revision of the form of resolutions

Rule 44

The General Committee may revise the resolutions adopted by the General Assembly, changing their form but not their substance. Any such changes shall be reported to the General Assembly for its consideration.

VII. Secretariat

Duties of the Secretary-General

Rule 45

The Secretary-General shall act in that capacity in all meetings of the General Assembly,[1] its committees and its subcommittees. He may designate a member of the Secretariat to act in his place at these meetings.

Rule 46

The Secretary-General shall provide and direct the staff required by the General Assembly and any committees or subsidiary organs which it may establish.

Duties of the Secretariat

Rule 47

The Secretariat shall receive, translate, print and distribute documents, reports and resolutions of the General Assembly, its committees and its organs; interpret speeches made at the meetings; prepare, print and circulate the records of the session; have the custody and proper preservation of the documents in the archives of the General Assembly; distribute all documents of the Assembly to the Members of the United Nations, and, generally, perform all other work which the Assembly may require.

Report of the Secretary-General on the work of the Organization

Rule 48

The Secretary-General shall make an annual report, and such supplementary reports as are required, to the General Assembly on the work of the Organization. He shall communicate the annual report to the Members of the United Nations at least forty-five days before the opening of the session.

Notification under Article 12 of the Charter

Rule 49[2]

The Secretary-General, with the consent of the Security Council, shall notify the General Assembly at each session of any matters relative to the maintenance of international peace and security which are being dealt with by the Security Council, and shall similarly notify the General Assembly, or the Members of the United Nations if the General Assembly is not in session, immediately the Security Council ceases to deal with such matters.

Regulations concerning the Secretariat

Rule 50[3]

The General Assembly shall establish regulations concerning the staff of the Secretariat.[4]

VIII. Languages

Official and working languages

Rule 51

Arabic, Chinese, English, French, Russian and Spanish shall be both the official and the working languages of the General Assembly, its committees and its subcommittees.

---

1 Rule based directly on a provision of the Charter (Art. 98).

2 Rule reproducing textually a provision of the Charter (Art. 12, para. 2).

3 Rule based directly on a provision of the Charter (Art. 101, para. 1).

4 For the Staff Regulations of the United Nations see ST/SGB/Staff Regulations/Rev.23.

Interpretation

Rule 52

Speeches made in any of the six languages of the General Assembly shall be interpreted into the other five languages.

Rule 53

Any representative may make a speech in a language other than the languages of the General Assembly. In this case, he shall himself provide for interpretation into one of the languages of the General Assembly or of the committee concerned. Interpretation into the other languages of the General Assembly or of the committee concerned by the interpreters of the Secretariat may be based on the interpretation given in the first such language.

Languages of verbatim and summary records

Rule 54

Verbatim or summary records shall be drawn up as soon as possible in the languages of the General Assembly.

Languages of the Journal of the United Nations

Rule 55

During the sessions of the General Assembly; the Journal of the United Nations shall be published in the languages of the Assembly.

Languages of resolutions and other documents

Rule 56

All resolutions and other documents shall be published in the languages of the General Assembly.

Publications in languages other than the languages of the General Assembly

Rule 57

Documents of the General Assembly, its committees and its subcommittees shall, if the Assembly so decides, be published in any language other than the languages of the Assembly or of the committee concerned.

IX Records

Records and sound recordings of meetings

Rule 58

(a) Verbatim records of the meetings of the General Assembly and of the Political and Security Committee (First Committee) shall be drawn up by the Secretariat and submitted to those organs after approval by the presiding officer. The General Assembly shall decide upon the form of the records of the meetings of the other Main Committees and, if any, of the subsidiary organs and of special meetings and conferences. No organ of the General Assembly shall have both verbatim and summary records.

(b) Sound recordings of the meetings of the General Assembly and of the Main Committees shall be made by the Secretariat. Such recordings shall also be made of the proceedings of subsidiary organs and special meetings and conferences when they so decide.

Resolutions Rule 59

Resolutions adopted by the General Assembly shall be communicated by the Secretary-General to the Members of the United Nations within fifteen days after the close of the session.

X. Public and private meetings of the General Assembly, its committees and its subcommittees

General principles

Rule 60

The meetings of the General Assembly and its Main Committees shall be held in public unless the organ concerned decides that exceptional circumstances require that the meeting be held in private. Meetings of other committees and subcommittees shall also be held in public unless the organ concerned decides otherwise.

Private meetings

Rule 61

All decisions of the General Assembly taken at a private meeting shall be announced at an early public meeting of the Assembly. At the close of each private meeting of the main Committees, other committees and subcommittees, the Chairman may issue a communiqué through the Secretary-General.

XI. Minute of silent prayer or meditation

Invitation to silent prayer or meditation

Rule 62

Immediately after the opening of the first plenary meeting and immediately preceding the closing of the final plenary meeting of each session of the General Assembly, the President shall invite the representatives to observe one minute of silence dedicated to prayer or meditation.

XII. Plenary Meetings

Conduct of Business

Emergency special sessions

Rule 63

Notwithstanding the provisions of any other rule and unless the General Assembly decides otherwise, the Assembly, in case of an emergency special session, shall convene in plenary meeting only and proceed directly to consider the item proposed for consideration in the request for the holding of the session, without previous reference to the General Committee or to any other committee; the President and Vice-Presidents for such emergency special sessions shall be, respectively, the chairmen of those delegations from which were elected the President and Vice-Presidents of the previous session.

Report of the Secretary-General

Rule 64

Proposals to refer any portion of the report of the Secretary-General to one of the Main Committees without debate shall be decided upon by the General Assembly without previous reference to the General Committee.

References to committees

Rule 65

The General Assembly shall not, unless it decides otherwise, make a final decision upon any item on the agenda until it has received the report of a committee on that item.

Discussion of reports of Main Committees

Rule 66

Discussion of a report of a Main Committee in a plenary meeting of the General Assembly shall take place if at least one third of the members present and voting at the plenary meeting consider such a discussion to be necessary. Any proposal to this effect shall not be debated but shall be immediately put to the vote.

Quorum

Rule 67 [108]

The President may declare a meeting open and permit the debate to proceed when at least one third of the members of the General Assembly are present. The presence of a majority of the members shall be required for any decision to be taken.

Speeches

Rule 68 [109]

No representative may address the General Assembly without having previously obtained the permission of the President. The President shall call upon speakers in the order in which they signify their desire to speak. The President may call a speaker to order if his remarks are not relevant to the subject under discussion.

Precedence

Rule 69 [111]

The Chairman and the Rapporteur of a committee may be accorded precedence for the purpose of explaining the conclusions arrived at by their committee.

Statements by the Secretariat

Rule 70 [112]

The Secretary-General, or a member of the Secretariat designated by him as his representative, may at any time make either oral or written statements to the General Assembly concerning any questions under consideration by it.

Points of order

Rule 71 [113]

During the discussion of any matter, a representative may rise to a point of order, and the point of order shall be immediately decided by the President in accordance with the rules of procedure. A representative may appeal against the ruling of the President. The appeal shall be immediately put to the vote, and the President's ruling shall stand unless overruled by a majority of the members present and voting. A representative rising to a point of order may not speak on the substance of the matter under discussion.

Time-limit on speeches

Rule 72 [114]

The General Assembly may limit the time to be allowed to each speaker and the number of times each representative may speak on any question. Before a decision is taken, two representatives may speak in favour of, and two against, a proposal to set such limits. When the debate is limited and a representative exceeds his alloted time, the President shall call him to order without delay.

Closing of list of speakers, right of reply

Rule 73 [115]

During the course of a debate, the President may announce the list of speakers and, with the consent of the General Assembly, declare the list closed. He may, however, accord the right of reply to any member if a speech delivered after he has declared the list closed makes this desirable.

Adjournment of debate

Rule 74 [116]

During the discussion of any matter, a representative may move the adjournment of the debate on the item under discussion. In addition to the proposer of the motion, two representatives may speak in favour of, and two against, the motion, after which the motion shall be immediately put to the vote. The President may limit the time to be allowed to speakers under this rule.

Closure of debate

Rule 75 [117]

A representative may at any time move the closure of the debate on the item under discussion, whether or not any other representative has signified his wish to speak. Permission to speak on the closure of the debate shall be accorded only to two speakers opposing the closure, after which the motion shall be immediately put to the vote. If the General Assembly is in favour of the closure, the President shall declare the closure of the debate. The President may limit the time to be allowed to speakers under this rule.

Suspension or adjournment of the meeting

Rule 76 [118]

During the discussion of any matter, a representative may move the suspension or the adjournment of the meeting. Such motions shall not be debated but shall be immediately put to the vote. The President may limit the time to be allowed to the speaker moving the suspension or adjournment of the meeting.

Order of procedural motions

Rule 77 [119]

Subject to rule 71, the motions indicated below shall have precedence in the following order over all other proposals or motions before the meeting:

(a) To suspend the meeting;

(b) To adjourn the meeting;

(c) To adjourn the debate on the item under discussion;

(d) To close the debate on the item under discussion.

Proposals and amendments

Rule 78 [120]

Proposals and amendments shall normally be submitted in writing to the Secretary-General, who shall circulate copies to the delegations. As a general rule, no proposal shall be discussed or put to the vote at any meeting of the General Assembly unless copies of it have been circulated to all delegations not later than the day preceding the meeting. The President may, however, permit the discussion and consideration of amendments, or of motions as to procedure, even though such amendments and motions have not been circulated or have only been circulated the same day.

Decisions on competence

Rule 79 [1211

Subject to rule 77, any motion calling for a decision on the competence of the General Assembly to adopt a proposal submitted to it shall be put to the vote before a vote is taken on the proposal in question.

Withdrawal of motions

Rule 80 1122]

A motion may be withdrawn by its proposer at any time before voting on it has commenced, provided that the motion has not been amended. A motion thus withdrawn may be reintroduced by any member.

Reconsideration of proposals

Rule 81 [123]

When a proposal has been adopted or rejected, it may not be reconsidered at the same session unless the General Assembly, by a two-thirds majority of the members present and voting, so decides. Permission to speak on a motion to reconsider shall be accorded only to two speakers opposing the motion, after which it shall be immediately put to the vote.

Voting

Voting rights

Rule 82[1] [124]

Each member of the General Assembly shall have one vote.

Two-thirds majority

Rule 83[1]

Decisions of the General Assembly on important questions shall be made by a two-thirds majority of the members present and voting. These questions shall include: recommendations with respect to the maintenance of international peace and security, the election of the non-permanent members of the Security Council, the election of the members of the Economic and social Council, the election of members of the Trusteeship Council in accordance with paragraph 1 c of Article 86 of the Charter, the admission of new Members to the United Nations, the suspension of the rights and privileges of membership, the expulsion of Members, questions relating to the operation of the trusteeship system, and budgetary questions.

Rule 84

Decisions of the General Assembly on amendments to proposals relating to important questions, and on parts of such proposals put to the vote separately, shall be made by a two-thirds majority of the members present and voting.

Rule 85[1] [125]

Decisions of the General Assembly on questions other than those provided for in rule 83, including the determination of additional categories of questions to be decided by a two-thirds majority, shall be made by a majority of the members present and voting.

Meaning of the phrase 'members present and voting'

Rule 86 [126]

For the purposes of these rules, the phrase 'members present and voting' means members casting an affirmative or negative vote. Members which abstain from voting are considered as not voting.

Method of voting

Rule 87 [127]

(a) The General Assembly shall normally vote by show of hands or by standing, but any representative may request a roll-call. The roll-call shall be taken in the English alphabetical order of the names of the members, beginning with the member whose name is drawn by lot by the President. The name of each member shall be called in any roll-call, and one of its representatives shall reply 'yes', 'no' or 'abstention'. The result of the voting shall be inserted in the record in the English alphabetical order of the names of the members.

(b) When the General Assembly votes by mechanical means, a non-recorded vote shall replace a vote by show of hands or by standing and a recorded vote shall replace a roll-call vote. Any representative may request a recorded vote. In the case of a recorded vote, the General Assembly shall, unless a representative requests otherwise, dispense with the procedure of calling out the names of the members; nevertheless, the result of the voting shall be inserted in the record in the same manner as that of a roll-call vote.

Conduct during voting

Rule 88 [128]

After the President has announced the beginning of voting, no representative shall interrupt the voting except on a point of order in connection with the actual conduct of the voting. The President may permit members to explain their votes, either before or after the voting, except when the vote is taken by secret ballot. The President may limit the time to be allowed for such explanations. The President shall not permit the proposer of a proposal or of an amendment to explain his vote on his own proposal or amendment.

Division of proposals and amendments

Rule 89 [129]

A representative may move that parts of a proposal or of an amendment should be voted on separately. If objection is made to the request for division, the motion for division shall be voted upon. Permission to speak on the motion for division shall be given only to two speakers in favour and two speakers against. If the motion for division is carried, those parts of the proposal or of the amendment which are approved shall then be put to the vote as a whole. If all operative parts of the proposal or of the amendment have been rejected, the proposal or the amendment shall be considered to have been rejected as a whole.

Rule 90 [130]

When an amendment is moved to a proposal, the amendment shall be voted on first. When two or more amendments are moved to a proposal, the General Assembly shall first vote on the amendment furthest removed in substance from the original proposal and then on the amendment next furthest removed therefrom, and so on until all the amendments have been put to the vote. Where, however, the adoption of one amendment necessarily implies the rejection of another amendment, the latter amendment shall not be put to the vote. If one or more amendments are adopted, the amended proposal shall then be voted upon. A motion is considered an amendment to a proposal if it merely adds to, deletes from or revises part of the proposal.

Voting on proposals

Rule 91 [131]

If two or more proposals relate to the same question, the General Assembly shall, unless it decides otherwise, vote on the proposals in the order in which they have been submitted. The General Assembly may, after each vote on a proposal, decide whether to vote on the next proposal.

Elections

Rule 92 [103]

All elections shall be held by secret ballot. There shall be no nominations.

Rule 93 [132]

When only one person or Member is to be elected and no candidate obtains in the first ballot the majority required, a second ballot shall be taken, which shall be restricted to the two candidates obtaining the largest number of votes. If in the second ballot the votes are equally divided, and a majority is required, the President shall decide between the candidates by drawing lots. If a two-thirds majority is required, the balloting shall be continued until one candidate secures two thirds of the votes cast; provided that, after the third inconclusive ballot, votes may be cast for any eligible person or Member. If three such unrestricted ballots are inconclusive, the next three ballots shall be restricted to the two candidates who obtained the greatest number of votes in the third of the unrestricted ballots, and the following three ballots thereafter shall be unrestricted, and so on until a person or Member is elected. These provisions shall not prejudice the application of rules 143, 144, 146 and 148.

Rule 94

When two or more elective places are to be filled at one time under the same conditions, those candidates obtaining in the first ballot the majority required shall be elected. If the number of candidates obtaining such majority is less than the number of persons or Members to be elected, there shall be additional ballots to fill the remaining places, the voting being restricted to the candidates obtaining the greatest number of votes in the previous ballot to a number not more

---

1 Rules 82, 83 and 85 reproduce the three paragraphs of Article 18 of the Charter.

than twice the places remaining to be filled; provided that, after the third inconclusive ballot, votes may be cast for any eligible person or Member. If three such unrestricted ballots are inconclusive, the next three ballots shall be restricted to the candidates who obtained the greatest number of votes in the third of the unrestricted ballots, to a number not more than twice the places remaining to be filled, and the following three ballots thereafter shall be unrestricted, and so on until all the places have been filled. These provisions shall not prejudice the application of rules 143, 144, 146 and 148.

Equally divided votes

Rule 95 [133]

If a vote is equally divided on matters other than elections, a second vote shall be taken at a subsequent meeting which shall be held within forty-eight hours of the first vote; and it shall be expressly mentioned in the agenda that a second vote will be taken on the matter in question. If this vote also results in equality, the proposal shall be regarded as rejected.

XIII. Committees

Establishment, officers, organization of work

Establishment of committees

Rule 96

The General Assembly may establish such committees as it deems necessary for the performance of its functions.

Categories of subjects

Rule 97

Items relating to the same category of subjects shall be referred to the committee or committees dealing with that category of subjects. Committees shall not introduce new items on their own initiative.

Main Committees

Rule 98

The Main Committees of the General Assembly are the following:

(a) Disarmament and International Security Committee (First Committee);

(b) Special Political and Decolonization Committee (Fourth Committee);

(c) Economic and Financial Committee (Second Committee);

(d) Social, Humanitarian and Cultural Committee (Third Committee);

(e) Administration and Budgetary Committee (Fifth Committee);

(f) Legal Committee (Sixth Committee).

Organization of work

Rule 99

(a) All the Main Committees shall, during the first week of the session, hold the elections provided for in rule 103.

(b) Each Main Committee, taking into account the closing date for the session fixed by the General Assembly on the recommendation of the General Committee, shall adopt its own priorities and meet as may be necessary to complete the consideration of the items referred to it. It shall at the beginning of the session adopt a programme of work indicating, if possible, a target date for the conclusion of its work, the approximate dates of consideration of items and the number of meetings to bc allocatcd to each item.

Representation of Members

Rule 100

Each member may be represented by one person on each Main Committee and on any other committee that may be established upon which all members have the right to be represented. It may also assign to these committees advisers, technical advisers, experts or persons of similar status.

Rule 101

Upon designation by the chairman of the delegation, advisers, technical advisers, experts or persons of similar status may act as members of committees. Persons of this status shall not, however, unless designated as alternative representatives, be eligible for election as Chairmen, Vice Chairmen or Reporters of committees or for seats in the General Assembly.

Subcommittees

Rule 102

Each committee may set up subcommittees, which shall elect their own officers.

Election of officers

Rule 103 [92]

Each Main Committee shall elect a Chairman, two Vice-Chairmen and a Rapporteur. In the case of other committees, each shall elect a Chairman, one or more Vice-Chairmen and a Rapporteur. These officers shall be elected on the basis of equitable geographical distribution, experience and personal competence. The elections shall be held by secret ballot unless the committee decides otherwise in an election where only one candidate is standing. The nomination of each candidate shall be limited to one speaker, after which the committee shall immediately proceed to the election.

The Chairman of a Main Committee shall not vote

Rule 104 [371

The Chairman of a Main Committee shall not vote, but another member of his delegation may vote in his place.

Absence of officers

Rule 105 [32-34]

If the Chairman finds it necessary to be absent during a meeting or any part thereof, he shall designate one of the Vice-Chairmen to take his place. A Vice-Chairman acting as Chairman shall have the same powers and duties as the Chairman. If any officer of the committee is unable to perform his functions, a new officer shall be elected for the unexpired term.

Functions of the Chairman

Rule 106 [35]

The Chairman shall declare the opening and closing of each meeting of the committee, direct its discussions, ensure observance of these rules, accord the right to speak, put questions and announce decisions. He shall rule on points of order and, subject to these rules, shall have complete control of the proceedings at any meeting and over the maintenance of order thereat. The Chairman may, in the course of the discussion of an item, propose to the committee the limitation of the time to be allowed to speakers, the limitation of the number of times each representative may speak, the closure of the list of speakers or the closure of the debate. He may also propose the suspension or the adjournment of the meeting or the adjournment of the debate on the item under discussion.

Rule 107 [36]

The Chairman, in the exercise of his functions, remains under thc authority of the committee.

Conduct of Business

Quorum

Rule 108 [67]

The Chairman may declare a meeting open and permit the debate to proceed when at least one quarter of the members of the committee are present. The presence of a majority of the members shall be required for any decision to be taken.

Speeches

Rule 109 [68]

No representative may address the committee without having previously obtained the permission of the Chairman. The Chairman shall call upon speakers in the order in which they signify their desire to speak. The Chairman may call a speaker to order if his remarks are not relevant to the subject under discussion.

Congratulations

Rule 110

Congratulations to the officers of a Main Committee shall not be expressed except by the Chairman of the previous session - or, in his absence, by a member of his delegation - after all the officers of the Committee have been elected.

Precedence

Rule 111 [69]

The Chairman and the Rapporteur of a committee or subcommittee may be accorded precedence for the purpose of explaining the conclusions arrived at by their committee or subcommittee.

Statements by the Secretariat

Rule 112 [70]

The Secretary-General, or a member of the Secretariat designated by him as his representative, may at any time make either oral or written statements to any committee or subcommittee concerning any question under consideration by it.

Points of order

Rule 113 [71]

During the discussion of any matter, a representative may rise to a point of order, and the point of order shall be immediately decided by the Chairman in accordance with the rules of procedure. A representative may appeal against the ruling of the chairman. The appeal shall be immediately put to the vote, and the Chairman's ruling shall stand unless overruled by a majority of the members present and voting. A representative rising to a point of order may not speak on the substance of the matter under discussion.

Time-limit on speeches

Rule 114 [72]

The committee may limit the time to be allowed to each speaker and the number of times each representative may speak on any question. Before a decision is taken, two representatives may speak in favour of, and two against, a proposal to set such limits. When the debate is limited and a representative exceeds his allotted time, the Chairman shall call him to order without delay.

Closing of list of speakers, right to reply

Rule 115 [73]

During the course of a debate, the Chairman may announce the list of speakers and, with the consent of the committee, declare the list closed. He may, however, accord the right of reply to any member if a speech delivered after he has declared the list closed makes this desirable.

Adjournment of debate

Rule 116 [74]

During the discussion of any matter, a representative may move the adjournment of the debate on the item under discussion. In addition to the proposer of the motion, two representatives may speak in favour of, and two against, the motion, after which the motion shall be immediately put to the vote. The Chairman may limit the time to be allowed to speakers under this rule.

Closure of debate

Rule 117 [75]

A representative may at any time move the closure of the debate on the item under discussion, whether or not any other representative has signified his wish to speak. Permission to speak on the closure of the debate shall be accorded only to two speakers opposing the closure, after which the motion shall be immediately put to the vote. If the committee is in favour of the closure, the Chairman shall declare the closure of the debate. The Chairman may limit the time to be allowed to speakers under this rule.

Suspension or adjournment of the meeting

Rule 118 [76]

During the discussion of any matter, a representative may move the suspension or the adjournment of the meeting. Such motions shall not be debated but shall be immediately put to the vote. The Chairman may limit the time to be allowed to the speaker moving the suspension or adjournment of the meeting.

Order of procedural motions

Rule 119 [77]

Subject to rule 113, the motions indicated below shall have precedence in the following order over all other proposals or motions before the meeting:

(a) To suspend the meeting;

(b) To adjourn the meeting;

(c) To adjourn the debate on the item under discussion;

(d) To close the debate on the item under discussion.

Proposals and amendments

Rule 120 [78]

Proposals and amendments shall normally be submitted in writing to the Secretary-General, who shall circulate copies to the delegations. As a general rule, no proposal shall be discussed or put to the vote at any meeting of the committee unless copies of it have been circulated to all delegations not later than the day preceding the meeting. The Chairman may, however, permit the discussion and consideration of amendments, or of motions as to procedure, even though such amendments and motions have not been circulated or have only been circulated the same day.

Decisions on competence

Rule 121 [79]

Subject to rule 119, any motion calling for a decision on the competence of the General Assembly or the committee to adopt a proposal submitted to it shall be put to the vote before a vote is taken on the proposal in question.

Withdrawal of motions

Rule 122 [80]

A motion may be withdrawn by its proposer at any time before voting on it has commenced, provided that the motion has not been amended. A motion thus withdrawn may be reintroduced by any member.

Reconsideration of proposals

Rule 123 [81]

When a proposal has been adopted or rejected, it may not be reconsidered at the same session unless the committee, by a two-thirds majority of the members present and voting, so decides. Permission to speak on a motion to reconsider shall be accorded only to two speakers opposing the motion, after which it shall be immediately put to the vote.

Voting

Voting rights

Rule 124 [82]

Each member of the committee shall have one vote.

Majority required

Rule 125 [85]

Decisions of committees shall be made by a majority of the members present and voting.

Meaning of the phrase 'members present and voting'

Rule 126 [86]

For the purposes of these rules, the phrase 'members present and voting' means members casting an affirmative or negative vote. Members which abstain from voting are considered as not voting.

Method of voting

Rule 127 [87]

(a) The committee shall normally vote by show of hands or by standing, but any representative may request a roll-call. The roll-call shall be taken in the English alphabetical order of the names of the members, beginning with the member whose name is drawn by lot by the Chairman. The name of each member shall be called in any roll-call, and its representative shall reply 'yes', 'no' or 'abstention'. The result of the voting shall be inserted in the record in the English alphabetical order of the names of the members.

(b) When the committee votes by mechanical means, a non-recorded vote shall replace a vote by show of hands or by standing and a recorded vote shall replace a roll-call vote. Any representative may request a recorded vote. In the case of a recorded vote, the committee shall, unless a representative requests otherwise, dispense with the procedure of calling out the names of the members; nevertheless, the result of the voting shall be inserted in the record in the same manner as that of a roll-call vote.

Conduct during voting

Rule 128 [88]

After the Chairman has announced the beginning of voting, no representative shall interrupt the voting except on a point of order in connection with the actual conduct of the voting. The Chairman may permit members to explain their votes, either before or after the voting, except when the vote is taken by secret ballot. The Chairman may limit the time to be allowed for such explanations. The Chairman shall not permit the proposer of a proposal or of an amendment to explain his vote on his own proposal or amendment.

Division of proposals and amendments

Rule 129 [89]

A representative may move that parts of a proposal or of an amendment should be voted on separately. If objection is made to the request for division, the motion for division shall be given only to two speakers in favour and two speakers against. If the motion for division is carried, those parts of the proposal or of the amendment which are approved shall then be put to the vote as a whole. If all operative parts of the proposal or of the amendment have been rejected, the proposal or the amendment shall be considered to have been rejected as a whole.

Voting on amendments

Rule 130 [90]

When an amendment is moved to a proposal, the amendment shall be voted on first. When two or more amendments are moved to a proposal, the committee shall first vote on the amendment furthest removed in substance from the original proposal and then on the amendment next furthest removed therefrom, and so on until all the amendments have been put to the vote. Where, however, the adoption of one amendment necessarily implies the rejection of another amendment, the latter amendment shall not be put to the vote. If one or more amendments are adopted, the amended proposal shall then be voted upon. A motion is considered an amendment to a proposal if it merely adds to, deletes from or revises part of the proposal.

Voting on proposals

Rule 131 [91]

If two or more proposals relate to the same question, the committee shall, unless it decides otherwise, vote on the proposals in the order in which they have been submitted. The committee may, after each vote on a proposal, decide whether to vote on the next proposal.

Elections

Rule 132 [93]

When only one person or Member is to be elected and no candidate obtains in the first ballot the majority required, a second ballot shall be taken, which shall be restricted to the two candidates obtaining the largest number of votes. If in the second ballot the votes are equally divided, and a majority is required, the Chairman shall decide between the candidates by drawing lots.

Equally divided votes

Rule 133 [95]

If a vote is equally divided on matters other than elections, the proposal shall be regarded as rejected.

XIV. Admission of new members to the United Nations

Applications

Rule 134

Any State which desires to become a Member of the United Nations shall submit an application to the Secretary-General. Such application shall contain a declaration, made in a formal instrument, that the State in question accepts the obligations contained in the Charter.

Notification of applications

Rule 135

The Secretary-General shall, for information, send a copy of the application to the General Assembly, or to the Members of the United Nations if the Assembly is not in session.

Consideration of applications and decision thereon

Rule 136

If the Security Council recommends the applicant State for membership, the General Assembly shall consider whether the applicant is a peace-loving State and is able and willing to carry out the obligations contained in the Charter and shall decide, by a two-thirds majority of the members present and voting, upon its application for membership.

Rule 137

If the Security Council does not recommend the applicant State for membership or postpones the consideration of the application, the General Assembly may, after full consideration of the special report of the Security Council, send the application back to the Council, together with a full record of the discussion in the Assembly, for further consideration and recommendation or report.

Notification of decision and effective date of membership

Rule 138

The Secretary-General shall inform the applicant State of the decision of the General Assembly. If the application is approved, membership shall become effective on the date on which the General Assembly takes its decision on the application.

XV. Elections to Principal Organs

General Provisions

Terms of office

Rule 139

Except as provided in rule 147, the term of office of members of Councils shall begin on 1 January following their election by the General Assembly and shall end on 31 December following the election of their successors.

By-elections

Rule 140

Should a member cease to belong to a Council before its term of office expires, a by-election shall be held separately at the next session of the General Assembly to elect a member for the unexpired term.

Secretary-General

Appointment of the Secretary-General

Rule 141

When the Security Council has submitted its recommendation on the appointment of the Secretary-General, the General Assembly shall consider the recommendation and vote upon it by secret ballot in private meeting.

Annual elections

Rule 142[1]

The General Assembly shall each year, in the course of its regular session, elect five non-permanent members of the Security Council for a term of two years.[2]

Qualifications for membership

Rule 143[3]

In the election of non-permanent members of the Security Council, due regard shall, in accordance with Article 23, paragraph 1, of the Charter, be specially paid, in the first instance, to the contribution of Members of the United Nations to the maintenance of international peace and security and to the other purposes of the Organization, and also to equitable geographical distribution.

Re-eligibility

Rule 144[4]

A retiring member of the Security Council shall not be eligible for immediate re-election.

Economic and Social Council

Annual elections

Rule 145[5]

The General Assembly shall each year, in the course of its regular session, elect eighteen members of the Economic and Social Council for a term of three years.[6]

Rule 146[7]

A retiring member of the Economic and Social Council shall be eligible for immediate re-election.

Trusteeship Council

Occasions for elections

Rule 147

When a Trusteeship Agreement has been approved and a Member of the United Nations has become an Administering Authority of a Trust Territory in accordance with Article 83 or Article 85 of the Charter, the General Assembly shall hold such election or elections to the Trusteeship Council as may be necessary, in accordance with Article 86. A Member or Members elected at any such election at a regular session shall take office immediately upon their election and shall complete their terms in accordance with the provisions of rule 139 as if they had begun their terms of office on 1 January following their election.

Terms of office and re-eligibility

Rule 148[8]

A non-administering member of the Trusteeship Council shall be elected for a term of three years and shall be eligible for immediate re-election.

Vacancies

Rule 149

At each session the General Assembly shall, in accordance with Article 86 of the Charter, elect members to fill any vacancies.

International Court of Justice

Method of election

Rule 150

The election of the members of the International Court of Justice shall take place in accordance with the Statute of the Court.

Rule 151

Any meeting of the General Assembly held in pursuance of the Statute of the International Court of Justice for the purpose of electing members of the court shall continue until as many candidates as are required for all the seats to be filled have obtained in one or more ballots an absolute majority of votes.

---

1 Rule based directly on a provision of the Charter (Art. 23, paral. 2, as amended under General Assembly resolution 1991 A (XVIII)).

2 Under paragraph 3 of resolution 1991 A (XVIII) of 17 December 1963, the General Assembly decided that "the ten non-permanent members of the Security Council shall be elected according to the following pattern:

"(a) Five from African and Asian States;

"(b) One from Eastern European States;

"(c) Two from Latin American States;

"(d) Two from Western European and other States".

3 Rule based directly on a provision of the Charter (Art. 23, para. 1).

4 Rule reproducing textually a provision of the Charter (Art. 23, para. 2, last sentence).

5 Rule based directly on a provision of the Charter (Art. 61, para. 2, as amended under General Assembly resolution 2847 (XXVI)).

6 Under parapgraph 4 of resolution 2847 (XXVI) of 20 December 1971, the General Assembly decided that "the members of the Economic and Social Council shall be elected according to the following pattern:

"(a) Fourteen members from African States;

"(b) Eleven members from Asian States;

"(c) Ten members from latin American States;

"(d) Thirteen members from Western European and other States;

"(e) Six members from socialist States of Eastern Europe".

7 Rule reproducing textually a provision of the Charter (Art. 62, para. 2, last sentence).

8 Rule based directly on a provision of the Charter (Art. 86, para. 1c).

XVI. Administrative and budgetary questions

General Provisions

Regulations for financial administration

Rule 152

The General Assembly shall establish regulations for the financial administration of the United Nations.[1]

Financial implications of resolutions

Rule 153

No resolution involving expenditure shall be recommended by a committee for approval by the General Assembly unless it is accompanied by an estimate of expenditures prepared by the Secretary-General. No resolution in respect of which expenditures are anticipated by the SecretaryGeneral shall be voted by the General Assembly until the Administrative and Budgetary Committee (Fifth Committee) has had an opportunity of stating the effect of the proposal upon the budget estimates of the United Nations.

Rule 154

The Secretary-General shall keep all committees informed of the detailed estimated cost of all resolutions which have been recommended by the committees for approval by the General Assembly.

Advisory Committee on administrative and budgetary questions

Appointment

Rule 155

The General Assembly shall appoint an Advisory Committee on Administrative and Budgetary Questions consisting of sixteen members, including at least three financial experts of recognized standing.

Composition

Rule 156

The members of the Advisory Committee on Administrative and Budgetary Questions, no two of whom shall be nationals of the same State, shall be selected on the basis of broad geographical representation, personal qualifications and experience and shall serve for a period of three years corresponding to three calendar years. Members shall retire by rotation and shall be eligible for reappointment. The three financial experts shall not retire simultaneously. The General Assembly shall appoint the members of the Advisory Committee at the regular session immediately preceding the expiration of the term of office of the members or, in case of vacancies, at the next session.

Functions

Rule 157

The Advisory Committee on Administrative and Budgetary Questions shall be responsible for expert examination of the programme budget of the United Nations and shall assist the Administrative and Budgetary Committee (Fifth Committee). At the beginning of each regular session at which the proposed programme budget for the following biennium is to be considered, it shall submit to the General Assembly a detailed report on the proposed programme budget for that biennium. It shall also submit, at such times as may be specified in the applicable provisions of the Financial Regulations and Rules of the United Nations,[2] a report on the accounts of the United Nations and all United Nations entities for which the Secretary-General has administrative responsibility. It shall examine on behalf of the General Assembly the administrative budgets of specialized agencies and proposals for financial and budgetary arrangements with such agencies. It shall perform such other duties as may be assigned to it under the Financial Regulations of the United Nations.

Committee on contributions

Appointment

Rule 158

The General Assembly shall appoint an expert Committee on Contributions consisting of eighteen members.

Composition

Rule 159

The members of the Committee on Contributions, no two of whom shall be nationals of the same State, shall be selected on the basis of broad geographical representation, personal qualifications and experience and shall serve for a period of three years corresponding to three calendar years. Members shall retire by rotation and shall be eligible for reappointment. The General Assembly shall appoint the members of the Committee on Contributions at the regular session immediately preceding the expiration of the term of office of the members or, in case of vacancies, at the next session.

Functions

Rule 160

The Committee on Contributions shall advise the General Assembly concerning the apportionment, under Article 17, paragraph 2, of the Charter, of the expenses of the Organization among Members, broadly according to capacity to pay. The scale of assessments, when once fixed by the General Assembly, shall not be subject to a general revision for at least three years unless it is clear that there have been substantial changes in relative capacity to pay. The Committee shall also advise the General Assembly on the assessments to be fixed for new Members, on appeals by members for a change of assessments and on the action to be taken with regard to the application of Article 19 of the Charter.

XVII. Subsidiary organs of the General Assembly

Establishment and rules of procedure

Rule 161

The General Assembly may establish such subsidiary organs as it deems necessary for the performance of its functions.[3] The rules relating to the procedure of committees of the General Assembly, as well as rules 45 and 60, shall apply to the procedure of any subsidiary organ unless the Assembly or the subsidiary organ decides otherwise.

XVIII. Interpretation and amendments

Italicized headings

Rule 162

The italicized headings of these rules, which were inserted for reference purposes only, shall be disregarded in the interpretation of the rules.

Method of amendment

Rule 163

These rules of procedure may be amended by a decision of the General Assembly, taken by a majority of the members present and voting, after a committee has reported on the proposed amendment.

[1] For the Financial Regulations of the United Nations, see ST/SGB/Financial Rules/1/Rev.3.

[2] ST/SGB/Financial Rules/1/Rev.3.

[3] Sentence reproducing textually a provision of the Charter (Art. 22).

Staff Regulations of the United Nations

Un Doc.: ST/SGB/Staff Regulations/Rev.23
Ref.: 590 (VI), 781 (VIII), 782 (VIII), 882 (IX), 887 (IX), 974 (X), 1095 (XI), 1225 (XII), 1234 (XII), 1295 (XIII), 1929 (XVIII), 2050 (XX), 2121 (XX), 2369 (XXII), 2481 (XXIII), 2485 (XXIII), 2742 (XXV), 2888 (XXVI), 2990 (XXVII), 3008 (XXVII), 3194 (XXVIII), 3353 (XXIX), 3358 B (XXIX), 31/141 B, 32/200, 32/450 B, 33/119, 33/433, 35/214, 36/459, 37/126, 37/235 C, 39/69, 39/236, 39/245, 40/467, 41/207, 41/209, 42/221, 42/225, 43/226, 44/185, 44/198, 45/241, 45/251, 45/259, 46/191, 47/216, 47/226, 48/224, 48/225, 49/222, 49/223.

Scope and purpose

The Staff Regulations embody the fundamental conditions of service and the basic rights, duties and obligations of the United Nations Secretariat. They represent the broad principles of personnel policy for the staffing and administration of the Secretariat. The Secretary-General, as the chief administrative officer, shall provide and enforce such staff rules consistent with these principles as he considers necessary.

Article I
Duties, obligations and privileges

Regulation 1.1: Members of the Secretariat are international civil servants. Their responsibilities are not national but exclusively international. By accepting appointment, they pledge themselves to discharge their functions and to regulate their conduct with the interests of the United Nations only in view.

Regulation 1.2: Staff members are subject to the authority of the Secretary-General and to assignment by him to any of the activities or offices of the United Nations. They are responsible to him in the exercise of their functions. The whole time of staff members shall be at the disposal of the Secretary-General. The Secretary-General shall establish a normal working week.

Regulation 1.3: In the performance of their duties members of the Secretariat shall neither seek nor accept instructions from any Government or from any other authority external to the Organization.

Regulation 1.4: Members of the Secretariat shall conduct themselves at all times in a manner befitting their status as international civil servants. They shall not engage in any activity that is incompatible with the proper discharge of their duties with the United Nations. They shall avoid any action and in particular any kind of public pronouncement that may adversely reflect on their status, or on the integrity, independence and impartiality that are required by that status. While they are not expected to give up their national sentiments or their political and religious convictions, they shall at all times bear in mind the reserve and tact incumbent upon them by reason of their international status.

Regulation 1.5: Staff members shall exercise the utmost discretion in regard to all matters of official business. They shall not communicate to any person any information known to them by reason of their official position that has not been made public, except in the course of their duties or by authorization of the Secretary-General. Nor shall they at any time use such information to private advantage. These obligations do not cease upon separation from the Secretariat.

Regulation 1.6: No staff member shall accept any honour, decoration, favour, gift or remuneration from any Government excepting for war service; nor shall a staff member accept any honour, decoration, favour, gift or remuneration from any source external to the Organization without first obtaining the approval of the Secretary-General. Approval shall be granted only in exceptional cases and where such acceptance is not incompatible with the terms of staff regulation 1.2 and with the individual's status as an international civil servant.

Regulation 1.7: Staff members may exercise the right to vote but shall not engage in any political activity that is inconsistent with or might reflect upon the independence and impartiality required by their status as international civil servants.

Regulation 1.8: The immunities and privileges attached to the United Nations by virtue of Article 105 of the Charter are conferred in the interests of the Organization. These privileges and immunities furnish no excuse to the staff members who enjoy them for non-performance of their private obligations or failure to observe laws and police regulations. In any case where these privileges and immunities arise, the staff member shall immediately report to the Secretary-General, with whom alone it rests to decide whether they shall be waived.

Regulation 1.9: Members of the Secretariat shall subscribe to the following oath or declaration:

> "I solemnly swear (undertake, affirm, promise) to exercise in all loyalty, discretion and conscience the functions entrusted to me as an international civil servant of the United Nations, to discharge these functions and regulate my conduct with the interests of the United Nations only in view, and not to seek or accept instructions in regard to the performance of my duties from any Government or other authority external to the Organization."

Regulation 1.10: The oath or declaration shall be made orally by the Secretary-General at a public meeting of the General Assembly. All other members of the Secretariat shall make the oath or declaration before the Secretary-General or his authorized representative.

Article II
Classification of posts and staff

Regulation 2.1: In conformity with principles laid down by the General Assembly, the Secretary-General shall make appropriate provision for the classification of posts and staff according to the nature of the duties and responsibilities required.

Article III
Salaries and related allowances

Regulation 3.1: Salaries of staff members shall be fixed by the Secretary-General in accordance with the provisions of annex I to the present Regulations.

Regulation 3.2: (*a*) The Secretary-General shall establish terms and conditions under which an education grant shall be available to a staff member serving outside his or her recognized home country whose dependent child is in full-time attendance at a school, university, or similar educational institution of a type that will, in the opinion of the Secretary-General, facilitate the child's reassimilation in the staff member's recognized home country. The grant shall be payable in respect of the child up to the end of the fourth year of post-secondary studies or the award of the first recognized degree, whichever is the earlier. The amount of the grant per scholastic year for each child shall be 75 per cent of the admissible educational expenses actually incurred, subject to a maximum grant as approved by the General Assembly. Travel costs of the child may also be paid for an outward and return journey once in each scholastic year between the educational institution and the duty station, except that in the case of staff members serving at designated duty stations where schools do not exist that provide schooling in the language or in the cultural tradition desired by staff members for their children, such travel costs may be paid twice in the year in which the staff member is not entitled to home leave. Such travel shall be by a route approved by the Secretary-General but not in an amount exceeding the cost of such a journey between the home country and the duty station;

(*b*) The Secretary-General shall also establish terms and conditions under which, at designated duty stations, an additional amount of 100 per cent of boarding costs subject to a maximum amount per year as approved by the General Assembly may be paid in respect of children in school attendance at the primary and secondary levels;

(*c*) The Secretary-General shall also establish terms and conditions under which an education grant shall be available to a staff member serving in a country whose language is different from his or her own and who is obliged to pay tuition for the teaching of the mother tongue to a dependent child attending a local school in which the instruction is given in a language other than his or her own;

(*d*) The Secretary-General shall also establish terms and conditions under which an education grant shall be available to a staff member whose child is unable, by reason of physical or mental disability, to attend a normal educational institution and therefore requires special teaching or training to prepare him or her for full integration into society or, while attending a normal educational institution, requires special teaching or training to assist him or her in overcoming the disability. The amount of this grant per year for each disabled child shall be equal to 100 per cent of the education expenses actually incurred, up to a maximum amount approved by the General Assembly;

(*e*) The Secretary-General may decide in each case whether the education grant shall extend to adopted children or stepchildren.

Regulation 3.3: (a) An assessment at the rates and under the conditions specified below shall be applied to the salaries and such other emoluments of staff members as are computed on the basis of salary, excluding post adjustments, provided that the Secretary-General may, where he deems it advisable, exempt from the assessment the salaries and emoluments of staff members engaged at locality rates;

(*b*) (i) The assessment shall be calculated at the following rates for staff members whose salary rates are set forth in paragraphs 1 and 3 of annex I to the present Regulations:

Total assessable payments (United States dollars)	Assessment (In percentages) Staff assessment rates for purposes of pensionable remuneration and pensions
First $ 15,000 per year	4
Next $ 10,000 per year	20
Next $ 10,000 per year	25
Next $ 20,000 per year	29
Next $ 20,000 per year	32
Next $ 20,000 per year	35
Next $ 30,000 per year	37
Remaining assessable payments	39

Staff assessment rates used in conjunction with gross base salaries

Total assessable payments (United States dollars)	Staff member with a dependent spouse or dependent child	Staff member with neither a dependent spouse nor a dependent child
First $ 15,000 per year	9.0	12.4
Next $ 5,000 per year	21.0	26.9
Next $ 5,000 per year	25.0	30.3
Next $ 5,000 per year	29.0	34.6
Next $ 5,000 per year	32.0	36.9
Next $ 10,000 per year	35.0	40.5
Next $ 10,000 per year	37.0	42.7
Next $ 10,000 per year	39.0	44.5
Next $ 10,000 per year	40.0	45.4
Next $ 15,000 per year	41.0	46.4
Next $ 20,000 per year	42.0	50.0
Remaining assessable payments	43.0	52.5

(ii) The assessment shall be calculated at the following rates for staff members whose salary rates are established under paragraph 7 of annex I to the present Regulations:

Total assessable payments (United States dollars)	Assessment (percentage)
First $ 2,000 per year	15
Next $ 2,000 per year	18
Next $ 2,000 per year	20
Next $ 2,000 per year	21
Next $ 4,000 per year	22
Next $ 4,000 per year	23
Next $ 4,000 per year	24
Next $ 6,000 per year	25
Next $ 6,000 per year	25.5
Next $ 6,000 per year	26
Next $ 8,000 per year	26.5
Next $ 8,000 per year	27
Next $ 8,000 per year	27.5
Next $ 8,000 per year	28
Remaining assessable payments	20

(iii) The Secretary-General shall determine which of the scales of assessment set out in subparagraphs (i) and (ii) above shall apply to each of the groups of personnel whose salary rates are established under paragraph 5 of annex I to the present Regulations;

(iv) In the case of staff members whose salary scales are established in currencies other than United States dollars, the relevant amounts to which the assessment applies shall be fixed at the local currency equivalent of the above-mentioned dollar amounts at the time the salary scales of the staff member concerned are approved;

(*c*) In the case of a person who is not employed by the United Nations for the whole of a calendar year or in cases where there is a change in the annual rate of payments made to a staff member, the rate of assessment shall be governed by the annual rate of each such payment made to him or her;

(*d*) The assessment computed under the foregoing provisions of the present regulation shall be collected by the United Nations by withholding it from payments. No part of the assessment so collected shall be refunded because of cessation of employment during the calendar year;

(*e*) Revenue derived from staff assessment not otherwise disposed of by specific resolution of the General Assembly shall be credited to the Tax Equalization Fund established by General Assembly resolution 973 A (X);

(*f*) Where a staff member is subject both to staff assessment under this plan and to national income taxation in respect of the salaries and emoluments paid to him or her by the United Nations, the Secretary-General is authorized to refund to him or her the amount of staff assessment collected from him or her provided that:

(i) The amount of such refund shall in no case exceed the amount of his or her income taxes paid and payable in respect of his or her United Nations income;

(ii) If the amount of such income taxes exceeds the amount of staff assessment, the Secretary-General may also pay to the staff member the amount of such excess;

(iii) Payments made in accordance with the provisions of the present regulation shall be charged to the Tax Equalization Fund;

(iv) A payment under the conditions prescribed in the three preceding subparagraphs is authorized in respect of dependency benefits and post adjustments, which are not subject to staff assessment but may be subject to national income taxation.

Regulation 3.4: (a) Staff members whose salary rates are set forth in paragraphs 1 and 3 of annex I to the present Regulations shall be entitled to receive dependency allowances for a dependent child, for a disabled child and for a secondary dependant at rates approved by the General Assembly as follows:

(i) The staff member shall receive an allowance for each dependent child, except that the allowance shall not be paid in respect of the first dependent child if the staff member has no dependent spouse, in which case the staff member shall be entitled to the dependency rate of staff assessment under subparagraph (b) (i) of regulation 3.3;

(ii) The staff member shall receive a special allowance for each disabled child. However, if the staff member has no dependent spouse and is entitled to the dependency rate of staff assessment under subparagraph (b) (i) of regulation 3.3 in respect of a disabled child, the allowance shall be the same as the allowance for a dependent child in (i) above;

(iii) Where there is no dependent spouse, a single annual allowance shall be paid for a secondary dependant in respect of either a dependent parent, a dependent brother or a dependent sister;

(*b*) If both husband and wife are staff members, one may claim, for dependent children, under subparagraph (a) (i) and (ii) above, in which case the other may claim only under subparagraph (a) (iii) above, if otherwise entitled;

(*c*) With a view to avoiding duplication of benefits and in order to achieve equality between staff members who receive dependency benefits under applicable laws in the form of governmental grants and staff members who do not receive such dependency benefits, the Secretary-General shall prescribe conditions under which the dependency allowance for a child specified in subparagraph (a) (i) above shall be payable only to the extent that the dependency benefits enjoyed by the staff member or his or her spouse under applicable laws amount to less than such a dependency allowance;

(*d*) Staff members whose salary rates are set by the Secretary-General under paragraph 5 or paragraph 6 of annex I to the present Regulations shall be entitled to receive dependency allowances at rates and under conditions determined by the Secretary-General, due regard being given to the circumstances in the locality in which the office is located;

(*e*) Claims for dependency allowances shall be submitted in writing and supported by evidence satisfactory to the Secretary-General. A separate claim for dependency allowances shall be made each year.

Article IV
Appointment and Promotion

Regulation 4.1: As stated in Article 101 of the Charter, the power of appointment of staff members rests with the Secretary-General. Upon appointment each staff member, including a staff member on secondment from government service, shall receive a letter of appointment in accordance with the provisions of annex II to the present Regulations and signed by the Secretary-General or by an official in the name of the Secretary-General.

Regulation 4.2: The paramount consideration in the appointment, transfer or promotion of the staff shall be the necessity for securing the highest standards of efficiency, competence and integrity. Due regard shall be paid to the importance of recruiting the staff on as wide a geographical basis as possible.

Regulation 4.3: In accordance with the principles of the Charter, selection of staff members shall be made without distinction as to race, sex or religion. So far as practicable, selection shall be made on a competitive basis.

Regulation 4.4: Subject to the provisions of Article 101, paragraph 3, of the Charter, and without prejudice to the recruitment of fresh talent at all levels, the fullest regard shall be had, in filling vacancies, to the requisite qualifications and experience of persons already in the service of the United Nations. This consideration shall also apply, on a reciprocal basis, to the specialized agencies brought into relationship with the United Nations.

Regulation 4.5: (*a*) Appointment of Under-Secretaries-General and of Assistant Secretaries-General shall normally be for a period of five years, subject to prolongation or renewal. Other staff members shall be granted either permanent or temporary appointments under such terms and conditions consistent with the present Regulations as the Secretary-General may prescribe;

(*b*) The Secretary-General shall prescribe which staff members are eligible for permanent appointments. The probationary period for granting or confirming a permanent appointment shall normally not exceed two years, provided that in individual cases the Secretary-General may extend the probationary period for not more than one additional year.

Regulation 4.6: The Secretary-General shall establish appropriate medical standards that staff members shall be required to meet before appointment.

Article V
Annual and special leave

Regulation 5.1: Staff members shall be allowed appropriate annual leave.

Regulation 5.2: Special leave may be authorized by the Secretary-General in exceptional cases.

Regulation 5.3: Eligible staff members shall be granted home leave once in every two years. However, in the case of service at designated duty stations having very difficult conditions of life and work, eligible staff members shall be granted home leave once in every twelve months. A staff member whose home country is the country of his or her official duty station or who continues to reside in his or her home country while performing his or her official duties shall not be eligible for home leave.

Article VI
Social security

Regulation 6.1: Provision shall be made for the participation of staff members in the United Nations Joint Staff Pension Fund in accordance with the regulations of that Fund.

Regulation 6.2: The Secretary-General shall establish a scheme of social security for the staff, including provisions for health protection, sick leave and maternity leave, and reasonable compensation in the event of illness, accident or death attributable to the performance of official duties on behalf of the United Nations.

Article VII
Travel and removal expenses

Regulation 7.1: Subject to conditions and definitions prescribed by the Secretary-General, the United Nations shall in appropriate cases pay the travel expenses of staff members, their spouses and dependent children.

Regulation 7.2: Subject to conditions and definitions prescribed by the Secretary-General, the United Nations shall pay removal costs for staff members.

Article VIII
Staff relations

Regulation 8.1: (*a*) The Secretary-General shall establish and maintain continuous contact and communication with the staff in order to ensure the effective participation of the staff in identifying, examining and resolving issues relating to staff welfare, including conditions of work, general conditions of life and other personnel policies;

(*b*) Staff representative bodies shall be established and shall be entitled to initiate proposals to the Secretary-General for the purpose set forth in subparagraph (a) above. They shall be organized in such a way as to afford equitable representation to all staff members, by means of elections that shall take place at least biennially under electoral regulations drawn up by the respective staff representative body and agreed to by the Secretary-General;

(*c*) Cancelled.

Regulation 8.2: The Secretary-General shall establish joint staff/management machinery at both local and Secretariat-wide levels to advise him regarding personnel policies and general questions of staff welfare as provided in regulation 8.1.

Article IX
Separation from service

Regulation 9.1: (*a*) The Secretary-General may terminate the appointment of a staff member who holds a permanent appointment and whose probationary period has been completed, if the necessities of the service require abolition of the post or reduction of the staff, if the services of the individual concerned prove unsatisfactory, or if he or she is, for reasons of health, incapacitated for further service;

The Secretary-General may also, giving his reasons therefor, terminate the appointment of a staff member who holds a permanent appointment:

(i) If the conduct of the staff member indicates that the staff member does not meet the highest standards of integrity required by Article 101, paragraph 3, of the Charter;

(ii) If facts anterior to the appointment of the staff member and relevant to his suitability come to light that, if they had been known at the time of his appointment, should, under the standards established in the Charter, have precluded his appointment;

No termination under subparagraphs (i) and (ii) shall take place until the matter has been considered and reported on by a special advisory board appointed for that purpose by the Secretary-General;

Finally, the Secretary-General may terminate the appointment of a staff member who holds a permanent appointment if such action would be in the interest of the good administration of the Organization and in accordance with the standards of the Charter, provided that the action is not contested by the staff member concerned;

(*b*) The Secretary-General may terminate the appointment of a staff member with a fixed-term appointment prior to the expiration date for any of the reasons specified in subparagraph (a) above, or for such other reason as may be specified in the letter of appointment;

(*c*) In the case of all other staff members, including staff members serving a probationary period for a permanent appointment, the Secretary-General may at any time terminate the appointment if, in his opinion, such action would be in the interest of the United Nations.

Regulation 9.2: Staff members may resign from the Secretariat upon giving the Secretary-General the notice required under the terms of their appointment.

Regulation 9.3: (*a*) If the Secretary-General terminates an appointment the staff member shall be given such notice and such indemnity payment as may be applicable under the Staff Regulations and Staff Rules. Payments of termination indemnity shall be made by the Secretary-General in accordance with the rates and conditions specified in annex III to the present Regulations;

(*b*) The Secretary-General may, where the circumstances warrant and he considers it justified, pay to a staff member terminated under the final paragraph of staff regulation 9.1 (a) a termination indemnity payment not more than 50 per cent higher than that which would otherwise be payable under the Staff Regulations.

Regulation 9.4: The Secretary-General shall establish a scheme for the payment of repatriation grants within the maximum rates and under the conditions specified in annex IV to the present Regulations.

Regulation 9.5: Staff members shall not be retained in active service beyond the age of sixty years or, if appointed on or after 1 January 1990, beyond the age of sixty-two years. The Secretary-General may, in the interest of the Organization, extend this age limit in exceptional cases.

Article X
Disciplinary measures

Regulation 10.1: The Secretary-General may establish administrative machinery with staff participation which will be available to advise him in disciplinary cases.

Regulation 10.2: The Secretary-General may impose disciplinary measures on staff members whose conduct is unsatisfactory.

He may summarily dismiss a member of the staff for serious misconduct.

Article XI
Appeals

Regulation 11.1: The Secretary-General shall establish administrative machinery with staff participation to advise him in case of any appeal by staff members against an administrative decision alleging the non-observance of their terms of appointment, including all pertinent regulations and rules.

Regulation 11.2: The United Nations Administrative Tribunal shall, under conditions prescribed in its statute, hear and pass judgement upon applications from staff members alleging non-observance of their terms of appointment, including all pertinent regulations and rules.

Article XII
General Provisions

Regulation 12.1: The present Regulations may be supplemented or amended by the General Assembly, without prejudice to the acquired rights of staff members.

Regulation 12.2: Such staff rules and amendments as the Secretary-General may make to implement the present Regulations shall be provisional until the requirements of regulations 12.3 and 12.4 below have been met.

Regulation 12.3: The full text of provisional staff rules and amendments shall be reported annually to the General Assembly. Should the Assembly find that a provisional rule and/or amendment is inconsistent with the intent and purpose of the Regulations, it may direct that the rule and/or amendment be withdrawn or modified.

Regulation 12.4: The provisional rules and amendments reported by the Secretary-General, taking into account such modifications and/or deletions that may be directed by the General Assembly, shall enter into full force and effect on 1 January following the year in which the report is made to the Assembly.

Regulation 12.5: Staff rules shall not give rise to acquired rights within the meaning of regulation 12.1 while they are provisional.

[...]

153 (II). Composition of the Secretariat and the Principle of Geographical Distribution

Committee: 5
Vote: unanimous
Ref.: 45/239A, 44/185A, 43/224A, 42/220A, 41/206A, 40/258A, 39/245, 38/231, 31/26, 3417(XXX), 3007(XXVII), 2736(XXV), 2539(XXIV), 2480(XXIII), 2369(XXII), 2359(XXII), 2241(XXI), 1928(XVIII), 1852(XVII), 1559(XV), 1436(XIV), 1294(XIII), 1226(XII), 1097(XI), 886(IX), 784(VIII), 233(III), 13(I)

Whereas it is desirable to attain a balanced geographical distribution in the composition of the Secretariat, thus improving the present distribution, which results from unavoidable difficulties encountered in the initial stages of organization;

Whereas the above consideration does not conflict with the paramount consideration of employment of the staff, as laid down in Article 101, paragraph 3, of the Charter, namely, the necessity of securing the highest standard of efficiency, competence and integrity;

Whereas, in view of its international character and in order to avoid undue predominance of national practices, the policies and administrative methods of the Secretariat should reflect, and profit to the highest degree from, assets of the various cultures and the technical competence of all Member nations,

The General Assembly

1. *Reaffirms* the principle of securing the highest standard of efficiency, competence and integrity in the staff of the Secretariat; as well as the importance of recruiting the staff on as wide a geographical basis as possible, and

2. *Requests* the Secretary-General

(*a*) To examine the recruitment policy that has been followed to date with a view to improving the present geographical distribution of the posts within the various Departments;

(*b*) To take, as soon as possible, the necessary steps with a view to engaging staff members from those countries which have not yet any of their nationals in the Secretariat;

(*c*) To review, in accordance with the recommendations of the Advisory Committee on Administrative and Budgetary Questions, the qualifications, background and experience of the present members of the staff, with a view to replacing those who do not reach the high standards fixed by the Charter;

(*d*) To take all practicable steps to ensure the improvement of the present geographical distribution of the staff, including the issuance of such rules and regulations as may be necessary to comply with the principles of the Charter as elaborated in this resolution;

(*e*) To present to the next regular session of the General Assembly a report of the action taken under this resolution.

Hundred and fifteenth plenary meeting
15 November 1947

258 (III). Reparation for Injuries Incurred in the Service of the United Nations

Committee: 6
Vote: unanimous

Whereas the series of tragic events which have lately befallen agents of the United Nations engaged in the performance of their duties raises, with greater urgency than ever, the question of the arrangements to be made by the United Nations with a view to ensuring to its agents the fullest measures of protection in the future and ensuring that reparation be made for the injuries suffered,[1] and

Whereas it is highly desirable that the Secretary General should be able to act, without question, as efficaciously as possible with a view to obtaining any reparation due,

The General Assembly

Decides to submit the following legal questions to the International Court of Justice for an advisory opinion:

"I. In the event of an agent of the United Nations in the Performance of his duties suffering injury in circumstances involving the responsibility of a State, has the United Nations, as an Organization, the capacity to bring an international claim against the responsible *de jure* or *de facto* Government with a view to obtaining the reparation due in respect of the damage caused (a) to the United Nations, (b) to the victim or to persons entitled through him?

"II. In the event of an affirmative reply on point I (b), how is action by the United Nations to be reconciled with such rights as may be possessed by the State of which the victim is a national?"

Instructs the Secretary-General, after the Court has given its opinion, to prepare proposals in the light of that opinion, and to submit them to the General Assembly at its next regular session.

Hundred and sixty-ninth plenary meeting
3 December 1948

365 (IV). Reparation for Injuries Incurred in the Service of the United Nations

Committee: 6
Vote: 48 - 5 - 1
Ref.: 690(VII), 476(V), 458(V)

The General Assembly,

Considering its request to the International Court of Justice for an advisory opinion, formulated in resolution 258 (III) of 3 December 1948 concerning reparation for injuries incurred in the service of the United Nations,

Having regarded to the advisory opinion[2] rendered by the International Court of Justice on 11 April 1949,

Considering that it is highly desirable that reparation be secured for injuries incurred in the service of the United Nations,

Considering that the Secretary-General has submitted in his report[3] of 23 August 1949 a number of proposals relating to the aforementioned advisory opinion,

Consequently

1. *Authorizes* the Secretary-General, in accordance with his proposals, to bring an international claim against the Government of a State, Member or non-member of the United Nations, alleged to be responsible, with a view to obtaining the reparation due in respect of the damage caused to the United Nations and in respect of the damage caused to the victim or to persons entitled through him and, if necessary, to submit to arbitration, under appropriate procedures, such claims as cannot be settled by negotiation;

2. *Authorizes* the Secretary-General to take the steps and to negotiate in each particular case the agreements necessary to reconcile action by the United Nations with such rights as may be possessed by the State of which the victim is a national;

3. *Requests* the Secretary-General to submit an annual report to subsequent sessions of the General Assembly on the status of claims for injuries incurred in the service of the United Nations, and proceedings in connexion with them.

262nd plenary meeting
1 December 1949

49/59. Convention on the Safety of United Nations and Associated Personnel

Committee: 6
Vote: Adopted without a vote

The General Assembly,

Considering that the codification and progressive development of international law contributes to the implementation of the purposes and principles set forth in Articles 1 and 2 of the Charter of the United Nations,

Gravely concerned at the increasing number of attacks on United Nations and associated personnel that have caused death or serious injury,

Bearing in mind that United Nations operations may be conducted in situations that entail risk to the safety of United Nations and associated personnel,

Recognizing the need to strengthen and to keep under review arrangements for the protection of United Nations and associated personnel,

Recalling its resolution 48/37 of 9 December 1993, by which it established the *Ad Hoc Committee* on the Elaboration of an International Convention Dealing with the Safety and Security of United Nations and Associated Personnel, with particular reference to responsibility for attacks on such personnel,

Taking into account the report of the *Ad Hoc Committee,*[4] in particular the revised negotiating text resulting from the work of the *Ad Hoc Committee,*

Recalling its decision, in accordance with the recommendation of the *Ad Hoc Committee*, to re-establish, at its current session, a working group within the framework of the Sixth Committee to continue consideration of the revised negotiating text and of proposals relating thereto,

Having considered the text of the draft convention prepared by the working group[5] and submitted to the Sixth Committee for consideration with a view to its adoption,

1. *Adopts* and opens for signature and ratification, acceptance or approval, or for accession, the Convention on the Safety of United Nations and Associated Personnel, the text of which is annexed to the present resolution;

2. *Urges* States to take all appropriate measures to ensure the safety and security of United Nations and associated personnel within their territory;

---

1 See document A/674; Appendix 7, p. 434.

2 See *Official Records of the fourth session of the General Assembly, Annex to the Sixth Committee,* document A/955.

3 *Ibid.*

4 *Official Records of the General Assembly, Forty-ninth Session, Supplement No. 22* (A/49/22).

5 A/C.6/49/L.4, annex.

3. *Recommends* that the safety and security of United Nations and associated personnel be kept under continuing review by all relevant bodies of the Organization;

4. *Underlines* the importance it attaches to the speedy conclusion of a comprehensive review of arrangements for compensation for death, disability, injury or illness attributable to peace-keeping service, with a view to developing equitable and appropriate arrangements and to ensuring expeditious reimbursement.

84th plenary meeting
9 December 1994

Annex

Convention on the Safety of United Nations and Associated Personnel

The States Parties to this Convention,

Deeply concerned over the growing number of deaths and injuries resulting from deliberate attacks against United Nations and associated personnel,

Bearing in mind that attacks against, or other mistreatment of, personnel who act on behalf of the United Nations are unjustifiable and unacceptable, by whomsoever committed,

Recognizing that United Nations operations are conducted in the common interest of the international community and in accordance with the principles and purposes of the Charter of the United Nations,

Acknowledging the important contribution that United Nations and associated personnel make in respect of United Nations efforts in the fields of preventive diplomacy, peacemaking, peace-keeping, peace-building and humanitarian and other operations,

Conscious of the existing arrangements for ensuring the safety of United Nations and associated personnel, including the steps taken by the principal organs of the United Nations, in this regard,

Recognizing none the less that existing measures of protection for United Nations and associated personnel are inadequate,

Acknowledging that the effectiveness and safety of United Nations operations are enhanced where such operations are conducted with the consent and cooperation of the host State,

Appealing to all States in which United Nations and associated personnel are deployed and to all others on whom such personnel may rely, to provide comprehensive support aimed at facilitating the conduct and fulfilling the mandate of United Nations operations,

Convinced that there is an urgent need to adopt appropriate and effective measures for the prevention of attacks committed against United Nations and associated personnel and for the punishment of those who have committed such attacks,

Have agreed as follows:

Article 1
Definitions

For the purposes of this Convention:

(*a*) "United Nations personnel" means:

(i) Persons engaged or deployed by the Secretary-General of the United Nations as members of the military, police or civilian components of a United Nations operation;

(ii) Other officials and experts on mission of the United Nations or its specialized agencies or the International Atomic Energy Agency who are present in an official capacity in the area where a United Nations operation is being conducted;

(*b*) "Associated personnel" means:

(i) Persons assigned by a Government or an intergovernmental organization with the agreement of the competent organ of the United Nations;

(ii) Persons engaged by the Secretary-General of the United Nations or by a specialized agency or by the International Atomic Energy Agency;

(iii) Persons deployed by a humanitarian non-governmental organization or agency under an agreement with the Secretary-General of the United Nations or with a specialized agency or with the International Atomic Energy Agency, to carry out activities in support of the fulfilment of the mandate of a United Nations operation;

(*c*) "United Nations operation" means an operation established by the competent organ of the United Nations in accordance with the Charter of the United Nations and conducted under United Nations authority and control:

(i) Where the operation is for the purpose of maintaining or restoring international peace and security; or

(ii) Where the Security Council or the General Assembly has declared, for the purposes of this Convention, that there exists an exceptional risk to the safety of the personnel participating in the operation;

(*d*) "Host State" means a State in whose territory a United Nations operation is conducted;

(*e*) "Transit State" means a State, other than the host State, in whose territory United Nations and associated personnel or their equipment are in transit or temporarily present in connection with a United Nations operation.

Article 2
Scope of application

1. This Convention applies in respect of United Nations and associated personnel and United Nations operations, as defined in article 1.

2. This Convention shall not apply to a United Nations operation authorized by the Security Council as an enforcement action under Chapter VII of the Charter of the United Nations in which any of the personnel are engaged as combatants against organized armed forces and to which the law of international armed conflict applies.

Article 3
Identification

1. The military and police components of a United Nations operation and their vehicles, vessels and aircraft shall bear distinctive identification. Other personnel, vehicles, vessels and aircraft involved in the United Nations operation shall be appropriately identified unless otherwise decided by the Secretary-General of the United Nations.

2. All United Nations and associated personnel shall carry appropriate identification documents.

Article 4
Agreements on the status of the operation

The host State and the United Nations shall conclude as soon as possible an agreement on the status of the United Nations operation and all personnel engaged in the operation including, *inter alia*, provisions on privileges and immunities for military and police components of the operation.

Article 5
Transit

A transit State shall facilitate the unimpeded transit of United Nations and associated personnel and their equipment to and from the host State.

Article 6
Respect for laws and regulations

1. Without prejudice to such privileges and immunities as they may enjoy or to the requirements of their duties, United Nations and associated personnel shall:

(*a*) Respect the laws and regulations of the host State and the transit State; and

(*b*) Refrain from any action or activity incompatible with the impartial and international nature of their duties.

2. The Secretary-General of the United Nations shall take all appropriate measures to ensure the observance of these obligations.

Article 7
Duty to ensure the safety and security of United Nations and associated personnel

1. United Nations and associated personnel, their equipment and premises shall not be made the object of attack or of any action that prevents them from discharging their mandate.

2. States Parties shall take all appropriate measures to ensure the safety and security of United Nations and associated personnel. In particular, States Parties shall take all appropriate steps to protect United Nations and associated personnel who are deployed in their territory from the crimes set out in article 9.

3. States Parties shall cooperate with the United Nations and other States Parties, as appropriate, in the implementation of this Convention, particularly in any case where the host State is unable itself to take the required measures.

Article 8
Duty to release or return United Nations and associated personnel captured or detained

Except as otherwise provided in an applicable status-of-forces agreement, if United Nations or associated personnel are captured or detained in the course of the performance of their duties and their identification has been established, they shall not be subjected to interrogation and they shall be promptly released and returned to United Nations or other appropriate authorities. Pending their release such personnel shall be treated in accordance with universally recognized standards of human rights and the principles and spirit of the Geneva Conventions of 1949.

Article 9
Crimes against United Nations and associated personnel

1. The intentional commission of:

(*a*) A murder, kidnapping or other attack upon the person or liberty of any United Nations or associated personnel;

(*b*) A violent attack upon the official premises, the private accommodation or the means of transportation of any United Nations or associated personnel likely to endanger his or her person or liberty;

(*c*) A threat to commit any such attack with the objective of compelling a physical or juridical person to do or to refrain from doing any act;

(*d*) An attempt to commit any such attack; and

(*e*) An act constituting participation as an accomplice in any such attack, or in an attempt to commit such attack, or in organizing or ordering others to commit such attack,

shall be made by each State Party a crime under its national law.

2. Each State Party shall make the crimes set out in paragraph 1 punishable by appropriate penalties which shall take into account their grave nature.

Article 10
Establishment of jurisdiction

1. Each State Party shall take such measures as may be necessary to establish its jurisdiction over the crimes set out in article 9 in the following cases:

(*a*) When the crime is committed in the territory of that State or on board a ship or aircraft registered in that State;

(*b*) When the alleged offender is a national of that State.

2. A State Party may also establish its jurisdiction over any such crime when it is committed:

(*a*) By a stateless person whose habitual residence is in that State; or

(*b*) With respect to a national of that State; or

(*c*) In an attempt to compel that State to do or to abstain from doing any act.

3. Any State Party which has established jurisdiction as mentioned in paragraph 2 shall notify the Secretary-General of the United Nations. If such State Party subsequently rescinds that jurisdiction, it shall notify the Secretary-General of the United Nations.

4. Each State Party shall take such measures as may be necessary to establish its jurisdiction over the crimes set out in article 9 in cases where the alleged offender is present in its territory and it does not extradite such person pursuant to article 15 to any of the States Parties which have established their jurisdiction in accordance with paragraph 1 or 2.

5. This Convention does not exclude any criminal jurisdiction exercised in accordance with national law.

Article 11
Prevention of crimes against United Nations and associated personnel

States Parties shall cooperate in the prevention of the crimes set out in article 9, particularly by:

(*a*) Taking all practicable measures to prevent preparations in their respective territories for the commission of those crimes within or outside their territories; and

(*b*) Exchanging information in accordance with their national law and coordinating the taking of administrative and other measures as appropriate to prevent the commission of those crimes.

Article 12
Communication of information

1. Under the conditions provided for in its national law, the State Party in whose territory a crime set out in article 9 has been committed shall, if it has reason to believe that an alleged offender has fled from its territory, communicate to the Secretary-General of the United Nations and, directly or through the Secretary-General, to the State or States concerned all the pertinent facts regarding the crime committed and all available information regarding the identity of the alleged offender.

2. Whenever a crime set out in article 9 has been committed, any State Party which has information concerning the victim and circumstances of the crime shall endeavour to transmit such information, under the conditions provided for in its national law, fully and promptly to the Secretary-General of the United Nations and the State or States concerned.

Article 13
Measures to ensure prosecution or extradition

1. Where the circumstances so warrant, the State Party in whose territory the alleged offender is present shall take the appropriate measures under its national law to ensure that person's presence for the purpose of prosecution or extradition.

2. Measures taken in accordance with paragraph 1 shall be notified, in conformity with national law and without delay, to the Secretary-General of the United Nations and, either directly or through the Secretary-General, to:

(*a*) The State where the crime was committed;

(*b*) The State or States of which the alleged offender is a national or, if such person is a stateless person, in whose territory that person has his or her habitual residence;

(*c*) The State or States of which the victim is a national; and

(*d*) Other interested States.

Article 14
Prosecution of alleged offenders

The State Party in whose territory the alleged offender is present shall, if it does not extradite that person, submit, without exception whatsoever and without undue delay, the case to its competent authorities for the purpose of prosecution, through proceedings in accordance with the law of that State. Those authorities shall take their decision in the same manner as in the case of an ordinary offence of a grave nature under the law of that State.

Article 15
Extradition of alleged offenders

1. To the extent that the crimes set out in article 9 are not extraditable offences in any extradition treaty existing between States Parties, they shall be deemed to be included as such therein. States Parties

undertake to include those crimes as extraditable offences in every extradition treaty to be concluded between them.

2. If a State Party which makes extradition conditional on the existence of a treaty receives a request for extradition from another State Party with which it has no extradition treaty, it may at its option consider this Convention as the legal basis for extradition in respect of those crimes. Extradition shall be subject to the conditions provided in the law of the requested State.

3. States Parties which do not make extradition conditional on the existence of a treaty shall recognize those crimes as extraditable offences between themselves subject to the conditions provided in the law of the requested State.

4. Each of those crimes shall be treated, for the purposes of extradition between States Parties, as if it had been committed not only in the place in which it occurred but also in the territories of the States Parties which have established their jurisdiction in accordance with paragraph 1 or 2 of article 10.

Article 16
Mutual assistance in criminal matters

1. States Parties shall afford one another the greatest measure of assistance in connection with criminal proceedings brought in respect of the crimes set out in article 9, including assistance in obtaining evidence at their disposal necessary for the proceedings. The law of the requested State shall apply in all cases.

2. The provisions of paragraph 1 shall not affect obligations concerning mutual assistance embodied in any other treaty.

Article 17
Fair treatment

1. Any person regarding whom investigations or proceedings are being carried out in connection with any of the crimes set out in article 9 shall be guaranteed fair treatment, a fair trial and full protection of his or her rights at all stages of the investigations or proceedings.

2. Any alleged offender shall be entitled:

(*a*) To communicate without delay with the nearest appropriate representative of the State or States of which such person is a national or which is otherwise entitled to protect that person's rights or, if such person is a stateless person, of the State which, at that person's request, is willing to protect that person's rights; and

(*b*) To be visited by a representative of that State or those States.

Article 18
Notification of outcome of proceedings

The State Party where an alleged offender is prosecuted shall communicate the final outcome of the proceedings to the Secretary-General of the United Nations, who shall transmit the information to other States Parties.

Article 19
Dissemination

The States Parties undertake to disseminate this Convention as widely as possible and, in particular, to include the study thereof, as well as relevant provisions of international humanitarian law, in their programmes of military instruction.

Article 20
Savings clauses

Nothing in this Convention shall affect:

(*a*) The applicability of international humanitarian law and universally recognized standards of human rights as contained in international instruments in relation to the protection of United Nations operations and United Nations and associated personnel or the responsibility of such personnel to respect such law and standards;

(*b*) The rights and obligations of States, consistent with the Charter of the United Nations, regarding the consent to entry of persons into their territories;

(*c*) The obligation of United Nations and associated personnel to act in accordance with the terms of the mandate of a United Nations operation;

(*d*) The right of States which voluntarily contribute personnel to a United Nations operation to withdraw their personnel from participation in such operation; or

(*e*) The entitlement to appropriate compensation payable in the event of death, disability, injury or illness attributable to peace-keeping service by persons voluntarily contributed by States to United Nations operations.

Article 21
Right of self-defence

Nothing in this Convention shall be construed so as to derogate from the right to act in self-defence.

Article 22
Dispute settlement

1. Any dispute between two or more States Parties concerning the interpretation or application of this Convention which is not settled by negotiation shall, at the request of one of them, be submitted to arbitration. If within six months from the date of the request for arbitration the parties are unable to agree on the organization of the arbitration, any one of those parties may refer the dispute to the International Court of Justice by application in conformity with the Statute of the Court.

2. Each State Party may at the time of signature, ratification, acceptance or approval of this Convention or accession thereto declare that it does not consider itself bound by all or part of paragraph 1. The other States Parties shall not be bound by paragraph 1 or the relevant part thereof with respect to any State Party which has made such a reservation.

3. Any State Party which has made a reservation in accordance with paragraph 2 may at any time withdraw that reservation by notification to the Secretary-General of the United Nations.

Article 23
Review meetings

At the request of one or more States Parties, and if approved by a majority of States Parties, the Secretary-General of the United Nations shall convene a meeting of the States Parties to review the implementation of the Convention, and any problems encountered with regard to its application.

Article 24
Signature

This Convention shall be open for signature by all States, until 31 December 1995, at United Nations Headquarters in New York.

Article 25
Ratification, acceptance or approval

This Convention is subject to ratification, acceptance or approval. Instruments of ratification, acceptance or approval shall be deposited with the Secretary-General of the United Nations.

Article 26
Accession

This Convention shall be open for accession by any State. The instruments of accession shall be deposited with the Secretary-General of the United Nations.

Article 27
Entry into force

1. This Convention shall enter into force thirty days after twenty-two instruments of ratification, acceptance, approval or accession have been deposited with the Secretary-General of the United Nations.

2. For each State ratifying, accepting, approving or acceding to the Convention after the deposit of the twenty-second instrument of ratification, acceptance, approval or accession, the Convention shall

enter into force on the thirtieth day after the deposit by such State of its instrument of ratification, acceptance, approval or accession.

Article 28
Denunciation

1. A State Party may denounce this Convention by written notification to the Secretary-General of the United Nations.

2. Denunciation shall take effect one year following the date on which notification is received by the Secretary-General of the United Nations.

Article 29
Authentic texts

The original of this Convention, of which the Arabic, Chinese, English, French, Russian and Spanish texts are equally authentic, shall be deposited with the Secretary-General of the United Nations, who shall send certified copies thereof to all States.

45/264. Restructuring and Revitalization of the United Nations in the Economic, Social and Related Fields

Committee: -
Vote: Adopted without a vote
Ref.: 48/218, 45/177, 44/103, 43/174, 39/88, 38/141, 36/187, 34/215, 34/214, 34/213, 34/21234/206, , 33/202, 2188(XXI), 2089(XX), 1675(XVI), 732(VIII)

The General Assembly,

Reaffirming its resolution 45/177 of 19 December 1990, on the restructuring and revitalization of the United Nations in the economic and social fields, and other relevant resolutions,

1. *Adopts* the text contained in the annex to the present resolution, including the basic principles and guidelines, goals and measures, as well as issues to be addressed in the future, for the restructuring and revitalization of the United Nations in the economic, social and related fields;

2. *Requests* the Secretary-General to implement the recommendations addressed to him in the annex to the present resolution and to report thereon as proposed;

3. *Invites* the specialized agencies, organs, organizations and bodies of the United Nations system to implement, as appropriate, those recommendations within their respective spheres of competence;

4. *Decides* to include in the provisional agenda of its forty-sixth session an item entitled "Restructuring and revitalization of the United Nations in the economic, social and related fields".

75th plenary meeting
13 May 1991

Annex

Restructuring and Revitalization of the United Nations in the Economic, Social and Related Fields

1. Given the role of the United Nations in the economic, social and related sectors as set out in the relevant provisions of the Charter of the United Nations, including Article 55, the overall objective of the restructuring and revitalization of the United Nations in the economic, social and related fields is defined in resolution 45/177 adopted by the General Assembly on 19 December 1990. In paragraph 3 of the resolution, the Assembly "stresses the need for more effective and efficient functioning of the intergovernmental machinery of the United Nations system in the economic, social and related fields in order to be more responsive to the needs of enhancing international economic cooperation and promoting the development of the developing countries". The restructuring and revitalization process should also take account of Assembly resolutions 32/197 of 20 December 1977 and 41/213 of 19 December 1986, and other relevant resolutions.

2. The objective in paragraph 1 of the present annex needs to be addressed through a concerted, deliberate and continuing process of restructuring and revitalization of the United Nations, encompassing all organs and bodies concerned in the economic, social and related fields. Such an approach should ensure orderly restructuring and revitalization of the economic, social and related fields and enhance the flexibility and adaptability of the Organization in the performance of its functions, and its ability to address the most urgent tasks and new demands, and should bear in mind the need for an efficient and effective United Nations system to deal with a number of global challenges in the economic, social and related fields in a world of growing interdependence, as well as enhance the interest taken by the international community in the work of the Organization. Thus it would also enhance the effectiveness and efficiency of the Organization.

I. Basic principles and guidelines for the restructuring and revitalization of the United Nations in the economic, social and related fields

3. The deliberations and decisions of the restructuring and revitalization process should be predicated on the following basic principles and guidelines, in order to ensure a successful outcome:

(*a*) Restructuring is primarily an intergovernmental responsibility and needs to be pursued in this context. The Secretary-General, in fulfilment of his responsibility as the chief administrative officer of the United Nations, in accordance with the provisions of the Charter, is requested to assist and cooperate in this regard;

(*b*) The process of restructuring and revitalization of the United Nations in the economic, social and related fields should be in accordance with the mandate set forth in General Assembly resolution 45/177, the provisions agreed upon at the resumed forty-fifth session of the Assembly, and other relevant resolutions;

(*c*) Political will is an essential prerequisite for enhancing international cooperation. The socio-economic goals of the United Nations will remain unachievable in the absence of the requisite political will of all States;

(*d*) The current restructuring and revitalization process should promote the achievement of the objectives and priorities of the United Nations in the economic, social and related fields as set forth in the relevant resolutions of the General Assembly;

(*e*) The restructuring and revitalization of the United Nations in the economic, social and related fields should aim at achieving greater complementarity between the bodies and organs of the United Nations with the General Assembly, while ensuring the latter's position as a principal organ of the United Nations;

(*f*) The restructuring and revitalization of the United Nations in the economic, social and related fields should preserve the democratic principles which underpin the decision-making process of the United Nations;

(*g*) Transparency and openness need to be preserved and strengthened in the functioning of the United Nations system in the economic, social and related fields;

(*h*) Restructuring and revitalization should be examined and pursued while ensuring the most efficient and effective use of the financial and human resources of the United Nations system in the economic, social and related fields;

(*i*) The ongoing process of revitalization of the Economic and Social Council, on the basis of all its relevant resolutions, as appropriate, remains valid.

II. Goals of the resumed forty-fifth session of the General Assembly

4. The reconvened session is a step in the process of restructuring and revitalization of the United Nations system in the economic, social and related fields, on the basis of the basic principles and guidelines set out in paragraph 3 of the present annex. The session is aimed at reaching agreement, *inter alia*, on the role and functioning of the Economic and Social Council in order to:

(*a*) Enable the Economic and Social Council to discharge the responsibilities entrusted to it by the Charter by enhancing its role as a central forum for major economic, social and related issues and policies and its coordinating functions relating to the United Nations system in the economic, social and related fields;

(*b*) Improve its effectiveness and efficiency in the consideration of and action on the reports of its subsidiary bodies and other relevant reports;

(*c*) Ensure greater complementarity with the work of the General Assembly, in accordance with Article 60 of the Charter;

(*d*) Avoid duplication with other organs of the United Nations;

(*e*) Follow an integrated approach to policy and programme aspects of the economic and social issues.

In addition, the session agreed on the agenda and the timetable for the continuation of the process of restructuring and revitalization of the United Nations in the economic, social and related fields, as specified in section IV of the present annex.

III. Measures for the restructuring and revitalization of the Economic and Social Council

5. The following measures are adopted:

(*a*) The continued implementation of the relevant resolutions of the General Assembly as well as Economic and Social Council resolutions 1988/77 of 29 July 1988, 1989/114 of 28 July 1989, 1990/69 of 27 July 1990 and Council decision 1990/205 of 9 February 1990, as appropriate;

(*b*) An organizational session not to exceed four days to be held in New York in early February to determine the annual agenda of the Council and related organizational matters, taking into account the relevant provisions of the resolutions and decision mentioned in paragraph 5 (a) of the present annex, particularly on the themes to be discussed in the high-level segment. This session will also select themes for the coordination segment, taking into account, *inter alia*, the recommendations of the joint meetings of the Committee for Programme and Coordination and the Administrative Committee on Coordination. Elections, appointments and confirmations to take place during a resumed organizational session of one or two days at the end of April;

(*c*) One substantive session of four to five weeks to take place in alternate years in New York and Geneva between May and July;

(*d*) The substantive session to be broadly organized, sequentially, along the following lines:

High-level segment

(i) A high-level segment of four days open to all Member States in accordance with Article 69 of the Charter, with ministerial participation, devoted to the consideration of one or more major economic and/or social policy themes to be determined at the organizational session, taking into account the Economic and Social Council multi-year work programme; adequate Secretariat preparation, including, in particular, one comprehensive background document for each theme; debate to follow an integrated and interdisciplinary approach; heads of the relevant organizations, agencies and other organs to participate actively;

One-day policy dialogue and discussion on important developments in the world economy and international economic cooperation. In this context, heads of multilateral financial and trade institutions of the United Nations system are invited to participate actively in this dialogue and discussion on matters of mutual interest with a view to building areas of understanding;

The main features of the deliberations of the high-level segment would be presented to the Economic and Social Council by its President in the form of a summary, which would be incorporated in its final report;

The deliberations of the high-level segment would provide political impetus for building areas of convergence and facilitate the consideration of the issues in question, including the emergence of new recommendations on the issues, in the relevant forums.

Coordination segment

(ii) Coordination of the activities of the specialized agencies, organs, organizations and bodies of the United Nations system in the economic, social and related fields, in accordance with Articles 63 and 64 of the Charter. This segment will consist of the following:

a. A segment of four to five days devoted to the coordination of the policies and activities of the specialized agencies, organs, organizations and bodies of the United Nations system relating to the achievement of the economic and social objectives of the United Nations. Discussion will be organized around one or more themes selected at the organizational session, and designed to focus attention on the activities of the United Nations system in the selected economic and social areas;

b. Discussion will take into account the report of the Secretary-General as Chairman of the Administrative Committee on Coordination, together with appropriate recommendations of the Committee for Programme and Coordination and the joint meetings of the Committee for Programme and Coordination and the Administrative Committee on Coordination. This report should contain a system-wide assessment of the status of coordination with regard to the themes and include recommendations, as appropriate;

c. The heads of concerned specialized agencies, organs, organizations and bodies of the United Nations system, including multilateral financial and trade institutions, are invited to participate actively, making contributions to the policy dialogue reflecting a global perspective on the agreed theme or themes, as well as their activities in the chosen themes;

d. Recommendations which result from these discussions shall be submitted to the General Assembly and forwarded, as appropriate, to the governing bodies of the specialized agencies, organs, organizations and bodies of the United Nations system as well as to the Committee for Programme and Coordination and the Administrative Committee on Coordination. In this context, the Secretary-General should arrange to apprise the next session of the Economic and Social Council of steps taken by the United Nations system to give effect to these recommendations.

Operational activities segment

(iii) A segment of two to three days devoted to operational activities of the United Nations system focusing, in particular, on the follow-up of policy recommendations and decisions of the General Assembly and coordination of operational activities on a system-wide basis, taking account of Economic and Social Council resolution 1988/77. The triennial review would continue to be undertaken by the General Assembly.

Committee segment

(iv) Consideration of specific economic, social and related issues, including their programme implications, in two separate committees meeting simultaneously to consider and take decisions on the reports of the subsidiary bodies of the Economic and Social Council and other relevant reports;[1] these reports should be arranged in clusters, as appropriate, for consideration; discussions to be decision-oriented focusing on specific recommendations and issues and not to involve a general debate. Review and monitoring of the implementation of the decisions of the General Assembly in the economic, social and related fields. Reports of the committees to be submitted to the plenary Council for approval.

(v) Adoption of the report.

(*e*) The above measures will come into effect in February 1992.

IV. Issues to be addressed in the future

6. The following non-exclusive list contains issues to be addressed in the future. The agenda and timetable for some further steps will be as follows:

---

1 The meetings of the Economic Committee will begin immediately after the operational activities segment. The work of the Social Committee will begin immediately after the completion of the coordination segment.

(1) *Complementarity between the work of the Economic and Social Council and the General Assembly*

Review at the forty-seventh session of the General Assembly of ways of enhancing the complementarity between the work of the Economic and Social Council and its own work, in accordance with Article 60 of the Charter.

(2) *Composition of the Economic and Social Council*

The process of restructuring and revitalization of the United Nations in the economic, social and related fields, undertaken with a view to enhancing its impact and effectiveness, shall include a review of the composition of the Economic and Social Council with due regard to equitable geographical representation and other relevant factors, in order to ensure the most effective participation of Member States, to be undertaken at a resumed forty-seventh session of the General Assembly.

(3) *Subsidiary machinery in the economic, social and related fields*

A review at the forty-sixth session of the General Assembly of the subsidiary bodies of the Economic and Social Council and the General Assembly, with the objective of possible restructuring and revitalization, and of their reporting responsibilities and procedures with a view to avoiding duplication, where possible. The review should be on the basis of, *inter alia*, the following criteria:

(*a*) Ensuring that programme delivery of a subsidiary body meets the needs of Member States and that it is consistent with the goals and priorities of the United Nations in the economic and social fields;

(*b*) Application of the same basic principles and guidelines for enhancing the effectiveness and efficiency of the subsidiary machinery as those set out in paragraph 3 of the present annex;

(*c*) Avoidance of subsuming highly technical functions of subsidiary bodies and expert groups into the Council;

(*d*) Ensuring that the subsidiary machinery in the economic, social and related fields is able to offer sound recommendations and advice as input into and not a substitute for the consideration and decisions by the Council and the Assembly.

The Secretary-General is requested to provide to the General Assembly at its forty-sixth session relevant information, including information on the status of subsidiary bodies and their reporting procedures, in order to facilitate the review of the subsidiary bodies of the Council and of the Assembly.

(4) *Secretariat*

A review of the Secretariat structure will be necessary on the basis of the agreements to be reached in the restructuring and revitalization process. In this context, the Secretary-General is requested to review the structure of the Secretariat in the economic, social and related fields, taking into account the outcome of the resumed forty-fifth session of the General Assembly, future work, and other relevant resolutions, as appropriate, and to report thereon with such recommendations as might be appropriate to the Assembly at its forty-seventh session.

Noting that management of the Secretariat is the responsibility of the Secretary-General, he is requested expeditiously to implement those measures within his purview, in accordance with the Charter and the relevant resolutions of the General Assembly, to streamline Secretariat operations in the economic, social and related fields in order to reinforce the restructuring and revitalization process directed by the Assembly, and to report thereon to the Assembly at its forty-sixth and forty-seventh sessions.

(5) *Progress report*

The Secretary-General is requested to submit an annual progress report to the General Assembly, starting with its forty-seventh session, on the implementation of the result of the restructuring and revitalization process in the economic, social and related fields, in which he is requested to provide information on any recommendation agreed upon which has not been implemented as scheduled.

(6) *Review*

As part of the restructuring and revitalization process the implementation of the measures in paragraph 5 above, including all organizational aspects of both the organizational and substantive sessions of the Economic and Social Council, will be reviewed at the forty-eighth session of the General Assembly in the light of the experience of the reforms agreed upon, with the view to enhancing the impact and effectiveness of the restructuring and revitalization of the United Nations in the economic, social and related fields.

50/52. Report of the Special Committee on the Charter of the United Nations and on the Strengthening of the Role of the Organization

Committee: 6
Vote: 155 - 0 - 3
Ref.: 3499(XXX); 31/28; 32/45; 33/94; 34/147; 35/164; 36/122; 37/114; 38/141; 39/88; 40/78; 41/83; 42/157; 43/170; 44/37; 45/44; 46/58; 47/38; 48/36; 49/58

The General Assembly,

Recalling its resolution 3499 (XXX) of 15 December 1975, by which it established the Special Committee on the Charter of the United Nations and on the Strengthening of the Role of the Organization, and its relevant resolutions adopted at subsequent sessions,

Recalling also its resolution 47/233 of 17 August 1993 on the revitalization of the work of the General Assembly,

Recalling further its resolution 47/62 of 11 December 1992 on the question of equitable representation on and increase in the membership of the Security Council,

Bearing in mind the provisions of its resolution 50/55 of 11 December 1995,

Conscious of the ongoing discussion in the open-ended working groups of the General Assembly dealing with the various aspects of the revitalization, strengthening and reform of the work of the United Nations,

Welcoming the report of the Open-ended Working Group on the Question of Equitable Representation on and Increase in the Membership of the Security Council and Other Matters Related to the Security Council,[1]

Bearing in mind the reports of the Secretary-General on the work of the Organization submitted to the General Assembly at its thirty-seventh,[2] thirty-ninth,[3] fortieth,[4] forty-first,[5] forty-second,[6] forty-third,[7] forty-fourth,[8] forty-fifth,[9] forty-sixth,[10] forty-seventh,[11] forty-eighth,[12] forty-ninth[13] and fiftieth[14] sessions, as well as the views and comments expressed on them by Member States,

Recalling the elements relevant to the work of the Special Committee contained in its resolution 47/120 B of 20 September 1993,

Mindful of the desirability for the Special Committee to carry out further work in the fields of the maintenance of international peace and security and the peaceful settlement of disputes between States,

---

1 *Official Records of the General Assembly, Forty-ninth Session, Supplement No. 47* (A/49/47).

2 *Ibid.*,Thirty-seventh Session, Supplement No. 1 (A/37/1).

3 *Ibid.*,Thirty-ninth Session, Supplement No. 1 (A/39/1).

4 *Ibid.*, Fortieth Session, Supplement No. 1 (A/40/1).

5 *Ibid.*, Forty-first Session, Supplement No. 1 (A/41/1).

6 *Ibid.*, Forty-second Session, Supplement No. 1 (A/42/1).

7 *Ibid.*, Forty-third Session, Supplement No. 1 (A/43/1).

8 *Ibid.*, Forty-fourth Session, Supplement No. 1 (A/44/1).

9 *Ibid.*, Forty-fifth Session, Supplement No. 1 (A/45/1).

10 *Ibid.*, Forty-sixth Session, Supplement No. 1 (A/46/1).

11 *Ibid.*, Forty-seventh Session, Supplement No. 1 (A/47/1).

12 *Ibid.*, Forty-eighth Session, Supplement No. 1 (A/48/1).

13 *Ibid.*, Forty-ninth Session, Supplement No. 1 (A/49/1).

14 *Ibid.*, Fiftieth Session, Supplement No. 1 (A/50/1).

Recalling its resolution 49/58 of 9 December 1994,

Having considered the report of the Special Committee on the work of its session held in 1995,[1]

Taking note of the recommendation of the Special Committee on the most appropriate legal action to be taken on the question of the deletion of the "enemy State" clauses from Articles 53, 77 and 107 of the Charter of the United Nations,[2]

Recognizing that, having regard to the substantial changes that have taken place in the world, the "enemy State" clauses in Articles 53, 77 and 107 of the Charter of the United Nations have become obsolete,

Noting that the States to which those clauses were directed are Members of the United Nations and represent a valuable asset in all the endeavours of the Organization,

Taking into account the complex process involved in amending the Charter,

1. *Takes note* of the report of the Special Committee on the Charter of the United Nations and on the Strengthening of the Role of the Organization;[3]

2. *Decides* that the Special Committee will hold its next session from 21 February to 5 March 1996;

3. *Expresses its intention* to initiate the procedure set out in Article 108 of the Charter of the United Nations to amend the Charter, with prospective effect, by the deletion of the "enemy State" clauses from Articles 53, 77 and 107 at its earliest appropriate future session;

4. *Requests* the Special Committee, at its session in 1996, in accordance with the provisions of paragraph 5 below:

(*a*) To accord appropriate time for the consideration of all proposals concerning the question of the maintenance of international peace and security in all its aspects in order to strengthen the role of the United Nations and, in this context, to consider other proposals relating to the maintenance of international peace and security already submitted or which might be submitted to the Special Committee at its session in 1996, including the proposal on the strengthening of the role of the Organization and enhancing its effectiveness and the revised proposal submitted with a view to enhancing the effectiveness of the Security Council in regard to the maintenance of international peace and security, and to consider recommending to the General Assembly the desired priorities for its further consideration;

(*b*) To continue to consider on a priority basis the question of the implementation of the provisions of the Charter related to assistance to third States affected by the application of sanctions under Chapter VII of the Charter, taking into consideration the report of the Secretary-General,[4] the proposals presented on this subject, the debate on this question which took place in the Sixth Committee at the fiftieth session of the General Assembly and, in particular, the implementation of the provisions of General Assembly resolution 50/51 of 11 December 1995;

(*c*) To continue its work on the question of the peaceful settlement of disputes between States, and in this context to continue its consideration of proposals relating to the peaceful settlement of disputes between States, including the proposal on the establishment of a dispute settlement service offering or responding with its services early in disputes and those proposals relating to the enhancement of the role of the International Court of Justice;

(*d*) To continue its consideration of the question of the enhancement of cooperation between the United Nations and regional arrangements or agencies in the maintenance of international peace and security;

(*e*) To consider proposals concerning the Trusteeship Council;

(*f*) To consider the status of the Repertory of Practice of United Nations Organs and the Repertoire of the Practice of the Security Council:[5]

5. *Decides* that the Special Committee shall henceforth be open to all States Members of the United Nations and that it will continue to operate on the basis of the practice of consensus;

6. *Decides also* that the Special Committee shall be authorized to accept the participation of observers of States other than States Members of the United Nations which are members of specialized agencies or of the International Atomic Energy Agency in its meetings, and further decides to invite intergovernmental organizations to participate in the debate in the plenary meetings of the Committee on specific items where it considers that such participation would assist in the work;

7. *Invites* the Special Committee at its session in 1996 to identify new subjects for consideration in its future work with a view to contributing to the revitalization of the work of the United Nations, and to discuss how to offer its assistance to the working groups of the General Assembly in this field;

8. *Requests* the Special Committee to submit a report on its work to the General Assembly at the fifty-first session;

9. *Decides* to include in the provisional agenda of its fifty-first session the item entitled "Report of the Special Committee on the Charter of the United Nations and on the Strengthening of the Role of the Organization".

87th plenary meeting
11 December 1995

---

1 *Ibid.*, Supplement No. 33 (A/50/33).

2 *Official Records of the General Assembly, Fiftieth-ninth Session, Supplement No. 33,* (A/50/33), para 65.

3 *Official Records of the General Assembly, Fiftieth Session, Supplement No. 33* (A/50/33).

4 A/50/361.

5 See A/C.6/50/SR.44.

11.30 FINANCIAL AND BUDGETARY QUESTIONS

456 (V). Financial Regulations of the United Nations

Committee: 5
Vote: unanimous
Ref.: 3149(XXVIII), 3049(XXVII), 3047(XXVII), 3043(XXVII), 2197(XVII), 1739(XV), 1096(XI), 950(X), 875(IX), 677(VII), 459(V), 353(IV), 163(II), 80(I), 14(I)

The General Assembly,

Taking note of the agreement reached in the Administrative Committee on Coordination to recommend a common set of financial regulations for the United Nations and the specialized agencies,

Approving the amendments[1] recommended by the Advisory Committee on Administrative and Budgetary Questions,

1. *Declares* that the Financial Regulations of the United Nations set out in the annex to the present resolution are adopted in place of those adopted by the General Assembly at its second session under resolution 163 (II);

2. *Expresses* the hope that Member States will support the adoption by the specialized agencies of the Financial Regulations approved herein for the United Nations, with only such alterations as are required to meet the constitutional provisions and organizational structure of the respective agencies.

305th plenary meeting
16 November 1950

Annex

Financial Regulations of the United Nations

Article I

Applicability

1.1 These regulations shall govern the financial administration of the United Nations, including the International Court of Justice.

Article II

The Financial Year

2.1 The financial year shall be the period 1 January to 31 December inclusive.

Article III

The Budget

3.1 The annual budget estimates shall be prepared by the Secretary-General.

3.2 The estimates shall cover income and expenditures for the financial year to which they relate, and shall be presented in United States dollars.

3.3 The annual budget estimates shall be divided into parts, sections, chapters and articles, and shall be accompanied by such information annexes and explanatory statements as may be requested by, or on behalf of, the General Assembly, and such further annexes or statements as the Secretary-General may deem necessary and useful.

3.4 The Secretary-General shall submit to the regular session of the General Assembly budget estimates for the following financial year. The estimates shall be transmitted to all Member States at least five weeks prior to the opening of the regular session of the General Assembly.

3.5 The Secretary-General shall, at least twelve weeks prior to the opening of the regular session of the General Assembly, submit the estimates to the Advisory Committee on Administrative and Budgetary Questions (hereinafter referred to as the "Advisory Committee") for examination.

3.6 The Advisory Committee shall prepare a report to the General Assembly on the estimates submitted by the Secretary-General. This report shall be transmitted to all Member States at the same time as the estimates.

3.7 The budget for the following financial year shall be adopted by the General Assembly after consideration and report on the estimates by the Administrative and Budgetary Committee of the Assembly.

3.8 Supplementary estimates may be submitted by the Secretary-General whenever necessary.

3.9 The Secretary-General shall prepare supplementary estimates in a form consistent with the annual estimates and shall submit such estimates to the General Assembly. The Advisory Committee shall review such estimates and report thereon.

Article IV

Appropriations

4.1 The appropriations voted by the General Assembly shall constitute an authorization to the Secretary-General to incur obligations and make payments for the purposes for which the appropriations were voted and up to the amounts so voted.

4.2 Appropriations shall be available for obligation during the financial year to which they relate.

4.3 Appropriations shall remain available for twelve months following the end of the financial year to which they relate to the extent that they are required to discharge obligations in respect of goods supplied and services rendered in the financial year and to liquidate any other outstanding legal obligation of the year. The balance of the appropriations shall be surrendered.

4.4 At the end of the twelve-month period provided in regulation 4.3 above, the then remaining balance of any appropriations retained will be surrendered. Any unliquidated prior year obligations shall at that time be cancelled or, where the obligation remains a valid charge, transferred as an obligation against current appropriations.

4.5 No transfer between appropriation sections may be made without authorization by the General Assembly.

Article V

Provision of Funds

5.1 The appropriations, subject to the adjustments effected in accordance with the provisions of regulation 5.2, shall be financed by contributions from Member States, according to the scale of assessments determined by the General Assembly. Pending the receipt of such contributions, the appropriations may be financed from the Working Capital Fund.

5.2 In the assessment of the contributions of Member States, adjustments shall be made to the amount of the appropriations approved by the General Assembly for the financial year in respect of:

(*a*) Supplementary appropriations for which contributions have not previously been assessed on the Member States;

(*b*) Miscellaneous income for which credits have not previously been taken into account, and any adjustments in estimated miscellaneous income previously taken into account;

(*c*) Contributions resulting from the assessment of new Member States under the provisions of regulation 5.8;

(*d*) Any balance of the appropriations surrendered under regulations 4.3 and 4.4.

5.3 After the General Assembly has adopted the budget and determined the amount of the Working Capital Fund, the Secretary-General shall:

(*a*) Transmit the relevant documents to Member States;

(*b*) Inform Member States of their commitments in respect of annual contributions and advances to the Working Capital Fund;

(*c*) Request them to remit their contributions and advances.

1 See document A/1412.

5.4 Contributions and advances shall be considered as due and payable in full within thirty days of the receipt of the communication of the Secretary-General referred to in regulation 5.3 above, or as of the first day of the financial year to which they relate, whichever is the later. As of 1 January of the following financial year, the unpaid balance of such contributions and advances shall be considered to be one year in arrears.

5.5 Annual contributions and advances to the Working Capital Fund of the United Nations shall be assessed and paid in United States dollars.

5.6 Payments made by a Member State shall be credited first to the Working Capital Fund and then to the contributions due in the order in which the Member was assessed.

5.7 The Secretary-General shall submit to the regular session of the General Assembly a report on the collection of contributions and advances to the Working Capital Fund.

5.8 New Members shall be required to make a contribution for the year in which they become Members and to provide their proportion of the total advances to the Working Capital Fund at rates to be determined by the General Assembly.

5.9 States which are not Members of the United Nations but which become parties to the Statute of the International Court of Justice or treaty bodies financed from United Nations appropriations shall contribute to the estimated expenses of such bodies at rates to be determined by the General Assembly. Such contributions shall be taken into account as miscellaneous income.

Article VI

Funds

6.1 There shall be established a General Fund for the purpose of accounting for the expenditures of the Organization. The contributions paid by Member States under regulation 5.1, miscellaneous income, and any advances made from the Working Capital Fund to finance general expenditures shall be credited to the General Fund.

6.2 There shall be established a Working Capital Fund in an amount and for purposes to be determined from time to time by the General Assembly. The source of monies of the Working Capital Fund shall be advances from Member States, and these advances, made in accordance with the scale of assessments as determined by the General Assembly for the apportionment of the expenses of the United Nations, shall be carried to the credit of the Member States which have made such advances.

6.3 Advances made from the Working Capital Fund to finance budgetary appropriations during a financial year shall be reimbursed to the Fund as soon as and to the extent that income is available for that purpose.

6.4 Except when such advances are recoverable from some other source, advances made from the Working Capital Fund for unforeseen and extraordinary expenses or other authorized purposes shall be reimbursed through the submission of supplementary estimates.

6.5 Income derived from investments of the Working Capital Fund shall be credited to miscellaneous income.

6.6 Trust Funds, Reserve and Special Accounts may be established by the Secretary-General and shall be reported to the Advisory Committee.

6.7 The purpose and limits of each Trust Fund, Reserve and Special Account shall be clearly defined by the appropriate authority. Unless otherwise provided by the General Assembly, such Funds and Accounts shall be administered in accordance with the present Regulations.

Article VII

Other Income

7.1 All other income, except:

(*a*) Contributions to the budget;

(*b*) Direct refunds of expenditures made during the financial year; and

(*c*) Advances or deposits to Funds, shall be classed as miscellaneous income, for credit to the General Fund.

7.2 Voluntary contributions, whether or not in cash, may be accepted by the Secretary-General provided that the purposes for which the contributions are made are consistent with the policies, aims and activities of the Organization and provided that the acceptance of such contributions which directly or indirectly involve additional financial liability for the Organization shall require the consent of the appropriate authority.

7.3 Monies accepted for purposes specified by the donor shall be treated as Trust Funds or Special Accounts under regulations 6.6 and 6.7.

7.4 Monies accepted in respect of which no purpose is specified shall be treated as miscellaneous income and reported as "gifts" in the annual accounts.

Article VIII

Custody of Funds

8.1 The Secretary-General shall designate the bank or banks in which the funds of the Organization shall be kept.

Article IX

Investment of Funds

9.1 The Secretary-General may make short-term investments of monies not needed for immediate requirements and shall inform the Advisory Committee periodically of such investments which he has made.

9.2 The Secretary-General may make long-term investments of monies standing to the credit of Trust Funds, Reserve and Special Accounts as may be provided by the appropriate authority in respect of each such Fund or Account.

9.3 Income derived from investments shall be credited as provided in the rules relating to each Fund or Account.

Article X

Internal Control

10.1 The Secretary-General shall:

(*a*) Establish detailed financial rules and procedures in order to ensure effective financial administration and the exercise of economy;

(*b*) Cause all payments to be made on the basis of supporting vouchers and other documents which ensure that the services or goods have been received, and that payments have not previously been made;

(*c*) Designate the officers who may receive monies, incur obligations and make payments on behalf of the Organization;

(*d*) Maintain an internal financial control which shall provide for an effective current examination and/or review of financial transactions in order to ensure:

(i) The regularity of the receipt, custody and disposal of all funds and other financial resources of the Organization;

(ii) The conformity of obligations and expenditures with the appropriations or other financial provisions voted by the General Assembly, or with the purposes and rules relating to Trust Funds and Special Accounts;

(iii) The economic use of the resources of the Organization.

10.2 No obligations shall be incurred until allotments or other appropriate authorizations have been made in writing under the authority of the Secretary-General.

10.3 The Secretary-General may make such *ex gratia* payments as he deems to be necessary in the interests of the Organization, provided that a statement of such payments shall be submitted to the General Assembly with the annual accounts.

10.4 The Secretary-General may, after full investigation, authorize the writing off of losses of cash, stores and other assets, provided that a statement of all such accounts written off shall be submitted to the Auditors with the annual accounts.

10.5 Tenders for equipment, supplies and other requirements shall be invited by advertisement, except where the Secretary-General deems that, in the interests of the Organization, a departure from the rule is desirable.

Article XI

The Accounts

11.1 The Secretary-General shall maintain such accounting records as are necessary and shall submit annual accounts showing for the financial year to which they relate:

(*a*) The income and expenditures of all Funds;

(*b*) The status of appropriations, including:

(i) The original budget appropriations;

(ii) The appropriations as modified by any transfers;

(iii) Credits, if any, other than the appropriations voted by the General Assembly;

(iv) The amounts charged against these appropriations and/or other credits;

(*c*) The assets and liabilities of the Organization.

He shall also give such other information as may be appropriate to indicate the current financial position of the Organization.

11.2 The annual accounts of the Organization shall be presented in United States dollars. Accounting records may, however, be kept in such currency or currencies as the Secretary-General may deem necessary.

11.3 Appropriate separate accounts shall be maintained for all Trust Funds, Reserve and Special Accounts.

11.4 The annual accounts shall be submitted by the Secretary-General to the Board of Auditors not later than 31 March following the end of the financial year.

Article XII

External Audit

12.1 Subject to any special direction of the General Assembly, each audit which the Board of Auditors established under resolution 74 (I) is required to make shall be conducted in accordance with the principles set out in the appendix to the present Regulations.

12.2 At the commencement of each financial year the Board of Auditors and the Advisory Committee shall be notified as to the sum provided to defray the cost of audit of each Trust Fund, Reserve and Special Account to be performed by the Board during the year. Thereupon, the Board shall consult the Advisory Committee relative to the scope of the several audits to be made by the Board.

12.3 The Board of Auditors may allocate, subject to the concurrence of the Advisory Committee, the audit work among the members of the Board, provided that two members shall jointly certify the annual accounts submitted by the Secretary-General in accordance with the provisions of regulation 11.4.

12.4 Whenever any financial statement is certified by only one member of the Board of Auditors, there shall be associated therewith a certificate of another member of the Board to the effect that the audit programme had been approved by the Board and that all special instructions given by the Board to the member were carried out.

12.5 Whenever it is necessary to make a local or special examination, the Board of Auditors may, subject to the budgetary provision for the audit concerned, arrange for the services of any national Auditor-General (or equivalent title) who is eligible to be appointed to the membership of the Board or of commercial public auditors of known repute.

Article XIII

Resolutions Involving Expenditures

13.1 No Council, commission or other competent body shall take a decision involving expenditure unless it has before it a report from the Secretary-General on the administrative and financial implications of the proposal.

13.2 Where, in the opinion of the Secretary-General, the proposed expenditure cannot be made from the existing appropriations, it shall not be incurred until the General Assembly has made the necessary appropriations, unless the Secretary-General certifies that provision can be made under the conditions of the resolution of the General Assembly relating to unforeseen and extraordinary expenses.

Article XIV

General Provisions

14.1 These regulations shall be effective as of the date of their approval by the General Assembly, and may be amended only by the General Assembly.

Article XV

Special Provisions

15.1 The estimates of the International Court of Justice shall be prepared by the Court, in consultation with the Secretary-General. These estimates shall be submitted to the General Assembly by the Secretary-General, together with such observations as he may deem desirable.

Appendix to the Financial Regulations

Principles to Govern the Audit Procedures of the United Nations

1. The Board of Auditors shall perform an audit of the accounts of the United Nations, including all Trust and Special Accounts, as it may deem necessary in order to certify:

(*a*) That the financial statements are in accord with the books and records of the Organization;

(*b*) That the financial transactions reflected in the statements have been in accordance with the rules and regulations, the budgetary provisions and other applicable directives;

(*c*) That the securities and monies on deposit and on hand have been verified by certificate received direct from the Organization's depositaries or by actual count.

2. Subject to the provisions of the Financial Regulations, the Board of Auditors shall be the sole judge as to the acceptance in whole or in part of certifications by the Secretariat and may proceed to such detailed examination and verification as it chooses of all financial records, including those relating to supplies and equipment.

3. The Board of Auditors may affirm by test the reliability of the internal audit and may make such reports with respect thereto as the Board may deem necessary, to the General Assembly or to the Advisory Committee on Administrative and Budgetary Questions, or to the Secretary-General.

4. The several members of the Board and staff working under its direction shall subscribe to such oath as may be approved by the Advisory Committee on Administrative and Budgetary Questions. Thereupon the members of the Board and its staff shall have free access at all convenient times to all books of account and records which are, in the opinion of the Board, necessary for the performance of the audit. Information classified as confidential in the records of the Secretariat, and which is required by the Board for the purposes of the audit shall be made available on application to the Assistant Secretary-General for Administrative and Financial Services. In the event that the Board is of the opinion that a duty rests on it to draw to the attention of the General Assembly any matter respecting which all or part of the documentation is classified as confidential, direct quotations should be avoided.

5. The Board of Auditors, in addition to certifying the accounts, may make such observations as it may deem necessary with respect to the efficiency of the financial procedures, the accounting system, the internal financial controls and, in general, the financial consequences of administrative practices.

6. In no case, however, shall the Board of Auditors include criticism in its audit report without first affording the Secretariat an opportu-

nity of explanation to the Board on the matter under observation. Audit objections to any items arising during the examination of the accounts shall be immediately communicated to the Assistant Secretary-General for Administrative and Financial Services.

7. The Board of Auditors shall prepare a report on the accounts certified in which it should mention:

(*a*) The extent and character of its examination or any important changes therein;

(*b*) Matters affecting the completeness or accuracy of the accounts, such as:

(i) Information necessary to the correct interpretation of the account,

(ii) Any amounts which ought to have been received but which have not been brought to account,

(iii) Expenditures not properly substantiated;

(*c*) Other matters which should be brought to the notice of the General Assembly such as:

(i) Cases of fraud or presumptive fraud,

(ii) Wasteful or improper expenditure of United Nations money or other assets (notwithstanding that the accounting for the transactions may be correct),

(iii) Expenditure likely to commit the United Nations to further outlay on a large scale,

(iv) Any defect in the general system or detailed regulations governing the control of receipts and expenditure, or of supplies and equipment,

(v) Expenditure not in accordance with the intention of the General Assembly, after making allowance for duly authorized transfers within the budget,

(vi) Expenditure in excess of appropriations as amended by duly authorized transfers within the budget,

(vii) Expenditure not in conformity with the authority which governs it;

(*d*) The accuracy or otherwise of the supplies and equipment records as determined by stock-taking and examination of the records;

In addition, the reports may contain reference to:

(*e*) Transactions accounted for in a previous year concerning which further information has been obtained, or transactions in a later year concerning which it seems desirable that the General Assembly should have early knowledge.

8. The Board of Auditors, or such of their officers as they may designate, shall certify the financial statements in the following terms:

"The financial statements of the United Nations for the financial year ended 31 December ... have been examined in accordance with our directions. We have obtained all the information and explanations that we have required, and we certify, as a result of the audit, that, in our opinion, the financial statements are correct",

adding, should it be necessary:

"subject to the observations in our report".

9. The Board of Auditors shall have no power to disallow items in the accounts but shall draw to the attention of the Secretary-General for appropriate action any transaction concerning which it entertains doubt as to legality or propriety.

10. A representative of the Board of Auditors shall be present when the Board's report is being considered by the General Assembly.

41/213. Review of the Efficiency of the Administrative and Financial Functioning of the United Nations

Committee: -
Vote: Adopted without a vote
Ref.: 48/218, 45/254, 40/237

The General Assembly,

Recalling its resolution 40/237 of 18 December 1985, by which it decided to establish the Group of High-level Intergovernmental Experts to Review the Efficiency of the Administrative and Financial Functioning of the United Nations,

Having considered the report of the Group[1] and the related report of the Fifth Committee,[2] as well as the comments on the report of the Group made by the Secretary-General[3] and the Administrative Committee on Coordination;[4]

Expressing its appreciation to the Group for its report,

Taking fully into account the views expressed during the consideration of this item at the current session,

Recognizing the need for measures to improve the efficiency of the administrative and financial functioning of the United Nations with a view to strengthening its effectiveness in dealing with political, economic and social issues,

Recognizing the need to improve the planning, programming and budgeting process in the Organization,

Reaffirming the requirement of all Member States to fulfil their financial obligations as set out in the Charter of the United Nations promptly and in full,

Recognizing the detrimental effect of the withholding of assessed contributions on the administrative and financial functioning of the United Nations,

Recognizing further that late payments of assessed contributions adversely affect the short-term financial situation of the Organization,

I

Recommendations of the Group of High-Level Intergovernmental Experts to Review the Efficiency of the Administrative and Financial Functioning of the United Nations

1. *Decides* that the recommendations as agreed upon and as contained in the report of the Group of High-Level Intergovernmental Experts to Review the Efficiency of the Administrative and Financial Functioning of the United Nations[5] should be implemented by the Secretary-General and the relevant organs and bodies of the United Nations in the light of the findings of the Fifth Committee[6] and subject to the following:

(*a*) The implementation of recommendation 5 should not prejudice the implementation of projects and programmes already approved by the General Assembly;

(*b*) The percentages referred to in recommendation 15, which were arrived at in a pragmatic manner, should be regarded as targets in the formulation of the Secretary-General's plans to be submitted to the General Assembly for implementation of the recommendation; further, the Secretary-General is requested to implement this recommendation with flexibility in order to avoid, *inter alia*, negative impact on programmes and on the structure and composition of the Secretariat, bearing in mind the necessity of securing the highest standards of efficiency, competence and integrity of the staff, with due regard to equitable geographical distribution;

(*c*) The Secretary-General should transmit to the International Civil Service Commission those recommendations having direct impact on the United Nations common system (recommendations 53 and 61), with the request that it report to the General Assembly at its forty-second session, so as to enable the Assembly to make a final decision; the expertise of the Commission should be availed of in dealing with the other recommendations over which the Commission has a mandate to advise and make recommendations;

---

1 *Official Records of the General Assembly, Forty-first Session, Supplement No. 49* (A/41/49).

2 A/41/795.

3 A/41/663.

4 A/41/763, annex.

5 *Official Records of the General Assembly, Forty-first Session, Supplement No. 49* (A/41/49).

6 A/41/795.

(*d*) The Secretary-General should take into consideration the relevant provisions of General Assembly resolution 35/210 of 17 December 1980, in implementing recommendations 55 and 57, to the extent they are agreed upon;

(*e*) The Economic and Social Council, assisted as and when required by relevant organs and bodies, in particular the Committee for Programme and Coordination, should carry out the study called for in recommendation 8;

(*f*) The Committee for Programme and Coordination, assisted as required by the Joint Inspection Unit and other bodies, shall evaluate the implementation of the recommendations relating to the intergovernmental machinery and its functioning, as indicated in recommendation 70;

(*g*) In the implementation of recommendation 24, the provisions of General Assembly resolution 41/201 of 8 December 1986 should be duly taken into account;

2. *Requests* the Secretary-General and the Committee for Programme and Coordination to report to the General Assembly as indicated in recommendations 69, 70 and 71 of the Group;

II

Planning, programming and budgeting process

1. *Decides* that the planning, programming and budgeting process shall be governed, *inter alia*, by the following principles:

(*a*) Strict adherence to the principles and provisions of the Charter of the United Nations, in particular Articles 17 and 18 thereof;

(*b*) Full respect for the prerogatives of the principal organs of the United Nations with respect to the planning, programming and budgeting process;

(*c*) Full respect for the authority and the prerogatives of the Secretary-General as the chief administrative officer of the Organization;

(*d*) Recognition of the need for Member States to participate in the budgetary preparation from its early stages and throughout the process;

2. *Reaffirms* the need to improve the planning, programming and budgeting process through, *inter alia*, the following:

(*a*) Full implementation of regulation 4.8 of the Regulations Governing Programme Planning, the Programme Aspects of the Budget, the Monitoring of Implementation and the Methods of Evaluation, which governs coordination between the Committee for Programme and Coordination and the Advisory Committee on Administrative and Budgetary Questions;

(*b*) Implementation of the recommendations contained in paragraphs 25 to 54 of the report of the Committee for Programme and Coordination on the work of its twenty-sixth session;[1]

(*c*) Ensuring follow-up of implementation of the recommendations of the Committee for Programme and Coordination;

(*d*) Improvement of the representation of Member States in the Committee for Programme and Coordination in conformity with the provisions of paragraph 46 of the annex to General Assembly resolution 32/197 of 20 December 1977;

3. *Resolves* to achieve improvement in the consultative process for the formulation of the medium-term plan through:

(*a*) Full implementation of the Regulations Governing Programme Planning, the Programme Aspects of the Budget, the Monitoring of Implementation and the Methods of Evaluation pertaining to the medium-term plan, as contained in the annex to General Assembly resolution 37/234 of 21 December 1982 and of the related Rules;

(*b*) Submission of the introduction to the medium-term plan, which constitutes an integral element in the planning process, to Member States for wide consultations;

(*c*) Consultations in a systematic way regarding the major programmes in the plan with sectoral, technical, regional and central bodies in the United Nations;

(*d*) Drawing up by the Secretary-General, in consultation with the Committee for Programme and Coordination and the Advisory Committee on Administrative and Budgetary Questions, of a calendar for such consultations;

4. *Approves* the budget process set forth in annex I to the present resolution;

5. *Reaffirms* that the decision-making process is governed by the provisions of the Charter of the United Nations and the rules of procedure of the General Assembly;[2]

6. *Agrees* that, without prejudice to paragraph 5 above, the Committee for Programme and Coordination should continue its existing practice of reaching decisions by consensus; explanatory views, if any, shall be presented to the General Assembly;[3]

7. *Considers it desirable* that the Fifth Committee, before submitting its recommendations on the outline of the programme budget to the General Assembly in accordance with the provisions of the Charter and the rules of procedure of the Assembly, should continue to make all possible efforts with a view to establishing the broadest possible agreement;[4]

8. *Requests* the Secretary-General to submit to the General Assembly, through the Committee for Programme and Coordination and the Advisory Committee on Administrative and Budgetary Questions, such supplementary rules and regulations as may be deemed necessary for the improvement in the planning, programming and budgeting process;

9. *Also requests* the Secretary-General to submit to the General Assembly at its forty-second session a proposal on the date for submission of the outline of the programme budget and also on the date for final approval of the outline by the Assembly;

10. *Further requests* the Secretary-General to report to the General Assembly at its forty-second session on the implementation of the present resolution.

102nd plenary meeting
19 December 1986

Annex I

Budget Process

A. Off-budget years

1. The Secretary-General shall submit an outline of the programme budget for the following biennium, which shall contain an indication of the following:

(*a*) Preliminary estimate of resources to accommodate the proposed programme of activities during the biennium;

(*b*) Priorities, reflecting general trends of a broad sectoral nature;

(*c*) Real growth, positive or negative, compared with the previous budget;

(*d*) Size of the contingency fund expressed as a percentage of the overall level of resources.

2. The Committee for Programme and Coordination, acting as a subsidiary organ of the General Assembly, shall consider the outline of the programme budget and submit, through the Fifth Committee, to the Assembly its conclusions and recommendations.

3. On the basis of a decision by the General Assembly, the Secretary-General shall prepare his proposed programme budget for the following biennium.

4. Throughout this process, the mandate and functions of the Advisory Committee on Administrative and Budgetary Questions shall be fully respected. The Advisory Committee shall consider the outline of the programme budget in accordance with its terms of reference.

---

1 *Official Records of the General Assembly, Forty-first Session, Supplement No. 38* (A/41/38 and Corr.2).

2 See annex II to the present resolution.

3 See annex II to the present resolution.

4 See annex II to the present resolution.

B. Budget years

5. The Secretary-General shall submit his proposed programme budget to the Committee for Programme and Coordination and the Advisory Committee on Administrative and Budgetary Questions in accordance with the existing procedures.

6. The Committee for Programme and Coordination and the Advisory Committee on Administrative and Budgetary Questions shall examine the proposed programme budget in accordance with their respective mandates and shall submit their conclusions and recommendations to the General Assembly, through the Fifth Committee, for the final approval of the programme budget.

C. Contingency fund and additional expenditures

7. The programme budget shall include expenditures related to political activities of a "perennial" character whose mandates are renewed annually, together with their related conference costs.

8. The programme budget shall include a contingency fund expressed as a percentage of the overall budget level, to accommodate additional expenditures relating to the biennium derived from legislative mandates not provided for in the proposed programme budget or, subject to the provisions of paragraph 11 below, from revised estimates.

9. If additional expenditures, as defined in paragraph 8 above, are proposed that exceed resources available within the contingency fund, such additional expenditures can only be included in the budget through redeployment of resources from low-priority areas or modifications of existing activities. Otherwise, such additional activities will have to be deferred until a later biennium.

10. A comprehensive solution to the Problem of all additional expenditures, including those deriving from inflation and currency fluctuation, is also necessary. It is desirable to accommodate these expenditures, within the overall level of the budget, either as a reserve or as a separate part of the contingency fund set up in paragraph 8 above. The Secretary-General should examine all aspects related to the question and report, through the Advisory Committee on Administrative and Budgetary Questions and the Committee for Programme and Coordination, to the General Assembly at its forty-second session.

11. Pending a decision by the General Assembly on the question dealt with in paragraph 10 above, the revised estimates arising from the impact of extraordinary expenses, including those relating to the maintenance of peace and security, as well as fluctuations in rates of exchange and inflation, shall not be covered by the contingency fund and shall continue to be treated in accordance with established procedures and under the relevant provisions of the Financial Regulations and Rules. The Secretary-General should nevertheless make efforts to absorb these expenditures, to the extent possible, through savings from the programme budget, without causing in any way a negative effect on programme delivery and without prejudice to the utilization of the contingency fund.

Annex II

Statement Made by the President of the General Assembly at the 102nd Plenary Meeting, on 19 December 1986[1]

... I have obtained a legal opinion from the Legal Counsel of the United Nations on three paragraphs of the draft resolution. The legal opinion reads as follows:

"You have requested our opinion on the legal consequences of three draft paragraphs which are under consideration for inclusion in a resolution to be adopted by the General Assembly on the United Nations budgetary process. These three paragraphs read as follows:

"5. *Reaffirms* that the decision-making process is governed by the provisions of the Charter of the United Nations and the rules of procedure of the General Assembly;

"6. *Agrees* that, without prejudice to paragraph 5 above, the Committee for Programme and Coordination should continue its existing practice of reaching decisions by consensus; explanatory views, if any, shall be presented to the General Assembly;

"7. *Considers it desirable* that the Fifth Committee, before submitting its recommendations on the outline of the programme budget to the General Assembly in accordance with the provisions of the Charter and the rules of procedure, should continue to make all possible efforts with a view to establishing the broadest possible agreement;

"It is our opinion that these draft paragraphs read separately or together do not in any way prejudice the provisions of Article 18 of the Charter of the United Nations or of the relevant rules of procedure of the General Assembly giving effect to that Article."

That coincides with the views expressed by all delegations.

I concur with the foregoing, and I take it that the General Assembly also agrees with it.

1 Annexed to the resolution following a decision by the General Assembly.

49/143. Financial Situation of the United Nations

Committee: -
Vote: Adopted without a vote
Ref.: 47/215, 45/236, 44/195, 43/215, 43/220, 42/212, 42/216, 41/204, 40/471, 40/472, 40/241, 39/239, 38/228, 37/13, 36/116, 35/113, 34/436D, 33/430D, 32/104, 31/191, 3538(XXX)

The General Assembly,

Recalling Article 17 of the Charter of the United Nations,

Expressing its profound concern about the financial situation of the Organization,

Noting the views expressed by Member States during the general debate on the financial difficulties of the Organization which have resulted, *inter alia*, from the failure of Member States to discharge their financial obligations to the Organization in full and on time,

Taking note of the report of the Secretary-General on the work of the Organization[2] and of his statement to the General Assembly on 12 October 1994 on the precariousness of the financial situation of the Organization,[3]

Noting also the views expressed by Member States during its consideration, in plenary meeting, of the financial situation of the Organization, under item 10 of the agenda of its forty-ninth session,

Aware of the importance and urgency of securing a viable financial basis for the Organization,

Aware also that the solution of the serious financial situation of the Organization calls for political efforts,

Reaffirming the role of the Fifth Committee of the General Assembly with regard to budgetary and financial matters and the importance of making every effort to establish the broadest possible agreement in accordance with the practice established in the Fifth Committee and in conformity with Assembly resolution 41/213 of 19 December 1986,

1. *Decides* to consider additional measures aimed at ensuring a sound and viable financial basis for the Organization;

2. *Also decides*, to this end, to establish a high-level open-ended working group under the chairmanship of the President of the General Assembly and with two vice-chairmen;

3. *Requests* the high-level working group to submit to it, through the Fifth Committee, a report on the progress of its work, with the broadest possible agreement, for review before the end of its forty-ninth session.

94th plenary meeting
23 December 1994

2 *Official Records of the General Assembly, Forty-ninth Session, Supplement No. 1* (A/49/1).

3 See *Official Records of the General Assembly, Forty-ninth Session, Plenary Meetings*, 28th meeting, and corrigendum.

11.40 ESTABLISHMENT AND FUNCTIONING OF CERTAIN SUBSIDIARY AND OTHER BODIES IN THE FIELD OF LAW

174 (II). Establishment of an International Law Commission

Committee: 6
Vote: 44 - 0 - 6
Ref.: 2927(XXVII), 2780(XXVI), 2634(XXV), 1647(XVI), 1106(XI), 1103(XI), 987(X), 986(X), 985(X), 984(X), 685(VII), 683(VII), 601(VI), 600(VI), 485(V), 484(V), 374(IV), 175(II)

The General Assembly,

Recognizing the need for giving effect to Article 13, paragraph 1, sub-paragraph a, of the Charter, stipulating that the General Assembly shall initiate studies and make recommendations for the purpose of encouraging the progressive development of international law and its codification;

Having studied the report[1] of the Committee directed by resolution 94(I)[2] of the General Assembly of 11 December 1946 to study:

(*a*) The methods by which the General Assembly should encourage the progressive development of international law and its eventual codification;

(*b*) Methods of securing the cooperation of the several organs of the United Nations to this end;

(*c*) Methods of enlisting the assistance of such national or international bodies as might aid in the attainment of this objective;

Recognizing the desirability of establishing a commission composed of persons of recognized competence in international law and representing as a whole the chief forms of civilization and the basic legal systems of the world,

Resolves to establish an "Intentional Law Commission", the members of which shall be elected at the third regular session of the General Assembly, and which shall be constituted and shall exercise its functions in accordance with the provisions of the annexed statute.

Hundred and twenty-third plenary meeting
21 November 1947

Statute of the International Law Commission

Article 1

1. The International Law Commission shall have for its object the promotion of the progressive development of international law and its codification.

2. The Commission shall concern itself primarily with public international law, but is not precluded from entering the field of private international law.

Chapter I.
Organization of the International Law Commission

Article 2

1. The Commission shall consist of fifteen members who shall be persons of recognized competence in international law.

2. No two members of the Commission shall be nationals of the same State.

3. In case of dual nationality a candidate shall be deemed to be a national of the State in which he ordinarily exercises civil and political rights.

Article 3

The members of the Commission shall be elected by the General Assembly from a list of candidates nominated by the Governments of States Members of the United Nations.

Article 4

Each Member may nominate for election not more than four candidates, of whom two may be nationals of the nominating State and two nationals of other States.

Article 5

The names of the candidates shall be submitted, in writing by the Governments to the Secretary-General by 1 June of the year in which an election is held, provided that a Government may in exceptional circumstances substitute for a candidate whom it has nominated before 1 June another candidate whom it shall name not later than thirty days before the opening of the General Assembly.

Article 6

The Secretary-General shall as soon as possible communicate to the Governments of States Members the names submitted, as well as any *curricula vitae* of candidates that may have been submitted by the nominating Governments.

Article 7

The Secretary-General shall prepare the list referred to in article 3 above, comprising in alphabetical order the names of all the candidates duly nominated, and shall submit this list to the General Assembly for the purposes of the election.

Article 8

At the election the electors shall bear in mind that the persons to be elected to the Commission should individually possess the qualifications required and that in the Commission as a whole representation of the main forms of civilization and of the principal legal systems of the world should be assured.

Article 9

1. The fifteen candidates who obtain the greatest number of votes and at least a majority of the votes of the Members present and voting shall be elected.

2. In the event of more than one national of the same State obtaining a sufficient number of votes for election, the one who obtains the greatest number of votes shall be elected and, if the votes are equally divided the elder or eldest candidate shall be elected.

Article 10

The members of the Commission shall be elected for three years. They shall be eligible for re-election.

Article 11

In the case of a vacancy, the Commission itself shall fill the vacancy having due regard to the provisions contained in articles 2 and 8 above.

Article 12

The Commission shall sit at the headquarters of the United Nations. The Commission shall, however, have the right to hold meetings at other places after consultation with the Secretary-General.

Article 13

Members of the Commission shall be paid travel expenses and shall also receive a *per diem* allowance at the same rate as the allowance

---

1 See document A/331. See appendix 12, p. 469.

2 See resolution*s adopted by the General Assembly during the second part of its first session,* p. 174-75.

paid to members of commissions of experts of the Economic and Social Council.

Article 14

The Secretary-General shall, so far as he is able, make available staff and facilities required by the Commission to fulfil its task.

Chapter II.
Functions of the International Law Commission

Article 15

In the following articles the expression "progressive development of international law" is used for convenience as meaning the preparation of draft conventions on subjects which have not yet been regulated by international law or in regard to which the law has not yet been sufficiently developed in the practice of States. Similarly, the expression "codification of international law" is used for convenience as meaning the more precise formulation and systematization of rules of international law in fields where there already has been extensive state practice, precedent and doctrine.

A. Progressive development of international law

Article 16

When the General Assembly refers to the Commission a proposal for the progressive development of international law, the Commission shall follow in general a procedure on the following lines:

(*a*) It shall appoint one of its members to be Rapporteur;

(*b*) It shall formulate a plan of work;

(*c*) It shall circulate a questionnaire to the Governments, and shall invite them to supply, within a fixed period of time, data and information relevant to items included in the plan of work;

(*d*) It may appoint some of its members to work with the Rapporteur on the preparation of drafts pending receipt of replies to this questionnaire;

(*e*) It may consult with scientific institutions and individual experts; these experts need not necessarily be nationals of Members of the United Nations. The Secretary-General will provide, when necessary and within the limits of the budget, for the expenses of these consultations of experts;

(*f*) It shall consider the drafts proposed by the Rapporteur;

(*g*) When the Commission considers a draft to be satisfactory, it shall request the Secretary-General to issue it as a Commission document. The Secretariat shall give all necessary publicity to this document which shall be accompanied by such explanations and supporting material as the Commission considers appropriate. The publication shall include any information supplied to the Commission in reply to the questionnaire referred to in sub-paragraph (*c*) above;

(*h*) The Commission shall invite the Governments to submit their comments on this document within a reasonable time;

(*i*) The Rapporteur and the members appointed for that purpose shall reconsider the draft, taking into consideration these comments, and shall prepare a final draft and explanatory report which they shall submit for consideration and adoption by the Commission;

(*j*) The Commission shall submit the draft so adopted with its recommendations through the Secretary-General to the General Assembly.

Article 17

1. The Commission shall also consider proposals and draft multilateral conventions submitted by Members of the United Nations, the principal organs of thc Unitcd Nations other than the General Assembly, specialized agencies, or official bodies established by intergovernmental agreement to encourage the progressive development of international law and its codification, and transmitted to it for that purpose by the Secretary-General.

2. If in such cases the Commission deems it appropriate to proceed with the study of such proposals or drafts, it shall follow in general procedure on the following lines:

(*a*) The Commission shall formulate a plan of work, and study such proposals or drafts and compare them with any other proposals and drafts on the same subjects;

(*b*) The Commission shall circulate a questionnaire to all Members of the United Nations and to the organs, specialized agencies and official bodies mentioned above which are concerned with the question, and shall invite them to transmit their comments within a reasonable time;

(*c*) The Commission shall submit a report and its recommendations to the General Assembly. By doing so, it may also, if it deems it desirable, make an interim report to the organ or agency which has submitted the proposal or draft;

(*d*) If the General Assembly should invite the Commission to proceed with its work in accordance with a suggested plan, the procedure outlined in article 16 above shall apply. The questionnaire referred to in paragraph (*c*) of that article may not, however, be necessary.

B. Codification of international law

Article 18

1. The Commission shall survey the whole field of international law with a view to selecting topics for codification, having in mind existing drafts, whether governmental or not.

2. When the Commission considers that the codification of a particular topic is necessary and desirable, it shall submit its recommendations to the General Assembly.

3. The Commission shall give priority to requests of the General Assembly to deal with any question.

Article 19

1. The Commission shall adopt a plan of work appropriate to each case.

2. The Commission shall, through the Secretary-General, address to Governments a detailed request to furnish the texts of laws, decrees, judicial decisions, treaties, diplomatic correspondence and other documents relevant to the topic being studied and which the Commission deems necessary.

Article 20

The Commission shall prepare its drafts in the form of articles and shall submit them to the General Assembly together with a commentary containing:

(*a*) Adequate presentation of precedents and other relevant data, including treaties, judicial decisions and doctrine;

(*b*) Conclusions defining:

(i) The extent of agreement on each point in the practice of States and in doctrine;

(ii) Divergencies and disagreements which exist, as well as arguments invoked in favour of one or another solution.

Article 21

1. When the Commission considers a draft to be satisfactory, it shall request the Secretary-General to issue it as a Commission document. The Secretariat shall give all necessary publicity to the document, including such explanations and supporting material as the Commission may consider appropriate. The publication shall include any information supplied to the Commission by Governments in accordance with article 19. The Commission shall decide whether the opinions of any scientific institution or individual experts consulted by the Commission shall be included in the publication.

2. The Commission shall request Governments to submit comments on this document within a reasonable time.

Article 22

Taking such comments into consideration, the Commission shall prepare a final draft and explanatory report, which it shall submit with its recommendations through the Secretary-General to the General Assembly.

Article 23

1. The Commission may recommend to the General Assembly:

(*a*) To take no action, the report having already been published;

(*b*) To take note of or adopt the report by resolution;

(*c*) To recommend the draft to Members with a view to the conclusion of a convention;

(*d*) To convoke a conference to conclude a convention.

2. Whenever it deems it desirable, the General Assembly may refer drafts back to the Commission for reconsideration or redrafting.

Article 24

The Commission shall consider ways and means for making the evidence of customary international law more readily available, such as the collection and publication of documents concerning State practice and of the decisions of national and international courts on questions of international law, and shall make a report to the General Assembly on this matter.

Chapter III.
Cooperation with other Bodies

Article 25

1. The Commission may consult, if it considers necessary, with any of the organs of the United Nations on any subject which is within the competence of that organ.

2. All documents of the Commission which are circulated to Governments by the Secretary-General shall also be circulated to such organs of the United Nations as are concerned. Such organs may furnish any information or make any suggestions to the Commission.

Article 26

1. The Commission may consult with any international or national organizations, official or non-official, on any subject entrusted to it if it believes that such a procedure might aid it in the performance of its functions.

2. For the purpose of distribution of documents of the Commission, the Secretary-General, after consultation with the Commission, shall draw up a list of national and international organizations concerned with questions of international law. The Secretary-General shall endeavour to include on this list at least one national organization of each Member of the United Nations.

3. In the application of the provisions of this article, the Commission and the Secretary-General shall comply with the resolutions of the General Assembly and the other principal organs of the United Nations concerning relations with Franco Spain and shall exclude both from consultations and from the list, organizations which have collaborated with the nazis and fascists.

4. The advisability of consultation by the Commission with intergovernmental organizations whose task is the codification of international law, such as those of the Pan-American Union, is recognized.

36/39. Enlargement of the International Law Commission: Amendments to Articles 2 and 9 of the Statute of the Commission

Committee: -
Vote: 122 - 21 - 2
Ref.: 1647(XVI)

The General Assembly,

Reaffirming the importance of the International Law Commission as the main permanent subsidiary organ of the General Assembly entrusted with the promotion of the progressive development of international law and its codification,

Recalling its resolution 1647 (XVI) of 6 November 1961, by which the membership of the International Law Commission was established at twenty-five members,

Noting that the membership of the United Nations has grown substantially since the adoption of that resolution,

Conscious of the increased interest shown by Member States, particularly those admitted to membership in the Organization since 1961, in the Commission's work on the progressive development of international law and its codification,

1. *Decides* to amend article 2, paragraph 1, of the Statute of the International Law Commission to read as follows:

"The Commission shall consist of thirty-four members who shall be persons of recognized competence in international law";

2. *Also decides* to amend article 9, paragraph 1, of the said Statute to read as follows:

"Those candidates, up to the maximum number prescribed for each regional group, who obtain the greatest number of votes and not less than a majority of the votes of the Members present and voting shall be elected";

3. *Decides further* that the thirty-four members of the International Law Commission shall be elected according to the following pattern:

(*a*) Eight nationals from African States;

(*b*) Seven nationals from Asian States;

(*c*) Three nationals from Eastern European States;

(*d*) Six nationals from Latin American States;

(*e*) Eight nationals from Western European or other States;

(*f*) One national from African States or Eastern European States in rotation, with the seat being allocated to a national of an African State in the first election held after the adoption of the present resolution;

(*g*) One national from Asian States or Latin American States in rotation, with the seat being allocated to a national of an Asian State in the first election held after the adoption of the present resolution;

4. *Decides*, by way of exception and in consequence of the enlargement of the Commission, to request the Secretary-General to include in the list of candidates for the election to be held at the current session, in addition to the nominations already received, such names as shall have been communicated to him in writing before 21 November 1981.

63rd plenary meeting
18 November 1981

351 (IV). Establishment of a United Nations Administrative Tribunal

Committee: 5
Vote: A: 48 - 0; B: Adopted without a vote
Ref.: 2490(XXIII), 957(X), 873(IX), 351(IV)

A

The General Assembly

Resolves that the following Statute shall be adopted for the United Nations Administrative Tribunal to come into force on 1 January 1950:

Statute of the United Nations Administrative Tribunal

Article 1

A Tribunal is established by the present Statute to be known as the United Nations Administrative Tribunal.

Article 2

1. The Tribunal shall be competent to hear and pass judgment upon applications alleging non-observance of contracts of employment of staff members of the Secretariat of the United Nations or of the terms of appointment of such staff members. The words "contracts" and "terms of appointment" include all pertinent regulations and rules in force at the time of alleged nonobservance, including the staff pension regulations.

2. The Tribunal shall be open:

(*a*) To any staff member of the Secretariat of the United Nations even after his employment has ceased, and to any person who has succeeded to the staff member's rights on his death;

(*b*) To any other person who can show that he is entitled to rights under any contract or terms of appointment, including the provisions of staff regulations and rules upon which the staff member could have relied.

3. In the event of a dispute as to whether the Tribunal has competence, the matter shall be settled by the decision of the Tribunal.

4. The Tribunal shall not be competent, however, to deal with any applications where the cause of complaint arose prior to 1 January 1950.

Article 3

1. The Tribunal shall be composed of seven members, no two of whom may be nationals of the same State. Only three shall sit in any particular case.

2. The members shall be appointed by the General Assembly for three years, and they may be re-appointed; provided, however, that of the members initially appointed, the terms of two members shall expire at the end of one year and the terms of two members shall expire at the end of two years. A member appointed to replace a member whose term of office has not expired shall hold office for the remainder of his predecessor's term.

3. The Tribunal shall elect its President and its two Vice-Presidents from among its members.

4. The Secretary-General shall provide the Tribunal with an Executive Secretary and such other staff as may be considered necessary.

5. No member of the Tribunal can be dismissed by the General Assembly unless the other members are of the unanimous opinion that he is unsuited for further service.

6. In case of a resignation of a member of the Tribunal, the resignation shall be addressed to the President of the Tribunal for transmission to the Secretary-General. This last notification makes the place vacant.

Article 4

The Tribunal shall hold ordinary sessions at dates to be fixed by its rules, subject to there being cases on its list which, in the opinion of the President, justify holding the session. Extraordinary sessions may be convoked by the President when required by the cases on the list.

Article 5

1. The Secretary-General of the United Nations shall make the administrative arrangements necessary for the functioning of the Tribunal.

2. The expenses of the Tribunal shall be borne by the United Nations.

Article 6

1. Subject to the provisions of the present Statute, the Tribunal shall establish its rules.

2. The rules shall include provisions concerning:

(*a*) Election of the President and Vice-Presidents;

(*b*) Composition of the Tribunal for its sessions;

(*c*) Presentation of applications and the procedure to be followed in respect to them;

(*d*) Intervention by persons to whom the Tribunal is open under paragraph 2 of article 2, whose rights may be affected by the judgment;

(*e*) Hearing, for purposes of information, of persons to whom the Tribunal is open under paragraph 2 of article 2, even though they are not parties to the case; and generally

(*f*) Other matters relating to the functioning of the Tribunal.

Article 7

1. An application shall not be receivable unless the person concerned has previously submitted the dispute to the joint appeals body provided for in the staff regulations and the latter has communicated its opinion to the Secretary-General, except where the Secretary-General and the applicant have agreed to submit the application directly to the Administrative Tribunal.

2. In the event of the joint body's recommendations being favourable to the application submitted to it, and in so far as this is the case, an application to the Tribunal shall be receivable if the Secretary-General has:

(*a*) Rejected the recommendations;

(*b*) Failed to take any action within the thirty days following the communication of the opinion; or

(*c*) Failed to carry out the recommendations within the thirty days following the communication of the opinion.

3. In the event that the recommendations made by the joint body and accepted by the Secretary-General are unfavourable to the applicant, and in so far as this is the case, the application shall be receivable, unless the joint body unanimously considers that it is frivolous.

4. An application shall not be receivable unless it is filed within ninety days reckoned from the respective dates and periods referred to in paragraph 2 above, or within ninety days reckoned from the date of the communication of the joint body's opinion containing recommendations unfavourable to the applicant. If the circumstances rendering the application receivable by the Tribunal, pursuant to paragraphs 2 and 3 above, is anterior to the date of announcement of the first session of the Tribunal, the time-limit of ninety days shall begin to run from that date. Nevertheless, the said time-limit on his behalf shall be extended to one year if the heirs of a deceased staff member or the trustee of a staff member who is not in a position to manage his own affairs, file the application in the name of the said staff member.

5. In any particular case the Tribunal may decide to suspend the provisions regarding time-limits.

6. The filing of an application shall not have the effect of suspending the execution of the decision contested.

7. Applications may be filed in any of the five official languages of the United Nations.

Article 8

The oral proceedings of the Tribunal shall be held in public unless the Tribunal decides that exceptional circumstances require that they be held in private.

Article 9

If the Tribunal finds that the application is well founded, it shall order the rescinding of the decision contested or the specific performance of the obligation invoked; but if, in exceptional circumstances, such rescinding or specific performance is, in the opinion of the Secretary-General, impossible or inadvisable, the Tribunal shall within a period of not more than sixty days order the payment to the applicant of compensation for the injury sustained. The applicant shall be entitled to claim compensation in lieu of rescinding of the contested decision or specific performance. In any case involving compensation, the amount awarded shall be fixed by the Tribunal and paid by the United Nations or, as appropriate, by the specialized agency participating under article 12.

Article 10

1. The Tribunal shall take all decisions by a majority vote.

2. The judgments shall be final and without appeal.

3. The judgments shall state the reasons on which they are based.

4. The judgments shall be drawn up, in any of the five official languages of the United Nations, in two originals which shall be deposited in the archives of the Secretariat of the United Nations.

5. A copy of the judgment shall be communicated to each of the parties in the case. Copies shall also be made available on request to interested persons.

Article 11

The present Statute may be amended by decisions of the General Assembly.

Article 12

The competence of the Tribunal may be extended to any specialized agency brought into relationship with the United Nations in accordance with the provisions of Articles 57 and 63 of the Charter upon the terms established by a special agreement to be made with each such agency by the Secretary-General of the United Nations. Each such special agreement shall provide that the agency concerned shall be bound by the judgments of the Tribunal and be responsible for the payment of any compensation awarded by the Tribunal in respect of a staff member of that agency and shall include, *inter alia*, provisions concerning the agency's participation in the administrative arrangements for the functioning of the Tribunal and concerning its sharing the expenses of the Tribunal.

255th plenary meeting
24 November 1949

B

The General Assembly

1. *Appoints* the following persons as members of the United Nations Administrative Tribunal in accordance with article 3 of the Statute of the Administrative Tribunal:

Madame Paul Bastid;
Sir Sydney Caine;
Lt. General His Highness Maharaja Jam Shri Digvijayasinhji Sahib;
Mr. Roland Andrews Egger;
Mr. Omar Loutfi;
Dr. Emilio N. Oribe;
Dr. Vladimir Outrata;

2. *Declares* the following members to be appointed for a three-year term, to commence on 1 January 1950:

Madame Paul Bastid;
Lt. General His Highness Maharaja Jam Shri Digvijayasinhji Sahib;
Mr. Omar Loutfi;

3. *Declares* the following members to be appointed for a two-year term, to commence on 1 January 1950:

Mr. Roland Andrews Egger;
Dr. Emilio N. Oribe;

4. *Declares* the following members to be appointed for a one-year term, to commence on 1 January 1950:

Sir Sydney Caine;
Dr. Vladimir Outrata.

274th plenary meeting
9 December 1949

50/46. Establishment of an International Criminal Court

Committee: 6
Vote: Adopted without a vote

The General Assembly,

Recalling its resolution 47/33 of 25 November 1992, in which it requested the International Law Commission to undertake the elaboration of a draft statute for an international criminal court,

Recalling also its resolution 48/31 of 9 December 1993, in which it requested the International Law Commission to continue its work on the question of the draft statute for an international criminal court, with a view to elaborating a draft statute for such a court, if possible at the Commission's forty-sixth session in 1994,

Recalling further that the International Law Commission adopted a draft statute for an international criminal court[1] at its forty-sixth session and decided to recommend that an international conference of plenipotentiaries be convened to study the draft statute and to conclude a convention on the establishment of an international criminal court,[2]

Recalling its resolution 49/53 of 9 December 1994, in which it decided to establish an *Ad Hoc* Committee, open to all States Members of the United Nations or members of specialized agencies, to review the major substantive and administrative issues arising out of the draft statute prepared by the International Law Commission and, in the light of that review, to consider arrangements for the convening of an international conference of plenipotentiaries,

Noting that the *Ad Hoc* Committee on the Establishment of an International Criminal Court has made considerable progress during its sessions on the review of the major substantive and administrative issues arising out of the draft statute prepared by the International Law Commission,

Noting also that the States participating in the *Ad Hoc* Committee still have different views on major substantive and administrative issues arising out of the draft statute prepared by the International Law Commission and that, therefore, further discussions are needed for reaching consensus on the above issues in the future,

Noting further that the *Ad Hoc* Committee is of the opinion that issues can be addressed most effectively by combining further discussions with the drafting of texts, with a view to preparing a consolidated text of a convention for an international criminal court as a next step towards consideration by a conference of plenipotentiaries,

Noting that the *Ad Hoc* Committee recommends that the General Assembly take up the organization of future work with a view to its early completion, given the interest of the international community in the establishment of an international criminal court,

Noting also that the *Ad Hoc* Committee encourages participation by the largest number of States in its future work in order to promote universality,

Expressing deep appreciation for the renewed offer of the Government of Italy to host a conference on the establishment of an international criminal court,

1. *Takes note* of the report of the *Ad Hoc* Committee on the Establishment of an International Criminal Court,[3] including the recommendations contained therein, and expresses its appreciation to the *Ad Hoc* Committee for the useful work done;

2. *Decides* to establish a preparatory committee open to all States Members of the United Nations or members of specialized agencies or of the International Atomic Energy Agency, to discuss further the major substantive and administrative issues arising out of the draft statute prepared by the International Law Commission and, taking into account the different views expressed during the meetings, to draft texts, with a view to preparing a widely acceptable consolidated text of a convention for an international criminal court as a next step towards consideration by a conference of plenipotentiaries, and also decides that the work of the Preparatory Committee should be based on the draft statute prepared by the International Law Commission and should take into account the report of the *Ad Hoc* Committee and the written comments submitted by States to the Secretary-General on the draft statute for an international criminal court pursuant to paragraph 4 of General Assembly resolution 49/53[4] and, as appropriate, contributions of relevant organizations;

3. *Also decides* that the Preparatory Committee will meet from 25 March to 12 April and from 12 to 30 August 1996 and submit its report to the General Assembly at the beginning of its fifty-first session, and requests the Secretary-General to provide the Preparatory Committee with the necessary facilities for the performance of its work;

4. *Urges* participation in the Preparatory Committee by the largest number of States in order to promote universal support for an international criminal court;

1 *Official Records of the General Assembly, Forty-ninth Session, Supplement No. 10* (A/49/10), para. 91.

2 *Ibid.*, para. 90.

3 *Official Records of the General Assembly, Fiftieth Session, Supplement No. 22* (A/50/22).

4 A/AC.244/1 and Add. 1-3.

5. *Decides* to include in the provisional agenda of its fifty-first session an item entitled "Establishment of an international criminal court", in order to study the report of the Preparatory Committee and, in the light of that report, to decide on the convening of an international conference of plenipotentiaries to finalize and adopt a convention on the establishment of an international criminal court, including on the timing and the duration of the conference.

87th plenary meeting
11 December 1995

11.50 MEMBERSHIP AND REPRESENTATION

11.51 MEMBERSHIP

35 (I). Question of the Re-Examination by the Security Council of Certain Applications for Admission to Membership in the United Nations

Committee: 1
Vote: unanimous

Applications for membership in the United Nations were submitted by the People's Republic of Albania, the Mongolian People's Republic, the Hashemite Kingdom of Transjordan, Ireland and Portugal;

The Security Council, which examined these applications, has not made any recommendations;

Since membership in the United Nations is open to all peace-loving States which accept the obligations contained in the Charter and which in the judgment of the Organization are able and willing to carry out these obligations, as stated in Article 4;

Therefore, the General Assembly recommends that the Security Council re-examine the applications for membership in the United Nations of the above-mentioned States on their respective merits as measured by the yardstick of the Charter, in accordance with Article 4.

Forty-ninth plenary meeting
19 November 1946

197 (III). Admission of New Members

Committee: P
Vote: A: 32 - 10 - 2; B: 33 - 0- 10; C: 39 - 6 - 1; D: 40 - 6 - 1; E: 37 - 6 - 1; F: 38 - 6 - 1; G: 38 - 6 - 1; H: 37 - 6 - 2; I: 41 - 6 - 0
Ref.: 113(II)

A

Whereas, pursuant to the provisions of Article 4, paragraph 2, of the Charter, admission to membership in the United Nations will be effected by a decision of the General Assembly upon the recommendation of the Security Council, and

Whereas the International Court of Justice in an advisory opinion of 28 May 1948[1] declared that:

(*a*) A Member of the United Nations which is called upon, in virtue of Article 4 of the Charter, to pronounce itself by its vote, either in the Security Council or in the General Assembly, on the admission of a State to membership in the United Nations, is not juridically entitled to make its consent to the admission dependent on conditions not expressly provided by paragraph 1 of the said Article; and

(*b*) In particular, a Member of the Organization cannot, while it recognizes the conditions set forth in that provision to be fulfilled by the State concerned, subject its affirmative vote to the additional condition that other States be admitted to membership in the United Nations together with that State,

The General Assembly,

Recommends that each member of the Security Council and of the General Assembly, in exercising its vote on the admission of new Members, should act in accordance with the foregoing opinion of the International Court of Justice.

Hundred and seventy-seventh plenary meeting
8 December 1948

B

The General Assembly,

Having noted the special reports of the Security Council on the question of the admission of new Members (A/617 and A/618),

Having noted the advisory opinion of the International Court of Justice of 28 May 1948,

Having noted the general sentiment in favour of the universality of the United Nations,

Asks the Security Council to reconsider, taking into account the circumstances in each particular case, the applications for membership in the United Nations of the States mentioned in the said special reports.

Hundred and seventy-seventh plenary meeting
8 December 1948

C

The General Assembly,

Recalling that nine members of the Security Council, on 18 August 1947,[2] supported a draft resolution recommending the admission to the United Nations of Portugal, and that no recommendation was made to the General Assembly because of the opposition of one of the permanent members of the Council,

Recalling resolution 113 (II), D, of 17 November 1947, requesting the Security Council to reconsider the application of Portugal,

Noting from the report of the Security Council that, since none of its members has changed its decision with regard to this application, the Security Council has adjourned its discussion on the matter indefinitely,[3]

Reaffirms its view that the opposition to the application of Portugal was based on grounds not included in Article 4 of the Charter;

Determines again that Portugal is, in its judgment, a peace-loving State within the meaning of Article 4 of the Charter, is able and willing to carry out the obligations of the Charter, and should therefore be admitted to membership in the United Nations;

Requests the Security Council to reconsider the application of Portugal, in the light of this determination of the Assembly and of the advisory opinion of the International Court of Justice of 28 May 1948.

Hundred and seventy-seventh plenary meeting
8 December 1948

---

1 See *Admission of a State to the United Nations (Charter, Article 4)*, Advisory Opinion, I. C. J. Reports, 1948, p. 57.

2 See *Official Records of the Security Council*, Second Year, 186th meeting.

3 See *Official Record of the third session of the General Assembly*, Supplement No. 2, p. 131.

D

The General Assembly,

Recalling that nine members of the Security Council, on 18 August 1947, supported a draft resolution recommending the admission to the United Nations of Transjordan, and that no recommendation was made to the General Assembly because of the opposition of one of the permanent members of the Council,

Recalling resolution 113 (II), E, of 17 November 1947, requesting the Security Council to reconsider the application of Transjordan,

Noting from the report of the Security Council that, since none of its members has changed its decision with regard to this application, the Security Council has adjourned its discussion on the matter indefinitely,

Reaffirms its view that the opposition to the application of Transjordan was based on grounds not included in Article 4 of the Charter;

Determines again that Transjordan is, in its judgment, a peace-loving State within the meaning of Article 4 of the Charter, is able and willing to carry out the obligations of the Charter, and should therefore be admitted to membership in the United Nations;

Requests the Security Council to reconsider the application of Transjordan, in the light of this determination of the Assembly and of the advisory opinion of the International Court of Justice of 28 May 1948.

Hundred and seventy-seventh plenary meeting
8 December 1948

E

The General Assembly,

Recalling that nine members of the Security Council, on 21 August 1947;[1] supported a draft resolution recommending the admission to the United Nations of Italy, and that no recommendation was made to the General Assembly because of the opposition of one of the permanent members of the Council, although that member had previously expressed the view that Italy was eligible for membership,

Recalling resolution 113 (II), F, of 17 November 1947, requesting the Security Council to reconsider the application of Italy,

Noting from the report of the Security Council that, on 10 April 1948,[2] nine members again supported a draft resolution recommending the admission to the United Nations of Italy, and that no recommendation was made to the Assembly because of the opposition of one of the permanent members of the Council,

Reaffirms its view that the opposition to the application of Italy was based on grounds not included in Article 4 of the Charter;

Determines again that Italy is, in its judgment, a peace-loving State within the meaning of Article 4 of the Charter, is able and willing to carry out the obligations of the Charter, and should therefore be admitted to membership in the United Nations;

Requests the Security Council to reconsider the application of Italy, in the light of this determination of the Assembly and of the advisory opinion of the International Court of Justice of 28 May 1948.

Hundred and seventy-seventh plenary meeting
8 December 1948

F

The General Assembly,

Recalling that nine members of the Security Council, on 18 August 1947, supported a draft resolution recommending the admission to the United Nations of Finland, and that no recommendation was made to the General Assembly because of the opposition of one of the permanent members of the Council, although that member had previously expressed the view that Finland was eligible for membership,

Recalling resolution 113 (II), G, of 17 November 1947, requesting the Security Council to reconsider the application of Finland,

Noting from the report of the Security Council that, since none of its members has changed its decision with regard to this application, the Security Council has adjourned its discussion on the matter indefinitely,

Reaffirms its view that the opposition to the application of Finland was based on grounds not included in Article 4 of the Charter;

Determines again that Finland is in its judgment a peace-loving State within the meaning of Article 4 of the Charter, is able and willing to carry out the obligations of the Charter, and should therefore be admitted to membership in the United Nations;

Requests the Security Council to reconsider the application of Finland, in the light of this determination of the Assembly and of the advisory opinion of the International Court of Justice of 28 May 1948.

Hundred and seventy-seventh plenary meeting
8 December 1948

G

The General Assembly,

Recalling that nine members of the Security Council, on 18 August 1947, supported a draft resolution recommending the admission to the United Nations of Ireland, and that no recommendation was made to the General Assembly because of the opposition of one of the permanent members of the Council,

Recalling resolution 113 (II), C, of 17 November 1947, requesting the Security Council to reconsider the application of Ireland,

Noting from the report of the Security Council that, since none of its members has changed its decision with regard to this application, the Security Council has adjourned its discussion on the matter indefinitely,

Reaffirms its view that the opposition to the application of Ireland was based on grounds not included in Article 4 of the Charter;

Determines again that Ireland is in its judgment a peace-loving State within the meaning of Article 4 of the Charter, is able and willing to carry out the obligations of the Charter, and should therefore be admitted to membership in the United Nations;

Requests the Security Council to reconsider the application of Ireland, in the light of this determination of the Assembly and of the advisory opinion of the International Court of Justice of March 1948.

Hundred and seventy-seventh plenary meeting
8 December 1948

H

The General Assembly,

Recalling that eight members of the Security Council, in August 1947[3], supported a draft resolution recommending the admission to the United Nations of Austria, at such time and under such conditions as the General Assembly might deem appropriate, but that no recommendation was made to the Assembly because of the opposition of one of the permanent members of the Council,

Recalling resolution 113 (II), H, of 17 November 1947, requesting the Security Council to reconsider the application of Austria,

Noting from the report of the Security Council that, since none of its members had changed its decision with regard to this application, the Security Council has adjourned its discussion on the matter indefinitely,

Reiterates its opinion that Austria is a peace-loving State within the meaning of Article 4 of the Charter; and consequently

---

1 See *Official Records of the Security Council*, Second Year, 190th meeting.

2 *Ibid.*, Third Year, No. 54.

3 See *Official Records of the Security Council*, Second Year, 190th meeting.

Requests the Security Council to reconsider the application of Austria, in the light of this expression of opinion of the Assembly and of the advisory opinion of the International Court of Justice of 28 May 1948.

Hundred and seventy-seventh plenary meeting
8 December 1948

I

The General Assembly,

Noting that nine members of the Security Council, on 18 August 1948[1] supported a draft resolution recommending the admission to the United Nations of Ceylon,

Considering that the records of the discussions in the *Ad Hoc* Political Committee reveal a unanimous opinion that Ceylon is a peace-loving State, is able and willing to carry out the obligations of the Charter, and should therefore be admitted to membership in the United Nations,

Requests the Security Council to reconsider at the earliest possible moment the application of Ceylon in the light of the present resolution and of the discussions in the *Ad Hoc* Political Committee.

Hundred and seventy-seventh plenary meeting
8 December 1948

918 (X). Admission of New Members to the United Nations

Committee: Ad hoc
Vote: 52 - 2 - 5
Ref.: 718(VIII), 506(VI), 296(IV)

The General Assembly,

Having noted the general sentiment which has been expressed on numerous occasions in favour of the widest possible membership of the United Nations,

Having received the preliminary report[2] of the Committee of Good Offices established by General Assembly resolution 718 (VIII) of 23 October 1953,

Taking into account the statements about the admission of new Members made by permanent members of the Security Council in the general debate at the present session of the General Assembly,

Believing that a broader representation in the membership of the United Nations will enable the Organization to play a more effective role in the current international situation,

1. *Expresses appreciation* of the work and efforts of the Committee of Good Offices;

2. *Requests* the Security Council to consider, in the light of the general opinion in favour of the widest possible membership of the United Nations, the pending applications for membership of all those eighteen countries about which no problem of unification arises;

3. *Requests further* that the Security Council make its report on these applications to the General Assembly during the present session.

552nd plenary meeting
8 December 1955

1144 (XII). Admission of New Members to the United Nations

Committee: P
Vote: A: 51 - 9 - 21; B: 49 - 9 - 23

A

The General Assembly,

Recalling its resolutions 296 G (IV) of 22 November 1949 and 1017 A (XI) of 28 February 1957 finding the Republic of Korea qualified for membership in the United Nations,

Noting with regret the continued inability of the Security Council to recommend the admission of the Republic of Korea to membership in the United Nations owing to the negative vote of a permanent member of the Council,

Reaffirms that the Republic of Korea is fully qualified for and should be admitted to membership in the United Nations.

709th plenary meeting
25 October 1957

B

The General Assembly,

Recalling its resolutions 620 C (VII) of 21 December 1952 and 1017 B (XI) of 28 February 1957 finding Viet-Nam qualified for membership in the United Nations,

Noting with regret the continued inability of the Security Council to recommend the admission of Viet-Nam to membership in the United Nations owing to the negative vote of a permanent member of the Council,

Reaffirms that Viet-Nam is fully qualified for and should be admitted to membership in the United Nations.

709th plenary meeting
25 October 1957

32/2. Admission of the Socialist Republic of Viet Nam to Membership in the United Nations

Committee: -
Vote: Adopted without a vote

The General Assembly,

Having received the recommendation of the Security Council of 20 July 1977 that the Socialist Republic of Viet Nam should be admitted to membership in the United Nations,[3]

Having considered the application for membership of the Socialist Republic of Viet Nam,[4]

Decides to admit the Socialist Republic of Viet Nam to membership in the United Nations.

1st plenary meeting
20 September 1977

46/1. Admission of the Democratic People's Republic of Korea and the Republic of Korea to Membership in the United Nations

Committee: -
Vote: Adopted without a vote

The General Assembly,

Having received the recommendation of the Security Council of 8 August 1991 that the Democratic People's Republic of Korea and the Republic of Korea should be admitted to membership in the United Nations,

Having considered separately the application for membership of the Democratic People's Republic of Korea and the application for membership of the Republic of Korea,

1. *Decides* to admit the Democratic People's Republic of Korea to membership in the United Nations;

2. *Decides* to admit the Republic of Korea to membership in the United Nations.

1st plenary meeting
17 September 1991

---

1 *Ibid.*, Third Year, No. 105.

2 *Official Records of the General Assembly, Tenth Session, Annexes*, agenda item 21, document A/2973. Appendix 43, p. 427.

3 *Official Records of the General Assembly, Thirty-second Session, Annexes*, agenda item 25, document A/32/152.

4 A/31/180-S/12183. For the printed text, see *Official Records of the Security Council, Thirty-first Year, Supplement for July, August and September 1976*.

47/225. Admission of the State whose Application is Contained in Document A/47/876-S/25147 to Membership in the United Nations

Committee: -
Vote: Adopted without a vote

The General Assembly,

Having received the recommendation of the Security Council of 7 April 1993 that the State whose application is contained in document A/47/876-S/25147 should be admitted to membership in the United Nations,[1]

Having considered the application for membership contained in document A/47/876-S/25147,

Decides to admit the State whose application is contained in document A/47/876-S/25147 to membership in the United Nations, this State being provisionally referred to for all purposes within the United Nations as "the former Yugoslav Republic of Macedonia" pending settlement of the difference that has arisen over the name of the State.

98th plenary meeting
8 April 1993

11.52 REPRESENTATION

396 (V). Recognition by the United Nations of the Representation of a Member State

Committee: P
Vote: 36 - 6 - 9

The General Assembly,

Considering that difficulties may arise regarding the representation of a Member State in the United Nations and that there is a risk that conflicting decisions may be reached by its various organs,

Considering that it is in the interest of the proper functioning of the Organization that there should be uniformity in the procedure applicable whenever more than one authority claims to be the government entitled to represent a Member State in the United Nations, and this question becomes the subject of controversy in the United Nations,

Considering that, in virtue of its composition, the General Assembly is the organ of the United Nations in which consideration can best be given to the views of all Member States in matters affecting the functioning of the Organization as a whole,

1. *Recommends* that, whenever more than one authority claims to be the government entitled to represent a Member State in the United Nations and this question becomes the subject of controversy in the United Nations, the question should be considered in the light of the Purposes and Principles of the Charter and the circumstances of each case;

2. *Recommends* that, when any such question arises, it should be considered by the General Assembly, or by the Interim Committee if the General Assembly is not in session;

3. *Recommends* that the attitude adopted by the General Assembly or its Interim Committee concerning any such question should be taken into account in other organs of the United Nations and in the specialized agencies;

4. *Declares* that the attitude adopted by the General Assembly or its Interim Committee concerning any such question shall not of itself affect the direct relations of individual Member States with the State concerned;

5. *Requests* the Secretary-General to transmit the present resolution to the other organs of the United Nations and to the specialized agencies for such action as may be appropriate.

325th plenary meeting
14 December 1950

1 A/47/923.

2642 (XXV). Representation of China in the United Nations

Committee: -
Vote: 66 - 52 - 7
Ref.: 2500(XXIV), 2389(XXIII), 2271(XXII), 2159(XXI), 2025(XX), 1668(XVI), 1493(XV), 1351(XIV), 1239(XIII), 1135(XII), 1108(XI), 990(X), 903(IX), 800(VIII), 501(V), 490(V)

The General Assembly,

Recalling the recommendation contained in its resolution 396 (V) of 14 December 1950 that, whenever more than one authority claims to be the Government entitled to represent a Member State in the United Nations and this question becomes the subject of controversy in the United Nations, the question should be considered in the light of the purposes and principles of the Charter of the United Nations and the circumstances of each case,

Recalling further its decision in resolution 1668 (XVI) of 15 December 1961, in accordance with Article 18 of the Charter, that any proposal to change the representation of China is an important question, which, in General Assembly resolutions 2025 (XX) of 17 November 1965, 2159 (XXI) of 29 November 1966, 2271 (XXII) of 28 November 1967, 2389 (XXIII) of 19 November 1968 and 2500 (XXIV) of 11 November 1969, was affirmed as remaining valid,

Affirms again that this decision remains valid.

1913th plenary meeting
20 November 1970

2758 (XXVI). Restoration of the Lawful Rights of the People's Republic of China in the United Nations

Committee: -
Vote: 76 - 35 - 17

The General Assembly,

Recalling the principles of the Charter of the United Nations,

Considering that the restoration of the lawful rights of the People's Republic of China is essential both for the protection of the Charter of the United Nations and for the cause that the United Nations must serve under the Charter,

Recognizing that the representatives of the Government of the People's Republic of China are the only lawful representatives of China to the United Nations and that the People's Republic of China is one of the five permanent members of the Security Council,

Decides to restore all its rights to the People's Republic of China and to recognize the representatives of its Government as the only legitimate representatives of China to the United Nations, and to expel forthwith the representatives of Chiang Kai-shek from the place which they unlawfully occupy at the United Nations and in all the organizations related to it.

1976th plenary meeting
25 October 1971

3238 (XXIX). Restoration of the Lawful Rights of the Royal Government of National Union of Cambodia in the United Nations

Committee: -
Vote: 54 - 54 - 24

The General Assembly,

Recalling the purposes and principles of the Charter of the United Nations,

Recognizing that the situation in Cambodia is of concern to all Member States and especially to the countries situated close to the area,

Taking into account that, while the Royal Government of National Union of Cambodia, presided over by Prince Norodom Sihanouk, exercises authority over a segment of Cambodia, the Government of the Khmer Republic still has control over a preponderant number of the Cambodian people,

Believing that the Cambodian people themselves should be allowed to solve their own political problems peacefully, free from outside interference,

Believing also that such political settlement should be reached by the indigenous parties concerned, without external influence,

1. *Calls upon* all the Powers which have been influencing the two parties to the conflict to use their good offices for conciliation between these two parties with a view to restoring peace in Cambodia;

2. *Requests* the Secretary-General, after due consultation, to lend appropriate assistance to the two contending parties claiming lawful rights in Cambodia and to report on the results to the General Assembly at its thirtieth session;

3. *Decides* not to press for any further action until Member States have an opportunity to examine the report of the Secretary-General.

2302nd plenary meeting
29 November 1974

50/83. Normalization of the Situation Concerning South Africa

Committee: -
Vote: Adopted without a vote

The General Assembly,

Recalling its resolution 48/258 A, adopted by consensus on 23 June 1994, the date on which South Africa was invited to resume its participation in the work of the General Assembly,

Noting that South Africa has since that date commenced payment of its assessed contributions.

Also recalling the exceptional circumstances pertaining to the resumption of South Africa's participation in the work of the General Assembly following the elimination of apartheid and the establishment of a democratic, non-racial South Africa,

Recognizing that, owing to the exceptional circumstances arising from apartheid, South Africa requested not to be held liable for contributions relating to the period from 30 September 1974 to 23 June 1994,

Recognizing also that the General Assembly took a moral and political decision to exclude South Africa from participation in its work,

Recognizing further that the exclusion of South Africa from the work of the General Assembly was unprecedented,

1. *Accepts* owing to these exceptional and unique circumstances, South Africa's request not to pay its contributions for the period from 30 September 1974 to 23 June 1994, and decides that the consequent burden for the Organization shall be borne by Member States pursuant to Article 17 of the Charter of the United Nations and the provisions of the present resolution;

2. *Welcomes and endorses* the statement of South Africa that it will waive any credits it would receive in the amount of $549,606, and $737,142 from budgetary surpluses retained in the regular budget and the peace-keeping special accounts, respectively, for the period from 30 September 1974 to 23 June 1994;

3. *Decides* to reduce the net amount of $122, 238,000 available as credits to Member States, arising from the implementation of resolutions 2947 A and B (XXVII) of 8 December 1972, 36/116 B of 10 December 1981, 40/241 B of 18 December 1985 and 42/216 of 21 December 1987, by $53,881,711 and to waive the share of the credits in the amount of $53,332,105 among other Member States on the basis of the respective scale of assessments contained in resolutions 34/6 A of 25 October 1979, 37/125 A of 17 December 1982 and 40/248 of 18 December 1985, in order to account for the reduction in outstanding contributions resulting from paragraph 1 above;

4. *Also decides* to reduce the amount of $173,392,935, available as credits to Member States, arising from the implementation of resolutions 33/13 E of 14 December 1978, 34/7 D and 34/9 E of 17 December 1979, 35/45 B of 1 December 1980, 35/115 B of 10 December 1980, 36/66 B of 30 November 1981, 36/138 B of 16 December 1981, 37/38 B of 30 November 1982, 37/127 B of 17 December 1982, 38/35 B of 1 December 1983, 38/38 B of 5 December 1983, 39/28 B of 30 November 1984, 39/71 B of 13 December 1984, 40/59 B of 2 December 1985, 40/246 B of 18 December 1985, 41/44 B of 3 December 1986, 41/179 B of 5 December 1986, 42/70 B of 3 December 1987, 42/223 of 21 December 1987, 43/228 and 43/229 of 21 December 1988, 44/187 and 44/188 of 21 December 1989, 46/194 of 20 December 1991, 47/204 and 47/205 of 22 December 1992 and 49/226 of 23 December 1994, by $40,905,714 and to waive the share of credits in the amount of $40,168,572 among other Member States on the basis of the respective scale of assessments for the period in which the surpluses arose, in order to account for the reduction in outstanding contributions resulting from paragraph 1 above;

5. *Further decides* that, owing to the unique and exceptional circumstances arising from apartheid, the decisions set out in paragraphs 3 and 4 of the present resolution shall under no circumstances constitute a precedent.

93rd plenary meeting
15 December 1995

11.60 NON-MEMBERS AND OBSERVERS

91 (I). Conditions on which Switzerland may Become a Party to the International Court of Justice

Committee: 6
Vote: unanimous
Ref.: 806(VIII), 805(VIII), 363(IV)

The Chief of the Swiss Federal Political Department, in a letter forwarded to the Secretary General of the United Nations on 26 October 1946, by the Swiss Consul-General in New York, expressed the desire of the Swiss Federal Council to ascertain the conditions on which Switzerland could, in pursuance of Article 93, paragraph 2, of the Charter, become a party to the Statute of the International Court of Justice.

Article 93, paragraph 2, of the Charter provides that a State which is not a member of the United Nations may become a party to the Statute of the Court on conditions to be determined in each case by the General Assembly upon the recommendation of the Security Council.

The Security Council considered and adopted at its eightieth meeting, held on 15 November 1946, a report and recommendation on this matter from its Committee of Experts. (Annex.)

The General Assembly has considered and adopted, on the recommendation of its Sixth Committee, the report and recommendation of the Security Council.

The General Assembly therefore determines, in pursuance of Article 93, paragraph 2, of the Charter, and upon the recommendation of the Security Council, the conditions on which Switzerland may become a party to the Statute of the International Court of Justice, as follows:

Switzerland will become a party to the Statute of the Court on the date of the deposit with the Secretary-General of the United Nations of an instrument, signed on behalf of the Government of Switzerland and ratified as may be required by Swiss constitutional law, containing:

(*a*) Acceptance of the provisions of the Statute of the International Court of Justice;

(*b*) Acceptance of all the obligations of a Member of the United Nations under Article 94 of the Charter;

(*c*) An undertaking to contribute to the expenses of the Court such equitable amount as the General Assembly shall assess from time to time after consultation with the Swiss Government.

Fifty-sixth plenary meeting
11 December 1946

Annex

Report and Recommendation of the Committee of Experts of the Security Council Concerning the Conditions on which Switzerland May Become a Party to the Statute of the International Court of Justice

(Adopted by the Security Council at its eightieth meeting on 15 November 1946)

1. The Committee has considered the letter from the Chief of the Swiss Federal Political Department which was forwarded to the Secretary-General on 26 October 1946 by the Swiss Consul-General in New York (document S/185). That letter expressed the desire of the Swiss Federal Council to know the conditions on which Switzerland could become a party to the Statute of the International Court of Justice. Under Article 93, paragraph 2, of the Charter, those conditions are to be determined by the General Assembly upon the recommendation of the Security Council.

2. The Committee advises the Security Council to send the following recommendation to the General Assembly:

"The Security Council recommends that the General Assembly, in accordance with Article 93, paragraph 2, of the Charter, determine the conditions on which Switzerland may become a party to the Statute of the International Court of Justice, as follows:

"Switzerland will become a party to the Statute of the Court on the date of the deposit with the Secretary-General of the United Nations of an instrument, signed on behalf of the Government of Switzerland and ratified as may be required by Swiss constitutional law, containing:

"(*a*) Acceptance of the provisions of the Statute of the International Court of Justice;

"(*b*) Acceptance of all the obligations of a Member of the United Nations under Article 94 of the Charter;

"(*c*) An undertaking to contribute to the expenses of the Court such equitable amount as the General Assembly shall assess from time to time after consultation with the Swiss Government."

3. The Committee decided that it is unnesessary to use in the first suggested condition the words in the Protocol of Signature of the Statute of the Permanent Court of International Justice (16 December 1920, Series D, No. 1, 4th edition, page 7) whereby signatories declared acceptance of "the jurisdiction of the Court in accordance with the terms and subject to the conditions of the Statute. In the opinion of the Committee, acceptance of the provisions of the Statute includes acceptance of any incidental jurisdiction exercisable by the Court under the provisions of the Statute.

4. The Committee desires to state that its intention in inserting the second suggested condition is the same as that which caused it to recommend the identical wording appearing in paragraph (I) of the resolution adopted by the Security Council on 15 October 1946 setting out the conditions under which the Court shall be open to States not parties to the Statute. The obligations imposed by Article 94 of the Charter upon a Member of the United Nations should, in the opinion of the Committee, apply equally to non-members of the United Nations which become parties to the Statute and to non-parties which are allowed access to the Court. In the opinion of the Committee, the obligations of a Member of the United Nations under Article 94 include the complementary obligations arising under Articles 25 and 103 of the Charter insofar as the provisions of those Articles may relate to the provisions of Article 94, and non-members of the United Nations which become parties to the Statute (and non-parties which have access to the Court) become bound by these complementary obligations under Articles 25 and 103 in relation to the provisions of Article 94 (but not otherwise), when they accept, "all the obligations of a Member of the United Nations under Article 94." The French text of this latter phrase in the recommendation in this report differs from the French text of the Council resolution of 15 October 1946 relating to access to the Court. The Committee believes that the present text states the meaning more accurately.

5. On the third suggested condition - contributions to the expenses of the Court - the Committee noted that the last sentence of Article 35, paragraph 3, of the Statute contemplates a general contribution (i.e., not one assessed in each case) towards the expenses of the Court by parties to the Statute which are not members of the United Nations. Although budgetary matters are within the competence of the Assembly, the obligation to contribute to the expenses of the Court must be imposed by the Assembly as a condition under Article 93, paragraph 2, upon the recommendation of the Security Council. The Committee therefore decided to recommend this condition.

6. The Committee desires to draw attention to the fact that under Article 93, paragraph 2, of the Charter the conditions on which a State which is not a member of the United Nations may become a party to the Statute are to be determined *in each case* by the General Assembly upon the recommendation of the Security Council. Accordingly, the conditions recommended above as appropriate to the case of Switzerland are not intended to constitute a precedent to be followed either by the Security Council or by the General Assembly in any future case under Article 93, paragraph 2, of the Charter.

7. The Committee points out that when Switzerland becomes a party to the Statute by accepting the conditions determined by the General Assembly under Article 93, paragraph 2, of the Charter, Switzerland may, under Articles 4 and 69 of the Statute, participate in electing members of the Court and in making amendments to the Statute, on conditions which the Assembly may prescribe upon the recommendation of the Security Council. In this connection, it is noted that, while Article 93, paragraph 2, of the Charter requires the setting of conditions of accession in each case, Articles 4 and 69 of the Statute permit the General Assembly, on the recommendation of the Security Council, to set generally applicable conditions on which non-member States parties to the Statute may participate in electing members of the Court and in the making of amendments to the Statute. The Committee advises that no special conditions on those matters should be prescribed in the case of Switzerland. It advises also that the Council should not now recommend to the Assembly generally applicable conditions under Articles 4 and 69 of the Statute, but should do so after Switzerland or some other non-member State has actually acceded to the Statute. At that time, the Council may wish to include in the generally applicable conditions provisions similar to those of Article 19 of the Charter in connection with the third condition of accession suggested in paragraph 2 above, if the General Assembly prescribes that condition and Switzerland accepts it.

264 (III). Conditions under which a State, a Party to the Statute of the International Court of Justice but not a Member of the United Nations, may Participate in the Elections of Members of the Court

Committee: -
Vote: Adopted without a vote

The General Assembly,

Having received the recommendations[1] of the Security Council with regard to the conditions under which a State which is a party to the Statute of the International Court of Justice but not a Member of the United Nations may participate in electing members of the Court,

Resolves

1. That such a State shall be on an equal footing with the Members of the United Nations in respect to those provisions of the Statute which regulate the nominations of candidates for election by the General Assembly;

2. That such a State shall participate, in the General Assembly, in electing the members of the Court in the same manner as the Members of the United Nations;

3. That such a State, when in arrears in the payment of its contribution to the expenses of the Court, shall not participate in electing the members of the Court in the General Assembly if the amount of its arrears equals or exceeds the amount of the contribution due from it for the preceding two full years. The General Assembly may, never-

---

1 Adopted at the 360th meeting on 28 September 1948. See *Official Records of the Security Council*, third year, No. 112.

theless, permit such a State to participate in the elections, if it is satisfied that the failure to pay is due to conditions beyond the control of that State (see Charter, Article 19).

Hundred and fiftieth plenary meeting
8 October 1948

2520 (XXIV). Participation of States which are Parties to the Statute of the International Court of Justice, but Are Not Members of the United Nations, in the Procedure for Effecting Amendments to the Statute

Committee: -
Vote: unanimous

The General Assembly,

Recalling that, under Article 69 of the Statute of the International Court of Justice, the Security Council may recommend to the General Assembly for adoption provisions concerning the participation of States which are parties to the Statute, but are not Members of the United Nations, in the procedure for effecting amendments to the Statute,

Having received the recommendations of the Security Council in this regard, contained in Council resolution 272 (1969) of 23 October 1969,

Decides that:

(*a*) A State which is a party to the Statute of the International Court of Justice, but is not a Member of the United Nations, may participate in the General Assembly in regard to amendments to the Statute in the same manner as the Members of the United Nations;

(*b*) Amendments to the Statute of the International Court of Justice shall come into force for all States which are parties to the Statute when they have been adopted by a vote of two thirds of the States which are parties to the Statute and ratified in accordance with their respective constitutional processes by two thirds of the States which are parties to the Statute and in accordance with the provisions of Article 69 of the Statute and Article 108 of the Charter of the United Nations.

1820th plenary meeting
4 December 1969

3208 (XXIX). Status of the European Economic Community in the General Assembly

Committee: -
Vote: Adopted without a vote
Ref.: 1470(XIV), 1330(XII)

The General Assembly,

Wishing to promote cooperation between the United Nations and the European Economic Community,

Requests the Secretary-General to invite the European Economic Community to participate in the sessions and work of the General Assembly in the capacity of observer.

2266th plenary meeting
11 October 1974

3237 (XXIX). Observer Status for the Palestine Liberation Organization

Committee: -
Vote: 95 - 17 - 19

The General Assembly,

Having considered the question of Palestine,

Taking into consideration the universality of the United Nations prescribed in the Charter,

Recalling its resolution 3102 (XXVIII) of 12 December 1973,

Taking into account Economic and Social Council resolutions 1835 (LVI) of 14 May 1974 and 1840 (LVI) of 15 May 1974,

Noting that the Diplomatic Conference on the Reaffirmation and Development of International Humanitarian Law Applicable in Armed Conflicts, the World Population Conference and the World Food Conference have in effect invited the Palestine Liberation Organization to participate in their respective deliberations,

Noting also that the Third United Nations Conference on the Law of the Sea has invited the Palestine Liberation Organization to participate in its deliberations as an observer,

1. *Invites* the Palestine Liberation Organization to participate in the sessions and the work of the General Assembly in the capacity of observer;

2. *Invites* the Palestine Liberation Organization to participate in the sessions and the work of all international conferences convened under the auspices of the General Assembly in the capacity of observer;

3. *Considers* that the Palestine Liberation Organization is entitled to participate as an observer in the sessions and the work of all international conferences convened under the auspices of other organs of the United Nations;

4. *Requests* the Secretary-General to take the necessary steps for the implementation of the present resolution.

2296th plenary meeting
22 November 1974

31/152. Observer Status for the South West Africa People's Organization

Committee: 4
Vote: 113 - 0 - 13

The General Assembly,

Having considered the question of Namibia,

Recognizing the crucial phase reached in the struggle of the Namibian people and the added demands and critical tasks imposed upon their liberation movement, the South West Africa People's Organization,

Taking into consideration the report of the United Nations Council for Namibia[1] and the recommendations contained therein,[2]

Reaffirming the resolutions and decisions of the General Assembly and the Security Council concerning the question of Namibia,

Recalling, in particular, its resolution 3111 (XXVIII) of 12 December 1973, by which it recognized the South West Africa People's Organization as the authentic representative of the Namibian people,

Noting that the Organization of African Unity and the non-aligned countries have recognized and invited the South West Africa People's Organization to participate in their meetings in an observer capacity,

1. *Invites* the South West Africa People's Organization to participate in the sessions and the work of the General Assembly in the capacity of observer;

2. *Invites* the South West Africa People's Organization to participate in the sessions and the work of all international conferences convened under the auspices of the General Assembly in the capacity of observer;

3. *Considers* that the South West Africa People's Organization is entitled to participate as an observer in the sessions and the work of all international conferences convened under the auspices of other organs of the United Nations;

4. *Requests* the Secretary-General to take the necessary steps for the implementation of the present resolution and to accord all the facilities as may be required.

105th plenary meeting
20 December 1976

---

1 *Official Records of the General Assembly, Thirty First Session, Supplement No. 24* (A/31/24).

2 *Ibid., Supplement No. 24* (A/31/24), vol. I, paras. 272 and 273.

45/6. Observer Status for the International Committee of the Red Cross, in Consideration of the Special Role and Mandates Conferred upon it by the Geneva Conventions of 12 August 1949

Committee: -
Vote: Adopted without a vote

The General Assembly,

Recalling the mandates conferred upon the International Committee of the Red Cross by the Geneva Conventions of 12 August 1949,[1]

Considering the special role carried on accordingly by the International Committee of the Red Cross in international humanitarian relations,

Desirous of promoting cooperation between the United Nations and the International Committee of the Red Cross,

1. *Decides* to invite the International Committee of the Red Cross to participate in the sessions and the work of the General Assembly in the capacity of observer;

2. *Requests* the Secretary-General to take the necessary action to implement the present resolution.

31st plenary meeting
16 October 1990

45/37. Observer Status of National Liberation Movements Recognized by the Organization of African Unity and/or by the League of Arab States

Committee: 6
Vote: 116 - 9 - 26
Ref.: 47/29

The General Assembly,

Recalling its resolutions 35/167 of 15 December 1980, 37/104 of 16 December 1982, 39/76 of 13 December 1984, 41/71 of 3 December 1986 and 43/160 B of 9 December 1988,

Recalling also its resolutions 3237 (XXIX) of 22 November 1974 and 3280 (XXIX) of 10 December 1974,

Taking note of the report of the Secretary-General,[2]

Bearing in mind the resolution of the United Nations Conference on the Representation of States in Their Relations with International Organizations relating to the observer status of national liberation movements recognized by the Organization of African Unity and/or by the League of Arab States,[3]

Noting that the Vienna Convention on the Representation of States in their Relations with International Organizations of a Universal Character, of 14 March 1975,[4] regulates only the representation of States in their relations with international organizations,

Taking into account the current practice of inviting the above-mentioned national liberation movements to participate as observers in the sessions of the General Assembly, specialized agencies and other organizations of the United Nations system and in the work of the conferences held under the auspices of such international organizations,

Convinced that the participation of the national liberation movements referred to above in the work of international organizations helps to strengthen international peace and cooperation,

Desirous of ensuring the effective participation of the above-mentioned national liberation movements as observers in the work of international organizations and of regulating, to that end, their status and the facilities, privileges and immunities necessary for the performance of their functions,

Noting that many States have recognized those national liberation movements and have granted them facilities, privileges and immunities in their countries,

1. *Urges* all States that have not done so, in particular those which are host to international organizations or to conferences convened by, or held under the auspices of, international organizations of a universal character, to consider as soon as possible the question of ratifying, or acceding to, the Vienna Convention on the Representation of States in Their Relations with International Organizations of a Universal Character;

2. *Calls once more upon* the States concerned to accord to the delegations of the national liberation movements recognized by the Organization of African Unity and/or by the League of Arab States and accorded observer status by international organizations, the facilities, privileges and immunities necessary for the performance of their functions, in accordance with the provisions of the Vienna Convention on the Representation of States in Their Relations with International Organizations of a Universal Character;

3. *Requests* the Secretary-General to report to the General Assembly at its forty-seventh session on the implementation of the present resolution.

48th plenary meeting
28 November 1990

---

1 United Nations, *Treaty Series*, vol. 75, Nos. 970-973.

2 A/45/438.

3 See *Official Records of the United Nations Conference on the Representation of States in Their Relations with International Organizations, Vienna, 4 February-14 March 1975,* vol. II (United Nations publication, Sales No. E.75.V.12), document A/CONF. 67/15, annex.

4 *Ibid.*, vol. II, p. 207.

11.70 DECLARATIONS ON THE OCCASIONS OF THE ANNIVERSARIES

2627 (XXV). Declaration on the Occasion of the Twenty-Fifth Anniversary of the United Nations

Committee: -
Vote: Adopted without a vote
Ref.: 2499(XXIV), 889(IX)

The General Assembly
Adopts the following Declaration:

Declaration on the Occasion of The Twenty-Fifth Anniversary of the United Nations

We, the representatives of the States Members of the United Nations, assembled at United Nations Headquarters on 24 October 1970 on the occasion of the twenty-fifth anniversary of the coming into force of the Charter of the United Nations, now solemnly declare that:

1. In furtherance of the anniversary objectives of peace, justice and progress, we reaffirm our dedication to the Charter of the United Nations and our will to carry out the obligations contained in the Charter.

2. The United Nations, despite its limitations, has, in its role as a centre for harmonizing the actions of nations in attaining the purposes mentioned in Article 1 of the Charter, made an important contribution to the maintenance of international peace and security, to developing friendly relations based on respect for the principle of equal rights and self-determination of peoples and to achieving international cooperation in economic, social, cultural and humanitarian fields. We reaffirm our deep conviction that the United Nations can provide a most effective means to strengthen the freedom and independence of nations.

3. In pursuance of the purposes of the Charter, we reaffirm our determination to respect the principles of international law concerning friendly relations and cooperation among States. We will exert our utmost efforts to develop such relations among all States, irrespective of their political, economic and social systems, on the basis of strict observance of the principles of the Charter, and in particular the principle of sovereign equality of States, the principle that States shall refrain in their international relations from the threat or use of force against the territorial integrity or political independence of any State, the principle that they shall settle their international disputes by peaceful means, the duty not to intervene in matters within the domestic jurisdiction of any State, the duty of States to cooperate with one another in accordance with the Charter, and the principle that States shall fulfil in good faith the obligations assumed by them in accordance with the Charter. The progressive development and codification of international law, in which important progress was made during the first twenty-five years of the United Nations, should be advanced in order to promote the rule of law among nations. In this connexion we particularly welcome the adoption today of the Declaration on Principles of International Law concerning Friendly Relations and Cooperation among States in accordance with the Charter of the United Nations.[1]

4. Despite the achievements of the United Nations, a grave situation of insecurity still confronts the Organization and armed conflicts occur in various parts of the world, while at the same time the arms race and arms expenditure continue and a large part of humanity is suffering from economic under-development. We reaffirm our determination to take concrete steps to fulfil the central task of the United Nations - the preservation of international peace and security - since the solution to many other crucial problems, notably those of disarmament and economic development, is inseparably linked thereto, and to reach agreement on more effective procedures for carrying out United Nations peace-keeping consistent with the Charter. We invite all Member States to resort more often to the peaceful settlement of international disputes and conflicts by the means provided for in the Charter, notably through negotiation, inquiry, mediation, conciliation, arbitration and judicial settlement, making use as appropriate of the relevant organs of the United Nations, as well as through resort to regional agencies or arrangements or other peaceful means of their own choice.

5. On the threshold of the Disarmament Decade, we welcome the important international agreements which have already been achieved in the limitation of armaments, especially nuclear arms. Conscious of the long and difficult search for ways to halt and reverse the arms race and of the grave threat to international peace posed by the continuing development of sophisticated weapons, we look forward to the early conclusion of further agreements of this kind and to moving forward from arms limitation to a reduction of armaments and to disarmament everywhere, particularly in the nuclear field, with the participation of all nuclear Powers. We call upon all Governments to renew their determination to make concrete progress towards the elimination of the arms race and the achievement of the final goal - general and complete disarmament under effective international control.

6. We acclaim the role of the United Nations in the past twenty-five years in the process of the liberation of peoples of colonial, Trust and other Non-Self-Governing Territories. As a result of this welcome development, the number of sovereign States in the Organization has been greatly increased and colonial empires have virtually disappeared. Despite these achievements, many Territories and peoples continue to be denied their right to self-determination and independence, particularly in Namibia, Southern Rhodesia, Angola, Mozambique and Guinea (Bissau), in deliberate and deplorable defiance of the United Nations and world opinion by certain recalcitrant States and by the illegal régime of Southern Rhodesia. We reaffirm the inalienable right of all colonial peoples to self-determination, freedom and independence and condemn all actions which deprive any people of these rights. In recognizing the legitimacy of the struggle of colonial peoples for their freedom by all appropriate means at their disposal, we call upon all Governments to comply in this respect with the provisions of the Charter, taking into account the Declaration on the Granting of Independence to Colonial Countries and Peoples adopted by the United Nations in 1960. We re-emphasize that these countries and peoples are entitled, in their just struggle, to seek and to receive all necessary moral and material help in accordance with the purposes and principles of the Charter.

7. We strongly condemn the evil policy of apartheid, which is a crime against the conscience and dignity of mankind and, like nazism, is contrary to the principles of the Charter. We reaffirm our determination to spare no effort, including support to those who struggle against it, in accordance with the letter and spirit of the Charter, to secure the elimination of apartheid in South Africa. We also condemn all forms of oppression and tyranny wherever they occur and racism and the practice of racial discrimination in all its manifestations.

8. The United Nations has endeavoured in its first twenty-five years to further the Charter objectives of promoting respect for, and observance of human rights and fundamental freedoms for all. The international conventions and declarations concluded under its auspices give expression to the moral conscience of mankind and represent humanitarian standards for all members of the international community. The Universal Declaration of Human Rights, the International Covenants on Human Rights, the International Convention on the Elimination of All Forms of Racial Discrimination and the Convention on the Prevention and Punishment of the Crime of Genocide constitute a landmark in international cooperation and in the recognition and protection of the rights of every individual without any distinction. Although some progress has been achieved, serious violations of human rights are still being committed against individuals and groups in several regions of the world. We pledge ourselves to a continued and determined struggle against all violations of the rights and fundamental freedoms of human beings, by eliminating the basic causes of such violations,

[1] Resolution 2625 (XXV).

by promoting universal respect for the dignity of all people without regard to race, colour, sex, language or religion, and in particular through greater use of the facilities provided by the United Nations in accordance with the Charter.

9. During the past twenty-five years, efforts have been made, by adopting specific measures and by fashioning and employing new institutions, to give concrete substance to the fundamental objectives enshrined in the Charter, to create conditions of stability and well-being and to ensure a minimum standard of living consistent with human dignity. We are convinced that such economic and social development is essential to peace, international security and justice. The nations of the world have, therefore, resolved to seek a better and more effective system of international cooperation whereby the prevailing disparities may be banished and prosperity secured for all. International efforts for economic and technical cooperation must be on a scale commensurate with that of the problem itself. In this context, the activities of the United Nations system designed to secure the economic and social progress of all countries, in particular the developing countries, which have grown significantly in the past twenty-five years, should be further strengthened and increased. Partial, sporadic and half-hearted measures will not suffice. On the occasion of this anniversary, we have proclaimed the 1970s to be the Second United Nations Development Decade, which coincides with and is linked to the Disarmament Decade, and have adopted the International Development Strategy for the Second United Nations Development Decade.[1] We urge all Governments to give their full support to its most complete and effective implementation in order to realize the fundamental objectives of the Charter.

10. The new frontiers of science and technology demand greater international cooperation. We reaffirm our intention to make full use, *inter alia*, through the United Nations, of the unprecedented opportunities created by advances in science and technology for the benefit of peoples everywhere in such fields as outer space, the peaceful uses of the seabed beyond national jurisdiction and the improvement of the quality of the environment, so that the developed and developing countries can share equitably scientific and technical advances, thus contributing to the acceleration of economic development throughout the world.

11. The great increase in the membership of the Organization since 1945 testifies to its vitality; however, universality in terms of membership in the Organization has not yet been achieved. We express the hope that in the near future all other peaceloving States which accept and, in the judgement of the Organization, are able and willing to carry out the obligations of the Charter will become Members. It is furthermore desirable to find ways and means to strengthen the Organization's effectiveness in dealing with the growing volume and complexity of its work in all areas of its activities, and notably those relating to the strengthening of international peace and security, including a more rational division and coordination of work among the various agencies and organizations of the United Nations system.

12. Mankind is confronted today by a critical and urgent choice: either increased peaceful cooperation and progress or disunity and conflict, even annihilation. We, the representatives of the States Members of the United Nations, solemnly observing the twenty-fifth anniversary of the United Nations, reaffirm our determination to do our utmost to ensure a lasting peace on earth and to observe the purposes and principles embodied in the Charter, and express full confidence that the actions of the United Nations will be conducive to the advancement of mankind along the road to peace, justice and progress.

1883rd plenary meeting
24 October 1970

1 Resolution 2626 (XXV).

50/6. Declaration on the Occasion of the Fiftieth Anniversary of the United Nations

Committee: -
Vote: Adopted without a vote
Ref.: 39/161

The General Assembly,

Adopts the following Declaration:

Declaration on the Occasion of the Fiftieth Anniversary of the United Nations

Fifty years ago the United Nations was born out of the sufferings caused by the Second World War. The determination, enshrined in the Charter of the United Nations, "to save succeeding generations from the scourge of war" is as vital today as it was fifty years ago. In this, as in other respects, the Charter gives expression to the common values and aspirations of humankind.

The United Nations has been tested by conflict, humanitarian crisis and turbulent change, yet it has survived and played an important role in preventing another global conflict and has achieved much for people all over the world. The United Nations has helped to shape the very structure of relations between nations in the modern age. Through the process of decolonization and the elimination of apartheid, hundreds of millions of human beings have been and are assured the exercise of the fundamental right of self-determination.

At this time, following the end of the cold war, and as the end of the century approaches, we must create new opportunities for peace, development, democracy and cooperation. The speed and extent of change in today's world point to a future of great complexity and challenge and to a sharp increase in the level of expectations of the United Nations.

Our resolve on this historic occasion is clear. The commemoration of the fiftieth anniversary of the United Nations must be seized as an opportunity to redirect it to greater service to humankind, especially to those who are suffering and are deeply deprived. This is the practical and moral challenge of our time. Our obligation to this end is found in the Charter. The need for it is manifest in the condition of humankind.

On the occasion of the fiftieth anniversary of the United Nations, we, the Member States and observers of the United Nations, representing the peoples of the world:

- Solemnly reaffirm the Purposes and Principles of the Charter of the United Nations and our commitments to them;
- Express our gratitude to all men and women who have made the United Nations possible, done its work and served its ideals, particularly those who have given their lives during service to the United Nations;
- Are determined that the United Nations of the future will work with renewed vigour and effectiveness in promoting peace, development, equality and justice and understanding among the peoples of the world;
- Will give to the twenty-first century a United Nations equipped, financed and structured to serve effectively the peoples in whose name it was established.

In fulfilment of these commitments we will be guided in our future cooperation by the following, with respect to peace, development, equality, justice and the United Nations Organization:

Peace

1. To meet these challenges, and while recognizing that action to secure global peace, security and stability will be futile unless the economic and social needs of people are addressed, we will:

- Promote methods and means for the peaceful settlement of disputes in accordance with the Charter of the United Nations and enhance the capabilities of the United Nations in conflict prevention, preventive diplomacy, peace-keeping and peace-building;

- Strongly support United Nations, regional and national efforts on arms control, limitation and disarmament and the non-proliferation of nuclear weapons, in all aspects, and other weapons of mass destruction, including biological and chemical weapons and other forms of particularly excessively injurious or indiscriminate weapons, in pursuit of our common commitment to a world free of all these weapons;
- Continue to reaffirm the right of self-determination of all peoples, taking into account the particular situation of peoples under colonial or other forms of alien domination or foreign occupation, and recognize the right of peoples to take legitimate action in accordance with the Charter of the United Nations to realize their inalienable right of self- determination. This shall not be construed as authorizing or encouraging any action that would dismember or impair, totally or in part, the territorial integrity or political unity of sovereign and independent States conducting themselves in compliance with the principle of equal rights and self-determination of peoples and thus possessed of a Government representing the whole people belonging to the territory without distinction of any kind;
- Act together to defeat the threats to States and people posed by terrorism, in all its forms and manifestations, and transnational organized crime and the illicit trade in arms and the production and consumption of and trafficking in illicit drugs;
- Strengthen consultation and cooperation between regional arrangements or agencies and the United Nations in the maintenance of international peace and security.

Development

2. A dynamic, vigorous, free and equitable international economic environment is essential to the well-being of humankind and to international peace, security and stability. This objective must be addressed, in greater measure and more effectively, by the United Nations system.

3. The United Nations has played an important role in the promotion of economic and social development and has, over the years, provided life- saving assistance to women, children and men around the world. But the pledge recorded in the Charter that all Members of the United Nations shall take joint and separate action in cooperation with the Organization for the achievement of higher standards of living, full employment and conditions of economic and social progress and development has not been adequately implemented.

4. It must be recognized that notwithstanding past efforts, the gap between the developed and developing countries remains unacceptably wide. The specific problems of countries with economies in transition with respect to their twofold transition to democracy and a market economy should also be recognized. In addition, accelerating globalization and interdependence in the world economy call for policy measures designed to ensure the maximization of the benefits from and the minimization of the negative effects of these trends for all countries.

5. Of greatest concern is that one fifth of the world's 5.7 billion people live in extreme poverty. Extraordinary measures by all countries, including strengthened international cooperation, are needed to address this and related problems.

6. In response to these facts and circumstances, the United Nations has convened a number of specifically focused global conferences in the last five years. From these conferences, a consensus has emerged, *inter alia,* that economic development, social development and environmental protection are interdependent and mutually reinforcing components of sustainable development, which is the framework of our efforts to achieve a higher quality of life for all people. At the core of this consensus is the recognition that the human person is the central subject of development and that people must be at the centre of our actions towards and concerns for sustainable development.

7. In this context, we reaffirm that democracy, development and respect for human rights and fundamental freedoms, including the right to development, are interdependent and mutually reinforcing.

8. In order to foster sustained economic growth, social development, environmental protection and social justice in fulfilment of the commitments we have made on international cooperation for development, we will:

- Promote an open and equitable, rule-based, predictable and non- discriminatory multilateral trading system and a framework for investment, transfers of technology and knowledge, as well as enhanced cooperation in the areas of development, finance and debt as critical conditions for development;
- Give particular attention to national and international action to enhance the benefits of the process of globalization for all countries and to avoid the marginalization from and promote the integration of the least developed countries and countries in Africa into the world economy;
- Improve the effectiveness and efficiency of the United Nations system for development and strengthen its role in all relevant fields of international economic cooperation;
- Invigorate the dialogue and partnership between all countries in order to secure the existence of a favourable political and economic environment for the promotion of international cooperation for development based on the imperatives of mutual benefit and interest and genuine interdependence, while recognizing that each country is ultimately responsible for its own development but reaffirming that the international community must create a supportive international environment for such development;
- Promote social development through decisive national and international action aimed at the eradication of poverty as an ethical, social, political and economic imperative of humankind and the promotion of full employment and social integration;
- Recognize that the empowerment and the full and equal participation of women is central to all efforts to achieve development;
- Reduce and eliminate unsustainable patterns of production and consumption and promote appropriate demographic policies in order to meet the needs of current generations without compromising the ability of future generations to meet their own needs, recognizing that environmental sustainability constitutes an integral part of the development process;
- Intensify cooperation on natural disaster reduction and major technological and man-made disasters, disaster relief, post-disaster rehabilitation and humanitarian assistance in order to enhance the capabilities of affected countries to cope with such situations.

Equality

9. We reiterate the affirmation by the Charter of the dignity and worth of the human person and the equal rights of men and women and reaffirm that all human rights are universal, indivisible, interdependent and interrelated.

10. While the significance of national and regional particularities and various historical, cultural and religious backgrounds must be borne in mind, it is the duty of all States, regardless of their political, economic and cultural systems, to promote and protect all human rights and fundamental freedoms, the universal nature of which is beyond question. It is also important for all States to ensure the universality, objectivity and non-selectivity of the consideration of human rights issues.

11. We will therefore:

- Promote and protect all human rights and fundamental freedoms, which are inherent to all human beings;
- Strengthen laws, policies and programmes that would ensure the full and equal participation of women in all spheres of political, civil, economic, social and cultural life as equal partners and the full realization of all human rights and fundamental freedoms for all women;
- Promote and protect the rights of the child;
- Ensure that the rights of persons who can be particularly vulnerable to abuse or neglect, including youth, persons with disabilities, the elderly and migrant workers, are protected;

- Promote and protect the rights of indigenous people;
- Ensure the protection of the rights of refugees and of displaced persons;
- Ensure that the rights of persons belonging to national, ethnic and other minorities are protected, and that such persons are able to pursue economic and social development and live in circumstances of full respect for their identity, traditions, forms of social organization and cultural and religious values.

Justice

12. The Charter of the United Nations has provided a durable framework for the promotion and development of international law. The continued promotion and development of international law must be pursued with a view to ensuring that relations between States are based on the principles of justice, sovereign equality, universally recognized principles of international law and respect for the rule of law. Such action should take account of developments under way in such areas as technology, transport information and resource-related fields and international financial markets, as well as the growing complexity of the work of the United Nations in the humanitarian and refugee assistance fields.

13. We are determined to:

- Build and maintain justice among all States in accordance with the principles of the sovereign equality and territorial integrity of States;
- Promote full respect for and implementation of international law;
- Settle international disputes by peaceful means;
- Encourage the widest possible ratification of international treaties and ensure compliance with the obligations arising from them;
- Promote respect for and the implementation of international humanitarian law;
- Promote the progressive development of international law in the field of development, including that which would foster economic and social progress;
- Promote respect for and implementation of international law in the field of human rights and fundamental freedoms and encourage ratification of or accession to international human rights instruments;
- Promote the further codification and progressive development of international law.

United Nations Organization

14. In order to be able to respond effectively to the challenges of the future and the expectations of the United Nations held by peoples around the world, it is essential that the United Nations itself be reformed and modernized. The work of the General Assembly, the universal organ of the States Members of the United Nations, should be revitalized. The Security Council should, *inter alia*, be expanded and its working methods continue to be reviewed in a way that will further strengthen its capacity and effectiveness, enhance its representative character and improve its working efficiency and transparency; as important differences on key issues continue to exist, further in-depth consideration of these issues is required. The role of the Economic and Social Council should be strengthened to enable it to carry out effectively, in the modern age, the tasks it has been assigned with respect to the well-being and standards of life of all people. These and other changes, within the United Nations system, should be made if we are to ensure that the United Nations of the future serves well the peoples in whose name it was established.

15. In order to carry out its work effectively, the United Nations must have adequate resources. Member States must meet, in full and on time, their obligation to bear the expenses of the Organization, as apportioned by the General Assembly. That apportionment should be established on the basis of criteria agreed to and considered to be fair by Member States.

16. The secretariats of the United Nations system must improve significantly their efficiency and effectiveness in administering and managing the resources allocated to them. For their part, Member States will pursue and take responsibility for reforming that system.

17. We recognize that our common work will be the more successful if it is supported by all concerned actors of the international community, including non-governmental organizations, multilateral financial institutions, regional organizations and all actors of civil society. We will welcome and facilitate such support, as appropriate.

LIST OF RESOLUTIONS IN NUMERICAL ORDER

The resolution adopted in a Special or Emergency Special Sessions that are not consequtively numbered appear at the end of the list.

INDEX

Page numbers that appear in bold print indicate the pages containing the main text of the relevant resolution. The other page numbers refer to resolutions in which the subject is only briefly discussed. If a subject is mentioned more than once in a resolution, the page number is quoted for the first reference only.